THE OXFORD
New Spanish Dictionary

Also Available

THE OXFORD
New Spanish Dictionary

Spanish—English
English—Spanish

Español—Inglés
Inglés—Español

CHRISTINE LEA

SECOND EDITION
edited by
Carol Styles Carvajal
Michael Britton
Jane Horwood

BERKLEY BOOKS, NEW YORK

THE OXFORD NEW SPANISH DICTIONARY

A Berkley Book / published in mass market paperback
by arrangement with Oxford University Press, Inc.

PRINTING HISTORY
Oxford University Press edition published 1994
Berkley edition / August 1997
Berkley second edition / August 1999

The Penguin Putnam Inc. World Wide Web site address is
http://www.penguinputnam.com

ISBN: 0-425-17090-X

BERKLEY®
Berkley Books are published by
The Berkley Publishing Group, a division of Penguin Putnam Inc.,
375 Hudson Street, New York, New York 10014.
BERKLEY and the "B" design are trademarks
belonging to Penguin Putnam Inc.

PRINTED IN THE UNITED STATES OF AMERICA

10 9 8 7 6 5

Contents
Índice

Introduction
Introducción

Introduction

This major new edition of the *Oxford Spanish Dictionary* is designed as an effective and practical reference tool for the student, adult learner, traveller, and business professional. It provides a user-friendly treatment of core vocabulary across a broad spectrum of written and spoken language.

The wordlist has been comprehensively revised to reflect recent additions to both languages and to cover such topics as computing and the Internet. A further new feature of the dictionary is the special status given to more complex grammatical words which provide the basic structure of both languages. Boxed entries in the text for these *function words* provide extended treatment, including notes to warn of possible pitfalls.

The dictionary has an easy-to-use, streamlined layout. Bullets separate each new part of speech within an entry. Nuances of sense or usage are pinpointed by indicators or by typical collocates with which the word frequently occurs. Extra help is given in the form of symbols to mark the register of words and phrases. An exclamation mark 🄸 indicates colloquial language, and a cross 🄧 indicates slang.

Each English headword is followed by its phonetic transcription between slashes. The symbols used are those of the International Phonetic Alphabet. Pronunciation is also shown for derivatives and compounds where it is not easily deduced from that of a headword. The rules for pronunciation of Spanish are given on page x.

The swung dash (∼) is used to replace a headword or that part of a headword preceding the vertical bar (|).

In both English and Spanish only irregular plurals are given. Normally Spanish nouns and adjectives ending in an unstressed vowel form the plural by adding *s* (e.g. *libro, libros*). Nouns and adjectives ending in a stressed vowel or a consonant add *es* (e.g. *rubí, rubíes, pared, paredes*). An accent on the final syllable is not required when *es* is added (e.g. *nación, naciones*). Final *z* becomes *ces* (e.g. *vez, veces*).

Spanish nouns and adjectives ending in *o* form the feminine by changing the final *o* to *a* (e.g. *hermano, hermana*). Most Spanish nouns and adjectives ending in anything other than final *o* do not have a separate feminine form, with the exception of those denoting nationality etc.; these add *a* to the masculine singular form (e.g. *español, española*). An accent on the final syllable is then not required (e.g. *inglés, inglesa*). Adjectives ending in *án, ón,* or *or* behave like those denoting nationality, with the following exceptions: *inferior, mayor, mejor, menor, peor, superior*, where the feminine has the same form as the masculine.

Spanish verb tables will be found in the appendix on pp. 467–473.

The Spanish alphabet

In Spanish *ñ* is considered a separate letter and in the Spanish–English section, therefore, is alphabetized after *ny*.

Introducción

Esta importante nueva edición del *Diccionario de Oxford* ha sido concebida a fin de proporcionar una herramienta de referencia práctica y eficaz al estudiante, joven y adulto, al viajero y a la persona de negocios. El diccionario ofrece un vocabulario básico, de uso fácil, dentro de una amplia gama del lenguaje escrito y hablado.

Se ha revisado exhaustivamente la lista de palabras con el objeto de incorporar nuevos términos en ambos idiomas y cubrir así temas tales como la informática e Internet. Otro nuevo aspecto del diccionario es la importancia especial que se da a palabras con una función más compleja dentro de la gramática y que proveen la estructura básica de ambos idiomas. Estos *vocablos clave* están contenidos en recuadros dentro del texto, donde se les da un tratamiento amplio y se incluyen notas para advertir sobre posibles escollos.

El diccionario tiene una presentación clara y es fácil de usar. Símbolos distintivos separan las diferentes categorías gramaticales dentro de cada entrada. Los matices de sentido y de uso se muestran con precisión mediante indicadores o por colocaciones típicas con las que la palabra se usa frecuentemente. Se encuentra ayuda adicional en los signos que indican el registro idiomático de las palabras y frases. Un signo de exclamación ⚠ señala el uso coloquial y una cruz ✖ el uso argot.

Cada palabra cabeza de artículo en inglés va seguida de su transcripción fonética entre barras oblicuas. Los símbolos que se usan son los del Alfabeto Fonético Internacional. También aparece la pronunciación de derivados y nombres compuestos cuando no es posible deducirla de la palabra cabeza de artículo. Las reglas sobre pronunciación española se encuentran en la página x.

La tilde (∼) se emplea para sustituir la palabra cabeza de artículo o aquella parte de tal palabra que precede a la barra vertical (|).

Tanto en inglés como en español se dan los plurales solamente si son irregulares. Para formar el plural regular en inglés se añade la letra *s* al sustantivo singular, pero se añade *es* cuando se trata de una palabra que termina en *ch, sh, s, ss, us, x, o, z* (p.ej. *sash, sashes*). En el caso de una palabra que termine en *y* precedida por una consonante, la *y* se transforma en *ies* (p.ej. *baby, babies*).

Para formar el tiempo pasado y el participio pasado se añade *ed* al infinitivo de los verbos regulares ingleses (p.ej. *last, lasted*). En el caso de los verbos ingleses que terminan en *e* muda se añade sólo la *d* (p.ej. *move, moved*). En el caso de los verbos ingleses que terminan en *y*, se debe cambiar la *y* por *ied* (p.ej. *carry, carried*).

Los verbos irregulares se encuentran en el diccionario por orden alfabético remitidos al infinitivo, y también en la lista del apéndice en las págs 474–478.

Pronunciation
Pronunciación

Pronunciation of Spanish

Vowels

a between pronunciation of *a* in English *cat* and *arm*
e like *e* in English *bed*
i like *ee* in English *see* but a little shorter
o like *o* in English *hot* but a little longer
u like *oo* in English *too*
y when a vowel is as Spanish **i**

Consonants

b (1) in initial position or after a nasal consonant is like English *b*
       (2) in other positions is between English *b* and English *v*
c (1) before **e** or **i** is like *th* in English *thin*. In Latin American
           Spanish is like English *s*.
       (2) in other positions is like *c* in English *cat*
ch like *ch* in English *chip*
d (1) in initial position, after nasal consonants and after **l** is like
           English *d*
       (2) in other positions is like *th* in English *this*
f like English *f*
g (1) before **e** or **i** is like *ch* in Scottish *loch*
       (2) in initial position is like *g* in English *get*
       (3) in other positions is like (2) but a little softer
h silent in Spanish but see also **ch**
j like *ch* in Scottish *loch*
k like English *k*
l like English *l* but see also **ll**
ll like *lli* in English *million*
m like English *m*
n like English *n*
ñ like *ni* in English *opinion*
p like English *p*
q like English *k*
r rolled or trilled
s like *s* in English *sit*
t like English *t*
v (1) in initial position or after a nasal consonant is like English *b*
       (2) in other positions is between English *b* and English *v*
w like Spanish **b** or **v**
x like English *x*
y like English *y*
z like *th* in English *thin*

Pronunciación Inglesa

Símbolos fonéticos

Vocales y diptongos

iː	see	ɔː	saw	əɪ	page	ɔɪ	join
ɪ	sit	ʊ	put	əʊ	home	ɪə	near
e	ten	uː	too	aɪ	five	eə	hair
æ	hat	ʌ	cup	aɪə	fire	ʊə	poor
ɑː	arm	ɜː	fur	aʊ	now		
ɒ	got	ə	ago	aʊə	flour		

Consonantes

p	pen	tʃ	chin	s	so	n	no
b	bad	dʒ	June	z	zoo	ŋ	sing
t	tea	f	fall	ʃ	she	l	leg
d	dip	v	voice	ʒ	measure	r	red
k	cat	θ	thin	h	how	j	yes
g	got	ð	then	m	man	w	wet

Abbreviations
Abreviaturas

Abbreviations
Abreviaturas

adjective	*a*	adjetivo
abbreviation	*abbr/abrev*	abreviatura
administration	*admin*	administración
adverb	*adv*	adverbio
American	*Amer*	americano
anatomy	*Anat*	anatomía
architecture	*Archit/Arquit*	arquitectura
definite article	*art def*	artículo definido
indefinite article	*art indef*	artículo indefinido
astrology	*Astr*	astrología
motoring	*Auto*	automóvil
auxiliary	*aux*	auxiliar
aviation	*Aviat/Aviac*	aviación
biology	*Biol*	biología
botany	*Bot*	botánica
British	*Brit*	británico
commerce	*Com*	comercio
conjunction	*conj*	conjunción
cookery	*Culin*	cocina
electricity	*Elec*	electricidad
school	*Escol*	enseñanza
Spain	*Esp*	España
feminine	*f*	femenino
familiar	*fam*	familiar
figurative	*fig*	figurado
philosophy	*Fil*	filosofía
photography	*Foto*	fotografía
geography	*Geog*	geografía
geology	*Geol*	geología
grammar	*Gram*	gramática
humorous	*hum*	humorístico
interjection	*int*	interjección
interrogative	*inter*	interrogativo
invariable	*invar*	invariable
legal, law	*Jurid*	jurídico
Latin American	*LAm*	latinoamericano
language	*Lang*	lengua(je)
masculine	*m*	masculino
mathematics	*Mat(h)*	matemáticas

mechanics	*Mec*	mecánica
medicine	*Med*	medicina
Mexico	*Mex*	México
military	*Mil*	militar
music	*Mus*	música
mythology	*Myth*	mitología
noun	*n*	nombre
nautical	*Naut*	náutica
oneself	*o. s.*	uno mismo, se
proprietary term	*P*	marca registrada
pejorative	*pej*	peyorativo
philosophy	*Phil*	filosofía
photography	*Photo*	fotografía
plural	*pl*	plural
politics	*Pol*	política
possessive	*poss*	posesivo
past participle	*pp*	participio pasado
prefix	*pref*	prefijo
preposition	*prep*	preposición
present participle	*pres p*	participio de presente
pronoun	*pron*	pronombre
psychology	*Psych*	psicología
past tense	*pt*	tiempo pasado
railroad	*Rail*	ferrocarril
relative	*rel*	relativo
religion	*Relig*	religión
school	*Schol*	enseñanza
singular	*sing*	singular
slang	*sl*	argot
someone	*s. o.*	alguien
something	*sth*	algo
subjunctive	*subj*	subjuntivo
technical	*Tec*	técnico
television	*TV*	televisión
university	*Univ*	universidad
auxiliary verb	*v aux*	verbo auxiliar
verb	*vb*	verbo
intransitive verb	*vi*	verbo intransitivo
pronominal verb	*vpr*	verbo pronominal
transitive verb	*vt*	verbo transitivo
transitive & intransitive verb	*vti*	verbo transitivo e intransitivo
vulgar	*vulg*	vulgar

Proprietary terms

This dictionary includes some words which have, or are asserted to have, proprietary status as trademarks. Their inclusion does not imply that they have acquired for legal purposes a non-proprietary or general significance, nor any other judgement concerning their legal status. In cases where the editorial staff have some evidence that a word has proprietary status this is indicated in the entry for that word by the symbol (P), but no judgement concerning the legal status of such words is made or implied thereby.

Marcas registradas

Este diccionario incluye algunas palabras que son o pretenden ser marcas registradas. No debe atribuirse ningún valor jurídico ni a la presencia ni a la ausencia de tal designación.

Spanish–English dictionary
Diccionario Español–Inglés

Aa

a

● *preposición*

Note that **a** followed by **el** becomes **al**, e.g. **vamos al cine**

····▸ (dirección) to. **fui a México** I went to Mexico. **muévete a la derecha** move to the right

····▸ (posición) **se sentaron a la mesa** they sat at the table. **al lado del banco** next to the bank. **a orillas del río** on the banks of the river

····▸ (distancia) **queda a 5 km** it's 5 km away. **a pocos metros de aquí** a few metres from here

····▸ (fecha) **hoy estamos a 5** today is the 5th. **¿a cuánto estamos?**, (LAm) **¿a cómo estamos?** what's the date?

····▸ (hora, momento) at. **a las 2** at 2 o'clock. **a fin de mes** at the end of the month. **a los 21 años** at the age of 21; (después de) after 21 years

····▸ (precio) **¿a cómo están las peras?** how much are the pears? **están a 500 pesetas el kilo** they're 500 pesetas a kilo. **salen a 30 pesetas cada uno** they work out at 30 pesetas each.

····▸ (medio, modo) **fuimos a pie** we went on foot. **hecho a mano** handmade. **pollo al horno** (LAm) roast chicken

····▸ (cuando precede al objeto directo de persona) *no se traduce*. **conocí a Juan** I met Juan. **quieren mucho a sus hijos** they love their children very much

····▸ (con objeto indirecto) to. **se lo di a Juan** I gave it to Juan. **le vendí el coche a mi amigo** I sold my friend the car, I sold the car to my friend. **se lo compré a mi madre** I bought it from my mother; (para) I bought it for my mother

⟹ Cuando la preposición **a** se emplea precedida de ciertos verbos como **empezar, faltar, ir, llegar** etc., ver bajo el respectivo verbo

ábaco *m* abacus

abadía *f* abbey

abajo *adv* (down) below; (dirección) down(wards); (en casa) downstairs. ● *int* down with. ~ **de** (LAm) under (neath). **calle** ~ down the street. **el** ~ **firmante** the undersigned. **escaleras** ~ down the stairs. **la parte de** ~ the bottom (part). **los de** ~ those at the bottom. **más** ~ further down

abalanzarse [10] *vpr* rush (**hacia** towards)

abanderado *m* standard-bearer; (Mex, en fútbol) linesman

abandon|ado *adj* abandoned; (descuidado) neglected; <*persona*> untidy. ~**ar** *vt* leave <*un lugar*>; abandon <*persona, cosa*>. ● *vi* give up. □ ~**arse** *vpr* give in; (descuidarse) let o.s. go. ~**o** *m* abandonment; (estado) neglect

abani|car [7] *vt* fan. ~**co** *m* fan

abaratar *vt* reduce

abarcar [7] *vt* put one's arms around, embrace; (comprender) embrace

abarrotar *vt* overfill, pack full

abarrotes *mpl* (LAm) groceries; (tienda) grocer's shop

abast|ecer [11] *vt* supply. ~**ecimiento** *m* supply; (acción) supplying. ~**o** *m* supply. **no dar** ~**o** be unable to cope (**con** with)

abati|do *a* depressed. ~**miento** *m* depression

abdicar [7] *vt* give up. ● *vi* abdicate

abdom|en *m* abdomen. ~**inal** *a* abdominal

abec|é *m* Ⅰ alphabet, ABC. ~**edario** *m* alphabet

abedul *m* birch (tree)

abej|a *f* bee. ~**orro** *m* bumble-bee

aberración *f* aberration

abertura *f* opening

abeto *m* fir (tree)

abierto *pp* ⇒ABRIR. ● *a* open

abism|al *a* abysmal; (profundo) deep. ~ar *vt* throw into an abyss; (fig, abatir) humble. □ ~**arse** *vpr* be absorbed (en in), be lost (en in). ~**o** *m* abyss; (fig, diferencia) world of difference

ablandar *vt* soften.□ ~**se** *vpr* soften

abnega|ción *f* self-sacrifice. ~**do** *a* self-sacrificing

abochornar *vt* embarrass. □ ~**se** *vpr* feel embarrassed

abofetear *vt* slap

aboga|cía *f* law. ~**do** *m* lawyer, solicitor; (ante tribunal superior) barrister (Brit), attorney (Amer). ~**r** [12] *vi* plead

abolengo *m* ancestry

aboli|ción *f* abolition. ~**cionismo** *m* abolitionism. ~**cionista** *m* & *f* abolitionist. ~**r** [24] *vt* abolish

abolla|dura *f* dent. ~**r** *vt* dent

abolsado *a* baggy

abomba|do *a* convex; (LAm, atontado) dopey. ~**r** *vt* make convex. □ ~**rse** *vpr* (LAm, descomponerse) go bad

abominable *a* abominable

abona|ble *a* payable. ~**do** *a* paid. ● *m* subscriber. ~**r** *vt* pay; (en agricultura) fertilize. □ ~**rse** *vpr* subscribe. ~**o** *m* payment; (estiércol) fertilizer; (a un periódico) subscription

aborda|ble *a* reasonable; <persona> approachable. ~**je** *m* boarding. ~**r** *vt* tackle <un asunto>; approach <una persona>; (Naut) come alongside; (Mex, Aviac) board

aborigen *a* & *m* native

aborrec|er [11] *vt* loathe. ~**ible** *a* loathsome. ~**ido** *a* loathed. ~**imiento** *m* loathing

abort|ar *vi* have a miscarriage. ~**ivo** *a* abortive. ~**o** *m* miscarriage; (voluntario) abortion. **hacerse un** ~**o** have an abortion

abotonar *vt* button (up). □ ~**se** *vpr* button (up)

abovedado *a* vaulted

abrasa|dor *a* burning. ~**r** *vt* burn. □ ~**rse** *vpr* burn

abraz|ar *vt* [10] embrace. ~**arse** *vpr* embrace. ~**o** *m* hug. **un fuerte**

~**o de** (en una carta) with best wishes from

abre|botellas *m invar* bottle-opener. ~**cartas** *m invar* paper-knife. ~**latas** *m invar* tin opener (Brit), can opener

abrevia|ción *f* abbreviation; (texto abreviado) abridged text. ~**do** *a* brief; <texto> abridged. ~**r** *vt* abbreviate; abridge <texto>; cut short <viaje etc>. ● *vi* be brief. ~**tura** *f* abbreviation

abrig|ado *a* <lugar> sheltered; <persona> well wrapped up. ~**ador** *a* (Mex, ropa) warm. ~**ar** [12] *vt* shelter; cherish <esperanza>; harbour <duda, sospecha>. □ ~**arse** *vpr* (take) shelter; (con ropa) wrap up. ~**o** *m* (over)coat; (lugar) shelter

abril *m* April. ~**eño** *a* April

abrillantar *vt* polish

abrir (*pp* **abierto**) *vt/i* open. □ ~**se** *vpr* open; (extenderse) open out; <el tiempo> clear

abrochar *vt* do up; (con botones) button up

abruma|dor *a* overwhelming. ~**r** *vt* overwhelm

abrupto *a* steep; (áspero) harsh

abrutado *a* brutish

absentismo *m* absenteeism

absolución *f* (Relig) absolution; (Jurid) acquittal

absolut|amente *adv* absolutely, completely. ~**o** *a* absolute. **en** ~**o** (not) at all. ~**orio** *a* of acquittal

absolver [2] (*pp* **absuelto**) *vt* (Relig) absolve; (Jurid) acquit

absor|bente *a* absorbent; (fig, interesante) absorbing. ~**ber** *vt* absorb. ~**ción** *f* absorption. ~**to** *a* absorbed

abstemio *a* teetotal. ● *m* teetotaller

absten|ción *f* abstention. □ ~**erse** [40] *vpr* abstain, refrain (de from)

abstinencia *f* abstinence

abstra|cción *f* abstraction. ~**cto** *a* abstract. ~**er** [41] *vt* abstract. □ ~**erse** *vpr* be lost in thought. ~**ído** *a* absent-minded

absuelto *a* (Relig) absolved; (Jurid) acquitted

absurdo *a* absurd. ● *m* absurd thing

abuche|ar *vt* boo. **~o** *m* booing

abuel|a *f* grandmother. **~o** *m* grandfather. **~os** *mpl* grandparents

ab|ulia *f* apathy. **~úlico** *a* apathetic

abulta|do *a* bulky. **~r** *vt* (fig, exagerar) exaggerate. ● *vi* be bulky

abunda|ncia *f* abundance. **nadar en la ~ncia** be rolling in money. **~nte** *a* abundant, plentiful. **~r** *vi* be plentiful

aburguesarse *vpr* become middle-class

aburri|do *a* (con estar) bored; (con ser) boring. **~dor** *a* (LAm) boring. **~miento** *m* boredom; (cosa pesada) bore. **~r** *vt* bore. □ **~rse** *vpr* get bored

abus|ar *vi* take advantage. **~ar de la bebida** drink too much. **~ivo** *a* excessive. **~o** *m* abuse

acá *adv* here. **~ y allá** here and there. **de ~ para allá** to and fro. **de ayer ~** since yesterday. **más ~** nearer

acaba|do *a* finished; (perfecto) perfect. ● *m* finish. **~r** *vt/i* finish. □ **~rse** *vpr* finish; (agotarse) run out; (morirse) die. **~r con** put an end to. **~r de** (+ *infinitivo*) have just (+ *pp*). **~ de llegar** he has just arrived. **~r por** (+ *infinitivo*) end up (+ *gerundio*). **¡se acabó!** that's it!

acabóse *m*. **ser el ~** be the end, be the limit

acad|emia *f* academy. **~émico** *a* academic

acallar *vt* silence

acalora|do *a* heated; <persona> hot. □ **~rse** *vpr* get hot; (fig, excitarse) get excited

acampar *vi* camp

acantilado *m* cliff

acapara|r *vt* hoard; (monopolizar) monopolize. **~miento** *m* hoarding; (monopolio) monopolizing

acariciar *vt* caress; <animal> stroke; <idea etc> nurture

ácaro *m* mite

acarre|ar *vt* transport; <desgracias etc> cause. **~o** *m* transport

acartona|do *a* <piel> wizened. □ **~rse** *vpr* (ponerse rígido) go stiff; <piel> become wizened

acaso *adv* maybe, perhaps. ● *m* chance. **~ llueva mañana** perhaps it will rain tomorrow. **por si ~** (just) in case

acata|miento *m* compliance (de with). **~r** *vt* comply with

acatarrarse *vpr* catch a cold, get a cold

acaudalado *a* well off

acceder *vi* agree; (tener acceso) have access

acces|ible *a* accessible; <persona> approachable. **~o** *m* access, entry; (Med, ataque) attack

accesorio *a* & *m* accessory

accident|ado *a* <terreno> uneven; (agitado) troubled; <persona> injured. **~al** *a* accidental. □ **~arse** *vpr* have an accident. **~e** *m* accident

acci|ón *f* (incl Jurid) action; (hecho) deed; (Com) share. **~onar** *vt* work. ● *vi* gesticulate. **~onista** *m* & *f* shareholder

acebo *m* holly (tree)

acech|ar *vt* lie in wait for. **~o** *m* spying. **al ~o** on the look-out

aceit|ar *vt* oil; (Culin) add oil to. **~e** *m* oil. **~e de oliva** olive oil. **~te de ricino** castor oil. **~era** *f* cruet; (para engrasar) oilcan. **~ero** *a* oil. **~oso** *a* oily

aceitun|a *f* olive. **~ado** *a* olive. **~o** *m* olive tree

acelera|dor *m* accelerator. **~r** *vt* accelerate; (fig) speed up, quicken

acelga *f* chard

acent|o *m* accent; (énfasis) stress. **~uación** *f* accentuation. **~uar** [21] *vt* stress; (fig) emphasize. □ **~uarse** *vpr* become noticeable

acepción *f* meaning, sense

acepta|ble *a* acceptable. **~ción** *f* acceptance; (éxito) success. **~r** *vt* accept

acequia *f* irrigation channel

acera *f* pavement (Brit), sidewalk (Amer)

acerca de *prep* about

acerca|miento *m* approach; (fig) reconciliation. ~**r** [7] *vt* bring near. □ ~**rse** *vpr* approach

acero *m* steel. ~ **inoxidable** stainless steel

acérrimo *a* (fig) staunch

acert|ado *a* right, correct; (apropiado) appropriate. ● ~**ar** [1] *vt* (adivinar) get right, guess. ● *vi* get right; (en el blanco) hit. ~**ar a** happen to. ~**ar con** hit on.~**ijo** *m* riddle

achacar [7] *vt* attribute

achacoso *a* sickly

achaque *m* ailment

achatar *vt* flatten

achicar [7] *vt* make smaller; (fig, 🄯, empequeñecer) belittle; (Naut) bale out. □ ~**rse** *vpr* become smaller; (humillarse) be intimidated

achicharra|r *vt* burn; (fig) pester. □ ~**rse** *vpr* burn

achichincle *m & f* (Mex) hanger-on

achicopalado *a* (Mex) depressed

achicoria *f* chicory

achiote *m* (LAm) annatto

achispa|do *a* tipsy. □ ~**rse** *vpr* get tipsy

achulado *a* cocky

acicala|do *a* dressed up. ~**r** *vt* dress up. □ ~**rse** *vpr* get dressed up

acicate *m* spur

acidez *f* acidity; (Med) heartburn

ácido *a* sour. ● *m* acid

acierto *m* success; (idea) good idea; (habilidad) skill

aclama|ción *f* acclaim; (aplausos) applause. ~**r** *vt* acclaim; (aplaudir) applaud

aclara|ción *f* explanation. ~**r** *vt* lighten *<colores>*; (explicar) clarify; (enjuagar) rinse. ● *vi* *<el tiempo>* brighten up. □ ~**rse** *vpr* become clear. ~**torio** *a* explanatory

aclimata|ción *f* acclimatization, acclimation (Amer). ~**r** *vt* acclimatize, acclimate (Amer). □ ~**rse** *vpr* become acclimatized, become acclimated (Amer)

acné *m* acne

acobardar *vt* intimidate. □ ~**se** *vpr* lose one's nerve

acocil *m* (Mex) freshwater shrimp

acog|edor *a* welcoming; *<ambiente>* friendly. ~**er** [14] *vt* welcome; (proteger) shelter; (recibir) receive. □ ~**erse** *vpr* take refuge. ~**ida** *f* welcome; (refugio) refuge

acolcha|do *a* quilted. ~**r** *vt* quilt, pad

acomedido *a* (Mex) obliging

acomet|er *vt* attack; (emprender) undertake ~**ida** *f* attack

acomod|ado *a* well off. ~**ador** *m* usher. ~**adora** *f* usherette. ~**ar** *vt* arrange; (adaptar) adjust. ● *vi* be suitable. □ ~**arse** *vpr* settle down; (adaptarse) conform

acompaña|miento *m* accompaniment. ~**nte** *m & f* companion; (Mus) accompanist. ~**r** *vt* go with; (hacer compañía) keep company; (adjuntar) enclose

acondicionar *vt* fit out; (preparar) prepare

aconseja|ble *a* advisable. ~**do** *a* advised. ~**r** *vt* advise. □ ~**rse** *vpr* ~**rse con** consult

acontec|er [11] *vi* happen. ~**imiento** *m* event

acopla|miento *m* coupling; (Elec) connection. ~**r** *vt* fit; (Elec) connect; (Rail) couple

acorazado *a* armour-plated. ● *m* battleship

acord|ar [2] *vt* agree (upon); (decidir) decide; (recordar) remind. □ ~**arse** *vpr* remember. ~**e** *a* in agreement; (Mus) harmonious. ● *m* chord

acorde|ón *m* accordion. ~**onista** *m & f* accordionist

acordona|do *a* *<lugar>* cordoned off; *<zapatos>* lace-up. ~**r** *vt* lace (up); (rodear) cordon off

acorralar *vt* round up *<animales>*; corner *<personas>*

acortar *vt* shorten; cut short *<permanencia>*. □ ~**se** *vpr* get shorter

acos|ar *vt* hound; (fig) pester. ~**o** *m* pursuit; (fig) pestering

acostar [2] *vt* put to bed; (Naut) bring alongside. ● *vi* (Naut) reach land. □ ~**se** *vpr* go to bed; (echarse) lie down. ~**se con** (fig) sleep with

acostumbra|do *a* (habitual) usual. ~do a used to. ~r *vt* get used. me ha ~do a levantarme por la noche he's got me used to getting up at night. ● *vi.* ~r a be accustomed to. **acostumbro a comer a la una** I usually have lunch at one o'clock. □ ~**rse** *vpr* become accustomed, get used

acota|ción *f* (nota) margin note; (en el teatro) stage direction; (cota) elevation mark. ~**miento** *m* (Mex) hard shoulder

acrecentar [1] *vt* increase. □ ~**se** *vpr* increase

acredita|do *a* reputable; (Pol) accredited. ~**r** *vt* prove; accredit <*diplomático*>; (garantizar) guarantee; (autorizar) authorize. □ ~**rse** *vpr* make one's name

acreedor *a* worthy (**de** of). ● *m* creditor

acribillar *vt* (a balazos) riddle (**a** with); (a picotazos) cover (**a** with); (fig, a preguntas etc) bombard (**a** with)

acr|obacia *f* acrobatics. ~**obacias aéreas** aerobatics. ~**óbata** *m & f* acrobat. ~**obático** *a* acrobatic

acta *f* minutes; (certificado) certificate

actitud *f* posture, position; (fig) attitude, position

activ|ar *vt* activate; (acelerar) speed up. ~**idad** *f* activity. ~**o** *a* active. ● *m* assets

acto *m* act; (ceremonia) ceremony. **en el** ~ immediately

act|or *m* actor. ~**riz** *f* actress

actuación *f* action; (conducta) behaviour; (Theat) performance

actual *a* present; <*asunto*> topical. ~**idad** *f* present; (de asunto) topicality. **en la** ~**idad** (en este momento) currently; (hoy en día) nowadays. ~**idades** *fpl* current affairs. ~**ización** *f* modernization. ~**izar** [10] *vt* modernize. ~**mente** *adv* now, at the present time

actuar [21] *vi* act. ~ **de** act as

acuarel|a *f* watercolour. ~**ista** *m & f* watercolourist

acuario *m* aquarium. A~ Aquarius

acuartelar *vt* quarter, billet; (mantener en cuartel) confine to barracks

acuático *a* aquatic

acuchillar *vt* slash; stab <*persona*>

acuci|ante *a* urgent. ~**ar** *vt* urge on; (dar prisa a) hasten. ~**oso** *a* keen

acudir *vi.* ~ **a** go to; (asistir) attend; turn up for <*a una cita*>. ~ **en auxilio de** <*a una cita*>. ~ **en auxilio** go to help

acueducto *m* aqueduct

acuerdo *m* agreement. ● *vb* ⇒ACORDAR. **¡de** ~**!** OK! **de** ~ **con** in accordance with. **estar de** ~ agree. **ponerse de** ~ agree

acuesto *vb* ⇒ACOSTAR

acumula|dor *m* accumulator. ~**r** *vt* accumulate. □ ~**rse** *vpr* accumulate

acunar *vt* rock

acuñar *vt* mint, coin

acupuntura *f* acupuncture

acurrucarse [7] *vpr* curl up

acusa|do *a* accused; (destacado) marked. ● *m* accused. ~**r** *vt* accuse; (mostrar) show; (denunciar) denounce; acknowledge <*recibo*>

acuse *m.* ~ **de recibo** acknowledgement of receipt

acus|ica *m & f* 🄵 telltale. ~**ón** *m* 🄵 telltale

acústic|a *f* acoustics. ~**o** *a* acoustic

adapta|ble *a* adaptable. ~**ción** *f* adaptation. ~**dor** *m* adapter. ~**r** *vt* adapt; (ajustar) fit. □ ~**rse** *vpr* adapt o.s.

adecua|do *a* suitable. ~**r** *vt* adapt, make suitable

adelant|ado *a* advanced; <*niño*> precocious; <*reloj*> fast. **por** ~**ado** in advance. ~**amiento** *m* advance (ment); (Auto) overtaking. ~**ar** *vt* advance, move forward; (acelerar) speed up; put forward <*reloj*>; (Auto) overtake. ● *vi* advance, go forward; <*reloj*> gain, be fast. □ ~**arse** *vpr* advance, move forward; <*reloj*> gain; (Auto) overtake. ~**e** *adv* forward. ● *int* come in!; (¡siga!) carry on! **más** ~**e** (lugar) further on; (tiempo) later on. ~**o** *m* advance; (progreso) progress

adelgaza|miento *m* slimming. ~**r** [10] *vt* make thin; lose <*kilos*>. ● *vi* lose weight; (adrede) slim. □ ~**rse** *vpr* lose weight; (adrede) slim

ademán *m* gesture. en ~ de as if to.
ademanes *mpl* (modales) manners.

además *adv* besides; (también) also; (lo que es más) what's more. ~ de besides

adentr|arse *vpr*. ~arse en penetrate into; study thoroughly *<tema etc>*. ~o *adv* in(side). ~ de (LAm) in(side). mar ~o out at sea. tierra ~o inland

adepto *m* supporter

aderez|ar [10] *vt* flavour *<bebidas>*; (condimentar) season; dress *<ensalada>*. ~o *m* flavouring; (con condimentos) seasoning; (para ensalada) dressing

adeud|ar *vt* owe. ~o *m* debit

adhe|rir [4] *vt/i* stick. □ ~rirse *vpr* stick; (fig) follow. ~sión *f* adhesion; (fig) support. ~sivo *a* & *m* adhesive

adici|ón *f* addition. ~onal *a* additional. ~onar *vt* add

adicto *a* addicted. ● *m* addict; (seguidor) follower

adiestra|do *a* trained. ~miento *m* training. ~r *vt* train. □ ~rse *vpr* practise

adinerado *a* wealthy

adiós *int* goodbye!; (al cruzarse con alguien) hello!

adit|amento *m* addition; (accesorio) accessory. ~ivo *m* additive

adivin|anza *f* riddle. ~ar *vt* foretell; (acertar) guess. ~o *m* fortuneteller

adjetivo *a* adjectival. ● *m* adjective

adjudica|ción *f* award. ~r [7] *vt* award. □ ~rse *vpr* appropriate. ~tario *m* winner of an award

adjunt|ar *vt* enclose. ~o *a* enclosed; (auxiliar) assistant. ● *m* assistant

administra|ción *f* administration; (gestión) management. ~dor *m* administrator; (gerente) manager. ~dora *f* administrator; manageress. ~r *vt* administer. ~tivo *a* administrative

admira|ble *a* admirable. ~ción *f* admiration. ~dor *m* admirer. ~r *vt* admire; (sorprender) amaze. □ ~rse *vpr* be amazed

admi|sibilidad *f* admissibility. ~sible *a* acceptable. ~sión *f* admission; (aceptación) acceptance. ~tir *vt* admit; (aceptar) accept

adobar *vt* (Culin) pickle; (condimentar) marinade

adobe *m* sun-dried brick

adobo *m* pickle; (condimento) marinade

adoctrinar *vt* indoctrinate

adolecer [11] *vi*. ~ de suffer from

adolescen|cia *f* adolescence. ~te *a* adolescent. ● *m* & *f* teenager, adolescent

adonde *adv* where

adónde *adv* where?

adop|ción *f* adoption. ~tar *vt* adopt. ~tivo *a* adoptive; *<hijo>* adopted; *<patria>* of adoption

adoqu|ín *m* paving stone; (imbécil) idiot. ~inado *m* paving. ~inar *vt* pave

adora|ción *f* adoration. ~r *vt* adore

adormec|er [11] *vt* send to sleep; (fig, calmar) calm, soothe. □ ~erse *vpr* fall asleep; *<un miembro>* go to sleep. ~ido *a* sleepy; *<un miembro>* numb

adormilarse *vpr* doze

adorn|ar *vt* adorn (con, de with). ~o *m* decoration

adosar *vt* lean (a against); (Mex, adjuntar) to enclose

adquiri|r [4] *vt* acquire; (comprar) purchase. ~sición *f* acquisition; (compra) purchase. ~sitivo *a* purchasing

adrede *adv* on purpose

adrenalina *f* adrenalin

aduan|a *f* customs. ~ero *a* customs. ● *m* customs officer

aducir [47] *vt* allege

adueñarse *vpr* take possession

adul|ación *f* flattery. ~ador *a* flattering. ● *m* flatterer. ~ar *vt* flatter

ad|ulterar *vt* adulterate. ~últero *a* adulterous. ~ulterio *m* adultery

adulto *a* & *m* adult, grown-up

advenedizo *a* & *m* upstart

advenimiento *m* advent, arrival; (subida al trono) accession

adverbio *m* adverb

advers|ario *m* adversary. **~idad** *f* adversity. **~o** *a* adverse, unfavourable

advert|encia *f* warning. **~ir** [4] *vt* warn; (notar) notice

adviento *m* Advent

adyacente *a* adjacent

aéreo *a* air; <foto> aerial; <ferrocarril> overhead

aeróbico *a* aerobic

aerodeslizador *m* hovercraft

aero|lito *m* meteorite. **~moza** *f* (LAm) flight attendant. **~puerto** *m* airport. **~sol** *m* aerosol

afab|ilidad *f* affability. **~le** *a* affable

afamado *a* famous

af|án *m* hard work; (deseo) desire. **~nador** *m* (Mex) cleaner. **~anar** *vt* 🗷 pinch 🗓. □ **~anarse** *vpr* strive (en, por to)

afear *vt* disfigure, make ugly; (censurar) censure

afecta|ción *f* affectation. **~do** *a* affected. **~r** *vt* affect

afect|ivo *a* sensitive. **~o** *m* (cariño) affection. ● *a.* **~o a** attached to. **~uoso** *a* affectionate. **con un ~uoso saludo** (en cartas) with kind regards. **suyo ~ísimo** (en cartas) yours sincerely

afeita|do *m* shave. **~dora** *f* electric razor. **~r** *vt* shave. □ **~rse** *vpr* shave, have a shave

afeminado *a* effeminate. ● *m* effeminate person

aferrar *vt* grasp. □ **~se** *vpr* to cling (a to)

afianza|miento *m* (refuerzo) strengthening; (garantía) guarantee. □ **~rse** [10] *vpr* become established

afiche *m* (LAm) poster

afici|ón *f* liking; (conjunto de aficionados) fans. **por ~ón** as a hobby. **~onado** *a* keen (a on), fond (a of). ● *m* fan. **~onar** *vt* make fond. □ **~onarse** *vpr* take a liking to

afila|do *a* sharp. **~dor** *m* knifegrinder. **~r** *vt* sharpen

afilia|ción *f* affiliation. **~do** *a* affiliated. □ **~rse** *vpr* become a member (a of)

afín *a* similar; (contiguo) adjacent; <personas> related

afina|ción *f* (Auto, Mus) tuning. **~do** *a* (Mus) in tune. **~dor** *m* tuner. **~r** *vt* (afilar) sharpen; (Auto, Mus) tune. □ **~rse** *vpr* become thinner

afincarse [7] *vpr* settle

afinidad *f* affinity; (parentesco) relationship by marriage

afirma|ción *f* affirmation. **~r** *vt* make firm; (asentir) affirm. □ **~rse** *vpr* steady o.s. **~tivo** *a* affirmative

aflicción *f* affliction

afligi|do *a* distressed. **~r** [14] *vt* distress. □ **~rse** *vpr* distress o.s.

aflojar *vt* loosen; (relajar) ease. ● *vi* let up. □ **~se** *vpr* loosen

aflu|encia *f* flow. **~ente** *a* flowing. ● *m* tributary. **~ir** [17] *vi* flow (a into)

afónico *a* hoarse

aforismo *m* aphorism

aforo *m* capacity

afortunado *a* fortunate, lucky

afrancesado *a* Frenchified

afrenta *f* insult; (vergüenza) disgrace

África *f* Africa. **~ del Sur** South Africa

africano *a & m* African

afrodisíaco, afrodisiaco *a & m* aphrodisiac

afrontar *vt* bring face to face; (enfrentar) face, confront

afuera *adv* out(side) **¡~!** out of the way! **~ de** (LAm) outside. **~s** *fpl* outskirts

agachar *vt* lower. □ **~se** *vpr* bend over

agalla *f* (de los peces) gill. **~s** *fpl* (fig) guts

agarradera *f* (LAm) handle

agarr|ado *a* (fig, 🗓) mean. **~ar** *vt* grasp; (esp LAm) take; (LAm, pillar) catch. □ **~arse** *vpr* hold on; (🗓, reñirse) have a fight. **~ón** *m* tug; (LAm 🗓, riña) row

agarrotar *vt* tie tightly; <el frío> stiffen; garotte <un reo>. □ **~se** *vpr* go stiff; (Auto) seize up

agasaj|ado *m* guest of honour. **~ar** *vt* look after well. **~o** *m* good treatment

agazaparse *vpr* crouch

agencia *f* agency. ~ **de viajes** travel agency. ~ **inmobiliaria** estate agency (Brit), real estate agency (Amer). □ ~**rse** *vpr* find (out) for o.s.

agenda *f* diary (Brit), appointment book (Amer); (programa) agenda

agente *m* agent; (de policía) policeman. ●*f* agent; (de policía) policewoman. ~ **de aduanas** customs officer. ~ **de bolsa** stockbroker

ágil *a* agile

agili|dad *f* agility. ~**zación** *f* speeding up. ~**zar** *vt* speed up

agita|ción *f* waving; (de un líquido) stirring; (intranquilidad) agitation. ~**do** *a* <el mar> rough; (fig) agitated. ~**dor** *m* (Pol) agitator

agitar *vt* wave; shake <botellas etc>; stir <líquidos>; (fig) stir up. □ ~**se** *vpr* wave; <el mar> get rough; (fig) get excited

aglomera|ción *f* agglomeration; (de tráfico) traffic jam. ~**r** *vt* amass. □ ~**rse** *vpr* form a crowd

agnóstico *a & m* agnostic

agobi|ante *a* <trabajo> exhausting; <calor> oppressive. ~**ar** *vt* weigh down; (fig, abrumar) overwhelm. ~**o** *m* weight; (cansancio) exhaustion; (opresión) oppression

agolparse *vpr* crowd together

agon|ía *f* death throes; (fig) agony. ~**izante** *a* dying; <luz> failing. ~**izar** [10] *vi* be dying

agosto *m* August. **hacer su** ~ feather one's nest

agota|do *a* exhausted; (todo vendido) sold out; <libro> out of print. ~**dor** *a* exhausting. ~**miento** *m* exhaustion. ~**r** *vt* exhaust. □ ~**rse** *vpr* be exhausted; <existencias> sell out; <libro> go out of print

agracia|do *a* attractive; (que tiene suerte) lucky. ~**r** *vt* make attractive

agrada|ble *a* pleasant, nice. ~**r** *vt/i* please. **esto me** ~ I like this

agradec|er [11] *vt* thank <persona>; be grateful for <cosa>. ~**ido** *a* grateful. **¡muy** ~**ido!** thanks a lot! ~**imiento** *m* gratitude

agrado *m* pleasure; (amabilidad) friendliness

agrandar *vt* enlarge; (fig) exaggerate. □ ~**se** *vpr* get bigger

agrario *a* agrarian, land; <política> agricultural

agrava|nte *a* aggravating. ●*f* additional problem. ~**r** *vt* aggravate; (aumentar el peso) make heavier. □ ~**rse** *vpr* get worse

agravi|ar *vt* offend; (perjudicar) wrong. ~**o** *m* offence

agredir [24] *vt* attack. ~ **de palabra** insult

agrega|do *m* aggregate; (diplomático) attaché. ~**r** [12] *vt* add; appoint <persona>. □ ~**rse** *vpr* to join

agres|ión *f* aggression; (ataque) attack. ~**ividad** *f* aggressiveness. ~**ivo** *a* aggressive. ~**or** *m* aggressor

agreste *a* country; <terreno> rough

agriar *regular, o raramente* [20] *vt* sour. □ ~**se** *vpr* turn sour; (fig) become embittered

agr|ícola *a* agricultural. ~**icultor** *m* farmer. ~**icultura** *f* agriculture, farming

agridulce *a* bitter-sweet; (Culin) sweet-and-sour

agrietar *vt* crack. □ ~**se** *vpr* crack; <piel> chap

agrio *a* sour. ~**s** *mpl* citrus fruits

agro|nomía *f* agronomy. ~**pecuario** *a* farming

agrupa|ción *f* group; (acción) grouping. ~**r** *vt* group. □ ~**rse** *vpr* form a group

agruras *fpl* (Mex) heartburn

agua *f* water; (lluvia) rain; (marea) tide; (vertiente del tejado) slope. ~ **abajo** downstream. ~ **arriba** upstream. ~ **bendita** holy water. ~ **corriente** running water. ~ **de colonia** eau-de-cologne. ~ **dulce** fresh water. ~ **mineral con gas** fizzy mineral water. ~ **mineral sin gas** still mineral water. ~ **potable** drinking water. ~ **salada** salt water. **hacer** ~ (Naut) leak. **se me hizo** ~ **la boca** (LAm) it made my mouth water

aguacate *m* avocado pear; (árbol) avocado pear tree

aguacero *m* downpour, heavy shower

aguado *a* watery; (Mex, aburrido) boring

agua|fiestas *m & f invar* spoilsport, wet blanket. ~**mala** *f* (Mex), ~**mar** *m* jellyfish. ~**marina** *f* aquamarine

aguant|ar *vt* put up with, bear; (sostener) support. ● *vi* hold out. □ ~**arse** *vpr* restrain o.s. ~**e** *m* patience; (resistencia) endurance

aguar [15] *vt* water down

aguardar *vt* wait for. ● *vi* wait

agua|rdiente *m* (cheap) brandy. ~**rrás** *m* turpentine, turps 🔲

agud|eza *f* sharpness; (fig, perspicacia) insight; (fig, ingenio) wit. ~**izar** [10] *vt* sharpen. □ ~**izarse** *vpr* <enfermedad> get worse. ~**o** *a* sharp; <ángulo, enfermedad> acute; <voz> high-pitched

agüero *m* omen. **ser de mal** ~ be a bad omen

aguijón *m* sting; (vara) goad

águila *f* eagle; (persona perspicaz) astute person; (Mex, de moneda) heads. **¿**~ **o sol?** heads or tails?

aguileño *a* aquiline

aguinaldo *m* Christmas box; (LAm, paga) Christmas bonus

aguja *f* needle; (del reloj) hand; (Arquit) steeple. ~**s** *fpl* (Rail) points

aguje|ear *vt* make holes in. ~**o** *m* hole

agujetas *fpl* stiffness; (Mex, de zapatos) shoe laces. **tener** ~ be stiff

aguzado *a* sharp

ah *int* ah!, oh!

ahí *adv* there. ~ **nomás** (LAm) just there. **de** ~ **que** that is why. **por** ~ that way; (aproximadamente) thereabouts

ahija|da *f* god-daughter, godchild. ~**do** *m* godson, godchild. ~**dos** *mpl* godchildren

ahínco *m* enthusiasm; (empeño) insistence

ahog|ado *a* (en el agua) drowned; (asfixiado) suffocated. ~**ar** [12] *vt* (en el agua) drown; (asfixiar) suffocate; put out <fuego>. □ ~**arse** *vpr* (en el agua) drown; (asfixiarse) suffocate. ~**o** *m* breathlessness; (fig, angustia) distress

ahondar *vt* deepen. ● *vi* go deep. ~ **en** (fig) examine in depth. □ ~**se** *vpr* get deeper

ahora *adv* now; (hace muy poco) just now; (dentro de poco) very soon. ~ **bien** however. ~ **mismo** right now. **de** ~ **en adelante** from now on, in future. **por** ~ for the time being

ahorcar [7] *vt* hang. □ ~**se** *vpr* hang o.s.

ahorita *adv* (esp LAm 🔲) now. ~ **mismo** right now

ahorr|ador *a* thrifty. ~**ar** *vt* save. □ ~**arse** *vpr* save o.s. ~**o** *m* saving. ~**os** *mpl* savings

ahuecar [7] *vt* hollow; fluff up <colchón>; deepen <la voz>

ahuizote *m* (Mex) scourge

ahuma|do *a* (Culin) smoked; (de colores) smoky. ~**r** *vt* (Culin) smoke; (llenar de humo) fill with smoke. ● *vi* smoke. □ ~**rse** *vpr* become smoky; <comida> acquire a smoky taste

ahuyentar *vt* drive away; banish <pensamientos etc>

aimará *a & m* Aymara. ● *m & f* Aymara indian

airado *a* annoyed

aire *m* air; (viento) breeze; (corriente) draught; (aspecto) appearance; (Mus) tune, air. ~ **acondicionado** air-conditioning. **al** ~ **libre** outdoors. **darse** ~**s** give o.s. airs. ~**ar** *vt* air; (ventilar) ventilate; (fig, publicar) make public. □ ~**arse** *vpr*. **salir para** ~**arse** go out for some fresh air

airoso *a* graceful; (exitoso) successful

aisla|do *a* isolated; (Elec) insulated. ~**dor** *a* (Elec) insulating. ~**nte** *a* insulating. ~**r** [23] *vt* isolate; (Elec) insulate

ajar *vt* crumple; (estropear) spoil

ajedre|cista *m & f* chess-player. ~**z** *m* chess

ajeno *a* (de otro) someone else's; (de otros) other people's; (extraño) alien

ajetre|ado *a* hectic, busy. ~**o** *m* bustle

ají *m* (LAm) chilli; (salsa) chilli sauce

aj|illo *m* garlic. **al** ~**illo** cooked with garlic. ~**o** *m* garlic. ~**onjolí** *m* sesame

ajuar *m* furnishings; (de novia) trousseau; (de bebé) layette

ajust|ado *a* right; <*vestido*> tight. ~ar *vt* fit; (adaptar) adapt; (acordar) agree; settle <*una cuenta*>; (apretar) tighten. ● *vi* fit. □ ~arse *vpr* fit; (adaptarse) adapt o.s.; (acordarse) come to an agreement. ~e *m* fitting; (adaptación) adjustment; (acuerdo) agreement; (de una cuenta) settlement

al = a + el

ala *f* wing; (de sombrero) brim.● *m* & *f* (deportes) winger

alaba|nza *f* praise. ~r *vt* praise

alacena *f* cupboard (Brit), closet (Amer)

alacrán *m* scorpion

alambr|ada *f* wire fence. ~ado *m* (LAm) wire fence. ~e *m* wire. ~e de púas barbed wire

alameda *f* avenue; (plantío de álamos) poplar grove

álamo *m* poplar. ~ temblón aspen

alarde *m* show. hacer ~ de boast of

alarga|do *a* long. ~dor *m* extension. ~r [12] *vt* lengthen; stretch out <*mano etc*>; (dar) give, pass. □ ~rse *vpr* get longer

alarido *m* shriek

alarm|a *f* alarm. ~ante *a* alarming. ~ar *vt* alarm, frighten. □ ~arse *vpr* be alarmed. ~ista *m* & *f* alarmist

alba *f* dawn

albacea *m* & *f* executor

albahaca *f* basil

albanés *a* & *m* Albanian

Albania *f* Albania

albañil *m* builder; (que coloca ladrillos) bricklayer

albarán *m* delivery note

albaricoque *m* apricot. ~ro *m* apricot tree

albedrío *m* will. libre ~ free will

alberca *f* tank, reservoir; (Mex, piscina) swimming pool

alberg|ar [12] *vt* (alojar) put up; <*vivienda*> house; (dar refugio) shelter. □ ~arse *vpr* stay; (refugiarse) shelter. ~ue *m* accommodation; (refugio) shelter. ~ue de juventud youth hostel

albino *a* & *m* albino

albóndiga *f* meatball, rissole

albornoz *m* bathrobe

alborot|ado *a* excited; (aturdido) hasty. ~ador *a* rowdy. ● *m* troublemaker. ~ar *vt* disturb, upset. ● *vi* make a racket. □ ~arse *vpr* get excited; <*el mar*> get rough. ~o *m* row, uproar

álbum *m* (*pl* ~es *o* ~s) album

alcachofa *f* artichoke

alcald|e *m* mayor. ~esa *f* mayoress. ~ía *f* mayoralty; (oficina) mayor's office

alcance *m* reach; (de arma, telescopio etc) range; (déficit) deficit

alcancía *f* money-box; (LAm, de niño) piggy bank

alcantarilla *f* sewer; (boca) drain

alcanzar [10] *vt* (llegar a) catch up; (coger) reach; catch <*un autobús*>; <*bala etc*> strike, hit. ● *vi* reach; (ser suficiente) be enough. ~ a manage

alcaparra *f* caper

alcázar *m* fortress

alcoba *f* bedroom

alcoh|ol *m* alcohol. ~ol desnaturalizado methylated spirits, meths ~ólico *a* & *m* alcoholic. ~olímetro *m* Breathalyser . ~olismo *m* alcoholism

alcornoque *m* cork-oak; (persona torpe) idiot

aldaba *f* door-knocker

aldea *f* village. ~ano *a* village. ● *m* villager

alea|ción *f* alloy. ~r *vt* alloy

aleatorio *a* uncertain

aleccionar *vt* instruct

aledaños *mpl* outskirts

alega|ción *f* allegation; (LAm, disputa) argument. ~r [12] *vt* claim; (Jurid) plead. ● *vi* (LAm) argue. ~ta *f* (Mex) argument. ~to *m* plea

alegoría *f* allegory

alegr|ar *vt* make happy; (avivar) brighten up. □ ~arse *vpr* be happy; (emborracharse) get merry. ~e *a* happy; (achispado) merry, tight. ~ía *f* happiness

aleja|do *a* distant. ~amiento *m* removal; (entre personas) estrangement; (distancia) distance. ∼**r** *vt* remove; (ahuyentar) get rid of; (fig, apartar) separate. □ ∼**rse** *vpr* move away

alemán *a* & *m* German

Alemania *f* Germany. ∼ **Occidental** (historia) West Germany. ∼ **Oriental** (historia) East Germany

alenta|dor *a* encouraging. ∼**r** [1] *vt* encourage. ● *vi* breathe

alerce *m* larch

al|ergia *f* allergy. ∼**érgico** *a* allergic

alero *m* (del tejado) eaves

alerta *a* alert. ¡∼! look out! estar ∼ be alert; (en guardia) be on the alert. ∼**r** *vt* alert

aleta *f* wing; (de pez) fin

aletarga|do *a* lethargic. ∼**r** [12] *vt* make lethargic. □ ∼**rse** *vpr* become lethargic

alet|azo *m* (de un ave) flap of the wings; (de un pez) flick of the fin. ∼**ear** *vi* flap its wings, flutter

alevosía *f* treachery

alfab|ético *a* alphabetical. ∼**etizar** [10] *vt* alphabetize; teach to read and write. ∼**eto** *m* alphabet. ∼**eto Morse** Morse code

alfalfa *f* alfalfa

alfarería *m* pottery. ∼**ero** *m* potter

alféizar *m* (window)sill

alférez *m* second lieutenant

alfil *m* (en ajedrez) bishop

alfile|r *m* pin. ∼**tero** *m* pincushion; (estuche) pin-case

alfombr|a *f* (grande) carpet; (pequeña) rug, mat. ∼**ado** *a* (LAm) carpeted. ∼**ar** *vt* carpet. ∼**illa** *f* rug, mat; (Med) type of measles

alforja *f* saddle-bag

algarabía *f* hubbub

algas *fpl* seaweed

álgebra *f* algebra

álgido *a* (fig) decisive

algo *pron* something; (en frases interrogativas, condicionales) anything. ● *adv* rather. ¿∼ **más?** anything else? ¿**quieres tomar** ∼? would you like a drink?; (de comer) would you like something to eat?

algod|ón *m* cotton. ∼**ón de azúcar** candy floss (Brit), cotton candy (Amer).

∼**ón hidrófilo** cotton wool. ∼**onero** *a* cotton. ● *m* cotton plant

alguacil *m* bailiff

alguien *pron* someone, somebody; (en frases interrogativas, condicionales) anyone, anybody

alguno *a* (delante de nombres masculinos en singular **algún**) some; (en frases interrogativas, condicionales) any; (pospuesto al nombre en frases negativas) at all. **no tiene idea alguna** he hasn't any idea at all. **alguna que otra vez** from time to time. **algunas veces, alguna vez** sometimes. ● *pron* one; (en plural) some; (alguien) someone

alhaja *f* piece of jewellery; (fig) treasure. ∼**s** *fpl* jewellery

alharaca *f* fuss

alhelí *m* wallflower

alia|do *a* allied. ● *m* ally. ∼**nza** *f* alliance; (anillo) wedding ring. ∼**r** [20] *vt* combine. □ ∼**rse** *vpr* be combined; (formar una alianza) form an alliance

alias *adv* & *m* alias

alicaído *a* (fig, débil) weak; (fig, abatido) depressed

alicates *mpl* pliers

aliciente *m* incentive; (de un lugar) attraction

alienado *a* mentally ill

aliento *m* breath; (ánimo) courage

aligerar *vt* make lighter; (aliviar) alleviate, ease; (apresurar) quicken

alijo *m* (de contrabando) consignment

alimaña *f* pest. ∼**s** *fpl* vermin

aliment|ación *f* diet; (acción) feeding. ∼**ar** *vt* feed; (nutrir) nourish. ● *vi* be nourishing. □ ∼**arse** *vpr* feed (con, de on). ∼**icio** *a* nourishing. **productos** *mpl* ∼**icios** foodstuffs. ∼**o** *m* food. ∼**os** *mpl* (Jurid) alimony

alinea|ción *f* alignment; (en deportes) line-up. ∼**r** *vt* align, line up

aliñ|ar *vt* (Culin) season; dress <*ensalada*>. ∼**o** *m* seasoning; (para ensalada) dressing

alioli *m* garlic mayonnaise

alisar *vt* smooth

alistar *vt* put on a list; (Mil) enlist. □ ∼**se** *vpr* enrol; (Mil) enlist; (LAm, prepararse) get ready

alivi|ar *vt* lighten; relieve <*dolor, etc*>; (⊠, hurtar) steal, pinch ⬛. □ ~**arse** *vpr* <*dolor*> diminish; <*persona*> get better. ~**o** *m* relief

aljibe *m* tank

allá *adv* (over) there. ¡~ él! that's his business. ~ **fuera** out there. ~ **por 1970** back in 1970. **el más** ~ the beyond. **más** ~ further on. **más** ~ **de** beyond. **por** ~ that way

allana|miento *m*. ~**miento** (de morada) breaking and entering; (LAm, por la autoridad) raid. ~**r** *vt* level; remove <*obstáculos*>; (fig) iron out <*dificultades etc*>; break into <*una casa*>; (LAm, por la autoridad) raid

allega|do *a* close. ● *m* close friend; (pariente) close relative. ~**r** [12] *vt* collect

allí *adv* there; (tiempo) then. ~ **fuera** out there. **por** ~ that way

alma *f* soul; (habitante) inhabitant

almac|én *m* warehouse; (LAm, tienda) grocer's shop; (de un arma) magazine. ~**enes** *mpl* department store. ~**enaje** *m* storage; (derechos) storage charges. ~**enar** *vt* store; stock up with <*provisiones*>

almanaque *m* almanac

almeja *f* clam

almendr|a *f* almond. ~**ado** *a* almond-shaped. ~**o** *m* almond tree

alm|íbar *m* syrup. ~**ibarar** *vt* cover in syrup

almid|ón *m* starch. ~**onado** *a* starched; (fig, estirado) starchy

almirante *m* admiral

almizcle *m* musk. ~**ra** *f* muskrat

almohad|a *f* pillow. **consultar con la** ~**a** sleep on it. ~**illa** *f* small cushion. ~**ón** *m* large pillow, bolster

almorranas *fpl* haemorrhoids, piles

alm|orzar [2 & 10] *vt* (a mediodía) have for lunch; (desayunar) have for breakfast. ● *vi* (a mediodía) have lunch; (desayunar) have breakfast. ~**uerzo** *m* (a mediodía) lunch; (desayuno) breakfast

alocado *a* scatter-brained

aloja|miento *m* accommodation. ~**r** *vt* put up. □ ~**rse** *vpr* stay

alondra *f* lark

alpaca *f* alpaca

alpargata *f* canvas shoe, espadrille

alpin|ismo *m* mountaineering, climbing. ~**ista** *m* & *f* mountaineer, climber. ~**o** *a* Alpine

alpiste *m* birdseed

alquil|ar *vt* (tomar en alquiler) hire <*vehículo*>, rent <*piso, casa*>; (dar en alquiler) hire (out) <*vehículo*>, rent (out) <*piso, casa*>. **se alquila** to let (Brit), for rent (Amer.) ~**er** *m* (acción — de alquilar un piso etc) renting; (— de alquilar un vehículo) hiring; (precio — por el que se alquila un piso etc) rent; (— por el que se alquila un vehículo) hire charge. **de** ~**er** for hire

alquimi|a *f* alchemy. ~**sta** *m* alchemist

alquitrán *m* tar

alrededor *adv* around. ~ **de** around; (con números) about. ~**es** *mpl* surroundings; (de una ciudad) outskirts

alta *f* discharge

altaner|ía *f* (arrogancia) arrogance. ~**o** *a* arrogant, haughty

altar *m* altar

altavoz *m* loudspeaker

altera|ble *a* changeable. ~**ción** *f* change, alteration. ~**r** *vt* change, alter; (perturbar) disturb; (enfadar) anger, irritate. □ ~**rse** *vpr* change, alter; (agitarse) get upset; (enfadarse) get angry; <*comida*> go off

altercado *m* argument

altern|ar *vt/i* alternate. □ ~**arse** *vpr* take turns. ~**ativa** *f* alternative. ~**ativo** *a* alternating. ~**o** *a* alternate; (Elec) alternating

Alteza *f* (título) Highness

altibajos *mpl* (de terreno) unevenness; (fig) ups and downs

altiplanicie *f*, **altiplano** *m* high plateau

altisonante *a* pompous

altitud *f* altitude

altiv|ez *f* arrogance. ~**o** *a* arrogant

alto *a* high; <*persona, edificio*> tall; <*voz*> loud; (fig, elevado) lofty; (Mus) <*nota*> high(-pitched); (Mus) <*voz, instrumento*> alto; <*horas*> early. ● *adv* high; (de sonidos) loud(ly). ● *m* height; (de un edificio) top floor; (viola)

viola; (voz) alto; (parada) stop. ● *int* halt!, stop! **en lo ~ de** on the top of. **tiene 3 metros de ~** it is 3 metres high

altoparlante *m* (esp LAm) loud-speaker

altruis|mo *m* altruism. **~ta** *a* altruistic. ● *m & f* altruist

altura *f* height; (Aviac, Geog) altitude; (de agua) depth; (fig, cielo) sky. **a estas ~s** at this stage. **tiene 3 metros de ~** it is 3 metres high

alubia *f* (haricot) bean

alucinación *f* hallucination

alud *m* avalanche

aludi|do *a* in question. **darse por ~do** take it personally. **no darse por ~do** turn a deaf ear. **~r** *vi* mention

alumbra|do *a* lit. ● *m* lighting. **~miento** *m* lighting; (parto) child-birth. **~r** *vt* light

aluminio *m* aluminium (Brit), aluminum (Amer)

alumno *m* pupil; (Univ) student

aluniza|je *m* landing on the moon. **~r** [10] *vi* land on the moon

alusi|ón *f* allusion. **~vo** *a* allusive

alza *f* rise. **~da** *f* (de caballo) height; (Jurid) appeal. **~do** *a* raised; (Mex, soberbio) vain; <*precio*> fixed. **~miento** *m* (Pol) uprising. **~r** [10] *vt* raise, lift (up); raise <*precios*>. □ **~rse** *vpr* (Pol) rise up

ama *f* lady of the house. **~ de casa** housewife. **~ de cría** wet-nurse. **~ de llaves** housekeeper

amab|ilidad *f* kindness. **~le** *a* kind; (simpático) nice

amaestra|do *a* trained. **~r** *vt* train

amag|ar [12] *vt* (mostrar intención de) make as if to; (Mex, amenazar) threaten. ● *vi* threaten; <*algo bueno*> be in the offing. **~o** *m* threat; (señal) sign; (Med) symptom

amainar *vi* let up

amalgama *f* amalgam. **~r** *vt* amalgamate

amamantar *vt/i* breast-feed; <*animal*> to suckle

amanecer *m* dawn. ● *vi* dawn; <*persona*> wake up. **al ~** at dawn, at daybreak. □ **~se** *vpr* (Mex) stay up all night

amanera|do *a* affected. □ **~rse** *vpr* become affected

amansar *vt* tame; break in <*un caballo*>; soothe <*dolor etc*>. □ **~se** *vpr* calm down

amante *a* fond. ● *m & f* lover

amapola *f* poppy

amar *vt* love

amara|je *m* landing on water; (de astronave) splash-down. **~r** *vi* land on water; <*astronave*> splash down

amarg|ado *a* embittered. **~ar** [12] *vt* make bitter; embitter <*persona*>. □ **~arse** *vpr* become bitter. **~o** *a* bitter. **~ura** *f* bitterness

amariconado *a* 🅣 effeminate

amarill|ento *a* yellowish; <*tez*> sallow. **~o** *a & m* yellow

amarra|s *fpl*. **soltar las ~s** cast off. **~do** *a* (LAm) mean. **~r** *vt* moor; (esp LAm, atar) tie. □ **~rse** *vpr* LAm tie up

amas|ar *vt* knead; (acumular) to amass. **~ijo** *m* dough; (acción) kneading; (fig, 🅣, mezcla) hotchpotch

amate *m* (Mex) fig tree

amateur *a & m & f* amateur

amazona *f* Amazon; (jinete) horse-woman

ámbar *m* amber

ambici|ón *f* ambition. **~onar** *vt* aspire to. **~onar ser** have an ambition to be. **~oso** *a* ambitious. ● *m* ambitious person

ambidextro *a* ambidextrous. ● *m* ambidextrous person

ambient|ar *vt* give an atmosphere to. □ **~arse** *vpr* adapt o.s. **~e** *m* atmosphere; (entorno) environment

ambig|üedad *f* ambiguity. **~uo** *a* ambiguous

ámbito *m* sphere; (alcance) scope

ambos *a & pron* both

ambulancia *f* ambulance

ambulante *a* travelling

ambulatorio *m* out-patients' department

amedrentar *vt* frighten, scare. □ **~se** *vpr* be frightened

amén *m* amen. ● *int* amen! **en un decir ~** in an instant

amenaza f threat. ~r [10] vt threaten

amen|idad f pleasantness. ~izar [10] vt brighten up. ~o a pleasant

América f America. ~ Central Central America. ~ del Norte North America. ~ del Sur South America. ~ Latina Latin America

american|a f jacket. ~ismo m Americanism. ~o a American

amerita|do a (LAm) meritorious. ~r vt (LAm) deserve

amerizaje m →AMARAJE

ametralla|dora f machine-gun. ~r vt machine-gun

amianto m asbestos

amig|a f friend; (novia) girl-friend; (amante) lover. ~able a friendly. ~ablemente adv amicably

am|ígdala f tonsil. ~igdalitis f tonsillitis

amigo a friendly. ● m friend; (novio) boyfriend; (amante) lover. ser ~ de be fond of. ser muy ~s be close friends

amilanar vt daunt. □ ~se vpr be daunted

aminorar vt lessen; reduce <velocidad>

amist|ad f friendship. ~ades fpl friends. ~oso a friendly

amn|esia f amnesia. ~ésico a amnesiac

amnist|ía f amnesty. ~iar [20] vt grant an amnesty to

amo m master; (dueño) owner

amodorrarse vpr feel sleepy

amoldar vt mould; (adaptar) adapt; (acomodar) fit. □ ~se vpr adapt

amonestar vt rebuke, reprimand; (anunciar la boda) publish the banns

amoniaco, **amoníaco** m ammonia

amontonar vt pile up; (fig, acumular) accumulate. □ ~se vpr pile up; <gente> crowd together

amor m love. ~es mpl (relaciones amorosas) love affairs. ~ propio pride. con mil ~es, de mil ~es with (the greatest of) pleasure. hacer el ~ make love. por (el) ~ de Dios for God's sake

amoratado a purple; (de frío) blue

amordazar [10] vt gag; (fig) silence

amorfo a amorphous, shapeless

amor|ío m affair. ~oso a loving; <cartas> love; (LAm), encantador) cute

amortajar vt shroud

amortigua|dor a deadening. ● m (Auto) shock absorber. ~r [15] vt deaden <ruido>; dim <luz>; cushion <golpe>; tone down <color>

amortiza|ble a redeemable. ~ción f (de una deuda) repayment; (de bono etc) redemption. ~r [10] vt repay <una deuda>

amotinar vt incite to riot. □ ~se vpr rebel; (Mil) mutiny

ampar|ar vt help; (proteger) protect. □ ~arse vpr seek protection; (de la lluvia) shelter. ~o m protection; (de la lluvia) shelter. al ~o de under the protection of

amperio m ampere, amp

amplia|ción f extension; (photo) enlargement. ~r [20] vt enlarge, extend; (photo) enlarge

amplifica|ción f amplification. ~dor m amplifier. ~r [7] amplify

ampli|o a wide; (espacioso) spacious; <ropa> loose-fitting. ~tud f extent; (espaciosidad) spaciousness; (espacio) space

ampolla f (Med) blister; (de medicamento) ampoule, phial

ampuloso a pompous

amputar vt amputate; (fig) delete

amueblar vt furnish

amuleto m charm, amulet

amuralla|do a walled. ~r vt build a wall around

anacr|ónico a anachronistic. ~onismo m anachronism

anales mpl annals

analfabet|ismo m illiteracy. ~o a & m illiterate

analgésico a analgesic. ● m painkiller

an|álisis m invar analysis. ~álisis de sangre blood test. ~alista m & f analyst. ~alítico a analytical. ~alizar [10] vt analyze

an|alogía f analogy. ~álogo a analogous

anaranjado a orangey

an|arquía f anarchy. **~árquico** a anarchic. **~arquismo** m anarchism. **~arquista** a anarchistic. ● m & f anarchist

anat|omía f anatomy. **~ómico** a anatomical

anca f haunch; (parte superior) rump; (🄵, nalgas) bottom. **en ~s** (LAm) on the crupper

ancestro m ancestor

ancho a wide; <ropa> loose-fitting; (fig) relieved; (demasiado grande) too big; (ufano) smug. ● m width; (Rail) gauge. **a mis anchas, a sus anchas** etc comfortable, relaxed. **tiene 3 metros de ~** it is 3 metres wide

anchoa f anchovy

anchura f width; (medida) measurement

ancian|o a elderly, old. ● m elderly man, old man. **~a** f elderly woman, old woman. **los ~os** old people

ancla f anchor. **echar ~s** drop anchor. **levar ~s** weigh anchor. **~r** vi anchor

andad|eras fpl (Mex) baby-walker. **~or** m baby-walker

Andalucía f Andalusia

andaluz a & m Andalusian

andamio m platform. **~s** mpl scaffolding

and|anzas fpl adventures. **~ar** [25] vt (recorrer) cover, go. ● vi walk; <máquina> go, work; (estar) be; (moverse) move. **~ar a caballo** (LAm) ride a horse. **~ar en bicicleta** (LAm) ride a bicycle. **¡anda!** go on!, come on! **~ar por** be about. □ **~arse** vpr (LAm, en imperativo) **¡ándate!** go away!. ● m walk. **~ariego** a fond of walking

andén m platform

Andes mpl. **los ~** the Andes

andin|o a Andean. **~ismo** m (LAm) mountaineering, climbing. **~ista** m & f (LAm) mountaineer, climber

andrajo m rag. **~so** a ragged

anduve vb ⇒ANDAR

anécdota f anecdote

anecdótico a anecdotal

anegar [12] vt flood. □ **~rse** vpr be flooded, flood

anejo a ⇒ANEXO

an|emia f anaemia. **~émico** a anaemic

anest|esia f anaesthesia; (droga) anaesthetic. **~esiar** vt anaesthetize. **~ésico** a & m anaesthetic. **~esista** m & f anaesthetist

anex|ar vt annex. **~o** a attached. ● m annexe

anfibio a amphibious. ● m amphibian

anfiteatro m amphitheatre; (en un teatro) upper circle

anfitri|ón m host. **~ona** f hostess

ángel m angel; (encanto) charm

angelical a, **angélico** a angelic

angina f. **~ de pecho** angina (pectoris). **tener ~s** have tonsillitis

anglicano a & m Anglican

angl|icismo m Anglicism. **~ófilo** a & m Anglophile. **~ohispánico** a Anglo-Spanish. **~osajón** a & m Anglo-Saxon

angosto a narrow

angu|ila f eel. **~la** f elver, baby eel

ángulo m angle; (rincón, esquina) corner; (curva) bend

angusti|a f anguish. **~ar** vt distress; (inquietar) worry. □ **~arse** vpr get distressed; (inquietarse) get worried. **~oso** a anguished; (que causa angustia) distressing

anhel|ar vt (+ nombre) long for; (+ verbo) long to. **~o** m (fig) yearning

anidar vi nest

anill|a f ring. **~o** m ring. **~o de boda** wedding ring

ánima f soul

anima|ción f (de personas) life; (de cosas) liveliness; (bullicio) bustle; (en el cine) animation. **~do** a lively; <sitio etc> busy. **~dor** m host. **~dora** f hostess; (de un equipo) cheerleader

animadversión f ill will

animal a animal; (fig, 🄵, torpe) stupid. ● m animal; (fig, 🄵, idiota) idiot; (fig, 🄵, bruto) brute

animar vt give life to; (dar ánimo) encourage; (dar vivacidad) liven up. □ **~se** vpr (decidirse) decide; (ponerse alegre) cheer up. **¿te animas a ir al cine?** do you feel like going to the cinema?

ánimo *m* soul; (mente) mind; (valor) courage; (intención) intention. ¡~! come on!, cheer up! **dar ~s** encourage

animos|idad *f* animosity. **~o** *a* brave; (resuelto) determined

aniquilar *vt* annihilate; (acabar con) ruin

anís *m* aniseed; (licor) anisette

aniversario *m* anniversary

anoche *adv* last night, yesterday evening

anochecer [11] *vi* get dark. **anochecí en Madrid** I was in Madrid at dusk. ● *m* nightfall, dusk. **al ~** at nightfall

anodino *a* bland

an|omalía *f* anomaly. **~ómalo** *a* anomalous

an|onimato *m* anonymity. **~ónimo** *a* anonymous; <sociedad> limited. ● *m* (carta) anonymous letter

anormal *a* abnormal. ● *m & f* 🔲 idiot. **~idad** *f* abnormality

anota|ción *f* (nota) note; (acción de poner notas) annotation. **~r** *vt* (poner nota) annotate; (apuntar) make a note of; (LAm) score <un gol>

anquilosa|miento *m* (fig) paralysis. □ **~rse** *vpr* become paralyzed

ansi|a *f* anxiety, worry; (anhelo) yearning. **~ar** [20] *vt* long for. **~edad** *f* anxiety. **~oso** *a* anxious; (deseoso) eager

antag|ónico *a* antagonistic. **~onismo** *m* antagonism. **~onista** *m & f* antagonist

antaño *adv* in days gone by

antártico *a & m* Antarctic

ante *prep* in front of, before; (frente a) in the face of; (en vista de) in view of. ● *m* elk; (piel) suede. **~anoche** *adv* the night before last. **~ayer** *adv* the day before yesterday. **~brazo** *m* forearm

antece|dente *a* previous. ● *m* antecedent. **~dentes** *mpl* history, background. **~dentes penales** criminal record. **~der** *vt* precede. **~sor** *m* predecessor; (antepasado) ancestor

antelación *f* (advance) notice. **con ~** in advance

antemano *adv*. **de ~** beforehand

antena *f* antenna; (radio, TV) aerial

antenoche *adv* (LAm) the night before last

anteoj|eras *fpl* blinkers. **~jo** *m* telescope. **~os** *mpl* binoculars; (LAm, gafas) glasses, spectacles. **~os de sol** sunglasses

ante|pasados *mpl* forebears, ancestors. **~poner** [34] *vt* put in front (**a** of); (fig) put before, prefer. **~proyecto** *m* preliminary sketch; (fig) blueprint

anterior *a* previous; (delantero) front. **~idad** *f*. **con ~idad** previously. **con ~idad a** prior to

antes *adv* before; (antiguamente) in the past; (mejor) rather; (primero) first. **~ de** before. **~ de ayer** the day before yesterday. **~ de que** + *subj* before. **~ de que llegue** before he arrives. **cuanto ~, lo ~ posible** as soon as possible

anti|aéreo *a* anti-aircraft. **~biótico** *a & m* antibiotic. **~ciclón** *m* anticyclone

anticip|ación *f*. **con ~ación** in advance. **con media hora de ~ación** half an hour early. **~ado** *a* advance. **por ~ado** in advance. **~ar** *vt* bring forward; advance <dinero>. □ **~arse** *vpr* be early. **~o** *m* (dinero) advance; (fig) foretaste

anti|conceptivo *a & m* contraceptive. **~congelante** *m* antifreeze

anticua|do *a* old-fashioned. **~rio** *m* antique dealer

anticuerpo *m* antibody

antídoto *m* antidote

anti|estético *a* ugly. **~faz** *m* mask

antig|ualla *f* old relic. **~uamente** *adv* formerly; (hace mucho tiempo) long ago. **~üedad** *f* antiquity; (objeto) antique; (en un empleo) length of service. **~uo** *a* old; <ruinas> ancient; <mueble> antique

Antillas *fpl*. **las ~** the West Indies

antílope *m* antelope

antinatural *a* unnatural

antip|atía *f* dislike; (cualidad de antipático) unpleasantness. **~ático** *a* unpleasant, unfriendly

anti|semita *m* & *f* anti-Semite. ∼**séptico** *a* & *m* antiseptic. ∼**social** *a* antisocial

antítesis *f invar* antithesis

antoj|adizo *a* capricious. ▢ ∼**arse** *vpr* fancy. **se le** ∼**a un caramelo** he fancies a sweet. ∼**itos** *mpl* (Mex) snacks bought at street stands. ∼**o** *m* whim; (de embarazada) craving

antología *f* anthology

antorcha *f* torch

antro *m* (fig) dump, hole. ∼ **de perversión** den of iniquity

antrop|ología *f* anthropology. ∼**ólogo** *m* anthropologist

anua|l *a* annual. ∼**lidad** *f* annuity. ∼**lmente** *adv* yearly. ∼**rio** *m* yearbook

anudar *vt* tie, knot. ▢ ∼**se** *vpr* tie

anula|ción *f* annulment, cancellation. ∼**r** *vt* annul, cancel. ● *a* <dedo> ring. ● *m* ring finger

anunci|ante *m* & *f* advertiser. ∼**ar** *vt* announce; advertise <producto comercial>; (presagiar) be a sign of. ∼**o** *m* announcement; (para vender algo) advertisement, advert Ⓔ; (cartel) poster

anzuelo *m* (fish)hook; (fig) bait. **tragar el** ∼ swallow the bait

añadi|dura *f* addition. **por** ∼**dura** in addition. ∼**r** *vt* add

añejo *a* <vino> mature

añicos *mpl*. **hacer(se)** ∼ smash to pieces

año *m* year. ∼ **bisiesto** leap year. ∼ **nuevo** new year. **al** ∼ per year, a year. **¿cuántos** ∼**s tiene?** how old is he? **tiene 5** ∼**s** he's 5 (years old). **el** ∼ **pasado** last year. **el** ∼ **que viene** next year. **entrado en** ∼**s** elderly. **los** ∼**s 60** the sixties

añora|nza *f* nostalgia. ∼**r** *vt* miss

apabulla|nte *a* overwhelming. ∼**r** *vt* overwhelm

apacible *a* gentle; <clima> mild

apaciguar [15] *vt* pacify; (calmar) calm; relieve <dolor etc>. ▢ ∼**se** *vpr* calm down

apadrinar *vt* sponsor; be godfather to <a un niño>

apag|ado *a* extinguished; <color> dull; <aparato eléctrico, luz> off;

<persona> lifeless; <sonido> muffled. ∼**ar** [12] *vt* put out <fuego, incendio>; turn off, switch off <aparato eléctrico, luz>; quench <sed>; muffle <sonido>. ▢ ∼**arse** *vpr* <fuego, luz> go out; <sonido> die away. ∼**ón** *m* blackout

apalabrar *vt* make a verbal agreement; (contratar) engage

apalear *vt* winnow <grano>; beat <alfombra, frutos, persona>

apantallar *vt* (Mex) impress

apañar *vt* (arreglar) fix; (remendar) mend; (agarrar) grasp, take hold of. ▢ ∼**se** *vpr* get along, manage

apapachar *vt* (Mex) cuddle

aparador *m* sideboard; (Mex, de tienda) shop window

aparato *m* apparatus; (máquina) machine; (doméstico) appliance; (teléfono) telephone; (radio, TV) set; (ostentación) show, pomp. ∼**so** *a* showy, ostentatious; <caída> spectacular

aparca|miento *m* car park (Brit), parking lot (Amer). ∼**r** [7] *vt/i* park

aparear *vt* mate <animales>. ▢ ∼**se** *vpr* mate

aparecer [11] *vi* appear. ▢ ∼**se** *vpr* appear

aparej|ado *a*. **llevar** ∼**ado, traer** ∼**ado** mean, entail. ∼**o** *m* (avíos) equipment; (de caballo) tack; (de pesca) tackle

aparent|ar *vt* (afectar) feign; (parecer) look. ● *vi* show off. ∼**a 20 años** she looks like she's 20. ∼**e** *a* apparent

apari|ción *f* appearance; (visión) apparition. ∼**encia** *f* appearance; (fig) show. **guardar las** ∼**encias** keep up appearances

apartado *a* separated; (aislado) isolated. ● *m* (de un texto) section. ∼ **(de correos)** post-office box, PO box

apartamento *m* apartment, flat (Brit)

apart|ar *vt* separate; (alejar) move away; (quitar) remove; (guardar) set aside. ▢ ∼**arse** *vpr* leave; (quitarse de en medio) get out of the way; (aislarse) cut o.s. off. ∼**e** *adv* apart; (por separado) separately; (además) besides. ● *m* aside; (párrafo) new paragraph. ∼**e de**

apart from. **dejar** ~**e** leave aside. **eso** ~**e** apart from that

apasiona|do *a* passionate; (entusiasta) enthusiastic; (falto de objetividad) biased. ● *m.* ~**do de** lover. ~**miento** *m* passion. ~**r** *vt* excite. □ ~**rse** *vpr* be mad (**por** about); (ser parcial) become biased

ap|atía *f* apathy. ~**ático** *a* apathetic

apea|dero *m* (Rail) halt. □ ~**rse** *vpr* get off

apechugar [12] *vi* 🗉 ~ **con** put up with

apedrear *vt* stone

apeg|ado *a* attached (**a** to). ~**o** *m* 🗉 attachment. **tener** ~**o a** be fond of

apela|ción *f* appeal. ~**r** *vi* appeal; (recurrir) resort (**a** to). ● *vt* (apodar) call. ~**tivo** *m* (nick)name

apellid|ar *vt* call. □ ~**arse** *vpr* be called. ¿**cómo te apellidas?** what's your surname? ~**o** *m* surname

apelmazarse *vpr* <lana> get matted

apenar *vt* sadden; (LAm, avergonzar) embarrass. □ ~**se** *vpr* be sad; (LAm, avergonzarse) be embarrassed

apenas *adv* hardly, scarcely; (Mex, sólo) only. ● *conj* (esp LAm, en cuanto) as soon as. ~ **si** 🗉 hardly

ap|éndice *m* appendix. ~**endicitis** *f* appendicitis

apergaminado *a* <piel> wrinkled

aperitivo *m* (bebida) aperitif; (comida) appetizer

aperos *mpl* implements; (de labranza) agricultural equipment; (LAm, de un caballo) tack

apertura *f* opening

apesadumbrar *vt* upset. □ ~**se** *vpr* sadden

apestar *vt* infect. ● *vi* stink (**a** of)

apet|ecer [11] *vi.* ¿**te** ~**ece una copa?** do you fancy a drink? do you feel like a drink?. **no me** ~**ece** I don't feel like it. ~**ecible** *a* attractive. ~**ito** *m* appetite; (fig) desire. ~**itoso** *a* appetizing

apiadarse *vpr* feel sorry (**de** for)

ápice *m* (nada, en frases negativas) anything. **no ceder un** ~ not give an inch

apilar *vt* pile up

apiñar *vt* pack in. □ ~**se** *vpr* <personas> crowd together; <cosas> be packed tight

apio *m* celery

aplacar [7] *vt* placate; soothe <dolor>

aplanar *vt* level. ~ **calles** (LAm 🗉) loaf around

aplasta|nte *a* overwhelming. ~**r** *vt* crush. □ ~**rse** *vpr* flatten o.s.

aplau|dir *vt* clap, applaud; (fig) applaud. ~**so** *m* applause; (fig) praise

aplaza|miento *m* postponement. ~**r** [10] *vt* postpone; defer <pago>

aplica|ble *a* applicable. ~**ción** *f* application. ~**do** *a* <persona> diligent. ~**r** [7] *vt* apply. ● *vi* (LAm, a un puesto) apply (for). □ ~**rse** *vpr* apply o.s.

aplom|ado *a* composed. ~**o** *m* composure

apocado *a* timid

apocar [7] *vt* belittle <persona>. □ ~**se** *vpr* feel small

apodar *vt* nickname

apodera|do *m* representative. □ ~**rse** *vpr* seize

apodo *m* nickname

apogeo *m* (fig) height

apolilla|do *a* moth-eaten. □ ~**rse** *vpr* get moth-eaten

apolítico *a* non-political

apología *f* defence

apoltronarse *vpr* settle o.s. down

apoplejía *f* stroke

aporrear *vt* hit, thump; beat up <persona>

aport|ación *f* contribution. ~**ar** *vt* contribute. ~**e** *m* (LAm) contribution

aposta *adv* on purpose

apostar[1] [2] *vt/i* bet

apostar[2] *vt* station. □ ~**se** *vpr* station o.s.

apóstol *m* apostle

apóstrofo *m* apostrophe

apoy|ar *vt* lean (**en** against); (descansar) rest; (asentar) base; (reforzar) support. □ ~**arse** *vpr* lean, rest. ~**o** *m* support

apreci|able *a* appreciable; (digno de estima) worthy. ~**ación** *f* appreci-

ation; (valoración) appraisal. ~**ar** *vt*
value; (estimar) appreciate. ~**o** *m* appraisal; (fig) esteem

apremi|ante *a* urgent, pressing.
~**ar** *vt* urge; (obligar) compel; (dar prisa
a) hurry up. ● *vi* be urgent. ~**o** *m*
urgency; (obligación) obligation

aprender *vt/i* learn. □ ~**se** *vpr*
learn

aprendiz *m* apprentice. ~**aje** *m*
learning; (período) apprenticeship

aprensi|ón *f* apprehension; (miedo)
fear. ~**vo** *a* apprehensive, fearful

apresar *vt* seize; (capturar) capture

aprestar *vt* prepare. □ ~**se** *vpr*
prepare

apresura|do *a* in a hurry; (hecho
con prisa) hurried. ~**r** *vt* hurry.
□ ~**rse** *vpr* hurry up

apret|ado *a* tight; (difícil) difficult;
(tacaño) stingy, mean. ~**ar** [1] *vt*
tighten; press <*botón*>; squeeze
<*persona*>; (comprimir) press down. ●
vi be too tight. □ ~**arse** *vpr* crowd
together. ~**ón** *m* squeeze. ~**ón de
manos** handshake

aprieto *m* difficulty. **verse en un** ~
be in a tight spot

aprisa *adv* quickly

aprisionar *vt* trap

aproba|ción *f* approval. ~**r** [2] *vt*
approve (of); pass <*examen*>. ● *vi*
pass

apropia|ción *f* appropriation.
~**do** *a* appropriate. ~**rse** *vpr*. ~**rse
de** appropriate, take

aprovecha|ble *a* usable. ~**do** *a*
(aplicado) diligent; (ingenioso) resourceful; (oportunista) opportunist. **bien
~do** well spent. ~**miento** *m* advantage; (uso) use. ~**r** *vt* take advantage
of; (utilizar) make use of. ● *vi* make
the most of it. **¡que aproveche!** enjoy
your meal! □ ~**rse** *vpr*. ~**rse de**
take advantage of

aprovisionar *vt* provision (con, de
with). □ ~**se** *vpr* stock up

aproxima|ción *f* approximation;
(proximidad) closeness; (en la lotería)
consolation prize. ~**damente** *adv*
roughly, approximately. ~**do** *a* approximate, rough. ~**r** *vt* bring near;

(fig) bring together <*personas*>.
□ ~**rse** *vpr* come closer, approach

apt|itud *f* suitability; (capacidad) ability. ~**o** *a* (capaz) capable; (adecuado)
suitable

apuesta *f* bet

apuesto *m* handsome. ● *vb* ⇒APOS-
TAR ¹

apuntalar *vt* shore up

apunt|ar *vt* aim <*arma*>; (señalar)
point at; (anotar) make a note of, note
down; (inscribir) enrol; (en el teatro)
prompt. ● *vi* (con un arma) to aim (a
at). □ ~**arse** *vpr* put one's name
down; score <*triunfo, tanto etc*>. ~**e**
m note; (bosquejo) sketch. **tomar** ~**s**
take notes

apuñalar *vt* stab

apur|ado *a* difficult; (sin dinero) hard
up; (LAm, con prisa) in a hurry. ~**ar** *vt*
(acabar) finish; drain <*vaso etc*>; (causar vergüenza) embarrass; (LAm, apresurar) hurry. □ ~**arse** *vpr* worry; (LAm,
apresurarse) hurry up. ~**o** *m* tight
spot, difficult situation; (vergüenza)
embarrassment; (estrechez) hardship,
want; (LAm, prisa) hurry

aquejar *vt* afflict

aquel *a* (*f* **aquella**, *mpl* **aquellos**,
fpl **aquellas**) that; (en plural) those

aquél *pron* (*f* **aquélla**, *mpl* **aquéllos**, *fpl* **aquéllas**) that one; (en plural) those

aquello *pron* that; (asunto) that business

aquí *adv* here. **de** ~ from here. **de** ~
a 15 días in a fortnight's time. ~
mismo right here. **de** ~ **para allá** to
and fro. **de** ~ **que** that is why. **hasta**
~ until now. **por** ~ around here

aquietar *vt* calm (down)

árabe *a* & *m* & *f* Arab; (lengua) Arabic

Arabia *f* Arabia. ~ **Saudita**, ~ **Saudí**
Saudi Arabia

arado *m* plough. ~**r** *m* ploughman

arancel *m* tariff; (impuesto) duty.
~**ario** *a* tariff

arandela *f* washer

araña *f* spider; (lámpara) chandelier.
~**r** *vt* scratch

arar *vt* plough

arbitra|je *m* arbitration; (en deportes) refereeing. **~r** *vt/i* arbitrate; (en fútbol etc) referee; (en tenis etc) umpire

arbitr|ariedad *f* arbitrariness. **~ario** *a* arbitrary. **~io** *m* (free) will

árbitro *m* arbitrator; (en fútbol etc) referee; (en tenis etc) umpire

árbol *m* tree; (eje) axle; (palo) mast. **~ genealógico** family tree. **~ de Navidad** Christmas tree

arbol|ado *m* trees. **~eda** *f* wood

arbusto *m* bush

arca *f* (caja) chest. **~ de Noé** Noah's ark

arcada *f* arcade; (de un puente) arch; (náuseas) retching

arcaico *a* archaic

arce *m* maple (tree)

arcén *m* (de autopista) hard shoulder; (de carretera) verge

archipiélago *m* archipelago

archiv|ador *m* filing cabinet. **~ar** *vt* file (away). **~o** *m* file; (de documentos históricos) archives

arcilla *f* clay

arco *m* arch; (Elec, Mat) arc; (Mus, arma) bow; (LAm, en fútbol) goal. **~ iris** rainbow

arder *vi* burn; (LAm, escocer) sting; (fig, de ira) seethe. **estar que arde** be very tense

ardid *m* trick, scheme

ardiente *a* burning

ardilla *f* squirrel

ardor *m* heat; (fig) ardour; (LAm, escozor) smarting. **~ de estómago** heartburn

arduo *a* arduous

área *f* area

arena *f* sand; (en deportes) arena; (en los toros) (bull)ring. **~ movediza** quicksand

arenoso *a* sandy

arenque *m* herring. **~ ahumado** kipper

arete *m* (Mex) earring

Argel *m* Algiers. **~ia** *f* Algeria

Argentina *f* Argentina

argentino *a* Argentinian, Argentine. ● *m* Argentinian

argolla *f* ring. **~ de matrimonio** (LAm) wedding ring

arg|ot *m* slang. **~ótico** *a* slang

argucia *f* cunning argument

argüir [19] *vt* (probar) prove, show; (argumentar) argue. ● *vi* argue

argument|ación *f* argument. **~ar** *vt/i* argue. **~o** *m* argument; (de libro, película etc) story, plot

aria *f* aria

aridez *f* aridity, dryness

árido *a* arid, dry. **~s** *mpl* dry goods

Aries *m* Aries

arisco *a* unfriendly

arist|ocracia *f* aristocracy. **~ócrata** *m* & *f* aristocrat. **~ocrático** *a* aristocratic

aritmética *f* arithmetic

arma *f* arm, weapon; (sección) section. **~ de fuego** firearm. **~da** *f* navy; (flota) fleet. **~do** *a* armed (de with). **~dura** *f* armour; (de gafas etc) frame; (Tec) framework. **~mentismo** *m* build up of arms. **~mento** *m* arms, armaments; (acción de armar) armament. **~r** *vt* arm (de with); (montar) put together. **~r un lío** kick up a fuss

armario *m* cupboard; (para ropa) wardrobe (Brit), closet (Amer)

armatoste *m* huge great thing

armazón *m* & *f* frame(work)

armiño *m* ermine

armisticio *m* armistice

armonía *f* harmony

armónica *f* harmonica, mouth organ

armoni|oso *a* harmonious. **~zar** [10] *vt* harmonize. ● *vi* harmonize; *<personas>* get on well (con with); *<colores>* go well (con with)

arn|és *m* armour. **~eses** *mpl* harness

aro *m* ring, hoop

arom|a *m* aroma; (de flores) scent; (de vino) bouquet. **~ático** *a* aromatic

arpa *f* harp

arpía *f* harpy; (fig) hag

arpillera *f* sackcloth, sacking

arpón *m* harpoon

arquear *vt* arch, bend. □ **~se** *vpr* arch, bend

arque|ología f archaeology. ~ológico a archaeological. ~ólogo m archaeologist

arquero m archer; (LAm, en fútbol) goalkeeper

arquitect|o m architect. ~ónico a architectural. ~ura f architecture

arrabal m suburb; (barrio pobre) poor area. ~es mpl outskirts. ~ero a suburban; (de modales groseros) common

arraiga|do a deeply rooted. ~r [12] vi take root. □ ~rse vpr take root; (fig) settle

arran|car [7] vt pull up <planta>; pull out <diente>; (arrebatar) snatch; (Auto) start. ● vi start. □ ~carse vpr pull out. ~que m sudden start; (Auto) start; (fig) outburst

arras fpl security; (en boda) coins

arrasar vt level, smooth; raze to the ground <edificio etc>; (llenar) fill to the brim. ● vi (en deportes) sweep to victory; (en política) win a landslide victory

arrastr|ar vt pull; (por el suelo) drag (along); give rise to <consecuencias>. ● vi trail on the ground. □ ~arse vpr crawl; (humillarse) grovel. ~e m dragging; (transporte) haulage. estar para el ~e 🔲 be done in

arre int gee up! ~ar vt urge on

arrebat|ado a (irreflexivo) impetuous. ~ar vt snatch (away); (fig) win (over); captivate <corazón etc>. □ ~arse vpr get carried away. ~o m (de cólera etc) fit; (éxtasis) extasy

arrech|ar vt (LAm 🔲, enfurecer) to infuriate. □ ~se vpr get furious. ~o a furious

arrecife m reef

arregl|ado a neat; (bien vestido) well-dressed; (LAm, amañado) fixed. ~ar vt arrange; (poner en orden) tidy up; sort out <asunto, problema etc>; (reparar) mend. □ ~arse vpr (solucionarse) get sorted out; (prepararse) get ready; (apañarse) manage, make do; (ponerse de acuerdo) come to an agreement. ~árselas manage, get by. ~o m (incl Mus) arrangement; (acción de reparar) repair; (acuerdo) agreement; (solución) solution. con ~o a according to

arrellanarse vpr settle o.s. (en into)

arremangar [12] vt roll up <mangas>; tuck up <falda>. □ ~se vpr roll up one's sleeves

arremeter vi charge (contra at); (atacar) attack

arremolinarse vpr mill about; <el agua> to swirl

arrenda|dor m landlord. ~dora f landlady. ~miento m renting; (contrato) lease; (precio) rent. ~r [1] vt (dar casa en alquiler) let; (dar cosa en alquiler) hire out; (tomar en alquiler) rent. ~tario m tenant

arreos mpl tack

arrepenti|miento m repentance, regret. ~rse [4] vpr (retractarse) to change one's mind; (lamentarse) be sorry. ~rse de regret; repent of <pecados>

arrest|ar vt arrest, detain; (encarcelar) imprison. ~o m arrest; (encarcelamiento) imprisonment

arriar [20] vt lower <bandera, vela>

arriba adv up; (dirección) up(wards); (en casa) upstairs. ● int up with; (¡levántate!) up you get!; (¡ánimo!) come on! ¡~ España! long live Spain! ~ de (LAm) on top of. ~ mencionado aforementioned. calle ~ up the street. de ~ abajo from top to bottom. de 100 pesetas para ~ over 100 pesetas. escaleras ~ upstairs. la parte de ~ the top part. los de ~ those at the top. más ~ higher up

arrib|ar vi <barco> reach port; (esp LAm, llegar) arrive. ~ista m & f social climber. ~o m (esp LAm) arrival

arriero m muleteer

arriesga|do a risky; <person> daring. ~r [12] vt risk; (aventurar) venture. □ ~rse vpr take a risk

arrim|ar vt bring close(r). □ ~arse vpr come closer, approach; (apoyarse) lean (a on). ~o m protection. al ~o de with the help of

arrincona|do a forgotten; (acorralado) cornered. ~r vt put in a corner; (perseguir) corner (arrumbar) put aside. □ ~rse vpr become a recluse

arrocero a rice

arrodillarse vpr kneel (down)

arrogan|cia *f* arrogance; (orgullo) pride. **~te** *a* arrogant; (orgulloso) proud

arroj|ar *vt* throw; (emitir) give off, throw out; (producir) produce. ● *vi* (esp LAm, vomitar) throw up. □ **~arse** *vpr* throw o.s. **~o** *m* courage

arrollar *vt* roll (up); (atropellar) run over; (vencer) crush

arropar *vt* wrap up; (en la cama) tuck up. □ **~se** *vpr* wrap (o.s.) up

arroy|o *m* stream; (de una calle) gutter. **~uelo** *m* small stream

arroz *m* rice. **~ con leche** rice pudding. **~al** *m* rice field

arruga *f* (en la piel) wrinkle, line; (en tela) crease. **~r** [12] *vt* wrinkle; crumple *<papel>*; crease *<tela>*. □ **~rse** *vpr* *<la piel>* become wrinkled; *<tela>* crease, get creased

arruinar *vt* ruin; (destruir) destroy. □ **~se** *vpr* *<persona>* be ruined

arrullar *vt* lull to sleep. ● *vi* *<palomas>* coo

arrumbar *vt* put aside

arsenal *m* (astillero) shipyard; (de armas) arsenal; (fig) mine

arsénico *m* arsenic

arte *m* (*f en plural*) art; (habilidad) skill; (astucia) cunning. **bellas ~s** fine arts. **con ~** skilfully. **malas ~s** trickery. **por amor al ~** for the fun of it

artefacto *m* device

arteria *f* artery; (fig, calle) main road

artesan|al *a* craft. **~ía** *f* handicrafts. **objeto** *m* **de ~ía** traditional craft object. **~o** *m* artisan, craftsman

ártico *a* Arctic. **Á~** *m*. **el Á~** the Arctic

articula|ción *f* joint; (pronunciación) articulation. **~do** *a* articulated; *<lenguaje>* articulate. **~r** *vt* articulate

artículo *m* article. **~s** *mpl* (géneros) goods. **~ de exportación** export product. **~ de fondo** editorial, leader

artífice *m & f* artist; (creador) architect

artifici|al *a* artificial. **~o** *m* (habilidad) skill; (dispositivo) device; (engaño) trick

artiller|ía *f* artillery. **~o** *m* artilleryman, gunner

artilugio *m* gadget

artimaña *f* trick

art|ista *m & f* artist. **~ístico** *a* artistic

artritis *f* arthritis

arveja *f* (LAm) pea

arzobispo *m* archbishop

as *m* ace

asa *f* handle

asado *a* roast(ed) ● *m* roast (meat), joint; (LAm, reunión) barbecue. **~ a la parrilla** grilled meat; (LAm) barbecued meat

asalariado *a* salaried. ● *m* employee

asalt|ante *m* attacker; (de un banco) robber. **~ar** *vt* storm *<fortaleza>*; attack *<persona>*; raid *<banco etc>*; (fig) *<duda>* assail; (fig) *<idea etc>* cross one's mind. **~o** *m* attack; (robo) robbery; (en boxeo) round

asamblea *f* assembly; (reunión) meeting

asar *vt* roast. □ **~se** *vpr* be very hot. **~ a la parrilla** grill; (LAm) barbecue. **~ al horno** (sin grasa) bake; (con grasa) roast

asbesto *m* asbestos

ascend|encia *f* descent; (LAm, influencia) influencia. **~ente** *a* ascending. **~er** [1] *vt* promote. ● *vi* go up, ascend; *<cuenta etc>* come to, amount to; (ser ascendido) be promoted. **~iente** *m & f* ancestor; (influencia) influence

ascens|ión *f* ascent; (de grado) promotion. **día** *m* **de la A~ión** Ascension Day. **~o** *m* ascent; (de grado) promotion

ascensor *m* lift (Brit), elevator (Amer). **~ista** *m & f* lift attendant (Brit), elevator operator (Amer)

asco *m* disgust. **dar ~** be disgusting; (fig, causar enfado) be infuriating. **estar hecho un ~** be disgusting. **me da ~** it makes me feel sick. **¡qué ~!** how disgusting! **ser un ~** be disgusting

ascua *f* ember. **estar en ~s** be on tenterhooks

asea|do *a* clean; (arreglado) neat. ~r *vt* (lavar) wash; (limpiar) clean; (arreglar) tidy up

asedi|ar *vt* besiege; (fig) pester. ~o *m* siege

asegura|do *a & m* insured. ~dor *m* insurer. ~r *vt* secure, make safe; (decir) assure; (concertar un seguro) insure; (preservar) safeguard. □ ~rse *vpr* make sure

asemejarse *vpr* be alike

asenta|do *a* situated; (arraigado) established. ~r [1] *vt* place; (asegurar) settle; (anotar) note down; (Mex, afirmar) state. □ ~rse *vpr* settle; (estar situado) be situated; (esp LAm, sentar cabeza) settle down

asentir [4] *vi* agree (a to). ~ con la cabeza nod

aseo *m* cleanliness. ~s *mpl* toilets

asequible *a* obtainable; <precio> reasonable; <persona> approachable

asesin|ar *vt* murder; (Pol) assassinate. ~ato *m* murder; (Pol) assassination. ~o *m* murderer; (Pol) assassin

asesor *m* adviser, consultant. ~ar *vt* advise. □ ~arse *vpr*. ~arse con consult. ~ía *f* consultancy; (oficina) consultant's office

asfalt|ado *a* asphalt. ~ar *vt* asphalt. ~o *m* asphalt

asfixia *f* suffocation. ~nte *a* suffocating. ~r *vt* suffocate. □ ~rse *vpr* suffocate

así *adv* (de esta manera) like this, like that. ● *a* such. ~ ~ so-so. ~ como just as. ~ como ~, (LAm) ~ nomás just like that. ~ ... como both ... and. ~ pues so. ~ que so; (en cuanto) as soon as. ~ sea so be it. ~ y todo even so. aun ~ even so. ¿no es ~? isn't that right? si es ~ if that is the case. y ~ (sucesivamente) and so on

Asia *f* Asia

asiático *a & m* Asian

asidero *m* handle; (fig, pretexto) excuse

asidu|amente *adv* regularly. ~o *a & m* regular

asiento *m* seat; (en contabilidad) entry. ~ delantero front seat. ~ trasero back seat

asignar *vt* assign; allot <porción, tiempo etc>

asignatura *f* subject. ~ pendiente (Escol) failed subject; (fig) matter still to be resolved

asil|ado *m* inmate; (Pol) refugee. ~o *m* asylum; (fig) shelter; (de ancianos etc) home. pedir ~o político ask for political asylum

asimétrico *a* asymmetrical

asimila|ción *f* assimilation. ~r *vt* assimilate

asimismo *adv* also; (igualmente) in the same way, likewise

asir [45] *vt* grasp

asist|encia *f* attendance; (gente) people (present); (en un teatro etc) audience; (ayuda) assistance. ~encia médica medical care. ~enta *f* (mujer de la limpieza) charwoman. ~ente *m & f* assistant. ~ente social social worker. ~ido *a* assisted. ~ir *vt* assist, help. ● *vi*. ~ir a attend, be present at

asm|a *f* asthma. ~ático *a & m* asthmatic

asno *m* donkey; (fig) ass

asocia|ción *f* association; (Com) partnership. ~do *a* associated; <socio> associate. ● *m* associate. ~r *vt* associate; (Com) take into partnership. □ ~rse *vpr* associate; (Com) become a partner

asolar [1] *vt* devastate

asomar *vt* show. ● *vi* appear, show. □ ~se *vpr* <persona> lean out (a, por of); <cosa> appear

asombr|ar *vt* (pasmar) amaze; (sorprender) surprise. □ ~arse *vpr* be amazed; (sorprenderse) be surprised. ~o *m* amazement, surprise. ~oso *a* amazing, astonishing

asomo *m* sign. ni por ~ by no means

aspa *f* cross, X-shape; (de molino) (windmill) sail. en ~ X-shaped

aspaviento *m* show, fuss. ~s *mpl* gestures. hacer ~s make a big fuss

aspecto *m* look, appearance; (fig) aspect

aspereza *f* roughness; (de sabor etc) sourness

áspero *a* rough; <sabor etc> bitter

aspersión *f* sprinkling

aspiración f breath; (deseo) ambition

aspirador m, **aspiradora** f vacuum cleaner

aspira|nte m & f candidate. **~r** vt breathe in; <máquina> suck up. ● vi breathe in; <máquina> suck. **~r a** aspire to

aspirina f aspirin

asquear vt sicken. ● vi be sickening. □ **~se** vpr be disgusted

asqueroso a disgusting

asta f spear; (de la bandera) flagpole; (cuerno) horn. **a media ~** at half-mast. **~bandera** f (Mex) flagpole

asterisco m asterisk

astilla f splinter. **~s** fpl firewood

astillero m shipyard

astringente a & m astringent

astr|o m star. **~ología** f astrology. **~ólogo** m astrologer. **~onauta** m & f astronaut. **~onave** f spaceship. **~onomía** f astronomy. **~ónomo** m astronomer

astu|cia f cleverness; (ardid) cunning trick. **~to** a astute; (taimado) cunning

asumir vt assume

asunción f assumption. **la A~** the Assumption

asunto m (cuestión) matter; (de una novela) plot; (negocio) business. **~s** mpl exteriores foreign affairs. **el ~ es que** the fact is that

asusta|dizo a easily frightened. **~r** vt frighten. □ **~rse** vpr be frightened

ataca|nte m & f attacker. **~r** [7] vt attack

atad|o a tied. ● m bundle. **~ura** f tie

ataj|ar vi take a short cut; (Mex, en tenis) pick up the balls. ● vt (LAm, agarrar) catch. **~o** m short cut

atañer [22] vt concern

ataque m attack; (Med) fit, attack. **~ al corazón** heart attack. **~ de nervios** fit of hysterics

atar vt tie. □ **~se** vpr tie up

atarantar vt (LAm) fluster. □ **~se** vpr (LAm) get flustered

atardecer [11] vi get dark. ● m dusk. **al ~** at dusk

atareado a busy

atasc|ar [7] vt block; (fig) hinder. □ **~arse** vpr get stuck; <tubo etc> block. **~o** m blockage; (Auto) traffic jam

ataúd m coffin

atav|iar [20] vt dress up. □ **~iarse** vpr dress up, get dressed up. **~ío** m dress, attire

atemorizar [10] vt frighten. □ **~se** vpr be frightened

atención f attention; (cortesía) courtesy, kindness; (interés) interest. **¡~!** look out!. **llamar la ~** attract attention, catch the eye; **prestar ~** pay attention

atender [1] vt attend to; (cuidar) look after. ● vi pay attention

atenerse [40] vpr abide (**a** by)

atentado m (ataque) attack; (afrenta) affront (**contra** to). **~ contra la vida de uno** attempt on s.o.'s life

atentamente adv attentively; (con cortesía) politely; (con amabilidad) kindly. **lo saluda ~** (en cartas) yours faithfully

atentar vi. **~ contra** threaten. **~ contra la vida de uno** make an attempt on s.o.'s life

atento a attentive; (cortés) polite; (amable) kind

atenua|nte a extenuating. ● f extenuating circumstance. **~r** [21] vt attenuate; (hacer menor) diminish, lessen

ateo a atheistic. ● m atheist

aterciopelado a velvety

aterra|dor a terrifying. **~r** vt terrify

aterriza|je m landing. **~je forzoso** emergency landing. **~r** [10] vt land

aterrorizar [10] vt terrify

atesorar vt hoard; amass <fortuna>

atesta|do a packed, full up. ● m sworn statement. **~r** vt fill up, pack; (Jurid) testify

atestiguar [15] vt testify to; (fig) prove

atiborrar vt fill, stuff. □ **~se** vpr stuff o.s.

ático m attic

atina|do *a* right; (juicioso) wise, sensible. ~**r** *vt/i* hit upon; (acertar) guess right

atizar [10] *vt* poke; (fig) stir up

atlántico *a* Atlantic. **el** (**océano**) **A**~ the Atlantic (Ocean)

atlas *m* atlas

atl|eta *m & f* athlete. ~**ético** *a* athletic. ~**etismo** *m* athletics

atmósfera *f* atmosphere

atole *m* (LAm) boiled maize drink

atolladero *m* bog; (fig) tight corner

atolondra|do *a* scatter-brained; (aturdido) stunned. ~**r** *vt* fluster; (pasmar) stun. □ ~**rse** *vpr* get flustered

at|ómico *a* atomic. ~**omizador** *m* spray, atomizer

átomo *m* atom

atónito *m* amazed

atonta|do *a* stunned; (tonto) stupid. ~**r** *vt* stun. □ ~**rse** *vpr* get confused

atorar *vt* (esp LAm) to block; (Mex, sujetar) secure. □ ~**rse** *vpr* (esp LAm, atragantarse) choke; (atascarse) get blocked; <*puerta*> get jammed

atormentar *vt* torture. □ ~**rse** *vpr* worry, torment o.s.

atornillar *vt* screw on

atosigar [12] *vt* pester

atraca|dor *m* mugger; (de banco) bank robber. ~**r** [7] *vt* dock; (arrimar) bring alongside; hold up <*banco*>; mug <*persona*>. ● *vi* <*barco*> dock

atracci|ón *f* attraction. ~**ones** *fpl* entertainment, amusements

atrac|o *m* hold-up, robbery. ~**ón** *m*. **darse un** ~**ón** stuff o.s. (**de** with)

atractivo *a* attractive. ● *m* attraction; (encanto) charm

atraer [41] *vt* attract

atragantarse *vpr* choke (**con** on). **la historia se me atraganta** I can't stand history

atrancar [7] *vt* bolt <*puerta*>. □ ~**se** *vpr* get stuck

atrapar *vt* catch; (encerrar) trap

atrás *adv* back; (tiempo) previously, before. **años** ~ years ago. ~ **de** (LAm) behind. **dar un paso** ~ step backwards. **hacia** ~, **para** ~ backwards

atras|ado *a* behind; <*reloj*> slow; (con deudas) in arrears; <*país*> back-

ward. **llegar** ~**ado** (esp LAm) arrive late. ~**ar** *vt* put back <*reloj*>; (demorar) delay, postpone. ● *vi* <*reloj*> be slow. □ ~**arse** *vpr* be late; <*reloj*> be slow; (quedarse atrás) fall behind. ~**o** *m* delay; (de un reloj) slowness; (de un país) backwardness. ~**os** *mpl* (Com) arrears

atravesa|do *a* lying across. ~**r** [1] *vt* cross; (traspasar) go through (poner transversalmente) lay across. □ ~**rse** *vpr* lie across; (en la garganta) get stuck, stick

atrayente *a* attractive

atrev|erse *vpr* dare. ~**erse con** tackle. ~**ido** *a* daring; (insolente) insolent. ~**imiento** *m* daring; (descaro) insolence

atribu|ción *f* attribution. ~**ciones** *fpl* authority. ~**ir** [17] *vt* attribute; confer <*función*>. □ ~**irse** *vpr* claim

atribulado *a* afflicted

atributo *m* attribute

atril *m* lectern; (Mus) music stand

atrocidad *f* atrocity. **¡qué** ~! how awful!

atrofiarse *vpr* atrophy

atropell|ado *a* hasty. ~**ar** *vt* knock down; (por encima) run over; (empujar) push aside; (fig) outrage, insult. □ ~**arse** *vpr* rush. ~**o** *m* (Auto) accident; (fig) outrage

atroz *a* appalling; (fig) atrocious

atuendo *m* dress, attire

atún *m* tuna (fish)

aturdi|do *a* bewildered; (por golpe) stunned. ~**r** *vt* bewilder; <*golpe*> stun; <*ruido*> deafen

auda|cia *f* boldness, audacity. ~**z** *a* bold

audi|ble *a* audible. ~**ción** *f* hearing; (prueba) audition. ~**encia** *f* audience; (tribunal) court; (sesión) hearing

auditor *m* auditor. ~**io** *m* audience; (sala) auditorium

auge *m* peak; (Com) boom

augur|ar *vt* predict; <*cosas*> augur. ~**io** *m* prediction. **con nuestros mejores** ~**ios para** with our best wishes for. **mal** ~ bad omen

aula *f* class-room; (Univ) lecture room

aull|ar [23] *vi* howl. ~**ido** *m* howl

aument|ar vt increase; magnify <imagen>. ● vi increase. ~o m increase; (de sueldo) rise

aun adv even. ~ así even so. ~ cuando although. **más** ~ even more. **ni** ~ not even

aún adv still, yet. ~ no ha llegado it still hasn't arrived, it hasn't arrived yet

aunar [23] vt join. □ ~se vpr join together

aunque conj although, (even) though

aúpa int up! **de** ~ wonderful

aureola f halo

auricular m (de teléfono) receiver. ~es mpl headphones

aurora f dawn

ausen|cia f absence. **en** ~cia de in the absence of. □ ~tarse vpr leave. ~te a absent. ● m & f absentee; (Jurid) missing person. ~tismo m (LAm) absenteeism

auspici|ador m sponsor. ~ar vt sponsor. ~o m sponsorship; (signo) omen. **bajo los** ~s de sponsored by

auster|idad f austerity. ~o a austere

austral a southern

Australia m Australia

australiano a & m Australian

Austria f Austria

austriaco, austríaco a & m Austrian

aut|enticar [7] authenticate. ~enticidad f authenticity. ~éntico a authentic

auto m (Jurid) decision; (orden) order; (Auto, Ⓜ) car. ~s mpl proceedings

auto|abastecimiento m self-sufficiency. ~biografía f autobiography

autobús m bus. **en** ~ by bus

autocar m (long-distance) bus, coach (Brit)

autocontrol m self-control

autóctono a indigenous

auto|determinación f self-determination. ~didacta a self-taught. ● m & f self-taught person. ~escuela f driving school. ~financiamiento m self-financing

autógrafo m autograph

autómata m robot

autom|ático a automatic. ● m press-stud. ~atización f automation

automotor m diesel train

autom|óvil a motor. ● m car. ~ovilismo m motoring. ~ovilista m & f driver, motorist

aut|onomía f autonomy. ~onómico a, ~ónomo a autonomous

autopista f motorway (Brit), freeway (Amer)

autopsia f autopsy

autor m author. ~a f author(ess)

autori|dad f authority. ~tario a authoritarian

autoriza|ción f authorization. ~do a authorized, official; <opinión etc> authoritative. ~r [10] vt authorize

auto|rretrato m self-portrait. ~servicio m self-service restaurant. ~stop m hitch-hiking. **hacer** ~stop hitch-hike

autosuficiente a self-sufficient

autovía f dual carriageway

auxili|ar a auxiliary; <profesor> assistant. ● m & f assistant. ● vt help. ~o m help. ¡~o! help! **en** ~o de in aid of. **pedir** ~o shout for help. **primeros** ~os first aid

Av. abrev (**Avenida**) Ave

aval m guarantee

avalancha f avalanche

avalar vt guarantee

aval|uar vt [21] (LAm) value. ~úo m valuation

avance m advance; (en el cine) trailer. ~s mpl (Mex) trailer

avanzar [10] vt move forward. ● vi advance

avar|icia f avarice. ~icioso a, ~iento a greedy; (tacaño) miserly. ~o a miserly. ● m miser

avasallar vt dominate

Avda. abrev (**Avenida**) Ave

ave f bird. ~ **de paso** (incl fig) bird of passage. ~ **de rapiña** bird of prey

avecinarse vpr approach

avejentar vt age

avellan|a *f* hazel-nut. **∼o** *m* hazel (tree)

avemaría *f* Hail Mary

avena *f* oats

avenida *f* (calle) avenue

avenir [53] *vt* reconcile. □ **∼se** *vpr* come to an agreement; (entenderse) get on well (**con** with)

aventaja|do *a* outstanding. **∼r** *vt* be ahead of; (superar) surpass

avent|ar [1] *vt* fan; winnow *<grano etc>*; (Mex, lanzar) throw; (Mex, empujar) push. □ **∼arse** *vpr* (Mex) throw o.s.; (atreverse) dare. **∼ón** *m* (Mex) ride, lift (Brit)

aventur|a *f* adventure. **∼a amorosa** love affair. **∼ado** *a* risky. **∼ero** *a* adventurous. ● *m* adventurer

avergonzar [10 & 16] *vt* shame; (abochornar) embarrass. □ **∼se** *vpr* be ashamed; (abochornarse) be embarrassed

aver|ía *f* (Auto) breakdown; (en máquina) failure. **∼iado** *a* broken down. □ **∼iarse** [20] *vpr* break down

averigua|ción *f* inquiry; (Mex, disputa) argument. **∼r** [15] *vt* find out. ● *vi* (Mex) argue

aversión *f* aversion (**a, hacia, por** to)

avestruz *m* ostrich

avia|ción *f* aviation; (Mil) air force. **∼dor** *m* (piloto) pilot

av|ícola *a* poultry. **∼icultura** *f* poultry farming

avidez *f* eagerness, greed

ávido *a* eager, greedy

avinagra|do *a* sour. □ **∼rse** *vpr* go sour; (fig) become embittered

avi|ón *m* aeroplane (Brit), airplane (Amer); (Mex, juego) hopscotch. **∼onazo** *m* (Mex) plane crash

avis|ar *vt* warn; (informar) notify, inform; call *<médico etc>*. **∼o** *m* warning; (comunicación) notice; (LAm, anuncio, cartel) advertisement; (en televisión) commercial. **estar sobre ∼o** be on the alert. **sin previo ∼o** without prior warning

avisp|a *f* wasp. **∼ado** *a* sharp. **∼ero** *m* wasps' nest; (fig) mess. **∼ón** *m* hornet

avistar *vt* catch sight of

avivar *vt* stoke up *<fuego>*; brighten up *<color>*; arouse *<interés, pasión>*; intensify *<dolor>*. □ **∼se** *vpr* revive; (animarse) cheer up; (LAm, despabilarse) wise up

axila *f* armpit, axilla

axioma *m* axiom

ay *int* (de dolor) ouch!; (de susto) oh!; (de pena) oh dear! **¡∼ de ti!** poor you!

aya *f* governess, child's nurse

ayer *adv* yesterday. ● *m* past. **antes de ∼** the day before yesterday. **∼ por la mañana**, (LAm) **∼ en la mañana** yesterday morning

ayuda *f* help, aid. **∼ de cámara** valet. **∼nta** *f*, **∼nte** *m* assistant; (Mil) adjutant. **∼r** *vt* help

ayun|ar *vi* fast. **∼as** *fpl*. **estar en ∼as** have had nothing to eat or drink; (fig, 🄸) be in the dark. **∼o** *m* fasting

ayuntamiento *m* town council, city council; (edificio) town hall

azabache *m* jet

azad|a *f* hoe. **∼ón** *m* (large) hoe

azafata *f* air hostess

azafate *m* (LAm) tray

azafrán *m* saffron

azahar *m* orange blossom; (del limonero) lemon blossom

azar *m* chance; (desgracia) misfortune. **al ∼** at random. **por ∼** by chance. **∼es** *mpl* ups and downs

azaros|amente *adv* hazardously. **∼o** *a* hazardous, risky; *<vida>* eventful

azorar *vt* embarrass. □ **∼rse** *vpr* be embarrassed

Azores *fpl*. **las ∼** the Azores

azotador *m* (Mex) caterpillar

azot|ar *vt* whip, beat; (Mex, puerta) slam. **∼e** *m* whip; (golpe) smack; (fig, calamidad) calamity

azotea *f* flat roof

azteca *a & m & f* Aztec

az|úcar *m & f* sugar. **∼ucarado** *a* sweet, sugary. **∼ucarar** *vt* sweeten. **∼ucarero** *m* sugar bowl

azucena *f* (white) lily

azufre *m* sulphur

azul *a & m & f* blue. **∼ado** *a* bluish. **∼ marino** navy blue

azulejo *m* tile

azuzar [10] *vt* urge on, incite

Bb

bab|a f spittle. **~ear** vi drool, slobber; <niño> dribble. **caérsele la ~a a uno** be delighted. **~eo** m drooling; (de un niño) dribbling. **~ero** m bib

babor m port. **a ~** to port, on the port side

babosa f slug

babosada f (Mex) drivel

babos|ear vt slobber over; <niño> dribble over. ● vi (Mex) day dream. **~o** a slimy; (LAm, tonto) silly

babucha f slipper

baca f luggage rack

bacalao m cod

bache m pothole; (fig) bad patch

bachillerato m school-leaving examination

bacteria f bacterium

bagaje m. **~ cultural** cultural knowledge; (de un pueblo) cultural heritage

bahía f bay

bail|able a dance. **~aor** m Flamenco dancer. **~ar** vt/i dance. **ir a ~ar** go dancing. **~arín** m dancer. **~arina** f dancer; (de ballet) ballerina. **~e** m dance; (actividad) dancing. **~e de etiqueta** ball

baja f drop, fall; (Mil) casualty. **~ por maternidad** maternity leave. **darse de ~** take sick leave. **~da** f slope; (acto de bajar) descent; (camino) way down. **~r** vt lower; (llevar abajo) get down; go down <escalera>; bow <la cabeza>. ● vi go down; <temperatura, precio> fall. □ **~rse** vpr pull down <pantalones>. **~r(se) de** get out of <coche>; get off <autobús, caballo, tren, bicicleta>

bajeza f vile deed

bajío m shallows; (de arena) sandbank; (LAm, terreno bajo) low-lying area

bajo a low; (de estatura) short, small; <cabeza, ojos> lowered; (humilde) humble, low; (vil) vile, low; <voz> low; (Mus) deep. ● m lowland; (Mus) bass. ● adv quietly; <volar> low. ● prep under. **~ cero** below zero. **~ la lluvia** in the rain. **los ~s** (LAm) ground floor (Brit), first floor (Amer); **los ~s fondos** the underworld

bajón m sharp drop; (de salud) sudden decline

bala f bullet; (de algodón etc) bale. (LAm, en atletismo) shot. **como una ~** like a shot. **lanzamiento de ~** (LAm) shot put

balada f ballad

balan|ce m balance; (documento) balance sheet; (resultado) outcome. **~cear** vt balance. □ **~cearse** vpr swing. **~ceo** m swinging. **~cín** m rocking chair; (de niños) seesaw. **~za** f scales; (Com) balance

balar vi bleat

balazo m (disparo) shot; (herida) bullet wound

balboa f (unidad monetaria panameña) balboa

balbuc|ear vt/i stammer; <niño> babble. **~eo** m stammering; (de niño) babbling. **~ir** [24] vt/i stammer; <niño> babble

balcón m balcony

balda f shelf

balde m bucket. **de ~** free (of charge). **en ~** in vain

baldío a <terreno> waste

baldosa f (floor) tile; (losa) flagstone

bale|ar a Balearic. **las (Islas) B~ares** the Balearics, the Balearic Islands. ● vt (LAm) to shoot. **~o** m (LAm, tiroteo) shooting

balero m (Mex) cup and ball toy; (rodamiento) bearing

balido m bleat; (varios sonidos) bleating

balística f ballistics

baliza f (Naut) buoy; (Aviac) beacon

ballena f whale

ballet /ba'le/ (pl ~s) m ballet

balneario m spa; (con playa) seaside resort

balompié m soccer, football (Brit)

bal|ón *m* ball. **~oncesto** *m* basketball. **~onmano** *m* handball. **~onvolea** *m* volleyball

balotaje *m* (LAm) voting

balsa *f* (de agua) pool; (plataforma flotante) raft

bálsamo *m* balsam; (fig) balm

baluarte *m* (incl fig) bastion

bambalina *f* drop curtain. **entre ~s** behind the scenes

bambole|ar *vi* sway. □ **~arse** *vpr* sway; <*mesa etc*> wobble; <*barco*> rock. **~o** *m* swaying; (de mesa etc) wobbling; (de barco) rocking

bambú *m* (*pl* **~es**) bamboo

banal *a* banal. **~idad** *f* banality

banan|a *f* (esp LAm) banana. **~ero** *a* banana. **~o** *m* (LAm) banana tree

banc|a *f* banking; (conjunto de bancos) banks; (en juegos) bank; (LAm, asiento) bench. **~ario** *a* bank, banking. **~arrota** *f* bankruptcy. **hacer ~arrota, ir a la ~arrota** go bankrupt. **~o** *m* (asiento) bench; (Com) bank; (bajío) sandbank; (de peces) shoal

banda *f* (incl Mus, Radio) band; (Mex, para el pelo) hair band; (raya ancha) stripe; (cinta ancha) sash; (grupo) gang, group. **~ sonora** sound-track. **~da** *f* (de pájaros) flock; (de peces) shoal

bandeja *f* tray

bandejón *m* (Mex) central reservation (Brit), median strip (Amer)

bander|a *f* flag. **~illa** *f* banderilla. **~ear** *vt* stick the banderillas in. **~ero** *m* banderillero. **~ín** *m* pennant, small flag

bandido *m* bandit

bando *m* edict, proclamation; (facción) camp, side. **~s** *mpl* banns. **pasarse al otro ~** go over to the other side

bandolero *m* bandit

bandoneón *m* large accordion

banjo *m* banjo

banquero *m* banker

banquete *m* banquet; (de boda) wedding reception

banquillo *m* bench; (Jurid) dock; (taburete) footstool

bañ|ador *m* (de mujer) swimming costume; (de hombre) swimming trunks. **~ar** *vt* bath <*niño*>; (Culin, recubrir) coat. □ **~arse** *vpr* go swimming, have a swim; (en casa) have a bath. **~era** *f* bath (tub). **~ista** *m & f* bather. **~o** *m* bath; (en piscina, mar etc) swim; (cuarto) bathroom; (LAm, wáter) toilet; (bañera) bath(tub); (capa) coat (ing)

baqueano, (LAm) **baquiano** *m* guide

bar *m* bar

baraja *f* pack of cards. **~r** *vt* shuffle; juggle <*cifras etc*>; consider <*posibilidades*>; (Mex, explicar) explain

baranda, barandilla *f* rail; (de escalera) banisters

barat|a *f* (Mex) sale. **~ija** *f* trinket. **~illo** *m* junk shop; (géneros) cheap goods. **~o** *a* cheap. ● *adv* cheap(ly)

barba *f* chin; (pelo) beard

barbacoa *f* barbecue; (carne) barbecued meat

barbari|dad *f* atrocity; (🔲, mucho) awful lot 🔲. **¡qué ~dad!** how awful! **~e** *f* barbarity; (fig) ignorance. **~smo** *m* barbarism

bárbaro *a* barbaric, cruel; (bruto) uncouth; (🔲, estupendo) terrific 🔲 ● *m* barbarian. **¡qué ~!** how marvellous!

barbear *vt* (Mex, lisonjear) suck up to

barbecho *m*. **en ~** fallow

barber|ía *f* barber's (shop). **~o** *m* barber; (Mex, adulador) creep

barbilla *f* chin

barbitúrico *m* barbiturate

barbudo *a* bearded

barca *f* (small) boat. **~ de pasaje** ferry. **~za** *f* barge

barcelonés *a* of Barcelona, from Barcelona. ● *m* native of Barcelona

barco *m* boat; (navío) ship. **~ cisterna** tanker. **~ de vapor** steamer. **~ de vela** sailing boat. **ir en ~** go by boat

barda *f* (Mex) wall; (de madera) fence

barítono *a & m* baritone

barman *m* (*pl* **~s**) barman

barniz *m* varnish; (para loza etc) glaze; (fig) veneer. **~ar** [10] *vt* varnish; glaze <*loza etc*>

barómetro *m* barometer

bar|ón *m* baron. **~onesa** *f* baroness

barquero *m* boatman

barquillo m wafer; (Mex, de helado) ice-cream cone

barra f bar; (pan) loaf of French bread; (palanca) lever; (de arena) sandbank; (LAm, de hinchas) supporters. ∼ **de labios** lipstick

barrabasada f mischief, prank

barraca f hut; (vivienda pobre) shack, shanty

barranco m ravine, gully; (despeñadero) cliff, precipice

barrer vt sweep; thrash <rival>

barrera f barrier. ∼ **del sonido** sound barrier

barriada f district; (LAm, barrio marginal) slum

barrial m (LAm) quagmire

barrida f sweep; (LAm, redada) police raid

barrig|a f belly. ∼**ón** a, ∼**udo** a pot-bellied

barril m barrel

barrio m district, area. ∼**s bajos** poor quarter, poor area. **el otro** ∼ (fig, ⊞) the other world. ∼**bajero** a vulgar, common

barro m mud; (arcilla) clay; (arcilla cocida) earthenware

barroco a Baroque. ● m Baroque style

barrote m bar

bartola f. **tirarse a la** ∼ take it easy

bártulos mpl things. **liar los** ∼ pack one's bags

barullo m racket; (confusión) confusion. **a** ∼ galore

basar vt base. □ ∼**se** vpr. ∼**se en** be based on

báscula f scales

base f base; (fig) basis, foundation. **a** ∼ **de** thanks to; (mediante) by means of; (en una receta) mainly consisting of. ∼ **de datos** database. **partiendo de la** ∼ **de, tomando como** ∼ on the basis of

básico a basic

basílica f basilica

básquetbol, basquetbol m (LAm) basketball

....

bastante

● adjetivo/pronombre

····▸ (suficiente) enough. **¿hay** ∼**s sillas?** are there enough chairs? **ya tengo** ∼ I have enough already

····▸ (mucho) quite a lot. **vino** ∼ **gente** quite a lot of people came. **tiene** ∼**s amigos** he has quite a lot of friends **¿te gusta?- sí,** ∼ do you like it? - yes, quite a lot

● adverbio

····▸ (suficientemente) enough. **no has estudiado** ∼ you haven't studied enough. **no es lo** ∼ **inteligente** he's not clever enough (**como para** to)

····▸ **bastante** + adjetivo/adverbio (modificando la intensidad) quite, fairly. **parece** ∼ **simpático** he looks quite friendly. **es** ∼ **fácil de hacer** it's quite easy to do. **canta** ∼ **bien** he sings quite well

····▸ **bastante** con verbo (considerablemente) quite a lot. **el lugar ha cambiado** ∼ the place has changed quite a lot

....

bastar vi be enough. **¡basta!** that's enough! **basta con decir que** suffice it to say that. **basta y sobra** that's more than enough

bastardilla f italics

bastardo a & m bastard

bastidor m frame; (Auto) chassis. ∼**es** mpl (en el teatro) wings. **entre** ∼**es** behind the scenes

basto a coarse. ∼**s** mpl (naipes) clubs

bast|ón m walking stick; (de esquí) ski pole. ∼**onazo** m blow with a stick; (de mando) staff of office

basur|a f rubbish, garbage (Amer); (en la calle) litter. ∼**al** m (LAm, lugar) rubbish dump. ∼**ero** m dustman (Brit), garbage collector (Amer); (sitio) rubbish dump; (Mex, recipiente) dustbin (Brit), garbage can (Amer)

bata f dressing-gown; (de médico etc) white coat; (esp LAm, de baño) bathrobe

batahola f (LAm) pandemonium

batall|a f battle. ∼**a campal** pitched battle. **de** ∼**a** everyday. ∼**ador** a fighting. ● m fighter. ∼**ar** vi battle, fight. ∼**ón** m battalion.

batata f sweet potato

bate *m* bat. ~**ador** *m* batter; (cricket) batsman. ~**ar** *vi* bat

batería *f* battery; (Mus) drums. ● *m* & *f* drummer. ~ **de cocina** kitchen utensils, pots and pans

baterista *m* & *f* drummer

batido *a* beaten; <*nata*> whipped. ● *m* batter; (bebida) milk shake. ~**ra** *f* (food) mixer

batir *vt* beat; break <*récord*>; whip <*nata*>. ~ **palmas** clap. □ ~**se** *vpr* fight

batuta *f* baton. llevar la ~ be in command, be the boss

baúl *m* trunk

bauti|smal *a* baptismal. ~**smo** *m* baptism, christening. ~**zar** [10] *vt* baptize, christen. ~**zo** *m* christening

baya *f* berry

bayeta *f* cloth

bayoneta *f* bayonet

baza *f* (naipes) trick; (fig) advantage. meter ~ interfere

bazar *m* bazaar

bazofia *f* revolting food; (fig) rubbish

beato *a* blessed; (piadoso) devout; (pey) overpious

bebé *m* baby

beb|edero *m* drinking trough; (sitio) watering place. ~**edizo** *m* potion; (veneno) poison. ~**edor** *m* heavy drinker. ~**er** *vt/i* drink. ~**ida** *f* drink. ~**ido** *a* drunk

beca *f* grant, scholarship. ~**do** *m* (LAm) scholarship holder, scholar. ~**r** [7] *vt* give a scholarship to. ~**rio** *m* scholarship holder, scholar

beige /beis, beʒ/ *a* & *m* beige

béisbol, (Mex) **beisbol** *m* baseball

belén *m* crib, nativity scene

belga *a* & *m* & *f* Belgian

Bélgica *f* Belgium

bélico *a*, **belicoso** *a* warlike

bell|eza *f* beauty. ~**o** *a* beautiful. ~**as artes** *fpl* fine arts

bellota *f* acorn

bemol *m* flat. tener (muchos) ~**es** be difficult

bend|ecir [46] (*pero imperativo* **bendice**, *futuro, condicional y pp*

regulares) *vt* bless. ~**ición** *f* blessing. ~**ito** *a* blessed; (que tiene suerte) lucky; (feliz) happy

benefactor *m* benefactor

benefic|encia *f* charity. de ~**encia** charitable. ~**iar** *vt* benefit. □ ~**iarse** *vpr* benefit. ~**iario** *m* beneficiary; (de un cheque etc) payee. ~**io** *m* benefit; (ventaja) advantage; (ganancia) profit, gain. ~**ioso** *a* beneficial

benéfico *a* beneficial; (de beneficencia) charitable

ben|evolencia *f* benevolence. ~**évolo** *a* benevolent

bengala *f* flare. luz *f* de ~ flare

benigno *a* kind; (moderado) gentle, mild; <*tumor*> benign

berberecho *m* cockle

berenjena *f* aubergine (Brit), eggplant (Amer)

berr|ear *vi* <*animales*> bellow; <*niño*> bawl. ~**ido** *m* bellow; (de niño) bawling

berrinche *m* temper; (de un niño) tantrum

berro *m* watercress

besamel(a) *f* white sauce

bes|ar *vt* kiss. □ ~**arse** *vpr* kiss (each other). ~**o** *m* kiss

bestia *f* beast; (bruto) brute; (idiota) idiot. ~ **de carga** beast of burden. ~**l** *a* bestial, animal; (fig, 🔲) terrific. ~**lidad** *f* (acción brutal) horrid thing; (insensatez) stupidity

besugo *m* red bream

besuquear *vt* cover with kisses

betabel *f* (Mex) beetroot

betún *m* (para el calzado) shoe polish

biberón *m* feeding-bottle

Biblia *f* Bible

bibliografía *f* bibliography

biblioteca *f* library; (mueble) bookcase. ~ **de consulta** reference library. ~**rio** *m* librarian

bicarbonato *m* bicarbonate

bicho *m* insect, bug; (animal) small animal, creature. ~ **raro** odd sort

bici *f* 🔲 bike. ~**cleta** *f* bicycle. ir en ~**cleta** cycle. ~**moto** (LAm) moped

bidé, **bidet** *m* /bi'ðe/ bidet

bidón *m* drum, can

bien *adv* well; (muy) very, quite; (correctamente) right; (de buena gana) willingly. ● *m* good; (efectos) property. ¡~! fine!, OK!, good! ~... (o) ~ either... or. ¡está ~! fine!, alright!; (basta) that is enough!. **más** ~ rather. ¡**muy** ~! good! **no** ~ as soon as. ¡**qué** ~! marvellous!, great! Ⓣ. **si** ~ although

bienal *a* biennial

bien|aventurado *a* fortunate. ~**estar** *m* well-being. ~**hablado** *a* well-spoken. ~**hechor** *m* benefactor. ~**intencionado** *a* well-meaning

bienio *m* two year-period

bienvenid|a *f* welcome. **dar la** ~**a a uno** welcome s.o. ~**o** *a* welcome. ¡~**o!** welcome!

bifurca|ción *f* junction. □ ~**rse** [7] *vpr* fork; (rail) branch off

b|igamia *f* bigamy. ~**ígamo** *a* bigamous. ● *m* bigamist

bigot|e *m* moustache. ~**ón** *a* (Mex), ~**udo** *a* with a big moustache

bikini *m* bikini

bilingüe *a* bilingual

billar *m* billiards

billete *m* ticket; (de banco) (bank) note (Brit), bill (Amer). ~ **de ida y vuelta** return ticket (Brit), round-trip ticket (Amer). ~ **sencillo** single ticket (Brit), one-way ticket (Amer). ~**ra** *f*, ~**ro** *m* wallet, billfold (Amer)

billón *m* billion (Brit), trillion (Amer)

bi|mensual *a* fortnightly, twice-monthly. ~**mestral** *a* two-monthly. ~**mestre** *m* two-month period. ~**motor** *a* twin-engined. ● *m* twin-engined plane

binoculares *mpl* binoculars

bi|ografía *f* biography. ~**ográfico** *a* biographical

bi|ología *f* biology. ~**ológico** *a* biological. ~**ólogo** *m* biologist

biombo *m* folding screen

biopsia *f* biopsy

biplaza *m* two-seater

biquini *m* bikini

birlar *vt* Ⓣ steal, pinch Ⓣ

bis *m* encore. ¡~! encore! **vivo en el 3** ~ I live at 3A

bisabuel|a *f* great-grandmother. ~**o** *m* great-grandfather. ~**os** *mpl* great-grandparents

bisagra *f* hinge

bisiesto *a*. **año** *m* ~ leap year

bisniet|a *f* great-granddaughter. ~**o** *m* great-grandson. ~**os** *mpl* great-grandchildren

bisonte *m* bison

bisoño *a* inexperienced

bisté, bistec *m* steak

bisturí *m* scalpel

bisutería *f* imitation jewellery, costume jewellery

bitácora *f* binnacle

bizco *a* cross-eyed

bizcocho *m* sponge (cake)

bizquear *vi* squint

blanc|a *f* white woman; (Mus) minim. ~**o** *a* white; <*tez*> fair. ● *m* white; (persona) white man; (espacio) blank; (objetivo) target. **dar en el** ~**o** hit the mark. **dejar en** ~**o** leave blank. **pasar la noche en** ~**o** have a sleepless night. ~**ura** *f* whiteness

blandir [24] *vt* brandish

bland|o *a* soft; <*carácter*> weak; (cobarde) cowardly; <*carne*> tender. ~**ura** *f* softness; (de la carne) tenderness

blanque|ar *vt* whiten; whitewash <*paredes*>; bleach <*tela*>; launder <*dinero*>. ● *vi* turn white. ~**o** *m* whitening; (de dinero) laundering

blasón *m* coat of arms

bledo *m*. **me importa un** ~ I couldn't care less

blinda|je *m* armour (plating). ~**r** *vt* armour(-plate)

bloc *m* (*pl* ~**s**) pad

bloque *m* block; (Pol) bloc. **en** ~ **en bloc**. ~**ar** *vt* block; (Mil) blockade; (Com) freeze. ~**o** *m* blockade; (Com) freezing

blusa *f* blouse

bob|ada *f* silly thing. **decir** ~**adas** talk nonsense. ~**ería** *f* silly thing

bobina *f* reel; (Elec) coil

bobo *a* silly, stupid. ● *m* idiot, fool

boca f mouth; (fig, entrada) entrance; (de buzón) slot; (de cañón) muzzle. ~ **abajo** face down. ~ **arriba** face up. **a** ~ **de jarro** point-blank. **con la** ~ **abierta** dumbfounded. **se me hizo la** ~ **agua** it made my mouth water

bocacalle f junction. **la primera** ~ **a la derecha** the first turning on the right

bocad|illo m (filled) roll; (🄴, comida ligera) snack. ~**o** m mouthful; (mordisco) bite; (de caballo) bit

boca|jarro. a ~**jarro** point-blank. ~**manga** f cuff

bocanada f puff; (de vino etc) mouthful; (ráfaga) gust

bocaza m & f invar big-mouth

boceto m sketch; (de proyecto) outline

bochinche m row; (alboroto) racket. ~**ro** a (LAm) rowdy

bochorno m sultry weather; (fig, vergüenza) embarrassment. **¡qué** ~**!** how embarrassing!. ~**so** a oppressive; (fig) embarrassing

bocina f horn; (LAm, auricular) receiver. **tocar la** ~ sound one's horn. ~**zo** m toot

boda f wedding

bodeg|a f cellar; (de vino) wine cellar; (LAm, almacén) warehouse; (de un barco) hold. ~**ón** m cheap restaurant; (pintura) still life

bodoque m & f (🄴, tonto) thickhead; (Mex, niño) kid

bofes mpl lights. **echar los** ~ slog away

bofet|ada f slap; (fig) blow. ~**ón** m punch

boga f (moda) fashion. **estar en** ~ be in fashion, be in vogue. ~**r** [12] vt row. ~**vante** m (crustáceo) lobster

Bogotá f Bogotá

bogotano a from Bogotá. ● m native of Bogotá

bohemio a & m Bohemian

bohío m (LAm) hut

boicot m (pl ~**s**) boycott. ~**ear** vt boycott. ~**eo** m boycott. **hacer un** ~ boycott

boina f beret

bola f ball; (canica) marble; (mentira) fib; (Mex, reunión desordenada) rowdy party; (Mex, montón). **una** ~ **de a** bunch of; (Mex, revolución) revolution; (Mex, brillo) shine

boleadoras (LAm) fpl bolas

bolear vt (Mex) polish, shine

bolera f bowling alley

bolero m (baile, chaquetilla) bolero; (fig, 🄴, mentiroso) liar; (Mex, limpiabotas) bootblack

bole|ta f (LAm, de rifa) ticket; (Mex, de notas) (school) report; (Mex, electoral) ballot paper. ~**taje** m (Mex) tickets. ~**tería** f (LAm) ticket office; (de teatro, cine) box office. ~**tero** m (LAm) ticket-seller

boletín m bulletin; (publicación periódica) journal; (de notas) report

boleto m (esp LAm) ticket; (Mex, de avión) (air) ticket. ~ **de ida y vuelta**, (Mex) ~ **redondo** return ticket (Brit), round-trip ticket (Amer). ~ **sencillo** single ticket (Brit), one-way ticket (Amer)

boli m 🄴 Biro (P), ball-point pen

boliche m (juego) bowls; (bolera) bowling alley

bolígrafo m Biro (P), ball-point pen

bolillo m bobbin; (Mex, pan) (bread) roll

bolívar m (unidad monetaria venezolana) bolívar

Bolivia f Bolivia

boliviano a Bolivian. ● m Bolivian; (unidad monetaria de Bolivia) boliviano

boll|ería f baker's shop. ~**o** m roll; (con azúcar) bun

bolo m skittle; (Mex, en bautizo) coins. ~**s** mpl (juego) bowling

bols|a f bag; (Mex, bolsillo) pocket; (Mex, de mujer) handbag; (Com) stock exchange; (cavidad) cavity. ~**a de agua caliente** hot-water bottle. ~**illo** m pocket. **de** ~**illo** pocket. ~**o** m (de mujer) handbag. ~**o de mano**, ~**o de viaje** (overnight) bag

bomba f bomb; (máquina) pump; (noticia) bombshell. ~ **de aceite** (Auto) oil pump. ~ **de agua** (Auto) water pump. **pasarlo** ~ have a marvellous time

bombachos mpl baggy trousers, baggy pants (Amer)

bombarde|ar *vt* bombard; (desde avión) bomb. **~o** *m* bombardment; (desde avión) bombing. **~ro** *m* (avión) bomber

bombazo *m* explosion

bombear *vt* pump

bombero *m* fireman. **cuerpo** *m* **de ~s** fire brigade (Brit), fire department (Amer)

bombilla *f* (light) bulb; (LAm, para mate) pipe for drinking maté

bombín *m* pump; (🆂, sombrero) bowler (hat) (Brit), derby (Amer)

bombo *m* (tambor) bass drum. **a ~ y platillos** with a lot of fuss

bomb|ón *m* chocolate; (Mex, malvavisco) marshmallow. **~ona** *f* gas cylinder

bonachón *a* easygoing; (bueno) good-natured

bonaerense *a* from Buenos Aires. ● *m* native of Buenos Aires

bondad *f* goodness; (amabilidad) kindness; (del clima) mildness. **tenga la ~ de** would you be kind enough to. **~oso** *a* kind

boniato *m* sweet potato

bonito *a* nice; (mono) pretty. ¡**muy ~!**, ¡**qué ~!** that's nice!, very nice!. ● *m* bonito

bono *m* voucher; (título) bond. **~ del Tesoro** government bond

boñiga *f* dung

boqueada *f* gasp. **dar la última ~** be dying

boquerón *m* anchovy

boquete *m* hole; (brecha) breach

boquiabierto *a* open-mouthed; (fig) amazed, dumbfounded. **quedarse ~** be amazed

boquilla *f* mouthpiece; (para cigarrillos) cigarette-holder; (filtro de cigarrillo) tip

borbotón *m*. **hablar a borbotones** gabble. **salir a borbotones** gush out

borda|do *a* embroidered. ● *m* embroidery. **~r** *vt* embroider

bord|e *m* edge; (de carretera) side; (de plato etc) rim; (de un vestido) hem. **al ~e de** on the edge of; (fig) on the brink of. **~ear** *vt* go round; (fig) border on. **~illo** *m* kerb (Brit), curb (esp Amer)

bordo. **a ~** on board

borla *f* tassel

borrach|era *f* drunkenness. **pegarse una ~era** get drunk. **~in** *m* drunk; (habitual) drunkard. **~o** *a* drunk. ● *m* drunkard. **estar ~o** be drunk. **ser ~o** be a drunkard

borrador *m* rough draft; (de contrato) draft; (para la pizarra) (black)board rubber; (goma) eraser

borrar *vt* rub out; (tachar) cross out; delete *<información>*

borrasc|a *f* depression; (tormenta) storm. **~oso** *a* stormy

borrego *m* year-old lamb; (Mex, noticia falsa) canard

borrico *m* donkey; (fig, 🆂) ass

borrón *m* smudge; (de tinta) inkblot. **~ y cuenta nueva** let's forget about it!

borroso *a* blurred; (fig) vague

bos|coso *a* wooded. **~que** *m* wood, forest

bosquej|ar *vt* sketch; outline *<plan>*. **~o** *m* sketch; (de plan) outline

bosta *f* dung

bostez|ar [10] *vi* yawn. **~o** *m* yawn

bota *f* boot; (recipiente) wineskin

botana *f* (Mex) snack, appetizer

botánic|a *f* botany. **~o** *a* botanical. ● *m* botanist

botar *vt* launch; bounce *<pelota>*; (esp LAm, tirar) throw away. ● *vi* bounce

botarate *m* irresponsible person; (esp LAm, derrochador) spendthrift

bote *m* boat; (de una pelota) bounce; (lata) tin, can; (vasija) jar. **~ de la basura** (Mex) rubbish bin (Brit), trash can (Amer). **~ salvavidas** lifeboat. **de ~ en ~** packed

botella *f* bottle

botica *f* chemist's (shop) (Brit), drugstore (Amer). **~rio** *m* chemist (Brit), druggist (Amer)

botijo *m* earthenware jug

botín *m* half boot; (de guerra) booty; (de ladrones) haul

botiquín *m* medicine chest; (de primeros auxilios) first aid kit

bot|ón m button; (yema) bud; (LAm, insignia) badge. ~**ones** m invar bellboy (Brit), bellhop (Amer)

bóveda f vault

boxe|ador m boxer. ~**ar** vi box. ~**o** m boxing

boya f buoy; (corcho) float. ~**nte** a buoyant

bozal m (de perro etc) muzzle; (de caballo) halter

bracear vi wave one's arms; (nadar) swim, crawl

bracero m seasonal farm labourer

braga(s) f(pl) panties, knickers (Brit)

bragueta f flies

bram|ar vi bellow. ~**ido** m bellowing

branquia f gill

bras|a f ember. **a la** ~**a** grilled. ~**ero** m brazier

brasier m (Mex) bra

Brasil m. (el) ~ Brazil

brasile|ño a & m Brazilian. ~**ro** a & m (LAm) Brazilian

bravío a wild

brav|o a fierce; (valeroso) brave; <mar> rough. ¡~! int well done! bravo! ~**ura** f ferocity; (valor) bravery

braz|a f fathom. **nadar a** ~**a** swim breast-stroke. ~**ada** f (en natación) stroke. ~**alete** m bracelet; (brazal) arm-band. ~**o** m arm; (de caballo) foreleg; (rama) branch. ~**o derecho** right-hand man. **del** ~**o** arm in arm

brea f tar, pitch

brebaje m potion; (pej) concoction

brecha f opening; (Mil) breach; (Med) gash. ~ **generacional** generation gap. **estar en la** ~ be in the thick of it

brega f struggle. **andar a la** ~ work hard

breva f early fig

breve a short. **en** ~ soon, shortly. **en** ~**s momentos** soon. ~**dad** f shortness

brib|ón m rogue, rascal. ~**onada** f dirty trick

brida f bridle

brigad|a f squad; (Mil) brigade. ~**ier** m brigadier (Brit), brigadier-general (Amer)

brill|ante a bright; (lustroso) shiny; <persona> brilliant. ●m diamond. ~**ar** vi shine; (centellear) sparkle. ~**o** m shine; (brillantez) brilliance; (centelleo) sparkle. **sacar** ~**o** polish. ~**oso** a (LAm) shiny

brinc|ar [7] vi jump up and down. ~**o** m jump. **dar un** ~**o**, **pegar un** ~**o** jump

brind|ar vt offer. ● vi. ~**ar por** toast, drink a toast to. ~**is** m toast

br|ío m energy; (decisión) determination. ~**ioso** a spirited; (garboso) elegant

brisa f breeze

británico a British. ● m Briton, British person

brocha f paintbrush; (para afeitarse) shaving-brush

broche m clasp, fastener; (joya) brooch; (Mex, para el pelo) hairslide (Brit), barrete (Amer)

brocheta f skewer; (plato) kebab

brócoli m broccoli

brom|a f joke. ~**a pesada** practical joke. **en** ~**a** in fun. **ni de** ~**a** no way. ~**ear** vi joke. ~**ista** a fond of joking. ● m & f joker

bronca f row; (represión) telling-off; (LAm, rabia) foul mood. **dar** ~ **a uno** bug s.o.

bronce m bronze; (LAm) brass. ~**ado** a bronze; (por el sol) tanned. ~**ar** vt tan <piel>. □ ~**arse** vpr get a suntan

bronquitis f bronchitis

brot|ar vi (plantas) sprout; (Med) break out; <líquido> gush forth; <lágrimas> well up. ~**e** m shoot; (Med) outbreak

bruces: **de** ~ face down(wards). **caer de** ~ fall flat on one's face

bruj|a f witch. ~**ería** f witchcraft. ~**o** m wizard, magician. ● a (Mex) broke

brújula f compass

brum|a f mist; (fig) confusion. ~**oso** a misty, foggy

brusco a (repentino) sudden; <persona> brusque

Bruselas f Brussels

brusquedad f roughness; (de movimiento) abruptness

brut|al a brutal. ~**alidad** f brutality; (estupidez) stupidity. ~**o** a ignorant; (tosco) rough; *<peso, sueldo>* gross

bucal a oral; *<lesión>* mouth

buce|ar vi dive; (nadar) swim under water. ~**o** m diving; (natación) underwater swimming

bucle m ringlet

budín m pudding

budis|mo m Buddhism. ~**ta** m & f Buddhist

buen ⇒BUENO

buenaventura f good luck; (adivinación) fortune

bueno a (delante de nombre masculino en singular **buen**) good; *<tiempo>* fine. ● int well!; (de acuerdo) OK!, very well! ¡buena la has hecho! you've gone and done it now! ¡buenas noches! good night! ¡buenas tardes! (antes del atardecer) good afternoon!; (después del atardecer) good evening! ¡~s días! good morning! estar de buenas be in a good mood. por las buenas willingly. ¡qué bueno! (LAm) great!

Buenos Aires m Buenos Aires

buey m ox

búfalo m buffalo

bufanda f scarf

bufar vi snort

bufete m (mesa) writing-desk; (despacho) lawyer's office

buf|o a comic. ~**ón** a comical. ● m buffoon; (Historia) jester

buhardilla f attic; (ventana) dormer window

búho m owl

buhonero m pedlar

buitre m vulture

bujía f (Auto) spark plug

bulbo m bulb

bulevar m avenue, boulevard

Bulgaria f Bulgaria

búlgaro a & m Bulgarian

bull|a f noise. ~**icio** m hubbub; (movimiento) bustle. ~**icioso** a bustling; (ruidoso) noisy

bullir [22] vi boil; (burbujear) bubble; (fig) bustle

bulto m (volumen) bulk; (forma) shape; (paquete) package; (maleta etc) piece of luggage; (protuberancia) lump

buñuelo m fritter

BUP abrev (**Bachillerato Unificado Polivalente**) secondary school education

buque m ship, boat

burbuj|a f bubble. ~**ear** vi bubble; *<vino>* sparkle

burdel m brothel

burdo a rough, coarse; *<excusa>* clumsy

burgu|és a middle-class, bourgeois. ● m middle-class person. ~**esía** f middle class, bourgeoisie

burla f taunt; (broma) joke; (engaño) trick. ~**r** vt evade. □ ~**rse** vpr. ~**rse de** mock, make fun of

burlesco a (en literatura) burlesque

burlón a mocking

bur|ocracia f bureaucracy; (Mex, funcionariado) civil service. ~**ócrata** m & f bureaucrat; (Mex, funcionario) civil servant. ~**ocrático** a bureaucratic; (Mex) *<empleado>* government

burro a stupid; (obstinado) pigheaded. ● m donkey; (fig) ass

bursátil a stock-exchange

bus m bus

busca f search. a la ~ de in search of. en ~ de in search of. ● m beeper

buscapleitos m & f invar (LAm) trouble-maker

buscar [7] vt look for. ● vi look. buscársela ask for it; ir a ~ a uno fetch s.o.

búsqueda f search

busto m bust

butaca f armchair; (en el teatro etc) seat

buzo m diver

buzón m postbox (Brit), mailbox (Amer)

Cc

C/ *abrev* (**Calle**) St, Rd

cabal *a* exact; (completo) complete. **no estar en sus ~es** not be in one's right mind

cabalga|dura *f* mount, horse. **~r** [12] *vt* ride. ● *vi* ride, go riding. **~ta** *f* ride; (desfile) procession

caballa *f* mackerel

caballerango *m* (Mex) groom

caballeresco *a* gentlemanly. **literatura** *f* **caballeresca** books of chivalry

caballer|ía *f* mount, horse. **~iza** *f* stable. **~izo** *m* groom

caballero *m* gentleman; (de orden de caballería) knight; (tratamiento) sir. **~so** *a* gentlemanly

caballete *m* (del tejado) ridge; (para mesa) trestle; (de pintor) easel

caballito *m* pony. **~ del diablo** dragonfly. **~ de mar** sea-horse. **~s** *mpl* (carrusel) merry-go-round

caballo *m* horse; (del ajedrez) knight; (de la baraja española) queen. **~ de fuerza** horsepower. **a ~** on horseback

cabaña *f* hut

cabaret /kaba're/ *m* (*pl* **~s**) nightclub

cabecear *vi* nod off; (en fútbol) head the ball; *<caballo>* toss its head

cabecera *f* (de la cama) headboard; (de la mesa) head; (en un impreso) heading

cabecilla *m* ringleader

cabello *m* hair. **~s** *mpl* hair

caber [28] *vi* fit (**en** into). **no cabe duda** there's no doubt

cabestr|illo *m* sling. **~o** *m* halter

cabeza *f* head; (fig, inteligencia) intelligence. **andar de ~** have a lot to do. **~da** *f* nod. **dar una ~da** nod off. **~zo** *m* butt; (en fútbol) header

cabida *f* capacity; (extensión) area; (espacio) room. **dar ~ a** have room for, accommodate

cabina *f* (de pasajeros) cabin; (de pilotos) cockpit; (electoral) booth; (de camión) cab. **~ telefónica** telephone box (Brit), telephone booth (Amer)

cabizbajo *a* crestfallen

cable *m* cable

cabo *m* end; (trozo) bit; (Mil) corporal; (mango) handle; (Geog) cape; (Naut) rope. **al ~ de** after. **de ~ a rabo** from beginning to end. **llevar a ~** carry out

cabr|a *f* goat. **~iola** *f* jump, skip. **~itilla** *f* kid. **~ito** *m* kid

cábula *m* (Mex) crook

cacahuate, (Mex) **cacahuete** *m* peanut

cacalote *m* (Mex) crow

cacao *m* (planta y semillas) cacao; (polvo) cocoa; (fig) confusion

cacarear *vt* boast about. ● *vi* *<gallo>* crow; *<gallina>* cluck

cacería *f* hunt. **ir de ~** go hunting

cacerola *f* saucepan, casserole

cacharro *m* (earthenware) pot; (coche estropeado) wreck; (cosa inútil) piece of junk; (chisme) thing. **~s** *mpl* pots and pans

cachear *vt* frisk

cachemir *m*, **cachemira** *f* cashmere

cacheo *m* frisking

cachetada *f* (LAm) slap

cache|te *m* slap; (esp LAm, mejilla) cheek. **~tear** *vt* (LAm) slap. **~tón** *a* (LAm) chubby-cheeked

cachimba *f* pipe

cachiporra *f* club, truncheon

cachivache *m* piece of junk. **~s** *mpl* junk

cacho *m* bit, piece; (LAm, cuerno) horn

cachondeo *m* 🅴 joking, joke

cachorro *m* (perrito) puppy; (de león, tigre) cub

cachucha *f* (Mex) cup

caciqu|e *m* cacique, chief; (Pol) local political boss; (hombre poderoso) tyrant. **~il** *a* despotic. **~ismo** *m* despotism

caco *m* thief

cacofonía *f* cacophony

cacto *m*, **cactus** *m invar* cactus

cada *a invar* each, every. ∼ **uno** each one, everyone. **uno de** ∼ **cinco** one in five. ∼ **vez más** more and more

cadáver *m* corpse

cadena *f* chain; (TV) channel. ∼ **de fabricación** production line. ∼ **de montañas** mountain range. ∼ **perpetua** life imprisonment

cadera *f* hip

cadete *m* cadet

caduc|ar [7] *vi* expire. ∼**idad** *f*. fecha *f* de ∼**idad** sell-by date. ∼**o** *a* outdated

cae|r [29] *vi* fall. **dejar** ∼**r** drop. **este vestido no me** ∼ **bien** this dress doesn't suit me. **hacer** ∼**r** knock over. **Juan me** ∼ **bien** I like Juan. **su cumpleaños cayó en martes** his birthday fell on a Tuesday. □ ∼**rse** *vpr* fall (over). **se le cayó** he dropped it

café *m* coffee; (cafetería) café; (Mex, marrón) brown. ● *a*. **color** ∼ coffee-coloured. ∼ **con leche** white coffee. ∼ **cortado** coffee with a little milk. ∼ **negro** (LAm) expresso. ∼ **solo** black coffee

cafe|ína *f* caffeine. ∼**tal** *m* coffee plantation. ∼**tera** *f* coffee-pot. ∼**tería** *f* café. ∼**tero** *a* coffee

caíd|a *f* fall; (disminución) drop; (pendiente) slope. ∼**o** *a* fallen

caigo *vb* ⇒CAER

caimán *m* cayman, alligator

caj|a *f* box; (de botellas) case; (ataúd) coffin; (en tienda) cash desk; (en supermercado) check-out; (en banco) cashier's desk. ∼**a de ahorros** savings bank. ∼**a de cambios** gearbox. ∼**a de caudales**, ∼**a fuerte** safe. ∼**a registradora** till. ∼**ero** *m* cashier. ∼**ero automático** cash dispenser. ∼**etilla** *f* packet. ∼**ita** *f* small box. ∼**ón** *m* (de mueble) drawer; (caja grande) crate; (LAm, ataúd) coffin; (Mex, en estacionamiento) parking space. **ser de** ∼**ón** be obvious. ∼**uela** *f* (Mex) boot (Brit), trunk (Amer)

cal *m* lime

cala *f* cove

calaba|cín *m*, ∼**cita** *f* (Mex) courgette (Brit), zucchini (Amer). ∼**za** *f* pumpkin; (fig, 🄵, idiota) idiot. **dar** ∼**zas a uno** give s.o. the brush-off

calabozo *m* prison; (celda) cell

calado *a* soaked. **estar** ∼ **hasta los huesos** be soaked to the skin. ● *m* (Naut) draught

calamar *m* squid

calambre *m* cramp

calami|dad *f* calamity, disaster. ∼**toso** *a* calamitous

calaña *f* sort

calar *vt* soak; (penetrar) pierce; (fig, penetrar) see through; (fruta) sample *<fruta>*. □ ∼**se** *vpr* get soaked; *<zapatos>* leak; (Auto) stall

calavera *f* skull; (Mex, Auto) taillight

calcar [7] *vt* trace; (fig) copy

calcet|a *f*. **hacer** ∼ knit. ∼**ín** *m* sock

calcetín *m* sock

calcinar *vt* burn

calcio *m* calcium

calcomanía *f* transfer

calcula|dor *a* calculating. ∼**dora** *f* calculator. ∼**r** *vt* calculate; (suponer) reckon, think; (imaginar) imagine

cálculo *m* calculation; (Med) stone

caldear *vt* heat, warm. □ ∼**se** *vpr* get hot

caldera *f* boiler

calderilla *f* small change

caldo *m* stock; (sopa) clear soup, broth

calefacción *f* heating. ∼ **central** central heating

caleidoscopio *m* kaleidoscope

calendario *m* calendar; (programa) schedule

calent|ador *m* heater. ∼**amiento** *m* warming; (en deportes) warm-up. ∼**ar** [1] *vt* heat; (templar) warm. □ ∼**arse** *vpr* get hot; (templarse) warm up; (LAm, enojarse) get mad. ∼**ura** *f* fever, (high) temperature. ∼**uriento** *a* feverish

calibr|ar *vt* calibrate; (fig) weigh up. ∼**e** *m* calibre; (diámetro) diameter; (fig) importance

calidad *f* quality; (condición) capacity. **en** ∼ **de** as

calidez f (LAm) warmth

cálido a warm

caliente a hot; <*habitación, ropa*> warm; (LAm, enojado) angry

califica|ción f qualification; (evaluación) assessment; (nota) mark. ~**do** a (esp LAm) qualified; (mano de obra) skilled. ~**r** [7] vt qualify; (evaluar) assess; mark <*examen etc*>. ~**r de** describe as, label

cáliz m chalice; (Bot) calyx

caliz|a f limestone. ~**o** a lime

calla|do a quiet. ~**r** vt silence; keep <*secreto*>; hush up <*asunto*>. ● vi be quiet, keep quiet, shut up 🅸. □ ~**rse** vpr be quiet, keep quiet, shut up 🅸 ¡**cállate!** be quiet!, shut up! 🅸

calle f street, road; (en deportes, autopista) lane. ~ **de dirección única** one-way street. ~ **mayor** high street, main street. **de** ~ everyday. ~**ja** f narrow street. ~**jear** vi hang out on the streets. ~**jero** a street. ● m street plan. ~**jón** m alley. ~**ón sin salida** dead end. ~**juela** f back street, side street

call|ista m & f chiropodist. ~**o** m corn, callus. ~**os** mpl tripe. ~**osidad** f callus

calm|a f calm. ¡~**a**! calm down!. **en** ~**a** calm. **perder la** ~**a** lose one's composure. ~**ante** m tranquilizer; (para el dolor) painkiller. ~**ar** vt calm; (aliviar) soothe. ● vi <*viento*> abate. □ ~**arse** vpr calm down; <*viento*> abate. ~**o** a calm. ~**oso** a calm; (🅸, flemático) slow

calor m heat; (afecto) warmth. **hace** ~ it's hot. **tener** ~ be hot. ~**ía** f calorie. ~**ífero** a heat-producing. ~**ico** a calorific

calumni|a f calumny; (oral) slander; (escrita) libel. ~**ar** vt slander; (por escrito) libel. ~**oso** a slanderous; <*cosa escrita*> libellous

caluroso a warm; <*clima*> hot

calv|a f bald head; (parte sin pelo) bald patch. ~**icie** f baldness. ~**o** a bald

calza f wedge

calzada f road; (en autopista) carriageway

calza|do a wearing shoes. ● m footwear, shoe. ~**dor** m shoehorn. ~**r** [10] vt put shoes on; (llevar) wear. **¿qué número calza Vd?** what size shoe do you take? ● vi wear shoes. □ ~**rse** vpr put on

calz|ón m shorts. ~**ones** mpl shorts; (LAm, ropa interior) panties. ~**oncillos** mpl underpants

cama f bed. ~ **de matrimonio** double bed. ~ **individual** single bed. **guardar** ~ stay in bed

camada f litter

camafeo m cameo

camaleón m chameleon

cámara f (aposento) chamber; (fotográfica) camera. ~ **fotográfica** camera. **a** ~ **lenta** in slow motion

camarad|a m & f colleague; (de colegio) schoolfriend; (Pol) comrade. ~**ería** f camaraderie

camarer|a f chambermaid; (de restaurante etc) waitress. ~**o** m waiter

camarógrafo m cameraman

camarón m shrimp

camarote m cabin

cambi|able a changeable; (Com etc) exchangeable. ~**ante** a variable; <*persona*> moody. ~**ar** vt change; (trocar) exchange. ● vi change. ~**ar de idea** change one's mind. □ ~**arse** vpr change. ~**o** m change; (Com) exchange rate; (moneda menuda) (small) change; (Auto) gear. **en** ~**o** on the other hand

camello m camel

camellón m (Mex) traffic island

camerino m dressing room

camilla f stretcher

camin|ante m traveller. ~**ar** vt/i walk. ~**ata** f long walk. ~**o** m road; (sendero) path, track; (dirección, ruta) way. ~**o de** towards, on the way to. **abrir** ~**o** make way. **a medio** ~**o, a la mitad del** ~**o** half-way. **de** ~**o** on the way

cami|ón m lorry; (Mex, autobús) bus. ~**onero** m lorry-driver; (Mex, de autobús) bus driver. ~**oneta** f van; (LAm, coche familiar) estate car

camis|a f shirt. ~ **de fuerza** straitjacket. ~**ería** f shirtmaker's. ~**eta**

f T-shirt; (ropa interior) vest. **~ón** *m* nightdress

camorra *f* ▣ row. **buscar ~** look for a fight

camote *m* (LAm) sweet potato

campamento *m* camp. **de ~** *a* camping

campan|a *f* bell. **~ada** *f* stroke. **~ario** *m* bell tower, belfry. **~illa** *f* bell

campaña *f* campaign

campe|ón *a* & *m* champion. **~onato** *m* championship

campes|ino *a* country. ● *m* peasant. **~tre** *a* country

camping /'kampin/ *m* (*pl* **~s**) camping; (lugar) campsite. **hacer ~** go camping

camp|iña *f* countryside. **~o** *m* country; (agricultura, fig) field; (de fútbol) pitch; (de golf) course. **~osanto** *m* cemetery

camufla|je *m* camouflage. **~r** *vt* camouflage

cana *f* grey hair, white hair. **peinar ~s** be getting old

Canadá *m*. **el ~** Canada

canadiense *a* & *m* & *f* Canadian

canal *m* (incl TV) channel; (artificial) canal; (del tejado) gutter. **~ de la Mancha** English Channel. **~ de Panamá** Panama Canal. **~ón** *m* (horizontal) gutter; (vertical) drain-pipe

canalla *f* rabble. ● *m* (fig, ▣) swine. **~da** *f* dirty trick

canapé *m* sofa, couch; (Culin) canapé

Canarias *fpl*. **las (islas) ~** the Canary Islands, the Canaries

canario *a* of the Canary Islands. ● *m* native of the Canary Islands; (pájaro) canary

canast|a *f* (large) basket **~illa** *f* small basket; (para un bebé) layette. **~illo** *m* small basket. **~o** *m* (large) basket

cancela|ción *f* cancellation. **~r** *vt* cancel; write off *<deuda>*

cáncer *m* cancer. **C~** Cancer

cancha *f* court; (LAm, de fútbol, rugby) pitch, ground

canciller *m* chancellor; (LAm, ministro) Minister of Foreign Affairs

canci|ón *f* song. **~ón de cuna** lullaby. **~onero** *m* song-book

candado *m* padlock

candel|a *f* candle. **~abro** *m* candelabra. **~ero** *m* candlestick

candente *a* (rojo) red-hot; (fig) burning

candidato *m* candidate

candidez *f* innocence; (ingenuidad) naivety

cándido *a* naive

candil *m* oil lamp. **~ejas** *fpl* footlights

candor *m* innocence; (ingenuidad) naivety

canela *f* cinnamon

cangrejo *m* crab. **~ de río** crayfish

canguro *m* kangaroo. ● *m* & *f* (persona) baby-sitter

caníbal *a* & *m* & *f* cannibal

canica *f* marble

canijo *a* weak; (Mex, terco) stubborn; (Mex, intenso) incredible

canilla *f* (LAm) shinbone

canino *a* canine. ● *m* canine (tooth)

canje *m* exchange. **~ar** *vt* exchange

cano *a* grey. **de pelo ~** grey-haired

canoa *f* canoe

can|ónigo *m* canon. **~onizar** [10] *vt* canonize

canoso *a* grey-haired

cansa|do *a* tired; (que cansa) tiring. **~dor** (LAm) tiring. **~ncio** *m* tiredness. **~r** *vt* tire; (aburrir) bore. ● *vi* be tiring; (aburrir) get boring. □ **~rse** *vpr* get tired

canta|nte *a* singing. ● *m* & *f* singer. **~or** *m* Flamenco singer. **~r** *vt/i* sing. **~rlas claras** speak frankly. ● *m* singing; (poema) poem

cántaro *m* pitcher. **llover a ~s** pour down

cante *m* folk song. **~ flamenco, ~ jondo** Flamenco singing

cantera *f* quarry

cantidad *f* quantity; (número) number; (de dinero) sum. **una ~ de** lots of

cantimplora *f* water-bottle

cantina *f* canteen; (Rail) buffet; (LAm, bar) bar

cant|inela *f* song. **~o** *m* singing; (canción) chant; (borde) edge; (de un cuchillo) blunt edge. ~**o rodado** boulder; (guijarro) pebble. **de** ~**o** on edge

canturre|ar vt/i hum. ~**o** m humming

canuto m tube

caña f (planta) reed; (del trigo) stalk; (del bambú) cane; (de pescar) rod; (de la bota) leg; (vaso) glass. ~ **de azúcar** sugar-cane. ~**da** f ravine; (camino) track; (LAm, arroyo) stream

cáñamo m hemp. ~ **indio** cannabis

cañ|ería f pipe; (tubería) piping. ~**o** m pipe, tube; (de fuente) jet. ~**ón** m (de pluma) quill; (de artillería) cannon; (de arma de fuego) barrel; (desfiladero) canyon. ~**onera** f gunboat

caoba f mahogany

ca|os m chaos. ~**ótico** a chaotic

capa f layer; (de pintura) coat; (Culin) coating; (prenda) cloak; (más corta) cape; (Geol) stratum

capaci|dad f capacity; (fig) ability. ~**tar** vt qualify, enable; (instruir) train

caparazón m shell

capataz m foreman

capaz a capable, able

capcioso a sly, insidious

capellán m chaplain

caperuza f hood; (de bolígrafo) cap

capilla f chapel

capital a capital, very important. ● m (dinero) capital. ● f (ciudad) capital. ~ **de provincia** county town. ~**ismo** (LAm) of/from the capital. ~**ismo** m capitalism. ~**ista** a & m & f capitalist. ~**izar** [10] vt capitalize

capit|án m captain; (de pesquero) skipper. ~**anear** vt lead, command; skipper <pesquero>; captain <un e-quipo>

capitel m (Arquit) capital

capitulaci|ón f surrender. ~**ones** fpl marriage contract

capítulo m chapter; (de serie) episode

capó m bonnet (Brit), hood (Amer)

capón m (pollo) capon

caporal m (Mex) foreman

capot|a f (de mujer) bonnet; (Auto) folding top; (de cochecito) hood. ~**e** m cape; (Mex, de coche) bonnet (Brit), hood (Amer)

capricho m whim. ~**so** a capricious, whimsical

Capricornio m Capricorn

cápsula f capsule

captar vt harness <agua>; grasp <sentido>; capture <atención>; win <confianza>; (radio) pick up

captura f capture. ~**r** vt capture

capucha f hood

capullo m bud; (de insecto) cocoon

caqui m khaki

cara f face; (de una moneda) heads; (de un objeto) side; (aspecto) look, appearance; (descaro) cheek. ~ **a** facing. ~ **a** ~ face to face. ~ **dura** ⇒ CARADURA. ~ **o cruz** heads or tails. **dar la** ~ **a** face up to. **hacer** ~ **a** face. **tener mala** ~ look ill. **volver la** ~ look the other way

carabela f caravel

carabina f carbine; (fig, 🔲, señora) chaperone

caracol m snail; (de mar) winkle; (LAm, concha) conch; (de pelo) curl. ¡~**es!** Good Heavens!. ~**a** f conch

carácter m (pl **caracteres**) character; (índole) nature. **con** ~ **de** as

característic|a f characteristic. ~**o** a characteristic, typical

caracteriza|do a characterized; (prestigioso) distinguished. ~**r** [10] vt characterize

caradura f cheek, nerve. ● m & f cheeky person

caramba int good heavens!

carambola f (en billar) cannon; (Mex, choque múltiple) pile-up. **de** ~ by pure chance

caramelo m sweet (Brit), candy (Amer); (azúcar fundido) caramel

caraqueño a from Caracas

carátula f (de disco) sleeve (Brit), jacket (Amer); (de video) case; (de libro) cover; (Mex, del reloj) face

caravana f caravan; (de vehículos) convoy; (Auto) long line, traffic jam; (remolque) caravan (Brit), trailer (Amer); (Mex, reverencia) bow

caray int 🔲 good heavens!

carb|ón m coal; (para dibujar) charcoal. ~ **de leña** charcoal. ~**oncillo** m charcoal. ~**onero** a coal. ● m coal-merchant. ~**onizar** [10] *vt* (fig) burn (to a cinder). ~**ono** *m* carbon

carbura|dor *m* carburettor. ~**nte** *m* fuel

carcajada *f* guffaw. **reírse a** ~**s** roar with laughter. **soltar una** ~ burst out laughing

cárcel *f* prison, jail

carcelero *m* jailer

carcom|er *vt* eat away; (fig) undermine. □ ~**erse** *vpr* be eaten away; (fig) waste away

cardenal *m* cardinal; (contusión) bruise

cardiaco, **cardíaco** *a* cardiac, heart

cardinal *a* cardinal

cardo *m* thistle

carear *vt* bring face to face <*personas*>; compare <*cosas*>

care|cer [11] *vi*. ~**cer de** lack. ~**cer de sentido** not to make sense. ~**ncia** *f* lack. ~**nte** *a* lacking

care|ro *a* pricey. ~**stía** *f* (elevado) high cost

careta *f* mask

carey *m* tortoiseshell

carga *f* load; (fig) burden; (acción) loading; (de barco, avión) cargo; (de tren) freight; (de arma) charge; (Elec, ataque) charge; (obligación) obligation. **llevar la** ~ **de algo** be responsible for sth. ~**da** *f* (Mex, Pol) supporters. ~**do** *a* loaded; (fig) burdened; <*atmósfera*> heavy; <*café*> strong; <*pila*> charged. ~**mento** *m* load; (acción) loading; (de un barco) cargo. ~**r** [12] *vt* load; (fig) burden; (Elec, atacar) charge; fill <*pluma etc*>. ● *vi* load. ~**r con** carry. □ ~**rse** *vpr* <*pila*> charge. ~**rse de** to load s.o. down with

cargo *m* (puesto) post; (acusación) charge. **a** ~ **de** in the charge of. **hacerse** ~ **de** take responsibility for. **tener a su** ~ be in charge of

carguero *m* (Naut) cargo ship

caria|do *a* decayed. □ ~**rse** *vpr* decay

caribeño *a* Caribbean

caricatura *f* caricature

caricia *f* caress; (a animal) stroke

caridad *f* charity. **¡por** ~**!** for goodness sake!

caries *f invar* tooth decay; (lesión) cavity

cariño *m* affection; (caricia) caress. ~ **mío** my darling. **con mucho** ~ (en carta) with love from. **tener** ~ **a** be fond of. **tomar** ~ **a** become fond of. ~**so** *a* affectionate

carisma *m* charisma

caritativo *a* charitable

cariz *m* look

carmesí *a* & *m* crimson

carmín *m* (de labios) lipstick; (color) red

carnal *a* carnal. **primo** ~ first cousin

carnaval *m* carnival. ~**esco** *a* carnival

carne *f* meat; (Anat, de frutos, pescado) flesh. ~ **de cerdo** pork. ~ **de cordero** lamb. ~ **de gallina** goose pimples. ~ **molida** (LAm), ~ **picada** mince (Brit), ground beef (Amer). ~ **de ternera** veal. ~ **de vaca** beef. **me pone la** ~ **de gallina** it gives me the creeps. **ser de** ~ **y hueso** be only human

carné, **carnet** *m* card. ~ **de conducir** driving licence (Brit), driver's license (Amer) ~ **de identidad** identity card. ~ **de manejar** (LAm) driving license (Brit), driver's license (Amer). ~ **de socio** membership card

carnero *m* ram

carnicer|ía *f* butcher's (shop); (fig) massacre. ~**o** *a* carnivorous. ● *m* butcher

carnívoro *a* carnivorous. ● *m* carnivore

carnoso *a* fleshy; <*pollo*> meaty

caro *a* expensive. ● *adv* dear, dearly. **costar** ~ **a uno** cost s.o. dear.

carpa *f* carp; (LAm, tienda) tent

carpeta *f* folder, file. ~**zo** *m*. **dar** ~**zo a** shelve

carpinter|ía *f* carpentry. ~**o** *m* carpenter, joiner

carraspe|ar *vi* clear one's throat. ~**ra** *f*. **tener** ~**ra** have a frog in one's throat

carrera *f* run; (prisa) rush; (concurso) race; (estudios) degree course; (profesión) career; (de taxi) journey

carreta f cart. ∼**da** f cartload

carrete m reel; (película) film

carretear vi (LAm) taxi

carretera f road. ∼ **de circunvala-ción** bypass, ring road. ∼ **nacional** A road (Brit), highway (Amer)

carretilla f wheelbarrow

carril m lane; (Rail) rail

carrito m (en supermercado, para equipaje) trolley (Brit), cart (Amer)

carro m cart; (LAm, coche) car; (Mex, vagón) coach. ∼ **de combate** tank. ∼**cería** f (Auto) bodywork

carroña f carrion

carroza f coach, carriage; (en desfile de fiesta) float

carruaje m carriage

carrusel m merry-go-round

cart|a f letter; (lista de platos) menu; (lista de vinos) list; (Geog) map; (naipe) card. ∼**a blanca** free hand. ∼**a de crédito** letter of credit. ∼**earse** vpr correspond

cartel m poster; (letrero) sign. ∼**era** f hoarding; (en periódico) listings; (LAm en escuela, oficina) notice board (Brit), bulletin board (Amer). **de** ∼ celebrated

carter|a f wallet; (de colegial) satchel; (para documentos) briefcase; (l Am, de mujer) handbag (Brit), purse (Amer). ∼**ista** m & f pickpocket

cartero m postman, mailman (Amer)

cartílago m cartilage

cartilla f first reading book. ∼ **de ahorros** savings book. **leerle la** ∼ **a uno** tell s.o. off

cartón m cardboard

cartucho m cartridge

cartulina f card

casa f house; (hogar) home; (empresa) firm. ∼ **de huéspedes** boarding-house. ∼ **de socorro** first aid post. **ir a** ∼ go home. **salir de** ∼ go out

casaca f jacket

casado a married. **los recién** ∼**os** the newly-wed

casa|mentero m matchmaker. ∼**miento** m marriage; (ceremonia) wedding. ∼**r** vt marry. □ ∼**rse** vpr get married

cascabel m small bell; (de serpiente) rattle

cascada f waterfall

casca|nueces m invar nutcrack-ers. ∼**r** [7] vt crack <nuez, huevo>; (pegar) beat. □ ∼**rse** vpr crack

cáscara f (de huevo, nuez) shell; (de naranja) peel; (de plátano) skin

cascarrabias a invar grumpy

casco m helmet; (de cerámica etc) piece, fragment; (cabeza) scalp; (de barco) hull; (envase) empty bottle; (de caballo) hoof; (de una ciudad) part, area

cascote m piece of rubble. ∼**s** mpl rubble

caserío m country house; (poblado) hamlet

casero a home-made; (doméstico) do-mestic; (amante del hogar) home-loving; <reunión> family. ● m owner; (vigilante) caretaker

caseta f hut; (puesto) stand. ∼ **de ba-ño** bathing hut

casete m & f cassette

casi adv almost, nearly; (en frases ne-gativas) hardly. ∼ ∼ very nearly. ∼ **nada** hardly any. ¡∼ **nada!** is that all? ∼ **nunca** hardly ever

casill|a f hut; (en ajedrez etc) square; (en formulario) box; (compartimento) pigeonhole. ∼ **electrónica** e-mail ad-dress. ∼**ero** m pigeonholes; (comparti-mento) pigeonhole

casino m casino; (club social) club

caso m case. **el** ∼ **es que** the fact is that. **en** ∼ **de** in the event of. **en cual-quier** ∼ in any case, whatever hap-pens. **en ese** ∼ in that case. **en todo** ∼ in any case. **en último** ∼ as a last resort. **hacer** ∼ **de** take notice of. **po-ner por** ∼ suppose

caspa f dandruff

casquivana f flirt

cassette m & f cassette

casta f (de animal) breed; (de persona) descent; (grupo social) caste

castaña f chestnut

castañetear vi <dientes> chatter

castaño a chestnut; <ojos> brown. ● m chestnut (tree)

castañuela f castanet

castellano *a* Castilian. ● *m* (persona) Castilian; (lengua) Castilian, Spanish. ~**parlante** *a* Castilian-speaking, Spanish-speaking. **¿habla Vd ~?** do you speak Spanish?

castidad *f* chastity

castig|ar [12] *vt* punish; (en deportes) penalize. ~**o** *m* punishment; (en deportes) penalty

castillo *m* castle

cast|izo *a* traditional; (puro) pure. ~**o** *a* chaste

castor *m* beaver

castrar *vt* castrate

castrense *m* military

casual *a* chance, accidental. ~**idad** *f* chance, coincidence. **dar la** ~**idad** happen. **de** ~**idad, por** ~**idad** by chance. **¡qué** ~**idad!** what a coincidence!. ~**mente** *adv* by chance; (precisamente) actually

cataclismo *m* cataclysm

catador *m* taster

catalán *a & m* Catalan

catalizador *m* catalyst

cat|alogar [12] *vt* catalogue; (fig) classify. ~**álogo** *m* catalogue

Cataluña *f* Catalonia

catamarán *m* catamaran

catapulta *f* catapult

catar *vt* taste, try

catarata *f* waterfall, falls; (Med) cataract

catarro *m* cold

cat|ástrofe *m* catastrophe. ~**astrófico** *a* catastrophic

catecismo *m* catechism

cátedra *f* (en universidad) professorship, chair; (en colegio) post of head of department

catedral *f* cathedral

catedrático *m* professor; (de colegio) teacher, head of department

categ|oría *f* category; (clase) class. **de** ~**oría** important. **de primera** ~**oría** first-class. ~**órico** *a* categorical

cat|olicismo *m* catholicism. ~**óli-co** *a* (Roman) Catholic ● *m* (Roman) Catholic

catorce *a & m* fourteen

cauce *m* river bed; (fig, artificial) channel

caucho *m* rubber

caudal *m* (de río) volume of flow; (riqueza) wealth. ~**oso** *a* <río> large

caudillo *m* leader

causa *f* cause; (motivo) reason; (Jurid) trial. **a** ~ **de, por** ~ **de** because of. ~**r** *vt* cause

cautel|a *f* caution. ~**oso** *a* cautious, wary

cauterizar [10] *vt* cauterize

cautiv|ar *vt* capture; (fig, fascinar) captivate. ~**erio** *m*, ~**idad** *f* captivity. ~**o** *a & m* captive

cauto *a* cautious

cavar *vt/i* dig

caverna *f* cave, cavern

caviar *m* caviare

cavidad *f* cavity

caza *f* hunting; (con fusil) shooting; (animales) game. ● *m* fighter. **andar a (la)** ~ **de** be in search of. ~ **mayor** game hunting. **dar** ~ chase, go after. **ir de** ~ go hunting/shooting. ~**dor** *m* hunter. ~**dora** *f* jacket. ~**r** [10] *vt* hunt; (con fusil) shoot; (fig) track down; (obtener) catch, get

caz|o *m* saucepan; (cucharón) ladle. ~**oleta** *f* (small) saucepan. ~**uela** *f* casserole

cebada *f* barley

ceb|ar *vt* fatten (up); bait *<anzuelo>*; prime *<arma de fuego>*. ~**o** *m* bait; (de arma de fuego) charge

cebol|la *f* onion. ~**eta** *f* spring onion (Brit), scallion (Amer). ~**ino** *m* chive

cebra *f* zebra

cece|ar *vi* lisp. ~**o** *m* lisp

cedazo *m* sieve

ceder *vt* give up; (transferir) transfer. ● *vi* give in; (disminuir) ease off; (romperse) give way, collapse. **ceda el paso** give way (Brit), yield (Amer)

cedro *m* cedar

cédula *f* bond. ~ **de identidad** identity card

CE(E) *abrev* (**Comunidad (Económica) Europea**) E(E)C

ceg|ador *a* blinding. ~**ar** [1 & 12] *vt* blind; (tapar) block up. □ ~**arse** *vpr* be blinded (**de** by). **∼uera** *f* blindness

ceja *f* eyebrow

cejar *vi* give way

celada *f* ambush; (fig) trap

cela|dor *m* (de cárcel) prison warder; (de museo etc) security guard. **∼r** *vt* watch

celda *f* cell

celebra|ción *f* celebration. **∼r** *vt* celebrate; (alabar) praise. □ **∼rse** *vpr* take place

célebre *a* famous

celebridad *f* fame; (persona) celebrity

celest|e *a* heavenly; *<vestido>* pale blue. **azul ∼e** sky-blue. **∼ial** *a* heavenly

celibato *m* celibacy

célibe *a* celibate

celo *m* zeal; (de las hembras) heat; (de los machos) rut; (cinta adhesiva) Sellotape (P) (Brit), Scotch (P) tape (Amer). **∼s** *mpl* jealousy. **dar ∼s** make jealous. **tener ∼s** be jealous

celofán *m* cellophane

celoso *a* conscientious; (que tiene celos) jealous

celta *a & m* (lengua) Celtic. ● *m & f* Celt

célula *f* cell

celular *a* cellular. ● *m* (LAm) mobile phone

celulosa *f* cellulose

cementerio *m* cemetery

cemento *m* cement; (hormigón) concrete; (LAm, cola) glue

cena *f* dinner; (comida ligera) supper

cenag|al *m* marsh, bog; (fig) tight spot. **∼oso** *a* boggy

cenar *vt* have for dinner; (en cena ligera) have for supper. ● *vi* have dinner; (tomar cena ligera) have supper

cenicero *m* ashtray

ceniza *f* ash

censo *m* census. **∼ electoral** electoral roll

censura *f* censure; (de prensa etc) censorship. **∼r** *vt* censure; censor *<prensa etc>*

centavo *a & m* hundredth; (moneda) centavo

centell|a *f* flash; (chispa) spark. **∼ar**, **∼ear** *vi* sparkle

centena *f* hundred. **∼r** *m* hundred. **a ∼res** by the hundred. **∼rio** *a* centenarian. ● *m* centenary; (persona) centenarian

centeno *m* rye

centésim|a *f* hundredth. **∼o** *a* hundredth

cent|ígrado *a* centigrade, Celsius. ● *m* centigrade. **∼igramo** *m* centigram. **∼ilitro** *m* centilitre. **∼ímetro** *m* centimetre

céntimo *a* hundredth. ● *m* cent

centinela *f* sentry

centolla *f*, **centollo** *m* spider crab

central *a* central. ● *f* head office. **∼ de correos** general post office. **∼ eléctrica** power station. **∼ nuclear** nuclear power station. **∼ telefónica** telephone exchange. **∼ita** *f* switchboard

centraliza|ción *f* centralization. **∼r** [10] *vt* centralize

centrar *vt* centre

céntrico *a* central

centrífugo *a* centrifugal

centro *m* centre. **∼ comercial** shopping centre (Brit), shopping mall (Amer)

Centroamérica *f* Central America

centroamericano *a & m* Central American

ceñi|do *a* tight. **∼r** [5 & 22] *vt* take *<corona>*; *<vestido>* cling to. □ **∼rse** *vpr* limit o.s. (**a** to)

ceñ|o *m* frown. **fruncir el ∼o** frown. **∼udo** *a* frowning

cepill|ar *vt* brush; (en carpintería) plane. **∼o** *m* brush; (en carpintería) plane. **∼o de dientes** toothbrush

cera *f* wax

cerámic|a *f* ceramics; (materia) pottery; (objeto) piece of pottery. **∼o** *a* ceramic

cerca *f* fence; (de piedra) wall. ● *adv* near, close. **∼ de** close to, close up, closely

cercan|ía f nearness, proximity. **~ías** fpl vicinity. **tren** m de **~ías** local train. **~o** a near, close.

cercar [7] vt fence in, enclose; <gente> surround; (asediar) besiege

cerciorar vt convince. □ **~se** vpr make sure

cerco m (asedio) siege; (círculo) ring; (LAm, valla) fence; (LAm, seto) hedge

cerdo m pig; (carne) pork

cereal m cereal

cerebr|al a cerebral. **~o** m brain; (persona) brains

ceremoni|a f ceremony. **~al** a ceremonial. **~oso** a ceremonious

cerez|a f cherry. **~o** m cherry tree

cerill|a f match. **~o** m (Mex) match

cern|er [1] vt sieve. □ **~erse** vpr hover. **~idor** m sieve

cero m nought, zero; (fútbol) nil (Brit), zero (Amer); (tenis) love; (persona) nonentity

cerquillo m (LAm, flequillo) fringe (Brit), bangs (Amer)

cerra|do a shut, closed; (espacio) shut in, enclosed; <cielo> overcast; <curva> sharp. **~dura** f lock; (acción de cerrar) shutting, closing. **~jero** m locksmith. **~r** [1] vt shut, close; (con llave) lock; (cercar) enclose; turn off <grifo>; block up <agujero etc>. ● vi shut, close. □ **~rse** vpr shut, close; <herida> heal. **~r con llave** lock

cerro m hill

cerrojo m bolt. **echar el ~** bolt

certamen m competition, contest

certero a accurate

certeza, certidumbre f certainty

certifica|do a <carta etc> registered. ● m certificate. **~r** [7] vt certify

certitud f certainty

cervatillo, cervato m fawn

cerve|cería f beerhouse, bar; (fábrica) brewery. **~za** f beer. **~za de barril** draught beer. **~za rubia** lager

cesa|ción f cessation, suspension. **~nte** a redundant. **~r** vt stop. ● vi stop, cease; (dejar un empleo) resign. **sin ~r** incessantly

cesárea f caesarian (section)

cese m cessation; (de un empleo) dismissal. **~ del fuego** (LAm) ceasefire

césped m grass, lawn

cest|a f basket. **~o** m basket. **~o de los papeles** waste-paper basket

chabacano a common; <chiste etc> vulgar. ● m (Mex, albaricoque) apricot

chabola f shack. **~s** fpl shanty town

cháchara f 🔳 chatter; (Mex, objetos sin valor) junk

chacharear vt (Mex) sell. ● vi 🔳 chatter

chacra f (LAm) farm

chal m shawl

chalado a 🔳 crazy

chalé m house (with a garden), villa

chaleco m waistcoat, vest (Amer). **~ salvavidas** life-jacket

chalet m (pl **~s**) house (with a garden), villa

chalote m shallot

chamac|a f (esp Mex) girl. **~o** m (esp Mex) boy

chamarra f sheepskin jacket; (Mex, chaqueta corta) jacket

chamb|a f (Mex, trabajo) work. **por ~a** by fluke. **~ear** vi (Mex, 🔳) work

champán m, **champaña** m & f champagne

champiñón m mushroom

champú m (pl **~es** o **~s**) shampoo

chamuscar [7] vt scorch

chance m (esp LAm) chance

chancho m (LAm) pig

chanchullo m 🔳 swindle, fiddle 🔳

chanclo m clog; (de caucho) rubber overshoe

chándal m (pl **~s**) tracksuit

chantaje m blackmail. **~ar** vt blackmail

chanza f joke

chapa f plate, sheet; (de madera) plywood; (de botella) metal top; (carrocería) bodywork; (LAm cerradura) lock. **~do** a plated. **~do a la antigua** old-fashioned. **~do en oro** gold-plated

chaparro a (LAm) short, squat

chaparrón m downpour

chapopote m (Mex) tar

chapotear *vi* splash

chapucero *a* <*persona*> slapdash; <*trabajo*> shoddy

chapulín *m* (Mex) locust; (saltamontes) grasshopper

chapurrar, **chapurrear** *vt* have a smattering of, speak a little

chapuza *f* botched job; (trabajo ocasional) odd job

chaquet|a *f* jacket. **cambiar de** ∼**a** change sides. ∼**ón** *m* three-quarter length coat

charc|a *f* pond, pool. ∼**o** *m* puddle, pool

charcutería *f* delicatessen

charla *f* chat; (conferencia) talk. ∼**dor** *a* talkative. ∼**r** *vi* 🛈 chat. ∼**tán** *a* talkative. ● *m* chatterbox; (vendedor) cunning hawker; (curandero) charlatan

charol *m* varnish; (cuero) patent leather. ∼**a** *f* (Mex) tray

charr|a *f* (Mex) horsewoman, cowgirl. ∼**o** *m* (Mex) horseman, cowboy

chascar [7] *vt* crack <*látigo*>; click <*lengua*>; snap <*dedos*>. ● *vi* <*madera*> creak. ∼ **con la lengua** click one's tongue

chasco *m* disappointment

chasis *m* (Auto) chassis

chasqu|ear *vt* crack <*látigo*>; click <*lengua*>; snap <*dedos*>. ● *vi* <*madera*> creak. ∼ **con la lengua** click one's tongue. ∼**ido** *m* crack; (de la lengua) click; (de los dedos) snap

chatarra *f* scrap iron; (fig) scrap

chato *a* <*nariz*> snub; <*objetos*> flat. ● *m* wine glass

chav|a *f* (Mex) girl, lass. ∼**al** *m* 🛈 boy, lad. ∼**o** *m* (Mex) boy, lad

checa|da *f* (Mex) check; (Mex, Med) checkup. ∼**r** [7] *vt* (Mex) check; (vigilar) check up on. ∼**r tarjeta** clock in

checo *a & m* Czech. ∼**slovaco** *a & m* (History) Czechoslovak

chelín *m* shilling

chelo *m* cello

cheque *m* cheque. ∼ **de viaje** traveller's cheque. ∼**ar** *vt* check; (LAm) check in <*equipaje*>. ∼**o** *m* check; (Med) checkup. ∼**ra** *f* chequebook

chévere *a* (LAm) great

chica *f* girl; (criada) maid, servant

chicano *a & m* Chicano, Mexican-American

chícharo *m* (Mex) pea

chicharra *f* cicada; (timbre) buzzer

chichón *m* bump

chicle *m* chewing-gum

chico *a* 🛈 small; (esp LAm, de edad) young. ● *m* boy. ∼**s** *mpl* children

chicoria *f* chicory

chifla|do *a* 🛈 crazy, daft. ∼**r** *vt* whistle at, boo. ● *vi* (LAm) whistle; (🛈, gustar mucho) **me chifla el chocolate** I'm mad about chocolate. □ ∼**rse** *vpr* be mad (**por** about)

chilango *a* (Mex) from Mexico City

chile *m* chilli

Chile *m* Chile

chileno *a & m* Chilean

chill|ar *vi* scream, shriek; <*ratón*> squeak; <*cerdo*> squeal. ∼**ido** *m* scream, screech. ∼**ón** *a* noisy; <*colores*> loud; <*sonido*> shrill

chimenea *f* chimney; (hogar) fireplace

chimpancé *m* chimpanzee

china *f* Chinese (woman)

China *f* China

chinche *m* drawing-pin (Brit), thumbtack (Amer); (insecto) bedbug; (fig) nuisance. ∼**eta** *f* drawing-pin (Brit), thumbtack (Amer)

chinela *f* slipper

chino *a* Chinese; (Mex rizado) curly. ● *m* Chinese (man); (Mex, de pelo rizado) curly-haired person

chipriota *a & m & f* Cypriot

chiquero *m* pen; (LAm, pocilga) pigsty (Brit), pigpen (Amer)

chiquillo *a* childish. ● *m* child, kid 🛈

chirimoya *f* custard apple

chiripa *f* fluke

chirri|ar [20] *vi* creak; <*frenos*> screech; <*pájaro*> chirp. ∼**do** *m* creaking; (de frenos) screech; (de pájaros) chirping

chis *int* sh!, hush!; (🛈, para llamar a uno) hey!, psst!

chism|e *m* gadget, thingumajig 🛈; (chismorreo) piece of gossip. ∼**es** *mpl* things, bits and pieces. **~orreo** *m* gossip. **~oso** *a* gossipy.● *m* gossip

chisp|a *f* spark; (pizca) drop; (gracia) wit; (fig) sparkle. **estar que echa ~a(s)** be furious. **~eante** *a* sparkling. **~ear** *vi* spark; (lloviznar) drizzle; (fig) sparkle. **~orrotear** *vt* throw out sparks; *<fuego>* crackle; *<aceite>* spit

chistar *vi.* **ni chistó** he didn't say a word. **sin ~** without saying a word

chiste *m* joke, funny story. **tener ~** be funny

chistera *f* top hat

chistoso *a* funny

chiva|rse *vpr* tip-off; *<niño>* tell. **~tazo** *m* tip-off. **~to** *m* informer; (niño) telltale

chivo *m* kid; (LAm, macho cabrío) billy goat

choca|nte *a* shocking; (Mex desagradable) unpleasant. **~r** [7] *vt* clink *<vasos>*; (LAm) crash *<vehículo>*. **¡chócala!** give me five! ● *vi* collide, hit. **~r con**, **~r contra** crash into

choch|ear *vi* be gaga. **~o** *a* gaga; (fig) soft

chocolate *m* chocolate. **tableta** *f* **de ~** bar of chocolate

chófer, (LAm) **chofer** *m* chauffeur; (conductor) driver

cholo *a & m* (LAm) half-breed

chopo *m* poplar

choque *m* collision; (fig) clash; (eléctrico) shock; (Auto, Rail etc) crash, accident; (sacudida) jolt

chorizo *m* chorizo

chorro *m* jet, stream; (caudal pequeño) trickle; (fig) stream. **a ~** *<avión>* jet. **a ~os** (fig) in abundance

chovinista *a* chauvinistic. ● *m & f* chauvinist

choza *f* hut

chubas|co *m* squall, heavy shower. **~quero** *m* raincoat, anorak

chuchería *f* trinket

chueco *a* (LAm) crooked

chufa *f* tiger nut

chuleta *f* chop

chulo *a* cocky; (bonito) lovely (Brit), neat (Amer); (Mex, atractivo) cute. ● *m* tough guy; (proxeneta) pimp

chup|ada *f* suck; (al helado) lick; (al cigarro) puff. **~ado** *a* skinny; (f, fácil) very easy. **~ar** *vt* suck; puff at *<cigarro etc>*; (absorber) absorb. **~ete** *m* dummy (Brit), pacifier (Amer). **~ón** *m* sucker; (LAm) dummy (Brit), pacifier (Amer); (Mex, del biberón) teat

churro *m* fritter; [mess

chusma *f* riff-raff

chut|ar *vi* shoot. **~e** *m* shot

cianuro *m* cyanide

cibernética *f* cibernetics

cicatriz *f* scar. **~ar** [10] *vt/i* heal. □ **~arse** *vpr* heal

cíclico *a* cyclic(al)

ciclis|mo *m* cycling. **~ta** *a* cycle. ● *m & f* cyclist

ciclo *m* cycle; (de películas, conciertos) season; (de conferencias) series

ciclomotor *m* moped

ciclón *m* cyclone

ciego *a* blind. ● *m* blind man, blind person. **a ciegas** in the dark

cielo *m* sky; (Relig) heaven; (persona) darling. **¡~s!** good heavens!, goodness me!

ciempiés *m invar* centipede

cien *a* a hundred. **~ por ~** one hundred per cent

ciénaga *f* bog, swamp

ciencia *f* science; (fig) knowledge. **~s** *fpl* (Univ etc) science. **~s empresariales** business studies. **a ~ cierta** for certain

cieno *m* mud

científico *a* scientific. ● *m* scientist

ciento *a & m* a hundred, one hundred. **~s de** hundreds of. **por ~** per cent

cierre *m* fastener; (acción de cerrar) shutting, closing; (LAm, cremallera) zip, zipper (Amer)

cierro *vb* ⇒CERRAR

cierto *a* certain; (verdad) true. **estar en lo ~** be right. **lo ~ es que** the fact is that. **no es ~** that's not true. **¿no es ~?** isn't that right? **por ~** by the way. **si bien es ~ que** although

ciervo *m* deer

cifra f figure, number; (cantidad) sum. **en ~** coded, in code. **~do** a coded. **~r** vt code; place *<esperanzas>*

cigala f crayfish

cigarra f cicada

cigarr|illera f cigarette box; (de bolsillo) cigarette case. **~illo** m cigarette. **~o** m (cigarrillo) cigarette; (puro) cigar

cigüeña f stork

cilantro m coriander

cil|índrico a cylindrical. **~indro** m cylinder

cima f top; (fig) summit

cimbr|ear vt shake. □ **~earse** vpr sway. **~onada** f, **~onazo** m (LAm) jolt; (de explosión) blast

cimentar [1] vt lay the foundations of; (fig, reforzar) strengthen

cimientos mpl foundations

cinc m zinc

cincel m chisel. **~ar** vt chisel

cinco a & m five; (en fechas) fifth

cincuent|a a & m fifty; (quincuagésimo) fiftieth. **~ón** a in his fifties

cine m cinema; (local) cinema (Brit), movie theater (Amer). **~asta** m & f film maker (Brit), movie maker (Amer). **~matográfico** a film (Brit), movie (Amer)

cínico a cynical. ● m cynic

cinismo m cynicism

cinta f ribbon; (película) film (Brit), movie (Amer); (para grabar, en carreras) tape. **~ aislante** insulating tape. **~ métrica** tape measure. **~ virgen** blank tape

cintur|a f waist. **~ón** m belt. **~ón de seguridad** safety belt. **~ón salvavidas** lifebelt

ciprés m cypress (tree)

circo m circus

circuito m circuit; (viaje) tour. **~ cerrado** closed circuit. **corto ~** short circuit

circula|ción f circulation; (vehículos) traffic. **~r** a circular. ● vi circulate; *<líquidos>* flow; (conducir) drive; (caminar) walk; *<autobús>* run

círculo m circle. **~ vicioso** vicious circle. **en ~** in a circle

circunci|dar vt circumcise. **~sión** f circumcision

circunferencia f circumference

circunflejo m circumflex

circunscri|bir (pp **circunscrito**) vt confine. □ **~birse** vpr confine o.s. (a to). **~pción** f (distrito) district. **~pción electoral** constituency

circunspecto a circumspect

circunstancia f circumstance

circunv|alar vt bypass. **~olar** vt [2] circle

cirio m candle

ciruela f plum. **~ pasa** prune

ciru|gía f surgery. **~jano** m surgeon

cisne m swan

cisterna f tank, cistern

cita f appointment; (entre chico y chica) date; (referencia) quotation. **~ción** f quotation; (Jurid) summons. **~do** a aforementioned. **~r** vt make an appointment with; (mencionar) quote; (Jurid) summons. □ **~rse** vpr arrange to meet

cítara f zither

ciudad f town; (grande) city. **~ balneario** (LAm) coastal resort. **~ perdida** (Mex) shanty town. **~ universitaria** university campus. **~anía** f citizenship; (habitantes) citizens. **~ano** a civic. ● m citizen, inhabitant

cívico a civic

civil a civil. ● m & f civil guard; (persona no militar) civilian

civiliza|ción f civilization. **~r** [10] vt civilize. □ **~rse** vpr become civilized

civismo m community spirit

clam|ar vi cry out, clamour. **~or** m clamour; (protesta) outcry. **~oroso** a noisy; (éxito) resounding

clandestino a clandestine, secret; *<periódico>* underground

clara f (de huevo) egg white

claraboya f skylight

clarear vi dawn; (aclarar) brighten up

clarete m rosé

claridad f clarity; (luz) light

clarifica|ción f clarification. **~r** [7] vt clarify

clar|ín m bugle. **~inete** m clarinet. **~inetista** m & f clarinettist

clarividen|cia f clairvoyance; (fig) far-sightedness. **~te** a clairvoyant; (fig) far-sighted

claro a clear; (luminoso) bright; <colores> light; <líquido> thin. ● m (en bosque etc) clearing; (espacio) gap. ● adv clearly. ● int of course! ¡~ que sí! yes, of course! ¡~ que no! of course not!

clase f class; (tipo) kind, sort; (aula) classroom. **~ media** middle class. **~ obrera** working class. **~ social** social class. **dar ~s** teach

clásico a classical; (típico) classic. ● m classic

clasifica|ción f classification; (deportes) league. **~r** [7] vt classify; (seleccionar) sort

claudicar [7] give in

claustro m cloister; (Univ) staff

claustrof|obia f claustrophobia. **~óbico** a claustrophobic

cláusula f clause

clausura f closure; (ceremonia) closing ceremony. **~r** vt close

clava|do a fixed; (con clavo) nailed. **es ~do a su padre** he's the spitting image of his father. ● m (LAm) dive. **~r** vt knock in <clavo>; stick in <cuchillo>; (fijar) fix; (juntar) nail together

clave f key; (Mus) clef; (instrumento) harpsichord. **~cín** m harpsichord

clavel m carnation

clavícula f collarbone, clavicle

clav|ija f peg; (Elec) plug. **~o** m nail; (Culin) clove

claxon m /'klakson/ (pl ~s) horn

clemencia f clemency, mercy

clementina f clementine

cleptómano m kleptomaniac

clerical a clerical

clérigo m priest

clero m clergy

cliché m cliché; (Foto) negative

cliente m customer; (de médico) patient; (de abogado) client. **~la** f clientele, customers; (de médico) patients

clim|a m climate; (ambiente) atmosphere. **~ático** a climatic. **~atizado** a air-conditioned

clínic|a f clinic. **~o** a clinical

cloaca f drain, sewer

cloro m chlorine

club m (pl ~s o ~es) club

coacci|ón f coercion. **~onar** vt coerce

coagular vt coagulate; clot <sangre>; curdle <leche>. □ **~se** vpr coagulate; <sangre> clot; <leche> curdle

coalición f coalition

coarta|da f alibi. **~r** vt hinder; restrict <libertad etc>

cobard|e a cowardly. ● m coward. **~ía** f cowardice

cobert|izo m shed. **~ura** f covering

cobij|a f (Mex, manta) blanket. **~as** fpl (LAm, ropa de cama) bedclothes. **~ar** vt shelter. □ **~arse** vpr (take) shelter. **~o** m shelter

cobra f cobra

cobra|dor m collector; (de autobús) conductor. **~r** vt collect; (ganar) earn; charge <precio>; cash <cheque>; (recuperar) recover. ● vi be paid

cobr|e m copper. **~izo** a coppery

cobro m collection; (de cheque) cashing; (pago) payment. **presentar al ~** cash

cocaína f cocaine

cocción f cooking; (Tec) firing

coc|er [2 & 9] vt/i cook; (hervir) boil; (Tec) fire. **~ido** m stew

coche m car, automobile (Amer); (de tren) coach, carriage; (de bebé) pram (Brit), baby carriage (Amer). **~cama** sleeper. **~ fúnebre** hearse. **~ restaurante** dining-car. **~s de choque** dodgems. **~ra** f garage; (de autobuses) depot

cochin|ada f dirty thing. **~o** a dirty, filthy. ● m pig

cociente m quotient. **~ intelectual** intelligence quotient, IQ

cocin|a f kitchen; (arte) cookery, cuisine; (aparato) cooker. **~a de gas** gas cooker. **~a eléctrica** electric cooker. **~ar** vt/i cook. **~ero** m cook

coco m coconut; (árbol) coconut palm; (cabeza) head; (que mete miedo) bogeyman. **comerse el ~** think hard

cocoa f (LAm) cocoa

cocodrilo m crocodile

cocotero m coconut palm

cóctel m (pl ~s o ~es) cocktail

cod|azo m nudge (with one's elbow). ~**ear** vt/i elbow, nudge. □ ~**arse** vpr rub shoulders (con with)

codici|a f greed. ~**ado** a coveted, sought after. ~**ar** vt covet. ~**oso** a greedy

código m code. ~ **de la circulación** Highway Code

codo m elbow; (dobladura) bend. ~ **a** ~ side by side. **hablar (hasta) por los** ~**s** talk too much

codorniz m quail

coeficiente m coefficient. ~ **intelectual** intelligence quotient, IQ

coerción f constraint

coetáneo a & m contemporary

coexist|encia f coexistence. ~**ir** vi coexist

cofradía f brotherhood

cofre m chest; (Mex, capó) bonnet (Brit), hood (Amer)

coger [14] vt (esp Esp) take; catch <tren, autobús, pelota, catarro>; (agarrar) take hold of; (del suelo) pick up; pick <frutos etc>. □ ~**se** vpr trap, catch; (agarrarse) hold on

cogollo m (de lechuga etc) heart; (brote) bud

cogote m nape; (LAm, cuello) neck

cohech|ar vt bribe. ~**o** m bribery

cohe|rente a coherent. ~**sión** f cohesion

cohete m rocket

cohibi|do a shy; (inhibido) awkward; (incómodo) awkward. ~**r** vt inhibit; (incomodar) make s.o. feel embarrassed. □ ~**rse** vpr feel inhibited

coincid|encia f coincidence. **dar la** ~**encia** happen. ~**ir** vt coincide

coje|ar vt limp; <mueble> wobble. ~**ra** f lameness

coj|ín m cushion. ~**inete** m small cushion

cojo a lame; <mueble> wobbly. ● m lame person

col f cabbage. ~**es de Bruselas** Brussel sprouts

cola f tail; (fila) queue; (para pegar) glue. **a la** ~ at the end. **hacer** ~ queue (up) (Brit), line up (Amer). **tener** ~, **traer** ~ have serious consequences

colabora|ción f collaboration. ~**dor** m collaborator. ~**r** vi collaborate

colada f washing. **hacer la** ~ do the washing

colador m strainer

colapso m collapse; (fig) standstill

colar [2] vt strain; pass <moneda falsa etc>. ● vi <líquido> seep through; (fig) be believed. □ ~**se** vpr slip; (en una cola) jump the queue; (en fiesta) gatecrash

colch|a f bedspread. ~**ón** m mattress. ~**oneta** f air bed; (en gimnasio) mat.

colear vi wag its tail; <asunto> not be resolved. **vivito y coleando** alive and kicking

colecci|ón f collection. ~**onar** vt collect. ~**onista** m & f collector

colecta f collection

colectivo a collective

colega m & f colleague

colegi|al m schoolboy. ~**ala** f schoolgirl. ~**o** m school; (de ciertas profesiones) college. ~**o mayor** hall of residence

cólera m cholera. ●f anger, fury. **montar en** ~ fly into a rage

colérico a furious, irate

colesterol m cholesterol

coleta f pigtail

colga|nte a hanging. ● m pendant. ~**r** [2 & 12] vt hang; hang out <ropa lavada>; hang up <abrigo etc>; put down <teléfono>. ● vi hang; (teléfono) hang up. □ ~**rse** vpr hang o.s. **dejar a uno** ~**do** let s.o. down

colibrí m hummingbird

cólico m colic

coliflor f cauliflower

colilla f cigarette end

colina f hill

colinda|nte a adjoining. ~**r** vt border (con on)

colisión f collision, crash; (fig) clash

collar m necklace; (de perro) collar

colmar vt fill to the brim; try <pa- ciencia>; (fig) fulfill. ~ a uno de aten- ciones lavish attention on s.o.

colmena f beehive, hive

colmillo m eye tooth, canine (tooth); (de elefante) tusk; (de carnívoro) fang

colmo m height. ser el ~ be the limit, be the last straw

coloca|ción f positioning; (empleo) job, position. ~r [7] vt put, place; (buscar empleo) find work for. □ ~rse vpr find a job

Colombia f Colombia

colombiano a & m Colombian

colon m colon

colón m (unidad monetaria de Costa Rica y El Salvador) colon

colon|ia f colony; (comunidad) com- munity; (agua de colonia) cologne; (Mex, barrio) residential suburb. ~a de verano holiday camp. ~iaje m (LAm) colonial period. ~ial a colo- nial. ~ialista m & f colonialist. ~ización f colonization. ~izar [10] colonize. ~o m colonist, settler; (labrador) tenant farmer

coloqui|al a colloquial. ~o m con- versation; (congreso) conference

color m colour. de ~ colour. en ~(es) <fotos, película> colour. ~ado a (rojo) red. ~ante m colouring. ~ear vt/i colour. ~ete m blusher. ~ido m colour

colosal a colossal; (fig, ⧉, magnífico) terrific

columna f column; (Anat) spine. ~ vertebral spinal column; (fig) back- bone

columpi|ar vt swing. □ ~arse vpr swing. ~o m swing

coma f comma; (Mat) point. ● m (Med) coma

comadre f (madrina) godmother; (amiga) friend. ~ar vi gossip

comadreja f weasel

comadrona f midwife

comal m (Mex) griddle

comand|ancia f command. ~ante m & f commander. ~o m command; (Mil, soldado) commando; (de terroristas) cell

comarca f area, region

comba f bend; (juguete) skipping- rope; (de viga) sag. saltar a la ~ skip. □ ~rse vpr bend; <viga> sag

combat|e m combat; (pelea) fight. ~iente m fighter. ~ir vt/i fight

combina|ción f combination; (enlace) connection; (prenda) slip. ~r vt combine; put together <colores>

combustible m fuel

comedia f comedy; (cualquier obra de teatro) play; (LAm, telenovela) soap (opera)

comedi|do a restrained; (LAm, atento) obliging. □ ~rse [5] vpr show restrain

comedor m dining-room; (restau- rante) restaurant

comensal m companion at table, fellow diner

comentar vt comment on; discuss <tema>; (mencionar) mention. ~io m commentary; (observación) comment. ~ios mpl gossip. ~ista m & f com- mentator

comenzar [1 & 10] vt/i begin, start

comer vt eat; (a mediodía) have for lunch; (esp LAm, cenar) have for din- ner; (corroer) eat away; (en ajedrez) take. ● vi eat; (a mediodía) have lunch; (esp LAm, cenar) have dinner. dar de ~ a feed. □ ~se vpr eat (up)

comerci|al a commercial; <ruta> trade; <nombre, trato> business. ● m (LAm) commercial, ad. ~ante m trader; (de tienda) shopkeeper. ~ar vi trade (con with, en in); (con otra perso- na) do business. ~o m commerce; (actividad) trade; (tienda) shop; (nego- cios) business

comestible a edible. ~s mpl food. tienda de ~s grocer's (shop) (Brit), grocery (Amer)

cometa m comet. ● f kite

comet|er vt commit; make <falta>. ~ido m task

comezón m itch

comicios mpl elections

cómico a comic; (gracioso) funny. ● m comic actor; (humorista) comedian

comida f food; (a mediodía) lunch; (esp LAm, cena) dinner; (acto) meal

comidilla f. ser la ~ del pueblo be the talk of the town

comienzo *m* beginning, start

comillas *fpl* inverted commas

comil|ón *a* greedy. ~**ona** *f* feast

comino *m* cumin. **(no) me importa un** ~ I couldn't care less

comisar|ía *f* police station. ~**io** *m* commissioner; (deportes) steward

comisión *f* assignment; (organismo) commission, committee; (Com) commission

comisura *f* corner. ~ **de los labios** corner of the mouth

comité *m* committee

como *prep* as; (comparación) like. ● *adv* about. ● *conj* as. ~ **quieras** as you like. ~ **si** as if

cómo

● *adverbio*

····▸ how. ¿~ **se llega?** how do you get there? ¿~ **es de alto?** how tall is it? **sé** ~ **pasó** I know how it happened

⚠ Cuando **cómo** va seguido del verbo **llamar** se traduce por *what*, p. ej. ¿~ **te llamas?** *what's your name?*

····▸ **cómo + ser** (sugiriendo descripción) ¿~ **es su marido?** what's her husband like?; (físicamente) what does her husband look like? **no sé** ~ **es la comida** I don't know what the food's like

····▸ (por qué) why. ¿~ **no actuaron antes?** why didn't they act sooner?

····▸ (pidiendo que se repita) sorry?, pardon? ¿~? **no te escuché** sorry? I didn't hear you

····▸ (en exclamaciones) ¡ ~ **llueve!** it's really pouring! ¡~! ¿**que no lo sabes?** what! you mean you don't know? ¡~ **no!** of course!

cómoda *f* chest of drawers

comodidad *f* comfort. **a su** ~ at your convenience

cómodo *a* comfortable; (conveniente) convenient

comoquiera *conj*. ~ **que sea** however it may be

compacto *a* compact; (denso) dense; *<líneas etc>* close

compadecer [11] *vt* feel sorry for. □ ~**se** *vpr*. ~**se de** feel sorry for

compadre *m* godfather; (amigo) friend

compañ|ero *m* companion; (de trabajo) colleague; (de clase) classmate; (pareja) partner. ~**ía** *f* company. **en** ~**ía de** with

compara|ble *a* comparable. ~**ción** *f* comparison. ~**r** *vt* compare. ~**tivo** *a & m* comparative

comparecer [11] *vi* appear

comparsa *f* group. ● *m & f* (en el teatro) extra

compartim(i)ento *m* compartment

compartir *vt* share

compás *m* (instrumento) (pair of) compasses; (ritmo) rhythm; (división) bar (Brit), measure (Amer); (Naut) compass. **a** ~ in time

compasi|ón *f* compassion, pity. **tener** ~**ón de** feel sorry for. ~**vo** *a* compassionate

compatib|ilidad *f* compatibility. ~**le** *a* compatible

compatriota *m & f* compatriot

compendio *m* summary

compensa|ción *f* compensation. ~**ción por despido** redundancy payment. ~**r** *vt* compensate

competen|cia *f* competition; (capacidad) competence; (poder) authority; (incumbencia) jurisdiction. ~**te** *a* competent

competi|ción *f* competition. ~**dor** *m* competitor. ~**r** [5] *vi* compete

compinche *m* accomplice; (🄴, amigo) friend, mate 🄴

complac|er [32] *vt* please. □ ~**erse** *vpr* be pleased. ~**iente** *a* obliging; *<marido>* complaisant

complej|idad *f* complexity. ~**o** *a & m* complex

complement|ario *a* complementary. ~**o** *m* complement; (Gram) object, complement

complet|ar *vt* complete. ~**o** *a* complete; (lleno) full; (exhaustivo) comprehensive

complexión *f* build

complica|ción f complication; (esp AmL, implicación) involvement. **~r** [7] vt complicate; involve <persona>. □ **~rse** vpr become complicated; (implicarse) get involved

cómplice m & f accomplice

complot m (pl ~s) plot

compon|ente a component. ● m component; (miembro) member. **~er** [34] vt make up; (Mus, Literatura etc) write, compose; (esp LAm, reparar) mend; (LAm) set <hueso>; settle <estómago>. □ **~erse** vpr be made up; (arreglarse) get better. **~érselas** manage

comporta|miento m behaviour. □ **~rse** vpr behave. **~rse mal** misbehave

composi|ción f composition. **~tor** m composer

compostura f composure; (LAm, arreglo) repair

compota f stewed fruit

compra f purchase. **~ a plazos** hire purchase. **hacer la(s) ~(s)** do the shopping. **ir de ~s** go shopping. **~dor** m buyer. **~r** vt buy. **~venta** f buying and selling; (Jurid) sale and purchase contract. **negocio** m **de ~venta** second-hand shop

compren|der vt understand; (incluir) include. **~sión** f understanding. **~sivo** a understanding

compresa f compress; (de mujer) sanitary towel

compr|esión f compression. **~imido** a compressed. ● m pill, tablet. **~imir** vt compress

comproba|nte m proof; (recibo) receipt. **~r** vt check; (demostrar) prove

comprom|eter vt compromise; (arriesgar) jeopardize. □ **~eterse** vpr compromise o.s.; (obligarse) agree to; <novios> get engaged. **~etido** a <situación> awkward, delicate; <autor> politically committed. **~iso** m obligation; (apuro) predicament; (cita) appointment; (acuerdo) agreement. **sin ~iso** without obligation

compuesto a compound; <persona> smart. ● m compound

computa|ción f (esp LAm) computing. **curso** m **de ~ción** computer course. **~dor** m, **~dora** f computer. **~r** vt calculate. **~rizar, computerizar** [10] vt computerize

cómputo m calculation

comulgar [12] vi take Communion

común a common; (compartido) joint. **en ~** in common. **por lo ~** generally. ● m. **el ~ de** most

comunal a communal

comunica|ción f communication. **~do** m communiqué. **~do de prensa** press release. **~r** [7] vt communicate; (informar) inform; (LAm, por teléfono) put through. **está ~ndo** <teléfono> it's engaged. □ **~rse** vpr communicate; (ponerse en contacto) get in touch. **~tivo** a communicative

comunidad f community. **~ de vecinos** residents' association. **C~ (Económica) Europea** European (Economic) Community. **en ~** together

comunión f communion; (Relig) (Holy) Communion

comunis|mo m communism. **~ta** a & m & f communist

con prep with; (+ infinitivo) by. **~ decir la verdad** by telling the truth. **~ que** so. **~ tal que** as long as

concebir [5] vt/i conceive

conceder vt concede, grant; award <premio>; (admitir) admit

concej|al m councillor. **~ero** m (LAm) councillor. **~o** m council

concentra|ción f concentration; (Pol) rally. **~r** vt concentrate; assemble <personas>. □ **~rse** vpr concentrate

concep|ción f conception. **~to** m concept; (opinión) opinion. **bajo ningún ~to** in no way

concerniente a. **en lo ~ a** with regard to

concertar [1] vt arrange; agree (upon) <plan>

concesión f concession

concha f shell; (carey) tortoiseshell

conciencia f conscience; (conocimiento) awareness. **~ limpia** clear conscience. **~ sucia** guilty conscience. **a ~ de que** fully aware that. **en ~** honestly. **tener ~ de** be aware of. **tomar** ~ **de** become aware of. ~**r** *vt* make aware. ~**rse** *vpr* become aware

concientizar [10] *vt* (esp LAm) make aware. □ ~**se** *vpr* become aware

concienzudo *a* conscientious

concierto *m* concert; (acuerdo) agreement; (Mus, composición) concerto

concilia|ción *f* reconciliation. ~**r** *vt* reconcile. ~ **el sueño** get to sleep. □ ~**rse** *vpr* gain

concilio *m* council

conciso *m* concise

conclu|ir [17] *vt* finish; (deducir) conclude. ● *vi* finish, end. ~**sión** *f* conclusion. ~**yente** *a* conclusive

concord|ancia *f* agreement. ~**ar** [2] *vt* reconcile. ● *vi* agree. ~**e** *a* in agreement. ~**ia** *f* harmony

concret|amente *adv* specifically, to be exact. ~**ar** *vt* make specific. ~**arse** *vpr* become definite; (limitarse) confine o.s. ~**o** *a* concrete; (determinado) specific, particular. **en** ~**o** definite; (concretamente) to be exact; (en resumen) in short. ● *m* (LAm, hormigón) concrete

concurr|encia *f* concurrence; (reunión) audience. ~**ido** *a* crowded, busy. ~**ir** *vi* meet; ; (coincidir) agree. ~ **a** (asistir a) attend

concurs|ante *m & f* competitor, contestant. ~**ar** *vi* compete, take part. ~**o** *m* competition; (ayuda) help

cond|ado *m* county. ~**e** *m* earl, count

condena *f* sentence. ~**ción** *f* condemnation. ~**do** *m* convicted person. ~**r** *vt* condemn; (Jurid) convict

condensa|ción *f* condensation. ~**r** *vt* condense

condesa *f* countess

condescende|ncia *f* condescension; (tolerancia) indulgence. ~**r** [1] *vi* agree; (dignarse) condescend

condici|ón *f* condition. **a** ~**ón de (que)** on condition that. ~**onal** *a* conditional. ~**onar** *vt* condition

condiment|ar *vt* season. ~**o** *m* seasoning

condolencia *f* condolence

condominio *m* joint ownership; (LAm, edificio) block of flats (Brit), condominium (esp Amer)

condón *m* condom

condonar *vt* (perdonar) reprieve; cancel <*deuda*>

conducir [47] *vt* drive <*vehículo*>; carry <*electricidad, gas, agua*>. ● *vi* drive; (fig, llevar) lead. **¿a qué conduce?** what's the point? □ ~**se** *vpr* behave

conducta *f* behaviour

conducto *m* pipe, tube; (Anat) duct. **por** ~ **de** through. ~**r** *m* driver; (jefe) leader; (Elec) conductor

conduzco *vb* ⇒CONDUCIR

conectar *vt/i* connect

conejo *m* rabbit

conexión *f* connection

confabularse *vpr* plot

confecci|ón *f* (de trajes) tailoring; (de vestidos) dressmaking. ~**ones** *fpl* clothing, clothes. **de** ~**ón** ready-to-wear. ~**onar** *vt* make

confederación *f* confederation

conferencia *f* conference; (al teléfono) long-distance call; (Univ) lecture. ~ **en la cima**, ~ **(en la) cumbre** summit conference. ~**nte** *m & f* lecturer

conferir [4] *vt* confer; award <*premio*>

confes|ar [1] *vt/i* confess. □ ~**arse** *vpr* confess. ~**ión** *f* confession. ~**ionario** *m* confessional. ~**or** *m* confessor

confeti *m* confetti

confia|do *a* trusting; (seguro de sí mismo) confident. ~**nza** *f* trust; (en sí mismo) confidence; (intimidad) familiarity. ~**r** [20] *vt* entrust. ● *vi*. ~**r en** trust

confiden|cia *f* confidence, secret. ~**cial** *a* confidential. ~**te** *m* confidant. ● *f* confidante

conf|ín *m* border. ~**ines** *mpl* outermost parts. ~**inar** *vt* confine; (desterrar) banish

confirma|ción *f* confirmation. ~**r** *vt* confirm

confiscar [7] *vt* confiscate

confit|ería *f* sweet-shop (Brit), candy store (Amer). ~**ura** *f* jam

conflict|ivo *a* difficult; *<época>* troubled; (polémico) controversial. **~o** *m* conflict

confluencia *f* confluence

conform|ación *f* conformation, shape. **~ar** *vt* (acomodar) adjust. ● *vi* agree. □ **~arse** *vpr* conform. **~e** *a* in agreement;(contento) happy, satisfied; (según) according (**con** to). **~e a** in accordance with, according to. ● *conj* as. ● *int* OK!. **~idad** *f* agreement; (tolerancia) resignation. **~ista** *m & f* conformist

conforta|ble *a* comfortable. **~nte** *a* comforting. **~r** *vt* comfort

confronta|ción *f* confrontation. **~r** *vt* confront

confu|ndir *vt* (equivocar) mistake, confuse; (mezclar) mix up, confuse; (turbar) embarrass. □ **~ndirse** *vpr* become confused; (equivocarse) make a mistake. **~sión** *f* confusion; (vergüenza) embarrassment. **~so** *a* confused; (borroso) blurred

congela|do *a* frozen. **~dor** *m* freezer. **~r** *vt* freeze

congeniar *vi* get on

congesti|ón *f* congestion. **~onado** *a* congested. □ **~onarse** *vpr* become congested

congoja *f* distress; (pena) grief

congraciarse *vpr* ingratiate o.s.

congratular *vt* congratulate

congrega|ción *f* gathering; (Relig) congregation. □ **~rse** [12] *vpr* gather, assemble

congres|ista *m & f* delegate, member of a congress. **~o** *m* congress, conference. **C~** Parliament. **C~o de los Diputados** Chamber of Deputies

cónico *a* conical

conífer|a *f* conifer. **~o** *a* coniferous

conjetura *f* conjecture, guess. **~r** *vt* conjecture, guess

conjuga|ción *f* conjugation. **~r** [12] *vt* conjugate

conjunción *f* conjunction

conjunto *a* joint. ● *m* collection; (Mus) band; (ropa) suit, outfit. **en ~** altogether

conjurar *vt* exorcise; avert *<peligro>*. ● *vi* plot, conspire

conllevar *vt* to entail

conmemora|ción *f* commemoration. **~r** *vt* commemorate

conmigo *pron* with me

conmo|ción *f* shock; (tumulto) upheaval. **~ cerebral** concussion. **~cionar** *vt* shock. **~ver** [2] *vt* shake; (emocionar) move

conmuta|dor *m* switch; (LAm, de teléfonos) switchboard. **~r** *vt* exchange

connota|ción *f* connotation. **~do** *a* (LAm, destacado) distinguished. **~r** *vt* connote

cono *m* cone

conoc|edor *a & m* expert. **~er** [11] *vt* know; (por primera vez) meet; (reconocer) recognize, know. **se conoce que** apparently. **dar a ~er** make known. □ **~erse** *vpr* know o.s.; *<dos personas>* know each other; (notarse) be obvious. **~ido** *a* well-known. ● *m* acquaintance. **~imiento** *m* knowledge; (sentido) consciousness. **sin ~imiento** unconscious. **tener ~imiento de** know about

conozco *vb* ⇒CONOCER

conque *conj* so

conquista *f* conquest. **~dor** *a* conquering. ● *m* conqueror; (de América) conquistador. **~r** *vt* conquer, win

consabido *a* usual, habitual

consagra|ción *f* consecration. **~r** *vt* consecrate; (fig) devote. □ **~rse** *vpr* devote o.s.

consanguíneo *m* blood relation

consciente *a* conscious

consecuen|cia *f* consequence; (coherencia) consistency. **a ~cia de** as a result of. **~te** *a* consistent

consecutivo *a* consecutive

conseguir [5 & 13] *vt* get, obtain; (lograr) manage; achieve *<objetivo>*

consej|ero *m* adviser; (miembro de consejo) member. **~o** *m* piece of advice; (Pol) council. **~o de ministros** cabinet

consenso *m* assent, consent

consenti|do *a* *<niño>* spoilt. **~miento** *m* consent. **~r** [4] *vt* allow; spoil *<niño>*. ● *vi* consent

conserje *m* porter, caretaker. **~ría** *f* porter's office

conserva f (mermelada) preserve; (en lata) tinned food. **en ~** tinned (Brit), canned. **~ción** f conservation; (de alimentos) preservation

conservador a & m (Pol) conservative

conservar vt keep; preserve <alimentos>. □ **~se** vpr keep; <costumbre> survive

conservatorio m conservatory

considera|ble a considerable. **~ción** f consideration; (respeto) respect. **de ~ción** serious. **de mi ~ción** (LAm, en cartas) Dear Sir. **~do** a considerate; (respetado) respected. **~r** vt consider; (respetar) respect

consigna f order; (para equipaje) left luggage office (Brit), baggage room (Amer); (eslogan) slogan

consigo pron (él) with him; (ella) with her; (Ud, Uds) with you; (uno mismo) with o.s.

consiguiente a consequent. **por ~** consequently

consist|encia f consistency. **~ente** a consisting (en of); (firme) solid; (LAm, congruente) consistent. **~ir** vi. **~ en** consist of; (radicar en) be due to

consola|ción f consolation. **~r** [2] vt console, comfort. □ **~rse** vpr console o.s.

consolidar vt consolidate. □ **~se** vpr consolidate

consomé m clear soup, consommé

consonante a consonant. ● f consonant

consorcio m consortium

conspira|ción f conspiracy. **~dor** m conspirator. **~r** vi conspire

consta|ncia f constancy; (prueba) proof; (LAm, documento) written evidence. **~nte** a constant. **~r** vi be clear; (figurar) appear, figure; (componerse) consist. **hacer ~r** state; (por escrito) put on record. **me ~ que** I'm sure that. **que conste que** believe me

constatar vt check; (confirmar) confirm

constipa|do m cold. ● a. **estar ~do** have a cold; (LAm, estreñido) be constipated. □ **~rse** vpr catch a cold

constitu|ción f constitution; (establecimiento) setting up. **~cional** a constitutional. **~ir** [17] vt constitute; (formar) form; (crear) set up, establish. □ **~irse** vpr set o.s. up (**en** as). **~tivo** a, **~yente** a constituent

constru|cción f construction. **~ctor** m builder. **~ir** [17] vt construct; build <edificio>

consuelo m consolation

consuetudinario a customary

cónsul m & f consul

consulado m consulate

consult|a f consultation. **horas** fpl **de ~a** surgery hours. **obra** f **de ~a** reference book. **~ar** vt consult. **~orio** m surgery

consumar vt complete; commit <crimen>; carry out <robo>; consummate <matrimonio>

consum|ición f consumption; (bebida) drink; (comida) food. **~ición mínima** minimum charge. **~ido** a <persona> skinny, wasted. **~idor** m consumer. **~ir** vt consume. □ **~irse** vpr <persona> waste away; <vela, cigarillo> burn down; <líquido> dry up. **~ismo** m consumerism. **~o** m consumption; (LAm, en restaurante etc) (bebida) drink; (comida) food. **~o mínimo** minimum charge

contab|ilidad f book-keeping; (profesión) accountancy. **~le** m & f accountant

contacto m contact. **ponerse en ~ con** get in touch with

conta|do a. **al ~** cash. **~s** a pl few. **tiene los días ~s** his days are numbered. **~dor** m meter; (LAm, persona) accountant

contagi|ar vt infect <persona>; pass on <enfermedad>; (fig) contaminate. **~o** m infection; (directo) contagion. **~oso** a infectious; (por contacto directo) contagious

contamina|ción f contamination, pollution. **~r** vt contaminate, pollute

contante a. **dinero** m **~** cash

contar [2] vt count; tell <relato>. **se cuenta que** it's said that. ● vi count. **~ con** rely on, count on. □ **~se** vpr be included (**entre** among)

contempla|ción *f* contemplation. **sin ~ciones** unceremoniously. **~r** *vt* look at; (fig) contemplate

contemporáneo *a & m* contemporary

conten|er [40] *vt* contain; hold <*respiración*>. □ **~erse** *vpr* contain o.s. **~ido** *a* contained. ● *m* contents

content|ar *vt* please. □ **~arse** *vpr*. **~arse con** be satisfied with, be pleased with. **~o** *a* (alegre) happy; (satisfecho) pleased

contesta|ción *f* answer. **~dor** *m*. **~ automático** answering machine. **~r** *vt/i* answer; (replicar) answer back

contexto *m* context

contienda *f* conflict; (lucha) contest

contigo *pron* with you

contiguo *a* adjacent

continen|tal *a* continental. **~te** *m* continent

continu|ación *f* continuation. **a ~ación** immediately after. **~ar** [21] *vt* continue, resume. ● *vi* continue. **~idad** *f* continuity. **~o** *a* continuous; (frecuente) continual. **corriente** *f* **~a** direct current

contorno *m* outline; (de árbol) girth; (de caderas) measurement. **~s** *mpl* surrounding area

contorsión *f* contortion

contra *prep* against. **en ~** against. ● *m* cons. ●*f* snag. **llevar la ~** contradict

contraata|car [7] *vt/i* counterattack. **~que** *m* counter-attack

contrabaj|ista *m & f* double-bass player. **~o** *m* double-bass; (persona) double-bass player

contraband|ista *m & f* smuggler. **~o** *m* contraband

contracción *f* contraction

contrad|ecir [46] *vt* contradict. **~icción** *f* contradiction. **~ictorio** *a* contradictory

contraer [41] *vt* contract. **~ matrimonio** marry. □ **~se** *vpr* contract

contralto *m* counter tenor. ● *f* contralto

contra|mano. **a ~** in the wrong direction. **~partida** *f* compensation. **~pelo**. **a ~** the wrong way

contrapes|ar *vt* counterweight. **~o** *m* counterweight

contraproducente *a* counterproductive

contrari|a *f*. **llevar la ~a** contradict. **~ado** *a* upset; (enojado) annoyed. **~ar** [20] *vt* upset; (enojar) annoy. **~edad** *f* setback; (disgusto) annoyance. **~o** *a* contrary (**a** to); <*dirección*> opposite. **al ~o** on the contrary. **al ~o de** contrary to. **de lo ~o** otherwise. **por el ~o** on the contrary. **ser ~o a** be opposed to, be against

contrarrestar *vt* counteract

contrasentido *m* contradiction

contraseña *f* (palabra) password; (en cine) stub

contrast|ar *vt* check, verify. ● *vi* contrast. **~e** *m* contrast; (en oro, plata) hallmark

contratar *vt* contract <*servicio*>; hire, take on <*empleados*>; sign up <*jugador*>

contratiempo *m* setback; (accidente) mishap

contrat|ista *m & f* contractor. **~o** *m* contract

contraven|ción *f* contravention. **~ir** [53] *vt* contravene

contraventana *f* shutter

contribu|ción *f* contribution; (tributo) tax. **~ir** [17] *vt/i* contribute. **~yente** *m & f* contributor; (que paga impuestos) taxpayer

contrincante *m* rival, opponent

control *m* control; (vigilancia) check; (lugar) checkpoint. **~ar** *vt* control; (vigilar) check. □ **~se** *vpr* control s.o.

controversia *f* controversy

contundente *a* <*arma*> blunt; <*argumento*> convincing

contusión *f* bruise

convalec|encia *f* convalescence. **~er** [11] *vi* convalesce. **~iente** *a & m & f* convalescent

convalidar *vt* recognize <*título*>

convenc|er [9] *vt* convince. **~imiento** *m* conviction

convenci|ón *f* convention. **~onal** *a* conventional

conveni|encia *f* convenience; (aptitud) suitability. **~ente** *a* suitable; (aconsejable) advisable; (provechoso) useful. **~o** *m* agreement. **~r** [53] *vt* agree. ● *vi* agree (**en** on); (ser conveniente) be convenient for, suit; (ser aconsejable) be advisable

convento *m* (de monjes) monastery; (de monjas) convent

conversa|ción *f* conversation. **~ciones** *fpl* talks. **~r** *vi* converse, talk

conver|sión *f* conversion. **~so** *a* converted. ● *m* convert. **~tible** *a* convertible. ● *m* (LAm) convertible. **~tir** [4] *vt* convert. □ **~tirse** *vpr*. **~tirse en** turn into; (Relig) convert

convic|ción *f* conviction. **~to** *a* convicted

convida|do *m* guest. **~r** *vt* invite

convincente *a* convincing

conviv|encia *f* coexistence; (de parejas) life together. **~ir** *vi* live together; (coexistir) coexist

convulsión *f* convulsion

convocar [7] *vt* call <*huelga, elecciones*>; convene <*reunión*>; summon <*personas*>

convulsión *f* convulsion

conyugal *a* marital, conjugal; <*vida*> married

cónyuge *m* spouse. **~s** *mpl* married couple

coñac *m* (*pl* **~s**) brandy

coopera|ción *f* cooperation. **~r** *vi* cooperate. **~tiva** *f* cooperative. **~tivo** *a* cooperative

coordinar *vt* coordinate

copa *f* glass; (deportes, fig) cup; (de árbol) top. **~s** *fpl* (naipes) hearts. **tomar una ~** have a drink

copia *f* copy. **~ en limpio** fair copy. **sacar una ~** make a copy. **~r** *vt* copy

copioso *a* copious; <*lluvia, nevada etc*> heavy

copla *f* verse; (canción) folksong

copo *m* flake. **~ de nieve** snowflake. **~s de maíz** cornflakes

coquet|a *f* flirt; (mueble) dressing-table. **~ear** *vi* flirt. **~o** *a* flirtatious

coraje *m* courage; (rabia) anger

coral *a* choral. ● *m* coral; (Mus) chorale

coraza *f* cuirass; (Naut) armour-plating; (de tortuga) shell

coraz|ón *m* heart; (persona) darling. **sin ~ón** heartless. **tener buen ~ón** be good-hearted. **~onada** *f* hunch; (impulso) impulse

corbata *f* tie, necktie (esp Amer). **~ de lazo** bow tie

corche|a *f* quaver. **~te** *m* fastener, hook and eye; (gancho) hook; (paréntesis) square bracket

corcho *m* cork. **~lata** *f* (Mex) (crown) cap

corcova *f* hump. **~do** *a* hunchbacked

cordel *m* cord, string

cordero *m* lamb

cordial *a* cordial, friendly. ● *m* tonic. **~idad** *f* cordiality, warmth

cordillera *f* mountain range

córdoba *m* (unidad monetaria de Nicaragua) córdoba

cordón *m* string; (de zapatos) lace; (cable) cord; (fig) cordon. **~ umbilical** umbilical cord

coreografía *f* choreography

corista *f* (bailarina) chorus girl

cornet|a *f* bugle; (Mex, de coche) horn. **~ín** *m* cornet

cornudo *a* horned. ● *m* cuckold

coro *m* (Arquit, Mus) choir; (en teatro) chorus

corona *f* crown; (de flores) wreath, garland. **~ción** *f* coronation. **~r** *vt* crown

coronel *m* colonel

coronilla *f* crown. **estar hasta la ~** be fed up

corpora|ción *f* corporation. **~l** *a* <*castigo*> corporal; <*trabajo*> physical

corpulento *a* stout

corral *m* farmyard. **aves** *fpl* **de ~** poultry

correa *f* strap; (de perro) lead; (cinturón) belt

correc|ción *f* correction; (cortesía) good manners. **~to** *a* correct; (cortés) polite

corre|dizo *a* running. **nudo** *m* **~dizo** slip knot. **puerta** *f* **~diza** sliding door. **~dor** *m* runner; (pasillo) corridor; (agente) agent, broker. **~dor de coches** racing driver

corregir [5 & 14] *vt* correct

correlación *f* correlation

correo *m* post, mail; (persona) courier; (LAm, oficina) post office. **~s** *mpl* post office. ● **electrónico** e-mail. **echar al ~** post

correr *vt* run; (mover) move; draw *<cortinas>*. ● *vi* run; *<agua, electricidad etc>* flow; *<tiempo>* pass. □ **~se** *vpr* (apartarse) move along; *<colores>* run

correspond|encia *f* correspondence. **~er** *vi* correspond; (ser adecuado) be fitting; (contestar) reply; (pertenecer) belong; (incumbir) fall to. □ **~erse** *vpr* (amarse) love one another. **~iente** *a* corresponding

corresponsal *m* correspondent

corrid|a *f* run. **~a de toros** bullfight. **de ~a** from memory. **~o** *a* (continuo) continuous

corriente *a* *<agua>* running; *<monedas, publicación, cuenta, año>* current; (ordinario) ordinary. ● *f* current; (de aire) draught; (fig) tendency. ● *m* current month. **al ~** (al día) up-to-date; (enterado) aware

corr|illo *m* small group. **~o** *m* circle

corroborar *vt* corroborate

corroer [24 & 37] *vt* corrode; (Geol) erode; (fig) eat away

corromper *vt* corrupt, rot *<materia>*. □ **~se** *vpr* become corrupted; *<materia>* rot; *<alimentos>* go bad

corrosi|ón *f* corrosion. **~vo** *a* corrosive

corrupción *f* corruption; (de materia etc) rot

corsé *m* corset

corta|do *a* cut; *<carretera>* closed; *<leche>* curdled; (avergonzado) embarrassed; (confuso) confused. ● *m* coffee with a little milk. **~dura** *f* cut. **~nte** *a* sharp; *<viento>* biting; *<frío>* bitter. **~r** *vt* cut; (recortar) cut out; (aislar, separar, interrumpir) cut off. ● *vi* cut; *<novios>* break up. □ **~rse** *vpr* cut o.s.; *<leche etc>* curdle; (fig) be embarrassed. **~rse el pelo** have one's

hair cut. **~rse las uñas** cut one's nails. **~uñas** *m invar* nail-clippers

corte *m* cut; (de tela) length. **~ de luz** power cut. **~ y confección** dressmaking. ● *f* court; (LAm, tribunal) Court of Appeal. **hacer la ~** court. **las C~s** the Spanish parliament. **la C~ Suprema** the Supreme Court

cortej|ar *vt* court. **~o** *m* (de rey etc) entourage. **~o fúnebre** cortège, funeral procession

cortés *a* polite

cortesía *f* courtesy

corteza *f* bark; (de queso) rind; (de pan) crust

cortijo *m* farm; (casa) farmhouse

cortina *f* curtain

corto *a* short; (apocado) shy. **~ de** short of. **~ de alcances** dim, thick. **~ de vista** short-sighted. **a la corta o a la larga** sooner or later. **quedarse ~** fall short; (miscalcular) underestimate. **~circuito** *m* short circuit

Coruña *f*. **La ~** Corunna

cosa *f* thing; (asunto) business; (idea) idea. **como si tal ~** just like that; (como si no hubiera pasado nada) as if nothing had happened. **decirle a uno cuatro ~s** tell s.o. a thing or two

cosecha *f* harvest; (de vino) vintage. **~r** *vt* harvest

coser *vt* sew; sew on *<botón>*; stitch *<herida>*. ● *vi* sew. □ **~se** *vpr* stick to s.o.

cosmético *a & m* cosmetic

cósmico *a* cosmic

cosmo|polita *a & m & f* cosmopolitan. **~s** *m* cosmos

cosquillas *fpl*. **dar ~** tickle. **hacer ~** tickle. **tener ~** be ticklish

costa *f* coast. **a ~ de** at the expense of. **a toda ~** at any cost

costado *m* side

costal *m* sack

costar [2] *vt* cost. ● *vi* cost; (resultar difícil) to be hard. **~ caro** be expensive. **cueste lo que cueste** at any cost

costarricense *a & m*, **costarriqueño** *a & m* Costa Rican

cost|as *fpl* (Jurid) costs. **~e** *m* cost. **~ear** *vt* pay for; (Naut) sail along the coast

costero *a* coastal

costilla *f* rib; (chuleta) chop

costo *m* cost. ∼**so** *a* expensive

costumbre *f* custom; (de persona) habit. **de** ∼ usual; (como adv) usually

costur|a *f* sewing; (línea) seam; (confección) dressmaking. ∼**era** *f* dressmaker. ∼**ero** *m* sewing box

cotejar *vt* compare

cotidiano *a* daily

cotille|ar *vt* gossip. ∼**o** *m* gossip

cotiza|ción *f* quotation, price. ∼**r** [10] *vt* (en la bolsa) quote. ● *vi* pay contributions. □ ∼**rse** *vpr* fetch; (en la bolsa) stand at; (fig) be valued

coto *m* enclosure; (de caza) preserve. ∼ **de caza** game preserve

cotorr|a *f* parrot; (fig) chatterbox. ∼**ear** *vi* chatter

coyuntura *f* joint

coz *f* kick

cráneo *m* skull

cráter *m* crater

crea|ción *f* creation. ∼**dor** *a* creative. ● *m* creator. ∼**r** *vt* create

crec|er [11] *vi* grow; (aumentar) increase; <*río*> rise. ∼**ida** *f* (de río) flood. ∼**ido** *a* <*persona*> grown-up; <*número*> large, considerable; <*plantas*> fully-grown. ∼**iente** *a* growing; <*luna*> crescent. ∼**imiento** *m* growth

credencial *f* document. ● *a*. **cartas** *fpl* ∼**es** credentials

credibilidad *f* credibility

crédito *m* credit; (préstamo) loan. **digno de** ∼ reliable

credo *m* creed

crédulo *a* credulous

cre|encia *f* belief. ∼**er** [18] *vt/i* believe; (pensar) think. ∼**o que no** I don't think so, I think not. ∼**o que sí** I think so. **no** ∼**o** I don't think so. ¡**ya lo** ∼**o!** I should think so!. □ ∼**erse** *vpr* consider o.s. **no me lo** ∼**o** I don't believe it. ∼**ible** *a* credible

crema *f* cream; (Culin) custard; (LAm, de la leche) cream. ∼ **batida** (LAm) whipped cream. ∼ **bronceadora** suntan cream

cremallera *f* zip (Brit), zipper (Amer)

crematorio *m* crematorium

crepitar *vi* crackle

crepúsculo *m* twilight

crespo *a* frizzy; (LAm, rizado) curly. ● *m* (LAm) curl

cresta *f* crest; (de gallo) comb

creyente *m* believer

cría *f* breeding; (animal) baby animal. **las** ∼**s** the young

cria|da *f* maid, servant. ∼**dero** *m* (de pollos etc) farm; (de ostras) bed; (Bot) nursery. ● *m* servant. ∼**dor** *m* breeder. ∼**nza** *f* breeding. ∼**r** [20] *vt* suckle; grow <*plantas*>; breed <*animales*>; (educar) bring up (Brit), raise (esp Amer). □ ∼**rse** *vpr* grow up

criatura *f* creature; (niño) baby

crim|en *m* (serious) crime; (asesinato) murder; (fig) crime. ∼**inal** *a & m & f* criminal

crin *f* mane

crío *m* child

criollo *a* Creole; (LAm, <*música, comida*> traditional. ● *m* Creole; (LAm, nativo) Peruvian, Chilean etc

crisantemo *m* chrysanthemum

crisis *f invar* crisis

crispar *vt* twitch; (Ⓕ, irritar) annoy. ∼**le los nervios a uno** get on s.o.'s nerves

cristal *m* crystal; (Esp, vidrio) glass; (Esp, de una ventana) pane of glass. **limpiar los** ∼**es** (Esp) clean the windows. ∼**ino** *a* crystalline; (fig) crystal-clear. ∼**izar** [10] crystallize. □ ∼**izarse** *vpr* crystallize

cristian|dad *f* Christendom. ∼**ismo** *m* Christianity. ∼**o** *a* Christian. **ser** ∼**o** be a Christian. ● *m* Christian

cristo *m* crucifix

Cristo *m* Christ

criterio *m* criterion; (discernimiento) judgement; (opinión) opinion

cr|ítica *f* criticism; (reseña) review. ∼**iticar** [7] *vt* criticize. ∼**ítico** *a* critical. ● *m* critic

croar *vi* croak

crom|ado *a* chromium-plated. ∼**o** *m* chromium, chrome

crónic|a *f* chronicle; (de radio, TV) report; (de periódico) feature. ∼**a deportiva** sport section. ∼**o** *a* chronic

cronista *m* & *f* reporter

cronología *f* chronology

cron|ometrar *vt* time. **~ómetro** *m* (en deportes) stop-watch

croqueta *f* croquette

cruce *m* crossing; (de calles, carreteras) crossroads; (de peatones) (pedestrian) crossing

crucial *a* crucial

crucifi|car [7] *vt* crucify. **~jo** *m* crucifix

crucigrama *m* crossword (puzzle)

crudo *a* raw; (fig) harsh. ● *m* crude (oil)

cruel *a* cruel. **~dad** *f* cruelty

cruji|do *m* (de seda, de hojas secas) rustle; (de muebles) creak. **~r** *vi* <seda, hojas secas> rustle; <muebles> creak

cruz *f* cross; (de moneda) tails. **~ gamada** swastika. **la C~ Roja** the Red Cross

cruza|da *f* crusade. **~r** [10] *vt* cross; exchange <palabras>. □ **~rse** *vpr* cross; (pasar en la calle) pass each other. **~rse con** pass

cuaderno *m* exercise book; (para apuntes) notebook

cuadra *f* (caballeriza) stable; (LAm, distancia) block

cuadrado *a* & *m* square

cuadragésimo *a* fortieth

cuadr|ar *vt* square. ● *vi* suit; <cuentas> tally. □ **~arse** *vpr* (Mil) stand to attention; (fig) dig one's heels in. **~ilátero** *m* quadrilateral; (Boxeo) ring

cuadrilla *f* group; (pandilla) gang

cuadro *m* square; (pintura) painting; (Teatro) scene; (de números) table; (de mando etc) panel; (conjunto del personal) staff. **~ de distribución** switchboard. **a ~s, de ~s** check. **¡qué ~!, ¡vaya un ~!** what a sight!

cuadrúpedo *m* quadruped

cuádruple *a* & *m* quadruple

cuajar *vt* congeal <sangre>; curdle <leche>; (llenar) fill up. ● *vi* <nieve> settle; (fig, 🔢) work out. **cuajado de** full of. □ **~se** *vpr* coagulate; <sangre> clot; <leche> curdle

cual *pron*. **el ~, la ~** etc (animales y cosas) that, which; (personas, sujeto) who, that; (personas, objeto) whom. ● *a* (LAm, qué) what. **~ si** as if. **cada ~** everyone. **lo ~** which. **por lo ~** because of which. **sea ~ sea** whatever

cuál *pron* which

cualidad *f* quality

cualquiera *a* (delante de nombres **cualquier,** *pl* **cualesquiera**) any. ● *pron* (*pl* **cualesquiera**) anyone, anybody; (cosas) whatever, whichever. **un ~** a nobody. **una ~** a slut

cuando *adv* when. ● *conj* when; (si) if. **~ más** at the most. **~ menos** at the least. **aun ~** even if. **de ~ en ~** from time to time

cuándo *adv* & *conj* when. **¿de ~ acá?, ¿desde ~?** since when? **¡~ no!** (LAm) as usual!, typical!

cuant|ía *f* quantity; (extensión) extent. **~ioso** *a* abundant. **~o** *a* as much ... as, as many ... as. ● *pron* as much as, as many as. ● *adv* as much as. **~o antes** as soon as possible. **~o más, mejor** the more the merrier. **en ~o** as soon as. **en ~o a** as for. **por ~o** since. **unos ~os** a few, some

cuánto *a* (interrogativo) how much?; (interrogativo en plural) how many?; (exclamativo) what a lot of! ● *pron* how much?; (en plural) how many? ● *adv* how much. **¿~ mides?** how tall are you? **¿~ tiempo?** how long? **¡~ tiempo sin verte!** it's been a long time! **¿a ~s estamos?** what's the date today? **un Sr. no sé ~s** Mr So-and-So

cuáquero *m* Quaker

cuarent|a *a* & *m* forty; (cuadragésimo) fortieth. **~ena** *f* (Med) quarantine. **~ón** *a* about forty

cuaresma *f* Lent

cuarta *f* (palmo) span

cuartel *m* (Mil) barracks. **~ general** headquarters

cuarteto *m* quartet

cuarto *a* fourth. ● *m* quarter; (habitación) room. **~ de baño** bathroom. **~ de estar** living room. **~ de hora** quarter of an hour. **estar sin un ~** be broke. **y ~** (a) quarter past

cuarzo *m* quartz

cuate *m* (Mex) twin; (amigo) friend; (🔲, tipo) guy

cuatro *a & m* four. ~**cientos** *a & m* four hundred

Cuba *f* Cuba

cuba|libre *m* rum and Coke (P). ~**no** *a & m* Cuban

cúbico *a* cubic

cubículo *m* cubicle

cubiert|a *f* cover; (neumático) tyre; (Naut) deck. ~**o** *a* covered; <*cielo*> overcast. ● *m* place setting, piece of cutlery; (en restaurante) cover charge. **a** ~**o** under cover

cubilete *m* bowl; (molde) mould; (para los dados) cup

cubis|mo *m* cubism. ~**ta** *a & m & f* cubist

cubo *m* bucket; (Mat) cube

cubrecama *m* bedspread

cubrir (*pp* **cubierto**) *vt* cover; fill <*vacante*>. □ ~**se** *vpr* cover o.s.; (ponerse el sombrero) put on one's hat; <*el cielo*> cloud over, become overcast

cucaracha *f* cockroach

cuchar|a *f* spoon. ~**ada** *f* spoonful. ~**adita** *f* teaspoonful. ~**illa**, ~**ita** *f* teaspoon. ~**ón** *m* ladle

cuchichear *vi* whisper

cuchill|a *f* large knife; (de carnicero) cleaver; (hoja de afeitar) razor blade. ~**ada** *f* stab; (herida) knife wound. ~**o** *m* knife

cuchitril *m* (fig) hovel

cuclillas: **en** ~ *adv* squatting

cuco *a* shrewd; (mono) pretty, nice. ● *m* cuckoo

cucurucho *m* cornet

cuello *m* neck; (de camisa) collar. **cortar(le) el** ~ **a uno** cut s.o.'s throat

cuenc|a *f* (del ojo) (eye) socket; (Geog) basin. ~**o** *m* hollow; (vasija) bowl

cuenta *f* count; (acción de contar) counting; (cálculo) calculation; (factura) bill; (en banco, relato) account; (de collar) bead. ~ **corriente** current account, checking account (Amer). **dar** ~ **de** give an account of. **darse** ~ **de** realize. **en resumidas** ~**s** in short. **por mi propia** ~ on my own account. **tener en** ~ bear in mind

cuentakilómetros *m invar* milometer

cuent|ista *m & f* story-writer; (de mentiras) fibber. ~**o** *m* story; (mentira) fib, tall story. ~ **de hadas** fairy tale. ● *vb* ⇒CONTAR

cuerda *f* rope; (más fina) string; (Mus) string. ~ **floja** tightrope. **dar** ~ **a** wind up <*un reloj*>

cuerdo *a* <*persona*> sane; <*acción*> sensible

cuerno *m* horn

cuero *m* leather; (piel) skin; (del grifo) washer. ~ **cabelludo** scalp. **en** ~**s** (vivos) stark naked

cuerpo *m* body

cuervo *m* crow

cuesta *f* slope, hill. ~ **abajo** downhill. ~ **arriba** uphill. **a** ~**s** on one's back

cuestión *f* matter; (problema) problem; (cosa) thing

cueva *f* cave

cuida|do *m* care; (preocupación) worry. ~**do!** watch out!. **tener** ~**do** be careful. ~**doso** *a* careful. ~**r** *vt* look after. ● *vi*. ~**r de** look after. □ ~**rse** *vpr* look after o.s. ~**rse de** be careful to

culata *f* (de revólver, fusil) butt. ~**zo** *m* recoil

culebr|a *f* snake. ~**ón** *m* soap opera

culinario *a* culinary

culminar *vi* culminate

culo *m* 🔲 bottom; (LAm vulg) arse (Brit vulg), ass (Amer vulg)

culpa *f* fault. **echar la** ~ blame. **por** ~ **de** because of. **tener la** ~ be to blame (de for). ~**bilidad** *f* guilt. ~**ble** *a* guilty. ● *m & f* culprit. ~**r** *vt* blame (de for)

cultiv|ar *vt* farm; grow <*plantas*>; (fig) cultivate. ~**o** *m* farming; (de plantas) growing

cult|o *a* <*persona*> educated. ● *m* cult; (homenaje) worship. ~**ura** *f* culture. ~**ural** *a* cultural

culturismo *m* body-building

cumbre *f* summit

cumpleaños *m invar* birthday

cumplido *a* perfect; (cortés) polite. ● *m* compliment. **de** ~ courtesy. **por**

~ out of a sense of duty. **~r** *a* reliable

cumpli|miento *m* fulfilment; (de ley) observance; (de orden) carrying out. **~r** *vt* carry out; observe *<ley>*; serve *<condena>*; reach *<años>*; keep *<promesa>*. **hoy cumple 3 años** he's 3 (years old) today. ● *vi* do one's duty. **por ~r** as a mere formality. □ **~rse** *vpr* expire; (realizarse) be fulfilled

cuna *f* cradle; (fig, nacimiento) birthplace

cundir *vi* spread; (rendir) go a long way

cuneta *f* ditch

cuña *f* wedge

cuñad|a *f* sister-in-law. **~o** *m* brother-in-law

cuño *m* stamp. **de nuevo ~** new

cuota *f* quota; (de sociedad etc) membership, fee; (LAm, plazo) instalment; (Mex, peaje) toll

cupe *vb* →CABER

cupo *m* cuota; (LAm, capacidad) room; (Mex, plaza) place

cupón *m* coupon

cúpula *f* dome

cura *f* cure; (tratamiento) treatment. ● *m* priest. **~ción** *f* healing. **~ndero** *m* faith-healer. **~r** *vt* (incl Culin) cure; dress *<herida>*; (tratar) treat; (fig) remedy; tan *<pieles>*. □ **~rse** *vpr* get better

curios|ear *vi* pry; (mirar) browse. **~idad** *f* curiosity. **~o** *a* curious; (raro) odd, unusual. ● *m* onlooker; (fisgón) busybody

curita *f* (LAm) (sticking) plaster

curriculum (vitae) *m* curriculum vitae, CV

cursar *vt* issue; (estudiar) study

cursi *a* pretentious, showy

cursillo *m* short course

cursiva *f* italics

curso *m* course; (Univ etc) year. **en ~** under way; *<año etc>* current

cursor *m* cursor

curtir *vt* tan; (fig) harden. □ **~se** *vpr* become tanned; (fig) become hardened

curv|a *f* curve; (de carretera) bend. **~ar** *vt* bend; bow *<estante>*. **~arse** *vpr* bend; *<estante>* bow; *<madera>* warp. **~ilíneo** *a* curvilinear; *<mujer>* curvaceous. **~o** *a* curved

cúspide *f* top; (fig) pinnacle

custodi|a *f* safe-keeping; (Jurid) custody. **~ar** *vt* guard; (guardar) look after. **~o** *m* guardian

cutáneo *a* skin

cutis *m* skin, complexion

cuyo *pron* (de persona) whose, of whom; (de cosa) whose, of which. **en ~ caso** in which case

Dd

dactilógrafo *m* typist

dado *m* dice. ● *a* given. **~ que** since, given that

daltónico *a* colour-blind

dama *f* lady. **~ de honor** bridesmaid. **~s** *fpl* draughts (Brit), checkers (Amer)

damasco *m* damask; (LAm, fruta) apricot

danés *a* Danish. ● *m* Dane; (idioma) Danish

danza *f* dance; (acción) dancing. **~r** [10] *vt/i* dance

dañ|ar *vt* damage. □ **~se** *vpr* get damaged. **~ino** *a* harmful. **~o** *m* damage; (a una persona) harm. **~os y perjuicios** damages. **hacer ~o a** harm, hurt. **hacerse ~o** hurt o.s.

dar [26] *vt* give; bear *<frutos>*; give out *<calor>*; strike *<la hora>*. ● *vi* give. **da igual** it doesn't matter. **¡dale!** go on! **da lo mismo** it doesn't matter. **~ a** *<ventana>* look on to; *<edificio>* face. **~ a luz** give birth. **~ con** meet *<persona>*; find *<cosa>*. **¿qué más da?** it doesn't matter! □ **~se** *vpr* have *<baño>*. **dárselas de** make o.s. out to be. **~se por** consider o.s.

dardo *m* dart

datar *vi*. **~ de** date from

dátil *m* date

dato *m* piece of information. ~s *mpl* data, information. ~s **personales** personal details

....

de

● *preposición*

Note that **de** before **el** becomes **del**, e.g. **es del norte**

····➤ (contenido, material) of. **un vaso de agua** a glass of water. **es de madera** it's made of wood

····➤ (pertenencia) **el coche de Juan** Juan's car. **es de ella** it's hers. **es de María** it's María's. **las llaves del coche** the car keys

····➤ (procedencia, origen, época) from. **soy de Madrid** I'm from Madrid. **una llamada de Lima** a call from Lima. **es del siglo V** it's from the 5th century

····➤ (causa, modo) **se murió de cáncer** he died of cancer. **temblar de miedo** to tremble with fear. **de dos en dos** two by two

····➤ (parte del día, hora) **de noche** at night. **de madrugada** early in the morning. **las diez de la mañana** ten (o'clock) in the morning. **de 9 a 12** from 9 to 12

····➤ (en oraciones pasivas) by. **rodeado de agua** surrounded by water. **va seguido de coma** it's followed by a comma. **es de Mozart** it's by Mozart

····➤ (al especificar) **el cajón de arriba** the top drawer. **la clase de inglés** the English lesson. **la chica de verde** the girl in green. **el de debajo** the one underneath

····➤ (en calidad de) as. **trabaja de oficinista** he works as a clerk. **vino de chaperón** he came as a chaperon

····➤ (en comparaciones) than. **pesa más de un kilo** it weighs more than a kilo

····➤ (con superlativo) **el más alto del mundo** the tallest in the world. **el mejor de todos** the best of all

····➤ (sentido condicional) if. **de haberlo sabido** if I had known. **de continuar así** if this goes on

➡ Cuando la preposición **de** se emplea como parte de expresiones como **de prisa, de acuerdo** etc., y de nombres

compuestos como **hombre de negocios, saco de dormir** etc., ver bajo el respectivo nombre

....

deambular *vi* roam (**por** about)

debajo *adv* underneath. ~ **de** under(neath). **el de** ~ the one underneath. **por** ~ underneath. **por** ~ **de** below

debat|e *m* debate. ~**ir** *vt* debate

deber *vt* owe. ● *v aux* have to, must; (en condicional) should. **debo marcharme** I must go, I have to go. ● *m* duty. ~**es** *mpl* homework. ☐ ~**se** *vpr.* ~**se a** be due to

debido *a* due; (correcto) proper. ~ **a** due to. **como es** ~ as is proper

débil *a* weak; <*sonido*> faint; <*luz*> dim

debili|dad *f* weakness. ~**tar** *vt* weaken. ☐ ~**tarse** *vpr* weaken, get weak

débito *m* debit. ~ **bancario** (LAm) direct debit

debutar *vi* make one's debut

década *f* decade

deca|dencia *f* decline. ~**dente** *a* decadent. ~**er** [29] *vi* decline; (debilitarse) weaken. ~**ído** *a* in low spirits. ~**imiento** *m* decline, weakening

decano *m* dean; (miembro más antiguo) senior member

decapitar *vt* behead

decena *f* ten. **una** ~ **de** about ten

decencia *f* decency

decenio *m* decade

decente *a* decent; (decoroso) respectable; (limpio) clean, tidy

decepci|ón *f* disappointment. ~**onar** *vt* disappoint

decidi|do *a* decided; <*persona*> determined, resolute. ~**r** *vt* decide; settle <*cuestión etc*>. ● *vi* decide. ☐ ~**rse** *vpr* make up one's mind

decimal *a & m* decimal

décimo *a & m* tenth. ● *m* (de lotería) tenth part of a lottery ticket

decir [46] *vt* say; (contar) tell. ● *m* saying. ~ **que no** say no. ~ **que sí** say yes. **dicho de otro modo** in other words. **dicho y hecho** no sooner said than done. **¿dígame?** can I help you? **¡dígame!** (al teléfono) hello! **digamos**

let's say. **es** ~ that is to say. **mejor dicho** rather. **¡no me digas!** you don't say!, really! **por así** ~, **por** ~**lo así** so to speak, as it were. **querer** ~ mean. **se dice que** it is said that, they say that

decisi|ón f decision. ~**vo** a decisive

declara|ción f declaration; (a autoridad, prensa) statement. ~**ción de renta** income tax return. ~**r** vt/i declare. □ ~**rse** vpr declare o.s.; <epidemia etc> break out

declinar vt turn down; (Gram) decline

declive m slope; (fig) decline. **en** ~ sloping

decola|je m (LAm) take-off. ~**r** vi (LAm) take off

decolorarse vpr become discoloured, fade

decora|ción f decoration. ~**do** m (en el teatro) set. ~**r** vt decorate. ~**tivo** a decorative

decoro m decorum. ~**so** a decent, respectable

decrépito a decrepit

decret|ar vt decree. ~**o** m decree

dedal m thimble

dedica|ción f dedication. ~**r** [7] vt dedicate; devote <tiempo>. □ ~**rse** vpr. ~**rse a** devote o.s. to. **¿a qué se dedica?** what does he do? ~**toria** f dedication

dedo m finger; (del pie) toe. ~ **anular** ring finger. ~ **corazón** middle finger. ~**gordo** thumb; (del pie) big toe. ~ **índice** index finger. ~ **meñique** little finger. ~ **pulgar** thumb

deduc|ción f deduction. ~**ir** [47] vt deduce; (descontar) deduct

defect|o m fault, defect. ~**uoso** a defective

defen|der [1] vt defend. ~**sa** f defence. □ ~**derse** vpr defend o.s. ~**sivo** a defensive. ~**sor** m defender. **abogado** m ~**sor** defence counsel

defeño m (Mex) person from the Federal District

deficien|cia f deficiency. ~**cia mental** mental handicap. ~**te** a poor, deficient. ● m & f. ~**te mental** mentally handicapped person

déficit m invar deficit

defini|ción f definition. ~**do** a defined. ~**r** vt define. ~**tivo** a definitive. **en** ~**tiva** all in all

deform|ación f deformation; (de imagen etc) distortion. ~**ar** vt deform; distort <imagen, metal>. □ ~**arse** vpr go out of shape. ~**e** a deformed

defraudar vt defraud; (decepcionar) disappoint

defunción f death

degenera|ción f degeneration; (cualidad) degeneracy. ~**do** a degenerate. ~**r** vi degenerate

degollar [16] vt cut s.o.'s throat

degradar vt degrade; (Mil) demote. □ ~**se** vpr demean o.s..

degusta|ción f tasting. ~**r** vt taste

dehesa f pasture

deja|dez f slovenliness; (pereza) laziness. ~**do** a slovenly; (descuidado) slack, negligent. ~**r** vt leave; (abandonar) abandon; give up <estudios>; (prestar) lend; (permitir) let. ~**r a un lado** leave aside. ~**r de** stop

dejo m aftertaste; (tonillo) slight accent; (toque) touch

del = **de** + **el**

delantal m apron

delante adv in front. ~ **de** in front of. **de** ~ front. ~**ra** f front; (de teatro etc) front row; (ventaja) lead; (de equipo) forward line. **llevar la** ~**ra** be in the lead. ~**ro** a front. ● m forward

delat|ar vt denounce. ~**or** m informer

delega|ción f delegation; (oficina) regional office; (Mex, comisaría) police station. ~**do** m delegate; (Com) agent, representative. ~**r** [12] vt delegate

deleit|ar vt delight. ~**e** m delight

deletrear vt spell (out)

delfín m dolphin

delgad|ez f thinness. ~**o** a thin; (esbelto) slim. ~**ucho** a skinny

delibera|ción f deliberation. ~**do** a deliberate. ~**r** vi deliberate (**sobre** on)

delicad|eza f gentleness; (fragilidad) frailty; (tacto) tact. **falta de** ~**eza** tactlessness. **tener la** ~ **de** have the courtesy to. **~o** *a* delicate; (refinado) refined; (sensible) sensitive

delici|a *f* delight. **~oso** *a* delightful; *<sabor etc>* delicious

delimitar *vt* delimit

delincuen|cia *f* delinquency. **~te** *m & f* criminal, delinquent

delinquir [8] *vi* commit a criminal offence

delir|ante *a* delirious. **~ar** *vi* be delirious; (fig) talk nonsense. **~io** *m* delirium; (fig) frenzy

delito *m* crime, offence

demacrado *a* haggard

demagogo *m* demagogue

demanda *f* demand; (Jurid) lawsuit. **~do** *m* defendant. **~nte** *m & f* (Jurid) plaintiff. **~r** *vt* (Jurid) sue; (LAm, requerir) require

demarcación *f* demarcation

demás *a* rest of the, other. ● *pron* rest, others. lo **~** the rest. por **~** extremely. por lo **~** otherwise

demas|ía *f*. en **~ía** in excess. **~iado** *a* too much; (en plural) too many. ● *adv* too much; (con adjetivo) too

demen|cia *f* madness. **~te** *a* demented, mad

dem|ocracia *f* democracy. **~ócrata** *m & f* democrat. **~ocrático** *a* democratic

demol|er [2] *vt* demolish. **~ición** *f* demolition

demonio *m* devil, demon. ¡**~s!** hell! ¿cómo **~s?** how the hell? ¡qué **~s!** what the hell!

demora *f* delay. **~r** *vt* delay. ● *vi* stay on. □ **~rse** *vpr* be too long; (LAm, cierto tiempo). se **~** una hora en llegar it takes him an hour to get there

demostra|ción *f* demonstration, show. **~r** [2] *vt* demonstrate; (mostrar) show; (probar) prove. **~tivo** *a* demonstrative

dengue *m* dengue fever

denigrar *vt* denigrate

dens|idad *f* density. **~o** *a* dense, thick

denta|dura *f* teeth. **~dura postiza** dentures, false teeth. **~l** *a* dental

dent|era *f*. darle **~era** a uno set s.o.'s teeth on edge. **~ífrico** *m* toothpaste. **~ista** *m & f* dentist

dentro *adv* inside; (de un edificio) indoors. **~** de in. **~** de poco soon. por **~** inside

denuncia *f* report; (acusación) accusation. **~r** *vt* report; *<periódico etc>* denounce

departamento *m* department; (LAm, apartamento) flat (Brit), apartment (Amer)

depend|encia *f* dependence; (sección) section; (oficina) office. **~encias** *fpl* buildings. **~er** *vi* depend (de on). **~ienta** *f* shop assistant. **~iente** *a* dependent (de on). ● *m* shop assistant

depila|r *vt* depilate. **~torio** *a* depilatory

deplora|ble *a* deplorable. **~r** *vt* deplore, regret

deponer [34] *vt* remove from office; depose *<rey>*; lay down *<armas>*. ● *vi* give evidence

deporta|ción *f* deportation. **~r** *vt* deport

deport|e *m* sport. hacer **~e** take part in sports. **~ista** *m* sportsman. ● *f* sportswoman. **~ivo** *a* sports. ● *m* sports car

dep|ositante *m & f* depositor. **~ositar** *vt* deposit; (poner) put, place. **~ósito** *m* deposit; (almacén) warehouse; (Mil) depot; (de líquidos) tank

depravado *a* depraved

deprecia|ción *f* depreciation. **~r** *vt* depreciate. □ **~rse** *vpr* depreciate

depr|esión *f* depression. **~imido** *a* depressed. **~imir** *vt* depress. □ **~imirse** *vpr* get depressed

depura|ción *f* purification. **~do** *a* refined. **~r** *vt* purify; (Pol) purge; refine *<estilo>*

derech|a *f* (mano) right hand; (lado) right. a la **~a** on the right; (hacia el lado derecho) to the right. **~ista** *a* right-winger. ● *m & f* right-winger. **~o** *a* right; (vertical) upright; (recto) straight. ● *adv* straight. todo **~o**

straight on. ● *m* right; (Jurid) law; (lado) right side. ~**os** *mpl* dues. ~**os de autor** royalties

deriva *f* drift. **a la ~** drifting, adrift

deriva|do *a* derived. ● *m* derivative, by-product. ~**r** *vt* divert. ● *vi*. ~**r de** derive from, be derived from. □ ~**rse** *vpr*. ~**se de** be derived from

derram|amiento *m* spilling. ~**amiento de sangre** bloodshed. ~**ar** *vt* spill; shed <*lágrimas*>. □ ~**arse** *vpr* spill. ~**e** *m* spilling; (pérdida) leakage; (Med) discharge; (Med, de sangre) haemorrhage

derretir [5] *vt* melt

derribar *vt* knock down; bring down, overthrow <*gobierno etc*>

derrocar [7] *vt* bring down, overthrow <*gobierno etc*>

derroch|ar *vt* squander. ~**e** *m* waste

derrot|a *f* defeat. ~**ar** *vt* defeat. ~**ado** *a* defeated. ~**ero** *m* course

derrumba|r *vt* knock down. □ ~**rse** *vpr* collapse; <*persona*> go to pieces

desabotonar *vt* unbutton, undo. □ ~**se** *vpr* come undone; <*persona*> undo

desabrido *a* tasteless; <*persona*> surly; (LAm) dull

desabrochar *vt* undo. □ ~**se** *vpr* come undone; <*persona*> undo

desacato *m* defiance; (Jurid) contempt of court

desac|ertado *a* ill-advised; (erróneo) wrong. ~**ierto** *m* mistake

desacreditar *vt* discredit

desactivar *vt* defuse

desacuerdo *m* disagreement

desafiar [20] *vt* challenge; (afrontar) defy

desafina|do *a* out of tune. ~**r** *vi* be out of tune. □ ~**rse** *vpr* go out of tune

desafío *m* challenge; (a la muerte) defiance; (combate) duel

desafortunad|amente *adv* unfortunately. ~**o** *a* unfortunate

desagrada|ble *a* unpleasant. ~**r** *vt* displease. ● *vi* be unpleasant. **me ~ el sabor** I don't like the taste

desagradecido *a* ungrateful

desagrado *m* displeasure. **con ~** unwillingly

desagüe *m* drain; (acción) drainage. **tubo *m* de ~** drain-pipe

desahog|ado *a* roomy; (acomodado) comfortable. ~**ar** [12] *vt* vent. □ ~**arse** *vpr* let off steam. ~**o** *m* comfort; (alivio) relief

desahuci|ar *vt* declare terminally ill <*enfermo*>; evict <*inquilino*>. ~**o** *m* eviction

desair|ar *vt* snub. ~**e** *m* snub

desajuste *m* maladjustment; (desequilibrio) imbalance

desal|entador *a* disheartening. ~**entar** [1] *vt* discourage. ~**iento** *m* discouragement

desaliñado *a* slovenly

desalmado *a* heartless

desalojar *vt* <*ocupantes*> evacuate; <*policía*> to clear; (LAm) evict <*inquilino*>

desampar|ado *a* helpless; <*lugar*> unprotected. ~**ar** *vt* abandon. ~**o** *m* helplessness; (abandono) lack of protection

desangrar *vt* bleed. □ ~**se** *vpr* bleed

desanima|do *a* down-hearted. ~**r** *vt* discourage. □ ~**rse** *vpr* lose heart

desapar|ecer [11] *vi* disappear; <*efecto*> wear off. ~**ecido** *a* missing. ● *m* missing person. ~**ición** *f* disappearance

desapego *m* indifference

desapercibido *a*. **pasar ~** go unnoticed

desaprobar [2] *vt* disapprove of

desarm|able *a* collapsible; <*estante*> easy to dismantle. ~**ar** *vt* disarm; (desmontar) dismantle; take apart; (LAm) take down <*carpa*>. ~**e** *m* disarmament

desarraig|ado *a* rootless. ~**ar** [12] *vt* uproot. ~**o** *m* uprooting

desarregl|ar *vt* mess up; (alterar) disrupt. ~**o** *m* disorder

desarroll|ar *vt* develop. □ ~**arse** *vpr* (incl Foto) develop; <*suceso*> take place. ~**o** *m* development

desaseado *a* dirty; (desordenado) untidy

desasosiego *m* anxiety; (intranquilidad) restlessness

desastr|ado *a* scruffy. ~**e** *m* disaster. ~**oso** *a* disastrous

desatar *vt* untie; (fig, soltar) unleash. □ ~**se** *vpr* come undone; to undo *<zapatos>*

desatascar [7] *vt* unblock

desaten|der [1] *vt* not pay attention to; neglect *<deber etc>*. ~**to** *a* inattentive; (descortés) discourteous

desatin|ado *a* silly. ~**o** *m* silliness; (error) mistake

desatornillar *vt* unscrew

desautorizar [10] *vt* declare unauthorized; discredit *<persona>*; (desmentir) deny

desavenencia *f* disagreement

desayun|ar *vt* have for breakfast. ● *vi* have breakfast. ~**o** *m* breakfast

desazón *m* (fig) unease

desbandarse *vpr* (Mil) disband; (dispersarse) disperse

desbarajust|ar *vt* mess up. ~**e** *m* mess

desbaratar *vt* spoil; (Mex) mess up *<papeles>*

desbloquear *vt* clear; release *<mecanismo>*; unfreeze *<cuenta>*

desbocado *a* *<caballo>* runaway; *<escote>* wide

desbordarse *vpr* overflow; *<río>* burst its banks

descabellado *a* crazy

descafeinado *a* decaffeinated. ● *m* decaffeinated coffee

descalabro *m* disaster

descalificar [7] *vt* disqualify; (desacreditar) discredit

descalz|ar [10] *vt* take off *<zapatos>*. ~**o** *a* barefoot

descampado *m* open ground. al ~ (LAm) in the open air

descans|ado *a* rested; *<trabajo>* easy. ~**ar** *vt/i* rest. ~**illo** *m* landing. ~**o** *m* rest; (del trabajo) break; (LAm, rellano) landing; (en deportes) half-time; (en el teatro etc) interval

descapotable *a* convertible

descarado *a* cheeky; (sin vergüenza) shameless

descarg|a *f* unloading; (Mil, Elec) discharge. ~**ar** [12] *vt* unload; (Mil, Elec) discharge; (Informática) download. ~**o** *m* (recibo) receipt; (Jurid) evidence

descaro *m* cheek, nerve

descarriarse [20] *vpr* go the wrong way; *<res>* stray; (fig) go astray

descarrila|miento *m* derailment. ~**r** *vi* be derailed. □ ~**se** *vpr* (LAm) be derailed

descartar *vt* rule out

descascararse *vpr* *<pintura>* peel; *<taza>* chip

descen|dencia *f* descent; (personas) descendants. ~**der** [1] *vt* go down *<escalera etc>*. ● *vi* go down; *<temperatura>* fall, drop; (provenir) be descended (de from). ~**diente** *m & f* descendent. ~**so** *m* descent; (de temperatura, fiebre etc) fall, drop

descifrar *vt* decipher; decode *<clave>*

descolgar [2 & 12] *vt* take down; pick up *<el teléfono>*. □ ~**se** *vpr* lower o.s.

descolor|ar *vt* discolour, fade. ~**ido** *a* discoloured, faded; *<persona>* pale

descomp|oner [34] *vt* break down; decompose *<materia>*; upset *<estómago>*; (esp LAm, estropear) break; (esp LAm, desarreglar) mess up. □ ~**onerse** *vpr* decompose; (esp LAm, estropearse) break down; *<persona>* feel sick. ~**ostura** *f* (esp LAm, de máquina) breakdown; (esp LAm, náuseas) sickness; (esp LAm, diarrea) diarrhoea; (LAm, falla) fault. ~**uesto** *a* decomposed; (encolerizado) angry; (esp LAm, estropeado) broken. **estar** ~**uesto** (del estómago) have diarrhoea

descomunal *a* enormous

desconc|ertante *a* disconcerting. ~**ertar** [1] *vt* disconcert; (dejar perplejo) puzzle. □ ~**ertarse** *vpr* be put out, be disconcerted

desconectar *vt* disconnect

desconfia|do *a* distrustful. ~**nza** *f* distrust, suspicion. ~**r** [20] *vi*. ~**r** **de** mistrust; (no creer) doubt

descongelar *vt* defrost; (Com) unfreeze

desconoc|er [11] *vt* not know, not recognize. ~**ido** *a* unknown; (cambiado) unrecognizable. ● *m* stranger. ~**imiento** *m* ignorance

desconsidera|ción *f* lack of consideration. ~**do** *a* inconsiderate

descons|olado *a* distressed. ~**uelo** *m* distress; (tristeza) sadness

desconta|do *a.* dar por ~**do** (que) take for granted (that). ~**r** [2] *vt* discount; deduct *<impuestos etc>*

descontento *a* unhappy (**con** with), dissatisfied (**con** with). ● *m* discontent

descorazonar *vt* discourage. □ ~**se** *vpr* lose heart

descorchar *vt* uncork

descorrer *vt* draw *<cortina>*. ~ **el cerrojo** unbolt the door

descort|és *a* rude, discourteous. ~**esía** *f* rudeness

descos|er *vt* unpick. □ ~**erse** *vpr* come undone. ~**ido** *a* unstitched

descrédito *m* disrepute. **ir en** ~ **de** damage the reputation of

descremado *a* skimmed

descri|bir (*pp* **descrito**) *vt* describe. ~**pción** *f* description

descuartizar [10] *vt* cut up

descubierto *a* discovered; (no cubierto) uncovered; *<vehículo>* open-top; *<piscina>* open-air; *<cielo>* clear; *<cabeza>* bare. ● *m* overdraft. **poner al** ~ expose

descubri|miento *m* discovery. ~**r** (*pp* **descubierto**) *vt* discover; (destapar) uncover; (revelar) reveal; unveil *<estatua>*. □ ~**rse** *vpr* (quitarse el sombrero) take off one's hat

descuento *m* discount; (del sueldo) deduction

descuid|ado *a* careless; *<aspecto etc>* untidy; (desprevenido) unprepared. ~**ar** *vt* neglect. ● *vi* not worry. ¡~**a**! don't worry!. □ ~**arse** *vpr* be careless ~**o** *m* carelessness; (negligencia) negligence

desde *prep* (lugar etc) from; (tiempo) since, from. ~ **ahora** from now on. ~ **hace un mes** for a month. ~ **luego** of course. ~ **Madrid hasta Barcelona** from Madrid to Barcelona. ~ **niño** since childhood

desdecirse [46] *vpr.* ~ **de** take back *<palabras etc>*; go back on *<promesa>*

desd|én *m* scorn. ~**eñable** *a* insignificant. **nada** ~**eñable** significant. ~**eñar** *vt* scorn

desdicha *f* misfortune. **por** ~ unfortunately. ~**do** *a* unfortunate

desdoblar *vt* (desplegar) unfold

desear *vt* want; wish *<suerte etc>*. **le deseo un buen viaje** I hope you have a good journey. ¿**qué desea Vd?** can I help you?

desech|able *a* disposable. ~**ar** *vt* throw out; (rechazar) reject. ~**o** *m* waste

desembalar *vt* unpack

desembarcar [7] *vt* unload. ● *vi* disembark

desemboca|dura *f* (de río) mouth; (de calle) opening. ~**r** [7] *vi.* ~**r en** *<río>* flow into; *<calle>* lead to

desembolso *m* payment

desembragar [12] *vi* declutch

desempaquetar *vt* unwrap

desempat|ar *vi* break a tie. ~**e** *m* tie-breaker

desempeñ|ar *vt* redeem; play *<papel>*; hold *<cargo>*; perform, carry out *<deber etc>*. □ ~**arse** *vpr* (LAm) perform. ~**arse bien** manage well. ~**o** *m* redemption; (de un deber, una función) discharge; (LAm, actuación) performance

desemple|ado *a* unemployed. ● *m* unemployed person. **los** ~**ados** the unemployed. ~**o** *m* unemployment

desencadenar *vt* unchain *<preso>*; unleash *<perro>*; (causar) trigger. □ ~**se** *vpr* be triggered off; *<guerra etc>* break out

desencajar *vt* dislocate; (desconectar) disconnect. □ ~**se** *vpr* become dislocated

desenchufar *vt* unplug

desenfad|ado *a* uninhibited; (desenvuelto) self-assured. ~**o** *m* lack of inhibition; (desenvoltura) self-assurance

desenfocado *a* out of focus

desenfren|ado *a* unrestrained. **~o** *m* licentiousness

desenganchar *vt* unhook; uncouple <*vagón*>

desengañ|ar *vt* disillusion. □ **~arse** *vpr* become disillusioned; (darse cuenta) realize. **~o** *m* disillusionment, disappointment

desenlace *m* outcome

desenmascarar *vt* unmask

desenredar *vt* untangle. □ **~se** *vpr* untangle

desenro|llar *vt* unroll, unwind. **~scar** [7] *vt* unscrew

desentend|erse [1] *vpr* want nothing to do with. **~ido** *m*. **hacerse el ~ido** (fingir no oír) pretend not to hear; (fingir ignorancia) pretend not to know

desenterrar [1] *vt* exhume; (fig) unearth

desentonar *vi* be out of tune; <*colores*> clash

desenvoltura *f* ease; (falta de timidez) confidence

desenvolver [2] (*pp* **desenvuelto**) *vt* unwrap; expound <*idea etc*>. □ **~se** *vpr* perform; (manejarse) manage

deseo *m* wish, desire. **~so** *a* eager. **estar ~so** de be eager to

desequilibr|ado *a* unbalanced. **~io** *m* imbalance

des|ertar *vt* desert; (Pol) defect. **~értico** *a* desert-like. **~ertor** *m* deserter; (Pol) defector

desespera|ción *f* despair. **~do** *a* desperate. **~nte** *a* infuriating. **~r** *vt* drive to despair. □ **~rse** *vpr* despair

desestimar *vt* (rechazar) reject

desfachat|ado *a* brazen, shameless. **~ez** *f* nerve, cheek

desfallec|er [11] *vt* weaken. ● *vi* become weak; (desmayarse) faint. **~imiento** *m* weakness; (desmayo) faint

desfasado *a* out of phase; <*idea*> outdated; <*persona*> out of touch

desfavorable *a* unfavourable

desfil|adero *m* narrow mountain pass; (cañón) narrow gorge. **~ar** *vi* march (past). **~e** *m* procession, parade. **~e de modelos** fashion show

desgana *f*, (LAm) **desgano** *m* (falta de apetito) lack of appetite; (Med) weakness, faintness; (fig) unwillingness

desgarr|ador *a* heart-rending. **~ar** *vt* tear; (fig) break <*corazón*>. **~o** *m* tear, rip

desgast|ar *vt* wear away; wear out <*ropa*>. □ **~arse** *vpr* wear away; <*ropa*> be worn out; <*persona*> wear o.s. out. **~e** *m* wear

desgracia *f* misfortune; (accidente) accident; **por ~** unfortunately. **¡qué ~!** what a shame!. **~do** *a* unlucky; (pobre) poor. ● *m* unfortunate person, poor devil 🆃

desgranar *vt* shell <*habas etc*>

desgreñado *a* ruffled, dishevelled

deshabitado *a* uninhabited; <*edificio*> unoccupied

deshacer [31] *vt* undo; strip <*cama*>; unpack <*maleta*>; (desmontar) take to pieces; break <*trato*>; (derretir) melt; (disolver) dissolve. □ **~se** *vpr* come undone; (disolverse) dissolve; (derretirse) melt. **~se de algo** get rid of sth. **~se en lágrimas** dissolve into tears. **~se por hacer algo** go out of one's way to do sth

desheredar *vt* disinherit

deshidratarse *vpr* become dehydrated

deshielo *m* thaw

deshilachado *a* frayed

deshincha|do *a* <*neumático*> flat. **~r** *vt* deflate; (Med) reduce the swelling in. □ **~rse** *vpr* go down

deshollinador *m* chimney sweep

deshon|esto *a* dishonest; (obsceno) indecent. **~ra** *f* disgrace. **~rar** *vt* dishonour

deshora *f*. **a ~** out of hours. **comer a ~s** eat between meals

deshuesar *vt* bone <*carne*>; stone <*fruta*>

desidia *f* slackness; <*pereza*> laziness

desierto *a* deserted. ● *m* desert

designar *vt* designate; (fijar) fix

desigual *a* unequal; <*terreno*> uneven; (distinto) different. **~dad** *f* inequality

desilusi|ón *f* disappointment; (pérdida de ilusiones) disillusionment. **~onar** *vt* disappoint; (quitar las ilusiones) disillusion. □ **~onarse** *vpr* be disappointed; (perder las ilusiones) become disillusioned

desinfecta|nte *m* disinfectant. **~r** *vt* disinfect

desinflar *vt* deflate. □ **~se** *vpr* go down

desinhibido *a* uninhibited

desintegrar *vt* disintegrate. □ **~se** *vpr* disintegrate

desinter|és *m* lack of interest; (generosidad) unselfishness. **~esado** *a* uninterested; (liberal) unselfish

desistir *vi.* **~ de** give up

desleal *a* disloyal. **~tad** *f* disloyalty

desligar [12] *vt* untie; (separar) separate; (fig, librar) free. □ **~se** *vpr* break away; (de un compromiso) free o.s. (**de** from)

desliza|dor *m* (Mex) hang glider. **~r** [10] *vt* slide, slip. □ **~se** *vpr* slide, slip; <patinador> glide; <tiempo> slip by, pass; (fluir) flow

deslucido *a* tarnished; (gastado) worn out; (fig) undistinguished

deslumbrar *vt* dazzle

desmadr|arse *vpr* get out of control. **~e** *m* excess

desmán *m* outrage

desmanchar *vt* (LAm) remove the stains from

desmantelar *vt* dismantle; (despojar) strip

desmaquillador *m* make-up remover

desmay|ado *a* unconscious. □ **~arse** *vpr* faint. **~o** *m* faint

desmedido *a* excessive

desmemoriado *a* forgetful

desmenti|do *m* denial. **~r** [4] *vt* deny; (contradecir) contradict

desmenuzar [10] *vt* crumble; shred <carne etc>

desmerecer [11] *vi.* no **~ de** compare favourably with

desmesurado *a* excessive; (enorme) enormous

desmonta|ble *a* collapsible; <armario> easy to dismantle; (separable) removable. **~r** *vt* (quitar) remove; (desarmar) dismantle, take apart. ● *vi* dismount

desmoralizar [10] *vt* demoralize

desmoronarse *vpr* crumble; <edificio> collapse

desnatado *a* skimmed

desnivel *m* unevenness; (fig) difference, inequality

desnud|ar *vt* strip; undress, strip <persona>. □ **~arse** *vpr* undress. **~ez** *f* nudity. **~o** *a* naked; (fig) bare. ● *m* nude

desnutri|ción *f* malnutrition. **~do** *a* undernourished

desobed|ecer [11] *vt* disobey. **~iencia** *f* disobedience

desocupa|do *a* <asiento etc> vacant, free; (sin trabajo) unemployed; (ocioso) idle. **~r** *vt* vacate; (vaciar) empty; (desalojar) clear

desodorante *m* deodorant

desolado *a* desolate; <persona> sorry, sad

desorbitante *a* excessive

desorden *m* disorder, untidiness; (confusión) confusion. **~ado** *a* untidy. **~ar** *vt* disarrange, make a mess of

desorganizar [10] *vt* disorganize; (trastornar) disturb

desorienta|do *a* confused. **~r** *vt* disorientate. □ **~rse** *vpr* lose one's bearings

despabila|do *a* wide awake; (listo) quick. **~r** *vt* (despertar) wake up; (avivar) wise up. □ **~rse** *vpr* wake up; (avivarse) wise up

despach|ar *vt* finish; (tratar con) deal with; (atender) serve; (vender) sell; (enviar) send; (despedir) fire. **~o** *m* dispatch; (oficina) office; (venta) sale; (de localidades) box office

despacio *adv* slowly

despampanante *a* stunning

desparpajo *m* confidence; (descaro) impudence

desparramar *vt* scatter; spill <líquidos>

despavorido *a* terrified

despecho *m* spite. **a ~ de** in spite of. **por ~** out of spite

despectivo *a* contemptuous; <*sentido etc*> pejorative

despedazar [10] *vt* tear to pieces

despedi|da *f* goodbye, farewell. **~da de soltero** stag-party. **~r** [5] *vt* say goodbye to, see off; dismiss <*empleado*>; evict <*inquilino*>; (arrojar) throw; give off <*olor etc*>. □ **~rse** *vpr* say goodbye (**de** to)

despeg|ar [12] *vt* unstick. ● *vi* <*avión*> take off. **~ue** *m* take-off

despeinar *vt* ruffle the hair of

despeja|do *a* clear; <*persona*> wide awake. **~r** *vt* clear; (aclarar) clarify. ● *vi* clear. □ **~rse** *vpr* (aclararse) become clear; <*tiempo*> clear up

despellejar *vt* skin

despensa *f* pantry, larder

despeñadero *m* cliff

desperdici|ar *vt* waste. **~o** *m* waste. **~os** *mpl* rubbish

desperta|dor *m* alarm clock. **~r** [1] *vt* wake (up); (fig) awaken. □ **~rse** *vpr* wake up

despiadado *a* merciless

despido *m* dismissal

despierto *a* awake; (listo) bright

despilfarr|ar *vt* waste. **~o** *m* squandering; (gasto innecesario) extravagance

despintarse *vpr* (Mex) run

despista|do *a* (con estar) confused; (con ser) absent-minded. **~r** *vt* throw off the scent; (fig) mislead. □ **~rse** *vpr* go wrong; (fig) get confused

despiste *m* mistake; (confusión) muddle

desplaza|miento *m* displacement; (de opinión etc) swing, shift. **~r** [10] *vt* displace. □ **~rse** *vpr* travel

desplegar [1 & 12] *vt* open out; spread <*alas*>; (fig) show

desplomarse *vpr* collapse

despoblado *m* deserted area

despoj|ar *vt* deprive <*persona*>; strip <*cosa*>. **~os** *mpl* remains; (de res) offal; (de ave) giblets

despreci|able *a* despicable; <*cantidad*> negligible. **~ar** *vt* des-

pise; (rechazar) scorn. **~o** *m* contempt; (desaire) snub

desprender *vt* remove; give off <*olor*>. □ **~se** *vpr* fall off; (fig) part with; (deducirse) follow

despreocupa|do *a* unconcerned; (descuidado) careless. □ **~rse** *vpr* not worry

desprestigiar *vt* discredit

desprevenido *a* unprepared. **pillar a uno ~** catch s.o. unawares

desproporcionado *a* disproportionate

desprovisto *a*. **~ de** lacking in, without

después *adv* after, afterwards; (más tarde) later; (a continuación) then. **~ de** after. **~ de comer** after eating. **~ de todo** after all. **~ (de) que** after. **poco ~** soon after

desquit|arse *vpr* get even (**de** with). **~e** *m* revenge

destaca|do *a* outstanding. **~r** [7] *vt* emphasize. ● *vi* stand out. □ **~rse** *vpr* stand out. **~se en** excel at

destajo *m*. **trabajar a ~** do piecework

destap|ar *vt* uncover; open <*botella*>. □ **~arse** *vpr* reveal one's true self. **~e** *m* (fig) permissiveness

destartalado *a* <*coche*> clapped-out; <*casa*> ramshackle

destello *m* sparkle; (de estrella) twinkle; (fig) glimmer

destemplado *a* discordant; <*nervios*> frayed

desteñir [5 & 22] *vt* fade. ● *vi* fade; <*color*> run. □ **~se** *vpr* fade; <*color*> run

desterra|do *m* exile. **~r** [1] *vt* banish

destetar *vt* wean

destiempo *m*. **a ~** at the wrong moment; (Mus) out of time

destierro *m* exile

destil|ar *vt* distil. **~ería** *f* distillery

destin|ar *vt* destine; (nombrar) post. **~atario** *m* addressee. **~o** *m* (uso) use, function; (lugar) destination; (suerte) destiny. **con ~o a** (going) to

destituir [17] *vt* dismiss

destornilla|dor *m* screwdriver. **~r** *vt* unscrew

destreza *f* skill

destroz|ar [10] *vt* destroy; (fig) shatter. **~os** *mpl* destruction, damage

destru|cción *f* destruction. **~ir** [17] *vt* destroy

desus|ado *a* old-fashioned; (insólito) unusual. **~o** *m* disuse. **caer en ~o** fall into disuse

desvalido *a* needy, destitute

desvalijar *vt* rob; ransack <*casa*>

desvalorizar [10] *vt* devalue

desván *m* loft

desvanec|er [11] *vt* make disappear; (borrar) blur; (fig) dispel. □ **~erse** *vpr* disappear; (desmayarse) faint. **~imiento** *m* (Med) faint

desvariar [20] *vi* be delirious; (fig) talk nonsense

desvel|ar *vt* keep awake. □ **~arse** *vpr* stay awake, have a sleepless night. **~o** *m* sleeplessness

desvencijado *a* <*mueble*> rickety

desventaja *f* disadvantage

desventura *f* misfortune. **~do** *a* unfortunate

desverg|onzado *a* impudent, cheeky. **~üenza** *f* impudence, cheek

desvestirse [5] *vpr* undress

desv|iación *f* deviation; (Auto) diversion. **~iar** [20] *vt* divert; deflect <*pelota*>. □ **~iarse** *vpr* <*carretera*> branch off; (del camino) make a detour; (del tema) stray. **~ío** *m* diversion

desvivirse *vpr.* **~se por** be completely devoted to; (esforzarse) go out of one's way to

detall|ar *vt* relate in detail. **~e** *m* detail; (fig) gesture. **al ~e** retail. **entrar en ~es** go into detail. **¡qué ~e!** how thoughtful! **~ista** *m & f* retailer

detect|ar *vt* detect. **~ive** *m* detective

deten|ción *f* stopping; (Jurid) arrest; (en la cárcel) detention. **~er** [40] *vt* stop; (Jurid) arrest; (encarcelar) detain; (retrasar) delay. □ **~erse** *vpr* stop; (entretenerse) spend a lot of time.

~idamente *adv* at length. **~ido** *a* (Jurid) under arrest. ● *m* prisoner

detergente *a & m* detergent

deterior|ar *vt* damage, spoil. □ **~arse** *vpr* deteriorate. **~o** *m* deterioration

determina|ción *f* determination; (decisión) decison. **~nte** *a* decisive. **~r** *vt* determine; (decidir) decide

detestar *vt* detest

detrás *adv* behind; (en la parte posterior) on the back. **~ de** behind. **por ~** at the back; (por la espalda) from behind

detrimento *m* detriment. **en ~ de** to the detriment of

deud|a *f* debt. **~or** *m* debtor

devalua|ción *f* devaluation. **~r** [21] *vt* devalue. □ **~se** *vpr* depreciate

devastador *a* devastating

devoción *f* devotion

devol|ución *f* return; (Com) repayment, refund. **~ver** [5] (*pp* **devuelto**) *vt* return; (Com) repay, refund. ● *vi* be sick

devorar *vt* devour

devoto *a* devout; <*amigo etc*> devoted. ● *m* admirer

di *vb* ⇒DAR, DECIR

día *m* day. **~ de fiesta** (public) holiday. **~ del santo** saint's day. **~ feriado** (LAm), **~ festivo** (public) holiday. **al ~** up to date. **al ~ siguiente** (on) the following day. **¡buenos ~s!** good morning! **de ~** by day. **el ~ de hoy** today. **el ~ de mañana** tomorrow. **un ~ sí y otro no** every other day. **vivir al ~** live from hand to mouth

diab|etes *f* diabetes. **~ético** *a* diabetic

diab|lo *m* devil. **~lura** *f* mischief. **~ólico** *a* diabolical

diadema *f* diadem

diáfano *a* diaphanous; <*cielo*> clear

diafragma *m* diaphragm

diagn|osis *f* diagnosis. **~osticar** [7] *vt* diagnose. **~óstico** *m* diagnosis

diagonal *a & f* diagonal

diagrama *m* diagram

dialecto *m* dialect

di|alogar [12] *vi* talk. **~álogo** *m* dialogue; (Pol) talks

diamante *m* diamond

diámetro *m* diameter

diana *f* reveille; (blanco) bull's-eye

diapositiva *f* slide, transparency

diario *a* daily. ● *m* newspaper; (libro) diary. **a ~o** daily. **de ~o** everyday, ordinary

diarrea *f* diarrhoea

dibuj|ante *m* draughtsman. ● *f* draughtswoman. **~ar** *vt* draw. **~o** *m* drawing. **~os animados** cartoons

diccionario *m* dictionary

dich|a *f* happiness. **por ~a** fortunately. **~o** *a* said; (tal) such. ● *m* saying. **~o y hecho** no sooner said than done. **mejor ~o** rather. **propiamente ~o** strictly speaking. **~oso** *a* happy; (afortunado) fortunate

diciembre *m* December

dicta|do *m* dictation. **~dor** *m* dictator. **~dura** *f* dictatorship. **~men** *m* opinion; (informe) report. **~r** *vt* dictate; pronounce *<sentencia etc>*; (LAm) give *<clase>*

didáctico *a* didactic

dieci|nueve *a & m* nineteen. **~ocho** *a & m* eighteen. **~séis** *a & m* sixteen. **~siete** *a & m* seventeen

diente *m* tooth; (de tenedor) prong; (de ajo) clove. **~ de león** dandelion. **hablar entre ~s** mumble

diestro *a* right-handed; (hábil) skillful

dieta *f* diet

diez *a & m* ten

diezmar *vt* decimate

difamación *f* (con palabras) slander; (por escrito) libel

diferen|cia *f* difference; (desacuerdo) disagreement. **~ciar** *vt* differentiate between. □ **~ciarse** *vpr* differ. **~te** *a* different; (diversos) various

diferido *a* (TV etc). **en ~** recorded

dif|ícil *a* difficult; (poco probable) unlikely. **~icultad** *f* difficulty. **~icultar** *vt* make difficult

difteria *f* diphtheria

difundir *vt* spread; (TV etc) broadcast

difunto *a* late, deceased. ● *m* deceased

difusión *f* spreading

dige|rir [4] *vt* digest. **~stión** *f* digestion. **~stivo** *a* digestive

digital *a* digital; (de los dedos) finger

dign|arse *vpr* deign to. **~atario** *m* dignitary. **~idad** *f* dignity. **~o** *a* honourable; (decoroso) decent; (merecedor) worthy (**de** of). **~ de elogio** praiseworthy

digo *vb* ⇒DECIR

dije *vb* ⇒DECIR

dilatar *vt* expand; (Med) dilate; (prolongar) prolong. □ **~se** *vpr* expand; (Med) dilate; (extenderse) extend; (Mex, demorarse) be late

dilema *m* dilemma

diligen|cia *f* diligence; (gestión) job; (carruaje) stagecoach. **~te** *a* diligent

dilucidar *vt* clarify; solve *<misterio>*

diluir [17] *vt* dilute

diluvio *m* flood

dimensión *f* dimension; (tamaño) size

diminut|ivo *a & m* diminutive. **~o** *a* minute

dimitir *vt/i* resign

Dinamarca *f* Denmark

dinamarqués *a* Danish. ● *m* Dane

dinámic|a *f* dynamics. **~o** *a* dynamic

dinamita *f* dynamite

dínamo *m* dynamo

dinastía *f* dynasty

diner|al *m* fortune. **~o** *m* money. **~o efectivo** cash. **~o suelto** change

dinosaurio *m* dinosaur

dios *m* god. **~a** *f* goddess. **¡D~ mío!** good heavens! **¡gracias a D~!** thank God!

diplom|a *m* diploma. **~acia** *f* diplomacy. **~ado** *a* qualified. □ **~arse** *vpr* (LAm) graduate. **~ático** *a* diplomatic. ● *m* diplomat

diptongo *m* diphthong

diputa|ción *f* delegation. **~ción provincial** county council. **~do** *m* deputy; (Pol, en España) member of the Cortes; (Pol, en Inglaterra) Member of Parliament; (Pol, en Estados Unidos) congressman

dique m dike

direc|ción f direction; (señas) address; (los que dirigen) management; (Pol) leadership; (Auto) steering. ~ción prohibida no entry. ~ción única one-way. ~ta f (Auto) top gear. ~tiva f board; (Pol) executive committee. ~tivas fpl guidelines. ~to a direct; <línea> straight; <tren> through. en ~to (TV etc) live. ~tor m director; (Mus) conductor; (de escuela) headmaster; (de periódico) editor; (gerente) manager. ~tora f (de escuela etc) headmistress. ~torio m board of directors; (LAm, de teléfonos) telephone directory

dirig|ente a ruling. ● m & f leader; (de empresa) manager. ~ir [14] vt direct; (Mus) conduct; run <empresa etc>; address <carta etc>. □ ~irse vpr make one's way; (hablar) address

disciplina f discipline. ~r vt discipline. ~rio a disciplinary

discípulo m disciple; (alumno) pupil

disco m disc; (Mus) record; (deportes) discus; (de teléfono) dial; (de tráfico) sign; (Rail) signal. ~ duro hard disk. ~ flexible floppy disk

disconforme a not in agreement

discord|e a discordant. ~ia f discord

discoteca f discothèque, disco 🛈; (colección de discos) record collection

discreción f discretion

discrepa|ncia f discrepancy; (desacuerdo) disagreement. ~r vi differ

discreto a discreet; (moderado) moderate

discrimina|ción f discrimination. ~r vt (distinguir) discriminate between; (tratar injustamente) discriminate against

disculpa f apology; (excusa) excuse. pedir ~s apologize. ~r vt excuse, forgive. □ ~rse vpr apologize

discurs|ar vi speak (sobre about). ~o m speech

discusión f discussion; (riña) argument

discuti|ble a debatable. ~r vt discuss; (contradecir) contradict. ● vi argue (por about)

disecar [7] vt stuff; (cortar) dissect

diseminar vt disseminate, spread

disentir [4] vi disagree (de with, en on)

diseñ|ador m designer. ~ar vt design. ~o m design; (fig) sketch

disertación f dissertation

disfraz m fancy dress; (para engañar) disguise. ~ar [10] vt dress up; (para engañar) disguise. □ ~arse vpr. ~arse de dress up as; (para engañar) disguise o.s. as.

disfrutar vt enjoy. ● vi enjoy o.s. ~ de enjoy

disgust|ar vt displease; (molestar) annoy. □ ~arse vpr get annoyed, get upset; <dos personas> fall out. ~o m annoyance; (problema) trouble; (riña) quarrel; (dolor) sorrow, grief

disidente a & m & f dissident

disimular vt conceal. ● vi pretend

disipar vt dissipate; (derrochar) squander

dislocarse [7] vpr dislocate

disminu|ción f decrease. ~ir [17] vi diminish

disolver [2] (pp **disuelto**) vt dissolve. □ ~se vpr dissolve

dispar a different

disparar vt fire; (Mex, pagar) buy. ● vi shoot (contra at)

disparate m silly thing; (error) mistake. decir ~s talk nonsense. ¡qué ~! how ridiculous!

disparidad f disparity

disparo m (acción) firing; (tiro) shot

dispensar vt give; (eximir) exempt. ● vi. ¡Vd dispense! forgive me

dispers|ar vt scatter, disperse. □ ~arse vpr scatter, disperse. ~ión f dispersion. ~o a scattered

dispon|er [34] vt arrange; (Jurid) order. ● vi. ~er de have; (vender etc) dispose of. □ ~erse vpr prepare (a to). ~ibilidad f availability. ~ible a available

disposición f arrangement; (aptitud) talent; (disponibilidad) disposal; (Jurid) order, decree. ~ de ánimo frame of mind. a la ~ de at the disposal of. a su ~ at your service

dispositivo m device

dispuesto *a* ready; *<persona>* disposed (**a** to); (servicial) helpful

disputa *f* dispute; (pelea) argument

disquete *m* diskette, floppy disk

dista|ncia *f* distance. **a ～ncia** from a distance. **guardar las ～ncias** keep one's distance. **～nciar** *vt* space out; distance *<amigos>*. □ **～nciarse** *vpr* *<dos personas>* fall out. **～nte** *a* distant. **～r** *vi* be away; (fig) be far. **～ 5 kilómetros** it's 5 kilometres away

distin|ción *f* distinction; (honor) award. **～guido** *a* distinguished. **～guir** [13] *vt/i* distinguish. □ **～guirse** *vpr* distinguish o.s.; (diferenciarse) differ. **～tivo** *a* distinctive. ● *m* badge. **～to** *a* different, distinct

distra|cción *f* amusement; (descuido) absent-mindedness, inattention. **～er** [41] *vt* distract; (divertir) amuse. □ **～erse** *vpr* amuse o.s.; (descuidarse) not pay attention. **～ido** *a* (desatento) absent-minded

distribu|ción *f* distribution. **～idor** *m* distributor. **～ir** [17] *vt* distribute

distrito *m* district

disturbio *m* disturbance

disuadir *vt* deter, dissuade

diurno *a* daytime

divagar [12] *vi* digress; (hablar sin sentido) ramble

diván *m* settee, sofa

diversi|dad *f* diversity. **～ficar** [7] *vt* diversify

diversión *f* amusement, entertainment; (pasatiempo) pastime

diverso *a* different

diverti|do *a* amusing; (que tiene gracia) funny. **～r** [4] *vt* amuse, entertain. □ **～rse** *vpr* enjoy o.s.

dividir *vt* divide; (repartir) share out

divino *a* divine

divisa *f* emblem. **～s** *fpl* currency

divisar *vt* make out

división *f* division

divorci|ado *a* divorced. ● *m* divorcee. **～ar** *vt* divorce. □ **～arse** *vpr* get divorced. **～o** *m* divorce

divulgar [12] *vt* spread; divulge *<secreto>*

dizque *adv* (LAm) apparently; (supuestamente) supposedly

do *m* C; (solfa) doh

dobl|adillo *m* hem; (de pantalón) turn-up (Brit), cuff (Amer). **～ar** *vt* double; (plegar) fold; (torcer) bend; turn *<esquina>*; dub *<película>*. ● *vi* turn; *<campana>* toll. □ **～arse** *vpr* double; (curvarse) bend. **～e** *a* double. ● *m* double. **el ～e** twice as much (**de**, **que** as). **～egar** [12] *vt* (fig) force to give in. □ **～egarse** *vpr* give in

doce *a & m* twelve. **～na** *f* dozen

docente *a* teaching. ● *m & f* teacher

dócil *a* obedient

doctor *m* doctor. **～ado** *m* doctorate

doctrina *f* doctrine

document|ación *f* documentation, papers. **～al** *a & m* documentary. **～o** *m* document. **D～o Nacional de Identidad** national identity card

dólar *m* dollar

dol|er [2] *vi* hurt, ache; (fig) grieve. **me duele la cabeza** I have a headache. **le duele el estómago** he has (a) stomach-ache. **～or** *m* pain; (sordo) ache; (fig) sorrow. **～or de cabeza** headache. **～or de muelas** toothache. **～oroso** *a* painful

domar *vt* tame; break in *<caballo>*

dom|esticar [7] *vt* domesticate. **～éstico** *a* domestic

domicili|ar *vt*. **～ar los pagos** pay by direct debit. **～o** *m* address. **～o particular** home address. **reparto a ～** home delivery service

domina|nte *a* dominant; *<persona>* domineering. **～r** *vt* dominate; (contener) control; (conocer) have a good command of. ● *vi* dominate. □ **～rse** *vpr* control o.s.

domingo *m* Sunday

dominio *m* authority; (territorio) domain; (fig) command

dominó *m* (*pl* **～s**) dominoes; (ficha) domino

don *m* talent, gift; (en un sobre) Mr. **～ Pedro** Pedro

donación *f* donation

donaire *m* grace, charm

dona|nte *m & f* (de sangre) donor. ~**r** *vt* donate

doncella *f* maiden; (criada) maid

donde *adv* where

dónde *adv* where?; (LAm, cómo) how; ¿hasta ~? how far? ¿por ~? whereabouts?; (por qué camino?) which way? ¿a ~ vas? where are you going? ¿de ~ eres? where are you from?

dondequiera *adv*. ~ **que** wherever. **por** ~ everywhere

doña *f* (en un sobre) Mrs. ~ **María** María

dora|do *a* golden; (cubierto de oro) gilt. ~**r** *vt* gilt; (Culin) brown

dormi|do *a* asleep. **quedarse** ~**do** fall asleep; (no despertar) oversleep. ~**r** [6] *vt* send to sleep. ~**r la siesta** have an afternoon nap, have a siesta. ● *vi* sleep. □ ~**rse** *vpr* fall asleep. ~**tar** *vi* doze. ~**torio** *m* bedroom

dors|al *a* back. ● *m* (en deportes) number. ~**o** *m* back. **nadar de** ~ (Mex) do (the) backstroke

dos *a & m* two. **de** ~ **en** ~ in twos, in pairs. **los** ~, **las** ~ both (of them). ~**cientos** *a & m* two hundred

dosi|ficar [7] *vt* dose; (fig) measure out. ~**s** *f invar* dose

dot|ado *a* gifted. ~**ar** *vt* give a dowry; (proveer) provide (**de** with). ~**e** *m* dowry

doy *vb* ⇒DAR

dragar [12] *vt* dredge

drama *m* drama; (obra de teatro) play. ~**turgo** *m* playwright

drástico *a* drastic

droga *f* drug. ~**dicto** *m* drug addict. ~**do** *m* drug addict. ~**r** [12] *vt* drug. □ ~**rse** *vpr* take drugs

droguería *f* hardware store

ducha *f* shower. □ ~**rse** *vpr* have a shower

dud|a *f* doubt. **poner en** ~**a** question. **sin** ~**a** (alguna) without a doubt. ~**ar** *vt/i* doubt. ~**oso** *a* doubtful; (sospechoso) dubious

duelo *m* duel; (luto) mourning

duende *m* imp

dueñ|a *f* owner, proprietress; (de una pensión) landlady. ~**o** *m* owner, proprietor; (de una pensión) landlord

duermo *vb* ⇒DORMIR

dul|ce *a* sweet; <agua> fresh; (suave) soft, gentle. ● *m* (LAm) sweet. ~**zura** *f* sweetness; (fig) gentleness

duna *f* dune

dúo *m* duet, duo

duplica|do *a* duplicated. **por** ~ in duplicate. ● *m* duplicate. ~**r** [7] *vt* duplicate. □ ~**rse** *vpr* double

duque *m* duke. ~**sa** *f* duchess

dura|ción *f* duration, length. ~**de-ro** *a* lasting. ~**nte** *prep* during; (medida de tiempo) for. ~ **todo el año** all year round. ~**r** *vi* last

durazno *m* (LAm, fruta) peach

dureza *f* hardness; (Culin) toughness; (fig) harshness

duro *a* hard; (Culin) tough; (fig) harsh. ● *adv* (esp LAm) hard. ● *m* five-peseta coin

Ee

e *conj* and

ebrio *a* drunk

ebullición *f* boiling

eccema *m* eczema

echar *vt* throw; post <carta>; give off <olor>; pour <líquido>; (expulsar) expel; (de recinto) throw out; fire <empleado>; (poner) put on; get <gasolina>; put out <raíces>; show <película>. ~ **a** start. ~ **a perder** spoil. ~ **de menos** miss. ~**se atrás** (fig) back down. **echárselas de** feign. □ ~**se** *vpr* throw o.s.; (tumbarse) lie down

eclesiástico *a* ecclesiastical

eclipse *m* eclipse

eco *m* echo. **hacerse** ~ **de** echo

ecolog|ía *f* ecology. ~**ista** *m & f* ecologist

economato *m* cooperative store

econ|omía *f* economy; (ciencia) economics. ~**ómico** *a* economic; (no caro) inexpensive. ~**omista** *m & f* economist. ~**omizar** [10] *vt/i* economize

ecuación *f* equation

ecuador *m* equator. **el E~** the Equator. **E~** (país) Ecuador

ecuánime *a* level-headed; (imparcial) impartial

ecuatoriano *a & m* Ecuadorian

ecuestre *a* equestrian

edad *f* age. **~ avanzada** old age. **E~ de Piedra** Stone Age. **E~ Media** Middle Ages. **¿qué ~ tiene?** how old is he?

edición *f* edition; (publicación) publication

edicto *m* edict

edific|ación *f* building. **~ante** *a* edifying. **~ar** [7] *vt* build; (fig) edify. **~io** *m* building; (fig) structure

edit|ar *vt* edit; (publicar) publish. **~or** *a* publishing. ● *m* editor; (que publica) publisher. **~orial** *a* editorial. ● *m* leading article. ● *f* publishing house

edredón *m* duvet

educa|ción *f* upbringing; (modales) (good) manners; (enseñanza) education. **falta de ~ción** rudeness, bad manners. **~do** *a* polite. **bien ~do** polite. **mal ~do** rude. **~r** [7] *vt* bring up; (enseñar) educate. **~tivo** *a* educational

edulcorante *m* sweetener

EE.UU. *abrev* (**Estados Unidos**) USA

efect|ivamente *adv* really; (por supuesto) indeed. **~ivo** *a* effective; (auténtico) real. ● *m* cash. **~o** *m* effect; (impresión) impression. **en ~o** really; (como respuesta) indeed. **~os** *mpl* belongings; (Com) goods. **~uar** [21] *vt* carry out; make <*viaje, compras etc*>

efervescente *a* effervescent; <*bebidas*> fizzy

efica|cia *f* effectiveness; (de persona) efficiency. **~z** *a* effective; <*persona*> efficient

eficien|cia *f* efficiency. **~te** *a* efficient

efímero *a* ephemeral

efusi|vidad *f* effusiveness. **~vo** *a* effusive; <*persona*> demonstrative

egipcio *a & m* Egyptian

Egipto *m* Egypt

ego|ísmo *m* selfishness, egotism. **~ista** *a* selfish

egresar *vi* (LAm) graduate; (de colegio) leave school, graduate Amer

eje *m* axis; (Tec) axle

ejecu|ción *f* execution; (Mus) performance. **~tar** *vt* carry out; (Mus) perform; (matar) execute. **~tivo** *m* executive

ejempl|ar *a* exemplary; (ideal) model. ● *m* specimen; (libro) copy; (revista) issue, number. **~ificar** [7] *vt* exemplify. **~o** *m* example. **dar (el) ~o** set an example. **por ~o** for example

ejerc|er [9] *vt* exercise; practise <*profesión*>; exert <*influencia*>. ● *vi* practise. **~icio** *m* exercise; (de profesión) practice. **hacer ~icios** take exercise. **~itar** *vt* exercise

ejército *m* army

ejido *m* (Mex) cooperative

ejote *m* (Mex) green bean

el

● *artículo definido masculino* (*pl* **los**)

> The masculine article **el** is also used before feminine nouns which begin with stressed **a** or **ha**, e.g. **el ala derecha**, **el hada madrina**. Also, preceded by **el de** becomes **del** and preceded by **a** becomes **al**

‥‥▸ the. **el tren de las seis** the six o'clock train. **el vecino de al lado** the next-door neighbour. **cerca del hospital** near the hospital

No se traduce en los siguientes casos:

‥‥▸ (con nombre abstracto, genérico) **el tiempo vuela** time flies. **odio el queso** I hate cheese. **el hilo es muy durable** linen is very durable

‥‥▸ (con colores, días de la semana) **el rojo está de moda** red is in fashion. **el lunes es fiesta** Monday is a holiday

‥‥▸ (con algunas instituciones) **termino el colegio mañana** I finish school tomorrow. **lo ingresaron en el hospital** he was admitted to hospital

‥‥▸ (con nombres propios) **el Sr. Díaz** Mr Díaz. **el doctor Lara** Doctor Lara

‥‥▸ (antes de infinitivo) **es muy cuidadosa en el vestir** she takes great care in the way she dresses. **me di cuenta al verlo** I realized when I saw him

····► (con partes del cuerpo, artículos personales) *se traduce por un posesivo*.
apretó el puño he clenched his fist.
tienes el zapato desatado your shoe
is undone

····► **el + de. es el de Pedro** it's Pedro's.
el del sombrero the one with the hat

····► **el + que** (persona) **el que me atendió** the one who served me. (cosa) **el
que se rompió** the one that broke.

····► **el + que** + *subjuntivo* (quienquiera)
whoever. **el que gane la lotería** whoever wins the lottery. (cualquiera)
whichever. **compra el que sea más
barato** buy whichever is cheaper

él *pron* (persona) he; (persona con prep)
him; (cosa) it. **es de ~** it's his

elabora|ción *f* elaboration; (fabrica-
ción) manufacture. **~r** *vt* elaborate;
manufacture *<producto>*; (producir)
produce

el|asticidad *f* elasticity. **~ástico**
a & m elastic

elec|ción *f* choice; (de político etc)
election. **~ciones** *fpl* (Pol) election.
~tor *m* voter. **~torado** *m* elector-
ate. **~toral** *a* electoral; *<campaña>*
election

electrici|dad *f* electricity. **~sta**
m & f electrician

eléctrico *a* electric; *<aparato>* electrical

electri|ficar [7] *vt*, electrify. **~zar**
[10] *vt* electrify

electrocutar *vt* electrocute.
□ **~se** *vpr* be electrocuted

electrodoméstico *a* electrical
appliance

electrónic|a *f* electronics. **~o** *a*
electronic

elefante *m* elephant

elegan|cia *f* elegance. **~te** *a* ele-
gant

elegía *f* elegy

elegi|ble *a* eligible. **~do** *a* chosen.
~r [5 & 14] *vt* choose; (por votación)
elect

element|al *a* elementary; (esencial)
fundamental. **~o** *m* element; (persona) person, bloke (Brit, 🆒). **~os** *mpl*
(nociones) basic principles

elenco *m* (en el teatro) cast

eleva|ción *f* elevation; (de precios)
rise, increase; (acción) raising. **~dor**
m (Mex) lift (Brit), elevator (Amer). **~r**
vt raise; (promover) promote

elimina|ción *f* elimination. **~r** *vt*
eliminate; (Informática) delete. **~to-
ria** *f* preliminary heat

élite /e'lit, e'lite/ *f* elite

ella *pron* (persona) she; (persona con
prep) her; (cosa) it. **es de ~** it's hers.
~s *pron pl* they; (con prep) them. **es
de ~s** it's theirs

ello *pron* it

ellos *pron pl* they; (con prep) them. **es
de ~** it's theirs

elocuen|cia *f* eloquence. **~te** *a*
eloquent

elogi|ar *vt* praise. **~o** *m* praise

elote *m* (Mex) corncob; (Culin) corn on
the cob

eludir *vt* avoid, elude

emanar *vi* emanate (de from); (origi-
narse) originate (de from, in)

emancipa|ción *f* emancipation.
~r *vt* emancipate. □ **~rse** *vpr* become emancipated

embadurnar *vt* smear

embajad|a *f* embassy. **~or** *m* am-
bassador

embalar *vt* pack

embaldosar *vt* tile

embalsamar *vt* embalm

embalse *m* reservoir

embaraz|ada *a* pregnant. ● *f*
pregnant woman. **~ar** [10] *vt* get
pregnant. **~o** *m* pregnancy; (apuro)
embarrassment; (estorbo) hindrance.
~oso *a* awkward, embarrassing

embar|cación *f* vessel. **~cadero**
m jetty, pier. **~car** [7] *vt* load *<mer-
cancías etc>*. □ **~carse** *vpr* board.
~carse en (fig) embark upon

embargo *m* embargo; (Jurid) seizure.
sin ~ however

embarque *m* loading; (de pasajeros)
boarding

embaucar [7] *vt* trick

embelesar *vt* captivate

embellecer [11] *vt* make beautiful

embesti|da *f* charge. **~r** [5] *vt/i*
charge

emblema *m* emblem

embolsarse *vpr* pocket

embonar *vt* (Mex) fit

emborrachar *vt* get drunk. □ ~**se** *vpr* get drunk

emboscada *f* ambush

embotar *vt* dull

embotella|miento *m* (de vehículos) traffic jam. ~**r** *vt* bottle

embrague *m* clutch

embriag|arse [12] *vpr* get drunk. ~**uez** *f* drunkenness

embrión *m* embryo

embroll|ar *vt* mix up; involve <*persona*>. □ ~**arse** *vpr* get into a muddle; (en un asunto) get involved. ~**o** *m* tangle; (fig) muddle

embruj|ado *a* bewitched; <*casa*> haunted. ~**ar** *vt* bewitch. ~**o** *m* spell

embrutecer [11] *vt* brutalize

embudo *m* funnel

embuste *m* lie. ~**ro** *a* deceitful. ● *m* liar

embuti|do *m* (Culin) sausage. ~**r** *vt* stuff

emergencia *f* emergency

emerger [14] *vi* appear, emerge

emigra|ción *f* emigration. ~**nte** *a & m & f* emigrant. ~**r** *vi* emigrate

eminen|cia *f* eminence. ~**te** *a* eminent

emisario *m* emissary

emi|sión *f* emission; (de dinero) issue; (TV etc) broadcast. ~**sor** *a* issuing; (TV etc) broadcasting. ~**sora** *f* radio station. ~**tir** *vt* emit, give out; (TV etc) broadcast; cast <*voto*>; (poner en circulación) issue

emoci|ón *f* emotion; (excitación) excitement. ¡qué ~**ón**! how exciting!. ~**onado** *a* moved. ~**onante** *a* exciting; (conmovedor) moving. ~**onar** *vt* move. □ ~**onarse** *vpr* get excited; (conmoverse) be moved

emotivo *a* emotional; (conmovedor) moving

empacar [7] *vt* (LAm) pack

empacho *m* indigestion

empadronar *vt* register. □ ~**se** *vpr* register

empalagoso *a* sickly; <*persona*> cloying

empalizada *f* fence

empalm|ar *vt* connect, join. ● *vi* meet. ~**e** *m* junction; (de trenes) connection

empan|ada *f* (savoury) pie; (LAm, individual) pasty. ~**adilla** *f* pasty

empantanarse *vpr* become swamped; <*coche*> get bogged down

empañar *vt* steam up; (fig) tarnish. □ ~**se** *vpr* steam up

empapar *vt* soak. □ ~**se** *vpr* get soaked

empapela|do *m* wallpaper. ~**r** *vt* wallpaper

empaquetar *vt* package

emparedado *m* sandwich

emparentado *a* related

empast|ar *vt* fill <*muela*>. ~**e** *m* filling

empat|ar *vi* draw. ~**e** *m* draw

empedernido *a* confirmed; <*bebedor*> inveterate

empedrar [1] *vt* pave

empeine *m* instep

empeñ|ado *a* in debt; (decidido) determined (en to). ~**ar** *vt* pawn; pledge <*palabra*>. □ ~**arse** *vpr* get into debt; (estar decidido a) be determined (en to). ~**o** *m* pledge; (resolución) determination. casa *f* de ~**s** pawnshop. ~**oso** *a* (LAm) hardworking

empeorar *vt* make worse. ● *vi* get worse. □ ~**se** *vpr* get worse

empequeñecer [11] *vt* become smaller; (fig) belittle

empera|dor *m* emperor. ~**triz** *f* empress

empezar [1 & 10] *vt/i* start, begin. para ~ to begin with

empina|do *a* <*cuesta*> steep. ~**r** *vt* raise. □ ~**rse** *vpr* <*persona*> stand on tiptoe

empírico *a* empirical

emplasto *m* plaster

emplaza|miento *m* (Jurid) summons; (lugar) site. ~**r** [10] *vt* summon; (situar) site

emple|ada *f* employee; (doméstica) maid. ~**ado** *m* employee. ~**ar** *vt* use; employ <*persona*>; spend <*tiempo*>. □ ~**arse** *vpr* get a job. ~**o** *m* use; (trabajo) employment; (puesto) job

empobrecer [11] *vt* impoverish. □ ~**se** *vpr* become poor

empoll|ar *vt* incubate <*huevos*>; (🅧, estudiar) cram 🅕. ●*vi* <*ave*> sit; <*estudiante*> 🅧 cram. ~**ón** *m* 🅧 swot (Brit 🅕), grind (Amer 🅕)

empolvarse *vpr* powder

empotra|do *a* built-in, fitted. ~**r** *vt* fit

emprende|dor *a* enterprising. ~**r** *vt* undertake; set out on <*viaje*>. ~**rla con uno** pick a fight with s.o.

empresa *f* undertaking; (Com) company, firm. ~**rio** *m* businessman; (patrón) employer; (de teatro etc) impresario

empuj|ar *vt* push. ~**e** *m* (fig) drive. ~**ón** *m* push, shove

empuña|dura *f* handle. ~**r** *vt* take up <*pluma, espada*>

emular *vt* emulate

en *prep* in; (sobre) on; (dentro) inside, in; (medio de transporte) by. ~ **casa** at home. ~ **coche** by car. ~ **10 días** in 10 days. **de pueblo** ~ **pueblo** from town to town

enagua *f* petticoat

enajena|ción *f* alienation. ~**ción mental** insanity. ~**r** *vt* alienate; (volver loco) derange

enamora|do *a* in love. ● *m* lover. ~**r** *vt* win the love of. □ ~**rse** *vpr* fall in love (**de** with)

enano *a* & *m* dwarf

enardecer [11] *vt* inflame. □ ~**se** *vpr* get excited (**por** about)

encabeza|do *m* (Mex) headline. ~**miento** *m* heading; (de periódico) headline. ~**r** [10] *vt* head; lead <*revolución etc*>

encabritarse *vpr* rear up

encadenar *vt* chain; (fig) tie down

encaj|ar *vt* fit; fit together <*varias piezas*>. ●*vi* fit; (cuadrar) tally. □ ~**arse** *vpr* put on. ~**e** *m* lace; (Com) reserve

encaminar *vt* direct. □ ~**se** *vpr* make one's way

encandilar *vt* dazzle; (estimular) stimulate

encant|ado *a* enchanted; <*persona*> delighted. ¡~**ado!** pleased to meet you! ~**ador** *a* charming. ~**amiento** *m* spell. ~**ar** *vt* bewitch; (fig) charm, delight. **me** ~**a la leche** I love milk. ~**o** *m* spell; (fig) delight

encapricharse *vpr*. ~ **con** take a fancy to

encarar *vt* face; (LAm) stand up to <*persona*>. □ ~**se** *vpr*. ~**se con** stand up to

encarcelar *vt* imprison

encarecer [11] *vt* put up the price of. □ ~**se** *vpr* become more expensive

encarg|ado *a* in charge. ● *m* manager, person in charge. ~**ar** [12] *vt* entrust; (pedir) order. □ ~**arse** *vpr* take charge (**de** of). ~**o** *m* job; (Com) order; (recado) errand. **hecho de** ~**o** made to measure

encariñarse *vpr*. ~ **con** take to, become fond of

encarna|ción *f* incarnation. ~**do** *a* incarnate; (rojo) red; <*uña*> ingrowing. ● *m* red

encarnizado *a* bitter

encarpetar *vt* file; (LAm, dar carpetazo) shelve

encarrilar *vt* put back on the rails; (fig) direct, put on the right track

encasillar *vt* classify; (fig) pigeonhole

encauzar [10] *vt* channel

enceguecer *vt* [11] (LAm) blind

encend|edor *m* lighter. ~**er** [1] *vt* light; switch on, turn on <*aparato eléctrico*>; start <*motor*>; (fig) arouse. □ ~**erse** *vpr* light; <*aparato eléctrico*> come on; (excitarse) get excited; (ruborizarse) blush. ~**ido** *a* lit; <*aparato eléctrico*> on; (rojo) bright red. ● *m* (Auto) ignition

encera|do *a* waxed. ● *m* (pizarra) blackboard. ~**r** *vt* wax

encerr|ar [1] *vt* shut in; (con llave) lock up; (fig, contener) contain. ~**ona** *f* trap

enchilar *vt* (Mex) add chili to

enchinar *vt* (Mex) perm

enchuf|ado *a* switched on. ~**ar** *vt* plug in; fit together <*tubos etc*>. ~**e** *m* socket; (clavija) plug; (de tubos etc) joint; (〈E〉, influencia) contact. **tener** ~**e** have friends in the right places

encía *f* gum

enciclopedia *f* encyclopaedia

encierro *m* confinement; (cárcel) prison

encim|a *adv* on top; (arriba) above. ~ **de** on, on top of; (sobre) over; (además de) besides, as well as. **por** ~ on top; (a la ligera) superficially. **por** ~ **de todo** above all. ~**ar** *vt* (Mex) stack up. ~**era** *f* worktop

encina *f* holm oak

encinta *a* pregnant

enclenque *a* weak; (enfermizo) sickly

encoger [14] *vt* shrink; (contraer) contract. □ ~**se** *vpr* shrink. ~**erse de hombros** shrug one's shoulders

encolar *vt* glue; (pegar) stick

encolerizar [10] *vt* make angry. □ ~**se** *vpr* get furious

encomendar [1] *vt* entrust

encomi|ar *vt* praise. ~**o** *m* praise. ~**oso** *a* (LAm) complimentary

encono *m* bitterness, ill will

encontra|do *a* contrary, conflicting. ~**r** [2] *vt* find; (tropezar con) meet. □ ~**rse** *vpr* meet; (hallarse) be. **no** ~**rse** feel uncomfortable

encorvar *vt* hunch. □ ~**se** *vpr* stoop

encrespa|do *a* <pelo> curly; <mar> rough. ~**r** *vt* curl <pelo>; make rough <mar>

encrucijada *f* crossroads

encuaderna|ción *f* binding. ~**dor** *m* bookbinder. ~**r** *vt* bind

encub|ierto *a* hidden. ~**rir** (*pp* **encubierto**) *vt* hide, conceal; cover up <delito>; shelter <delincuente>

encuentro *m* meeting; (en deportes) match; (Mil) encounter

encuesta *f* survey; (investigación) inquiry

encumbrado *a* eminent; (alto) high

encurtidos *mpl* pickles

endeble *a* weak

endemoniado *a* possessed; (muy malo) wretched

enderezar [10] *vt* straighten out; (poner vertical) put upright; (fig, arreglar) put right, sort out; (dirigir) direct. □ ~**se** *vpr* straighten out

endeudarse *vpr* get into debt

endiablado *a* possessed; (malo) terrible; (difícil) difficult

endosar *vt* endorse <cheque>

endulzar [10] *vt* sweeten; (fig) soften

endurecer [11] *vt* harden. □ ~**se** *vpr* harden

enemi|go *a* enemy. ● *m* enemy. ~**stad** *f* enmity. ~**star** *vt* make an enemy of. □ ~**starse** *vpr* fall out (**con** with)

en|ergía *f* energy. ~**érgico** *a* <persona> lively; <decisión> forceful

energúmeno *m* madman

enero *m* January

enésimo *a* nth, umpteenth 〈E〉

enfad|ado *a* angry; (molesto) annoyed. ~**ar** *vt* make cross, anger; (molestar) annoy. □ ~**arse** *vpr* get angry; (molestarse) get annoyed. ~**o** *m* anger; (molestia) annoyance

énfasis *m invar* emphasis, stress. **poner** ~ stress, emphasize

enfático *a* emphatic

enferm|ar *vi* fall ill. □ ~**arse** *vpr* (LAm) fall ill. ~**edad** *f* illness. ~**era** *f* nurse. ~**ería** *f* sick bay; (carrera) nursing. ~**ero** *m* (male) nurse ~**izo** *a* sickly. ~**o** *a* ill. ● *m* patient

enflaquecer [11] *vt* make thin. ● *vi* lose weight

enfo|car [7] *vt* shine on; focus <lente>; (fig) approach. ~**que** *m* focus; (fig) approach

enfrentar *vt* face, confront; (poner frente a frente) bring face to face. □ ~**se** *vpr*. ~**se con** confront; (en deportes) meet

enfrente *adv* opposite. ~ **de** opposite. **de** ~ opposite

enfria|miento *m* cooling; (catarro) cold. ~**r** [20] *vt* cool (down); (fig) cool down. □ ~**rse** *vpr* go cold; (fig) cool off

enfurecer [11] *vt* infuriate. □ ~**se** *vpr* get furious

engalanar *vt* adorn. □ ~**se** *vpr* dress up

enganchar vt hook; hang up <ropa>. □ ~se vpr get caught; (Mil) enlist

engañ|ar vt deceive, trick; (ser infiel) be unfaithful. □ ~arse vpr be wrong, be mistaken; (no admitir la verdad) deceive o.s. ~o m deceit, trickery; (error) mistake. ~oso a deceptive; <persona> deceitful

engarzar [10] vt string <cuentas>; set <joyas>

engatusar vt 🗓 coax

engendr|ar vt father; (fig) breed. ~o m (monstruo) monster; (fig) brainchild

englobar vt include

engomar vt glue

engordar vt fatten, gain <kilo>. ● vi get fatter, put on weight

engorro m nuisance

engranaje m (Auto) gear

engrandecer [11] vt (enaltecer) exalt, raise

engrasar vt grease; (con aceite) oil; (ensuciar) get grease on

engreído a arrogant

engullir [22] vt gulp down

enhebrar vt thread

enhorabuena f congratulations. dar la ~ congratulate

enigm|a m enigma. ~ático a enigmatic

enjabonar vt soap. □ ~se vpr to soap o.s.

enjambre m swarm

enjaular vt put in a cage

enjuag|ar [12] vt rinse. ~ue m rinsing; (para la boca) mouthwash

enjugar [12] vt wipe (away)

enjuiciar vt pass judgement on

enjuto a <persona> skinny

enlace m connection; (matrimonial) wedding

enlatar vt tin, can

enlazar [10] vt link; tie together <cintas>; (Mex, casar) marry

enlodar vt, **enlodazar** [10] vt cover in mud

enloquecer [11] vt drive mad. ● vi go mad. □ ~se vpr go mad

enlosar vt (con losas) pave; (con baldosas) tile

enmarañar vt tangle (up), entangle; (confundir) confuse. □ ~se vpr get into a tangle; (confundirse) get confused

enmarcar [7] vt frame

enm|endar vt correct. □ ~endarse vpr mend one's way. ~ienda f correction; (de ley etc) amendment

enmohecerse [11] vpr (con óxido) go rusty; (con hongos) go mouldy

enmudecer [11] vi be dumbstruck; (callar) fall silent

ennegrecer [11] vt blacken

ennoblecer [11] vt ennoble; (fig) add style to

enoj|adizo a irritable. ~ado a angry; (molesto) annoyed. ~ar vt anger; (molestar) annoy. □ ~arse vpr get angry; (molestarse) get annoyed. ~o m anger; (molestia) annoyance. ~oso a annoying

enorgullecerse [11] vpr be proud

enorm|e a huge, enormous. ~emente adv enormously. ~idad f immensity; (de crimer) enormity

enraizado a deeply rooted

enrarecido a rarefied

enred|adera f creeper. ~ar vt tangle (up), entangle; (confundir) confuse; (involucrar) involve. □ ~arse vpr get tangled; (confundirse) get confused; <persona> get involved (con with). ~o m tangle; (fig) muddle, mess

enrejado m bars

enriquecer [11] vt make rich; (fig) enrich. □ ~se vpr get rich

enrojecerse [11] vpr <persona> go red, blush

enrolar vt enlist

enrollar vt roll (up), wind <hilo etc>

enroscar [7] vt coil; (atornillar) screw in

ensalad|a f salad. armar una ~a make a mess. ~era f salad bowl. ~illa f Russian salad

ensalzar [10] vt praise; (enaltecer) exalt

ensambla|dura f, **ensamblaje** m (acción) assembling; (efecto) joint. ~r vt join

ensanch|ar *vt* widen; (agrandar) enlarge. □ **~arse** *vpr* get wider. **~e** *m* widening

ensangrentar [1] *vt* stain with blood

ensañarse *vpr*. **~ con** treat cruelly

ensartar *vt* string *<cuentas etc>*

ensay|ar *vt* test; rehearse *<obra de teatro etc>*. **~o** *m* test, trial; (composición literaria) essay

enseguida *adv* at once, immediately

ensenada *f* inlet, cove

enseña|nza *f* education; (acción de enseñar) teaching. **~nza media** secondary education. **~r** *vt* teach; (mostrar) show

enseres *mpl* equipment

ensillar *vt* saddle

ensimismarse *vpr* be lost in thought

ensombrecer [11] *vt* darken

ensordecer [11] *vt* deafen. ● *vi* go deaf

ensuciar *vt* dirty. □ **~se** *vpr* get dirty

ensueño *m* dream

entablar *vt* (empezar) start

entablillar *vt* put in a splint

entallar *vt* tailor *<un vestido>*. ● *vi* fit

entarimado *m* parquet; (plataforma) platform

ente *m* entity, being; (🅵, persona rara) weirdo; (Com) firm, company

entend|er [1] *vt* understand; (opinar) believe, think. ● *vi* understand. **~er de** know about. **a mi ~er** in my opinion. **dar a ~er** hint. **darse a ~er** (LAm) make o.s. understood. □ **~erse** *vpr* make o.s. understood; (comprenderse) be understood. **~erse con** get on with. **~ido** *a* understood; (enterado) well-informed. **no darse por ~ido** pretend not to understand. ● *interj* agreed!, OK! 🅵. **~imiento** *m* understanding

entera|do *a* well-informed; (que sabe) aware. **darse por ~do** take the hint. **~r** *vt* inform (de of). □ **~rse** *vpr*. **~rse de** find out about, hear of. ¡entérate! listen! ¿**te ~s?** do you understand?

entereza *f* (carácter) strength of character

enternecer [11] *vt* (fig) move, touch. □ **~se** *vpr* be moved, be touched

entero *a* entire, whole. **por ~** entirely, completely

enterra|dor *m* gravedigger. **~r** [1] *vt* bury

entibiar *vt* (enfriar) cool; (calentar) warm (up). □ **~se** *vpr* (enfriarse) cool down; (fig) cool; (calentarse) get warm

entidad *f* entity; (organización) organization; (Com) company; (importancia) significance

entierro *m* burial; (ceremonia) funeral

entona|ción *f* intonation. **~r** *vt* intone; sing *<nota>*. ● *vi* (Mus) be in tune; *<colores>* match. □ **~rse** *vpr* (emborracharse) get tipsy

entonces *adv* then. **en aquel ~** at that time, then

entorn|ado *a* *<puerta>* ajar; *<ventana>* slightly open. **~o** *m* environment; (en literatura) setting

entorpecer [11] *vt* dull; slow down *<tráfico>*; (dificultar) hinder

entra|da *f* entrance; (incorporación) admission, entry; (para cine etc) ticket; (de datos, Tec) input; (de una comida) starter. **de ~da** right away. **~do** *a*. **~do en años** elderly. **ya ~da la noche** late at night. **~nte** *a* next, coming

entraña *f* (fig) heart. **~s** *fpl* entrails; (fig) heart. **~ble** *a* *<cariño>* deep; *<amigo>* close. **~r** *vt* involve

entrar *vt* (traer) bring in; (llevar) take in. ● *vi* go in, enter; (venir) come in, enter; (empezar) start, begin; (incorporarse) join. **~ en**, (LAm) **~ a** go into

entre *prep* (dos personas o cosas) between; (más de dos) among(st)

entre|abierto *a* half-open. **~abrir** (*pp* **entreabierto**) *vt* half open. **~acto** *m* interval. **~cejo** *m* forehead. **fruncir el ~cejo** frown. **~cerrar** [1] *vt* (LAm) half close. **~cortado** *a* *<voz>* faltering; *<respiración>* laboured. **~cruzar** [10] *vt* intertwine

entrega *f* handing over; (de mercancías etc) delivery; (de novela etc) instalment; (dedicación) commitment. ~**r** [12] *vt* deliver; (dar) give; hand in *<deberes>*; hand over *<poder>*. □ ~**rse** *vpr* surrender, give o.s. up; (dedicarse) devote o.s. (**a** to)

entre|lazar [10] *vt* intertwine. ~**més** *m* hors-d'oeuvre; (en el teatro) short comedy. ~**mezclar** *vt* intermingle

entrena|dor *m* trainer. ~**miento** *m* training. ~**r** *vt* train. □ ~**rse** *vpr* train

entre|pierna *f* crotch. ~**piso** *m* (LAm) mezzanine. ~**sacar** [7] *vt* pick out. ~**suelo** *m* mezzanine. ~**tanto** *adv* meanwhile. ~**tejer** *vt* interweave

entrepiso *m* (LAm) mezzanine

entresacar [7] *vt* pick out

entresuelo *m* mezzanine

entretanto *adv* meanwhile

entretejer *vt* interweave

entreten|ción *f* (LAm) entertainment. ~**er** [40] *vt* entertain, amuse; (detener) delay, keep. □ ~**erse** *vpr* amuse o.s.; (tardar) delay, linger. ~**ido** *a* (con ser) entertaining; (con estar) busy. ~**imiento** *m* entertainment

entrever [43] *vt* make out, glimpse

entrevista *f* interview; (reunión) meeting. □ ~**rse** *vpr* have an interview

entristecer [11] *vt* sadden, make sad. □ ~**se** *vpr* grow sad

entromet|erse *vpr* interfere. ~**ido** *a* interfering

entumec|erse [11] *vpr* go numb. ~**ido** *a* numb

enturbiar *vt* cloud

entusi|asmar *vt* fill with enthusiasm; (gustar mucho) delight. □ ~**asmarse**. ~**asmarse con** get enthusiastic about. ~**asmo** *m* enthusiasm. ~**asta** *a* enthusiastic. ● *m* & *f* enthusiast

enumerar *vt* enumerate

envalentonar *vt* encourage. □ ~**se** *vpr* become bolder

envas|ado *m* packaging; (en latas) canning; (en botellas) bottling. ~**ar** *vt* package; (en latas) tin, can; (en botellas) bottle. ~**e** *m* packing; (lata) tin, can; (botella) bottle

envejec|er [11] *vt* make (look) older. ● *vi* age, grow old. □ ~**erse** *vpr* age, grow old

envenenar *vt* poison

envergadura *f* importance

envia|do *m* envoy; (de la prensa) correspondent. ~**r** [20] *vt* send

enviciarse *vpr* become addicted (**con** to)

envidi|a *f* envy; (celos) jealousy. ~**ar** *vt* envy, be envious of. ~**oso** *a* envious; (celoso) jealous. **tener** ~**a** a envy

envío *m* sending, dispatch; (de mercancías) consignment; (de dinero) remittance. ~ **contra reembolso** cash on delivery. **gastos** *mpl* **de** ~ postage and packing (costs)

enviudar *vi* be widowed

env|oltura *f* wrapping. ~**olver** [2] (*pp* **envuelto**) *vt* wrap; (cubrir) cover; (rodear) surround; (fig, enredar) involve. ~**uelto** *a* wrapped (up)

enyesar *vt* plaster; (Med) put in plaster

épica *f* epic

épico *a* epic

epid|emia *f* epidemic. ~**émico** *a* epidemic

epil|epsia *f* epilepsy. ~**éptico** *a* epileptic

epílogo *m* epilogue

episodio *m* episode

epístola *f* epistle

epitafio *m* epitaph

época *f* age; (período) period. **hacer** ~ make history, be epoch-making

equidad *f* equity

equilibr|ado *a* (well-)balanced. ~**ar** *vt* balance. ~**io** *m* balance; (de balanza) equilibrium. ~**ista** *m* & *f* tightrope walker

equinoccio *m* equinox

equipaje *m* luggage (esp Brit), baggage (esp Amer)

equipar *vt* equip; (de ropa) fit out

equiparar *vt* make equal; (comparar) compare

equipo *m* equipment; (de personas) team

equitación *f* riding

equivale|nte *a* equivalent. **~r** [42] *vi* be equivalent; (significar) mean

equivoca|ción *f* mistake, error. **~do** *a* wrong. □ **~rse** *vpr* make a mistake; (estar en error) be wrong, be mistaken. **~rse de** be wrong about. **~rse de número** dial the wrong number. **si no me equivoco** if I'm not mistaken

equívoco *a* equivocal; (sospechoso) suspicious ● *m* misunderstanding; (error) mistake

era *f* era. ● *vb* ⇒SER

erario *m* treasury

erección *f* erection

eres *vb* ⇒SER

erguir [48] *vt* raise. □ **~se** *vpr* raise

erigir [14] *vt* erect. □ **~se** *vpr.* **~se en** set o.s. up as; (llegar a ser) become

eriza|do *a* prickly. □ **~rse** [10] *vpr* stand on end; (LAm) *<persona>* get goose pimples

erizo *m* hedgehog; (de mar) sea urchin. **~ de mar** sea urchin

ermita *f* hermitage. **~ño** *m* hermit

erosi|ón *f* erosion. **~onar** *vt* erode

er|ótico *a* erotic. **~otismo** *m* eroticism

err|ar [1] (*la* **i** *inicial pasa a ser* **y**) *vt* miss. ● *vi* wander; (equivocarse) make a mistake, be wrong. **~ata** *f* misprint. **~óneo** *a* erroneous, wrong. **~or** *m* error, mistake. **estar en un ~or** be wrong, be mistaken

eruct|ar *vi* belch. **~o** *m* belch

erudi|ción *f* learning, erudition. **~to** *a* learned; *<palabra>* erudite

erupción *f* eruption; (Med) rash

es *vb* ⇒SER

esa *a* ⇒ESE

ésa *pron* ⇒ÉSE

esbelto *a* slender, slim

esboz|ar [10] *vt* sketch, outline. **~o** *m* sketch, outline

escabeche *m* brine. **en ~** pickled

escabroso *a* *<terreno>* rough; *<asunto>* difficult; (atrevido) crude

escabullirse [22] *vpr* slip away

escafandra *f* diving-suit

escala *f* scale; (escalera de mano) ladder; (Aviac) stopover. **hacer ~ en** stop at. **vuelo sin ~s** non-stop flight. **~da** *f* climbing; (Pol) escalation. **~r** *vt* climb; break into *<una casa>*. ● *vi* climb, go climbing

escaldar *vt* scald

escalera *f* staircase, stairs; (de mano) ladder. **~ de caracol** spiral staircase. **~ de incendios** fire escape. **~ de tijera** step-ladder. **~ mecánica** escalator

escalfa|do *a* poached. **~r** *vt* poach

escalinata *f* flight of steps

escalofrío *m* shiver. **tener ~s** be shivering

escalón *m* step, stair; (de escala) rung

escalope *m* escalope

escam|a *f* scale; (de jabón, de la piel) flake. **~oso** *a* scaly; *<piel>* flaky

escamotear *vt* make disappear; (robar) steal, pinch

escampar *vi* stop raining

esc|andalizar [10] *vt* scandalize, shock. □ **~andalizarse** *vpr* be shocked. **~ándalo** *m* scandal; (alboroto) commotion, racket. **armar un ~** make a scene. **~andaloso** *a* scandalous; (alborotador) noisy

escandinavo *a* & *m* Scandinavian

escaño *m* bench; (Pol) seat

escapa|da *f* escape; (visita) flying visit. **~r** *vi* escape. **dejar ~r** let out. □ **~rse** *vpr* escape; *<líquido, gas>* leak

escaparate *m* (shop) window

escap|atoria *f* (fig) way out. **~e** *m* (de gas, de líquido) leak; (fuga) escape; (Auto) exhaust

escarabajo *m* beetle

escaramuza *f* skirmish

escarbar *vt* scratch; pick *<dientes, herida>*; (fig, escudriñar) pry (**en** into). □ **~se** *vpr* pick

escarcha *f* frost. **~do** *a* *<fruta>* crystallized

escarlat|a *a invar* scarlet. **~ina** *f* scarlet fever

escarm|entar [1] *vt* teach a lesson to. ● *vi* learn one's lesson. **~iento** *m* punishment; (lección) lesson

escarola *f* endive

escarpado *a* steep

escas|ear *vi* be scarce. ~**ez** *f* scarcity, shortage; (pobreza) poverty. ~**o** *a* scarce; (poco) little; (muy justo) barely. ~**o de** short of

escatimar *vt* be sparing with

escayola *f* plaster

esc|ena *f* scene; (escenario) stage. ~**enario** *m* stage; (fig) scene. ~**énico** *a* stage. ~**enografía** *f* set design

esc|epticismo *m* scepticism. ~**éptico** *a* sceptical. ● *m* sceptic

esclarecer [11] *vt* (fig) throw light on, clarify

esclav|itud *f* slavery. ~**izar** [10] *vt* enslave. ~**o** *m* slave

esclusa *f* lock; (de presa) floodgate

escoba *f* broom

escocer [2 & 9] *vi* sting

escocés *a* Scottish. ● *m* Scot

Escocia *f* Scotland

escog|er [14] *vt* choose. ~**ido** *a* chosen; <mercancía> choice; <clientela> select

escolar *a* school. ● *m* schoolboy. ● *f* schoolgirl

escolta *f* escort

escombros *mpl* rubble

escond|er *vt* hide. □ ~**erse** *vpr* hide. ~**idas** *fpl* (LAm, juego) hide-and-seek. **a** ~**idas** secretly. ~**ite** *m* hiding place; (juego) hide-and-seek. ~**rijo** *m* hiding place

escopeta *f* shotgun

escoria *f* slag; (fig) dregs

escorpión *m* scorpion

Escorpión *m* Scorpio

escot|ado *a* low-cut. ~**e** *m* low neckline. **pagar a** ~**e** share the expenses

escozor *m* stinging

escri|bano *m* clerk. ~**bir** (*pp* **escrito**) *vt/i* write. ~**bir a máquina** type. **¿cómo se escribe...?** how do you spell...? □ ~**birse** *vpr* write to each other. ~**to** *a* written. **por** ~**to** in writing. ● *m* document. ~**tor** *m* writer. ~**torio** *m* desk; (oficina) office; (LAm, en una casa) study. ~**tura** *f* (hand)writing; (Jurid) deed

escr|úpulo *m* scruple. ~**upuloso** *a* scrupulous

escrut|ar *vt* scrutinize; count <votos>. ~**inio** *m* count

escuadr|a *f* (instrumento) square; (Mil) squad; (Naut) fleet. ~**ón** *m* squadron

escuálido *a* skinny

escuchar *vt* listen to; (esp LAm, oír) hear. ● *vi* listen

escudo *m* shield. ~ **de armas** coat of arms

escudriñar *vt* examine

escuela *f* school. ~ **normal** teachers' training college

escueto *a* simple

escuincle *m* (Mex 🄵) kid 🄵

escul|pir *vt* sculpture. ~**tor** *m* sculptor. ~**tora** *f* sculptress. ~**tura** *f* sculpture

escupir *vt/i* spit

escurr|eplatos *m invar* plate rack. ~**idizo** *a* slippery. ~**ir** *vt* drain; wring out <ropa>. ● *vi* drain; <ropa> drip. □ ~**irse** *vpr* slip

ese *a* (*f* **esa**) that; (*mpl* **esos**, *fpl* **esas**) those

ése *pron* (*f* **ésa**) that one: (*mpl* **ésos**, *fpl* **ésas**) those; (primero de dos) the former

esencia *f* essence. ~**l** *a* essential. **lo** ~**l** the main thing

esf|era *f* sphere; (de reloj) face. ~**érico** *a* spherical

esf|orzarse [2 & 10] *vpr* make an effort. ~**uerzo** *m* effort

esfumarse *vpr* fade away; <persona> vanish

esgrim|a *f* fencing. ~**ir** *vt* brandish; (fig) use

esguince *m* sprain

eslabón *m* link

eslavo *a* Slavic, Slavonic

eslogan *m* slogan

esmalt|ar *vt* enamel. ~**e** *m* enamel. ~**e de uñas** nail polish

esmerado *a* careful; <persona> painstaking

esmeralda *f* emerald

esmer|arse *vpr* take care (**en** over). ~**o** *m* care

esmero *m* care

esmoquin (*pl* **esmóquines**) *m* dinner jacket, tuxedo (Amer)

esnob *a invar* snobbish. ● *m & f* (*pl* ~s) snob. ~**ismo** *m* snobbery

esnórkel *m* snorkel

eso *pron* that. ¡~ es! that's it! ~ mismo exactly. a ~ de about. en ~ at that moment. ¿no es ~? isn't that right? por ~ that's why. y ~ que even though

esos *a pl* ⇒ESE

ésos *pron pl* ⇒ÉSE

espabila|do *a* bright; (despierto) awake. ~**r** *vt* (avivar) brighten up; (despertar) wake up. □ ~**rse** *vpr* wake up; (avivarse) wise up; (apresurarse) hurry up

espaci|al *a* space. ~**ar** *vt* space out. ~**o** *m* space. ~**oso** *a* spacious

espada *f* sword. ~**s** *fpl* (en naipes) spades

espaguetis *mpl* spaghetti

espald|a *f* back. a ~**as de uno** behind s.o.'s back. **volver la(s)** ~**a(s) a uno** give s.o. the cold shoulder. ~**illa** *f* shoulder-blade

espant|ajo *m*, ~**apájaros** *m invar* scarecrow. ~**ar** *vt* frighten; (ahuyentar) frighten away. □ ~**arse** *vpr* be frightened; (ahuyentarse) be frightened away. ~**o** *m* terror; (horror) horror. **¡qué** ~**o!** how awful! ~**oso** *a* horrific; (terrible) terrible

España *f* Spain

español *a* Spanish. ● *m* (persona) Spaniard; (lengua) Spanish. **los** ~**es** the Spanish. ~**izado** *a* Hispanicized

esparadrapo *m* (sticking) plaster

esparcir [9] *vt* scatter; (difundir) spread. □ ~**rse** *vpr* be scattered; (difundirse) spread; (divertirse) enjoy o.s.

espárrago *m* asparagus

espasm|o *m* spasm. ~**ódico** *a* spasmodic

espátula *f* spatula; (en pintura) palette knife

especia *f* spice

especial *a* special. **en** ~ especially. ~**idad** *f* speciality (Brit), specialty (Amer). ~**ista** *a & m & f* specialist. ~**ización** *f* specialization. □ ~**izarse** [10] *vpr* specialize. ~**mente** *adv* especially

especie *f* kind, sort; (Biol) species. **en** ~ in kind

especifica|ción *f* specification. ~**r** [7] *vt* specify

específico *a* specific

espect|áculo *m* sight; (de circo etc) show. ~**acular** *a* spectacular. ~**ador** *m & f* spectator

espectro *m* spectre; (en física) spectrum

especula|dor *m* speculator. ~**r** *vi* speculate

espej|ismo *m* mirage. ~**o** *m* mirror. ~**o retrovisor** (Auto) rear-view mirror

espeluznante *a* horrifying

espera *f* wait. **a la** ~ waiting (**de** for). ~**nza** *f* hope. ~**r** *vt* hope; (aguardar) wait for; expect <*visita, carta, bebé*>. **espero que no** I hope not. **espero que sí** I hope so. ● *vi* (aguardar) wait. □ ~**rse** *vpr* hang on; (prever) expect

esperma *f* sperm

esperpento *m* fright

espes|ar *vt/i* thicken. □ ~**arse** *vpr* thicken. ~**o** *a* thick. ~**or** *m* thickness

espetón *m* spit

esp|ía *f* spy. ~**iar** [20] *vt* spy on. ● *vi* spy

espiga *f* (de trigo etc) ear

espina *f* thorn; (de pez) bone; (Anat) spine. ~ **dorsal** spine

espinaca *f* spinach

espinazo *m* spine

espinilla *f* shin; (Med) blackhead; (LAm, grano) spot

espino *m* hawthorn. ~**so** *a* thorny; (fig) difficult

espionaje *m* espionage

espiral *a & f* spiral

espiritista *m & f* spiritualist. ~**iritu** *m* spirit; (mente) mind. ~**iritual** *a* spiritual

espl|éndido *a* splendid; <*persona*> generous. ~**endor** *m* splendour

espolear *vt* spur (on)

espolvorear *vt* sprinkle

esponj|a *f* sponge. ~**oso** *a* spongy

espont|aneidad *f* spontaneity. ~**áneo** *a* spontaneous

esporádico *a* sporadic

espos|a f wife. ~**as** fpl handcuffs. ~**ar** vt handcuff. ~**o** m husband

espuela f spur; (fig) incentive

espum|a f foam; (en bebidas) froth; (de jabón) lather; (de las olas) surf. **echar** ~**a** foam, froth. ~**oso** a <vino> sparkling

esqueleto m skeleton; (estructura) framework

esquema m outline

esqu|í m (pl ~**is**, ~**íes**) ski; (deporte) skiing. ~**iar** [20] vi ski

esquilar vt shear

esquimal a & m Eskimo

esquina f corner

esquiv|ar vt avoid; dodge <golpe>. ~**o** a elusive

esquizofrénico a & m schizophrenic

esta a ⇒ESTE

ésta pron ⇒ÉSTE

estab|ilidad f stability. ~**le** a stable

establec|er [11] vt establish. □ ~**erse** vpr settle; (Com) set up. ~**imiento** m establishment

establo m cattleshed

estaca f stake

estación f station; (del año) season. ~ **de invierno** winter (sports) resort. ~ **de servicio** service station

estaciona|miento m parking; (LAm, lugar) car park (Brit), parking lot (Amer). ~**r** vt station; (Auto) park. ~**rio** a stationary

estadía f (LAm) stay

estadio m stadium; (fase) stage

estadista m statesman. ● f stateswoman

estadístic|a f statistics; (cifra) statistic. ~**o** a statistical

estado m state; (Med) condition. ~ **civil** marital status. ~ **de ánimo** frame of mind. ~ **de cuenta** bank statement. ~ **mayor** (Mil) staff. **en buen** ~ in good condition

Estados Unidos mpl United States

estadounidense a American, United States. ● m & f American

estafa f swindle. ~**r** vt swindle

estafeta f (oficina de correos) (sub-) post office

estala|ctita f stalactite. ~**gmita** f stalagmite

estall|ar vi explode; <olas> break; <guerra etc> break out; (fig) burst. ~**ar en llanto** burst into tears. ~**ar de risa** burst out laughing. ~**ido** m explosion; (de guerra etc) outbreak

estamp|a f print; (aspecto) appearance. ~**ado** a printed. ● m printing; (motivo) pattern; (tela) cotton print. ~**ar** vt stamp; (imprimir) print

estampido m bang

estampilla f (LAm, de correos) (postage) stamp

estanca|do a stagnant. ~**r** [7] vt stem. □ ~**rse** vpr stagnate

estancia f stay; (cuarto) large room

estanco a watertight. ● m tobacconist's (shop)

estandarte m standard, banner

estanque m pond; (depósito de agua) (water) tank

estanquero m tobacconist

estante m shelf. ~**ría** f shelves; (para libros) bookcase

estaño m tin

estar [27]

● verbo intransitivo

····➤ to be. ¿**cómo estás?** how are you?. **estoy enfermo** I'm ill. **está muy cerca** it's very near. ¿**está Pedro?** is Pedro in? ¿**cómo está el tiempo?** what's the weather like? **ya estamos en invierno** it's winter already

····➤ (quedarse) to stay. **sólo** ~**é una semana** I'll only be staying for a week. **estoy en un hotel** I'm staying in a hotel

····➤ (con fecha) ¿**a cuánto estamos?** what's the date today? **estamos a 8 de mayo** it's the 8th of May.

····➤ (en locuciones) ¿**estamos?** all right? ¡**ahí está!** that's it! ~ **por** (apoyar a) to support; (LAm, encontrarse a punto de) to be about to; (quedar por) **eso está por verse** that remains to be seen. **son cuentas que están por pa-gar** they're bills still to be paid

● verbo auxiliar

····▶ (con gerundio) **estaba estudiando** I was studying

····▶ (con participio) **está condenado a muerte** he's been sentenced to death. **está mal traducido** it's wrongly translated.

▢ **estarse** *verbo pronominal* to stay. **no se está quieto** he won't stay still

⟹ Cuando el verbo **estar** forma parte de expresiones como **estar de acuerdo, estar a la vista, estar constipado**, etc., ver bajo el respectivo nombre o adjetivo

estatal *a* state

estático *a* static

estatua *f* statue

estatura *f* height

estatuto *m* statute; (norma) rule

este *a* <*región*> eastern; <*viento, lado*> east. ● *m* east. ● *a* (*f* **esta**) this; (*mpl* **estos**, *fpl* **estas**) these; (LAm, como muletilla) well, er

éste *pron* (*f* **ésta**) this one; (*mpl* **éstos**, *fpl* **éstas**) these; (segundo de dos) the latter

estela *f* wake; (de avión) trail; (Arquit) carved stone

estera *f* mat; (tejido) matting

est|éreo *a* stereo. **~ereofónico** *a* stereo, stereophonic

estereotipo *m* stereotype

estéril *a* sterile; <*terreno*> barren

esterilla *f* mat

esterlina *a*. **libra** *f* **~** pound sterling

estético *a* aesthetic

estiércol *m* dung; (abono) manure

estigma *m* stigma. **~s** *mpl* (Relig) stigmata

estil|arse *vpr* be used. **~o** *m* style; (en natación) stroke. **~ mariposa** butterfly. **~ pecho** (LAm) breaststroke. **por el ~o** of that sort

estilográfica *f* fountain pen

estima *f* esteem. **~do** *a* <*amigo, colega*> valued. **~do señor** (en cartas) Dear Sir. **~r** *vt* esteem; have great respect for <*persona*>; (valorar) value; (juzgar) consider

est|imulante *a* stimulating. ● *m* stimulant. **~imular** *vt* stimulate; (incitar) incite. **~ímulo** *m* stimulus

estir|ado *a* stretched; <*persona*> haughty. **~ar** *vt* stretch; (fig) stretch out. **~ón** *m* pull, tug; (crecimiento) sudden growth

estirpe *m* stock

esto *pron neutro* this; (este asunto) this business. **en ~** at this point. **en ~ de** in this business of. **por ~** therefore

estofa|do *a* stewed. ● *m* stew. **~r** *vt* stew

estómago *m* stomach. **dolor** *m* **de ~** stomach ache

estorb|ar *vt* obstruct; (molestar) bother. ● *vi* be in the way. **~o** *m* hindrance; (molestia) nuisance

estornud|ar *vi* sneeze. **~o** *m* sneeze

estos *a mpl* ⇒ESTE

éstos *pron mpl* ⇒ÉSTE

estoy *vb* ⇒ESTAR

estrabismo *m* squint

estrado *m* stage; (Mus) bandstand

estrafalario *a* eccentric; <*ropa*> outlandish

estrago *m* devastation. **hacer ~os** devastate

estragón *m* tarragon

estrambótico *a* eccentric; <*ropa*> outlandish

estrangula|dor *m* strangler; (Auto) choke. **~r** *vt* strangle

estratagema *f* stratagem

estrat|ega *m* & *f* strategist. **~egia** *f* strategy. **~égico** *a* strategic

estrato *m* stratum

estrech|ar *vt* make narrower; take in <*vestido*>; embrace <*persona*>. **~ar la mano a uno** shake hands with s.o. ▢ **~arse** *vpr* become narrower; (abrazarse) embrace. **~ez** *f* narrowness. **~eces** *fpl* financial difficulties. **~o** *a* narrow; <*vestido etc*> tight; (fig, íntimo) close. **~o de miras** narrow-minded. ● *m* strait(s)

estrella *f* star. **~ de mar** starfish. **~ado** *a* starry

estrellar *vt* smash; crash <*coche*>. ▢ **~se** *vpr* crash (**contra** into)

estremec|er [11] *vt* shake. □ ~**erse** *vpr* shake; (de emoción etc) tremble (**de** with). ~**imiento** *m* shaking

estren|ar *vt* wear for the first time <*vestido etc*>; show for the first time <*película*>. □ ~**arse** *vpr* make one's début. ~**o** *m* (de película) première; (de obra de teatro) first night; (de persona) debut

estreñi|do *a* constipated. ~**miento** *m* constipation

estrés *m* stress

estría *f* groove; (de la piel) stretch mark

estribillo *m* (incl Mus) refrain

estribo *m* stirrup; (de coche) step. perder los ~s lose one's temper

estribor *m* starboard

estricto *a* strict

estridente *a* strident, raucous

estrofa *f* stanza, verse

estropajo *m* scourer

estropear *vt* damage; (plan) spoil; ruin <*ropa*>. □ ~**se** *vpr* be damaged; (averiarse) break down; <*ropa*> get ruined; <*fruta etc*> go bad; (fracasar) fail

estructura *f* structure. ~**l** *a* structural

estruendo *m* roar; (de mucha gente) uproar

estrujar *vt* squeeze; wring (out) <*ropa*>; (fig) drain

estuario *m* estuary

estuche *m* case

estudi|ante *m & f* student. ~**antil** *a* student. ~**ar** *vt* study. ~**o** *m* study; (de artista) studio. ~**oso** *a* studious

estufa *f* heater; (Mex, cocina) cooker

estupefac|iente *m* narcotic. ~**to** *a* astonished

estupendo *a* marvellous; <*persona*> fantastic; ¡~! that's great!

est|upidez *f* stupidity; (acto) stupid thing. ~**úpido** *a* stupid

estupor *m* amazement

estuve *vb* ⇒ESTAR

etapa *f* stage. por ~s in stages

etc *abrev* (**etcétera**) etc. ~**étera** *adv* et cetera

etéreo *a* ethereal

etern|idad *f* eternity. ~**o** *a* eternal

étic|a *f* ethics. ~**o** *a* ethical

etimología *f* etymology

etiqueta *f* ticket, tag; (ceremonial) etiquette. **de** ~ formal

étnico *a* ethnic

eucalipto *m* eucalyptus

eufemismo *m* euphemism

euforia *f* euphoria

Europa *f* Europe

europeo *a & m* European

eutanasia *f* euthanasia

evacua|ción *f* evacuation. ~**r** [21] *vt* evacuate

evadir *vt* avoid; evade <*impuestos*>. □ ~**se** *vpr* escape

evaluar [21] *vt* assess; evaluate <*datos*>

evangeli|o *m* gospel. ~**sta** *m & f* evangelist; (Mex, escribiente) scribe

evapora|ción *f* evaporation. □ ~**rse** *vpr* evaporate; (fig) disappear

evasi|ón *f* evasion; (fuga) escape. ~**vo** *a* evasive

evento *m* event; (caso) case

eventual *a* possible. ~**idad** *f* eventuality

eviden|cia *f* evidence. poner en ~cia a uno show s.o. up. ~**ciar** *vt* show. □ ~**ciarse** *vpr* be obvious. ~**te** *a* obvious. ~**temente** *adv* obviously

evitar *vt* avoid; (ahorrar) spare; (prevenir) prevent

evocar [7] *vt* evoke

evoluci|ón *f* evolution. ~**onar** *vi* evolve; (Mil) manoeuvre

ex *pref* ex-, former

exacerbar *vt* exacerbate

exact|amente *adv* exactly. ~**itud** *f* exactness. ~**o** *a* exact; (preciso) accurate; (puntual) punctual. ¡~! exactly!

exagera|ción *f* exaggeration. ~**do** *a* exaggerated. ~**r** *vt/i* exaggerate

exalta|do *a* exalted; (excitado) (over-)excited; (fanático) hot-headed. ~**r** *vt* exalt. □ ~**rse** *vpr* get excited

exam|en *m* exam, examination. **∼inar** *vt* examine. □ **∼inarse** *vpr* take an exam

exasperar *vt* exasperate. □ **∼se** *vpr* get exasperated

excarcela|ción *f* release (from prison). **∼r** *vt* release

excava|ción *f* excavation. **∼dora** *f* digger. **∼r** *vt* excavate

excede|ncia *f* leave of absence. **∼nte** *a & m* surplus. **∼r** *vi* exceed. □ **∼rse** *vpr* go too far

excelen|cia *f* excellence; (tratamiento) Excellency. **∼te** *a* excellent

exc|entricidad *f* eccentricity. **∼éntrico** *a & m* eccentric

excepci|ón *f* exception. **∼onal** *a* exceptional. **a ∼ón de, con ∼ón de** except (for)

except|o *prep* except (for). **∼uar** [21] *vt* except

exces|ivo *a* excessive. **∼o** *m* excess. **∼o de equipaje** excess luggage (esp Brit), excess baggage (esp Amer)

excita|ción *f* excitement. **∼r** *vt* excite; (incitar) incite. □ **∼rse** *vpr* get excited

exclama|ción *f* exclamation. **∼r** *vi* exclaim

exclu|ir [17] *vt* exclude. **∼sión** *f* exclusion. **∼siva** *f* sole right; (reportaje) exclusive (story). **∼sivo** *a* exclusive

excomu|lgar [12] *vt* excommunicate. **∼nión** *f* excommunication

excremento *m* excrement

excursi|ón *f* excursion, outing. **∼onista** *m & f* day-tripper

excusa *f* excuse; (disculpa) apology. **presentar sus ∼s** apologize. **∼r** *vt* excuse

exento *a* exempt; (libre) free

exhalar *vt* exhale, breath out; give off <color etc>

exhaust|ivo *a* exhaustive. **∼o** *a* exhausted

exhibi|ción *f* exhibition; (demostración) display. **∼cionista** *m & f* exhibitionist. **∼r** *vt* exhibit. □ **∼rse** *vpr* show o.s.; (hacerse notar) draw attention to o.s.

exhumar *vt* exhume; (fig) dig up

exig|encia *f* demand. **∼ente** *a* demanding. **∼ir** [14] *vt* demand

exiguo *a* meagre

exil|(i)ado *a* exiled. ● *m* exile. □ **∼(i)arse** *vpr* go into exile. **∼io** *m* exile

exim|ente *m* reason for exemption; (Jurid) grounds for acquittal. **∼ir** *vt* exempt

existencia *f* existence. **∼s** *fpl* stock. **∼lismo** *m* existentialism

exist|ente *a* existing. **∼ir** *vi* exist

éxito *m* success. **no tener ∼** fail. **tener ∼** be successful

exitoso *a* successful

éxodo *m* exodus

exonerar *vt* exonerate

exorbitante *a* exorbitant

exorci|smo *m* exorcism. **∼zar** [10] *vt* exorcise

exótico *a* exotic

expan|dir *vt* expand; (fig) spread. □ **∼dirse** *vpr* expand. **∼sión** *f* expansion. **∼sivo** *a* expansive

expatria|do *a & m* expatriate. □ **∼rse** *vpr* emigrate; (exiliarse) go into exile

expectativa *f* prospect; (esperanza) expectation. **estar a la ∼** be waiting

expedi|ción *f* expedition; (de documento) issue; (de mercancías) dispatch. **∼ente** *m* record, file; (Jurid) proceedings. **∼r** [5] *vt* issue; (enviar) dispatch, send. **∼to** *a* clear; (LAm, fácil) easy

expeler *vt* expel

expend|edor *m* dealer. **∼dor automático** vending machine. **∼io** *m* (LAm) shop; (venta) sale

expensas *fpl* (Jurid) costs. **a ∼ de** at the expense of. **a mis ∼** at my expense

experiencia *f* experience

experiment|al *a* experimental. **∼ar** *vt* test, experiment with; (sentir) experience. **∼o** *m* experiment

experto *a & m* expert

expiar [20] *vt* atone for

expirar *vi* expire

explanada *f* levelled area; (paseo) esplanade

explayarse *vpr* speak at length; (desahogarse) unburden o.s. (**con** to)

explica|ción f explanation. **~r** [7] vt explain. □ **~rse** vpr understand; (hacerse comprender) explain o.s. **no me lo explico** I can't understand it

explícito a explicit

explora|ción f exploration. **~dor** m explorer; (muchacho) boy scout. **~r** vt explore

explosi|ón f explosion; (fig) outburst. **~onar** vt blow up. **~vo** a & m explosive

explota|ción f working; (abuso) exploitation. **~r** vt work <mina>; farm <tierra>; (abusar) exploit. ● vi explode

expone|nte m exponent. **~r** [34] vt expose; display <mercancías>; present <tema>; set out <hechos>; exhibit <cuadros etc>; (arriesgar) risk. ● vi exhibit. □ **~rse** vpr. **~se a que** run the risk of

exporta|ción f export. **~dor** m exporter. **~r** vt export

exposición f exposure; (de cuadros etc) exhibition; (de hechos) exposition

expres|ar vt express. □ **~arse** vpr express o.s. **~ión** f expression. **~ivo** a expressive; (cariñoso) affectionate

expreso a express. ● m express; (café) expresso

exprimi|dor m squeezer. **~r** vt squeeze

expropiar vt expropriate

expuesto a on display; <lugar etc> exposed; (peligroso) dangerous. **estar ~ a** be exposed to

expuls|ar vt expel; throw out <persona>; send off <jugador>. **~ión** f expulsion

exquisito a exquisite; (de sabor) delicious

éxtasis m invar ecstasy

extend|er [1] vt spread (out); (ampliar) extend; issue <documento>. □ **~erse** vpr spread; <paisaje etc> extend, stretch. **~ido** a spread out; (generalizado) widespread; <brazos> outstretched

extens|amente adv widely; (detalladamente) in full. **~ión** f extension; (área) expanse; (largo) length. **~o** a extensive

extenuar [21] vt exhaust

exterior a external, exterior; (del extranjero) foreign; <aspecto etc> outward. ● m outside, exterior; (países extranjeros) abroad

extermin|ación f extermination. **~ar** vt exterminate. **~io** m extermination

externo a external; <signo etc> outward. ● m day pupil

extin|ción f extinction. **~guidor** m (LAm) fire extinguisher. **~guir** [13] vt extinguish. □ **~guirse** vpr die out; <fuego> go out. **~to** a <raza etc> extinct. **~tor** m fire extinguisher

extirpar vt eradicate; remove <tumor>

extorsión f extortion

extra a invar extra; (de buena calidad) good-quality; <huevos> large. **paga f ~** bonus

extracto m extract

extradición f extradition

extraer [41] vt extract

extranjero a foreign. ● m foreigner; (países) foreign countries. **del ~** from abroad. **en el ~, por el ~** abroad

extrañ|ar vt surprise; (encontrar extraño) find strange; (LAm, echar de menos) miss. □ **~arse** vpr be surprised (de at). **~eza** f strangeness; (asombro) surprise. **~o** a strange. ● m stranger

extraoficial a unofficial

extraordinario a extraordinary

extrarradio m outlying districts

extraterrestre a extraterrestrial. ● m alien

extravagan|cia f oddness, eccentricity. **~te** a odd, eccentric

extrav|iado a lost. **~iar** [20] vt lose. □ **~iarse** vpr get lost; <objetos> go missing. **~ío** m loss

extremar vt take extra <precauciones>; tighten up <vigilancia>. □ **~se** vpr make every effort

extremeño a from Extremadura

extrem|idad f end. **~idades** fpl extremities. **~ista** a & m & f extremist. **~o** a extreme. ● m end; (colmo) extreme. **en ~o** extremely. **en último ~o** as a last resort

extrovertido *a & m* extrovert
exuberan|cia *f* exuberance. **~te** *a* exuberant
eyacular *vt/i* ejaculate

Ff

fa *m* F; (solfa) fah
fabada *f* bean and pork stew
fábrica *f* factory. **marca** *f* **de ~** trade mark
fabrica|ción *f* manufacture. **~ción en serie** mass production. **~nte** *m & f* manufacturer. **~r** [7] *vt* manufacture
fábula *f* fable; (mentira) fabrication
fabuloso *a* fabulous
facci|ón *f* faction. **~ones** *fpl* (de la cara) features
faceta *f* facet
facha *f* (⬛, aspecto) look. **~da** *f* façade
fácil *a* easy; (probable) likely
facili|dad *f* ease; (disposición) aptitude. **~dades** *fpl* facilities. **~tar** *vt* facilitate; (proporcionar) provide
factible *a* feasible
factor *m* factor
factura *f* bill, invoice. **~r** *vt* (hacer la factura) invoice; (Aviat) check in
faculta|d *f* faculty; (capacidad) ability; (poder) power. **~tivo** *a* optional
faena *f* job. **~s domésticas** housework
faisán *m* pheasant
faja *f* (de tierra) strip; (corsé) corset; (Mil etc) sash
fajo *m* bundle; (de billetes) wad
falda *f* skirt; (de montaña) side
falla *f* fault; (defecto) flaw. **~ humana** (LAm) human error. **~r** *vi* fail. **me falló** he let me down. **sin ~r** without fail. ● *vt* (errar) miss
fallec|er [11] *vi* die. **~ido** *m* deceased
fallido *a* vain; (fracasado) unsuccessful

fallo *m* (defecto) fault; (error) mistake. **~ humano** human error; (en certamen) decision; (Jurid) ruling

falluca *f* (Mex) smuggled goods

fals|ear *vt* falsify, distort. **~ificación** *f* forgery. **~ificador** *m* forger. **~ificar** [7] *vt* forge. **~o** *a* false; (falsificado) forged; <joya> fake

falt|a *f* lack; (ausencia) absence; (escasez) shortage; (defecto) fault, defect; (culpa) fault; (error) mistake; (en fútbol etc) foul; (en tenis) fault. **a ~a de** for lack of. **echar en ~a** miss. **hacer ~a** be necessary. **me hace ~a** I need. **sacar ~as** find fault. **~o** *a* lacking (**de** in

faltar

● *verbo intransitivo*

❗ Cuando el verbo **faltar** va precedido del complemento indirecto **le** (o **les, nos** etc) el sujeto en español pasa a ser el objeto en inglés p.ej: **les falta experiencia** *they lack experience*

····▶ (no estar) to be missing **¿quién falta?** who's missing? **falta una de las chicas** one of the girls is missing. **al abrigo le faltan 3 botones** the coat has three buttons missing. **~ a algo** (no asistir) to be absent from sth; (no acudir) to miss sth

····▶ (no haber suficiente) **va a ~ leche** there won't be enough milk. **nos faltó tiempo** we didn't have enough time

····▶ (no tener) **le falta cariño** he lacks affection

····▶ (hacer falta) **le falta sal** it needs more salt. **¡es lo que nos faltaba!** that's all we needed!

····▶ (quedar) **¿te falta mucho?** are you going to be much longer? **falta poco para Navidad** it's not long until Christmas. **aún falta mucho** (distancia) there's a long way to go yet **¡no faltaba más!** of course!

fama *f* fame; (reputación) reputation

famélico *a* starving

familia *f* family; (hijos) children. ∼ **numerosa** large family. ∼**r** *a* familiar; (de la familia) family; (sin ceremonia) informal; *<lenguaje>* colloquial. ● *m* & *f* relative. ∼**ridad** *f* familiarity. □ ∼**rizarse** [10] *vpr* become familiar (con with)

famoso *a* famous

fanático *a* fanatical. ● *m* fanatic

fanfarr|ón *a* boastful. ● *m* braggart. ∼**onear** *vi* show off

fango *m* mud. ∼**so** *a* muddy

fantasía *f* fantasy. de ∼ fancy; *<joya>* imitation

fantasma *m* ghost

fantástico *a* fantastic

fardo *m* bundle

faringe *f* pharynx

farmac|éutico *m* chemist (Brit), pharmacist, druggist (Amer). ∼**ia** *f* (ciencia) pharmacy; (tienda) chemist's (shop) (Brit), pharmacy

faro *m* lighthouse; (Aviac) beacon; (Auto) headlight

farol *m* lantern; (de la calle) street lamp. ∼**a** *f* street lamp

farr|a *f* partying. ∼**ear** *vi* (LAm) go out partying

farsa *f* farce. ∼**nte** *m* & *f* fraud

fascículo *m* instalment

fascinar *vt* fascinate

fascis|mo *m* fascism. ∼**ta** *a* & *m* & *f* fascist

fase *f* phase

fastidi|ar *vt* annoy; (estropear) spoil. □ ∼**arse** *vpr* *<máquina>* break down; hurt *<pierna>*; (LAm, molestarse) get annoyed. ¡para que te ∼**es!** so there!. ∼**o** *m* nuisance; (aburrimiento) boredom. ∼**oso** *a* annoying

fatal *a* fateful; (mortal) fatal; (🔲, pésimo) terrible. ∼**idad** *f* fate; (desgracia) misfortune

fatig|a *f* fatigue. ∼**ar** [12] *vt* tire. □ ∼**arse** *vpr* get tired. ∼**oso** *a* tiring

fauna *f* fauna

favor *m* favour. a ∼ de, en ∼ de in favour of. haga el ∼ de would you be so kind as to, please. por ∼ please

favorec|er [11] *vt* favour; *<vestido, peinado etc>* suit. ∼**ido** *a* favoured

favorito *a* & *m* favourite

faz *f* face

fe *f* faith. dar ∼ de certify. de buena ∼ in good faith

fealdad *f* ugliness

febrero *m* February

febril *a* feverish

fecha *f* date. a estas ∼**s** now; (todavía) still. hasta la ∼ so far. poner ∼ date. ∼**r** *vt* date

fecund|ación *f* fertilization. ∼**ación artificial** artificial insemination. ∼**ar** *vt* fertilize. ∼**o** *a* fertile; (fig) prolific

federa|ción *f* federation. ∼**l** *a* federal

felici|dad *f* happiness. ∼**dades** *fpl* best wishes; (congratulaciones) congratulations. ∼**tación** *f* letter of congratulation. ¡∼**taciones!** (LAm) congratulations! ∼**tar** *vt* congratulate

feligrés *m* parishioner

feliz *a* happy; (afortunado) lucky. ¡Felices Pascuas! Happy Christmas! ¡F∼ Año Nuevo! Happy New Year!

felpudo *m* doormat

fem|enil *a* (Mex) women's. ∼**inino** *a* feminine; *<equipo>* women's; (Biol, Bot) female. ● *m* feminine. ∼**inista** *a* & *m* & *f* feminist

fen|omenal *a* phenomenal. ∼**ómeno** *m* phenomenon; (monstruo) freak

feo *a* ugly; (desagradable) nasty. ● *adv* (LAm, mal) bad

feria *f* fair; (verbena) carnival; (Mex, cambio) small change. ∼**do** *m* (LAm) public holiday

ferment|ar *vt/i* ferment. ∼**o** *m* ferment

fero|cidad *f* ferocity. ∼**z** *a* fierce

férreo *a* iron; *<disciplina>* strict

ferreter|ía *f* hardware store, ironmonger's (Brit). ∼**o** *m* hardware dealer, ironmonger (Brit)

ferro|carril *m* railway (Brit), railroad (Amer). ∼**viario** *a* rail. ● *m* railwayman (Brit), railroader (Amer)

fértil *a* fertile

fertili|dad *f* fertility. ∼**zante** *m* fertilizer. ∼**zar** [10] *vt* fertilize

ferv|iente *a* fervent. **~or** *m* fervour

festej|ar *vt* celebrate; entertain *<persona>*. **~o** *m* celebration

festiv|al *m* festival. **~idad** *f* festivity. **~o** *a* festive. ● *m* public holiday

fétido *a* stinking

feto *m* foetus

fiable *a* reliable

fiado *m*. al **~** on credit. **~r** *m* (Jurid) guarantor

fiambre *m* cold meat. **~ria** *f* (LAm) delicatessen

fianza *f* (dinero) deposit; (objeto) surety. **bajo ~** on bail

fiar [20] *vt* (vender) sell on credit. ● *vi* give credit. **ser de ~** be trustworthy. □ **~se** *vpr*. **~se de** trust

fibra *f* fibre. **~ de vidrio** fibreglass

fic|ción *f* fiction. **~ticio** *a* fictitious; (falso) false

fich|a *f* token; (tarjeta) index card; (en juegos) counter. **~ar** *vt* open a file on. **estar ~ado** have a (police) record. **~ero** *m* card index

fidedigno *a* reliable

fidelidad *f* faithfulness. **alta ~** hi-fi 🆃, high fidelity

fideos *mpl* noodles

fiebre *f* fever. **~ del heno** hay fever. **tener ~** have a temperature

fiel *a* faithful; *<memoria, relato etc>* reliable. ● *m* believer; (de balanza) needle. **los ~es** the faithful

fieltro *m* felt

fier|a *f* wild animal. **~o** *a* fierce

fierro *m* (LAm) metal bar; (hierro) iron

fiesta *f* party; (día festivo) holiday. **~s** *fpl* celebrations

figura *f* figure; (forma) shape. **~r** *vi* appear; (destacar) show off. □ **~rse** *vpr* imagine. **¡figúrate!** just imagine!

fij|ación *f* fixing; (obsesión) fixation. **~ar** *vt* fix; establish *<residencia>*. □ **~arse** *vpr* (poner atención) pay attention; (percatarse) notice. **¡fíjate!** just imagine! **~o** *a* fixed; (firme) stable; (permanente) permanent. ● *adv*. **mirar ~o** stare

fila *f* line; (de soldados etc) file; (en el teatro, cine etc) row; (cola) queue. **ponerse en ~** line up

filántropo *m* philanthropist

filat|elia *f* stamp collecting, philately. **~élico** *a* philatelic. ● *m* stamp collector, philatelist

filete *m* fillet

filial *a* filial. ● *f* subsidiary

Filipinas *fpl*. **las (islas) ~** the Philippines

filipino *a* Philippine, Filipino

filmar *vt* film; shoot *<película>*

filo *m* edge; (de hoja) cutting edge. **al ~ de las doce** at exactly twelve o'clock. **sacar ~ a** sharpen

filología *f* philology

filón *m* vein; (fig) gold-mine

fil|osofía *f* philosophy. **~ósofo** *m* philosopher

filtr|ar *vt* filter. □ **~arse** *vpr* filter; *<dinero>* disappear; *<noticia>* leak. **~o** *m* filter; (bebida) philtre. **~ solar** sunscreen

fin *m* end; (objetivo) aim. **~ de semana** weekend. **a ~ de** in order to. **a ~ de cuentas** at the end of the day. **a ~ de que** in order that. **a ~es de** at the end of. **al ~** finally. **al ~ y al cabo** after all. **dar ~ a** end. **en ~** in short. **por ~** finally. **sin ~** endless

final *a* final. ● *m* end. ● *f* final. **~idad** *f* aim. **~ista** *m & f* finalist. **~izar** [10] *vt* finish. ● *vi* end

financi|ación *f* financing; (fondos) funds; (facilidades) credit facilities. **~ar** *vt* finance. **~ero** *a* financial. ● *m* financier

finca *f* property; (tierras) estate; (rural) farm; (de recreo) country house

fingir [14] *vt* feign; (simular) simulate. ● *vi* pretend. □ **~se** *vpr* pretend to be

finlandés *a* Finnish. ● *m* (persona) Finn; (lengua) Finnish

Finlandia *f* Finland

fino *a* fine; (delgado) thin; *<oído>* acute; (de modales) refined; (sútil) subtle

firma *f* signature; (acto) signing; (empresa) firm

firmar *vt/i* sign

firme *a* firm; (estable) stable, steady; *<color>* fast. ● *m* (pavimento) (road) surface. ● *adv* hard. **~za** *f* firmness

fisc|al a fiscal, tax. ● m & f public prosecutor. ~**o** m treasury

fisg|ar [12] vi snoop (around). ~**ón** a nosy. ● m snooper

físic|a f physics. ~**o** a physical. ● m physique; (persona) physicist

fisonomista m & f. **ser buen** ~ be good at remembering faces

fistol m (Mex) tiepin

flaco a thin, skinny; (débil) weak

flagelo m scourge

flagrante a flagrant. **en** ~ redhanded

flama f (Mex) flame

flamante a splendid; (nuevo) brandnew

flamear vi flame; <bandera etc> flap

flamenco a flamenco; (de Flandes) Flemish. ● m (ave) flamingo; (música etc) flamenco; (idioma) Flemish

flan m crème caramel

flaqueza f thinness; (debilidad) weakness

flauta f flute

flecha f arrow. ~**zo** m love at first sight

fleco m fringe; (Mex, en el pelo) fringe (Brit), bangs (Amer)

flem|a f phlegm. ~**ático** a phlegmatic

flequillo m fringe (Brit), bangs (Amer)

fletar vt charter; (LAm, transportar) transport

flexible a flexible

flirte|ar vi flirt. ~**o** m flirting

floj|ear vi flag; (holgazanear) laze around. ~**o** a loose; (poco fuerte) weak; (perezoso) lazy

flor f flower. **la** ~ **y nata** the cream. ~**a** f flora. ~**ecer** [11] vi flower, bloom; (fig) flourish. ~**eciente** a (fig) flourishing. ~**ero** m flower vase. ~**ista** m & f florist

flot|a f fleet. ~**ador** m float; (de niño) rubber band. ~**ar** vi float. ~**e. a** ~**e** afloat

fluctua|ción f fluctuation. ~**r** [21] vi fluctuate

flu|idez f fluidity; (fig) fluency. ~**ido** a fluid; (fig) fluent. ● m fluid. ~**ir** [17] vi flow

fluoruro m fluoride

fluvial a river

fobia f phobia

foca f seal

foco m focus; (lámpara) floodlight; (LAm, de coche) (head)light; (Mex, bombilla) light bulb

fogón m cooker; (LAm, fogata) bonfire

folio m sheet

folklórico a folk

follaje m foliage

follet|ín m newspaper serial. ~**o** m pamphlet

follón m ⊞ mess; (alboroto) row; (problema) trouble

fomentar vt promote; boost <ahorro>; stir up <odio>

fonda f (pensión) boarding-house; (LAm, restaurant) cheap restaurant

fondo m bottom; (de calle, pasillo) end; (de sala etc) back; (de escenario, pintura etc) background. ~**s** mpl funds, money. **a** ~ thoroughly. **en el** ~ deep down

fonétic|a f phonetics. ~**o** a phonetic

fontanero m plumber

footing /'futin/ m jogging

forastero m stranger

forcejear vi struggle

forense a forensic. ● m & f forensic scientist

forjar vt forge. □ ~**se** vpr forge; build up <ilusiones>

forma f form; (contorno) shape; (modo) way; (Mex, formulario) form. ~**s** fpl conventions. **de todas** ~**s** anyway. **estar en** ~ be in good form. ~**ción** f formation; (educación) training. ~**l** a formal; (de fiar) reliable; (serio) serious. ~**lidad** f formality; (fiabilidad) reliability; (seriedad) seriousness. ~**r** vt form; (componer) make up; (enseñar) train. □ ~**rse** vpr form; (desarrollarse) develop; (educarse) to be educated. ~**to** m format

formidable a formidable; (muy grande) enormous

fórmula f formula; (sistema) way. ~ **de cortesía** polite expression

formular vt formulate; make <queja etc>. ~**io** m form

fornido a well-built

forr|ar vt (en el interior) line; (en el exterior) cover. ~**o** m lining; (cubierta) cover

fortale|cer [11] vt strengthen. ~**za** f strength; (Mil) fortress; (fuerza moral) fortitude

fortuito a fortuitous; <encuentro> chance

fortuna f fortune; (suerte) luck

forz|ar [2 & 10] vt force; strain <vista>. ~**osamente** adv necessarily. ~**oso** a necessary

fosa f ditch; (tumba) grave. ~**s nasales** nostrils

fósforo m phosphorus; (cerilla) match

fósil a & m fossil

foso m ditch; (en castillo) moat; (de teatro) pit

foto f photo. sacar ~**s** take photos

fotocopia f photocopy. ~**dora** f photocopier. ~**r** vt photocopy

fotogénico a photogenic

fot|ografía f photography; (Foto) photograph. ~**ografiar** [20] vt photograph. ~**ógrafo** m photographer

foul /faʊl/ m (pl ~**s**) (LAm) foul

frac m (pl ~**s** o **fraques**) tails

fracas|ar vi fail. ~**o** m failure

fracción f fraction; (Pol) faction

fractura f fracture. ~**r** vt fracture. □ ~**rse** vpr fracture

fragan|cia f fragrance. ~**te** a fragrant

frágil a fragile

fragmento m fragment; (de canción etc) extract

fragua f forge. ~**r** [15] vt forge; (fig) concoct. ● vi set

fraile m friar; (monje) monk

frambuesa f raspberry

franc|és a French. ● m (persona) Frenchman; (lengua) French. ~**esa** f Frenchwoman

Francia f France

franco a frank; (evidente) marked; (Com) free. ● m (moneda) franc

francotirador m sniper

franela f flannel

franja f border; (banda) stripe; (de terreno) strip

franque|ar vt clear; (atravesar) cross; pay the postage on <carta>. ~**o** m postage

franqueza f frankness

frasco m bottle; (de mermelada etc) jar

frase f phrase; (oración) sentence. ~ **hecha** set phrase

fratern|al a fraternal. ~**idad** f fraternity

fraud|e m fraud. ~**ulento** a fraudulent

fray m brother, friar

frecuen|cia f frequency. con ~**cia** frequently. ~**tar** vt frequent. ~**te** a frequent

frega|dero m sink. ~**r** [1 & 12] vt scrub; wash <los platos>; mop <el suelo>; (LAm, 🄵, molestar) annoy

freír [51] (pp **frito**) vt fry. □ ~**se** vpr fry; <persona> roast

frenar vt brake; (fig) check

frenético a frenzied; (furioso) furious

freno m (de caballería) bit; (Auto) brake; (fig) check

frente m front. ~ a opposite. ~ a ~ face to face. al ~ at the head; (hacia delante) forward. chocar de ~ crash head on. de ~ a (LAm) facing. hacer ~ a face <cosa>; stand up to <persona>. ● f forehead. arrugar la ~ frown

fresa f strawberry

fresc|o a (frío) cool; (reciente) fresh; (descarado) cheeky. ● m fresh air; (frescor) coolness; (mural) fresco; (persona) impudent person. al ~**o** in the open air. hacer ~**o** be cool. tomar el ~**o** get some fresh air. ~**or** m coolness. ~**ura** f freshness; (frío) coolness; (descaro) cheek

frialdad f coldness; (fig) indifference

fricci|ón f rubbing; (fig, Tec) friction; (masaje) massage. ~**onar** vt rub

frigidez f frigidity

frígido a frigid

frigorífico m fridge, refrigerator

frijol m (LAm) bean. ~**es refritos** (Mex) fried purée of beans

frío a & m cold. tomar ~ catch cold. hacer ~ be cold. tener ~ be cold

frito a fried; (🄵, harto) fed up. me tiene ~ I'm sick of him

fr|ivolidad f frivolity. **~ívolo** a frivolous

fronter|a f border, frontier. **~izo** a border; <país> bordering

frontón m pelota court; (pared) fronton

frotar vt rub; strike <cerilla>

fructífero a fruitful

fruncir [9] vt gather <tela>. **~ el ceño** frown

frustra|ción f frustration. **~r** vt frustrate. □ **~rse** vpr (fracasar) fail. **quedar ~do** be disappointed

frut|a f fruit. **~al** a fruit. **~ería** f fruit shop. **~ero** m fruit seller; (reci-piente) fruit bowl. **~icultura** f fruit-growing. **~o** m fruit

fucsia f fuchsia. ● m fuchsia

fuego m fire. **~s artificiales** fireworks. **a ~ lento** on a low heat. **tener ~** have a light

fuente f fountain; (manantial) spring; (plato) serving dish; (fig) source

fuera adv out; (al exterior) outside; (en otra parte) away; (en el extranjero) abroad. **~ de** outside; (excepto) except for, besides. **por ~** on the outside. ● vb ⇒IR y SER

fuerte a strong; <color> bright; <so-nido> loud; <dolor> severe; (duro) hard; (grande) large; <lluvia, nevada> heavy. ● m fort; (fig) strong point. ● adv hard; (con hablar en) loudly; <llover> heavily; (mucho) a lot

fuerza f strength; (poder) power; (en física) force; (Mil) forces. **~ de vo-luntad** will-power. **a ~ de** by (dint of). **a la ~** by necessity. **por ~** by force; (por necesidad) by necessity. **te-ner ~s para** have the strength to

fuese vb ⇒IR y SER

fug|a f flight, escape; (de gas etc) leak; (Mus) fugue. □ **~arse** [12] vpr flee, escape. **~az** a fleeting. **~itivo** a & m fugitive

fui vb ⇒IR, SER

fulano m so-and-so. **~, mengano y zu-tano** every Tom, Dick and Harry

fulminar vt (fig, con mirada) look daggers at

fuma|dor a smoking. ● m smoker. **~r** vt/i smoke. **~r en pipa** smoke a pipe. □ **~rse** vpr smoke. **~rada** f puff of smoke

funci|ón f function; (de un cargo etc) duty; (de teatro) show, performance. **~onal** a functional. **~onar** vi work, function. **no ~ona** out of order. **~onario** m civil servant

funda f cover. **~ de almohada** pillow-case

funda|ción f foundation. **~mental** a fundamental. **~mentar** vt base (en on). **~mento** m foundation; (fig) base. □ **~rse** vpr be based

fundi|ción f melting; (de metales) smelting; (taller) foundry. **~r** vt melt; smelt <metales>; cast <objeto>; blend <colores>; (fusionar) merge; (Elec) blow; (LAm) seize up <motor>. □ **~rse** vpr melt; (unirse) merge

fúnebre a funeral; (sombrío) gloomy

funeral a funeral. ● m funeral. **~es** mpl funeral

funicular a & m funicular

furg|ón m van. **~oneta** f van

fur|ia f fury; (violencia) violence. **~ibundo** a furious. **~ioso** a furious. **~or** m fury

furtivo a furtive. **cazador ~** poacher

furúnculo m boil

fusible m fuse

fusil m rifle. **~ar** vt shoot

fusión f melting; (unión) fusion; (Com) merger

fútbol m, (Mex) **futbol** m football

futbolista m & f footballer

futur|ista a futuristic. ● m & f futur-ist. **~o** a & m future

Gg

gabardina f raincoat

gabinete m (Pol) cabinet; (en museo etc) room; (de dentista, médico etc) consulting room

gaceta f gazette

gafa f hook. **~s** fpl glasses, spectacles. **~s de sol** sunglasses

gaf|ar *vt* 🔲 bring bad luck to. **~e** *m* jinx

gaita *f* bagpipes

gajo *m* segment

gala *f* gala. **~s** *fpl* finery, best clothes. **estar de ~** be dressed up. **hacer ~ de** show off

galán *m* (en el teatro) (romantic) hero; (enamorado) lover

galante *a* gallant. **~ar** *vt* court. **~ría** *f* gallantry

galápago *m* turtle

galardón *m* award

galaxia *f* galaxy

galera *f* galley

galer|ía *f* gallery. **~ía comercial** (shopping) arcade. **~ón** *m* (Mex) hall

Gales *m* Wales. **país de ~** Wales

gall|és *a* Welsh. ● *m* Welshman; (lengua) Welsh. **~esa** *f* Welshwoman

galgo *m* greyhound

Galicia *f* Galicia

galimatías *m invar* gibberish

gallard|ía *f* elegance. **~o** *a* elegant

gallego *a* & *m* Galician

galleta *f* biscuit (Brit), cookie (Amer)

gall|ina *f* hen, chicken; (fig, 🔲) coward. **~o** *m* cock

galón *m* gallon; (cinta) braid; (Mil) stripe

galop|ar *vi* gallop. **~e** *m* gallop

gama *f* scale; (fig) range

gamba *f* prawn (Brit), shrimp (Amer)

gamberro *m* hooligan

gamuza *f* (piel) chamois leather; (de otro animal) suede

gana *f* wish, desire; (apetito) appetite. **de buena ~** willingly. **de mala ~** reluctantly. **no me da la ~** I don't feel like it. **tener ~s de** (+ *infinitivo*) feel like (+ *gerundio*)

ganad|ería *f* cattle raising; (ganado) livestock. **~o** *m* livestock. **~o lanar** sheep. **~o porcino** pigs. **~o vacuno** cattle

gana|dor *a* winning. ● *m* winner. **~ncia** *f* gain; (Com) profit. **~r** *vt* earn; (en concurso, juego etc) win; (alcanzar) reach. ● *vi* (vencer) win; (mejorar) improve. **~rle a uno** beat s.o. **~rse la vida** earn a living. **salir ~ndo** come out better off

ganch|illo *m* crochet. **hacer ~illo** crochet. **~o** *m* hook; (LAm, colgador) hanger. **tener ~o** be very attractive

ganga *f* bargain

ganso *m* goose

garabat|ear *vt/i* scribble. **~o** *m* scribble

garaje *m* garage

garant|e *m* & *f* guarantor. **~ía** *f* guarantee. **~izar** [10] *vt* guarantee

garapiña *f* (Mex) pineapple squash. **~do** *a.* **almendras** *fpl* **~das** sugared almonds

garbanzo *m* chick-pea

garbo *m* poise; (de escrito) style. **~so** *a* elegant

garganta *f* throat; (Geog) gorge

gárgaras *fpl.* **hacer ~** gargle

garita *f* hut; (de centinela) sentry box

garra *f* (de animal) claw; (de ave) talon

garrafa *f* carafe

garrafal *a* huge

garrapata *f* tick

garrapat|ear *vi* scribble. **~o** *m* scribble

garrote *m* club, cudgel; (tormento) garrotte

gar|úa *f* (LAm) drizzle. **~uar** *vi* [21] (LAm) drizzle

garza *f* heron

gas *m* gas. **con ~** fizzy. **sin ~** still

gasa *f* gauze

gaseosa *f* fizzy drink

gas|óleo *m* diesel. **~olina** *f* petrol (Brit), gasoline (Amer), gas (Amer). **~olinera** *f* petrol station (Brit), gas station (Amer)

gast|ado *a* spent; <*vestido etc*> worn out. **~ador** *m* spendthrift. **~ar** *vt* spend; (consumir) use; (malgastar) waste; (desgastar) wear out; wear <*vestido etc*>; crack <*broma*>. □ **~arse** *vpr* wear out. **~o** *m* expense; (acción de gastar) spending

gastronomía *f* gastronomy

gat|a *f* cat. **a ~as** on all fours. **~ear** *vi* crawl

gatillo *m* trigger

gat|ito *m* kitten. **~o** *m* cat. **dar ~o por liebre** take s.o. in

gaucho *m* Gaucho

gaveta *f* drawer

gaviota *f* seagull

gazpacho *m* gazpacho

gelatina *f* gelatine; (jalea) jelly

gema *f* gem

gemelo *m* twin. ~**s** *mpl* (anteojos) binoculars; (de camisa) cuff-links

gemido *m* groan

Géminis *m* Gemini

gemir [5] *vi* moan; <*animal*> whine, howl

gen *m*, **gene** *m* gene

geneal|ogía *f* genealogy. ~**ógico** *a* genealogical. árbol *m* ~**ógico** family tree

generaci|ón *f* generation. ~**onal** *a* generation

general *a* general. en ~ in general. por lo ~ generally. ~**izar** [10] *vt/i* generalize. ~**mente** *adv* generally

generar *vt* generate

género *m* type, sort; (Biol) genus; (Gram) gender; (en literatura etc) genre; (producto) product; (tela) material. ~**s** de punto knitwear. ~ humano mankind

generos|idad *f* generosity. ~**o** *a* generous

genétic|a *f* genetics. ~**o** *a* genetic

geni|al *a* brilliant; (divertido) funny. ~**o** *m* temper; (carácter) nature; (talento, persona) genius

genital *a* genital. ~**es** *mpl* genitals

gente *f* people; (nación) nation; (🄰, familia) family, folks; (Mex, persona) person. ● *a* (LAm) respectable; (amable) kind

gentil *a* charming. ~**eza** *f* kindness. tener la ~**eza** de be kind enough to

gentío *m* crowd

genuflexión *f* genuflection

genuino *a* genuine

ge|ografía *f* geography. ~**ográfico** *a* geographical.

ge|ología *f* geology. ~**ólogo** *m* geologist

geom|etría *f* geometry. ~**étrico** *a* geometrical

geranio *m* geranium

geren|cia *f* management. ~**ciar** *vt* (LAm) manage. ~**te** *m* & *f* manager

germen *m* germ

germinar *vi* germinate

gestación *f* gestation

gesticula|ción *f* gesticulation. ~**r** *vi* gesticulate

gesti|ón *f* step; (administración) management. ~**onar** *vt* take steps to arrange; (dirigir) manage

gesto *m* expression; (ademán) gesture; (mueca) grimace

gibraltareño *a* & *m* Gibraltarian

gigante *a* gigantic. ● *m* giant. ~**sco** *a* gigantic

gimn|asia *f* gymnastics. ~**asio** *m* gymnasium, gym 🄰. ~**asta** *m* & *f* gymnast. ~**ástic** *a* gymnastic

gimotear *vi* whine

ginebra *f* gin

ginecólogo *m* gynaecologist

gira *f* tour. ~**r** *vt* spin; draw <*cheque*>; transfer <*dinero*>. ● *vi* rotate, go round; <*en camino*> turn

girasol *m* sunflower

gir|atorio *a* revolving. ~**o** *m* turn; (Com) draft; (locución) expression. ~**o** postal money order

gitano *a* & *m* gypsy

glacia|l *a* icy. ~**r** *m* glacier

glándula *f* gland

glasear *vt* glaze; (Culin) ice

glob|al *a* global; (fig) overall. ~**o** *m* globe; (aerostato, juguete) balloon

glóbulo *m* globule

gloria *f* glory; (placer) delight. □ ~**rse** *vpr* boast (de about)

glorieta *f* square; (Auto) roundabout (Brit), (traffic) circle (Amer)

glorificar [7] *vt* glorify

glorioso *a* glorious

glotón *a* gluttonous. ● *m* glutton

gnomo /'nomo/ *m* gnome

gob|ernación *f* government. Ministerio *m* de la G~ernación Home Office (Brit), Department of the Interior (Amer). ~**ernador** *a* governing. ● *m* governor. ~**ernante** *a* governing. ● *m* & *f* leader. ~**ernar** [1] *vt* govern. ~**ierno** *m* government

goce *m* enjoyment

gol *m* goal

golf *m* golf

golfo *m* gulf; (niño) urchin; (holgazán) layabout

golondrina f swallow

golos|ina f titbit; (dulce) sweet. **∼o** a fond of sweets

golpe m blow; (puñetazo) punch; (choque) bump; (de emoción) shock; (🅇, atraco) job 🅣; (en golf, en tenis, de remo) stroke. **∼ de estado** coup d'etat. **∼ de fortuna** stroke of luck. **∼ de vista** glance. **∼ militar** military coup. **de ∼** suddenly. **de un ∼** in one go. **∼ar** vt hit; (dar varios golpes) beat; (con mucho ruido) bang; (con el puño) punch. **●** vi knock

goma f rubber; (para pegar) glue; (banda) rubber band; (de borrar) eraser. **∼a de mascar** chewing gum. **∼a espuma** foam rubber

gord|a f (Mex) small thick tortilla. **∼o** a <persona> (con ser) fat; (con estar) have put on weight; <carne> fatty; (grueso) thick; (grande) large, big. **●** m first prize. **∼ura** f fatness; (grasa) fat

gorila f gorilla

gorje|ar vi chirp. **∼o** m chirping

gorra f cap. **∼ de baño** (LAm) bathing cap

gorrión m sparrow

gorro m cap; (de niño) bonnet. **∼ de baño** bathing cap

got|a f drop; (Med) gout. **ni ∼a** nothing. **∼ear** vi drip. **∼era** f leak

gozar [10] vt enjoy. **●** vi. **∼ de** enjoy

gozne m hinge

gozo m pleasure; (alegría) joy. **∼so** a delighted

graba|ción f recording. **∼do** m engraving, print; (en libro) illustration. **∼dora** f tape-recorder. **∼r** vt engrave; record <discos etc>

graci|a f grace; (favor) favour; (humor) wit. **∼as** fpl thanks. **¡∼as!** thank you!, thanks! **dar las ∼as** thank. **hacer ∼a** amuse; (gustar) please. **¡muchas ∼as!** thank you very much! **tener ∼a** be funny. **∼oso** a funny. **●** m fool, comic character

grad|a f step. **∼as** fpl stand(s). **∼ación** f gradation. **∼o** m degree; (Escol) year (Brit), grade (Amer). **de buen ∼o** willingly

gradua|ción f graduation; (de alcohol) proof. **∼do** m graduate. **∼l** a

gradual. **∼r** [21] vt graduate; (regular) adjust. □ **∼rse** vpr graduate

gráfic|a f graph. **∼o** a graphic. **●** m graph

gram|ática f grammar. **∼atical** a grammatical

gramo m gram, gramme (Brit)

gran a véase GRANDE

grana f (color) deep red

granada f pomegranate; (Mil) grenade

granate m (color) maroon

Gran Bretaña f Great Britain

grande a (delante de nombre en singular **gran**) big, large; (alto) tall; (fig) great; (LAm, de edad) grown up. **∼za** f greatness

grandioso a magnificent

granel m. **a ∼** in bulk; (suelto) loose; (fig) in abundance

granero m barn

granito m granite; (grano) small grain

graniz|ado m iced drink. **∼ar** [10] vi hail. **∼o** m hail

granj|a f farm. **∼ero** m farmer

grano m grain; (semilla) seed; (de café) bean; (Med) spot. **∼s** mpl cereals

granuja m & f rogue

grapa f staple. **∼r** vt staple

gras|a f grease; (Culin) fat. **∼iento** a greasy

gratifica|ción f (de sueldo) bonus (recompensa) reward. **∼r** [7] vt reward

grat|is adv free. **∼itud** f gratitude. **∼o** a pleasant **∼uito** a free; (fig) uncalled for

grava|men m tax; (carga) burden; (sobre inmueble) encumbrance. **∼r** vt tax; (cargar) burden

grave a serious; <voz> deep; <sonido> low; <acento> grave. **∼dad** f gravity

gravilla f gravel

gravitar vi gravitate; (apoyarse) rest (sobre on); <peligro> hang (sobre over)

gravoso a costly

graznar vi <cuervo> caw; <pato> quack; honk <ganso>

Grecia f Greece

gremio m union

greña *f* mop of hair

gresca *f* rumpus; (riña) quarrel

griego *a & m* Greek

grieta *f* crack

grifo *m* tap, faucet (Amer)

grilletes *mpl* shackles

grillo *m* cricket. **~s** *mpl* shackles

gringo *m* (LAm) foreigner; (norteamericano) Yankee 🅣

gripe *f* flu

gris *a* grey. ● *m* grey; (🅣, policía) policeman

grit|ar *vi* shout. **~ería** *f*, **~erío** *m* uproar. **~o** *m* shout; (de dolor, sorpresa) cry; (chillido) scream. **dar ~s** shout

grosella *f* redcurrant. **~ negra** blackcurrant

groser|ía *f* rudeness; (ordinariez) coarseness; (comentario etc) coarse remark; (palabra) swearword. **~o** *a* coarse; (descortés) rude

grosor *m* thickness

grotesco *a* grotesque

grúa *f* crane

grueso *a* thick; *<persona>* fat, stout. ● *m* thickness; (fig) main body

grumo *m* lump

gruñi|do *m* grunt; (de perro) growl. **~r** [22] *vi* grunt; *<perro>* growl

grupa *f* hindquarters

grupo *m* group

gruta *f* grotto

guacamole *m* guacamole

guadaña *f* scythe

guaje *m* (Mex) gourd

guajolote *m* (Mex) turkey

guante *m* glove

guapo *a* good-looking; *<chica>* pretty; (elegante) smart

guarda *m & f* guard; (de parque etc) keeper. **~barros** *m invar* mudguard. **~bosque** *m* gamekeeper. **~costas** *m invar* coastguard vessel. **~espaldas** *m invar* bodyguard. **~meta** *m* goalkeeper. **~r** *vt* keep; (proteger) protect; (en un lugar) put away; (reservar) save, keep. □ **~rse** *vpr*. **~rse de** (+ *infinitivo*) avoid (+ *gerundio*). **~rropa** *m* wardrobe; (en local público) cloakroom. **~vallas** *m invar* (LAm) goalkeeper

guardería *f* nursery

guardia *f* guard; (policía) policewoman; (de médico) shift. **G~** Civil Civil Guard. **~ municipal** police. **estar de ~** be on duty. **estar en ~** be on one's guard. **montar la ~** mount guard. ● *m* policeman. **~ jurado** *m & f* security guard. **~ de tráfico** *m* traffic policeman. ● *f* traffic policewoman

guardián *m* guardian; (de parque etc) keeper; (de edificio) security guard

guar|ecer [11] *vt* (albergar) give shelter to. □ **~ecerse** *vpr* take shelter. **~ida** *f* den, lair; (de personas) hideout

guarn|ecer [11] *vt* (adornar) adorn; (Culin) garnish. **~ición** *m* adornment; (de caballo) harness; (Culin) garnish; (Mil) garrison; (de piedra preciosa) setting

guas|a *f* joke. **~ón** *a* humorous. ● *m* joker

Guatemala *f* Guatemala

guatemalteco *a & m* Guatemalan

guateque *m* party, bash

guayab|a *f* guava; (dulce) guava jelly. **~era** *f* lightweight jacket

gubernatura *f* (Mex) government

güero *a* (Mex) fair

guerr|a *f* war; (método) warfare. **dar ~a** annoy. **~ero** *a* warlike; (belicoso) fighting. ● *m* warrior. **~illa** *f* band of guerrillas. **~illero** *m* guerrilla

guía *m & f* guide. ● *f* guidebook; (de teléfonos) directory

guiar [20] *vt* guide; (llevar) lead; (Auto) drive. □ **~se** *vpr* be guided (**por** by)

guijarro *m* pebble

guillotina *f* guillotine

guind|a *f* morello cherry. **~illa** *f* chilli

guiñapo *m* rag; (fig, persona) wreck

guiñ|ar *vt/i* wink. **~o** *m* wink. **hacer ~os** wink

gui|ón *m* hyphen, dash; (de película etc) script. **~onista** *m & f* scriptwriter

guirnalda *f* garland

guisado *m* stew

guisante *m* pea. **~ de olor** sweet pea

guis|ar *vt/i* cook. **~o** *m* stew

guitarr|a f guitar. **~ista** m & f guitarist

gula f gluttony

gusano m worm; (larva de mosca) maggot

---

gustar

● *verbo intransitivo*

! Cuando el verbo **gustar** va precedido del complemento indirecto **le** (o **les, nos** etc), el sujeto en español pasa a ser el objeto en inglés. **me gusta mucho la música** *I like music very much*. **le gustan los helados** *he likes ice cream*. **a Juan no le gusta** *Juan doesn't like it* (or *her* etc)

····▸ gustar + *infinitivo*. **les gusta ver televisión** they like watching television

····▸ gustar que + *subjuntivo*. **me ~ía que vinieras** I'd like you to come. **no le gusta que lo corrijan** he doesn't like being corrected. **¿te ~ía que te lo comprara?** would you like me to buy it for you?

····▸ gustar de algo to like sth. **gustan de las fiestas** they like parties

····▸ (tener acogida) to go down well. **ese tipo de cosas siempre gusta** those sort of things always go down well. **el libro no gustó** the book didn't go down well

····▸ (en frases de cortesía) to wish. **como guste** as you wish. **cuando gustes** whenever you wish

● *verbo transitivo*

····▸ (LAm, querer) **¿gusta un café?** would you like a coffee? **¿gustan pasar?** would you like to come in?

□ **gustarse** *verbo pronominal* to like each other

---

gusto m taste; (placer) pleasure. **a ~** comfortable. **a mi ~** to my liking. **buen ~** good taste. **con mucho ~** with pleasure. **dar ~** please. **mucho ~** pleased to meet you. **~so** a tasty; (de buen grado) willingly

gutural a guttural

Hh

---

ha *vb* ⇒HABER

haba f broad bean

Habana f. La ~ Havana

habano m (puro) Havana

haber v aux [30] have. ● v impersonal (presente s & pl **hay**, imperfecto s & pl **había**, pretérito s & pl **hubo**). **hay una carta para ti** there's a letter for you. **hay 5 bancos en la plaza** there are 5 banks in the square. **hay que hacerlo** it must be done, you have to do it. **he aquí** here is, here are. **no hay de qué** don't mention it, not at all. **¿qué hay?** (¿qué pasa?) what's the matter?; (¿qué tal?) how are you?

habichuela f bean

hábil a skilful; (listo) clever; <día> working; (Jurid) competent

habili|dad f skill; (astucia) cleverness; (Jurid) competence. **~tar** vt qualify

habita|ción f room; (dormitorio) bedroom; (en biología) habitat. **~ción de matrimonio**, **~ción doble** double room. **~ción individual**, **~ción sencilla** single room. **~do** a inhabited. **~nte** m inhabitant. **~r** vt live in. ● vi live

hábito m habit

habitua|l a usual, habitual; <cliente> regular. **~r** [21] vt accustom. □ **~rse** vpr. **~rse a** get used to

habla f speech; (idioma) language; (dialecto) dialect. **al ~** (al teléfono) speaking. **ponerse al ~ con** get in touch with. **~dor** a talkative. ● m chatterbox. **~duría** f rumour. **~durías** fpl gossip. **~nte** a speaking. ● m & f speaker. **~r** vt speak. ● vi speak, talk (con to); (Mex, por teléfono) call. **¡ni ~r!** out of the question! **se ~ español** Spanish spoken

hacend|ado m landowner; (LAm) farmer. **~oso** a hard-working

hacer [31]

● *verbo transitivo*

••••▸ to do. ¿**qué haces?** what are you doing? ∼ **los deberes** to do one's homework. **no sé qué** ∼ I don't know what to do. **hazme un favor** can you do me a favour?

••••▸ (fabricar, preparar, producir) to make. **me hizo un vestido** she made me a dress. ∼ **un café** to make a (cup of) coffee. **no hagas tanto ruido** don't make so much noise

••••▸ (construir) to build <*casa, puente*>

••••▸ **hacer que uno haga algo** to make s.o. do sth. **haz que se vaya** make him leave. **hizo que se equivocara** he made her go wrong

••••▸ **hacer hacer algo** to have sth done. **hizo arreglar el techo** he had the roof repaired

⇨ Cuando el verbo **hacer** se emplea en expresiones como **hacer una pregunta, hacer trampa** etc., ver bajo el respectivo nombre

● *verbo intransitivo*

••••▸ (actuar, obrar) to do. **hiciste bien en llamar** you did the right thing to call. ¿**cómo haces para parecer tan joven?** what do you do to look so young?

••••▸ (fingir, simular) **hacer como que** to pretend. **hizo como que no me conocía** he pretended to not to know me. **haz como que estás dormido** pretend you're asleep

••••▸ **hacer de** (en teatro) to play the part of; (ejercer la función de) to act as

••••▸ (LAm, sentar) **tanta sal hace mal** so much salt is not good for you. **dormir le hizo bien** the sleep did him good. **el pepino me hace mal** cucumber doesn't agree with me

● *verbo impersonal*

••••▸ (hablando del tiempo atmosférico) to be. **hace sol** it's sunny. **hace 3 grados** it's 3 degrees

••••▸ (con expresiones temporales) **hace una hora que espero** I've been waiting for an hour. **llegó hace 3 días** he arrived 3 days ago. **hace mucho tiempo** a long time ago. **hasta hace poco** until recently

□ **hacerse** *verbo pronominal*

••••▸ (para sí) to make o.s. <*falda, café*>

••••▸ (hacer que otro haga) **se hizo la permanente** she had her hair permed. **me hice una piscina** I had a swimming pool built

••••▸ (convertirse en) to become. **se hicieron amigos** they became friends

••••▸ (acostumbrarse) ∼**se a algo** to get used to sth

••••▸ (fingirse) to pretend. ∼**se el enfermo** to pretend to be ill

••••▸ (moverse) to move. **hazte para atrás** move back

••••▸ **hacerse de** (LAm) to make <*amigo, dinero*>

hacha *f* axe; (antorcha) torch

hacia *prep* towards; (cerca de) near; (con tiempo) at about. ∼ **abajo** downwards. ∼ **arriba** upwards. ∼ **atrás** backwards. ∼ **las dos** (at) about two o'clock

hacienda *f* country estate; (en LAm) ranch; **la** ∼ **pública** the Treasury. **Ministerio** *m* **de H**∼ Ministry of Finance; (en Gran Bretaña) Exchequer; (en Estados Unidos) Treasury

hada *f* fairy. **el** ∼ **madrina** the fairy godmother

hago *vb* ⇒HACER

Haití *m* Haiti

halag|ar [12] *vt* flatter. ∼**üeño** *a* flattering; (esperanzador) promising

halcón *m* falcon

halla|r *vt* find; (descubrir) discover. □ ∼**rse** *vpr* be. ∼**zgo** *m* discovery

hamaca *f* hammock; (asiento) deckchair

hambr|e *f* hunger; (de muchos) famine. **tener** ∼**e** be hungry. ∼**iento** *a* starving

hamburguesa *f* hamburger

harag|án *a* lazy, idle. ● *m* layabout. ∼**anear** *vi* laze around

harap|iento *a* in rags. ∼**o** *m* rag

harina *f* flour

hart|ar *vt* (fastidiar) annoy. **me estás** ∼**ando** you're annoying me. □ ∼**arse** *vpr* (llenarse) gorge o.s. (de on); (cansarse) get fed up (de with).

∼o a full; (cansado) tired; (fastidiado) fed up (de with). ● adv (LAm) (muy) very; (mucho) a lot

hasta prep as far as; (en el tiempo) until, till; (Mex) not until. ● adv even. ¡∼ **la vista!** goodbye!, see you! Ⓣ ¡∼ **luego!** see you later! ¡∼ **mañana!** see you tomorrow! ¡∼ **pronto!** see you soon!

hast|iar [20] vt (cansar) weary, tire; (aburrir) bore. □ ∼**iarse** vpr get fed up (de with). ∼**ío** m weariness; (aburrimiento) boredom

haya f beech (tree). ● vb ⇒HABER

hazaña f exploit

hazmerreír m laughing stock

he vb ⇒HABER

hebilla f buckle

hebra f thread; (fibra) fibre

hebreo a & m Hebrew

hechi|cera f witch. ∼**cería** f witchcraft. ∼**cero** m wizard. ∼**zar** [10] vt cast a spell on; (fig) captivate. ∼**zo** m spell; (fig) charm

hech|o pp de hacer. ● a (manufacturado) made; (terminado) done; <vestidos etc> ready-made; (Culin) done. ● m fact; (acto) deed; (cuestión) matter; (suceso) event. **de** ∼**o** in fact. ∼**ura** f making; (forma) form; (del cuerpo) build; (calidad de fabricación) workmanship

hed|er [1] vi stink. ∼**iondez** f stench. ∼**iondo** a stinking, smelly. ∼**or** m stench

hela|da f frost. ∼**dera** f (LAm) fridge, refrigerator. ∼**dería** f ice-cream shop. ∼**do** a freezing; (congelado) frozen; (LAm, bebida) chilled. ● m ice-cream. ∼**r** [1] vt/i freeze. **anoche heló** there was a frost last night. □ ∼**rse** vpr freeze

helecho m fern

hélice f propeller

helicóptero m helicopter

hembra f female; (mujer) woman

hemorr|agia f haemorrhage. ∼**oides** fpl haemorrhoids

hendidura f crack, split; (Geol) fissure

heno m hay

heráldica f heraldry

hered|ar vt/i inherit. ∼**era** f heiress. ∼**ero** m heir. ∼**itario** a hereditary

herej|e m heretic. ∼**ía** f heresy

herencia f inheritance; (fig) heritage

heri|da f injury; (con arma) wound. ∼**do** a injured; (con arma) wounded; (fig) hurt. ● m injured person. ∼**r** [4] vt injure; (con arma) wound; (fig) hurt. □ ∼**rse** vpr hurt o.s.

herman|a f sister. ∼**a política** sister-in-law. ∼**astra** f stepsister. ∼**astro** m stepbrother. ∼**o** m brother. ∼**o político** brother-in-law. ∼**os** mpl brothers; (chicos y chicas) brothers and sisters. ∼**os gemelos** twins

hermético a hermetic; (fig) watertight

hermos|o a beautiful; (espléndido) splendid. ∼**ura** f beauty

héroe m hero

hero|ico a heroic. ∼**ína** f heroine; (droga) heroin. ∼**ísmo** m heroism

herr|adura f horseshoe. ∼**amienta** f tool. ∼**ero** m blacksmith

herv|idero m (fig) hotbed; (multitud) throng. ∼**ir** [4] vt/i boil. ∼**or** m (fig) ardour. **romper el** ∼ come to the boil

hiberna|ción f hibernation. ∼**r** vi hibernate

híbrido a & m hybrid

hice vb ⇒HACER

hidalgo m nobleman

hidrata|nte a moisturizing. ∼**r** vt hydrate; <crema etc> moisturize

hidráulico a hydraulic

hid|roavión m seaplane. ∼**oeléctrico** a hydroelectric. ∼**ofobia** f rabies. ∼**ófobo** a rabid. ∼**ógeno** m hydrogen

hiedra f ivy

hielo m ice

hiena f hyena

hierba f grass; (Culin, Med) herb. **mala** ∼ weed. ∼**buena** f mint

hierro m iron

hígado m liver

higi|ene f hygiene. ∼**énico** a hygienic

hig|o m fig. ∼**uera** f fig tree

hij|a f daughter. **~astra** f stepdaughter. **~astro** m stepson. **~o** m son. **~os** mpl sons; (chicos y chicas) children

hilar vt spin. **~ delgado** split hairs

hilera f row; (Mil) file

hilo m thread; (Elec) wire; (de líquido) trickle; (lino) linen

hilv|án m tacking. **~anar** vt tack; (fig) put together

himno m hymn. **~ nacional** anthem

hincapié m. hacer **~ en** stress, insist on

hincar [7] vt drive <estaca> (en into). □ **~se** vpr. **~se de rodillas** kneel down

hincha f □ grudge. ● m & f (□, aficionado) fan

hincha|do a inflated; (Med) swollen. **~r** vt inflate, blow up. □ **~rse** vpr swell up; (fig, □, comer mucho) gorge o.s. **~zón** f swelling

hinojo m fennel

hiper|mercado m hypermarket. **~sensible** a hypersensitive. **~tensión** f high blood pressure

hípic|a f horse racing. **~o** a horse

hipn|osis f hypnosis. **~otismo** m hypnotism. **~otizar** [10] vt hypnotize

hipo m hiccup. **tener ~** have hiccups

hipo|alérgeno a hypoallergenic. **~condríaco** a & m hypochondriac

hip|ocresía f hypocrisy. **~ócrita** a hypocritical. ● m & f hypocrite

hipódromo m racecourse

hipopótamo m hippopotamus

hipoteca f mortgage. **~r** [7] vt mortgage

hip|ótesis f invar hypothesis. **~otético** a hypothetical

hiriente a offensive, wounding

hirsuto a <barba> bristly; <pelo> wiry

hispánico a Hispanic

Hispanoamérica f Spanish America

hispano|americano a Spanish American. **~hablante** a Spanish-speaking

hist|eria f hysteria. **~érico** a hysterical

hist|oria f history; (relato) story; (excusa) tale, excuse. **pasar a la ~oria** go down in history. **~oriador** m historian. **~órico** a historical. **~orieta** f tale; (con dibujos) strip cartoon

hito m milestone

hizo vb ➡HACER

hocico m snout

hockey /'(x)oki/ m hockey. **~ sobre hielo** ice hockey

hogar m home; (chimenea) hearth. **~eño** a domestic; <persona> home-loving

hoguera f bonfire

hoja f leaf; (de papel, metal etc) sheet; (de cuchillo, espada etc) blade. **~ de afeitar** razor blade. **~lata** f tin

hojaldre m puff pastry

hojear vt leaf through

hola int hello!

Holanda f Holland

holand|és a Dutch. ● m Dutchman; (lengua) Dutch. **~esa** f Dutchwoman. **los ~eses** the Dutch

holg|ado a loose; (fig) comfortable. **~ar** [2 & 12] vi. **huelga decir que** needless to say. **~azán** a lazy. ● m idler. **~ura** f looseness; (fig) comfort

hollín m soot

hombre m man; (especie humana) man(kind). ● int Good Heavens!; (de duda) well. **~ de negocios** businessman. **~ rana** frogman

hombr|era f shoulder pad. **~o** m shoulder

homenaje m homage, tribute. **rendir ~ a** pay tribute to

home|ópata m homoeopath. **~opatía** f homoeopathy. **~opático** a homoeopathic

homicid|a a murderous. ● m & f murderer. **~io** m murder

homosexual a & m & f homosexual. **~idad** f homosexuality

hond|o a deep. **~onada** f hollow

Honduras f Honduras

hondureño a & m Honduran

honest|idad f honesty. **~o** a honest

hongo m fungus; (LAm, Culin) mushroom; (venenoso) toadstool

hon|or *m* honour. **~orable** *a* honourable. **~orario** *a* honorary. **~orarios** *mpl* fees. **~ra** *f* honour; (buena fama) good name. **~radez** *f* honesty. **~rado** *a* honest. **~rar** *vt* honour

hora *f* hour; (momento puntual) time; (cita) appointment. **~ pico, ~ punta** rush hour. **~s** *fpl* **de trabajo** working hours. **~s** *fpl* **extraordinarias** overtime. **~s** *fpl* **libres** free time. **a estas ~s** now. **¿a qué ~?** (at) what time? **a última ~** at the last moment. **de última ma ~** last-minute. **en buena ~** at the right time. **media ~** half an hour. **pedir ~** to make an appointment. **¿qué ~ es?** what time is it?

horario *a* hourly. ● *m* timetable. **~ de trabajo** working hours

horca *f* gallows

horcajadas *fpl*. **a ~** astride

horchata *f* tiger-nut milk

horizont|al *a* & *f* horizontal. **~e** *m* horizon

horma *f* mould; (para fabricar calzado) last; (para conservar su forma) shoe-tree. **de ~ ancha** broad-fitting

hormiga *f* ant

hormigón *m* concrete

hormigue|ar *vi* tingle; (bullir) swarm. **me ~a la mano** I've got pins and needles in my hand. **~o** *m* tingling; (fig) anxiety

hormiguero *m* anthill; (de gente) swarm

hormona *f* hormone

horn|ada *f* batch. **~illa** *f* (LAm) burner. **~illo** *m* burner; (cocina portátil) portable electric cooker. **~o** *m* oven; (para cerámica etc) kiln; (Tec) furnace

horóscopo *m* horoscope

horquilla *f* pitchfork; (para el pelo) hairpin

horr|endo *a* awful. **~ible** *a* horrible. **~ipilante** *a* terrifying. **~or** *m* horror; (atrocidad) atrocity. **¡qué ~or!** how awful!. **~orizar** [10] *vt* horrify. □ **~orizarse** *vpr* be horrified. **~oroso** *a* horrifying

hort|aliza *f* vegetable. **~elano** *m* market gardener

hosco *a* surly

hospeda|je *m* accommodation. **~r** *vt* put up. □ **~rse** *vpr* stay

hospital *m* hospital. **~ario** *a* hospitable. **~idad** *f* hospitality

hostal *m* boarding-house

hostería *f* inn

hostia *f* (Relig) host

hostigar [12] *vt* whip; (fig, molestar) pester

hostil *a* hostile. **~idad** *f* hostility

hotel *m* hotel. **~ero** *a* hotel. ● *m* hotelier

hoy *adv* today. **~ (en) día** nowadays. **~ por ~** at the present time. **de ~ en adelante** from now on

hoy|o *m* hole. **~uelo** *m* dimple

hoz *f* sickle

hube *vb* ⇒HABER

hucha *f* money box

hueco *a* hollow; *<palabras>* empty; *<voz>* resonant; *<persona>* superficial. ● *m* hollow; (espacio) space; (vacío) gap

huelg|a *f* strike. **~a de brazos caídos** sit-down strike. **~a de hambre** hunger strike. **declararse en ~a** come out on strike. **~uista** *m* & *f* striker

huella *f* footprint; (de animal, vehículo etc) track. **~ digital** fingerprint

huelo *vb* ⇒OLER

huérfano *a* orphaned. ● *m* orphan. **~ de** without

huert|a *f* market garden (Brit), truck farm (Amer); (terreno de regadío) irrigated plain. **~o** *m* vegetable garden; (de árboles frutales) orchard

hueso *m* bone; (de fruta) stone

huésped *m* guest; (que paga) lodger

huesudo *a* bony

huev|a *f* roe. **~o** *m* egg. **~o duro** hard-boiled egg. **~o escalfado** poached egg. **~o estrellado, ~o frito** fried egg. **~o pasado por agua** boiled egg. **~o revueltos** scrambled eggs. **~o tibio** (Mex) boiled egg

hui|da *f* flight, escape. **~dizo** *a* (tímido) shy; (esquivo) elusive

huipil *m* (Mex) traditional embroidered smock

huir *vi* [17] flee, run away; (evitar). **~ de** avoid. **me huye** he avoids me

huitlacoche *m* (Mex) edible black fungus

hule *m* oilcloth; (Mex, goma) rubber

human|idad *f* mankind; (fig) humanity. **~itario** *a* humanitarian. **~o** *a* human; (benévolo) humane

humareda *f* cloud of smoke

humed|ad *f* dampness; (en meteorología) humidity; (gotitas de agua) moisture. **~ecer** [11] *vt* moisten. □ **~ecerse** *vpr* become moist

húmedo *a* damp; <*clima*> humid; <*labios*> moist; (mojado) wet

humi|ldad *f* humility. **~lde** *a* humble. **~llación** *f* humiliation. **~llar** *vt* humiliate. □ **~llarse** *vpr* lower o.s.

humo *m* smoke; (vapor) steam; (gas nocivo) fumes. **~s** *mpl* airs

humor *m* mood, temper; (gracia) humour. **estar de mal ~** be in a bad mood. **~ista** *m & f* humorist. **~ístico** *a* humorous

hundi|miento *m* sinking. **~r** *vt* sink; destroy <*persona*>. □ **~rse** *vpr* sink; <*edificio*> collapse

húngaro *a & m* Hungarian

Hungría *f* Hungary

huracán *m* hurricane

huraño *a* unsociable

hurgar [12] *vi* rummage (**en** through). □ **~se** *vpr*. **~se la nariz** pick one's nose

hurra *int* hurray!

hurtadillas *fpl*. **a ~** stealthily

hurt|ar *vt* steal. **~o** *m* theft; (cosa robada) stolen object

husmear *vt* sniff out; (fig) pry into

huyo *vb* ⇒HUIR

. . . .

I i

. . . .

iba *vb* ⇒IR

ibérico *a* Iberian

iberoamericano *a & m* Latin American

iceberg /iθ'ber/ *m* (*pl* **~s**) iceberg

ictericia *f* jaundice

ida *f* outward journey; (partida) departure. **de ~ y vuelta** <*billete*> return (Brit), round-trip (Amer); <*viaje*> round

idea *f* idea; (opinión) opinion. **cambiar de ~** change one's mind. **no tener la más remota ~, no tener la menor ~** not have the slightest idea, not have a clue 𝔽

ideal *a & m* ideal. **~ista** *m & f* idealist. **~izar** [10] *vt* idealize

idear *vt* think up, conceive; (inventar) invent

ídem *pron & adv* the same

idéntico *a* identical

identi|dad *f* identity. **~ficación** *f* identification. **~ficar** [7] *vt* identify. □ **~ficarse** *vpr* identify o.s. **~ficarse con** identify with

ideolog|ía *f* ideology. **~ógico** *a* ideological

idílico *a* idyllic

idilio *m* idyll

idiom|a *m* language. **~ático** *a* idiomatic

idiosincrasia *f* idiosyncrasy

idiot|a *a* idiotic. ● *m & f* idiot. **~ez** *f* stupidity

idolatrar *vt* worship; (fig) idolize

ídolo *m* idol

idóneo *a* suitable (**para** for)

iglesia *f* church

iglú *m* igloo

ignora|ncia *f* ignorance. **~nte** *a* ignorant. ● *m* ignoramus. **~r** *vt* not know, be unaware of; (no hacer caso de) ignore

igual *a* equal; (mismo) the same; (similar) like; (llano) even; (liso) smooth. ● *adv* the same. ● *m* equal. **~** as (the same) as. **al ~ que** the same as. **da ~, es ~** it doesn't matter. **sin ~** unequalled

igual|ar *vt* make equal; equal <*éxito, récord*>; (allanar) level. □ **~arse** *vpr* be equal. **~dad** *f* equality. **~mente** *adv* equally; (también) also, likewise; (respuesta de cortesía) the same to you

ilegal *a* illegal

ilegible *a* illegible

ilegítimo *a* illegitimate

ileso *a* unhurt

ilícito *a* illicit

ilimitado *a* unlimited

ilógico *a* illogical

ilumina|ción *f* illumination; (alumbrado) lighting. **∼r** *vt* light (up). □ **∼rse** *vpr* light up

ilusi|ón *f* illusion; (sueño) dream; (alegría) joy. **hacerse ∼ones** build up one's hopes. **me hace ∼ón** I'm thrilled; I'm looking forward to *<algo en el futuro>*. **∼onado** *a* excited. **∼onar** *vt* give false hope. □ **∼onarse** *vpr* have false hopes

ilusionis|mo *m* conjuring. **∼ta** *m & f* conjurer

iluso *a* naive. ● *m* dreamer. **∼rio** *a* illusory

ilustra|ción *f* learning; (dibujo) illustration. **∼do** *a* learned; (con dibujos) illustrated. **∼r** *vt* explain; (instruir) instruct; (añadir dibujos etc) illustrate. □ **∼rse** *vpr* acquire knowledge. **∼tivo** *a* illustrative

ilustre *a* illustrious

imagen *f* image; (TV etc) picture

imagina|ble *a* imaginable. **∼ción** *f* imagination. **∼r** *vt* imagine. □ **∼rse** *vpr* imagine. **∼rio** *m* imaginary. **∼tivo** *a* imaginative

imán *m* magnet

imbécil *a* stupid. ● *m & f* idiot

imborrable *a* indelible; *<recuerdo etc>* unforgettable

imita|ción *f* imitation. **∼r** *vt* imitate

impacien|cia *f* impatience. □ **∼tarse** *vpr* lose one's patience. **∼te** *a* impatient

impacto *m* impact; (huella) mark. **∼ de bala** bullet hole

impar *a* odd

imparcial *a* impartial. **∼idad** *f* impartiality

impartir *vt* impart, give

impasible *a* impassive

impávido *a* fearless; (impasible) impassive

impecable *a* impeccable

impedi|do *a* disabled. **∼mento** *m* impediment. **∼r** [5] *vt* prevent; (obstruir) hinder

impenetrable *a* impenetrable

impensa|ble *a* unthinkable. **∼do** *a* unexpected

impera|r *vi* prevail. **∼tivo** *a* imperative; *<necesidad>* urgent

imperceptible *a* imperceptible

imperdible *m* safety pin

imperdonable *a* unforgivable

imperfec|ción *f* imperfection. **∼to** *a* imperfect

imperi|al *a* imperial. **∼alismo** *m* imperialism. **∼o** *m* empire; (poder) rule. **∼oso** *a* imperious

impermeable *a* waterproof. ● *m* raincoat

impersonal *a* impersonal

impertinen|cia *f* impertinence. **∼te** *a* impertinent

imperturbable *a* imperturbable

ímpetu *m* impetus; (impulso) impulse; (violencia) force

impetuos|idad *f* impetuosity. **∼o** *a* impetuous

implacable *a* implacable

implantar *vt* introduce

implica|ción *f* implication. **∼r** [7] *vt* implicate; (significar) imply

implícito *a* implicit

implorar *vt* implore

impon|ente *a* imposing; 🆃 terrific. **∼er** [34] *vt* impose; (requerir) demand; deposit *<dinero>*. □ **∼erse** *vpr* (hacerse obedecer) assert o.s.; (hacerse respetar) command respect; (prevalecer) prevail. **∼ible** *a* taxable

importa|ción *f* importation; (artículo) import. **∼ciones** *fpl* imports. **∼dor** *a* importing. ● *m* importer

importa|ncia *f* importance. **∼nte** *a* important; (en cantidad) considerable. **∼r** *vt* import; (ascender a) amount to. ● *vi* be important, matter. **¿le ∼ría...?** would you mind...? **no ∼** it doesn't matter

importe *m* price; (total) amount

importun|ar *vt* bother. **∼o** *a* troublesome; (inoportuno) inopportune

imposib|ilidad *f* impossibility. **∼le** *a* impossible. **hacer lo ∼le para** do all one can to

imposición *f* imposition; (impuesto) tax

impostor *m* impostor

impoten|cia f impotence. ∼**te** a impotent

impracticable a impracticable; (intransitable) unpassable

imprecis|ión f vagueness; (error) inaccuracy. ∼**o** a imprecise

impregnar vt impregnate; (empapar) soak

imprenta f printing; (taller) printing house, printer's

imprescindible a indispensable, essential

impresi|ón f impression; (acción de imprimir) printing; (tirada) edition; (huella) imprint. ∼**onable** a impressionable. ∼**onante** a impressive; (espantoso) frightening. ∼**onar** vt impress; (negativamente) shock; (conmover) move; (Foto) expose. □ ∼**onarse** vpr be impressed; (negativamente) be shocked; (conmover) be moved

impresionis|mo m impressionism. ∼**ta** a & m & f impressionist

impreso a printed. ● m form. ∼**s** mpl printed matter. ∼**ra** f printer

imprevis|ible a unforeseeable. ∼**to** a unforeseen

imprimir (pp **impreso**) vt print <libro etc>

improbab|ilidad f improbability. ∼**le** a unlikely, improbable

improcedente a inadmissible; <conducta> improper; <despido> unfair

improductivo a unproductive

improperio m insult. ∼**s** mpl abuse

impropio a improper

improvis|ación f improvisation. ∼**ado** a improvised. ∼**ar** vt improvise. ∼**o** a. de ∼**o** unexpectedly

impruden|cia f imprudence. ∼**te** a imprudent

imp|udicia f indecency; (desvergüenza) shamelessness. ∼**údico** a indecent; (desvergonzado) shameless. ∼**udor** m indecency; (desvergüenza) shamelessness

impuesto a imposed. ● m tax. ∼ a la renta income tax. ∼ sobre el valor agregado (LAm), ∼ sobre el valor añadido VAT, value added tax

impuls|ar vt propel; drive <persona>; boost <producción etc>. ∼**ivi-dad** f impulsiveness. ∼**ivo** a impulsive. ∼**o** m impulse

impun|e a unpunished. ∼**idad** f impunity

impur|eza f impurity. ∼**o** a impure

imputa|ción f charge. ∼**r** vt attribute; (acusar) charge

inaccesible a inaccessible

inaceptable a unacceptable

inactiv|idad f inactivity. ∼**o** a inactive

inadaptado a maladjusted

inadecuado a inadequate; (inapropiado) unsuitable

inadmisible a inadmissible; (inaceptable) unacceptable

inadvertido a distracted. pasar ∼ go unnoticed

inagotable a inexhaustible

inaguantable a unbearable

inaltera|ble a impassive; <color> fast; <convicción> unalterable. ∼**do** a unchanged

inapreciable a invaluable; (imperceptible) imperceptible

inapropiado a inappropriate

inasequible a out of reach

inaudito a unprecedented

inaugura|ción f inauguration. ∼**l** a inaugural. ∼**r** vt inaugurate

inca a & m & f Inca. ∼**ico** a Inca

incalculable a incalculable

incandescente a incandescent

incansable a tireless

incapa|cidad f incapacity; (física) disability. ∼**citado** a disabled. ∼**citar** vt incapacitate. ∼**z** a incapable

incauto a unwary; (fácil de engañar) gullible

incendi|ar vt set fire to. □ ∼**arse** vpr catch fire. ∼**ario** a incendiary. ● m arsonist. ∼**o** m fire

incentivo m incentive

incertidumbre f uncertainty

incesante a incessant

incest|o m incest. ∼**uoso** a incestuous

inciden|cia f incidence; (efecto) impact; (incidente) incident. ∼**tal** a incidental. ∼**te** m incident

incidir *vi* fall (**en** into); (influir) influence

incienso *m* incense

incierto *a* uncertain

incinera|dor *m* incinerator. **~r** *vt* incinerate; cremate *<cadáver>*

incipiente *a* incipient

incisi|ón *f* incision. **~vo** *a* incisive. ● *m* incisor

incitar *vt* incite

inclemen|cia *f* harshness. **~te** *a* harsh

inclina|ción *f* slope; (de la cabeza) nod; (fig) inclination. **~r** *vt* tilt; (inducir) incline. **~rse** *vpr* lean; (en saludo) bow; (tender) be inclined (**a** to)

inclu|ido *a* included; *<precio>* inclusive. **~ir** [17] *vt* include; (en cartas) enclose. **~sión** *f* inclusion. **~sive** *adv* inclusive. **hasta el lunes ~sive** up to and including Monday. **~so** *adv* even

incógnito *a* unknown. **de ~** incognito

incoheren|cia *f* incoherence. **~te** *a* incoherent

incoloro *a* colourless

incomestible *a*, **incomible** *a* uneatable, inedible

incomodar *vt* inconvenience; (causar vergüenza) make feel uncomfortable. □ **~se** *vpr* feel uncomfortable; (enojarse) get angry

incómodo *a* uncomfortable; (inconveniente) inconvenient

incomparable *a* incomparable

incompatib|ilidad *f* incompatibility. **~le** *a* incompatible

incompeten|cia *f* incompetence. **~te** *a & m & f* incompetent

incompleto *a* incomplete

incompren|dido *a* misunderstood. **~sible** *a* incomprehensible. **~sión** *f* incomprehension

incomunicado *a* cut off; *<preso>* in solitary confinement

inconcebible *a* inconceivable

inconcluso *a* unfinished

incondicional *a* unconditional

inconfundible *a* unmistakable

incongruente *a* incoherent; (contradictorio) inconsistent

inconmensurable *a* immeasurable

inconscien|cia *f* unconsciousness; (irreflexión) recklessness. **~te** *a* unconscious; (irreflexivo) reckless

inconsecuente *a* inconsistent

inconsistente *a* flimsy

inconsolable *a* unconsolable

inconstan|cia *f* lack of perseverance. **~te** *a* changeable; *<persona>* lacking in perseverance; (voluble) fickle

incontable *a* countless

incontenible *a* irrepressible

incontinen|cia *f* incontinence. **~te** *a* incontinent

inconvenien|cia *f* inconvenience. **~te** *a* inconvenient; (inapropiado) inappropriate; (incorrecto) improper. ● *m* problem; (desventaja) drawback

incorpora|ción *f* incorporation. **~r** *vt* incorporate; (Culin) add. □ **~rse** *vpr* sit up; join *<sociedad, regimiento etc>*

incorrecto *a* incorrect; (descortés) discourteous

incorregible *a* incorrigible

incorruptible *a* incorruptible

incrédulo *a* sceptical; *<mirada, gesto>* incredulous

increíble *a* incredible

increment|ar *vt* increase. **~o** *m* increase

incriminar *vt* incriminate

incrustar *vt* encrust

incuba|ción *f* incubation. **~dora** *f* incubator. **~r** *vt* incubate; (fig) hatch

incuestionable *a* unquestionable

inculcar [7] *vt* inculcate

inculpar *vt* accuse

inculto *a* uneducated

incumplimiento *m* non-fulfilment; (de un contrato) breach

incurable *a* incurable

incurrir *vi*. **~ en** incur *<gasto>*; fall into *<error>*; commit *<crimen>*

incursión *f* raid

indagar [12] *vt* investigate

indebido *a* unjust; *<uso>* improper

indecen|cia *f* indecency. **~te** *a* indecent

indecible *a* indescribable

indecis|ión *f* indecision. **~o** *a* (con ser) indecisive; (con estar) undecided

indefenso *a* defenceless

indefini|ble *a* indefinable. **~do** *a* indefinite; (impreciso) undefined

indemnizar [10] *vt* compensate

independ|encia *f* independence. **~iente** *a* independent. **~izarse** [10] *vpr* become independent

indes|cifrable *a* indecipherable. **~criptible** *a* indescribable

indeseable *a* undesirable

indestructible *a* indestructible

indetermina|ble *a* indeterminable. **~do** *a* indeterminate; <tiempo> indefinite

India *f*. la **~** India

indica|ción *f* indication; (señal) signal. **~ciones** *fpl* directions. **~dor** *m* indicator; (Tec) gauge. **~r** [7] *vt* show, indicate; (apuntar) point at; (hacer saber) point out; (aconsejar) advise. **~tivo** *a* indicative. ● *m* indicative; (al teléfono) dialling code

índice *m* index; (dedo) index finger; (catálogo) catalogue; (indicación) indication; (aguja) pointer

indicio *m* indication, sign; (vestigio) trace

indiferen|cia *f* indifference. **~te** *a* indifferent. me es **~te** it's all the same to me

indígena *a* indigenous. ● *m & f* native

indigen|cia *f* poverty. **~te** *a* needy

indigest|ión *f* indigestion. **~o** *a* indigestible

indign|ación *f* indignation. **~ado** *a* indignant. **~ar** *vt* make indignant. □ **~arse** *vpr* become indignant. **~o** *a* unworthy; (despreciable) contemptible

indio *a & m* Indian

indirect|a *f* hint. **~o** *a* indirect

indisciplinado *a* undisciplined

indiscre|ción *f* indiscretion. **~to** *a* indiscreet

indiscutible *a* unquestionable

indisoluble *a* indissoluble

indispensable *a* indispensable

indisp|oner [34] *vt* (enemistar) set against. □ **~onerse** *vpr* fall out; (ponerse enfermo) fall ill. **~osición** *f* indisposition. **~uesto** *a* indisposed

individu|al *a* individual; <cama> single. ● *m* (en tenis etc) singles. **~alidad** *f* individuality. **~alista** *m & f* individualist. **~alizar** [10] *vt* individualize. **~o** *m* individual

índole *f* nature; (clase) type

indolen|cia *f* indolence. **~te** *a* indolent

indoloro *a* painless

indomable *a* untameable

inducir [47] *vt* induce. **~ a error** be misleading

indudable *a* undoubted

indulgen|cia *f* indulgence. **~te** *a* indulgent

indult|ar *vt* pardon. **~o** *m* pardon

industria *f* industry. **~l** *a* industrial. ● *m & f* industrialist. **~lización** *f* industrialization. **~lizar** [10] *vt* industrialize

inédito *a* unpublished; (fig) unknown

inefable *a* indescribable

ineficaz *a* ineffective; <sistema etc> inefficient

ineficiente *a* inefficient

ineludible *a* inescapable, unavoidable

inept|itud *f* ineptitude. **~o** *a* inept

inequívoco *a* unequivocal

inercia *f* inertia

inerte *a* inert; (sin vida) lifeless

inesperado *a* unexpected

inestable *a* unstable

inestimable *a* inestimable

inevitable *a* inevitable

inexistente *a* non-existent

inexorable *a* inexorable

inexper|iencia *f* inexperience. **~to** *a* inexperienced

inexplicable *a* inexplicable

infalible *a* infallible

infam|ar *vt* defame. **~atorio** *a* defamatory. **~e** *a* infamous; (fig, ⊞, muy malo) awful. **~ia** *f* infamy

infancia *f* infancy

infant|a *f* infanta, princess. **~e** *m* infante, prince. **~eria** *f* infantry. **~il** *a* children's; *<población>* child; *<actitud etc>* childish, infantile

infarto *m* heart attack

infec|ción *f* infection. **~cioso** *a* infectious. **~tar** *vt* infect. □ **~tarse** *vpr* become infected. **~to** *a* infected; ⚡ disgusting

infeli|cidad *f* unhappiness. **~z** *a* unhappy

inferior *a* inferior. ● *m & f* inferior. **~idad** *f* inferiority

infernal *a* infernal, hellish

infestar *vt* infest; (fig) inundate

infi|delidad *f* unfaithfulness. **~el** *a* unfaithful

infierno *m* hell

infiltra|ción *f* infiltration. □ **~rse** *vpr* infiltrate

ínfimo *a* lowest; *<calidad>* very poor

infini|dad *f* infinity. **~tivo** *m* infinitive. **~to** *a* infinite. ● *m*. el **~to** the infinite; (en matemáticas) infinity. **~dad de** countless

inflación *f* inflation

inflama|ble *a* (in)flammable **~ción** *f* inflammation. **~r** *vt* set on fire; (fig, Med) inflame. □ **~rse** *vpr* catch fire; (Med) become inflamed

inflar *vt* inflate; blow up *<globo>*; (fig, exagerar) exaggerate

inflexi|ble *a* inflexible. **~ón** *f* inflexion

influ|encia *f* influence (en on). **~ir** [17] *vt* influence. ● *vi*. **~ en** influence. **~jo** *m* influence. **~yente** *a* influential

informa|ción *f* information; (noticias) news; (en aeropuerto etc) information desk; (de teléfonos) directory enquiries. **~dor** *m* informant

informal *a* informal; *<persona>* unreliable

inform|ante *m & f* informant. **~ar** *vt/i* inform. □ **~arse** *vpr* find out. **~ática** *f* information technology, computing. **~ativo** *a* informative; *<programa>* news. **~atizar** [10] *vt* computerize

informe *a* shapeless. ● *m* report. **~s** *fpl* references, information

infracción *f* infringement. **~ de tráfico** traffic offence

infraestructura *f* infrastructure

infranqueable *a* impassable; (fig) insuperable

infrarrojo *a* infrared

infringir [14] *vt* infringe

infructuoso *a* fruitless

ínfulas *fpl*. darse **~** give o.s. airs. tener **~ de** fancy o.s. as

infundado *a* unfounded

infu|ndir *vt* instil. **~sión** *f* infusion

ingeni|ar *vt* invent. **~árselas para** find a way to

ingenier|ía *f* engineering. **~o** *m* engineer

ingenio *m* ingenuity; (agudeza) wit; (LAm, de azúcar) refinery. **~so** *a* ingenious

ingenu|idad *f* naivety. **~o** *a* naive

Inglaterra *f* England

ingl|és *a* English. ● *m* Englishman; (lengua) English. **~esa** *f* Englishwoman. **los ~eses** the English

ingrat|itud *f* ingratitude. **~o** *a* ungrateful; (desagradable) thankless

ingrediente *m* ingredient

ingres|ar *vt* deposit. ● *vi*. **~ar en** come in, enter; join *<sociedad>*. **~o** *m* entrance; (de dinero) deposit; (en sociedad, hospital) admission. **~os** *mpl* income

inh|ábil *a* unskilful; (no apto) unfit. **~abilidad** *f* unskilfulness; (para cargo) ineligibility

inhabitable *a* uninhabitable

inhala|dor *m* inhaler. **~r** *vt* inhale

inherente *a* inherent

inhibi|ción *f* inhibition. **~r** *vt* inhibit

inhóspito *a* inhospitable

inhumano *a* inhuman

inici|ación *f* beginning. **~al** *a & f* initial. **~ar** *vt* initiate; (comenzar) begin, start. **~ativa** *f* initiative. **~o** *m* beginning

inigualado *a* unequalled

ininterrumpido *a* uninterrupted

injert|ar *vt* graft. **~to** *m* graft

injuri|a *f* insult. **~ar** *vt* insult. **~oso** *a* insulting

injust|icia f injustice. **~o** a unjust, unfair

inmaculado a immaculate

inmaduro a unripe; *<persona>* immature

inmediaciones fpl. **las ~** the vicinity, the surrounding area

inmediat|amente adv immediately. **~o** a immediate; (contiguo) next. **de ~o** immediately

inmejorable a excellent

inmemorable a immemorial

inmens|idad f immensity. **~o** a immense

inmersión f immersion

inmigra|ción f immigration. **~nte** a & m & f immigrant. **~r** vt immigrate

inminen|cia f imminence. **~te** a imminent

inmiscuirse [17] vpr interfere

inmobiliario a property

inmolar vt sacrifice

inmoral a immoral. **~idad** f immorality

inmortal a immortal. **~izar** [10] vt immortalize

inmóvil a immobile

inmueble a. **bienes ~s** property

inmund|icia f filth. **~o** a filthy

inmun|e a immune. **~idad** f immunity. **~ización** f immunization. **~izar** [10] vt immunize

inmuta|ble a unchangeable. □ **~rse** vpr be perturbed. **sin ~rse** unperturbed

innato a innate

innecesario a unnecessary

innegable a undeniable

innova|ción f innovation. **~r** vi innovate. ● vt make innovations in

innumerable a innumerable

inocen|cia f innocence. **~tada** f practical joke. **~te** a innocent. **~tón** a naïve

inocuo a innocuous

inodoro a odourless. ● m toilet

inofensivo a inoffensive

inolvidable a unforgettable

inoperable a inoperable

inoportuno a untimely; *<comentario>* ill-timed

inoxidable a stainless

inquiet|ar vt worry. □ **~arse** vpr get worried. **~o** a worried; (agitado) restless. **~ud** f anxiety

inquilino m tenant

inquirir [4] vt enquire into, investigate

insaciable a insatiable

insalubre a unhealthy

insatisfecho a unsatisfied; (descontento) dissatisfied

inscri|bir (pp **inscrito**) vt (en registro) register; (en curso) enrol; (grabar) inscribe. □ **~birse** vpr register. **~pción** f inscription; (registro) registration

insect|icida m insecticide. **~o** m insect

insegur|idad f insecurity. **~o** a insecure; *<ciudad>* unsafe, dangerous

insemina|ción f insemination. **~r** vt inseminate

insensato a foolish

insensible a insensitive

inseparable a inseparable

insertar vt insert

insidi|a f malice. **~oso** a insidious

insigne a famous

insignia f badge; (bandera) flag

insignificante a insignificant

insinu|ación f insinuation. **~ante** a insinuating. **~ar** [21] vt imply; insinuate *<algo ofensivo>*. □ **~arse** vpr. **~árse a** make a pass at

insípido a insipid

insist|encia f insistence. **~ente** a insistent. **~ir** vi insist; (hacer hincapié) stress

insolación f sunstroke

insolen|cia f rudeness, insolence. **~te** a rude, insolent

insólito a unusual

insolven|cia f insolvency. **~te** a & m & f insolvent

insomn|e a sleepless. ● m & f insomniac. **~io** m insomnia

insondable a unfathomable

insoportable a unbearable

insospechado a unexpected

insostenible *a* untenable

inspec|ción *f* inspection. **~cio-nar** *vt* inspect. **~tor** *m* inspector

inspira|ción *f* inspiration. **~r** *vt* inspire. □ **~rse** *vpr* be inspired

instala|ción *f* installation. **~r** *vt* install. □ **~rse** *vpr* settle

instancia *f* request. **en última ~** as a last resort

instant|ánea *f* snapshot. **~áneo** *a* instantaneous; *<café etc>* instant. **~e** *m* instant. **a cada ~e** constantly. **al ~e** immediately

instaura|ción *f* establishment. **~r** *vt* establish

instiga|ción *f* instigation. **~dor** *m* instigator. **~r** [12] *vt* instigate; (incitar) incite

instint|ivo *a* instinctive. **~o** *m* instinct

institu|ción *f* institution. **~cional** *a* institutional. **~ir** [17] *vt* establish. **~to** *m* institute; (Escol) (secondary) school. **~triz** *f* governess

instru|cción *f* education; (Mil) training. **~cciones** *fpl* instruction. **~ctivo** *a* instructive; *<película etc>* educational. **~ctor** *m* instructor. **~ir** [17] *vt* instruct, teach; (Mil) train

instrument|ación *f* instrumentation. **~al** *a* instrumental. **~o** *m* instrument; (herramienta) tool

insubordina|ción *f* insubordination. **~r** *vt* stir up. □ **~rse** *vpr* rebel

insuficien|cia *f* insufficiency; (inadecuación) inadequacy. **~te** *a* insufficient

insufrible *a* insufferable

insular *a* insular

insulina *f* insulin

insulso *a* tasteless; (fig) insipid

insult|ar *vt* insult. **~o** *m* insult

insuperable *a* insuperable; (inmejorable) unbeatable

insurgente *a* insurgent

insurrec|ción *f* insurrection. **~to** *a* insurgent

intachable *a* irreproachable

intacto *a* intact

intangible *a* intangible

integra|ción *f* integration. **~l** *a* integral; (completo) complete; (incorporado) built-in; *<pan>* wholemeal (Brit), wholewheat (Amer). **~r** *vt* make up

integridad *f* integrity; (entereza) wholeness

íntegro *a* complete; (fig) upright

intelect|o *m* intellect. **~ual** *a & m & f* intellectual

inteligen|cia *f* intelligence. **~te** *a* intelligent

inteligible *a* intelligible

intemperie *f.* **a la ~** in the open

intempestivo *a* untimely

intenci|ón *f* intention. **con doble ~ón** implying sth else. **~onado** *a* deliberate. **bien ~onado** well-meaning. **mal ~onado** malicious. **~onal** *a* intentional

intens|idad *f* intensity. **~ificar** [7] *vt* intensify. **~ivo** *a* intensive. **~o** *a* intense

intent|ar *vt* try. **~o** *m* attempt; (Mex, propósito) intention

inter|calar *vt* insert. **~cambio** *m* exchange. **~ceder** *vt* intercede

interceptar *vt* intercept

interdicto *m* ban

inter|és *m* interest; (egoísmo) self-interest. **~esado** *a* interested; (parcial) biassed; (egoísta) selfish. **~esante** *a* interesting. **~esar** *vt* interest; (afectar) concern. ● *vi* be of interest. □ **~esarse** *vpr* take an interest (por in)

interfer|encia *f* interference. **~ir** [4] *vi* interfere

interfono *m* intercom

interino *a* temporary; *<persona>* acting. ● *m* stand-in; (médico) locum

interior *a* interior; *<comercio etc>* domestic. ● *m* inside. **Ministerio del I~** Home Office (Brit), Department of the Interior (Amer)

interjección *f* interjection

inter|locutor *m* speaker. **~mediario** *a & m* intermediary. **~medio** *a* intermediate. ● *m* interval

interminable *a* interminable

intermitente *a* intermittent. ● *m* indicator

internacional *a* international

intern|ado *m* (Escol) boarding-school. **~ar** *vt* (en manicomio) commit; (en hospital) admit. □ **~arse** *vpr* penetrate

Internet *m* Internet

interno *a* internal; (Escol) boarding. ● *m* (Escol) boarder

interponer [34] *vt* interpose. □ **~se** *vpr* intervene

int|erpretación *f* interpretation. **~erpretar** *vt* interpret; (Mús etc) play. **~érprete** *m* interpreter; (Mus) performer

interroga|ción *f* interrogation; (signo) question mark. **~r** [12] *vt* question. **~tivo** *a* interrogative

interru|mpir *vt* interrupt; cut off *<suministro>*; cut short *<viaje etc>*; block *<tráfico>*. **~pción** *f* interruption. **~ptor** *m* switch

inter|sección *f* intersection. **~urbano** *a* inter-city; *<llamada>* long-distance

intervalo *m* interval; (espacio) space. **a ~s** at intervals

interven|ir [53] *vt* control; (Med) operate on. ● *vi* intervene; (participar) take part. **~tor** *m* inspector; (Com) auditor

intestino *m* intestine

intim|ar *vi* become friendly. **~idad** *f* intimacy

intimidar *vt* intimidate

íntimo *a* intimate; *<amigo>* close. ● *m* close friend

intolera|ble *a* intolerable. **~nte** *a* intolerant

intoxicar [7] *vt* poison

intranquilo *a* worried

intransigente *a* intransigent

intransitable *a* impassable

intransitivo *a* intransitive

intratable *a* impossible

intrépido *a* intrepid

intriga *f* intrigue. **~nte** *a* intriguing. **~r** [12] *vt* intrigue

intrincado *a* intricate

intrínseco *a* intrinsic

introduc|ción *f* introduction. **~ir** [47] *vt* introduce; (meter) insert. □ **~irse** *vpr* get into

intromisión *f* interference

introvertido *a* introverted. ● *m* introvert

intruso *m* intruder

intui|ción *f* intuition. **~r** [17] *vt* sense. **~tivo** *a* intuitive

inunda|ción *f* flooding. **~r** *vt* flood

inusitado *a* unusual

in|útil *a* useless; (vano) futile. **~utilidad** *f* uselessness

invadir *vt* invade

inv|alidez *f* invalidity; (Med) disability. **~álido** *a & m* invalid

invariable *a* invariable

invas|ión *f* invasion. **~or** *a* invading. ● *m* invader

invencible *a* invincible

inven|ción *f* invention. **~tar** *vt* invent

inventario *m* inventory

invent|iva *f* inventiveness. **~ivo** *a* inventive. **~or** *m* inventor

invernadero *m* greenhouse

invernal *a* winter

inverosímil *a* implausible

inversión *f* inversion; (Com) investment

inverso *a* inverse; (contrario) opposite. **a la inversa** the other way round. **a la inversa de** contrary to

invertir [4] *vt* reverse; (Com) invest; put in *<tiempo>*

investidura *f* investiture

investiga|ción *f* investigation; (Univ) research. **~dor** *m* investigator; (Univ) researcher. **~r** [12] *vt* investigate; (Univ) research

investir [5] *vt* invest

invicto *a* unbeaten

invierno *m* winter

inviolable *a* inviolate

invisible *a* invisible

invita|ción *f* invitation. **~do** *m* guest. **~r** *vt* invite. **te invito a una copa** I'll buy you a drink

invocar [7] *vt* invoke

involuntario *a* involuntary

invulnerable *a* invulnerable

inyec|ción *f* injection. **~tar** *vt* inject

ir [49]

● *verbo intransitivo*

····▸ to go. **fui a verla** I went to see her. **ir a pie** to go on foot. **ir en coche** to go by car. **vamos a casa** let's go home. **fue (a) por el pan** he went to get some bread

▌ Cuando la acción del verbo **ir**
■ significa trasladarse hacia o con el interlocutor la traducción es *to come,* p.ej: **¡ya voy!** *I'm coming!* **yo voy contigo** *I'll come with you*

····▸ (estar) to be. **iba con su novio** she was with her boyfriend. **¿cómo te va?** how are you?

····▸ (sentar) to suit. **ese color no le va** that colour doesn't suit her. **no me va ni me viene** I don't mind at all

····▸ (Méx, apoyar) **irle a** to support. **le va al equipo local** he supports the local team

····▸ (en exclamaciones) **¡vamos!** come on! **¡vaya!** what a surprise!; (contrariedad) oh, dear! **¡vaya noche!** what a night! **¡qué va!** nonsense!

➡ Cuando el verbo intransitivo se emplea con expresiones como **ir de paseo, ir de compras, ir tirando** etc., ver bajo el respectivo nombre, verbo etc.

● *verbo auxiliar*

····▸ **ir a** + *infinitivo* (para expresar futuro, propósito) to be going to + *infinitive;* (al prevenir) **no te vayas a caer** be careful you don't fall. **no vaya a ser que llueva** in case it rains. (en sugerencias) **vamos a dormir** let's go to sleep. **vamos a ver** let's see

····▸ **ir** + *gerundio.* **ve arreglándote** start getting ready. **el tiempo va mejorando** the weather is gradually getting better.

□ **irse** *verbo pronominal*

····▸ to go. **vete a la cama** go to bed. **se ha ido a casa** he's gone home

····▸ (marcharse) to leave. **se fue sin despedirse** he left without saying goodbye. **se fue de casa** she left home

ira *f* anger. **∼cundo** *a* irascible
Irak *m* Iraq
Irán *m* Iran
iraní *a & m & f* Iranian
iraquí *a & m & f* Iraqi
iris *m* (Anat) iris
Irlanda *f* Ireland
irland|és *a* Irish. ● *m* Irishman; (lengua) Irish. **∼esa** *f* Irishwoman. **los ∼eses** the Irish
ir|onía *f* irony. **∼ónico** *a* ironic
irracional *a* irrational
irradiar *vt* radiate
irreal *a* unreal. **∼idad** *f* unreality
irrealizable *a* unattainable
irreconciliable *a* irreconcilable
irreconocible *a* unrecognizable
irrecuperable *a* irretrievable
irreflexión *f* impetuosity
irregular *a* irregular. **∼idad** *f* irregularity
irreparable *a* irreparable
irreprimible *a* irrepressible
irreprochable *a* irreproachable
irresistible *a* irresistible
irrespetuoso *a* disrespectful
irresponsable *a* irresponsible
irriga|ción *f* irrigation. **∼r** [12] *vt* irrigate
irrisorio *a* derisory
irrita|ble *a* irritable. **∼ción** *f* irritation. **∼r** *vt* irritate. □ **∼rse** *vpr* get annoyed
irrumpir *vi* burst (en in)
isla *f* island. **las I∼s Británicas** the British Isles
islámico *a* Islamic
islandés *a* Icelandic. ● *m* Icelander; (lengua) Icelandic
Islandia *f* Iceland
isleño *a* island. ● *m* islander
Israel *m* Israel
israelí *a & m* Israeli
Italia *f* Italy
italiano *a & m* Italian
itinerario *a* itinerary
IVA *abrev* (**impuesto sobre el valor agregado** (LAm), **impuesto sobre el valor añadido**) VAT

izar [10] *vt* hoist

izquierd|a *f.* **la ~a** the left hand; (Pol) left. **a la ~a** on the left; (con movimiento) to the left. **de ~a** left-wing. **~ista** *m & f* leftist. **~o** *a* left

Jj

ja *int* ha!

jabalí *m* (*pl* **~es**) wild boar

jabalina *f* javelin

jab|ón *m* soap. **~onar** *vt* soap. **~onoso** *a* soapy

jaca *f* pony

jacinto *m* hyacinth

jactarse *vpr* boast

jadea|nte *a* panting. **~r** *vi* pant

jaguar *m* jaguar

jaiba *f* (LAm) crab

jalar *vt* (LAm) pull

jalea *f* jelly

jaleo *m* row, uproar. **armar un ~** kick up a fuss

jalón *m* (LAm, tirón) pull; (Mex ▣, trago) drink; (Mex, tramo) stretch

jamás *adv* never. **nunca ~** never ever

jamelgo *m* nag

jamón *m* ham. **~ de York** boiled ham. **~ serrano** cured ham

Japón *m.* **el ~** Japan

japonés *a & m* Japanese

jaque *m* check. **~ mate** checkmate

jaqueca *f* migraine

jarabe *m* syrup

jardín *m* garden. **~ de la infancia**, (Mex) **~ de niños** kindergarten, nursery school

jardiner|ía *f* gardening. **~o** *m* gardener

jarr|a *f* jug. **en ~as** with hands on hips. **~o** *m* jug. **caer como un ~o de agua fría** come as a shock. **~ón** *m* vase

jaula *f* cage

jauría *f* pack of hounds

jazmín *m* jasmine

jef|a *f* boss. **~atura** *f* leadership; (sede) headquarters. **~e** *m* boss; (Pol etc) leader. **~e de camareros** head waiter. **~e de estación** station-master. **~e de ventas** sales manager

jengibre *m* ginger

jer|arquía *f* hierarchy. **~árquico** *a* hierarchical

jerez *m* sherry. **al ~** with sherry

jerga *f* coarse cloth; (argot) jargon

jerigonza *f* jargon; (galimatías) gibberish

jeringa *f* syringe; (LAm ▣, molestia) nuisance. **~r** [12] *vt* (fig, ▣, molestar) annoy

jeroglífico *m* hieroglyph(ic)

jersey *m* (*pl* **~s**) jersey

Jesucristo *m* Jesus Christ. **antes de ~** BC, before Christ

jesuita *a & m* Jesuit

Jesús *m* Jesus. ● *int* good heavens!; (al estornudar) bless you!

jícara *f* (Mex) gourd

jilguero *m* goldfinch

jinete *m & f* rider

jipijapa *m* panama hat

jirafa *f* giraffe

jirón *m* shred, tatter

jitomate *m* (Mex) tomato

jorna|da *f* working day; (viaje) journey; (etapa) stage. **~l** *m* day's wage. **~lero** *m* day labourer

joroba *f* hump. **~do** *a* hunchbacked. ● *m* hunchback. **~r** *vt* ▣ annoy

jota *f* letter J; (danza) jota, popular dance. **ni ~** nothing

joven (*pl* **jóvenes**) *a* young. ● *m* young man. ● *f* young woman

jovial *a* jovial

joy|a *f* jewel. **~as** *fpl* jewellery. **~ería** *f* jeweller's (shop). **~ero** *m* jeweller; (estuche) jewellery box

juanete *m* bunion

jubil|ación *f* retirement. **~ado** *a* retired. **~ar** *vt* pension off. □ **~arse** *vpr* retire. **~eo** *m* jubilee

júbilo *m* joy

judaísmo *m* Judaism

judía *f* Jewish woman; (alubia) bean. **~ blanca** haricot bean. **~ escarlata** runner bean. **~ verde** French bean

judicial *a* judicial

judío *a* Jewish. ● *m* Jewish man

judo *m* judo

juego *m* play; (de mesa, niños) game; (de azar) gambling; (conjunto) set. **estar en** ~ be at stake. **estar fuera de** ~ be offside. **hacer** ~ match. ~**s** *mpl* ma-labares juggling. **J**~**s** *mpl* **Olímpicos** Olympic Games. ● *vb* ⇒JUGAR

juerga *f* spree

jueves *m invar* Thursday

juez *m* judge. ~ **de instrucción** examining magistrate. ~ **de línea** linesman

juga|dor *m* player; (habitual, por dine-ro) gambler. ~**r** [3] *vt* play. ● *vi* play; (apostar fuerte) gamble. □ ~**rse** *vpr* risk. ~**r al fútbol**, (LAm) ~**r fútbol** play football

juglar *m* minstrel

jugo *m* juice; (de carne) gravy; (fig) substance. ~**so** *a* juicy; (fig) substantial

juguet|e *m* toy. ~**ear** *vi* play. ~**ón** *a* playful

juicio *m* judgement; (opinión) opinion; (razón) reason. **a mi** ~ in my opinion. ~**so** *a* wise

juliana *f* vegetable soup

julio *m* July

junco *m* rush, reed

jungla *f* jungle

junio *m* June

junt|a *f* meeting; (consejo) board, committee; (Pol) junta; (Tec) joint. ~**ar** *vt* join; (reunir) collect. □ ~**arse** *vpr* join; <gente> meet. ~**o** *a* joined; (en plural) together. ~**o a** next to. ~**ura** *f* joint

jura|do *a* sworn. ● *m* jury; (miembro de jurado) juror. ~**mento** *m* oath. **prestar** ~**mento** take an oath. ~**r** *vt/i* swear. ~**r en falso** commit perjury. **jurárselas a uno** have it in for s.o.

jurel *m* (type of) mackerel

jurídico *a* legal

juris|dicción *f* jurisdiction. ~**prudencia** *f* jurisprudence

justamente *a* exactly; (con justicia) fairly

justicia *f* justice

justifica|ción *f* justification. ~**r** [7] *vt* justify

justo *a* fair, just; (exacto) exact; <ro-pa> tight. ● *adv* just. ~ **a tiempo** just in time

juven|il *a* youthful. ~**tud** *f* youth; (gente joven) young people

juzga|do *m* (tribunal) court. ~**r** [12] *vt* judge. **a** ~**r por** judging by

Kk

kilo *m*, **kilogramo** *m* kilo, kilogram

kil|ometraje *m* distance in kilometres, mileage. ~**ométrico** *a* 🚇 endless. ~**ómetro** *m* kilometre. ~**ómetro cuadrado** square kilometre

kilovatio *m* kilowatt

kiosco *m* kiosk

Ll

la

● *artículo definido femenino* (*pl* **las**)

····▸ the. **la flor azul** the blue flower. **la casa de al lado** the house next door. **cerca de la iglesia** near the church

No se traduce en los siguientes casos:

····▸ (con nombre abstracto, genérico) **la paciencia es una virtud** patience is a virtue. **odio la leche** I hate milk. **la madera es muy versátil** wood is very versatile

····▸ (con algunas instituciones) **termino la universidad mañana** I finish university tomorrow. **no va nunca a la iglesia** he never goes to church. **está en la cárcel** he's in jail

····▸ (con nombres propios) **la Sra. Díaz** Mrs Díaz. **la doctora Lara** doctor Lara

····▸ (antes de infinitivo) **es muy cuidadosa en el vestir** she takes great care in the way she dresses. **me di cuenta al** verla I realized when I saw her

····▸ (con partes del cuerpo, artículos personales) *se traduce por un posesivo*. **apretó la mano** he clenched his fist. **tienes la camisa desabrochada** your shirt is undone

····▸ **la + de. es la de Ana** it's Ana's. **la del sombrero** the one with the hat

····▸ **la + que** (persona) **la que me atendió** the one who served me. (cosa) **la que se rompió** the one that broke

····▸ **la + que +** *subjuntivo* (quienquiera) whoever. **la que gane pasará a la final** whoever wins will go to the final. (cualquiera) whichever. **compra la que sea más barata** buy whichever is cheaper

laberinto *m* labyrinth, maze

labia *f* gift of the gab

labio *m* lip

labor *f* work. ~**es de aguja** needlework. ~**es de ganchillo** crochet. ~**es de punto** knitting. ~**es domésticas** housework. ~**able** *a* working. ~**ar** *vi* work

laboratorio *m* laboratory

laborioso *a* laborious

laborista *a* Labour. ● *m & f* member of the Labour Party

labra|do *a* worked; *<madera>* carved; *<metal>* wrought; *<tierra>* ploughed. ~**dor** *m* farmer; (obrero) farm labourer. ~**nza** *f* farming. ~**r** *vt* work; carve *<madera>*; cut *<piedra>*; till *<la tierra>*. □ ~**rse** *vpr*. ~**rse un porvenir** carve out a future for o.s.

labriego *m* peasant

laca *f* lacquer

lacayo *m* lackey

lacio *a* straight; (flojo) limp

lacón *m* shoulder of pork

lacónico *a* laconic

lacr|ar *vt* seal. ~**e** *m* sealing wax

lactante *a* *<niño>* still on milk

lácteo *a* milky. **productos** *mpl* ~**s** dairy products

ladear *vt* tilt. □ ~**se** *vpr* lean

ladera *f* slope

ladino *a* astute

lado *m* side. **al** ~ near. **al** ~ **de** next to, beside. **de** ~ sideways. **en todos** ~**s** everywhere. **los de al** ~ the next door neighbours. **por otro** ~ on the other hand. **por todos** ~**s** everywhere. **por un** ~ on the one hand

ladr|ar *vi* bark. ~**ido** *m* bark

ladrillo *m* brick

ladrón *m* thief, robber; (de casas) burglar

lagart|ija *f* (small) lizard. ~**o** *m* lizard

lago *m* lake

lágrima *f* tear

lagrimoso *a* tearful

laguna *f* small lake; (fig, omisión) gap

laico *a* lay

lament|able *a* deplorable; (que da pena) pitiful; *<pérdida>* sad. ~**ar** *vt* be sorry about. □ ~**arse** *vpr* lament; (quejarse) complain. ~**o** *m* moan

lamer *vt* lick

lámina *f* sheet; (ilustración) plate; (estampa) picture card

lamina|do *a* laminated. ~**r** *vt* laminate

lámpara *f* lamp. ~ **de pie** standard lamp

lamparón *m* stain

lampiño *a* beardless; *<cuerpo>* hairless

lana *f* wool. **de** ~ wool(len)

lanceta *f* lancet

lancha *f* boat. ~ **motora** motor boat. ~ **salvavidas** lifeboat

langost|a *f* (de mar) lobster; (insecto) locust. ~**ino** *m* king prawn

languide|cer [11] *vi* languish. ~**z** *f* languor

lánguido *a* languid; (decaído) listless

lanilla *f* nap; (tela fina) flannel

lanudo *a* woolly; *<perro>* shaggy

lanza *f* lance, spear

lanza|llamas *m* *invar* flamethrower. ~**miento** *m* throw; (acción de lanzar) throwing; (de proyectil, de producto) launch. ~**miento de peso**, (LAm) ~**miento de bala** shot put. ~**r** [10] *vt* throw; (de un avión) drop; launch *<proyectil, producto>*. □ ~**rse** *vpr* throw o.s.

lapicero *m* (propelling) pencil

lápida f tombstone; (placa conmemorativa) memorial tablet

lapidar vt stone

lápiz m pencil. ~ **de labios** lipstick. a ~ in pencil

lapso m lapse

larg|a f. **a la** ~**a** in the long run. **dar** ~**as** put off. ~**ar** [12] vt (Naut) let out; (🔟, dar) give; 🔟 deal <*bofetada etc*>. □ ~**arse** vpr 🔟 beat it 🔟. ~**o** a long. ● m length. **¡**~**o!** go away! **a lo** ~**o** lengthwise. **a lo** ~**o de** along. **tener 100 metros de** ~**o** be 100 metres long

laring|e f larynx. ~**itis** f laryngitis

larva f larva

las art def fpl the. véase tb LA. ● pron them. ~ **de** those, the ones. ~ **de Vd** your ones, yours. ~ **que** whoever, the ones

láser m laser

lástima f pity; (queja) complaint. **da** ~ **verlo así** it's sad to see him like that. **ella me da** ~ I feel sorry for her. **¡qué** ~**!** what a pity!

lastim|ado a hurt. ~**ar** vt hurt. □ ~**arse** vpr hurt o.s. ~**ero** a doleful. ~**oso** a pitiful

lastre m ballast; (fig) burden

lata f tinplate; (envase) tin (esp Brit), can; (🔟, molestia) nuisance. **dar la** ~ be a nuisance. **¡qué** ~**!** what a nuisance!

latente a latent

lateral a side, lateral

latido m beating; (cada golpe) beat

latifundio m large estate

latigazo m (golpe) lash; (chasquido) crack

látigo m whip

latín m Latin. **saber** ~ 🔟 know what's what 🔟

latino a Latin. **L**~**américa** f Latin America. ~**americano** a & m Latin American

latir vi beat; <*herida*> throb

latitud f latitude

latón m brass

latoso a annoying; (pesado) boring

laúd m lute

laureado a honoured; (premiado) prize-winning

laurel m laurel; (Culin) bay

lava f lava

lava|ble a washable. ~**bo** m washbasin; (retrete) toilet. ~**dero** m sink. ~**do** m washing. ~**do de cerebro** brainwashing. ~**do en seco** dry-cleaning. ~**dora** f washing machine. ~**ndería** f laundry. ~**ndería automática** launderette, laundromat (esp Amer). ~**platos** m & f invar dishwasher. ● m (Mex, fregadero) sink. ~**r** vt wash. ~**r en seco** dry-clean. □ ~**rse** vpr have a wash. ~**rse las manos** (incl fig) wash one's hands. ~**tiva** f enema. ~**vajillas** m invar dishwasher; (detergente) washing-up liquid (Brit), dishwashing liquid (Amer)

laxante a & m laxative

lazada f bow

lazarillo m guide for a blind person

lazo m knot; (lazada) bow; (fig, vínculo) tie; (con nudo corredizo) lasso; (Mex, cuerda) rope

le pron (acusativo, él) him; (acusativo, Vd) you; (dativo, él) (to) him; (dativo, ella) (to) her; (dativo, cosa) (to) it; (dativo, Vd) (to) you

leal a loyal; (fiel) faithful. ~**tad** f loyalty; (fidelidad) faithfulness

lección f lesson

leche f milk; (golpe) bash. ~ **condensada** condensed milk. ~ **desnatada** skimmed milk. ~ **en polvo** powdered milk. ~ **sin desnatar** whole milk. **tener mala** ~ be spiteful. ~**ra** f (vasija) milk jug. ~**ría** f dairy. ~**ro** a milk, dairy. ● m milkman

lecho m (en literatura) bed. ~ **de río** river bed

lechoso a milky

lechuga f lettuce

lechuza f owl

lect|or m reader; (Univ) language assistant. ~**ura** f reading

leer [18] vt/i read

legación f legation

legado m legacy; (enviado) legate

legajo m bundle, file

legal a legal. ~**idad** f legality. ~**izar** [10] vt legalize; (certificar) authenticate. ~**mente** adv legally

legar [12] vt bequeath

legible *a* legible

legi|ón *f* legion. ∿**onario** *m* legionary

legisla|ción *f* legislation. ∿**dor** *m* legislator. ∿**r** *vi* legislate. ∿**tura** *f* term (of office); (año parlamentario) session; (LAm, cuerpo) legislature

leg|itimidad *f* legitimacy. ∿**ítimo** *a* legitimate; (verdadero) real

lego *a* lay; (ignorante) ignorant. ● *m* layman

legua *f* league

legumbre *f* vegetable

lejan|ía *f* distance. ∿**o** *a* distant

lejía *f* bleach

lejos *adv* far. ∿ **de** far from. **a lo** ∿ in the distance. **desde** ∿ from a distance, from afar

lema *m* motto

lencería *f* linen; (de mujer) lingerie

lengua *f* tongue; (idioma) language. **irse de la** ∿ talk too much. **morderse la** ∿ hold one's tongue

lenguado *m* sole

lenguaje *m* language

lengüeta *f* (de zapato) tongue. ∿**da** *f*, ∿**zo** *m* lick

lente *f* lens. ∿**s** *mpl* glasses. ∿**s de contacto** contact lenses

lentej|a *f* lentil. ∿**uela** *f* sequin

lentilla *f* contact lens

lent|itud *f* slowness. ∿**o** *a* slow

leñ|a *f* firewood. ∿**ador** *m* woodcutter. ∿**o** *m* log

Leo *m* Leo

le|ón *m* lion. ∿**ona** *f* lioness

leopardo *m* leopard

leotardo *m* thick tights

lepr|a *f* leprosy. ∿**oso** *m* leper

lerdo *a* dim; (torpe) clumsy

les *pron* (acusativo) them; (acusativo, Vds) you; (dativo) (to) them; (dativo, Vds) (to) you

lesbiana *f* lesbian

lesi|ón *f* wound. ∿**onado** *a* injured. ∿**onar** *vt* injure; (dañar) damage

letal *a* lethal

let|árgico *a* lethargic. ∿**argo** *m* lethargy

letr|a *f* letter; (escritura) handwriting; (de una canción) words, lyrics. ∿**a de** cambio bill of exchange. ∿**a de imprenta** print. ∿**ado** *a* learned. ∿**ero** *m* notice; (cartel) poster

letrina *f* latrine

leucemia *f* leukaemia

levadura *f* yeast. ∿ **en polvo** baking powder

levanta|miento *m* lifting; (sublevación) uprising. ∿**r** *vt* raise, lift; (construir) build; (recoger) pick up. □ ∿**rse** *vpr* get up; (ponerse de pie) stand up; (erguirse, sublevarse) rise up

levante *m* east; (viento) east wind

levar *vt.* ∿ **anclas** weigh anchor

leve *a* light; <sospecha etc> slight; <enfermedad> mild; (de poca importancia) trivial. ∿**dad** *f* lightness; (fig) slightness

léxico *m* vocabulary

lexicografía *f* lexicography

ley *f* law; (parlamentaria) act

leyenda *f* legend

liar [20] *vt* tie; (envolver) wrap up; roll <cigarrillo>; (fig, confundir) confuse; (fig, enredar) involve. □ ∿**se** *vpr* get involved

libanés *a & m* Lebanese

libelo *m* (escrito) libellous article; (Jurid) petition

libélula *f* dragonfly

libera|ción *f* liberation. ∿**dor** *a* liberating. ● *m* liberator

liberal *a & m & f* liberal. ∿**idad** *f* liberality

liber|ar *vt* free. ∿**tad** *f* freedom. ∿**tad de cultos** freedom of worship. ∿**tad de imprenta** freedom of the press. ∿**tad provisional** bail. **en** ∿**tad** free. ∿**tador** *m* liberator. ∿**tar** *vt* free

libertino *m* libertine

libido *f* libido

libio *a & m* Libyan

libra *f* pound. ∿ **esterlina** pound sterling

Libra *m* Libra

libra|dor *m* (Com) drawer. ∿**r** *vt* free; (de un peligro) save. □ ∿**rse** *vpr* free o.s. ∿**rse de** get rid of

libre *a* free. **estilo** ∿ (en natación) freestyle. ∿ **de impuestos** tax-free

librea *f* livery

libr|ería f bookshop (Brit), bookstore (Amer); (mueble) bookcase. **~ero** m bookseller; (Mex, mueble) bookcase. **~eta** f notebook. **~o** m book. **~o de bolsillo** paperback. **~o de ejercicios** exercise book. **~o de reclamaciones** complaints book

licencia f permission; (documento) licence. **~do** m graduate; (Mex, abogado) lawyer. **~ para manejar** (Mex) driving licence. **~r** vt (Mil) discharge; (echar) dismiss. **~tura** f degree

licencioso a licentious

licitar vt bid for

lícito a legal; (permisible) permissible

licor m liquor; (dulce) liqueur

licua|dora f blender. **~r** [21] liquefy; (Culin) blend

lid f fight. **en buena ~** by fair means. **~es** fpl matters

líder m leader

liderato m, **liderazgo** m leadership

lidia f bullfighting; (lucha) fight. **~r** vt/i fight

liebre f hare

lienzo m linen; (del pintor) canvas; (muro, pared) wall

liga f garter; (alianza) league; (LAm, goma) rubber band. **~dura** f bond; (Mus) slur; (Med) ligature. **~mento** m ligament. **~r** [12] vt bind; (atar) tie; (Mus) slur. ● vi mix. **~r con** (fig) pick up. □ **~rse** vpr (fig) commit o.s.

liger|eza f lightness; (agilidad) agility; (rapidez) swiftness; (de carácter) fickleness. **~o** a light; (rápido) quick; (ágil) agile; (superficial) superficial; (de poca importancia) slight. ● adv quickly. **a la ~a** lightly, superficially

liguero m suspender belt

lija f dogfish; (papel de lija) sandpaper. **~r** vt sand

lila f lilac. ● m (color) lilac

lima f file; (fruta) lime. **~duras** fpl filings. **~r** vt file (down)

limita|ción f limitation. **~do** a limited. **~r** vt limit. **~r con** border on. **~tivo** a limiting

límite m limit. **~ de velocidad** speed limit

limítrofe a bordering

lim|ón m lemon; (Mex) lime. **~ona-da** f lemonade

limosn|a f alms. **pedir ~a** beg. **~ear** vi beg

limpia|botas m invar bootblack. **~parabrisas** m invar windscreen wiper (Brit), windshield wiper (Amer). **~pipas** m invar pipe-cleaner. **~r** vt clean; (enjugar) wipe. **~vidrios** m invar (LAm) window cleaner.

limpi|eza f cleanliness; (acción de limpiar) cleaning. **~eza en seco** dry-cleaning. **~o** a clean; <cielo> clear; (fig, honrado) honest; (neto) net. **pasar a ~o**, (LAm) **pasar en ~o** make a fair copy. ● adv fairly. **jugar ~o** play fair

linaje m lineage; (fig, clase) kind

lince m lynx

linchar vt lynch

lind|ar vi border (**con** on). **~e** f boundary. **~ero** m border

lindo a pretty, lovely. **de lo ~** 🆎 a lot

línea f line. **en ~s generales** broadly speaking. **guardar la ~** watch one's figure

lingote m ingot

lingü|ista m & f linguist. **~ística** f linguistics. **~ístico** a linguistic

lino m flax; (tela) linen

linterna f lantern; (de bolsillo) torch, flashlight (Amer)

lío m bundle; (jaleo) fuss; (embrollo) muddle; (amorío) affair

liquida|ción f liquidation; (venta especial) sale. **~r** vt liquify; (Com) liquidate; settle <cuenta>

líquido a liquid; (Com) net. ● m liquid; (Com) cash

lira f lyre; (moneda italiana) lira

líric|a f lyric poetry. **~o** a lyric(al)

lirio m iris

lirón m dormouse; (fig) sleepyhead. **dormir como un ~** sleep like a log

lisiado a crippled

liso a smooth; <pelo> straight; <tierra> flat; (sencillo) plain

lisonj|a f flattery. **~eador** a flattering. ● m flatterer. **~ear** vt flatter. **~ero** a flattering

lista f stripe; (enumeración) list. **~ de correos** poste restante. **a ~s** striped.

pasar ~ take the register. **~do** *a* striped

listo *a* clever; (preparado) ready

listón *m* strip; (en saltos) bar; (Mex, cinta) ribbon

litera *f* (en barco, tren) berth; (en habitación) bunk bed

literal *a* literal

litera|rio *a* literary. **~tura** *f* literature

litig|ar [12] *vi* dispute; (Jurid) litigate. **~io** *m* dispute; (Jurid) litigation

litografía *f* (arte) lithography; (cuadro) lithograph

litoral *a* coastal. ● *m* coast

litro *m* litre

lituano *a & m* Lithuanian

liturgia *f* liturgy

liviano *a* fickle; (LAm, de poco peso) light

lívido *a* livid

llaga *f* wound; (úlcera) ulcer

llama *f* flame; (animal) llama

llamada *f* call

llama|do *a* called. ● *m* (LAm) call. **~miento** *m* call. **~r** *vt* call; (por teléfono) phone. ● *vi* call; (golpear en la puerta) knock; (tocar el timbre) ring. **~r por teléfono** phone, telephone. □ **~rse** *vpr* be called. **¿cómo te ~s?** what's your name?

llamarada *f* sudden blaze; (fig, de pasión etc) outburst

llamativo *a* flashy; *<color>* loud; *<persona>* striking

llamear *vi* blaze

llano *a* flat, level; *<persona>* natural; (sencillo) plain. ● *m* plain

llanta *f* (Auto) (wheel) rim; (LAm, neumático) tyre

llanto *m* crying

llanura *f* plain

llave *f* key; (para tuercas) spanner; (LAm, del baño etc) tap (Brit), faucet (Amer); (Elec) switch. ~ **inglesa** monkey wrench. **cerrar con ~** lock. **echar la ~** lock up. **~ro** *m* key-ring

llega|da *f* arrival. **~r** [12] *vi* arrive, come; (alcanzar) reach; (bastar) be enough. **~r a** (conseguir) manage to. **~r a saber** find out. **~r a ser** become. **~r hasta** go as far as

llen|ar *vt* fill (up); (rellenar) fill in; (cubrir) cover (de with). **~o** *a* full. ● *m* (en el teatro etc) full house. **de ~** entirely

lleva|dero *a* tolerable. **~r** *vt* carry; (inducir, conducir) lead; (acompañar) take; wear *<ropa>*. **¿cuánto tiempo ~s aquí?** how long have you been here? **llevo 3 años estudiando inglés** I've been studying English for 3 years. □ **~rse** *vpr* take away; win *<premio etc>*; (comprar) take. **~rse bien** get on well together

llor|ar *vi* cry; *<ojos>* water. **~iquear** *vi* whine. **~iqueo** *m* whining. **~o** *m* crying. **~ón** *a* whining. ● *m* crybaby. **~oso** *a* tearful

llov|er [2] *vi* rain. **~izna** *f* drizzle. **~iznar** *vi* drizzle

llueve *vb* ⇒LLOVER

lluvi|a *f* rain; (fig) shower. **~oso** *a* rainy; *<clima>* wet

lo *art def neutro*. ~ **importante** what is important, the important thing. ● *pron* (él) him; (cosa) it. ~ **que** what, that which

loa *f* praise. **~ble** *a* praiseworthy. **~r** *vt* praise

lobo *m* wolf

lóbrego *a* gloomy

lóbulo *m* lobe

local *a* local. ● *m* premises. **~idad** *f* locality; (de un espectáculo) seat; (entrada) ticket. **~izar** [10] *vt* find, locate

loción *f* lotion

loco *a* mad, crazy. ● *m* lunatic. ~ **de alegría** mad with joy. **estar ~ por** be crazy about. **volverse ~** go mad

locomo|ción *f* locomotion. **~tora** *f* locomotive

locuaz *a* talkative

locución *f* expression

locura *f* madness; (acto) crazy thing. **con ~** madly

locutor *m* broadcaster

lod|azal *m* quagmire. **~o** *m* mud

lógic|a *f* logic. **~o** *a* logical

logr|ar *vt* get; win *<premio>*. ~ **hacer** manage to do. **~o** *m* achievement; (de premio) winning; (éxito) success

loma *f* small hill

lombriz *f* worm

lomo *m* back; (de libro) spine. ~ de cerdo loin of pork

lona *f* canvas

loncha *f* slice; (de tocino) rasher

londinense *a* from London. ● *m* Londoner

Londres *m* London

loneta *f* thin canvas

longaniza *f* sausage

longev|idad *f* longevity. ~o *a* long-lived

longitud *f* length; (Geog) longitude

lonja *f* slice; (de tocino) rasher; (Com) market

lord *m* (*pl* **lores**) lord

loro *m* parrot

los *art def mpl* the. *véase tb* EL. ● *pron* them. ~ de Antonio Antonio's. ~ que whoever, the ones

losa *f* (baldosa) flagstone. ~ sepulcral tombstone

lote *m* share; (de productos) batch; (terreno) plot (Brit), lot (Amer)

lotería *f* lottery

loto *m* lotus

loza *f* crockery; (fina) china

lozano *a* fresh; <vegetación> lush; <persona> healthy-looking

lubrica|nte *a* lubricating. ● *m* lubricant. ~r [7] *vt* lubricate

lucero *m* bright star. ~ del alba morning star

lucha *f* fight; (fig) struggle. ~dor *m* fighter. ~r *vi* fight; (fig) struggle

lucid|ez *f* lucidity. ~o *a* splendid

lúcido *a* lucid

luciérnaga *f* glow-worm

lucimiento *m* brilliance

lucir [11] *vt* (fig) show off. ● *vi* shine; <joya> sparkle; (LAm, mostrarse) look. □ ~se *vpr* (fig) shine, excel; (presumir) show off

lucr|ativo *a* lucrative. ~o *m* gain

luego *adv* then; (más tarde) later (on); (Mex, pronto) soon. ● *conj* therefore. ~ que as soon as. desde ~ of course

lugar *m* place; (espacio libre) room. ~ común cliché. dar ~ a give rise to. en ~ de instead of. en primer ~ first. hacer ~ make room. tener ~ take place. ~eño *a* local, village

lugarteniente *m* deputy

lúgubre *a* gloomy

lujo *m* luxury. de ~ luxury. ~so *a* luxurious

lujuria *f* lust

lumbago *m* lumbago

lumbre *f* fire; (luz) light

luminoso *a* luminous; (fig) bright; <letrero> illuminated

luna *f* moon; (espejo) mirror. ~ de miel honeymoon. claro de ~ moonlight. estar en la ~ be miles away. ~r *a* lunar. ● *m* mole; (en tela) spot

lunes *m invar* Monday

lupa *f* magnifying glass

lustr|abotas *m invar* (LAm) bootblack. ~ar *vt* shine, polish. ~e *m* shine; (fig, esplendor) splendour. dar ~e a, sacar ~e a polish. ~oso *a* shining

luto *m* mourning. estar de ~ be in mourning

luz *f* light; (electricidad) electricity. luces altas (LAm) headlights on full beam. luces bajas (LAm), luces cortas dipped headlights. luces antiniebla fog light. luces largas headlights on full beam. a la ~ de in the light of. a todas luces obviously. dar a ~ give birth. hacer la ~ sobre shed light on. sacar a la ~ bring to light

M m

macabro *a* macabre

macaco *m* macaque (monkey)

macanudo *a* 🏴 great🏴

macarrones *mpl* macaroni

macerar *vt* macerate <fruta>; marinade <carne etc>

maceta *f* mallet; (tiesto) flowerpot

machacar [7] *vt* crush. ● *vi* go on (sobre about)

machamartillo. a ~ *adj* ardent; (como adv) firmly

machet|azo *m* blow with a machete; (herida) wound from a machete. ~e *m* machete

mach|ista *m* male chauvinist. ∼**o** *a* male; (varonil) macho

machu|car [7] *vt* bruise; (aplastar) crush. ∼**cón** *m* (LAm) bruise

macizo *a* solid. ● *m* mass; (de plantas) bed

madeja *f* skein

madera *m* (vino) Madeira. ● *f* wood; (naturaleza) nature. ∼**ble** *a* yielding timber. ∼**men** *m* woodwork

madero *m* log; (de construcción) timber

madona *f* Madonna

madr|astra *f* stepmother. ∼**e** *f* mother. ∼**eperla** *f* mother-of-pearl. ∼**eselva** *f* honeysuckle

madrigal *m* madrigal

madriguera *f* den; (de conejo) burrow

madrileño *a* of Madrid. ● *m* person from Madrid

madrina *f* godmother; (en una boda) matron of honour

madrug|ada *f* dawn. de ∼ada at dawn. ∼**ador** *a* who gets up early. ● *m* early riser. ∼**ar** [12] *vi* get up early

madur|ación *f* maturing; (de fruta) ripening. ∼**ar** *vt/i* mature; <fruta> ripen. ∼**ez** *f* maturity; (de fruta) ripeness. ∼**o** *a* mature; <fruta> ripe

maestr|ía *f* skill; (Univ) master's degree. ∼**o** *m* master; (de escuela) schoolteacher

mafia *f* mafia

magdalena *f* fairy cake (Brit), cup cake (Amer)

magia *f* magic

mágico *a* magic; (maravilloso) magical

magist|erio *m* teaching (profession); (conjunto de maestros) teachers. ∼**rado** *m* magistrate; (juez) judge. ∼**ral** *a* teaching; (bien hecho) masterly. ∼**ratura** *f* magistracy

magn|animidad *f* magnanimity. ∼**ánimo** *a* magnanimous. ∼**ate** *m* magnate, tycoon

magnavoz *m* (Mex) megaphone

magnético *a* magnetic

magneti|smo *m* magnetism. ∼**zar** [10] *vt* magnetize

magn|ificar *vt* extol; (LAm) magnify <objeto>. ∼**ificencia** *f* magnificence. ∼**ífico** *a* magnificent. ∼**itud** *f* magnitude

magnolia *f* magnolia

mago *m* magician; (en cuentos) wizard

magro *a* lean; <tierra> poor

magulla|dura *f* bruise. ∼**r** *vt* bruise. □ ∼**rse** *vpr* bruise

mahometano *a* Islamic

maíz *m* maize, corn (Amer)

majada *f* sheepfold; (estiércol) manure; (LAm) flock of sheep

majader|ía *f* silly thing. ∼**o** *m* idiot. ● *a* stupid

majest|ad *f* majesty. ∼**uoso** *a* majestic

majo *a* nice

mal *adv* badly; (poco) poorly; (difícilmente) hardly; (equivocadamente) wrongly; (desagradablemente) bad. ● *a*. **estar** ∼ be ill; (anímicamente) be in a bad way; (incorrecto) be wrong. **estar** ∼ **de** (escaso de) be short of. *véase tb* MALO. ● *m* evil; (daño) harm; (enfermedad) illness. ∼ **que bien** somehow (or other). **de** ∼ **en peor** from bad to worse. **hacer** ∼ **en** be wrong to. **¡menos** ∼**!** thank goodness!

malabaris|mo *m* juggling. ∼**ta** *m* & *f* juggler

mala|consejado *a* ill-advised. ∼**costumbrado** *a* spoilt. ∼**crianza** *f* (LAm) rudeness. ∼**gradecido** *a* ungrateful

malagueño *a* of Málaga. ● *m* person from Málaga

malaria *f* malaria

Malasia *f* Malaysia

malavenido *a* incompatible

malaventura *a* unfortunate

malayo *a* Malay(an)

malbaratar *vt* sell off cheap; (malgastar) squander

malcarado *a* nasty looking

malcriado *a* <niño> spoilt

maldad *f* evil; (acción) wicked thing

maldecir [46] (*pero imperativo* **maldice**, *futuro y condicional regulares, pp* **maldecido** *o* **maldito**) *vt* curse. ● *vi* curse; speak ill (**de** of)

maldi|ciente *a* backbiting; (que blasfema) foul-mouthed. **∼ción** *f* curse. **∼to** *a* damned. **¡∼to sea!** damn (it)!

maleab|ilidad *f* malleability. **∼le** *a* malleable

malea|nte *m* criminal. **∼r** *vt* damage; (pervertir) corrupt. □ **∼rse** *vpr* be spoilt; (pervertirse) be corrupted

malecón *m* breakwater; (embarcadero) jetty; (Rail) embankment; (LAm, paseo marítimo) seafront

maledicencia *f* slander

mal|eficio *m* curse. **∼éfico** *a* evil

malestar *m* discomfort; (fig) uneasiness

malet|a *f* (suit)case. **hacer la ∼a** pack (one's case). **∼ero** *m* porter; (Auto) boot, trunk (Amer). **∼ín** *m* small case; (para documentos) briefcase

mal|evolencia *f* malevolence. **∼évolo** *a* malevolent

maleza *f* weeds; (matorral) undergrowth

mal|gastar *vt* waste. **∼hablado** *a* foul-mouthed. **∼hechor** *m* criminal. **∼humorado** *a* bad-tempered

malici|a *f* malice; (picardía) mischief. □ **∼arse** *vpr* suspect. **∼oso** *a* malicious; (pícaro) mischievous

maligno *a* malignant; *<persona>* evil

malintencionado *a* malicious

malla *f* mesh; (de armadura) mail; (de gimnasia) leotard

Mallorca *f* Majorca.

mallorquín *a & m* Majorcan

malmirado *a* (con estar) frowned upon

malo *a* (*delante de nombre masculino en singular* **mal**) bad; (enfermo) ill. **∼ de** difficult to. **estar de malas** (malhumorado) be in a bad mood; (LAm, con mala suerte) be out of luck. **lo ∼ es que** the trouble is that. **por las malas** by force

malogr|ar *vt* waste; (estropear) spoil. □ **∼arse** *vpr* fall through

maloliente *a* smelly

malpensado *a* nasty, malicious

malsano *a* unhealthy

malsonante *a* ill-sounding; (grosero) offensive

malt|a *f* malt. **∼eada** *f* (LAm) milk shake. **∼ear** *vt* malt

maltr|atar *vt* ill-treat; (pegar) batter; mistreat *<juguete etc>*. **∼echo** *a* battered

malucho *a* 🄘 under the weather

malva *f* mallow. (**color de**) **∼** *a invar* mauve

malvado *a* wicked

malvavisco *m* marshmallow

malversa|ción *f* embezzlement. **∼dor** *a* embezzling. ● *m* embezzler. **∼r** *vt* embezzle

Malvinas *fpl.* **las (islas) ∼** the Falklands, the Falkland Islands

mama *f* mammary gland; (de mujer) breast

mamá *f* mum; (usado por niños) mummy

mama|da *f* sucking. **∼r** *vt* suck; (fig) grow up with. ● *vi* *<bebé>* feed; *<animal>* suckle. **dar de ∼** breastfeed

mamario *a* mammary

mamarracho *m* clown; (cosa ridícula) (ridiculous) sight; (cosa mal hecha) botch; (cosa fea) mess. **ir hecho un ∼** look a sight

mameluco *m* (LAm) overalls; (de niño) rompers

mamífero *a* mammalian. ● *m* mammal

mamila *f* (Mex) feeding bottle

mamotreto *m* (libro) hefty volume; (armatoste) huge thing

mampara *f* screen

mampostería *f* masonry

mamut *m* mammoth

manada *f* herd; (de lobos) pack; (de leones) pride. **en ∼** in crowds

mana|ntial *m* spring; (fig) source. **∼r** *vi* flow; (fig) abound. ● *vt* drip with

manaza *f* big hand

mancha *f* stain; (en la piel) blotch. **∼do** *a* stained; (sucio) dirty; *<animal>* spotted. **∼r** *vt* stain; (ensuciar) dirty. □ **∼rse** *vpr* get stained; (ensuciarse) get dirty

manchego *a* of la Mancha. ● *m* person from la Mancha

manchón *m* large stain

mancilla *f* blemish. **~r** *vt* stain

manco *a* (de una mano) one-handed; (de las dos manos) handless; (de un brazo) one-armed; (de los dos brazos) armless

mancomun|adamente *adv* jointly. **~ar** *vt* unite; (Jurid) make jointly liable. □ **~arse** *vpr* unite. **~idad** *f* union

manda *f* (Mex) religious offering

manda|dero *m* messenger. **~do** *m* (LAm) shopping; (diligencia) errand. **hacer los ~dos** (LAm) do the shopping. **~miento** *m* order; (Relig) commandment. **~r** *vt* order; (enviar) send; (gobernar) rule. ● *vi* be in command. **¿mande?** (Mex) pardon?

mandarin|a *f* (naranja) mandarin (orange). **~o** *m* mandarin tree

mandat|ario *m* attorney; (Pol) head of state. **~o** *m* mandate; (Pol) term of office

mandíbula *f* jaw

mando *m* command. **~ a distancia** remote control. **al ~ de** in charge of. **altos ~s** *mpl* high-ranking officers

mandolina *f* mandolin

mandón *a* bossy

manducar [7] *vt* 🄳 stuff oneself with

manecilla *f* hand

manej|able *a* manageable. **~ar** *vt* use; handle *<asunto etc>*; (fig) manage; (LAm, conducir) drive. □ **~arse** *vpr* get by. **~o** *m* handling. **~os** *mpl* scheming

manera *f* way. **~s** *fpl* manners. **de alguna ~** somehow. **de ~ que** so (that). **de ninguna ~** by no means. **de otra ~** otherwise. **de todas ~s** anyway

manga *f* sleeve; (tubo de goma) hose; (red) net; (para colar) filter; (LAm, de langostas) swarm

mango *m* handle; (fruta) mango. **~near** *vt* boss about. ● *vi* (entrometerse) interfere

manguera *f* hose(pipe)

manguito *m* muff

maní *m* (*pl* **~es**) (LAm) peanut

manía *f* mania; (antipatía) dislike. **tener la ~ de** have an obsession with

maniaco *a*, **maníaco** *a* maniac (al). ● *m* maniac

maniatar *vt* tie s.o.'s hands

maniático *a* maniac(al); (obsesivo) obsessive; (loco) crazy; (delicado) finicky

manicomio *m* lunatic asylum

manicura *f* manicure; (mujer) manicurist

manido *a* stale

manifesta|ción *f* manifestation, sign; (Pol) demonstration. **~nte** *m* demonstrator. **~r** [1] *vt* show; (Pol) state. □ **~rse** *vpr* show; (Pol) demonstrate

manifiesto *a* clear; *<error>* obvious; *<verdad>* manifest. ● *m* manifesto

manilargo *a* light-fingered

manilla *f* (de cajón etc) handle; (de reloj) hand. **~r** *m* handlebar(s)

maniobra *f* manoeuvre. **~r** *vt* operate; (Rail) shunt. ● *vt/i* manoeuvre. **~s** *fpl* (Mil) manoeuvres

manipula|ción *f* manipulation. **~r** *vt* manipulate

maniquí *m* dummy. ● *m & f* model

mani|rroto *a & m* spendthrift. **~ta** *f*, (LAm) **~to** *m* little hand

manivela *f* crank

manjar *m* delicacy

mano *f* hand; (de animales) front foot; (de perros, gatos) front paw. **~ de obra** work force. **~s arriba!** hands up! **a ~** by hand; (próximo) handy. **a ~ derecha** on the right. **de segunda ~** second hand. **echar una ~** lend a hand. **tener buena ~ para** be good at. ● *m* (LAm, 🄳) mate (Brit), buddy (Amer)

manojo *m* bunch

manose|ar *vt* handle. **~o** *m* handling

manotada *f*, **manotazo** *m* slap

manote|ar *vi* gesticulate. **~o** *m* gesticulation

mansalva: **a ~** *adv* without risk

mansarda *f* attic

mansión *f* mansion. **~ señorial** stately home

manso *a* gentle; *<animal>* tame

manta *f* blanket

mantec|a *f* fat. **~oso** *a* greasy

mantel m tablecloth; (del altar) altar cloth. ~ería f table linen

manten|er [40] vt support; (conservar) keep; (sostener) maintain. □ ~erse vpr support o.s.; (permanecer) remain. ~se de/con live off. ~imiento m maintenance

mantequ|era f butter churn. ~illa f butter

mant|illa f mantilla. ~o m cloak. ~ón m shawl

manual a & m manual

manubrio m crank; (LAm, de bicicleta) handlebars

manufactura f manufacture. ~r vt manufacture, make

manuscrito a handwritten. ● m manuscript

manutención f maintenance

manzana f apple; (de edificios) block. ~ de Adán (LAm) Adam's apple. ~r m (apple) orchard

manzan|illa f camomile tea. ● m manzanilla, pale dry sherry. ~o m apple tree

maña f skill. ~s fpl cunning

mañan|a f morning. ~a por la ~a tomorrow morning. pasado ~a the day after tomorrow. en la ~a (LAm), por la ~a in the morning. ● m future. ● adv tomorrow. ~ero a who gets up early. ● m early riser

mañoso a clever; (astuto) crafty; (LAm, caprichoso) difficult

mapa m map

mapache m racoon

maqueta f scale model

maquiladora f (Mex) cross-border assembly plant

maquilla|je m make-up. ~r vt make up. □ ~rse vpr make up

máquina f machine; (Rail) engine. ~ de afeitar shaver. ~ de escribir typewriter. ~ fotográfica camera

maquin|ación f machination. ~al a mechanical. ~aria f machinery. ~ista m & f operator; (Rail) engine driver

mar m & f sea. alta ~ high seas. la ~ de Ⅱ lots of

maraña f thicket; (enredo) tangle; (embrollo) muddle

maratón m & f marathon

maravill|a f wonder. a las mil ~as, de ~as marvellously. contar/decir ~as de speak wonderfully of. hacer ~as work wonders. ~ar vt astonish. □ ~arse vpr be astonished (de at). ~oso a marvellous, wonderful

marca f mark; (de coches etc) make; (de alimentos, cosméticos) brand; (Deportes) record. ~ de fábrica trade mark. de ~ brand name; (fig) excellent. de ~ mayor Ⅱ absolute. ~do a marked. ~dor m marker; (Deportes) scoreboard. ~r [7] vt mark; (señalar) show; score <un gol>; dial <número de teléfono>. ● vi score

marcha f (incl Mus) march; (Auto) gear; (desarrollo) course; (partida) departure. a toda ~ at full speed. dar/hacer ~ atrás put into reverse. poner en ~ start; (fig) set in motion

marchante m (f **marchanta**) art dealer; (Mex, en mercado) stall holder

marchar vi go; (funcionar) work, go; (Mil) march. □ ~se vpr leave

marchit|ar vt wither. □ ~arse vpr wither. ~o a withered

marcial a martial

marciano a & m Martian

marco m frame; (moneda alemana) mark; (deportes) goal-posts

marea f tide. ~do a sick; (en el mar) seasick; (aturdido) dizzy; (borracho) drunk. ~r vt make feel sick; (aturdir) make feel dizzy; (confundir) confuse. □ ~rse vpr feel sick; (en un barco) get seasick; (estar aturdido) feel dizzy; (irse la cabeza) feel faint; (emborracharse) get slightly drunk; (confundirse) get confused

marejada f swell; (fig) wave

mareo m sickness; (en el mar) seasickness; (aturdimiento) dizziness; (confusión) muddle

marfil m ivory

margarina f margarine

margarita f daisy; (cóctel) margarita

marg|en m margin; (de un camino) side. ● f (de un río) bank. ~inado a excluded. ● m outcast. al ~en (fig) outside. ~inal a marginal. ~inar vt (excluir) exclude; (fijar márgenes) set margins

mariachi *m* (Mex) (música popular de Jalisco) Mariachi music; (conjunto) Mariachi band; (músico) Mariachi musician

maric|a *m* 🏳 sissy 🏳. **~ón** *m* 🏳 homosexual, queer 🏳; (LAm, cobarde) wimp

marido *m* husband

mariguana *f*, **marihuana** *f* marijuana

marimacho *f* mannish woman

marimba *f* (type of) drum (LAm, especie de xilofón) marimba

marin|a *f* navy; (barcos) fleet; (cuadro) seascape. **~a de guerra** navy. **~a mercante** merchant navy. **~ería** *f* seamanship; (marineros) sailors. **~ero** *a* marine; <barco> seaworthy. ● *m* sailor. **a la ~era** in tomato and garlic sauce. **~o** *a* marine

marioneta *f* puppet. **~s** *fpl* puppet show

maripos|a *f* butterfly. **~a nocturna** moth. **~ear** *vi* be fickle; (galantear) flirt. **~ón** *m* flirt

mariquita *f* ladybird (Brit), ladybug (Amer). ● *m* 🏳 sissy 🏳

mariscador *m* shell-fisher

mariscal *m* marshal

maris|car *vt* fish for shellfish. **~co** *m* seafood, shellfish. **~quero** *m* (pescador de mariscos) seafood fisherman; (vendedor de mariscos) seafood seller

marital *a* marital; <vida> married

marítimo *a* maritime; <ciudad etc> coastal, seaside

marmita *f* cooking pot

mármol *m* marble

marmota *f* marmot

maroma *f* rope; (Mex, voltereta) somersault

marqu|és *m* marquess. **~esa** *f* marchioness. **~esina** *f* glass canopy; (en estadio) roof

marran|a *f* sow. **~ada** *f* filthy thing; (cochinada) dirty trick. **~o** *a* filthy. ● *m* hog

marrón *a* & *m* brown

marroqu|í *a* & *m* & *f* Moroccan. ● *m* (leather) morocco. **~inería** *f* leather goods

Marruecos *m* Morocco

marsopa *f* porpoise

marsupial *a* & *m* marsupial

marta *f* marten

martajar *vt* (Mex) crush <maíz>

Marte *m* Mars

martes *m invar* Tuesday. **~ de carnaval** Shrove Tuesday

martill|ar *vt* hammer. **~azo** *m* blow with a hammer. **~ear** *vt* hammer. **~eo** *m* hammering. **~o** *m* hammer

martín pescador *m* kingfisher

martinete *m* (del piano) hammer; (ave) heron

martingala *f* (ardid) trick

mártir *m* & *f* martyr

martir|io *m* martyrdom; (fig) torment. **~izar** [10] *vt* martyr; (fig) torment, torture

marxis|mo *m* Marxism. **~ta** *a* & *m* & *f* Marxist

marzo *m* March

más *adv* & *a* (comparativo) more; (superlativo) most. **~ caro** dearer. **~ doloroso** more painful. **el ~ caro** the dearest; (de dos) the dearer. **el ~ curioso** the most curious; (de dos) the more curious. ● *prep* plus. ● *m* plus (sign). **~ bien** rather. **~ de** (cantidad indeterminada) more than. **~ o menos** more or less. **~ que** more than. **~ y ~** more and more. **a lo ~** at (the) most. **dos ~ dos** two plus two. **de ~** too many. **es ~** moreover. **nadie ~** nobody else. **no ~** no more

masa *f* mass; (Culin) dough. **en ~** en masse

masacre *f* massacre

masaj|e *m* massage. **~ear** *vt* massage. **~ista** *m* masseur. ● *f* masseuse

mascada *f* (Mex) scarf

mascar [7] *vt* chew

máscara *f* mask

mascar|ada *f* masquerade. **~illa** *f* mask. **~ón** *m* (Naut) figurehead

mascota *f* mascot

masculin|idad f masculinity. ~o a masculine; <sexo> male. ● m masculine

mascullar [3] vt mumble

masilla f putty

masivo a massive, large-scale

mas|ón m Freemason. ~onería f Freemasonry. ~ónico a Masonic

masoquis|mo m masochism. ~ta a masochistic. ● m & f masochist

mastica|ción f chewing. ~r [7] vt chew

mástil m (Naut) mast; (de bandera) flagpole; (de guitarra, violín) neck

mastín m mastiff

mastodonte m mastodon; (fig) giant

masturba|ción f masturbation. □ ~rse vpr masturbate

mata f (arbusto) bush; (LAm, planta) plant

matad|ero m slaughterhouse. ~or a killing. ● m (torero) matador

matamoscas m invar fly swatter

mata|nza f killing. ~r vt kill <personas>; slaughter <reses>. ~rife m butcher. □ ~rse vpr kill o.s.; (en un accidente) be killed; (Mex, para un examen) cram. ~rse trabajando work like mad

mata|polillas m invar moth killer. ~rratas m invar rat poison

matasanos m invar quack

matasellos m invar postmark

mate a matt. ● m (ajedrez) (check) mate (LAm, bebida) maté

matemátic|as fpl mathematics, maths (Brit), math (Amer). ~o a mathematical. ● m mathematician

materia f matter; (material) material; (LAm, asignatura) subject. ~ prima raw material. en ~ de on the question of

material a & m material. ~idad f material nature. ~ismo m materialism. ~ista a materialistic. ● m & f materialist; (Mex, constructor) building contractor. ~izar [10] vt materialize. □ ~izarse vpr materialize. ~mente adv materially; (absolutamente) absolutely

matern|al a maternal; <amor> motherly. ~idad f motherhood; (hospital) maternity hospital; (sala) maternity ward. ~o a motherly; <lengua> mother

matin|al a morning. ~ée m matinée

matiz m shade; (fig) nuance. ~ación f combination of colours. ~ar [10] vt blend <colores>; (introducir variedad) vary; (teñir) tinge (de with)

mat|ón m bully; (de barrio) thug. ~onismo m bullying; (de barrio) thuggery

matorral m scrub; (conjunto de matas) thicket

matraca f rattle. dar ~ pester

matraz m flask

matriarca f matriarch. ~do m matriarchy. ~l a matriarchal

matr|ícula f (lista) register, list; (inscripción) registration; (Auto) registration number; (placa) licence plate. ~icular vt register. □ ~icularse vpr enrol, register

matrimoni|al a matrimonial. ~o m marriage; (pareja) married couple

matriz f matrix; (molde) mould; (Anat) womb, uterus

matrona f matron; (partera) midwife

matutino a morning

maull|ar vi miaow. ~ido m miaow

mausoleo m mausoleum

maxilar a maxillary. ● m jaw(bone)

máxim|a f maxim. ~e adv especially. ~o a maximum; <punto> highest. ● m maximum

maya f daisy. ● a Mayan. ● m & f (persona) Maya

mayo m May

mayonesa f mayonnaise

mayor a (más grande, comparativo) bigger; (más grande, superlativo) biggest; (de edad, comparativo) older; (de edad, superlativo) oldest; (adulto) grown-up; (principal) main, major; (Mus) major. ● m & f (adulto) adult. al por ~ wholesale. ~al m foreman. ~azgo m entailed estate

mayordomo m butler

mayor|ía _f_ majority. **~ista** _m_ & _f_ wholesaler. **~itario** _a_ majority; <_so-cio_> principal. **~mente** _adv_ especially

mayúscul|a _f_ capital (letter). **~o** _a_ capital; (fig, grande) big

mazacote _m_ hard mass

mazapán _m_ marzipan

mazmorra _f_ dungeon

mazo _m_ mallet; (manojo) bunch; (LAm, de naipes) pack (Brit), deck (Amer)

mazorca _f_ cob. **~ de maíz** corncob

me _pron_ (acusativo) me; (dativo) (to) me; (reflexivo) (to) myself

mecánic|a _f_ mechanics. **~o** _a_ mechanical. ● _m_ mechanic

mecani|smo _m_ mechanism. **~za-ción** _f_ mechanization. **~zar** [10] _vt_ mechanize

mecanograf|ía _f_ typing. **~iado** _a_ typed, typewritten. **~iar** [20] _vt_ type

mecanógrafo _m_ typist

mecate _m_ (Mex) string; (más grueso) rope

mecedora _f_ rocking chair

mecenas _m_ & _f invar_ patron

mecer [9] _vt_ rock; swing <_columpio_>. □**~se** _vpr_ rock; (en un columpio) swing

mecha _f_ (de vela) wick; (de explosivo) fuse. **~s** _fpl_ highlights

mechar _vt_ stuff, lard

mechero _m_ (cigarette) lighter

mechón _m_ (de pelo) lock

medall|a _f_ medal. **~ón** _m_ medallion; (relicario) locket

media _f_ stocking; (promedio) average. **a ~s** half each

mediación _f_ mediation

mediado _a_ half full; (a mitad de) halfway through. **~s** _mpl_. **a ~s de marzo** in mid-March

mediador _m_ mediator

medialuna _f_ (_pl_ **mediaslunas**) croissant

median|amente _adv_ fairly. **~a** _f_ (Auto) central reservation (Brit), median strip (Amer). **~era** _f_ party wall. **~ero** _a_ <_muro_> party. **~o** _a_ medium; (mediocre) average, mediocre

medianoche _f_ (_pl_ **mediasno-ches**) midnight; (Culin) _type of roll_

mediante _prep_ through, by means of

mediar _vi_ mediate; (llegar a la mitad) be halfway through; (interceder) intercede (**por** for)

medic|ación _f_ medication. **~amento** _m_ medicine. **~ina** _f_ medicine. **~inal** _a_ medicinal

medición _f_ measurement

médico _a_ medical. ● _m_ doctor. **~ de cabecera** GP, general practitioner

medid|a _f_ measurement; (unidad) measure; (disposición) measure, step; (prudencia) moderation. **a la ~a** made to measure. **a ~a que** as. **en cierta ~a** to a certain extent. **~or** _m_ (LAm) meter

medieval _a_ medieval. **~ista** _m_ & _f_ medievalist

medio _a_ half (a); (mediano) average. **dos horas y media** two and a half hours. **~ litro** half a litre. **las dos y media** half past two. ● _m_ middle; (Math) half; (manera) means; (en deportes) half(-back). **en ~** in the middle (de of). **por ~ de** through. **~ ambiente** _m_ environment

medioambiental _a_ environmental

mediocr|e _a_ mediocre. **~idad** _f_ mediocrity

mediodía _m_ midday, noon; (sur) south

medioevo _m_ Middle Ages

Medio Oriente _m_ Middle East

medir [5] _vt_ measure; weigh up <_palabras etc_>. ● _vi_ measure, be. **¿cuánto mide de alto?** how tall is it? □**~se** _vpr_ (moderarse) measure o.s.; (Mex, probarse) try on

medita|bundo _a_ thoughtful. **~ción** _f_ meditation. **~r** _vt_ think about. ● _vi_ meditate

mediterráneo _a_ Mediterranean

Mediterráneo _m_ Mediterranean

médium _m_ & _f_ medium

médula _f_ marrow

medusa _f_ jellyfish

megáfono _m_ megaphone

megalómano _m_ megalomaniac

mejicano _a_ & _m_ Mexican

Méjico _m_ Mexico

mejilla *f* cheek

mejillón *m* mussel

mejor *a* & *adv* (comparativo) better; (superlativo) best. ~ **dicho** rather. **a lo** ~ perhaps. **tanto** ~ so much the better. ~**a** *f* improvement. ~**able** *a* improvable. ~**amiento** *m* improvement

mejorana *f* marjoram

mejorar *vt* improve, better. ● *vi* get better. □ ~**se** *vpr* get better

mejunje *m* mixture

melanc|olía *f* melancholy. ~**ólico** *a* melancholic

melaza *f* molasses

melen|a *f* long hair; (de león) mane. ~**udo** *a* long-haired

melindr|es *mpl* affectation. **hacer** ~**es con la comida** be picky about food. ~**oso** *a* affected

mellizo *a* & *m* twin

melocot|ón *m* peach. ~**onero** *m* peach tree

mel|odía *f* melody. ~**ódico** *a* melodic. ~**odioso** *a* melodious

melodram|a *m* melodrama. ~**ático** *a* melodramatic

melómano *m* music lover

melón *m* melon

meloso *a* sickly-sweet; *<canción>* slushy

membran|a *f* membrane. ~**oso** *a* membranous

membrete *m* letterhead

membrill|ero *m* quince tree. ~**o** *m* quince

memo *a* stupid. ● *m* idiot

memorable *a* memorable

memorando *m*, **memorándum** *m* notebook; (nota) memorandum, memo

memori|a *f* memory; (informe) report; (tesis) thesis. ~**as** *fpl* (autobiografía) memoirs. **de** ~**a** by heart; *<citar>* from memory. ~**al** *m* memorial. ~**ón** *m* good memory. ~**zación** *f* memorizing. ~**zar** [10] *vt* memorize

menaje *m* household goods. ~ **de cocina** kitchenware

menci|ón *f* mention. ~**onado** *a* aforementioned. ~**onar** *vt* mention

mendi|cidad *f* begging. ~**gar** [12] *vt* beg for. ● *vi* beg. ~**go** *m* beggar

mendrugo *m* piece of stale bread

mene|ar *vt* wag *<rabo>*; shake *<cabeza>*; wiggle *<caderas>*. □ ~**arse** *vpr* move; (con inquietud) fidget; (balancearse) swing. ~**o** *m* movement; *<sacudida>* shake

menester *m* occupation. **ser** ~ be necessary. ~**oso** *a* needy

menestra *f* vegetable stew

mengano *m* so-and-so

mengua *f* decrease; (falta) lack. ~**do** *a* diminished. ~**nte** *a* *<luna>* waning; *<marea>* ebb. ~**r** [15] *vt/i* decrease, diminish

meningitis *f* meningitis

menjurje *m* mixture

menopausia *f* menopause

menor *a* (más pequeño, comparativo) smaller; (más pequeño, superlativo) smallest; (más joven, comparativo) younger; (más joven, superlativo) youngest; (Mus) minor. ● *m* & *f* (menor de edad) minor. **al por** ~ retail

menos *a* (comparativo) less; (comparativo, con plural) fewer; (superlativo) least; (superlativo, con plural) fewest. ● *adv* (comparativo) less; (superlativo) least. ● *prep* except. **al** ~ at least. **a** ~ **que** unless. **las dos** ~ **diez** ten to two. **ni mucho** ~ far from it. **por lo** ~ at least. ~**cabar** *vt* lessen; (fig, estropear) damage. ~**cabo** *m* lessening. ~**preciable** *a* contemptible. ~**preciar** *vt* despise. ~**precio** *m* contempt

mensaje *m* message. ~**ro** *m* messenger

menso *a* (LAm, 🔲) stupid

menstru|ación *f* menstruation. ~**al** *a* menstrual. ~**ar** [21] *vi* menstruate

mensual *a* monthly. ~**idad** *f* monthly pay; (cuota) monthly payment

mensurable *a* measurable

menta *f* mint

mental *a* mental. ~**idad** *f* mentality. ~**mente** *adv* mentally

mentar [1] *vt* mention, name

mente *f* mind

mentecato *a* stupid. ● *m* idiot

mentir [4] *vi* lie. ~**a** *f* lie. ~**ijillas** *fpl.* de ~**ijillas** for a joke. ~**oso** *a* lying. ● *m* liar

mentís *m invar* denial

mentor *m* mentor

menú *m* menu

menud|ear *vi* happen frequently; (Mex, Com) sell retail. ~**encia** *f* trifle. ~**encias** *fpl* (LAm) giblets. ~**eo** *m* (Mex) retail trade. ~**illos** *mpl* giblets. ~**o** *a* small; <*lluvia*> fine. **a** ~**o** often. ~**os** *mpl* giblets

meñique *a* <*dedo*> little. ● *m* little finger

meollo *m* (médula) marrow; (de tema etc) heart

merca|chifle *m* hawker; (fig) profiteer. ~**der** *m* merchant. ~**dería** *f* (LAm) merchandise. ~**do** *m* market. M~**do Común** Common Market. ~**do negro** black market

mercan|cía(s) *f(pl)* goods, merchandise. ~**te** *a* merchant. ● *m* merchant ship. ~**til** *a* mercantile, commercial. ~**tilismo** *m* mercantilism

merced *f* favour. **su/vuestra** ~ your honour

mercenario *a* & *m* mercenary

mercer|ía *f* haberdashery (Brit), notions (Amer). ~**io** *m* mercury

mercurial *a* mercurial

Mercurio *m* Mercury

merec|edor *a* worthy (de of). ~**er** [11] *vt* deserve. □ ~**erse** *vpr* deserve. ~**idamente** *adv* deservedly. ~**ido** *a* well deserved. ~**imiento** *m* (mérito) merit

merend|ar [1] *vt* have as an afternoon snack. ● *vi* have an afternoon snack. ~**ero** *m* snack bar; (lugar) picnic area

merengue *m* meringue

meridi|ano *a* midday; (fig) dazzling. ● *m* meridian. ~**onal** *a* southern. ● *m* southerner

merienda *f* afternoon snack

merino *a* merino

mérito *m* merit; (valor) worth

meritorio *a* praiseworthy. ● *m* unpaid trainee

merluza *f* hake

merma *f* decrease. ~**r** *vt/i* decrease, reduce

mermelada *f* jam

mero *a* mere; (Mex, verdadero) real. ● *adv* (Mex, precisamente) exactly; (Mex, casi) nearly. ● *m* grouper

merode|ador *m* prowler. ~**ar** *vi* prowl

mes *m* month

mesa *f* table; (para escribir o estudiar) desk. **poner la** ~ lay the table

mesarse *vpr* tear at one's hair

meser|a *f* (LAm) waitress. ~**o** *m* (LAm) waiter

meseta *f* plateau; (descansillo) landing

Mesías *m* Messiah

mesilla *f*, **mesita** *f* small table. ~ **de noche** bedside table

mesón *m* inn

mesoner|a *f* landlady. ~**o** *m* landlord

mestiz|aje *m* crossbreeding. ~**o** *a* <*persona*> half-caste; <*animal*> cross-bred. ● *m* (persona) half-caste; (animal) cross-breed

mesura *f* moderation. ~**do** *a* moderate

meta *f* goal; (de una carrera) finish

metabolismo *m* metabolism

metafísic|a *f* metaphysics. ~**o** *a* metaphysical

met|áfora *f* metaphor. ~**afórico** *a* metaphorical

met|al *m* metal; (de la voz) timbre. ~**ales** *mpl* (instrumentos de latón) brass. ~**álico** *a* <*objeto*> metal; <*sonido*> metallic

metal|urgia *f* metallurgy. ~**úrgico** *a* metallurgical

metamorfosis *f invar* metamorphosis

metedura de pata *f* blunder

mete|órico *a* meteoric. ~**orito** *m* meteorite. ~**oro** *m* meteor. ~**orología** *f* meteorology. ~**orológico** *a* meteorological. ~**orólogo** *m* meteorologist

meter *vt* put; score <*un gol*>; (enredar) involve; (causar) make. □ ~**se** *vpr* get involved (**en** in); (entrometerse) meddle. ~se con uno pick a quarrel with s.o.

meticulos|idad f meticulousness. ~o a meticulous

metida de pata f (LAm) blunder

metido m reprimand. ● a. ~ en años getting on. estar ~ en algo be involved in sth. estar muy ~ con uno be well in with s.o.

metódico a methodical

metodis|mo m Methodism. ~ta a & m & f Methodist

método m method

metodología f methodology

metraje m length. de largo ~ <película> feature

metrall|a f shrapnel. ~eta f submachine gun

métric|a f metrics. ~o a metric; <verso> metrical

metro m metre; (tren) underground (Brit), subway (Amer). ~ cuadrado square metre

metrónomo m metronome

metr|ópoli f metropolis. ~opolitano a metropolitan. ● m metropolitan; (tren) underground (Brit), subway (Amer)

mexicano a & m Mexican

México m Mexico. ~ D. F. Mexico City

mezcal m (Mex) mescal

mezc|la f (acción) mixing; (substancia) mixture; (argamasa) mortar. ~lador m mixer. ~lar vt mix; shuffle <los naipes>. □ ~larse vpr mix; (intervenir) interfere. ~olanza f mixture

mezquin|dad f meanness. ~o a mean; (escaso) meagre. ● m mean person

mezquita f mosque

mi a my. ● m (Mus) E; (solfa) mi

mí pron me

miau m miaow

mica f (silicato) mica

mico m (long-tailed) monkey

microbio m microbe

micro|biología f microbiology. ~cosmos m invar microcosm. ~film(e) m microfilm

micrófono m microphone

microonda f microwave. ~s m invar microwave oven

microordenador m microcomputer

micros|cópico a microscopic. ~copio m microscope. ~urco m long-playing record

miedo m fear (a for). dar ~ frighten. morirse de ~ be scared to death. tener ~ be frightened. ~so a fearful

miel f honey

miembro m limb; (persona) member

mientras conj while. ● adv meanwhile. ~ que whereas. ~ tanto in the meantime

miércoles m invar Wednesday. ~ de ceniza Ash Wednesday

mierda f (vulgar) shit

mies f ripe, grain

miga f crumb; (fig, meollo) essence. ~jas fpl crumbs; (sobras) scraps. ~r [12] vt crumble

migra|ción f migration. ~torio a migratory

mijo m millet

mil a & m a/one thousand. ~es de thousands of. ~ novecientos noventa y nueve nineteen ninety-nine. ~ pesetas a thousand pesetas

milagro m miracle. ~so a miraculous

milen|ario a millenial. ~io m millennium

milésimo a & m thousandth

mili f [I] military service. ~cia f soldiering; (gente armada) militia

mili|gramo m milligram. ~litro m millilitre

milímetro m millimetre

militante a & m & f activist

militar a military. ● m soldier. ~ismo m militarism. ~ista a militaristic. ● m & f militarist. ~izar [10] vt militarize

milla f mile

millar m thousand. a ~es by the thousand

mill|ón m million. un ~ón de libros a million books. ~onada f fortune. ~onario m millionaire. ~onésimo a & m millionth

milonga *f popular dance and music from the River Plate region*

milpa *f* (Mex) maize field, cornfield (Amer)

milpies *m invar* woodlouse

mimar *vt* spoil

mimbre *m & f* wicker. □ ~**arse** *vpr* sway. ~**ra** *f* osier. ~**ral** *m* osier-bed

mimetismo *m* mimicry

mímic|a *f* mime. ~**o** *a* mimic

mimo *m* mime; (*a un niño*) spoiling; (*caricia*) cuddle

mimosa *f* mimosa

mina *f* mine. ~**r** *vt* mine; (fig) undermine

minarete *m* minaret

mineral *m* mineral; (*mena*) ore. ~**ogía** *f* mineralogy. ~**ogista** *m & f* mineralogist

miner|ía *f* mining. ~**o** *a* mining. ● *m* miner

miniatura *f* miniature

minifundio *m* smallholding

minimizar [10] *vt* minimize

mínim|o *a & m* minimum. **como** ~ at least. ~**um** *m* minimum

minino *m* 🔢 cat, puss 🔢

minist|erial *a* ministerial; <*reunión*> cabinet. ~**erio** *m* ministry. ~**ro** *m* minister

minor|ía *f* minority. ~**idad** *f* minority. ~**ista** *m & f* retailer

minuci|a *f* trifle. ~**osidad** *f* thoroughness. ~**oso** *a* thorough; (*detallado*) detailed

minúscul|a *f* lower case letter. ~**o** *a* tiny

minuta *f* draft copy; (*de abogado*) bill

minut|ero *m* minute hand. ~**o** *m* minute

mío *a & pron* mine. **un amigo** ~ a friend of mine

miop|e *a* short-sighted. ● *m & f* short-sighted person. ~**ía** *f* short-sightedness

mira *f* sight; (fig, *intención*) aim. **a la** ~ on the lookout. **con** ~**s a** with a view to. ~**da** *f* look. **echar una** ~**da a** glance at. ~**do** *a* careful with money; (*comedido*) considerate. **bien** ~**do** highly regarded. **no estar bien** ~**do** be frowned upon. ~**dor** *m*

viewpoint. ~**miento** *m* consideration. ~**r** *vt* look at; (*observar*) watch; (*considerar*) consider. ~**r fijamente a** stare at. ● *vi* look <*edificio etc*>. ~ **hacia** face. □ ~**rse** *vpr* <*personas*> look at each other

mirilla *f* peephole

miriñaque *m* crinoline

mirlo *m* blackbird

mirón *a* nosey. ● *m* nosey-parker; (*espectador*) onlooker

mirto *m* myrtle

misa *f* mass. ~**l** *m* missal

misántropo *m* misanthropist

miscelánea *f* miscellany; (Mex, *tienda*) corner shop (Brit), small general store (Amer)

miser|able *a* very poor; (*lastimoso*) miserable; (*tacaño*) mean. ~**ia** *f* extreme poverty; (*suciedad*) squalor

misericordi|a *f* pity; (*piedad*) mercy. ~**oso** *a* merciful

mísero *a* miserable; (*tacaño*) mean; (*malvado*) wicked

misil *m* missile

misi|ón *f* mission. ~**onero** *m* missionary

misiva *f* missive

mism|ísimo *a* very same. ~**o** *a* same; (*después de pronombre personal*) myself, yourself, himself, herself, itself, ourselves, yourselves, themselves; (*enfático*) very. ● *adv.* **ahora** ~ right now. **aquí** ~ right here. **lo** ~ the same

misterio *m* mystery. ~**so** *a* mysterious

místic|a *f* mysticism. ~**o** *a* mystical. ● *m* mystic

mistifica|ción *f* mystification. ~**r** [7] *vt* mystify

mitad *f* half; (*centro*) middle. **cortar algo por la** ~ cut sth in half

mitigar [12] *vt* mitigate; quench <*sed*>; relieve <*dolor etc*>

mitin *m*, **mitín** *m* meeting

mito *m* myth. ~**logía** *f* mythology. ~**lógico** *a* mythological

mitón *m* mitten

mitote *m* (Mex) Aztec dance

mixt|o *a* mixed. **educación mixta** coeducation

mobiliario *m* furniture

moce|dad *f* youth. **~río** *m* young people. **~tón** *m* strapping lad. **~tona** *f* strapping girl

mochales *a invar.* **estar ~** be round the bend

mochila *f* rucksack

mocho *a* blunt. ● *m* butt end

mochuelo *m* little owl

moción *f* motion

moco *m* mucus. **limpiarse los ~s** blow one's nose

moda *f* fashion. **estar de ~** be in fashion. **~l** *a* modal. **~les** *mpl* manners. **~lidad** *f* kind

model|ado *m* modelling. **~ador** *m* modeller. **~ar** *vt* model; (fig, configurar) form. **~o** *m & f* model

módem *m* modem

modera|ción *f* moderation. **~do** *a* moderate. **~r** *vt* moderate; reduce <*velocidad*>. □ **~rse** *vpr* control oneself

modern|idad *f* modernity. **~ismo** *m* modernism. **~ista** *m & f* modernist. **~izar** [10] *vt* modernize. **~o** *a* modern; (a la moda) fashionable

modest|ia *f* modesty. **~o** *a* modest

módico *a* moderate

modifica|ción *f* modification. **~r** [7] *vt* modify

modismo *m* idiom

modist|a *f* dressmaker. **~o** *m* designer

modo *m* manner, way; (Gram) mood; (Mus) mode. **~ de ser** character. **de ~ que** so that. **de ningún ~** certainly not. **de todos ~s** anyhow. **ni ~** (LAm) no way

modorra *f* drowsiness

modula|ción *f* modulation. **~dor** *m* modulator. **~r** *vt* modulate

módulo *m* module

mofa *f* mockery. □ **~rse** *vpr*. **~rse de** make fun of

mofeta *f* skunk

moflet|e *m* chubby cheek. **~udo** *a* with chubby cheeks

mohín *m* grimace. **hacer un ~** pull a face

moho *m* mould; (óxido) rust. **~so** *a* mouldy; <*metales*> rusty

moisés *m* Moses basket

mojado *a* wet

mojar *vt* wet; (empapar) soak; (humedecer) moisten, dampen

mojigat|ería *f* prudishness. **~o** *m* prude. ● *a* prudish

mojón *m* boundary post; (señal) signpost

molar *m* molar

mold|e *m* mould; (aguja) knitting needle. **~ear** *vt* mould, shape; (fig) form. **~ura** *f* moulding

mole *f* mass, bulk. ● *m* (Mex, salsa) chili sauce with chocolate and sesame

mol|écula *f* molecule. **~ecular** *a* molecular

mole|dor *a* grinding. ● *m* grinder. **~r** [2] grind

molest|ar *vt* annoy; (incomodar) bother. **¿le ~a que fume?** do you mind if I smoke? ● *vi* be a nuisance. **no ~ar** do not disturb. □ **~arse** *vpr* bother; (ofenderse) take offence. **~ia** *f* bother, nuisance; (inconveniente) inconvenience; (incomodidad) discomfort. **~o** *a* annoying; (inconveniente) inconvenient; (ofendido) offended

molicie *f* softness; (excesiva comodidad) easy life

molido *a* ground; (fig, muy cansado) worn out

molienda *f* grinding

molin|ero *m* miller. **~ete** *m* toy windmill. **~illo** *m* mill; (juguete) toy windmill. **~o** *m* mill. **~ de agua** watermill. **~o de viento** windmill

molleja *f* gizzard

mollera *f* (de la cabeza) crown; (fig, sesera) brains

molusco *m* mollusc

moment|áneamente *adv* momentarily. **~áneo** *a* (breve) momentary; (pasajero) temporary. **~o** *m* moment; (ocasión) time. **al ~o** at once. **de ~o** for the moment

momi|a *f* mummy. **~ficar** [7] *vt* mummify. □ **~ficarse** *vpr* become mummified

monacal *a* monastic

monada *f* beautiful thing; (niño bonito) cute kid; (acción tonta) silliness

monaguillo *m* altar boy

mon|arca *m* & *f* monarch. **~arquía** *f* monarchy. **~árquico** *a* monarchical

monasterio *m* monastery

monda *f* peeling; (piel) peel. **~dientes** *m invar* toothpick. **~adura** *f* peeling; (piel) peel. **~ar** *vt* peel *<fruta etc>*. **~o** *a* (sin pelo) bald

mondongo *m* innards

moned|a *f* coin; (de un país) currency. **~ero** *m* purse (Brit), change purse (Amer)

monetario *a* monetary

mongolismo *m* Down's syndrome

monigote *m* weak character; (muñeco) rag doll; (dibujo) doodle

monitor *m* monitor

monj|a *f* nun. **~e** *m* monk. **~il** *a* nun's; (como de monja) like a nun

mono *m* monkey; (sobretodo) overalls. ● *a* pretty

monocromo *a* & *m* monochrome

monóculo *m* monocle

mon|ogamia *f* monogamy. **~ógamo** *a* monogamous

monogra|fía *f* monograph. **~ma** *m* monogram

mon|ologar [12] *vi* soliloquize. **~ólogo** *m* monologue

monoplano *m* monoplane

monopoli|o *m* monopoly. **~zar** [10] *vt* monopolize

monos|ilábico *a* monosyllabic. **~ílabo** *m* monosyllable

monoteís|mo *m* monotheism. **~ta** *a* monotheistic. ● *m* & *f* monotheist

mon|otonía *f* monotony. **~ótono** *a* monotonous

monseñor *m* monsignor

monstruo *m* monster. **~sidad** *f* monstrosity; (atrocidad) atrocity. **~so** *a* monstrous

monta *f* mounting; (valor) total value

montacargas *m invar* service lift (Brit), service elevator (Amer)

monta|dor *m* fitter. **~je** *m* assembly; (Cine) montage; (teatro) staging, production

montañ|a *f* mountain. **~a rusa** roller coaster. **~ero** *a* mountaineer.

~és *a* mountain. ● *m* highlander. **~ismo** *m* mountaineering. **~oso** *a* mountainous

montaplatos *m invar* dumb waiter

montar *vt* ride; (subirse a) get on; (ensamblar) assemble; cock *<arma>*; set up *<una casa, un negocio>*. ● *vi* ride; (subirse) mount. **~ a caballo** ride a horse

monte *m* (montaña) mountain; (terreno inculto) scrub; (bosque) woodland. **~ de piedad** pawnshop

montepío *m* charitable fund for dependents

montés *a* wild

montevideano *a* & *m* Montevidean

montículo *m* hillock

montón *m* heap, pile. **a montones** in abundance. **un ~ de** loads of

montura *f* mount; (silla) saddle

monument|al *a* monumental; (fig, muy grande) enormous. **~o** *m* monument

monzón *m* & *f* monsoon

moñ|a *f* ribbon. **~o** *m* bun; (LAm, lazo) bow

moque|o *m* runny nose. **~ro** *m* 🄴 handkerchief

moqueta *f* fitted carpet

moquillo *m* distemper

mora *f* mulberry; (de zarzamora) blackberry; (Jurid) default

morada *f* dwelling

morado *a* purple

morador *m* inhabitant

moral *m* mulberry tree. ● *f* morals. ● *a* moral. **~eja** *f* moral. **~idad** *f* morality. **~ista** *m* & *f* moralist. **~izador** *a* moralizing. ● *m* moralist. **~izar** [10] *vt* moralize

morar *vi* live

moratoria *f* moratorium

mórbido *a* soft; (malsano) morbid

morbo *m* illness. **~sidad** *f* morbidity. **~so** *a* unhealthy

morcilla *f* black pudding

morda|cidad *f* sharpness. **~z** *a* scathing

mordaza *f* gag

morde|dura f bite. **~r** [2] vt bite; (Mex, exigir soborno a) extract a bribe from. ● vi bite. □ **~rse** vpr bite o.s. **~rse las uñas** bite one's nails

mordi|da f (Mex) bribe. **~sco** m bite. **~squear** vt nibble (at)

moreno a (con ser) dark; (de pelo obscuro) dark-haired; (de raza negra) dark-skinned; (con estar) brown, tanned

morera f white mulberry tree

moretón m bruise

morfema m morpheme

morfin|a f morphine. **~ómano** m morphine addict

morfol|ogía f morphology. **~ógico** a morphological

moribundo a dying

morir [6] (pp **muerto**) vi die; (fig, extinguirse) die away; (fig, terminar) end. **~ ahogado** drown. □ **~se** vpr die. **~se de hambre** starve to death; (fig) be starving. **se muere por una flauta** she's dying to have a flute

morisco a Moorish. ● m Moor

morm|ón m Mormon. **~ónico** a Mormon. **~onismo** m Mormonism

moro a Moorish. ● m Moor

morral m (mochila) rucksack; (de cazador) gamebag; (para caballos) nosebag

morrillo m nape of the neck

morriña f homesickness

morro m snout

morrocotudo a 🗉 (tremendo) terrible; (estupendo) terrific 🗉

morsa f walrus

mortaja f shroud

mortal a & m & f mortal. **~idad** f mortality. **~mente** adv mortally

mortandad f loss of life; (Mil) carnage

mortecino a failing; <color> pale

mortero m mortar

mortífero a deadly

mortifica|ción f mortification. **~r** [7] vt (atormentar) torment. □ **~rse** vpr distress o.s.

mortuorio a death

mosaico m mosaic; (Mex, baldosa) floor tile

mosca f fly. **~rda** f blowfly. **~rdón** m botfly; (de cuerpo azul) bluebottle

moscatel a muscatel

moscón m botfly; (mosca de cuerpo azul) bluebottle

moscovita a & m & f Muscovite

mosque|arse vpr get cross. **~o** m resentment

mosquete m musket. **~ro** m musketeer

mosquit|ero m mosquito net. **~o** m mosquito

mostacho m moustache

mostaza f mustard

mosto m must, grape juice

mostrador m counter

mostrar [2] vt show. □ **~se** vpr (show oneself to) be. **se mostró muy amable** he was very kind

mota f spot, speck

mote m nickname

motea|do a speckled. **~r** vt speckle

motejar vt call

motel m motel

motete m motet

motín m riot; (de tropas, tripulación) mutiny

motiv|ación f motivation. **~ar** vt motivate. **~o** m reason. **con ~o de** because of

motocicl|eta f motor cycle, motor bike 🗉. **~ista** m & f motorcyclist

motoneta f (LAm) (motor) scooter

motor a motor. ● m motor, engine. **~ de arranque** starter motor. **~a** f motor boat. **~ismo** m motorcycling. **~ista** m & f motorist; (de una moto) motorcyclist. **~izar** [10] vt motorize

motriz a motor

move|dizo a movable; (poco firme) unstable; <persona> fickle. **~r** [2] vt move; shake <la cabeza>; (provocar) cause. □ **~rse** vpr move; (darse prisa) hurry up

movi|ble a movable. **~do** a moved; (Foto) blurred

móvil a mobile. ● m motive

movili|dad f mobility. **~zación** f mobilization. **~zar** [10] vt mobilize

movimiento m movement, motion; (agitación) bustle

moza f young girl. **~lbete** m lad

mozárabe a Mozarabic. ● m & f Mozarab

moz|o *m* young boy. **~uela** *f* young girl. **~uelo** *m* young boy/lad

mucam|a *f* (LAm) servant. **~o** *m* (LAm) servant

muchach|a *f* girl; (sirvienta) servant, maid. **~o** *m* boy, lad

muchedumbre *f* crowd

mucho *a* a lot of; (en negativas, preguntas) much, a lot of. **~s** a lot of; (en negativas, preguntas) many, a lot of. ● *pron* a lot; (personas) many (people). **como ~** at the most. **ni ~ menos** by no means. **por ~ que** however much. ● *adv* a lot, very much; (tiempo) long, a long time

mucos|idad *f* mucus. **~o** *a* mucous

muda *f* change of clothing; (de animales) shedding. **~ble** *a* changeable; <*personas*> fickle. **~nza** *f* move, removal (Brit). **~r** *vt* change; shed <*piel*>. **~rse** *vpr* (de ropa) change one's clothes; (de casa) move (house)

mudéjar *a* & *m* & *f* Mudejar

mud|ez *f* dumbness. **~o** *a* dumb; (callado) silent

mueble *a* movable. ● *m* piece of furniture. **~s** *mpl* furniture

mueca *f* grimace, face. **hacer una ~** pull a face

muela *f* back tooth, molar; (piedra de afilar) grindstone; (piedra de molino) millstone. **~ del juicio** wisdom tooth

muelle *a* soft. ● *m* spring; (Naut) wharf; (malecón) jetty

muérdago *m* mistletoe

muero *vb* ⇒MORIR

muert|e *f* death; (homicidio) murder. **~o** *a* dead. ● *m* dead person

muesca *f* nick; (ranura) slot

muestra *f* sample; (prueba) proof; (modelo) model; (señal) sign. **~rio** *m* collection of samples

muestro *vb* ⇒MOSTRAR

muevo *vb* ⇒MOVER

mugi|do *m* moo. **~r** [14] *vi* moo

mugr|e *m* dirt. **~iento** *a* dirty, filthy

mugrón *m* sucker

mujer *f* woman; (esposa) wife. ● *int* my dear! **~iego** *a* fond of the women. ● *m* womanizer. **~zuela** *f* prostitute

mula *f* mule. **~da** *f* drove of mules

mulato *a* of mixed race (black and white). ● *m* person of mixed race

mulero *m* muleteer

muleta *f* crutch; (toreo) stick with a red flag

mulli|do *a* soft. **~r** [22] *vt* soften

mulo *m* mule

multa *f* fine. **~r** *vt* fine

multi|color *a* multicoloured. **~copista** *m* duplicator. **~forme** *a* multiform. **~lateral** *a* multilateral. **~lingüe** *a* multilingual. **~millonario** *m* multimillionaire

múltiple *a* multiple

multiplic|ación *f* multiplication. **~ar** [7] *vt* multiply. □ **~arse** *vpr* multiply. **~idad** *f* multiplicity

múltiplo *m* multiple

multitud *f* multitude, crowd. **~inario** *a* mass; <*concierto*> with mass audience

mund|ano *a* wordly; (de la sociedad elegante) society. **~ial** *a* world-wide. **la segunda guerra ~ial** the Second World War. **~illo** *m* world, circles. **~o** *m* world. **todo el ~o** everybody

munición *f* ammunition; (provisiones) supplies

municip|al *a* municipal. **~alidad** *f* municipality. **~io** *m* municipality; (ayuntamiento) town council

muñe|ca *f* (Anat) wrist; (juguete) doll; (maniquí) dummy. **~co** *m* doll. **~quera** *f* wristband

muñón *m* stump

mura|l *a* mural, wall. ● *m* mural. **~lla** *f* (city) wall. **~r** *vt* wall

murciélago *m* bat

murga *f* street band

murmullo *m* (incl fig) murmur

murmura|ción *f* gossip. **~dor** *a* gossiping. ● *m* gossip. **~r** *vi* murmur; (criticar) gossip

muro *m* wall

murria *f* depression

mus *m* card game

musa *f* muse

musaraña *f* shrew

muscula|r *a* muscular. **~tura** *f* muscles

músculo *m* muscle

musculoso *a* muscular

muselina *f* muslin

museo *m* museum. **~ de arte** art gallery

musgo *m* moss. **~so** *a* mossy

música *f* music

musical *a & m* musical

músico *a* musical. ● *m* musician

music|ología *f* musicology. **~ólogo** *m* musicologist

muslo *m* thigh

mustio *a* <plantas> withered; <cosas> faded; <personas> gloomy; (Mex, hipócrita) two-faced

musulmán *a & m* Muslim

muta|bilidad *f* mutability. **~ción** *f* mutation

mutila|ción *f* mutilation. **~do** *a* crippled. ● *m* cripple. **~r** *vt* mutilate; maim <persona>

mutis *m* (en el teatro) exit. **~mo** *m* silence

mutu|alidad *f* mutuality; (asociación) friendly society. **~amente** *adv* mutually. **~o** *a* mutual

muy *adv* very; (demasiado) too

....

Nn

....

nabo *m* turnip

nácar *m* mother-of-pearl

nac|er [11] *vi* be born; <pollito> hatch out; <planta> sprout. **~ido** *a* born. **recien ~ido** newborn. **~iente** *a* <sol> rising. **~imiento** *m* birth; (de río) source; (belén) crib. **lugar** *m* **de ~imiento** place of birth

naci|ón *f* nation. **~onal** *a* national. **~onalidad** *f* nationality. **~onalismo** *m* nationalism. **~onalista** *m & f* nationalist. **~onalizar** [10] *vt* nationalize. □ **~onalizarse** *vpr* become naturalized

nada *pron* nothing, not anything. ● *adv* not at all. **¡~ de eso!** nothing of the sort! **antes que ~** first of all. **¡de ~!** (después de 'gracias') don't mention it! **para ~** (not) at all. **por ~ del mundo** not for anything in the world

nada|dor *m* swimmer. **~r** *vi* swim. **~r de espalda(s)** do (the) backstroke

nadería *f* trifle

nadie *pron* no one, nobody

nado *m* (Mex) swimming. ● *adv* **a ~** swimming

naipe *m* (playing) card. **juegos** *mpl* **de ~s** card games

nalga *f* buttock. **~s** *fpl* bottom. **~da** *f* (Mex) smack on the bottom

nana *f* lullaby

naranj|a *f* orange. **~ada** *f* orangeade. **~al** *m* orange grove. **~ero** *m* orange tree

narcótico *a & m* narcotic

nariz *f* nose. **¡narices!** rubbish!

narra|ción *f* narration. **~dor** *m* narrator. **~r** *vt* tell. **~tivo** *a* narrative

nasal *a* nasal

nata *f* cream

natación *f* swimming

natal *a* native; <pueblo etc> home. **~idad** *f* birth rate

natillas *fpl* custard

nativo *a & m* native

nato *a* born

natural *a* natural. ● *m* native. **~eza** *f* nature. **~eza muerta** still life. **~idad** *f* naturalness. **~ista** *m & f* naturalist. **~izar** [10] *vt* naturalize. □ **~izarse** *vpr* become naturalized. **~mente** *adv* naturally. ● *int* of course!

naufrag|ar [12] *vi* <barco> sink; <persona> be shipwrecked; (fig) fail. **~io** *m* shipwreck

náufrago *a* shipwrecked. ● *m* shipwrecked person

náuseas *fpl* nausea. **dar ~s a uno** make s.o. feel sick. **sentir ~s** feel sick

náutico *a* nautical

navaja *f* penknife; (de afeitar) razor. **~zo** *m* slash

naval *a* naval

nave f ship; (de iglesia) nave. ~ **espacial** spaceship. **quemar las** ~s burn one's boats

navega|ble a navigable; <barco> seaworthy. ~**ción** f navigation; (tráfico) shipping. ~**dor** m (Informática) browser. ~**nte** m & f navigator. ~**r** [12] vi sail; (Informática) browse

Navid|ad f Christmas. ~**eño** a Christmas. **en** ~**ades** at Christmas. **¡feliz** ~**ad!** Happy Christmas! **por** ~**ad** at Christmas

nazi a & m & f Nazi. ~**smo** m Nazism

neblina f mist

nebuloso a misty; (fig) vague

necedad f foolishness. **decir** ~**es** talk nonsense. **hacer una** ~ do sth stupid

necesari|amente adv necessarily. ~**o** a necessary

necesi|dad f need; (cosa esencial) necessity; (pobreza) poverty. ~**dades** fpl hardships. **no hay** ~**dad** there's no need. **por** ~**dad** (out) of necessity. ~**tado** a in need (de of). ~**tar** vt need. ● vi. ~**tar de** need

necio a silly. ● m idiot

néctar m nectar

nectarina f nectarine

nefasto a unfortunate; <consecuencia> disastrous; <influencia> harmful

nega|ción f denial; (Gram) negative. ~**do** a useless. ~**r** [1 & 12] vt deny; (rehusar) refuse. □ ~**rse** vpr refuse (a to). ~**tiva** f (acción) denial; (acción de rehusar) refusal. ~**tivo** a & m negative

negligen|cia f negligence. ~**te** a negligent

negoci|able a negotiable. ~**ación** f negotiation. ~**ante** m & f dealer. ~**ar** vt/i negotiate. ~**ar en** trade in. ~**o** m business; (Com, trato) deal. ~**os** mpl business. **hombre** m **de** ~**os** businessman

negr|a f black woman; (Mus) crotchet. ~**o** a black; <ojos> dark. ● m (color) black; (persona) black man. ~**ura** f blackness. ~**uzco** a blackish

nen|a f little girl. ~**o** m little boy

nenúfar m water lily

neocelandés a from New Zealand. ● m New Zealander

neón m neon

nepotismo m nepotism

nervio m nerve; (tendón) sinew; (Bot) vein. ~**sidad** f, ~**sismo** m nervousness; (impaciencia) impatience. ~**so** a nervous; (de temperamento) highly-strung. **ponerse** ~**so** get nervous

neto a clear; <verdad> simple; (Com) net

neumático a pneumatic. ● m tyre

neumonía f pneumonia

neur|algia f neuralgia. ~**ología** f neurology. ~**ólogo** m neurologist. ~**osis** f neurosis. ~**ótico** a neurotic

neutr|al a neutral. ~**alidad** f neutrality. ~**alizar** [10] vt neutralize. ~**o** a neutral; (Gram) neuter

neva|da f snowfall. ~**r** [1] vi snow. ~**sca** f blizzard

nevera f refrigerator, fridge (Brit)

nevisca f light snowfall

nexo m link

ni conj. ~**...** ~ neither... nor. ~ **aunque** not even if. ~ **siquiera** not even. **sin...** ~ **...** without ... or...

Nicaragua f Nicaragua

nicaragüense a & m & f Nicaraguan

nicho m niche

nicotina f nicotine

nido m nest; (de ladrones) den

niebla f fog. **hay** ~ it's foggy. **un día de** ~ a foggy day

niet|a f granddaughter. ~**o** m grandson. ~**os** mpl grandchildren

nieve f snow; (Mex, helado) sorbet

niki m polo shirt

nimi|edad f triviality. ~**o** a insignificant

ninfa f nymph

ningún ⇒ NINGUNO

ninguno a (delante de nombre masculino en singular **ningún**) no; (con otro negativo) any. **de ninguna manera, de ningún modo** by no means. **en ninguna parte** nowhere. **sin ningún amigo** without any friends.

●*pron* (de dos) neither; (de más de dos) none; (nadie) no-one, nobody

niñ|a *f* (little) girl. **~era** *f* nanny. **~ería** *f* childish thing. **~ez** *f* childhood. **~o** *a* childish. ● *m* (little) boy **de ~o** as a child. **desde ~o** from childhood

níquel *m* nickel

níspero *m* medlar

nitidez *f* clarity; (de foto, imagen) sharpness

nítido *a* clear; (foto, imagen) sharp

nitrógeno *m* nitrogen

nivel *m* level; (fig) standard. **~ de vida** standard of living. **~ar** *vt* level. □ **~arse** *vpr* become level

no *adv* not; (como respuesta) no. **¿~?** isn't it? **¡a que ~!** I bet you don't! **¡cómo ~!** of course! **Felipe ~ tiene hijos** Felipe has no children. **¡que ~!** certainly not!

nob|iliario *a* noble. **~le** *a & m & f* noble. **~leza** *f* nobility

noche *f* night. **~ vieja** New Year's Eve. **de ~** at night. **hacerse de ~** get dark. **hacer ~** spend the night. **media ~** midnight. **en la ~** (LAm), **por la ~** at night

Nochebuena *f* Christmas Eve

noción *f* notion. **nociones** *fpl* rudiments

nocivo *a* harmful

nocturno *a* nocturnal; *<clase>* evening; *<tren etc>* night. ● *m* nocturne

nodriza *f* wet nurse

nogal *m* walnut tree; (madera) walnut

nómada *a* nomadic. ● *m & f* nomad

nombr|ado *a* famous; (susodicho) aforementioned. **~amiento** *m* appointment. **~ar** *vt* appoint; (citar) mention. **~e** *m* name; (Gram) noun; (fama) renown. **~e de pila** Christian name. **en ~e de** in the name of. **no tener ~e** be unspeakable. **poner de ~e** call

nomeolvides *m invar* forget-me-not

nómina *f* payroll

nomina|l *a* nominal. **~tivo** *a & m* nominative. **~tivo** *a* *<cheque etc>* made out to

non *a* odd. ● *m* odd number. **pares y ~es** odds and evens

nono *a* ninth

nordeste *a* *<región>* north-eastern; *<viento>* north-easterly. ● *m* north-east

nórdico *a* Nordic. ● *m* Northern European

noria *f* water-wheel; (en una feria) big wheel (Brit), Ferris wheel (Amer)

norma *f* rule

normal *a* normal. ● *f* teachers' training college. **~idad** *f* normality (Brit), normalcy (Amer). **~izar** [10] *vt* normalize. **~mente** *adv* normally, usually

noroeste *a* *<región>* north-western; *<viento>* north-westerly. ● *m* north-west

norte *a* *<región>* northern; *<viento, lado>* north. ● *m* north; (fig, meta) aim

Norteamérica *f* (North) America

norteamericano *a & m* (North) American

norteño *a* northern. ● *m* northerner

Noruega *f* Norway

noruego *a & m* Norwegian

nos *pron* (acusativo) us; (dativo) (to) us; (reflexivo) (to) ourselves; (recíproco) (to) each other

nosotros *pron* we; (con prep) us

nost|algia *f* nostalgia; (de casa, de patria) homesickness. **~álgico** *a* nostalgic

nota *f* note; (de examen etc) mark. **de ~** famous. **de mala ~** notorious. **digno de ~** notable. **~ble** *a* notable. **~ción** *f* notation. **~r** *vt* notice. **es de ~r** it should be noted. **hacerse ~r** stand out

notario *m* notary

notici|a *f* (piece of) news. **~as** *fpl* news. **atrasado de ~as** behind with the news. **tener ~as de** hear from. **~ario**, (LAm) **~ero** *m* news

notifica|ción *f* notification. **~r** [7] *vt* notify

notori|edad *f* notoriety. **~o** *a* well-known; (evidente) obvious; (notable) marked

novato a inexperienced. ● m novice

novecientos a & m nine hundred

noved|ad f newness; (cosa nueva) innovation; (cambio) change; (moda) latest fashion. **llegar sin ~ad** arrive safely. **~oso** a novel

novel|a f novel. **~ista** m & f novelist

noveno a ninth

noventa a & m ninety; (nonagésimo) ninetieth

novia f girlfriend; (prometida) fiancée; (en boda) bride. **~r** vi (LAm) go out together. **~zgo** m engagement

novicio m novice

noviembre m November

novill|a f heifer. **~o** m bullock. hacer **~os** play truant

novio m boyfriend; (prometido) fiancé; (en boda) bridegroom. **los ~s** the bride and groom

nub|arrón m large dark cloud. **~e** f cloud; (de insectos etc) swarm. **~lado** a cloudy, overcast. ● m cloud. **~lar** vt cloud. □ **~larse** vpr become cloudy; <vista> cloud over. **~oso** a cloudy

nuca f back of the neck

nuclear a nuclear

núcleo m nucleus

nudillo m knuckle

nudis|mo m nudism. **~ta** m & f nudist

nudo m knot; (de asunto etc) crux. **te-ner un ~ en la garganta** have a lump in one's throat. **~so** a knotty

nuera f daughter-in-law

nuestro a our. ● pron ours. **~ amigo** our friend. **un coche ~** a car of ours

nueva f (piece of) news. **~s** fpl news. **~mente** adv again

Nueva Zelanda, (LAm) **Nueva Zelandia** f New Zealand

nueve a & m nine

nuevo a new. **de ~** again. **estar ~** be as good as new

nuez f walnut. **~ de Adán** Adam's apple. **~ moscada** nutmeg

nul|idad f nullity; (🅴, persona) dead loss 🅴. **~o** a useless; (Jurid) null and void

num|eración f numbering. **~eral** a & m numeral. **~erar** vt number. **~érico** a numerical

número m number; (arábigo, romano) numeral; (de zapatos etc) size; (billete de lotería) lottery ticket; (de publicación) issue. **sin ~** countless

numeroso a numerous

nunca adv never. **~ (ja)más** never again. **casi ~** hardly ever. **como ~** like never before. **más que ~** more than ever

nupcial a nuptial. **banquete ~** wedding breakfast

nutria f otter

nutri|ción f nutrition. **~do** a nourished, fed; (fig) large; <aplausos> loud; <fuego> heavy. **~r** vt nourish, feed; (fig) feed. **~tivo** a nutritious. **valor** m **~tivo** nutritional value

nylon m nylon

ñapa f (LAm) extra goods given free

ñato adj (LAm) snub-nosed

ñoñ|ería f, **~ez** f insipidity. **~o** a insipid; (tímido) bashful; (quisquilloso) prudish

o conj or. **~ bien** rather. **~... ~** either ... or

oasis m invar oasis

obed|ecer [11] vt/i obey. **~iencia** f obedience. **~iente** a obedient

obes|idad f obesity. **~o** a obese

obispo m bishop

obje|ción f objection. **~tar** vt/i object

objetivo *a* objective. ● *m* objective; (foto etc) lens

objeto *m* object. ~**r** *m* objector. ~**r de conciencia** conscientious objector

oblicuo *a* oblique

obliga|ción *f* obligation; (Com) bond. ~**do** *a* obliged; (forzoso) obligatory; ~**r** [12] *vt* force, oblige. □ ~**rse** *vpr*. ~**rse a** undertake to. □ ~**torio** *a* obligatory

oboe *m* oboe. ● *m & f* (músico) oboist

obra *f* work; (acción) deed; (de teatro) play; (construcción) building work. ~ **maestra** masterpiece. **en** ~**s** under construction. **por** ~ **de** thanks to. ~**r** *vt* do

obrero *a* labour; *<clase>* working. ● *m* workman; (de fábrica, construcción) worker

obscen|idad *f* obscenity. ~**o** *a* obscene

obscu... ⇨ OSCU...

obsequi|ar *vt* lavish attention on. ~**ar con** give, present with. ~**o** *m* gift, present; (agasajo) attention. ~**oso** *a* obliging

observa|ción *f* observation. **hacer una** ~**ción** make a remark. ~**dor** *m* observer. ~**ncia** *f* observance. ~**r** *vt* observe; (notar) notice. ~**torio** *m* observatory

obses|ión *f* obsession. ~**ionar** *vt* obsess. ~**ivo** *a* obsessive. ~**o** *a* obsessed

obst|aculizar [10] *vt* hinder; hold up *<tráfico>*. ~**áculo** *m* obstacle

obstante: **no** ~ *adv* however, nevertheless; (como prep) in spite of

obstar *vi*. **eso no obsta para que vaya** that should not prevent him from going

obstina|do *a* obstinate. □ ~**rse** *vpr*. ~**rse en** (+ *infinitivo*) insist on (+ *gerundio*)

obstru|cción *f* obstruction. ~**ir** [17] *vt* obstruct

obtener [40] *vt* get, obtain

obtura|dor *m* (Foto) shutter. ~**r** *vt* plug; fill *<muela etc>*

obvio *a* obvious

oca *f* goose

ocasi|ón *f* occasion; (oportunidad) opportunity. **aprovechar la** ~**ón** take the opportunity. **con** ~**ón de** on the occasion of. **de** ~**ón** bargain; (usado) second-hand. **en** ~**ones** sometimes. **perder una** ~**ón** miss a chance. ~**onal** *a* chance. ~**onar** *vt* cause

ocaso *m* sunset; (fig) decline

occident|al *a* western. ● *m & f* westerner. ~**e** *m* west

océano *m* ocean

ochenta *a & m* eighty

ocho *a & m* eight. ~**cientos** *a & m* eight hundred

ocio *m* idleness; (tiempo libre) leisure time. ~**sidad** *f* idleness. ~**so** *a* idle; (inútil) pointless

oct|agonal *a* octagonal. ~**ágono** *m* octagon

octano *m* octane

octav|a *f* octave. ~**o** *a & m* eighth

octogenario *a & m* octogenarian

octubre *m* October

ocular *a* eye

oculista *m & f* ophthalmologist, ophthalmic optician

ocult|ar *vt* hide. □ ~**arse** *vpr* hide. ~**o** *a* hidden; (secreto) secret

ocupa|ción *f* occupation. ~**do** *a* occupied; *<persona>* busy. **estar** ~**do** *<asiento>* be taken; *<línea telefónica>* be engaged (Brit), be busy (Amer). ~**nte** *m & f* occupant. ~**r** *vt* occupy, take up *<espacio>*. □ ~**rse** *vpr* look after

ocurr|encia *f* occurrence, event; (idea) idea; (que tiene gracia) witty remark. ~**ir** *vi* happen. **¿qué** ~**e?** what's the matter? □ ~**irse** *vpr* occur. **se me** ~**e que** it occurs to me that

oda *f* ode

odi|ar *vt* hate. ~**o** *m* hatred. ~**oso** *a* hateful; *<persona>* horrible

oeste *a <región>* western; *<viento, lado>* west. ● *m* west

ofen|der *vt* offend; (insultar) insult. □ ~**derse** *vpr* take offence. ~**sa** *f* offence. ~**siva** *f* offensive. ~**sivo** *a* offensive

oferta *f* offer; (en subasta) bid. ~**s de empleo** situations vacant. **en** ~ on (special) offer

oficial *a* official. ● *m* skilled worker; (Mil) officer

oficin|a *f* office. **~a de colocación** employment office. **~a de turismo** tourist office. **horas** *fpl* **de ~a** business hours. **~ista** *m* & *f* office worker

oficio *m* trade. **~so** *a* (no oficial) unofficial

ofrec|er [11] *vt* offer; give *<fiesta, banquete etc>*; (prometer) promise. □ **~erse** *vpr* *<persona>* volunteer. **~imiento** *m* offer

ofrenda *f* offering. **~r** *vt* offer

ofuscar [7] *vt* blind; (confundir) confuse. □ **~se** *vpr* get worked up

oí|ble *a* audible. **~do** *m* hearing; (Anat) ear. **al ~do** in one's ear. **de ~das** by hearsay. **conocer de ~das** have heard of. **de ~do** by ear. **duro de ~do** hard of hearing

oigo *vb* ⇒**oír**

oír [50] *vt* hear. **¡oiga!** listen!; (al teléfono) hello!

ojal *m* buttonhole

ojalá *int* I hope so! ● *conj* if only

ojea|da *f* glance. **dar una ~da a, echar una ~da a** have a quick glance at. **~r** *vt* have a look at

ojeras *fpl* rings under one's eyes

ojeriza *f* ill will. **tener ~ a** have a grudge against

ojo *m* eye; (de cerradura) keyhole; (de un puente) span. **¡~!** careful!

ola *f* wave

olé *int* bravo!

olea|da *f* wave. **~je** *m* swell

óleo *m* oil; (cuadro) oil painting

oleoducto *m* oil pipeline

oler [2] (*las formas que empezarían por* **ue** *se escriben* **hue**) *vt* smell. ● *vi* smell (**a** of). **me huele mal** (fig) it sounds fishy to me

olfat|ear *vt* sniff; scent *<rastro>*. **~o** *m* (sense of) smell (fig) intuition

olimpiada *f*, **olimpíada** *f* Olympic games, Olympics

olímpico *a* Olympic; (fig, 🔲) total

oliv|a *f* olive. **~ar** *m* olive grove. **~o** *m* olive tree

olla *f* pot, casserole. **~ a/de presión**, **~ exprés** pressure cooker

olmo *m* elm (tree)

olor *m* smell. **~oso** *a* sweet-smelling

olvid|adizo *a* forgetful. **~ar** *vt* forget. □ **~arse** *vpr* forget. **~arse de** forget. **se me ~ó** I forgot. **~o** *m* oblivion; (acto) omission

ombligo *m* navel

omi|sión *f* omission. **~tir** *vt* omit

ómnibus *a* omnibus

omnipotente *a* omnipotent

omóplato *m*, **omoplato** *m* shoulder blade

once *a* & *m* eleven

ond|a *f* wave. **~a corta** short wave. **~a larga** long wave. **longitud** *f* **de ~a** wavelength. **~ear** *vi* wave; *<agua>* ripple. **~ulación** *f* undulation; (del pelo) wave. **~ular** *vi* wave

onomásti|co *a* *<índice>* of names. ● *m* (LAm) saint's day. **~ca** *f* saint's day

ONU *abrev* (**Organización de las Naciones Unidas**) UN

opac|ar [7] (LAm) make opaque; (deslucir) mar; (anular) overshadow. **~o** *a* opaque; (fig) dull

opci|ón *f* option. **~onal** *a* optional

ópera *f* opera

opera|ción *f* operation; (Com) transaction. **~dor** *m* operator; (TV) cameraman; (Mex, obrero) machinist. **~r** *vt* operate on; work *<milagro etc>*; (Mex) operate *<máquina>*. ● *vi* operate; (Com) deal. **~rio** *m* machinist. □ **~rse** *vpr* take place; (Med) have an operation. **~torio** *a* operative

opereta *f* operetta

opin|ar *vi* express one's opinion. ● *vt* think. **~ que** think that. **¿qué opinas?** what do you think? **~ión** *f* opinion. **la ~ión pública** public opinion

opio *m* opium

opone|nte *a* opposing. ● *m* & *f* opponent. **~r** *vt* oppose; offer *<resistencia>*; raise *<objeción>*. □ **~rse** *vpr* be opposed; *<dos personas>* oppose each other

oporto *m* port (wine)

oportun|idad *f* opportunity; (cualidad de oportuno) timeliness; (LAm, ocasión) occasion. **~ista** *m* & *f* opportunist. **~o** *a* opportune; (apropiado) suitable

oposi|ción *f* opposition. **~ciones** *fpl* public examination. **~tor** *m* candidate; (Pol) opponent

opres|ión *f* oppression; (ahogo) difficulty in breathing. **~ivo** *a* oppressive. **~or** *m* oppressor

oprimir *vt* squeeze; press *<botón etc>*; *<ropa>* be too tight for; (fig) oppress

optar *vi* choose. **~ por** opt for

óptic|a *f* optics; (tienda) optician's (shop). **~o** *a* optic(al). ● *m* optician

optimis|mo *m* optimism. **~ta** *a* optimistic. ● *m & f* optimist

óptimo *a* ideal; *<condiciones>* perfect

opuesto *a* opposite; *<opiniones>* conflicting

opulen|cia *f* opulence. **~to** *a* opulent

oración *f* prayer; (Gram) sentence

ora|dor *m* speaker. **~l** *a* oral

órale *int* (Mex) come on!; (de acuerdo) OK!

orar *vi* pray (por for)

órbita *f* orbit

orden *f* order. **~ del día** agenda. **órdenes** *fpl* **sagradas** Holy Orders. **a sus órdenes** (esp Mex) can I help you? **~ de arresto** arrest warrant. **en ~** in order. **por ~** in turn. **~ado** *a* tidy

ordenador *m* computer

ordena|nza *f* ordinance. ● *m* (Mil) orderly. **~r** *vt* put in order; (mandar) order; (Relig) ordain; (LAm, en restaurante) order

ordeñar *vt* milk

ordinario *a* ordinary; (grosero) common; (de mala calidad) poor-quality

orear *vt* air

orégano *m* oregano

oreja *f* ear

orfanato *m* orphanage

orfebre *m* goldsmith, silversmith

orfeón *m* choral society

orgánico *a* organic

organillo *m* barrel-organ

organismo *m* organism

organista *m & f* organist

organiza|ción *f* organization. **~dor** *m* organizer. **~r** [10] *vt* organize. □ **~rse** *vpr* get organized

órgano *m* organ

orgasmo *m* orgasm

orgía *f* orgy

orgullo *m* pride. **~so** *a* proud

orientación *f* orientation; (guía) guidance; (Archit) aspect

oriental *a & m & f* oriental

orientar *vt* position; advise *<persona>*. □ **~se** *vpr* point; *<persona>* find one's bearings

oriente *m* east

orificio *m* hole

orig|en *m* origin. **dar ~en a** give rise to. **~inal** *a* original; (excéntrico) odd. **~inalidad** *f* originality. **~inar** *vt* give rise to. **~inario** *a* original; (nativo) native. **ser ~inario de** come from. □ **~inarse** *vpr* originate; *<incendio>* start

orilla *f* (del mar) shore; (de río) bank; (borde) edge. **a ~s del mar** by the sea

orina *f* urine. **~l** *m* chamber-pot. **~r** *vi* urinate

oriundo *a* native. **ser ~ de** *<persona>* come from; *<especie etc>* native to

ornamental *a* ornamental

ornitología *f* ornithology

oro *m* gold. **~s** *mpl* Spanish card suit. **~ de ley** 9 carat gold. **hacerse de ~** make a fortune. **prometer el ~ y el moro** promise the moon

orquesta *f* orchestra. **~l** *a* orchestral. **~r** *vt* orchestrate

orquídea *f* orchid

ortiga *f* nettle

ortodoxo *a* orthodox

ortografía *f* spelling

ortopédico *a* orthopaedic

oruga *f* caterpillar

orzuelo *m* sty

os *pron* (acusativo) you; (dativo) (to) you; (reflexivo) (to) yourselves; (recíproco) (to) each other

osad|ía *f* boldness. **~o** *a* bold

oscila|ción *f* swinging; (de precios) fluctuation; (Tec) oscillation. **~r** *vi* swing; *<precio>* fluctuate; (Tec) oscillate

oscur|ecer [11] *vi* get dark. ● *vt* darken; (fig) obscure. □ **~ecerse** *vpr* grow dark; (nublarse) cloud over. **~idad** *f* darkness; (fig) obscurity. **~o** *a* dark; (fig) obscure. **a ~as** in the dark

óseo *a* bone

oso *m* bear. **~ de felpa, ~ de peluche** teddy bear

ostensible *a* obvious

ostent|ación *f* ostentation. **~ar** *vt* show off; (mostrar) show. **~oso** *a* ostentatious

osteópata *m* & *f* osteopath

ostión *m* (esp Mex) oyster

ostra *f* oyster

ostracismo *m* ostracism

Otan *abrev* (**Organización del Tratado del Atlántico Norte**) NATO, North Atlantic Treaty Organization

otitis *f* inflammation of the ear

otoño *m* autumn (Brit), fall (Amer)

otorga|miento *m* granting. **~r** [12] *vt* give; grant <*préstamo*>; (Jurid) draw up <*testamento*>

otorrinolaringólogo *m* ear, nose and throat specialist

otro, otra

● *adjetivo*

····➤ another; (con artículo, posesivo) other. **come ~ pedazo** have another piece. **el ~ día** the other day. **mi ~ coche** my other car. **otra cosa** something else. **otra persona** somebody else. **otra vez** again

····➤ (en plural) other; (con numeral) another. **en otras ocasiones** on other occasions. **~s 3 vasos** another 3 glasses

····➤ (siguiente) next. **al ~ día** the next day. **me bajo en la otra estación** I get off at the next station

● *pronombre*

····➤ (cosa) another one. **lo cambié por ~** I changed it for another one

····➤ (persona) someone else. **invitó a ~** she invited someone else

····➤ (en plural) (some) others. **tengo ~s en casa** I have (some) others at home. **~s piensan lo contrario** others think the opposite

····➤ (con artículo) **el ~** the other one. **los ~s** the others. **uno detrás del ~** one after the other. **los ~s no vinieron** the others didn't come. **esta semana no, la otra** not this week, next week. **de un día para el ~** from one day to the next

➡ Para usos complementarios ver **uno, tanto**

ovación *f* ovation

oval *a*, **ovalado** *a* oval

óvalo *m* oval

ovario *m* ovary

oveja *f* sheep; (hembra) ewe

overol *m* (LAm) overalls

ovillo *m* ball. **hacerse un ~** curl up

OVNI *abrev* (**objeto volante no identificado**) UFO

ovulación *f* ovulation

oxida|ción *f* rusting. **~r** *vi* rust. □ **~rse** *vpr* go rusty

óxido *m* rust; (en química) oxide

oxígeno *m* oxygen

oye *vb* ➪ OÍR

oyente *a* listening. ● *m* & *f* listener; (Univ) occasional student

ozono *m* ozone

Pp

pabellón *m* pavilion; (en jardín) summerhouse; (en hospital) block; (de instrumento) bell; (bandera) flag

pacer [11] *vi* graze

pachucho *a* <*fruta*> overripe; <*persona*> poorly

pacien|cia *f* patience. **perder la ~cia** lose patience. **~te** *a* & *m* & *f* patient

pacificar [7] *vt* pacify. □ **~se** *vpr* calm down

pacífico *a* peaceful. **el (Océano) P~** the Pacific (Ocean)

pacifis|mo *m* pacifism. **~ta** *a* & *m* & *f* pacifist

pact|ar *vi* agree, make a pact. **~o** *m* pact, agreement

padec|er [11] *vt/i* suffer (**de** from); (soportar) bear. **∼cer del corazón** have heart trouble. **∼imiento** *m* suffering

padrastro *m* stepfather

padre *a* 🅣 terrible; (Mex, estupendo) great. ● *m* father. **∼s** *mpl* parents

padrino *m* godfather; (en boda) *man who gives away the bride*

padrón *m* register. **∼ electoral** (LAm) electoral roll

paella *f* paella

paga *f* payment; (sueldo) pay. **∼dero** *a* payable

pagano *a* & *m* pagan

pagar [12] *vt* pay; pay for *<compras>*. ● *vi* pay. **∼é** *m* IOU

página *f* page

pago *m* payment

país *m* country; (ciudadanos) nation. **∼ natal** native land. **el P∼ Vasco** the Basque Country. **los P∼es Bajos** the Low Countries

paisaje *m* landscape, scenery

paisano *m* compatriot

paja *f* straw; (en texto) padding

pájaro *m* bird. **∼ carpintero** woodpecker

paje *m* page

pala *f* shovel; (para cavar) spade; (para basura) dustpan; (de pimpón) bat

palabr|a *f* word; (habla) speech. **pedir la ∼a** ask to speak. **tomar la ∼a** take the floor. **∼ota** *f* swear-word. **decir ∼otas** swear

palacio *m* palace

paladar *m* palate

palanca *f* lever; (fig) influence. **∼ de cambio** (**de velocidades**) gear lever (Brit), gear shift (Amer)

palangana *f* washbasin (Brit), washbowl (Amer)

palco *m* (en el teatro) box

palestino *a* & *m* Palestinian

paleta *f* (de pintor) palette; (de albañil) trowel

paleto *m* yokel

paliativo *a* & *m* palliative

palide|cer [11] *vi* turn pale. **∼z** *f* paleness

pálido *a* pale. **ponerse ∼** turn pale

palillo *m* (de dientes) toothpick; (para comer) chopstick

paliza *f* beating

palma *f* (de la mano) palm; (árbol) palm (tree); (de dátiles) date palm. **dar ∼s** clap. **∼da** *f* pat; (LAm) slap. **∼das** *fpl* applause

palmera *f* palm tree

palmo *m* span; (fig) few inches. **∼ a ∼** inch by inch

palmote|ar *vi* clap. **∼o** *m* clapping, applause

palo *m* stick; (de valla) post; (de golf) club; (golpe) blow; (de naipes) suit; (mástil) mast

paloma *f* pigeon; (blanca, símbolo) dove

palomitas *fpl* popcorn

palpar *vt* feel

palpita|ción *f* palpitation. **∼nte** *a* throbbing. **∼r** *vi* beat; (latir con fuerza) pound; *<vena, sien>* throb

palta *f* (LAm) avocado (pear)

paludismo *m* malaria

pamp|a *f* pampas. **∼ero** *a* of the pampas

pan *m* bread; (barra) loaf. **∼ integral** wholewheat bread, wholemeal bread (Brit). **∼ tostado** toast. **∼ rallado** breadcrumbs. **ganarse el ∼** earn one's living

pana *f* corduroy

panader|ía *f* bakery; (tienda) baker's (shop). **∼o** *m* baker

panal *m* honeycomb

panameño *a* & *m* Panamanian

pancarta *f* banner, placard

panda *m* panda

pander|eta *f* (small) tambourine **∼o** *m* tambourine

pandilla *f* gang

panecillo *m* (bread) roll

panel *m* panel

panfleto *m* pamphlet

pánico *m* panic. **tener ∼** be terrified (**a** of)

panor|ama *m* panorama. **∼ámico** *a* panoramic

panque *m* (Mex) sponge cake

pantaletas *fpl* (Mex) panties, knickers (Brit)

pantalla f screen; (de lámpara) (lamp) shade

pantalón m, **pantalones** mpl trousers

pantano m marsh; (embalse) reservoir. ~**so** a marshy

pantera f panther

panti m, (Mex) **pantimedias** fpl tights (Brit), pantyhose (Amer)

pantomima f pantomime

pantorrilla f calf

pantufla f slipper

panz|a f belly. ~**udo** a pot-bellied

pañal m nappy (Brit), diaper (Amer)

paño m material; (de lana) woollen cloth; (trapo) cloth. ~**o de cocina** dishcloth; (para secar) tea towel. ~**o higiénico** sanitary towel. **en** ~**os menores** in one's underclothes

pañuelo m handkerchief; (de cabeza) scarf

papa m pope. ● f (LAm) potato. ~**s fritas** (LAm) chips (Brit), French fries (Amer); (de paquete) crisps (Brit), chips (Amer)

papá m dad(dy). ~**s** mpl parents. **P**~ **Noel** Father Christmas

papada f (de persona) double chin

papagayo m parrot

papalote m (Mex) kite

papanatas m invar simpleton

paparrucha f (tontería) silly thing

papaya f papaya, pawpaw

papel m paper; (en el teatro etc) role. ~ **carbón** carbon paper. ~ **de calcar** tracing paper. ~ **de envolver** wrapping paper. ~ **de plata** silver paper. ~ **higiénico** toilet paper. ~ **pintado** wallpaper. ~ **secante** blotting paper. ~**eo** m paperwork. ~**era** f wastepaper basket. ~**ería** f stationer's (shop). ~**eta** f (para votar) (ballot) paper

paperas fpl mumps

paquete m packet; (bulto) parcel; (LAm, de papas fritas) bag; (Mex, problema) headache. ~ **postal** parcel

Paquistán m Pakistan

paquistaní a & m Pakistani

par a <número> even. ● m couple; (dos cosas iguales) pair. **a** ~**es** two by two. **de** ~ **en** ~ wide open. ~**es y nones** odds and evens. **sin** ~ without equal. ● f par. **a la** ~ (Com) at par. **a la** ~ **que** at the same time

para

● preposición

····▸ for. **es** ~ **ti** it's for you. ~ **siempre** for ever. **¿**~ **qué?** what for? ~ **mi cumpleaños** for my birthday

····▸ (con infinitivo) to. **es muy tarde** ~ **llamar** it's too late to call. **salió** ~ **para divertirse** he went out to have fun. **lo hago** ~ **ahorrar** I do it (in order) to save money

····▸ (dirección) **iba** ~ **la oficina** he was going to the office. **empújalo** ~ **atrás** push it back. **¿vas** ~ **casa?** are you going home?

····▸ (tiempo) by. **debe estar listo** ~ **el 5** it must be ready by the 5th. ~ **entonces** by then

····▸ (LAm, hora) to. **son 5 para la una** it's 5 to one

····▸ **para que** so (that). **grité** ~ **que me oyera** I shouted so (that) he could hear me.

Note that **para que** is always followed by a verb in the subjunctive

parabienes mpl congratulations

parábola f (narración) parable

parabólica f satellite dish

para|brisas m invar windscreen (Brit), windshield (Amer). ~**caídas** m invar parachute. ~**caidista** m & f parachutist; (Mil) paratrooper. ~**choques** m invar bumper (Brit), fender (Amer) (Rail) buffer

parad|a f (acción) stop; (lugar) bus stop; (de taxis) rank; (Mil) parade. ~**ero** m whereabouts; (LAm, lugar) bus stop. ~**o** a stationary; <desempleado> unemployed. **estar** ~ (LAm, de pie) be standing

paradoja f paradox

parador m state-owned hotel

parafina f paraffin

paraguas m invar umbrella

Paraguay m Paraguay

paraguayo a & m Paraguayan

paraíso m paradise; (en el teatro) gallery

paralel|a *f* parallel (line). **~as** *fpl* parallel bars. **~o** *a & m* parallel

par|álisis *f invar* paralysis. **~alítico** *a* paralytic. **~alizar** [10] *vt* paralyse

paramilitar *a* paramilitary

páramo *m* bleak upland

parangón *m* comparison.

paraninfo *m* main hall

paranoi|a *f* paranoia. **~co** *a* paranoiac

parar *vt/i* stop. **sin ~** continuously. □ **~se** *vpr* stop; (LAm, ponerse de pie) stand

pararrayos *m invar* lightning conductor

parásito *a* parasitic. ● *m* parasite

parcela *f* plot. **~r** *vt* divide into plots

parche *m* patch

parcial *a* partial. **a tiempo ~** part-time. **~idad** *f* prejudice

parco *a* laconic; (sobrio) sparing, frugal

parear *vt* put into pairs

parec|er *m* opinion. **al ~er** apparently. **a mi ~er** in my opinion. ● *vi* [11] seem; (asemejarse) look like; (tener aspecto de) look. **me ~e** I think. **~e fácil** it looks easy. **¿qué te ~e?** what do you think? **según ~e** apparently. □ **~erse** *vpr* resemble, look like. **~ido** *a* similar. **bien ~ido** good-looking. ● *m* similarity

pared *f* wall. **~ por medio** next door. **~ón** *m* (de fusilamiento) wall. **llevar al ~ón** shoot

parej|a *f* pair; (hombre y mujer) couple; (compañero) partner. **~o** *a* the same; (LAm, sin desniveles) even; (LAm, liso) smooth; (Mex, equitativo) equal. ● *adv* (LAm) evenly

parente|la *f* relations. **~sco** *m* relationship

paréntesis *m invar* parenthesis, bracket (Brit); (intervalo) break. **entre ~** in brackets (Brit), in parenthesis; (fig) by the way

paria *m & f* outcast

paridad *f* equality; (Com) parity

pariente *m & f* relation, relative

parir *vt* give birth to. ● *vi* give birth

parisiense *a & m & f*, **parisino** *a & m* Parisian

parking /'parkin/ *m* car park (Brit), parking lot (Amer)

parlament|ar *vi* talk. **~ario** *a* parliamentary. ● *m* member of parliament (Brit), congressman (Amer). **~o** *m* parliament

parlanchín *a* talkative. ● *m* chatterbox

parlante *m* (LAm) loudspeaker

paro *m* stoppage; (desempleo) unemployment; (subsidio) unemployment benefit; (LAm, huelga) strike. **~ cardíaco** cardiac arrest

parodia *f* parody

parpadear *vi* blink; <*luz*> flicker

párpado *m* eyelid

parque *m* park. **~ de atracciones** funfair. **~ infantil** playground. **~ zoológico** zoo, zoological gardens

parquímetro *m* parking meter

parra *f* grapevine

párrafo *m* paragraph

parrilla *f* grill; (LAm, Auto) luggage rack. **a la ~** grilled. **~da** *f* grill

párroco *m* parish priest

parroquia *f* parish; (iglesia) parish church. **~no** *m* parishioner; (cliente) customer

parte *m* (informe) report. **dar ~** report. **de mi ~** for me ● *f* part; (porción) share; (Jurid) party; (Mex, repuesto) spare (part). **de ~ de** from. **¿de ~ de quién?** (al teléfono) who's speaking? **en cualquier ~** anywhere. **en gran ~** largely. **en ~** partly. **en todas ~s** everywhere. **la mayor ~** the majority. **la ~ superior** the top. **ninguna ~** nowhere. **por otra ~** on the other hand. **por todas ~s** everywhere

partera *f* midwife

partición *f* division; (Pol) partition

participa|ción *f* participation; (noticia) announcement; (de lotería) share. **~nte** *a* participating. ● *m & f* participant. **~r** *vt* announce. ● *vi* take part

participio *m* participle

particular *a* particular; <*clase*> private. **nada de ~** nothing special. ● *m* private individual.

partida f departure; (en registro) entry; (documento) certificate; (de mercancías) consignment; (juego) game; (de gente) group

partidario a & m partisan. ~ de in favour of

parti|do m (Pol) party; (encuentro) match, game; (LAm, de ajedrez) game. ~r vt cut; (romper) break; crack <nueces>. ● vi leave. a ~r de from. ~ de start from. □ ~rse vpr (romperse) break; (dividirse) split

partitura f (Mus) score

parto m labour. **estar de** ~ be in labour

parvulario m kindergarten, nursery school (Brit)

pasa f raisin. ~ **de Corinto** currant

pasa|da f passing; (de puntos) row. **de** ~**da** in passing. ~**dero** a passable. ~**dizo** m passage. ~**do** a past; <día, mes etc> last; (anticuado) old-fashioned; <comida> bad, off. ~**do maña-na** the day after tomorrow. ~**dos tres días** after three days. ~**dor** m bolt; (de pelo) hair-slide

pasaje m passage; (pasajeros) passengers; (LAm, de avión etc) ticket. ~**ro** a passing. ● m passenger

pasamano(s) m handrail; (barandilla de escalera) banister(s)

pasamontañas m invar balaclava

pasaporte m passport

pasar vt pass; (atravesar) go through; (filtrar) strain; spend <tiempo>; show <película>; (tolerar) tolerate; give <mensaje, enfermedad>. ● vi pass; (suceder) happen; (ir) go; (venir) come; <tiempo> go by. ~ de have no interest in. ~**lo bien** have a good time. ~ **frío** be cold. ~ **la aspiradora** vacuum. ~ **por alto** leave out. **lo que pasa es que** the fact is that. **pase lo que pase** whatever happens. **¡pase Vd!** come in!, go in! **¡que lo pases bien!** have a good time! **¿qué pasa?** what's the matter?, what's happening? □ ~**se** vpr pass; <dolor> go away; <flores> wither; <comida> go bad; spend <tiempo>; (excederse) go too far

pasarela f footbridge; (Naut) gangway

pasatiempo m hobby, pastime

Pascua f (fiesta de los hebreos) Passover; (de Resurrección) Easter; (Navidad) Christmas. ~**s** fpl Christmas

pase m pass

pase|ante m & f passer-by. ~**ar** vt walk <perro>; (exhibir) show off. ● vi walk. **ir a** ~**ar, salir a** ~**ar** walk. □ ~**arse** vpr walk. ~**o** m walk; (en coche etc) ride; (calle) avenue. ~**o marítimo** promenade. **dar un** ~**o, ir de** ~ go for a walk. **¡vete a** ~**o!** get lost! 🅃

pasillo m corridor; (de cine, avión) aisle

pasión f passion

pasivo a passive

pasm|ar vt astonish. □ ~**arse** vpr be astonished

paso m step; (acción de pasar) passing; (camino) way; (entre montañas) pass; (estrecho) strait(s). ~ **a nivel** level crossing (Brit), grade crossing (Amer). ~ **de cebra** zebra crossing. ~ **de peatones** pedestrian crossing. ~ **elevado** flyover (Brit), overpass (Amer). **a cada** ~ at every turn. **a dos** ~**s** very near. **de** ~ in passing. **de** ~ **por** just passing through. **oír** ~**s** hear footsteps. **prohibido el** ~ no entry

pasota m & f drop-out

pasta f paste; (masa) dough; (🅇, dinero) dough 🅇. ~**s** fpl pasta; (pasteles) pastries. ~ **de dientes,** ~ **dentífrica** toothpaste

pastel m cake; (empanada) pie; (lápiz) pastel. ~**ería** f cake shop

pasteurizado a pasteurized

pastilla f pastille; (de jabón) bar; (de chocolate) piece

pasto m pasture; (hierba) grass; (LAm, césped) lawn. ~**r** m shepherd; (Relig) minister. ~**ra** f shepherdess

pata f leg; (pie de perro, gato) paw; (de ave) foot. ~**s arriba** upside down. **a cuatro** ~**s** on all fours. **meter la** ~ put one's foot in it. **tener mala** ~ have bad luck. ~**da** f kick. ~**lear** vi stamp one's feet; <niño pequeño> kick

patata f potato. ~**s fritas** chips (Brit), French fries (Amer); (de bolsa) (potato) crisps (Brit), (potato) chips (Amer)

patente *a* obvious. ● *f* licence

patern|al *a* paternal; <*cariño etc*> fatherly. **~idad** *f* paternity. **~o** *a* paternal; <*cariño etc*> fatherly

patético *a* moving

patillas *fpl* sideburns

patín *m* skate; (con ruedas) roller skate

patina|dor *m* skater. **~je** *m* skating. **~r** *vi* skate; (resbalar) slide; <*coche*> skid

patio *m* patio. **~** de butacas stalls (Brit), orchestra (Amer)

pato *m* duck

patológico *a* pathological

patoso *a* clumsy

patraña *f* hoax

patria *f* homeland

patriarca *m* patriarch

patrimonio *m* patrimony; (fig) heritage

patri|ota *a* patriotic. ● *m & f* patriot. **~otismo** *m* patriotism

patrocin|ar *vt* sponsor. **~io** *m* sponsorship

patrón *m* (jefe) boss; (de pensión etc) landlord; (en costura) pattern

patrulla *f* patrol; (fig, cuadrilla) group. **~r** *vt/i* patrol

pausa *f* pause. **~do** *a* slow

pauta *f* guideline

paviment|ar *vt* pave. **~o** *m* pavement

pavo *m* turkey. **~** real peacock

pavor *m* terror

payas|ada *f* buffoonery. **~o** *m* clown

paz *f* peace

peaje *m* toll

peatón *m* pedestrian

peca *f* freckle

peca|do *m* sin; (defecto) fault. **~dor** *m* sinner. **~minoso** *a* sinful. **~r** [7] *vi* sin

pech|o *m* chest; (de mujer) breast; (fig, corazón) heart. dar el **~o** a un niño breast-feed a child. tomar a **~o** take to heart. **~uga** *f* breast

pecoso *a* freckled

peculiar *a* peculiar, particular. **~idad** *f* peculiarity

pedal *m* pedal. **~ear** *vi* pedal

pedante *a* pedantic

pedazo *m* piece, bit. a **~s** in pieces. hacer(se) **~s** smash

pediatra *m & f* paediatrician

pedicuro *m* chiropodist

pedi|do *m* order; (LAm, solicitud) request. **~r** [5] *vt* ask for; (Com, en restaurante) order. ● *vi* ask. **~r** prestado borrow

pega|dizo *a* catchy. **~joso** *a* sticky

pega|mento *m* glue. **~r** [12] *vt* stick (on); (coser) sew on; give <*enfermedad etc*>; (juntar) join; (golpear) hit; (dar) give. **~r** fuego a set fire to. ● *vi* stick. □ **~rse** *vpr* stick; (pelearse) hit each other. **~tina** *f* sticker

pein|ado *m* hairstyle. **~ar** *vt* comb. □ **~arse** *vpr* comb one's hair. **~e** *m* comb. **~eta** *f* ornamental comb

p.ej. *abrev* (**por ejemplo**) e.g.

pelado *a* <*fruta*> peeled; <*cabeza*> bald; <*terreno*> bare

pela|je *m* (de animal) fur; (fig, aspecto) appearance. **~mbre** *m* (de animal) fur; (de persona) thick hair

pelar *vt* peel; shell <*habas*>; skin <*tomates*>; pluck <*ave*>

peldaño *m* step; (de escalera de mano) rung

pelea *f* fight; (discusión) quarrel. **~r** *vi* fight; (discutir) quarrel. □ **~rse** *vpr* fight; (discutir) quarrel

peletería *f* fur shop

peliagudo *a* difficult, tricky

pelícano *m* pelican

película *f* film (esp Brit), movie (esp Amer). **~** de dibujos animados cartoon (film)

peligro *m* danger; (riesgo) hazard, risk. poner en **~** endanger. **~so** *a* dangerous

pelirrojo *a* red-haired

pellejo *m* skin

pellizc|ar [7] *vt* pinch. **~o** *m* pinch

pelma *m & f*, **pelmazo** *m* bore, nuisance

pelo *m* hair. no tener **~os** en la lengua be outspoken. tomar el **~o** a uno pull s.o.'s leg

pelota *f* ball. **~** vasca pelota. hacer la **~** a uno suck up to s.o.

pelotera f squabble

peluca f wig

peludo a hairy

peluquer|ía f hairdresser's. ~o m hairdresser

pelusa f down

pena f sadness; <*lástima*> pity; (LAm, vergüenza) embarrassment; (Jurid) sentence. ~ **de muerte** death penalty. **a duras** ~s with difficulty. **da** ~ **que** it's a pity that. **me da** ~ it makes me sad. **merecer la** ~ be worthwhile. **pasar** ~s suffer hardship. ¡**qué** ~! what a pity! **valer la** ~ be worthwhile

penal a penal; <*derecho*> criminal. ● m prison; (LAm, penalty) penalty. ~**idad** f suffering; (Jurid) penalty. ~**ty** m penalty

pendiente a hanging; <*cuenta*> outstanding; <*asunto etc*> pending. ● m earring. ● f slope

péndulo m pendulum

pene m penis

penetra|nte a penetrating; <*sonido*> piercing; <*viento*> bitter. ~**r** vt penetrate; (fig) pierce. ● vi. ~**r en** penetrate; (entrar) go into

penicilina f penicillin

pen|ínsula f peninsula. ~**insular** a peninsular

penique m penny

penitencia f penitence; (castigo) penance

penoso a painful; (difícil) difficult; (LAm, tímido) shy; (LAm, embarazoso) embarrassing

pensa|do a. **bien** ~**do** all things considered. **menos** ~**do** least expected. ~**dor** m thinker. ~**miento** m thought. ~**r** [1] vt think; (considerar) consider. **cuando menos se piensa** when least expected. ¡**ni** ~**rlo**! no way! **pienso que sí** I think so. ● vi think. ~**r en** think about. ~**tivo** a thoughtful

pensi|ón f pension; (casa de huéspedes) guest-house. ~**ón completa** full board. ~**onista** m & f pensioner; (huésped) lodger

penúltimo a & m penultimate, last but one

penumbra f half-light

penuria f shortage. **pasar** ~s suffer hardship

peñ|a f rock; (de amigos) group; (LAm, club) folk club. ~**ón** m rock. **el P**~**ón de Gibraltar** The Rock (of Gibraltar)

peón m labourer; (en ajedrez) pawn; (en damas) piece

peonza f (spinning) top

peor a (comparativo) worse; (superlativo) worst. ● adv worse. **de mal en** ~ from bad to worse. **lo** ~ the worst thing. **tanto** ~ so much the worse

pepin|illo m gherkin. ~**o** m cucumber. (**no**) **me importa un** ~**o** I couldn't care less

pepita f pip; (de oro) nugget

pequeñ|ez f smallness; (minucia) trifle. ~**o** a small, little; (de edad) young; (menor) younger. ● m little one. **es el** ~**o** he's the youngest

pera f (fruta) pear. ~**l** m pear (tree)

percance m mishap

percatarse vpr. ~ **de** notice

perc|epción f perception. ~**ibir** vt perceive; earn <*dinero*>

percha f hanger; (de aves) perch

percusión f percussion

perde|dor a losing. ● m loser. ~**r** [1] vt lose; (malgastar) waste; miss <*tren etc*>. ● vi lose. □ ~**rse** vpr get lost; (desaparecer) disappear; (desperdiciarse) be wasted; (estropearse) be spoilt. **echar(se) a** ~**r** spoil

pérdida f loss; (de líquido) leak; (de tiempo) waste

perdido a lost

perdiz f partridge

perd|ón m pardon, forgiveness. **pedir** ~**ón** apologize. ● int sorry! ~**onar** vt excuse, forgive; (Jurid) pardon. ¡~**one** (**Vd**)! sorry!

perdura|ble a lasting. ~**r** vi last

perece|dero a perishable. ~**r** [11] vi perish

peregrin|ación f pilgrimage. ~**o** a strange. ● m pilgrim

perejil m parsley

perengano m so-and-so

perenne a everlasting; (Bot) perennial

perez|a f laziness. ~**oso** a lazy

perfec|ción f perfection. **a la** ~**ción** perfectly, to perfection. ~**cionar** vt perfect; (mejorar) improve. ~**cionista** m & f perfectionist. ~**to** a perfect; (completo) complete

perfil m profile; (contorno) outline. ~**ado** a well-shaped

perfora|ción f perforation. ~**dora** f punch. ~**r** vt pierce, perforate; punch <papel, tarjeta etc>

perfum|ar vt perfume. □ ~**arse** vpr put perfume on. ~**e** m perfume, scent. ~**ería** f perfumery

pericia f skill

perif|eria f (de ciudad) outskirts. ~**érico** a <barrio> outlying. ● m (Mex, carretera) ring road

perilla f (barba) goatee

perímetro m perimeter

periódico a periodic(al). ● m newspaper

periodis|mo m journalism. ~**ta** m & f journalist

período m, **periodo** m period

periquito m budgerigar

periscopio m periscope

perito a & m expert

perju|dicar [7] vt damage; (desfavorecer) not suit. ~**dicial** a damaging. ~**icio** m damage. **en** ~**icio de** to the detriment of

perla f pearl. **de** ~**s** adv very well

permane|cer [11] vi remain. ~**ncia** f permanence; (estancia) stay. ~**nte** a permanent. ● f perm. ● m (Mex) perm

permi|sivo a permissive. ~**so** m permission; (documento) licence; (Mil etc) leave. ~**so de conducir** driving licence (Brit), driver's license (Amer). **con** ~**so** excuse me. ~**tir** vt allow, permit. **¿me** ~**te?** may I? □ ~**tirse** vpr allow s.o.

pernicioso a pernicious; <persona> wicked

perno m bolt

pero conj but. ● m fault; (objeción) objection

perogrullada f platitude

perpendicular a & f perpendicular

perpetrar vt perpetrate

perpetu|ar [21] vt perpetuate. ~**o** a perpetual

perplejo a perplexed

perr|a f (animal) bitch; (moneda) coin, penny (Brit), cent (Amer); (rabieta) tantrum. **estar sin una** ~**a** be broke. ~**era** f dog pound; (vehículo) dog catcher's van. ~**o** a awful. ● m dog. ~**o galgo** greyhound. **de** ~**os** awful

persa a & m & f Persian

perse|cución f pursuit; (política etc) persecution. ~**guir** [5 & 13] vt pursue; (por ideología etc) persecute

persevera|nte a persevering. ~**r** vi persevere

persiana f blind; (LAm, contraventana) shutter

persignarse vpr cross o.s.

persist|ente a persistent. ~**ir** vi persist

person|a f person. ~**as** fpl people. ~**aje** m (persona importante) important figure; (de obra literaria) character. ~**al** a personal. ● m staff. ~**alidad** f personality. □ ~**arse** vpr appear in person. ~**ificar** [7] vt personify

perspectiva f perspective

perspica|cia f shrewdness; (de vista) keen eyesight. ~**z** a shrewd; <vista> keen

persua|dir vt persuade. ~**sión** f persuasion. ~**sivo** a persuasive

pertenecer [11] vi belong

pértiga f pole. **salto** m **con** ~ pole vault

pertinente a relevant

perturba|ción f disturbance. ~**ción del orden público** breach of the peace. ~**r** vt disturb; disrupt <orden>

Perú m. **el** ~ Peru

peruano a & m Peruvian

perver|so a evil. ● m evil person. ~**tir** [4] vt pervert

pesa f weight. ~**dez** f weight; (de cabeza etc) heaviness; (lentitud) sluggishness; (cualidad de fastidioso) tediousness; (cosa fastidiosa) bore, nuisance

pesadilla f nightmare

pesado *a* heavy; *<sueño>* deep; *<viaje>* tiring; (duro) hard; (aburrido) boring, tedious

pésame *m* sympathy, condolences

pesar *vt* weigh. ● *vi* be heavy. ● *m* sorrow; (remordimiento) regret. **a ~ de (que)** in spite of. **pese a (que)** in spite of

pesca *f* fishing; (peces) fish; (pescado) catch. **ir de ~** go fishing. **~da** *f* hake. **~dería** *f* fish shop. **~dilla** *f* whiting. **~do** *m* fish. **~dor** *a* fishing. ● *m* fisherman. **~r** [7] *vt* catch. ● *vi* fish

pescuezo *m* neck

pesebre *m* manger

pesero *m* (Mex) minibus

peseta *f* peseta

pesimista *a* pessimistic. ● *m & f* pessimist

pésimo *a* very bad, awful

peso *m* weight; (moneda) peso. **~ bruto** gross weight. **~ neto** net weight. **al ~** by weight. **de ~** influential

pesquero *a* fishing

pestañ|a *f* eyelash. **~ear** *vi* blink

pest|e *f* plague; (hedor) stench. **~icida** *m* pesticide

pestillo *m* bolt; (de cerradura) latch

petaca *f* cigarette case; (Mex, maleta) suitcase

pétalo *m* petal

petardo *m* firecracker

petición *f* request; (escrito) petition

petirrojo *m* robin

petrificar [7] *vt* petrify

petr|óleo *m* oil. **~olero** *a* oil. ● *m* oil tanker

petulante *a* smug

peyorativo *a* pejorative

pez *f* fish; (substancia negruzca) pitch. **~ espada** swordfish

pezón *m* nipple

pezuña *f* hoof

piadoso *a* compassionate; (devoto) devout

pian|ista *m & f* pianist. **~o** *m* piano. **~o de cola** grand piano

piar [20] *vi* chirp

picad|a *f*. **caer en ~a** (LAm) nosedive. **~o** *a* perforated; *<carne>* minced (Brit), ground (Amer); (ofendido)

offended; *<mar>* choppy; *<diente>* bad. ● *m*. **caer en ~o** nosedive. **~ura** *f* bite, sting; (de polilla) moth hole

picaflor *m* (LAm) hummingbird

picante *a* hot; *<chiste etc>* risqué

picaporte *m* door-handle; (aldaba) knocker

picar [7] *vt* *<ave>* peck; *<insecto, pez>* bite; *<abeja, avispa>* sting; (comer poco) pick at; mince (Brit), grind (Amer) *<carne>*; chop (up) *<cebolla etc>*; (Mex, pinchar) prick. ● *vi* itch; *<ave>* peck; *<insecto, pez>* bite; *<sol>* scorch; *<comida>* be hot

picardía *f* craftiness; (travesura) naughty thing

pícaro *a* crafty; *<niño>* mischievous. ● *m* rogue

picazón *f* itch

pichón *m* pigeon; (Mex, novato) beginner

pico *m* beak; (punta) corner; (herramienta) pickaxe; (cima) peak. **y ~** (con tiempo) a little after; (con cantidad) a little more than. **~tear** *vt* peck; (🄸, comer) pick at

picudo *a* pointed

pido *vb* ⇨PEDIR

pie *m* foot; (Bot, de vaso) stem. **~ cuadrado** square foot. **a cuatro ~s** on all fours. **al ~ de la letra** literally. **a ~** on foot. **a ~(s) juntillas** (fig) firmly. **buscarle tres ~s al gato** split hairs. **de ~** standing (up). **de ~s a cabeza** from head to toe. **en ~** standing (up). **ponerse de ~** stand up

piedad *f* pity; (Relig) piety

piedra *f* stone; (de mechero) flint

piel *f* skin; (cuero) leather

pienso *vb* ⇨PENSAR

pierdo *vb* ⇨PERDER

pierna *f* leg

pieza *f* piece; (parte) part; (obra teatral) play; (moneda) coin; (habitación) room. **~ de recambio** spare part

pijama *m* pyjamas

pila *f* (montón) pile; (recipiente) basin; (eléctrica) battery. **~ bautismal** font. **~r** *m* pillar

píldora *f* pill

pilla|je *m* pillage. **~r** *vt* catch

pillo *a* wicked. ● *m* rogue

pilot|ar *vt* pilot. **~o** *m* pilot

pim|entero *m* (vasija) pepperpot. **~entón** *m* paprika; (LAm, fruto) pepper. **~ienta** *f* pepper. **grano** *m* de **~ienta** peppercorn. **~iento** *m* pepper

pináculo *m* pinnacle

pinar *m* pine forest

pincel *m* paintbrush. **~ada** *f* brushstroke. **la última ~ada** (fig) the finishing touch

pinch|ar *vt* pierce, prick; puncture <neumático>; (fig, incitar) push; (Med, 🔲) give an injection to. **~azo** *m* prick; (en neumático) puncture. **~itos** *mpl* kebab(s); (tapas) savoury snacks. **~o** *m* point

ping-pong *m* table tennis, pingpong

pingüino *m* penguin

pino *m* pine (tree)

pint|a *f* spot; (fig, aspecto) appearance. **tener ~a de** look like. **~ada** *f* graffiti. **~ar** *vt* paint. **no ~a nada** (fig) it doesn't count. □ **~arse** *vpr* put on make-up. **~or** *m* painter. **~oresco** *a* picturesque. **~ura** *f* painting; (material) paint

pinza *f* (clothes-)peg (Brit), clothespin (Amer); (de cangrejo etc) claw. **~s** *fpl* tweezers

piñ|a *f* pine cone; (fruta) pineapple. **~ón** *m* (semilla) pine nut

pío *a* pious. ● *m* chirp. **no decir ni ~** not say a word

piojo *m* louse

pionero *m* pioneer

pipa *f* pipe; (semilla) seed; (de girasol) sunflower seed

pique *m* resentment; (rivalidad) rivalry. **irse a ~** sink

piquete *m* picket; (Mex, herida) prick; (Mex, de insecto) sting

piragua *f* canoe

pirámide *f* pyramid

pirata *a invar* pirate. ● *m* & *f* pirate

Pirineos *mpl* **los ~** the Pyrenees

piropo *m* flattering comment

pirueta *f* pirouette

pirulí *m* lollipop

pisa|da *f* footstep; (huella) footprint. **~papeles** *m invar* paperweight. **~r** *vt* tread on. ● *vi* tread

piscina *f* swimming pool

Piscis *m* Pisces

piso *m* floor; (vivienda) flat (Brit), apartment (Amer); (de autobús) deck

pisotear *vt* trample (on)

pista *f* track; (fig, indicio) clue. **~ de aterrizaje** runway. **~ de baile** dance floor. **~ de carreras** racing track. **~ de hielo** ice-rink. **~ de tenis** tennis court

pistol|a *f* pistol. **~era** *f* holster. **~ero** *m* gunman

pistón *m* piston

pit|ar, (LAm) **~ear** *vt* whistle at; <conductor> hoot at; award <falta>. ● *vi* blow a whistle; (Auto) sound one's horn. **~ido** *m* whistle

pitill|era *f* cigarette case. **~o** *m* cigarette

pito *m* whistle; (Auto) horn

pitón *m* python

pitorre|arse *vpr*. **~arse de** make fun of. **~o** *m* teasing

pitorro *m* spout

piyama *m* (LAm) pyjamas

pizarr|a *f* slate; (en aula) blackboard. **~ón** *m* (LAm) blackboard

pizca *f* 🔲 tiny piece; (de sal) pinch. **ni ~** not at all

placa *f* plate; (con inscripción) plaque; (distintivo) badge. **~ de matrícula** number plate

place|ntero *a* pleasant. **~r** [32] *vi*. **haz lo que te plazca** do as you please. **me ~ hacerlo** I'm pleased to do it. ● *m* pleasure

plácido *a* placid

plaga *f* (also fig) plague. **~do** *a*. **~do de** filled with

plagio *m* plagiarism

plan *m* plan. **en ~ de** as

plana *f* page. **en primera ~** on the front page

plancha *f* iron; (lámina) sheet. **a la ~** grilled. **tirarse una ~** put one's foot in it. **~do** *m* ironing. **~r** *vt* iron. ● *vi* do the ironing

planeador *m* glider

planear *vt* plan. ● *vi* glide

planeta *m* planet

planicie *f* plain

planifica|ción *f* planning. **~r** [7] *vt* plan

planilla *f* (LAm) payroll; (personal) staff

plano *a* flat. ● *m* plane; (de edificio) plan; (de ciudad) street plan. **primer ~** foreground; (Foto) close-up

planta *f* (Anat) sole; (Bot, fábrica) plant; (plano) ground plan; (piso) floor. **~ ba-ja** ground floor (Brit), first floor (Amer)

planta|ción *f* plantation. **~r** *vt* plant; deal *<golpe>*. **~r en la calle** throw out. □ **~rse** *vpr* stand; (fig) stand firm

plantear *vt* (exponer) expound; (causar) create; raise *<cuestión>*

plantilla *f* insole; (nómina) payroll; (personal) personnel

plaqué *m* plating. **de ~** plated

plástico *a & m* plastic

plata *f* silver; (fig, 🄸, dinero) money. **~ de ley** hallmarked silver

plataforma *f* platform

plátano *m* plane (tree); (fruta) banana. **platanero** *m* banana tree

platea *f* stalls (Brit), orchestra (Amer)

plateado *a* silver-plated; (color de plata) silver

pl|ática *f* talk. **~aticar** [7] *vi* (Mex) talk. ● *vt* (Mex) tell

platija *f* plaice

platillo *m* saucer; (Mus) cymbal. **~ volador** (LAm), **~ volante** flying saucer

platino *m* platinum. **~s** *mpl* (Auto) points

plato *m* plate; (comida) dish; (parte de una comida) course

platónico *a* platonic

playa *f* beach; (fig) seaside

plaza *f* square; (mercado) market (place); (sitio) place; (empleo) job. **~ de toros** bullring

plazco *vb* ⇒PLACER

plazo *m* period; (pago) instalment; (fecha) date. **comprar a ~s** buy on hire purchase (Brit), buy on the installment plan (Amer)

plazuela *f* little square

pleamar *f* high tide

pleb|e *f* common people. **~eyo** *a & m* plebeian. **~iscito** *m* plebiscite

plega|ble *a* pliable; *<silla>* folding. **~r** [1 & 12] *vt* fold. □ **~rse** *vpr* bend; (fig) yield

pleito *m* (court) case; (fig) dispute

plenilunio *m* full moon

plen|itud *f* fullness; (fig) height. **~o** *a* full. **en ~o día** in broad daylight. **en ~o verano** at the height of the summer

plieg|o *m* sheet. **~ue** *m* fold; (en ropa) pleat

plisar *vt* pleat

plom|ero *m* (LAm) plumber. **~o** *m* lead; (Elec) fuse. **con ~o** leaded. **sin ~o** unleaded

pluma *f* feather; (para escribir) pen. **~ atómica** (Mex) ballpoint pen. **~ estilográfica** fountain pen. **~je** *m* plumage

plum|ero *m* feather duster; (para plumas, lápices etc) pencil-case. **~ón** *m* down; (edredón) down-filled quilt

plural *a & m* plural. **en ~** in the plural

pluriempleo *m* having more than one job

plus *m* bonus

pluscuamperfecto *m* pluperfect

plusvalía *f* capital gain

pluvial *a* rain

pobla|ción *f* population; (ciudad) city, town; (pueblo) village. **~do** *a* populated. ● *m* village. **~r** [2] *vt* populate; (habitar) inhabit. □ **~rse** *vpr* get crowded

pobre *a* poor. ● *m & f* poor person; (fig) poor thing. **¡~cito!** poor (little) thing! **¡~ de mí!** poor (old) me! **~za** *f* poverty

pocilga *f* pigsty

poción *f* potion

··

poco

● *adjetivo/pronombre*

····▸ poco, poca little, not much. **tiene poca paciencia** he has little patience. **¿cuánta leche queda? - poca** how much milk is there left? - not much

····▸ **pocos, pocas** few. **muy** ∼**s días** very few days. **unos** ∼**s dólares** a few dollars. **compré unos** ∼**s** I bought a few. **aceptaron a muy** ∼**s** very few (people) were accepted

····▸ **a** ∼ **de llegar** soon after he arrived. **¡a** ∼ **!** (Mex) really? **dentro de** ∼ **soon.** ∼ **a** ∼**, (LAm) de a** ∼ gradually, little by little. **hace** ∼ recently, not long ago. **por** ∼ nearly. **un** ∼ (cantidad) a little; (tiempo) a while. **un** ∼ **de** a (little) bit of, a little, some

● *adverbio*

····▸ (con verbo) not much. **lee muy** ∼ he doesn't read very much

····▸ (con adjetivo) **un lugar** ∼ **conocido** a little known place. **es** ∼ **inteligente** he's not very intelligent

> ! Cuando **poco** modifica a un adjetivo, muchas veces el inglés prefiere el uso del prefijo *un-*, p. ej. **poco amistoso** *unfriendly.* **poco agradecido** *ungrateful*

podar *vt* prune

poder [33] *v aux* be able to. **no voy a** ∼ **terminar** I won't be able to finish. **no pudo venir** he couldn't come. **¿puedo hacer algo?** can I do anything? **¿puedo pasar?** may I come in?. **no** ∼ **con** not be able to cope with; (no aguantar) not be able to stand. **no** ∼ **más** be exhausted; (estar harto de algo) not be able to manage any more. **no** ∼ **menos que** have no alternative but. **puede que** it is possible that. **puede ser** it is possible. **¿se puede ...?** may I...? ● *m* power. **en el** ∼ in power. ∼**es** *mpl* **públicos** authorities. ∼**oso** *a* powerful

podrido *a* rotten

po|ema *m* poem. ∼**esía** *f* poetry; (poema) poem. ∼**eta** *m & f* poet. ∼**ético** *a* poetic

polaco *a* Polish. ● *m* Pole; (lengua) Polish

polar *a* polar. **estrella** ∼ polestar

polea *f* pulley

pol|émica *f* controversy. ∼**emizar** [10] *vi* argue

polen *m* pollen

policía *f* police (force); (persona) policewoman. ● *m* policeman. ∼**co** *a* police; *<novela etc>* detective

polícromo *a*, **polícromo** *a* polychrome

polideportivo *m* sports centre

polietileno *m* polythene

poligamia *f* polygamy

polígono *m* polygon

polilla *f* moth

polio(mielitis) *f* polio(myelitis)

polític|a *f* politics; (postura) policy; (mujer) politician. ∼ **interior** domestic policy. ∼**o** *a* political. **familia** ∼**a** in-laws. ● *m* politician

póliza *f* (de seguros) policy

poll|o *m* chicken; (gallo joven) chick. ∼**uelo** *m* chick

polo *m* pole; (helado) ice lolly (Brit), Popsicle (P) (Amer); (juego) polo. **P**∼ **norte** North Pole

Polonia *f* Poland

poltrona *f* armchair

polución *f* pollution

polv|areda *f* dust cloud; (fig, escándalo) uproar. ∼**era** *f* compact. ∼**o** *m* powder; (suciedad) dust. ∼**os** *mpl* powder. **en** ∼**o** powdered. **estar hecho** ∼**o** be exhausted. **quitar el** ∼**o** dust

pólvora *f* gunpowder; (fuegos artificiales) fireworks

polvoriento *a* dusty

pomada *f* ointment

pomelo *m* grapefruit

pómez *a.* **piedra** *f* ∼ pumice stone

pomp|a *f* bubble; (esplendor) pomp. ∼**as fúnebres** funeral. ∼**oso** *a* pompous; (espléndido) splendid

pómulo *m* cheekbone

ponchar *vt* (Mex) puncture

ponche *m* punch

poncho *m* poncho

ponderar *vt* (alabar) speak highly of

poner [34] *vt* put; put on *<ropa, obra de teatro, TV etc>*; lay *<la mesa, un huevo>*; set *<examen, deberes>*; (contribuir) contribute; give *<nombre>*; make *<nervioso>*; pay *<atención>*; show *<película, interés>*; open *<una tienda>*; equip *<una casa>.* ∼ **con** (al teléfono) put through to. ∼ **por escrito**

put into writing. ~ **una multa** fine. **pongamos** let's suppose. ● *vi* lay. □ ~**se** *vpr* put o.s.; (volverse) get; put on *<ropa>*; *<sol>* set. ~**se a** start to. ~**se a mal con uno** fall out with s.o.

pongo *vb* ⇒PONER

poniente *m* west; (viento) west wind

pont|ificar [7] *vi* pontificate. ~**ífice** *m* pontiff

popa *f* stern

popote *m* (Mex) (drinking) straw

popul|acho *m* masses. ~**ar** *a* popular; *<costumbre>* traditional; *<lenguaje>* colloquial. ~**aridad** *f* popularity. ~**arizar** [10] *vt* popularize.

póquer *m* poker

poquito *m*. **un** ~ a little bit. ● *adv* a little

por

● *preposición*

····▸ for. **es** ~ **tu bien** it's for your own good. **lo compró** ~ **5 dólares** he bought it for 5 dollars. **si no fuera** ~ **ti** if it weren't for you. **vino** ~ **una semana** he came for a week

⇨ Para expresiones como **por la mañana, por la noche** etc., ver bajo el respectivo nombre

····▸ (causa) because of. **se retrasó** ~ **la lluvia** he was late because of the rain. **no hay trenes** ~ **la huelga** there aren't any trains because of the strike

····▸ (medio, agente) by. **lo envié** ~ **correo** I sent it by post. **fue destruida** ~ **las bombas** it was destroyed by the bombs

····▸ (a través de) through. **entró** ~ **la ventana** he got in through the window. **me enteré** ~ **un amigo** I found out through a friend. ~ **todo el país** throughout the country

····▸ (a lo largo de) along. **caminar** ~ **la playa** to walk along the beach. **cortar** ~ **la línea de puntos** cut along the dotted line

····▸ (proporción) per. **cobra 30 dólares** ~ **hora** he charges 30 dollars per hour. **uno** ~ **persona** one per person. **10** ~ **ciento** 10 per cent

····▸ (Mat) times. **dos** ~ **dos (son) cuatro** two times two is four

····▸ (modo) in. ~ **escrito** in writing. **pagar** ~ **adelantado** to pay in advance

⇨ Para expresiones como **por dentro, por fuera** etc., ver bajo el respectivo adverbio

····▸ (en locuciones) ~ **más que** no matter how much. **¿** ~ **qué?** why? ~ **si** in case. ~ **supuesto** of course

porcelana *f* china

porcentaje *m* percentage

porcino *a* pig

porción *f* portion; (de chocolate) piece

pordiosero *m* beggar

porfia|do *a* stubborn. ~**r** [20] *vi* insist

pormenor *m* detail

pornogr|afía *f* pornography. ~**áfico** *a* pornographic

poro *m* pore; (Mex, puerro) leek. ~**so** *a* porous

porque *conj* because; (para que) so that

porqué *m* reason

porquería *f* filth; (basura) rubbish; (grosería) dirty trick

porra *f* club

porrón *m* wine jug (with a long spout)

portaaviones *m invar* aircraft carrier

portada *f* (de libro) title page; (de revista) cover

portadocumentos *m invar* (LAm) briefcase

portador *m* bearer

portaequipaje(s) *m invar* boot (Brit), trunk (Amer); (encima del coche) roof-rack

portal *m* hall; (puerta principal) main entrance. ~**es** *mpl* arcade

porta|ligas *m invar* suspender belt. ~**monedas** *m invar* purse

portarse *vpr* behave

portátil *a* portable

portavoz *m* spokesman. ● *f* spokeswoman

portazo *m* bang. **dar un** ~ slam the door

porte *m* transport; (precio) carriage; (LAm, tamaño) size. ∼**ador** *m* carrier

portento *m* marvel

porteño *a* (from Buenos Aires

porter|ía *f* porter's lodge; (en deportes) goal. ∼**o** *m* caretaker, porter; (en deportes) goalkeeper. ∼**o automático** entryphone

pórtico *m* portico

portorriqueño *a* & *m* Puerto Rican

Portugal *m* Portugal

portugués *a* & *m* Portuguese

porvenir *m* future

posada *f* inn. **dar** ∼ give shelter

posar *vt* put. ● *vi* pose. □ ∼**se** *vpr* <*pájaro*> perch; <*avión*> land

posdata *f* postscript

pose|edor *m* owner; (de récord, billete, etc) holder. ∼**er** [18] *vt* own; hold <*récord*>; have <*conocimientos*>. ∼**sión** *f* possession. □ ∼**sionarse** *vpr*. ∼**sionarse de** take possession of. ∼**sivo** *a* possessive

posgraduado *a* & *m* postgraduate

posguerra *f* post-war years

posib|ilidad *f* possibility. ∼**le** *a* possible. **de ser** ∼**le** if possible. **en lo** ∼**le** as far as possible. **si es** ∼**le** if possible

posición *f* position; (en sociedad) social standing

positivo *a* positive

poso *m* sediment

posponer [34] *vt* put after; (diferir) postpone

posta *f*. **a** ∼ on purpose

postal *a* postal. ● *f* postcard

poste *m* pole; (de valla) post

póster *m* (*pl* ∼**s**) poster

postergar [12] *vt* pass over; (diferir) postpone

posteri|dad *f* posterity. ∼**or** *a* back; <*años*> later; <*capítulos*> subsequent. ∼**ormente** *adv* later

postigo *m* door; (contraventana) shutter

postizo *a* false, artificial. ● *m* hairpiece

postrarse *vpr* prostrate o.s.

postre *m* dessert, pudding (Brit)

postular *vt* postulate; (LAm) nominate <*candidato*>

póstumo *a* posthumous

postura *f* position, stance

potable *a* drinkable; <*agua*> drinking

potaje *m* vegetable stew

potasio *m* potassium

pote *m* pot

poten|cia *f* power. ∼**cial** *a* & *m* potential. ∼**te** *a* powerful

potro *m* colt; (en gimnasia) horse

pozo *m* well; (hoyo seco) pit; (de mina) shaft; (fondo común) pool

práctica *f* practice. **en la** ∼ in practice

practica|nte *m* & *f* nurse. ∼**r** [7] *vt* practise; play <*deportes*>; (ejecutar) carry out

práctico *a* practical; (conveniente, útil) handy. ● *m* practitioner

prad|era *f* meadow; (terreno grande) prairie. ∼**o** *m* meadow

pragmático *a* pragmatic

preámbulo *m* preamble

precario *a* precarious; <*medios*> scarce

precaución *f* precaution; (cautela) caution. **con** ∼ cautiously

precaverse *vpr* take precautions

precede|ncia *f* precedence; (prioridad) priority. ∼**nte** *a* preceding. ● *m* precedent. ∼**r** *vt/i* precede

precepto *m* precept. ∼**r** *m* tutor

precia|do *a* valued; <*don*> valuable. □ ∼**rse** *vpr*. ∼**rse de** pride o.s. on

precio *m* price. ∼ **de venta al público** retail price. **al** ∼ **de** at the cost of. **no tener** ∼ be priceless. **¿qué** ∼ **tiene?** how much is it?

precios|idad *f* (cosa preciosa) beautiful thing. **¡es una** ∼**idad!** it's beautiful! ∼**o** *a* precious; (bonito) beautiful

precipicio *m* precipice

precipita|ción *f* precipitation; (prisa) rush. ∼**damente** *adv* hastily. ∼**do** *a* hasty. ∼**r** *vt* (apresurar) hasten; (arrojar) hurl. □ ∼**rse** *vpr* throw o.s.; (correr) rush; (actuar sin reflexionar) act rashly

precis|amente a exactly. **~ar** vt require; (determinar) determine. **~ión** f precision. **~o** a precise; (necesario) necessary. **si es ~o** if necessary

preconcebido a preconceived

precoz a early; <niño> precocious

precursor m forerunner

predecesor m predecessor

predecir [46], (pero imperativo **pre-dice**, futuro y condicional regulares) vt foretell

predestinado a predestined

prédica f sermon

predicar [7] vt/i preach

predicción f prediction; (del tiempo) forecast

predilec|ción f predilection. **~to** a favourite

predisponer [34] vt predispose

predomin|ante a predominant. **~ar** vi predominate. **~io** m predominance

preeminente a pre-eminent

prefabricado a prefabricated

prefacio m preface

prefer|encia f preference; (Auto) right of way. **de ~encia** preferably. **~ente** a preferential. **~ible** a preferable. **~ido** a favourite. **~ir** [4] vt prefer

prefijo m prefix; (telefónico) dialling code

pregonar vt announce

pregunta f question. **hacer una ~** ask a question. **~r** vt/i ask (por about). □ **~rse** vpr wonder

prehistórico a prehistoric

preju|icio m prejudice. **~zgar** [12] vt prejudge

preliminar a & m preliminary

preludio m prelude

premarital a, **prematrimonial** a premarital

prematuro a premature

premedita|ción f premeditation. **~r** vt premeditate

premi|ar vt give a prize to; (recompensar) reward. **~o** m prize; (recompensa) reward. **~o gordo** jackpot

premonición f premonition

prenatal a antenatal

prenda f garment; (garantía) surety; (en juegos) forfeit. **en ~ de** as a token of. **~r** vt captivate. □ **~rse** vpr fall in love (**de** with)

prende|dor m brooch. **~r** vt capture; (sujetar) fasten; light <cigarrillo>; (LAm) turn on <gas, radio, etc>. ● vi catch; (arraigar) take root. □ **~se** vpr (encenderse) catch fire

prensa f press. **~r** vt press

preñado a pregnant; (fig) full

preocupa|ción f worry. **~do** a worried. **~r** vt worry. □ **~rse** vpr worry. **~rse de** look after

prepara|ción f preparation. **~do** a prepared. ● m preparation. **~r** vt prepare. □ **~rse** vpr get ready. **~tivos** mpl preparations. **~torio** a preparatory

preposición f preposition

prepotente a arrogant; <actitud> high-handed

prerrogativa f prerogative

presa f (cosa) prey; (embalse) dam

presagi|ar vt presage. **~o** m omen

presb|iteriano a & m Presbyterian. **~ítero** m priest

prescindir vi. **~ de** do without; (deshacerse de) dispense with

prescri|bir (pp **prescrito**) vt prescribe. **~pción** f prescription

presencia f presence; (aspecto) appearance. **en ~ de** in the presence of. **~r** vt be present at; (ver) witness

presenta|ble a presentable. **~ción** f presentation; (de una persona a otra) introduction. **~dor** m presenter. **~r** vt present; (ofrecer) offer; (entregar) hand in; (hacer conocer) introduce; show <película>. □ **~rse** vpr present o.s.; (hacerse conocer) introduce o.s.; (aparecer) turn up

presente a present; (actual) this. ● m present. **los ~s** those present. **tener ~** remember

presenti|miento m premonition. **~r** [4] vt have a feeling (**que** that)

preserva|r vt preserve. **~tivo** m condom

presiden|cia f presidency; (de asamblea) chairmanship. **~cial** a presidential. **~ta** f (woman) president. **~te** m president; (de asamblea) chairman. **~te del gobierno** prime minister

presidi|ario *m* convict. **~o** *m* prison

presidir *vt* be president of; preside over *<tribunal>*; chair *<reunión, comité>*

presi|ón *f* pressure. **a ~ón** under pressure. **hacer ~ón** press. **~onar** *vt* press; (fig) put pressure on

preso *a*. **estar ~** be in prison. **llevarse ~ a uno** take s.o. away under arrest. ● *m* prisoner

presta|do *a* (de uno) lent; (a uno) borrowed. **pedir ~do** borrow. **~mista** *m & f* moneylender

préstamo *m* loan; (acción de pedir prestado) borrowing; (acción de prestar) lending

prestar *vt* lend; give *<ayuda etc>*; pay *<atención>*. □ **~se** *vpr*. **~se a** be open to; (ser apto) be suitable (**para** for)

prestidigita|ción *f* conjuring. **~dor** *m* conjurer

prestigio *m* prestige. **~so** *a* prestigious

presu|mido *a* conceited. **~mir** *vi* show off. boast (**de** about). **~nción** *f* conceit; (suposición) presumption. **~nto** *a* alleged. **~ntuoso** *a* conceited

presup|oner [34] *vt* presuppose. **~uesto** *m* budget; (precio estimado) estimate

preten|cioso *a* pretentious. **~der** *vt* try to; (afirmar) claim; (solicitar) apply for; (cortejar) court. **~diente** *m* pretender; (a una mujer) suitor. **~sión** *f* pretension; (aspiración) aspiration

pretérito *m* preterite, past

pretexto *m* pretext. **con el ~ de** on the pretext of

prevalecer [11] *vi* prevail (**sobre** over)

preven|ción *f* prevention; (prejuicio) prejudice. **~ido** *a* ready; (precavido) cautious. **~ir** [53] *vt* prevent; (advertir) warn. **~tiva** *f* (Mex) amber light. **~tivo** *a* preventive

prever [43] *vt* foresee; (planear) plan

previo *a* previous

previs|ible *a* predictable. **~ión** *f* forecast; (prudencia) precaution

prima *f* (pariente) cousin; (cantidad) bonus

primario *a* primary

primavera *f* spring. **~l** *a* spring

primer *a* ⇒PRIMERO. **~a** *f* (Auto) first (gear); (en tren etc) first class. **~o** *a* (*delante de nombre masculino en singular* **primer**) first; (mejor) best; (principal) leading. **la ~a fila** the front row. **lo ~o es** the most important thing is. **~a enseñanza** primary education. **a ~os de** at the beginning of. **de ~a** first-class. ● *n* (the) first. ● *adv* first

primitivo *a* primitive

primo *m* cousin; ⊡ fool. **hacer el ~** be taken for a ride

primogénito *a & m* first-born, eldest

primor *m* delicacy; (cosa) beautiful thing

primordial *a* fundamental; *<interés>* paramount

princesa *f* princess

principal *a* main. **lo ~ es que** the main thing is that

príncipe *m* prince

principi|ante *m & f* beginner. **~o** *m* beginning; (moral, idea) principle; (origen) origin. **al ~o** at first. **a ~o(s) de** at the beginning of. **desde el ~o** from the start. **en ~o** in principle. **~os** *mpl* (nociones) rudiments

prioridad *f* priority

prisa *f* hurry, haste. **a ~** quickly. **a toda ~** as quickly as possible. **darse ~** hurry (up). **de ~** quickly. **tener ~** be in a hurry

prisi|ón *f* prison; (encarcelamiento) imprisonment. **~onero** *m* prisoner

prismáticos *mpl* binoculars

priva|ción *f* deprivation. **~da** *f* (Mex) private road. **~do** *a* (particular) private. **~r** *vt* deprive (**de** of). **~tivo** *a* exclusive (**de** to)

privilegi|ado *a* privileged; (muy bueno) exceptional. **~o** *m* privilege

pro *prep*. **en ~ de** for, in favour of. ● *m* advantage. **los ~s y los contras** the pros and cons

proa *f* bow

probab|ilidad f probability. ~**le** a probable, likely. ~**lemente** adv probably

proba|dor m fitting-room. ~**r** [2] vt try; try on <ropa>; (demostrar) prove. ● vi try. □ ~**rse** vpr try on

probeta f test-tube

problema m problem. **hacerse** ~**as** (LAm) worry

procaz a indecent

proced|encia f origin. ~**ente** a (razonable) reasonable. ~**ente de** (coming) from. ~**er** m conduct. ● vi proceed. ~**er contra** start legal proceedings against. ~**er de** come from. ~**imiento** m procedure; (sistema) process; (Jurid) proceedings

proces|ador m. ~ **de textos** word processor. ~**al** a procedural. **costas** ~**ales** legal costs. ~**amiento** m processing; (Jurid) prosecution. ~**amiento de textos** word-processing. ~**ar** vt process; (Jurid) prosecute

procesión f procession

proceso m process; (Jurid) trial; (transcurso) course

proclamar vt proclaim

procrea|ción f procreation. ~**r** vt procreate

procura|dor m attorney, solicitor; (asistente) clerk (Brit), paralegal (Amer). ~**r** vt try; (obtener) obtain

prodigar [12] vt lavish

prodigio m prodigy; (maravilla) wonder; (milagro) miracle. ~**oso** a prodigious

pródigo a prodigal

produc|ción f production. ~**ir** [47] vt produce; (causar) cause. □ ~**irse** vpr (suceder) happen. ~**tivo** a productive. ~**to** m product. ~**tos agrícolas** farm produce. ~**tos alimenticios** foodstuffs. ~**tos de belleza** cosmetics. ~**tos de consumo** consumer goods. ~**tor** m producer.

proeza f exploit

profan|ación f desecration. ~**ar** vt desecrate. ~**o** a profane

profecía f prophecy

proferir [4] vt utter; hurl <insultos etc>

profes|ión f profession. ~**ional** a professional. ~**or** m teacher; (en universidad) lecturer. ~**orado** m teaching profession; (conjunto de profesores) staff

prof|eta m prophet. ~**etizar** [10] vt/i prophesize

prófugo a & m fugitive

profund|idad f depth. ~**o** a deep; (fig) profound. **poco** ~ shallow

progenitor m ancestor

programa m programme; (de estudios) syllabus. ~ **concurso** quiz show. ~ **de entrevistas** chat show. ~**ción** f programming; (TV etc) programmes; (en periódico) TV guide. ~**r** vt programme. ~**dor** m computer programmer

progres|ar vi (make) progress. ~**ión** f progression. ~**ista** a progressive. ~**ivo** a progressive. ~**o** m progress. **hacer** ~**os** make progress

prohibi|ción f prohibition. ~**do** a forbidden. **prohibido fumar** no smoking. ~**r** vt forbid. ~**tivo** a prohibitive

prójimo m fellow man

prole f offspring

proletari|ado m proletariat. ~**o** a & m proletarian

prol|iferación f proliferation. ~**iferar** vi proliferate. ~**ífico** a prolific

prolijo a long-winded

prólogo m prologue

prolongar [12] vt prolong; (alargar) lengthen. □ ~**se** vpr go on

promedio m average. **como** ~ on average

prome|sa f promise. ~**ter** vt promise. ● vi show promise. □ ~**terse** vpr <novios> get engaged. ~**tida** f fiancée. ~**tido** a promised; <novios> engaged. ● m fiancé

prominente f prominence

promiscu|idad f promiscuity. ~**o** a promiscuous

promo|ción f promotion. ~**tor** m promoter. ~**ver** [2] vt promote; (causar) cause

promulgar [12] vt promulgate

pronombre m pronoun

pron|osticar [7] vt predict; forecast <tiempo>. ~**óstico** m prediction; (del tiempo) forecast; (Med) prognosis

pront|itud f promptness. **~o** a quick. ● adv quickly; (dentro de poco) soon; (temprano) early. **de ~o** suddenly. **por lo ~o** for the time being. **tan ~o como** as soon as

pronuncia|ción f pronunciation. **~miento** m revolt. **~r** vt pronounce; deliver *<discurso>*. □ **~rse** vpr (declararse) declare o.s.; (sublevarse) rise up

propagación f propagation

propaganda f propaganda; (anuncios) advertising

propagar [12] vt/i propagate. □ **~se** vpr spread

propasarse vpr go too far

propens|ión f inclination. **~o** a inclined

propici|ar vt favour; (provocar) bring about. **~o** a favourable

propie|dad f property. **~tario** m owner

propina f tip

propio a own; (característico) typical; (natural) natural; (apropiado) proper. **el ~ médico** the doctor himself

proponer [34] vt propose; put forward *<persona>*. □ **~se** vpr. **~se hacer** intend to do

proporci|ón f proportion. **~onado** a proportioned. **~onal** a proportional. **~onar** vt provide

proposición f proposition

propósito m intention. **a ~** (adrede) on purpose; (de paso) by the way. **a ~ de** with regard to

propuesta f proposal

propuls|ar vt propel; (fig) promote. **~ión** f propulsion. **~ión a chorro** jet propulsion

prórroga f extension

prorrogar [12] vt extend

prosa f prose. **~ico** a prosaic

proscri|bir (pp **proscrito**) vt exile; (prohibir) ban. **~to** a banned. ● m exile; (bandido) outlaw

proseguir [5 & 13] vt/i continue

prospecto m prospectus; (de fármaco) directions for use

prosper|ar vi prosper; *<persona>* do well. **~idad** f prosperity

próspero a prosperous. **¡P~ Año Nuevo!** Happy New Year!

prostit|ución f prostitution. **~uta** f prostitute

protagonista m & f protagonist

prote|cción f protection. **~ctor** a protective. ● m protector; (benefactor) patron. **~ger** [14] vt protect. **~gida** f protegée. **~gido** a protected. ● m protegé

proteína f protein

protesta f protest; (manifestación) demonstration; (Mex, promesa) promise; (Mex, juramento) oath

protestante a & m & f Protestant

protestar vt/i protest

protocolo m protocol

provecho m benefit. **¡buen ~!** enjoy your meal! **de ~** useful. **en ~ de** to the benefit of. **sacar ~ de** benefit from

proveer [18] (pp **proveído** y **provisto**) vt supply, provide

provenir [53] vi come (**de** from)

proverbi|al a proverbial. **~o** m proverb

provincia f province. **~l** a, **~no** a provincial

provisional a provisional

provisto a provided (**de** with)

provoca|ción f provocation. **~r** [7] vt provoke; (causar) cause. **~tivo** a provocative

proximidad f proximity

próximo a next; (cerca) near

proyec|ción f projection. **~tar** vt hurl; cast *<luz>*; show *<película>*. **~til** m missile. **~to** m plan. **~to de ley** bill. **en ~to** planned. **~tor** m projector

pruden|cia f prudence; (cuidado) caution. **~te** a prudent, sensible

prueba f proof; (examen) test; (de ropa) fitting. **a ~** on trial. **a ~ de** proof against. **a ~ de agua** waterproof. **poner a ~** test

pruebo vb ⇒PROBAR

psicoan|álisis f psychoanalysis. **~alista** m & f psychoanalyst. **~alizar** [10] vt psychoanalyse

psic|ología f psychology. **~ológico** a psychological. **~ólogo** m psychologist. **~ópata** m & f psychopath. **~osis** f invar psychosis

psiqu|e f psyche. **~iatra** m & f psychiatrist. **~iátrico** a psychiatric

psíquico a psychic

ptas, pts abrev (**pesetas**) pesetas

púa f sharp point; (Bot) thorn; (de erizo) quill; (de peine) tooth; (Mus) plectrum

pubertad f puberty

publica|ción f publication. **~r** [7] vt publish

publici|dad f publicity; (Com) advertising. **~tario** a advertising

público a public. ● m public; (de espectáculo etc) audience

puchero m cooking pot; (guisado) stew. **hacer ~s** (fig, 🄵) pout

pude vb ⇒PODER

pudor m modesty. **~oso** a modest

pudrir (pp **podrido**) vt rot; (fig, molestar) annoy. □ **~se** vpr rot

puebl|ecito m small village. **~erino** m country bumpkin. **~o** m town; (aldea) village; (nación) nation, people

puedo vb ⇒PODER

puente m bridge; (fig, 🄵) long weekend. **~ colgante** suspension bridge. **~ levadizo** drawbridge. **hacer ~** 🄵 have a long weekend

puerco a filthy; (grosero) coarse. ● m pig. **~ espín** porcupine

puerro m leek

puerta f door; (en deportes) goal; (de ciudad, en jardín) gate. **~ principal** main entrance. **a ~ cerrada** behind closed doors

puerto m port; (fig, refugio) refuge; (entre montañas) pass. **~ franco** free port

puertorriqueño a & m Puerto Rican

pues adv (entonces) then; (bueno) well. ● conj since

puest|a f setting; (en juegos) bet. **~a de sol** sunset. **~a en escena** staging. **~a en marcha** starting. **~o** a put; (vestido) dressed. ● m place; (empleo) position, job; (en mercado etc) stall. ● conj. **~o que** since

pugna f struggle. **~r** vi. **~r por** strive to

puja f struggle (por to); (en subasta) bid. **~r** vt struggle; (en subasta) bid

pulcro a neat

pulga f flea. **tener malas ~s** be bad-tempered

pulga|da f inch. **~r** m thumb; (del pie) big toe

puli|do a polished; <modales> refined. **~r** vt polish; (suavizar) smooth

pulla f gibe

pulm|ón m lung. **~onar** a pulmonary. **~onía** f pneumonia

pulpa f pulp

pulpería f (LAm) grocer's shop (Brit), grocery store (Amer)

púlpito m pulpit

pulpo m octopus

pulque m (Mex) pulque, alcoholic Mexican drink. **~ría** f bar

pulsa|ción f pulsation. **~dor** m button. **~r** vt press; (Mus) pluck

pulsera f bracelet

pulso m pulse; (firmeza) steady hand. **echar un ~** arm wrestle. **tomar el ~ a uno** take s.o.'s pulse

pulular vi teem with

puma m puma

puna f puna, high plateau

punitivo a punitive

punta f point; (extremo) tip. **estar de ~** be in a bad mood. **ponerse de ~ con uno** fall out with s.o. **sacar ~ a** sharpen

puntada f stitch

puntaje m (LAm) score

puntal m prop, support

puntapié m kick

puntear vt mark; (Mus) pluck; (LAm, en deportes) lead

puntería f aim; (destreza) markmanship

puntiagudo a pointed; (afilado) sharp

puntilla f (encaje) lace. **en ~s** (LAm), **de ~s** on tiptoe

punto m point; (señal, trazo) dot; (de examen) mark; (lugar) spot, place; (de taxis) stand; (momento) moment; (punto final) full stop (Brit), period (Amer); (puntada) stitch. **~ de vista** point of view. ~ **final** full stop (Brit), period (Amer). ~ **muerto** (Auto) neutral (gear). ~ **y aparte** full stop, new paragraph (Brit), period, new paragraph (Amer). ~ **y coma** semicolon. **a** ~ on time; (listo) ready. **a** ~ **de** on the point of. **de** ~ knitted. **dos** ~**s** colon. **en** ~ exactly. **hacer** ~ knit. **hasta cierto** ~ to a certain extent

puntuación f punctuation; (en deportes, acción) scoring; (en deportes, número de puntos) score

puntual a punctual; (exacto) accurate. ~**idad** f punctuality; (exactitud) accuracy

puntuar [21] vt punctuate; mark (Brit), grade (Amer) <examen>. ● vi score (points)

punza|da f sharp pain; (fig) pang. ~**nte** a sharp. ~**r** [10] vt prick

puñado m handful. **a** ~**s** by the handful

puñal m dagger. ~**ada** f stab

puñ|etazo m punch. ~**o** m fist; (de ropa) cuff; (mango) handle. **de su** ~**o** **(y letra)** in his own handwriting

pupa f (🄵, en los labios) cold sore

pupila f pupil

pupitre m desk

puré m purée; (sopa) thick soup. ~ **de papas** (LAm), ~ **de patatas** mashed potatoes

pureza f purity

purga f purge. ~**torio** m purgatory

puri|ficación f purification. ~**ificar** [7] vt purify. ~**sta** m & f purist. ~**tano** a puritanical. ● m puritan

puro a pure; <cielo> clear. **de pura casualidad** by sheer chance. **de** ~ **tonto** out of sheer stupidity. ● m cigar

púrpura f purple

pus m pus

puse vb ⇒PONER

pusilánime a fainthearted

puta f (vulg) whore

Qq

que pron rel (personas, sujeto) who; (personas, complemento) whom; (cosas) which, that. ● conj that. **¡**~ **tengan Vds buen viaje!** have a good journey! **¡**~ **venga!** let him come! ~ **venga o no venga** whether he comes or not. **creo** ~ **tiene razón** I think (that) he is right. **más** ~ more than. **lo** ~ what. **yo** ~ **tú** if I were you

qué a (con sustantivo) what; (con a o adv) how. ● pron what. **¡**~ **bonito!** how nice!. **¿en** ~ **piensas?** what are you thinking about?

quebra|da f gorge; (paso) pass. ~**dizo** a fragile. ~**do** a broken; (Com) bankrupt. ● m (Math) fraction. ~**ntar** vt break; disturb <paz>. ~**nto** m (pérdida) loss; (daño) damage. ~**r** [1] vt break. ● vi break; (Com) go bankrupt. □ ~**rse** vpr break

quechua a Quechua. ● m & f Quechan. ● m (Lang) Quecha

quedar vi stay, remain; (estar) be; (haber todavía) be left. ~ **bien** come off well. □ ~**se** vpr stay. ~ **con** arrange to meet. ~ **en** agree to. ~ **en nada** come to nothing. ~ **por** (+ infinitivo) remain to be (+ pp)

quehacer m work. ~**es domésticos** household chores

quej|a f complaint; (de dolor) moan. □ ~**arse** vpr complain (de about); (gemir) moan. ~**ido** m moan

quema|do a burnt; (LAm, bronceado) tanned; (fig) annoyed. ~**dor** m burner. ~**dura** f burn. ~**r** vt/i burn. □ ~**rse** vpr burn o.s.; (consumirse) burn up; (con el sol) get sunburnt. ~**rropa** adv. **a** ~**rropa** point-blank

quena f Indian flute

quepo vb ⇒CABER

querella f (riña) quarrel, dispute; (Jurid) criminal action

quer|er [35] vt want; (amar) love; (necesitar) need. ~**er decir** mean. ● m love; (amante) lover. **como quiera que** however. **cuando quiera que**

whenever. **donde quiera** wherever. **¿quieres darme ese libro?** would you pass me that book? **¿quieres un helado?** would you like an ice-cream? **quisiera ir a la playa** I'd like to go to the beach. **sin ~er** without meaning to. **~ido** a dear; (amado) loved

querosén m, **queroseno** m kerosene

querubín m cherub

ques|adilla f (Mex) tortilla filled with cheese. **~o** m cheese

quetzal m (unidad monetaria ecuatoriana) quetzal

quicio m frame. **sacar de ~ a uno** infuriate s.o.

quiebra f (Com) bankruptcy

quien pron rel (sujeto) who; (complemento) whom

quién pron interrogativo (sujeto) who; (tras preposición) **¿con ~?** who with ?, to whom? **¿de ~ son estos libros?** whose are these books?

quienquiera pron whoever

quiero vb ⇒QUERER

quiet|o a still; (inmóvil) motionless; <carácter etc> calm. **~ud** f stillness

quijada f jaw

quilate m carat

quilla f keel

quimera f (fig) illusion

químic|a f chemistry. **~o** a chemical. ● m chemist

quince a & m fifteen. **~ días** a fortnight. **~na** f fortnight. **~nal** a fortnightly

quincuagésimo a fiftieth

quiniela f pools coupon. **~s** fpl (football) pools

quinientos a & m five hundred

quinquenio m (period of) five years

quinta f (casa) villa

quintal m a hundred kilograms

quinteto m quintet

quinto a & m fifth

quiosco m kiosk; (en jardín) summerhouse; (en parque etc) bandstand

quirúrgico a surgical

quise vb ⇒QUERER

quisquill|a f trifle; (camarón) shrimp. **~oso** a irritable; (exigente) fussy

quita|esmalte m nail polish remover. **~manchas** m invar stain remover. **~nieves** m invar snow plough. **~r** vt remove, take away; take off <ropa>; (robar) steal. **~ndo** (fam, a excepción de) apart from. □ **~rse** vpr get rid of <dolor>; take off <ropa>. **~rse de** (no hacerlo más) stop. **~rse de en medio** get out of the way. **~sol** m sunshade

quizá(s) adv perhaps

quórum m quorum

Rr

rábano m radish. **~ picante** horseradish. **me importa un ~** I couldn't care less

rabi|a f rabies; (fig) rage. **~ar** vi (de dolor) be in great pain; (estar enfadado) be furious. **dar ~a** infuriate. **~eta** f tantrum

rabino m rabbi

rabioso a rabid; (furioso) furious

rabo m tail

racha f gust of wind; (fig) spate. **pasar por una mala ~** go through a bad patch

racial a racial

racimo m bunch

ración f share, ration; (de comida) portion

racional a rational. **~lizar** [10] vt rationalize. **~r** vt (limitar) ration; (repartir) ration out

racis|mo m racism. **~ta** a racist

radar m radar

radiación f radiation

radiactiv|idad f radioactivity. **~o** a radioactive

radiador m radiator

radiante a radiant; (brillante) brilliant

radical a & m & f radical

radicar [7] *vi* lie (en in). □ ~**se** *vpr* settle

radio *m* radius; (de rueda) spoke; (LAm) radio. ● *f* radio. ~**actividad** *f* radioactivity. ~**activo** *a* radioactive. ~**difusión** *f* broadcasting. ~**emisora** *f* radio station. ~**escucha** *m & f* listener. ~**grafía** *f* radiography

radi|ólogo *m* radiologist. ~**oterapia** *f* radiotherapy

radioyente *m & f* listener

raer [36] *vt* scrape; (quitar) scrape off

ráfaga *f* (de viento) gust; (de ametralladora) burst

rafia *f* raffia

raído *a* threadbare

raíz *f* root. **a** ~ **de** as a result of. **echar raíces** (fig) settle

raja *f* split; (Culin) slice. ~**r** *vt* split. □ ~**rse** *vpr* split; (fig) back out

rajatabla. a ~ rigorously

ralea *f* sort

ralla|dor *m* grater. ~**r** *vt* grate

ralo *a* <pelo> thin

rama *f* branch. ~**je** *m* branches. ~**l** *m* branch

rambla *f* watercourse; (avenida) avenue

ramera *f* prostitute

ramifica|ción *f* ramification. □ ~**rse** [7] *vpr* branch out

ram|illete *m* bunch. ~**o** *m* branch; (de flores) bunch, bouquet

rampa *f* ramp, slope

rana *f* frog

ranch|era *f* (Mex) folk song. ~**ero** *m* cook; (Mex, hacendado) rancher. ~**o** *m* (LAm, choza) hut; (LAm, casucha) shanty; (Mex, hacienda) ranch

rancio *a* rancid; <vino> old; (fig) ancient

rango *m* rank

ranúnculo *m* buttercup

ranura *f* groove; (para moneda) slot

rapar *vt* shave; crop <pelo>

rapaz *a* rapacious; <ave> of prey

rapidez *f* speed

rápido *a* fast, quick. ● *adv* quickly. ● *m* (tren) express. ~**s** *mpl* rapids

rapiña *f* robbery. **ave** *f* **de** ~ bird of prey

rapsodia *f* rhapsody

rapt|ar *vt* kidnap. ~**o** *m* kidnapping; (de ira etc) fit

raqueta *f* racquet

rar|eza *f* rarity; (cosa rara) oddity. ~**o** *a* rare; (extraño) odd. **es** ~**o que** it is strange that. **¡qué** ~**o!** how strange!

ras. a ~ **de** level with

rasca|cielos *m invar* skyscraper. ~**r** [7] *vt* scratch; (raspar) scrape

rasgar [12] *vt* tear

rasgo *m* characteristic; (gesto) gesture; (de pincel) stroke. ~**s** *mpl* (facciones) features

rasguear *vt* strum

rasguñ|ar *vt* scratch. ~**o** *m* scratch

raso *a* <cucharada etc> level; <vuelo etc> low. **al** ~ in the open air. ● *m* satin

raspa|dura *f* scratch; (acción) scratching. ~**r** *vt* scratch; (rozar) scrape

rastr|a. a ~**as** dragging. ~**ear** *vt* track. ~**ero** *a* creeping. ~**illar** *vt* rake. ~**illo** *m* rake. ~**o** *m* track; (señal) sign. **ni** ~**o** not a trace

rata *f* rat

ratero *m* petty thief

ratifica|ción *f* ratification. ~**r** [7] *vt* ratify

rato *m* moment, short time. ~**s libres** spare time. **a** ~**s** at times. **a cada** ~ (LAm) always. **hace un** ~ a moment ago. **pasar un mal** ~ have a rough time

rat|ón *m* mouse. ~**onera** *f* mousetrap; (madriguera) mouse hole

raudal *m* torrent. **a** ~**les** in abundance

raya *f* line; (lista) stripe; (de pelo) parting. **a** ~**s** striped. **pasarse de la** ~ go too far. ~**r** *vt* scratch. ~**r en** border on

rayo *m* ray; (descarga eléctrica) lightning. ~ **de luna** moonbeam. ~ **láser** laser beam. ~**s X** X-rays

raza *f* race; (de animal) breed. **de** ~ <caballo> thoroughbred; <perro> pedigree

raz|ón *f* reason. **a** ~**ón de** at the rate of. **perder la** ~**ón** go out of one's

mind. **tener** ~**ón** be right. ~**onable**
a reasonable. ~**onamiento** *m* reasoning. ~**onar** *vt* reason out. ● *vi*
reason

re *m* D; (solfa) re

reac|ción *f* reaction; (LAm, Pol) right
wing. ~**ción en cadena** chain reaction. ~**cionario** *a & m* reactionary.
~**tor** *m* reactor; (avión) jet

real *a* real; (de rey etc) royal; <*hecho*>
true. ● *m* real, old Spanish coin

realidad *f* reality; (verdad) truth. **en**
~ in fact. **hacerse** ~ come true

realis|mo *m* realism. ~**ta** *a* realistic. ● *m & f* realist

realiza|ción *f* fulfilment. ~**r** [10] *vt*
carry out; make <*viaje*>; fulfil <*ilusión*>; (vender) sell. □ ~**rse** *vpr* <*sueño, predicción etc*> come true; <*persona*> fulfil o.s.

realzar [10] *vt* (fig) enhance

reanimar *vt* revive. □ ~**se** *vpr* revive

reanudar *vt* resume; renew <*amistad*>

reavivar *vt* revive

rebaja *f* reduction. **en** ~**s** in the
sale. ~**do** *a* <*precio*> reduced. ~**r** *vt*
lower; lose <*peso*>

rebanada *f* slice

rebaño *m* herd; (de ovejas) flock

rebasar *vt* exceed; (dejar atrás) leave
behind; (Mex, Auto) overtake

rebatir *vt* refute

rebel|arse *vpr* rebel. ~**de** *a* rebellious; <*grupo*> rebel. ● *m* rebel.
~**día** *f* rebelliousness. ~**ión** *f* rebellion

rebosa|nte *a* brimming (**de** with).
~**r** *vi* overflow; (abundar) abound

rebot|ar *vt* bounce; (rechazar) repel.
● *vi* bounce; <*bala*> ricochet. ~**e** *m*
bounce, rebound. **de** ~**e** on the rebound

reboz|ar [10] *vt* wrap up; (Culin) coat
in batter. ~**o** *m* (LAm) shawl

rebusca|do *a* affected; (complicado)
over-elaborate. ~**r** [7] *vt* search
through

rebuznar *vi* bray

recado *m* errand; (mensaje) message

reca|er [29] *vi* fall back; (Med) relapse; (fig) fall. ~**ida** *f* relapse

recalcar [7] *vt* stress

recalcitrante *a* recalcitrant

recalentar [1] *vt* reheat; (demasiado)
overheat

recámara *f* small room; (de arma de
fuego) chamber; (Mex, dormitorio) bedroom

recambio *m* (Mec) spare (part); (de
pluma etc) refill. **de** ~ spare

recapitular *vt* sum up

recarg|ar [12] *vt* overload; (aumentar)
increase; recharge <*batería*>. ~**o** *m*
increase

recat|ado *a* modest. ~**o** *m* prudence; (modestia) modesty. **sin** ~**o**
openly

recauda|ción *f* (cantidad) takings.
~**dor** *m* tax collector. ~**r** *vt* collect

recel|ar *vt* suspect. ● *vi* be suspicious (**de** of). ~**o** *m* distrust; (temor)
fear. ~**oso** *a* suspicious

recepci|ón *f* reception. ~**onista**
m & f receptionist

receptáculo *m* receptacle

receptor *m* receiver

recesión *f* recession

receta *f* recipe; (Med) prescription

rechaz|ar [10] *vt* reject; defeat <*moción*>; repel <*ataque*>; (no aceptar)
turn down. ~**o** *m* rejection

rechifla *f* booing

rechinar *vi* squeak. **le rechinan los
dientes** he grinds his teeth

rechoncho *a* stout

recib|imiento *m* (acogida) welcome. ~**ir** *vt* receive; (acoger) welcome. ● *vi* entertain. □ ~**irse** *vpr*
graduate. ~**o** *m* receipt. **acusar** ~**o**
acknowledge receipt

reci|én *adv* recently; (LAm, hace poco)
just. ~ **casado** newly married. ~
nacido newborn. ~**ente** *a* recent;
(Culin) fresh

recinto *m* enclosure; (local) premises

recio *a* strong; <*voz*> loud. ● *adv*
hard; (en voz alta) loudly

recipiente *m* receptacle. ● *m & f*
recipient

recíproco *a* reciprocal; <*sentimiento*> mutual

recita|l *m* recital; (de poesías) reading. **~r** *vt* recite

reclama|ción *f* claim; (queja) complaint. **~r** *vt* claim. ● *vi* appeal

réclame *m* (LAm) advertisement

reclamo *m* (LAm) complaint

reclinar *vi* lean. □ **~se** *vpr* lean

reclus|ión *f* imprisonment. **~o** *m* prisoner

recluta *m & f* recruit. **~miento** *m* recruitment. **~r** *vt* recruit

recobrar *vt* recover. □ **~se** *vpr* recover

recodo *m* bend

recog|er [14] *vt* collect; pick up <*cosa caída*>; (cosechar) harvest. □ **~erse** *vpr* withdraw; (ir a casa) go home; (acostarse) go to bed. **~ida** *f* collection; (cosecha) harvest

recomenda|ción *f* recommendation. **~r** [1] *vt* recommend; (encomendar) entrust

recomenzar [1 & 10] *vt/i* start again

recompensa *f* reward. **~r** *vt* reward

reconcilia|ción *f* reconciliation. **~r** *vt* reconcile. □ **~rse** *vpr* be reconciled

reconoc|er [11] *vt* recognize; (admitir) acknowledge; (examinar) examine. **~imiento** *m* recognition; (admisión) acknowledgement; (agradecimiento) gratitude; (examen) examination

reconozco *vb* ⇒RECONOCER

reconquista *f* reconquest. **~r** *vt* reconquer; (fig) win back

reconsiderar *vt* reconsider

reconstruir [17] *vt* reconstruct

récord /'rekor/ *m* (*pl* **~s**) record

recordar [2] *vt* remember; (hacer acordar) remind. ● *vi* remember. **que yo recuerde** as far as I remember. **si mal no recuerdo** if I remember rightly

recorr|er *vt* tour <*país*>; go round <*zona, museo*>; cover <*distancia*>. **~ mundo** travel all around the world. **~ido** *m* journey; (trayecto) route

recort|ar *vt* cut (out). **~e** *m* cutting (out); (de periódico etc) cutting

recostar [2] *vt* lean. □ **~se** *vpr* lie down

recoveco *m* bend; (rincón) nook

recre|ación *f* recreation. **~ar** *vt* recreate; (divertir) entertain. □ **~arse** *vpr* amuse o.s. **~ativo** *a* recreational. **~o** *m* recreation; (Escol) break

recrudecer [11] *vi* intensify

recta *f* straight line. **~ final** home stretch

rect|angular *a* rectangular. **~ángulo** *a* rectangular; <*triángulo*> right-angled. ● *m* rectangle

rectifica|ción *f* rectification. **~r** [7] *vt* rectify

rect|itud *f* straightness; (fig) honesty. **~o** *a* straight; (fig, justo) fair; (fig, honrado) honest. **todo ~o** straight on. ● *m* rectum

rector *a* governing. ● *m* rector

recubrir (*pp* **recubierto**) *vt* cover (con, de with)

recuerdo *m* memory; (regalo) souvenir. **~s** *mpl* (saludos) regards. ● *vb* ⇒RECORDAR

recupera|ción *f* recovery. **~r** *vt* recover. **~r el tiempo perdido** make up for lost time. □ **~rse** *vpr* recover

recur|rir *vi*. **~rir a** resort to <*cosa*>; turn to <*persona*>. **~so** *m* resort; (medio) resource; (Jurid) appeal. **~sos** *mpl* resources

red *f* network; (malla) net; (para equipaje) luggage rack; (Com) chain; (Elec, gas) mains. **la R~** the Net

redac|ción *f* writing; (lenguaje) wording; (conjunto de redactores) editorial staff; (oficina) editorial office; (Escol, Univ) essay. **~tar** *vt* write. **~tor** *m* writer; (de periódico) editor

redada *f* catch; (de policía) raid

redecilla *f* small net; (para el pelo) hairnet

redentor *a* redeeming

redimir *vt* redeem

redoblar *vt* redouble; step up <*vigilancia*>

redomado *a* utter

redond|a *f* (de imprenta) roman (type); (Mus) semibreve (Brit), whole note (Amer). **a la ~a** around. **~ear** *vt* round off. **~el** *m* circle; (de plaza de toros) arena. **~o** *a* round; (completo) complete; (Mex, boleto) return, round-trip (Amer). **en** ~**o** round; (categóricamente) flatly

reduc|ción f reduction. ~**ido** a reduced; (limitado) limited; (pequeño) small; <precio> low. ~**ir** [47] vt reduce. □ ~**irse** vpr be reduced; (fig) amount

reduje vb ⇒REDUCIR

redundan|cia f redundancy. ~**te** a redundant

reduzco vb ⇒REDUCIR

reembols|ar vt reimburse. ~**o** m repayment. **contra** ~**o** cash on delivery

reemplaz|ar [10] vt replace. ~**o** m replacement

refacci|ón f (LAm) refurbishment; (Mex, Mec) spare part. ~**onar** vt (LAm) refurbish. ~**onaria** f (Mex) repair shop

referencia f reference; (información) report. **con** ~ **a** with reference to. **hacer** ~ **a** refer to

referéndum m (pl ~**s**) referendum

referir [4] vt tell; (remitir) refer. □ ~**se** vpr refer. **por lo que se refiere a** as regards

refiero vb ⇒REFERIR

refilón. de ~ obliquely

refin|amiento m refinement. ~**ar** vt refine. ~**ería** f refinery

reflector m reflector; (proyector) searchlight

reflej|ar vt reflect. ~**o** a reflex. ● m reflection; (Med) reflex; (en el pelo) highlights

reflexi|ón f reflection. **sin** ~**ón** without thinking. ~**onar** vi reflect. ~**vo** a <persona> thoughtful; (Gram) reflexive

reforma f reform. ~**s** fpl (reparaciones) repairs. ~**r** vt reform. □ ~**rse** vpr reform

reforzar [2 & 10] vt reinforce

refrac|ción f refraction. ~**tario** a heat-resistant

refrán m saying

refregar [1 & 12] vt scrub

refresc|ar [7] vt refresh; (enfriar) cool. ● vi get cooler. □ ~**arse** vpr

refresh o.s. ~**o** m cold drink. ~**os** mpl refreshments

refrigera|ción f refrigeration; (aire acondicionado) air-conditioning; (de motor) cooling. ~**r** vt refrigerate; air-condition <lugar>; cool <motor>. ~**dor** m refrigerator

refuerzo m reinforcement

refugi|ado m refugee. □ ~**arse** vpr take refuge. ~**o** m refuge, shelter

refunfuñar vi grumble

refutar vt refute

regadera f watering-can; (Mex, ducha) shower

regala|do a as a present, free; (cómodo) comfortable. ~**r** vt give

regalo m present, gift

regañ|adientes. a ~**adientes** reluctantly. ~**ar** vt scold. ● vi moan; (dos personas) quarrel. ~**o** m (reprensión) scolding

regar [1 & 12] vt water

regata f boat race; (serie) regatta

regate|ar vt haggle over; (economizar) economize on. ● vi haggle; (en deportes) dribble. ~**o** m haggling; (en deportes) dribbling

regazo m lap

regenerar vt regenerate

régimen m (pl **regímenes**) regime; (Med) diet; (de lluvias) pattern

regimiento m regiment

regi|ón f region. ~**onal** a regional

regir [5 & 14] vt govern. ● vi apply, be in force

registr|ado a registered. ~**ar** vt register; (Mex) check in <equipaje>; (grabar) record; (examinar) search. □ ~**arse** vpr register; (darse) be reported. ~**o** m (acción de registrar) registration; (libro) register; (cosa anotada) entry; (inspección) search. ~**o civil** (oficina) registry office

regla f ruler; (norma) rule; (menstruación) period. **en** ~ in order. **por** ~ **general** as a rule. ~**mentación** f regulation. ~**mentar** vt regulate. ~**mentario** a regulation; <horario> set. ~**mento** m regulations

regocij|arse vpr be delighted. ~**o** m delight

regode|arse *vpr* (+ *gerundio*) delight in (+ *gerund*). **~o** *m* delight

regordete *a* chubby

regres|ar *vi* return; (LAm) send back <*persona*>. □ **~arse** *vpr* (LAm) return. **~ivo** *a* backward. **~o** *m* return

regula|ble *a* adjustable. **~dor** *m* control. **~r** *a* regular; (mediano) average; (no bueno) so-so. ● *vt* regulate; adjust <*volumen etc*>. **~ridad** *f* regularity. con **~ridad** regularly

rehabilita|ción *f* rehabilitation; (en empleo etc) reinstatement. **~r** *vt* rehabilitate; (en cargo) reinstate

rehacer [31] *vt* redo; (repetir) repeat; rebuild <*vida*>. □ **~se** *vpr* recover

rehén *m* hostage

rehogar [12] *vt* sauté

rehuir [17] *vt* avoid

rehusar *vt/i* refuse

reimpr|esión *f* reprinting. **~imir** (*pp* **reimpreso**) *vt* reprint

reina *f* queen. **~do** *m* reign. **~nte** *a* ruling; (fig) prevailing. **~r** *vi* reign; (fig) prevail

reincidir *vi* (Jurid) reoffend

reino *m* kingdom. R**~** **Unido** United Kingdom

reintegr|ar *vt* reinstate <*persona*>; refund <*cantidad*>. □ **~arse** *vpr* return. **~o** *m* refund

reír [51] *vi* laugh. □ **~se** *vpr* laugh. **~se de** laugh at. **echarse a ~** burst out laughing

reivindica|ción *f* claim. **~r** [7] *vt* claim; (rehabilitar) restore

rej|a *f* grille; (verja) railing. **entre ~as** behind bars. **~illa** *f* grille, grating; (red) luggage rack

rejuvenecer [11] *vt/i* rejuvenate. □ **~se** *vpr* be rejuvenated

relaci|ón *f* connection; (trato) relation(ship); (relato) account; (lista) list. **con ~ón a, en ~ón a** in relation to. **~onado** *a* related. **bien ~onado** well-connected. **~onar** *vt* relate (con to). □ **~onarse** *vpr* be connected; (tratar) mix (**con** with)

relaja|ción *f* relaxation; (aflojamiento) slackening. **~do** *a* relaxed. **~r** *vt* relax; (aflojar) slacken. □ **~rse** *vpr* relax

relamerse *vpr* lick one's lips

relámpago *m* (flash of) lightning

relatar *vt* tell, relate

relativ|idad *f* relativity. **~o** *a* relative

relato *m* tale; (relación) account

relegar [12] *vt* relegate. **~ al olvido** consign to oblivion

relev|ante *a* outstanding. **~ar** *vt* relieve; (substituir) replace. **~o** *m* relief. **carrera** *f* **de ~os** relay race

relieve *m* relief; (fig) importance. **de ~** important. **poner de ~** emphasize

religi|ón *f* religion. **~osa** *f* nun. **~oso** *a* religious. ● *m* monk

relinch|ar *vi* neigh. **~o** *m* neigh

reliquia *f* relic

rellano *m* landing

rellen|ar *vt* refill; (Culin) stuff; fill in <*formulario*>. **~o** *a* full up; (Culin) stuffed. ● *m* filling; (Culin) stuffing

reloj *m* clock; (de bolsillo o pulsera) watch. **~ de caja** grandfather clock. **~ de pulsera** wrist-watch. **~ de sol** sundial. **~ despertador** alarm clock. **~ería** *f* watchmaker's (shop). **~ero** *m* watchmaker

reluci|ente *a* shining. **~r** [11] *vi* shine; (destellar) sparkle

relumbrar *vi* shine

remach|ar *vt* rivet. **~e** *m* rivet

remangar [12] *vt* roll up

remar *vi* row

remat|ado *a* (total) complete. **~ar** *vt* finish off; (agotar) use up; (Com) sell off cheap; (LAm, subasta) auction; (en tenis) smash. **~e** *m* end; (fig) finishing touch; (LAm, subastar) auction; (en tenis) smash. **de ~e** completely

remedar *vt* imitate

remedi|ar *vt* remedy; repair <*daño*>; (fig, resolver) solve. **no lo pude ~ar** I couldn't help it. **~o** *m* remedy; (fig) solution; (LAm, medicamento) medicine. **como último ~o** as a last resort. **no hay más ~o** there's no other way. **no tener más ~o** have no choice

remedo *m* poor imitation

rem|endar [1] *vt* repair. **~iendo** *m* patch

remilg|ado *a* fussy; (afectado) affected. **~o** *m* fussiness; (afectación) affectation. **~oso** *a* (Mex) fussy

reminiscencia *f* reminiscence

remisión *f* remission; (envío) sending; (referencia) reference

remit|e *m* sender's name and address. **~ente** *m* sender. **~ir** *vt* send; (referir) refer ● *vi* diminish

remo *m* oar

remoj|ar *vt* soak; (fig, 🖪) celebrate. **~o** *m* soaking. **poner a ~o** soak

remolacha *f* beetroot. **~ azucarera** sugar beet

remolcar [7] *vt* tow

remolino *m* swirl; (de aire etc) whirl

remolque *m* towing; (cabo) towrope; (vehículo) trailer. **a ~** on tow. **dar ~ a** tow

remontar *vt* overcome. **~ el vuelo** soar up; *<avión>* gain height. □ **~se** *vpr* soar up; (en el tiempo) go back to

remord|er [2] *vi*. **eso le remuerde** he feels guilty for it. **me remuerde la conciencia** I have a guilty conscience. **~imiento** *m* remorse. **tener ~imientos** feel remorse

remoto *a* remote; *<época>* distant

remover [2] *vt* stir *<líquido>*; turn over *<tierra>*; (quitar) remove; (fig, activar) revive

remunera|ción *f* remuneration. **~r** *vt* remunerate

renac|er [11] *vi* be reborn; (fig) revive. **~imiento** *m* rebirth. **R~imiento** Renaissance

renacuajo *m* tadpole; (fig) tiddler

rencilla *f* quarrel

rencor *m* bitterness. **guardar ~ a** have a grudge against. **~oso** *a* resentful

rendi|ción *f* surrender. **~do** *a* submissive; (agotado) exhausted

rendija *f* crack

rendi|miento *m* performance; (Com) yield. **~r** [5] *vt* yield; (agotar) exhaust; pay *<homenaje>*; present *<informe>*. ● *vi* pay; (producir) produce. □ **~rse** *vpr* surrender

renegar [1 & 12] *vt* deny. ● *vi* grumble. **~r de** renounce *<fe etc>*; disown *<personas>*

renglón *m* line; (Com) item. **a ~ seguido** straight away

reno *m* reindeer

renombr|ado *a* renowned. **~e** *m* renown

renova|ción *f* renewal; (de edificio) renovation; (de mobiliario) complete change. **~r** *vt* renew; renovate *<edificio>*; change *<mobiliario>*

rent|a *f* income; (Mex, alquiler) rent. **~a vitalicia** (life) annuity. **~able** *a* profitable. **~ar** *vt* yield; (Mex, alquilar) rent, hire. **~ista** *m & f* person of independent means

renuncia *f* renunciation; (dimisión) resignation. **~r** *vi*. **~r a** renounce, give up; (dimitir) resign

reñi|do *a* hard-fought. **estar ~do con** be incompatible with *<cosa>*; be on bad terms with *<persona>*. **~r** [5 & 22] *vt* scold. ● *vi* quarrel

reo *m & f* (Jurid) accused; (condenado) convicted offender

reojo. mirar de ~ look out of the corner of one's eye at

reorganizar [10] *vt* reorganize

repar|ación *f* repair; (acción) repairing (fig, compensación) reparation. **~ar** *vt* repair; (fig) make amends for; (notar) notice. ● *vi*. **~ar en** notice; (hacer caso de) pay attention to. **~o** *m* fault; (objeción) objection. **poner ~os** raise objections

repart|ición *f* distribution. **~idor** *m* delivery man. **~imiento** *m* distribution. **~ir** *vt* distribute, share out; deliver *<cartas, leche etc>*; hand out *<folleto, premio>*. **~o** *m* distribution; (de cartas, leche etc) delivery; (actores) cast

repas|ar *vt* go over; check *<cuenta>*; revise *<texto>*; (leer a la ligera) glance through; (coser) mend. ● *vi* revise. **~o** *m* revision; (de ropa) mending. **dar un ~o** look through

repatria|ción *f* repatriation. **~r** *vt* repatriate

repele|nte *a* repulsive. ● *m* insect repellent. **~r** *vt* repel

repent|e. de ~ suddenly. **~ino** *a* sudden

repercu|sión f repercussion. ~**tir** vi reverberate; (fig) have repercussions (**en** on)

repertorio m repertoire

repeti|ción f repetition; (de programa) repeat. ~**damente** adv repeatedly. ~**r** [5] vt repeat; have a second helping of <plato>; (imitar) copy. ● vi have a second helping of

repi|car [7] vt ring <campanas>. ~**que** m peal

repisa f shelf. ~ **de chimenea** mantlepiece

repito vb ⇒REPETIR

replegarse [1 & 12] vpr withdraw

repleto a full up. ~ **de gente** packed with people

réplica a reply; (copia) replica

replicar [7] vi reply

repollo m cabbage

reponer [34] vt replace; revive <obra de teatro>; (contestar) reply. □ ~**se** vpr recover

report|aje m report; (LAm, entrevista) interview. ~**ar** vt yield; (LAm, denunciar) report. ~**e** m (Mex, informe) report; (Mex, queja) complaint. ~**ero** m reporter

repos|ado a quiet; (sin prisa) unhurried. ~**ar** vi rest; <líquido> settle. ~**o** m rest

repost|ar vt replenish. ● vi (Aviac) refuel; (Auto) fill up. ~**ería** f pastrymaking

reprender vt reprimand

represalia f reprisal. **tomar** ~**s** retaliate

representa|ción f representation; (en el teatro) performance. **en** ~**ción de** representing. ~**nte** m representative. ~**r** vt represent; perform <obra de teatro>; play <papel>; (aparentar) look. □ ~**rse** vpr imagine. ~**tivo** a representative

represi|ón f repression. ~**vo** a repressive

reprimenda f reprimand

reprimir vt supress. □ ~**se** vpr control o.s.

reprobar [2] vt condemn; (LAm, Univ, etc) fail

reproch|ar vt reproach. ~**e** m reproach

reproduc|ción f reproduction. ~**ir** [47] vt reproduce. ~**tor** a reproductive; <animal> breeding

reptil m reptile

rep|ública f republic. ~**ublicano** a & m republican

repudiar vt condemn; (Jurid) repudiate

repuesto m (Mec) spare (part). **de** ~ spare

repugna|ncia f disgust. ~**nte** a repugnant; <olor> disgusting. ~**r** vt disgust

repuls|a f rebuff. ~**ión** f repulsion. ~**ivo** a repulsive

reputa|ción f reputation. ~**do** a reputable. ~**r** vt consider

requeri|miento m request; (necesidad) requirement. ~**r** [4] vt require; summons <persona>

requesón m curd cheese

requete... pref extremely

requis|a f requisition; (confiscación) seizure; (inspección) inspection; (Mil) requisition. ~**ar** vt requisition; (confiscar) seize; (inspeccionar) inspect. ~**ito** m requirement

res f animal. ~ **lanar** sheep. ~ **vacuna** (vaca) cow; (toro) bull; (buey) ox. **carne de** ~ (Mex) beef

resabido a well-known; <persona> pedantic

resaca f undercurrent; (después de beber) hangover

resaltar vi stand out. **hacer** ~ emphasize

resarcir [9] vt repay; (compensar) compensate. □ ~**se** vpr make up for

resbal|adilla f (Mex) slide. ~**adizo** a slippery. ~**ar** vi slip; (Auto) skid; <líquido> trickle. □ ~**arse** vpr slip; (Auto) skid; <líquido> trickle. ~**ón** m slip; (de vehículo) skid. ~**oso** a (LAm) slippery

rescat|ar vt rescue; (fig) recover. ~**e** m ransom; (recuperación) recovery; (salvamento) rescue

rescoldo m embers

resecar [7] vt dry up. □ ~**se** vpr dry up

resenti|do *a* resentful. **~miento** *m* resentment. □ **~rse** *vpr* feel the effects; (debilitarse) be weakened; (ofenderse) take offence (**de** at)

reseña *f* summary; (de persona) description; (en periódico) report, review. **~r** *vt* describe; (en periódico) report on, review

reserva *f* reservation; (provisión) reserve(s). **de ~** in reserve. **~ción** *f* (LAm) reservation. **~do** *a* reserved. **~r** *vt* reserve; (guardar) keep, save. □ **~rse** *vpr* save o.s.

resfria|do *m* cold. □ **~rse** *vpr* catch a cold

resguard|ar *vt* protect. □ **~arse** *vpr* protect o.s.; (fig) take care. **~o** *m* protection; (garantía) guarantee; (recibo) receipt

resid|encia *f* residence; (Univ) hall of residence (Brit), dormitory (Amer); (de ancianos etc) home. **~encial** *a* residential. **~ente** *a* & *m* & *f* resident. **~ir** *vi* reside; (fig) lie (**en** in)

residu|al *a* residual. **~o** *m* residue. **~os** *mpl* waste

resigna|ción *f* resignation. □ **~rse** *vpr* resign o.s. (**a** to)

resist|encia *f* resistence. **~ente** *a* resistent. **~ir** *vt* resist; (soportar) bear. ● *vi* resist. **ya no resisto más** I can't take it any more

resol|ución *f* resolution; (solución) solution; (decisión) decision. **~ver** [2] (*pp* **resuelto**) resolve; solve <*problema etc*>. □ **~verse** *vpr* resolve itself; (resultar bien) work out; (decidir) decide

resona|ncia *f* resonance. **tener ~ncia** cause a stir. **~nte** *a* resonant; (fig) resounding. **~r** [2] *vi* resound

resorte *m* spring; (Mex, elástico) elastic. **tocar (todos los) ~s** (fig) pull strings

respald|ar *vt* back; (escribir) endorse. □ **~arse** *vpr* lean back. **~o** *m* backing; (de asiento) back

respect|ar *vi*. **en lo que ~a a** with regard to. **en lo que a mí ~a** as far as I'm concerned. **~ivo** *a* respective. **~o** *m* respect. **al ~o** on this matter. (**con**) **~o a** with regard to

respet|able *a* respectable. ● *m* audience. **~ar** *vt* respect. **~o** *m* respect. **faltar al ~o a** be disrespectful to. **~uoso** *a* respectful

respir|ación *f* breathing; (ventilación) ventilation. **~ar** *vi* breathe; (fig) breathe a sigh of relief. **~o** *m* breathing; (fig) rest

respland|ecer [11] *vi* shine. **~eciente** *a* shining. **~or** *m* brilliance; (de llamas) glow

responder *vi* answer; (replicar) answer back; (reaccionar) respond. **~ de** be responsible for. **~ por uno** vouch for s.o.

responsab|ilidad *f* responsibility. **~le** *a* responsible

respuesta *f* reply, answer

resquebrajar *vt* crack. □ **~se** *vpr* crack

resquemor *m* (fig) uneasiness

resquicio *m* crack; (fig) possibility

resta *f* subtraction

restablecer [11] *vt* restore. □ **~se** *vpr* recover

rest|ante *a* remaining. **lo ~nte** the rest. **~ar** *vt* take away; (substraer) subtract. ● *vi* be left

restaura|ción *f* restoration. **~nte** *m* restaurant. **~r** *vt* restore

restitu|ción *f* restitution. **~ir** [17] *vt* return; (restaurar) restore

resto *m* rest, remainder; (en matemática) remainder. **~s** *mpl* remains; (de comida) leftovers

restorán *m* restaurant

restregar [1 & 12] *vt* rub

restri|cción *f* restriction. **~ngir** [14] *vt* restrict, limit

resucitar *vt* resuscitate; (fig) revive. ● *vi* return to life

resuello *m* breath; (respiración) heavy breathing

resuelto *a* resolute

resulta|do *m* result (**en** in). **~r** *vi* result; (salir) turn out; (dar resultado) work; (ser) be; (costar) come to

resum|en *m* summary. **en ~en** in short. **~ir** *vt* summarize; (recapitular) sum up

resur|gir [14] *vi* reemerge; (fig) revive. **~gimiento** *m* resurgence. **~rección** *f* resurrection

retaguardia *f* (Mil) rearguard

retahíla *f* string

retar *vt* challenge

retardar *vt* slow down; (demorar) delay

retazo *m* remnant; (fig) piece, bit

reten|ción *f* retention. **~er** [40] *vt* keep; (en la memoria) retain; (no dar) withhold

reticencia *f* insinuation; (reserva) reluctance

retina *f* retina

retir|ada *f* withdrawal. **~ado** *a* remote; <*vida*> secluded; (jubilado) retired. **~ar** *vt* move away; (quitar) remove; withdraw <*dinero*>; (jubilar) pension off. □ **~arse** *vpr* draw back; (Mil) withdraw; (jubilarse) retire; (acostarse) go to bed. **~o** *m* retirement; (pensión) pension; (lugar apartado) retreat; (LAm, de apoyo, fondos) withdrawal

reto *m* challenge

retocar [7] *vt* retouch

retoño *m* shoot; (fig) kid

retoque *m* (acción) retouching; (efecto) finishing touch

retorc|er [2 & 9] *vt* twist; wring <*ropa*>. □ **~erse** *vpr* get twisted up; (de dolor) writhe. **~ijón** *m* (LAm) stomach cramp

retóric|a *f* rhetoric; (grandilocuencia) grandiloquence. **~o** *m* rhetorical

retorn|ar *vt/i* return. **~o** *m* return

retortijón *m* twist; (de tripas) stomach cramp

retractarse *vpr* retract. **~se de lo dicho** withdraw what one said

retransmitir *vt* repeat; (radio, TV) broadcast. **~ en directo** broadcast live

retras|ado *a* (con ser) mentally handicapped; (con estar) behind; <*reloj*> slow; (poco desarrollado) backward; (anticuado) old-fashioned. **~ar** *vt* delay; put back <*reloj*>; (retardar) slow down; (posponer) postpone. ● *vi* <*reloj*> be slow. □ **~arse** *vpr* be late; <*reloj*> be slow. **~o** *m* delay; (poco desarrollo) backwardness; (de reloj) slow-

ness. **traer ~o** be late. **~os** *mpl* arrears

retrato *m* portrait; (fig, descripción) description. **ser el vivo ~o de** be the living image of

retrete *m* toilet

retribu|ción *f* payment; (recompensa) reward. **~ir** [17] *vt* pay; (recompensar) reward; (LAm) return <*favor*>

retroce|der *vi* move back; (fig) back down. **~so** *m* backward movement; (de arma de fuego) recoil; (Med) relapse

retrógrado *a & m* (Pol) reactionary

retrospectivo *a* retrospective

retrovisor *m* rear-view mirror

retumbar *vt* echo; <*trueno etc*> boom

reum|a *m*, **reúma** *m* rheumatism. **~ático** *a* rheumatic. **~atismo** *m* rheumatism

reuni|ón *f* meeting; (entre amigos) reunion. **~r** [23] *vt* join together; (recoger) gather (together); raise <*fondos*>. □ **~rse** *vpr* meet; <*amigos etc*> get together

revalidar *vt* confirm; (Mex, estudios) validate

revalorizar [10] *vt*, (LAm) **revaluar** [21] *vt* revalue; increase <*pensiones*>. □ **~se** *vpr* appreciate

revancha *f* revenge; (en deportes) return match. **tomar la ~** get one's own back

revela|ción *f* revelation. **~do** *m* developing. **~dor** *a* revealing. **~r** *vt* reveal; (Foto) develop

revent|ar [1] *vi* burst; (tener ganas) be dying to. □ **~arse** *vpr* burst. **~ón** *m* burst; (Auto) blow out; (Mex, fiesta) party

reveren|cia *f* reverence; (de hombre, niño) bow; (de mujer) curtsy. **~ciar** *vt* revere. **~do** *a* (Relig) reverend. **~te** *a* reverent

revers|ible *a* reversible. **~o** *m* reverse; (de papel) back

revertir [4] *vi* revert (**a** to)

revés *m* wrong side; (de prenda) inside; (contratiempo) setback; (en deportes) backhand. **al ~** the other way round; (con lo de arriba abajo) upside down; (con lo de dentro fuera) inside out

revesti|miento *m* coating. **~r** [5] *vt* cover

revis|ar *vt* check; overhaul *<mecanismo>*; service *<coche etc>*; (LAm, equipaje) search. **~ión** *f* check(ing)); (Med) checkup; (de coche etc) service; (LAm, de equipaje) inspection. **~or** *m* inspector

revista *f* magazine; (inspección) inspection; (artículo) review; (espectáculo) revue. **pasar ~ a** inspect

revivir *vi* revive

revolcar [2 & 7] *vt* knock over. □ **~se** *vpr* roll around

revolotear *vi* flutter

revoltijo *m*, **revoltillo** *m* mess

revoltoso *a* rebellious; *<niño>* naughty

revoluci|ón *f* revolution. **~onar** *vt* revolutionize. **~onario** *a & m* revolutionary

revolver [2] (*pp* **revuelto**) *vt* mix; stir *<líquido>*; (desordenar) mess up

revólver *m* revolver

revuelo *m* fluttering; (fig) stir

revuelt|a *f* revolt; (conmoción) disturbance. **~o** *a* mixed up; *<líquido>* cloudy; *<mar>* rough; *<tiempo>* unsettled; *<huevos>* scrambled

rey *m* king. **los ~es** the king and queen. **los R~es Magos** the Three Wise Men

reyerta *f* brawl

rezagarse [12] *vpr* fall behind

rez|ar [10] *vt* say. ● *vi* pray; (decir) say. **~o** *m* praying; (oración) prayer

rezongar [12] *vi* grumble

ría *f* estuary

riachuelo *m* stream

riada *f* flood

ribera *f* bank

ribete *m* border; (fig) embellishment

rico *a* rich; (Culin, 🔟) good, nice. ● *m* rich person

rid|ículo *a* ridiculous. **~iculizar** [10] *vt* ridicule

riego *m* watering; (irrigación) irrigation

riel *m* rail

rienda *f* rein

riesgo *m* risk. **correr (el) ~ de** run the risk of

rifa *f* raffle. **~r** *vt* raffle

rifle *m* rifle

rigidez *f* rigidity; (fig) inflexibility

rígido *a* rigid; (fig) inflexible

rig|or *m* strictness; (exactitud) exactness; (de clima) severity. **de ~or** compulsory. **en ~or** strictly speaking. **~uroso** *a* rigorous

rima *f* rhyme. **~r** *vt/i* rhyme

rimbombante *a* resounding; *<lenguaje>* pompous; (fig, ostentoso) showy

rímel *m* mascara

rin *m* (Mex) rim

rincón *m* corner

rinoceronte *m* rhinoceros

riña *f* quarrel; (pelea) fight

riñón *m* kidney

río *m* river; (fig) stream. **~ abajo** downstream. **~ arriba** upstream. ● *vb* ⇒REÍR

riqueza *f* wealth; (fig) richness. **~s** *fpl* riches

ris|a *f* laugh. **desternillarse de ~a** split one's sides laughing. **la ~a** laughter. **~otada** *f* guffaw. **~ueño** *a* smiling; (fig) cheerful

rítmico *a* rhythmic(al)

ritmo *m* rhythm; (fig) rate

rit|o *m* rite; (fig) ritual. **~ual** *a & m* ritual

rival *a & m & f* rival. **~idad** *f* rivalry. **~izar** [10] *vi* rival

riz|ado *a* curly. **~ar** [10] *vt* curl; ripple *<agua>*. **~o** *m* curl; (en agua) ripple

róbalo *m* bass

robar *vt* steal *<cosa>*; rob *<banco>*; (raptar) kidnap

roble *m* oak (tree)

robo *m* theft; (de banco, museo) robbery; (en vivienda) burglary

robusto *a* robust

roca *f* rock

roce *m* rubbing; (señal) mark; (fig, entre personas) regular contact; (Pol) friction. **tener un ~ con uno** have a brush with s.o.

rociar [20] *vt* spray

rocín *m* nag

rocío *m* dew

rodaballo *m* turbot

rodaja *f* slice. **en ~s** sliced

roda|je *m* (de película) shooting; (de coche) running in. **~r** [2] *vt* shoot *<película>*; run in *<coche>*. ● *vi* roll; *<coche>* run; (hacer una película) shoot

rode|ar *vt* surround; (LAm) round up *<ganado>*. □ **~arse** *vpr* surround o.s. (**de** with). **~o** *m* detour; (de ganado) round-up. **andar con ~os** beat about the bush. **sin ~os** plainly

rodill|a *f* knee. **ponerse de ~as** kneel down. **~era** *f* knee-pad

rodillo *m* roller; (Culin) rolling-pin

roe|dor *m* rodent. **~r** [37] *vt* gnaw

rogar [2 & 12] *vt/i* beg; (Relig) pray; **se ruega a los Sres. pasajeros...** passengers are requested.... **se ruega no fumar** please do not smoke

roj|izo *a* reddish. **~o** *a* & *m* red. **ponerse ~o** blush

roll|izo *a* plump; *<bebé>* chubby. **~o** *m* roll; (de cuerda) coil; (Culin, rodillo) rolling-pin; (fig, 🔲, pesadez) bore

romance *a* Romance. ● *m* (idilio) romance; (poema) ballad

romano *a* & *m* Roman. **a la ~a** (Culin) (deep-)fried in batter

rom|anticismo *m* romanticism. **~ántico** *a* romantic

romería *f* pilgrimage; (LAm, multitud) mass

romero *m* rosemary

romo *a* blunt; *<nariz>* snub

rompe|cabezas *m invar* puzzle; (de piezas) jigsaw (puzzle). **~olas** *m invar* breakwater

romp|er (*pp* **roto**) *vt* break; tear *<hoja, camisa etc>*; break off *<relaciones etc>*. ● *vi* break; *<novios>* break up. **~er a** burst out. □ **~erse** *vpr* break

ron *m* rum

ronc|ar [7] *vi* snore. **~o** *a* hoarse

roncha *f* lump; (por alergia) rash

ronda *f* round; (patrulla) patrol; (serenata) serenade. **~r** *vt* patrol. ● *vi* be on patrol; (merodear) hang around

ronqu|era *f* hoarseness. **~ido** *m* snore

ronronear *vi* purr

roñ|a *f* (suciedad) grime. **~oso** *a* dirty; (oxidado) rusty; (tacaño) mean

rop|a *f* clothes, clothing. **~a blanca** linen, underwear. **~a de cama** bedclothes. **~a interior** underwear. **~aje** *m* robes; (excesivo) heavy clothing. **~ero** *m* wardrobe

ros|a *a invar* pink. ● *f* rose. ● *m* pink. **~áceo** *a* pinkish. **~ado** *a* pink; *<mejillas>* rosy. ● *m* (vino) rosé. **~al** *m* rose-bush

rosario *m* rosary; (fig) series

ros|ca *f* (de tornillo) thread; (de pan) roll; (bollo) type of doughnut. **~co** *m* roll. **~quilla** *f* type of doughnut

rostro *m* face

rota|ción *f* rotation. **~r** *vt/i* rotate. □ **~rse** *vpr* take turns. **~tivo** *a* rotary

roto *a* broken

rótula *f* kneecap

rotulador *m* felt-tip pen

rótulo *m* sign; (etiqueta) label; (logotipo) logo

rotundo *a* categorical

rotura *f* tear; (grieta) crack

rozadura *f* scratch

rozagante *a* (LAm) healthy

rozar [10] *vt* rub against; (ligeramente) brush against; (raspar) graze. □ **~se** *vpr* rub; (con otras personas) mix

Rte. *abrev* (**Remite(nte)**) sender

rubéola *f* German measles

rubí *m* ruby

rubicundo *a* ruddy

rubio *a* *<pelo>* fair; *<persona>* fairhaired; *<tabaco>* Virginia

rubor *m* blush; (Mex, cosmético) blusher. □ **~izarse** [10] *vpr* blush

rúbrica *f* (de firma) flourish; (firma) signature; (título) heading

rudeza *f* roughness

rudiment|ario *a* rudimentary. **~os** *mpl* rudiments

rueca *f* distaff

rueda *f* wheel; (de mueble) castor; (de personas) ring; (Culin) slice. **~ de prensa** press conference

ruedo *m* edge; (redondel) bullring

ruego *m* request; (súplica) entreaty. ● *vb* ⇒ROGAR

rufián *m* pimp; (granuja) rogue

rugby *m* rugby

rugi|do *m* roar. ~**r** [14] *vi* roar

ruibarbo *m* rhubarb

ruido *m* noise. ~**so** *a* noisy; (fig) sensational

ruin *a* despicable; (tacaño) mean

ruin|a *f* ruin; (colapso) collapse. ~**oso** *a* ruinous

ruiseñor *m* nightingale

ruleta *f* roulette

rulo *m* curler

rumano *a & m* Romanian

rumbo *m* direction; (fig) course; (fig, esplendidez) lavishness. **con** ~ **a** in the direction of. ~**so** *a* lavish

rumia|nte *a & m* ruminant. ~**r** *vt* chew; (fig) brood over. ● *vi* ruminate

rumor *m* rumour; (ruido) murmur. ~**ear** *vt*. **se** ~**ea que** rumour has it that. ~**oso** *a* murmuring

runrún *m* (de voces) murmur; (de motor) whirr

ruptura *f* breakup; (de relaciones etc) breaking off; (de contrato) breach

rural *a* rural

ruso *a & m* Russian

rústico *a* rural; (de carácter) coarse. **en rústica** paperback

ruta *f* route; (fig) course

rutina *f* routine. ~**rio** *a* routine; <trabajo> monotonous

Ss

S.A. *abrev* (**Sociedad Anónima**) Ltd, plc, Inc (Amer)

sábado *m* Saturday

sábana *f* sheet

sabañón *m* chilblain

sabático *a* sabbatical

sab|elotodo *m & f invar* know-all 🛈. ~**er** [38] *vt* know; (ser capaz de) be able to, know how to; (enterarse de) find out. ● *vi* know. ~**er a** taste of. **hacer** ~**er** let know. **¡qué sé yo!** how should I know? **que yo sepa** as far as I know. **¿~es nadar?** can you swim?

un no sé qué a certain sth. **¡yo qué sé!** how should I know? **¡vete a** ~**er!** who knows? ~**er** *m* knowledge. ~**ido** *a* well-known. ~**iduría** *f* wisdom; (conocimientos) knowledge

sabi|endas. a ~ knowingly; (a propósito) on purpose. ~**hondo** *m* know-all 🛈. ~**o** *a* learned; (prudente) wise

sabor *m* taste, flavour; (fig) flavour. ~**ear** *vt* taste; (fig) savour

sabot|aje *m* sabotage. ~**eador** *m* saboteur. ~**ear** *vt* sabotage

sabroso *a* tasty; <chisme> juicy; (LAm, agradable) pleasant

sabueso *m* (perro) bloodhound; (fig, detective) detective

saca|corchos *m invar* corkscrew. ~**puntas** *m invar* pencil-sharpener

sacar [7] *vt* take out; put out <parte del cuerpo>; (quitar) remove; take <foto>; win <premio>; get <billete, entrada>; withdraw <dinero>; reach <solución>; draw <conclusión>; make <copia>. ~ **adelante** bring up <niño>; carry on <negocio>

sacarina *f* saccharin

sacerdo|cio *m* priesthood. ~**te** *m* priest

saciar *vt* satisfy; quench <sed>

saco *m* sack; (LAm, chaqueta) jacket. ~ **de dormir** sleeping-bag

sacramento *m* sacrament

sacrific|ar [7] *vt* sacrifice; slaughter <res>; put to sleep <perro, gato>. □ ~**arse** *vpr* sacrifice o.s. ~**io** *m* sacrifice; (de res) slaughter

sacr|ilegio *m* sacrilege. ~**ílego** *a* sacrilegious

sacudi|da *f* shake; (movimiento brusco) jolt, jerk; (fig) shock. ~**da eléctrica** electric shock. ~**r** *vt* shake; (golpear) beat. □ ~**rse** *vpr* shake off; (fig) get rid of

sádico *a* sadistic. ● *m* sadist

sadismo *m* sadism

safari *m* safari

sagaz *a* shrewd

Sagitario *m* Sagittarius

sagrado *a* <lugar> holy, sacred; <altar, escrituras> holy; (fig) sacred

sal *f* salt. ● *vb* ⇒SALIR

sala *f* room; (en casa) living room; (en hospital) ward; (para reuniones etc) hall; (en teatro) house; (Jurid) courtroom. ∼ **de embarque** departure lounge. ∼ **de espera** waiting room. ∼ **de estar** living room. ∼ **de fiestas** nightclub

salado *a* salty; *<agua del mar>* salt; (no dulce) savoury; (fig) witty

salario *m* wage

salchich|a *f* (pork) sausage. ∼**ón** *m* salami

sald|ar *vt* settle *<cuenta>*; (vender) sell off. ∼**o** *m* balance. ∼**os** *mpl* sales. **venta de** ∼**os** clearance sale

salero *m* salt-cellar

salgo *vb* ⇒SALIR

sali|da *f* departure; (puerta) exit, way out; (de gas, de líquido) leak; (de astro) rising; (Com, venta) sale; (chiste) witty remark; (fig) way out; ∼**da de emergencia** emergency exit. ∼**ente** *a* (Archit) projecting; *<pómulo etc>* prominent. ∼**r** [52] *vi* leave; (ir afuera) go out; (Informática) exit; *<revista etc>* be published; (resultar) turn out; *<astro>* rise; (aparecer) appear. ∼**r adelante** get by. □ ∼**rse** *vpr* leave; *<recipiente, líquido etc>* leak. ∼**rse con la suya** get one's own way

saliva *f* saliva

salmo *m* psalm

salm|ón *m* salmon. ∼**onete** *m* red mullet

salón *m* living-room, lounge. ∼ **de actos** assembly hall. ∼ **de clases** classroom. ∼ **de fiestas** dancehall

salpica|dera *f* (Mex) mudguard. ∼**dero** *m* (Auto) dashboard. ∼**dura** *f* splash; (acción) splashing. ∼**r** [7] *vt* splash; (fig) sprinkle

sals|a *f* sauce; (para carne asada) gravy; (Mus) salsa. ∼**a verde** parsley sauce. ∼**era** *f* sauce-boat

salt|amontes *m invar* grasshopper. ∼**ar** *vt* jump (over); (fig) miss out. ● *vi* jump; (romperse) break; *<líquido>* spurt out; (desprenderse) come off; *<pelota>* bounce. (estallar) explode. ∼**eador** *m* highwayman. ∼**ear** *vt* (Culin) sauté

salt|o *m* jump; (al agua) dive. ∼**o de agua** waterfall. ∼ **mortal** somersault.

de un ∼**o** with one jump. ∼**ón** *a* *<ojos>* bulging

salud *f* health. ● *int* cheers!; (LAm, al estornudar) bless you! ∼**able** *a* healthy

salud|ar *vt* greet, say hello to; (Mil) salute. **lo** ∼**a atentamente** (en cartas) yours faithfully. ∼ **con la mano** wave. ∼**o** *m* greeting; (Mil) salute. ∼**os** *mpl* best wishes

salva *f* salvo. **una** ∼ **de aplausos** a burst of applause

salvación *f* salvation

salvado *m* bran

salvaguardia *f* safeguard

salvaje *a* (planta, animal) wild; (primitivo) savage. ● *m & f* savage

salva|mento *m* rescue. ∼**r** *vt* save, rescue; (atravesar) cross (recorrer); travel (fig) overcome. □ ∼**rse** *vpr* save o.s. ∼**vidas** *m & f invar* lifeguard. ● *m* lifebelt. **chaleco** *m* ∼**vidas** life-jacket

salvo *a* safe. ● *adv & prep* except (for). **a** ∼ out of danger. **poner a** ∼ put in a safe place. ∼ **que** unless. ∼**conducto** *m* safe-conduct

San *a* Saint, St. ∼ **Miguel** St Michael

sana|r *vt* cure. ● *vi* recover; heal *<herida>*. ∼**torio** *m* sanatorium

sanci|ón *f* sanction. ∼**onar** *vt* sanction

sandalia *f* sandal

sandía *f* watermelon

sándwich /'saŋgwitʃ/ *m* (*pl* ∼**s,** ∼**es**) sandwich

sangr|ante *a* bleeding; (fig) flagrant ∼**ar** *vt/i* bleed. ∼**e** *f* blood. **a** ∼**e fría** in cold blood

sangría *f* (bebida) sangria

sangriento *a* bloody

sangu|ijuela *f* leech. ∼**íneo** *a* blood

san|idad *f* health. ∼**itario** *a* sanitary. ● *m* (Mex) toilet. ∼**o** *a* healthy; *<mente>* sound. ∼**o y salvo** safe and sound. **cortar por lo** ∼**o** settle things once and for all

santiamén *m*. **en un** ∼ in an instant

sant|idad *f* sanctity. ∼**ificar** [7] *vt* sanctify. □ ∼**iguarse** [15] *vpr* cross o.s. **~o** *a* holy; (delante de nombre) Saint, St. ● *m* saint; (día) saint's day, name day. **~uario** *m* sanctuary. **~urrón** *a* sanctimonious

saña *f* viciousness. **con ~** viciously

sapo *m* toad

saque *m* (en tenis) service; (inicial en fútbol) kick-off. **~ de banda** throw-in; (en rugby) line-out. **~ de esquina** corner (kick)

saque|ar *vt* loot. **~o** *m* looting

sarampión *m* measles

sarape *m* (Mex) colourful blanket

sarc|asmo *m* sarcasm. **~ástico** *a* sarcastic

sardina *f* sardine

sargento *m* sergeant

sarpullido *m* rash

sartén *f or m* frying-pan (Brit), frypan (Amer)

sastre *m* tailor. **~ría** *f* tailoring; (tienda) tailor's (shop)

Sat|anás *m* Satan. **~ánico** *a* satanic

satélite *m* satellite

satinado *a* shiny

sátira *f* satire

satírico *a* satirical. ● *m* satirist

satisf|acción *f* satisfaction. **~acer** [31] *vt* satisfy; (pagar) pay; (gustar) please; meet *<gastos, requisitos>*. □ **~acerse** *vpr* satisfy o.s.; (vengarse) take revenge. **~actorio** *a* satisfactory. **~echo** *a* satisfied. **~echo de sí mismo** smug

satura|ción *f* saturation. **~r** *vt* saturate

Saturno *m* Saturn

sauce *m* willow. **~ llorón** weeping willow

sauna *f*, (LAm) **sauna** *m* sauna

saxofón *m*, **saxófono** *m* saxophone

sazona|do *a* ripe; (Culin) seasoned. **~r** *vt* ripen; (Culin) season

....

se

● *pronombre*

····▸ (en lugar de le, les) **se lo di** (a él) I gave it to him; (a ella) I gave it to her; (a usted, ustedes) I gave it to you; (a ellos, ellas) I gave it to them. **se lo**

compré I bought it for him (*or* her *etc*). **se lo quité** I took it away from him (*or* her *etc*). **se lo dije** I told him (*or* her *etc*)

····▸ (reflexivo) **se secó** (él) he dried himself; (ella) she dried herself; (usted) you dried yourself; (sujeto no humano) it dried itself. **se secaron** (ellos, ellas) they dried themselves; (ustedes) you dried yourselves. (con partes del cuerpo) **se lavó la cara** (él) he washed his face. (con efectos personales) **se limpian los zapatos** they clean their shoes

····▸ (recíproco) each other, one another. **se ayudan mucho** they help each other a lot. **no se hablan** they don't speak to each other

····▸ (cuando otro hace la acción) **va a operarse** she's going to have an operation. **se cortó el pelo** he had his hair cut

····▸ (enfático) **se bebió el café** he drank his coffee. **se subió al tren** he got on the train

➡ **se** also forms part of certain pronominal verbs such as equivocarse, arrepentirse, caerse etc., which are treated under the respective entries

····▸ (voz pasiva) **se construyeron muchas casas** many houses were built. **se vendió rápidamente** it was sold very quickly

····▸ (impersonal) **antes se escuchaba más radio**) people used to listen to the radio more in the past. **no se puede entrar** you can't get in. **se está bien aquí** it's very nice here

····▸ (en instrucciones) **sírvase frío** serve cold

....

sé *vb* ⇒SABER *y* SER

sea *vb* ⇒SER

seca|dor *m* drier; (de pelo) hairdrier. **~nte** *a* drying. ● *m* blotting-paper. **~r** [7] *vt* dry. □ **~rse** *vpr* dry; *<río etc>* dry up; *<persona>* dry o.s.

sección *f* section

seco *a* dry; *<frutos, flores>* dried; (flaco) thin; *<respuesta>* curt. **a secas** just. **en ~** (bruscamente) suddenly. **lavar en ~** dry-clean

secretar|ía f secretariat; (Mex, ministerio) ministry. **∼io** m secretary; (Mex, Pol) minister

secreto a & m secret

secta f sect. **∼rio** a sectarian

sector m sector

secuela f consequence

secuencia f sequence

secuestr|ar vt confiscate; kidnap *<persona>*; hijack *<avión>*. **∼o** m seizure; (de persona) kidnapping; (de avión) hijack(ing)

secundar vt second, help. **∼io** a secondary

sed f thirst. ● vb ⇒SER. **tener ∼** be thirsty. **tener ∼ de** (fig) be hungry for

seda f silk. **∼ dental** dental floss

sedante a & m sedative

sede f seat; (Relig) see; (de organismo) headquarters; (de congreso, juegos etc) venue

sedentario a sedentary

sedici|ón f sedition. **∼oso** a seditious

sediento a thirsty

seduc|ción f seduction. **∼ir** [47] vt seduce; (atraer) attract. **∼tor** a seductive. ● m seducer

seglar a secular. ● m layman

segrega|ción f segregation. **∼r** [12] vt segregate

segui|da f. **en ∼da** immediately. **∼do** a continuous; (en plural) consecutive. **∼ de** followed by. ● adv straight; (LAm, a menudo) often. **todo ∼do** straight ahead. **∼dor** m follower; (en deportes) supporter. **∼r** [5 & 13] vt follow. ● vi (continuar) continue; (por un camino) go on. **∼ adelante** carry on

según prep according to. ● adv it depends; (a medida que) as

segunda f (Auto) second gear; (en tren, avión etc) second class. **∼o** a & m second

segur|amente adv certainly; (muy probablemente) surely. **∼idad** f security; (ausencia de peligro) safety; (certeza) certainty; (aplomo) confidence. **∼idad en sí mismo** self-confidence. **∼idad social** social security. **∼o** a safe; (cierto) certain, sure; (estable) secure; (de fiar) reliable. ● adv for certain. ●

m insurance; (dispositivo de seguridad) safety device. **∼o de sí mismo** self-confident. **∼o contra terceros** third-party insurance

seis a & m six. **∼cientos** a & m six hundred

seísmo m earthquake

selec|ción f selection. **∼cionar** vt select, choose. **∼tivo** a selective. **∼to** a selected; (fig) choice

sell|ar vt stamp; (cerrar) seal. **∼o** m stamp; (precinto) seal; (fig, distintivo) hallmark; (LAm, en moneda) reverse

selva f forest; (jungla) jungle

semáforo m (Auto) traffic lights; (Rail) signal; (Naut) semaphore

semana f week. **S∼** Santa Holy Week. **∼l** a weekly. **∼rio** a & m weekly

semántic|a f semantics. **∼o** a semantic

semblante m face; (fig) look

sembrar [1] vt sow; (fig) scatter

semeja|nte a similar; (tal) such. ● m fellow man. **∼nza** f similarity. **a ∼nza de** like. **∼r** vi. **∼ a** resemble

semen m semen. **∼tal** a stud. ● m stud animal

semestr|al a half-yearly. **∼e** m six months

semi|circular a semicircular. **∼círculo** m semicircle. **∼final** f semifinal

semill|a f seed. **∼ero** m seedbed; (fig) hotbed

seminario m (Univ) seminar; (Relig) seminary

sémola f semolina

senado m senate. **∼r** m senator

sencill|ez f simplicity. **∼o** a simple; (para viajar) single ticket; (disco) single; (LAm, dinero suelto) change

senda f, **sendero** m path

sendos a pl each

seno m bosom. **∼ materno** womb

sensaci|ón f sensation; (percepción, impresión) feeling. **∼onal** a sensational

sensat|ez f good sense. **∼o** a sensible

sensi|bilidad f sensibility. **~ble** a sensitive; (notable) notable; (lamentable) lamentable. **~tivo** a <órgano> sense

sensual a sensual. **~idad** f sensuality

senta|do a sitting (down); **dar algo por ~do** take something for granted. **~dor** a (LAm) flattering. **~r** [1] vt sit; (establecer) establish. ● vi suit; (de medidas) fit; <comida> agree with. □ **~rse** vpr sit (down)

sentencia f (Jurid) sentence. **~r** vt sentence (**a** to)

sentido a heartfelt; (sensible) sensitive. ● m sense; (dirección) direction; (conocimiento) consciousness. **~ común** common sense. **~ del humor** sense of humour. **~ único** one-way. **doble ~** double meaning. **no tener ~** not make sense. **perder el ~** faint. **sin ~** senseless

sentim|ental a sentimental. **~iento** m feeling; (sentido) sense; (pesar) regret

sentir [4] vt feel; (oír) hear; (lamentar) be sorry for. **lo siento mucho** I'm really sorry. ● m (opinión) opinion. □ **~se** vpr feel; (Mex, ofenderse) be offended

seña f sign. **~s** fpl (dirección) address; (descripción) description. **dar ~s de** show signs of

señal f signal; (letrero, aviso) sign; (telefónica) tone; (Com) deposit. **dar ~es de** show signs of. **en ~ de** as a token of. **~ado** a <hora, día> appointed. **~ar** vt signal; (poner señales en) mark; (apuntar) point out; <manecilla, aguja> point to; (determinar) fix. □ **~arse** vpr stand out

señor m man, gentleman; (delante de nombre propio) Mr; (tratamiento directo) sir. **~a** f lady, woman; (delante de nombre propio) Mrs; (esposa) wife; (tratamiento directo) madam. **el ~ Mr. muy ~ mío** Dear Sir. **¡no ~!** certainly not!. **~ial** a <casa> stately. **~ita** f young lady; (delante de nombre propio) Miss; (tratamiento directo) miss. **~ito** m young gentleman

señuelo m lure

sepa vb ⇒SABER

separa|ción f separation. **~do** a separate. **por ~do** separately. **~r** vt separate; (de empleo) dismiss. □ **~rse** vpr separate; <amigos> part. **~tista** a & m & f separatist

septentrional a north(ern)

septiembre m September

séptimo a seventh

sepulcro m sepulchre

sepult|ar vt bury. **~ura** f burial; (tumba) grave. **~urero** m gravedigger

sequ|edad f dryness. **~ía** f drought

séquito m entourage; (fig) train

ser [39]

● verbo intransitivo

···▸ to be. **es bajo** he's short. **es abogado** he's a lawyer. **ábreme, soy yo** open up, it's me. **¿cómo es?** (como persona) what's he like?; (físicamente) what does he look like? **era invierno** it was winter

···▸ **ser de** (indicando composición) to be made of. **es de hierro** it's made of iron. (provenir de) to be from. **es de México** he's from Mexico. (pertenecer a) to belong to. **el coche es de Juan** the car belongs to Juan, it's Juan's car

···▸ (sumar) **¿cuánto es todo?** how much is that altogether? **son 40 dólares** that's 40 dollars. **somos 10** there are 10 of us

···▸ (con la hora) **son las 3** it's 3 o'clock. **~ía la una** it must have been one o'clock

···▸ (tener lugar) to be held. **~á en la iglesia** it will be held in the church

···▸ (ocurrir) to happen **¿dónde fue el accidente?** where did the accident happen? **me contó cómo fue** he told me how it happened

···▸ (en locuciones) **a no ~ que** unless. **como sea** no matter what. **cuando sea** whenever. **donde sea** wherever. **¡eso es!** that's it! **es que** the thing is. **lo que sea** anything. **no sea que, no vaya a ~ que** in case. **o sea** in other words. **sea ... sea ...** either ... or ... **sea como sea** at all costs

● nombre masculino

····▸ being; (persona) person. **el ~ humano** the human being. **un ~ amargado** a bitter person. **los ~es queridos** the loved ones

seren|ar *vt* calm down. □**~arse** *vpr* calm down. **~ata** *f* serenade. **~idad** *f* serenity. **~o** *a* serene; <*cielo*> clear; <*mar*> calm. ● *m* night watchman. **al ~o** in the open

seri|al *m* serial. **~e** *f* series. **fuera de ~e** (fig) out of this world. **producción *f* en ~e** mass production

seri|edad *f* seriousness. **~o** *a* serious; (confiable) reliable; **en ~o** seriously. **poco ~o** frivolous

sermón *m* sermon; (fig) lecture

serp|enteante *a* winding. **~entear** *vi* wind. **~iente** *f* snake. **~iente de cascabel** rattlesnake

serr|ar [1] *vt* saw. **~ín** *m* sawdust. **~uchar** *vt* (LAm) saw. **~ucho** *m* (hand)saw

servi|cial *a* helpful. **~cio** *m* service; (conjunto) set; (aseo) toilet; **~cio a domicilio** delivery service. **~dor** *m* servant. **su (seguro) ~dor** (en cartas) yours faithfully. **~dumbre** *f* servitude; (criados) servants, staff. **~l** *a* servile

servilleta *f* napkin, serviette

servir [5] *vt* serve; (en restaurante) wait on. ● *vi* serve; (ser útil) be of use. □ **~se** *vpr* help o.s.. **~se de** use. **no ~ de nada** be useless. **para ~le** at your service. **sírvase sentarse** please sit down

sesent|a *a & m* sixty. **~ón** *a & m* sixty-year-old

seseo *m* pronunciation of the Spanish *c* as an *s*

sesión *f* session; (en el cine, teatro)

seso *m* brain

seta *f* mushroom

sete|cientos *a & m* seven hundred. **~nta** *a & m* seventy. **~ntón** *a & m* seventy-year-old

setiembre *m* September

seto *m* fence; (de plantas) hedge. **~ vivo** hedge

seudónimo *m* pseudonym

sever|idad *f* severity; (de profesor etc) strictness. **~o** *a* severe; <*profesor etc*> strict

sevillan|as *fpl* popular dance from Seville. **~o** *m* person from Seville

sexo *m* sex

sext|eto *m* sextet. **~o** *a* sixth

sexual *a* sexual. **~idad** *f* sexuality

si *m* (Mus) B; (solfa) te. ● *conj* if; (dubitativo) whether; **~ no** otherwise. **por ~ (acaso)** in case

sí[1] *pron reflexivo* (él) himself; (ella) herself; (de cosa) itself; (uno) oneself; (Vd) yourself; (ellos, ellas) themselves; (Vds) yourselves; (recíproco) each other

sí[2] *adv* yes. ● *m* consent

sida *m* Aids

sidra *f* cider

siembra *f* sowing; (época) sowing time

siempre *adv* always; (LAm, todavía) still; (Mex, por fin) after all. **~ que** if; (cada vez) whenever. **como ~** as usual. **de ~** (acostumbrado) usual. **lo de ~** the usual thing. **para ~** for ever

sien *f* temple

siento *vb* ⇒SENTAR *y* SENTIR

sierra *f* saw; (cordillera) mountain range

siesta *f* nap, siesta

siete *a & m* seven

sífilis *f* syphilis

sifón *m* U-bend; (de soda) syphon

sigilo *m* stealth; (fig) secrecy

sigla *f* abbreviation

siglo *m* century; (época) age. **hace ~s que no escribe** he hasn't written for ages

significa|ción *f* significance. **~do** *a* (conocido) well-known. ● *m* meaning; (importancia) significance. **~r** [7] *vt* mean; (expresar) express. **~tivo** *a* meaningful; (importante) significant

signo *m* sign. **~ de admiración** exclamation mark. **~ de interrogación** question mark

sigo *vb* ⇒SEGUIR

siguiente *a* following, next. **lo ~** the following

sílaba *f* syllable

silb|ar *vt/i* whistle. **~ato** *m*, **~ido** *m* whistle

silenci|ador *m* silencer. **~ar** *vt* hush up. **~o** *m* silence. **~oso** *a* silent

sill|a *f* chair; (de montar) saddle (Relig) see **~a de ruedas** wheelchair. **~ín** *m* saddle. **~ón** *m* armchair

silueta *f* silhouette; (dibujo) outline

silvestre *a* wild

simb|ólico *a* symbolic(al). **~olismo** *m* symbolism. **~olizar** [10] *vt* symbolize

símbolo *m* symbol

sim|etría *f* symmetry. **~étrico** *a* symmetric(al)

similar *a* similar (a to)

simp|atía *f* friendliness; (cariño) affection. **~ático** *a* nice, likeable; <*ambiente*> pleasant. **~atizante** *m* & *f* sympathizer. **~atizar** [10] *vi* get on (well together)

simpl|e *a* simple; (mero) mere. **~eza** *f* simplicity; (tontería) stupid thing; (insignificancia) trifle. **~icidad** *f* simplicity. **~ificar** [7] *vt* simplify. **~ista** *a* simplistic. **~ón** *m* simpleton

simula|ción *f* simulation. **~r** *vt* simulate; (fingir) feign

simultáneo *a* simultaneous

sin *prep* without. **~ saber** without knowing. **~ querer** accidentally

sinagoga *f* synagogue

sincer|idad *f* sincerity. **~o** *a* sincere

sincronizar [10] *vt* synchronize

sindica|l *a* (trade-)union. **~lista** *m* & *f* trade-unionist. **~to** *m* trade union

síndrome *m* syndrome

sinfín *m* endless number (de of)

sinfonía *f* symphony

singular *a* singular; (excepcional) exceptional. □ **~izarse** *vpr* stand out

siniestro *a* sinister. ● *m* disaster; (accidente) accident

sinnúmero *m* endless number (de of)

sino *m* fate. ● *conj* but

sinónimo *a* synonymous. ● *m* synonym (de for)

sintaxis *f* syntax

síntesis *f invar* synthesis; (resumen) summary

sint|ético *a* synthetic. **~etizar** [10] *vt* synthesize; (resumir) summarize

síntoma *f* sympton

sintomático *a* symptomatic

sinton|ía *f* tuning; (Mus) signature tune. **~izar** [10] *vt* (con la radio) tune (in) to

sinvergüenza *m* & *f* crook

siquiera *conj* even if. ● *adv* at least. **ni ~** not even

sirena *f* siren; (en cuentos) mermaid

sirio *a* & *m* Syrian

sirvient|a *f* maid. **~e** *m* servant

sirvo *vb* ⇒SERVIR

sísmico *a* seismic

sismo *m* earthquake

sistem|a *m* system. **por ~a** as a rule. **~ático** *a* systematic

sitiar *vt* besiege; (fig) surround

sitio *m* place; (espacio) space; (Mil) siege; (Mex, parada de taxi) taxi rank. **en cualquier ~** anywhere. **~ web** website

situa|ción *f* situation; (estado, condición) position. **~r** [21] *vt* place, put; lócate <*edificio*>. □ **~rse** *vpr* be successful, establish o.s.

slip /es'lip/ *m* (*pl* **~s**) underpants, briefs

smoking /es'mokin/ *m* (*pl* **~s**) dinner jacket (Brit), tuxedo (Amer)

sobaco *m* armpit

sobar *vt* handle; knead <*masa*>

soberan|ía *f* sovereignty. **~o** *a* sovereign; (fig) supreme. ● *m* sovereign

soberbi|a *f* pride; (altanería) arrogance. **~o** *a* proud; (altivo) arrogant

soborn|ar *vt* bribe. **~o** *m* bribe

sobra *f* surplus. **de ~** more than enough. **~s** *fpl* leftovers. **~do** *a* more than enough. **~nte** *a* surplus. **~r** *vi* be left over; (estorbar) be in the way

sobre *prep* on; (encima de) on top of; (más o menos) about; (por encima de) above; (sin tocar) over. **~ todo** above all, especially. ● *m* envelope. **~car-**

gar [12] *vt* overload. ~**coger** [14] *vt* startle; (conmover) move. ~**cubierta** *f* dustcover. ~**dosis** *f invar* overdose. ~**entender** [1] *vt* understand, infer. ~**girar** *vt* (LAm) overdraw. ~**giro** *m* (LAm) overdraft. ~**humano** *a* superhuman. ~**llevar** *vt* bear. ~**mesa** *f*. de ~**mesa** after-dinner. ~**natural** *a* supernatural. ~**nombre** *m* nickname. ~**pasar** *vt* exceed. ~**peso** *m* (LAm) excess baggage. ~**poner** [34] *vt* superimpose. □ ~**ponerse** *vpr* overcome. ~**saliente** *a* (fig) outstanding. ● *m* excellent mark. ~**salir** [52] *vi* stick out; (fig) stand out. ~**saltar** *vt* startle. ~**salto** *m* fright. ~**sueldo** *m* bonus. ~**todo** *m* overcoat. ~**venir** [53] *vi* happen. ~**viviente** *a* surviving. ● *m* & *f* survivor. ~**vivir** *vi* survive. ~**volar** *vt* fly over

sobriedad *f* moderation; (de estilo) simplicity

sobrin|a *f* niece. ~**o** *m* nephew. ~**os** (varones) nephews; (varones y mujeres) nieces and nephews

sobrio *a* moderate, sober

socavar *vt* undermine

soci|able *a* sociable. ~**al** *a* social. ~**aldemócrata** *m* & *f* social democrat. ~**alismo** *m* socialism. ~**alista** *a* & *m* & *f* socialist. ~**edad** *f* society; (Com) company. ~**edad anónima** limited company. ~**o** *m* member; (Com) partner. ~**ología** *f* sociology. ~**ólogo** *m* sociologist

socorr|er *vt* help. ~**o** *m* help

soda *f* (bebida) soda (water)

sodio *m* sodium

sofá *m* sofa, settee

sofistica|ción *f* sophistication. ~**do** *a* sophisticated

sofo|cante *a* suffocating; (fig) stifling. ~**r** [7] *vt* smother <*fuego*>; (fig) stifle. □ ~**rse** *vpr* get upset

soga *f* rope

soja *f* soya (bean)

sojuzgar [12] *vt* subdue

sol *m* sun; (luz) sunlight; (Mus) G; (solfa) soh. al ~ in the sun. día *m* de ~ sunny day. hace ~, hay ~ it is sunny. tomar el ~ sunbathe

solamente *adv* only

solapa *f* lapel; (de bolsillo etc) flap. ~**do** *a* sly

solar *a* solar. ● *m* plot

solariego *a* <*casa*> ancestral

soldado *m* soldier. ~ **raso** private

solda|dor *m* welder; (utensilio) soldering iron. ~**r** [2] *vt* weld, solder

soleado *a* sunny

soledad *f* solitude; (aislamiento) loneliness

solemn|e *a* solemn. ~**idad** *f* solemnity

soler [2] *vi* be in the habit of. **suele despertarse a las 6** he usually wakes up at 6 o'clock

sol|icitar *vt* request, ask for; apply for <*empleo*>. ~**icito** *a* solicitous. ~**icitud** *f* request; (para un puesto) application; (formulario) application form; (preocupación) concern

solidaridad *f* solidarity

solid|ez *f* solidity; (de argumento etc) soundness. □ ~**ificarse** [7] *vpr* solidify

sólido *a* solid; <*argumento etc*> sound. ● *m* solid

soliloquio *m* soliloquy

solista *m* & *f* soloist

solitario *a* solitary; (aislado) lonely. ● *m* loner; (juego, diamante) solitaire

solloz|ar [10] *vi* sob. ~**o** *m* sob

solo *a* (sin compañía) alone; (aislado) lonely; (sin ayuda) by oneself; (único) only; (Mus) solo; <*café*> black. ● *m* solo; (juego) solitaire. **a solas** alone

sólo *adv* only. ~ **que** except that. **no** ~... **sino también** not only... but also.... **tan** ~ only

solomillo *m* sirloin

soltar [2] *vt* let go of; (dejar ir) release; (dejar caer) drop; (dejar salir, decir) let out; give <*golpe etc*>. □ ~**se** *vpr* come undone; (librarse) break loose

solter|a *f* single woman. ~**o** *a* single. ● *m* bachelor

soltura *f* looseness; (fig) ease, fluency

solu|ble *a* soluble. ~**ción** *f* solution. ~**cionar** *vt* solve; settle <*huelga, asunto*>

solvente *a* & *m* solvent

sombr|a *f* shadow; (lugar sin sol) shade. **a la ~a** in the shade. **~eado** *a* shady

sombrero *m* hat. **~ hongo** bowler hat

sombrío *a* sombre

somero *a* superficial

someter *vt* subdue; subject <*persona*>; (presentar) submit. □ **~se** *vpr* give in

somn|oliento *a* sleepy. **~ífero** *m* sleeping-pill

somos *vb* ⇒SER

son *m* sound. ● *vb* ⇒SER

sonámbulo *m* sleepwalker. **ser ~** walk in one's sleep

sonar [2] *vt* blow; ring <*timbre*>. ● *vi* sound; <*timbre, teléfono etc*> ring; <*despertador*> go off; (Mus) play; (fig, ser conocido) be familiar. **~ a** sound like. □ **~se** *vpr* blow one's nose

sonde|ar *vt* sound out; explore <*espacio*>; (Naut) sound. **~o** *m* poll; (Naut) sounding

soneto *m* sonnet

sonido *m* sound

sonoro *a* sonorous; (ruidoso) loud

sonr|eír [51] *vi* smile. □ **~eírse** *vpr* smile. **~isa** *f* smile

sonroj|arse *vpr* blush. **~o** *m* blush

sonrosado *a* rosy, pink

sonsacar [7] *vt* wheedle out

soñ|ado *a* dream. **~ador** *m* dreamer. **~ar** [2] *vi* dream (**con** of). **¡ni ~arlo!** not likely!

sopa *f* soup

sopesar *vt* (fig) weigh up

sopl|ar *vt* blow; blow out <*vela*>; blow off <*polvo*>; (inflar) blow up. ● *vi* blow. **~ete** *m* blowlamp. **~o** *m* puff

soport|al *m* porch. **~ales** *mpl* arcade. **~ar** *vt* support; (fig) bear, put up with. **~e** *m* support

soprano *f* soprano

sor *f* sister

sorb|er *vt* sip; (con ruido) slurp; (absorber) absorb. **~ por la nariz** sniff. **~ete** *m* sorbet, water-ice. **~o** *m* (pequeña cantidad) sip; (trago grande) gulp

sordera *f* deafness

sórdido *a* squalid; <*asunto*> sordid

sordo *a* deaf; <*ruido etc*> dull. ● *m* deaf person. **hacerse el ~** turn a deaf ear. **~mudo** *a* deaf and dumb

soroche *m* (LAm) mountain sickness

sorpre|ndente *a* surprising. **~nder** *vt* surprise. □ **~nderse** *vpr* be surprised. **~sa** *f* surprise

sorte|ar *vt* draw lots for; (fig) avoid. **~o** *m* draw. **por ~o** by drawing lots

sortija *f* ring; (de pelo) ringlet

sortilegio *m* sorcery; (embrujo) spell

sos|egar [1 & 12] *vt* calm. **~iego** *m* calmness

soslayo. de ~ sideways

soso *a* tasteless; (fig) dull

sospech|a *f* suspicion. **~ar** *vt* suspect. ● *vi*. **~ de** suspect. **~oso** *a* suspicious. ● *m* suspect

sost|én *m* support; (prenda femenina) bra Ⓣ, brassière. **~ener** [40] *vt* support; bear <*peso*>; (sujetar) hold; (sustentar) maintain; (alimentar) sustain. □ **~enerse** *vpr* support o.s.; (continuar) remain. **~enido** *a* sustained; (Mus) sharp. ● *m* (Mus) sharp

sota *f* (de naipes) jack

sótano *m* basement

soviético *a* (Historia) Soviet

soy *vb* ⇒SER

Sr. *abrev* (**Señor**) Mr. **~a.** *abrev* (**Señora**) Mrs. **~ta.** *abrev* (**Señorita**) Miss

su *a* (de él) his; (de ella) her; (de animal, objeto) its; (de uno) one's; (de Vd) your; (de ellos, de ellas) their; (de Vds) your

suav|e *a* smooth; (fig) gentle; <*color, sonido*> soft; <*tabaco, sedante*> mild. **~idad** *f* smoothness, softness. **~izante** *m* conditioner; (para ropa) softener. **~izar** [10] *vt* smooth, soften

subalimentado *a* underfed

subarrendar [1] *vt* sublet

subasta *f* auction. **~r** *vt* auction

sub|campeón *m* runner-up. **~consciencia** *f* subconscious. **~consciente** *a* & *m* subconscious. **~continente** *m* subcontinent. **~desarrollado** *a* under-developed. **~director** *m* assistant manager

súbdito *m* subject

sub|dividir *vt* subdivide. **~esti-mar** *vt* underestimate

subi|da *f* rise; (a montaña) ascent; (pendiente) slope. **~do** *a* <color> intense. **~r** *vt* go up; climb <mountain>; (llevar) take up; (aumentar) raise; turn up <radio, calefacción>. ● *vi* go up. **~r a** get into <coche>; get on <autobús, avión, barco, tren>; (aumentar) rise. **~ a pie** walk up. □ **~rse** *vpr* climb up. **~rse a** get on <tren etc>

súbito *a* sudden. **de ~** suddenly

subjetivo *a* subjective

subjuntivo *a & m* subjunctive

subleva|ción *f* uprising. □ **~rse** *vpr* rebel

sublim|ar *vt* sublimate. **~e** *a* sublime

submarino *a* underwater. ● *m* submarine

subordinado *a & m* subordinate

subrayar *vt* underline

subsanar *vt* rectify; overcome <dificultad>; make up for <carencia>

subscri|bir *vt* (*pp* **subscrito**) sign. □ **~birse** *vpr* subscribe (a to). **~pción** *f* subscription

subsidi|ario *a* subsidiary. **~o** *m* subsidy. **~o de desempleo, ~ de paro** unemployment benefit

subsiguiente *a* subsequent

subsist|encia *f* subsistence. **~ir** *vi* subsist; (perdurar) survive

substraer [41] *vt* take away

subterráneo *a* underground

subtítulo *m* subtitle

suburb|ano *a* suburban. **~io** *m* suburb; (barrio pobre) depressed area

subvenci|ón *f* subsidy. **~onar** *vt* subsidize

subver|sión *f* subversion. **~sivo** *a* subversive. **~tir** [4] *vt* subvert

succi|ón *f* suction. **~onar** *vt* suck

suce|der *vi* happen; (seguir) **~ a** follow. ● *vt* (substituir) succeed. **lo que ~de es que** the trouble is that. **¿qué ~de?** what's the matter? **~sión** *f* succession. **~sivo** *a* successive; (consecutivo) consecutive. **en lo ~sivo** in future. **~so** *m* event; (incidente) incident. **~sor** *m* successor

suciedad *f* dirt; (estado) dirtiness

sucinto *a* concise; <prenda> scanty

sucio *a* dirty; <conciencia> guilty. **en ~** in rough

sucre *m* (unidad monetaria del Ecuador) sucre

suculento *a* succulent

sucumbir *vi* succumb (a to)

sucursal *f* branch (office)

Sudáfrica *f* South Africa

sudafricano *a & m* South African

Sudamérica *f* South America

sudamericano *a & m* South American

sudar *vi* sweat

sud|este *m* south-east. **~oeste** *m* south-west

sudor *m* sweat

Suecia *f* Sweden

sueco *a* Swedish. ● *m* (persona) Swede; (lengua) Swedish. **hacerse el ~** pretend not to hear

suegr|a *f* mother-in-law. **~o** *m* father-in-law. **mis ~os** my in-laws

suela *f* sole

sueldo *m* salary

suelo *m* ground; (dentro de edificio) floor; (territorio) soil; (en la calle etc) road surface. ● *vb* ⇒SOLER

suelto *a* loose; <cordones> undone; (sin pareja) odd; <lenguaje> fluent. **con el pelo ~** with one's hair down. ● *m* change

sueño *m* sleep; (lo soñado, ilusión) dream. **tener ~** be sleepy

suerte *f* luck; (destino) fate; (azar) chance. **de otra ~** otherwise. **de ~ que so. echar ~s** draw lots. **por ~** fortunately. **tener ~** be lucky

suéter *m* sweater, jersey

suficien|cia *f* (aptitud) aptitude; (presunción) smugness. **~te** *a* enough, sufficient; (presumido) smug. **~temente** *adv* sufficiently

sufijo *m* suffix

sufragio *m* (voto) vote

sufrimiento *m* suffering. **~r** *vt* suffer; undergo <cambio>; have <accident>. ● *vi* suffer

suge|rencia *f* suggestion. **~rir** [4] *vt* suggest. **~stión** *f* (Psych) suggestion. **es pura ~stión** it's all in one's mind. **~stionable** *a* impressionable. **~stionar** *vt* influence. **~stivo** *a* (estimulante) stimulating; (atractivo) sexy

suicid|a *a* suicidal. ● *m & f* suicide victim; (fig) maniac. □ **~arse** *vpr* commit suicide. **~io** *m* suicide

Suiza *f* Switzerland

suizo *a & m* Swiss

suje|ción *f* subjection. **con ~** a in accordance with. **~tador** *m* bra 🇮, brassière. **~tapapeles** *m invar* paper-clip. **~tar** *vt* fasten; (agarrar) hold. □ **~tarse** *vpr*. **~se a** hold on to; (someterse) abide by. **~to a** fastened; (susceptible) subject (**a** to). ● *m* individual; (Gram) subject.

suma *f* sum; (Math) addition; (combinación) combination. **en ~** in short. **~mente** *adv* extremely. **~r** *vt* add (up); (totalizar) add up to. ● *vi* add up. □ **~rse** *vpr*. **~rse a** join in

sumario *a* brief; (Jurid) summary. ● *m* table of contents; (Jurid) pre-trial proceedings

sumergi|ble *a* submersible. **~r** [14] *vt* submerge

suministr|ar *vt* supply. **~o** *m* supply; (acción) supplying

sumir *vt* sink; (fig) plunge

sumis|ión *f* submission. **~o** *a* submissive

sumo *a* great; (supremo) supreme. **a lo ~** at the most

suntuoso *a* sumptuous

supe *vb* ⇒SABER

superar *vt* surpass; (vencer) overcome; beat <*marca*>; (dejar atrás) get over. □ **~se** *vpr* better o.s.

superchería *f* swindle

superfici|al *a* superficial. **~e** *f* surface; (extensión) area. **de ~e** surface

superfluo *a* superfluous

superior *a* superior; (más alto) higher; (mejor) better; <*piso*> upper. ● *m* superior. **~idad** *f* superiority

superlativo *a & m* superlative

supermercado *m* supermarket

supersti|ción *f* superstition. **~oso** *a* superstitious

supervis|ar *vt* supervise. **~ión** *f* supervision. **~or** *m* supervisor

superviv|encia *f* survival. **~iente** *a* surviving. ● *m & f* survivor

suplantar *vt* supplant

suplement|ario *a* supplementary. **~o** *m* supplement

suplente *a & m & f* substitute

súplica *f* entreaty; (Jurid) request

suplicar [7] *vt* beg

suplicio *m* torture

suplir *vt* make up for; (reemplazar) replace

supo|ner [34] *vt* suppose; (significar) mean; involve <*gasto, trabajo*>. **~sición** *f* supposition

suprem|acía *f* supremacy. **~o** *a* supreme

supr|esión *f* suppression; (de impuesto) abolition; (de restricción) lifting. **~imir** *vt* suppress; abolish <*impuesto*>; lift <*restricción*>; delete <*párrafo*>

supuesto *a* supposed; <*falso*> false. ● *m* assumption. **¡por ~!** of course!

sur *m* south; (viento) south wind

surc|ar [7] *vt* plough; cut through <*agua*>. **~o** *m* furrow; (de rueda) rut

surfear *vi* (Informática) surf

surgir [14] *vi* spring up; (elevarse) loom up; (aparecer) appear; <*dificultad, oportunidad*> arise

surrealis|mo *m* surrealism. **~ta** *a & m & f* surrealist

surti|do *a* well-stocked; (variado) assorted. ● *m* assortment, selection. **~dor** *m* (de gasolina) petrol pump (Brit), gas pump (Amer). **~r** *vt* supply; have <*efecto*>. □ **~rse** *vpr* provide o.s. (**de** with)

susceptib|ilidad *f* sensitivity. **~le** *a* susceptible; (sensible) sensitive

suscitar *vt* provoke; arouse <*curiosidad, interés*>

suscr... ⇒SUBSCR...

susodicho *a* aforementioned

suspen|der *vt* suspend; stop <*tratamiento*>; call off <*viaje*>; (Escol) fail; (colgar) hang (**de** from). **~se** *m* suspense. **novela de ~se** thriller. **~sión** *f* suspension. **~so** *m* fail; (LAm, en libro, película) suspense. **en ~so** suspended

suspir|ar *vi* sigh. **~o** *m* sigh

sust... ⇨SUBST...

sustanci|a f substance. **~al** a substantial. **~oso** a substantial

sustantivo m noun

sustent|ación f support. **~ar** vt support; (alimentar) sustain; (mantener) maintain. **~o** m support; (alimento) sustenance

sustitu|ción f substitution; (permanente) replacement. **~ir** [17] vt substitute, replace. **~to** m substitute; (permanente) replacement

susto m fright

susurr|ar vi <persona> whisper; <agua> murmur; <hojas> rustle

sutil a fine; (fig) subtle. **~eza** f subtlety

suyo a & pron (de él) his; (de ella) hers; (de animal) its; (de Vd) yours; (de ellos, de ellas) theirs; (de Vds) yours. un amigo **~** a friend of his, a friend of theirs, etc

T t

tabac|alera f (state) tobacco monopoly. **~o** m tobacco; (cigarrillos) cigarettes

tabern|a f bar. **~ero** m barman; (dueño) landlord

tabique m partition wall; (Mex, ladrillo) brick

tabl|a f plank; (del suelo) floorboard; (de vestido) pleat; (índice) index; (gráfico, en matemática etc) table. hacer **~as** (en ajedrez) draw. **~a de surf** surfboard. **~ado** m platform; (en el teatro) stage. **~ao** m place where flamenco shows are held. **~ero** m board. **~ero de mandos** dashboard

tableta f tablet; (de chocolate) bar

tabl|illa f splint; (Mex, de chocolate) bar. **~ón** m plank. **~ón de anuncios** notice board (esp Brit), bulletin board (Amer)

tabú m (pl ~es, ~s) taboo

tabular vt tabulate

taburete m stool

tacaño a mean

tacha f stain, blemish. sin **~** unblemished; <conducta> irreproachable. **~r** vt (con raya) cross out; (Jurid) impeach. **~ de** accuse of

tácito a tacit

taciturno a taciturn; (triste) glum

taco m plug; (LAm, tacón) heel; (de billar) cue; (de billetes) book; (fig, ⚠, lío) mess; (palabrota) swearword; (Mex, Culin) taco, filled tortilla

tacón m heel

táctic|a f tactics. **~o** a tactical

táctil a tactile

tacto m touch; (fig) tact

tahúr m card-sharp

Tailandia f Thailand

tailandés a & m Thai

taimado a sly

taj|ada f slice. sacar **~ada** profit. **~ante** a categorical; <tono> sharp. **~ear** vt (LAm) slash. **~o** m cut; (en mina) face

tal a such. de **~** manera in such a way. un **~** someone called. ● pron. como **~** as such. y **~** and things like that. ● adv. con **~** de que as long as. **~** como the way. **~** para cual ⚠ two of a kind. **~** vez maybe. ¿qué **~**? how are you? ¿qué **~** es ella? what's she like?

taladr|ar vt drill. **~o** m drill

talante m mood. de buen **~** <estar> in a good mood; <ayudar> willingly

talar vt fell

talco m talcum powder

talega f, **talego** m sack

talento m talent; (fig) talented person

talismán m talisman

talla f carving; (de diamante etc) cutting; (estatura) height; (tamaño) size. **~do** m carving; (de diamante etc) cutting. **~dor** m carver; (cortador) cutter; (LAm, de naipes) dealer. **~r** vt carve; sculpt <escultura>; cut <diamante>; (Mex, restregar) scrub. ▢ **~rse** vpr (Mex) rub o.s.

tallarín m noodle

talle m waist; (figura) figure

taller m workshop; (de pintor etc) studio; (Auto) garage

tallo m stem, stalk

tal|ón m heel; (recibo) counterfoil; (cheque) cheque. **~onario** m receipt book; (de cheques) cheque book

tamal m (LAm) tamale

tamaño a such a. ● m size. **de ~** natural life-size

tambalearse vpr (persona) stagger; <cosa> wobble

también adv also, too

tambor m drum. **~ del freno** brake drum. **~ilear** vi drum

tamiz m sieve. **~ar** [10] vt sieve

tampoco adv neither, nor, not either. **yo ~ fui** I didn't go either

tampón m tampon; (para entintar) ink-pad

tan adv so. **~... como** as... as. **¿qué ~...?** (LAm) how...?

tanda f group; (de obreros) shift

tang|ente a & f tangent. **~ible** a tangible

tango m tango

tanque m tank

tante|ar vt estimate; sound up <persona>; (ensayar) test; (fig) weigh up; (LAm, palpar) feel. ● vi (LAm) feel one's way. **~o** m estimate; (prueba) test; (en deportes) score

tanto a (en singular) so much; (en plural) so many; (comparación en singular) as much; (comparación en plural) as many. ●pron so much; (en plural) so many. ●adv so; (con verbo) so much. **hace ~ tiempo** it's been so long. **~... como** both...and. **¿qué ~...?** (LAm) how much...? **~ como** as well as; (cantidad) as much as. **~ más... cuanto que** all the more ... because. **~ si... como si** whether ... or. **a ~s de** sometime in. **en ~** meanwhile. **en ~ que** while. **entre ~** meanwhile. **hasta ~ que** until. **no es para ~** it's not as bad as all that. **otro ~** the same; (el doble) as much again. **por (lo) ~** therefore. ●m certain amount; (punto) point; (gol) goal. **estar al ~ de** be up to date with

tañer [22] vi peal

tapa f lid; (de botella) top; (de libro) cover. **~s** fpl savoury snacks. **~dera** f cover, lid; (fig) cover. **~r** vt cover; (abrigar) wrap up; (obturar) plug. **~rrabo(s)** m invar loincloth

tapete m (de mesa) table cover; (Mex, alfombra) rug

tapia f wall. **~r** vt enclose

tapi|cería f tapestry; (de muebles) upholstery. **~z** m tapestry. **~ar** [10] vt upholster <muebles>

tapón m stopper; (Tec) plug

taqu|igrafía f shorthand. **~ígrafo** m shorthand writer

taquill|a f ticket office; (fig, dinero) takings. **~ero** a box-office

tara f (peso) tare; (defecto) defect

tarántula f tarantula

tararear vt/i hum

tarda|nza f delay. **~r** vt take. ● vi (retrasarse) be late; (emplear mucho tiempo) take a long time. **a más ~r** at the latest. **sin ~r** without delay

tard|e adv late. ● f (antes del atardecer) afternoon; (después del atardecer) evening. **~e o temprano** sooner or later. **de ~e en ~e** from time to time. **en la ~e** (LAm), **por la ~e** in the afternoon. **~ío** a late

tarea f task, job

tarifa f rate; (en transporte) fare; (lista de precios) tariff

tarima f dais

tarjeta f card. **~ de crédito** credit card. **~ postal** postcard

tarro m jar; (Mex, taza) mug

tarta f cake; (con base de masa) tart. **~ helada** ice-cream gateau

tartamud|ear vi stammer. **~o** a. **es ~o** he stammers

tasa f valuation; (impuesto) tax; (índice) rate. **~r** vt value; (limitar) ration

tasca f bar

tatarabuel|a f great-great-grandmother. **~o** m great-great-grandfather. **~os** mpl great-great-grandparents

tatua|je m (acción) tattooing; (dibujo) tattoo. **~r** [21] vt tattoo

taurino a bullfighting

Tauro m Taurus

tauromaquia f bullfighting

taxi m taxi. **~ista** m & f taxi-driver

taz|a f cup. **~ón** m bowl

te pron (acusativo) you; (dativo) (to) you; (reflexivo) (to) yourself

té m tea; (LAm, reunión) tea party

teatr|al a theatre; (exagerado) theatrical. ~**o** m theatre; (literatura) drama

tebeo m comic

tech|ado m roof. ~**ar** vt roof. ~**o** m (interior) ceiling; (LAm, tejado) roof. ~**umbre** f roof

tecl|a f key. ~**ado** m keyboard. ~**ear** vt key in

técnica f technique

tecnicismo m technical nature; (palabra) technical term

técnico a technical. ● m technician; (en deportes) trainer

tecnol|ogía f technology. ~**ógico** a technological

tecolote m (Mex) owl

teja f tile. ~**s de pizarra** slates. ~**do** m roof. **a toca ~** cash

teje|dor m weaver. ~**r** vt weave; (hacer punto) knit

tejemaneje m 🅸 intrigue. ~**s** mpl scheming

tejido m material; (Anat, fig) tissue. ~**s** mpl textiles

tejón m badger

tela f material, fabric; (de araña) web; (en líquido) skin

telar m loom. ~**es** mpl textile mill

telaraña f spider's web, cobweb

tele f 🅸 TV, telly

tele|comunicación f telecommunication. ~**diario** m television news. ~**dirigido** a remote-controlled; <misil> guided. ~**férico** m cable-car

tel|efonear vt/i telephone. ~**efónico** a telephone. ~**efonista** m & f telephonist. ~**éfono** m telephone. **al ~éfono** on the phone

tel|egrafía f telegraphy. ~**égrafo** m telegraph. ~**egrama** m telegram

telenovela f television soap opera

teleobjetivo m telephoto lens

telep|atía f telepathy. ~**ático** a telepathic

telesc|ópico a telescopic. ~**opio** m telescope

telesilla m & f chair-lift

telespectador m viewer

telesquí m ski-lift

televi|dente m & f viewer. ~**sar** vt televise. ~**sión** f television. ~**sor** m television (set)

télex m invar telex

telón m curtain

tema m subject; (Mus) theme

tembl|ar [1] vi shake; (de miedo) tremble; (de frío) shiver. ~**or** m shaking; (de miedo) trembling; (de frío) shivering; ~**or de tierra** earth tremor. ~**oroso** a trembling

tem|er vt be afraid (of). ● vi be afraid. □ ~**erse** vpr be afraid. ~**erario** a reckless. ~**eroso** a frightened. ~**ible** a fearsome. ~**or** m fear

témpano m floe

temperamento m temperament

temperatura f temperature

tempest|ad f storm. ~**uoso** a stormy

templ|ado a (tibio) warm; <clima, tiempo> mild; (valiente) courageous. ~**anza** f mildness. ~**ar** vt temper; (calentar) warm up. ~**e** m tempering; <coraje> courage; (humor) mood

templo m temple

tempora|da f season. ~**l** a temporary. ● m storm

tempran|ero a <frutos> early. **ser ~ero** be an early riser. ~**o** a & adv early

tenacidad f tenacity

tenacillas fpl tongs

tenaz a tenacious

tenaza f, **tenazas** fpl pliers; (de chimenea, Culin) tongs; (de cangrejo) pincer

tende|ncia f tendency. ~**nte** a. ~**nte a** aimed at. ~**r** [1] vt spread (out); hang out <ropa a secar>; (colocar) lay. ● vi tend (a to). □ ~**rse** vpr lie down

tender|ete m stall. ~**o** m shopkeeper

tendido a spread out; <ropa> hung out; <persona> lying down. ● m (en plaza de toros) front rows

tendón m tendon

tenebroso a gloomy; <asunto> sinister

tenedor m fork; (poseedor) holder

tener [40]

● *verbo transitivo*

> ❗ El presente del verbo **tener** admite dos traducciones: *to have* y *to have got*, este último de uso más extendido en el inglés británico

····▸ to have. **¿tienen hijos?** do you have any children?, have you got any children? **no tenemos coche** we don't have a car, we haven't got a car. **tiene gripe** he has (the) flu, he's got (the) flu

····▸ to be <*dimensiones, edad*>. **tiene 1 metro de largo** it's 1 metre long. **tengo 20 años** I'm 20 (years old)

····▸ (sentir) **tener** + *nombre* to be + *adjective*. ~ **celos** to be jealous. ~ **frío** to be cold

····▸ (sujetar, sostener) to hold. **tenme la escalera** hold the ladder for me

····▸ (indicando estado) **tiene las manos sucias** his hands are dirty. **me tiene preocupada** I'm worried about him. **me tuvo esperando** he kept me waiting

····▸ (llevar puesto) to be wearing, to have on. **¡qué zapatos más elegantes tienes!** those are very smart shoes you're wearing! **tienes el suéter al revés** you have your sweater on inside out

····▸ (considerar) ~ **a uno por algo** to think s.o. is sth. **lo tenía por tímido** I thought he was shy

● *verbo auxiliar*

····▸ ~ **que hacer algo** to have to do sth. **tengo que irme** I have to go

····▸ **tener** + *participio pasado*. **tengo pensado comprarlo** I'm thinking of buying it. **tenía entendido otra cosa** I understood something else

····▸ (LAm, con expresiones temporales) **tienen 2 años de estar aquí** they've been here for 2 months. **tiene mucho tiempo sin verlo** she hasn't seen him for a long time

····▸ (en locuciones) **aquí tiene** here you are. **¿qué tienes?** what's the matter with you? **¿y eso qué tiene?** (LAm) and what's wrong with that?

◻ **tenerse** *verbo pronominal*

····▸ (sostenerse) **no podía** ~**se en pie** (de cansancio) he was dead on his feet; (de borracho) he could hardly stand

····▸ (considerarse) to consider o.s. **se tiene por afortunado** he considers himself lucky

tengo *vb* ⇒TENER

teniente *m* lieutenant

tenis *m* tennis. ~ **de mesa** table tennis. ~**ta** *m & f* tennis player

tenor *m* sense; (Mus) tenor. **a** ~ **de** according to

tens|ión *f* tension; (arterial) blood pressure; (Elec) voltage; (estrés) strain. ~**o** *a* tense

tentación *f* temptation

tentáculo *m* tentacle

tenta|dor *a* tempting. ~**r** [1] *vt* tempt; (palpar) feel

tentativa *f* attempt

tenue *a* thin; <*luz, voz*> faint; <*color*> subdued

teñi|r [5 & 22] *vt* dye; (fig) tinge (**de** with). ◻ ~**rse** *vpr* dye one's hair

teología *f* theology

te|oría *f* theory. ~**órico** *a* theoretical

tequila *f* tequila

terap|euta *m & f* therapist. ~**éutico** *a* therapeutic. ~**ia** *f* therapy

terc|er *a* véase TERCERO. ~**era** *f* (Auto) third (gear). ~**ero** *a* (*delante de nombre masculino en singular* **tercer**) third. ● *m* third party. ~**io** *m* third

terciopelo *m* velvet

terco *a* obstinate

tergiversar *vt* distort

termal *a* thermal

térmico *a* thermal

termina|ción *f* ending; (conclusión) conclusion. ~**l** *a & m* terminal. ~**nte** *a* categorical. ~**r** *vt* finish, end. ~**r por** end up. ◻ ~**rse** *vpr* come to an end

término *m* end; (palabra) term; (plazo) period. ~ **medio** average. **dar** ~ **a** finish off. **en primer** ~ first of all. **en último** ~ as a last resort. **estar en**

buenos ∼s con be on good terms with. **llevar a** ∼ carry out

terminología f terminology

termita f termite

termo m Thermos (P) flask, flask

termómetro m thermometer

termo|nuclear a thermonuclear. ∼**stato** m thermostat

terner|a f (carne) veal. ∼**o** m calf

ternura f tenderness

terquedad f stubbornness

terrado m flat roof

terraplén m embankment

terrateniente m & f landowner

terraza f terrace; (balcón) balcony; (terrado) flat roof

terremoto m earthquake

terre|no a earthly. ● m land; (solar) plot (fig) field. ∼**stre** a land; (Mil) ground

terrible a terrible. ∼**mente** adv awfully

territori|al a territorial. ∼**o** m territory

terrón m (de tierra) clod; (Culin) lump

terror m terror. ∼**ífico** a terrifying. ∼**ismo** m terrorism. ∼**ista** m & f terrorist

terso a smooth

tertulia f gathering

tesina f dissertation

tesón m tenacity

tesor|ería f treasury. ∼**ero** m treasurer. ∼**o** m treasure; (tesorería) treasury; (libro) thesaurus

testaferro m figurehead

testa|mento m will. T∼mento (Relig) Testament. ∼**r** vi make a will

testarudo a stubborn

testículo m testicle

testi|ficar [7] vt/i testify. ∼**go** m witness. ∼**go ocular**, ∼**go presencial** eyewitness. **ser** ∼**go de** witness. ∼**monio** m testimony

teta f tit (🔲 o vulg); (de biberón) teat

tétanos m tetanus

tetera f (para el té) teapot

tetilla f nipple; (de biberón) teat

tétrico a gloomy

textil a & m textile

text|o m text. ∼**ual** a textual; ‹traducción› literal; ‹palabras› exact

textura f texture

tez f complexion

ti pron you

tía f aunt; 🔲 woman

tiara f tiara

tibio a lukewarm

tiburón m shark

tiempo m time; (atmosférico) weather; (Mus) tempo; (Gram) tense; (en partido) half. **a su** ∼ in due course. **a** ∼ in time. **¿cuánto** ∼? how long? **hace buen** ∼ the weather is fine. **hace** ∼ some time ago. **mucho** ∼ a long time. **perder el** ∼ waste time

tienda f shop (esp Brit), store (esp Amer); (de campaña) tent. ∼ **de comestibles**, ∼ **de ultramarinos** grocer's (shop) (Brit), grocery store (Amer)

tiene vb ⇒TENER

tienta. **andar a** ∼s feel one's way

tierno a tender; (joven) young

tierra f land; (planeta, Elec) earth; (suelo) ground; (Geol) soil, earth; (LAm, polvo) dust. **por** ∼ overland, by land

tieso a stiff; (engreído) conceited

tiesto m flowerpot

tifón m typhoon

tifus m typhus; (fiebre tifoidea) typhoid (fever)

tigre m tiger. ∼**sa** f tigress

tijera f, **tijeras** fpl scissors; (de jardín) shears

tijeretear vt snip

tila f (infusión) lime tea

tild|ar vt. ∼**ar de** (fig) brand as. ∼**e** f tilde

tilo m lime(-tree)

timar vt swindle

timbal m kettledrum; (Culin) timbale, meat pie. ∼**es** mpl (Mus) timpani

timbr|ar vt stamp. ∼**e** m (sello) fiscal stamp; (Mex) postage stamp; (Elec) bell; (sonido) timbre

timidez f shyness

tímido a shy

timo m swindle

timón m rudder; (rueda) wheel; (fig) helm

tímpano *m* eardrum

tina *f* tub. **~co** *m* (Mex) water tank. **~ja** *f* large earthenware jar

tinglado *m* mess; (asunto) racket

tinieblas *fpl* darkness; (fig) confusion

tino *f* good sense; (tacto) tact

tint|a *f* ink. **de buena ~a** on good authority. **~e** *m* dyeing; (color) dye; (fig) tinge. **~ero** *m* ink-well

tintinear *vi* tinkle; *<vasos>* chink, clink

tinto *a* *<vino>* red

tintorería *f* dry cleaner's

tintura *f* dyeing; (color) dye

tío *m* uncle; 🇪 man. **~s** *mpl* uncle and aunt

tiovivo *m* merry-go-round

típico *a* typical

tipo *m* type; (🇪, persona) person; (figura de mujer) figure; (figura de hombre) build; (Com) rate

tip|ografía *f* typography. **~ográfico** *a* typographic(al)

tira *f* strip. **la ~ de** lots of

tirabuzón *m* corkscrew; (de pelo) ringlet

tirad|a *f* distance; (serie) series; (de periódico etc) print-run. **de una ~a** in one go. **~o** *a* (barato) very cheap; (🇪, fácil) very easy. **~or** *m* (asa) handle

tiran|ía *f* tyranny. **~izar** [10] *vt* tyrannize. **~o** *a* tyrannical. ● *m* tyrant

tirante *a* tight; (fig) tense; *<relaciones>* strained. ● *m* strap. **~s** *mpl* braces (esp Brit), suspenders (Amer)

tirar *vt* throw; (desechar) throw away; (derribar) knock over; drop *<bomba>*; fire *<cohete>*; (imprimir) print. ● *vi* (disparar) shoot. **~ a** tend to (be); (parecerse a) resemble. **~ abajo** knock down. **~ de** pull. **a todo ~** at the most. **ir tirando** get by. □ **~se** *vpr* throw o.s.; (tumbarse) lie down

tirita *f* (sticking) plaster

tiritar *vi* shiver (**de** with)

tiro *m* throw; (disparo) shot. **~ libre** free kick. **a ~** within range. **errar el ~** miss. **pegarse un ~** shoot o.s.

tiroides *m* thyroid (gland)

tirón *m* tug. **de un ~** in one go

tirote|ar *vt* shoot at. **~o** *m* shooting

tisana *f* herb tea

tisú *m* (*pl* **~s**, **~es**) tissue

títere *m* puppet. **~s** *mpl* puppet show

titilar *vi* *<estrella>* twinkle

titiritero *m* puppeteer; (acróbata) acrobat

titube|ante *a* faltering; (fig) hesitant. **~ar** *vi* falter. **~o** *m* hesitation

titula|do *a* *<libro>* entitled; *<persona>* qualified. **~r** *m* headline; (persona) holder. ● *vt* call. □ **~rse** *vpr* be called; *<persona>* graduate

título *m* title; (académico) qualification; (Univ) degree. **a ~ de** as, by way of

tiza *f* chalk

tiz|nar *vt* dirty. **~ne** *m* soot

toall|a *f* towel. **~ero** *m* towel-rail

tobillo *m* ankle

tobogán *m* slide; (para la nieve) toboggan

tocadiscos *m* *invar* record-player

toca|do *a* touched 🇪. ● *m* head-dress. **~dor** *m* dressing-table. **~nte** *a*. **en lo ~nte a** with regard to. **~r** [7] *vt* touch; (palpar) feel; (Mus) play; ring *<timbre>*; (mencionar) touch on; *<barco>* stop at. ● *vi* ring; (corresponder a uno). **te ~ a ti** it's your turn. **en lo que ~ a** as for. □ **~rse** *vpr* touch; *<personas>*; touch each other

tocayo *m* namesake

tocino *m* bacon

tocólogo *m* obstetrician

todavía *adv* still; (con negativos) yet. **~ no** not yet

todo, toda

● *adjetivo*

⸱⸱⸱▸ (la totalidad) all. **~ el vino** all the wine. **~s los edificios** all the buildings. **~ ese dinero** all that money. **~ el mundo** everyone. (como adv) **está toda sucia** it's all dirty

⸱⸱⸱▸ (entero) whole. **~ el día** the whole day, all day. **toda su familia** his whole family. **~ el tiempo** the whole time, all the time

····▸ (cada, cualquiera) every. ~ **tipo de coche** every type of car. ~**s los días** every day

····▸ (enfático) **a toda velocidad** at top speed. **es ~ un caballero** he's a real gentleman

····▸ (en locuciones) **ante ~** above all. **a ~ esto** meanwhile. **con ~** even so. **del ~** totally. **~ lo contrario** quite the opposite

⟹ Para expresiones como **todo recto, todo seguido** etc., ver bajo el respectivo adjetivo

● *pronombre*

····▸ all; (todas las cosas) everything. **eso es ~** that's all. **lo perdieron ~** they lost everything. **quiere comprar ~** he wants to buy everything

····▸ **todos, todas** all; (todo el mundo) everyone. **los compró ~s** he bought them all, he bought all of them. **~s queríamos ir** we all wanted to go. **vinieron ~s** everyone came

● *nombre masculino*

····▸ **el/un ~** the/a whole

toldo *m* awning

tolera|ncia *f* tolerance. **~nte** *a* tolerant. **~r** *vt* tolerate

toma *f* taking; (de universidad etc) occupation; (Med) dose; (de agua) intake; (Elec) socket; (LAm, acequia) irrigation channel. ● *int* well!, fancy that! **~ de corriente** power point. **~dura** *f*. **~dura de pelo** hoax. **~r** *vt* take; catch <*autobús, tren*>; occupy <*universidad etc*>; (beber) drink, have; (comer) eat, have. ● *vi* take; (esp LAm, beber) drink; (LAm, dirigirse) go. **~r a bien** take well. **~r a mal** take badly. **~r en serio** take seriously. **~rla con uno** pick on s.o. **~r por** take for. **~ y daca** give and take. **¿qué va a ~r?** what would you like? ◻ **~rse** *vpr* take; (beber) drink, have; (comer) eat, have

tomate *m* tomato

tomillo *m* thyme

tomo *m* volume

ton: **sin ~ ni son** without rhyme or reason

tonad|a *f* tune; (canción) popular song; (LAm, acento) accent. **~illa** *f* tune

tonel *m* barrel. **~ada** *f* ton. **~aje** *m* tonnage

tónic|a *f* trend; (bebida) tonic water. **~o** *a* tonic; <*sílaba*> stressed. ● *m* tonic

tonificar [7] *vt* invigorate

tono *m* tone; (Mus, modo) key; (color) shade

tont|ería *f* silliness; (cosa) silly thing; (dicho) silly remark. **dejarse de ~erías** stop fooling around. **~o** *a* silly. ● *m* fool, idiot; (payaso) clown. **hacer el ~o** act the fool. **hacerse el ~o** act dumb

topacio *m* topaz

topar *vi*. **~ con** run into

tope *a* maximum. ● *m* end; (de tren) buffer; (Mex, Auto) speed bump. **hasta los ~s** crammed full. **ir a ~** go flat out

tópico *a* trite. **de uso ~** (Med) for external use only. ● *m* cliché

topo *m* mole

topogr|afía *f* topography. **~áfico** *a* topographical

toque *m* touch; (sonido) sound; (de campana) peal; (de reloj) stroke. **~ de queda** curfew. **dar los últimos ~s** put the finishing touches. **~tear** *vt* fiddle with

toquilla *f* shawl

tórax *m invar* thorax

torcer [2 & 9] *vt* twist; (doblar) bend; wring out <*ropa*>. ● *vi* turn. ◻ **~se** *vpr* twist

tordo *a* dapple grey. ● *m* thrush

tore|ar *vt* fight; (evitar) dodge. ● *vi* fight (bulls). **~o** *m* bullfighting. **~ro** *m* bullfighter

torment|a *f* storm. **~o** *m* torture. **~oso** *a* stormy

tornado *m* tornado

tornasolado *a* irridescent

torneo *m* tournament

tornillo *m* screw

torniquete *m* (Med) tourniquet; (entrada) turnstile

torno *m* lathe; (de alfarero) wheel. **en ~ a** around

toro *m* bull. **~s** *mpl* bullfighting. **ir a los ~s** go to a bullfight

toronja *f* (LAm) grapefruit

torpe *a* clumsy; (estúpido) stupid

torpedo *m* torpedo

torpeza *f* clumsiness; (de inteligencia) slowness. **una ~** a blunder

torre *f* tower; (en ajedrez) castle, rook; (Elec) pylon; (edificio) tower block (Brit), apartment block (Amer)

torren|cial *a* torrential. **~te** *m* torrent; (circulatorio) bloodstream; (fig) flood

tórrido *a* torrid

torsión *f* twisting

torso *m* torso

torta *f* tart; (LAm, de verduras) pie; (golpe) slap, punch; (Mex, bocadillo) filled roll. **no entender ni ~** not understand a thing. **~zo** *m* slap, punch. **pegarse un ~zo** have a bad accident

tortícolis *f* stiff neck

tortilla *f* omelette; (Mex, de maíz) tortilla

tórtola *f* turtle-dove

tortuga *f* tortoise; (de mar) turtle

tortuoso *a* winding; (fig) devious

tortura *f* torture. **~r** *vt* torture

tos *f* cough. **~ ferina** whooping cough

tosco *a* crude; <persona> coarse

toser *vi* cough

tost|ada *f* piece of toast. **~adas** *fpl* toast; (Mex, de tortilla) fried tortillas. **~ado** *a* <pan> toasted; <café> roasted; <persona, color> tanned. **~ar** *vt* toast <pan>; roast <café>; tan <piel>

total *a* total. ● *adv* after all. **~ que** so, to cut a long story short. ● *m* total; (totalidad) whole. **~idad** *f* whole. **~itario** *a* totalitarian. **~izar** [10] *vt* total

tóxico *a* toxic

toxi|cómano *m* drug addict. **~na** *f* toxin

tozudo *a* stubborn

traba *f* catch; (fig, obstáculo) obstacle. **poner ~s a** hinder

trabaj|ador *a* hard-working. ● *m* worker. **~ar** *vt* work; knead <masa>. ● *vi* work (**de** as); <actor> act. **¿en qué ~as?** what do you do? **~o** *m* work. **costar ~o** be difficult. **~oso** *a* hard

trabalenguas *m invar* tongue-twister

traba|r *vt* (sujetar) fasten; (unir) join; (entablar) strike up. □ **~rse** *vpr* get stuck. **trabársele la lengua** get tongue-tied

trácala *m* (Mex) cheat. ● *f* (Mex) trick

tracción *f* traction

tractor *m* tractor

tradici|ón *f* tradition. **~onal** *a* traditional

traduc|ción *f* translation. **~ir** [47] *vt* translate (**a** into). **~tor** *m* translator

traer [41] *vt* bring; (llevar) carry; (causar) cause. **traérselas** be difficult

trafica|nte *m & f* dealer. **~r** [7] *vi* deal

tráfico *m* traffic; (Com) trade

traga|luz *m* skylight. **~perras** *f invar* slot-machine. **~r** [12] *vt* swallow; (comer mucho) devour; (soportar) put up with. **no lo trago** I can't stand him. □ **~rse** *vpr* swallow; (fig) swallow up

tragedia *f* tragedy

trágico *a* tragic. ● *m* tragedian

trag|o *m* swallow, gulp; (pequeña porción) sip; (fig, disgusto) blow; (LAm, bebida alcohólica) drink. **echar(se) un ~o** have a drink. **~ón** *a* greedy. ● *m* glutton

trai|ción *f* treachery; (Pol) treason. **~cionar** *vt* betray. **~cionero** *a* treacherous. **~dor** *a* treacherous. ● *m* traitor

traigo *vb* ⇒TRAER

traje *m* dress; (de hombre) suit. **~ de baño** swimming-costume. **~ de etiqueta** evening dress. **~ de noche** evening dress. ● *vb* ⇒TRAER

traj|ín *m* coming and going; (ajetreo) hustle and bustle. **~inar** *vi* bustle about

trama *f* weft; (fig, argumento) plot. **~r** *vt* weave; (fig) plot

tramitar *vt* negotiate

trámite *m* step. **~s** *mpl* procedure

tramo *m* (parte) section; (de escalera) flight

tramp|a *f* trap; (fig) trick. **hacer ~a** cheat. **~illa** *f* trapdoor

trampolín *m* trampoline; (de piscina) springboard; (rígido) diving board

tramposo *a* cheating. ● *m* cheat

tranca *f* bar. **~r** *vt* bar

trance *m* moment; (hipnótico etc) trance

tranco *m* stride

tranquil|idad *f* peace; (de espíritu) peace of mind. **con ~** calmly. **~izar** [10] *vt* calm down; (reconfortar) re- assure. **~o** *a* calm; *<lugar>* quiet; *<conciencia>* clear. **estáte ~o** don't worry

transa|cción *f* transaction; (acuer- do) settlement. **~r** *vi* (LAm) comprom- ise

transatlántico *a* transatlantic. ● *m* (ocean) liner

transbord|ador *m* ferry. **~ar** *vt* transfer. **~o** *m* transfer. **hacer ~o** change (**en** at)

transcri|bir (*pp* **transcrito**) *vt* transcribe. **~pción** *f* transcription

transcur|rir *vi* pass. **~so** *m* course

transeúnte *m & f* passer-by

transfer|encia *f* transfer. **~ir** [4] *vt* transfer

transforma|ción *f* transform- ation. **~dor** *m* transformer. **~r** *vt* transform

transfusión *f* transfusion

transgre|dir *vt* transgress. **~sión** *f* transgression

transición *f* transition

transigir [14] *vi* give in, comprom- ise

transistor *m* transistor

transita|ble *a* passable. **~r** *vi* go

transitivo *a* transitive

tránsito *m* transit; (tráfico) traffic

transitorio *a* transitory

transmi|sión *f* transmission; (radio, TV) broadcast **~sor** *m* transmitter. **~sora** *f* broadcasting station. **~tir** *vt* transmit; (radio, TV) broadcast; (fig) pass on

transparen|cia *f* transparency. **~tar** *vt* show. **~te** *a* transparent

transpira|ción *f* perspiration. **~r** *vi* transpire; (sudar) sweat

transport|ar *vt* transport. **~e** *m* transport. **empresa** *f* **de ~es** re- movals company

transversal *a* transverse. **una calle ~ a la Gran Vía** a street which crosses the Gran Vía

tranvía *m* tram

trapear *vt* (LAm) mop

trapecio *m* trapeze; (Math) trapez- ium

trapo *m* cloth. **~s** *mpl* rags; (⊞, ropa) clothes. **a todo ~** out of control

tráquea *f* windpipe, trachea

traquete|ar *vt* bang, rattle; *<perso- na>* rush around. **~o** *m* banging, rattle

tras *prep* after; (detrás) behind

trascende|ncia *f* significance; (alcance) implication. **~ntal** *a* tran- scendental; (importante) important. **~r** [1] *vi* (saberse) become known; (exten- derse) spread

trasero *a* back, rear. ● *m* (Anat) bot- tom

trasfondo *m* background

traslad|ar *vt* move; transfer *<em- pleado etc>*; (aplazar) postpone. **~o** *m* transfer; (copia) copy. (mudanza) re- moval. **dar ~o** notify

trasl|úcido *a* translucent. □ **~ucirse** [11] *vpr* be translucent; (dejarse ver) show through; (fig, reve- larse) be revealed. **~uz** *m*. **al ~uz** against the light

trasmano. **a ~** out of the way

trasnochar *vt* (acostarse tarde) go to bed late; (no acostarse) stay up all night; (no dormir) be unable to sleep

traspas|ar *vt* go through; (transferir) transfer; go beyond *<límite>*. **se ~a** for sale. **~o** *m* transfer

traspié *m* trip; (fig) slip. **dar un ~** stumble; (fig) slip up

trasplant|ar *vt* transplant. **~e** *m* transplant

trastada *f* prank; (jugada) dirty trick

traste *m* fret. **dar al ~ con** ruin. **ir al ~** fall through. **~s** *mpl* (Mex) junk

trastero *m* storeroom

trasto *m* piece of junk. ● **~s** *mpl* junk

trastorn|ado *a* mad. **~ar** *vt* upset; (volver loco) drive mad; (fig, 🔲, gustar mucho) delight. □ **~arse** *vpr* get upset; (volverse loco) go mad. **~o** *m* (incl Med) upset; (Pol) disturbance; (fig) confusion

trat|able *a* friendly; (Med) treatable. **~ado** *m* treatise; (acuerdo) treaty. **~amiento** *m* treatment; (título) title. **~ante** *m* & *f* dealer. **~ar** *vt* (incl Med) treat; deal with *<asunto etc>*; (manejar) handle; (de tú, de Vd) address (de as). ● *vi* deal (with). **~ar con** have to do with; (Com) deal in. **~ar de** be about; (intentar) try. ¿de qué se **~a?** what's it about? **~o** *m* treatment; (acuerdo) agreement; (título) title; (relación) relationship. ¡**~o** hecho! agreed! **~os** *mpl* dealings

traum|a *m* trauma. **~ático** *a* traumatic

través: a **~ de** through; (de lado a lado) crossways

travesaño *m* crossbeam; (de portería) crossbar

travesía *f* crossing; (calle) side-street

trav|esura *f* prank. **~ieso** *a* *<niño>* mischievous, naughty

trayecto *m* (tramo) stretch; (ruta) route; (viaje) journey. **~ria** *f* trajectory; (fig) course

traz|a *f* (aspecto) appearance. **~as** *fpl* signs. **~ado** *m* plan. **~ar** [10] *vt* draw; (bosquejar) sketch. **~o** *m* stroke; (línea) line

trébol *m* clover. **~es** *mpl* (en naipes) clubs

trece *a* & *m* thirteen

trecho *m* stretch; (distancia) distance; (tiempo) while. **a ~s** here and there. **de ~ en ~** at intervals

tregua *f* truce; (fig) respite

treinta *a* & *m* thirty

tremendo *a* terrible; (extraordinario) terrific

tren *m* train. **~ de aterrizaje** landing gear. **~ de vida** lifestyle

tren|cilla *f* braid. **~za** *f* braid; (de pelo) plait. **~zar** [10] *vt* plait

trepa|dor *a* climbing. **~dora** *f* climber. **~r** *vt/i* climb. □ **~rse** *vpr*. **~rse a** climb *<árbol>*; climb onto *<silla etc>*

tres *a* & *m* three. **~cientos** *a* & *m* three hundred. **~illo** *m* three-piece suite; (Mus) triplet

treta *f* trick

tri|angular *a* triangular. **~ángulo** *m* triangle

trib|al *a* tribal. **~u** *f* tribe

tribuna *f* platform; (de espectadores) stand. **~l** *m* court; (de examen etc) board; (fig) tribunal

tribut|ar *vt* pay. **~o** *m* tribute; (impuesto) tax

triciclo *m* tricycle

tricolor *a* three-coloured

tricotar *vt/i* knit

tridimensional *a* three-dimensional

trig|al *m* wheat field. **~o** *m* wheat

trigésimo *a* thirtieth

trigueño *a* olive-skinned; *<pelo>* dark blonde

trilla|do *a* (fig, manoseado) trite; (fig, conocido) well-known. **~r** *vt* thresh

trilogía *f* trilogy

trimestr|al *a* quarterly. **~e** *m* quarter; (Escol, Univ) term

trinar *vi* warble. **estar que trina** be furious

trinchar *vt* carve

trinchera *f* ditch; (Mil) trench; (abrigo) trench coat

trineo *m* sledge

trinidad *f* trinity

trino *m* warble

trío *m* trio

tripa *f* intestine; (fig, vientre) tummy, belly. **~s** *fpl* (de máquina etc) parts, workings. **revolver las ~s** turn one's stomach

tripl|e *a* triple. ● *m*. **el ~e (de)** three times as much (as). **~icado** *a*. **por ~icado** in triplicate. **~icar** [7] *vt* treble

tripula|ción *f* crew. **~nte** *m* & *f* member of the crew. **~r** *vt* man

tris *m*. **estar en un ~** be on the point of

triste *a* sad; *<paisaje, tiempo etc>* gloomy; (fig, insignificante) miserable. **~za** *f* sadness

triturar *vt* crush

triunf|al *a* triumphal. **~ante** *a* triumphant. **~ar** *vi* triumph (**de, sobre** over). **~o** *m* triumph

trivial *a* trivial. **~idad** *f* triviality

trizas. **hacer algo ~** smash sth to pieces. **hacerse ~** smash

trocear *vt* cut up, chop

trocha *f* narrow path; (LAm, rail) gauge

trofeo *m* trophy

tromba *f* whirlwind; (marina) waterspout. **~ de agua** heavy downpour

trombón *m* trombone

trombosis *f invar* thrombosis

trompa *f* horn; (de orquesta) French horn; (de elefante) trunk; (hocico) snout; (Anat) tube. **coger una ~** 🔢 get drunk. **~zo** *m* bump

trompet|a *f* trumpet; (músico) trumpet player; (Mil) trumpeter. **~illa** *f* ear-trumpet

trompo *m* (juguete) (spinning) top

tronar *vt* (Mex) shoot. ● *vi* thunder

tronchar *vt* bring down; (fig) cut short. **~se de risa** laugh a lot

tronco *m* trunk. **dormir como un ~** sleep like a log

trono *m* throne

trop|a *f* troops. **~el** *m* mob

tropez|ar [1 & 10] *vi* trip; (fig) slip up. **~ar con** run into. **~ón** *m* stumble; (fig) slip

tropical *a* tropical

trópico *a* tropical. ● *m* tropic

tropiezo *m* slip; (desgracia) hitch

trot|ar *vi* trot. **~e** *m* trot; (fig) toing and froing. **al ~e** at a trot; (de prisa) in a rush. **de mucho ~e** hard-wearing

trozo *m* piece, bit. **a ~s** in bits

trucha *f* trout

truco *m* trick. **coger el ~** get the knack

trueno *m* thunder; (estampido) bang

trueque *m* exchange; (Com) barter

trufa *f* truffle

truhán *m* rogue

truncar [7] *vt* truncate; (fig) cut short

tu *a* your

tú *pron* you

tuba *f* tuba

tubérculo *m* tuber

tuberculosis *f* tuberculosis

tub|ería *f* pipes; (oleoducto etc) pipeline. **~o** *m* tube. **~o de ensayo** test tube. **~o de escape** (Auto) exhaust (pipe). **~ular** *a* tubular

tuerca *f* nut

tuerto *a* one-eyed, blind in one eye. ● *m* one-eyed person

tuétano *m* marrow; (fig) heart. **hasta los ~s** completely

tufo *m* stench

tugurio *m* hovel

tul *m* tulle

tulipán *m* tulip

tulli|do *a* paralysed. **~r** [22] *vt* cripple

tumba *f* grave, tomb

tumb|ar *vt* knock over, knock down *<estructura>*; (fig, 🔢, en examen) fail. □ **~arse** *vpr* lie down. **~o** *m* jolt. **dar un ~o** tumble. **~ona** *f* sun lounger

tumor *m* tumour

tumulto *m* turmoil; (Pol) riot

tuna *f* prickly pear; (de estudiantes) student band

tunante *m & f* rogue

túnel *m* tunnel

túnica *f* tunic

tupé *m* toupee; (fig) nerve

tupido *a* thick

turba *f* peat; (muchedumbre) mob

turbado *a* upset

turbante *m* turban

turbar *vt* upset; (molestar) disturb. □ **~se** *vpr* be upset

turbina *f* turbine

turbi|o *a* cloudy; *<vista>* blurred; *<asunto etc>* shady. **~ón** *m* squall

turbulen|cia *f* turbulence; (disturbio) disturbance. **~te** *a* turbulent

turco *a* Turkish. ● *m* Turk; (lengua) Turkish

tur|ismo *m* tourism; (coche) car. **hacer ~** travel around. **~ista** *m & f* tourist. **~ístico** *a* tourist

turn|arse *vpr* take turns (**para** to). **~o** *m* turn; (de trabajo) shift. **de ~** on duty

turquesa *f* turquoise

Turquía *f* Turkey

turrón *m* nougat

tutear *vt* address as *tú*. □ **~se** *vpr* be on familiar terms

tutela *f* (Jurid) guardianship; (fig) protection

tutor *m* guardian; (Escol) form master

tuve *vb* →TENER

tuyo *a* & *pron* yours. **un amigo ~** a friend of yours

Uu

u *conj* or

ubic|ar *vt* (LAm) place; (localizar) find. □ **~arse** *vpr* (LAm) be situated; (orientarse) find one's way around

ubre *f* udder

Ud. *abrev* (**Usted**) you

uf *int* phew!; (de repugnancia) ugh!

ufan|arse *vpr* be proud (con, de of); (jactarse) boast (con, de about). **~o** *a* proud

úlcera *f* ulcer

ulterior *a* later; *<lugar>* further

últimamente *adv* (recientemente) recently; (finalmente) finally

ultim|ar *vt* complete; (LAm, matar) kill. **~átum** *m* ultimatum

último *a* last; (más reciente) latest; (más lejano) furthest; (más alto) top; (más bajo) bottom; (definitivo) final. ● *m* last one. **estar en las últimas** be on one's last legs; (sin dinero) be down to one's last penny. **por ~** finally. **vestido a la última** dressed in the latest fashion

ultra *a* ultra, extreme

ultraj|ante *a* offensive. **~e** *m* insult, outrage

ultramar *m*. **de ~** overseas; *<productos>* foreign. **~inos** *mpl* groceries. **tienda de ~inos** grocer's (shop) (Brit), grocery store (Amer)

ultranza. **a ~** (con decisión) decisively; (extremo) out-and-out

ultravioleta *a invar* ultraviolet

umbilical *a* umbilical

umbral *m* threshold

un, una

● *artículo indefinido*

> **!** The masculine article **un** is also used before feminine nouns which begin with stressed **a** or **ha**, e.g. **un alma piadosa, un hada madrina**

····▶ (en sing) a; (antes de sonido vocálico) an. **un perro** a dog. **una hora** an hour

····▶ **unos, unas** (cantidad incierta) some. **compré ~os libros** I bought some books. (cantidad cierta) **tiene ~os ojos preciosos** she has beautiful eyes. **tiene ~os hijos muy buenos** her children are very good. (en aproximaciones) about. **en ~as 3 horas** in about 3 hours

⟹ For further information see **uno**

un|ánime *a* unanimous. **~animidad** *f* unanimity

undécimo *a* eleventh

ungüento *m* ointment

únic|amente *adv* only. **~o** *a* only; (fig, incomparable) unique

unicornio *m* unicorn

unid|ad *f* unit; (cualidad) unity. **~ad de disco** disk drive. **~o** *a* united

unifica|ción *f* unification. **~r** [7] *vt* unite, unify

uniform|ar *vt* standardize. **~e** *a* & *m* uniform. **~idad** *f* uniformity

unilateral *a* unilateral

uni|ón *f* union; (cualidad) unity; (Tec) joint. **~r** *vt* join; mix *<líquidos>*. □ **~rse** *vpr* join together; *<caminos>* converge; *<compañías>* merge

unísono *m* unison. **al ~** in unison

univers|al *a* universal. **~idad** *f* university. **~itario** *a* university. **~o** *m* universe

uno, una

● *adjetivo*

Note that **uno** becomes **un** before masculine nouns

····▶ one. **una peseta** one peseta. **un dólar** one dollar. **ni una persona** not one person, not a single person. **treinta y un años** thirty one years

● *pronombre*

····▶ one. **~ es mío** one (of them) is mine. **es la una** it's one o'clock. **se ayudan el ~ al otro** they help one another, they help each other. **lo que sienten el ~ por el otro** what they feel for each other

····▶ (🔲, alguien) someone. **le pregunté a ~** I asked someone

····▶ **unos, unas** some. **no tenía vasos así es que le presté ~s** she didn't have any glasses so I lent her some. **a ~s les gusta, a otros no** some like it, others don't. **los ~s a los otros** one another, each other.

····▶ (impersonal) you. **~ no sabe qué decir** you don't know what to say

untar *vt* grease; (cubrir) spread; (fig, 🔲, sobornar) bribe

uña *f* nail; (de animal) claw; (casco) hoof

uranio *m* uranium

Urano *m* Uranus

urban|idad *f* politeness. **~ismo** *m* town planning. **~ización** *f* development. **~izar** [10] *vt* develop. **~o** *a* urban

urbe *f* big city

urdir *vt* (fig) plot

urg|encia *f* urgency; (emergencia) emergency. **~ente** *a* urgent; <carta> express. **~ir** [14] *vi* be urgent.

urinario *m* urinal

urna *f* urn; (Pol) ballot box

urraca *f* magpie

URSS *abrev* (Historia) (**Unión de Repúblicas Socialistas Soviéticas**) USSR

Uruguay *m*. el ~ Uruguay

uruguayo *a & m* Uruguayan

us|ado *a* (con estar) used; <ropa etc> worn; (con ser) secondhand. **~ar** *vt* use; (llevar) wear. □ **~arse** *vpr* (LAm) be in fashion. **~o** *m* use; (costumbre) custom. **al ~o de** in the style of

usted *pron* you. **~es** you

usual *a* usual

usuario *a* user

usur|a *f* usury. **~ero** *m* usurer

usurpar *vt* usurp

utensilio *m* utensil; (herramienta) tool

útero *m* womb, uterus

útil *a* useful. **~es** *mpl* implements; (equipo) equipment

utili|dad *f* usefulness. **~dades** *fpl* (LAm) profits. **~zación** *f* use, utilization. **~zar** [10] *vt* use, utilize

utopía *f* Utopia

uva *f* grape. **~ pasa** raisin. **mala ~** bad mood

Vv

vaca *f* cow. **carne de ~** beef

vacaciones *fpl* holiday(s), vacation(s) (Amer). **de ~** on holiday, on vacation (Amer)

vacante *a* vacant. ● *f* vacancy

vaciar [20] *vt* empty; (ahuecar) hollow out; (en molde) cast

vacila|ción *f* hesitation. **~nte** *a* unsteady; (fig) hesitant. **~r** *vi* hesitate (🔲, bromear) tease; (LAm, divertirse) have fun

vacío *a* empty; (frívolo) frivolous. ● *m* empty space; (estado) emptiness; (en física) vacuum; (fig) void

vacuna *f* vaccine. **~ción** *f* vaccination. **~r** *vt* vaccinate

vacuno *a* bovine

vad|ear *vt* ford. **~o** *m* ford

vaga|bundear *vi* wander. **~bundo** *a* vagrant; <perro> stray. **niño ~** street urchin. ● *m* tramp, vagrant. **~ncia** *f* vagrancy; (fig) laziness. **~r** [12] *vi* wander (about)

vagina *f* vagina

vago *a* vague; (holgazán) lazy. ● *m* layabout

vag|ón *m* coach, carriage; (de mercancías) wagon. ∼**ón restaurante** dining-car. ∼**oneta** *f* small freight wagon; (Mex, para pasajeros) van

vaho *m* breath; (vapor) steam. ∼**s** *mpl* inhalation

vain|a *f* sheath; (Bot) pod. ∼**illa** *f* vanilla

vaiv|én *m* swinging; (de tren etc) rocking. ∼**enes** *mpl* (fig, de suerte) swings

vajilla *f* dishes, crockery

vale *m* voucher; (pagaré) IOU. ∼**dero** *a* valid

valenciano *a* from Valencia

valentía *f* bravery, courage

valer [42] *vt* be worth; (costar) cost; (fig, significar) mean. ● *vi* be worth; (costar) cost; (servir) be of use; (ser valedero) be valid; (estar permitido) be allowed. ∼ **la pena** be worthwhile, be worth it. **¿cuánto vale?** how much is it? **no** ∼ **para nada** be useless. **eso no me vale** (Mex, 🅣) I don't give a damn about that. **¡vale!** all right!, OK! 🅣

valeroso *a* courageous

valgo *vb* ⇒ VALER

valía *f* worth

validez *f* validity. **dar** ∼ **a** validate

válido *a* valid

valiente *a* brave; (en sentido irónico) fine. ● *m* brave person

valija *f* suitcase. ∼ **diplomática** diplomatic bag

valioso *a* valuable

valla *f* fence; (en atletismo) hurdle

valle *m* valley

valor *m* value, worth; (coraje) courage. **objetos** *mpl* **de** ∼ valuables. **sin** ∼ worthless. ∼**es** *mpl* securities. ∼**ación** *f* valuation. ∼**ar** *vt* value

vals *m invar* waltz

válvula *f* valve

vampiro *m* vampire

vanagloriarse *vpr* boast

vandalismo *m* vandalism

vándalo *m* & *f* vandal

vanguardia *f* vanguard. **de** ∼ (en arte, música etc) avant-garde

vani|dad *f* vanity. ∼**doso** *a* vain. ∼**o** *a* vain; (inútil) futile; *<palabras>* empty. **en** ∼ in vain

vapor *m* steam, vapour; (Naut) steamer. **al** ∼ (Culin) steamed. ∼**iza-dor** *m* vaporizer. ∼**izar** [10] vaporize

vaquer|o *m* cowherd, cowboy. ∼**os** *mpl* jeans

vara *f* stick; (de autoridad) staff (medida) yard

varar *vi* run aground

varia|ble *a* & *f* variable. ∼**ción** *f* variation. ∼**do** *a* varied. ∼**nte** *f* variant; (Auto) by-pass. ∼**ntes** *fpl* hors d'oeuvres. ∼**r** [20] *vt* change; (dar variedad a) vary. ● *vi* vary; (cambiar) change

varicela *f* chickenpox

variedad *f* variety

varilla *f* stick; (de metal) rod

varios *a* several

varita *f* wand

variz *f* (*pl* **varices**, (LAm) **várices**) varicose vein

var|ón *a* male. ● *m* man; (niño) boy. ∼**onil** *a* manly

vasco *a* & *m* Basque

vaselina *f* Vaseline (P), petroleum jelly

vasija *f* vessel, pot

vaso *m* glass; (Anat) vessel

vástago *m* shoot; (descendiente) descendant

vasto *a* vast

vaticin|ar *vt* forecast. ∼**io** *m* prediction, forecast

vatio *m* watt

vaya *vb* ⇒IR

Vd. *abrev* (**Usted**) you

vecin|al *a* local. ∼**dad** *f* neighbourhood; (vecinos) residents; (Mex, edificio) tenement house. ∼**dario** *m* neighbourhood; (vecinos) residents. ∼**o** *a* neighbouring. ● *m* neighbour; (de barrio, edificio) resident

veda *f* close season. ∼**do** *m* reserve. ∼**do de caza** game preserve. ∼**r** *vt* prohibit

vega *f* fertile plain

vegeta|ción f vegetation. **~l** a & m plant, vegetable. **~r** vi grow; <persona> vegetate. **~riano** a & m vegetarian

vehemente a vehement

vehículo m vehicle

veinte a & m twenty

veinti|cinco a & m twenty-five. **~cuatro** a & m twenty-four. **~dós** a & m twenty-two. **~nueve** a & m twenty-nine; **~ocho** a & m twenty-eight. **~séis** a & m twenty-six. **~siete** a & m twenty-seven. **~trés** a & m twenty-three. **~uno** a & m (delante de nombre masculino **veintún**) twenty-one

vejar vt ill-treat

veje|storio m old crock; (LAm, cosa) old relic. **~z** f old age

vejiga f bladder

vela f (Naut) sail; (de cera) candle; (vigilia) vigil. **pasar la noche en ~** have a sleepless night

velada f evening

vela|do a veiled; (Foto) exposed. **~r** vt watch over; hold a wake over <difunto>; (encubrir) veil; (Foto) expose. ● vi stay awake. **~r por** look after. □ **~rse** vpr (Foto) get exposed

velero m sailing-ship

veleta f weather vane

vell|o m hair; (pelusa) down. **~ón** m fleece

velo m veil

veloc|idad f speed; (Auto, Mec) gear. **a toda ~idad** at full speed. **~ímetro** m speedometer. **~ista** m & f sprinter

velódromo m cycle-track

veloz a fast, quick

vena f vein; (en madera) grain. **estar de/en ~** be in the mood

venado m deer; (Culin) venison

vencedor a winning. ● m winner

venc|er [9] vt defeat; (superar) overcome. ● vi win; <pasaporte> expire. □ **~erse** vpr collapse; (LAm, pasaporte) expire. **~ido** a beaten; <pasaporte> expired; (Com, atrasado) in arrears. **darse por ~ido** give up. **~imiento** m due date; (de pasaporte) expiry date

venda f bandage. **~je** m dressing. **~r** vt bandage

vendaval m gale

vende|dor a selling. ● m seller; (en tienda) salesperson. **~dor ambulante** pedlar. **~r** vt sell. **se ~** for sale. □ **~rse** vpr <persona> sell out

vendimia f grape harvest

veneciano a Venetian

veneno m poison; (malevolencia) venom. **~so** a poisonous

venera|ble a venerable. **~ción** f reverence. **~r** vt revere

venéreo a venereal

venezolano a & m Venezuelan

Venezuela f Venezuela

venga|nza f revenge. **~r** [12] vt avenge. □ **~rse** vpr take revenge (de, por for) (en on). **~tivo** a vindictive

vengo vb ⇒VENIR

venia f (permiso) permission. **~l** a venial

veni|da f arrival; (vuelta) return. **~dero** a coming. **~r** [53] vi come. **~r bien** suit. **la semana que viene** next week. **¡venga!** come on!

venta f sale; (posada) inn. **en ~** for sale

ventaj|a f advantage. **~oso** a advantageous

ventan|a f (inc informática) window; (de la nariz) nostril. **~illa** f window

ventarrón m strong wind

ventila|ción f ventilation. **~dor** m fan. **~r** vt air

vent|isca f blizzard. **~olera** f gust of wind. **~osa** f sucker. **~osidad** f wind, flatulence. **~oso** a windy

ventrílocuo m ventriloquist

ventur|a f happiness; (suerte) luck. **a la ~a** with no fixed plan. **echar la buena ~a a uno** tell s.o.'s fortune. **por ~a** fortunately; (acaso) perhaps. **~oso** a happy, lucky

Venus m Venus

ver [43] vt see; watch <televisión>. ● vi see. **a mi modo de ~** in my view. **a ~** let's see. **dejarse ~** show. **no lo puedo ~** I can't stand him. **no tener nada que ~ con** have nothing to do with. **vamos a ~** let's see. **ya lo veo**

that's obvious. **ya ~emos** we'll see. □ **~se** *vpr* see o.s.; (encontrarse) find o.s.; <*dos personas*> meet; (LAm, parecer) look

veran|eante *m & f* holidaymaker, vacationer (Amer). **~ear** *vi* spend one's summer holiday. **~eo** *m*. **ir de ~eo** spend one's summer holiday. **lugar** *m* **de ~eo** summer resort. **~iego** *a* summer. **~o** *m* summer

vera|s. de ~s really; (verdadero) real. **~z** *a* truthful

verbal *a* verbal

verbena *f* (fiesta) fair; (baile) dance

verbo *m* verb. **~so** *a* verbose

verdad *f* truth. **¿~?** isn't it?, aren't they?, won't it? etc. **a decir ~** to tell the truth. **de ~** really. **~eramente** *adv* really. **~ero** *a* true; (fig) real

verd|e *a* green; <*fruta*> unripe; <*chiste*> dirty. ● *m* green; (hierba) grass. **~or** *m* greenness

verdugo *m* executioner; (fig) tyrant

verdu|lería *f* greengrocer's (shop). **~lero** *m* greengrocer

vereda *f* path; (LAm, acera) pavement (Brit), sidewalk (Amer)

veredicto *m* verdict

verg|onzoso *a* shameful; (tímido) shy. **~üenza** *f* shame; (bochorno) embarrassment. **¡es una ~üenza!** it's a disgrace! **me da ~üenza** I'm ashamed/embarrassed. **tener ~üenza** be ashamed/embarrassed

verídico *a* true

verifica|ción *f* verification. **~r** [7] *vt* check. □ **~rse** *vpr* take place; (resultar verdad) come true

verja *f* (cerca) railings; (puerta) iron gate

vermú *m*, **vermut** *m* vermouth

verosímil *a* likely; <*relato*> credible

verruga *f* wart

versa|do *a* versed. **~r** *vi.* **~ sobre** deal with

versátil *a* versatile; (fig) fickle

versión *f* version; (traducción) translation

verso *m* verse; (poema) poem

vértebra *f* vertebra

verte|dero *m* dump; (desagüe) drain **~r** [1] *vt* pour; (derramar) spill ● *vi* flow

vertical *a & f* vertical

vértice *f* vertex

vertiente *f* slope

vertiginoso *a* dizzy

vértigo *m* (Med) vertigo. **dar ~** make dizzy

vesícula *f* vesicle. **~ biliar** gall bladder

vespertino *a* evening

vestíbulo *m* hall; (de hotel, teatro) foyer

vestido *m* dress

vestigio *m* trace. **~s** *mpl* remains

vest|imenta *f* clothes. **~ir** [5] *vt* (llevar) wear; dress <*niño etc*>. ● *vi* dress. **~ir de** wear. □ **~irse** *vpr* get dressed. **~irse de** wear; (disfrazarse) dress up as. **~uario** *m* wardrobe; (en gimnasio etc) changing room (Brit), locker room (Amer)

vetar *vt* veto

veterano *a* veteran

veterinari|a *f* veterinary science. **~o** *a* veterinary. ● *m* vet ⫐, veterinary surgeon (Brit), veterinarian (Amer)

veto *m* veto

vez *f* time; (turno) turn. **a la ~** at the same time. **alguna ~** sometimes; (en preguntas) ever. **algunas veces** sometimes. **a su ~** in turn. **a veces** sometimes. **cada ~** each time. **cada ~ más** more and more. **de una ~** in one go. **de una ~ para siempre** once and for all. **de ~ en cuando** from time to time. **dos veces** twice. **en ~ de** instead of. **érase una ~, había una ~** once upon a time there was. **otra ~** again. **pocas veces, rara ~** seldom. **una ~ (que)** once

vía *f* road; (Rail) line; (Anat) tract; (fig) way. **estar en ~s de** be in the process of. ● *prep* via. **~ aérea** by air. **~ de comunicación** means of communication. **~ férrea** railway (Brit), railroad (Amer). **~ rápida** fast lane

viab|ilidad *f* viability. **~le** *a* viable

viaducto *m* viaduct

viaj|ante *m & f* commercial traveller. **~ar** *vi* travel. **~e** *m* journey; (corto) trip. **∼e de novios** honeymoon. **¡buen ∼e!** have a good journey!. **estar de ∼** be away. **salir de ∼** go on a trip. **∼ero** *m* traveller; (pasajero) passenger

víbora *f* viper

vibra|ción *f* vibration. **∼nte** *a* vibrant. **∼r** *vt/i* vibrate

vicario *m* vicar

viceversa *adv* vice versa

vici|ado *a* <*texto*> corrupt; <*aire*> stale. **∼ar** *vt* corrupt; (estropear) spoil. **∼o** *m* vice; (mala costumbre) bad habit. **∼oso** *a* dissolute; <*círculo*> vicious

víctima *f* victim; (de un accidente) casualty

victori|a *f* victory. **∼oso** *a* victorious

vid *f* vine

vida *f* life; (duración) lifetime. **¡∼ mía!** my darling! **de por ∼** for life. **en mi ∼** never (in my life). **estar con ∼** be still alive

vídeo *m*, (LAm) **video** *m* video; (cinta) videotape; (aparato) video recorder

videojuego *m* video game

vidri|era *f* stained glass window; (puerta) glass door; (LAm, escaparate) shop window. **∼ería** *f* glass works. **∼ero** *m* glazier. **∼o** *m* glass; (LAm, en ventana) window pane. **limpiar los ∼os** clean the windows. **∼oso** *a* glassy

vieira *f* scallop

viejo *a* old. ● *m* old person

viene *vb* ⇒VENIR

viento *m* wind. **hacer ∼** be windy

vientre *m* stomach; (cavidad) abdomen; (matriz) womb; (intestino) bowels; (de vasija etc) belly

viernes *m invar* Friday. **V∼ Santo** Good Friday

viga *f* beam; (de metal) girder

vigen|cia *f* validity. **∼te** *a* valid; <*ley*> in force. **entrar en ∼cia** come into force

vigésimo *a* twentieth

vigía *f* watch-tower. ● *m & f* (persona) lookout

vigil|ancia *f* vigilance. **∼ante** *a* vigilant. ● *m & f* security guard;

(nocturno) watchman. **∼ar** *vt* keep an eye on. ● *vi* be vigilant; <*vigía*> keep watch. **∼ia** *f* vigil; (Relig) fasting

vigor *m* vigour; (vigencia) force. **entrar en ∼** come into force. **∼oso** *a* vigorous

vil *a* vile. **∼eza** *f* vileness; (acción) vile deed

villa *f* (casa) villa; (Historia) town. **la V∼** Madrid

villancico *m* (Christmas) carol

villano *a* villanous; (Historia) peasant

vilo. en ∼ in the air

vinagre *m* vinegar. **∼ra** *f* vinegar bottle. **∼ras** *fpl* cruet. **∼ta** *f* vinaigrette

vincular *vt* bind

vínculo *m* tie, bond

vindicar [7] *vt* (rehabilitar) vindicate

vine *vb* ⇒VENIR

vinicult|or *m* wine-grower. **∼ura** *f* wine growing

vino *m* wine. **∼ de la casa** house wine. **∼ de mesa** table wine. **∼ tinto** red wine

viñ|a *f* vineyard. **∼atero** *m* (LAm) wine-grower. **∼edo** *m* vineyard

viola *f* viola

viola|ción *f* violation; (de una mujer) rape. **∼r** *vt* violate; break <*ley*>; rape <*mujer*>

violen|cia *f* violence; (fuerza) force. □ **∼tarse** *vpr* get embarrassed. **∼to** *a* violent; (fig) awkward

violeta *a invar & f* violet

viol|ín *m* violin. ● *m & f* (músico) violinist. **∼inista** *m & f* violinist. **∼ón** *m* double bass. **∼onc(h)elista** *m & f* cellist. **∼onc(h)elo** *m* cello

vira|je *m* turn. **∼r** *vt* turn. ● *vi* turn; (fig) change direction. **∼r bruscamente** swerve

virg|en *a*. **ser ∼en** be a virgin. ● *f* virgin. **∼inal** *a* virginal. **∼inidad** *f* virginity

Virgo *m* Virgo

viril *a* virile. **∼idad** *f* virility

virtu|al *a* virtual. **∼d** *f* virtue; (capacidad) power. **en ∼d de** by virtue of. **∼oso** *a* virtuous. ● *m* virtuoso

viruela *f* smallpox

virulento *a* virulent

virus *m invar* virus

visa *f* (LAm) visa. **~ado** *m* visa. **~r** *vt* endorse

vísceras *fpl* entrails

viscoso *a* viscous

visera *f* visor; (de gorra) peak

visib|ilidad *f* visibility. **~le** *a* visible

visillo *m* (cortina) net curtain

visi|ón *f* vision; (vista) sight. **~onario** *a & m* visionary

visita *f* visit; (visitante) visitor; (invitado) guest. **~nte** *m & f* visitor. **~r** *vt* visit

vislumbrar *vt* glimpse

viso *m* sheen; (aspecto) appearance

visón *m* mink

visor *m* viewfinder

víspera *f* day before, eve

vista *f* sight, vision; (aspecto, mirada) look; (panorama) view. **apartar la ~** look away. **a primera ~, a simple ~** at first sight. **con ~s a** with a view to. **en ~ de** in view of. **estar a la ~** be obvious. **hacer la ~ gorda** turn a blind eye. **perder la ~** lose one's sight. **tener a la ~** have in front of one. **volver la ~ atrás** look back. **~zo** *m* glance. **dar/echar un ~zo a** glance at

visto *a* seen; (poco original) common (considerado) considered. **~ que** since. **bien ~** acceptable. **está ~ que** it's obvious that. **mal ~** unacceptable. **por lo ~** apparently. **●** *vb* ⇒VESTIR. **~ bueno** *m* approval. **~so** *a* colourful, bright

visual *a* visual. **campo ~** field of vision

vital *a* vital. **~icio** *a* life; *<cargo>* held for life. **~idad** *f* vitality

vitamina *f* vitamin

viticult|or *m* wine-grower. **~ura** *f* wine growing

vitorear *vt* cheer

vítreo *a* vitreous

vitrina *f* showcase; (en casa) glass cabinet; (LAm, escaparate) shop window

viud|a *f* widow. **~ez** *f* widowhood. **~o** *a* widowed. **●** *m* widower

viva *m* cheer. **~cidad** *f* liveliness. **~mente** *adv* vividly. **~z** *a* lively

víveres *mpl* supplies

vivero *m* nursery; (de peces) hatchery; (de moluscos) bed

viveza *f* vividness; (de inteligencia) sharpness; (de carácter) liveliness

vívido *a* vivid

vividor *m* pleasure seeker

vivienda *f* housing; (casa) house; (piso) flat (Brit), apartment (esp Amer). **sin ~** homeless

viviente *a* living

vivificar [7] *vt* (animar) enliven

vivir *vt* live through. **●** *vi* live; (estar vivo) be alive. **¡viva!** hurray! **¡viva el rey!** long live the king! **●** *m* life. **~ de** live on. **de mal ~** dissolute

vivisección *f* vivisection

vivo *a* alive; (viviente) living; *<color>* bright; (listo) clever; (fig) lively. **●** *m* sharp operator

vocab|lo *m* word. **~ulario** *m* vocabulary

vocación *f* vocation

vocal *a* vocal. **●** *f* vowel. **●** *m & f* member. **~ista** *m & f* vocalist

voce|ar *vt* call *<mercancías>*; (fig) proclaim; (Mex) page *<persona>*. **●** *vi* shout. **~río** *m* shouting. **~ro** *m* (LAm) spokeperson

vociferar *vi* shout

vola|dor *a* flying. **●** *m* rocket. **~ndas. en ~ndas** in the air. **~nte** *a* flying. **●** *m* (Auto) steering-wheel; (nota) note; (rehilete) shuttlecock. **~r** [2] *vt* blow up. **●** *vi* fly; (🄵, desaparecer) disappear

volátil *a* volatile

volcán *m* volcano. **~ico** *a* volcanic

volcar [2 & 7] *vt* knock over; (vaciar) empty out; turn over *<molde>*. **●** *vi* overturn. **□ ~se** *vpr* fall over; *<vehículo>* overturn; (fig) do one's utmost. **~se en** throw o.s. into

vóleibol *m*, (Mex) **volibol** *m* volleyball

voltaje *m* voltage

volte|ar *vt* turn over; (en el aire) toss; ring *<campanas>*; (LAm) turn over *<colchón etc>*. **□ ~arse** *vpr* (LAm) turn around; *<carro>* overturn. **~reta** *f* somersault

voltio *m* volt

voluble *a* (fig) fickle

volum|en *m* volume. **~inoso** *a* voluminous

voluntad *f* will; (fuerza de voluntad) willpower; (deseo) wish; (intención) intention. **buena ~** goodwill. **mala ~** ill will

voluntario *a* voluntary. ● *m* volunteer

voluptuoso *a* voluptuous

volver [2] (*pp* **vuelto**) *vt* turn; (de arriba a abajo) turn over; (devolver) restore. ● *vi* return; (fig) revert. **~ a hacer algo** do sth again. **~ en sí** come round. □ **~se** *vpr* turn round; (hacerse) become

vomit|ar *vt* bring up. ● *vi* be sick, vomit. **~ivo** *a* disgusting

vómito *m* vomit; (acción) vomiting

voraz *a* voracious

vos *pron* (LAm) you. **~otros** *pron* you; (reflexivo) yourselves

vot|ación *f* voting; (voto) vote. **~ante** *m & f* voter. **~ar** *vt* vote for. ● *vi* vote (**por** for). **~o** *m* vote; (Relig) vow

voy *vb* ⇒IR

voz *f* voice; (rumor) rumour; (palabra) word. **~ pública** public opinion. **a media ~** softly. **a una ~** unanimously. **dar voces** shout. **en ~ alta** loudly

vuelco *m* upset. **el corazón me dio un ~** my heart missed a beat

vuelo *m* flight; (acción) flying; (de ropa) flare. **al ~** in flight; (fig) in passing

vuelta *f* turn; (curva) bend; (paseo) walk; (revolución) revolution; (regreso) return; (dinero) change. **a la ~** on one's return. **a la ~ de la esquina** round the corner. **dar la ~ al mundo** go round the world. **dar una ~** go for a walk. **estar de ~** be back

vuelvo *vb* ⇒VOLVER

vuestro *a* your. ● *pron* yours. **un amigo ~** a friend of yours

vulg|ar *a* vulgar; ‹*persona*› common. **~aridad** *f* vulgarity. **~arizar** [10] *vt* popularize. **~o** *m* common people

vulnerable *a* vulnerable

Ww

wáter /'(g)water/ *m* toilet

Web *m* /'(g)web/. **el ~** the Web

whisky /'(g)wiski/ *m* whisky

Xx

xenofobia *f* xenophobia

xilófono *m* xylophone

Yy

y *conj* and

ya *adv* already; (ahora) now; (con negativos) any more; (para afirmar) yes, sure; (en seguida) immediately; (pronto) soon. **~ mismo** (LAm) right away. ● *int* of course! **~ no** no longer. **~ que** since. **¡~!, ~!** oh sure!

yacaré *m* (LAm) alligator

yac|er [44] *vi* lie. **~imiento** *m* deposit; (de petróleo) oilfield

yanqui *m & f* American, Yank(ee)

yate *m* yacht

yegua *f* mare

yelmo *m* helmet

yema *f* (Bot) bud; (de huevo) yolk; (golosina) sweet. **~ del dedo** fingertip

yerba *f* (LAm) grass; (Med) herb

yergo *vb* ⇒ERGUIR

yermo *a* uninhabited; (no cultivable) barren. ● *m* wasteland

yerno *m* son-in-law

yerro *m* mistake. ● *vb* ⇒ERRAR

yeso *m* plaster; (mineral) gypsum

yo *pron* I. ∼ **mismo** myself. ¿quién, ∼? who, me? **soy** ∼ it's me

yodo *m* iodine

yoga *m* yoga

yogur *m* yog(h)urt

yuca *f* yucca

yugo *m* yoke

Yugoslavia *f* Yugoslavia

yugoslavo *a* & *m* Yugoslav

yunque *m* anvil

yunta *f* yoke

Zz

zafarrancho *m* (confusión) mess; (riña) quarrel

zafarse *vpr* escape; get out of <*obligación etc*>; (Mex, dislocarse) dislocate

zafiro *m* sapphire

zaga *f* rear; (en deportes) defence. **a la** ∼ behind

zaguán *m* hall

zaherir [4] *vt* hurt

zahorí *m* dowser

zaino *a* <*caballo*> chestnut; <*vaca*> black

zalamer|ía *f* flattery. ∼**o** *a* flattering. ● *m* flatterer

zamarra *f* (piel) sheepskin; (prenda) sheepskin jacket

zamarrear *vt* shake

zamba *f* South American dance

zambulli|da *f* dive; (baño) dip. □ ∼**rse** *vpr* dive

zamparse *vpr* gobble up

zanahoria *f* carrot

zancad|a *f* stride. ∼**illa** *f* trip. **hacer una** ∼**illa a uno** trip s.o. up

zanc|o *m* stilt. ∼**udo** *a* long-legged; <*ave*> wading. ● *m* (LAm) mosquito

zanganear *vi* idle

zángano *m* drone. ● *m* & *f* (persona) idler

zangolotear *vt* shake. ● *vi* rattle; <*persona*> fidget

zanja *f* ditch; (para tuberías etc) trench. ∼**r** *vt* (fig) settle

zapat|ear *vi* tap with one's feet. ∼**ería** *f* shoe shop; (arte) shoemaking. ∼**ero** *m* shoemaker; (el que remienda zapatos) cobbler. ∼**illa** *f* slipper; (de deportes) trainer. ∼ **de ballet** ballet shoe. ∼**o** *m* shoe

zarand|a *f* sieve. ∼**ear** *vt* (sacudir) shake

zarcillo *m* earring

zarpa *f* paw

zarpar *vi* set sail, weigh anchor

zarza *f* bramble. ∼**mora** *f* blackberry

zarzuela *f* Spanish operetta

zigzag *m* zigzag. ∼**uear** *vi* zigzag

zinc *m* zinc

zócalo *m* skirting-board; (pedestal) plinth; (Mex, plaza) main square

zodiaco *m*, **zodíaco** *m* zodiac

zona *f* zone; (área) area

zoo *m* zoo. ∼**logía** *f* zoology. ∼**lógico** *a* zoological

zoólogo *m* zoologist

zopenco *a* stupid. ● *m* idiot

zoquete *m* blockhead

zorr|a *f* vixen ∼**illo** *m* (LAm) skunk.. ∼**o** *m* fox

zorzal *m* thrush

zozobra *f* (fig) anxiety. ∼**r** *vi* founder

zueco *m* clog

zumb|ar *vt* Ⅰ give <*golpe etc*>. ● *vi* buzz. ∼**ido** *m* buzzing

zumo *m* juice

zurci|do *m* darning. ∼**r** [9] *vt* darn

zurdo *a* left-handed; <*mano*> left

zurrar *vt* (fig, Ⅰ, dar golpes) beat (up)

zutano *m* so-and-so

English-Spanish dictionary
Diccionario Inglés-Español

Aa

a /ə/, *stressed form* /eɪ/

before vowel sound or silent 'h' **an**

● *indefinite article*

····▸ un (*m*), una (*f*). **a problem** un problema. **an apple** una manzana. **have you got a pencil?** ¿tienes un lápiz?

! Feminine singular nouns beginning with stressed or accented *a* or *ha* take the article *un* instead of *una*, e.g. *un águila, un hada*

····▸ (when talking about prices and quantities) por. **30 miles an hour** 30 millas por hora. **twice a week** dos veces por semana, dos veces a la semana

! There are many cases in which **a** is not translated, such as when talking about people's professions, in exclamations, etc: **she's a lawyer** *es abogada*. **what a beautiful day!** *¡qué día más precioso!*. **have you got a car?** ¿tienes coche? **half a cup** *media taza*

aback /ə'bæk/ *adv*. **be taken ∼** quedar desconcertado

abandon /ə'bændən/ *vt* abandonar. ● *n* abandono *m*, desenfado *m*. **∼ed** *a* abandonado. **∼ment** *n* abandono *m*

abashed /ə'bæʃt/ *a* confuso

abate /ə'beɪt/ *vi* disminuir; <storm etc> calmarse

abattoir /'æbətwɑ:(r)/ *n* matadero *m*

abbess /'æbɪs/ *n* abadesa *f*

abbey /'æbɪ/ *n* abadía *f*

abbot /'æbət/ *n* abad *m*

abbreviat|e /ə'bri:vɪeɪt/ *vt* abreviar. **∼ion** /-'eɪʃn/ *n* abreviatura *f*; (act) abreviación *f*

abdicat|e /'æbdɪkeɪt/ *vt/i* abdicar. **∼ion** /-'eɪʃn/ *n* abdicación *f*

abdom|en /'æbdəmən/ *n* abdomen *m*. **∼inal** /-'dɒmɪnl/ *a* abdominal

abduct /æb'dʌkt/ *vt* secuestrar. **∼ion** /-ʃn/ *n* secuestro *m*

abhor /əb'hɔ:(r)/ *vt* (*pt* **abhorred**) aborrecer. **∼rence** /-'hɒrəns/ *n* aborrecimiento *m*. **∼rent** /-'hɒrənt/ *a* aborrecible

abide /ə'baɪd/ *vt* (*pt* **abided**) soportar. ● *vi* (old use, *pt* **abode**) morar. □ **∼ by** *vt* atenerse a; cumplir <promise>

ability /ə'bɪlətɪ/ *n* capacidad *f*; (cleverness) habilidad *f*

abject /'æbdʒekt/ *a* (wretched) miserable

ablaze /ə'bleɪz/ *a* en llamas

able /'eɪbl/ *a* (-er, -est) capaz. **be ∼** poder; (know how to) saber. **∼-bodied** /-'bɒdɪd/ *a* sano, no discapacitado

ably /'eɪblɪ/ *adv* hábilmente

abnormal /æb'nɔ:ml/ *a* anormal. **∼ity** /-'mælətɪ/ *n* anormalidad *f*

aboard /ə'bɔ:d/ *adv* a bordo. ● *prep* a bordo de

abode /ə'bəʊd/ ⇒ABIDE. ● *n* (old use) domicilio *m*

aboli|sh /ə'bɒlɪʃ/ *vt* abolir. **∼tion** /æbə'lɪʃn/ *n* abolición *f*

abominable /ə'bɒmɪnəbl/ *a* abominable

aborigin|al /æbə'rɪdʒənl/ *a & n* aborigen (*m & f*), indígena (*m & f*). **∼es** /-i:z/ *npl* aborígenes *mpl*

abort /ə'bɔ:t/ *vt* hacer abortar. **∼ion** /-ʃn/ *n* aborto *m* provocado; (fig) aborto *m*. **have an ∼ion** hacerse un aborto. **∼ive** *a* fracasado

abound /ə'baʊnd/ *vi* abundar (**in** en)

about /ə'baʊt/ *adv* (approximately) alrededor de; (here and there) por todas partes; (in existence) por aquí. **∼ here** por aquí. **be ∼ to** estar a punto de. ● *prep* sobre; (around) alrededor de; (somewhere in) en. **talk ∼** hablar de. **∼-face**, **∼-turn** *n* (fig) cambio *m* rotundo

above /ə'bʌv/ *adv* arriba. ● *prep* encima de; (more than) más de. ~ **all** sobre todo. ~ **board** *a* legítimo. ● *adv* abiertamente. ~**-mentioned** *a* susodicho

abrasi|on /ə'breɪʒn/ *n* abrasión *f*. ~**ve** /-sɪv/ *a* abrasivo

abreast /ə'brest/ *adv*. march four ~ marchar en columna de cuatro en fondo. **keep** ~ **of** mantenerse al corriente de

abroad /ə'brɔːd/ *adv* (be) en el extranjero; (go) al extranjero; (far and wide) por todas partes

abrupt /ə'brʌpt/ *a* brusco. ~**ly** *adv* (suddenly) repentinamente; (curtly) bruscamente

abscess /'æbsɪs/ *n* absceso *m*

abscond /əb'skɒnd/ *vi* fugarse

absen|ce /'æbsəns/ *n* ausencia *f*; (lack) falta *f*. ~**t** /'æbsənt/ *a* ausente. ~**t-minded** /-'maɪndɪd/ *a* distraído. ~**t-mindedness** *n* distracción *f*, despiste *m*. ~**tee** /-'tiː/ *n* ausente *m* & *f*. ~**teeism** *n* absentismo *m*, ausentismo (LAm)

absolute /'æbsəluːt/ *a* absoluto. ~**ly** *adv* absolutamente

absolve /əb'zɒlv/ *vt* (from sin) absolver; (from obligation) liberar

absor|b /əb'zɔːb/ *vt* absorber. ~**bent** /-bent/ *a* absorbente. ~**bent cotton** *n* (Amer) algodón *m* hidrófilo. ~**ption** /əb'zɔːpʃən/ *n* absorción *f*

abstain /əb'steɪn/ *vi* abstenerse (from de)

abstemious /əb'stiːmɪəs/ *a* abstemio

abstention /əb'stenʃn/ *n* abstención *f*

abstract /'æbstrækt/ *a* abstracto. ● *n* (summary) resumen *m*; (painting) cuadro *m* abstracto. ● /əb'strækt/ *vt* extraer; (summarize) resumir. ~**ion** /-ʃn/ *n* abstracción *f*

absurd /əb'sɜːd/ *a* absurdo. ~**ity** *n* absurdo *m*, disparate *m*

abundan|ce /ə'bʌndəns/ *n* abundancia *f*. ~**t** *a* abundante

abus|e /ə'bjuːz/ *vt* (misuse) abusar de; (ill-treat) maltratar; (insult) insultar. ● /ə'bjuːs/ *n* abuso *m*; (insults) insultos *mpl*. ~**ive** /ə'bjuːsɪv/ *a* injurioso

abysmal /ə'bɪzməl/ *a* 🄴 pésimo

abyss /ə'bɪs/ *n* abismo *m*

academic /ækə'demɪk/ *a* académico; (pej) teórico. ● *n* universitario *m*, catedrático *m*

academy /ə'kædəmɪ/ *n* academia *f*.

accelerat|e /ək'seləreɪt/ *vt* acelerar. ● *vi* acelerar; (Auto) apretar el acelerador. ~**ion** /-'reɪʃn/ *n* aceleración *f*. ~**or** *n* acelerador *m*

accent /'æksənt/ *n* acento *m*

accept /ək'sept/ *vt* aceptar. ~**able** *a* aceptable. ~**ance** *n* aceptación *f*; (approval) aprobación *f*

access /'ækses/ *n* acceso *m*. ~**ible** /ək'sesəbl/ *a* accesible; *<person>* tratable

accession /æk'seʃn/ *n* (to power, throne etc) ascenso *m*; (thing added) adquisición *f*

accessory /ək'sesərɪ/ *a* accesorio. ● *n* accesorio *m*, complemento *m*; (Jurid) cómplice *m* & *f*

accident /'æksɪdənt/ *n* accidente *m*; (chance) casualidad *f*. **by** ~ sin querer; (by chance) por casualidad. ~**al** /-'dentl/ *a* accidental, fortuito. ~**ally** /-'dentəlɪ/ *adv* sin querer; (by chance) por casualidad. ~**-prone** *a* propenso a los accidentes

acclaim /ə'kleɪm/ *vt* aclamar. ● *n* aclamación *f*

accolade /'ækəleɪd/ *n* (praise) encomio *m*

accommodat|e /ə'kɒmədeɪt/ *vt* (give hospitality to) alojar; (adapt) acomodar; (oblige) complacer. ~**ing** *a* complaciente. ~**ion** /-'deɪʃn/ *n*, ~**ions** *npl* (Amer) alojamiento *m*

accompan|iment /ə'kʌmpənɪmənt/ *n* acompañamiento *m*. ~**ist** *n* acompañante *m* & *f*. ~**y** /ə'kʌmpənɪ/ *vt* acompañar

accomplice /ə'kʌmplɪs/ *n* cómplice *m* & *f*

accomplish /ə'kʌmplɪʃ/ *vt* (complete) acabar; (achieve) realizar; (carry out) llevar a cabo. ~**ed** *a* consumado. ~**ment** *n* realización *f*; (ability) talento *m*; (thing achieved) triunfo *m*, logro *m*

accord /ə'kɔːd/ *vi* concordar. ● *vt* conceder. ● *n* acuerdo *m*; (harmony) armonía *f.* **of one's own ~** espontáneamente. **~ance** *n.* **in ~ance with** de acuerdo con. **~ing** *adv.* **~ing to** según. **~ingly** *adv* en conformidad; (therefore) por consiguiente

accordion /əˈkɔːdɪən/ *n* acordeón *m*

accost /əˈkɒst/ *vt* abordar

account /əˈkaʊnt/ *n* cuenta *f*; (description) relato *m*. **~s** *npl* (in business) contabilidad *f*. **on ~ of** a causa de. **on no ~** de ninguna manera. **on this ~** por eso. **take into ~** tener en cuenta. ● *vt* considerar. □ **~ for** *vt* dar cuenta de, explicar

accountan|cy /əˈkaʊntənsɪ/ *n* contabilidad *f*. **~t** *n* contable *m & f*, contador *m* (LAm)

accumulat|e /əˈkjuːmjʊleɪt/ *vt* acumular. ● *vi* acumularse. **~ion** /-ˈleɪʃn/ *n* acumulación *f*

accura|cy /ˈækjərəsɪ/ *n* exactitud *f*, precisión *f*. **~te** /-ət/ *a* exacto, preciso

accus|ation /ækjuːˈzeɪʃn/ *n* acusación *f*. **~e** /əˈkjuːz/ *vt* acusar

accustom /əˈkʌstəm/ *vt* acostumbrar. **~ed** *a.* **be ~ed (to)** estar acostumbrado (a). **get ~ed (to)** acostumbrarse (a)

ace /eɪs/ *n* as *m*

ache /eɪk/ *n* dolor *m*. ● *vi* doler. **my leg ~s** me duele la pierna

achieve /əˈtʃiːv/ *vt* realizar; lograr *<success>*. **~ment** *n* realización *f*; (feat) proeza *f*; (thing achieved) logro *m*

acid /ˈæsɪd/ *a & n* ácido (*m*). **~ic** *a* /əˈsɪdɪk/ *a* ácido. **~ rain** *n* lluvia *f* ácida

acknowledge /əkˈnɒlɪdʒ/ *vt* reconocer. **~ receipt of** acusar recibo de. **~ment** *n* reconocimiento *m*; (Com) acuse *m* de recibo

acne /ˈæknɪ/ *n* acné *m*

acorn /ˈeɪkɔːn/ *n* bellota *f*

acoustic /əˈkuːstɪk/ *a* acústico. **~s** *npl* acústica *f*

acquaint /əˈkweɪnt/ *vt.* **~ s.o. with** poner a uno al corriente de. **be ~ed with** conocer *<person>*; saber *<fact>*. **~ance** *n* conocimiento *m*; (person) conocido *m*

acquiesce /ækwɪˈes/ *vi* consentir (in en). **~nce** *n* aquiescencia *f*, consentimiento *m*

acqui|re /əˈkwaɪə(r)/ *vt* adquirir; aprender *<language>*. **~re a taste for** tomar gusto a. **~sition** /ækwɪˈzɪʃn/ *n* adquisición *f*. **~sitive** /əˈkwɪ zətɪv/ *a* codicioso

acquit /əˈkwɪt/ *vt* (*pt* **acquitted**) absolver. **~tal** *n* absolución *f*

acre /ˈeɪkə(r)/ *n* acre *m*

acrid /ˈækrɪd/ *a* acre

acrimonious /ækrɪˈməʊnɪəs/ *a* cáustico, mordaz

acrobat /ˈækrəbæt/ *n* acróbata *m & f*. **~ic** /-ˈbætɪk/ *a* acrobático. **~ics** *npl* acrobacia *f*

acronym /ˈækrənɪm/ *n* acrónimo *m*, siglas *fpl*

across /əˈkrɒs/ *adv & prep* (side to side) de un lado al otro; (on other side) al otro lado de; (crosswise) a través. **it is 20 metres ~** tiene 20 metros de ancho. **go** *or* **walk ~** atravesar, cruzar

act /ækt/ *n* acto *m*; (action) acción *f*; (in variety show) número *m*; (decree) decreto *m*. ● *vt* hacer *<part, role>*. ● *vi* actuar; (pretend) fingir. **~ as** actuar de; *<object>* servir de. **~ for** representar. **~ing** *a* interino. ● *n* (of play) representación *f*; (by actor) interpretación *f*; (profession) profesión *f* de actor

action /ˈækʃn/ *n* acción *f*; (Jurid) demanda *f*; (plot) argumento *m*. **out of ~** (on sign) no funciona. **put out of ~** inutilizar. **take ~** tomar medidas **~ replay** *n* repetición *f* de la jugada

activate /ˈæktɪveɪt/ *vt* activar

activ|e /ˈæktɪv/ *a* activo; (energetic) lleno de energía; *<volcano>* en actividad. **~ist** *n* activista *m & f*. **~ity** /-ˈtɪvətɪ/ *n* actividad *f*

act|or /ˈæktə(r)/ *n* actor *m*. **~ress** /-trɪs/ *n* actriz *f*

actual /ˈæktʃʊəl/ *a* verdadero. **~ly** *adv* en realidad, efectivamente; (even) incluso

acute /əˈkjuːt/ *a* agudo. **~ly** *adv* agudamente

ad /æd/ *n* 🔲 anuncio *m*, aviso *m* (LAm)

AD /eɪˈdiː/ *abbr* (= **Anno Domini**) d. de J.C.

Adam's apple /ˈædəmzˈæpl/ *n* nuez *f* (de Adán)

adapt /əˈdæpt/ *vt* adaptar. ● *vi* adaptarse. ~**ability** /-əˈbɪləti/ *n* adaptabilidad *f*. ~**able** /-əbl/ *a* adaptable. ~**ation** /ædæpˈteɪʃn/ *n* adaptación *f*; (of book etc) versión *f*. ~**or** /əˈdæptə(r)/ *n* (Elec, with several sockets) enchufe *m* múltiple; (Elec, for different sockets) adaptador *m*

add /æd/ *vt* añadir. ● *vi* sumar. □ ~ **up** *vt* sumar; (fig) tener sentido. ~ **up to** equivaler a

adder /ˈædə(r)/ *n* víbora *f*

addict /ˈædɪkt/ *n* adicto *m*; (fig) entusiasta *m & f*. ~**ed** /əˈdɪktɪd/ *a*. ~**ed to** adicto a; (fig) fanático de. ~**ion** /əˈdɪkʃn/ *n* (Med) dependencia *f*; (fig) afición *f*. ~**ive** /əˈdɪktɪv/ *a* que crea adicción; (fig) que crea hábito

addition /əˈdɪʃn/ *n* suma *f*. **in** ~ además. ~**al** *a* suplementario

address /əˈdres/ *n* dirección *f*; (on form) domicilio *m*; (speech) discurso *m*. ● *vt* poner la dirección en; (speak to) dirigirse a. ~ **book** *n* libreta *f* de direcciones. ~**ee** /ædreˈsiː/ *n* destinatario *m*

adept /ˈædept/ *a & n* experto (*m*)

adequa|cy /ˈædɪkwəsɪ/ *n* suficiencia *f*. ~**te** /-ət/ *a* suficiente, adecuado. ~**tely** *adv* suficientemente, adecuadamente

adhere /ədˈhɪə(r)/ *vi* adherirse (**to** a); observar <*rule*>. ~**nce** /-rəns/ *n* adhesión *f*; (to rules) observancia *f*

adhesi|on /ədˈhiːʒn/ *n* adherencia *f*. ~**ve** /-sɪv/ *a & n* adhesivo (*m*)

adjacent /əˈdʒeɪsnt/ *a* contiguo

adjective /ˈædʒɪktɪv/ *n* adjetivo *m*

adjourn /əˈdʒɜːn/ *vt* aplazar; suspender <*meeting etc*>. ● *vi* suspenderse

adjust /əˈdʒʌst/ *vt* ajustar <*machine*>; (arrange) arreglar. ● *vi*. ~ (**to**) adaptarse (a). ~**able** *a* ajustable. ~**ment** *n* adaptación *f*; (Tec) ajuste *m*

administer /ədˈmɪnɪstə(r)/ *vt* administrar

administrat|ion /ədmɪnɪˈstreɪʃn/ *n* administración *f*. ~**ive** /ədˈmɪnɪstrətɪv/ *a* administrativo.

~**or** /ədˈmɪnɪstreɪtə(r)/ *n* administrador *m*

admirable /ˈædmərəbl/ *a* admirable

admiral /ˈædmərəl/ *n* almirante *m*

admir|ation /ædməˈreɪʃn/ *n* admiración *f*. ~**e** /ədˈmaɪə(r)/ *vt* admirar. ~**er** /ədˈmaɪərə(r)/ *n* admirador *m*

admission /ədˈmɪʃn/ *n* admisión *f*; (entry) entrada *f*

admit /ədˈmɪt/ *vt* (*pt* **admitted**) dejar entrar; (acknowledge) admitir, reconocer. ~ **to** confesar. **be** ~**ted** (to hospital etc) ingresar. ~**tance** *n* entrada *f*. ~**tedly** *adv* es verdad que

admonish /ədˈmɒnɪʃ/ *vt* reprender; (advise) aconsejar

ado /əˈduː/ *n* alboroto *m*; (trouble) dificultad *f*. **without more** *or* **further** ~ en seguida, sin más

adolescen|ce /ædəˈlesns/ *n* adolescencia *f*. ~**t** *a & n* adolescente (*m & f*)

adopt /əˈdɒpt/ *vt* adoptar. ~**ed** *a* <*child*> adoptivo. ~**ion** /-ʃn/ *n* adopción *f*

ador|able /əˈdɔːrəbl/ *a* adorable. ~**ation** /ædəˈreɪʃn/ *n* adoración *f*. ~**e** /əˈdɔː(r)/ *vt* adorar

adorn /əˈdɔːn/ *vt* adornar. ~**ment** *n* adorno *m*

adrift /əˈdrɪft/ *a & adv* a la deriva

adult /ˈædʌlt/ *a & n* adulto (*m*)

adulter|er /əˈdʌltərə(r)/ *n* adúltero *m*. ~**ess** /-ɪs/ *n* adúltera *f*. ~**y** *n* adulterio *m*

advance /ədˈvɑːns/ *vt* adelantar. ● *vi* adelantarse. ● *n* adelanto *m*. **in** ~ con anticipación, por adelantado. ~**d** *a* avanzado; <*studies*> superior

advantage /ədˈvɑːntɪdʒ/ *n* ventaja *f*. **take** ~ **of** aprovecharse de; abusar de <*person*>. ~**ous** /ædvənˈteɪdʒəs/ *a* ventajoso

advent /ˈædvənt/ *n* venida *f*. **A**~ *n* adviento *m*

adventur|e /ədˈventʃə(r)/ *n* aventura *f*. ~**er** *n* aventurero *m*. ~**ous** *a* <*person*> aventurero; <*thing*> arriesgado; (fig, bold) audaz

adverb /ˈædvɜːb/ *n* adverbio *m*

adversary /'ædvəsərɪ/ n adversario m

advers|e /'ædvɜːs/ a adverso, contrario, desfavorable. ~**ity** /əd'vɜːsətɪ/ n infortunio m

advert /'ædvɜːt/ n Ⓔ anuncio m, aviso m (LAm). ~**ise** /'ædvətaɪz/ vt anunciar. ● vi hacer publicidad; (seek, sell) poner un anuncio. ~**isement** /əd'vɜːtɪsmənt/ n anuncio m, aviso m (LAm). ~**iser** /'ædvətaɪzə(r)/ n anunciante m & f

advice /əd'vaɪs/ n consejo m; (report) informe m

advis|able /əd'vaɪzəbl/ a aconsejable. ~**e** /əd'vaɪz/ vt aconsejar; (inform) avisar. ~**e against** aconsejar en contra de. ~**er** n consejero m; (consultant) asesor m. ~**ory** a consultivo

advocate /'ædvəkət/ n defensor m; (Jurid) abogado m. ● /'ædvəkeɪt/ vt recomendar

aerial /'eərɪəl/ a aéreo. ● n antena f

aerobics /eə'rəʊbɪks/ npl aeróbica f

aerodrome /'eərədrəʊm/ n aeródromo m

aerodynamic /eərəʊdaɪ'næmɪk/ a aerodinámico

aeroplane /'eərəpleɪn/ n avión m

aerosol /'eərəsɒl/ n aerosol m

aesthetic /iːs'θetɪk/ a estético

afar /ə'fɑː(r)/ adv lejos

affable /'æfəbl/ a afable

affair /ə'feə(r)/ n asunto m. (love) ~ aventura f, amorío m. ~**s** npl (business) negocios mpl

affect /ə'fekt/ vt afectar; (pretend) fingir. ~**ation** /æfek'teɪʃn/ n afectación f. ~**ed** a afectado, amanerado

affection /ə'fekʃn/ n cariño m. ~**ate** /-ət/ a cariñoso

affiliate /ə'fɪlɪeɪt/ vt afiliar

affirm /ə'fɜːm/ vt afirmar. ~**ative** /-ətɪv/ a afirmativo. ● n respuesta f afirmativa

afflict /ə'flɪkt/ vt afligir. ~**ion** /-ʃn/ n aflicción f, pena f

affluen|ce /'æfluəns/ n riqueza f. ~**t** a rico.

afford /ə'fɔːd/ vt permitirse; (provide) dar. **he can't** ~ **a car** no le alcanza el dinero para comprar un coche

affront /ə'frʌnt/ n afrenta f, ofensa f. ● vt afrentar, ofender

afield /ə'fiːld/ adv. **far** ~ muy lejos

afloat /ə'fləʊt/ adv a flote

afraid /ə'freɪd/ a. **be** ~ tener miedo (**of** a); (be sorry) sentir, lamentar

afresh /ə'freʃ/ adv de nuevo

Africa /'æfrɪkə/ n África f. ~**n** a & n africano (m). ~**n-American** a & n norteamericano (m) de origen africano

after /'ɑːftə(r)/ adv después; (behind) detrás. ● prep después de; (behind) detrás de. **it's twenty** ~ **four** (Amer) son las cuatro y veinte. **be** ~ (seek) andar en busca de. ● conj después de que. ● a posterior. ~**-effect** n consecuencia f, efecto m secundario. ~**math** /'ɑːftəmæθ/ n secuelas fpl. ~**noon** /-'nuːn/ n tarde f. ~**shave** n loción f para después de afeitarse. ~**thought** n ocurrencia f tardía. ~**wards** /-wədz/ adv después

again /ə'gen/ adv otra vez; (besides) además. **do** ~ volver a hacer, hacer otra vez. ~ **and** ~ una y otra vez

against /ə'genst/ prep contra; (in opposition to) en contra de, contra

age /eɪdʒ/ n edad f. **at four years of** ~ a los cuatro años. **under** ~ menor de edad. ~**s** npl Ⓔ siglos mpl. ● vt/i (pres p **ageing**) envejecer. ~**d** /'eɪdʒd/ a de ... años. ~**d 10** de 10 años. ~**d** /'eɪdʒɪd/ a viejo, anciano

agency /'eɪdʒənsɪ/ n agencia f; (department) organismo m

agenda /ə'dʒendə/ n orden m del día

agent /'eɪdʒənt/ n agente m & f; (representative) representante m & f

aggravat|e /'ægrəveɪt/ vt agravar; (Ⓔ, irritate) irritar. ~**ion** /-'veɪʃn/ n agravación f; (Ⓔ, irritation) irritación f

aggress|ion /ə'greʃn/ n agresión f. ~**ive** a agresivo. ~**iveness** n agresividad f. ~**or** n agresor m

aggrieved /ə'griːvd/ a apenado, ofendido

aghast /ə'gɑːst/ a horrorizado

agil|e /ˈædʒaɪl/ a ágil. ~**ity** /əˈdʒɪlətɪ/ n agilidad f

aging /ˈeɪdʒɪŋ/ a envejecido. ●n envejecimiento m

agitat|e /ˈædʒɪteɪt/ vt agitar. ~**ed** a nervioso. ~**ion** /-ˈteɪʃn/ n agitación f, excitación f. ~**or** n agitador m

ago /əˈgəʊ/ adv. a long time ~ hace mucho tiempo. **3 days** ~ hace 3 días

agon|ize /ˈægənaɪz/ vi atormentarse. ~**izing** a <pain> atroz; <experience> angustioso. ~**y** n dolor m (agudo); (mental) angustia f

agree /əˈgriː/ vt acordar. ●vi estar de acuerdo; (of figures) concordar; (get on) entenderse. □ ~ **on** vt acordar <date, details>. □ ~ **with** vt (of food etc) sentarle bien a. ~**able** /əˈgriːəbl/ a agradable. **be** ~**able** (willing) estar de acuerdo. ~**d** a <time, place> convenido. ~**ment** /-mənt/ n acuerdo m. **in** ~**ment** de acuerdo

agricultur|al /ægrɪˈkʌltʃərəl/ a agrícola. ~**e** /ˈægrɪkʌltʃə(r)/ n agricultura f

aground /əˈgraʊnd/ adv. **run** ~ (of ship) varar, encallar

ahead /əˈhed/ adv delante; (in time) antes de. **be** ~ ir delante

aid /eɪd/ vt ayudar. ●n ayuda f. **in** ~ **of** a beneficio de

AIDS /eɪdz/ n sida m

ailment /ˈeɪlmənt/ n enfermedad f

aim /eɪm/ vt apuntar; (fig) dirigir. ●vi apuntar; (fig) pretender. ●n puntería f; (fig) objetivo m. ~**less** a, ~**lessly** adv sin objeto, sin rumbo

air /eə(r)/ n aire m. **be on the** ~ (Radio, TV) estar en el aire. **put on** ~s darse aires. ●vt airear. ~ **bag** n (Auto) bolsa f de aire. ~ **base** n base f aérea. ~**borne** a en el aire; (Mil) aerotransportado. ~-**conditioned** a climatizado, con aire acondicionado. ~ **conditioning** n aire m acondicionado. ~**craft** n (pl invar) avión m. ~**craft carrier** n portaaviones m. ~**field** n aeródromo m. **A~ Force** n fuerzas fpl aéreas. ~ **freshener** n ambientador m. ~**gun** n escopeta f de aire comprimido. ~ **hostess** n azafata f, aeromoza f (LAm). ~**line** n línea f aérea.

~ **mail** n correo m aéreo. ~**plane** n (Amer) avión m. ~**port** n aeropuerto m. ~**sick** a mareado (en un avión). ~**tight** a hermético. ~ **traffic controller** n controlador m aéreo. ~**y** a (-ier, -iest) aireado; <manner> desenfadado

aisle /aɪl/ n nave f lateral; (gangway) pasillo m

ajar /əˈdʒɑː(r)/ a entreabierto

alarm /əˈlɑːm/ n alarma f. ●vt asustar. ~ **clock** n despertador m. ~**ist** n alarmista m & f

Albania /ælˈbeɪnɪə/ n Albania f. ~**n** a & n albanés (m)

albatross /ˈælbətrɒs/ n albatros m

album /ˈælbəm/ n álbum m

alcohol /ˈælkəhɒl/ n alcohol m. ~**ic** /-ˈhɒlɪk/ a & n alcohólico (m)

alcove /ˈælkəʊv/ n nicho m

ale /eɪl/ n cerveza f

alert /əˈlɜːt/ a vivo; (watchful) vigilante. ●n alerta f. **on the** ~ alerta. ●vt avisar

algebra /ˈældʒɪbrə/ n álgebra f

Algeria /ælˈdʒɪərɪə/ n Argelia f. ~**n** a & n argelino (m)

alias /ˈeɪlɪəs/ n (pl -**ases**) alias m. ●adv alias

alibi /ˈælɪbaɪ/ n (pl -**is**) coartada f

alien /ˈeɪlɪən/ n extranjero m. ●a ajeno. ~**ate** /-eɪt/ vt enajenar. ~**ation** /-ˈneɪʃn/ n enajenación f

alienat|e /ˈeɪlɪəneɪt/ vt enajenar. ~**ion** /-ˈneɪʃn/ n enajenación f

alight /əˈlaɪt/ a ardiendo; <light> encendido

align /əˈlaɪn/ vt alinear. ~**ment** n alineación f

alike /əˈlaɪk/ a parecido, semejante. **look** or **be** ~ parecerse. ●adv de la misma manera

alive /əˈlaɪv/ a vivo. ~ **with** lleno de

alkali /ˈælkəlaɪ/ n (pl -**is**) álcali m. ~**ne** a alcalino

all /ɔːl/

● adjective

····▸ todo, -da; (pl) todos, -das. ~ **day** todo el día. ~ **the windows** todas las ventanas. ~ **four of us went** fuimos los cuatro

● *pronoun*

····▸ (everything) todo. **that's ~** eso es todo. **I did ~ I could to persuade her** hice todo lo que pude para convencerla

····▸ (after pronoun) todo, -da; (pl) todos, -das. **he helped us ~** nos ayudó a todos

····▸ **all of** todo, -da, (pl) todos, -das. **~ of the paintings** todos los cuadros. **~ of the milk** toda la leche

····▸ (in phrases) **all in all** en general. **not at all** (in no way) de ninguna manera; (after thanks) de nada, no hay de qué. **it's not at ~ bad** no está nada mal. **I don't like it at ~** no me gusta nada

● *adverb*

····▸ (completely) completamente. **she was ~ alone** estaba completamente sola. **I got ~ dirty** me ensucié todo/toda. **I don't know him ~ that well** no lo conozco tan bien

····▸ (in scores) **the score was one ~** iban empatados uno a uno

····▸ (in phrases) **to be all for sth** estar completamente a favor de algo. **to be all in** 🔲 estar rendido

all-around /ɔːləˈraʊnd/ *a* (Amer) completo

allay /əˈleɪ/ *vt* aliviar *<pain>*; aquietar *<fears etc>*

all-clear /ɔːlˈklɪə(r)/ *n* fin *m* de (la) alarma; (permission) visto *m* bueno

alleg|ation /ælɪˈɡeɪʃn/ *n* alegato *m*. **~e** /əˈledʒ/ *vt* alegar. **~edly** /-ɪdlɪ/ *adv* según se dice, supuestamente

allegiance /əˈliːdʒəns/ *n* lealtad *f*

allegory /ˈælɪɡərɪ/ *n* alegoría *f*

allerg|ic /əˈlɜːdʒɪk/ *a* alérgico (**to** a). **~y** /ˈælədʒɪ/ *n* alergia *f*

alleviate /əˈliːvɪeɪt/ *vt* aliviar

alley /ˈælɪ/ (*pl* **-eys**), **~way** *ns* calle-juela *f*

alliance /əˈlaɪəns/ *n* alianza *f*

alligator /ˈælɪɡeɪtə(r)/ *n* caimán *m*

allocat|e /ˈæləkeɪt/ *vt* asignar; (share out) repartir. **~ion** /-ˈkeɪʃn/ *n* asignación *f*; (distribution) reparto *m*

allot /əˈlɒt/ *vt* (*pt* **allotted**) asignar. **~ment** *n* asignación *f*; (land) parcela *f*

allow /əˈlaʊ/ *vt* permitir; (grant) conceder; (reckon on) prever; (agree)

admitir. □ **~ for** *vt* tener en cuenta. **~ance** /əˈlaʊəns/ *n* concesión *f*; (pension) pensión *f*; (Com) rebaja *f*. **make ~ances for** ser indulgente con *<person>*; (take into account) tener en cuenta

alloy /ˈælɔɪ/ *n* aleación *f*

all: ~ right *adj & adv* bien. ● *int* ¡vale!, ¡okey! (esp LAm), ¡órale! (Mex). **~-round** *a* completo

allusion /əˈluːʒn/ *n* alusión *f*

ally /ˈælaɪ/ *n* aliado *m*. ● /əˈlaɪ/ *vt*. **~ o.s.** aliarse (**with** con)

almighty /ɔːlˈmaɪtɪ/ *a* todopoderoso

almond /ˈɑːmənd/ *n* almendra *f*

almost /ˈɔːlməʊst/ *adv* casi

alms *npl* limosnas *fpl*

alone /əˈləʊn/ *a* solo. ● *adv* sólo, solamente

along /əˈlɒŋ/ *prep* por, a lo largo de. ● *adv*. **~ with** junto con. **all ~** todo el tiempo. **come ~** venga. **~side** /-ˈsaɪd/ *adv* (Naut) al costado. ● *prep* al lado de

aloof /əˈluːf/ *adv* apartado. ● *a* reservado

aloud /əˈlaʊd/ *adv* en voz alta

alphabet /ˈælfəbet/ *n* alfabeto *m*. **~ical** /-ˈbetɪkl/ *a* alfabético

Alps /ælps/ *npl*. **the ~** los Alpes

already /ɔːlˈredɪ/ *adv* ya

Alsatian /ælˈseɪʃn/ *n* pastor *m* alemán

also /ˈɔːlsəʊ/ *adv* también; (moreover) además

altar /ˈɔːltə(r)/ *n* altar *m*

alter /ˈɔːltə(r)/ *vt* cambiar. ● *vi* cambiarse. **~ation** /-ˈreɪʃn/ *n* modificación *f*; (to garment) arreglo *m*

alternate /ɔːlˈtɜːnət/ *a* alterno; (Amer) ⇒ALTERNATIVE. ● /ˈɔːltəneɪt/ *vt/i* alternar. **~ly** /ɔːlˈtɜːnətlɪ/ *adv* alternativamente

alternative /ɔːlˈtɜːnətɪv/ *a* alternativo. ● *n* alternativa *f*. **~ly** *adv* en cambio, por otra parte

although /ɔːlˈðəʊ/ *conj* aunque

altitude /ˈæltɪtjuːd/ *n* altitud *f*

altogether /ɔːltəˈɡeðə(r)/ *adv* completamente; (on the whole) en total

aluminium /ˌæljʊˈmɪnɪəm/, **aluminum** /əˈluːmɪnəm/ (Amer) *n* aluminio *m*

always /ˈɔːlweɪz/ *adv* siempre

am /æm/ ⇒BE

a.m. *abbr* (= **ante meridiem**) de la mañana

amalgamate /əˈmælɡəmeɪt/ *vt* amalgamar. ● *vi* amalgamarse

amass /əˈmæs/ *vt* acumular

amateur /ˈæmətə(r)/ *a & n* amateur (*m & f*). **~ish** (a) (pej) torpe, chapucero

amaz|e /əˈmeɪz/ *vt* asombrar. **~ed** *a* asombrado, estupefacto. be **~ed** at quedarse asombrado de, asombrarse de. **~ement** *n* asombro *m*. **~ing** *a* increíble

ambassador /æmˈbæsədə(r)/ *n* embajador *m*

ambigu|ity /æmbɪˈɡjuːətɪ/ *n* ambigüedad *f*. **~ous** /æmˈbɪɡjʊəs/ *a* ambiguo

ambiti|on /æmˈbɪʃn/ *n* ambición *f*. **~ous** /-ʃəs/ *a* ambicioso

ambivalent /æmˈbɪvələnt/ *a* ambivalente

amble /ˈæmbl/ *vi* andar despacio, andar sin prisa

ambulance /ˈæmbjʊləns/ *n* ambulancia *f*

ambush /ˈæmbʊʃ/ *n* emboscada *f*. ● *vt* tender una emboscada a

amen /ɑːˈmen/ *int* amén

amend /əˈmend/ *vt* enmendar. **~ment** *n* enmienda *f*. **~s** *npl*. make **~s** reparar

amenities /əˈmiːnətɪz/ *npl* servicios *mpl*; (of hotel, club) instalaciones *fpl*

America /əˈmerɪkə/ *n* (continent) América; (North America) Estados *mpl* Unidos, Norteamérica *f*. **~n** *a & n* americano (*m*); (North American) estadounidense (*m & f*), norteamericano (*m*). **~nism** *n* americanismo *m*

amiable /ˈeɪmɪəbl/ *a* simpático

amicable /ˈæmɪkəbl/ *a* amistoso

amid(st) /əˈmɪd(st)/ *prep* entre, en medio de

ammonia /əˈməʊnɪə/ *n* amoníaco *m*, amoniaco *m*

ammunition /æmjʊˈnɪʃn/ *n* municiones *fpl*

amnesty /ˈæmnəstɪ/ *n* amnistía *f*

amok /əˈmɒk/ *adv*. run **~** volverse loco

among(st) /əˈmʌŋ(st)/ *prep* entre

amount /əˈmaʊnt/ *n* cantidad *f*; (total) total *m*, suma *f*. □ **~ to** *vt* sumar; (fig) equivaler a, significar

amp(ere) /ˈamp(eə(r))/ *n* amperio *m*

amphibi|an /æmˈfɪbɪən/ *n* anfibio *m*. **~ous** /-əs/ *a* anfibio

amphitheatre /ˈæmfɪθɪətə(r)/ *n* anfiteatro *m*

ampl|e /ˈæmpl/ *a* (**-er, -est**) amplio; (enough) suficiente; (plentiful) abundante. **~y** *adv* ampliamente, bastante

amplif|ier /ˈæmplɪfaɪə(r)/ *n* amplificador *m*. **~y** /ˈæmplɪfaɪ/ *vt* amplificar

amputat|e /ˈæmpjʊteɪt/ *vt* amputar. **~ion** /-ˈteɪʃn/ *n* amputación *f*

amus|e /əˈmjuːz/ *vt* divertir. **~ed** *a* <*expression*> divertido. keep s.o. **~ed** entretener a uno. **~ement** *n* diversión *f*. **~ing** *a* divertido

an /ən, æn/ ⇒A

anaemi|a /əˈniːmɪə/ *n* anemia *f*. **~c** *a* anémico

anaesthe|tic /ænɪsˈθetɪk/ *n* anestésico *m*. **~tist** /əˈniːsθɪtɪst/ *n* anestesista *m & f*

anagram /ˈænəɡræm/ *n* anagrama *m*

analogy /əˈnælədʒɪ/ *n* analogía *f*

analy|se /ˈænəlaɪz/ *vt* analizar. **~sis** /əˈnæləsɪs/ *n* (*pl* **-ses** /-siːz/) análisis *m*. **~st** /ˈænəlɪst/ *n* analista *m & f*. **~tic(al)** /ænəˈlɪtɪk(əl)/ *a* analítico

anarch|ist /ˈænəkɪst/ *n* anarquista *m & f*. **~y** *n* anarquía *f*

anatom|ical /ænəˈtɒmɪkl/ *a* anatómico. **~y** /əˈnætəmɪ/ *n* anatomía *f*

ancest|or /ˈænsestə(r)/ *n* antepasado *m*. **~ral** /-ˈsestrəl/ *a* ancestral. **~ry** /ˈænsestrɪ/ *n* ascendencia *f*

anchor /ˈæŋkə(r)/ *n* ancla *f*. ● *vt* anclar; (fig) sujetar. ● *vi* anclar.

~**man** *n* (on TV) presentador *m*.
~**woman** *n* (on TV) presentadora *f*.

ancient /'eɪnʃənt/ *a* antiguo, viejo

ancillary /æn'sɪlərɪ/ *a* auxiliar

and /ənd, ænd/ *conj* y; (before **i-** and **hi-**) e. **bread** ~ **butter** pan *m* con mantequilla. **go** ~ **see him** ve a verlo. **more** ~ **more** cada vez más. **try** ~ **come** trata de venir

anecdot|al /ænɪk'dəʊtl/ *a* anecdótico. ~**e** /'ænɪkdəʊt/ *n* anécdota *f*

anew /ə'nju:/ *adv* de nuevo

angel /'eɪndʒl/ *n* ángel *m*. ~**ic** /æn'dʒelɪk/ *a* angélico

anger /'æŋgə(r)/ *n* ira *f*. ● *vt* enfadar, (esp LAm) enojar

angle /'æŋgl/ *n* ángulo *m*; (fig) punto *m* de vista. ~**r** /'æŋglə(r)/ *n* pescador *m*

Anglican /'æŋglɪkən/ *a* & *n* anglicano (*m*)

angr|ily /'æŋgrɪlɪ/ *adv* con enfado, (esp LAm) con enojo. ~**y** /'æŋgrɪ/ *a* (-**ier**, -**iest**) enfadado, (esp LAm) enojado. **get** ~**y** enfadarse, enojarse (esp LAm)

anguish /'æŋgwɪʃ/ *n* angustia *f*

animal /'ænɪməl/ *a* & *n* animal (*m*)

animat|e /'ænɪmeɪt/ *vt* animar. ~**ion** /-'meɪʃn/ *n* animación *f*

animosity /ænɪ'mɒsətɪ/ *n* animosidad *f*

ankle /'æŋkl/ *n* tobillo *m*. ~ **boot** botín *m*. ~ **sock** calcetín *m* corto

annexe /'æneks/ *n* anexo *m*

annihilat|e /ə'naɪəleɪt/ *vt* aniquilar. ~**ion** /-'leɪʃn/ *n* aniquilación *f*

anniversary /ænɪ'vɜːsərɪ/ *n* aniversario *m*

announce /ə'naʊns/ *vt* anunciar, comunicar. ~**ment** *n* anuncio *m*; (official) comunicado *m*. ~**r** *n* (Radio, TV) locutor *m*

annoy /ə'nɔɪ/ *vt* molestar. ~**ance** *n* molestia *m*. ~**ed** *a* enfadado, enojado (LAm). ~**ing** *a* molesto

annual /'ænjʊəl/ *a* anual. ● *n* anuario *m*. ~**ly** *adv* cada año

annul /ə'nʌl/ *vt* (*pt* **annulled**) anular. ~**ment** *n* anulación *f*

anonymous /ə'nɒnɪməs/ *a* anónimo

anorak /'ænəræk/ *n* anorac *m*

another /ə'nʌðə(r)/ *a* & *pron* otro. ~ **10 minutes** 10 minutos más. **in** ~ **way** de otra manera. **one** ~ el uno al otro; (*pl*) unos a otros

answer /'ɑːnsə(r)/ *n* respuesta *f*; (solution) solución *f*. ● *vt* contestar; escuchar, oír <*prayer*>. ~ **the door** abrir la puerta. ● *vi* contestar. □ ~ **back** *vi* contestar. □ ~ **for** *vt* ser responsable de. ~**able** *a* responsable. ~**ing machine** *n* contestador *m* automático

ant /ænt/ *n* hormiga *f*

antagoni|sm /æn'tægənɪzəm/ *n* antagonismo *m*. ~**stic** /-'nɪstɪk/ *a* antagónico, opuesto. ~**ze** /æn'tægənaɪz/ *vt* provocar la enemistad de

Antarctic /æn'tɑːktɪk/ *a* antártico. ● **n the** ~ **la** región antártica

antelope /'æntɪləʊp/ *n* antílope *m*

antenatal /'æntɪneɪtl/ *a* prenatal

antenna /æn'tenə/ (*pl* -**nae** /-niː/) (of insect etc) *n* antena *f*; (*pl* -**nas**) (of radio, TV) antena *f*

anthem /'ænθəm/ *n* himno *m*

anthology /æn'θɒlədʒɪ/ *n* antología *f*

anthropolog|ist /ænθrə'pɒlədʒɪst/ *n* antropólogo *m*. ~**y** *n* antropología *f*

anti-... /æntɪ/ *pref* anti... ~**aircraft** /-'eəkrɑːft/ *a* antiaéreo

antibiotic /æntɪbaɪ'ɒtɪk/ *a* & *n* antibiótico (*m*)

anticipat|e /æn'tɪsɪpeɪt/ *vt* anticiparse a; (foresee) prever; (forestall) prevenir. ~**ion** /-'peɪʃn/ *n* (foresight) previsión *f*; (expectation) expectativa *f*

anti: ~**climax** /-'klaɪmæks/ *n* decepción *f*. ~**clockwise** /-'klɒkwaɪz/ *adv* & *a* en sentido contrario al de las agujas del reloj

antidote /'æntɪdəʊt/ *m* antídoto *m*

antifreeze /'æntɪfriːz/ *n* anticongelante *m*

antiperspirant /æntɪ'pɜːspɪrənt/ *n* antitranspirante *m*

antiquated /'æntɪkweɪtɪd/ *a* anticuado

antique /æn'tiːk/ a antiguo. ●n antigüedad f. ~ **dealer** anticuario m. ~ **shop** tienda f de antigüedades

antiquity /æn'tɪkwətɪ/ n antigüedad f

anti: ~**septic** /-'septɪk/ a & n antiséptico (m). ~**social** /-'səʊʃl/ a antisocial

antlers /'æntləz/ npl cornamenta f

anus /'eɪnəs/ n ano m

anvil /'ænvɪl/ n yunque m

anxi|ety /æn'zaɪətɪ/ n ansiedad f; (worry) inquietud f; (eagerness) anhelo m. ~**ous** /'æŋkʃəs/ a inquieto; (eager) deseoso. ~**ously** adv con inquietud; (eagerly) con impaciencia

any /'enɪ/ a algún; (negative) ningún m; (whatever) cualquier; (every) todo. **at** ~ **moment** en cualquier momento. **have you** ~ **wine?** ¿tienes vino? ●pron alguno; (negative) ninguno. **have we** ~? ¿tenemos algunos? **not** ~ ninguno. ●adv (a little) un poco, algo. **is it** ~ **better?** ¿está algo mejor?

anybody /'enɪbɒdɪ/ pron alguien; (after negative) nadie. ~ **can do it** cualquiera puede hacerlo

anyhow /'enɪhaʊ/ adv de todas formas; (in spite of all) a pesar de todo; (badly) de cualquier manera

anyone /'enɪwʌn/ pron ⇒ANYBODY

anything /'enɪθɪŋ/ pron algo; (whatever) cualquier cosa; (after negative) nada. ~ **but** todo menos

anyway /'enɪweɪ/ adv de todas formas

anywhere /'enɪweə(r)/ adv en cualquier parte; (after negative) en ningún sitio. ~ **else** en cualquier otro lugar. ~ **you go** dondequiera que vayas

apart /ə'pɑːt/ adv aparte; (separated) separado. ~ **from** aparte de. **come** ~ romperse. **take** ~ desmontar

apartheid /ə'pɑːtheɪt/ n apartheid m

apartment /ə'pɑːtmənt/ n (Amer) apartamento m, piso m. ~ **building** n (Amer) edificio m de apartamentos, casa f de pisos

apath|etic /æpə'θetɪk/ apático. ~**y** /'æpəθɪ/ n apatía f

ape /eɪp/ n mono m. ●vt imitar

aperitif /ə'perətɪf/ n aperitivo m

aperture /'æpətʃʊə(r)/ n abertura f

apex /'eɪpeks/ n ápice m

aphrodisiac /æfrə'dɪzɪæk/ a & n afrodisíaco (m), afrodisiaco (m)

apolog|etic /əpɒlə'dʒetɪk/ a lleno de disculpas. **be** ~**etic** disculparse. ~**ize** /ə'pɒlədʒaɪz/ vi disculparse (for de). ~**y** /ə'pɒlədʒɪ/ n disculpa f

apostle /ə'pɒsl/ n apóstol m

apostrophe /ə'pɒstrəfɪ/ n apóstrofo m

appal /ə'pɔːl/ vt (pt **appalled**) horrorizar. ~**ling** a espantoso

apparatus /æpə'reɪtəs/ n aparato m

apparel /ə'pærəl/ n (Amer) ropa f

apparent /ə'pærənt/ a aparente; (clear) evidente. ~**ly** adv por lo visto

apparition /æpə'rɪʃn/ n aparición f

appeal /ə'piːl/ vi apelar; (attract) atraer. ●n llamamiento m; (attraction) atractivo m; (Jurid) apelación f. ~**ing** a atrayente

appear /ə'pɪə(r)/ vi aparecer; (seem) parecer; (in court) comparecer. ~**ance** n aparición f; (aspect) aspecto m; (in court) comparecencia f

appease /ə'piːz/ vt aplacar; (pacify) apaciguar

append /ə'pend/ vt adjuntar

appendicitis /əpendɪ'saɪtɪs/ n apendicitis f

appendix /ə'pendɪks/ n (pl **-ices** /-ɪsiːz/) (of book) apéndice m. (pl **-ixes**) (Anat) apéndice m

appetite /'æpɪtaɪt/ n apetito m

applau|d /ə'plɔːd/ vt/i aplaudir. ~**se** /ə'plɔːz/ n aplausos mpl. **round of** ~**se** aplauso m

apple /'æpl/ n manzana f. ~ **tree** n manzano m

appliance /ə'plaɪəns/ n aparato m. **electrical** ~ electrodoméstico m

applic|able /'æplɪkəbl/ a aplicable; (relevant) pertinente. ~**ant** /'æplɪkənt/ n candidato m, solicitante m & f. ~**ation** /æplɪ'keɪʃn/ n aplicación f; (request) solicitud f. ~**ation form** formulario m (de solicitud)

appl|ied /ə'plaɪd/ a aplicado. ∼y /ə'plaɪ/ vt aplicar. ● vi aplicarse; (ask) presentar una solicitud. ∼y for solicitar <job etc>

appoint /ə'pɔɪnt/ vt nombrar; (fix) señalar. ∼ment n cita f

apprais|al /ə'preɪzl/ n evaluación f. ∼e /ə'preɪz/ vt evaluar

appreciable /ə'pri:ʃəbl/ a (considerable) considerable

appreciat|e /ə'pri:ʃɪeɪt/ vt (value) apreciar; (understand) comprender; (be grateful for) agradecer. ∼ion /-'eɪʃn/ n aprecio m; (gratitude) agradecimiento m. ∼ive /ə'pri:ʃɪətɪv/ a agradecido

apprehen|sion /æprɪ'henʃn/ n (fear) recelo f. ∼sive a aprensivo

apprentice /ə'prentɪs/ n aprendiz m. ● vt. be ∼d to s.o. estar de aprendiz con uno. ∼ship n aprendizaje m

approach /ə'prəʊtʃ/ vt acercarse a. ● vi acercarse. ● n acercamiento m; (to problem) enfoque m; (access) acceso m

appropriate /ə'prəʊprɪət/ a apropiado. ● /ə'prəʊprɪeɪt/ vt apropiarse de. ∼ly /-ətlɪ/ adv apropiadamente

approv|al /ə'pru:vl/ n aprobación f. on ∼al a prueba. ∼e /ə'pru:v/ vt/i aprobar. ∼ingly adv con aprobación

approximat|e /ə'prɒksɪmət/ a aproximado. ● /ə'prɒksɪmeɪt/ vt aproximarse a. ∼ely /-ətlɪ/ adv aproximadamente. ∼ion /-'meɪʃn/ n aproximación f

apricot /'eɪprɪkɒt/ n albaricoque m, chabacano m (Mex)

April /'eɪprəl/ n abril m. ∼ fool! ¡inocentón!

apron /'eɪprən/ n delantal m

apt /æpt/ a apropiado. be ∼ to tener tendencia a. ∼itude /'æptɪtjuːd/ n aptitud f. ∼ly adv acertadamente

aquarium /ə'kweərɪəm/ n (pl -ums) acuario m

Aquarius /ə'kweərɪəs/ n Acuario m

aquatic /ə'kwætɪk/ a acuático

aqueduct /'ækwɪdʌkt/ n acueducto m

Arab /'ærəb/ a & n árabe (m & f). ∼ian /ə'reɪbɪən/ a árabe. ∼ic /'ærəbɪk/ a & n árabe (m). ∼ic numerals números mpl arábigos

arable /'ærəbl/ a cultivable

arbitrary /'ɑ:bɪtrərɪ/ a arbitrario

arbitrat|e /'ɑ:bɪtreɪt/ vi arbitrar. ∼ion /-'treɪʃn/ n arbitraje m. ∼or n árbitro m

arc /ɑ:k/ n arco m

arcade /ɑ:'keɪd/ n arcada f; (around square) soportales mpl; (shops) galería f

arch /ɑ:tʃ/ n arco m. ● vt arquear. ● vi arquearse

archaeolog|ical /ɑ:kɪə'lɒdʒɪkl/ a arqueológico. ∼ist /ɑ:kɪ'ɒlədʒɪst/ n arqueólogo m. ∼y /ɑ:kɪ'ɒlədʒɪ/ n arqueología f

archaic /ɑ:'keɪɪk/ a arcaico

archbishop /ɑ:tʃ'bɪʃəp/ n arzobispo m

archer /'ɑ:tʃə(r)/ n arquero m. ∼y n tiro m con arco

architect /'ɑ:kɪtekt/ n arquitecto m. ∼ure /-tʃə(r)/ n arquitectura f. ∼ural /-'tektʃərəl/ a arquitectónico

archives /'ɑ:kaɪvz/ npl archivo m

archway /'ɑ:tʃweɪ/ n arco m

Arctic /'ɑ:ktɪk/ a ártico. ● n. the ∼ el Ártico

ard|ent /'ɑ:dənt/ a fervoroso; <supporter, lover> apasionado. ∼our /'ɑ:də(r)/ n fervor m; (love) pasión f

arduous /'ɑ:djʊəs/ a arduo

are /ɑ:(r)/ ⇒BE

area /'eərɪə/ n (Math) superficie f; (of country) zona f; (of city) barrio m

arena /ə'ri:nə/ n arena f; (scene of activity) ruedo m

aren't /ɑ:nt/ = are not

Argentin|a /ɑ:dʒən'ti:nə/ n Argentina f. ∼ian /-'tɪnɪən/ a & n argentino (m)

argu|able /'ɑ:gjʊəbl/ a discutible. ∼e /'ɑ:gju:/ vi discutir; (reason) razonar. ∼ment /'ɑ:gjʊmənt/ n disputa f; (reasoning) argumento m. ∼mentative /ɑ:gjʊ'mentətɪv/ a discutidor

arid /'ærɪd/ a árido

Aries /'eəri:z/ n Aries m

arise /ə'raɪz/ vi (pt arose, pp arisen) surgir (from de)

aristocra|cy /ˌærɪ'stɒkrəsɪ/ *n* aristocracia *f*. **~t** /'ærɪstəkræt/ *n* aristócrata *m & f*. **~tic** /-'krætɪk/ *a* aristocrático

arithmetic /ə'rɪθmətɪk/ *n* aritmética *f*

ark /ɑːk/ *n* (Relig) arca *f*

arm /ɑːm/ *n* brazo *m*; (of garment) manga *f*. **~s** *npl* armas *fpl*. ● *vt* armar

armament /'ɑːməmənt/ *n* armamento *m*

arm: ~band *n* brazalete *m*. **~chair** *n* sillón *m*

armed /ɑːmd/ *a* armado. **~ robbery** *n* robo *m* a mano armada

armful /'ɑːmfʊl/ *n* brazada *f*

armour /'ɑːmə(r)/ *n* armadura *f*. **~ed** /'ɑːməd/ *a* blindado. **~y** /'ɑːmərɪ/ *n* arsenal *m*

armpit /'ɑːmpɪt/ *n* sobaco *m*, axila *f*

army /'ɑːmɪ/ *n* ejército *m*

aroma /ə'rəʊmə/ *n* aroma *m*

arose /ə'rəʊz/ ⇒ARISE

around /ə'raʊnd/ *adv* alrededor; (near) cerca. **all ~** por todas partes. ● *prep* alrededor de; (with time) a eso de

arouse /ə'raʊz/ *vt* despertar

arrange /ə'reɪndʒ/ *vt* arreglar; (fix) fijar. **~ment** *n* arreglo *m*; (agreement) acuerdo *m*. **~ments** *npl* (plans) preparativos *mpl*

arrears /ə'rɪəz/ *npl* atrasos *mpl*. **in ~** atrasado en el pago (**with** de)

arrest /ə'rest/ *vt* detener. ● *n* detención *f*. **under ~** detenido

arriv|al /ə'raɪvl/ *n* llegada *f*. **new ~al** recién llegado *m*. **~e** /ə'raɪv/ *vi* llegar

arrogan|ce /'ærəgəns/ *n* arrogancia *f*. **~t** *a* arrogante. **~tly** *adv* con arrogancia

arrow /'ærəʊ/ *n* flecha *f*

arse /ɑːs/ *n* (vulg) culo *m*

arsenal /'ɑːsənl/ *n* arsenal *m*

arsenic /'ɑːsnɪk/ *n* arsénico *m*

arson /'ɑːsn/ *n* incendio *m* provocado. **~ist** *n* incendiario *m*

art¹ /ɑːt/ *n* arte *m*. **A~s** *npl* (Univ) Filosofía y Letras *fpl*. **fine ~s** bellas artes *fpl*

art² /ɑːt/ (*old use, with* thou) ⇒ARE

artery /'ɑːtərɪ/ *n* arteria *f*

art gallery *n* museo *m* de arte, pinacoteca *f*; <*commercial*> galería *f* de arte

arthritis /ɑː'θraɪtɪs/ *n* artritis *f*

article /'ɑːtɪkl/ *n* artículo *m*. **~ of clothing** prenda *f* de vestir

articulat|e /ɑː'tɪkjʊlət/ *a* <*utterance*> articulado; <*person*> que sabe expresarse. ● /ɑː'tɪkjʊleɪt/ *vt/i* articular. **~ed lorry** *n* camión *m* articulado. **~ion** /-'leɪʃn/ *n* articulación *f*

artificial /ɑːtɪ'fɪʃl/ *a* artificial. **~ respiration** respiración *f* artificial

artillery /ɑː'tɪlərɪ/ *n* artillería *f*

artist /'ɑːtɪst/ *n* artista *m & f*. **~tic** /ɑː'tɪstɪk/ *a* artístico. **~ry** /'ɑːtɪstrɪ/ *n* arte *m*, habilidad *f*

as /æz, əz/ *adv & conj* como; (since) ya que; (while) mientras. **~ big ~** tan grande como. **~ far ~** (distance) hasta; (qualitative) en cuanto a. **~ far ~ I know** que yo sepa. **~ if** como si. **~ long ~** mientras. **~ much ~** tanto como. **~ soon ~** tan pronto como. **~ well** también

asbestos /æz'bestɒs/ *n* amianto *m*, asbesto *m*

ascen|d /ə'send/ *vt/i* subir. **A~sion** /ə'senʃn/ *n*. the **A~sion** la Ascensión. **~t** /ə'sent/ *n* subida *f*

ascertain /æsə'teɪn/ *vt* averiguar

ash /æʃ/ *n* ceniza *f*. ● *n*. **~** (tree) fresno *m*

ashamed /ə'ʃeɪmd/ *a* avergonzado (**of** de). **be ~ of** s.o. avergonzarse de uno

ashore /ə'ʃɔː(r)/ *adv* a tierra. **go ~** desembarcar

ash: ~tray *n* cenicero *m*. **A~ Wednesday** *n* Miércoles *m* de Ceniza

Asia /'eɪʃə/ *n* Asia *f*. **~n** *a & n* asiático (*m*). **~tic** /-ɪ'ætɪk/ *a* asiático

aside /ə'saɪd/ *adv* a un lado. ● *n* (in theatre) aparte *m*

ask /ɑːsk/ *vt* pedir; hacer <*question*>; (invite) invitar. **~ about** enterarse de. **~ s.o. to do something** pedirle a uno que haga algo. □ **~ after** *vt* preguntar por. □ **~ for** *vt*. **~ for help**

pedir ayuda. ~ **for trouble** buscarse problemas. □ ~ **in** *vt.* ~ **s.o.** in invitar a uno a pasar

askew /ə'skju:/ *adv & a* torcido

asleep /ə'sli:p/ *adv & a* dormido. **fall** ~ dormirse

asparagus /ə'spærəgəs/ *n* espárrago *m*

aspect /'æspekt/ *n* aspecto *m*

asphalt /'æsfælt/ *n* asfalto *m*. ● *vt* asfaltar

aspir|ation /æspə'reɪʃn/ *n* aspiración *f*. ~**e** /əs'paɪə(r)/ *vi* aspirar

aspirin /'æsprɪn/ *n* aspirina *f*

ass /æs/ *n* asno *m*; (fig, 🄴) imbécil *m*; (Amer vulg) culo *m*

assassin /ə'sæsɪn/ *n* asesino *m*. ~**ate** /-eɪt/ *vt* asesinar. ~**ation** /-'eɪʃn/ *n* asesinato *m*

assault /ə'sɔ:lt/ *n* (Mil) ataque *m*; (Jurid) atentado *m*. ● *vt* asaltar

assembl|e /ə'sembl/ *vt* reunir; (Mec) montar. ● *vi* reunirse. ~**y** *n* reunión *f*; (Pol etc) asamblea *f*. ~**y line** *n* línea *f* de montaje

assent /ə'sent/ *n* asentimiento *m*. ● *vi* asentir

assert /ə'sɜ:t/ *vt* afirmar; hacer valer *<one's rights>*. ~**ion** /-ʃn/ *n* afirmación *f*. ~**ive** *a* positivo, firme

assess /ə'ses/ *vt* evaluar; (determine) determinar; fijar *<tax etc>*. ~**ment** *n* evaluación *f*

asset /'æset/ *n* (advantage) ventaja *f*. ~**s** *npl* (Com) bienes *mpl*

assign /ə'saɪn/ *vt* asignar; (appoint) nombrar. ~**ment** *n* asignación *f*; (mission) misión *f*; (task) función *f*; (for school) trabajo *m*

assimilate /ə'sɪmɪleɪt/ *vt* asimilar. ● *vi* asimilarse

assist /ə'sɪst/ *vt/i* ayudar. ~**ance** *n* ayuda *f*. ~**ant** *n* ayudante *m & f*; (shop) dependienta *f*, dependiente *m*. ● *a* auxiliar, adjunto

associat|e /ə'səʊʃɪeɪt/ *vt* asociar. ● *vi* asociarse. ● /ə'səʊʃɪət/ *a* asociado. ● *n* colega *m & f*; (Com) socio *m*. ~**ion** /-'eɪʃn/ *n* asociación *f*.

assort|ed /ə'sɔ:tɪd/ *a* surtido. ~**ment** *n* surtido *m*

assum|e /ə'sju:m/ *vt* suponer; tomar *<power, attitude>*; asumir *<role, burden>*. ~**ption** /ə'sʌmpʃn/ *n* suposición *f*

assur|ance /ə'ʃʊərəns/ *n* seguridad *f*; (insurance) seguro *m*. ~**e** /ə'ʃʊə(r)/ *vt* asegurar. ~**ed** *a* seguro

asterisk /'æstərɪsk/ *n* asterisco *m*

asthma /'æsmə/ *n* asma *f*. ~**tic** /-'mætɪk/ *a & n* asmático (*m*)

astonish /ə'stɒnɪʃ/ *vt* asombrar. ~**ed** *adj* asombrado. ~**ing** *a* asombroso. ~**ment** *n* asombro *m*

astound /ə'staʊnd/ *vt* asombrar. ~**ed** *adj* atónito. ~**ing** *adj* increíble

astray /ə'streɪ/ *adv.* **go** ~ extraviarse. **lead** ~ llevar por mal camino

astrology /ə'strɒlədʒɪ/ *n* astrología *f*

astronaut /'æstrənɔ:t/ *n* astronauta *m & f*

astronom|er /ə'strɒnəmə(r)/ *n* astrónomo *m*. ~**ical** /æstrə'nɒmɪkl/ *a* astronómico. ~**y** /ə'strɒnəmɪ/ *n* astronomía *f*

astute /ə'stju:t/ *a* astuto

asylum /ə'saɪləm/ *n* asilo *m*. **lunatic** ~ manicomio *m*

at /æt/, *unstressed form* /ət/

● *preposition*

····▸ (location) en. **she's at the office** está en la oficina. **at home** en casa. **call me at the office** llámame a la oficina

⇒ For translations of phrases such as **at the top, at the front of, at the back of** see entries **top, front** etc

····▸ (at the house of) en casa de. **I'll be at Rachel's** estaré en casa de Rachel, voy a estar donde Rachel (LAm)

····▸ (talking about time) **at 7 o'clock** a las siete. **at night** por la noche, de noche, en la noche (LAm) **at Christmas** en Navidad

····▸ (talking about age) a. **at six (years of age)** a los seis años

····▸ (with measurements, numbers etc) a. **at 60 miles an hour** a 60 millas por hora. **at a depth of** a una profundidad de. **three at a time** de tres en tres

⇒ For translations of phrasal verbs with **at**, such as **look at**, see entries for those verbs

ate /et/ ⇒EAT

atheis|m /'eɪθɪɪzəm/ n ateísmo m. ∼**t** n ateo m

athlet|e /'æθliːt/ n atleta m & f. ∼**ic** /-'letɪk/ a atlético. ∼**ics** npl atletismo m; (Amer, Sport) deportes mpl

Atlantic /ət'læntɪk/ a atlántico. ● n. the ∼ (Ocean) el (Océano) Atlántico

atlas /'ætləs/ n atlas m

ATM abbr (= **automated teller machine**) cajero m automático

atmospher|e /'ætməsfɪə(r)/ n atmósfera f; (fig) ambiente m. ∼**ic** /-'ferɪk/ a atmosférico

atom /'ætəm/ n átomo m. ∼**ic** /ə'tɒmɪk/ a atómico

atroci|ous /ə'trəʊʃəs/ a atroz. ∼**ty** /ə'trɒsəti/ n atrocidad f

attach /ə'tætʃ/ vt sujetar; adjuntar <document etc>. be ∼ed to (be fond of) tener cariño a. ∼**ment** n (affection) cariño m; (tool) accesorio m

attack /ə'tæk/ n ataque m. ● vt/i atacar. ∼**er** n agresor m

attain /ə'teɪn/ vt conseguir. ∼**able** a alcanzable

attempt /ə'tempt/ vt intentar. ● n tentativa f; (attack) atentado m

attend /ə'tend/ vt asistir a; (escort) acompañar. ● vi prestar atención. □ ∼ **to** vt (look after) ocuparse de. ∼**ance** n asistencia f; (people present) concurrencia f

atten|tion /ə'tenʃn/ n atención f. ∼**tion!** (Mil) ¡firmes! pay ∼**tion** prestar atención. ∼**tive** a atento

attic /'ætɪk/ n desván m

attire /ə'taɪə(r)/ n atavío m. ● vt ataviar

attitude /'ætɪtjuːd/ n postura f

attorney /ə'tɜːnɪ/ n (pl **-eys**) (Amer) abogado m

attract /ə'trækt/ vt atraer. ∼**ion** /-ʃn/ n atracción f; (charm) atractivo m. ∼**ive** a atractivo; (interesting) atrayente

attribute /ə'trɪbjuːt/ vt atribuir. ● /'ætrɪbjuːt/ n atributo m

aubergine /'əʊbəʒiːn/ n berenjena f

auction /'ɔːkʃn/ n subasta f. ● vt subastar. ∼**eer** /-ə'nɪə(r)/ n subastador m

audaci|ous /ɔː'deɪʃəs/ a audaz. ∼**ty** /ɔː'dæsəti/ n audacia f

audible /'ɔːdəbl/ a audible

audience /'ɔːdɪəns/ n (at play, film) público m; (TV) audiencia f; (interview) audiencia f

audiovisual /ɔːdɪəʊ'vɪʒʊəl/ a audiovisual

audit /'ɔːdɪt/ n revisión f de cuentas. ● vt revisar

audition /ɔː'dɪʃn/ n audición f. ● vt hacerle una audición a. ● vi dar una audición (for para)

auditor /'ɔːdɪtə(r)/ n interventor m de cuentas

auditorium /ɔːdɪ'tɔːrɪəm/ (pl **-riums** or **-ria** /-rɪə/) n sala f, auditorio m

augment /ɔːg'ment/ vt aumentar

augur /'ɔːgə(r)/ vt augurar. it ∼s well es de buen agüero

August /'ɔːgəst/ n agosto m

aunt /ɑːnt/ n tía f

au pair /əʊ'peə(r)/ n chica f au pair

aura /'ɔːrə/ n aura f, halo m

auster|e /ɔː'stɪə(r)/ a austero. ∼**ity** /ɔː'sterəti/ n austeridad f

Australia /ɒ'streɪlɪə/ n Australia f. ∼**n** a & n australiano (m)

Austria /'ɒstrɪə/ n Austria f. ∼**n** a & n austríaco (m)

authentic /ɔː'θentɪk/ a auténtico. ∼**ate** /-keɪt/ vt autenticar. ∼**ity** /-ən'tɪsəti/ n autenticidad f

author /'ɔːθə(r)/ n autor m. ∼**ess** /-ɪs/ n autora f

authoritative /ɔː'θɒrɪtətɪv/ a autorizado; (manner) autoritario

authority /ɔː'θɒrəti/ n autoridad f; (permission) autorización f

authoriz|ation /ɔːθəraɪ'zeɪʃn/ n autorización f. ∼**e** /'ɔːθəraɪz/ vt autorizar

autobiography /ɔːtəʊbar'ɒgrəfɪ/ n autobiografía f

autograph /'ɔːtəgrɑːf/ n autógrafo m. ● vt firmar, autografiar

automat|e /'ɔːtəmeɪt/ vt automatizar. ∼**ic** /-'mætɪk/ a automático. ∼**ion** /-'meɪʃn/ n automatización f. ∼**on** /ɔː'tɒmətən/ n (pl **-tons** or **-ta** /-tə/) autómata m

automobile /'ɔːtəməbiːl/ *n* (Amer) coche *m*, carro *m* (LAm), automóvil *m*

autonom|ous /ɔː'tɒnəməs/ *a* autónomo. **~y** *n* autonomía *f*

autopsy /'ɔːtɒpsɪ/ *n* autopsia *f*

autumn /'ɔːtəm/ *n* otoño *m*. **~al** /ɔː'tʌmnəl/ *a* otoñal

auxiliary /ɔːg'zɪlɪərɪ/ *a & n* auxiliar (*m & f*)

avail /ə'veɪl/ *n*. **to no ~** inútil

availab|ility /əveɪlə'bɪlətɪ/ *n* disponibilidad *f*. **~le** /ə'veɪləbl/ *a* disponible

avalanche /'ævəlɑːnʃ/ *n* avalancha *f*

avaric|e /'ævərɪs/ *n* avaricia *f*. **~ious** /-'rɪʃəs/ *a* avaro

avenue /'ævənjuː/ *n* avenida *f*; (fig) vía *f*

average /'ævərɪdʒ/ *n* promedio *m*. **on ~** por término medio. ● *a* medio

avers|e /ə'vɜːs/ *a*. **be ~e** to ser reacio a. **~ion** /-ʃn/ *n* repugnancia *f*

avert /ə'vɜːt/ *vt* (turn away) apartar; (ward off) desviar

aviation /eɪvɪ'eɪʃn/ *n* aviación *f*

avid /'ævɪd/ *a* ávido

avocado /ævə'kɑːdəʊ/ *n* (*pl* **-os**) aguacate *m*

avoid /ə'vɔɪd/ *vt* evitar. **~able** *a* evitable. **~ance** *n* el evitar

await /ə'weɪt/ *vt* esperar

awake /ə'weɪk/ *vt/i* (*pt* **awoke**, *pp* **awoken**) despertar. ● *a* despierto. **wide ~** completamente despierto; (fig) despabilado. **~n** /ə'weɪkən/ *vt/i* despertar. **~ning** *n* el despertar

award /ə'wɔːd/ *vt* otorgar; (Jurid) adjudicar. ● *n* premio *m*; (Jurid) adjudicación *f*; (scholarship) beca *f*

aware /ə'weə(r)/ *a*. **be ~ of sth** ser consciente de algo, darse cuenta de algo

awash /ə'wɒʃ/ *a* inundado

away /ə'weɪ/ *adv* (absent) fuera. **far ~** muy lejos. ● *a* **~ match** partido *m* fuera de casa

awe /ɔː/ *n* temor *m*. **~-inspiring** *a* impresionante. **~some** /-səm/ *a* imponente

awful /'ɔːfʊl/ *a* terrible, malísimo. **feel ~** sentirse muy mal

awkward /'ɔːkwəd/ *a* difícil; (inconvenient) inoportuno; (clumsy) desmañado; (embarrassed) incómodo. **~ness** *n* dificultad *f*; (discomfort) molestia *f*; (clumsiness) torpeza *f*

awning /'ɔːnɪŋ/ *n* toldo *m*

awoke /ə'wəʊk/, **awoken** /ə'wəʊkən/ ⇒AWAKE

axe /æks/ *n* hacha *f*. ● *vt* (*pres p* **axing**) cortar con hacha; (fig) recortar

axis /'æksɪs/ *n* (*pl* **axes** /-iːz/) eje *m*

axle /'æksl/ *n* eje *m*

Bb

BA /biː'eɪ/ *abbr* ⇒BACHELOR

babble /'bæbl/ *vi* balbucir; (chatter) parlotear; <stream> murmullar.

baboon /bə'buːn/ *n* mandril *m*

baby /'beɪbɪ/ *n* niño *m*, bebé *m*. **~ buggy**, **~ carriage** *n* (Amer) cochecito *m*. **~ish** /'beɪbɪɪʃ/ *a* infantil. **~-sit** *vi* cuidar a los niños, hacer de canguro. **~-sitter** *n* baby sitter *m & f*, canguro *m & f*

bachelor /'bætʃələ(r)/ *n* soltero *m*. **B~ of Arts** (BA) licenciado *m* en filosofía y letras. **B~ of Science** (BSc) licenciado *m* en ciencias

back /bæk/ *n* espalda *f*; (of car) parte *f* trasera; (of chair) respaldo *m*; (of cloth) revés *m*; (of house) parte *f* de atrás; (of animal, book) lomo *m*; (of hand, document) dorso *m*; (football) defensa *m & f*. **in the ~ of beyond** en el quinto infierno. ● *a* trasero. **the ~ door** la puerta trasera. ● *adv* atrás; (returned) de vuelta. ● *vt* apoyar; (betting) apostar a; dar marcha atrás a <car>. ● *vi* retroceder; <car> dar marcha atrás. □ **~ down** *vi* volverse atrás. □ **~ out** *vi* retirarse. □ **~ up** *vt* apoyar; (Comp) hacer una copia de seguridad de. **~ache** *n* dolor *m* de espalda. **~bone** *n* columna *f* vertebral; (fig) pilar *m*. **~date** /-'deɪt/ *vt* antedatar. **~er** *n* partidario *m*; (Com) financiador *m*. ∼**fire** /-'faɪə(r)/ *vi* (Auto) petardear; (fig) fallar. **his plan** ∼**fired on him** le salió el tiro por la culata. ∼**ground** *n* fondo *m*; (environment) antecedentes *mpl*. ∼**hand** *n* (Sport) revés *m*. ∼**ing** *n* apoyo *m*. ∼**lash** *n* reacción *f*. ∼**log** *n* atrasos *mpl*. ∼**side** /-'saɪd/ *n* 🏴 trasero *m*. ∼**stage** /-'steɪdʒ/ *a* de bastidores. ● *adv* entre bastidores. ∼**stroke** *n* (tennis etc) revés *m*; (swimming) estilo *m* espalda, estilo *m* dorso (Mex). ∼**up** *n* apoyo *m*; (Comp) copia *f* de seguridad. ∼**ward** /-wəd/ *a* <*step etc*> hacia atrás; (retarded) retrasado; (undeveloped) atrasado. ● *adv* (Amer) ⇒BACK-WARDS. ∼**wards** *adv* hacia atrás; (fall) de espaldas; (back to front) al revés. **go** ∼**wards and forwards** ir de acá para allá. ∼**water** *n* agua *f* estancada; (fig) lugar *m* apartado

bacon /'beɪkən/ *n* tocino *m*

bacteria /bæk'tɪərɪə/ *npl* bacterias *fpl*

bad /bæd/ *a* (**worse, worst**) malo, (before masculine singular noun) mal; (serious) grave; (harmful) nocivo; <*language*> indecente. **feel** ∼ sentirse mal

bade /beɪd/ ⇒BID

badge /bædʒ/ *n* distintivo *m*, chapa *f*

badger /'bædʒə(r)/ *n* tejón *m*. ● *vt* acosar

bad: ∼**ly** *adv* mal. **want** ∼**ly** desear muchísimo. ∼**ly injured** gravemente herido. ∼**ly off** mal de dinero. ∼**-mannered** /-'mænəd/ *a* mal educado

badminton /'bædmɪntən/ *n* bádminton *m*

bad-tempered /bæd'tempəd/ *a* (always) de mal carácter; (temporarily) de mal humor

baffle /'bæfl/ *vt* desconcertar. ∼**d** *a* perplejo

bag /bæg/ *n* bolsa *f*; (handbag) bolso *m*. ● *vt* (*pt* **bagged**) ensacar; (take) coger (esp Spain), agarrar (LAm). ∼**s** *npl* (luggage) equipaje *m*. ∼**s of** 🏴 montones de

baggage /'bægɪdʒ/ *n* equipaje *m*. ∼**room** *n* (Amer) consigna *f*

baggy /'bægɪ/ *a* <*clothes*> holgado

bagpipes /'bægpaɪps/ *npl* gaita *f*

bail¹ /beɪl/ *n* fianza *f*. ● *vt* poner en libertad bajo fianza. ∼ **s.o. out** pagar la fianza a uno

bail² *vt*. ∼ **out** (Naut) achicar

bait /beɪt/ *n* cebo *m*

bak|e /beɪk/ *vt* cocer al horno. ● *vi* cocerse. ∼**er** *n* panadero *m*. ∼**ery** *n* panadería *f*

balance /'bæləns/ *n* equilibrio *m*; (Com) balance *m*; (sum) saldo *m*; (scales) balanza *f*; (remainder) resto *m*. ● *vt* equilibrar <*load*>; mantener en equilibrio <*object*>; nivelar <*budget*>. ● *vi* equilibrarse; (Com) cuadrar. ∼**d** *a* equilibrado

balcony /'bælkənɪ/ *n* balcón *m*

bald /bɔːld/ *a* (**-er, -est**) calvo, pelón (Mex)

bale /beɪl/ *n* bala *f*, fardo *m*. ● *vi*. ∼ **out** lanzarse en paracaídas

Balearic /bælɪ'ærɪk/ *a*. **the** ∼ **Islands** las Islas *fpl* Baleares

ball /bɔːl/ *n* bola *f*; (tennis etc) pelota *f*; (football etc) balón *m*, pelota *f* (esp LAm); (of yarn) ovillo *m*; (dance) baile *m*

ballad /'bæləd/ *n* balada *f*

ballast /'bæləst/ *n* lastre *m*

ball bearing *n* cojinete *m* de bolas

ballerina /bælə'riːnə/ *f* bailarina *f*

ballet /'bæleɪ/ *n* ballet *m*. ∼ **dancer** *n* bailarín *m* de ballet, bailarina *f* de ballet

balloon /bə'luːn/ *n* globo *m*

ballot /'bælət/ *n* votación *f*. ∼ **box** *n* urna *f*. ∼ **paper** *n* papeleta *f*.

ball: ∼**point** *n*. ∼**point (pen)** bolígrafo *m*, pluma *f* atómica (Mex). ∼**room** *n* salón *m* de baile

bamboo /bæm'buː/ *n* bambú *m*

ban /bæn/ *vt* (*pt* **banned**) prohibir. ∼ **s.o. from sth** prohibir algo a uno. ● *n* prohibición *f*

banal /bə'nɑːl/ *a* banal. ∼**ity** /bə'nælətɪ/ *n* banalidad *f*

banana /bə'nɑːnə/ *n* plátano *m*

band /bænd/ *n* (strip) banda *f*. ● *n* (Mus) orquesta *f*; (military, brass) banda *f*. □ ∼ **together** *vi* juntarse

bandage /'bændɪdʒ/ n venda f. ● vt vendar

Band-Aid /'bændeɪd/ n (Amer, P) tirita f, curita f (LAm)

B & B /'biːənbi:/ abbr (= **bed and breakfast**) cama f y desayuno; (place) pensión f

bandit /'bændɪt/ n bandido m

band: ∼**stand** n quiosco m de música. ∼**wagon** n. jump on the ∼**wagon** (fig) subirse al carro

bandy /'bændɪ/ a (-ier, -iest) patizambo

bang /bæŋ/ n (noise) ruido m; (blow) golpe m; (of gun) estampido m; (of door) golpe m. ● vt (strike) golpear. ∼ **the door** dar un portazo. ● adv exactamente. ● int ¡pum! ∼s npl (Amer) flequillo m, cerquillo m (LAm), fleco m (Mex)

banger /'bæŋə(r)/ n petardo m; (⊤, Culin) salchicha f

bangle /'bæŋgl/ n brazalete m

banish /'bænɪʃ/ vt desterrar

banisters /'bænɪstəz/ npl pasamanos m

banjo /'bændʒəʊ/ n (pl -os) banjo m

bank /bæŋk/ n (Com) banco m; (of river) orilla f. ● vt depositar. ● vi (Aviat) ladearse. □ ∼ **on** vt contar con. □ ∼ **with** vi tener una cuenta con. ∼ **card** n tarjeta f bancaria; (Amer) tarjeta f de crédito (expedida por un banco). ∼**er** n banquero m. ∼ **holiday** n día m festivo, día m feriado (LAm). ∼**ing** n (Com) banca f. ∼**note** n billete m de banco

bankrupt /'bæŋkrʌpt/ a & n quebrado (m). go ∼ quebrar. ● vt hacer quebrar. ∼**cy** /-rʌpsɪ/ n bancarrota f, quiebra f

bank statement n estado m de cuenta

banner /'bænə(r)/ n bandera f; (in demonstration) pancarta f

banquet /'bæŋkwɪt/ n banquete m

banter /'bæntə(r)/ n chanza f

bap /bæp/ n panecillo m blando

baptism /'bæptɪzəm/ n bautismo m; (act) bautizo m

Baptist /'bæptɪst/ n bautista m & f

baptize /bæp'taɪz/ vt bautizar

bar /bɑː(r)/ n barra f; (on window) reja f; (of chocolate) tableta f; (of soap) pastilla f; (pub) bar m; (Mus) compás m; (Jurid) abogacia f; (fig) obstáculo m. ● vt (pt **barred**) atrancar <door>; (exclude) excluir; (prohibit) prohibir. ● prep excepto

barbar|ian /bɑː'beərɪən/ a & n bárbaro (m). ∼**ic** /bɑː'bærɪk/ a bárbaro

barbecue /'bɑːbɪkjuː/ n barbacoa f. ● vt asar a la parrilla

barbed wire /bɑːbd 'waɪə(r)/ n alambre m de púas

barber /'bɑːbə(r)/ n peluquero m, barbero m

barbwire /'bɑːb'waɪə(r)/ n (Amer) ⇒BARBED WIRE

bare /beə(r)/ a (-er, -est) desnudo; (room) con pocos muebles; (mere) simple; (empty) vacío. ● vt desnudar; (uncover) descubrir. ∼ **one's teeth** mostrar los dientes. ∼**back** adv a pelo. ∼**faced** a descarado. ∼**foot** a descalzo. ∼**headed** /-'hedɪd/ a descubierto. ∼**ly** adv apenas

bargain /'bɑːgɪn/ n (agreement) pacto m; (good buy) ganga f. ● vi negociar; (haggle) regatear. □ ∼ **for** vt esperar, contar con

barge /bɑːdʒ/ n barcaza f. ● vi. ∼ **in** irrumpir

baritone /'bærɪtəʊn/ n barítono m

bark /bɑːk/ n (of dog) ladrido m; (of tree) corteza f. ● vi ladrar

barley /'bɑːlɪ/ n cebada f

bar: ∼**maid** n camarera f. ∼**man** /-mən/ n camarero m, barman m

barmy /'bɑːmɪ/ a 🅇 chiflado

barn /bɑːn/ n granero m

barometer /bə'rɒmɪtə(r)/ n barómetro m

baron /'bærən/ n barón m. ∼**ess** /-ɪs/ n baronesa f

barracks /'bærəks/ npl cuartel m

barrage /'bærɑːʒ/ n (Mil) barrera f; (dam) presa f. **a** ∼ **of questions** un aluvión de preguntas

barrel /'bærəl/ n barril m; (of gun) cañón m

barren /'bærən/ a estéril

barrette /bə'ret/ n (Amer) pasador m

barricade /ˈbærɪˈkeɪd/ n barricada f. ● vt cerrar con barricadas

barrier /ˈbærɪə(r)/ n barrera f

barring /ˈbɑːrɪŋ/ prep salvo

barrister /ˈbærɪstə(r)/ n abogado m

bartender /ˈbɑːtendə(r)/ n (Amer) (male) camarero m, barman m; (female) camarera f

barter /ˈbɑːtə(r)/ n trueque m. ● vt trocar

base /beɪs/ n base f. ● vt basar. ∼**ball** n béisbol m, beisbol m (Mex)

basement /ˈbeɪsmənt/ n sótano m

bash /bæʃ/ vt golpear. ● n golpe m. have a ∼ 🄸 probar

bashful /ˈbæʃfl/ a tímido

basic /ˈbeɪsɪk/ a básico, fundamental. ∼**ally** adv fundamentalmente

basin /ˈbeɪsn/ n (for washing) palangana f; (for food) cuenco m; (Geog) cuenca f

basis /ˈbeɪsɪs/ n (pl **bases** /-siːz/) base f

bask /bɑːsk/ vi asolearse; (fig) gozar (in de)

basket /ˈbɑːskɪt/ n cesta f; (big) cesto m. ∼**ball** n baloncesto m, básquetbol m (LAm)

bass /beɪs/ a bajo. ● n (Mus) bajo m

bassoon /bəˈsuːn/ n fagot m

bastard /ˈbɑːstəd/ n bastardo m. you ∼! (🄴 or vulg) ¡cabrón! (🄴 or vulg)

bat /bæt/ n (for baseball, cricket) bate m; (for table tennis) raqueta f; (mammal) murciélago m. off one's own ∼ por sí solo. ● vt (pt batted) golpear. without ∼ting an eyelid sin pestañear. ● vi batear

batch /bætʃ/ n (of people) grupo m; (of papers) pila f; (of goods) remesa f; (of bread) hornada f; (Comp) lote m

bated /ˈbeɪtɪd/ a. with ∼ breath con aliento entrecortado

bath /bɑːθ/ n (pl -s /bɑːðz/) baño m; (tub) bañera f, tina f (LAm). ∼s npl (swimming pool) piscina f, alberca f (LAm). have a ∼, take a ∼ (Amer) bañarse. ● vt bañar. ● vi bañarse

bathe /beɪð/ vt bañar. ● vi bañarse. ● n baño m. ∼**r** n bañista m & f

bathing /ˈbeɪðɪŋ/ n baños mpl. ∼ **costume**, ∼ **suit** n traje m de baño

bathroom /ˈbɑːθrʊm/ n cuarto m de baño; (Amer, toilet) servicio m, baño m (LAm)

batsman /ˈbætsmən/ n (pl -**men**) bateador m

battalion /bəˈtæliən/ n batallón m

batter /ˈbætə(r)/ vt (beat) apalear; (cover with batter) rebozar. ● n batido m para rebozar; (Amer, for cake) masa f. ∼**ed** /ˈbætəd/ a <car etc> estropeado; <wife etc> maltratada

battery /ˈbætərɪ/ n (Mil, Auto) batería f; (of torch, radio) pila f

battle /ˈbætl/ n batalla f; (fig) lucha f. ● vi luchar. ∼**field** n campo m de batalla. ∼**ship** n acorazado m

bawl /bɔːl/ vt/i gritar

bay /beɪ/ n (Geog) bahía f. keep at ∼ mantener a raya

bayonet /ˈbeɪənet/ n bayoneta f

bay window /beɪ ˈwɪndəʊ/ n ventana f salediza

bazaar /bəˈzɑː(r)/ n bazar m

BC abbr (= **before Christ**) a. de C., antes de Cristo

------

be /biː/

present **am**, **are**, **is**; past **was**, **were**; past participle **been**

● intransitive verb

❗ Spanish has two verbs
■ meaning be, ser and estar.
■ See those entries for further information about the differences between them.

⋯➤ (position, changed condition or state) estar. **where is the library?** ¿dónde está la biblioteca? **she's tired** está cansada. **how are you?** ¿cómo estás?

⋯➤ (identity, nature or permanent characteristics) ser. **she's tall** es alta. **he's Scottish** es escocés. **I'm a journalist** soy periodista. **he's very kind** es muy bondadoso

⋯➤ (feel) **to be** + adjective tener + sustantivo. **to be cold/hot** tener frío/calor. **he's hungry/thirsty** tiene hambre/sed

⋯➤ (age) **he's thirty** tiene treinta años

·····➤ (weather) **it's cold/hot** hace frío/calor. **it was 40 degrees** hacía 40 grados

● *auxiliary verb*

·····➤ (in tenses) estar. **I'm working** estoy trabajando. **they were singing** estaban cantando, cantaban

·····➤ (in tag questions) **it's a beautiful house, isn't it?** es una casa preciosa, ¿verdad? *or* ¿no? *or* ¿no es cierto?

·····➤ (in short answers) **are you disappointed? - yes, I am** ¿estás desilusionado? - sí (,lo estoy). **I'm surprised, aren't you?** estoy sorprendido, ¿tú no?

·····➤ (in passive sentences) **it was built in 1834** fue construido en 1834, se construyó en 1834. **she was told that ...** le dijeron que..., se le dijo que ...

> ▌ Note that passive sentences
> ▌ in English are often translated
> ▌ using the pronoun *se* or using
> ┊ the third person plural.

beach /biːtʃ/ *n* playa *f*

beacon /ˈbiːkən/ *n* faro *m*

bead /biːd/ *n* cuenta *f*; (of glass) abalorio *m*

beak /biːk/ *n* pico *m*

beaker /ˈbiːkə(r)/ *n* taza *f* (alta y sin asa)

beam /biːm/ *n* (of wood) viga *f*; (of light) rayo *m*; (Naut) bao *m*. ● *vt* emitir. ● *vi* irradiar; (smile) sonreír

bean /biːn/ *n* alubia *f*, frijol *m* (LAm); (broad bean) haba *f*; (of coffee) grano *m*

bear /beə(r)/ *vt* (*pt* **bore**, *pp* **borne**) llevar; parir <*niño*>; (endure) soportar. ∼ **right** torcer a la derecha. ∼ **in mind** tener en cuenta. □ ∼ **with** *vt* tener paciencia con. ● *n* oso *m*. ∼**able** *a* soportable

beard /biəd/ *n* barba *f*. ∼**ed** *a* barbudo

bearer /ˈbeərə(r)/ *n* portador *m*; (of passport) titular *m* & *f*

bearing /ˈbeərɪŋ/ *n* comportamiento *m*; (relevance) relación *f*; (Mec) cojinete *m*. **get one's** ∼**s** orientarse. **lose one's** ∼**s** desorientarse

beast /biːst/ *n* bestia *f*; (person) bruto *m*. ∼**ly** *a* (**-ier, -iest**) bestial; ⊞ horrible

beat /biːt/ *vt* (*pt* **beat**, *pp* **beaten**) (hit) pegar; (Culin) batir; (defeat) derrotar; (better) sobrepasar; batir <*record*>; (baffle) dejar perplejo. ∼ **it** ⊞ largarse. ● *vi* <*heart*> latir. ● *n* latido *m*; (Mus) ritmo *m*; (of policeman) ronda *f*. □ ∼ **up** *vt* darle una paliza a; (Culin) batir. ∼ **up on** (Amer, ⊞) darle una paliza a.. ∼**er** *n* batidor *m*. ∼**ing** *n* paliza *f*

beautician /bjuːˈtɪʃn/ *n* esteticista *m* & *f*

beautiful /ˈbjuːtɪfl/ *a* hermoso. ∼**ly** *adv* maravillosamente

beauty /ˈbjuːtɪ/ *n* belleza *f*. ∼ **salon**, ∼ **shop** (Amer) *n* salón *m* de belleza. ∼ **spot** *n* (on face) lunar *m*; (site) lugar *m* pintoresco

beaver /ˈbiːvə(r)/ *n* castor *m*

became /bɪˈkeɪm/ ⇒BECOME

because /bɪˈkɒz/ *conj* porque. ● *adv*. ∼ **of** por, a causa de

beckon /ˈbekən/ *vt/i*. ∼ **(to)** hacer señas (a)

become /bɪˈkʌm/ *vi* (*pt* **became**, *pp* **become**) hacerse, llegar a ser, volverse, convertirse en. **what has** ∼ **of her?** ¿qué es de ella?

bed /bed/ *n* cama *f*; (layer) estrato *m*; (of sea, river) fondo *m*; (of flowers) macizo *m*. **go to** ∼ acostarse. ● *vi* (*pt* **bedded**). ∼ **and breakfast** (B & B) cama y desayuno; (place) pensión *f*. ∼**bug** *n* chinche *f*. ∼**clothes** *npl*, ∼**ding** *n* ropa *f* de cama, cobijas *fpl* (LAm)

bed: ∼**room** *n* dormitorio *m*, cuarto *m*, habitación *f*, recámara *f* (Mex). ∼**-sitter** /-ˈsɪtə(r)/ *n* habitación *f* con cama y uso de cocina y baño compartidos, estudio *m*. ∼**spread** *n* colcha *f*. ∼**time** *n* hora *f* de acostarse

bee /biː/ *n* abeja *f*; (Amer, social gathering) círculo *m*

beech /biːtʃ/ *n* haya *f*

beef /biːf/ *n* carne *f* de vaca, carne *f* de res (Mex). ● *vi* ⊞ quejarse. ∼**burger** *n* hamburguesa *f*. ∼**y** *a* (**-ier, -iest**) musculoso

bee: ∼**hive** *n* colmena *f*. ∼**line** *n*. **make a** ∼**line for** ir en línea recta hacia

been /biːn/ ⇒BE

beer /bɪə(r)/ n cerveza f

beet /biːt/ n (Amer) remolacha f, betabel f (Mex)

beetle /'biːtl/ n escarabajo m

beetroot /'biːtruːt/ n invar remolacha f, betabel f (Mex)

befall /bɪ'fɔːl/ vt (pt **befell**, pp **befallen**) ocurrirle a. ● vi ocurrir

before /bɪ'fɔː(r)/ prep (time) antes de; (place) delante de. ~ **leaving** antes de marcharse. ● adv (place) delante; (time) antes. **a week** ~ una semana antes. **the week** ~ la semana anterior. ● conj (time) antes de que. ~ **he leaves** antes de que se vaya. ~**hand** adv de antemano

befriend /bɪ'frend/ vt hacerse amigo de

beg /beg/ vt/i (pt **begged**) mendigar; (entreat) suplicar; (ask) pedir. ~ **s.o.'s pardon** pedir perdón a uno. I ~ **your pardon!** ¡perdone Vd! I ~ **your pardon?** ¿cómo?

began /bɪ'gæn/ ⇒BEGIN

beggar /'begə(r)/ n mendigo m

begin /bɪ'gɪn/ vt/i (pt **began**, pp **begun**, pres p **beginning**) comenzar, empezar. ~**ner** n principiante m & f. ~**ning** n principio m

begrudge /bɪ'grʌdʒ/ vt envidiar; (give) dar de mala gana

begun /bɪ'gʌn/ ⇒BEGIN

behalf /bɪ'hɑːf/ n. **on** ~ **of, in** ~ **of** (Amer) de parte de, en nombre de

behav|e /bɪ'heɪv/ vi comportarse, portarse. ~**e** (o.s.) portarse bien. ~**iour** /bɪ'heɪvjə(r)/ n comportamiento m

behead /bɪ'hed/ vt decapitar

behind /bɪ'haɪnd/ prep detrás de, atrás de (LAm). ● adv detrás; (late) atrasado. ● n 🅴 trasero m

beige /beɪʒ/ a & n beige (m)

being /'biːɪŋ/ n ser m. **come into** ~ nacer

belated /bɪ'leɪtɪd/ a tardío

belch /beltʃ/ vi eructar. ▫ ~ **out** vt arrojar <smoke>

belfry /'belfrɪ/ n campanario m

Belgi|an /'beldʒən/ a & n belga (m & f). ~**um** /'beldʒəm/ n Bélgica f

belie|f /bɪ'liːf/ n (trust) fe f; (opinion) creencia f. ~**ve** /bɪ'liːv/ vt/i creer. ~**ve in** creer en. **make** ~**ve** fingir

belittle /bɪ'lɪtl/ vt menospreciar <achievements>; denigrar <person>

bell /bel/ n campana f; (on door, bicycle) timbre m

belligerent /bɪ'lɪdʒərənt/ a beligerante

bellow /'beləʊ/ vt gritar. ● vi bramar. ~**s** npl fuelle m

bell pepper n (Amer) pimiento m

belly /'belɪ/ n barriga f

belong /bɪ'lɒŋ/ vi pertenecer (**to** a); (club) ser socio (**to** de); (have as usual place) ir. ~**ings** /bɪ'lɒŋɪŋz/ npl pertenencias fpl. **personal** ~**ings** efectos mpl personales

beloved /bɪ'lʌvɪd/ a querido

below /bɪ'ləʊ/ prep debajo de, abajo de (LAm); (fig) inferior a. ● adv abajo

belt /belt/ n cinturón m; (area) zona f. ● vt (fig) rodear; 🅴 darle una paliza a. ~**way** n (Amer) carretera f de circunvalación

bench /bentʃ/ n banco m

bend /bend/ n curva f. ● vt (pt & pp **bent**) doblar; torcer <arm, leg>. ● vi doblarse; <road> torcerse. ▫ ~ **down** vi inclinarse ▫ ~ **over** vi agacharse

beneath /bɪ'niːθ/ prep debajo de; (fig) inferior a. ● adv abajo

beneficial /benɪ'fɪʃl/ a provechoso

beneficiary /benɪ'fɪʃərɪ/ n beneficiario m

benefit /'benɪfɪt/ n provecho m, ventaja f; (allowance) prestación f; (for unemployed) subsidio m; (perk) beneficio m. ● vt (pt **benefited**, pres p **benefiting**) beneficiar. ● vi beneficiarse

benevolent /bə'nevələnt/ a benévolo

benign /bɪ'naɪn/ a benigno

bent /bent/ ⇒BEND. ● n inclinación f. ● a torcido; (🅴, corrupt) corrompido

bereave|d /bɪ'riːvd/ n. **the** ~**d** la familia del difunto. ~**ment** n pérdida f; (mourning) luto m

beret /'bereɪ/ n boina f

berry /'berɪ/ n baya f

berserk /bə'sɜːk/ *a.* **go ~** volverse loco

berth /bɜːθ/ *n* litera *f*; (anchorage) amarradero *m.* **give a wide ~ to** evitar. ● *vt/i* atracar

beside /bɪ'saɪd/ *prep* al lado de. **be ~ o.s.** estar fuera de sí

besides /bɪ'saɪdz/ *prep* además de; (except) excepto. ● *adv* además

besiege /bɪ'siːdʒ/ *vt* sitiar, asediar; (fig) acosar

best /best/ *a* (el) mejor. **the ~ thing is to...** lo mejor es... ● *adv* mejor. **like ~** preferir. ● *n* lo mejor. **at ~** a lo más. **do one's ~** hacer todo lo posible. **make the ~ of** contentarse con. **~ man** *n* padrino *m* (de boda)

bestow /bɪ'stəʊ/ *vt* conceder

bestseller /best'selə(r)/ *n* éxito *m* de librería, bestséller *m*

bet /bet/ *n* apuesta *f.* ● *vt/i* (*pt* **bet** *or* **betted**) apostar

betray /bɪ'treɪ/ *vt* traicionar. **~al** *n* traición *f*

better /'betə(r)/ *a & adv* mejor. **~ off** en mejores condiciones; (richer) más rico. **get ~** mejorar. **all the ~** tanto mejor. **I'd ~ be off** me tengo que ir. **the ~ part of** la mayor parte de. ● *vt* mejorar; (beat) sobrepasar. **~ o.s.** superarse. ● *n* superior *m.* **get the ~ of** vencer a. **my ~s** mis superiores *mpl*

between /bɪ'twiːn/ *prep* entre. ● *adv* en medio

beverage /'bevərɪdʒ/ *n* bebida *f*

beware /bɪ'weə(r)/ *vi* tener cuidado. ● *int* ¡cuidado!

bewilder /bɪ'wɪldə(r)/ *vt* desconcertar. **~ment** *n* aturdimiento *m*

bewitch /bɪ'wɪtʃ/ *vt* hechizar; (delight) cautivar

beyond /bɪ'jɒnd/ *prep* más allá de; (fig) fuera de. **~ doubt** sin lugar a duda. ● *adv* más allá

bias /'baɪəs/ *n* tendencia *f*; (prejudice) prejuicio *m.* ● *vt* (*pt* **biased**) influir en. **~ed** *a* parcial

bib /bɪb/ *n* babero *m*

Bible /'baɪbl/ *n* Biblia *f*

biblical /'bɪblɪkl/ *a* bíblico

bibliography /bɪblɪ'ɒɡrəfɪ/ *n* bibliografía *f*

biceps /'baɪseps/ *n invar* bíceps *m*

bicker /'bɪkə(r)/ *vi* altercar

bicycle /'baɪsɪkl/ *n* bicicleta *f*

bid /bɪd/ *n* (offer) oferta *f*; (attempt) tentativa *f.* ● *vi* hacer una oferta. ● *vt* (*pt & pp* **bid**, *pres p* **bidding**) ofrecer; (*pt* **bid**, *pp* **bidden**, *pres p* **bidding**) mandar; dar <*welcome, good day etc*>. **~der** *n* postor *m.* **~ding** *n* (at auction) ofertas *fpl*; (order) mandato *m*

bide /baɪd/ *vt.* **~ one's time** esperar el momento oportuno

bifocals /baɪ'fəʊklz/ *npl* gafas *fpl* bifocales, anteojos *mpl* bifocales (LAm)

big /bɪɡ/ *a* (**bigger**, **biggest**) grande, (before singular noun) gran. ● *adv.* **talk ~** fanfarronear

bigam|ist /'bɪɡəmɪst/ *n* bígamo *m.* **~ous** /'bɪɡəməs/ *a* bígamo. **~y** *n* bigamia *f*

big-headed /-'hedɪd/ *a* engreído

bigot /'bɪɡət/ *n* fanático *m.* **~ed** *a* fanático

bike /baɪk/ *n* 🅕 bici *f* 🅕

bikini /bɪ'kiːnɪ/ *n* (*pl* **-is**) bikini *m*

bile /baɪl/ *n* bilis *f*

bilingual /baɪ'lɪŋɡwəl/ *a* bilingüe

bill /bɪl/ *n* cuenta *f*; (invoice) factura *f*; (notice) cartel *m*; (Amer, banknote) billete *m*; (Pol) proyecto *m* de ley; (of bird) pico *m*

billet /'bɪlɪt/ *n* (Mil) alojamiento *m.* ● *vt* alojar

billfold /'bɪlfəʊld/ *n* (Amer) cartera *f*, billetera *f*

billiards /'bɪlɪədz/ *n* billar *m*

billion /'bɪlɪən/ *n* billón *m*; (Amer) mil millones *mpl*

bin /bɪn/ *n* recipiente *m*; (for rubbish) cubo *m* de basura, bote *m* de basura (Mex); (for waste paper) papelera *f*

bind /baɪnd/ *vt* (*pt* **bound**) atar; encuadernar <*book*>; (Jurid) obligar. ● *n* 🅕 lata *f.* **~ing** *n* (of books) encuadernación *f*; (braid) ribete *m*

binge /bɪndʒ/ *n* 🅧 (of food) comilona *f*; (of drink) borrachera *f.* **go on a ~** ir de juerga

bingo /'bɪŋɡəʊ/ *n* bingo *m*

binoculars /bɪ'nɒkjʊləz/ *npl* gemelos *mpl*

biograph|er /baɪˈɒgrəfə(r)/ n biógrafo m. **~y** n biografía f

biolog|ical /baɪəˈlɒdʒɪkl/ a biológico. **~ist** /baɪˈɒlədʒɪst/ n biólogo m. **~y** /baɪˈɒlədʒɪ/ n biología f

birch /bɜːtʃ/ n (tree) abedul m

bird /bɜːd/ n ave f; (small) pájaro m; (☒, girl) chica f

Biro /ˈbaɪərəʊ/ n (pl **-os**) (P) bolígrafo m

birth /bɜːθ/ n nacimiento m. give **~** dar a luz. **~ certificate** n partida f de nacimiento. **~ control** n control m de la natalidad. **~day** n cumpleaños m. **~mark** n marca f de nacimiento. **~place** n lugar m de nacimiento. **~ rate** n natalidad f

biscuit /ˈbɪskɪt/ n galleta f

bisect /baɪˈsekt/ vt bisecar

bishop /ˈbɪʃəp/ n obispo m; (Chess) alfil m

bit /bɪt/ ⇒BITE. ● n trozo m; (quantity) poco m; (of horse) bocado m; (Mec) broca f; (Comp) bit m

bitch /bɪtʃ/ n perra f; (☒, woman) bruja f ☒

bit|e /baɪt/ vt/i (pt **bit**, pp **bitten**) morder; (insect) picar. **~e one's nails** morderse las uñas. ● n mordisco m; (mouthful) bocado m; (of insect etc) picadura f. **~ing** /ˈbaɪtɪŋ/ a mordaz

bitter /ˈbɪtə(r)/ a amargo; (of weather) glacial. ● n cerveza f amarga. **~ly** adv amargamente. it's **~ly cold** hace un frío glacial. **~ness** n amargor m; (resentment) amargura f

bizarre /bɪˈzɑː(r)/ a extraño

black /blæk/ a (**-er**, **-est**) negro. **~ and blue** amoratado. ● n negro m; (coffee) solo, negro (LAm). ● vt ennegrecer; limpiar <shoes>. **~ out** vi desmayarse. **~ and white** n blanco y negro m. **~-and-white** adj en blanco y negro. **~berry** /-bərɪ/ n zarzamora f. **~bird** n mirlo m. **~board** n pizarra f. **~currant** /-ˈkʌrənt/ n grosella f negra. **~en** vt ennegrecer. **~ eye** n ojo m morado. **~list** vt poner en la lista negra. **~mail** n chantaje m. ● vt chantajear. **~mailer** n chantajista m & f.

~out n apagón m; (Med) desmayo m; (of news) censura f. **~smith** n herrero m

bladder /ˈblædə(r)/ n vejiga f

blade /bleɪd/ n (of knife, sword) hoja f. **~ of grass** brizna f de hierba

blame /bleɪm/ vt echar la culpa a. be to **~** tener la culpa. ● n culpa f. **~less** a inocente

bland /blænd/ a (**-er**, **-est**) suave

blank /blæŋk/ a <page, space> en blanco; <cassette> virgen; <cartridge> sin bala; (fig) vacío. ● n blanco m

blanket /ˈblæŋkɪt/ n manta f, cobija f (LAm), frazada (LAm); (fig) capa f. ● vt (pt **blanketed**) (fig) cubrir (**in**, **with** de)

blare /bleə(r)/ vi sonar muy fuerte. ● n estrépito m

blasphem|e /blæsˈfiːm/ vt/i blasfemar. **~ous** /ˈblæsfəməs/ a blasfemo. **~y** /ˈblæsfəmɪ/ n blasfemia f

blast /blɑːst/ n explosión f; (gust) ráfaga f; (sound) toque m. ● vt volar. **~ed** a maldito. **~-off** n (of missile) despegue m

blatant /ˈbleɪtnt/ a patente; (shameless) descarado

blaze /bleɪz/ n llamarada f; (of light) resplandor m; (fig) arranque m. ● vi arder en llamas; (fig) brillar

blazer /ˈbleɪzə(r)/ n chaqueta f

bleach /bliːtʃ/ n lejía f, cloro m (LAm), blanqueador m (LAm). ● vt blanquear; decolorar <hair>.

bleak /bliːk/ a (**-er**, **-est**) desolado; (fig) sombrío

bleat /bliːt/ n balido m. ● vi balar

bleed /bliːd/ vt/i (pt **bled** /bled/) sangrar

bleep /bliːp/ n pitido m

blemish /ˈblemɪʃ/ n mancha f

blend /blend/ n mezcla f. ● vt mezclar. ● vi combinarse. **~er** n licuadora f

bless /bles/ vt bendecir. **~ you!** (on sneezing) ¡Jesús!, ¡salud! (Mex). **~ed** /ˈblesɪd/ a bendito. **~ing** n bendición f; (advantage) ventaja f

blew /bluː/ ⇒BLOW

blight /blaɪt/ n añublo m, tizón m; (fig) plaga f. ● vt añublar, atizonar; (fig) destrozar

blind /blaɪnd/ a ciego. ~ **alley** callejón m sin salida. ● n persiana f; (fig) pretexto m. ● vt dejar ciego; (dazzle) deslumbrar. ~**fold** a & adv con los ojos vendados. ● n venda f. ● vt vendar los ojos a. ~**ly** adv a ciegas. ~**ness** n ceguera f

blink /blɪŋk/ vi parpadear; <light> centellear. ~**ers** npl (on horse) anteojeras fpl

bliss /blɪs/ n felicidad f. ~**ful** a feliz

blister /'blɪstə(r)/ n ampolla f

blizzard /'blɪzəd/ n ventisca f

bloated /'bləʊtɪd/ a hinchado (with de)

blob /blɒb/ n (drip) gota f; (stain) mancha f

bloc /blɒk/ n (Pol) bloque m

block /blɒk/ n bloque m; (of wood) zoquete m; (of buildings) manzana f, cuadra f (LAm). **in ~ letters** en letra de imprenta. ~ **of flats** edificio m de apartamentos, casa f de pisos. ● vt bloquear. ~**ade** /blɒ'keɪd/ n bloqueo m. ● vt bloquear. ~**age** /-ɪdʒ/ n obstrucción f. ~**head** n 🔢 zopenco m

bloke /bləʊk/ n 🔢 tipo m, tío m 🔢

blond /blɒnd/ a & n rubio (m), güero (m) (Mex 🔢). ~**e** a & n rubia (f), güera (f) (Mex 🔢)

blood /blʌd/ n sangre f. ~**bath** n masacre m. ~**curdling** /-ke:dlɪŋ/a horripilante. ~**hound** n sabueso m. ~ **pressure** n tensión f arterial. **high ~ pressure** hipertensión f. ~**shed** n derramamiento m de sangre. ~**shot** a sanguinolento; <eye> inyectado de sangre. ~**stream** n torrente m sanguíneo. ~**thirsty** a sanguinario. ~**y** a (**-ier, -iest**) sangriento; (stained) ensangrentado; 🔀 maldito

bloom /blu:m/ n flor f. ● vi florecer

blossom /'blɒsəm/ n flor f. ● vi florecer. ~ (**out**) **into** (fig) llegar a ser

blot /blɒt/ n borrón m. ● vt (pt **blotted**) manchar; (dry) secar. □ ~ **out** vt oscurecer

blotch /blɒtʃ/ n mancha f. ~**y** a lleno de manchas

blotting-paper /'blɒtɪŋ/ n papel m secante

blouse /blaʊz/ n blusa f

blow /bləʊ/ vt (pt **blew**, pp **blown**) soplar; fundir <fuse>; tocar <trumpet>. ● vi soplar; <fuse> fundirse; (sound) sonar. ● n golpe m. □ ~ **down** vt derribar. □ ~ **out** vi apagar <candle>. □ ~ **over** vi pasar. □ ~ **up** vt inflar; (explode) volar; (Photo) ampliar. vi (explode) estallar; (burst) reventar. ~**dry** vt secar con secador. ~**lamp** n soplete m. ~**out** n (of tyre) reventón m. ~ **torch** n soplete m

blue /blu:/ a (**-er, -est**) azul; <joke> verde. ● n azul m. **out of the ~** totalmente inesperado. ~**s** npl. **have the ~s** tener tristeza. ~**bell** n campanilla f. ~**bottle** n moscarda f. ~**print** n plano m; (fig, plan) programa m

bluff /blʌf/ n (poker) farol m, bluff m (LAm), blof m (Mex). ● vt engañar. ● vi tirarse un farol, hacer un bluf (LAm), blofear (Mex)

blunder /'blʌndə(r)/ vi cometer un error. ● n metedura f de pata

blunt /blʌnt/ a desafilado; <person> directo, abrupto. ● vt desafilar. ~**ly** adv francamente

blur /blɜ:(r)/ n impresión f indistinta. ● vt (pt **blurred**) hacer borroso

blurb /blɜ:b/ n resumen m publicitario

blurt /blɜ:t/ vt. ~ **out** dejar escapar

blush /blʌʃ/ vi ruborizarse. ● n rubor m

boar /bɔ:(r)/ n verraco m. **wild ~** jabalí m

board /bɔ:d/ n tabla f, tablero m; (for notices) tablón m de anuncios, tablero m de anuncios (LAm); (blackboard) pizarra f; (food) pensión f; (Admin) junta f. ~ **and lodging** casa y comida. **full ~** pensión f completa. **go by the ~** ser abandonado. ● vt alojar; ~ **a ship** embarcarse. ● vi alojarse (**with** en casa de); (at school) ser interno. ~**er** n huésped m & f; (school) interno m. ~**ing card** n tarjeta f de embarque.

~**ing house** n casa f de huéspedes, pensión f. ~**ing pass** n ⇒~ING CARD. ~**ing school** n internado m

boast /bəʊst/ vt enorgullecerse de. ● vi jactarse. ● n jactancia f. ~**ful** a jactancioso

boat /bəʊt/ n barco m; (small) bote m, barca f

bob /bɒb/ vi (pt **bobbed**) menearse, subir y bajar. □ ~ **up** vi presentarse súbitamente

bobbin /'bɒbɪn/ n carrete m; (in sewing machine) canilla f, bobina f

bobby pin /'bɒbɪ/ n (Amer) horquilla f, pasador m (Mex). ~ **sox** /sɒks/ npl (Amer) calcetines mpl cortos

bobsleigh /'bɒbsleɪ/ n bob(sleigh) m

bode /bəʊd/ vi. ~ **well/ill** ser de buen/mal agüero

bodice /'bɒdɪs/ n corpiño m

bodily /'bɒdɪlɪ/ a físico, corporal. ● adv físicamente

body /'bɒdɪ/ n cuerpo m; (dead) cadáver m. ~**guard** n guardaespaldas m. ~**work** n carrocería f

bog /bɒg/ n ciénaga f. □ ~ **down** vt (pt **bogged**). get ~**ged down** empantanarse

boggle /'bɒgl/ vi sobresaltarse. the mind ~s uno se queda atónito

bogus /'bəʊgəs/ a falso

boil /bɔɪl/ vt/i hervir. be ~**ing hot** estar ardiendo; <weather> hacer mucho calor. ● n furúnculo m. □ ~ **away** vi evaporarse. □ ~ **down to** vt reducirse a. □ ~ **over** vi rebosar. ~**ed** a hervido; <egg> pasado por agua. ~**er** n caldera f. ~**er suit** n mono m, overol m (LAm)

boisterous /'bɔɪstərəs/ a ruidoso, bullicioso

bold /bəʊld/ a (-er, -est) audaz. ~**ly** adv con audacia, audazmente

Bolivia /bə'lɪvɪə/ n Bolivia f. ~**n** a & n boliviano (m)

bolster /'bəʊlstə(r)/ □ ~ **up** vt sostener

bolt /bəʊlt/ n (on door) cerrojo m; (for nut) perno m; (lightning) rayo m; (leap) fuga f. ● vt echar el cerrojo a <door>; engullir <food>. ● vi fugarse. ● adv. ~ **upright** rígido

bomb /bɒm/ n bomba f. ● vt bombardear. ~**ard** /bɒm'bɑːd/ vt bombardear ~**er** /'bɒmə(r)/ n (plane) bombardero m; (terrorist) terrorista m & f. ~**ing** /'bɒmɪŋ/ n bombardeo m. ~**shell** n bomba f

bond /bɒnd/ n (agreement) obligación f; (link) lazo m; (Com) bono m. ● vi (stick) adherirse. ~**age** /-ɪdʒ/ n esclavitud f

bone /bəʊn/ n hueso m; (of fish) espina f. ● vt deshuesar; quitar las espinas a <fish>. ~**-dry** a completamente seco. ~ **idle** a holgazán

bonfire /'bɒnfaɪə(r)/ n hoguera f, fogata f

bonnet /'bɒnɪt/ n gorra f; (Auto) capó m, capote m (Mex)

bonus /'bəʊnəs/ n (payment) bonificación f; (fig) ventaja f

bony /'bəʊnɪ/ a (-ier, -iest) huesudo; <fish> lleno de espinas

boo /buː/ int ¡bu! ● vt/i abuchear

boob /buːb/ n (🄴, mistake) metedura f de pata. ● vi 🄴 meter la pata

booby /'buːbɪ/ **: ~ prize** n premio m al peor. ~ **trap** n trampa f; (bomb) bomba f trampa.

book /bʊk/ n libro m; (of cheques etc) talonario m, chequera f; (notebook) libreta f; (exercise book) cuaderno m. ~**s** (mpl) (Com) cuentas fpl. ● vt (enter) registrar; (reserve) reservar. ● vi reservar. ~**case** n biblioteca f, librería f, librero m (Mex). ~**ing** n reserva f, reservación f (LAm). ~**ing office** n (in theatre) taquilla f, boletería f (LAm). ~**keeping** n contabilidad f. ~**let** /'bʊklɪt/ n folleto m. ~**maker** n corredor m de apuestas. ~**mark** n señal f. ~**seller** n librero m. ~**shop**, (Amer) ~**store** n librería f. ~**worm** n (fig) ratón m de biblioteca

boom /buːm/ vi retumbar; (fig) prosperar. ● n estampido m; (Com) boom m

boost /buːst/ vt estimular; reforzar <morale>. ● n empuje m. ~**er** n (Med) revacunación f. ~**er cable** n (Amer) cable m de arranque

boot /buːt/ n bota f; (Auto) maletero m, cajuela f (Mex). □ ~ **up** vt (Comp) cargar

booth /bu:ð/ *n* cabina *f*; (at fair) puesto *m*

booze /bu:z/ *vi* 🔊 beber mucho. ● *n* 🔊 alcohol *m*

border /'bɔːdə(r)/ *n* borde *m*; (frontier) frontera *f*; (in garden) arriate *m*. □ ~ **on** *vt* lindar con. ~**line** *n* línea *f* divisoria. ~**line case** *n* caso *m* dudoso

bor|e /bɔː(r)/ ⇒BEAR. ● *vt* (annoy) aburrir; (Tec) taladrar. ● *vi* taladrar. ● *n* (person) pelmazo *m*; (thing) lata *f*. ~**ed** *a* aburrido. be ~ed estar aburrido. get ~ed aburrirse. ~**edom** /'bɔːdəm/ *n* aburrimiento *m*. ~**ing** *a* aburrido, pesado

born /bɔːn/ *a* nato. be ~ nacer

borne /bɔːn/ ⇒BEAR

borough /'bʌrə/ *n* municipio *m*

borrow /'bɒrəʊ/ *vt* pedir prestado

Bosnia /'bɒznɪə/: ~ **Herzegovina** /hɜːtsəgəʊ'viːnə/ *n* Bosnia Herzegovina *f*. ~**n** *a* & *n* bosnio (*m*)

boss /bɒs/ *n* 🔊 jefe *m*. ● *vt*. ~ (about) 🔊 dar órdenes a. ~**y** *a* mandón

botan|ical /bə'tænɪkl/ *a* botánico. ~**ist** /'bɒtənɪst/ *n* botánico *m*. ~**y** /'bɒtənɪ/ *n* botánica *f*

both /bəʊθ/ *a* & *pron* ambos (*mpl*), los dos (*mpl*). ● *adv* al mismo tiempo, a la vez. ~ **Ann and Brian** came tanto Ann como Bob vinieron

bother /'bɒðə(r)/ *vt* (inconvenience) molestar; (worry) preocupar. ~ **it!** ¡caramba! ● *vi* molestarse. ~ **about** preocuparse de. ~ **doing** tomarse la molestia de hacer. ● *n* molestia *f*

bottle /'bɒtl/ *n* botella, mamila *f* (Mex); (for baby) biberón *m*. ● *vt* embotellar. □ ~ **up** *vt* (fig) reprimir. ~**neck** *n* (traffic jam) embotellamiento *m*. ~ **opener** *n* abrebotellas *m*, destapador *m* (LAm)

bottom /'bɒtəm/ *n* fondo *m*; (of hill) pie *m*; (buttocks) trasero *m*. ● *a* de más abajo; <price> más bajo; <lip, edge> inferior. ~**less** *a* sin fondo

bough /baʊ/ *n* rama *f*

bought /bɔːt/ ⇒BUY

boulder /'bəʊldə(r)/ *n* canto *m*

bounce /baʊns/ *vt* hacer rebotar. ● *vi* rebotar; <person> saltar; 🔊

<cheque> ser rechazado. ● *n* rebote *m*

bound /baʊnd/ ⇒BIND. ● *vi* saltar. ● *n* (jump) salto *m*. ~**s** *npl* (limits) límites *mpl*. out of ~s zona *f* prohibida. ● *a*. be ~ for dirigirse a. ~ **to** obligado a; (certain) seguro de

boundary /'baʊndərɪ/ *n* límite *m*

bouquet /bʊ'keɪ/ *n* ramo *m*; (of wine) buqué *m*, aroma *m*

bout /baʊt/ *n* período *m*; (Med) ataque *m*; (Sport) encuentro *m*

bow[1] /bəʊ/ *n* (weapon, mus) arco *m*; (knot) lazo *m*, moño *m* (LAm)

bow[2] /baʊ/ *n* reverencia *f*; (Naut) proa *f*. ● *vi* inclinarse. ● *vt* inclinar

bowels /'baʊəlz/ *npl* intestinos *mpl*; (fig) entrañas *fpl*

bowl /bəʊl/ *n* (container) cuenco *m*; (for washing) palangana *f*; (ball) bola *f*. ● *vt* (cricket) arrojar. ● *vi* (cricket) arrojar la pelota. □ ~ **over** *vt* derribar

bowl: ~**er** *n* (cricket) lanzador *m*. ~**er** (hat) sombrero *m* de hongo, bombín *m*. ~**ing** *n* bolos *mpl*. ~**ing alley** *n* bolera *f*

bow tie /bəʊ 'taɪ/ *n* corbata *f* de lazo, pajarita *f*

box /bɒks/ *n* caja *f*; (for jewels etc) estuche *m*; (in theatre) palco *m*. ● *vt* boxear contra. ~ **s.o.'s ears** dar una manotada a uno. ● *vi* boxear. ~**er** *n* boxeador *m*. ~**ing** *n* boxeo *m*. **B~ing Day** *n* el 26 de diciembre. ~ **office** *n* taquilla *f*, boletería *f* (LAm). ~**room** *n* trastero *m*

boy /bɔɪ/ *n* chico *m*, muchacho *m*; (young) niño *m*

boycott /'bɔɪkɒt/ *vt* boicotear. ● *n* boicoteo *m*

boy: ~**friend** *n* novio *m*. ~**hood** *n* niñez *f*. ~**ish** *a* de muchacho; (childish) infantil

bra /brɑː/ *n* sostén *m*, sujetador *m*, brasier *m* (Mex)

brace /breɪs/ *n* abrazadera *f*. ● *vt* asegurar. ~ **o.s.** prepararse. ~**s** *npl* tirantes *mpl*; (Amer, dental) aparato(s) *m(pl)*

bracelet /'breɪslɪt/ *n* pulsera *f*

bracken /'brækən/ *n* helecho *m*

bracket /'brækɪt/ *n* soporte *m*; (group) categoría *f*; (parenthesis) paréntesis *m*. **square ~s** corchetes *mpl*. ● *vt* poner entre paréntesis; (join together) agrupar

brag /bræg/ *vi* (*pt* **bragged**) jactarse (**about** de)

braid /breɪd/ *n* galón *m*; (Amer, in hair) trenza *f*

brain /breɪn/ *n* cerebro *m*. ● *vt* romper la cabeza a. **~child** *n* invento *m*. **~ drain** *n* 🏛 fuga *f* de ce-rebros. **~storm** *n* ataque *m* de lo-cura; (Amer, brainwave) idea *f* genial. **~wash** *vt* lavar el cerebro. **~wave** *n* idea *f* genial. **~y** *a* (**-ier, -iest**) inteligente

brake /breɪk/ *n* freno *m*. ● *vt/i* frenar. **~ fluid** *n* líquido *m* de freno. **~ lights** *npl* luces *fpl* de freno

bramble /'bræmbl/ *n* zarza *f*

bran /bræn/ *n* salvado *m*

branch /brɑːntʃ/ *n* rama *f*; (of road) bifurcación *f*; (Com) sucursal *m*; (fig) ramo *m*. □ **~ off** *vi* bifurcarse. □ **~ out** *vi* ramificarse

brand /brænd/ *n* marca *f*. ● *vt* marcar; (label) tildar de

brandish /'brændɪʃ/ *vt* blandir

brand: ~ name *n* marca *f*. **~-new** /-'njuː/ *a* flamante

brandy /'brændɪ/ *n* coñac *m*

brash /bræʃ/ *a* descarado

brass /brɑːs/ *n* latón *m*. **get down to ~ tacks** (fig) ir al grano. **~ band** *n* banda *f* de música

brassière /'bræsjeə(r)/ *n* ⇒BRA

brat /bræt/ *n* (pej) mocoso *m*

bravado /brə'vɑːdəʊ/ *n* bravata *f*

brave /breɪv/ *a* (**-er, -est**) valiente. ● *n* (North American Indian) guerrero *m* indio. **the ~** *npl* los valientes. ● *vt* afrontar. **~ry** /-ərɪ/ *n* valentía *f*, valor *m*

brawl /brɔːl/ *n* alboroto *m*. ● *vi* pelearse

brazen /'breɪzn/ *a* descarado

Brazil /brə'zɪl/ *n* Brasil *m*. **~ian** /-jən/ *a & n* brasileño (*m*)

breach /briːtʃ/ *n* infracción *f*, violación *f*; (of contract) incumplimiento *m*; (gap) brecha *f*. **~ of the peace** alteración *f* del orden público. ● *vt* abrir una brecha en

bread /bred/ *n* pan *m*. **a loaf of ~** un pan. **~crumbs** *npl* migajas *fpl*; (Culin) pan *m* rallado, pan *m* molido (Mex)

breadth /bredθ/ *n* anchura *f*

breadwinner /'bredwɪnə(r)/ *n* sostén *m* de la familia

break /breɪk/ *vt* (*pt* **broke**, *pp* **broken**) romper; infringir, violar *<law>*; batir *<record>*; comunicar *<news>*; interrumpir *<journey>*. ● *vi* romperse; *<news>* divulgarse. ● *n* ruptura *f*; (interval) intervalo *m*; (🏛, chance) oportunidad *f*; (in weather) cambio *m*. □ **~ away** *vi* escapar. □ **~ down** *vt* derribar; analizar *<figures>*. *vi* estropearse, descomponerse (LAm); (Auto) averiarse; (cry) deshacerse en lágrimas. □ **~ in** *vi* *<intruder>* entrar (para robar). □ **~ into** *vt* entrar en (para robar) *<house etc>*; (start doing) ponerse a. □ **~ off** *vi* interrumpirse. □ **~ out** *vi* *<war, disease>* estallar; (run away) escaparse. □ **~ up** *vi* romperse; *<band, lovers>* separarse; *<schools>* terminar. **~able** *a* frágil. **~age** /-ɪdʒ/ *n* rotura *f*. **~down** *n* (Tec) falla *f*; (Med) colapso *m*, crisis *f* nerviosa; (of figures) análisis *f*. **~er** *n* (wave) ola *f* grande

breakfast /'brekfəst/ *n* desayuno *m*. **have ~** desayunar

break: ~through *n* adelanto *m*. **~water** *n* rompeolas *m*

breast /brest/ *n* pecho *m*; (of chicken etc) pechuga *f*. (estilo *m*) **~stroke** *n* braza *f*, (estilo *m*) pecho *m* (LAm)

breath /breθ/ *n* aliento *m*, respiración *f*. **be out of ~** estar sin aliento. **hold one's ~** aguantar la respiración. **under one's ~** a media voz

breath|e /briːð/ *vt/i* respirar. **~er** *n* descanso *m*, pausa *f*. **~ing** *n* respiración *f*

breathtaking /'breθteɪkɪŋ/ *a* impresionante

bred /bred/ ⇒BREED

breed /briːd/ *vt* (*pt* **bred**) criar; (fig) engendrar. ● *vi* reproducirse. ● *n* raza *f*

breez|e /briːz/ *n* brisa *f*. **~y** *a* de mucho viento

brew /bruː/ vt hacer *<beer>*; preparar *<tea>*. ●vi hacer cerveza; *<tea>* reposar; (fig) prepararse. ●n infusión f. ∼**er** n cervecero m. ∼**ery** n cervecería f, fábrica f de cerveza

bribe /braɪb/ n soborno m. ●vt sobornar. ∼**ry** /'braɪbərɪ/ n soborno m

brick /brɪk/ n ladrillo m. ∼**layer** n albañil m

bridal /'braɪdl/ a nupcial

bride /braɪd/ m novia f. ∼**groom** n novio m. ∼**smaid** /'braɪdzmeɪd/ n dama f de honor

bridge /brɪdʒ/ n puente m; (of nose) caballete m; (Cards) bridge m. ●vt tender un puente sobre. ∼ a gap llenar un vacío

bridle /'braɪdl/ n brida f. ∼ **path** n camino m de herradura

brief /briːf/ a (**-er, -est**) breve. ●n (Jurid) escrito m. ●vt dar instrucciones a. ∼**case** n maletín m, portafolio(s) m (LAm). ∼**ly** adv brevemente. ∼**s** npl (man's) calzoncillos mpl; (woman's) bragas fpl, calzones mpl (LAm), pantaletas fpl (Mex)

brigade /brɪ'geɪd/ n brigada f

bright /braɪt/ a (**-er, -est**) brillante, claro; (clever) listo; (cheerful) alegre. ∼**en** vt aclarar; hacer más alegre *<house etc>*. ●vi (weather) aclararse; *<face>* illuminarse

brillian|ce /'brɪljəns/ n brillantez f, brillo m. ∼**t** a brillante

brim /brɪm/ n borde m; (of hat) ala f. □ ∼ **over** vi (pt **brimmed**) desbordarse

brine /braɪn/ n salmuera f

bring /brɪŋ/ vt (pt **brought**) traer; (lead) llevar. □ ∼ **about** vt causar. □ ∼ **back** vt devolver. □ ∼ **down** vt derribar. □ ∼ **off** vt lograr. □ ∼ **on** vt causar. □ ∼ **out** vt sacar; lanzar *<product>*; publicar *<book>*. □ ∼ **round/to** vt hacer volver en sí. □ ∼ **up** vt (Med) vomitar; educar *<children>*; plantear *<question>*

brink /brɪŋk/ n borde m

brisk /brɪsk/ a (**-er, -est**) enérgico, vivo

bristle /'brɪsl/ n cerda f. ●vi erizarse

Brit|ain /'brɪtən/ n Gran Bretaña f. ∼**ish** /'brɪtɪʃ/ a británico. ●npl the ∼**ish** los británicos. ∼**on** /'brɪtən/ n británico m

Brittany /'brɪtənɪ/ n Bretaña f

brittle /'brɪtl/ a frágil, quebradizo

broach /brəʊtʃ/ vt abordar

broad /brɔːd/ a (**-er, -est**) ancho. in ∼ **daylight** a plena luz del día. ∼**bean** n haba f ∼**cast** n emisión f. ●vt (pt **broadcast**) emitir. ●vi hablar por la radio. ∼**caster** n locutor m. ∼**casting** n radio-difusión f. ∼**en** vt ensanchar. ●vi ensancharse. ∼**ly** adv en general. ∼**-minded** /-'maɪndɪd/ a de miras amplias, tolerante

broccoli /'brɒkəlɪ/ n invar brécol m

brochure /'brəʊʃə(r)/ n folleto m

broil /brɔɪl/ vt (Amer) asar a la parrilla. ∼**er** n (Amer) parrilla f

broke /brəʊk/ ➾BREAK. ●a 🅘 sin blanca, en la ruina

broken /'brəʊkən/ ➾BREAK. ●a roto

broker /'brəʊkə(r)/ n corredor m

brolly /'brɒlɪ/ n 🅘 paraguas m

bronchitis /brɒn'kaɪtɪs/ n bronquitis f

bronze /brɒnz/ n bronce m. ●a de bronce

brooch /brəʊtʃ/ n broche m

brood /bruːd/ n cría f; (hum) prole m. ●vi empollar; (fig) meditar

brook /brʊk/ n arroyo m. ●vt soportar

broom /bruːm/ n escoba f. ∼**stick** n palo m de escoba

broth /brɒθ/ n caldo m

brothel /'brɒθl/ n burdel m

brother /'brʌðə(r)/ n hermano m. ∼**hood** n fraternidad f. ∼**-in-law** (pl ∼**s-in-law**) n cuñado m. ∼**ly** a fraternal

brought /brɔːt/ ➾BRING

brow /braʊ/ n frente f; (of hill) cima f. ∼**beat** vt (pt **-beaten**, pp **-beat**) intimidar

brown /braʊn/ a (**-er, -est**) marrón, café (Mex); *<hair>* castaño; *<skin>*

moreno; (tanned) bronceado. ● *n* marrón *m*, café *m* (Mex). ● *vt* poner moreno; (Culin) dorar. ~ **bread** *n* pan *m* integral ~ **sugar** /braʊn 'ʃʊgə(r)/ *n* azúcar *m* moreno, azúcar *f* morena

browse /braʊz/ *vi* (in a shop) curiosear; <*animal*> pacer; (Comp) navegar. ~**r** (Comp) browser *m*, navegador *m*

bruise /bruːz/ *n* magulladura *f*. ● *vt* magullar; machucar <*fruit*>

brunch /brʌntʃ/ *n* 🔲 desayuno *m* tardío

brunette /bruːˈnet/ *n* morena *f*

brunt /brʌnt/ *n*. bear *o* take the ~ of sth sufrir algo

brush /brʌʃ/ *n* cepillo *m*; (large) escoba; (for decorating) brocha *f*; (artist's) pincel; (skirmish) escaramuza *f*. ● *vt* cepillar. □ ~ **against** *vt* rozar. □ ~ **aside** *vt* rechazar. □ ~ **off** *vt* (rebuff) desairar. □ ~ **up (on)** *vt* refrescar

brusque /bruːsk/ *a* brusco. ~**ly** *adv* bruscamente

Brussels /ˈbrʌslz/ *n* Bruselas *f*. ~ **sprout** *n* col *f* de Bruselas

brutal /ˈbruːtl/ *a* brutal. ~**ity** /-ˈtæləti/ *n* brutalidad *f*. ~**ly** *adv* brutalmente

brute /bruːt/ *n* bestia *f*. ~ **force** fuerza *f* bruta

BSc *abbr* ⇒BACHELOR

bubbl|e /ˈbʌbl/ *n* burbuja *f*. ● *vi* burbujear. □ ~ **over** *vi* desbordarse. ~**ly** *a* burbujeante

buck /bʌk/ *a* macho. ● *n* (deer) ciervo *m*; (Amer 🔲) dólar *m*. **pass the** ~ pasar la pelota

bucket /ˈbʌkɪt/ *n* balde *m*, cubo *m*, cubeta *f* (Mex)

buckle /ˈbʌkl/ *n* hebilla *f*. ● *vt* abrochar. ● *vi* torcerse

bud /bʌd/ *n* brote *m*. ● *vi* (*pt* **budded**) brotar.

Buddhis|m /ˈbʊdɪzəm/ *n* budismo *m*. ~**t** *a* & *n* budista (*m* & *f*)

budding /ˈbʌdɪŋ/ *a* (fig) en ciernes

buddy /ˈbʌdɪ/ *n* 🔲 amigo *m*, cuate *m* (Mex)

budge /bʌdʒ/ *vt* mover. ● *vi* moverse

budgerigar /ˈbʌdʒərɪgɑː(r)/ *n* periquito *m*

budget /ˈbʌdʒɪt/ *n* presupuesto *m*

buffalo /ˈbʌfələʊ/ *n* (*pl* **-oes** *or* **-o**) búfalo *m*

buffer /ˈbʌfə(r)/ *n* parachoques *m*

buffet¹ /ˈbʊfeɪ/ *n* (meal) buffet *m*; (in train) bar *m*

buffet² /ˈbʌfɪt/ *n* golpe *m*; (slap) bofetada *f*. ● *vt* (*pt* **buffeted**) golpear

bug /bʌg/ *n* bicho *m*; 🔲, (germ) microbio *m*; (device) micrófono *m* oculto. ● *vt* (*pt* **bugged**) ocultar un micrófono en; (🔲, bother) molestar

buggy /ˈbʌgɪ/ *n*. **baby** ~ sillita *f* de paseo (plegable); (Amer) cochecito *m*

bugle /ˈbjuːgl/ *n* corneta *f*

build /bɪld/ *vt*/*i* (*pt* **built**) construir. ● *n* (of person) figura *f*, tipo *m*. □ ~ **up** *vt*/*i* fortalecer; (increase) aumentar. ~**er** *n* (contractor) contratista *m* & *f*; (labourer) albañil *m*. ~**ing** *n* edificio *m*; (construction) construcción *f*. ~**up** *n* aumento *m*; (of gas etc) acumulación *f*

built /bɪlt/ ⇒BUILD. ~**-in** *a* empotrado. ~**-up area** *n* zona *f* urbanizada

bulb /bʌlb/ *n* bulbo *m*; (Elec) bombilla *f*, foco *m* (Mex)

Bulgaria /bʌlˈgeərɪə/ *n* Bulgaria *f*. ~**n** *a* & *n* búlgaro (*m*)

bulg|e /bʌldʒ/ *n* protuberancia *f*. ● *vi* pandearse. ~**ing** *a* abultado; <*eyes*> saltón

bulk /bʌlk/ *n* bulto *m*, volumen *m*. in ~ a granel; (loose) suelto. **the** ~ **of** la mayor parte de. ~**y** *a* voluminoso

bull /bʊl/ *n* toro *m*. ~**dog** *n* bulldog *m*. ~**dozer** /-dəʊzə(r)/ *n* bulldozer *m*

bullet /ˈbʊlɪt/ *n* bala *f*

bulletin /ˈbʊlətɪn/ *n* anuncio *m*; (journal) boletín *m*. ~ **board** *n* (Amer) tablón *m* de anuncios, tablero *m* de anuncios (LAm)

bulletproof /ˈbʊlɪtpruːf/ *a* a prueba de balas

bullfight /ˈbʊlfaɪt/ *n* corrida *f* (de toros). ~**er** *n* torero *m*. ~**ing** *n* (deporte *m* de) los toros

bull: ~**ring** *n* plaza *f* de toros. ~**'s-eye** *n* diana *f*. ~**shit** *n* (vulg) sandeces *fpl* 🔲, gilipolleces *fpl* 🞪

bully /'bʊlɪ/ n matón m. ● vt intimidar. ∼**ing** n intimidación f

bum /bʌm/ n (🇬🇧, backside) trasero m; (Amer 🇺🇸) holgazán m

bumblebee /'bʌmblbiː/ n abejorro m

bump /bʌmp/ vt chocar contra. ● vi dar sacudidas. ● n (blow) golpe m; (jolt) sacudida f. □ ∼ **into** vt chocar contra; (meet) encontrar.

bumper /'bʌmpə(r)/ n parachoques m. ● a récord. ∼ **edition** n edición f especial

bun /bʌn/ n bollo m; (bread roll) panecillo m, bolillo m (Mex); (hair) moño m, chongo m (Mex)

bunch /bʌntʃ/ n (of people) grupo m; (of bananas, grapes) racimo m; (of flowers) ramo m

bundle /'bʌndl/ n bulto m; (of papers) legajo m. □ ∼ **up** vt atar

bungalow /'bʌŋgələʊ/ n casa f de un solo piso

bungle /'bʌŋgl/ vt echar a perder

bunk /bʌŋk/ n litera f

bunker /'bʌŋkə(r)/ n carbonera f; (Golf, Mil) búnker m

bunny /'bʌnɪ/ n conejito m

buoy /bɔɪ/ n boya f. □ ∼ **up** vt hacer flotar; (fig) animar

buoyant /'bɔɪənt/ a flotante; (fig) optimista

burden /'bɜːdn/ n carga f. ● vt cargar (**with** de)

bureau /'bjʊərəʊ/ n (pl **-eaux** /-əʊz/) agencia f; (desk) escritorio m; (Amer, chest of drawers) cómoda f

bureaucra|cy /bjʊə'rɒkrəsɪ/ n burocracia f. ∼**t** /'bjʊərəkræt/ n burócrata m & f. ∼**tic** /-'krætɪk/ a burocrático

burger /'bɜːgə(r)/ n 🇺🇸 hamburguesa f

burgl|ar /'bɜːglə(r)/ n ladrón m. ∼**ar alarm** n alarma f antirrobo. ∼**ary** n robo m (en casa o edificio). ∼**e** /'bɜːgl/ vt entrar a robar en. **we were** ∼**ed** nos entraron a robar

burial /'berɪəl/ n entierro m

burly /'bɜːlɪ/ a (**-ier, -iest**) corpulento

burn /bɜːn/ vt (pt **burned** or **burnt**) quemar. ● vi quemarse. ● n quemadura f. □ ∼ **down** vt incendiar. vi incendiarse

burnt /bɜːnt/ ⇒BURN

burp /bɜːp/ n 🇺🇸 eructo m. ● vi 🇺🇸 eructar

burrow /'bʌrəʊ/ n madriguera f. ● vt excavar

burst /bɜːst/ vt (pt **burst**) reventar. ● vi reventarse. ∼ **into tears** echarse a llorar. ∼ **out laughing** echarse a reír. ● n (Mil) ráfaga f; (of activity) arrebato; (of applause) salva f

bury /'berɪ/ vt enterrar; (hide) ocultar

bus /bʌs/ n (pl **buses**) autobús m, camión m (Mex)

bush /bʊʃ/ n arbusto m; (land) monte m. ∼**y** a espeso

business /'bɪznɪs/ n negocio m; (Com) negocios mpl; (profession) ocupación f; (fig) asunto m. **mind one's own** ∼ ocuparse de sus propios asuntos. ∼**like** a práctico, serio. ∼**man** /-mən/ n hombre m de negocios. ∼**woman** n mujer f de negocios

busker /'bʌskə(r)/ n músico m ambulante

bus stop n parada f de autobús, paradero m de autobús (LAm)

bust /bʌst/ n busto m; (chest) pecho m. ● vt (pt **busted** or **bust**) 🇺🇸 romper. ● vi romperse. ● a roto. **go** ∼ 🇺🇸 quebrar

bust-up /'bʌstʌp/ n 🇺🇸 riña f

busy /'bɪzɪ/ a (**-ier, -iest**) ocupado; <street> concurrido. **be** ∼ (Amer) <phone> estar comunicando, estar ocupado (LAm). ● vt. ∼ **o.s. with** ocuparse de. ∼**body** n entrometido m

but /bʌt/ conj pero; (after negative) sino. ● prep menos. ∼ **for** si no fuera por. **last** ∼ **one** penúltimo

butcher /'bʊtʃə(r)/ n carnicero m. ● vt matar; (fig) hacer una carnicería con

butler /'bʌtlə(r)/ n mayordomo m

butt /bʌt/ n (of gun) culata f; (of cigarette) colilla f; (target) blanco m; (Amer 🇺🇸, backside) trasero m. ● vi topar. □ ∼ **in** vi interrumpir

butter /'bʌtə(r)/ n mantequilla f. ● vt untar con mantequilla. ~**cup** n ranúnculo m. ~**fingers** n manazas m, torpe m. ~**fly** n mariposa f; (swimming) estilo m mariposa

buttock /'bʌtək/ n nalga f

button /'bʌtn/ n botón m. ● vt abotonar. ● vi abotonarse. ~**hole** n ojal m. ● vt (fig) detener

buy /baɪ/ vt/i (pt **bought**) comprar. ● n compra f. ~**er** n comprador m

buzz /bʌz/ n zumbido m. ● vi zumbar. □ ~ **off** vi ⊠ largarse. ~**er** n timbre m

by /baɪ/ prep por; (near) cerca de; (before) antes de; (according to) según. ~ **and large** en conjunto, en general. ~ **car** en coche. ~ **oneself** por sí solo

bye /baɪ/, **bye-bye** /'baɪbaɪ/ int ⊡ ¡adiós!

by: ~**-election** n elección f parcial. ~**-law** n reglamento m (local). ~**pass** n carretera f de circunvalación. ● vt eludir; <road> circunvalar. ~**product** n subproducto m. ~**stander** /-stændə(r)/ n espectador m

byte /baɪt/ n (Comp) byte m, octeto m

Cc

cab /kæb/ n taxi m; (of lorry, train) cabina f

cabaret /'kæbəreɪ/ n cabaret m

cabbage /'kæbɪdʒ/ n col f, repollo m

cabin /'kæbɪn/ n (house) cabaña f; (in ship) camarote m; (in plane) cabina f

cabinet /'kæbɪnɪt/ n (cupboard) armario m; (for display) vitrina f. **C**~ (Pol) gabinete m

cable /'keɪbl/ n cable m. ~ **car** n teleférico m. ~ **TV** n televisión f por cable, cablevisión f (LAm)

cackle /'kækl/ n (of hen) cacareo m; (laugh) risotada f. ● vi cacarear; (laugh) reírse a carcajadas

cactus /'kæktəs/ n (pl **-ti** /-taɪ/ or **-tuses**) cacto m

caddie, caddy /'kædɪ/ n (golf) portador m de palos

cadet /kə'det/ n cadete m

cadge /kædʒ/ vt/i gorronear

café /'kæfeɪ/ n cafetería f

cafeteria /kæfɪ'tɪərɪə/ n restaurante m autoservicio

caffeine /'kæfiːn/ n cafeína f

cage /keɪdʒ/ n jaula f. ● vt enjaular

cake /keɪk/ n pastel m, tarta f; (sponge) bizcocho m. ~ **of soap** pastilla f de jabón

calamity /kə'læmətɪ/ n calamidad f

calcium /'kælsɪəm/ n calcio m

calculat|e /'kælkjʊleɪt/ vt/i calcular. ~**ion** /-'leɪʃn/ n cálculo m. ~**or** n calculadora f

calculus /'kælkjʊləs/ n (Math) cálculo m

calendar /'kælɪndə(r)/ n calendario m

calf /kɑːf/ n (pl **calves**) (animal) ternero m; (of leg) pantorrilla f

calibre /'kælɪbə(r)/ n calibre m

call /kɔːl/ vt/i llamar. ● n llamada f; (shout) grito m; (visit) visita f. **be on** ~ estar de guardia. **long-distance** ~ llamada f de larga distancia, conferencia f. □ ~ **back** vt hacer volver; (on phone) volver a llamar. vi volver; (on phone) volver a llamar. □ ~ **for** vt pedir; (fetch) ir a buscar. □ ~ **off** vt suspender. □ ~ **on** vt pasar a visitar. □ ~ **out** vi dar voces. □ ~ **together** vt convocar. □ ~ **up** vt (Mil) llamar al servicio militar; (phone) llamar. ~ **box** n cabina f telefónica. ~**er** n visita f; (phone) el que llama m. ~**ing** n vocación f

callous /'kæləs/ a insensible, cruel

calm /kɑːm/ a (**-er, -est**) tranquilo; <sea> en calma. ● n tranquilidad f, calma f. ● vt calmar. ● vi calmarse. ~ **down** vi tranquilizarse. vt calmar. ~**ly** adv con calma

calorie /'kælərɪ/ n caloría f

calves /kɑːvz/ npl ⇒CALF

camcorder /'kæmkɔːdə(r)/ n videocámara f, camcórder m

came /keɪm/ ⇒COME

camel /'kæml/ n camello m

camera /'kæmərə/ n cámara f, máquina f fotográfica ∼**man** /-mən/ n camarógrafo m, cámara m

camouflage /'kæməflɑːʒ/ n camuflaje m. ● vt camuflar

camp /kæmp/ n campamento m. ● vi acampar. go ∼ing hacer camping

campaign /kæm'peɪn/ n campaña f. ● vi hacer campaña

camp: ∼**bed** n catre m de tijera. ∼**er** n campista m & f; (vehicle) cámper m. ∼**ground** n (Amer) ⇒∼SITE. ∼**ing** n camping m. ∼**site** n camping m

campus /'kæmpəs/ n (pl -puses) campus m, ciudad f universitaria

can[1] /kæn/, unstressed form /kən/

negative **can't, cannot** (formal);
past **could**

● auxiliary verb

····▶ (be able to) poder. I ∼'t lift it no lo puedo levantar. she says she ∼ come dice que puede venir

····▶ (be allowed to) poder. ∼ I smoke? ¿puedo fumar?

····▶ (know how to) saber. ∼ you swim? ¿sabes nadar?

····▶ (with verbs of perception) not translated. I ∼'t see you no te veo. I ∼ hear you better now ahora te oigo mejor

····▶ (in requests) ∼ I have a glass of water, please? ¿me trae un vaso de agua, por favor?. ∼ I have a kilo of cheese, please? ¿me da un kilo de queso, por favor?

····▶ (in offers) ∼ I help you? ¿te ayudo?; (in shop) ¿lo/la atienden?

can[2] /kæn/ n lata f, bote m. ● vt (pt canned) enlatar. ∼ned music música f grabada

Canad|a /'kænədə/ n (el) Canadá m. ∼**ian** /kə'neɪdɪən/ a & n canadiense (m & f)

canal /kə'næl/ n canal m

Canaries /kə'neərɪz/ npl = CANARY ISLANDS

canary /kə'neərɪ/ n canario m. **C**∼ **Islands** npl. the **C**∼ **Islands** las Islas Canarias

cancel /'kænsl/ vt (pt **cancelled**) cancelar; anular <command, cheque>; (delete) tachar. ∼**lation** /-'leɪʃn/ n cancelación f

cancer /'kænsə(r)/ n cáncer m. **C**∼ n (Astr) Cáncer m. ∼**ous** a canceroso

candid /'kændɪd/ a franco

candidate /'kændɪdeɪt/ n candidato m

candle /'kændl/ n vela f. ∼**stick** n candelero m

candour /'kændə(r)/ n franqueza f

candy /'kændɪ/ n (Amer) caramelo m, dulce f (LAm). ∼**floss** /-flɒs/ n algodón m de azúcar

cane /keɪn/ n caña f; (for baskets) mimbre m; (stick) bastón m; (for punishment) palmeta f. ● vt castigar con palmeta

canister /'kænɪstə(r)/ n bote m

cannabis /'kænəbɪs/ n cáñamo m índico, hachís m, cannabis m

cannibal /'kænɪbl/ n caníbal m. ∼**ism** n canibalismo m

cannon /'kænən/ n invar cañón m. ∼ **ball** n bala f de cañón

cannot /'kænət/ ⇒CAN[1]

canoe /kə'nuː/ n canoa f, piragua f. ● vi ir en canoa

canon /'kænən/ n canon m; (person) canónigo m. ∼**ize** vt canonizar

can opener n abrelatas m

canopy /'kænəpɪ/ n dosel m

can't /kɑːnt/ ⇒CAN[1]

cantankerous /kæn'tæŋkərəs/ a mal humorado

canteen /kæn'tiːn/ n cantina f; (of cutlery) juego m de cubiertos

canter /'kæntə(r)/ n medio galope m. ● vi ir a medio galope

canvas /'kænvəs/ n lona f; (artist's) lienzo m

canvass /'kænvəs/ vi hacer campaña, solicitar votos. ∼**ing** n solicitación f (de votos)

canyon /'kænjən/ n cañón m

cap /kæp/ n gorra f; (lid) tapa f; (of cartridge) cápsula f; (of pen) capuchón m.

● *vt* (*pt* **capped**) tapar, poner cápsula a; (outdo) superar

capab|ility /keɪpə'bɪlətɪ/ *n* capacidad *f*. ~**le** /'keɪpəbl/ *a* capaz

capacity /kə'pæsətɪ/ *n* capacidad *f*; (function) calidad *f*

cape /keɪp/ *n* (cloak) capa *f*; (Geog) cabo *m*

capital /'kæpɪtl/ *a* capital. ~ **letter** mayúscula *f*. ●*n* (town) capital *f*; (money) capital *m*. ~**ism** *n* capitalismo *m*. ~**ist** *a & n* capitalista (*m & f*.) ~**ize** *vt* capitalizar; escribir con mayúsculas *<word>*. ●*vi*. ~**ize on** aprovechar

capitulat|e /kə'pɪtʃʊleɪt/ *vi* capitular. ~**ion** /-'leɪʃn/ *n* capitulación *f*

Capricorn /'kæprɪkɔːn/ *n* Capricornio *m*

capsize /kæp'saɪz/ *vt* hacer volcar. ●*vi* volcarse

capsule /'kæpsjuːl/ *n* cápsula *f*

captain /'kæptɪn/ *n* capitán *m*; (of plane) comandante *m & f*. ●*vt* capitanear

caption /'kæpʃn/ *n* (heading) título *m*; (of cartoon etc) leyenda *f*

captivate /'kæptɪveɪt/ *vt* encantar

captiv|e /'kæptɪv/ *a & n* cautivo (*m*). ~**ity** /-'tɪvətɪ/ *n* cautiverio *m*, cautividad *f*

capture /'kæptʃə(r)/ *vt* capturar; atraer *<attention>*; (Mil) tomar. ●*n* apresamiento *m*; (Mil) toma *f*

car /kɑː(r)/ *n* coche *m*, carro *m* (LAm); (Amer, of train) vagón *m*

caramel /'kærəmel/ *n* azúcar *m* quemado; (sweet) caramelo *m*, dulce *m* (LAm)

caravan /'kærəvæn/ *n* caravana *f*

carbohydrate /kɑːbəʊ'haɪdreɪt/ *n* hidrato *m* de carbono

carbon /'kɑːbən/ *n* carbono *m*; (paper) carbón *m*. ~ **copy** copia *f* al carbón. ~ **dioxide** /daɪ'ɒksaɪd/ *n* anhídrido *m* carbónico. ~ **monoxide** /mə'nɒksaɪd/ *n* monóxido de carbono

carburettor /kɑːbjʊ'retə(r)/ *n* carburador *m*

carcass /'kɑːkəs/ *n* cuerpo *m* de animal muerto; (for meat) res *f* muerta

card /kɑːd/ *n* tarjeta *f*; (for games) carta *f*; (membership) carnet *m*; (records) ficha *f*. ~**board** *n* cartón *m*

cardigan /'kɑːdɪgən/ *n* chaqueta *f* de punto, rebeca *f*

cardinal /'kɑːdɪnəl/ *a* cardinal. ●*n* cardenal *m*

care /keə(r)/ *n* cuidado *m*; (worry) preocupación *f*; (protection) cargo *m*. ~ **of** a cuidado de, en casa de. take ~ tener cuidado. take ~ of cuidar de *<person>*; ocuparse de *<matter>*. ●*vi* interesarse. I don't ~ me da igual. □ ~ **about** *vt* preocuparse por. □ ~ **for** *vt* cuidar de; (like) querer

career /kə'rɪə(r)/ *n* carrera *f*. ●*vi* correr a toda velocidad

care: ~**free** *a* despreocupado. ~**ful** *a* cuidadoso; (cautious) prudente. be ~**ful** tener cuidado. ~**fully** *adv* con cuidado. ~**less** *a* negligente; (not worried) indiferente. ~**lessly** *adv* descuidadamente. ~**lessness** *n* descuido *m*

caress /kə'res/ *n* caricia *f*. ●*vt* acariciar

caretaker /'keəteɪkə(r)/ *n* vigilante *m*; (of flats etc) portero *m*

car ferry *n* transbordador *m* de coches

cargo /'kɑːgəʊ/ *n* (*pl* -**oes**) carga *f*

Caribbean /kærɪ'biːən/ *a* caribeño. **the** ~ (**Sea**) *n* el mar Caribe

caricature /'kærɪkətʃʊə(r)/ *n* caricatura *f*. ●*vt* caricaturizar

carnage /'kɑːnɪdʒ/ *n* carnicería *f*, matanza *f*

carnation /kɑː'neɪʃn/ *n* clavel *m*

carnival /'kɑːnɪvl/ *n* carnaval *m*

carol /'kærəl/ *n* villancico *m*

carousel /kærə'sel/ *n* tiovivo *m*, carrusel *m* (LAm); (for baggage) cinta *f* transportadora

carp /kɑːp/ *n* invar carpa *f*. □ ~ **at** *vi* quejarse de

car park *n* aparcamiento *m*, estacionamiento *m*

carpent|er /'kɑːpɪntə(r)/ *n* carpintero *m*. ~**ry** /-trɪ/ *n* carpintería *f*

carpet /'kɑːpɪt/ *n* alfombra *f*. ~ **sweeper** *n* cepillo *m* mecánico

carriage /'kærɪdʒ/ n coche m; (Mec) carro m; (transport) transporte m; (cost, bearing) porte m; (of train) vagón m. ~**way** n calzada f, carretera f

carrier /'kærɪə(r)/ n transportista m & f; (company) empresa f de transportes; (Med) portador m. ~ **bag** n bolsa f

carrot /'kærət/ n zanahoria f

carry /'kærɪ/ vt llevar; transportar <goods>; (involve) llevar consigo, implicar. ● vi <sounds> llegar, oírse. □ ~ **off** vt llevarse. □ ~ **on** vi seguir, continuar. □ ~ **out** vt realizar; cumplir <promise, threat>. ~ **cot** n cuna f portátil

carsick /'kɑːsɪk/ a mareado (por viajar en coche)

cart /kɑːt/ n carro m; (Amer, in supermarket, airport) carrito m. ● vt acarrear; (🖳, carry) llevar

carton /'kɑːtən/ n caja f de cartón

cartoon /kɑː'tuːn/ n caricatura f, chiste m; (strip) historieta f; (film) dibujos mpl animados

cartridge /'kɑːtrɪdʒ/ n cartucho m

carve /kɑːv/ vt tallar; trinchar <meat>

cascade /kæs'keɪd/ n cascada f. ● vi caer en cascadas

case /keɪs/ n caso m; (Jurid) proceso m; (crate) cajón m; (box) caja f; (suitcase) maleta f, petaca f (Mex). in any ~ en todo caso. in ~ he comes por si viene. in ~ of en caso de

cash /kæʃ/ n dinero m efectivo. pay (in) ~ pagar al contado. ● vt cobrar. ~ **in** (on) aprovecharse de. ~ **desk** n caja f. ~ **dispenser** n cajero m automático

cashier /kæ'ʃɪə(r)/ n cajero m

cashpoint /'kæʃpɔɪnt/ n cajero m automático

casino /kə'siːnəʊ/ n (pl -os) casino m

cask /kɑːsk/ n barril m

casket /'kɑːskɪt/ n cajita f; (Amer) ataúd m, cajón m (LAm)

casserole /'kæsərəʊl/ n cacerola f; (stew) guiso m, guisado m (Mex)

cassette /kə'set/ n cassette m & f

cast /kɑːst/ vt (pt cast) arrojar; fundir <metal>; emitir <vote>. ● n

lanzamiento m; (in play) reparto m; (mould) molde m

castanets /kæstə'nets/ npl castañuelas fpl

castaway /'kɑːstəweɪ/ n náufrago m

caster /'kɑːstə(r)/ n ruedecita f. ~ **sugar** n azúcar m extrafino

Castil|e /kæ'stiːl/ n Castilla f. ~**ian** /kæ'stɪlɪən/ a & n castellano (m)

cast: ~ **iron** n hierro m fundido. ~-**iron** a (fig) sólido

castle /'kɑːsl/ n castillo m; (Chess) torre f

cast-offs /'kɑːstɒfs/ npl desechos mpl

castrat|e /kæ'streɪt/ vt castrar. ~**ion** /-ʃn/ n castración f

casual /'kæʒʊəl/ a casual; <meeting> fortuito; <work> ocasional; <attitude> despreocupado; <clothes> informal, de sport. ~**ly** adv de paso

casualt|y /'kæʒʊəltɪ/ n (injured) herido m; (dead) víctima f; (in hospital) urgencias fpl. ~**ies** npl (Mil) bajas fpl

cat /kæt/ n gato m

Catalan /'kætəlæn/ a & n catalán (m)

catalogue /'kætəlɒg/ n catálogo m. ● vt catalogar

Catalonia /kætə'ləʊnɪə/ n Cataluña f

catalyst /'kætəlɪst/ n catalizador m

catamaran /kætəmə'ræn/ n catamarán m

catapult /'kætəpʌlt/ n catapulta f; (child's) tirachinas f, resortera f (Mex)

catarrh /kə'tɑː(r)/ n catarro m

catastroph|e /kə'tæstrəfɪ/ n catástrofe m. ~**ic** /kætə'strɒfɪk/ a catastrófico

catch /kætʃ/ vt (pt caught) coger (esp Spain), agarrar; tomar <train, bus>; (unawares) sorprender, pillar; (understand) entender; contagiarse de <disease>. ~ **a cold** resfriarse. ~ **sight of** avistar. ● vi (get stuck) engancharse; <fire> prenderse. ● n (by goalkeeper) parada f; (of fish) pesca f; (on door) pestillo m; (on window) cerradura f. □ ~ **on** vi 🖳 hacerse popular. □ ~

up *vi* poner al día. ~ **up with** alcanzar; ponerse al corriente de *<news etc>*. ~**ing** *a* contagioso. ~**y** *a* pegadizo

categor|ical /kætɪˈɡɒrɪkl/ *a* categórico. ~**y** /ˈkætɪɡəri/ *n* categoría *f*

cater /ˈkeɪtə(r)/ *vi* encargarse del servicio de comida. ~ **for** proveer a *<needs>*. ~**er** *n* proveedor *m*

caterpillar /ˈkætəpɪlə(r)/ *n* oruga *f*, azotador *m* (Mex)

cathedral /kəˈθiːdrəl/ *n* catedral *f*

catholic /ˈkæθəlɪk/ *a* universal. **C~** *a* & *n* católico (*m*). **C~ism** /kəˈθɒlɪsɪzəm/ *n* catolicismo *m*

cat: ~**nap** *n* sueñecito *m*. **C~seyes** *npl* (P) cataforas *mpl*

cattle /ˈkætl/ *npl* ganado *m*

catwalk *n* pasarela *f*

Caucasian /kɔːˈkeɪʒən/ *n*. **a male** ~ (Amer) un hombre de raza blanca

caught /kɔːt/ ⇒CATCH

cauliflower /ˈkɒlɪflaʊə(r)/ *n* coliflor *f*

cause /kɔːz/ *n* causa *f*, motivo *m*. ● *vt* causar

cautio|n /ˈkɔːʃn/ *n* cautela *f*; (warning) advertencia *f*. ● *vt* advertir; (Jurid) amonestar. ~**us** /-ʃəs/ *a* cauteloso, prudente

cavalry /ˈkævlrɪ/ *n* caballería *f*

cave /keɪv/ *n* cueva *f*. □ ~ **in** *vi* hundirse. ~**man** *n* troglodita *m*

cavern /ˈkævən/ *n* caverna *f*

caviare /ˈkævɪɑː(r)/ *n* caviar *m*

cavity /ˈkævɪtɪ/ *n* cavidad *f*; (in tooth) caries *f*

CD *abbr* (= **compact disc**) CD *m*. ~ **player** (reproductor *m* de) compact-disc *m*. ~**-ROM** *n* CD-ROM

cease /siːs/ *vt/i* cesar. ~**fire** *n* alto *m* el fuego, cese *m* del fuego (LAm)

cedar /ˈsiːdə(r)/ *n* cedro *m*

ceiling /ˈsiːlɪŋ/ *n* techo *m*

celebrat|e /ˈselɪbreɪt/ *vt* celebrar. ● *vi* divertirse. ~**ed** *a* célebre. ~**ion** /-ˈbreɪʃn/ *n* celebración *f*; (party) fiesta *f*

celebrity /sɪˈlebrətɪ/ *n* celebridad *f*

celery /ˈselərɪ/ *n* apio *m*

cell /sel/ *n* celda *f*; (Biol, Elec) célula *f*

cellar /ˈselə(r)/ *n* sótano *m*; (for wine) bodega *f*

cello /ˈtʃeləʊ/ *n* (*pl* **-os**) violonc(h)elo *m*, chelo *m*

Cellophane /ˈseləfeɪn/ *n* (P) celofán *m* (P)

celluloid /ˈseljʊlɔɪd/ *n* celuloide *m*

Celsius /ˈselsɪəs/ *a*. **20 degrees** ~ 20 grados centígrados *or* Celsio(s)

cement /sɪˈment/ *n* cemento *m*. ● *vt* cementar

cemetery /ˈsemətrɪ/ *n* cementerio *m*

cens|or /ˈsensə(r)/ *n* censor *m*. ● *vt* censurar. ~**ship** *n* censura *f*. ~**ure** /ˈsenʃə(r)/ *vt* censurar

census /ˈsensəs/ *n* censo *m*

cent /sent/ *n* centavo *m*

centenary /senˈtiːnərɪ/ *n* centenario *m*

centi|grade /ˈsentɪɡreɪd/ *a* centígrado. ~**litre** *n* centilitro *m*. ~**metre** *n* centímetro *m*. ~**pede** /-piːd/ *n* ciempiés *m*

central /ˈsentrəl/ *a* central; (of town) céntrico. ~ **heating** *n* calefacción *f* central. ~**ize** *vt* centralizar

centre /ˈsentə(r)/ *n* centro *m*. ● *vt* (*pt* **centred**) centrar. ● *vi* centrarse (on en)

century /ˈsentʃərɪ/ *n* siglo *m*

cereal /ˈsɪərɪəl/ *n* cereal *m*

ceremon|ial /serɪˈməʊnɪəl/ *a* & *n* ceremonial (*m*). ~**y** /ˈserɪmənɪ/ *n* ceremonia *f*

certain /ˈsɜːtn/ *a* cierto. **for** ~ seguro. **make** ~ **of** asegurarse de. ~**ly** *adv* desde luego. ~**ty** *n* certeza *f*

certificate /səˈtɪfɪkət/ *n* certificado *m*; (of birth, death etc) partida *f*

certify /ˈsɜːtɪfaɪ/ *vt* certificar

chafe /tʃeɪf/ *vt* rozar. ● *vi* rozarse

chaffinch /ˈtʃæfɪntʃ/ *n* pinzón *m*

chagrin /ˈʃæɡrɪn/ *n* disgusto *m*

chain /tʃeɪn/ *n* cadena *f*. ● *vt* encadenar. ~ **reaction** *n* reacción *f* en cadena. ~**-smoker** *n* fumador *m* que siempre tiene un cigarrillo encendido. ~ **store** *n* tienda *f* de una cadena

chair /tʃeə(r)/ *n* silla *f*; (Univ) cátedra *f*. ● *vt* presidir. ~**lift** *n* telesquí *m*, telesilla *m* (LAm). ∼**man** /-mən/ *n* presidente *m*

chalet /'ʃæleɪ/ *n* chalé *m*

chalk /tʃɔːk/ *n* (Geol) creta *f*; (stick) tiza *f*, gis *m* (Mex)

challeng|e /'tʃælɪndʒ/ *n* desafío *m*; (fig) reto *m*. ● *vt* desafiar; (question) poner en duda. ∼**ing** *a* estimulante

chamber /'tʃeɪmbə(r)/ *n* (old use) cámara *f*. ∼**maid** *n* camarera *f*. ∼**pot** *n* orinal *m*

champagne /ʃæm'peɪn/ *n* champaña *m*, champán *m*

champion /'tʃæmpɪən/ *n* campeón *m*. ● *vt* defender. ∼**ship** *n* campeonato *m*

chance /tʃɑːns/ *n* casualidad *f*; (likelihood) posibilidad *f*; (opportunity) oportunidad *f*; (risk) riesgo *m*. **by** ∼ por casualidad. ● *a* fortuito

chancellor /'tʃɑːnsələ(r)/ *n* canciller *m*; (Univ) rector *m*. **C**∼ **of the Exchequer** Ministro *m* de Hacienda

chandelier /ʃændə'lɪə(r)/ *n* araña *f* (de luces)

chang|e /tʃeɪndʒ/ *vt* cambiar; (substitute) reemplazar. ∼ **one's mind** cambiar de idea. ● *vi* cambiarse. ● *n* cambio *m*; (coins) cambio *m*, sencillo *m* (LAm), feria *f* (Mex); (money returned) cambio *m*, vuelta *f*, vuelto *m* (LAm). ∼**eable** *a* cambiable; <weather> variable. ∼**ing room** *n* (Sport) vestuario *m*, vestidor *m* (Mex); (in shop) probador *m*

channel /'tʃænl/ *n* canal *m*; (fig) medio *m*. ● *vt* (pt **channelled**) acanalar; (fig) encauzar. **the (English) C**∼ el Canal de la Mancha. **C**∼ **Islands** *npl*. **the C**∼ **Islands** las islas Anglonormandas. **C**∼ **Tunnel** *n*. **the C**∼ **Tunnel** el Eurotúnel

chant /tʃɑːnt/ *n* canto *m*. ● *vt/i* cantar

chao|s /'keɪɒs/ *n* caos *m*. ∼**tic** /-'ɒtɪk/ *a* caótico

chap /tʃæp/ *n* 🄸 tipo *m*, tío *m* 🄸. ● *vt* (pt **chapped**) agrietar. ● *vi* agrietarse

chapel /'tʃæpl/ *n* capilla *f*

chaperon /'ʃæpərəʊn/ *n* acompañante *f*

chapter /'tʃæptə(r)/ *n* capítulo *m*

char /tʃɑː(r)/ *vt* (pt **charred**) carbonizar

character /'kærəktə(r)/ *n* carácter *m*; (in book, play) personaje *m*. **in** ∼ característico. ∼**istic** /-'rɪstɪk/ *a* típico. ● *n* característica *f*. ∼**ize** *vt* caracterizar

charade /ʃə'rɑːd/ *n* farsa *f*. ∼**s** *npl* (game) charada *f*

charcoal /'tʃɑːkəʊl/ *n* carbón *m* vegetal; (for drawing) carboncillo *m*

charge /tʃɑːdʒ/ *n* precio *m*; (Elec, Mil) carga *f*; (Jurid) acusación *f*; (task, custody) encargo *m*; (responsibility) responsabilidad *f*. **in** ∼ **of** responsable de, encargado de. **the person in** ∼ la persona responsable. **take** ∼ **of** encargarse de. ● *vt* pedir; (Elec, Mil) cargar; (Jurid) acusar. ● *vi* cargar; <animal> embestir (**at** contra)

charit|able /'tʃærɪtəbl/ *a* caritativo. ∼**y** /'tʃærɪtɪ/ *n* caridad *f*; (society) institución *f* benéfica

charm /tʃɑːm/ *n* encanto *m*; (spell) hechizo *m*; (on bracelet) dije *m*, amuleto *m*. ● *vt* encantar. ∼**ing** *a* encantador

chart /tʃɑːt/ *n* (Aviat, Naut) carta *f* de navegación; (table) tabla *f*

charter /'tʃɑːtə(r)/ *n* carta *f*. ● *vt* alquilar <bus, train>; fletar <plane, ship>. ∼ **flight** *n* vuelo *m* chárter

chase /tʃeɪs/ *vt* perseguir. ● *vi* correr (after tras). ● *n* persecución *f*. □ ∼ **away**, ∼ **off** *vt* ahuyentar

chassis /'ʃæsɪ/ *n* chasis *m*

chastise /tʃæs'taɪz/ *vt* castigar

chastity /'tʃæstətɪ/ *n* castidad *f*

chat /tʃæt/ *n* charla *f*, conversación *f* (LAm), plática *f* (Mex). ● *vi* (pt **chatted**) charlar, conversar (LAm), platicar (Mex)

chatter /'tʃætə(r)/ *n* charla *f*. ● *vi* charlar. **his teeth are** ∼**ing** le castañetean los dientes. ∼**box** *n* parlanchín *m*

chauffeur /'ʃəʊfə(r)/ *n* chófer *m*

chauvinis|m /'ʃəʊvɪnɪzəm/ *n* patriotería *f*; (male) machismo *m*. ∼**t** *n* patriotero *m*; (male) machista *m*

cheap /tʃiːp/ *a* (**-er**, **-est**) barato; (poor quality) de baja calidad; <rate>

económico. ~**(ly)** *adv* barato, a bajo precio

cheat /'tʃiːt/ *vt* defraudar; (deceive) engañar. ●*vi* (at cards) hacer trampas. ●*n* trampa *f*; (person) tramposo *m*

check /tʃek/ *vt* comprobar; (examine) inspeccionar; (curb) frenar. ●*vi* comprobar. ●*n* comprobación *f*; (of tickets) control *m*; (curb) freno *m*; (Chess) jaque *m*; (pattern) cuadro *m*; (Amer, bill) cuenta *f*; (Amer, cheque) cheque *m*. □~ **in** *vi* registrarse; (at airport) facturar el equipaje, chequear el equipaje (LAm), registrar el equipaje (Mex). □~ **out** *vi* pagar la cuenta y marcharse. □~ **up** *vi* confirmar. □~ **up on** *vt* investigar. ~**book** *n* (Amer) ⇒CHEQUEBOOK. ~**ered** /'tʃekəd/ *a* (Amer) ⇒CHEQUERED

checkers /'tʃekəz/ *n* (Amer) damas *fpl*

check: ~**mate** *n* jaque *m* mate. ●*vt* dar mate a. ~**out** *n* caja *f*. ~**point** control *m*. ~**up** *n* chequeo *m*, revisión

cheek /tʃiːk/ *n* mejilla *f*; (fig) descaro *m*. ~**bone** *n* pómulo *m*. ~**y** *a* descarado

cheep /tʃiːp/ *vi* piar

cheer /tʃɪə(r)/ *n* alegría *f*; (applause) viva *m*. ~**s!** ¡salud!.● *vt* alegrar; (applaud) aplaudir. ●*vi* alegrarse; (applaud) aplaudir. ~ **up!** ¡anímate! ~**ful** *a* alegre

cheerio /tʃɪərɪ'əʊ/ *int* 🔲 ¡adiós!, ¡hasta luego!

cheerless /'tʃɪəlɪs/ *a* triste

cheese /tʃiːz/ *n* queso *m*

cheetah /'tʃiːtə/ *n* guepardo *m*

chef /ʃef/ *n* jefe *m* de cocina

chemical /'kemɪkl/ *a* químico. ●*n* producto *m* químico

chemist /'kemɪst/ *n* farmacéutico *m*; (scientist) químico *m*. ~**ry** *n* química *f*. ~'**s (shop)** *n* farmacia *f*

cheque /tʃek/ *n* cheque *m*, talón *m*. ~**book** *n* chequera *f*, talonario *m*

cherish /'tʃerɪʃ/ *vt* cuidar; (love) querer; abrigar <*hope*>

cherry /'tʃerɪ/ *n* cereza *f*. ~ **tree** *n* cerezo *m*

chess /tʃes/ *n* ajedrez *m*. ~**board** *n* tablero *m* de ajedrez

chest /tʃest/ *n* pecho *m*; (box) cofre *m*, cajón *m*

chestnut /'tʃesnʌt/ *n* castaña *f*. ●*a* castaño. ~ **tree** *n* castaño *m*

chest of drawers *n* cómoda *f*

chew /tʃuː/ *vt* masticar. ~**ing gum** *n* chicle *m*

chic /ʃiːk/ *a* elegante

chick /tʃɪk/ *n* polluelo *m*. ~**en** /'tʃɪkɪn/ *n* pollo *m*. ●*a* 🔲 cobarde. □~**en out** *vi* 🔲 acobardarse. ~**en-pox** /'tʃɪkɪnpɒks/ *n* varicela *f*. ~**pea** *n* garbanzo *m*

chicory /'tʃɪkərɪ/ *n* (in coffee) achicoria *f*; (in salad) escarola *f*

chief /tʃiːf/ *n* jefe *m*. ●*a* principal. ~**ly** *adv* principalmente

chilblain /'tʃɪlbleɪn/ *n* sabañón *m*

child /tʃaɪld/ *n* (*pl* **children** /'tʃɪldrən/) niño *m*; (offspring) hijo *m*. ~**birth** *n* parto *m*. ~**hood** *n* niñez *f*. ~**ish** *a* infantil. ~**less** *a* sin hijos. ~**like** *a* ingenuo, de niño

Chile /'tʃɪlɪ/ *n* Chile *m*. ~**an** *a* & *n* chileno (*m*)

chill /tʃɪl/ *n* frío *m*; (illness) resfriado *m*. ●*a* frío. ●*vt* enfriar; refrigerar <*food*>

chilli /'tʃɪlɪ/ *n* (*pl* -**ies**) chile *m*

chilly /'tʃɪlɪ/ *a* frío

chime /tʃaɪm/ *n* carillón *m*. ●*vt* tocar <*bells*>; dar <*hours*>. ●*vi* repicar

chimney /'tʃɪmnɪ/ *n* (*pl* -**eys**) chimenea *f*. ~ **sweep** *n* deshollinador *m*

chimpanzee /tʃɪmpæn'ziː/ *n* chimpancé *m*

chin /tʃɪn/ *n* barbilla *f*

china /'tʃaɪnə/ *n* porcelana *f*

Chin|a /'tʃaɪnə/ *n* China *f*. ~**ese** /-'niːz/ *a* & *n* chino (*m*)

chink /tʃɪŋk/ *n* (crack) grieta *f*; (sound) tintín *m*. ●*vi* tintinear

chip /tʃɪp/ *n* pedacito *m*; (splinter) astilla *f*; (Culin) patata *f* frita, papa *f* frita (LAm); (in gambling) ficha *f*; (Comp) chip *m*. **have a ~ on one's shoulder** guardar rencor. ●*vt* (*pt* **chipped**) desportillar. □~ **in** *vi* 🔲 interrumpir; (with money) contribuir

chiropodist /kɪˈrɒpədɪst/ n callista m & f, pedicuro m

chirp /tʃɜːp/ n pío m. ● vi piar. ~**y** a alegre

chisel /ˈtʃɪzl/ n formón m. ● vt (pt **chiselled**) cincelar

chivalr|ous /ˈʃɪvəlrəs/ a caballeroso. ~**y** /-rɪ/ n caballerosidad f

chlorine /ˈklɔːriːn/ n cloro m

chock /tʃɒk/ n cuña f. ~**-a-block** a, ~**-full** a atestado

chocolate /ˈtʃɒklət/ n chocolate m; (individual sweet) bombón m, chocolate m (LAm)

choice /tʃɔɪs/ n elección f; (preference) preferencia f. ● a escogido

choir /ˈkwaɪə(r)/ n coro m

choke /tʃəʊk/ vt sofocar. ● vi sofocarse. ● n (Auto) choke m, estárter m, ahogador m (Mex)

cholera /ˈkɒlərə/ n cólera m

cholesterol /kəˈlestərɒl/ n colesterol m

choose /tʃuːz/ vt/i (pt **chose**, pp **chosen**) elegir, escoger. ~**y** a 🄸 exigente

chop /tʃɒp/ vt (pt **chopped**) cortar. ● n (Culin) chuleta f. □ ~ **down** vt talar. □ ~ **off** vt cortar. ~**per** n hacha f; (butcher's) cuchilla f. ~**py** a picado

chord /kɔːd/ n (Mus) acorde m

chore /tʃɔː(r)/ n tarea f, faena f. **household** ~**s** npl quehaceres mpl domésticos

chorus /ˈkɔːrəs/ n coro m; (of song) estribillo m

chose /tʃəʊz/, **chosen** /ˈtʃəʊzn/ ⇒CHOOSE

Christ /kraɪst/ n Cristo m

christen /ˈkrɪsn/ vt bautizar. ~**ing** n bautizo m

Christian /ˈkrɪstjən/ a & n cristiano (m). ~**ity** /krɪstɪˈrænətɪ/ n cristianismo m. ~ **name** n nombre m de pila

Christmas /ˈkrɪsməs/ n Navidad f. **Merry** ~! ¡Feliz Navidad!, ¡Felices Pascuas! **Father** ~ Papá m Noel. ● a de Navidad, navideño. ~ **card** n tarjeta f de Navidad f. ~ **day** n día m de Navidad. ~ **Eve** n Nochebuena f. ~ **tree** n árbol m de Navidad

chrom|e /krəʊm/ n cromo m. ~**ium** /ˈkrəʊmɪəm/ n cromo m

chromosome /ˈkrəʊməsəʊm/ n cromosoma m

chronic /ˈkrɒnɪk/ a crónico; (🄸, bad) terrible

chronicle /ˈkrɒnɪkl/ n crónica f. ● vt historiar

chronological /krɒnəˈlɒdʒɪkl/ a cronológico

chubby /ˈtʃʌbɪ/ a (**-ier, -iest**) regordete; <person> gordinflón 🄸

chuck /tʃʌk/ vt 🄸 tirar. □ ~ **out** vt tirar

chuckle /ˈtʃʌkl/ n risa f ahogada. ● vi reírse entre dientes

chug /tʃʌg/ vi (pt **chugged**) (of motor) traquetear

chum /tʃʌm/ n amigo m, compinche m, cuate m (Mex)

chunk /tʃʌŋk/ n trozo m grueso. ~**y** a macizo

church /ˈtʃɜːtʃ/ n iglesia f. ~**yard** n cementerio m

churn /ˈtʃɜːn/ n (for milk) lechera f, cántara f; (for making butter) mantequera f. ● vt agitar. □ ~ **out** vt producir en profusión

chute /ʃuːt/ n tobogán m

cider /ˈsaɪdə(r)/ n sidra f

cigar /sɪˈgɑː(r)/ n puro m

cigarette /sɪgəˈret/ n cigarrillo m. ~ **end** n colilla f. ~ **holder** n boquilla f. ~ **lighter** n mechero m, encendedor m

cinecamera /ˈsɪnɪkæmərə/ n tomavistas m, filmadora f (LAm)

cinema /ˈsɪnəmə/ n cine m

cipher /ˈsaɪfə(r)/ n (Math, fig) cero m; (code) clave f

circle /ˈsɜːkl/ n círculo m; (in theatre) anfiteatro m. ● vt girar alrededor de. ● vi dar vueltas

circuit /ˈsɜːkɪt/ n circuito m

circular /ˈsɜːkjʊlə(r)/ a & n circular (f)

circulat|e /ˈsɜːkjʊleɪt/ vt hacer circular. ● vi circular. ~**ion** /-ˈleɪʃn/ n circulación f; (number of copies) tirada f

circumcise /ˈsɜːkəmsaɪz/ vt circuncidar

circumference /sə'kʌmfərəns/ n circunferencia f

circumstance /'sɜːkəmstəns/ n circunstancia f. ~s (means) npl situación f económica

circus /'sɜːkəs/ n circo m

cistern /'sɪstən/ n cisterna f

cite /saɪt/ vt citar

citizen /'sɪtɪzn/ n ciudadano m; (inhabitant) habitante m & f

citrus /'sɪtrəs/ n. ~ fruits cítricos mpl

city /'sɪtɪ/ n ciudad f; the C~ el centro m financiero de Londres

civic /'sɪvɪk/ a cívico

civil /'sɪvl/ a civil; (polite) cortés

civilian /sɪ'vɪlɪən/ a & n civil (m & f)

civiliz|ation /sɪvɪlaɪ'zeɪʃn/ n civilización f. ~ed /'sɪvəlaɪzd/ a civilizado.

civil: ~ **servant** n funcionario m (del Estado), burócrata m & f (Mex). ~ **service** n administración f pública. ~ **war** n guerra f civil

clad /klæd/ ⇒CLOTHE

claim /kleɪm/ vt reclamar; (assert) pretender. ●n reclamación f; (right) derecho m; (Jurid) demanda f

clairvoyant /kleə'vɔɪənt/ n clarividente m & f

clam /klæm/ n almeja f. ●vi (pt clammed). ~ up 🔲 ponerse muy poco comunicativo

clamber /'klæmbə(r)/ vi trepar a gatas

clammy /'klæmɪ/ a (-ier, -iest) húmedo

clamour /'klæmə(r)/ n clamor m. ●vi. ~ for pedir a gritos

clamp /klæmp/ n abrazadera f; (Auto) cepo m. ●vt sujetar con abrazadera; poner cepo a <car>. ▫~ **down on** vt reprimir

clan /klæn/ n clan m

clang /klæŋ/ n sonido m metálico

clap /klæp/ vt (pt clapped) aplaudir; batir <hands>. ●vi aplaudir. ●n palmada f; (of thunder) trueno m

clarif|ication /klærɪfɪ'keɪʃn/ n aclaración f. ~y /'klærɪfaɪ/ vt aclarar. ●vi aclararse

clarinet /klærɪ'net/ n clarinete m

clarity /'klærətɪ/ n claridad f

clash /klæʃ/ n choque m; (noise) estruendo m; (contrast) contraste m; (fig) conflicto m. ●vt golpear. ●vi encontrarse; <colours> desentonar

clasp /klɑːsp/ n cierre m. ●vt agarrar; apretar <hand>

class /klɑːs/ n clase f. **evening** ~ n clase nocturna. ●vt clasificar

classic /'klæsɪk/ a & n clásico (m). ~al a clásico. ~s npl estudios mpl clásicos

classif|ication /klæsɪfɪ'keɪʃn/ n clasificación f. ~y /'klæsɪfaɪ/ vt clasificar

class: ~**room** n aula f, clase f. ~**y** a 🔲 elegante

clatter /'klætə(r)/ n ruido m; (of train) traqueteo m. ●vi hacer ruido

clause /klɔːz/ n cláusula f; (Gram) oración f

claustrophobia /klɔːstrə'fəʊbɪə/ n claustrofobia f

claw /klɔː/ n garra f; (of cat) uña f; (of crab) pinza f. ●vt arañar

clay /kleɪ/ n arcilla f

clean /kliːn/ a (-er, -est) limpio; <stroke> bien definido. ●adv completamente. ●vt limpiar. ●vi limpiar. ▫~ **up** vt hacer la limpieza. ~**er** n persona f que hace la limpieza. ~**liness** /'klenlɪnɪs/ n limpieza f

cleans|e /klenz/ vt limpiar. ~**er** n producto m de limpieza; (for skin) crema f de limpieza. ~**ing cream** n crema f de limpieza

clear /klɪə(r)/ a (-er, -est) claro; (transparent) transparente; (without obstacles) libre; <profit> neto; <sky> despejado. **keep** ~ **of** evitar. ●adv claramente. ●vt despejar; liquidar <goods>; (Jurid) absolver; (jump over) saltar por encima de; quitar, levantar (LAm) <table>. ▫~ **off** vi 🔀, ~ **out** vi 🔲, (go away) largarse. ▫~ **up** vt (tidy) ordenar; aclarar <mystery>. vi <weather> despejarse. ~**ance** n (removal of obstructions) despeje m; (authorization) permiso m; (by security) acreditación f. ~**ing** n claro m. ~**ly** adv evidentemente.

~**way** *n* carretera *f* en la que no se permite parar

cleavage /'kliːvɪdʒ/ *n* escote *m*

clef /klef/ *n* (Mus) clave *f*

clench /klentʃ/ *vt* apretar

clergy /'klɜːdʒɪ/ *n* clero *m*. ~**man** /-mən/ *n* clérigo *m*

cleric /'klerɪk/ *n* clérigo *m*. ~**al** *a* clerical; (of clerks) de oficina

clerk /klɑːk/ *n* empleado *m*; (Amer, salesclerk) dependiente *m*, vendedor *m*

clever /'klevə(r)/ *a* (**-er, -est**) inteligente; (skilful) hábil. ~**ly** *adv* inteligentemente; (with skill) hábilmente. ~**ness** *n* inteligencia *f*

cliché /'kliːʃeɪ/ *n* lugar *m* común, cliché *m*

click /klɪk/ *n* golpecito *m*. ● *vi* chascar; Ⅰ llevarse bien. ● *vt* chasquear

client /'klaɪənt/ *n* cliente *m*

cliff /klɪf/ *n* acantilado *m*

climat|e /'klaɪmət/ *n* clima *m*. ~**ic** /-'mætɪk/ *a* climático

climax /'klaɪmæks/ *n* clímax *m*; (orgasm) orgasmo *m*

climb /klaɪm/ *vt* subir *<stairs>*; trepar *<tree>*; escalar *<mountain>*. ● *vi* subir. ● *n* subida *f*. □ ~ **down** *vi* bajar; (fig) ceder. ~**er** *n* (Sport) alpinista *m* & *f*, andinista *m* & *f* (LAm); (plant) trepadora *f*

clinch /klɪntʃ/ *vt* cerrar *<deal>*

cling /klɪŋ/ *vi* (*pt* **clung**) agarrarse; (stick) pegarse

clinic /'klɪnɪk/ *n* centro *m* médico; (private hospital) clínica *f*. ~**al** *a* clínico

clink /klɪŋk/ *n* tintineo *m*. ● *vt* hacer tintinear. ● *vi* tintinear

clip /klɪp/ *n* *<fastener>* clip *m*; (for paper) sujetapapeles *m*; (for hair) horquilla *f*. ● *vt* (*pt* **clipped**) (cut) cortar; (join) sujetar. ~**pers** /'klɪpəz/ *npl* (for hair) maquinilla *f* para cortar el pelo; (for nails) cortaúñas *m*. ~**ping** *n* recorte *m*

cloak /kləʊk/ *n* capa *f*. ~**room** *n* guardarropa *m*; (toilet) lavabo *m*, baño *m* (LAm)

clock /klɒk/ *n* reloj *m*. ~**wise** *a/adv* en el sentido de las agujas del re-

loj. ~**work** *n* mecanismo *m* de relojería. **like** ~**work** con precisión

clog /klɒg/ *n* zueco *m*. ● *vt* (*pt* **clogged**) atascar

cloister /'klɔɪstə(r)/ *n* claustro *m*

close[1] /kləʊs/ *a* (**-er, -est**) cercano; (together) apretado; *<friend>* íntimo; *<weather>* bochornoso; *<link etc>* estrecho; *<game, battle>* reñido. **have a** ~ **shave** (fig) escaparse de milagro. ● *adv* cerca. ● *n* recinto *m*

close[2] /kləʊz/ *vt* cerrar. ● *vi* cerrarse; (end) terminar. ~ **down** *vt/i* cerrar. ● *n* fin *m*. ~**d** *a* cerrado

closely /'kləʊslɪ/ *adv* estrechamente; (at a short distance) de cerca; (with attention) detenidamente; (precisely) rigurosamente

closet /'klɒzɪt/ *n* (Amer) armario *m*; (for clothes) armario *m*, closet *m* (LAm)

close-up /'kləʊsʌp/ *n* (Cinema etc) primer plano *m*

closure /'kləʊʒə(r)/ *n* cierre *m*

clot /klɒt/ *n* (Med) coágulo *m*; Ⅰ tonto *m*. ● *vi* (*pt* **clotted**) cuajarse; *<blood>* coagularse

cloth /klɒθ/ *n* tela *f*; (duster) trapo *m*; (tablecloth) mantel *m*

cloth|e /kləʊð/ *vt* (*pt* **clothed** *or* **clad**) vestir. ~**es** /kləʊðz/ *npl* ropa. ~**espin**, ~**espeg** (Amer) *n* pinza *f* (para tender la ropa). ~**ing** *n* ropa *f*

cloud /klaʊd/ *n* nube *f*. ● ~ **over** *vi* nublarse. ~**y** *a* (**-ier, -iest**) nublado; *<liquid>* turbio

clout /klaʊt/ *n* bofetada *f*. ● *vt* abofetear

clove /kləʊv/ *n* clavo *m*. ~ **of garlic** *n* diente *m* de ajo

clover /'kləʊvə(r)/ *n* trébol *m*

clown /klaʊn/ *n* payaso *m*. ● *vi* hacer el payaso

club /klʌb/ *n* club *m*; (weapon) porra *f*; (golf club) palo *m* de golf; (at cards) trébol *m*. ● *vt* (*pt* **clubbed**) apo-rrear. □ ~ **together** *vi* contribuir con dinero (**to para**)

cluck /klʌk/ *vi* cloquear

clue /kluː/ *n* pista *f*; (in crosswords) indicación *f*. **not to have a** ~ no tener la menor idea

clump /klʌmp/ *n* grupo *m*. ● *vt* agrupar

clums|iness /ˈklʌmzɪnɪs/ n torpeza f. ~**y** /ˈklʌmzɪ/ a (**-ier, -iest**) torpe

clung /klʌŋ/ ⇒CLING

cluster /ˈklʌstə(r)/ n grupo m. ● vi agruparse

clutch /klʌtʃ/ vt agarrar. ● n (Auto) embrague m

clutter /ˈklʌtə(r)/ n desorden m. ● vt. ~ (**up**) abarrotar. ~**ed** /ˈklʌtəd/ a abarratado de cosas

coach /kəʊtʃ/ n autocar m, autobús m; (of train) vagón m; (horse-drawn) coche m; (Sport) entrenador m. ● vt (Sport) entrenar

coal /kəʊl/ n carbón m

coalition /kəʊəˈlɪʃn/ n coalición f

coarse /kɔːs/ a (**-er, -est**) grueso; <material> basto; (person, language) ordinario

coast /kəʊst/ n costa f. ● vi (with cycle) deslizarse sin pedalear; (with car) ir en punto muerto. ~**al** a costero. ~**guard** n guardacostas m. ~**line** n litoral m

coat /kəʊt/ n abrigo m; (jacket) chaqueta f; (of animal) pelo m; (of paint) mano f. ● vt cubrir, revestir. ~**hanger** n percha f, gancho m (LAm). ~**ing** n capa f. ~ **of arms** n escudo m de armas

coax /kəʊks/ vt engatusar

cobbler /ˈkɒblə(r)/ n zapatero m (remendón)

cobblestone /ˈkɒbəlstəʊn/ n adoquín m

cobweb /ˈkɒbweb/ n telaraña f

cocaine /kəˈkeɪn/ n cocaína f

cock /kɒk/ n (cockerel) gallo m; (male bird) macho m. ● vt amartillar <gun>; aguzar <ears>. ~**erel** /ˈkɒkərəl/ n gallo m. ~**-eyed** /-aɪd/ a 🔲 torcido

cockney /ˈkɒknɪ/ a & n (pl **-eys**) londinense (m & f) (del este de Londres)

cockpit /ˈkɒkpɪt/ n (in aircraft) cabina f del piloto

cockroach /ˈkɒkrəʊtʃ/ n cucaracha f

cocktail /ˈkɒkteɪl/ n cóctel m

cock-up /ˈkɒkʌp/ n 🔲 lío m

cocky /ˈkɒkɪ/ a (**-ier, -iest**) engreído

cocoa /ˈkəʊkəʊ/ n cacao m; (drink) chocolate m, cocoa f (LAm)

coconut /ˈkəʊkənʌt/ n coco m

cocoon /kəˈkuːn/ n capullo m

cod /kɒd/ n invar bacalao m

code /kəʊd/ n código m; (secret) clave f; in ~ en clave

coeducational /kəʊedʒʊˈkeɪʃənl/ a mixto

coerce /kəʊˈɜːs/ vt coaccionar. ~**ion** /-ʃn/ n coacción f

coffee /ˈkɒfɪ/ n café m. ~ **bean** n grano m de café. ~ **maker** n cafetera f. ~**pot** n cafetera f

coffin /ˈkɒfɪn/ n ataúd m, cajón m (LAm)

cog /kɒg/ n diente m; (fig) pieza f

coherent /kəʊˈhɪərənt/ a coherente

coil /kɔɪl/ vt enrollar. ● n rollo m; (one ring) vuelta f

coin /kɔɪn/ n moneda f. ● vt acuñar

coincide /kəʊɪnˈsaɪd/ vi coincidir. ~**nce** /kəʊˈɪnsɪdəns/ n casualidad f. ~**ntal** /kəʊɪnsɪˈdentl/ a casual

coke /kəʊk/ n (coal) coque m. **C**~ (P) Coca-Cola f (P)

colander /ˈkʌləndə(r)/ n colador m

cold /kəʊld/ a (**-er, -est**) frío. be ~ <person> tener frío. it is ~ (weather) hace frío. ● n frío m; (Med) resfriado m. have a ~ estar resfriado. ~**-blooded** /-ˈblʌdɪd/ a <animal> de sangre fría; <murder> a sangre fría. ~**-shoulder** /-ˈʃəʊldə(r)/ vt tratar con frialdad. ~ **sore** n herpes m labial. ~ **storage** n conservación f en frigorífico

coleslaw /ˈkəʊlslɔː/ n ensalada f de col

collaborat|e /kəˈlæbəreɪt/ vi colaborar. ~**ion** /-ˈreɪʃn/ n colaboración f. ~**or** n colaborador m

collaps|e /kəˈlæps/ vi derrumbarse; (Med) sufrir un colapso. ● n derrumbamiento m; (Med) colapso m. ~**ible** /-əbl/ a plegable

collar /ˈkɒlə(r)/ n cuello m; (for animals) collar m. ● vt 🔲 hurtar. ~**bone** n clavícula f

colleague /ˈkɒliːg/ n colega m & f

collect /kə'lekt/ vt reunir; (hobby) coleccionar, juntar (LAm); (pick up) recoger; cobrar <rent>. ● vi <people> reunirse; <things> acumularse. **~ion** /-ʃn/ n colección f; (in church) colecta f; (of post) recogida f. **~or** n coleccionista m & f

college /'kɒlɪdʒ/ n colegio m; (of art, music etc) escuela f; (Amer) universidad f

colli|de /kə'laɪd/ vi chocar. **~sion** /-'lɪʒn/ n choque m

colloquial /kə'ləʊkwɪəl/ a coloquial

Colombia /kə'lʌmbɪə/ n Colombia f. **~n** a & n colombiano (m)

colon /'kəʊlən/ n (Gram) dos puntos mpl; (Med) colon m

colonel /'kɜ:nl/ n coronel m

colon|ial /kə'ləʊnɪəl/ a colonial. **~ize** /'kɒlənaɪz/ vt colonizar. **~y** /'kɒlənɪ/ n colonia f

colossal /kə'lɒsl/ a colosal

colour /'kʌlə(r)/ n color m. off **~** (fig) indispuesto. ● a de color(es), en color(es) ● vt colorear; (dye) teñir. **~-blind** a daltoniano. **~ed** /'kʌləd/ a de color. **~ful** a lleno de color; (fig) pintoresco. **~ing** n color; (food colouring) colorante m. **~less** a incoloro

column /'kɒləm/ n columna f. **~ist** n columnista m & f

coma /'kəʊmə/ n coma m

comb /kəʊm/ n peine m. ● vt (search) registrar. **~** one's hair peinarse

combat /'kɒmbæt/ n combate m. ● vt (pt **combated**) combatir

combination /kɒmbɪ'neɪʃn/ n combinación f

combine /kəm'baɪn/ vt combinar. ● vi combinarse. ● /'kɒmbaɪn/ n asociación f. **~ harvester** n cosechadora f

combustion /kəm'bʌstʃən/ n combustión f

come /kʌm/ vi (pt **came**, pp **come**) venir; (occur) pasar. □ **~ across** vt encontrarse con <person>; encontrar <object>. □ **~ apart** vi deshacerse. □ **~ away** vi (leave) salir; (become detached) salirse. □ **~ back** vi volver. □ **~ by** vt obtener. □ **~ down** vi bajar. □ **~ in** vi

entrar; (arrive) llegar. □ **~ into** vt entrar en; heredar <money>. □ **~ off** vi desprenderse; (succeed) tener éxito. vt. **~ off it!** ⊡ ¡no me vengas con eso! □ **~ on** vi (start to work) encenderse. **~ on, hurry up!** ¡vamos, date prisa! □ **~ out** vi salir. □ **~ round** vi (after fainting) volver en sí; (be converted) cambiar de idea; (visit) venir. □ **~ to** vt llegar a <decision etc>. □ **~ up** vi subir; (fig) surgir. □ **~ up with** vt proponer <idea>. **~back** n retorno m; (retort) réplica f

comedian /kə'mi:dɪən/ n cómico m

comedy /'kɒmədɪ/ n comedia f

comet /'kɒmɪt/ n cometa m

comfort /'kʌmfət/ n comodidad f; (consolation) consuelo m. ● vt consolar. **~able** a cómodo. **~er** n (for baby) chupete m, chupón m (LAm); (Amer, for bed) edredón m

comic /'kɒmɪk/ a cómico. ● n cómico m; (periodical) revista f de historietas, tebeo m. **~al** a cómico. **~ strip** n tira f cómica

coming /'kʌmɪŋ/ n llegada f. **~s and goings** idas fpl y venidas. ● a próximo; <week, month etc> que viene

comma /'kɒmə/ n coma f

command /kə'mɑ:nd/ n orden f; (mastery) dominio m. ● vt ordenar; imponer <respect>

commandeer /kɒmən'dɪə(r)/ vt requisar

command: ~er n comandante m. **~ing** a imponente. **~ment** n mandamiento m

commando /kə'mɑ:ndəʊ/ n (pl **-os**) comando m

commemorat|e /kə'meməreɪt/ vt conmemorar. **~ion** /-'reɪʃn/ n conmemoración f. **~ive** /-ətɪv/ a conmemorativo

commence /kə'mens/ vt dar comienzo a. ● vi iniciarse

commend /kə'mend/ vt alabar. **~able** a loable. **~ation** /kɒmen'deɪʃn/ n elogio m

comment /'kɒment/ n observación f. ● vi hacer observaciones (**on** sobre)

commentary /'kɒməntrɪ/ n comentario m; (Radio, TV) reportaje m

commentat|e /'kɒmənteɪt/ vi narrar. ~**or** n (Radio, TV) locutor m

commerc|e /'kɒmɜːs/ n comercio m. ~**ial** /kə'mɜːʃl/ a comercial. ●n anuncio m; aviso m (LAm). ~**ialize** vt comercializar

commiserat|e /kə'mɪzəreɪt/ vi compadecerse (**with** de). ~**ion** /-'reɪʃn/ n conmiseración f

commission /kə'mɪʃn/ n comisión f. **out of** ~ fuera de servicio. ●vt encargar; (Mil) nombrar oficial

commissionaire /kəmɪʃə'neə(r)/ n portero m

commit /kə'mɪt/ vt (pt **committed**) cometer; (entrust) confiar. ~ **o.s.** comprometerse. ~**ment** n compromiso m

committee /kə'mɪtɪ/ n comité m

commodity /kə'mɒdətɪ/ n producto m, artículo m

common /'kɒmən/ a (-**er**, -**est**) común; (usual) corriente; (vulgar) ordinario. ●n. **in** ~ en común. ~**er** n plebeyo m. ~ **law** n derecho m consuetudinario. ~**ly** adv comúnmente. **C**~ **Market** n Mercado m Común. ~**place** a banal. ●n banalidad f. ~ **room** n sala f común, salón m común. **C**~**s** n. **the (House of) C**~**s** la Cámara de los Comunes. ~ **sense** n sentido m común. **C**~**wealth** n. **the C**~**wealth** la Mancomunidad f Británica

commotion /kə'məʊʃn/ n confusión f

commune /'kɒmjuːn/ n comuna f

communicat|e /kə'mjuːnɪkeɪt/ vt comunicar. ●vi comunicarse. ~**ion** /-'keɪʃn/ n comunicación f. ~**ive** /-ətɪv/ a comunicativo

communion /kə'mjuːnɪən/ n comunión f

communis|m /'kɒmjʊnɪsəm/ n comunismo m. ~**t** n comunista m & f

community /kə'mjuːnətɪ/ n comunidad f. ~ **centre** n centro m social

commute /kə'mjuːt/ vi viajar diariamente (entre el lugar de residencia y el trabajo). ●vt (Jurid) conmutar. ~**r** n viajero m diario

compact /kəm'pækt/ a compacto. ●/'kɒmpækt/ n (for powder) polvera f. ~ **disc**, ~ **disk** /'kɒmpækt/ n disco m compacto, compact-disc m. ~ **disc player** n (reproductor m de) compact-disc

companion /kəm'pænɪən/ n compañero m. ~**ship** n compañía f

company /'kʌmpənɪ/ n compañía f; (guests) visita f; (Com) sociedad f

compar|able /'kɒmpərəbl/ a comparable. ~**ative** /kəm'pærətɪv/ a comparativo; (fig) relativo. ●n (Gram) comparativo m. ~**e** /kəm'peə(r)/ vt comparar. ~**ison** /kəm'pærɪsn/ n comparación f

compartment /kəm'pɑːtmənt/ n compartim(i)ento m

compass /'kʌmpəs/ n brújula f. ~**es** npl compás m

compassion /kəm'pæʃn/ n compasión f. ~**ate** /-ət/ a compasivo

compatible /kəm'pætəbl/ a compatible

compel /kəm'pel/ vt (pt **compelled**) obligar. ~**ling** a irresistible

compensat|e /'kɒmpənseɪt/ vt compensar; (for loss) indemnizar. ●vi. ~**e for sth** compensar algo. ~**ion** /-'seɪʃn/ n compensación f; (financial) indemnización f

compère /'kɒmpeə(r)/ n presentador m. ●vt presentar

compete /kəm'piːt/ vi competir

competen|ce /'kɒmpətəns/ n competencia f. ~**t** a competente

competit|ion /kɒmpə'tɪʃn/ n (contest) concurso m; (Sport) competición f, competencia f (LAm); (Com) competencia f. ~**ive** /kəm'petətɪv/ a competidor; <price> competitivo. ~**or** /kəm'petɪtə(r)/ n competidor m; (in contest) concursante m & f

compile /kəm'paɪl/ vt compilar

complacen|cy /kəm'pleɪsənsɪ/ n autosuficiencia f. ~**t** a satisfecho de sí mismo

complain /kəm'pleɪn/ vi. ~ (**about**) quejarse (de). ●vt. ~ **that** quejarse de que. ~**t** n queja f; (Med) enfermedad f

complement /'kɒmplɪmənt/ n complemento m. ● vt complementar. ~ary /-'mentrɪ/ a complementario

complet|e /kəm'pliːt/ a completo; (finished) acabado; (downright) total. ● vt acabar; llenar <a form>. ~ely adv completamente. ~ion /-ʃn/ n finalización f

complex /'kɒmpleks/ a complejo. ● n complejo m

complexion /kəm'plekʃn/ n tez f; (fig) aspecto m

complexity /kəm'pleksətɪ/ n complejidad f

complicat|e /'kɒmplɪkeɪt/ vt complicar. ~ed a complicado. ~ion /-'keɪʃn/ n complicación f

compliment /'kɒmplɪmənt/ n cumplido m; (amorous) piropo m. ● vt felicitar. ~ary /-'mentrɪ/ a halagador; (given free) de regalo. ~s npl saludos mpl

comply /kəm'plaɪ/ vi. ~ with conformarse con

component /kəm'pəʊnənt/ a & n componente (m)

compos|e /kəm'pəʊz/ vt componer. be ~ed of estar compuesto de. ~er n compositor m. ~ition /kɒmpə'zɪʃn/ n composición f

compost /'kɒmpɒst/ n abono m

composure /kəm'pəʊʒə(r)/ n serenidad f

compound /'kɒmpaʊnd/ n compuesto m; (enclosure) recinto m. ● a compuesto; <fracture> complicado

comprehen|d /kɒmprɪ'hend/ vt comprender. ~sion /kɒmprɪ'henʃn/ n comprensión f. ~sive /kɒmprɪ'hensɪv/ a extenso; <insurance> contra todo riesgo. ~sive (school) n instituto m de enseñanza secundaria

compress /'kɒmpres/ n (Med) compresa f. ● /kəm'pres/ vt comprimir. ~ion /-'preʃn/ n compresión f

comprise /kəm'praɪz/ vt comprender

compromis|e /'kɒmprəmaɪz/ n acuerdo m, compromiso m, arreglo m. ● vt comprometer. ● vi llegar a un acuerdo. ~ing a <situation> comprometido

compuls|ion /kəm'pʌlʃn/ n (force) coacción f; (obsession) compulsión f. ~ive /kəm'pʌlsɪv/ a compulsivo. ~ory /kəm'pʌlsərɪ/ a obligatorio

comput|er /kəm'pjuːtə(r)/ n ordenador m, computadora f (LAm). ~er-ize vt computarizar, computeri-zar. ~er studies n, ~ing n informática f, computación f

comrade /'kɒmreɪd/ n camarada m & f

con /kɒn/ vt (pt conned) 🅘 estafar. ● n (fraud) estafa f; (objection) ⇒PRO

concave /'kɒnkeɪv/ a cóncavo

conceal /kən'siːl/ vt ocultar

concede /kən'siːd/ vt conceder

conceit /kən'siːt/ n vanidad f. ~ed a engreído

conceiv|able /kən'siːvəbl/ a concebible. ~e /kən'siːv/ vt/i concebir

concentrat|e /'kɒnsəntreɪt/ vt concentrar. ● vi concentrarse (on en). ~ion /-'treɪʃn/ n concentración f

concept /'kɒnsept/ n concepto m

conception /kən'sepʃn/ n concepción f

concern /kən'sɜːn/ n asunto m; (worry) preocupación f; (Com) empresa f. ● vt tener que ver con; (deal with) tratar de. as far as I'm ~ed en cuanto a mí. be ~ed about preocuparse por. ~ing prep acerca de

concert /'kɒnsət/ n concierto m. ~ed /kən'sɜːtɪd/ a concertado

concertina /kɒnsə'tiːnə/ n concertina f

concerto /kən'tʃɜːtəʊ/ n (pl -os or -ti /-tɪ/) concierto m

concession /kən'seʃn/ n concesión f

concise /kən'saɪs/ a conciso

conclu|de /kən'kluːd/ vt/i concluir. ~ding a final. ~sion /-ʃn/ n conclusión f.. ~sive /-sɪv/ a decisivo. ~sively adv concluyentemente

concoct /kən'kɒkt/ vt confeccionar; (fig) inventar. ~ion /-ʃn/ n mezcla f; (drink) brebaje m

concrete /'kɒŋkriːt/ n hormigón m, concreto m (LAm). ● a concreto

concussion /kən'kʌʃn/ n conmoción f cerebral

condemn /kən'dem/ vt condenar. ∼**ation** /kɒndem'neɪʃn/ n condena f

condens|ation /kɒnden'seɪʃn/ n condensación f. ∼**e** /kən'dens/ vt condensar. ● vi condensarse

condescend /kɒndɪ'send/ vi dignarse (to a). ∼**ing** a superior

condition /kən'dɪʃn/ n condición f. on ∼ that a condición de que. ● vt condicionar. ∼**al** a condicional. ∼**er** n (for hair) suavizante m, enjuague m (LAm)

condo /'kɒndəʊ/ n (pl -os) (Amer 🄸) ⇒CONDOMINIUM

condolences /kən'dəʊlənsɪz/ npl pésame m

condom /'kɒndɒm/ n condón m

condominium /kɒndə'mɪnɪəm/ n (Amer) apartamento m, piso m (en régimen de propiedad horizontal)

condone /kən'dəʊn/ vt condonar

conduct /kən'dʌkt/ vt llevar a cabo <business, experiment>; conducir <electricity>; dirigir <orchestra>. ● /'kɒndʌkt/ n conducta f. ∼**or** /kən'dʌktə(r)/ n director m; (of bus) cobrador m. ∼**ress** /kən'dʌktrɪs/ n cobradora f

cone /kəʊn/ n cono m; (for ice cream) cucurucho m, barquillo m (Mex)

confectionery /kən'fekʃənrɪ/ n productos mpl de confitería

confederation /kənfedə'reɪʃn/ n confederación f

confess /kən'fes/ vt confesar. ● vi confesarse. ∼**ion** /-ʃn/ n confesión f

confetti /kən'fetɪ/ n confeti m

confide /kən'faɪd/ vt/i confiar

confiden|ce /'kɒnfɪdəns/ n confianza f; (self-confidence) confianza f en sí mismo; (secret) confidencia f. ∼**ce trick** n estafa f, timo m. ∼**t** /'kɒnfɪdənt/ a seguro de sí mismo. be ∼**t** of confiar en

confidential /kɒnfɪ'denʃl/ a confidencial. ∼**ity** /-denʃɪ'ælətɪ/ n confidencialidad f

confine /kən'faɪn/ vt confinar; (limit) limitar. ∼**ment** n (imprisonment) prisión f

confirm /kən'fɜːm/ vt confirmar. ∼**ation** /kɒnfə'meɪʃn/ n confirmación f. ∼**ed** a inveterado

confiscat|e /'kɒnfɪskeɪt/ vt confiscar. ∼**ion** /-'keɪʃn/ n confiscación f

conflict /'kɒnflɪkt/ n conflicto m. ● /kən'flɪkt/ vi chocar. ∼**ing** /kən'flɪktɪŋ/ a contradictorio

conform /kən'fɔːm/ vi conformarse. ∼**ist** n conformista m & f

confound /kən'faʊnd/ vt confundir. ∼**ed** a 🄸 maldito

confront /kən'frʌnt/ vt hacer frente a; (face) enfrentarse con. ∼**ation** /kɒnfrʌn'teɪʃn/ n confrontación f

confus|e /kən'fjuːz/ vt confundir. ∼**ed** a confundido. get ∼**ed** confundirse. ∼**ing** a confuso. ∼**ion** /-ʒn/ n confusión f

congeal /kən'dʒiːl/ vi coagularse

congest|ed /kən'dʒestɪd/ a congestionado. ∼**ion** /-tʃən/ n congestión f

congratulat|e /kən'grætjʊleɪt/ vt felicitar. ∼**ions** /-'leɪʃnz/ npl enhorabuena f, felicitaciones fpl (LAm)

congregat|e /'kɒŋgrɪgeɪt/ vi congregarse. ∼**ion** /-'geɪʃn/ n asamblea f; (Relig) fieles mpl, feligreses mpl

congress /'kɒŋgres/ n congreso m. C∼ (Amer) el Congreso. ∼**man** /-mən/ n (Amer) miembro m del Congreso. ∼**woman** n (Amer) miembro f del Congreso.

conifer /'kɒnɪfə(r)/ n conífera f

conjugat|e /'kɒndʒʊgeɪt/ vt conjugar. ∼**ion** /-'geɪʃn/ n conjugación f

conjunction /kən'dʒʌŋkʃn/ n conjunción f

conjur|e /'kʌndʒə(r)/ vi hacer juegos de manos. ● vt. ▢ ∼**e up** vt evocar. ∼**er**, ∼**or** n prestidigitador m

conk /kɒŋk/ vi. ∼ out 🄸 fallar; <person> desmayarse

conker /'kɒŋkə(r)/ n 🄸 castaña f de Indias

conman /'kɒnmæn/ n (pl -men) 🄸 estafador m, timador m

connect /kə'nekt/ vt conectar; (associate) relacionar. ● vi (be fitted) estar conectado (to a). ▢ ∼ **with** vt <train> enlazar con. ∼**ed** a unido;

(related) relacionado. **be ~ed with** tener que ver con, estar emparentado con. **~ion** /-ʃn/ n conexión f; (Rail) enlace m; (fig) relación f. **in ~ion with** a propósito de, con respecto a

connive /kə'naɪv/ vi. **~e at** ser cómplice en

connoisseur /kɒnə'sɜː(r)/ n experto m

connotation /kɒnə'teɪʃn/ n connotación f

conquer /'kɒŋkə(r)/ vt conquistar; (fig) vencer. **~or** n conquistador m

conquest /'kɒŋkwest/ n conquista f

conscience /'kɒnʃəns/ n conciencia f

conscientious /kɒnʃɪ'enʃəs/ a concienzudo

conscious /'kɒnʃəs/ a consciente; (deliberate) intencional. **~ly** adv a sabiendas. **~ness** n conciencia f; (Med) conocimiento m

conscript /'kɒnskrɪpt/ n recluta m & f, conscripto m (LAm). ● /kən'skrɪpt/ vt reclutar. **~ion** /kən'skrɪpʃn/ n reclutamiento m, conscripción f (LAm)

consecrate /'kɒnsɪkreɪt/ vt consagrar

consecutive /kən'sekjʊtɪv/ a sucesivo

consensus /kən'sensəs/ n consenso m

consent /kən'sent/ vi consentir. ● n consentimiento m

consequen|ce /'kɒnsɪkwəns/ n consecuencia f. **~t** a consiguiente. **~tly** adv por consiguiente

conservation /kɒnsə'veɪʃn/ n conservación f, preservación f. **~ist** n conservacionista m & f

conservative /kən'sɜːvətɪv/ a conservador; (modest) prudente, moderado. **C~** a & n conservador (m)

conservatory /kən'sɜːvətrɪ/ n invernadero m

conserve /kən'sɜːv/ vt conservar

consider /kən'sɪdə(r)/ vt considerar; (take into account) tomar en cuenta. **~able** a considerable. **~ably** adv considerablemente

considerat|e /kən'sɪdərət/ a considerado. **~ion** /-'reɪʃn/ n consideración f. **take sth into ~ion** tomar algo en cuenta

considering /kən'sɪdərɪŋ/ prep teniendo en cuenta. ● conj. **~ (that)** teniendo en cuenta que

consign /kən'saɪn/ vt consignar; (send) enviar. **~ment** n envío m

consist /kən'sɪst/ vi. **~ of** consistir en. **~ency** n consistencia f; (fig) coherencia f. **~ent** a coherente; (unchanging) constante. **~ent with** compatible con. **~ently** adv constantemente

consolation /kɒnsə'leɪʃn/ n consuelo m

console /kən'səʊl/ vt consolar. ● /'kɒnsəʊl/ n consola f

consolidate /kən'sɒlɪdeɪt/ vt consolidar

consonant /'kɒnsənənt/ n consonante f

conspicuous /kən'spɪkjʊəs/ a (easily seen) visible; (showy) llamativo; (noteworthy) notable

conspir|acy /kən'spɪrəsɪ/ n conspiración f. **~ator** /kən'spɪrətə(r)/ n conspirador m. **~e** /kən'spaɪə(r)/ vi conspirar

constable /'kʌnstəbl/ n agente m & f de policía

constant /'kɒnstənt/ a constante. **~ly** adv constantemente

constellation /kɒnstə'leɪʃn/ n constelación f

consternation /kɒnstə'neɪʃn/ n consternación f

constipat|ed /'kɒnstɪpeɪtɪd/ a estreñido. **~ion** /-'peɪʃn/ n estreñimiento m

constituen|cy /kən'stɪtjʊənsɪ/ n distrito m electoral. **~t** n (Pol) elector m. ● a constituyente, constitutivo

constitut|e /'kɒnstɪtjuːt/ vt constituir. **~ion** /-'tjuːʃn/ n constitución f. **~ional** /-'tjuːʃənl/ a constitucional. ● n paseo m

constrict /kən'strɪkt/ vt apretar. **~ion** /-ʃn/ n constricción f

construct /kən'strʌkt/ vt construir. **~ion** /-ʃn/ n construcción f. **~ive** a constructivo

consul /'kɒnsl/ n cónsul m & f. ∼**ate** /'kɒnsjʊlət/ n consulado m

consult /kən'sʌlt/ vt/i consultar. ∼**ancy** n asesoría. ∼**ant** n asesor m; (Med) especialista m & f; (Tec) consejero m técnico. ∼**ation** /kɒnsəl'teɪʃn/ n consulta f

consume /kən'sjuːm/ vt consumir. ∼**r** n consumidor m. ● a de consumo

consummate /'kɒnsəmət/ a consumado. ● /'kɒnsəmeɪt/ vt consumar

consumption /kən'sʌmpʃn/ n consumo m

contact /'kɒntækt/ n contacto m. ● vt ponerse en contacto con. ∼ **lens** n lentilla f, lente f de contacto (LAm)

contagious /kən'teɪdʒəs/ a contagioso

contain /kən'teɪn/ vt contener. ∼ **o.s.** contenerse. ∼**er** n recipiente m; (Com) contenedor m

contaminat|e /kən'tæmɪneɪt/ vt contaminar. ∼**ion** /-'neɪʃn/ n contaminación f

contemplate /'kɒntəmpleɪt/ vt contemplar; (consider) considerar

contemporary /kən'tempərərɪ/ a & n contemporáneo (m)

contempt /kən'tempt/ n desprecio m. ∼**ible** a despreciable. ∼**uous** /-tjʊəs/ a desdeñoso

contend /kən'tend/ vt competir. ∼**er** n aspirante m & f (for a)

content /kən'tent/ a satisfecho. ● /'kɒntent/ n contenido m. ● /kən'tent/ vt contentar. ∼**ed** /kən'tentɪd/ a satisfecho. ∼**ment** /kən'tentmənt/ n satisfacción f. ∼**s** /'kɒntents/ n contenido m; (of book) índice m de materias

contest /'kɒntest/ n (competition) concurso m; (Sport) competición f, competencia f (LAm). ● /kən'test/ vt disputar. ∼**ant** /kən'testənt/ n concursante m & f

context /'kɒntekst/ n contexto m

continent /'kɒntɪnənt/ n continente m. the C∼ Europa f. ∼**al** /-'nentl/ a continental. ∼**al quilt** n edredón m

contingen|cy /kən'tɪndʒənsɪ/ n contingencia f. ∼**t** a & n contingente (m)

continu|al /kən'tɪnjʊəl/ a continuo. ∼**ally** adv continuamente. ∼**ation** /-'eɪʃn/ n continuación f. ∼**e** /kən'tɪnjuː/ vt/i continuar, seguir. ∼**ed** a continuo. ∼**ity** /kɒntɪ'njuːətɪ/ n continuidad f. ∼**ous** /kən'tɪnjʊəs/ a continuo. ∼**ously** adv continuamente

contort /kən'tɔːt/ vt retorcer. ∼**ion** /-ʃn/ n contorsión f. ∼**ionist** /-ʃənɪst/ n contorsionista m & f

contour /'kɒntʊə(r)/ n contorno m

contraband /'kɒntrəbænd/ n contrabando m

contracepti|on /kɒntrə'sepʃn/ n anticoncepción f. ∼**ve** /-tɪv/ a & n anticonceptivo (m)

contract /'kɒntrækt/ n contrato m. ● /kən'trækt/ vt contraer. ● vi contraerse. ∼**ion** /kən'trækʃn/ n contracción f. ∼**or** /kən'træktə(r)/ n contratista m & f

contradict /kɒntrə'dɪkt/ vt contradecir. ∼**ion** /-ʃn/ n contradicción f. ∼**ory** a contradictorio

contraption /kən'træpʃn/ n 🄴 artilugio m

contrary /'kɒntrərɪ/ a contrario. the ∼ lo contrario. on the ∼ al contrario. ● adv. ∼ to contrariamente a. ● /kən'treərɪ/ a (obstinate) terco

contrast /'kɒntrɑːst/ n contraste m. ● /kən'trɑːst/ vt/i contrastar. ∼**ing** a contrastante

contravene /kɒntrə'viːn/ vt contravenir

contribut|e /kən'trɪbjuːt/ vt contribuir con. ● vi contribuir. ∼**e to** escribir para <newspaper>. ∼**ion** /kɒntrɪ'bjuːʃn/ n contribución f. ∼**or** n contribuyente m & f; (to newspaper) colaborador m

contrite /'kɒntraɪt/ a arrepentido, pesaroso

contriv|e /kən'traɪv/ vt idear. ∼**e to** conseguir. ∼**ed** a artificioso

control /kən'trəʊl/ vt (pt **controlled**) controlar. ● n control m.

~**ler** *n* director *m.* ~**s** *npl* (Mec) mandos *mpl*

controvers|ial /kɒntrə'vɜ:ʃl/ controvertido. ~**y** /'kɒntrəvɜ:sɪ/ *n* controversia *f*

conundrum /kə'nʌndrəm/ *n* adivinanza *f*

convalesce /kɒnvə'les/ *vi* convalecer. ~**nce** *n* convalecencia *f*

convector /kən'vektə(r)/ *n* estufa *f* de convección

convene /kən'vi:n/ *vt* convocar. ● *vi* reunirse

convenien|ce /kən'vi:nɪəns/ *n* conveniencia *f*, comodidad *f.* **all modern** ~**ces** todas las comodidades. **at your** ~**ce** según le convenga. ~**ces** *npl* servicios *mpl*, baños *mpl* (LAm). ~**t** *a* conveniente; *<place>* bien situado; *<time>* oportuno. **be** ~**t** convenir. ~**tly** *adv* convenientemente

convent /'kɒnvənt/ *n* convento *m*

convention /kən'venʃn/ *n* convención *f.* ~**al** *a* convencional

converge /kən'vɜ:dʒ/ *vi* converger

conversation /kɒnvə'seɪʃn/ *n* conversación *f.* ~**al** *a* familiar, coloquial.

converse /kən'vɜ:s/ *vi* conversar. ● /'kɒnvɜ:s/ *a* inverso. ● *n* lo contrario. ~**ly** *adv* a la inversa

conver|sion /kən'vɜ:ʃn/ *n* conversión *f.* ~**t** /kən'vɜ:t/ *vt* convertir. ● /'kɒnvɜ:t/ *n* converso *m.* ~**tible** /kən'vɜ:tɪbl/ *a* convertible. ● *n* (Auto) descapotable *m*, convertible *m* (LAm)

convex /'kɒnveks/ *a* convexo

convey /kən'veɪ/ *vt* transportar *<goods, people>*; comunicar *<idea, feeling>*. ~**or belt** *n* cinta *f* transportadora, banda *f* transportadora (LAm)

convict /kən'vɪkt/ *vt* condenar. ● /'kɒnvɪkt/ *n* presidiario *m.* ~**ion** /kən'vɪkʃn/ *n* condena *f*; (belief) creencia *f*

convinc|e /kən'vɪns/ *vt* convencer. ~**ing** *a* convincente

convoluted /'kɒnvəlu:tɪd/ *a <argument>* intrincado

convoy /'kɒnvɔɪ/ *n* convoy *m*

convuls|e /kən'vʌls/ *vt* convulsionar. **be** ~**ed with laughter** desternillarse de risa. ~**ion** /-ʃn/ *n* convulsión *f*

coo /ku:/ *vi* arrullar

cook /kʊk/ *vt* hacer, preparar. ● *vi* cocinar; *<food>* hacerse. ● *n* cocinero *m.* □ ~ **up** *vt* Ⓘ inventar. ~**book** *n* libro *m* de cocina. ~**er** *n* cocina *f*, estufa *f* (Mex). ~**ery** *n* cocina *f*

cookie /'kʊkɪ/ *n* (Amer) galleta *f*

cool /ku:l/ *a* (**-er, -est**) fresco; (calm) tranquilo; (unfriendly) frío. ● *n* fresco *m*; Ⓧ calma *f.* ● *vt* enfriar. ● *vi* enfriarse. □ ~ **down** *vi <person>* calmarse. ~**ly** *adv* tranquilamente

coop /ku:p/ *n* gallinero *m.* □ ~ **up** *vt* encerrar

co-op /'kəʊɒp/ *n* cooperativa *f*

cooperat|e /kəʊ'ɒpəreɪt/ *vi* cooperar. ~**ion** /-'reɪʃn/ *n* cooperación *f.* ~**ive** /kəʊ'ɒpərətɪv/ *a* cooperativo. ● *n* cooperativa *f*

co-opt /kəʊ'ɒpt/ *vt* cooptar

co-ordinat|e /kəʊ'ɔ:dɪneɪt/ *vt* coordinar. ● /kəʊ'ɔ:dɪnət/ *n* (Math) coordenada *f.* ~**es** *npl* prendas *fpl* para combinar. ~**ion** /kəʊɔ:dɪ'neɪʃn/ *n* coordinación *f*

cop /kɒp/ *n* Ⓘ poli *m* & *f* Ⓘ, tira *m* & *f* (Mex, Ⓘ)

cope /kəʊp/ *vi* arreglárselas. ~ **with** hacer frente a

copious /'kəʊpɪəs/ *a* abundante

copper /'kɒpə(r)/ *n* cobre *m*; (coin) perra *f*; Ⓘ poli *m* & *f* Ⓘ, tira *m* & *f* (Mex, Ⓘ). ● *a* de cobre

copy /'kɒpɪ/ *n* copia *f*; (of book, newspaper) ejemplar *m.* ● *vt* copiar. ~**right** *n* derechos *mpl* de reproducción

coral /'kɒrəl/ *n* coral *m*

cord /kɔ:d/ *n* cuerda *f*; (fabric) pana *f*; (Amer, Elec) cordón *m*, cable *m*

cordial /'kɔ:dɪəl/ *a* cordial. ● *n* refresco *m* (concentrado)

cordon /'kɔ:dn/ *n* cordón *m.* □ ~ **off** *vt* acordonar

core /kɔ:(r)/ *n* (of apple) corazón *m*; (of Earth) centro *m*; (of problem) meollo *m*

cork /kɔ:k/ *n* corcho *m.* ~**screw** *n* sacacorchos *m*

corn /kɔːn/ n (wheat) trigo m; (Amer) maíz m; (hard skin) callo m

corned beef /kɔːnd 'biːf/ n carne f de vaca en lata

corner /'kɔːnə(r)/ n ángulo m; (inside) rincón m; (outside) esquina f; (football) córner m. ● vt arrinconar; (Com) acaparar

cornet /'kɔːnɪt/ n (Mus) corneta f; (for ice cream) cucurucho m, barquillo m (Mex)

corn: ~**flakes** npl copos mpl de maíz. ~**flour** n maizena f (P)

Cornish /'kɔːnɪʃ/ a de Cornualles

cornstarch /'kɔːnstɑːtʃ/ n (Amer) maizena f (P)

corny /'kɔːnɪ/ a (🅕, trite) gastado

coronation /kɒrə'neɪʃn/ n coronación f

coroner /'kɒrənə(r)/ n juez m de primera instancia

corporal /'kɔːpərəl/ n cabo m. ● a corporal

corporate /'kɔːpərət/ a corporativo

corporation /kɔːpə'reɪʃn/ n corporación f; (Amer) sociedad f anónima

corps /kɔː(r)/ n (pl corps /kɔːz/) cuerpo m

corpse /kɔːps/ n cadáver m

corpulent /'kɔːpjʊlənt/ a corpulento

corral /kə'rɑːl/ n (Amer) corral m

correct /kə'rekt/ a correcto; <time> exacto. ● vt corregir. ~**ion** /-ʃn/ n corrección f

correspond /kɒrɪ'spɒnd/ vi corresponder; (write) escribirse. ~**ence** n correspondencia f. ~**ent** n corresponsal m & f

corridor /'kɒrɪdɔː(r)/ n pasillo m

corro|de /kə'rəʊd/ vt corroer. ● vi corroerse. ~**sion** /-ʒn/ n corrosión f. ~**sive** /-sɪv/ a corrosivo

corrugated /'kɒrəgeɪtɪd/ a ondulado. ~ **iron** n chapa f de zinc

corrupt /kə'rʌpt/ a corrompido. ● vt corromper. ~**ion** /-ʃn/ n corrupción f

corset /'kɔːsɪt/ n corsé m

cosmetic /kɒz'metɪk/ a & n cosmético (m)

cosmic /'kɒzmɪk/ a cósmico

cosmopolitan /kɒzmə'pɒlɪtən/ a & n cosmopolita (m & f)

cosmos /'kɒzmɒs/ n cosmos m

cosset /'kɒsɪt/ vt (pt cosseted) mimar

cost /kɒst/ vt (pt cost) costar; (pt costed) calcular el coste de, calcular el costo de (LAm). ● n coste m, costo m (LAm). at all ~s cueste lo que cueste. to one's ~ a sus expensas. ~s npl (Jurid) costas fpl

Costa Rica /kɒstə'riːkə/ n Costa f Rica. ~**n** a & n costarricense (m & f), costarriqueño (m & f)

cost: ~**effective** a rentable. ~**ly** a (-ier, -iest) costoso

costume /'kɒstjuːm/ n traje m; (for party, disguise) disfraz m

cosy /'kəʊzɪ/ a (-ier, -iest) acogedor. ● n cubreteras m

cot /kɒt/ n cuna f

cottage /'kɒtɪdʒ/ n casita f. ~ **cheese** n requesón m. ~ **pie** n pastel m de carne cubierta con puré

cotton /'kɒtn/ n algodón m; (thread) hilo m; (Amer) ⇒~ WOOL. □ ~ **on** vi 🅕 comprender. ~ **bud** n bastoncillo m, cotonete m (Mex). ~ **candy** n (Amer) algodón m de azúcar. ~ **swab** n (Amer) ⇒~ BUD. ~ **wool** n algodón m hidrófilo

couch /kaʊtʃ/ n sofá m

cough /kɒf/ vi toser. ● n tos f. □ ~ **up** vt 🅕 pagar. ~ **mixture** n jarabe m para la tos

could /kʊd/ pt of CAN¹

couldn't /'kʊdnt/ = **could not**

council /'kaʊnsl/ n consejo m; (of town) ayuntamiento m. ~ **house** n vivienda f subvencionada. ~**lor** n concejal m

counsel /'kaʊnsl/ n consejo m; (pl invar) (Jurid) abogado m. ● vt (pt counselled) aconsejar. ~**ling** n terapia f de apoyo. ~**lor** n consejero m

count /kaʊnt/ n recuento m; (nobleman) conde m. ● vt/i contar. □ ~ **on** vt contar. ~**down** n cuenta f atrás

counter /'kaʊntə(r)/ n (in shop) mostrador m; (in bank, post office) ventanilla f; (token) ficha f. ● adv. ~ **to** en contra de. ● a opuesto. ● vt oponerse a; parar <blow>

counter... /'kaʊntə(r)/ *pref* contra.... ~**act** /-'ækt/ *vt* contrarrestar. ~**attack** *n* contraataque *m*. ● *vt/i* contraatacar. ~**balance** *n* contrapeso *m*. ● *vt/i* contrapesar. ~**clockwise** /-'klɒkwaɪz/ *a/adv* (Amer) en sentido contrario al de las agujas del reloj

counterfeit /'kaʊntəfɪt/ *a* falsificado. ● *n* falsificación *f*. ● *vt* falsificar

counterfoil /'kaʊntəfɔɪl/ *n* matriz *f*, talón *m* (LAm)

counter-productive /kaʊntə prə'dʌktɪv/ *a* contraproducente

countess /'kaʊntɪs/ *n* condesa *f*

countless /'kaʊntlɪs/ *a* innumerable

country /'kʌntrɪ/ *n* (native land) país *m*; (countryside) campo *m*; (Mus) (música *f*) country *m*. ~**-and-western** /-en'westən/ (música *f*) country *m*. ~**man** /-mən/ *n* (of one's own country) compatriota *m*. ~**side** *n* campo *m*; (landscape) paisaje *m*

county /'kaʊntɪ/ *n* condado *m*

coup /ku:/ *n* golpe *m*

couple /'kʌpl/ *n* (of things) par *m*; (of people) pareja *f*; (married) matrimonio *m*. **a** ~ **of** un par de

coupon /'ku:pɒn/ *n* cupón *m*

courage /'kʌrɪdʒ/ *n* valor *m*. ~**ous** /kə'reɪdʒəs/ *a* valiente

courgette /kʊə'ʒet/ *n* calabacín *m*

courier /'kʊrɪə(r)/ *n* mensajero *m*; (for tourists) guía *m & f*

course /kɔ:s/ *n* curso *m*; (behaviour) conducta *f*; (Aviat, Naut) rumbo *m*; (Culin) plato *m*; (for golf) campo *m*. **in due** ~ a su debido tiempo. **in the** ~ **of** en el transcurso de, durante. **of** ~ claro, por supuesto. **of** ~ **not** claro que no, por supuesto que no

court /kɔ:t/ *n* corte *f*; (tennis) pista *f*, cancha *f* (LAm); (Jurid) tribunal *m*. ● *vt* cortejar; buscar <*danger*>

courteous /'kɜ:tɪəs/ *a* cortés

courtesy /'kɜ:təsɪ/ *n* cortesía *f*

courtier /'kɔ:tɪə(r)/ *n* (old use) cortesano *m*

court: ~ **martial** *n* (*pl* ~**s martial**) consejo *m* de guerra. ~**-martial** *vt* (*pt* ~**-martialled**) juzgar en

consejo de guerra. ~**ship** *n* cortejo *m*. ~**yard** *n* patio *m*

cousin /'kʌzn/ *n* primo *m*. **first** ~ primo carnal. **second** ~ primo segundo

cove /kəʊv/ *n* ensenada *f*, cala *f*

Coventry /'kɒvntrɪ/ *n*. **send s.o. to** ~ hacer el vacío a uno

cover /'kʌvə(r)/ *vt* cubrir. ● *n* cubierta *f*; (shelter) abrigo *m*; (lid) tapa *f*; (for furniture) funda *f*; (pretext) pretexto *m*; (of magazine) portada *f*. □ ~ **up** *vt* cubrir; (fig) ocultar. ~ **charge** *n* precio *m* del cubierto. ~**ing** *n* cubierta *f*. ~**ing letter** *n* carta *f* adjunta

covet /'kʌvɪt/ *vt* codiciar

cow /kaʊ/ *n* vaca *f*

coward /'kaʊəd/ *n* cobarde *m*. ~**ice** /'kaʊədɪs/ *n* cobardía *f*. ~**ly** *a* cobarde.

cowboy /'kaʊbɔɪ/ *n* vaquero *m*

cower /'kaʊə(r)/ *vi* encogerse, acobardarse

coxswain /'kɒksn/ *n* timonel *m*

coy /kɔɪ/ *a* (**-er, -est**) (shy) tímido; (evasive) evasivo

crab /kræb/ *n* cangrejo *m*, jaiba *f* (LAm)

crack /kræk/ *n* grieta *f*; (noise) crujido *m*; (of whip) chasquido *m*; (drug) crack *m*. ● *a* 🄸 de primera. ● *vt* agrietar; chasquear <*whip, fingers*>; cascar <*nut*>; gastar <*joke*>; resolver <*problem*>. ● *vi* agrietarse. **get** ~**ing** 🄸 darse prisa. □ ~ **down on** *vt* 🄸 tomar medidas enérgicas contra

cracker /'krækə(r)/ *n* (Culin) cracker *f*, galleta *f* (salada); (Christmas cracker) sorpresa *f* (*que estalla al abrirla*)

crackle /'krækl/ *vi* crepitar. ● *n* crepitación *f*, crujido *m*

crackpot /'krækpɒt/ *n* 🄸 chiflado *m*

cradle /'kreɪdl/ *n* cuna *f*. ● *vt* acunar

craft /krɑ:ft/ *n* destreza *f*; (technique) arte *f*; (cunning) astucia *f*. ● *n invar* (boat) barco *m*

craftsman /'krɑ:ftsmən/ *n* (*pl* **-men**) artesano *m*. ~**ship** *n* artesanía *f*

crafty /'krɑ:ftɪ/ *a* (**-ier, -iest**) astuto

cram /kræm/ *vt* (*pt* **crammed**) rellenar. ~ **with** llenar de. ● *vi* (for exams) memorizar, empollar, zambutir (Mex)

cramp /kræmp/ *n* calambre *m*

cramped /kræmpt/ *a* apretado

crane /kreɪn/ *n* grúa *f*. ● *vt* estirar <*neck*>

crank /kræŋk/ *n* manivela *f*; (person) excéntrico *m*. ~**y** *a* excéntrico

cranny /kræni/ *n* grieta *f*

crash /kræʃ/ *n* accidente *m*; (noise) estruendo *m*; (collision) choque *m*; (Com) quiebra *f*. ● *vt* estrellar. ● *vi* quebrar con estrépito; (have accident) tener un accidente; <*car etc*> estrellarse, chocar; (fail) fracasar. ~ **course** *n* curso *m* intensivo. ~ **helmet** *n* casco *m* protector. ~**land** *vi* hacer un aterrizaje forzoso

crass /kræs/ *a* craso, burdo

crate /kreɪt/ *n* cajón *m*. ● *vt* embalar

crater /kreɪtə(r)/ *n* cráter *m*

crav|e /kreɪv/ *vt* ansiar. ~**ing** *n* ansia *f*

crawl /krɔːl/ *vi* <*baby*> gatear; (move slowly) avanzar lentamente; (drag o.s.) arrastrarse. ~ **to** humillarse ante. ~ **with** hervir de. ● *n* (swimming) crol *m*. at a ~ a paso lento

crayon /kreɪən/ *n* lápiz *m* de color; (made of wax) lápiz *m* de cera, crayola *f* (P), crayón *m* (Mex)

craz|e /kreɪz/ *n* manía *f*. ~**y** /kreɪzi/ *a* (**-ier, -iest**) loco. be ~**y** about estar loco por

creak /kriːk/ *n* crujido *m*; (of hinge) chirrido *m*. ● *vi* crujir; <*hinge*> chirriar

cream /kriːm/ *n* crema *f*; (fresh) nata *f*, crema *f* (LAm). ● *a* (colour) color crema. ● *vt* (beat) batir. ~ **cheese** *n* queso *m* para untar, queso *m* crema (LAm). ~**y** *a* cremoso

crease /kriːs/ *n* raya *f*, pliegue *m* (Mex); (crumple) arruga *f*. ● *vt* plegar; (wrinkle) arrugar. ● *vi* arrugarse

creat|e /kriːˈeɪt/ *vt* crear. ~**ion** /-ʃn/ *n* creación *f*. ~**ive** *a* creativo. ~**or** *n* creador *m*

creature /kriːtʃə(r)/ *n* criatura *f*

crèche /kreʃ/ *n* guardería *f* (infantil)

credib|ility /kredəˈbɪlətɪ/ *n* credibilidad *f*. ~**le** /kredəbl/ *a* creíble

credit /kredɪt/ *n* crédito *m*; (honour) mérito *m*. take the ~ for atribuirse el mérito de. ● *vt* (*pt* **credited**) acreditar; (believe) creer. ~ **s.o. with** atribuir a uno. ~ **card** *n* tarjeta *f* de crédito. ~**or** *n* acreedor *m*

creed /kriːd/ *n* credo *m*

creek /kriːk/ *n* ensenada *f*. up the ~ ⊠ en apuros

creep /kriːp/ *vi* (*pt* **crept**) arrastrarse; (plant) trepar. ● *n* ⊞ adulador. ~**s** /kriːps/ *npl*. give s.o. the ~**s** poner los pelos de punta a uno. ~**er** *n* enredadera *f*

cremat|e /krɪˈmeɪt/ *vt* incinerar. ~**ion** /-ʃn/ *n* cremación *f*. ~**orium** /kreməˈtɔːrɪəm/ *n* (*pl* **-ia** /-ɪə/) crematorio *m*

crept /krept/ ⇒CREEP

crescendo /krɪˈʃendəʊ/ *n* (*pl* **-os**) crescendo *m*

crescent /kresnt/ *n* media luna *f*; (street) calle *f* en forma de media luna

crest /krest/ *n* cresta *f*; (on coat of arms) emblema *m*

crevice /krevɪs/ *n* grieta *f*

crew /kruː/ *n* tripulación *f*; (gang) pandilla *f*. ~ **cut** *n* corte *m* al rape

crib /krɪb/ *n* (Amer) cuna *f*; (Relig) belén *m*. ● *vt/i* (*pt* **cribbed**) copiar

crick /krɪk/ *n* calambre *m*; (in neck) tortícolis *f*

cricket /krɪkɪt/ *n* (Sport) críquet *m*; (insect) grillo *m*

crim|e /kraɪm/ *n* delito *m*; (murder) crimen *m*; (acts) delincuencia *f*. ~**inal** /krɪmɪnl/ *a* & *n* criminal (*m* & *f*)

crimson /krɪmzn/ *a* & *n* carmesí (*m*)

cringe /krɪndʒ/ *vi* encogerse; (fig) humillarse

crinkle /krɪŋkl/ *vt* arrugar. ● *vi* arrugarse. ● *n* arruga *f*

cripple /krɪpl/ *n* lisiado *m*. ● *vt* lisiar; (fig) paralizar

crisis /kraɪsɪs/ *n* (*pl* **crises** /-siːz/) crisis *f*

crisp /krɪsp/ *a* (**-er, -est**) (Culin) crujiente; <*air*> vigorizador. ~**s** *npl* pa-

tatas *fpl* fritas, papas *fpl* fritas (LAm)
(de bolsa)

crisscross /'krɪskrɒs/ *a* entrecruzado. ● *vt* entrecruzar. ● *vi* entrecruzarse

criterion /kraɪ'tɪərɪən/ *n* (*pl* **-ia** /-ɪə/) criterio *m*

critic /'krɪtɪk/ *n* crítico *m*. ~**al** *a* crítico. ~**ally** *adv* críticamente; (ill) gravemente

critici|sm /'krɪtɪsɪzəm/ *n* crítica *f*. ~**ze** /'krɪtɪsaɪz/ *vt/i* criticar

croak /krəʊk/ *n* (of person) gruñido *m*; (of frog) canto *m*. ● *vi* gruñir; *<frog>* croar

Croat /'krəʊæt/ *n* croata *m* & *f*. ~**ia** /krəʊ'eɪʃə/ *n* Croacia *f*. ~**ian** *a* croata

crochet /'krəʊʃeɪ/ *n* crochet *m*, ganchillo *m*. ● *vt* tejer a crochet *or* a ganchillo

crockery /'krɒkərɪ/ *n* loza *f*

crocodile /'krɒkədaɪl/ *n* cocodrilo *m*. ~ **tears** *npl* lágrimas *fpl* de cocodrilo

crocus /'krəʊkəs/ *n* (*pl* **-es**) azafrán *m* de primavera

crook /krʊk/ *n* 🖻 sinvergüenza *m* & *f*. ~**ed** /'krʊkɪd/ *a* torcido, chueco (LAm); (winding) tortuoso; (dishonest) deshonesto

crop /krɒp/ *n* cosecha *f*; (haircut) corte *m* de pelo muy corto. ● *vt* (*pt* **cropped**) cortar. □ ~ **up** *vi* surgir

croquet /'krəʊkeɪ/ *n* croquet *m*

cross /krɒs/ *n* cruz *f*; (of animals) cruce *m*. ● *vt* cruzar; (oppose) contrariar. ~ **s.o.'s mind** ocurrírsele a uno. ● *vi* cruzar. ~ **o.s.** santiguarse. ● *a* enfadado, enojado (esp LAm). □ ~ **out** *vt* tachar. ~**bar** *n* travesaño *m*. ~**examine** /-ɪg'zæmɪn/ *vt* interrogar. ~**eyed** *a* bizco. ~**fire** *n* fuego *m* cruzado. ~**ing** *n* (by boat) travesía *f*; (on road) cruce *m* peatonal. ~**ly** *adv* con enfado, con enojo (esp LAm). ~**purposes** /-'pɜːpəsɪz/ *npl*. **talk at** ~**purposes** hablar sin entenderse. ~**reference** /-'refrəns/ *n* remisión *f*. ~**roads** *n invar* cruce *m*. ~**section** /-'sekʃn/ *n* sección *f* transversal; (fig) muestra *f* representativa. ~**walk** *n* (Amer) paso de peatones.

~**word** *n* ~**word** (**puzzle**) crucigrama *m*

crotch /krɒtʃ/ *n* entrepiernas *fpl*

crouch /kraʊtʃ/ *vi* agacharse

crow /krəʊ/ *n* cuervo *m*. **as the** ~ **flies** en línea recta. ● *vi* cacarear. ~**bar** *n* palanca *f*

crowd /kraʊd/ *n* muchedumbre *f*. ● *vt* amontonar; (fill) llenar. ● *vi* amontonarse; (gather) reunirse. ~**ed** *a* atestado

crown /kraʊn/ *n* corona *f*; (of hill) cumbre *f*; (of head) coronilla *f*. ● *vt* coronar

crucial /'kruːʃl/ *a* crucial

crucifix /'kruːsɪfɪks/ *n* crucifijo *m*. ~**ion** /-'fɪkʃn/ *n* crucifixión *f*

crucify /'kruːsɪfaɪ/ *vt* crucificar

crude /kruːd/ *a* (**-er, -est**) (raw) crudo; (rough) tosco; (vulgar) ordinario

cruel /'krʊəl/ *a* (**crueller, cruellest**) cruel. ~**ty** *n* crueldad *f*

cruet /'kruːɪt/ *n* vinagrera *f*

cruise /kruːz/ *n* crucero *m*. ● *vi* hacer un crucero; (of car) circular lentamente. ~**r** *n* crucero *m*

crumb /krʌm/ *n* miga *f*

crumble /'krʌmbl/ *vt* desmenuzar. ● *vi* desmenuzarse; (collapse) derrumbarse

crummy /'krʌmɪ/ *a* (**-ier, -iest**) 🖻 miserable

crumpet /'krʌmpɪt/ *n* bollo *m* blando

crumple /'krʌmpl/ *vt* arrugar. ● *vi* arrugarse

crunch /krʌntʃ/ *vt* hacer crujir; (bite) masticar. ~**y** *a* crujiente

crusade /kruː'seɪd/ *n* cruzada *f*. ~**r** *n* cruzado *m*

crush /krʌʃ/ *vt* aplastar; arrugar *<clothes>*. ● *n* (crowd) aglomeración *f*. **have a** ~ **on** 🖻 estar chiflado por

crust /krʌst/ *n* corteza *f*. ~**y** *a* *<bread>* de corteza dura

crutch /krʌtʃ/ *n* muleta *f*; (Anat) entrepiernas *fpl*

crux /krʌks/ *n* (*pl* **cruxes**). **the** ~ (**of the matter**) el quid (de la cuestión)

cry /kraɪ/ *n* grito *m*. **be a far** ~ **from** (fig) distar mucho de. ● *vi* llorar; (call out) gritar. □ ~ **off** *vi* echarse atrás, rajarse. ~**baby** *n* llorón *m*

crypt /krɪpt/ *n* cripta *f*

cryptic /'krɪptɪk/ *a* enigmático

crystal /'krɪstl/ *n* cristal *m*. ~**lize** *vi* cristalizarse

cub /kʌb/ *n* cachorro *m*. **C~** (Scout) *n* lobato *m*

Cuba /'kjuːbə/ *n* Cuba *f*. ~**n** *a & n* cubano (*m*)

cubbyhole /'kʌbɪhəʊl/ *n* cuchitril *m*

cub|e /kjuːb/ *n* cubo *m*. ~**ic** *a* cúbico

cubicle /'kjuːbɪkl/ *n* cubículo *m*; (changing room) probador *m*

cuckoo /'kʊkuː/ *n* cuco *m*, cuclillo *m*

cucumber /'kjuːkʌmbə(r)/ *n* pepino *m*

cuddl|e /'kʌdl/ *vt* abrazar. ● *vi* abrazarse. ● *n* abrazo *m*. ~**y** *a* adorable

cue /kjuː/ *n* (Mus) entrada *f*; (in theatre) pie *m*; (in snooker) taco *m*

cuff /kʌf/ *n* puño *m*; (Amer, of trousers) vuelta *f*, dobladillo *m*; (blow) bofetada *f*. speak off the ~ hablar de improviso. ● *vt* abofetear. ~**link** *n* gemelo *m*, mancuerna *f* (Mex)

cul-de-sac /'kʌldəsæk/ *n* callejón *m* sin salida

culinary /'kʌlɪnərɪ/ *a* culinario

cull /kʌl/ *vt* sacrificar en forma selectiva *<animals>*

culminat|e /'kʌlmɪneɪt/ *vi* culminar. ~**ion** /-'neɪʃn/ *n* culminación *f*

culprit /'kʌlprɪt/ *n* culpable *m & f*

cult /kʌlt/ *n* culto *m*

cultivat|e /'kʌltɪveɪt/ *vt* cultivar. ~**ion** /-'veɪʃn/ *n* cultivo *m*

cultur|al /'kʌltʃərəl/ *a* cultural. ~**e** /'kʌltʃə(r)/ *n* cultura *f*; (Bot etc) cultivo *m*. ~**ed** *a* cultivado; *<person>* culto

cumbersome /'kʌmbəsəm/ *a* incómodo; (heavy) pesado

cunning /'kʌnɪŋ/ *a* astuto. ● *n* astucia *f*

cup /kʌp/ *n* taza *f*; (trophy) copa *f*

cupboard /'kʌbəd/ *n* armario *m*

curator /kjʊə'reɪtə(r)/ *n* (of museum) conservador *m*

curb /kɜːb/ *n* freno *m*; (Amer) bordillo *m* (de la acera), borde *m* de la banqueta (Mex). ● *vt* refrenar

curdle /'kɜːdl/ *vt* cuajar. ● *vi* cuajarse; (go bad) cortarse

cure /kjʊə(r)/ *vt* curar. ● *n* cura *f*

curfew /'kɜːfjuː/ *n* toque *m* de queda

curio|sity /kjʊərɪ'ɒsətɪ/ *n* curiosidad *f*. ~**us** /'kjʊərɪəs/ *a* curioso

curl /kɜːl/ *vt* rizar, enchinar (Mex). ~ **o.s. up** acurrucarse. ● *vi* *<hair>* rizarse, enchinarse (Mex); *<paper>* ondularse. ● *n* rizo *m*, chino *m* (Mex). ~**er** *n* rulo *m*, chino *m* (Mex). ~**y** *a* (-**ier**, -**iest**) rizado, chino (Mex)

currant /'kʌrənt/ *n* pasa *f* de Corinto

currency /'kʌrənsɪ/ *n* moneda *f*

current /'kʌrənt/ *a & n* corriente (*f*); (existing) actual. ~ **affairs** *npl* sucesos de actualidad. ~**ly** *adv* actualmente

curriculum /kə'rɪkjʊləm/ *n* (*pl* -**la**) programa *m* de estudios. ~ **vitae** *n* currículum *m* vitae

curry /'kʌrɪ/ *n* curry *m*. ● *vt* preparar al curry

curse /kɜːs/ *n* maldición *f*; (oath) palabrota *f*. ● *vt* maldecir. ● *vi* decir palabrotas

cursory /'kɜːsərɪ/ *a* superficial

curt /kɜːt/ *a* brusco

curtain /'kɜːtn/ *n* cortina *f*; (in theatre) telón *m*

curtsey, **curtsy** /'kɜːtsɪ/ *n* reverencia *f*. ● *vi* hacer una reverencia

curve /kɜːv/ *n* curva *f*. ● *vi* estar curvado; *<road>* torcerse

cushion /'kʊʃn/ *n* cojín *m*, almohadón *m*. ● *vt* amortiguar *<blow>*; (fig) proteger

cushy /'kʊʃɪ/ *a* (-**ier**, -**iest**) 🔲 fácil

custard /'kʌstəd/ *n* natillas *fpl*

custody /'kʌstədɪ/ *n* custodia *f*. **be in ~** (Jurid) estar detenido

custom /'kʌstəm/ *n* costumbre *f*; (Com) clientela *f*. ~**ary** /-ərɪ/ *a* acostumbrado. ~**er** *n* cliente *m*. ~**s** *npl* aduana *f*. ~**s officer** *n* aduanero *m*

cut /kʌt/ *vt/i* (*pt* **cut**, *pres p* **cutting**) cortar; reducir *<prices>*. ● *n* corte *m*; (reduction) reducción *f*. □ ~ **across** *vt* cortar camino por. □ ~ **back**, ~ **down** *vt* reducir. □ ~ **in** *vi* interrumpir. □ ~ **off** *vt* cortar; (phone) desconectar; (fig) aislar. □ ~ **out** *vt* recortar; (omit) suprimir. □ ~ **through** *vt* cortar camino por. □ ~ **up** *vt* cortar en pedazos

cute /kjuːt/ *a* (**-er**, **-est**) 🆒 mono, amoroso (LAm); (Amer, attractive) guapo, buen mozo (LAm)

cutlery /'kʌtləri/ *n* cubiertos *mpl*

cutlet /'kʌtlɪt/ *n* chuleta *f*

cut: ~**-price**, (Amer) ~**-rate** *a* a precio reducido. ~**-throat** *a* despiadado. ~**ting** *a* cortante; *<remark>* mordaz. ● *n* (from newspaper) recorte *m*; (of plant) esqueje *m*

CV *n* (= **curriculum vitae**) currículum *m* (vitae)

cycl|e /'saɪkl/ *n* ciclo *m*; (bicycle) bicicleta *f*. ● *vi* ir en bicicleta. ~**ing** *f* ciclismo *m*. ~**ist** *n* ciclista *m & f*

cylind|er /'sɪlɪndə(r)/ *n* cilindro *m*. ~**er head** (Auto) *n* culata *f*. ~**rical** /-'lɪndrɪkl/ *a* cilíndrico

cymbal /'sɪmbl/ *n* címbalo *m*

cynic /'sɪnɪk/ *n* cínico *m*. ~**al** *a* cínico. ~**ism** /-sɪzəm/ *n* cinismo *m*

Czech /tʃek/ *a & n* checo (*m*). ~**oslovakia** /-əslə'vækɪə/ *n* (History) Checoslovaquia *f*. ~ **Republic** *n*. the ~ **Republic** *n* la República Checa

Dd

dab /dæb/ *vt* (*pt* **dabbed**) tocar ligeramente. ● *n* toque *m* suave. **a** ~ **of** un poquito de

dad /dæd/ *n* 🆒 papá *m*. ~**dy** *n* papi *m*. ~**dy-long-legs** *n invar* (cranefly) típula *f*; (Amer, harvestman) segador *m*, falangio *m*

daffodil /'dæfədɪl/ *n* narciso *m*

daft /dɑːft/ *a* (**-er**, **-est**) 🆒 tonto

dagger /'dægə(r)/ *n* daga *f*, puñal *m*

daily /'deɪli/ *a* diario. ● *adv* diariamente, cada día

dainty /'deɪnti/ *a* (**-ier**, **-iest**) delicado

dairy /'deəri/ *n* vaquería *f*; (shop) lechería *f*

daisy /'deɪzi/ *n* margarita *f*

dam /dæm/ *n* presa *f*, represa *f* (LAm)

damag|e /'dæmɪdʒ/ *n* daño *m*; ~**s** (*npl*, Jurid) daños *mpl* y perjuicios *mpl*. ● *vt* (fig) dañar, estropear. ~**ing** *a* perjudicial

dame /deɪm/ *n* (old use) dama *f*; (Amer, 🆒) chica *f*

damn /dæm/ *vt* condenar; (curse) maldecir. ● *int* 🆒 ¡caray! 🆒. ● *a* maldito. ● *n* **I don't give a** ~ (no) me importa un comino

damp /dæmp/ *n* humedad *f*. ● *a* (**-er**, **-est**) húmedo. ● *vt* mojar. ~**ness** *n* humedad *f*

danc|e /dɑːns/ *vt/i* bailar. ● *n* baile *m*. ~**e hall** *n* salón *m* de baile. ~**er** *n* bailador *m*; (professional) bailarín *m*. ~**ing** *n* baile *m*

dandelion /'dændɪlaɪən/ *n* diente *m* de león

dandruff /'dændrʌf/ *n* caspa *f*

dandy /'dændi/ *n* petimetre *m*

Dane /deɪn/ *n* danés *m*

danger /'deɪndʒə(r)/ *n* peligro *m*; (risk) riesgo *m*. ~**ous** *a* peligroso

dangle /'dæŋgl/ *vt* balancear. ● *vi* suspender, colgar

Danish /'deɪnɪʃ/ *a* danés. ● *m* (Lang) danés *m*

dar|e /deə(r)/ *vt* desafiar. ● *vi* atreverse a. **I** ~ **say** probablemente. ● *n* desafío *m*. ~**edevil** *n* atrevido *m*. ~**ing** *a* atrevido

dark /dɑːk/ *a* (**-er**, **-est**) oscuro; *<skin, hair>* moreno. ● *n* oscuridad *f*; (nightfall) atardecer. **in the** ~ a oscuras. ~**en** *vt* oscurecer. ● *vi* oscurecerse. ~**ness** *n* oscuridad *f*. ~**room** *n* cámara *f* oscura

darling /'dɑːlɪŋ/ *a* querido. ● *n* cariño *m*

darn /dɑːn/ *vt* zurcir

dart /dɑːt/ *n* dardo *m*. ● *vi* lanzarse; (run) precipitarse. ~**board** *n* diana *f*. ~**s** *npl* los dardos *mpl*

dash /dæʃ/ *vi* precipitarse. ● *vt* tirar; (break) romper; defraudar <hopes>. ● *n* (small amount) poquito *m*; (punctuation mark) guión *m*. □ ~ **off** *vi* marcharse apresuradamente. ~ **out** *vi* salir corriendo. ~**board** *n* tablero *m* de mandos

data /'deɪtə/ *npl* datos *mpl*. ~**base** *n* base *f* de datos. ~ **processing** *n* proceso *m* de datos

date /deɪt/ *n* fecha *f*; (appointment) cita *f*; (fruit) dátil *m*. **to** ~ hasta la fecha. ● *vt* fechar. ● *vi* datar; datar <remains>; (be old-fashioned) quedar anticuado. ~**d** *a* pasado de moda

daub /dɔːb/ *vt* embadurnar

daughter /'dɔːtə(r)/ *n* hija *f*. ~**in-law** *n* nuera *f*

dawdle /'dɔːdl/ *vi* andar despacio; (waste time) perder el tiempo

dawn /dɔːn/ *n* amanecer *m*. ● *vi* amanecer; (fig) nacer. **it** ~**ed on me that** caí en la cuenta de que

day /deɪ/ *n* día *m*; (whole day) jornada *f*; (period) época *f*. ~**break** *n* amanecer *m*. ~ **care center** *n* (Amer) guardería *f* infantil. ~**dream** *n* ensueño *m*. ● *vi* soñar despierto. ~**light** *n* luz *f* del día. ~**time** *n* día *m*

daze /deɪz/ *vt* aturdir. ● *n* aturdimiento *m*. **in a** ~ aturdido. ~**d** *a* aturdido

dazzle /'dæzl/ *vt* deslumbrar

dead /ded/ *a* muerto; (numb) dormido. ● *adv* justo; (🆃, completely) completamente. ~ **beat** rendido. ~ **slow** muy lento. **stop** ~ parar en seco. ~**en** *vt* amortiguar <sound, blow>; calmar <pain>. ~ **end** *n* callejón *m* sin salida. ~**line** *n* fecha *f* tope, plazo *m* de entrega. ~**lock** *n* punto *m* muerto. ~**ly** *a* (**-ier, -iest**) mortal

deaf /def/ *a* (**-er, -est**) sordo. ~**en** *vt* ensordecer. ~**ness** *n* sordera *f*

deal /diːl/ *n* (agreement) acuerdo *m*; (treatment) trato *m*. **a good** ~ bastante. **a great** ~ **(of)** muchísimo. ● *vt* (*pt* **dealt**) dar <a blow, cards>. ● *vi* (cards) dar, repartir. □ ~ **in** *vt* comerciar en. □ ~ **out** *vt* repartir, distribuir. □ ~ **with** *vt* tratar con <person>; tratar de <subject>; ocu-

parse de <problem>. ~**er** *n* comerciante *m*. **drug** ~**er** traficante *m* & *f* de drogas

dean /diːn/ *n* deán *m*; (Univ) decano *m*

dear /dɪə(r)/ *a* (**-er, -est**) querido; (expensive) caro. ● *n* querido *m*. ● *adv* caro. ● *int.* oh ~! ¡ay por Dios! ~ **me!** ¡Dios mío! ~**ly** *adv* (pay) caro; (very much) muchísimo

death /deθ/ *n* muerte *f*. ~ **sentence** *n* pena *f* de muerte. ~ **trap** *n* lugar *m* peligroso

debat|able /dɪ'beɪtəbl/ *a* discutible. ~**e** /dɪ'beɪt/ *n* debate *m*. ● *vt* debatir, discutir

debauchery /dɪ'bɔːtʃərɪ/ *vt* libertinaje *m*

debit /'debɪt/ *n* débito *m*. ● *vt* debitar, cargar. ~ **card** *n* tarjeta *f* de cobro automático

debris /'debriː/ *n* escombros *mpl*

debt /det/ *n* deuda *f*. **be in** ~ tener deudas. ~**or** *n* deudor *m*

decade /'dekeɪd/ *n* década *f*

decaden|ce /'dekədəns/ *n* decadencia *f*. ~**t** *a* decadente

decay /dɪ'keɪ/ *vi* descomponerse; <tooth> cariarse. ● *n* descomposición *f*; (of tooth) caries *f*

deceased /dɪ'siːst/ *a* difunto

deceit /dɪ'siːt/ *n* engaño *m*. ~**ful** *a* falso. ~**fully** *adv* falsamente

deceive /dɪ'siːv/ *vt* engañar

December /dɪ'sembə(r)/ *n* diciembre *m*

decen|cy /'diːsənsɪ/ *n* decencia *f*. ~**t** *a* decente; (🆃, good) bueno; (🆃, kind) amable. ~**tly** *adv* decentemente

decepti|on /dɪ'sepʃn/ *n* engaño *m*. ~**ve** /-tɪv/ *a* engañoso

decibel /'desɪbel/ *n* decibel(io) *m*

decide /dɪ'saɪd/ *vt/i* decidir. ~**d** *a* resuelto; (unquestionable) indudable. ~**dly** *adv* decididamente; (unquestionably) indudablemente

decimal /'desɪml/ *a* & *n* decimal (*m*). ~ **point** *n* coma *f* (decimal), punto *m* decimal

decipher /dɪ'saɪfə(r)/ *vt* descifrar

decis|ion /dɪ'sɪʒn/ *n* decisión *f*. ~**ive** /dɪ'saɪsɪv/ *a* decisivo; <manner> decidido

deck /dek/ n (Naut) cubierta f; (Amer, of cards) baraja f; (of bus) piso m. ● vt adornar. ~**chair** n tumbona f, silla f de playa

declar|ation /deklə'reɪʃn/ n declaración f. ~**e** /dɪ'kleə(r)/ vt declarar

decline /dɪ'klaɪn/ vt rehusar; (Gram) declinar. ● vi disminuir; (deteriorate) deteriorarse. ● n decadencia f; (decrease) disminución f

decode /diː'kəʊd/ vt descifrar

decompose /diːkəm'pəʊz/ vi descomponerse

décor /'deɪkɔː(r)/ n decoración f

decorat|e /'dekəreɪt/ vt adornar, decorar (LAm); empapelar y pintar *<room>*. ~**ion** /-'reɪʃn/ n (act) decoración f; (ornament) adorno m. ~**ive** /-ətɪv/ a decorativo. ~**or** n pintor m decorador

decoy /'diːkɔɪ/ n señuelo m. ● /dɪ'kɔɪ/ vt atraer con señuelo

decrease /dɪ'kriːs/ vt/i disminuir. ● /'diːkriːs/ n disminución f

decree /dɪ'kriː/ n decreto m. ● vt decretar

decrepit /dɪ'krepɪt/ a decrépito

dedicat|e /'dedɪkeɪt/ vt dedicar. ~**ion** /-'keɪʃn/ n dedicación f

deduce /dɪ'djuːs/ vt deducir

deduct /dɪ'dʌkt/ vt deducir. ~**ion** /-ʃn/ n deducción f

deed /diːd/ n hecho m; (Jurid) escritura f

deem /diːm/ vt juzgar, considerar

deep /diːp/ a (**-er, -est**) adv profundo. ● adv profundamente. be ~ **in thought** estar absorto en sus pensamientos. ~**en** vt hacer más profundo. ● vi hacerse más profundo. ~**freeze** n congelador m, freezer m (LAm). ~**ly** adv profundamente

deer /dɪə(r)/ n invar ciervo m

deface /dɪ'feɪs/ vt desfigurar

default /dɪ'fɔːlt/ vi faltar. ● n. by ~ en rebeldía

defeat /dɪ'fiːt/ vt vencer; (frustrate) frustrar. ● n derrota f. ~**ism** n derrotismo m. ~**ist** n derrotista a & (m & f)

defect /'diːfekt/ n defecto m. ● /dɪ'fekt/ vi desertar. ~ **to** pasar a.

~**ion** /dɪ'fekʃn/ n (Pol) defección f. ~**ive** /dɪ'fektɪv/ a defectuoso

defence /dɪ'fens/ n defensa f. ~**less** a indefenso

defen|d /dɪ'fend/ vt defender. ~**dant** n (Jurid) acusado m. ~**sive** /-sɪv/ a defensivo. ● n defensiva f

defer /dɪ'fɜː(r)/ vt (pt **deferred**) aplazar. ~**ence** /'defərəns/ n deferencia f. ~**ential** /defə'renʃl/ a deferente

defian|ce /dɪ'faɪəns/ n desafío m. in ~**ce of** a despecho de. ~**t** a desafiante. ~**tly** adv con actitud desafiante

deficien|cy /dɪ'fɪʃənsɪ/ n falta f. ~**t** a deficiente. be ~**t in** carecer de

deficit /'defɪsɪt/ n déficit m

define /dɪ'faɪn/ vt definir

definite /'defɪnɪt/ a (final) definitivo; (certain) seguro; (clear) claro; (firm) firme. ~**ly** adv seguramente; (definitively) definitivamente

definition /defɪ'nɪʃn/ n definición f

definitive /dɪ'fɪnətɪv/ a definitivo

deflate /dɪ'fleɪt/ vt desinflar. ● vi desinflarse

deflect /dɪ'flekt/ vt desviar

deform /dɪ'fɔːm/ vt deformar. ~**ed** a deforme. ~**ity** n deformidad f

defrost /diː'frɒst/ vt descongelar. ● vi descongelarse

deft /deft/ a (**-er, -est**) hábil. ~**ly** adv hábilmente f

defuse /diː'fjuːz/ vt desactivar *<bomb>*; (fig) calmar

defy /dɪ'faɪ/ vt desafiar

degenerate /dɪ'dʒenəreɪt/ vi degenerar. ● /dɪ'dʒenərət/ a & n degenerado (m)

degrad|ation /degrə'deɪʃn/ n degradación f. ~**e** /dɪ'greɪd/ vt degradar

degree /dɪ'griː/ n grado m; (Univ) licenciatura f; (rank) rango m. to a cer-tain ~ hasta cierto punto

deign /deɪn/ vi. ~ **to** dignarse

deity /'diːɪtɪ/ n deidad f

deject|ed /dɪ'dʒektɪd/ a desanimado. ~**ion** /-ʃn/ n abatimiento m

delay /dɪ'leɪ/ vt retrasar, demorar (LAm). ● vi tardar, demorar (LAm). ● n retraso m, demora f (LAm)

delegat|e /'delɪgeɪt/ *vt/i* delegar. ● /'delɪgət/ *n* delegado *m*. ~**ion** /-'geɪʃn/ *n* delegación *f*

delet|e /dɪ'li:t/ *vt* tachar. ~**ion** /-ʃn/ *n* supresión *f*

deliberat|e /dɪ'lɪbəreɪt/ *vt/i* deliberar. ● /dɪ'lɪbərət/ *a* intencionado; <*steps etc*> pausado. ~**ely** *adv* a propósito. ~**ion** /-'reɪʃn/ *n* deliberación *f*

delica|cy /'delɪkəsɪ/ *n* delicadeza *f*; (food) manjar *m*. ~**te** /'delɪkət/ *a* delicado

delicatessen /delɪkə'tesn/ *n* charcutería *f*, salchichonería *f* (Mex)

delicious /dɪ'lɪʃəs/ *a* delicioso

delight /dɪ'laɪt/ *n* placer *m*. ● *vt* encantar. ● *vi* deleitarse. ~**ed** *a* encantado. ~**ful** *a* delicioso

deliri|ous /dɪ'lɪrɪəs/ *a* delirante. ~**um** /-əm/ *n* delirio *m*

deliver /dɪ'lɪvə(r)/ *vt* entregar; (distribute) repartir; (aim) lanzar; (Med) he ~**ed** the baby la asistió en el parto. ~**ance** *n* liberación *f*. ~**y** *n* entrega *f*; (of post) reparto *m*; (Med) parto *m*

delta /'deltə/ *n* (Geog) delta *m*

delude /dɪ'lu:d/ *vt* engañar. ~ **o.s.** engañarse

deluge /'delju:dʒ/ *n* diluvio *m*

delusion /dɪ'lu:ʒn/ *n* ilusión *f*

deluxe /dɪ'lʌks/ *a* de lujo

delve /delv/ *vi* hurgar. ~ **into** (investigate) ahondar en

demand /dɪ'mɑ:nd/ *vt* exigir. ● *n* petición *f*, pedido *m* (LAm); (claim) exigencia *f*; (Com) demanda *f*. **in** ~ muy popular, muy solicitado. **on** ~ a solicitud. ~**ing** *a* exigente. ~**s** *npl* exigencias *fpl*

demented /dɪ'mentɪd/ *a* demente

demo /'deməʊ/ *n* (*pl* -**os**) 🔲 manifestación *f*

democra|cy /dɪ'mɒkrəsɪ/ *n* democracia *f*. ~**t** /'deməkræt/ *n* demócrata *m* & *f*. **D~t** *a* & *n* (in US) demócrata (*m* & *f*). ~**tic** /demə'krætɪk/ *a* democrático

demoli|sh /dɪ'mɒlɪʃ/ *vt* derribar. ~**tion** /demə'lɪʃn/ *n* demolición *f*

demon /'di:mən/ *n* demonio *m*

demonstrat|e /'demənstreɪt/ *vt* demostrar. ● *vi* manifestarse, hacer

una manifestación. ~**ion** /-'streɪʃn/ *n* demostración *f*; (Pol) manifestación *f*. ~**or** /'demənstreɪtə(r)/*n* (Pol) manifestante *m* & *f*; (marketing) demostrador *m*

demoralize /dɪ'mɒrəlaɪz/ *vt* desmoralizar

demote /dɪ'məʊt/ *vt* bajar de categoría

demure /dɪ'mjʊə(r)/ *a* recatado

den /den/ *n* (of animal) guarida *f*, madriguera *f*

denial /dɪ'naɪəl/ *n* denegación *f*; (statement) desmentimiento *m*

denim /'denɪm/ *n* tela *f* vaquera *or* de jeans, mezclilla (Mex) *f*. ~**s** *npl* vaqueros *mpl*, jeans *mpl*, tejanos *mpl*, pantalones *mpl* de mezclilla (Mex)

Denmark /'denmɑ:k/ *n* Dinamarca *f*

denote /dɪ'nəʊt/ *vt* denotar

denounce /dɪ'naʊns/ *vt* denunciar

dens|e /dens/ *a* (-**er**, -**est**) espeso; <*person*> torpe. ~**ely** *adv* densamente. ~**ity** *n* densidad *f*

dent /dent/ *n* abolladura *f*. ● *vt* abollar

dental /'dentl/ *a* dental. ~ **floss** /flɒs/ *n* hilo *m or* seda *f* dental. ~ **surgeon** *n* dentista *m* & *f*

dentist /'dentɪst/ *n* dentista *m* & *f*. ~**ry** *n* odontología *f*

dentures /'dentʃəz/ *npl* dentadura *f* postiza

deny /dɪ'naɪ/ *vt* negar; desmentir <*rumour*>; denegar <*request*>

deodorant /dɪ'əʊdərənt/ *a* & *n* desodorante (*m*)

depart /dɪ'pɑ:t/ *vi* partir, salir. ~ **from** (deviate from) apartarse de

department /dɪ'pɑ:tment/ *n* departamento *m*; (Pol) ministerio *m*, secretaría *f* (Mex). ~ **store** *n* grandes almacenes *mpl*, tienda *f* de departamentos (Mex)

departure /dɪ'pɑ:tʃə(r)/ *n* partida *f*; (of train etc) salida *f*

depend /dɪ'pend/ *vi* depender. ~ **on** depender de. ~**able** *a* digno de confianza. ~**ant** /dɪ'pendənt/ *n* familiar *m* & *f* dependiente. ~**ence** *n* dependencia *f*. ~**ent** *a* dependiente. **be** ~**ent on** depender de

depict /dɪ'pɪkt/ vt representar; (in words) describir

deplete /dɪ'pliːt/ vt agotar

deplor|able /dɪ'plɔːrəbl/ a deplorable. ~e /dɪ'plɔː(r)/ vt deplorar

deploy /dɪ'plɔɪ/ vt desplegar

deport /dɪ'pɔːt/ vt deportar. ~ation /-'teɪʃn/ n deportación f

depose /dɪ'pəʊz/ vt deponer

deposit /dɪ'pɒzɪt/ vt (pt **deposited**) depositar. ● n depósito m

depot /'depəʊ/ n depósito m; (Amer) estación f de autobuses

deprav|ed /dɪ'preɪvd/ a depravado. ~ity /dɪ'prævətɪ/ n depravación f

depress /dɪ'pres/ vt deprimir; (press down) apretar. ~ed a deprimido. ~ing a deprimente. ~ion /-ʃn/ n depresión f

depriv|ation /deprɪ'veɪʃn/ n privación f. ~e /dɪ'praɪv/ vt. ~e of privar de. ~d a carenciado

depth /depθ/ n profundidad f. be out of one's ~ perder pie; (fig) meterse en honduras. in ~ a fondo

deput|ize /'depjʊtaɪz/ vi. ~ize for sustituir a. ~y /'depjʊtɪ/ n sustituto m. ~y **chairman** n vicepresidente m

derail /dɪ'reɪl/ vt hacer descarrilar. ~ment n descarrilamiento m

derelict /'derəlɪkt/ a abandonado y en ruinas

deri|de /dɪ'raɪd/ vt mofarse de. ~sion /dɪ'rɪʒn/ n mofa f. ~sive /dɪ'raɪsɪv/ a burlón. ~sory /dɪ'raɪsərɪ/ a <offer etc> irrisorio

deriv|ation /derɪ'veɪʃn/ n derivación f. ~ative /-'rɪvətɪv/ n derivado m. ~e /dɪ'raɪv/ vt/i derivar

derogatory /dɪ'rɒgətrɪ/ a despectivo

descen|d /dɪ'send/ vt/i descender, bajar. ~dant n descendiente m & f. ~t n descenso m, bajada f; (lineage) ascendencia f

descri|be /dɪs'kraɪb/ vt describir. ~ption /-'krɪpʃn/ n descripción f. ~ptive /-'krɪptɪv/ a descriptivo

desecrate /'desɪkreɪt/ vt profanar

desert¹ /dɪ'zɜːt/ vt abandonar. ● vi (Mil) desertar. ~er /dɪ'zɜːtə(r)/ n desertor m

desert² /'dezət/ a & n desierto (m)

deserts /dɪ'zɜːts/ npl lo merecido. get one's just ~ llevarse su merecido

deserv|e /dɪ'zɜːv/ vt merecer. ~ing a <cause> meritorio

design /dɪ'zaɪn/ n diseño m; (plan) plan m. ~s (intentions) propósitos mpl. ● vt diseñar; (plan) planear

designate /'dezɪgneɪt/ vt designar

designer /dɪ'zaɪnə(r)/ n diseñador m; (fashion ~) diseñador m de modas. ● a <clothes> de diseño exclusivo

desirable /dɪ'zaɪərəbl/ a deseable

desire /dɪ'zaɪə(r)/ n deseo m. ● vt desear

desk /desk/ n escritorio m; (at school) pupitre m; (in hotel) recepción f; (Com) caja f. ~top publishing n autoedición f, edición f electrónica

desolat|e /'desəlat/ a desolado; (uninhabited) deshabitado. ~ion /-'leɪʃn/ n desolación f

despair /dɪ'speə(r)/ n desesperación f. be in ~ estar desesperado. ● vi. ~ of desesperarse de

despatch /dɪ'spætʃ/ vt, n ⇒DISPATCH

desperat|e /'despərət/ a desesperado. ~ely adv desesperadamente. ~ion /-'reɪʃn/ n desesperación f

despicable /dɪ'spɪkəbl/ a despreciable

despise /dɪ'spaɪz/ vt despreciar

despite /dɪ'spaɪt/ prep a pesar de

despondent /dɪ'spɒndənt/ a abatido

despot /'despɒt/ n déspota m

dessert /dɪ'zɜːt/ n postre m. ~spoon n cuchara f de postre

destination /destɪ'neɪʃn/ n destino m

destiny /'destɪnɪ/ n destino m

destitute /'destɪtjuːt/ a indigente

destroy /dɪ'strɔɪ/ vt destruir. ~er n destructor m

destructi|on /dɪ'strʌkʃn/ n destrucción f. ~ve /-ɪv/ a destructivo

desultory /'desəltrɪ/ a desganado

detach /dɪ'tætʃ/ vt separar. ~able a separable. ~ed a (aloof) distante; (house) no adosado. ~ment n desprendimiento *m*; (Mil) desta-camento *m*; (aloofness) indiferencia *f*

detail /'di:teɪl/ *n* detalle *m*. **explain sth in** ~ explicar algo detalla-damente. ● *vt* detallar; (Mil) destacar. ~**ed** *a* detallado

detain /dɪ'teɪn/ *vt* detener; (delay) re-tener. ~**ee** /di:teɪ'ni:/ *n* detenido *m*

detect /dɪ'tekt/ *vt* percibir; (discover) descubrir. ~**ive** *n* (private) detective *m*; (in police) agente *m* & *f*. ~**or** *n* de-tector *m*

detention /dɪ'tenʃn/ *n* detención *f*

deter /dɪ'tɜ:(r)/ *vt* (*pt* **deterred**) di-suadir; (prevent) impedir

detergent /dɪ'tɜ:dʒənt/ *a* & *n* de-tergente (*m*)

deteriorat|e /dɪ'tɪərɪəreɪt/ *vi* dete-riorarse. ~**ion** /-'reɪʃn/ *n* deterioro *m*

determin|ation /dɪtɜ:mɪ'neɪʃn/ *n* determinación *f*. ~**e** /dɪ'tɜ:mɪn/ *vt* determinar; (decide) decidir. ~**ed** *a* determinado; (resolute) decidido

deterrent /dɪ'terənt/ *n* fuerza *f* de disuasión

detest /dɪ'test/ *vt* aborrecer. ~**able** *a* odioso

detonat|e /'detəneɪt/ *vt* hacer de-tonar. ● *vi* detonar. ~**ion** /-'neɪʃn/ *n* detonación *f*. ~**or** *n* detonador *m*

detour /'di:tʊə(r)/ *n* rodeo *m*; (Amer, of transport) desvío *m*, desviación *f*. ● *vt* (Amer) desviar

detract /dɪ'trækt/ *vi*. ~ **from** dismi-nuir

detriment /'detrɪmənt/ *n*. **to the** ~ **of** en perjuicio de. ~**al** /-'mentl/ *a* perjudicial

devalue /di:'vælju:/ *vt* desvalorizar

devastat|e /'devəsteɪt/ *vt* devastar. ~**ing** *a* devastador; (fig) arrollador. ~**ion** /-'steɪʃn/ *n* devastación *f*

develop /dɪ'veləp/ *vt* desarrollar; contraer *<illness>*; urbanizar *<land>*. ● *vi* desarrollarse; (appear) surgir. ~**ing** *a* *<country>* en vías de desa-rrollo. ~**ment** *n* desarrollo *m*. (new) ~**ment** novedad *f*

deviant /'di:vɪənt/ *a* desviado

deviat|e /'di:vɪeɪt/ *vi* desviarse. ~**ion** /-'eɪʃn/ *n* desviación *f*

device /dɪ'vaɪs/ *n* dispositivo *m*; (scheme) estratagema *f*

devil /'devl/ *n* diablo *m*

devious /'di:vɪəs/ *a* taimado

devise /dɪ'vaɪz/ *vt* idear

devoid /dɪ'vɔɪd/ *a*. **be** ~ **of** carecer de

devolution /di:və'lu:ʃn/ *n* descen-tralización *f*; (of power) delegación *f*

devot|e /dɪ'vəʊt/ *vt* dedicar. ~**ed** *a* *<couple>* unido; *<service>* leal. ~**ee** /devə'ti:/ *n* partidario *m*. ~**ion** /-ʃn/ *n* devoción *f*

devour /dɪ'vaʊə(r)/ *vt* devorar

devout /dɪ'vaʊt/ *a* devoto

dew /dju:/ *n* rocío *m*

dexterity /dek'sterətɪ/ *n* destreza *f*

diabet|es /daɪə'bi:ti:z/ *n* diabetes *f*. ~**ic** /-'betɪk/ *a* & *n* diabético (*m*)

diabolical /daɪə'bɒlɪkl/ *a* diabólico

diagnos|e /'daɪəgnəʊz/ *vt* diag-nosticar. ~**is** /-'nəʊsɪs/ *n* (*pl* -**oses** /-si:z/) diagnóstico *m*

diagonal /daɪ'ægənl/ *a* & *n* diago-nal (*f*)

diagram /'daɪəgræm/ *n* diagrama *m*

dial /'daɪəl/ *n* cuadrante *m*; (on clock, watch) esfera *f*; (on phone) disco *m*. ● *vt* (*pt* **dialled**) marcar, discar (LAm)

dialect /'daɪəlekt/ *n* dialecto *m*

dialling: ~ **code** *n* prefijo *m*, códi-go *m* de la zona (LAm). ~ **tone** *n* tono *m* de marcar, tono *m* de discado (LAm)

dialogue /'daɪəlɒg/ *n* diálogo *m*

dial tone *n* (Amer) ⇒DIALLING TONE

diameter /daɪ'æmɪtə(r)/ *n* diáme-tro *m*

diamond /'daɪəmənd/ *n* diamante *m*; (shape) rombo *m*. ~**s** *npl* (Cards) diamantes *mpl*

diaper /'daɪəpə(r)/ *n* (Amer) pañal *m*

diaphragm /'daɪəfræm/ *n* diafrag-ma *m*

diarrhoea /daɪə'rɪə/ *n* diarrea *f*

diary /'daɪərɪ/ *n* diario *m*; (book) agenda *f*

dice /daɪs/ *n invar* dado *m*. ● *vt* (Culin) cortar en cubitos

dictat|e /dɪk'teɪt/ *vt/i* dictar. ~**ion** /dɪk'teɪʃn/ *n* dictado *m*. ~**or** *n* dicta-dor *m*. ~**orship** *n* dictadura *f*

dictionary /'dɪkʃənərɪ/ n diccionario m

did /dɪd/ ⇒DO

didn't /'dɪdnt/ = **did not**

die /daɪ/ vi (pres p **dying**) morir. be dying to morirse por. □ ~ **down** vi irse apagando. □ ~ **out** vi extinguirse

diesel /'di:zl/ n (fuel) gasóleo m. ~ **engine** n motor m diesel

diet /'daɪət/ n alimentación f; (restricted) régimen m. be on a ~ estar a régimen. ● vi estar a régimen

differ /'dɪfə(r)/ vi ser distinto; (disagree) no estar de acuerdo. ~**ence** /'dɪfrəns/ n diferencia f; (disagreement) desacuerdo m. ~**ent** /'dɪfrənt/ a distinto, diferente. ~**ently** adv de otra manera

difficult /'dɪfɪkəlt/ a difícil. ~**y** n dificultad f

diffus|e /dɪ'fju:s/ a difuso. ● /dɪ'fju:z/ vt difundir. ● vi difundirse. ~**ion** /-ʒn/ n difusión f

dig /dɪg/ n (poke) empujón m; (poke with elbow) codazo m; (remark) indirecta f. ~**s** npl 🄵 alojamiento m ● vt (pt **dug**, pres p **digging**) cavar; (thrust) empujar. ● vi cavar. □ ~ **out** vt extraer. □ ~ **up** vt desenterrar

digest /'daɪdʒest/ n resumen m. ● /dar'dʒest/ vt digerir. ~**ion** /-'dʒestʃn/ n digestión f. ~**ive** /-'dʒestɪv/ a digestivo

digger /'dɪgə(r)/ n (Mec) excavadora f

digit /'dɪdʒɪt/ n dígito m; (finger) dedo m. ~**al** /'dɪdʒɪtl/ a digital

dignified /'dɪgnɪfaɪd/ a solemne

dignitary /'dɪgnɪtərɪ/ n dignatario m

dignity /'dɪgnətɪ/ n dignidad f

digress /daɪ'gres/ vi divagar. ~ from apartarse de. ~**ion** /-ʃn/ n digresión f

dike /daɪk/ n dique m

dilapidated /dɪ'læpɪdeɪtɪd/ a ruinoso

dilate /daɪ'leɪt/ vt dilatar. ● vi dilatarse

dilemma /daɪ'lemə/ n dilema m

diligent /'dɪlɪdʒənt/ a diligente

dilute /daɪ'lju:t/ vt diluir

dim /dɪm/ a (**dimmer, dimmest**) <light> débil; <room> oscuro; (🄵, stupid) torpe. ● vt (pt **dimmed**) atenuar. ~ one's headlights (Amer) poner las (luces) cortas or de cruce, poner las (luces) bajas (LAm). ● vi <light> irse atenuando

dime /daɪm/ n (Amer) moneda de diez centavos

dimension /daɪ'menʃn/ n dimensión f

diminish /dɪ'mɪnɪʃ/ vt/i disminuir

dimple /'dɪmpl/ n hoyuelo m

din /dɪn/ n jaleo m

dine /daɪn/ vi cenar. ~**r** n comensal m & f; (Amer, restaurant) cafetería f

dinghy /'dɪŋgɪ/ n bote m; (inflatable) bote m neumático

dingy /'dɪndʒɪ/ a (**-ier, -iest**) miserable, sucio

dining: /'daɪnɪŋ/~ **car** n coche m restaurante. ~ **room** n comedor m

dinner /'dɪnə(r)/ n cena f, comida f (LAm). have ~ cenar, comer (LAm). ~ **party** n cena f, comida f (LAm)

dinosaur /'daɪnəsɔ:(r)/ n dinosaurio m

dint /dɪnt/ n. by ~ of a fuerza de

dip /dɪp/ vt (pt **dipped**) meter; (in liquid) mojar. ~ one's headlights poner las (luces) cortas or de cruce, poner las (luces) bajas (LAm). ● vi bajar. ● n (slope) inclinación f; (in sea) baño m. □ ~ **into** vt hojear <book>

diphthong /'dɪfθɒŋ/ n diptongo m

diploma /dɪ'pləʊmə/ n diploma m

diploma|cy /dɪ'pləʊməsɪ/ n diplomacia f. ~**t** /'dɪpləmæt/ n diplomático m. ~**tic** /-'mætɪk/ a diplomático

dipstick /'dɪpstɪk/ n (Auto) varilla f del nivel de aceite

dire /daɪə(r)/ a (**-er, -est**) terrible; <need, poverty> extremo

direct /dɪ'rekt/ a directo. ● adv directamente. ● vt dirigir; (show the way) indicar. ~**ion** /-ʃn/ n dirección f. ~**ions** npl instrucciones fpl. ~**ly** adv directamente; (at once) en seguida. ● conj 🄵 en cuanto. ~**or** n director m; (of company) directivo m

directory /dɪ'rektərɪ/ n guía f; (Comp) directorio m

dirt /dɜːt/ *n* suciedad *f*. ~**y** *a* (**-ier**, **-iest**) sucio. ● *vt* ensuciar

disab|ility /dɪsə'bɪlətɪ/ *n* invalidez *f*. ~**le** /dɪs'eɪbl/ *vt* incapacitar. ~**led** *a* minusválido

disadvantage /dɪsəd'vɑːntɪdʒ/ *n* desventaja *f*. ~**d** *a* desfavorecido

disagree /dɪsə'griː/ *vi* no estar de acuerdo (**with** con). ~ **with** <*food, climate*> sentarle mal a. ~**able** *a* desagradable. ~**ment** *n* desacuerdo *m*; (quarrel) riña *f*

disappear /dɪsə'pɪə(r)/ *vi* desaparecer. ~**ance** *n* desaparición *f*

disappoint /dɪsə'pɔɪnt/ *vt* decepcionar. ~**ing** *a* decepcionante. ~**ment** *n* decepción *f*

disapprov|al /dɪsə'pruːvl/ *n* desaprobación *f*. ~**e** /dɪsə'pruːv/ *vi*. ~**e of** desaprobar. ~**ing** *a* de reproche

disarm /dɪs'ɑːm/ *vt* desarmar. ● *vi* desarmarse. ~**ament** *n* desarme *m*

disarray /dɪsə'reɪ/ *n* desorden *m*

disast|er /dɪ'zɑːstə(r)/ *n* desastre *m*. ~**rous** /-strəs/ *a* catastrófico

disband /dɪs'bænd/ *vt* disolver. ● *vi* disolverse

disbelief /dɪsbɪ'liːf/ *n* incredulidad *f*

disc /dɪsk/ *n* disco *m*

discard /dɪs'kɑːd/ *vt* descartar; abandonar <*beliefs etc*>

discern /dɪ'sɜːn/ *vt* percibir. ~**ing** *a* exigente; <*ear, eye*> educado

discharge /dɪs'tʃɑːdʒ/ *vt* descargar; cumplir <*duty*>; (Mil) licenciar. ● /'dɪstʃɑːdʒ/ *n* descarga *f*; (Med) secreción *f*; (Mil) licenciamiento *m*

disciple /dɪ'saɪpl/ *n* discípulo *m*

disciplin|ary /dɪsə'plɪnərɪ/ *a* disciplinario. ~**e** /'dɪsɪplɪn/ *n* disciplina *f*. ● *vt* disciplinar; (punish) sancionar

disc jockey /'dɪskdʒɒkɪ/ *n* pinchadiscos *m & f*

disclaim /dɪs'kleɪm/ *vt* desconocer. ~**er** *n* (Jurid) descargo *m* de responsabilidad

disclos|e /dɪs'kləʊz/ *vt* revelar. ~**ure** /-ʒə(r)/ *n* revelación *f*

disco /'dɪskəʊ/ *n* (*pl* **-os**) 🔲 discoteca *f*

discolour /dɪs'kʌlə(r)/ *vt* decolorar. ● *vi* decolorarse

discomfort /dɪs'kʌmfət/ *n* malestar *m*; (lack of comfort) incomodidad *f*

disconcert /dɪskən'sɜːt/ *vt* desconcertar

disconnect /dɪskə'nekt/ *vt* separar; (Elec) desconectar

disconsolate /dɪs'kɒnsələt/ *a* desconsolado

discontent /dɪskən'tent/ *n* descontento *m*. ~**ed** *a* descontento

discontinue /dɪskən'tɪnjuː/ *vt* interrumpir

discord /'dɪskɔːd/ *n* discordia *f*; (Mus) disonancia *f*. ~**ant** /-'skɔːdənt/ *a* discorde; (Mus) disonante

discotheque /'dɪskətek/ *n* discoteca *f*

discount /'dɪskaʊnt/ *n* descuento *m*. ● /dɪs'kaʊnt/ *vt* hacer caso omiso de; (Com) descontar

discourag|e /dɪs'kʌrɪdʒ/ *vt* desanimar; (dissuade) disuadir. ~**ing** *a* desalentador

discourteous /dɪs'kɜːtɪəs/ *a* descortés

discover /dɪs'kʌvə(r)/ *vt* descubrir. ~**y** *n* descubrimiento *m*

discredit /dɪs'kredɪt/ *vt* (*pt* **discredited**) desacreditar. ● *n* descrédito *m*

discreet /dɪs'kriːt/ *a* discreto. ~**ly** *adv* discretamente

discrepancy /dɪ'skrepənsɪ/ *n* discrepancia *f*

discretion /dɪ'skreʃn/ *n* discreción *f*

discriminat|e /dɪs'krɪmɪneɪt/ *vt* discriminar. ~**e between** distinguir entre. ~**ing** *a* perspicaz. ~**ion** /-'neɪʃn/ *n* discernimiento *m*; (bias) discriminación *f*

discus /'dɪskəs/ *n* disco *m*

discuss /dɪ'skʌs/ *vt* discutir. ~**ion** /-ʃn/ *n* discusión *f*

disdain /dɪs'deɪn/ *n* desdén *m*. ~**ful** *a* desdeñoso

disease /dɪ'ziːz/ *n* enfermedad *f*

disembark /dɪsɪm'bɑːk/ *vi* desembarcar

disenchant|ed /dɪsɪnˈtʃɑːntɪd/ a desilusionado. **~ment** n desencanto m

disentangle /dɪsɪnˈtæŋgl/ vt desenredar

disfigure /dɪsˈfɪgə(r)/ vt desfigurar

disgrace /dɪsˈgreɪs/ n vergüenza f. ● vt deshonrar. **~ful** a vergonzoso

disgruntled /dɪsˈgrʌntld/ a descontento

disguise /dɪsˈgaɪz/ vt disfrazar. ● n disfraz m. in ~ disfrazado

disgust /dɪsˈgʌst/ n repugnancia f, asco m. ● vt dar asco a. **~ed** a indignado; (stronger) asqueado. **~ing** a repugnante, asqueroso

dish /dɪʃ/ n plato m. wash or do the **~es** fregar los platos, lavar los trastes (Mex). □ ~ **up** vt/i servir. **~cloth** n bayeta f

disheartening /dɪsˈhɑːtnɪŋ/ a desalentador

dishonest /dɪsˈɒnɪst/ a deshonesto. **~y** n falta f de honradez

dishonour /dɪsˈɒnə(r)/ n deshonra f

dish: ~ **soap** n (Amer) lavavajillas m. ~ **towel** n paño m de cocina. **~washer** n lavaplatos m, lavavajillas m. **~washing liquid** n (Amer) ⇒~ SOAP

disillusion /dɪsɪˈluːʒn/ vt desilusionar. **~ment** n desilusión f

disinfect /dɪsɪnˈfekt/ vt desinfectar. **~ant** n desinfectante m

disintegrate /dɪsˈɪntɪgreɪt/ vt desintegrar. ● vi desintegrarse

disinterested /dɪsˈɪntrəstɪd/ a desinteresado

disjointed /dɪsˈdʒɔɪntɪd/ a inconexo

disk /dɪsk/ n disco m. ~ **drive** (Comp) unidad f de discos. **~ette** /dɪsˈket/ n disquete m

dislike /dɪsˈlaɪk/ n aversión f. ● vt. **I ~ dogs** no me gustan los perros

dislocate /ˈdɪsləkeɪt/ vt dislocar(se) <limb>

dislodge /dɪsˈlɒdʒ/ vt sacar

disloyal /dɪsˈlɔɪəl/ a desleal. **~ty** n deslealtad f

dismal /ˈdɪzməl/ a triste; (bad) fatal

dismantle /dɪsˈmæntl/ vt desmontar

dismay /dɪsˈmeɪ/ n consternación f. ● vt consternar

dismiss /dɪsˈmɪs/ vt despedir; (reject) rechazar. **~al** n despido m; (of idea) rechazo m

dismount /dɪsˈmaʊnt/ vi desmontar

disobe|dience /dɪsəˈbiːdɪəns/ n desobediencia f. **~dient** a desobediente. **~y** /dɪsəˈbeɪ/ vt/i desobedecer

disorder /dɪsˈɔːdə(r)/ n desorden m; (ailment) afección f. **~ly** a desordenado

disorganized /dɪsˈɔːgənaɪzd/ a desorganizado

disorientate /dɪsˈɔːrɪənteɪt/ vt desorientar

disown /dɪsˈəʊn/ vt repudiar

disparaging /dɪsˈpærɪdʒɪŋ/ a despreciativo

dispatch /dɪsˈpætʃ/ vt despachar. ● n despacho m. ~ **rider** n mensajero m

dispel /dɪsˈpel/ vt (pt **dispelled**) disipar

dispens|able /dɪsˈpensəbl/ a prescindible. **~e** vt distribuir; (Med) preparar. □ ~ **with** vt prescindir de

dispers|al /dɪˈspɜːsl/ n dispersión f. **~e** /dɪˈspɜːs/ vt dispersar. ● vi dispersarse

dispirited /dɪsˈpɪrɪtɪd/ a desanimado

display /dɪsˈpleɪ/ vt exponer <goods>; demostrar <feelings>. ● n exposición f; (of feelings) demostración f

displeas|e /dɪsˈpliːz/ vt desagradar. be **~ed with** estar disgustado con. **~ure** /-ˈpleʒə(r)/ n desagrado m

dispos|able /dɪsˈpəʊzəbl/ a desechable. **~al** /dɪsˈpəʊzl/ n (of waste) eliminación f. at s.o.'s **~al** a la disposición de uno. **~e of** /dɪsˈpəʊz/ vt deshacerse de

disproportionate /dɪsprəˈpɔːʃənət/ a desproporcionado

disprove /dɪsˈpruːv/ vt desmentir <claim>; refutar <theory>

dispute /dɪs'pjuːt/ vt discutir. ● n disputa f. in ~ disputado

disqualif|ication /dɪskwɒlɪfɪ'keɪʃn/ n descalificación f. ~y /dɪs'kwɒlɪfaɪ/ vt incapacitar; (Sport) descalificar

disregard /dɪsrɪ'gɑːd/ vt no hacer caso de. ● n indiferencia f (for a)

disreputable /dɪs'repjʊtəbl/ a de mala fama

disrespect /dɪsrɪ'spekt/ n falta f de respeto

disrupt /dɪs'rʌpt/ vt interrumpir; trastornar <plans>. ~ion /-ʃn/ n trastorno m. ~ive a <influence> perjudicial, negativo

dissatis|faction /dɪsætɪs'fækʃn/ n descontento m. ~fied /dɪ'sætɪsfaɪd/ a descontento

dissect /dɪ'sekt/ vt disecar

dissent /dɪ'sent/ vi disentir. ● n disentimiento m

dissertation /dɪsə'teɪʃn/ n (Univ) tesis f

dissident /'dɪsɪdənt/ a & n disidente (m & f)

dissimilar /dɪ'sɪmɪlə(r)/ a distinto

dissolute /'dɪsəluːt/ a disoluto

dissolve /dɪ'zɒlv/ vt disolver. ● vi disolverse

dissuade /dɪ'sweɪd/ vt disuadir

distan|ce /'dɪstəns/ n distancia f. from a ~ce desde lejos. in the ~ce a lo lejos. ~t a distante, lejano; (aloof) distante

distaste /dɪs'teɪst/ n desagrado m. ~ful a desagradable

distil /dɪs'tɪl/ vt (pt distilled) destilar. ~lery /dɪs'tɪlərɪ/ n destilería f

distinct /dɪs'tɪŋkt/ a distinto; (clear) claro; (marked) marcado. ~ion /-ʃn/ n distinción f; (in exam) sobresaliente m. ~ive a distintivo

distinguish /dɪs'tɪŋgwɪʃ/ vt/i distinguir. ~ed a distinguido

distort /dɪs'tɔːt/ vt torcer. ~ion /-ʃn/ n deformación f

distract /dɪs'trækt/ vt distraer. ~ed a distraído. ~ion /-ʃn/ n distracción f; (confusion) aturdimiento m

distraught /dɪs'trɔːt/ a consternado, angustiado

distress /dɪs'tres/ n angustia f. ● vt afligir. ~ed a afligido. ~ing a penoso

distribut|e /dɪ'strɪbjuːt/ vt repartir, distribuir. ~ion /-'bjuːʃn/ n distribución f. ~or n distribuidor m; (Auto) distribuidor m (del encendido)

district /'dɪstrɪkt/ n zona f, región f; (of town) barrio m

distrust /dɪs'trʌst/ n desconfianza f. ● vt desconfiar de

disturb /dɪs'tɜːb/ vt molestar; (perturb) inquietar; (move) desordenar; (interrupt) interrumpir. ~ance n disturbio m; (tumult) alboroto m. ~ed a trastornado. ~ing a inquietante

disused /dɪs'juːzd/ a fuera de uso

ditch /dɪtʃ/ n zanja f; (for irrigation) acequia f. ● vt 🆃 abandonar

dither /'dɪðə(r)/ vi vacilar

ditto /'dɪtəʊ/ adv ídem

divan /dɪ'væn/ n diván m

dive /daɪv/ vi tirarse (al agua), zambullirse; (rush) meterse (precipitadamente). ● n (into water) zambullida f; (Sport) salto m (de trampolín); (of plane) descenso m en picado, descenso m en picada (LAm); (🆃, place) antro m. ~r n saltador m; (underwater) buzo m

diverge /daɪ'vɜːdʒ/ vi divergir. ~nt a divergente

divers|e /daɪ'vɜːs/ a diverso. ~ify vt diversificar. ~ity n diversidad f

diver|sion /daɪ'vɜːʃn/ n desvío m; desviación f; (distraction) diversión f. ~t /daɪ'vɜːt/ vt desviar; (entertain) divertir

divide /dɪ'vaɪd/ vt dividir. ● vi dividirse. ~d highway n (Amer) autovía f, carretera f de doble pista

dividend /'dɪvɪdend/ n dividendo m

divine /dɪ'vaɪn/ a divino

diving /'daɪvɪŋ/: ~ board n trampolín m. ~ suit n escafandra f

division /dɪ'vɪʒn/ n división f

divorce /dɪ'vɔːs/ n divorcio m. ● vt divorciarse de. get ~d divorciarse. ● vi divorciarse. ~e /dɪvɔː'siː/ n divorciado m

divulge /daɪ'vʌldʒ/ vt divulgar

DIY abbr ⇒DO-IT-YOURSELF

dizz|iness /'dɪzɪnɪs/ n vértigo m.
~y a (**-ier, -iest**) mareado. **be** or
feel ~y marearse

DJ abbr ⇒DISC JOCKEY

do /duː/, unstressed forms /dʊ, də/

3rd pers sing present **does**; past
did; past participle **done**

● transitive verb

••••➤ hacer. **he does what he wants** hace lo que quiere. **to do one's homework** hacer los deberes. **to do the
cooking** preparar la comida, cocinar. **well done!** ¡muy bien!

••••➤ (clean) lavar <dishes>. limpiar
<windows>

••••➤ (as job) **what does he do?** ¿en qué
trabaja?

••••➤ (swindle) estafar. **I've been done!**
¡me han estafado!

••••➤ (achieve) **she's done it!** ¡lo ha logra-
do!

● intransitive verb

••••➤ hacer. **do as you're told!** ¡haz lo
que se te dice!

••••➤ (fare) **how are you doing?** (with a
task) ¿qué tal te va? **how do you do?**
(as greeting) mucho gusto, encantado

••••➤ (perform) **she did well/badly** le fue
bien/mal

••••➤ (be suitable) **will this do?** ¿esto
sirve?

••••➤ (be enough) ser suficiente, bastar.
one box will do con una caja basta,
con una caja es suficiente

● auxiliary verb

••••➤ (to form interrogative and negative) **do
you speak Spanish?** ¿hablas espa-
ñol?. **I don't want to** no quiero. **don't
shut the door** no cierres la puerta

••••➤ (in tag questions) **you eat meat, don't
you?** ¿comes carne, ¿verdad? or ¿no?
he lives in London, doesn't he? vive
en Londres, ¿no? or ¿verdad? or ¿no
es cierto?

••••➤ (in short answers) **do you like it?** -
yes, I do ¿te gusta? - sí. **who wrote it?**
- I did ¿quién lo escribió? - yo

••••➤ (emphasizing) **do come in!** ¡pase Ud!.
you do exaggerate! ¡cómo exageras!

▫ **do away with** vt abolir. ▫ **do in**
vt (⊠, kill) eliminar. ▫ **do up** vt abrochar <coat etc>; arreglar <house>.
▫ **do with** vt (need) (with can, could)
necesitar; (expressing connection) **it has
nothing to do with that** no tiene nada
que ver con eso. ▫ **do without** vt
prescindir de

docile /'dəʊsaɪl/ a dócil

dock /dɒk/ n (Naut) dársena f; (wharf,
quay) muelle m; (Jurid) banquillo m de
los acusados. **~s** npl (port) puerto m.
● vt cortar <tail>; atracar <ship>.
● vi <ship> atracar. **~er** n estibador
m. **~yard** n astillero m

doctor /'dɒktə(r)/ n médico m, doctor m

doctrine /'dɒktrɪn/ n doctrina f

document /'dɒkjʊmənt/ n documento m. **~ary** /-'mentrɪ/ a & n
documental (m)

dodg|e /dɒdʒ/ vt esquivar. ● vi
esquivarse. ● n treta f. **~ems**
/'dɒdʒəmz/ npl autos mpl de choque.
~y a (**-ier, -iest**) ⊞ (awkward) difícil

does /dʌz/ ⇒DO

doesn't /'dʌznt/ = **does not**

dog /dɒg/ n perro m. ● vt (pt **dogged**) perseguir

dogged /'dɒgɪd/ a obstinado

doghouse /'dɒghaʊs/ n (Amer) casa
f del perro. **in the ~** ⊞ en desgracia

dogma /'dɒgmə/ n dogma m. **~tic**
/-'mætɪk/ a dogmático

do|ings npl actividades fpl. **~-it-
yourself** /duːɪtjɔː'self/ n bricolaje m

dole /dəʊl/ n ⊞ subsidio m de paro,
subsidio m de desempleo. **on the ~**
parado, desempleado. ▫ **~ out** vt
distribuir

doleful /'dəʊlfl/ a triste

doll /dɒl/ n muñeca f

dollar /'dɒlə(r)/ n dólar m

dollop /'dɒləp/ n ⊞ porción f

dolphin /'dɒlfɪn/ n delfín m

domain /dəʊ'meɪn/ n dominio m;
(fig) campo m

dome /dəʊm/ n cúpula f

domestic /də'mestɪk/ a doméstico;
<trade, flights, etc> nacional. **~ated**

/dəˈmestɪkeɪtɪd/ a <animal> domesticado. ~ **science** n economía f doméstica

domin|ance /ˈdɒmɪnəns/ n dominio m. ~**ant** a dominante. ~**ate** /-eɪt/ vt/i dominar. ~**ation** /-ˈneɪʃn/ n dominación f. ~**eering** a dominante

Dominican Republic /dəˈmɪnɪkən/ n República f Dominicana

dominion /dəˈmɪnjən/ n dominio m

domino /ˈdɒmɪnəʊ/ n (pl -**oes**) ficha f de dominó. ~**es** npl (game) dominó m

donat|e /dəʊˈneɪt/ vt donar. ~**ion** /-ʃn/ n donativo m, donación f

done /dʌn/ ⇒DO

donkey /ˈdɒŋkɪ/ n burro m, asno m. ~**'s years** 🄸 siglos mpl

donor /ˈdəʊnə(r)/ n donante m & f

don't /dəʊnt/ = **do not**

doodle /ˈduːdl/ vi/t garrapatear

doom /duːm/ n destino m; (death) muerte f. ● vt. be ~ed to ser condenado a

door /dɔː(r)/ n puerta f. ~**bell** n timbre m. ~ **knob** n pomo m (de la puerta). ~**mat** n felpudo m. ~**step** n peldaño m. ~**way** n entrada f

dope /dəʊp/ n 🄸 droga f; (🄸, idiot) imbécil m. ● vt 🄸 drogar

dormant /ˈdɔːmənt/ a aletargado, <volcano> inactivo

dormice /ˈdɔːmaɪs/ n ⇒DORMOUSE

dormitory /ˈdɔːmɪtrɪ/ n dormitorio m

dormouse /ˈdɔːmaʊs/ n (pl -**mice**) lirón m

DOS /dɒs/ abbr (= **disc-operating system**) DOS m

dos|age /ˈdəʊsɪdʒ/ n dosis f. ~**e** /dəʊs/ n dosis f

dot /dɒt/ n punto m. on the ~ en punto

dote /dəʊt/ vi. ~ on adorar

dotty /ˈdɒtɪ/ a (-**ier**, -**iest**) 🄸 chiflado

double /ˈdʌbl/ a doble. ● adv el doble. ● n doble m; (person) doble m & f. at the ~ corriendo. ● vt doblar; redoblar <efforts etc>. ● vi doblarse.

~ **bass** /beɪs/ n contrabajo m. ~ **bed** n cama f de matrimonio, cama f de doa plazas (LAm). ~ **chin** n papada f. ~**cross** /-ˈkrɒs/ vt traicionar. ~**decker** /-ˈdekə(r)/ n autobús m de dos pisos. ~ **Dutch** n 🄸 chino m. ~ **glazing** /-gleɪzɪŋ/ n doble ventana f. ~**s** npl (tennis) dobles mpl

doubly /ˈdʌblɪ/ adv doblemente

doubt /daʊt/ n duda f. ● vt dudar; (distrust) dudar de. ~**ful** a dudoso. ~**less** adv sin duda

dough /dəʊ/ n masa f; (🄸, money) pasta f 🄸, lana f (LAm 🄸). ~**nut** n donut m, dona f (Mex)

dove /dʌv/ n paloma f

down /daʊn/ adv abajo. ~ **with** abajo. come ~ bajar. go ~ bajar; <sun> ponerse. ● prep abajo. ● a 🄸 deprimido. ● vt derribar; (🄸, drink) beber. ● n (feathers) plumón m. ~ **and out** a en la miseria. ~**cast** a abatido. ~**fall** n perdición f; (of king, dictator) caída f. ~**hearted** /-ˈhɑːtɪd/ a abatido. ~**hill** /-ˈhɪl/ adv cuesta abajo. ~**load** /-ˈləʊd/ vt (Comp) trasvasar. ~**market** /-ˈmɑːkɪt/ a <newspaper> popular; <store> barato. ~ **payment** n depósito m. ~**pour** n aguacero m. ~**right** a completo. ● adv completamente. ~**s** npl colinas fpl. ~**stairs** /-ˈsteəz/ adv abajo. ● /-steəz/ a de abajo. ~**stream** adv río abajo. ~**-to-earth** /-tuˈɜːθ/ a práctico. ~**town** /-ˈtaʊn/ n centro m (de la ciudad). ● adv. go ~**town** ir al centro. ~ **under** adv en las antípodas; (in Australia) en Australia. ~**ward** /-wəd/ a & adv, ~**wards** adv hacia abajo

dowry /ˈdaʊərɪ/ n dote f

doze /dəʊz/ vi dormitar. □ ~ **off** vi dormirse

dozen /ˈdʌzn/ n docena f. a ~ **eggs** una docena de huevos. ~**s of** 🄸 miles de, muchos

Dr /ˈdɒktə(r)/ abbr (= **Doctor**) Dr ~. **Broadley** (el) Doctor Broadley

drab /dræb/ a monótono

draft /drɑːft/ n borrador m; (Com) letra f de cambio; (Amer, Mil) reclutamiento m; (Amer, of air) corriente f de aire. ● vt redactar el borrador de; (Amer, conscript) reclutar

drag /dræg/ *vt* (*pt* **dragged**) arrastrar. ● *n* Ⓘ lata *f*

dragon /'drægən/ *n* dragón *m*. ∼**fly** *n* libélula *f*

drain /dreɪn/ *vt* vaciar <*tank, glass*>; drenar <*land*>; (fig) agotar. ● *vi* escurrirse. ● *n* (pipe) sumidero *m*, resumidero *m* (LAm); (plughole) desagüe *m*. ∼**board** (Amer), ∼**ing board** *n* escurridero *m*

drama /'drɑːmə/ *n* drama *m*; (art) arte *m* teatral. ∼**tic** /drə'mætɪk/ *a* dramático. ∼**tist** /'dræmətɪst/ *n* dramaturgo *m*. ∼**tize** /'dræmətaɪz/ *vt* adaptar al teatro; (fig) dramatizar

drank /dræŋk/ ⇒DRINK

drape /dreɪp/ *vt* cubrir; (hang) colgar. ∼**s** *npl* (Amer) cortinas *fpl*

drastic /'dræstɪk/ *a* drástico

draught /drɑːft/ *n* corriente *f* de aire. ∼ **beer** *n* cerveza *f* de barril. ∼**s** *npl* (game) juego *m* de damas *fpl*. ∼**y** *a* lleno de corrientes de aire

draw /drɔː/ *vt* (*pt* **drew**, *pp* **drawn**) tirar; (attract) atraer; dibujar <*picture*>; trazar <*line*>. ∼ **the line** trazar el límite. ● *vi* (Art) dibujar; (Sport) empatar; ∼ **near** acercarse. ● *n* (Sport) empate *m*; (in lottery) sorteo *m*. □ ∼ **in** *vi* <*days*> acortarse. □ ∼ **out** *vt* sacar <*money*>. □ ∼ **up** *vi* pararse. *vt* redactar <*document*>; acercar <*chair*>. ∼**back** *n* desventaja *f*. ∼**bridge** *n* puente *m* levadizo

drawer /drɔː(r)/ *n* cajón *m*, gaveta *f* (Mex). ∼**s** *npl* calzones *mpl*

drawing /'drɔːɪŋ/ *n* dibujo *m*. ∼ **pin** *n* tachuela *f*, chincheta *f*, chinche *f*. ∼ **room** *n* salón *m*

drawl /drɔːl/ *n* habla *f* lenta

drawn /drɔːn/ ⇒DRAW

dread /dred/ *n* terror *m*. ● *vt* temer. ∼**ful** *a* terrible. ∼**fully** *adv* terriblemente

dream /driːm/ *n* sueño *m*. ● *vt/i* (*pt* **dreamed** *or* **dreamt** /dremt/) soñar. □ ∼ **up** *vt* idear. *a* ideal. ∼**er** *n* soñador *m*

dreary /'drɪərɪ/ *a* (**-ier, -iest**) triste; (boring) monótono

dredge /dredʒ/ *n* draga *f*. ● *vt* dragar. ∼**r** *n* draga *f*

dregs /dregz/ *npl* posos *mpl*, heces *fpl*; (fig) hez *f*

drench /drentʃ/ *vt* empapar

dress /dres/ *n* vestido *m*; (clothing) ropa *f*. ● *vt* vestir; (decorate) adornar; (Med) vendar. ● *vi* vestirse. □ ∼ **up** *vi* ponerse elegante. ∼ **up as** disfrazarse de. ∼ **circle** *n* primer palco *m*

dressing /'dresɪŋ/ *n* (sauce) aliño *m*; (bandage) vendaje *m*. ∼**-down** /-'daʊn/ *n* rapapolvo *m*, reprensión *f*. ∼ **gown** *n* bata *f*. ∼ **room** *n* vestidor *m*; (in theatre) camarín *m*. ∼ **table** *n* tocador *m*

dress: ∼**maker** *n* modista *m* & *f*. ∼**making** *n* costura *f*. ∼ **rehearsal** *n* ensayo *m* general

drew /druː/ ⇒DRAW

dribble /'drɪbl/ *vi* <*baby*> babear; (in football) driblar, driblear

drie|d /draɪd/ *a* <*food*> seco; <*milk*> en polvo. ∼**r** /'draɪə(r)/ *n* secador *m*

drift /drɪft/ *vi* ir a la deriva; <*snow*> amontonarse. ● *n* (movement) dirección *f*; (of snow) montón *m*

drill /drɪl/ *n* (tool) taladro *m*; (of dentist) torno *m*; (training) ejercicio *m*. ● *vt* taladrar, perforar; (train) entrenar. ● *vi* entrenarse

drink /drɪŋk/ *vt/i* (*pt* **drank**, *pp* **drunk**) beber, tomar (LAm). ● *n* bebida *f*. ∼**able** *a* bebible; <*water*> potable. ∼**er** *n* bebedor *m*. ∼**ing water** *n* agua *f* potable

drip /drɪp/ *vi* (*pt* **dripped**) gotear. ● *n* gota *f*; (Med) goteo *m* intravenoso; (Ⓧ, person) soso *m*. ∼**-dry** /-'draɪ/ *a* de lava y pon. ∼**ping** *a*. be ∼**ping wet** estar chorreando

drive /draɪv/ *vt* (*pt* **drove**, *pp* **driven**) conducir, manejar (LAm) <*car etc*>. ∼ **s.o. mad** volver loco a uno. ∼ **s.o. to do sth** llevar a uno a hacer algo. ● *vi* conducir, manejar (LAm). ∼ **at** querer decir. ∼ **in** (in car) entrar en coche. ● *n* paseo *m*; (road) calle *f*; (private road) camino *m* de entrada; (fig) empuje *m*. ∼**r** *n* conductor *m*, chofer *m* (LAm). ∼**r's licence** *n* (Amer) ⇒DRIVING LICENSE

drivel /'drɪvl/ *n* tonterías *fpl*

driving /'draɪvɪŋ/ *n* conducción *f*. ∼ **licence** *n* permiso *m* de conducir,

licencia f de conducción (LAm), licencia f (de manejar) (Mex). ~ **test** n examen m de conducir, examen m de manejar (LAm)

drizzle /'drɪzl/ n llovizna f. ● vi lloviznar

drone /drəʊn/ n zumbido m. ● vi zumbar

drool /druːl/ vi babear

droop /druːp/ vi inclinarse; <flowers> marchitarse

drop /drɒp/ n gota f; (fall) caída f; (decrease) descenso m. ● vt (pt **dropped**) dejar caer; (lower) bajar. ● vi caer. □ ~ **in on** vt pasar por casa de. □ ~ **off** vi (sleep) dormirse. □ ~ **out** vi retirarse; <student> abandonar los estudios. ~**out** n marginado m

drought /draʊt/ n sequía f

drove /drəʊv/ ⇒DRIVE. ● n manada f

drown /draʊn/ vt ahogar. ● vi ahogarse

drowsy /'draʊzɪ/ a soñoliento

drudgery /'drʌdʒərɪ/ n trabajo m pesado

drug /drʌɡ/ n droga f; (Med) medicamento m. ● vt (pt **drugged**) drogar. ~ **addict** n drogadicto m. ~**gist** n (Amer) farmacéutico m. ~**store** n (Amer) farmacia f (que vende otros artículos también)

drum /drʌm/ n tambor m; (for oil) bidón m. ● vi (pt **drummed**) tocar el tambor. ● vt. ~ **sth into s.o.** hacerle aprender algo a uno a fuerza de repetírselo. ~**mer** n tambor m; (in group) batería f. ~**s** npl batería f. ~**stick** n baqueta f; (Culin) muslo m

drunk /drʌŋk/ ⇒DRINK. ● a borracho. **get** ~ emborracharse. ● n borracho m. ~**ard** /-əd/ n borracho m. ~**en** a borracho

dry /draɪ/ a (**drier**, **driest**) seco. ● vt secar. ● vi secarse. □ ~ **up** vi <stream> secarse; <funds> agotarse. ~**-clean** vt limpiar en seco. ~**-cleaner's** tintorería f. ~**er** n ⇒DRIER

dual /'djuːəl/ a doble. ~ **carriageway** n autovía f, carretera f de doble pista

dub /dʌb/ vt (pt **dubbed**) doblar <film>

dubious /'djuːbɪəs/ a dudoso; <person> sospechoso

duchess /'dʌtʃɪs/ n duquesa f

duck /dʌk/ n pato m. ● vt sumergir; bajar <head>. ● vi agacharse. ~**ling** /'dʌklɪŋ/ n patito m

duct /dʌkt/ n conducto m

dud /dʌd/ a inútil; <cheque> sin fondos

due /djuː/ a debido; (expected) esperado. ~ **to** debido a. ● adv. ~ **north** derecho hacia el norte. ~**s** npl derechos mpl

duel /'djuːəl/ n duelo m

duet /djuː'et/ n dúo m

duffel, **duffle** /'dʌfl/: ~ **bag** n bolsa f de lona. ~ **coat** n trenca f

dug /dʌɡ/ ⇒DIG

duke /djuːk/ n duque m

dull /dʌl/ a (**-er**, **-est**) <weather> gris; <colour> apagado; <person, play, etc> pesado; <sound> sordo

dumb /dʌm/ a (**-er**, **-est**) mudo; 🄸 estúpido. ~**found** /dʌm'faʊnd/ vt pasmar

dummy /'dʌmɪ/ n muñeco m; (of tailor) maniquí m; (for baby) chupete m. ● a falso. ~ **run** prueba f

dump /dʌmp/ vt tirar, botar (LAm). ● n vertedero m; (Mil) depósito m; 🄸 lugar m desagradable. **be down in the** ~**s** estar deprimido

dumpling /'dʌmplɪŋ/ n bola f de masa hervida

Dumpster /'dʌmpstə(r)/ n (Amer, P) contenedor m (para escombros)

dumpy /'dʌmpɪ/ a (**-ier**, **-iest**) regordete

dunce /dʌns/ n burro m

dung /dʌŋ/ n (manure) estiércol m

dungarees /dʌŋɡə'riːz/ npl mono m, peto m

dungeon /'dʌndʒən/ n calabozo m

dunk /dʌŋk/ vt remojar

dupe /djuːp/ vt engañar. ● n inocentón m

duplicat|e /'djuːplɪkət/ a & n duplicado (m). ● /'djuːplɪkeɪt/ vt duplicar;

(on machine) reproducir. **~ing machine**, **~or** *n* multicopista *f*

durable /'djʊərəbl/ *a* durable

duration /dju'reɪʃn/ *n* duración *f*

duress /dju'res/ *n*. **under ~** bajo coacción

during /'djʊərɪŋ/ *prep* durante

dusk /dʌsk/ *n* anochecer *m*

dust /dʌst/ *n* polvo *m*. ● *vt* quitar el polvo a; (sprinkle) espolvorear (**with** con). **~bin** *n* cubo *m* de la basura, bote *m* de la basura (Mex). **~ cloth** (Amer), **~er** *n* trapo *m*. **~jacket** *n* sobrecubierta *f*. **~man** /-mən/ *n* basurero *m*. **~pan** *n* recogedor *m*. **~y** *a* (**-ier, -iest**) polvoriento

Dutch /dʌtʃ/ *a* holandés. ● *n* (Lang) holandés *m*. **the ~** (people) los holandeses. **~man** /-mən/ *m* holandés *m*. **~woman** *n* holandesa *f*

duty /'dju:tɪ/ *n* deber *m*; (tax) derechos *mpl* de aduana. **on ~** de servicio. **~-free** /-'fri:/ *a* libre de impuestos

duvet /'dju:veɪ/ *n* edredón *m*

dwarf /dwɔːf/ *n* (*pl* **-s** or **dwarves**) enano *m*

dwell /dwel/ *vi* (*pt* **dwelt** or **dwelled**) morar.□ **~ on** *vt* detenerse en. **~ing** *n* morada *f*

dwindle /'dwɪndl/ *vi* disminuir

dye /daɪ/ *vt* (*pres p* **dyeing**) teñir. ● *n* tinte *m*

dying /'daɪɪŋ/ ⇨DIE

dynamic /daɪ'næmɪk/ *a* dinámico. **~s** *npl* dinámica *f*

dynamite /'daɪnəmaɪt/ *n* dinamita *f*. ● *vt* dinamitar

dynamo /'daɪnəməʊ/ *n* (*pl* **-os**) dinamo *f*, dínamo *f*, dinamo *m* (LAm), dínamo *m* (LAm)

dynasty /'dɪnəstɪ/ *n* dinastía *f*

Ee

E *abbr* (= **East**) E

each /iːtʃ/ *a* cada. ● *pron* cada uno. **~ one** cada uno. **~ other** uno a otro, el uno al otro. **they love ~ other** se aman

eager /'iːgə(r)/ *a* impaciente; (enthusiastic) ávido. **~ness** *n* impaciencia *f*; (enthusiasm) entusiasmo *m*

eagle /'iːgl/ *n* águila *f*

ear /ɪə(r)/ *n* oído *m*; (outer) oreja *f*; (of corn) espiga *f*. **~ache** *n* dolor *m* de oído. **~drum** *n* tímpano *m*

earl /ɜːl/ *n* conde *m*

early /'ɜːlɪ/ *a* (**-ier, -iest**) temprano; (before expected time) prematuro. ● *adv* temprano; (ahead of time) con anticipación

earn /ɜːn/ *vt* ganar; (deserve) merecer

earnest /'ɜːnɪst/ *a* serio. **in ~** en serio

earnings /'ɜːnɪŋz/ *npl* ingresos *mpl*; (Com) ganancias *fpl*

ear: ~phone *n* audífono *m*. **~ring** *n* pendiente *m*, arete *m* (LAm). **~shot** *n*. **within ~shot** al alcance del oído

earth /ɜːθ/ *n* tierra *f*. **the E~** (planet) la Tierra. ● *vt* (Elec) conectar a tierra. **~quake** *n* terremoto *m*

earwig /'ɪəwɪg/ *n* tijereta *f*

ease /iːz/ *n* facilidad *f*; (comfort) tranquilidad *f*. **at ~** a gusto; (Mil) en posición de descanso. **ill at ~** molesto. **with ~** fácilmente. ● *vt* calmar; aliviar *<pain>*. ● *vi* calmarse; (lessen) disminuir

easel /'iːzl/ *n* caballete *m*

easily /'iːzɪlɪ/ *adv* fácilmente

east /iːst/ *n* este *m*. ● *a* este, oriental; *<wind>* del este. ● *adv* hacia el este.

Easter /'iːstə(r)/ *n* Semana *f* Santa; (Relig) Pascua *f* de Resurrección. **~ egg** *n* huevo *m* de Pascua

east: ~erly /-əlɪ/ *a* *<wind>* del este. **~ern** /-ən/ *a* este, oriental. **~ward**

/-wəd/, **~wards** *adv* hacia el este

easy /'i:zɪ/ *a* (**-ier, -iest**) fácil. ● *adv.*
go ~ on sth 🔲 no pasarse con algo.
take it ~ tomarse las cosas con
calma. ● *int* ¡despacio! **~ chair** *n* sillón *m*. **~going** /-'gəʊɪŋ/ *a* acomo-
dadizo

eat /i:t/ *vt/i* (*pt* **ate**, *pp* **eaten**) comer. □ **~ into** *vt* corroer. **~er** *n* comedor *m*

eaves /i:vz/ *npl* alero *m*. **~drop** *vi*
(*pt* **-dropped**). **~drop (on)** escuchar
a escondidas

ebb /eb/ *n* reflujo *m*. ● *vi* bajar; (fig)
decaer

ebony /'ebənɪ/ *n* ébano *m*

EC /i:'si:/ *abbr* (= **European Community**) CE *f* (Comunidad *f* Europea)

eccentric /ɪk'sentrɪk/ *a* & *n*
excéntrico (*m*). **~ity** /eksen'trɪsətɪ/
n excentricidad *f*

echo /'ekəʊ/ *n* (*pl* **-oes**) eco *m*. ● *vi*
hacer eco

eclipse /ɪ'klɪps/ *n* eclipse *m*. ● *vt*
eclipsar

ecolog|ical /i:kə'lɒdʒɪkl/ *a* ecológi-
co. **~y** /ɪ'kɒlədʒɪ/ *n* ecología *f*

econom|ic /i:kə'nɒmɪk/ *a* económi-
co. **~ical** *a* económico. **~ics** *n*
economía *f*. **~ist** /ɪ'kɒnəmɪst/ *n*
economista *m* & *f*. **~ize**
/ɪ'kɒnəmaɪz/ *vi* economizar. **~ize on
sth** economizar algo. **~y** /ɪ'kɒnəmɪ/
n economía *f*

ecsta|sy /'ekstəsɪ/ *n* éxtasis *f*. **~tic**
/ɪk'stætɪk/ *a* extático

Ecuador /'ekwədɔː(r)/ *n* Ecuador *m*.
~ean /ekwə'dɔːrɪən/ *a* & *n* ecuatoriano (*m*)

edg|e /edʒ/ *n* borde *m*; (of knife) filo *m*;
(of town) afueras *fpl*. **have the ~e on**
🔲 llevar la ventaja a. **on ~e** nervioso. ● *vt* ribetear; (move) mover poco a
poco. ● *vi* avanzar cautelosamente.
~eways *adv* de lado. **~y** *a* nervioso

edible /'edɪbl/ *a* comestible

edit /'edɪt/ *vt* dirigir <*newspaper*>;
preparar una edición de <*text*>; edi-
tar <*film*>. **~ion** /ɪ'dɪʃn/ *n* edición *f*.
~or *n* (of newspaper) di-rector *m*; (of
text) redactor *m*.

~orial /edɪ'tɔːrɪəl/ *a* editorial. ● *n*
artículo *m* de fondo

educat|e /'edʒʊkeɪt/ *vt* educar.
~ed *a* culto. **~ion** /-'keɪʃn/ *n* educación *f*; (knowledge, culture) cultura *f*.
~ional /-'keɪʃənl/ *a* instructivo

EEC /i:i:'si:/ *abbr* (= **European
Economic Community**) CEE *f*
(Comunidad *f* Económica Europea)

eel /i:l/ *n* anguila *f*

eerie /'ɪərɪ/ *a* (**-ier, -iest**) misterioso

effect /ɪ'fekt/ *n* efecto *m*. **in ~** efectivamente. **take ~** entrar en vigor.
~ive *a* eficaz; (striking) impresionante; (real) efectivo. **~ively** *adv* efi-
cazmente. **~iveness** *n* eficacia *f*

effeminate /ɪ'femɪnət/ *a* afeminado

efficien|cy /ɪ'fɪʃənsɪ/ *n* eficiencia *f*;
(Mec) rendimiento *m*. **~t** *a* eficiente.
~tly *adv* eficientemente

effort /'efət/ *n* esfuerzo *m*. **~less** *a*
fácil

e.g. /i:'dʒi:/ *abbr* (= **exempli gra-
tia**) p.ej., por ejemplo

egg /eg/ *n* huevo *m*. □ **~ on** *vt* 🔲
incitar. **~cup** *n* huevera *f*. **~plant**
n (Amer) berenjena *f*. **~shell** *n* cáscara *f* de huevo

ego /'i:gəʊ/ *n* (*pl* **-os**) yo *m*. **~ism** *n*
egoísmo *m*. **~ist** *n* egoísta *m* & *f*.
~centric /i:gəʊ'sentrɪk/ *a*
egocéntrico. **~tism** *n* egotismo *m*.
~tist *n* egotista *m* & *f*

eh /eɪ/ *int* 🔲 ¡eh!

eiderdown /'aɪdədaʊn/ *n* edredón
m

eight /eɪt/ *a* & *n* ocho (*m*). **~een**
/eɪ'tiːn/ *a* & *n* dieciocho (*m*).
~eenth *a* decimoctavo. ● *n* dieci-
chavo *m*. **~h** /eɪtθ/ *a* & *n* octavo (*m*)
~ieth /'eɪtɪəθ/ *a* octogésimo. ● *n*
ochentavo *m*. **~y** /'eɪtɪ/ *a* & *n*
ochenta (*m*)

either /'aɪðə(r)/ *a* cualquiera de los
dos; (negative) ninguno de los dos;
(each) cada. ● *pron* uno u otro; (with
negative) ni uno ni otro. ● *adv* (negative) tampoco. ● *conj* o. **~ Tuesday or
Wednesday** o el martes o el miércoles; (with negative) ni el martes ni el
miércoles

eject /ɪ'dʒekt/ *vt* expulsar

eke /i:k/ *vt.* ~ **out** hacer alcanzar <*resources*>. ~ **a living** ganarse la vida a duras penas

elaborate /ɪ'læbərət/ *a* complicado. ●/ɪ'læbəreɪt/ *vt* elaborar. ●/ɪ'læbəreɪt/ *vi* explicarse

elapse /ɪ'læps/ *vi* transcurrir

elastic /ɪ'læstɪk/ *a & n* elástico (*m*). ~ **band** *n* goma *f* (elástica), liga *f* (Mex)

elat|ed /ɪ'leɪtɪd/ *a* regocijado. ~**ion** /-ʃn/ *n* regocijo *m*

elbow /'elbəʊ/ *n* codo *m*. ● *vt* dar un codazo a

elder /'eldə(r)/ *a* mayor. ● *n* mayor *m & f*; (tree) saúco *m*. ~**ly** /'eldəlɪ/ *a* mayor, anciano

eldest /'eldɪst/ *a & n* mayor (*m & f*)

elect /ɪ'lekt/ *vt* elegir. ~ **to do** decidir hacer. ● *a* electo. ~**ion** /-ʃn/ *n* elección *f*. ~**or** *n* elector *m*. ~**oral** *a* electoral. ~**orate** /-ət/ *n* electorado *m*

electric /ɪ'lektrɪk/ *a* eléctrico. ~**al** *a* eléctrico. ~ **blanket** *n* manta *f* eléctrica. ~**ian** /ɪlek'trɪʃn/ *n* electricista *m & f*. ~**ity** /ɪlek'trɪsətɪ/ *n* electricidad *f*

electrify /ɪ'lektrɪfaɪ/ *vt* electrificar; (fig) electrizar

electrocute /ɪ'lektrəkju:t/ *vt* electrocutar

electrode /ɪ'lektrəʊd/ *n* electrodo *m*

electron /ɪ'lektrɒn/ *n* electrón *m*

electronic /ɪlek'trɒnɪk/ *a* electrónico. ~ **mail** *n* correo *m* electrónico. ~**s** *n* electrónica *f*

elegan|ce /'elɪgəns/ *n* elegancia *f*. ~**t** *a* elegante. ~**tly** *adv* elegantemente

element /'elɪmənt/ *n* elemento *m*. ~**ary** /-'mentrɪ/ *a* elemental. ~**ary school** *n* (Amer) escuela *f* primaria

elephant /'elɪfənt/ *n* elefante *m*

elevat|e /'elɪveɪt/ *vt* elevar. ~**ion** /-'veɪʃn/ *n* elevación *f*. ~**or** *n* (Amer) ascensor *m*

eleven /ɪ'levn/ *a & n* once (*m*). ~**th** *a* undécimo. ● *n* onceavo *m*

elf /elf/ *n* (*pl* **elves**) duende *m*

eligible /'elɪdʒəbl/ *a* elegible. **be ~ for** tener derecho a

eliminat|e /ɪ'lɪmɪneɪt/ *vt* eliminar. ~**ion** /-'neɪʃn/ *n* eliminación *f*

élite /eɪ'li:t/ *n* elite *f*, élite *f*

ellip|se /ɪ'lɪps/ *n* elipse *f*. ~**tical** *a* elíptico

elm /elm/ *n* olmo *m*

elope /ɪ'ləʊp/ *vi* fugarse con el amante

eloquen|ce /'eləkwəns/ *n* elocuencia *f*. ~**t** *a* elocuente

El Salvador /el'sælvədɔ:(r)/ *n* El Salvador

else /els/ *adv.* **somebody** ~ otra persona. **everybody** ~ todos los demás. **nobody** ~ ningún otro, nadie más. **nothing** ~ nada más. **or** ~ o bien. **somewhere** ~ en otra parte. ~**where** *adv* en otra parte

elu|de /ɪ'lu:d/ *vt* eludir. ~**sive** /-sɪv/ *a* esquivo

elves /elvz/ ⇒ELF

emaciated /ɪ'meɪʃɪeɪtɪd/ *a* consumido

email, e-mail /'i:meɪl/ *n* correo *m* electrónico, correo-e *m*. ● *vt* mandar por correo electrónico, emailear. ~ **address** *n* casilla *f* electrónica, dirección *f* de correo electrónico

emancipat|e /ɪ'mænsɪpeɪt/ *vt* emancipar. ~**ion** /-'peɪʃn/ *n* emancipación *f*

embankment /ɪm'bæŋkmənt/ *n* terraplén *m*; (of river) dique *m*

embargo /ɪm'bɑ:gəʊ/ *n* (*pl* **-oes**) embargo *m*

embark /ɪm'bɑ:k/ *vi* embarcarse. ~ **on** (fig) emprender. ~**ation** /embɑ:'keɪʃn/ *n* embarque *m*

embarrass /ɪm'bærəs/ *vt* avergonzar. ~**ed** *a* avergonzado. ~**ing** *a* embarazoso. ~**ment** *n* vergüenza *f*

embassy /'embəsɪ/ *n* embajada *f*

embellish /ɪm'belɪʃ/ *vt* adornar. ~**ment** *n* adorno *m*

embers /'embəz/ *npl* ascuas *fpl*

embezzle /ɪm'bezl/ *vt* desfalcar. ~**ment** *n* desfalco *m*

emblem /'embləm/ *n* emblema *m*

embrace /ɪm'breɪs/ *vt* abrazar; (fig) abarcar. ● *vi* abrazarse. ● *n* abrazo *m*

embroider /ɪmˈbrɔɪdə(r)/ vt bordar. ~y n bordado m

embroil /ɪmˈbrɔɪl/ vt enredar

embryo /ˈembrɪəʊ/ n (pl -os) embrión m. ~nic /-ˈɒnɪk/ a embrionario

emend /ɪˈmend/ vt enmendar

emerald /ˈemərəld/ n esmeralda f

emerge /ɪˈmɜːdʒ/ vi salir. ~nce /-əns/ n aparición f

emergency /ɪˈmɜːdʒənsɪ/ n emergencia f; (Med) urgencia f. in an ~ en caso de emergencia. ~ exit n salida f de emergencia

emigra|nt /ˈemɪɡrənt/ n emigrante m & f. ~te /ˈemɪɡreɪt/ vi emigrar. ~tion /-ˈɡreɪʃn/ n emigración f

eminen|ce /ˈemɪnəns/ n eminencia f. ~t a eminente. ~tly adv eminentemente

emi|ssion /ɪˈmɪʃn/ n emisión f. ~t vt (pt emitted) emitir

emoti|on /ɪˈməʊʃn/ n emoción f. ~onal a emocional; <person> emotivo; (moving) conmovedor. ~ve /ɪˈməʊtɪv/ a emotivo

empathy /ˈempəθɪ/ n empatía f

emperor /ˈempərə(r)/ n emperador m

empha|sis /ˈemfəsɪs/ n (pl ~ses /-siːz/) énfasis m. ~size /ˈemfəsaɪz/ vt enfatizar. ~tic /ɪmˈfætɪk/ a <gesture> enfático; <assertion> categórico

empire /ˈempaɪə(r)/ n imperio m

empirical /ɪmˈpɪrɪkl/ a empírico

employ /ɪmˈplɔɪ/ vt emplear. ~ee /emplɔɪˈiː/ n empleado m. ~er n patrón m. ~ment n empleo m. ~ment agency n agencia f de trabajo

empower /ɪmˈpaʊə(r)/ vt autorizar (to do a hacer)

empress /ˈemprɪs/ n emperatriz f

empty /ˈemptɪ/ a vacío; <promise> vano. on an ~y stomach con el estómago vacío. ●n 🖭 envase m (vacío). ●vt vaciar. ●vi vaciarse

emulate /ˈemjʊleɪt/ vt emular

emulsion /ɪˈmʌlʃn/ n emulsión f

enable /ɪˈneɪbl/ vt. ~ s.o. to do sth permitir a uno hacer algo

enact /ɪˈnækt/ vt (Jurid) decretar; (in theatre) representar

enamel /ɪˈnæml/ n esmalte m. ●vt (pt enamelled) esmaltar

enchant /ɪnˈtʃɑːnt/ vt encantar. ~ing a encantador. ~ment n encanto m

encircle /ɪnˈsɜːkl/ vt rodear

enclave /ˈenkleɪv/ n enclave m

enclos|e /ɪnˈkləʊz/ vt cercar <land>; (Com) adjuntar. ~ed a <space> cerrado; (Com) adjunto. ~ure /ɪnˈkləʊʒə(r)/ n cercamiento m

encode /ɪnˈkəʊd/ vt codificar, cifrar

encore /ˈɒŋkɔː(r)/ int ¡otra! ●n bis m, repetición f

encounter /ɪnˈkaʊntə(r)/ vt encontrar. ●n encuentro m

encourag|e /ɪnˈkʌrɪdʒ/ vt animar; (stimulate) fomentar. ~ement n ánimo m. ~ing a alentador

encroach /ɪnˈkrəʊtʃ/ vi. ~ on invadir <land>; quitar <time>

encyclopaedi|a /ɪnsaɪkləˈpiːdɪə/ n enciclopedia f. ~c a enciclopédico

end /end/ n fin m; (furthest point) extremo m. in the ~ por fin. make ~s meet poder llegar a fin de mes. put an ~ to poner fin a. no ~ of muchísimos. on ~ de pie; (consecutive) seguido. ●vt/i terminar, acabar

endanger /ɪnˈdeɪndʒə(r)/ vt poner en peligro. ~ed a <species> en peligro

endearing /ɪnˈdɪərɪŋ/ a simpático

endeavour /ɪnˈdevə(r)/ n esfuerzo m, intento m. ●vi. ~ to esforzarse por

ending /ˈendɪŋ/ n fin m

endless /ˈendlɪs/ a interminable

endorse /ɪnˈdɔːs/ vt endosar; (fig) aprobar. ~ment n endoso m; (fig) aprobación f; (Auto) nota f de inhabilitación

endur|ance /ɪnˈdjʊərəns/ n resistencia f. ~e /ɪnˈdjʊə(r)/ vt aguantar. ~ing a perdurable

enemy /ˈenəmɪ/ n & a enemigo (m)

energ|etic /enəˈdʒetɪk/ a enérgico. ~y /ˈenədʒɪ/ n energía f

enforce /ɪnˈfɔːs/ vt hacer cumplir *<law>*; hacer valer *<claim>*. **~d** a forzado

engag|e /ɪnˈɡeɪdʒ/ vt emplear *<staff>*; captar *<attention>*; (Mec) hacer engranar. ● vi (Mec) engranar. **~e in** dedicarse a. **~ed** a prometido, comprometido (LAm); (busy) ocupado. **be ~ed** (of phone) estar comunicando, estar ocupado (LAm). **get ~ed** prometerse, comprometerse (LAm). **~ement** n compromiso m

engine /ˈendʒɪn/ n motor m; (of train) locomotora f. **~ driver** n maquinista m

engineer /endʒɪˈnɪə(r)/ n ingeniero m; (mechanic) mecánico m; (Amer, Rail) maquinista m. ● vt (contrive) fraguar. **~ing** n ingeniería f

England /ˈɪŋɡlənd/ n Inglaterra f

English /ˈɪŋɡlɪʃ/ a inglés. ● n (Lang) inglés m. ● npl. **the ~** los ingleses. **~man** /-mən/ n inglés m. **~woman** n inglesa f

engrav|e /ɪnˈɡreɪv/ vt grabar. **~ing** n grabado m

engrossed /ɪnˈɡrəʊst/ a absorto

engulf /ɪnˈɡʌlf/ vt envolver

enhance /ɪnˈhɑːns/ vt realzar; aumentar *<value>*

enigma /ɪˈnɪɡmə/ n enigma m. **~tic** /enɪɡˈmætɪk/ a enigmático

enjoy /ɪnˈdʒɔɪ/ vt. **I ~ reading** me gusta la lectura. **~ o.s.** divertirse. **~able** a agradable. **~ment** n placer m

enlarge /ɪnˈlɑːdʒ/ vt agrandar; (Photo) ampliar. ● vi agrandarse. **~ upon** extenderse sobre. **~ment** n (Photo) ampliación f

enlighten /ɪnˈlaɪtn/ vt ilustrar. **~ment** n. **the E~ment** el siglo de la luces

enlist /ɪnˈlɪst/ vt alistar; conseguir *<support>*. ● vi alistarse

enliven /ɪnˈlaɪvn/ vt animar

enorm|ity /ɪˈnɔːmətɪ/ n enormidad f. **~ous** /ɪˈnɔːməs/ a enorme. **~ously** adv enormemente

enough /ɪˈnʌf/ a & adv bastante. ● n bastante m, suficiente m. ● int ¡basta!

enquir|e /ɪnˈkwaɪə(r)/ vt/i preguntar. **~e about** informarse de. **~y** n pregunta f; (investigation) investigación f

enrage /ɪnˈreɪdʒ/ vt enfurecer

enrol /ɪnˈrəʊl/ vt (pt **enrolled**) inscribir, matricular *<student>*. ● vi inscribirse, matricularse

ensue /ɪnˈsjuː/ vi seguir

ensure /ɪnˈʃʊə(r)/ vt asegurar

entail /ɪnˈteɪl/ vt suponer; acarrear *<expense>*

entangle /ɪnˈtæŋɡl/ vt enredar. **~ment** n enredo m

enter /ˈentə(r)/ vt entrar en, entrar a (esp LAm); presentarse a *<competition>*; inscribirse en *<race>*; (write) escribir. ● vi entrar

enterpris|e /ˈentəpraɪz/ n empresa f; (fig) iniciativa f. **~ing** a emprendedor

entertain /entəˈteɪn/ vt entretener; recibir *<guests>*; abrigar *<ideas, hopes>*; (consider) considerar. **~ing** a entretenido. **~ment** n entretenimiento m; (show) espectáculo m

enthral /ɪnˈθrɔːl/ vt (pt **enthralled**) cautivar

enthuse /ɪnˈθjuːz/ vi. **~ over** entusiasmarse por

enthusias|m /ɪnˈθjuːzɪæzəm/ n entusiasmo m. **~t** n entusiasta m & f. **~tic** /-ˈæstɪk/ a entusiasta. **~tically** adv con entusiasmo

entice /ɪnˈtaɪs/ vt atraer

entire /ɪnˈtaɪə(r)/ a entero. **~ly** adv completamente. **~ty** /ɪnˈtaɪərətɪ/ n. **in its ~ty** en su totalidad

entitle /ɪnˈtaɪtl/ vt titular; (give a right) dar derecho a. **be ~d to** tener derecho a. **~ment** n derecho m

entity /ˈentətɪ/ n entidad f

entrails /ˈentreɪlz/ npl entrañas fpl

entrance /ˈentrəns/ n entrada f. ● /ɪnˈtrɑːns/ vt encantar

entrant /ˈentrənt/ n participante m & f; (in exam) candidato m

entreat /ɪnˈtriːt/ vt suplicar. **~y** n súplica f

entrenched /ɪnˈtrentʃt/ a *<position>* afianzado

entrust /ɪnˈtrʌst/ vt confiar

entry /'entrɪ/ n entrada f

entwine /ɪn'twaɪn/ vt entrelazar

enumerate /ɪ'nju:mǝreɪt/ vt enumerar

envelop /ɪn'velǝp/ vt envolver

envelope /'envǝlǝʊp/ n sobre m

enviable /'envɪǝbl/ a envidiable

envious /'envɪǝs/ a envidioso

environment /ɪn'vaɪǝrǝnmǝnt/ n medio m ambiente. ∼al /-'mentl/ a ambiental

envisage /ɪn'vɪzɪdʒ/ vt prever; (imagine) imaginar

envision /ɪn'vɪʒn/ vt (Amer) prever

envoy /'envɔɪ/ n enviado m

envy /'envɪ/ n envidia f. ● vt envidiar

enzyme /'enzaɪm/ n enzima f

ephemeral /ɪ'femǝrǝl/ a efímero

epic /'epɪk/ n épica f. ● a épico

epidemic /epɪ'demɪk/ n epidemia f. ● a epidémico

epilep|sy /'epɪlepsɪ/ n epilepsia f. ∼tic /-'leptɪk/ a & n epiléptico (m)

epilogue /'epɪlɒg/ n epílogo m

episode /'epɪsǝʊd/ n episodio m

epitaph /'epɪtɑːf/ n epitafio m

epitom|e /ɪ'pɪtǝmɪ/ n personificación f, epítome m. ∼ize vt ser la personificación de

epoch /'iːpɒk/ n época f

equal /'iːkwǝl/ a & n igual (m & f). ∼ to (a task) a la altura de. ● vt (pt **equalled**) ser igual a; (Math) ser. ∼ity /ɪ'kwɒlǝtɪ/ n igualdad f. ∼ize vt igualar. ● vi (Sport) emapatar. ∼izer n (Sport) gol m del empate. ∼ly adv igualmente; <share> por igual

equation /ɪ'kweɪʒn/ n ecuación f

equator /ɪ'kweɪtǝ(r)/ n ecuador m. ∼ial /ekwǝ'tɔːrɪǝl/ a ecuatorial

equilibrium /iːkwɪ'lɪbrɪǝm/ n equilibrio m

equinox /'iːkwɪnɒks/ n equinoccio m

equip /ɪ'kwɪp/ vt (pt **equipped**) equipar. ∼ with proveer algo de. ∼ment n equipo m

equivalen|ce /ɪ'kwɪvǝlǝns/ n equivalencia f. ∼t a & n equivalente (m). be ∼t to equivaler

equivocal /ɪ'kwɪvǝkl/ a equívoco

era /'ɪǝrǝ/ n era f

eradicate /ɪ'rædɪkeɪt/ vt erradicar, extirpar

erase /ɪ'reɪz/ vt borrar. ∼r n goma f (de borrar)

erect /ɪ'rekt/ a erguido. ● vt levantar. ∼ion /-ʃn/ n construcción f; (Anat) erección f

ero|de /ɪ'rǝʊd/ vt erosionar. ∼sion /-ʒn/ n erosión f

erotic /ɪ'rɒtɪk/ a erótico

err /ɜː(r)/ vi errar; (sin) pecar

errand /'erǝnd/ n recado m, mandado m (LAm)

erratic /ɪ'rætɪk/ a desigual; <person> voluble

erroneous /ɪ'rǝʊnɪǝs/ a erróneo

error /'erǝ(r)/ n error m

erudit|e /'eruːdaɪt/ a erudito. ∼ion /-'dɪʃn/ n erudición f

erupt /ɪ'rʌpt/ vi entrar en erupción; (fig) estallar. ∼ion /-ʃn/ n erupción f

escalat|e /'eskǝleɪt/ vt intensificar. ● vi intensificarse. ∼ion /-'leɪʃn/ n intensificación f. ∼or n escalera f mecánica

escapade /eskǝ'peɪd/ n aventura f

escap|e /ɪ'skeɪp/ vi escaparse. ● vt evitar. ● n fuga f; (of gas, water) escape m. have a narrow ∼e escapar por un pelo. ∼ism /-ɪzǝm/ n escapismo m

escort /'eskɔːt/ n acompañante m; (Mil) escolta f. ● /ɪ'skɔːt/ vt acompañar; (Mil) escoltar

Eskimo /'eskɪmǝʊ/ n (pl **-os** or invar) esquimal m & f

especial /ɪ'speʃl/ a especial. ∼ly adv especialmente

espionage /'espɪǝnɑːʒ/ n espionaje m

Esq. /ɪ'skwaɪǝ(r)/ abbr (= **Esquire**) (in address) E. Ashton, ∼ Sr. Don E. Ashton

essay /'eseɪ/ n ensayo m; (at school) composición f

essence /'esns/ n esencia f. in ∼ esencialmente

essential /ɪ'senʃl/ a esencial. ● n elemento m esencial. ∼ly adv esencialmente

establish /ɪˈstæblɪʃ/ vt establecer. **~ment** n establecimiento m. **the E~ment** los que mandan, el sistema

estate /ɪˈsteɪt/ n finca f; (housing estate) complejo m habitacional, urbanización f, fraccionamiento m (Mex); (possessions) bienes mpl. **~ agent** n agente m inmobiliario. **~ car** n ranchera f, (coche m) familiar m, camioneta f (LAm)

esteem /ɪˈstiːm/ n estimación f, estima f

estimat|e /ˈestɪmət/ n cálculo m; (Com) presupuesto m. ● /ˈestɪmeɪt/ vt calcular. **~ion** /-ˈmeɪʃn/ n estima f, estimación f; (opinion) opinión f

estranged /ɪsˈtreɪndʒd/ a alejado

estuary /ˈestʃʊərɪ/ n estuario m

etc /etˈsetrə/ abbr (= **et cetera**) etc., etcétera

etching /ˈetʃɪŋ/ n aguafuerte m

etern|al /ɪˈtɜːnl/ a eterno. **~ity** /-ətɪ/ n eternidad f

ether /ˈiːθə(r)/ n éter m

ethic /ˈeθɪk/ n ética f. **~al** a ético. **~s** npl ética f

ethnic /ˈeθnɪk/ a étnico

ethos /ˈiːθɒs/ n carácter m distintivo

etiquette /ˈetɪket/ n etiqueta f

etymology /etɪˈmɒlədʒɪ/ n etimología f

euphemism /ˈjuːfəmɪzəm/ n eufemismo m

euphoria /juːˈfɔːrɪə/ n euforia f

Europe /ˈjʊərəp/ n Europa f. **~an** /-ˈpɪən/ a & n europeo (m). **~an Union** n Unión f Europea

euthanasia /juːθəˈneɪzɪə/ n eutanasia f

evacuat|e /ɪˈvækjʊeɪt/ vt evacuar; desocupar <building>. **~ion** /-ˈeɪʃn/ n evacuación f

evade /ɪˈveɪd/ vt evadir

evaluate /ɪˈvæljʊeɪt/ vt evaluar

evangelical /iːvænˈdʒelɪkl/ a evangélico

evaporat|e /ɪˈvæpəreɪt/ vi evaporarse. **~ion** /-ˈreɪʃn/ n evaporación f

evasi|on /ɪˈveɪʒn/ n evasión f. **~ve** /ɪˈveɪsɪv/ a evasivo

eve /iːv/ n víspera f

even /ˈiːvn/ a (flat, smooth) plano; <colour> uniforme; <distribution> equitativo; <number> par. **get ~ with** desquitarse con. ● vt nivelar. □ **~ up** vt equilibrar. ● adv aun, hasta, incluso. **~ if** aunque. **~ so** aun así. **not ~** ni siquiera

evening /ˈiːvnɪŋ/ n tarde f; (after dark) noche f. **~ class** n clase f nocturna

event /ɪˈvent/ n acontecimiento m; (Sport) prueba f. **in the ~ of** en caso de. **~ful** a lleno de acontecimientos

eventual /ɪˈventʃʊəl/ a final, definitivo. **~ity** /-ˈælɪtɪ/ n eventualidad f. **~ly** adv finalmente

ever /ˈevə(r)/ adv (negative) nunca, jamás; (at all times) siempre. **have you ~ been to Greece?** ¿has estado (alguna vez) en Grecia? **~ after** desde entonces. **~ since** desde entonces. **~ so** Ⓔ muy. **for ~** para siempre. **hardly ~** casi nunca. **~green** a de hoja perenne. ● n árbol m de hoja perenne. **~lasting** a eterno.

every /ˈevrɪ/ a cada, todo. **~ child** todos los niños. **~ one** cada uno. **~ other day** un día sí y otro no. **~body** pron todos, todo el mundo. **~day** a de todos los días. **~one** pron todos, todo el mundo. **~thing** pron todo. **~where** adv (be) en todas partes, (go) a todos lados

evict /ɪˈvɪkt/ vt desahuciar. **~ion** /-ʃn/ n desahucio m

eviden|ce /ˈevɪdəns/ n evidencia f; (proof) pruebas fpl; (Jurid) testimonio m; **give ~ce** prestar declaración. **~ce of** señales de. **in ~ce** visible. **~t** a evidente. **~tly** adv evidentemente

evil /ˈiːvl/ a malvado. ● n mal m

evo|cative /ɪˈvɒkətɪv/ a evocador. **~ke** /ɪˈvəʊk/ vt evocar

evolution /iːvəˈluːʃn/ n evolución f

evolve /ɪˈvɒlv/ vt desarrollar. ● vi evolucionar

ewe /juː/ n oveja f

exact /ɪɡˈzækt/ a exacto. ● vt exigir (from a). **~ing** a exigente. **~ly** adv exactamente

exaggerat|e /ɪgˈzædʒəreɪt/ vt exagerar. ~**ion** /-ˈreɪʃn/ n exageración f

exam /ɪgˈzæm/ n examen m. ~**ination** /ɪgzæmɪˈneɪʃn/ n examen m. ~**ine** /ɪgˈzæmɪn/ vt examinar; interrogar <witness>. ~**iner** n examinador m

example /ɪgˈzɑːmpl/ n ejemplo m. **for** ~ por ejemplo. **make an** ~ **of s.o.** darle un castigo ejemplar a uno

exasperat|e /ɪgˈzæspəreɪt/ vt exasperar. ~**ing** a exasperante. ~**ion** /-ˈreɪʃn/ n exasperación f

excavat|e /ˈekskəveɪt/ vt excavar. ~**ion** /-ˈveɪʃn/ n excavación f

exceed /ɪkˈsiːd/ vt exceder. ~**ingly** adv sumamente

excel /ɪkˈsel/ vi (pt **excelled**) sobresalir. ● vt. ~ **o.s.** lucirse. ~**lence** /ˈeksələns/ n excelencia f. ~**lent** a excelente

except /ɪkˈsept/ prep menos, excepto. ~ **for** si no fuera por. ● vt exceptuar. ~**ing** prep con excepción de

exception /ɪkˈsepʃən/ n excepción f. **take** ~ **to** ofenderse por. ~**al** a excepcional. ~**ally** adv excepcionalmente

excerpt /ˈeksɜːpt/ n extracto m

excess /ɪkˈses/ n exceso m. ● /ˈekses/ a excedente. ~ **fare** suplemento m. ~ **luggage** exceso m de equipaje. ~**ive** a excesivo

exchange /ɪksˈtʃeɪndʒ/ vt cambiar. ● n intercambio m; (of money) cambio m. (**telephone**) ~ central f telefónica

excise /ˈeksaɪz/ n impuestos mpl interos. ● /ekˈsaɪz/ vt quitar

excit|able /ɪkˈsaɪtəbl/ a excitable. ~**e** /ɪkˈsaɪt/ vt emocionar; (stimulate) excitar. ~**ed** a entusiasmarse. **get** ~**ed** entusiasmarse. ~**ement** n emoción f; (enthusiasm) entusiasmo m. ~**ing** a emocionante

excla|im /ɪkˈskleɪm/ vi/t exclamar. ~**mation** /ekskləˈmeɪʃn/ n exclamación f. ~**mation mark** n signo m de admiración f

exclu|de /ɪkˈskluːd/ vt excluir. ~**sion** /-ʒən/ n exclusión f. ~**sive** /ɪkˈskluːsɪv/ a exclusivo; <club> selecto. ~**sive of** excluyendo. ~**sively** adv exclusivamente

excruciating /ɪkˈskruːʃieɪtɪŋ/ a atroz, insoportable

excursion /ɪkˈskɜːʃn/ n excursión f

excus|able /ɪkˈskjuːzəbl/ a perdonable. ~**e** /ɪkˈskjuːz/ vt perdonar. ~**e from** dispensar de. ~**e me!** ¡perdón! ● /ɪkˈskjuːs/ n excusa f

ex-directory /eksdɪˈrektərɪ/ a que no figura en la guía telefónica, privado (Mex)

execut|e /ˈeksɪkjuːt/ vt ejecutar. ~**ion** /eksɪˈkjuːʃn/ n ejecución f. ~**ioner** n verdugo m

executive /ɪgˈzekjʊtɪv/ a & n ejecutivo (m)

exempt /ɪgˈzempt/ a exento (**from** de). ● vt dispensar. ~**ion** /-ʃn/ n exención f

exercise /ˈeksəsaɪz/ n ejercicio m. ● vt ejercer. ● vi hacer ejercicio. ~ **book** n cuaderno m

exert /ɪgˈzɜːt/ vt ejercer. ~ **o.s.** hacer un gran esfuerzo. ~**ion** /-ʃn/ n esfuerzo m

exhale /eksˈheɪl/ vt/i exhalar

exhaust /ɪgˈzɔːst/ vt agotar. ● n (Auto) tubo m de escape. ~**ed** a agotado. ~**ion** /-stʃən/ n agotamiento m. ~**ive** a exhaustivo

exhibit /ɪgˈzɪbɪt/ vt exponer; (fig) mostrar. ● n objeto m expuesto; (Jurid) documento m. ~**ion** /eksɪˈbɪʃn/ n exposición. ~**ionist** n exhibicionista m & f. ~**or** /ɪgˈzɪbɪtə(r)/ n expositor m

exhilarat|ing /ɪgˈzɪləreɪtɪŋ/ a excitante. ~**ion** /-ˈreɪʃn/ n regocijo m

exhort /ɪgˈzɔːt/ vt exhortar

exile /ˈeksaɪl/ n exilio m; (person) exiliado m. ● vt desterrar

exist /ɪgˈzɪst/ vi existir. ~**ence** n existencia f. **in** ~**ence** existente

exit /ˈeksɪt/ n salida f

exorbitant /ɪgˈzɔːbɪtənt/ a exorbitante

exorcis|e /ˈeksɔːsaɪz/ vt exorcizar. ~**m** /-sɪzəm/ n exorcismo m. ~**t** n exorcista m & f

exotic /ɪgˈzɒtɪk/ a exótico

expand /ɪk'spænd/ *vt* expandir; (develop) desarrollar. ● *vi* expandirse

expanse /ɪk'spæns/ *n* extensión *f*

expansion /ɪk'spænʃn/ *n* expansión *f*

expatriate /eks'pætrɪət/ *a & n* expatriado (*m*)

expect /ɪk'spekt/ *vt* esperar; (suppose) suponer; (demand) contar con. **I ~ so** supongo que sí. **~ancy** *n* esperanza *f*. **life ~ancy** esperanza *f* de vida. ● **~ant** *a* expectante. **~ant mother** *n* futura madre *f*

expectation /ekspek'teɪʃn/ *n* expectativa *f*

expedient /ɪk'spiːdɪənt/ *a* conveniente. ● *n* expediente *m*

expedition /ekspɪ'dɪʃn/ *n* expedición *f*

expel /ɪk'spel/ *vt* (*pt* **expelled**) expulsar

expend /ɪk'spend/ *vt* gastar. **~able** *a* prescindible. **~iture** /-ɪtʃə(r)/ *n* gastos *mpl*

expens|e /ɪk'spens/ *n* gasto *m*. **at s.o.'s ~e** a costa de uno. **~es** *npl* (Com) gastos *mpl*. **~ive** *a* caro

experience /ɪk'spɪərɪəns/ *n* experiencia. ● *vt* experimentar. **~d** *a* con experiencia; *<driver>* experimentado

experiment /ɪk'sperɪmənt/ *n* experimento *m*. ● *vi* experimentar. **~al** /-'mentl/ *a* experimental

expert /'ekspɜːt/ *a & n* experto (*m*). **~ise** /eksps'tiːz/ *n* pericia *f*. **~ly** *adv* hábilmente

expir|e /ɪk'spaɪə(r)/ *vi* *<passport, ticket>* caducar; *<contract>* vencer. **~y** *n* vencimiento *m*, caducidad *f*

expla|in /ɪk'spleɪn/ *vt* explicar. **~nation** /eksplə'neɪʃn/ *n* explicación *f*. **~natory** /ɪks'plænətərɪ/ *a* explicativo

explicit /ɪk'splɪsɪt/ *a* explícito

explode /ɪk'spləʊd/ *vt* hacer explotar. ● *vi* estallar

exploit /'eksplɔɪt/ *n* hazaña *f*. ● /ɪk'splɔɪt/ *vt* explotar. **~ation** /eksplɔɪ'teɪʃn/ *n* explotación *f*

explor|ation /eksplə'reɪʃn/ *n* exploración *f*. **~atory** /ɪk'splɒrətrɪ/

a exploratorio. **~e** /ɪk'splɔː(r)/ *vt* explorar. **~er** *n* explorador *m*

explosi|on /ɪk'spləʊʒn/ *n* explosión *f*. **~ve** /-sɪv/ *a & n* explosivo (*m*)

export /ɪk'spɔːt/ *vt* exportar. ● /'ekspɔːt/ *n* exportación *f*; (item) artículo *m* de exportación. **~er** /ɪks'pɔːtə(r)/ exportador *m*

expos|e /ɪk'spəʊz/ *vt* exponer; (reveal) descubrir. **~ure** /-ʒə(r)/ *n* exposición *f*. **die of ~ure** morir de frío

express /ɪk'spres/ *vt* expresar. ● *a* expreso; *<letter>* urgente. ● *adv* (by express post) por correo urgente. ● *n* (train) rápido *m*, expreso *m*. **~ion** *n* expresión *f*. **~ive** *a* expresivo. **~ly** *adv* expresadamente. **~way** *n* (Amer) autopista *f*

expulsion /ɪk'spʌlʃn/ *n* expulsión *f*

exquisite /'ekskwɪzɪt/ *a* exquisito

exten|d /ɪk'stend/ *vt* extender; (prolong) prolongar; ampliar *<house>*. ● *vi* extenderse. **~sion** /-ʃn/ *n* extensión *f*; (of road, time) prolongación *f*; (building) anejo *m*. **~sive** /-sɪv/ *a* extenso. **~sively** *adv* extensamente. **~t** *n* extensión *f*; (fig) alcance *m*. **to a certain ~t** hasta cierto punto

exterior /ɪk'stɪərɪə(r)/ *a & n* exterior (*m*)

exterminat|e /ɪk'stɜːmɪneɪt/ *vt* exterminar. **~ion** /-'neɪʃn/ *n* exterminio *m*

external /ɪk'stɜːnl/ *a* externo

extinct /ɪk'stɪŋkt/ *a* extinto. **~ion** /-ʃn/ *n* extinción *f*

extinguish /ɪk'stɪŋgwɪʃ/ *vt* extinguir. **~er** *n* extintor *m*, extinguidor *m* (LAm)

extol /ɪk'stəʊl/ *vt* (*pt* **extolled**) alabar

extort /ɪk'stɔːt/ *vt* sacar por la fuerza. **~ion** /-ʃn/ *n* exacción *f*. **~ionate** /-ənət/ *a* exorbitante

extra /'ekstrə/ *a* de más. ● *adv* extraordinariamente. ● *n* suplemento *m*; (Cinema) extra *m & f*

extract /'ekstrækt/ *n* extracto *m*. ● /ɪk'strækt/ *vt* extraer. **~ion** /ɪk'strækʃn/ *n* extracción *f*

extradit|e /'ekstrədaɪt/ *vt* extraditar. **~ion** /-'dɪʃn/ *n* extradición *f*

extra: ∼**ordinary** /ɪk'strɔ:dnrɪ/ *a* extraordinario. ∼**-sensory** /ekstrə'sensərɪ/ *a* extrasensorial

extravagan|ce /ɪk'strævəgəns/ *n* prodigalidad *f*; (of gestures, dress) extravagancia *f*. ∼**t** *a* pródigo; <*behaviour*> extravagante. ∼**za** *n* gran espectáculo *m*

extrem|e /ɪk'stri:m/ *a & n* extremo (*m*). ∼**ely** *adv* extremadamente. ∼**ist** *n* extremista *m & f*

extricate /'ekstrɪkeɪt/ *vt* desenredar, librar

extrovert /'ekstrəvɜ:t/ *n* extrovertido *m*

exuberan|ce /ɪg'zju:bərəns/ *n* exuberancia *f*. ∼**t** *a* exuberante

exude /ɪg'zju:d/ *vt* rezumar

exult /ɪg'zʌlt/ *vi* exultar. ∼**ation** /egzʌl'teɪʃn/ *n* exultación *f*

eye /aɪ/ *n* ojo *m*. **keep an** ∼ **on** no perder de vista. **see** ∼ **to** ∼ **with s.o.** estar de acuerdo con uno. ● *vt* (*pt* **eyed**, *pres p* **eyeing**) mirar. ∼**ball** *n* globo *m* ocular. ∼**brow** *n* ceja *f*. ∼**drops** *npl* colirio *m*. ∼**lash** *n* pestaña *f*. ∼**lid** *n* párpado *m*. ∼**-opener** *n* 🅣 revelación *f*. ∼**-shadow** *n* sombra *f* de ojos. ∼**sight** *n* vista *f*. ∼**sore** *n* (fig, 🅣) monstruosidad *f*, adefesio *m*. ∼**witness** *n* testigo *m* ocular

Ff

fable /'feɪbl/ *n* fábula *f*

fabric /'fæbrɪk/ *n* tejido *m*, tela *f*

fabricate /'fæbrɪkeɪt/ *vt* inventar. ∼**ation** /-'keɪʃn/ *n* invención *f*

fabulous /'fæbjʊləs/ *a* fabuloso

facade /fə'sɑ:d/ *n* fachada *f*

face /feɪs/ *n* cara *f*, rostro *m*; (of watch) esfera *f*, carátula *f* (Mex); (aspect) aspecto *m*. ∼ **down(wards)** boca abajo. ∼ **up(wards)** boca arriba. **in the** ∼ **of** frente a. **lose** ∼ quedar mal. **pull** ∼**s** hacer muecas. ● *vt* mirar hacia; <*house*> dar a; (confront) enfrentarse con. ● *vi* volverse. ◻ ∼ **up to** *vt* enfrentarse con. ∼ **flannel** *n* paño *m* (para lavarse la cara). ∼**less** *a* anónimo. ∼ **lift** *n* cirugía *f* estética en la cara

facetious /fə'si:ʃəs/ *a* burlón

facial /'feɪʃl/ *a* facial

facile /'fæsaɪl/ *a* superficial, simplista

facilitate /fə'sɪlɪteɪt/ *vt* facilitar

facility /fə'sɪlɪtɪ/ *n* facilidad *f*

fact /fækt/ *n* hecho *m*. **as a matter of** ∼, **in** ∼ en realidad, de hecho

faction /'fækʃn/ *n* facción *f*

factor /'fæktə(r)/ *n* factor *m*

factory /'fæktərɪ/ *n* fábrica *f*

factual /'fæktʃʊəl/ *a* basado en hechos, factual

faculty /'fækəltɪ/ *n* facultad *f*

fad /fæd/ *n* manía *f*, capricho *m*

fade /feɪd/ *vi* <*colour*> desteñirse; <*flowers*> marchitarse; <*light*> apagarse; <*memory, sound*> desvanecerse

fag /fæg/ *n* (🅔, chore) faena *f*; (🅧, cigarette) cigarillo *m*, pitillo *m*

Fahrenheit /'færənhaɪt/ *a* Fahrenheit

fail /feɪl/ *vi* fracasar; <*brakes*> fallar; (in an exam) suspender, ser reprobado (LAm). **he** ∼**ed to arrive** no llegó. ● *vt* suspender, ser reprobado en (LAm) <*exam*>; suspender, reprobar (LAm) <*candidate*>. ● *n*. **without** ∼ sin falta. ∼**ing** *n* defecto *m*. ● *prep*. ∼**ing that,** ... si eso no resulta.... ∼**ure** /'feɪljə(r)/ *n* fracaso *m*

faint /feɪnt/ *a* (**-er, -est**) (weak) débil; (indistinct) indistinto. **feel** ∼ estar mareado. **the** ∼**est idea** la más remota idea. ● *vi* desmayarse. ● *n* desmayo *m*. ∼**-hearted** /-'hɑ:tɪd/ *a* pusilánime, cobarde. ∼**ly** *adv* (weakly) débilmente; (indistinctly) indistintamente; (slightly) ligeramente

fair /feə(r)/ *a* (**-er, -est**) (just) justo; <*weather*> bueno; <*amount*> razonable; <*hair*> rubio, güero (Mex 🅣); <*skin*> blanco. ● *adv* limpio. ● *n* feria *f*. ∼**-haired** /-'heəd/ *a* rubio, güero (Mex 🅣). ∼**ly** *adv* (justly) justamente; (rather) bastante. ∼**ness**

n justicia *f*. **in all ~ness** since-ramente. **~ play** *n* juego *m* limpio

fairy /'feərɪ/ *n* hada *f*. **~ story, ~ tale** *n* cuento *m* de hadas

faith /feɪθ/ *n* (trust) confianza *f*; (Relig) fe *f*. **~ful** *a* fiel. **~fully** *adv* fielmente. **yours ~fully** (in letters) (le saluda) atentamente

fake /feɪk/ *n* falsificación *f*; (person) farsante *m*. ● *a* falso. ● *vt* falsificar

falcon /'fɔːlkən/ *n* halcón *m*

Falkland Islands /'fɔːlklənd/ *npl*. **the Falkland Islands, the Falklands** las (Islas) Malvinas

fall /fɔːl/ *vi* (*pt* **fell**, *pp* **fallen**) caer; (decrease) bajar. ● *n* caída *f*; (Amer, autumn) otoño *m*; (in price) bajada *f*. □ ~ **apart** *vi* deshacerse. □ ~ **back on** *vt* recurrir a. □ ~ **down** *vi* (fall) caerse. □ ~ **for** *vt* 🔲 enamorarse de <*person*>; dejarse engañar por <*trick*>. □ ~ **in** *vi* (Mil) formar filas. □ ~ **off** *vi* caerse; (diminish) disminuir. □ ~ **out** *vi* (quarrel) reñir (**with** con); (drop out) caerse; (Mil) romper filas. □ ~ **over** *vi* caerse. *vt* tropezar con. □ ~ **through** *vi* no salir adelante

fallacy /'fæləsɪ/ *n* falacia *f*

fallible /'fælɪbl/ *a* falible

fallout /'fɔːlaʊt/ *n* lluvia *f* radiactiva. **~ shelter** *n* refugio *m* antinuclear

fallow /'fæləʊ/ *a* en barbecho

false /fɔːls/ *a* falso. **~ alarm** *n* falsa alarma. **~hood** *n* mentira *f*. **~ly** *adv* falsamente. **~ teeth** *npl* dentadura *f* postiza

falsify /'fɔːlsɪfaɪ/ *vt* falsificar

falter /'fɔːltə(r)/ *vi* vacilar

fame /feɪm/ *n* fama *f*. **~d** *a* famoso

familiar /fə'mɪlɪə(r)/ *a* familiar. **the name sounds ~** el nombre me suena. **be ~ with** conocer. **~ity** /-'ærətɪ/ *n* familiaridad *f*. **~ize** *vt* familiarizar

family /'fæməlɪ/ *n* familia *f*. ● *a* de (la) familia, familiar. **~ tree** *n* árbol *m* genealógico

famine /'fæmɪn/ *n* hambre *f*, hambruna *f*

famished /'fæmɪʃt/ *a* hambriento

famous /'feɪməs/ *a* famoso

fan /fæn/ *n* abanico *m*; (Mec) ventilador *m*; (enthusiast) aficionado *m*; (of group, actor) fan *m* & *f*; (of sport, team) hincha *m* & *f*. ● *vt* (*pt* **fanned**) abanicar; avivar <*interest*>. □ ~ **out** *vi* desparramarse en forma de abanico

fanatic /fə'nætɪk/ *n* fanático *m*. **~al** *a* fanático. **~ism** /-sɪzəm/ *n* fanatismo *m*

fan belt *n* correa *f* de ventilador, banda *f* del ventilador (Mex)

fanciful /'fænsɪfl/ *a* (imaginative) imaginativo; (impractical) extravagante

fancy /'fænsɪ/ *n* imaginación *f*; (liking) gusto *m*. **take a ~ to** tomar cariño a <*person*>; aficionarse a <*thing*>. ● *a* de lujo. ● *vt* (imagine) imaginar; (believe) creer; (🔲, want) apetecer a. **~ dress** *n* disfraz *m*

fanfare /'fænfeə(r)/ *n* fanfarria *f*

fang /fæŋ/ *n* (of animal) colmillo *m*; (of snake) diente *m*

fantasize /'fæntəsaɪz/ *vi* fantasear

fantastic /fæn'tæstɪk/ *a* fantástico

fantasy /'fæntəsɪ/ *n* fantasía *f*

far /fɑː(r)/ *adv* lejos; (much) mucho. **as ~ as** hasta. **as ~ as I know** que yo sepa. **by ~** con mucho. ● *a* (**further**, **furthest** *or* **farther**, **farthest**) lejano. **~ away** lejano

farc|e /fɑːs/ *n* farsa *f*. **~ical** *a* ridículo

fare /feə(r)/ *n* (on bus) precio *m* del billete, precio *m* del boleto (LAm); (on train, plane) precio *m* del billete, precio *m* del pasaje (LAm); (food) comida *f*

Far East /fɑː'riːst/ *n* Extremo *or* Lejano Oriente *m*

farewell /feə'wel/ *int* & *n* adiós (*m*)

far-fetched /fɑː'fetʃt/ *a* improbable

farm /fɑːm/ *n* granja *f*. ● *vt* cultivar. □ ~ **out** *vt* encargar (*a terceros*). ● *vi* ser agricultor. **~er** *n* agricultor *m*, granjero *m*. **~house** *n* granja *f*. **~ing** *n* agricultura *f*. **~yard** *n* corral *m*

far: ~-off *a* lejano. **~-reaching** /fɑː'riːtʃɪŋ/ *a* trascendental. **~-sighted** /fɑː'saɪtɪd/ *a* con visión del futuro; (Med, Amer) hipermétrope

farther, **farthest** /ˈfɑːðə(r),
ˈfɑːðəst/ ⇒FAR

fascinat|e /ˈfæsɪneɪt/ vt fascinar.
~**ed** a fascinado. ~**ing** a fascinante. ~**ion** /-ˈneɪʃn/ n fascinación f

fascis|m /ˈfæʃɪzəm/ n fascismo m.
~**t** a & n fascista (m & f)

fashion /ˈfæʃn/ n (manner) manera f;
(vogue) moda f. **be in/out of** ~ estar de
moda/estar pasado de moda. ~**able**
a de moda

fast /fɑːst/ a (-er, -est) rápido;
<clock> adelantado; (secure) fijo; <col-
ours> sólido. ● adv rápidamente; (se-
curely) firmemente. ~ **asleep** profundamente dormido. ● vi ayunar.
● n ayuno m

fasten /ˈfɑːsn/ vt sujetar; cerrar
<case>; abrochar <belt etc>. ● vi
<case> cerrar; <belt etc> cerrarse.
~**er**, ~**ing** n (on box, window) cierre
m; (on door) cerrojo m

fat /fæt/ n grasa f. ● a (**fatter, fat-
test**) gordo; <meat> que tiene mucha grasa; (thick) grueso. **get** ~ engordar

fatal /ˈfeɪtl/ a mortal; (fateful) fatídico.
~**ity** /fəˈtælətɪ/ muerto m. ~**ly** adv
mortalmente

fate /feɪt/ n destino m; (one's lot) suerte f. ~**d** a predestinado. ~**ful** a
fatídico

father /ˈfɑːðə(r)/ n padre m. ~**hood**
m paternidad f. ~**-in-law** m (pl ~**s-
in-law**) m suegro m. ~**ly** a pa-ternal

fathom /ˈfæðəm/ n braza f. ● vt. ~
(out) comprender

fatigue /fəˈtiːg/ n fatiga f. ● vt fa-
tigar

fat|ten vt. ~**ten** (up) cebar <animal>.
~**tening** a que engorda. ~**ty** a gra-
so, grasoso (LAm). ● n Ⓘ gordinflón
m

fatuous /ˈfætjʊəs/ a fatuo

faucet /ˈfɔːsɪt/ n (Amer) grifo m, llave
f (LAm)

fault /fɔːlt/ n defecto m; (blame) culpa
f; (tennis) falta f; (Geol) falla f. **at** ~
culpable. ● vt encontrarle defectos a.
~**less** a impecable. ~**y** a defectuoso

favour /ˈfeɪvə(r)/ n favor m. ● vt fa-
vorecer; (support) estar a favor de;

(prefer) preferir. ~**able** a favorable.
~**ably** adv favorablemente. ~**ite** a
& n preferido (m). ~**itism** n favori-
tismo m

fawn /fɔːn/ n cervato m. ● a beige,
beis. ● vi. ~ **on** adular

fax /fæks/ n fax m. ● vt faxear

fear /fɪə(r)/ n miedo m. ● vt temer.
~**ful** a (frightening) espantoso; (frightened) temeroso. ~**less** a intrépido.
~**some** /-səm/ a espantoso

feasib|ility /fiːzəˈbɪlətɪ/ n viabi-
lidad f. ~**le** /ˈfiːzəbl/ a factible; (likely) posible

feast /fiːst/ n (Relig) fiesta f; (meal)
banquete m

feat /fiːt/ n hazaña f

feather /ˈfeðə(r)/ n pluma f.
~**weight** n peso m pluma

feature /ˈfiːtʃə(r)/ n (on face) rasgo
m; (characteristic) característica f; (in
newspaper) artículo m; ~ (film) película f principal, largometraje m. ● vt
presentar; (give prominence to) destacar

February /ˈfebrʊərɪ/ n febrero m

fed /fed/ ⇒FEED

feder|al /ˈfedərəl/ a federal. ~**ation**
/fedəˈreɪʃn/ n federación f

fed up a Ⓘ harto (**with** de)

fee /fiː/ n (professional) honorarios
mpl; (enrolment) derechos mpl; (club)
cuota f

feeble /ˈfiːbl/ a (-er, -est) débil

feed /fiːd/ vt (pt fed) dar de comer a;
(supply) alimentar. ● vi comer. ● n
(for animals) pienso m; (for babies) comida f. ~**back** n reacción f

feel /fiːl/ vt (pt felt) sentir; (touch) tocar; (think) considerar. **do you** ~ **it's a
good idea?** ¿te parece buena idea? ~
as if tener la impresión de que. ~
hot/hungry tener calor/hambre. ~
like (Ⓘ, want) tener ganas de. ● n
sensación f. **get the** ~ **of sth** acostumbrarse a algo. ~**er** n (of insect)
antena f. ~**ing** n sentimiento m;
(physical) sensación f

feet /fiːt/ ⇒FOOT

feign /feɪn/ vt fingir

feint /feɪnt/ n finta f

fell /fel/ ⇒FALL. ● vt derribar; talar

fellow /'feləʊ/ n 🔲 tipo m; (comrade) compañero m; (of society) socio m. ~ **countryman** n compatriota m. ~ **passenger/traveller** n compañero m de viaje

felony /'felən/ n delito m grave

felt /felt/ n ⇒FEEL. ● n fieltro m

female /'fi:meɪl/ a hembra; <voice, sex etc> femenino. ● n mujer f; (animal) hembra f

femini|ne /'femənɪn/ a & n femenino (m). ~**nity** /-'nɪnəti/ n feminidad f. ~**st** a & n feminista m & f

fenc|e /fens/ n cerca f, cerco m (LAm). ● vt. ~**e (in)** encerrar, cercar. ● vi (Sport) practicar la esgrima. ~**er** n esgrimidor m. ~**ing** n (Sport) esgrima f

fend /fend/ vi. ~ **for o.s.** valerse por sí mismo. □ ~ **off** vt defenderse de

fender /'fendə(r)/ n rejilla f; (Amer, Auto) guardabarros m, salpicadera f (Mex)

ferment /fə'ment/ vt/i fermentar. ~**ation** /-'teɪʃn/ n fermentación f

fern /fɜːn/ n helecho m

feroci|ous /fə'rəʊʃəs/ a feroz. ~**ty** /fə'rɒsəti/ n ferocidad f

ferret /'ferɪt/ n hurón m. ● vi (pt **ferreted**) ~ **about** husmear. ● vt. ~ **out** descubrir

ferry /'ferɪ/ n ferry m. ● vt transportar

fertil|e /'fɜːtaɪl/ a fértil. ~**ity** /-'tɪləti/ n fertilidad f. ~**ize** /'fɜːtəlaɪz/ vt fecundar, abonar <soil>. ~**izer** n fertilizante m

ferv|ent /'fɜːvənt/ a ferviente. ~**our** /-və(r)/ n fervor m

fester /'festə(r)/ vi enconarse

festival /'festəvl/ n fiesta f; (of arts) festival m

festiv|e /'festɪv/ a festivo. **the ~e season** n las Navidades. ~**ity** /fe'stɪvəti/ n festividad f

fetch /fetʃ/ vt (go for) ir a buscar; (bring) traer; (be sold for) venderse en. ~**ing** a atractivo

fête /feɪt/ n fiesta f. ● vt festejar

fetish /'fetɪʃ/ n fetiche m

fetter /'fetə(r)/ vt encadenar

feud /fju:d/ n contienda f

feudal /'fju:dl/ a feudal. ~**ism** n feudalismo m

fever /'fi:və(r)/ n fiebre f. ~**ish** a febril

few /fju:/ a pocos. **a ~ houses** algunas casas. ● n pocos mpl. **a ~** unos (pocos). **a good ~, quite a ~** 🔲 muchos. ~**er** a & n menos. ~**est** a el menor número de

fiancé /fɪ'ɒnseɪ/ n novio m. ~**e** /fɪ'ɒnseɪ/ n novia f

fiasco /fɪ'æskəʊ/ n (pl -**os**) fiasco m

fib /fɪb/ n 🔲 mentirilla f. ● vi 🔲 mentir, decir mentirillas

fibre /'faɪbə(r)/ n fibra f. ~**glass** n fibra f de vidrio

fickle /'fɪkl/ a inconstante

ficti|on /'fɪkʃn/ n ficción f. (**works of**) ~**on** novelas fpl. ~**onal** a novelesco. ~**tious** /fɪk'tɪʃəs/ a ficticio

fiddle /'fɪdl/ n 🔲 violín m; (🔲, swindle) trampa f. ● vt 🔲 falsificar. ~ **with** juguetear con

fidget /'fɪdʒɪt/ vi (pt **fidgeted**) moverse, ponerse nervioso. ~ **with** juguetear con. ● n persona f inquieta. ~**y** a inquieto

field /fi:ld/ n campo m. ~ **day** n. **have a ~ day** hacer su agosto. ~ **glasses** npl gemelos mpl. F~ **Marshal** n mariscal m de campo. ~ **trip** n viaje m de estudio. ~**work** n investigaciones fpl en el terreno

fiend /fi:nd/ n demonio m. ~**ish** a diabólico

fierce /fɪəs/ a (-**er**, -**est**) feroz; <attack> violento. ~**ly** adv <growl> con ferocidad; <fight> con fiereza

fiery /'faɪərɪ/ a (-**ier**, -**iest**) ardiente; <temper> exaltado

fifteen /fɪf'ti:n/ a & n quince (m). ~**th** a decimoquinto. ● n quinceavo m

fifth /fɪfθ/ a & n quinto (m)

fift|ieth /'fɪftɪəθ/ a quincuagésimo. ● n cincuentavo m. ~**y** a & n cincuenta (m). ~**y-~y** adv mitad y mitad, a medias. ● a. **a ~y-~y** chance una posibilidad de cada dos

fig /fɪg/ n higo m

fight /faɪt/ vi (pt **fought**) luchar; (quarrel) disputar. ● vt luchar contra. ● n pelea m; (struggle) lucha f; (quarrel) disputa *f*; (Mil) combate *m*. □ **~ back** *vi* defenderse. □ **~ off** *vt* rechazar *<attack>*; luchar contra *<illness>*. **~er** *n* luchador *m*; (aircraft) avión *m* de caza. **~ing** *n* luchas *fpl*

figment /'fɪgmənt/ *n*. **~ of the imagination** producto *m* de la imaginación

figurative /'fɪgjʊrətɪv/ *a* figurado

figure /'fɪgə(r)/ *n* (number) cifra *f*; (person) figura *f*; (shape) forma *f*; (of woman) tipo *m*. ● *vt* imaginar; (Amer 🇺🇸, reckon) calcular. ● *vi* figurar. **that ~s** 🇺🇸 es lógico. □ **~ out** *vt* entender. **~head** *n* testaferro *m*, mascarón *m* de proa. **~ of speech** *n* figura *f* retórica

filch /fɪltʃ/ *vt* 🇺🇸 hurtar

file /faɪl/ *n* (tool, for nails) lima *f*; (folder) carpeta *f*; (set of papers) expediente *m*; (Comp) archivo *m*; (row) fila *f*. **in single ~** en fila india. ● *vt* archivar *<papers>*; limar *<metal, nails>*. ● **~ in** *vi* entrar en fila. **~ past** *vt* desfilar ante

filing cabinet /'faɪlɪŋ/ *n* archivador *m*

fill /fɪl/ *vt* llenar. ● *vi* llenarse. ● *n*. **eat one's ~** hartarse de comer. **have had one's ~ of** estar harto de □ **~ in** *vt* rellenar *<form, hole>*. □ **~ out** *vt* rellenar *<form>*. *vi* (get fatter) engordar. □ **~ up** *vt* llenar. *vi* llenarse

fillet /'fɪlɪt/ *n* filete *m*. ● *vt* (*pt* **filleted**) cortar en filetes *<meat>*; quitar la espina a *<fish>*

filling /'fɪlɪŋ/ *n* (in tooth) empaste *m*, tapadura *f* (Mex). **~ station** *n* gasolinera *f*

film /fɪlm/ *n* película *f*. ● *vt* filmar. **~ star** *n* estrella *f* de cine

filter /'fɪltə(r)/ *n* filtro *m*. ● *vt* filtrar. ● *vi* filtrarse. **~-tipped** *a* con filtro

filth /fɪlθ/ *n* mugre *f*. **~y** *a* mugriento

fin /fɪn/ *n* aleta *f*

final /'faɪnl/ *a* último; (conclusive) decisivo. ● *n* (Sport) final *f*. **~s** *npl* (Schol) exámenes *mpl* de fin de curso

finale /fɪ'nɑːlɪ/ *n* final *m*

final|ist *n* finalista *m & f*. **~ize** *vt* ultimar. **~ly** *adv* (lastly) finalmente, por fin

financ|e /'faɪnæns/ *n* finanzas *fpl*. ● *vt* financiar. **~ial** /faɪ'nænʃl/ *a* financiero; *<difficulties>* económico

find /faɪnd/ *vt* (*pt* **found**) encontrar. **~ out** *vt* descubrir. ● *vi* (learn) enterarse. **~ings** *npl* conclusiones *fpl*

fine /faɪn/ *a* (**-er, -est**) (delicate) fino; (excellent) excelente. ● *adv* muy bien. ● *n* multa *f*. ● *vt* multar. **~ arts** *npl* bellas artes *fpl*. **~ly** *adv* (cut) en trozos pequeños; *<adjust>* con precisión

finger /'fɪŋgə(r)/ *n* dedo *m*. ● *vt* tocar. **~nail** *n* uña *f*. **~print** *n* huella *f* digital. **~tip** *n* punta *f* del dedo

finish /'fɪnɪʃ/ *vt/i* terminar, acabar. **~ doing** terminar de hacer. ● *n* fin *m*; (of race) llegada *f*

finite /'faɪnaɪt/ *a* finito

Fin|land /'fɪnlənd/ *n* Finlandia *f*. **~n** *n* finlandés *m*. **~nish** *a & n* finlandés (*m*)

fiord /fjɔːd/ *n* fiordo *m*

fir /fɜː(r)/ *n* abeto *m*

fire /faɪə(r)/ *n* fuego *m*; (conflagration) incendio *m*. ● *vt* disparar *<gun>*; (dismiss) despedir; avivar *<imagination>*. ● *vi* disparar. **~ alarm** *n* alarma *f* contra incendios. **~arm** *n* arma *f* de fuego. **~ brigade**, **~ department** (Amer) *n* cuerpo *m* de bomberos. **~ engine** *n* coche *m* de bomberos, carro *m* de bomberos (Mex). **~escape** *n* escalera *f* de incendios. **~ extinguisher** *n* extintor *m*, extinguidor *m* (LAm). **~fighter** *n* bombero *m*. **~man** /-mən/ *n* bombero *m*. **~place** *n* chimenea *f*. **~side** *n* hogar *m*. **~ truck** *n* (Amer) ⇒**~** ENGINE. **~wood** *n* leña *f*. **~work** *n* fuego *m* artificial

firm /fɜːm/ *n* empresa *f*. ● *a* (**-er, -est**) firme. **~ly** *adv* firmemente

first /fɜːst/ *a* primero, (before masculine singular noun) primer. **at ~ hand** directamente. ● *n* primero *m*. ● *adv* primero; (first time) por primera vez. **~ of all** primero. **~ aid** *n* primeros auxilios *mpl*. **~ aid kit** *n* botiquín *m*. **~ class** /-'klɑːs/ *adv* *<travel>* en primera clase. **~-class** *a* de primera clase. **~ floor** *n* primer piso *m*; (Amer) planta *f* baja. **F~ Lady** *n* (Amer) Primera Dama *f*. **~ly** *adv* en primer lugar. **~ name** n nombre m de pila. **~-rate** /-'reɪt/ a excelente

fish /fɪʃ/ n (pl invar or **-es**) pez m; (as food) pescado m. ● vi pescar. **go ~ing** ir de pesca. □ **~ out** vt sacar. **~erman** n pescador m. **~ing** n pesca f. **~ing pole** (Amer), **~ing rod** n caña f de pesca. **~monger** n pescadero m. **~ shop** n pescadería f. **~y** a <smell> a pescado; (🄻, questionable) sospechoso

fission /'fɪʃn/ n fisión f

fist /fɪst/ n puño m

fit /fɪt/ a (**fitter**, **fittest**) (healthy) en forma; (good enough) adecuado; (able) capaz. ● n (attack) ataque; (of clothes) corte m. ● vt (pt **fitted**) (adapt) adaptar; (be the right size for) quedarle bien a; (install) colocar. ● vi encajar; (in certain space) caber; <clothes> quedarle bien a uno. □ **~ in** vi caber. **~ful** a irregular. **~ness** n salud f; (Sport) (buena) forma f física. **~ting** a apropiado. ● n (of clothes) prueba f. **~ting room** n probador m

five /faɪv/ a & n cinco (m)

fix /fɪks/ vt fijar; (mend, deal with) arreglar. ● n. **in a ~** en un aprieto. **~ed** a fijo. **~ture** /'fɪkstʃə(r)/ n (Sport) partido m

fizz /fɪz/ vi burbujear. ● n efervescencia f. **~le** /fɪzl/ vi. **~le out** fracasar. **~y** a efervescente; <water> con gas

fjord /fjɔːd/ n fiordo m

flabbergasted /'flæbəgɑːstɪd/ a estupefacto

flabby /'flæbɪ/ a flojo

flag /flæg/ n bandera f. ● vi (pt **flagged**) (weaken) flaquear; <conver­sation> languidecer

flagon /'flægən/ n botella f grande, jarro m

flagpole /'flægpəʊl/ n asta f de bandera

flagrant /'fleɪgrənt/ a flagrante

flair /fleə(r)/ n don m (**for** de)

flak|e /fleɪk/ n copo m; (of paint, metal) escama f. ● vi desconcharse. **~y** a escamoso

flamboyant /flæm'bɔɪənt/ a <clothes> vistoso; <manner> extravagante

flame /fleɪm/ n llama f. **go up in ~s** incendiarse

flamingo /flə'mɪŋgəʊ/ n (pl **-o(e)s**) flamenco m

flammable /'flæməbl/ a inflamable

flan /flæn/ n tartaleta f

flank /flæŋk/ n (of animal) ijada f; (of person) costado m; (Mil, Sport) flanco m

flannel /'flænl/ n franela f; (for face) paño m (para lavarse la cara).

flap /flæp/ vi (pt **flapped**) ondear; <wings> aletear. ● vt batir <wings>; agitar <arms>. ● n (cover) tapa f; (of pocket) cartera f; (of table) ala f. **get into a ~** 🄻 ponerse nervioso

flare /fleə(r)/ ● n llamarada f; (Mil) bengala f; (in skirt) vuelo m. □ **~ up** vi llamear; <fighting> estallar; <per­son> encolerizarse

flash /flæʃ/ ● vi destellar. ● vt (aim torch) dirigir; (flaunt) hacer ostentación de. **~ past** pasar como un rayo. ● n destello m; (Photo) flash m. **~back** n escena f retrospectiva. **~light** n (Amer, torch) linterna f. **~y** a ostentoso

flask /flɑːsk/ n frasco m; (vacuum flask) termo m

flat /flæt/ a (**flatter**, **flattest**) plano; <tyre> desinflado; <refusal> categórico; <fare, rate> fijo; (Mus) bemol. ● adv (Mus) demasiado bajo. **~ out** (at top speed) a toda velocidad. ● n (rooms) apartamento m, piso m; (Auto, esp Amer) 🄻 pinchazo m; (Mus) bemol m. **~ly** adv categóricamente. **~ten** vt allanar, aplanar

flatter /flætə(r)/ vt adular. **~ing** a <person> lisonjero; <clothes> favorecedor. **~y** n adulación f

flaunt /flɔːnt/ vt hacer ostentación de

flavour /'fleɪvə(r)/ n sabor m. ● vt sazonar. **~ing** n condimento m

flaw /flɔː/ n defecto m. **~less** a perfecto

flea /fliː/ n pulga f

fleck /flek/ n mancha f, pinta f

fled /fled/ ⇨FLEE

flee /fliː/ vi (pt **fled**) huir. ● vt huir de

fleece /fliːs/ n vellón m. ● vt 🄻 desplumar

fleet /fliːt/ n flota f; (of cars) parque m móvil

fleeting /'fliːtɪŋ/ a fugaz

Flemish /'flemɪʃ/ a & n flamenco (m)

flesh /fleʃ/ n carne f. **in the ~** en persona

flew /fluː/ ⇒FLY

flex /fleks/ vt doblar; flexionar <muscle>. ● n (Elec) cable m

flexib|ility /fleksə'bɪlətɪ/ n flexibilidad f. **~le** /'fleksəbl/ a flexible

flexitime /'fleksɪtaɪm/, (Amer) **flextime** /'flekstaɪm/ n horario m flexible

flick /flɪk/ n golpecito m. ● vt dar un golpecito a. □ **~ through** vt hojear

flicker /'flɪkə(r)/ vi parpadear. ● n parpadeo m; (of hope) resquicio m

flies /flaɪz/ npl (ⓘ, on trousers) bragueta f

flight /flaɪt/ n vuelo m; (fleeing) huida f, fuga f. **~ of stairs** tramo m de escalera f. **take (to) ~** darse a la fuga. **~ attendant** n (male) sobrecargo m, aeromozo m (LAm); (female) azafata f, aeromoza f (LAm). **~-deck** n cubierta f de vuelo

flimsy /'flɪmzɪ/ a (-ier, -iest) flojo, débil, poco sólido

flinch /flɪntʃ/ vi retroceder (from ante)

fling /flɪŋ/ vt (pt **flung**) arrojar. ● n (love affair) aventura f; (wild time) juerga f

flint /flɪnt/ n pedernal m; (for lighter) piedra f

flip /flɪp/ vt (pt **flipped**) dar un golpecito a. ● n golpecito m. □ **~ through** vt hojear.

flippant /'flɪpənt/ a poco serio

flipper /'flɪpə(r)/ n aleta f

flirt /flɜːt/ vi coquetear. ● n (woman) coqueta f; (man) coqueto m

flit /flɪt/ vi (pt **flitted**) revolotear

float /fləʊt/ vi flotar. ● vt hacer flotar; introducir en Bolsa <company>. ● n flotador m; (cash) caja f chica

flock /flɒk/ n (of birds) bandada f; (of sheep) rebaño m. ● vi congregarse

flog /flɒg/ vt (pt **flogged**) (beat) azotar; (ⓘ, sell) vender

flood /flʌd/ n inundación f; (fig) avalancha f. ● vt inundar. ● vi <building etc> inundarse; <river> desbordar. **~light** n foco m. ● vt (pt **~lit**) iluminar (con focos)

floor /flɔː(r)/ n suelo m; (storey) piso m; (for dancing) pista f. ● vt derribar; (baffle) confundir

flop /flɒp/ vi (pt **flopped**) dejarse caer pesadamente; (ⓘ, fail) fracasar. ● n ⓘ fracaso m. **~py** a flojo. ● n ⇒**~PY DISK. ~py disk** n disquete m, floppy (disk) m

floral /'flɔːrəl/ a floral

florid /'flɒrɪd/ a florido

florist /'flɒrɪst/ n florista m & f

flounder /'flaʊndə(r)/ vi (in water) luchar para mantenerse a flote; <speaker> quedar sin saber qué decir

flour /flaʊə(r)/ n harina f

flourish /'flʌrɪʃ/ vi florecer; <business> prosperar. ● vt blandir. ● n ademán m elegante; (in handwriting) rasgo m. **~ing** a próspero

flout /flaʊt/ vt burlarse de

flow /fləʊ/ vi fluir; <blood> correr; (hang loosely) caer. ● n flujo m; (stream) corriente f; (of traffic, information) circulación f. **~ chart** n organigrama m

flower /'flaʊə(r)/ n flor f. ● vi florecer, florear (Mex). **~ bed** n macizo m de flores. **~y** a florido

flown /fləʊn/ ⇒FLY

flu /fluː/ n gripe f

fluctuat|e /'flʌktjʊeɪt/ vi fluctuar. **~ion** /-'eɪʃn/ n fluctuación f

flue /fluː/ n tiro m

fluen|cy /'fluːənsɪ/ n fluidez f. **~t** a <style> fluido; <speaker> elocuente. **be ~t in a language** hablar un idioma con fluidez. **~tly** adv con fluidez

fluff /flʌf/ n pelusa f. **~y** a (-ier, -iest) velloso

fluid /'fluːɪd/ a & n fluido (m)

flung /flʌŋ/ ⇒FLING

fluorescent /flʊə'resnt/ a fluorescente

flush /flʌʃ/ vi ruborizarse. ● vt. **~ the toilet** tirar de la cadena, jalarle a la cadena (LAm). ● n (blush) rubor m

fluster /'flʌstə(r)/ vt poner nervioso

flute /fluːt/ n flauta f

flutter /'flʌtə(r)/ *vi* ondear; *<bird>* revolotear. ● *n* (of wings) revoloteo *m*; (fig) agitación *f*

flux /flʌks/ *n* flujo *m*. **be in a state of** ~ estar siempre cambiando

fly /flaɪ/ *vi* (*pt* **flew**, *pp* **flown**) volar; *<passenger>* ir en avión; *<flag>* flotar; (rush) correr. ● *vt* pilotar, pilotear (LAm) *<aircraft>*; transportar en avión *<passengers, goods>*; izar *<flag>*. ● *n* mosca *f*; (of trousers) ⇒FLIES. ~**ing** *a* volante. ~**ing** **visit** visita *f* relámpago. ● *n* (activity) aviación *f*. ~**leaf** *n* guarda *f*. ~**over** *n* paso *m* elevado

foal /fəʊl/ *n* potro *m*

foam /fəʊm/ *n* espuma *f*. ● *vi* espumar. ~ **rubber** *n* goma *f* espuma, hule *m* espuma (Mex)

fob /fɒb/ *vt* (*pt* **fobbed**). ~ **sth off onto s.o.** (palm off) encajarle algo a uno

focal /'fəʊkl/ *a* focal

focus /'fəʊkəs/ *n* (*pl* **-cuses** *or* **-ci** /-saɪ/) foco *m*; (fig) centro *m*. **in** ~ enfocado. **out of** ~ desenfocado. ● *vt* (*pt* **focused**) enfocar (fig) concentrar. ● *vi* enfocar; (fig) concentrarse (**on** en)

fodder /'fɒdə(r)/ *n* forraje *m*

foe /fəʊ/ *n* enemigo *m*

foetus /'fiːtəs/ *n* (*pl* **-tuses**) feto *m*

fog /fɒg/ *n* niebla *f*

fog|gy *a* (**-ier**, **-iest**) nebuloso. **it is** ~**gy** hay niebla. ~**horn** *n* sirena *f* de niebla

foible /'fɔɪbl/ *n* punto *m* débil

foil /fɔɪl/ *vt* (thwart) frustrar. ● *n* papel *m* de plata

foist /fɔɪst/ *vt* encajar (**on** a)

fold /fəʊld/ *vt* doblar; cruzar *<arms>*. ● *vi* doblarse; (fail) fracasar. ● *n* pliegue *m*. (for sheep) redil *m*. ~**er** *n* carpeta *f*. ~**ing** *a* plegable

foliage /'fəʊlɪɪdʒ/ *n* follaje *m*

folk /fəʊk/ *n* gente *f*. ● *a* popular. ~**lore** /-lɔː(r)/ *n* folklore *m*. ~ **music** *n* música *f* folklórica; (modern) música *f* folk. ~**s** *npl* (one's relatives) familia *f*

follow /'fɒləʊ/ *vt/i* seguir. □ ~ **up** *vt* seguir. ~**er** *n* seguidor *m*. ~**ing** *n*

partidarios *mpl*. ● *a* siguiente. ● *prep* después de

folly /'fɒlɪ/ *n* locura *f*

fond /fɒnd/ *a* (**-er**, **-est**) (loving) cariñoso; *<hope>* vivo. **be** ~ **of s.o.** tener(le) cariño a uno. **be** ~ **of sth** ser aficionado a algo

fondle /'fɒndl/ *vt* acariciar

fondness /'fɒndnɪs/ *n* cariño *m*; (for things) afición *f*

font /fɒnt/ *n* pila *f* bautismal

food /fuːd/ *n* comida *f*. ~ **processor** *n* robot *m* de cocina

fool /fuːl/ *n* idiota *m & f* ● *vt* engañar. □ ~ **about** *vi* hacer payasadas. ~**hardy** *a* temerario. ~**ish** *a* tonto. ~**ishly** *adv* tontamente. ~**ishness** *n* tontería *f*. ~**proof** *a* infalible

foot /fʊt/ *n* (*pl* **feet**) pie *m*; (measure) pie *m* (= 30,48cm); (of animal, furniture) pata *f*. **get under s.o.'s feet** estorbar a uno. **on** ~ a pie. **on/to one's feet** de pie. **put one's** ~ **in it** meter la pata. ● *vt* pagar *<bill>*. ~**age** /-ɪdʒ/ *n* (of film) secuencia *f*. ~**ball** *n* (ball) balón *m*; (game) fútbol *m*, futbol *m* (Mex); (American ~ball) fútbol *m* americano, futbol *m* americano (Mex). ~**baller** *n* futbolista *m & f*. ~**bridge** *n* puente *m* para peatones. ~**hills** *npl* estribaciones *fpl*. ~**hold** *n* punto *m* de apoyo. ~**ing** *n* pie *m*. **on an equal** ~**ing** en igualdad de condiciones. ~**lights** *npl* candilejas *fpl*. ~**man** /-mən/ *n* lacayo *m*. ~**note** *n* nota *f* (al pie de la página). ~**path** *n* (in country) senda *f*; (in town) acera *f*, banqueta *f* (Mex). ~**print** *n* huella *f*. ~**step** *n* paso *m*. ~**wear** *n* calzado *m*

---

for /fɔː(r)/, *unstressed form* /fə(r)/

● *preposition*

····▷ (intended for) para. **it's** ~ **my mother** es para mi madre. **she works** ~ **a multinational** trabaja para una multinacional

····▷ (on behalf of) por. **I did it** ~ **you** lo hice por ti

⇨ See entries **para** and **por** for further information

····▷ (expressing purpose) para. **I use it** ~ **washing the car** lo uso para limpiar el coche. **what ~?** ¿para qué?. **to go out ~ a meal** salir a comer fuera

····▸ (in favour of) a favor de. **are you ~ or against the idea?** estás a favor o en contra de la idea?

····▸ (indicating cost, in exchage for) por. **I bought it ~ 30 pounds** lo compré por 30 libras. **she left him ~ another man** lo dejó por otro. **thanks ~ everything** gracias por todo. **what's the Spanish ~ 'toad'?** ¿cómo se dice 'toad' en español?

····▸ (expressing duration) **he read ~ two hours** leyó durante dos horas. **how long are you going ~?** ¿por cuánto tiempo vas? **I've been waiting ~ three hours** hace tres horas que estoy esperando, llevo tres horas esperando

····▸ (in the direction of) para. **the train ~ Santiago** el tren para Santiago

● *conjunction*

····▸ (because) porque, pues (literary usage). **she left at once, ~ it was getting late** se fue en seguida, porque *or* pues se hacía tarde

forage /'fɒrɪdʒ/ *vi* forrajear. ● *n* forraje *m*

forbade /fəˈbæd/ ⇒FORBID

forbearance /fɔːˈbeərəns/ *n* paciencia *f*

forbid /fəˈbɪd/ *vt* (*pt* **forbade**, *pp* **forbidden**) prohibir (**s.o. to do a uno hacer**). **~ s.o. sth** prohibir algo a uno. **~ding** *a* imponente

force /fɔːs/ *n* fuerza *f*. **by ~** a la fuerza. **come into ~** entrar en vigor. **the ~s** las fuerzas *fpl* armadas. ● *vt* forzar; (compel) obligar (**s.o. to do sth** a uno a hacer algo). **~ on** imponer a. **~ open** forzar. **~d** *a* forzado. **~-feed** *vt* alimentar a la fuerza. **~ful** *a* enérgico

forceps /'fɔːseps/ *n* fórceps *m*

forcibl|e /'fɔːsəbl/ *a* a la fuerza. **~y** *adv* a la fuerza

ford /fɔːd/ *n* vado *m* ● *vt* vadear

fore /fɔː(r)/ *a* anterior. ● *n*. **come to the ~** hacerse evidente

forearm /'fɔːrɑːm/ *n* antebrazo *m*

foreboding /fɔːˈbəʊdɪŋ/ *n* presentimiento *m*

forecast /'fɔːkɑːst/ *vt* (*pt* **forecast**) pronosticar <*weather*>; prever <*result*>. ● *n* pronóstico *m*. **weather ~** pronóstico *m* del tiempo

forecourt /'fɔːkɔːt/ *n* patio *m* delantero

forefinger /'fɔːfɪŋgə(r)/ *n* (dedo *m*) índice *m*

forefront /'fɔːfrʌnt/ *n* vanguardia *f*. **in the ~** a la vanguardia

forego /fɔːˈgəʊ/ *vt* (*pt* **forewent**, *pp* **foregone**) ⇒FORGO

foregone /'fɔːgɒn/ *a*. **~ conclusion** resultado *m* previsto

foreground /'fɔːgraʊnd/ *n*. **in the ~** en primer plano

forehead /'fɒrɪd/ *n* frente *f*

foreign /'fɒrən/ *a* extranjero; <*trade*> exterior; <*travel*> al extranjero, en el extranjero. **~er** *n* extranjero *m*

foreman /'fɔːmən/ (*pl* **-men** /-mən/) *n* capataz *m*

foremost /'fɔːməʊst/ *a* primero. ● *adv*. **first and ~** ante todo

forerunner /'fɔːrʌnə(r)/ *n* precursor *m*

foresee /fɔːˈsiː/ *vt* (*pt* **-saw**, *pp* **-seen**) prever. **~able** *a* previsible

foresight /'fɔːsaɪt/ *n* previsión *f*

forest /'fɒrɪst/ *n* bosque *m*

forestall /fɔːˈstɔːl/ *vt* (prevent) prevenir; (preempt) anticiparse a

forestry /'fɒrɪstrɪ/ *n* silvicultura *f*

foretaste /'fɔːteɪst/ *n* anticipo *m*

foretell /fɔːˈtel/ *vt* (*pt* **foretold**) predecir

forever /fəˈrevə(r)/ *adv* para siempre; (always) siempre

forewarn /fɔːˈwɔːn/ *vt* advertir

forewent /fɔːˈwent/ ⇒FOREGO

foreword /'fɔːwɜːd/ *n* prefacio *m*

forfeit /'fɔːfɪt/ *n* (penalty) pena *f*; (in game) prenda *f*. ● *vt* perder; perder el derecho a <*property*>

forgave /fəˈgeɪv/ ⇒FORGIVE

forge /fɔːdʒ/ *n* fragua *f*. ● *vt* fraguar; (copy) falsificar. □ **~ ahead** *vi* adelantarse rápidamente. **~r** *n* falsificador *m*. **~ry** *n* falsificación *f*

forget /fəˈget/ *vt* (*pt* **forgot**, *pp* **forgotten**) olvidar, olvidarse de. ● *vi* olvidarse (**about** de). **I forgot** se me olvidó. **~ful** *a* olvidadizo

forgive /fə'gɪv/ *vt* (*pt* **forgave**, *pp* **forgiven**) perdonar. **~ s.o. for sth** perdonar algo a uno. **~ness** *n* perdón *m*

forgo /fɔː'gəʊ/ *vt* (*pt* **forwent**, *pp* **forgone**) renunciar a

fork /fɔːk/ *n* tenedor *m*; (for digging) horca *f*; (in road) bifurcación *f*. ● *vi* <*road*> bifurcarse. □ **~ out** *vt* ▣ desembolsar, aflojar ▣. **~lift truck** *n* carretilla *f* elevadora

forlorn /fə'lɔːn/ *a* <*hope, attempt*> desesperado; <*smile*> triste

form /fɔːm/ *n* forma *f*; (document) formulario *m*; (Schol) clase *f*. ● *vt* formar. ● *vi* formarse

formal /'fɔːml/ *a* formal; <*person*> formalista; <*dress*> de etiqueta. **~ity** /-'mælətɪ/ *n* formalidad *f*. **~ly** *adv* oficialmente

format /'fɔːmæt/ *n* formato *m*. ● *vt* (*pt* **formatted**) (Comp) formatear

formation /fɔː'meɪʃn/ *n* formación *f*

former /'fɔːmə(r)/ *a* anterior; (first of two) primero. ● *n*. **the ~** el primero *m*, la primera *f*, los primeros *mpl*, las primeras *fpl*. **~ly** *adv* antes

formidable /'fɔːmɪdəbl/ *a* formidable

formula /'fɔːmjʊlə/ *n* (*pl* **-ae** /-iː/ or **-as**) fórmula *f*. **~te** /-leɪt/ *vt* formular

forsake /fə'seɪk/ *vt* (*pt* **forsook**, *pp* **forsaken**) abandonar

fort /fɔːt/ *n* fuerte *m*

forth /fɔːθ/ *adv*. **and so ~** y así sucesivamente. **~coming** /-'kʌmɪŋ/ *a* próximo, venidero; (sociable) comunicativo. **~right** *a* directo. **~with** /-'wɪθ/ *adv* inmediatamente

fortieth /'fɔːtɪɪθ/ *a* cuadragésimo. ● *n* cuadragésima parte *f*

fortnight /'fɔːtnaɪt/ *n* quince días *mpl*, quincena *f*. **~ly** *a* bimensual. ● *adv* cada quince días

fortress /'fɔːtrɪs/ *n* fortaleza *f*

fortunate /'fɔːtʃənət/ *a* afortunado. **be ~** tener suerte. **~ly** *adv* afortunadamente

fortune /'fɔːtʃuːn/ *n* fortuna *f*. **~-teller** *n* adivino *m*

forty /'fɔːtɪ/ *a* & *n* cuarenta (*m*). **~ winks** un sueñecito

forum /'fɔːrəm/ *n* foro *m*

forward /'fɔːwəd/ *a* <*movement*> hacia adelante; (advanced) precoz; (pert) impertinente. ● *n* (Sport) delantero *m*. ● *adv* adelante. **go ~** avanzar. ● *vt* hacer seguir <*letter*>; enviar <*goods*>. **~s** *adv* adelante

forwent /fɔː'went/ ⇒FORGO

fossil /'fɒsl/ *a* & *n* fósil (*m*)

foster /'fɒstə(r)/ *vt* (promote) fomentar; criar <*child*>. **~ child** *n* hijo *m* adoptivo

fought /fɔːt/ ⇒FIGHT

foul /faʊl/ *a* (**-er, -est**) <*smell*> nauseabundo; <*weather*> pésimo; <*person*> asqueroso; (dirty) sucio; <*language*> obsceno. ● *n* (Sport) falta *f*. ● *vt* contaminar; (entangle) enredar. **~ play** *n* (Sport) jugada *f* sucia; (crime) delito *m*

found /faʊnd/ ⇒FIND. ● *vt* fundar.

foundation /faʊn'deɪʃn/ *n* fundación *f*; (basis) fundamento. (cosmetic) base *f* (de maquillaje). **~s** *npl* (Archit) cimientos *mpl*

founder /'faʊndə(r)/ *n* fundador *m*. ● *vi* <*ship*> hundirse

fountain /'faʊntɪn/ *n* fuente *f*. **~ pen** *n* pluma *f* (estilográfica) *f*, estilográfica *f*

four /fɔː(r)/ *a* & *n* cuatro (*m*). **~fold** *a* cuádruple. ● *adv* cuatro veces. **~some** /-səm/ *n* grupo *m* de cuatro personas **~teen** /'fɔːtiːn/ *a* & *n* catorce (*m*). **~teenth** *a* & *n* decimocuarto (*m*). **~th** /fɔːθ/ *a* & *n* cuarto (*m*). **~-wheel drive** *n* tracción *f* integral

fowl /faʊl/ *n* ave *f*

fox /fɒks/ *n* zorro *m*, zorra *f*. ● *vt* ▣ confundir

foyer /'fɔɪeɪ/ *n* (of theatre) foyer *m*; (of hotel) vestíbulo *m*

fraction /'frækʃn/ *n* fracción *f*

fracture /'fræktʃə(r)/ *n* fractura *f*. ● *vt* fracturar. ● *vi* fracturarse

fragile /'frædʒaɪl/ *a* frágil

fragment /'frægmənt/ *n* fragmento *m*. **~ary** /-ərɪ/ *a* fragmentario

fragran|ce /'freɪgrəns/ *n* fragancia *f*. **~t** *a* fragante

frail /freɪl/ a (**-er, -est**) frágil

frame /freɪm/ n (of picture, door, window) marco m; (of spectacles) montura f; (fig, structure) estructura f. ● vt enmarcar <picture>; formular <plan, question>; ⊡, (incriminate unjustly) incriminar falsamente. ~**work** n estructura f; (context) marco m

France /frɑːns/ n Francia f

frank /fræŋk/ a franco. ● vt franquear. ~**ly** adv francamente

frantic /'fræntɪk/ a frenético. ~ **with** loco de

fratern|al /frə'tɜːnl/ a fraternal. ~**ity** /frə'tɜːnɪti/ n fraternidad f; (club) asociación f. ~**ize** /'frætənaɪz/ vi fraternizar

fraud /frɔːd/ n fraude m; (person) impostor m. ~**ulent** /-julənt/a fraudulento

fraught /frɔːt/ a (tense) tenso. ~ **with** cargado de

fray /freɪ/ n riña f

freak /friːk/ n fenómeno m; (monster) monstruo m. ● a anormal. ~**ish** a anormal

freckle /'frekl/ n peca f. ~**d** a pecoso

free /friː/ a (**freer** /'friːə(r)/, **freest** /'friːɪst/) libre; (gratis) gratuito. ~ **of charge** gratis. ● vt (pt **freed**) (set at liberty) poner en libertad; (relieve from) liberar (**from/of** de); (untangle) desenredar. ~**dom** n libertad f. ~**hold** n propiedad f absoluta. ~ **kick** n tiro m libre. ~**lance** a & adv por cuenta propia. ~**ly** adv libremente. ~**mason** n masón m. ~-**range** a <eggs> de granja. ~ **speech** n libertad f de expresión. ~**style** n estilo m libre. ~**way** n (Amer) autopista f

freez|e /'friːz/ vt (pt **froze**, pp **frozen**) helar; congelar <food, wages>. ● vi helarse; (become motionless) quedarse inmóvil. ● n (on wages, prices) congelación f. ~**er** n congelador m. ~**ing** a glacial. ● n. ~**ing** (point) punto m de congelación f. **below** ~**ing** bajo cero

freight /freɪt/ n (goods) mercancías fpl. ~**er** n buque m de carga

French /frentʃ/ a francés. ● n (Lang) francés m. ● npl. the ~ (people) los

franceses. ~ **fries** npl patatas fpl fritas, papas fpl fritas (LAm). ~**man** /-mən/ n francés m. ~ **window** n puerta f ventana. ~**woman** f francesa f

frenz|ied /'frenzɪd/ a frenético. ~**y** n frenesí m

frequency /'friːkwənsɪ/ n frecuencia f

frequent /frɪ'kwent/ vt frecuentar. ● /'friːkwənt/ a frecuente. ~**ly** adv frecuentemente

fresh /freʃ/ a (**-er, -est**) fresco; (different, additional) nuevo; <water> dulce. ~**en** vi refrescar. □ ~**en up** vi <person> refrescarse. ~**er** n ⊡ ⇒~MAN. ~**ly** adv recientemente. ~**man** n /-mən/ estudiante m de primer año. ~**ness** n frescura f

fret /fret/ vi (pt **fretted**) preocuparse. ~**ful** a (discontented) quejoso; (irritable) irritable

friction /'frɪkʃn/ n fricción f

Friday /'fraɪdeɪ/ n viernes m

fridge /frɪdʒ/ n ⊡ frigorífico m, nevera f, refrigerador m (LAm)

fried /fraɪd/ ⇒FRY. ● a frito

friend /frend/ n amigo m. ~**liness** n simpatía f. ~**ly** a (**-ier, -iest**) simpático. ~**ship** n amistad f

fries /fraɪz/ npl ⇒FRENCH FRIES

frieze /friːz/ n friso m

frigate /'frɪgət/ n fragata f

fright /fraɪt/ n miedo m; (shock) susto m. ~**en** vt asustar. □ ~ **off** vt ahuyentar. ~**ened** a asustado. **be** ~**ened** tener miedo (**of** de.) ~**ful** a espantoso, horrible. ~**fully** adv terriblemente

frigid /'frɪdʒɪd/ a frígido

frill /frɪl/ n volante m, olán m (Mex). ~**s** npl (fig) adornos mpl. **with no** ~**s** sencillo

fringe /frɪndʒ/ n (sewing) fleco m; (ornamental border) franja f; (of hair) flequillo m, cerquillo m (LAm), fleco m (Mex); (of area) periferia f; (of society) margen m

fritter /'frɪtə(r)/ vt. □ ~ **away** vt desperdiciar <time>; malgastar <money>

frivol|ity /frɪ'vɒlətɪ/ n frivolidad f. ~**ous** /'frɪvələs/ a frívolo

fro /frəʊ/ ⇒TO AND FRO

frock /frɒk/ n vestido m

frog /frɒg/ n rana f. **have a ∼ in one's throat** tener carraspera. **∼man** /-mən/ n hombre m rana. **∼spawn** n huevos mpl de rana

frolic /'frɒlɪk/ vi (pt **frolicked**) retozar

from /frɒm/, unstressed /frəm/ prep de; (indicating starting point) desde; (habit, conviction) por; **∼ then on** a partir de ahí

front /frʌnt/ n parte f delantera; (of building) fachada f; (of clothes) delantera f; (Mil, Pol) frente f; (of book) principio m; (fig, appearance) apariencia f; (seafront) paseo m marítimo, malecón m (LAm). **in ∼ of** delante de. ● a delantero; (first) primero. **∼al** a frontal; <attack> de frente. **∼ door** n puerta f principal

frontier /'frʌntɪə(r)/ n frontera f

front page n (of newspaper) primera plana f

frost /frɒst/ n (freezing) helada f; (frozen dew) escarcha f. **∼bite** n congelación f. **∼bitten** a congelado. **∼ed** a <glass> esmerilado. **∼ing** n (Amer) glaseado m. **∼y** a <weather> helado; <night> de helada; (fig) glacial

froth /frɒθ/ n espuma f. ● vi espumar. **∼y** a espumoso

frown /fraʊn/ vi fruncir el entrecejo ● n ceño m. □ **∼ on** vt desaprobar

froze /frəʊz/ ⇒FREEZE. **∼n** /'frəʊzn/ ⇒FREEZE. ● a congelado; <region> helado

frugal /'fru:gl/ a frugal

fruit /fru:t/ n (Bot, on tree, fig) fruto m; (as food) fruta f. **∼ful** /'fru:tfl/ a fértil; (fig) fructífero. **∼ion** /fru:'ɪʃn/ n. **come to ∼ion** realizarse. **∼less** a infructuoso. **∼ salad** n macedonia f de frutas. **∼y** a que sabe a fruta

frustrat|e /frʌ'streɪt/ vt frustrar. **∼ion** /-ʃn/ n frustración f. **∼ed** a frustrado. **∼ing** a frustrante

fry /fraɪ/ vt (pt **fried**) freír. ● vi freírse. **∼ing pan** n sartén f, sartén m (LAm)

fudge /fʌdʒ/ n dulce m de azúcar

fuel /'fju:əl/ n combustible m

fugitive /'fju:dʒɪtɪv/ a & n fugitivo (m)

fulfil /fʊl'fɪl/ vt (pt **fulfilled**) cumplir (con) <promise, obligation>; satisfacer <condition>; hacer realidad <ambition>. **∼ment** n (of promise, obligation) cumplimiento m; (of conditions) satisfacción f; (of hopes, plans) realización f

full /fʊl/ a (**-er**, **-est**) lleno; <bus, hotel> completo; <account> detallado. **at ∼ speed** a máxima velocidad. **be ∼ (up)** (with food) no poder más. ● n. **in ∼** sin quitar nada. **to the ∼** completamente. **write in ∼** escribir con todas las letras. **∼back** n (Sport) defensa m & f. **∼-blown** /fʊl'bləʊn/ a verdadero. **∼-fledged** /-'fledʒd/ a (Amer) ⇒FULLY-FLEDGED. **∼ moon** n luna f llena. **∼-scale** /-'skeɪl/ a <drawing> de tamaño natural; (fig) amplio. **∼ stop** n punto m. **∼-time** a <employment> de jornada completa. ● /-'taɪm/ adv a tiempo completo. **∼y** adv completamente. **∼-fledged** /-'fledʒd/ a <chick> capaz de volar; <lawyer, nurse> hecho y derecho

fulsome /'fʊlsəm/ a excesivo

fumble /'fʌmbl/ vi buscar (a tientas)

fume /fju:m/ vi despedir gases; (fig, be furious) estar furioso. **∼s** npl gases mpl

fumigate /'fju:mɪgeɪt/ vt fumigar

fun /fʌn/ n (amusement) diversión f; (merriment) alegría f. **for ∼** en broma. **have ∼** divertirse. **make ∼ of** burlarse de

function /'fʌŋkʃn/ n (purpose, duty) función f; (reception) recepción f. ● vi funcionar. **∼al** a funcional

fund /fʌnd/ n fondo m. ● vt financiar

fundamental /fʌndə'mentl/ a fundamental. **∼ist** a & n fundamentalista (m & f)

funeral /'fju:nərəl/ n entierro m, funerales mpl. **∼ director** n director m de pompas fúnebres

funfair /'fʌnfeə(r)/ n feria f; (permanent) parque m de atracciones, parque m de diversiones (LAm)

fungus /'fʌŋgəs/ n (pl **-gi** /-gaɪ/) hongo m

funnel /'fʌnl/ n (for pouring) embudo m; (of ship) chimenea f

funn|ily /'fʌnɪlɪ/ adv (oddly) curiosamente. ~y a (-ier, -iest) divertido, gracioso; (odd) curioso, raro

fur /fɜ:(r)/ n pelo m; (pelt) piel f

furious /'fjʊərɪəs/ a furioso. ~ly adv furiosamente

furlough /'fɜ:ləʊ/ n (Amer) permiso m. on ~ de permiso

furnace /'fɜ:nɪs/ n horno m

furnish /'fɜ:nɪʃ/ vt amueblar, amoblar (LAm); (supply) proveer. ~ings npl muebles mpl, mobiliario m

furniture /'fɜ:nɪtʃə(r)/ n muebles mpl, mobiliario m. a piece of ~ un mueble

furrow /'fʌrəʊ/ n surco m

furry /'fɜ:rɪ/ a peludo

furthe|r /'fɜ:ðə(r)/ a más lejano; (additional) nuevo. ● adv más lejos; (more) además. ● vt fomentar. ~rmore adv además. ~st a más lejano. ● adv más lejos

furtive /'fɜ:tɪv/ a furtivo

fury /'fjʊərɪ/ n furia f

fuse /fju:z/ vt (melt) fundir; (fig, unite) fusionar. ~ the lights fundir los plomos. ● vi fundirse; (fig) fusionarse. ● n fusible m, plomo m; (of bomb) mecha f. ~box n caja f de fusibles

fuselage /'fju:zəlɑ:ʒ/ n fuselaje m

fusion /'fju:ʒn/ n fusión f

fuss /fʌs/ n (commotion) jaleo m. kick up a ~ armar un lío, armar una bronca. make a ~ of tratar con mucha atención. ● vi preocuparse. ~y a (-ier, -iest) (finicky) remilgado; (demanding) exigente

futil|e /'fju:taɪl/ a inútil, vano. ~ity /fju:'tɪlətɪ/ n inutilidad f

futur|e /'fju:tʃə(r)/ a futuro. ● n futuro m. in ~e de ahora en adelante. ~istic /fju:tʃə'rɪstɪk/ a futurista

fuzz /fʌz/ n pelusa f. ~y a <hair> crespo; <photograph> borroso

Gg

gab /gæb/ n. have the gift of the ~ tener un pico de oro

gabardine /gæbə'di:n/ n gabardina f

gabble /'gæbl/ vi hablar atropelladamente

gable /'geɪbl/ n aguilón m

gad /gæd/ vi (pt gadded). ~ about callejear

gadget /'gædʒɪt/ n chisme m

Gaelic /'geɪlɪk/ a & n gaélico (m)

gaffe /gæf/ n plancha f, metedura f de pata, metida f de pata (LAm)

gag /gæg/ n mordaza f; (joke) chiste m. ● vt (pt gagged) amordazar. ● vi hacer arcadas

gaiety /'geɪətɪ/ n alegría f

gaily /'geɪlɪ/ adv alegremente

gain /geɪn/ vt ganar; (acquire) adquirir; (obtain) conseguir. ● vi <clock> adelantar. ● n ganancia f; (increase) aumento m

gait /geɪt/ n modo m de andar

gala /'gɑ:lə/ n fiesta f. ~ performance (función f de) gala f

galaxy /'gæləksɪ/ n galaxia f

gale /geɪl/ n vendaval m

gall /gɔ:l/ n bilis f; (fig) hiel f; (impudence) descaro m

gallant /'gælənt/ a (brave) valiente; (chivalrous) galante. ~ry n valor m

gall bladder /'gɔ:lblædə(r)/ n vesícula f biliar

gallery /'gælərɪ/ n galería f

galley /'gælɪ/ n (ship) galera f; (ship's kitchen) cocina f. ~ (proof) n galerada f

gallivant /'gælɪvænt/ vi 🄴 callejear

gallon /'gælən/ n galón m (imperial = 4,546l; Amer = 3,785l)

gallop /'gæləp/ n galope m. ● vi (pt galloped) galopar

gallows /'gæləʊz/ n horca f

galore /gə'lɔ:(r)/ a en abundancia

galvanize /'gælvənaɪz/ vt galvanizar

gambl|e /'gæmbl/ vi jugar. ~e on contar con. ● vt jugarse. ● n (venture) empresa f arriesgada; (bet) apuesta f; (risk) riesgo m. ~er n jugador m. ~ing n juego m

game /geɪm/ n juego m; (match) partido m; (animals, birds) caza f. ● a valiente. ~ for listo para. ~keeper n guardabosque m. ~s n (in school) deportes mpl

gammon /'gæmən/ n jamón m fresco

gamut /'gæmət/ n gama f

gander /'gændə(r)/ n ganso m

gang /gæŋ/ n pandilla f; (of workmen) equipo m. □ ~ up vi unirse (on contra)

gangling /'gæŋglɪŋ/ a larguirucho

gangrene /'gæŋgriːn/ n gangrena f

gangster /'gæŋstə(r)/ n bandido m, gángster m & f

gangway /'gæŋweɪ/ n pasillo m; (of ship) pasarela f

gaol /dʒeɪl/ n cárcel f. ~er n carcelero m

gap /gæp/ n espacio m; (in fence, hedge) hueco m; (in time) intervalo m; (in knowledge) laguna f; (difference) diferencia f

gap|e /geɪp/ vi quedarse boquiabierto; (be wide open) estar muy abierto. ~ing a abierto; (person) boquiabierto

garage /'gærɑːʒ/ n garaje m, garage m (LAm), cochera f (Mex); (petrol station) gasolinera f; (for repairs, sales) taller m, garage m (LAm)

garbage /'gɑːbɪdʒ/ n basura f. ~ can n (Amer) cubo m de la basura, bote m de la basura (Mex). ~ collector, ~ man n (Amer) basurero m

garble /'gɑːbl/ vt tergiversar, embrollar

garden /'gɑːdn/ n (of flowers) jardín m; (of vegetables/fruit) huerto m. ● vi trabajar en el jardín. ~er /'gɑːdnə(r)/ n jardinero m. ~ing n jardinería f; (vegetable growing) horticultura f

gargle /'gɑːgl/ vi hacer gárgaras

gargoyle /'gɑːgɔɪl/ n gárgola f

garish /'geərɪʃ/ a chillón

garland /'gɑːlənd/ n guirnalda f

garlic /'gɑːlɪk/ n ajo m

garment /'gɑːmənt/ n prenda f (de vestir)

garnish /'gɑːnɪʃ/ vt adornar, decorar. ● n adorno m

garret /'gærət/ n buhardilla f

garrison /'gærɪsn/ n guarnición f

garrulous /'gærələs/ a hablador

garter /'gɑːtə(r)/ n liga f

gas /gæs/ n (pl gases) gas m; (anaesthetic) anestésico m; (Amer, petrol) gasolina f. ● vt (pt gassed) asfixiar con gas

gash /gæʃ/ n tajo m. ● vt hacer un tajo de

gasket /'gæskɪt/ n junta f

gas: ~ mask n careta f antigás. **~ meter** n contador m de gas

gasoline /'gæsəliːn/ n (Amer) gasolina f

gasp /gɑːsp/ vi jadear; (with surprise) dar un grito ahogado. ● n exclamación f, grito m

gas: ~ ring n hornillo m de gas. **~ station** n (Amer) gasolinera f

gastric /'gæstrɪk/ a gástrico

gate /geɪt/ n puerta f; (of metal) verja f; (barrier) barrera f

gate: ~crash vt colarse en. **~crasher** n intruso m (que ha entrado sin ser invitado). **~way** n puerta f

gather /'gæðə(r)/ vt reunir <people, things>; (accumulate) acumular; (pick up) recoger; recoger <flowers>; (fig, infer) deducir; (sewing) fruncir. **~ speed** acelerar. ● vi <people> reunirse; <things> acumularse. **~ing** n reunión f

gaudy /'gɔːdɪ/ a (-ier, -iest) chillón

gauge /geɪdʒ/ n (measurement) medida f; (Rail) entrevía f; (instrument) indicador m. ● vt medir; (fig) estimar

gaunt /gɔːnt/ a descarnado; (from illness) demacrado

gauntlet /'gɔːntlɪt/ n. run the ~ of aguantar el acoso de

gauze /gɔːz/ n gasa f

gave /geɪv/ ⇒GIVE

gawky /'gɔːkɪ/ a (-ier, -iest) torpe

gawp /gɔ:p/ vi. ~ at mirar como un tonto

gay /geɪ/ a (-er, -est) (🆃, homosexual) homosexual, gay 🆃; (dated; joyful) alegre

gaze /geɪz/ vi. ~ (at) mirar (fijamente). ● n mirada f (fija)

gazelle /gə'zel/ n (pl invar or -s) gacela f

GB abbr ⇒GREAT BRITAIN

gear /gɪə(r)/ n equipo m; (Tec) engranaje m; (Auto) marcha f, cambio m. in ~ engranado. out of ~ desengranado. change ~, shift ~ (Amer) cambiar de marcha. ● vt adaptar. ~**box** n (Auto) caja f de cambios

geese /gi:s/ ⇒GOOSE

gel /dʒel/ n gel m

gelatine /'dʒeləti:n/ n gelatina f

gelignite /'dʒelɪgnaɪt/ n gelignita f

gem /dʒem/ n piedra f preciosa

Gemini /'dʒemɪnaɪ/ n Géminis mpl

gender /'dʒendə(r)/ n género m

gene /dʒi:n/ n gen m, gene m

genealogy /dʒi:nɪ'ælədʒɪ/ n genealogía f

general /'dʒenərəl/ a general. ● n general m. in ~ en general. ~ **election** fpl elecciones fpl generales. ~**ization** /-'zeɪʃn/ n generalización f. ~**ize** vt/i generalizar. ~ **knowledge** n cultura f general. ~**ly** adv generalmente. ~ **practitioner** n médico m de cabecera

generat|e /'dʒenəreɪt/ vt generar. ~**ion** /-'reɪʃn/ n generación f. ~**ion gap** n brecha f generacional. ~**or** n generador m

genero|sity /dʒenə'rɒsətɪ/ n generosidad f. ~**us** /'dʒenərəs/ a generoso; (plentiful) abundante

genetic /dʒɪ'netɪk/ a genético. ~**s** n genética f

Geneva /dʒɪ'ni:və/ n Ginebra f

genial /'dʒi:nɪəl/ a simpático, afable

genital /'dʒenɪtl/ a genital. ~**s** npl genitales mpl

genitive /'dʒenɪtɪv/ a & n genitivo (m)

genius /'dʒi:nɪəs/ n (pl -**uses**) genio m

genocide /'dʒenəsaɪd/ n genocidio m

genre /ʒɑ:ŋr/ n género m

gent /dʒent/ n 🆃 señor m. ~**s** n aseo m de caballeros

genteel /dʒen'ti:l/ a distinguido

gentl|e /'dʒentl/ a (-er, -est) <person> dulce; <murmur, breeze> suave; <hint> discreto. ~**eman** n señor m; (well-bred) caballero m. ~**eness** n amabilidad f. ~**y** adv amablemente

genuine /'dʒenjuɪn/ a verdadero; <person> sincero

geograph|er /dʒɪ'ɒɡrəfə(r)/ n geógrafo m. ~**ical** /dʒɪə'ɡræfɪkl/ a geográfico. ~**y** /dʒɪ'ɒɡrəfɪ/ n geografía f

geolog|ical /dʒɪə'lɒdʒɪkl/ a geológico. ~**ist** /dʒɪ'ɒlədʒɪst/ n geólogo m. ~**y** /dʒɪ'ɒlədʒɪ/ n geología f

geometr|ic(al) /dʒɪə'metrɪk(l)/ a geométrico. ~**y** /dʒɪ'ɒmətrɪ/ n geometría f

geranium /dʒə'reɪnɪəm/ n geranio m

geriatric /dʒerɪ'ætrɪk/ a <patient> anciano; <ward> de geriatría. ~**s** n geriatría f

germ /dʒɜ:m/ n microbio m, germen m

German /'dʒɜ:mən/ a & n alemán (m). ~**ic** /dʒɜ:'mænɪk/ a germánico. ~ **measles** n rubéola f. ~**y** n Alemania f

germinate /'dʒɜ:mɪneɪt/ vi germinar

gesticulate /dʒe'stɪkjʊleɪt/ vi hacer ademanes, gesticular

gesture /'dʒestʃə(r)/ n gesto m, ademán m; (fig) gesto m. ● vi hacer gestos

....

get /get/

past **got**; past participle **got**, **gotten** (Amer); present participle **getting**

● transitive verb

····▸ (obtain) conseguir, obtener. **did you get the job?** ¿conseguiste el trabajo?

····▸ (buy) comprar. **I got it in the sales** lo compré en las rebajas

····▸ (achieve, win) sacar. **she got very good marks** sacó muy buenas notas

····▸ (receive) recibir. **I got a letter from Alex** recibí una carta de Alex

····▸ (fetch) ir a buscar. **~ your coat** vete a buscar tu abrigo

····▸ (experience) llevarse. **I got a terrible shock** me llevé un shock espantoso

····▸ (①, understand) entender. **I don't ~ what you mean** no entiendo lo que quieres decir

····▸ (ask or persuade) **to ~ s.o. to do sth** hacer que uno haga algo

Note that *hacer que* is followed by the subjunctive form of the verb

····▸ (cause to be done or happen) **I must ~ this watch fixed** tengo que llevar a arreglar este reloj. **they got the roof mended** hicieron arreglar el techo

● *intransitive verb*

····▸ (arrive, reach) llegar. **I got there late** llegué tarde. **how do you ~ to Paddington?** ¿cómo se llega a Paddington?

····▸ (become) **to ~ tired** cansarse. **she got very angry** se puso furiosa. **it's ~ting late** se está haciendo tarde

➡ For translations of expressions such as **get better, get old** see entries **better, old** etc. See also **got**

····▸ **to get to do sth** (manage to) llegar a. **did you ~ to see him?** ¿llegaste a verlo?

□ **get along** *vi* (manage) arreglárselas; (progress) hacer progresos. □ **get along with** *vt* llevarse bien con. □ **get at** *vt* (reach) llegar a; (imply) querer decir. □ **get away** *vi* salir; (escape) escaparse. □ **get back** *vi* volver. *vt* (recover) recobrar. □ **get by** *vi* (manage) arreglárselas; (pass) pasar. □ **get down** *vi* bajar. *vt* (make depressed) deprimir. □ **get in** *vi* entrar. □ **get into** *vt* entrar en; subir a *<car>*. □ **get off** *vt* bajar(se) de *<train etc>*. *vi* (from train etc) bajarse; (Jurid) salir absuelto. □ **get on** *vi* (progress) hacer progresos; (succeed) tener éxito. *vt* subirse a *<train etc>*. □ **get on with** *vt* (be on good terms

with) llevarse bien con; (continue) seguir con. □ **get out** *vi* salir. *vt* (take out) sacar. □ **get out of** *vt* (fig) librarse de. □ **get over** *vt* reponerse de *<illness>*. □ **get round** *vt* soslayar *<difficulty etc>*; engatusar *<person>*. □ **get through** *vi* pasar; (on phone) comunicarse (**to** con). □ **get together** *vi* (meet up) reunirse. *vt* (assemble) reunir. □ **get up** *vi* levantarse; (climb) subir

geyser /'giːzə(r)/ *n* géiser *m*

ghastly /'gɑːstlɪ/ *a* (**-ier**, **-iest**) horrible

gherkin /'gɜːkɪn/ *n* pepinillo *m*

ghetto /'getəʊ/ *n* (*pl* **-os**) gueto *m*

ghost /gəʊst/ *n* fantasma *m*. **~ly** *a* espectral

giant /'dʒaɪənt/ *n* gigante *m*. ● *a* gigantesco

gibberish /'dʒɪbərɪʃ/ *n* jerigonza *f*

gibe /dʒaɪb/ *n* pulla *f*

giblets /'dʒɪblɪts/ *npl* menudillos *mpl*

gidd|iness /'gɪdɪnɪs/ *n* vértigo *m*. **~y** *a* (**-ier**, **-iest**) mareado. **be/feel ~y** estar/sentirse mareado

gift /gɪft/ *n* regalo *m*; (ability) don *m*. **~ed** *a* dotado de talento. **~-wrap** *vt* envolver para regalo

gigantic /dʒaɪˈgæntɪk/ *a* gigantesco

giggle /'gɪgl/ *vi* reírse tontamente. ● *n* risita *f*

gild /gɪld/ *vt* dorar

gills /gɪlz/ *npl* agallas *fpl*

gilt /gɪlt/ *n* dorado *m*. ● *a* dorado

gimmick /'gɪmɪk/ *n* truco *m*

gin / dʒɪn/ *n* ginebra *f*

ginger /'dʒɪndʒə(r)/ *n* jengibre *m*. ● *a* rojizo. **he has ~ hair** es pelirrojo. **~bread** *n* pan *m* de jengibre

gipsy /'dʒɪpsɪ/ *n* gitano *m*

giraffe /dʒɪˈrɑːf/ *n* jirafa *f*

girder /'gɜːdə(r)/ *n* viga *f*

girdle /'gɜːdl/ *n* (belt) cinturón *m*; (corset) corsé *m*

girl /gɜːl/ *n* chica *f*, muchacha *f*; (child) niña *f*. **~friend** *n* amiga *f*; (of boy) novia *f*. **~ish** *a* de niña; *<boy>* afeminado. **~ scout** *n* (Amer) exploradora *f*, guía *f*

giro /'dʒaɪrəʊ/ *n* (*pl* **-os**) giro *m* (bancario)

girth /gɜ:θ/ *n* circunferencia *f*

gist /dʒɪst/ *n* lo esencial

give /gɪv/ *vt* (*pt* **gave**, *pp* **given**) dar; (deliver) entregar; regalar *‹present›*; prestar *‹aid, attention›*. ~ **o.s. to** darse a. ●*vi* dar; (yield) ceder; (stretch) dar de sí. ●*n* elasticidad *f*. □~ **away** *vt* regalar; revelar *‹secret›*. □~ **back** *vt* devolver. □~ **in** *vi* ceder. □~ **off** *vt* emitir. □~ **out** *vt* distribuir. (become used up) agotarse. □~ **up** *vt* renunciar a; (yield) ceder. ~ **up doing sth** dejar de hacer algo. ~ **o.s. up** entregarse (**to** a). *vi* rendirse. ~**n** /'gɪvn/ ⇒GIVE. ●*a* dado. ~**n name** *n* nombre *m* de pila

glacier /'glæsɪə(r)/ *n* glaciar *m*

glad /glæd/ *a* contento. **be** ~ alegrarse (**about** de). ~**den** *vt* alegrar

gladly /'glædlɪ/ *adv* alegremente; (willingly) con mucho gusto

glamo|rous /'glæmərəs/ *a* glamoroso. ~**ur** /'glæmə(r)/ *n* glamour *m*

glance /glɑːns/ *n* ojeada *f*. ●*vi*. ~ **at** dar un vistazo a

gland /glænd/ *n* glándula *f*

glar|e /gleə(r)/ *vi* *‹light›* deslumbrar; (stare angrily) mirar airadamente. ●*n* resplandor *m*; (stare) mirada *f* airada. ~**ing** *a* deslumbrante; (obvious) manifiesto

glass /glɑːs/ *n* (material) cristal *m*, vidrio *m*; (without stem or for wine) vaso *m*; (with stem) copa *f*; (for beer) caña *f*; (mirror) espejo *m*. ~**es** *npl* (spectacles) gafas *fpl*, lentes *fpl* (LAm), anteojos *mpl* (LAm). ~**y** *a* vítreo

glaze /gleɪz/ *vt* poner cristal(es) or vidrio(s) a *‹windows, doors›*; vidriar *‹pottery›*. ●*vi*. ~ (**over**) *‹eyes›* vidriarse. ●*n* barniz *m*; (for pottery) esmalte *m*

gleam /gliːm/ *n* destello *m*. ●*vi* destellar

glean /gliːn/ *vt* espigar; recoger *‹information›*

glee /gliː/ *n* regocijo *m*

glib /glɪb/ *a* de mucha labia; *‹reply›* fácil

glid|e /glaɪd/ *vi* deslizarse; (plane) planear. ~**er** *n* planeador *m*. ~**ing** *n* planeo *m*

glimmer /'glɪmə(r)/ *n* destello *m*. ●*vi* destellar

glimpse /glɪmps/ *n*. **catch a** ~ **of** vislumbrar, ver brevemente. ●*vt* vislumbrar

glint /glɪnt/ *n* destello *m*. ●*vi* destellar

glisten /'glɪsn/ *vi* brillar

glitter /'glɪtə(r)/ *vi* brillar. ●*n* brillo *m*

gloat /gləʊt/ *vi*. ~ **on/over** regodearse sobre

glob|al /'gləʊbl/ *a* (worldwide) mundial; (all-embracing) global. ~**al warming** *n* calentamiento *m* global. ~**e** /gləʊb/ *n* globo *m*

gloom /gluːm/ *n* oscuridad *f*; (sadness, fig) tristeza *f*. ~**y** *a* (**-ier**, **-iest**) triste; (pessimistic) pesimista

glor|ify /'glɔːrɪfaɪ/ *vt* glorificar. ~**ious** /'glɔːrɪəs/ *a* espléndido; *‹deed, hero etc›* glorioso. ~**y** /'glɔːrɪ/ *n* gloria *f*

gloss /glɒs/ *n* lustre *m*. ~ (**paint**) (pintura *f* al or de) esmalte *m*. □~ **over** *vt* (make light of) minimizar; (cover up) encubrir

glossary /'glɒsərɪ/ *n* glosario *m*

glossy /'glɒsɪ/ *a* brillante

glove /glʌv/ *n* guante *m*. ~ **compartment** *n* (Auto) guantera *f*, gaveta *f*

glow /gləʊ/ *vi* brillar. ●*n* brillo *m*. ~**ing** /'gləʊɪŋ/ *a* incandescente; *‹account›* entusiasta; *‹complexion›* rojo

glucose /'gluːkəʊs/ *n* glucosa *f*

glue /gluː/ *n* cola *f*, goma *f* de pegar. ●*vt* (*pres p* **gluing**) pegar

glum /glʌm/ *a* (**glummer**, **glummest**) triste

glutton /'glʌtn/ *n* glotón *m*

gnarled /nɑːld/ *a* nudoso

gnash /næʃ/ *vt*. ~ **one's teeth** rechinar los dientes

gnat /næt/ *n* jején *m*, mosquito *m*

gnaw /nɔː/ *vt* roer. ●*vi*. ~ **at** roer

gnome /nəʊm/ *n* gnomo *m*

go /gəʊ/

3rd pers sing present **goes**; past
went; past participle **gone**

● *intransitive verb*

····➤ ir. **I'm going to France** voy a Francia. **to go shopping** ir de compras. **to
go swimming** ir a nadar

····➤ (leave) irse. **we're going on Friday**
nos vamos el viernes

····➤ (work, function) <*engine, clock*> funcionar

····➤ (become) **to go deaf** quedarse
sordo. **to go mad** volverse loco. **his
face went red** se puso colorado

····➤ (stop) <*headache, pain*> irse (+ *me/
te/le*). **the pain's gone** se me ha ido el
dolor

····➤ (turn out, progress) ir. **everything's
going very well** todo va muy bien.
how did the exam go? ¿qué tal te fue
en el examen?

····➤ (match, suit) combinar. **the jacket
and the trousers go well together** la
chaqueta y los pantalones combinan
bien.

····➤ (cease to function) <*bulb, fuse*> fundirse. **the brakes have gone** los fre-
nos no funcionan

● *auxiliary verb*
to be going to + *infinitive* ir a + *infinitivo*. **it's going to rain** va a llover.
she's going to win! ¡va a ganar!

● *noun* (*pl* **goes**)

····➤ (turn) turno *m*. **you have three
goes** tienes tres turnos. **it's your go**
te toca a ti

····➤ (attempt) **to have a go at doing sth**
intentar hacer algo. **have another go**
inténtalo de nuevo

····➤ (energy, drive) empuje *m*. **she has a
lot of go** tiene mucho empuje

····➤ (in phrases) **I've been on the go all
day** no he parado en todo el día. **to
make a go of sth** sacar algo adelante
□ **go across** *vt/vi* cruzar. □ **go
after** *vt* perseguir. □ **go away** *vi*
irse. □ **go back** *vi* volver. □ **go
back on** *vt* faltar a <*promise etc*>.
□ **go by** *vi* pasar. □ **go down** *vi* bajar; <*sun*> ponerse. □ **go for** *vt* (🔢,
attack) atacar. □ **go in** *vi* entrar.

□ **go in for** *vt* presentarse para
□ **go in for** *vt* presentarse para
<*exam*>; participar en <*competition*>.
□ **go off** *vi* (leave) irse; (go bad) pasarse; (explode) estallar; <*lights*> apagarse. □ **go on** *vi* seguir; (happen) pasar; (be switched on) encenderse,
prenderse (LAm). □ **go out** *vi* salir;
<*fire, light*> apagarse. □ **go over** *vt*
(check) revisar; (revise) repasar. □ **go
through** *vt* pasar por; (search) registrar; (check) examinar. □ **go up**
vi/vt subir. □ **go without** *vt* pasar
sin

goad /gəʊd/ *vt* aguijonear
go-ahead /'gəʊəhed/ *n* luz *f* verde.
● *a* dinámico
goal /gəʊl/ *n* (Sport) gol *m*; (objective)
meta *f*. ~**ie** /'gəʊlɪ/ *n* 🔢, ~**keeper**
n portero *m*, arquero *m* (LAm).
~**post** *n* poste *m* de la portería,
poste *m* del arco (LAm)
goat /gəʊt/ *n* cabra *f*
gobble /'gɒbl/ *vt* engullir
goblin /'gɒblɪn/ *n* duende *m*
god /gɒd/ *n* dios *m*. **G~** *n* Dios *m*.
~**child** *n* ahijado *m*. ~**daughter** *n*
ahijada *f*. ~**dess** /'gɒdes/ *n* diosa *f*.
~**father** *n* padrino *m*. ~**forsaken**
a olvidado de Dios. ~**mother** *n*
madrina *f*. ~**send** *n* beneficio *m*
inesperado. ~**son** *n* ahijado *m*
going /'gəʊɪŋ/ *n* camino *m*; (racing)
(estado *m* del) terreno *m*. **it is slow/
hard ~** es lento/difícil. ● *a* <*price*>
actual; <*concern*> en funcionamiento
gold /gəʊld/ *n* oro *m*. ● *a* de oro.
~**en** *a* de oro; (in colour) dorado; <*opportunity*> único. ~**en wedding** *n*
bodas *fpl* de oro. ~**fish** *n invar* pez
m de colores. ~**mine** *n* mina *f* de
oro; (fig) fuente *f* de gran riqueza.
~**plated** /-'pleɪtɪd/ *a* chapado en
oro. ~**smith** *n* orfebre *m*
golf /gɒlf/ *n* golf *m*. ~**ball** *n* pelota *f* de
golf. ~ **club** *n* palo *m* de golf; (place)
club *m* de golf. ~**course** *n* campo *m*
de golf. ~**er** *n* jugador *m* de golf
gondola /'gɒndələ/ *n* góndola *f*
gone /gɒn/ ⇒GO. ● *a* pasado. ~ **six
o'clock** después de las seis
gong /gɒŋ/ *n* gong(o) *m*
good /gʊd/ *a* (**better**, **best**) bueno,
(*before masculine singular noun*)

buen. ~ **afternoon** buenas tardes. ~
evening (before dark) buenas tardes;
(after dark) buenas noches. ~ **morning**
buenos días. ~ night buenas noches.
as ~ as (almost) casi. **feel ~** sentirse
bien. **have a ~ time** divertirse. ● *n*
bien *m*. **for ~** para siempre. **it is no**
~ shouting es inútil gritar *etc*.
~bye /-'baɪ/ *int* ¡adiós! ● *n* adiós *m*.
say ~bye to despedirse de. **~-for-**
nothing /-fənʌθɪŋ/ *a & n* inútil (*m*).
G~ Friday *n* Viernes *m* Santo.
~-looking /-'lʊkɪŋ/ *a* guapo, buen
mozo *m* (LAm), buena moza *f* (LAm).
~ness *n* bondad *f*. **~ness!**, **~ness**
gracious!, **~ness me!**, **my ~ness!**
¡Dios mío! **~s** *npl* mercancías *fpl*.
~will /-'wɪl/ *n* buena voluntad *f*. **~y**
n (Culin, 🇬🇧) golosina *f*; (in film) bueno
m

gooey /'guːɪ/ *a* (**gooier, gooiest**)
🇬🇧 pegajoso; (fig) sentimental

goofy /'guːfɪ/ *a* (Amer) necio

goose /guːs/ *n* (*pl* **geese**) oca *f*,
ganso *m*. **~berry** /'gʊzbərɪ/ *n* uva *f*
espina, grosella *f* espinosa. **~-flesh**
n, **~-pimples** *npl* carne *f* de gallina

gore /gɔː(r)/ *n* sangre *f*. ● *vt* cornear

gorge /gɔːdʒ/ *n* (Geog) garganta *f*.
● *vt*. **~ o.s.** hartarse (**on** de)

gorgeous /'gɔːdʒəs/ *a* precioso;
(splendid) magnífico

gorilla /gə'rɪlə/ *n* gorila *m*

gorse /gɔːs/ *n* aulaga *f*

gory /'gɔːrɪ/ *a* (**-ier, -iest**) 🇬🇧 sangriento

gosh /gɒʃ/ *int* ¡caramba!

go-slow /gəʊ'sləʊ/ *n* huelga *f* de celo, huelga *f* pasiva

gospel /'gɒspl/ *n* evangelio *m*

gossip /'gɒsɪp/ *n* (chatter) chismorreo *m*; (person) chismoso *m*. ● *vi* (*pt*
gossiped) (chatter) chismorrear; (repeat scandal) conta chismes

got /gɒt/ ⇒GET. **have ~** tener. **I've ~**
to do it tengo que hacerlo.

gotten /'gɒtn/ ⇒GET

gouge /gaʊdʒ/ *vt* abrir <*hole*>. □ **~**
out *vt* sacar

gourmet /'gʊəmeɪ/ *n* gastrónomo *m*

govern /'gʌvən/ *vt/i* gobernar.
~ess *n* institutriz *f*. **~ment** *n* gobierno *m*. **~or** *n* gobernador *m*

gown /gaʊn/ *n* vestido *m*; (of judge,
teacher) toga *f*

GP *abbr* ⇒GENERAL PRACTITIONER

grab /græb/ *vt* (*pt* **grabbed**) agarrar

grace /greɪs/ *n* gracia *f*. **~ful** *a* elegante

gracious /'greɪʃəs/ *a* (kind) amable;
(elegant) elegante

grade /greɪd/ *n* clase *f*, categoría *f*;
(of goods) clase *f*, calidad *f*; (on scale)
grado *m*; (school mark) nota *f*; (Amer,
class) curso *m*, año *m*

gradient /'greɪdɪənt/ *n* pendiente *f*,
gradiente *f* (LAm)

gradual /'grædʒʊəl/ *a* gradual. **~ly**
adv gradualmente, poco a poco

graduat|e /'grædʒʊət/ *n* (Univ) li-
cenciado. ● /'grædʒʊeɪt/ *vi* licenciar-
se. **~ion** /-'eɪʃn/ *n* graduación *f*

graffiti /grə'fiːtɪ/ *npl* graffiti *mpl*,
pintadas *fpl*

graft /grɑːft/ *n* (Med, Bot) injerto *m*;
(Amer 🇬🇧, bribery) chanchullos *mpl*.
● *vt* injertar

grain /greɪn/ *n* grano *m*

gram /græm/ *n* gramo *m*

gramma|r /'græmə(r)/ *n* gramática
f. **~tical** /grə'mætɪkl/ *a* gramatical

gramme /græm/ *n* gramo *m*

grand /grænd/ *a* (**-er, -est**) magnífico; (🇬🇧, excellent) estupendo. **~child** *n*
nieto *m*. **~daughter** *n* nieta *f*.
~eur /'grændʒə(r)/ *n* grandiosidad
f. **~father** *n* abuelo *m*. **~father**
clock *n* reloj *m* de caja. **~iose**
/'grændɪəʊs/ *a* grandioso.
~mother *n* abuela *f*. **~parents**
npl abuelos *mpl*. **~ piano** *n* piano *m*
de cola. **~son** *n* nieto *m*. **~stand**
/'grænstænd/ *n* tribuna *f*

granite /'grænɪt/ *n* granito *m*

granny /'grænɪ/ *n* 🇬🇧 abuela *f*

grant /grɑːnt/ *vt* conceder; (give) do-
nar; (admit) admitir (**that** que). **take**
for ~ed dar por sentado. ● *n* concesión *f*; (Univ) beca *f*

granule /'grænuːl/ *n* gránulo *m*

grape /greɪp/ *n* uva *f*. **~fruit** *n invar*
pomelo *m*, toronja *f* (LAm)

graph 307 **grip**

graph /grɑːf/ n gráfica f

graphic /'græfɪk/ a gráfico. ~s npl diseño m gráfico; (Comp) gráficos mpl

grapple /'græpl/ vi. ~ **with** forcejear con; (mentally) lidiar con

grasp /grɑːsp/ vt agarrar. ● n (hold) agarro m; (fig) comprensión f. ~ing a avaro

grass /grɑːs/ n hierba f. ~hopper n saltamontes m. ~ **roots** npl base f popular. ● a de las bases. ~y a cubierto de hierba

grate /greɪt/ n rejilla f; (fireplace) chimenea f. ● vt rallar. ● vi rechinar; (be irritating) ser crispante

grateful /'greɪtfl/ a agradecido. ~ly adv con gratitud

grater /'greɪtə(r)/ n rallador m

gratif|ied /'grætɪfaɪd/ a contento. ~y /'grætɪfaɪ/ vt satisfacer; (please) agradar a. ~ying a agradable

grating /'greɪtɪŋ/ n reja f

gratitude /'grætɪtjuːd/ n gratitud f

gratuitous /grə'tjuːɪtəs/ a gratuito

gratuity /grə'tjuːətɪ/ n (tip) propina f

grave /greɪv/ n sepultura f. ● a (-er, -est) (serious) grave

gravel /'grævl/ n grava f

gravely /'greɪvlɪ/ adv (seriously) seriamente; (solemnly) con gravedad

grave: ~**stone** n lápida f. ~**yard** n cementerio m

gravitate /'græviteɪt/ vi gravitar

gravity /'grævəti/ n gravedad f

gravy /'greɪvɪ/ n salsa f

gray /greɪ/ a & n (Amer) ⇒GREY

graze /greɪz/ vi (eat) pacer. ● vt (touch) rozar; (scrape) raspar. ● n rasguño m

greas|e /griːs/ n grasa f. ● vt engrasar. ~**eproof paper** n papel m encerado or de cera. ~y a <hands> grasiento; <food> graso; <hair, skin> graso, grasoso (LAm)

great /greɪt/ a (-er, -est) grande, (before singular noun) gran; (🔲, very good) estupendo. **G~ Britain** n Gran Bretaña f. ~**grandfather** /-'græn fɑːðə(r)/ n bisabuelo m. ~**grandmother** /-'grænmʌðə(r)/ n bisabuela f. ~**ly** adv (very) muy; (much) mucho

Greece /griːs/ n Grecia f

greed /griːd/ n avaricia f; (for food) glotonería f. ~y a avaro; (for food) glotón

Greek /griːk/ a & n griego (m)

green /griːn/ a (-er, -est) verde. ● n verde m; (grass) césped m. ~ **belt** n zona f verde. ~ **card** n (Amer) permiso m de residencia y trabajo. ~**ery** n verdor m. ~**gage** /-geɪdʒ/ n claudia f. ~**grocer** n verdulero m. ~**house** n invernadero m. **the** ~**house effect** el efecto invernadero. ~ **light** n luz f verde. ~**s** npl verduras fpl

greet /griːt/ vt saludar; (receive) recibir. ~**ing** n saludo m

gregarious /grɪ'geərɪəs/ a gregario; <person> sociable

grenade /grɪ'neɪd/ n granada f

grew /gruː/ ⇒GROW

grey /greɪ/ a (-er, -est) gris. **have** ~ **hair** ser canoso. ● n gris m. ~**hound** n galgo m

grid /grɪd/ n reja f; (Elec, network) red f; (on map) cuadriculado m

grief /griːf/ n dolor m. **come to** ~ <person> acabar mal; (fail) fracasar

grievance /'griːvns/ n queja f formal

grieve /griːv/ vt apenar. ● vi afligirse. ~ **for** llorar

grievous /'griːvəs/ a doloroso; (serious) grave. ~ **bodily harm** (Jurid) lesiones fpl (corporales) graves

grill /grɪl/ n parrilla f. ● vt asar a la parrilla; ((🔲, interrogate) interrogar

grille /grɪl/ n rejilla f

grim /grɪm/ a (**grimmer**, **grimmest**) severo

grimace /'grɪməs/ n mueca f. ● vi hacer muecas

grim|e /graɪm/ n mugre f. ~y a mugriento

grin /grɪn/ vt (pt **grinned**) sonreír. ● n sonrisa f (abierta)

grind /graɪnd/ vt (pt **ground**) moler <coffee, corn etc>; (pulverize) pulverizar; (sharpen) afilar; (Amer) picar, moler <meat>

grip /grɪp/ vt (pt **gripped**) agarrar; (interest) captar. ● n (hold) agarro m; (strength of hand) apretón m; (hairgrip) horquilla *f*, pasador *m* (Mex). **come to ~s with** entender *<subject>*

grisly /'grɪzlɪ/ *a* (**-ier, -iest**) horrible

gristle /'grɪsl/ *n* cartílago *m*

grit /grɪt/ *n* arenilla *f*; (fig) agallas *fpl*. ● *vt* (*pt* **gritted**) echar arena en *<road>*. **~ one's teeth** (fig) acorazarse

groan /grəʊn/ *vi* gemir. ● *n* gemido *m*

grocer /'grəʊsə(r)/ *n* tendero *m*, abarrotero *m* (Mex). **~ies** *npl* comestibles *mpl*. **~y** *n* tienda *f* de comestibles, tienda *f* de abarrotes (Mex)

groggy /'grɒgɪ/ *a* (weak) débil; (unsteady) inseguro; (ill) malucho

groin /grɔɪn/ *n* ingle *f*

groom /gru:m/ *n* mozo *m* de caballos; (bridegroom) novio *m*. ● *vt* almohazar *<horses>*; (fig) preparar

groove /gru:v/ *n* ranura *f*; (in record) surco *m*

grope /grəʊp/ *vi* (find one's way) moverse a tientas. **~ for** buscar a tientas

gross /grəʊs/ *a* (**-er, -est**) (coarse) grosero; (Com) bruto; (fat) grueso; (flagrant) flagrante. ● *n invar* gruesa *f*. **~ly** *adv* (very) enormemente

grotesque /grəʊ'tesk/ *a* grotesco

ground /graʊnd/ ➾GRIND. ● *n* suelo *m*; (area) terreno *m*; (reason) razón *f*; (Amer, Elec) toma *f* de tierra. ● *vt* fundar *<theory>*; retirar del servicio *<aircraft>*. **~s** *npl* jardines *mpl*; (sediment) poso *m*. **~ beef** *n* (Amer) carne *f* picada, carne *f* molida. **~ cloth** *n* (Amer) ➾~SHEET. **~ floor** *n* planta *f* baja. **~ing** *n* base *f*, conocimientos *mpl* (in de). **~less** *a* infundado. **~sheet** *n* suelo *m* impermeable (de una tienda de campaña). **~work** *n* trabajo *m* preparatorio

group /gru:p/ *n* grupo *m*. ● *vt* agrupar. ● *vi* agruparse

grouse /graʊs/ *n invar* (bird) urogallo *m*. ● *vi* Ⓔ rezongar

grovel /'grɒvl/ *vi* (*pt* **grovelled**) postrarse; (fig) arrastrarse

grow /grəʊ/ *vi* (*pt* **grew**, *pp* **grown**) crecer; (become) volverse, ponerse. ● *vt* cultivar. **~ a beard** dejarse (crecer) la barba. □ **~ up** *vi* hacerse mayor. **~ing** *a <quantity>* cada vez mayor; *<influence>* creciente

growl /graʊl/ *vi* gruñir. ● *n* gruñido *m*

grown /grəʊn/ ➾GROW. ● *a* adulto. **~-up** *a & n* adulto (*m*)

growth /grəʊθ/ *n* crecimiento *m*; (increase) aumento *m*; (development) desarrollo *m*; (Med) bulto *m*, tumor *m*

grub /grʌb/ *n* (larva) larva *f*; (🆎, food) comida *f*

grubby /'grʌbɪ/ *a* (**-ier, -iest**) mugriento

grudg|e /grʌdʒ/ *vt* ➾BEGRUDGE. ● *n* rencilla *f*. **bear/have a ~e against s.o.** guardarle rencor a uno. **~ingly** *adv* de mala gana

gruelling /'gru:əlɪŋ/ *a* agotador

gruesome /'gru:səm/ *a* horrible

gruff /grʌf/ *a* (**-er, -est**) *<manners>* brusco; *<voice>* ronco

grumble /'grʌmbl/ *vi* rezongar

grumpy /'grʌmpɪ/ *a* (**-ier, -iest**) malhumorado

grunt /grʌnt/ *vi* gruñir. ● *n* gruñido *m*

guarant|ee /gærən'ti:/ *n* garantía *f*. ● *vt* garantizar. **~or** *n* garante *m* & *f*

guard /gɑ:d/ *vt* proteger; (watch) vigilar. ● *n* (vigilance, Mil group) guardia *f*; (person) guardia *m*; (on train) jefe *m* de tren. □ **~ against** *vt* evitar; protegerse contra *<risk>*. **~ed** *a* cauteloso. **~ian** /-ɪən/ *n* guardián *m*; (of orphan) tutor *m*

Guatemala /gwɑ:tə'mɑ:lə/ *n* Guatemala *f*. **~n** *a & n* guatemalteco (*m*)

guer(r)illa /gə'rɪlə/ *n* guerrillero *m*. **~ warfare** *n* guerrilla *f*

guess /ges/ *vt* adivinar; (Amer, suppose) suponer. ● *n* conjetura *f*. **~work** *n* conjeturas *fpl*

guest /gest/ *n* invitado *m*; (in hotel) huésped *m*. **~house** *n* casa *f* de huéspedes

guffaw /gʌ'fɔ:/ *n* carcajada *f*. ● *vi* reírse a carcajadas

guidance /'gaɪdəns/ *n* (advice) consejos *mpl*; (information) información *f*

guide /gaɪd/ *n* (person) guía *m* & *f*; (book) guía *f*. **Girl G~** exploradora *f*,

guía f. ● vt guiar. ~**book** n guía f. ~**dog** n perro m guía, perro m lazarillo. ~**d missile** n proyectil m teledirigido. ~**lines** npl pauta f

guild /gɪld/ n gremio m

guile /gaɪl/ n astucia f

guillotine /'gɪlətiːn/ n guillotina f

guilt /gɪlt/ n culpa f; (Jurid) culpabilidad f. ~**y** a culpable

guinea pig /'gɪnɪ/ n (also fig) cobaya f

guitar /gɪ'tɑː(r)/ n guitarra f. ~**ist** n guitarrista m & f

gulf /gʌlf/ n (part of sea) golfo m; (gap) abismo m

gull /gʌl/ n gaviota f

gullet /'gʌlɪt/ n garganta f, gaznate m 🔟

gullible /'gʌləbl/ a crédulo

gully /'gʌlɪ/ n (ravine) barranco m

gulp /gʌlp/ vt. □ ~ (down) tragarse de prisa. ● vi tragar saliva. ● n trago m

gum /gʌm/ n (Anat) encía f; (glue) goma f de pegar; (for chewing) chicle m. ● vt (pt gummed) engomar

gun /gʌn/ n (pistol) pistola f; (rifle) fusil m, escopeta f; (artillery piece) cañón m. ● vt (pt gunned). □ ~ down vt abatir a tiros. ~**fire** n tiros mpl

gun: ~**man** /-mən/ n pistolero m, gatillero m (Mex). ~**powder** n pólvora f. ~**shot** n disparo m

gurgle /'gɜːgl/ vi <liquid> gorgotear; <baby> gorjear

gush /gʌʃ/ vi. ~ (out) salir a borbotones. ● n (of liquid) chorro m; (fig) torrente m

gusset /'gʌsɪt/ n entretela f

gust /gʌst/ n ráfaga f

gusto /'gʌstəʊ/ n entusiasmo m

gusty /'gʌstɪ/ a borrascoso

gut /gʌt/ n intestino m. ● vt (pt gutted) destripar; <fire> destruir. ~**s** npl tripas fpl; (🔟, courage) agallas fpl

gutter /'gʌtə(r)/ n (on roof) canalón m, canaleta f; (in street) cuneta f; (fig, 🔀) arroyo m

guttural /'gʌtərəl/ a gutural

guy /gaɪ/ n (🔟, man) tipo m 🔟, tío m 🔟

guzzle /'gʌzl/ vt (drink) chupar 🔟; (eat) tragarse

gym /dʒɪm/ n 🔟 (gymnasium) gimnasio m; (gymnastics) gimnasia f

gymnasium /dʒɪm'neɪzɪəm/ n gimnasio m

gymnast /'dʒɪmnæst/ n gimnasta m & f. ~**ics** /dʒɪm'næstɪks/ npl gimnasia f

gymslip /'dʒɪmslɪp/ n túnica f (de gimnasia)

gynaecolog|ist /gaɪnɪ'kɒlədʒɪst/ n ginecólogo m. ~**y** n ginecología f

gypsy /'dʒɪpsɪ/ n gitano m

gyrate /dʒaɪə'reɪt/ vi girar

Hh

haberdashery /'hæbədæʃərɪ/ n mercería f; (Amer, clothes) ropa f y accesorios mpl para caballeros

habit /'hæbɪt/ n costumbre f; (Relig, costume) hábito m. be in the ~ of (+ gerund) tener la costumbre de (+ infinitivo), soler (+ infinitivo). get into the ~ of (+ gerund) acostumbrarse a (+ infinitivo)

habitable /'hæbɪtəbl/ a habitable

habitat /'hæbɪtæt/ n hábitat m

habitation /hæbɪ'teɪʃn/ n habitación f

habitual /hə'bɪtjʊəl/ a habitual; <liar> inveterado. ~**ly** adv de costumbre

hack /hæk/ n (old horse) jamelgo m; (writer) escritorzuelo m. ● vt cortar. ~**er** n (Comp) pirata m informático

hackneyed /'hæknɪd/ a manido

had /hæd/ ⇒HAVE

haddock /'hædək/ n invar eglefino m

haemorrhage /'hemərɪdʒ/ n hemorragia f

haemorrhoids /'hemərɔɪdz/ npl hemorroides fpl

hag /hæg/ n bruja f

haggard /'hægəd/ a demacrado

hail /heɪl/ n granizo m. ● vi granizar.
● vt (greet) saludar; llamar <taxi>.
□ ~ **from** vt venir de. ~**stone** n
grano m de granizo

hair /heə(r)/ n pelo m. ~**band** n
cinta f, banda f (Mex). ~**brush** n cepillo m (para el pelo). ~**cut** n corte
m de pelo. **have a** ~**cut** cortarse el
pelo. ~**do** n 🔲 peinado m.
~**dresser** n peluquero m. ~**dresser's** (**shop**) n peluquería f.
~**dryer** n secador m, secadora f
(Mex). ~**grip** n horquilla f, pasador
m (Mex). ~**pin** n horquilla f. ~**pin
bend** n curva f cerrada. ~**raising**
a espeluznante. ~**spray** n laca f, fi-
jador m (para el pelo). ~**style** n peinado m. ~**y** a (**-ier, -iest**) peludo

half /hɑːf/ n (pl **halves**) mitad f. ● a
medio. ~ **a dozen** media docena f. ~
an hour media hora f. ● adv medio, a
medias. ~**-hearted** /-'hɑːtɪd/ a poco
entusiasta. ~**-mast** /-'mɑːst/ n. at
~**-mast** a media asta. ~ **term** n vacaciones fpl de medio trimestre.
~**-time** n (Sport) descanso m, medio
tiempo m (LAm). ~**way** a medio.
● adv a medio camino

hall /hɔːl/ n (entrance) vestíbulo m; (for
public events) sala f, salón m. ~ **of resi-
dence** residencia f universitaria, colegio m mayor. ~**mark** /-mɑːk/ n (on
gold, silver) contraste m; (fig) sello m
(distintivo)

hallo /hə'ləʊ/ int ⇒HELLO

Hallowe'en /ˌhæləʊ'iːn/ n víspera f
de Todos los Santos

hallucination /həluːsɪ'neɪʃn/ n
alucinación f

halo /'heɪləʊ/ n (pl **-oes**) aureola f

halt /hɔːlt/ n. **come to a** ~ pararse.
● vt parar. ● vi pararse

halve /hɑːv/ vt reducir a la mitad;
(divide into halves) partir por la mitad

halves /hɑːvz/ ⇒HALF

ham /hæm/ n jamón m

hamburger /'hæmbɜːɡə(r)/ n
hamburguesa f

hammer /'hæmə(r)/ n martillo m.
● vt martill(e)ar

hammock /'hæmək/ n hamaca f

hamper /'hæmpə(r)/ n cesta f. ● vt
estorbar

hamster /'hæmstə(r)/ n hámster m

hand /'hænd/ n mano f; (of clock,
watch) manecilla f; (worker) obrero m.
by ~ a mano. **lend a** ~ echar una
mano. **on** ~ a mano. **on the one** ~...
on the other ~ por un lado... por
otro. **out of** ~ fuera de control. **to** ~
a mano. ● vt pasar. □ ~ **down** vt pasar. □ ~ **in** vt entregar. □ ~ **over** vt
entregar. □ ~ **out** vt distribuir.
~**bag** n bolso m, cartera f (LAm),
bolsa f (Mex). ~**brake** n (in car) freno
m de mano. ~**cuffs** npl esposas fpl.
~**ful** n puñado m; (🔲, person) persona f difícil

handicap /'hændɪkæp/ n desventaja f; (Sport) hándicap m. ~**ped** a mi-
nusválido

handicraft /'hændɪkrɑːft/ n artesanía f

handkerchief /'hæŋkətʃɪf/ n (pl
-fs or **-chieves** /-'tʃiːvz/) pañuelo m

handle /'hændl/ n (of door) picaporte
m; (of drawer) tirador m; (of implement)
mango m; (of cup, bag, jug) asa f. ● vt
manejar; (touch) tocar. ~**bars** npl
manillar m, manubrio m (LAm)

hand: ~**out** n folleto m; (of money,
food) dádiva f. ~**shake** n apretón m
de manos

handsome /'hænsəm/ a (good-looking) guapo, buen mozo, buena moza
(LAm); (generous) generoso

handwriting /'hændraɪtɪŋ/ n letra
f

handy /'hændɪ/ a (**-ier, -iest**) (useful)
práctico; <person> diestro; (near) a
mano. **come in** ~ venir muy bien.
~**man** n hombre m habilidoso

hang /hæŋ/ vt (pt **hung**) colgar; (pt
hanged) (capital punishment) ahorcar.
● vi colgar; <clothing> caer. ● n. **get
the** ~ **of sth** coger el truco de algo.
□ ~ **about**, ~ **around** vi holgazanear. □ ~ **on** vi (wait) esperar. □ ~
out vt tender <washing>. □ ~ **up** vi
(also telephone) colgar

hangar /'hæŋə(r)/ n hangar m

hang: ~**er** n (for clothes) percha f.
~**glider** n alta f delta, deslizador m
(Mex). ~**over** n (after drinking) resaca f.
~**up** n 🔲 complejo m

hankie, hanky /'hæŋkɪ/ n 🔲 pañuelo m

haphazard /hæp'hæzəd/ *a* fortuito. ∼**ly** *adv* al azar

happen /'hæpən/ *vi* pasar, suceder, ocurrir. **if he** ∼**s to come** si acaso viene. ∼**ing** *n* acontecimiento *m*

happ|ily /'hæpɪlɪ/ *adv* alegremente; (fortunately) afortunadamente. ∼**i-ness** *n* felicidad *f*. ∼**y** *a* (**-ier, -iest**) feliz; (satisfied) contento

harass /'hærəs/ *vt* acosar. ∼**ment** *n* acoso *m*

harbour /'hɑːbə(r)/ *n* puerto *m*

hard /hɑːd/ *a* (**-er, -est**) duro; (difficult) difícil. ● *adv* <*work*> mucho; (pull) con fuerza. ∼ **done by** tratado injustamente. ∼**-boiled egg** /-'bɔɪld/ *n* huevo *m* duro. ∼ **disk** *n* disco *m* duro. ∼**en** *vt* endurecer. ● *vi* endurecerse. ∼**-headed** /-'hedɪd/ *a* realista

hardly /'hɑːdlɪ/ *adv* apenas. ∼ **ever** casi nunca

hard: ∼**ness** *n* dureza *f*. ∼**ship** *n* apuro *m*. ∼ **shoulder** *n* arcén *m*, acotamiento *m* (Mex). ∼**ware** *n* /-weə(r)/ ferretería *f*; (Comp) hardware *m*. ∼**ware store** *n* (Amer) ferretería *f*. ∼**-working** /-'wɜːkɪŋ/ *a* trabajador

hardy /'hɑːdɪ/ *a* (**-ier, -iest**) fuerte; (Bot) resistente

hare /heə(r)/ *n* liebre *f*

hark /hɑːk/ *vi* escuchar. □ ∼ **back to** *vt* volver a

harm /hɑːm/ *n* daño *m*. **there is no** ∼ **in asking** con preguntar no se pierde nada. ● *vt* hacer daño a <*person*>; dañar <*thing*>; perjudicar <*interests*>. ∼**ful** *a* perjudicial. ∼**less** *a* inofensivo

harmonica /hɑːˈmɒnɪkə/ *n* armónica *f*

harmon|ious /hɑːˈməʊnɪəs/ *a* armonioso. ∼**y** /'hɑːmənɪ/ *n* armonía *f*

harness /'hɑːnɪs/ *n* arnés *m*. ● *vt* poner el arnés a <*horse*>; (fig) aprovechar

harp /hɑːp/ *n* arpa *f*. ● *vi*. ∼ **on** (**about**) machacar (con)

harpoon /hɑːˈpuːn/ *n* arpón *m*

harpsichord /'hɑːpsɪkɔːd/ *n* clavicémbalo *m*, clave *m*

harrowing /'hærəʊɪŋ/ *a* desgarrador

harsh /hɑːʃ/ *a* (**-er, -est**) duro, severo; <*light*> fuerte; <*climate*> riguroso. ∼**ly** *adv* severamente. ∼**ness** *n* severidad *f*

harvest /'hɑːvɪst/ *n* cosecha *f*. ● *vt* cosechar

has /hæz/ ⇒HAVE

hassle /'hæsl/ *n* 🄵 lío *m* 🄵, rollo *m* 🄵. ● *vt* (harass) fastidiar

hast|e /heɪst/ *n* prisa *f*, apuro *m* (LAm). **make** ∼**e** darse prisa. ∼**ily** /'heɪstɪlɪ/ *adv* de prisa. ∼**y** /'heɪstɪ/ *a* (**-ier, -iest**) rápido; (rash) precipitado

hat /hæt/ *n* sombrero *m*

hatch /hætʃ/ *n* (for food) ventanilla *f*; (Naut) escotilla *f*. ● *vt* empollar <*eggs*>; tramar <*plot*>. ● *vi* salir del cascarón. ∼**back** *n* coche *m* con tres/cinco puertas; (door) puerta *f* trasera

hatchet /'hætʃɪt/ *n* hacha *f*

hat|e /heɪt/ *n* odio *m*. ● *vt* odiar. ∼**eful** *a* odioso. ∼**red** /'heɪtrɪd/ *n* odio *m*

haughty /'hɔːtɪ/ *a* (**-ier, -iest**) altivo

haul /hɔːl/ *vt* arrastrar; transportar <*goods*>. ● *n* (catch) redada *f*; (stolen goods) botín *m*; (journey) recorrido *m*. ∼**age** /-ɪdʒ/ *n* transporte *m*. ∼**er** (Amer), ∼**ier** *n* transportista *m & f*

haunt /hɔːnt/ *vt* frecuentar; <*ghost*> rondar. ● *n* sitio *m* preferido. ∼**ed** *a* <*house*> embrujado; <*look*> angustiado

....

have /hæv/, *unstressed forms* /həv, əv/

3rd pers sing present **has**; past **had**

● *transitive verb*

••••▸ tener. I ∼ **three sisters** tengo tres hermanas. **do you** ∼ **a credit card?** ¿tiene una tarjeta de crédito?

••••▸ (in requests) **can I** ∼ **a kilo of apples, please?** ¿me da un kilo de manzanas, por favor?

••••▸ (eat) comer. **I had a pizza** comí una pizza

····➤ (drink) tomar. **come and ∼ a drink** ven a tomar una copa

····➤ (smoke) fumar <*cigarette*>

····➤ (hold, organize) hacer <*party, meeting*>

····➤ (get, receive) **I had a letter from Tony yesterday** recibí una carta de Tony ayer. **we've had no news of her** no hemos tenido noticias suyas

····➤ (illness) tener <*flu, headache*>. **to ∼ a cold** estar resfriado, tener catarro

····➤ **to have sth done: we had it painted** lo hicimos pintar. **I had my hair cut** me corté el pelo

····➤ **to have it in for s.o.** tenerle manía a uno

● *auxiliary verb*

····➤ haber. **I've seen her already** ya la he visto, ya la vi (LAm)

····➤ **to have just done sth** acabar de hacer algo. **I've just seen her** acabo de verla

····➤ **to have to do sth** tener que hacer algo. **I ∼ to** *or* **I've got to go to the bank** tengo que ir al banco

····➤ (in tag questions) **you've met her, ∼n't you?** ya la conoces, ¿no? *or* ¿verdad? *or* ¿no es cierto?

····➤ (in short answers) **you've forgotten something - have I?** has olvidado algo - ¿sí?

haven /'heɪvn/ n puerto m; (refuge) refugio m

haversack /'hævəsæk/ n mochila f

havoc /'hævək/ n estragos mpl

hawk /hɔːk/ n halcón m

hawthorn /'hɔːθɔːn/ n espino m

hay /heɪ/ n heno m. **∼ fever** n fiebre f del heno. **∼stack** n almiar m. **∼wire** a. **go ∼wire** (plans) desorganizarse; <*machine*> estropearse

hazard /'hæzəd/ n riesgo m. **∼ous** a arriesgado

haze /heɪz/ n neblina f

hazel /'heɪzl/ n avellano m. **∼nut** n avellana f

hazy /'heɪzɪ/ a (**-ier, -iest**) nebuloso

he /hiː/ pron él

head /hed/ n cabeza f; (of family, government) jefe m; (of organization) director m; (of beer) espuma f. **∼s or tails** cara o cruz. ● a principal. ● vt encabezar, cabecear <*ball*>. □ **∼ for** vt dirigirse a. **∼ache** n dolor m de cabeza. **∼er** n (football) cabezazo m. **∼first** /-'fɜːst/ adv de cabeza. **∼ing** n título m, encabezamiento m. **∼lamp** n faro m, foco m (LAm). **∼land** /-lənd/ n promontorio m. **∼line** n titular m. **the news ∼lines** el resumen informativo. **∼long** adv de cabeza; (precipitately) precipitadamente. **∼master** n director m. **∼mistress** n directora f. **∼-on** /-'ɒn/ a & adv de frente. **∼phones** npl auriculares mpl, cascos mpl. **∼quarters** /-'kwɔːtəz/ n (of business) oficina f central; (Mil) cuartel m general. **∼strong** a testarudo. **∼teacher** /-'tiːtʃə(r)/ n director m. **∼y** a (**-ier, -iest**) <*scent*> embriagador

heal /hiːl/ vt curar. ● vi cicatrizarse

health /helθ/ n salud f. **∼y** a sano

heap /hiːp/ n montón m. ● vt amontonar.

hear /hɪə(r)/ vt/i (pt **heard** /hɜːd/) oír. **∼, ∼!** ¡bravo! **∼ about** oír hablar de. **∼ from** recibir noticias de. **∼ing** n oído m; (Jurid) vista f. **∼ing-aid** n audífono m. **∼say** n rumores mpl

hearse /hɜːs/ n coche m fúnebre

heart / hɑːt/ n corazón m. **at ∼** en el fondo. **by ∼** de memoria. **lose ∼** descorazonarse. **∼ache** n congoja f. **∼ attack** n ataque m al corazón, infarto m. **∼break** n congoja f. **∼breaking** a desgarrador. **∼burn** n ardor m de estómago. **∼felt** a sincero

hearth /hɑːθ/ n hogar m

heart: ∼ily adv de buena gana. **∼less** a cruel. **∼y** a (welcome) caluroso; <*meal*> abundante

heat /hiːt/ n calor m; (contest) (prueba f) eliminatoria f. ● vt calentar. ● vi calentarse. **∼ed** a (fig) acalorado. **∼er** n calentador m

heath /hiːθ/ n brezal m, monte m

heathen /'hiːðn/ n & a pagano (m)

heather /'heðə(r)/ n brezo m

heat: ∼ing n calefacción f. **∼stroke** n insolación f. **∼wave** n ola f de calor

heave /hiːv/ *vt* (lift) levantar; exhalar *<sigh>*; (🔲, throw) tirar. ● *vi* (pull) tirar, jalar (LAm); (🔲, retch) dar arcadas

heaven /'hevn/ *n* cielo *m*. ~**ly** *a* celestial; (astronomy) celeste; (🔲, excellent) divino

heav|ily /'hevɪlɪ/ *adv* pesadamente; (smoke, drink) mucho. ~**y** *a* (-ier, -iest) pesado; *<rain>* fuerte; *<traffic>* denso. ~**yweight** *n* peso *m* pesado

heckle /'hekl/ *vt* interrumpir

hectic /'hektɪk/ *a* febril

he'd /hiːd/ = **he had, he would**

hedge /hedʒ/ *n* seto *m* (vivo). ● *vi* escaparse por la tangente. ~**hog** *n* erizo *m*

heed /hiːd/ *vt* hacer caso de. ● *n*. take ~ tener cuidado

heel /hiːl/ *n* talón *m*; (of shoe) tacón *m*

hefty /'heftɪ/ *a* (-ier, -iest) (sturdy) fuerte; (heavy) pesado

heifer /'hefə(r)/ *n* novilla *f*

height /haɪt/ *n* altura *f*; (of person) estatura *f*; (of fame, glory) cumbre *f*. ~**en** *vt* elevar; (fig) aumentar

heir /eə(r)/ *n* heredero *m*. ~**ess** *n* heredera *f*. ~**loom** *n* reliquia *f* heredada

held /held/ ⇒HOLD

helicopter /'helɪkɒptə(r)/ *n* helicóptero *m*

hell /hel/ *n* infierno *m*

he'll /hiːl/ = **he will**

hello /hə'ləʊ/ *int* ¡hola!; (Telephone, caller) ¡oiga!, ¡bueno! (Mex); (Telephone, person answering) ¡diga!, ¡bueno! (Mex). say ~ to saludar

helm /helm/ *n* (Naut) timón *m*

helmet /'helmɪt/ *n* casco *m*

help /help/ *vt/i* ayudar. he cannot ~ laughing no puede menos de reír. ~ o.s. to servirse. it cannot be ~ed no hay más remedio. ● *n* ayuda *f*. ● *int* ¡socorro! ~**er** *n* ayudante *m*. ~**ful** *a* útil; *<person>* amable. ~**ing** *n* porción *f*. ~**less** *a* (unable to manage) incapaz; (defenceless) indefenso

hem /hem/ *n* dobladillo *m*

hemisphere /'hemɪsfɪə(r)/ *n* hemisferio *m*

hen /hen/ *n* (chicken) gallina *f*; (female bird) hembra *f*

hence /hens/ *adv* de aquí. ~**forth** *adv* de ahora en adelante

henpecked /'henpekt/ *a* dominado por su mujer

her /hɜː(r)/ *pron* (direct object) la; (indirect object) le; (after prep) ella. I know ~ la conozco. ● *a* su, sus *pl*

herb /hɜːb/ *n* hierba *f*. ~**al** *a* de hierbas

herd /hɜːd/ *n* (of cattle, pigs) manada *f*; (of goats) rebaño *m*. ● *vt* arrear. ~ **together** reunir

here /hɪə(r)/ *adv* aquí, acá (esp LAm). ~! (take this) ¡tenga! ~**abouts** /-ə'baʊts/ *adv* por aquí. ~**after** /-'ɑːftə(r)/ *adv* en el futuro. ~**by** /-'baɪ/ *adv* por este medio

heredit|ary /hɪ'redɪtərɪ/ *a* hereditario

here|sy /'herəsɪ/ *n* herejía *f*. ~**tic** *n* hereje *m* & *f*

herewith /hɪə'wɪð/ *adv* adjunto

heritage /'herɪtɪdʒ/ *n* herencia *f*; (fig) patrimonio *m*

hermetically /hɜː'metɪklɪ/ *adv*. ~ sealed herméticamente cerrado

hermit /'hɜːmɪt/ *n* ermitaño *m*, eremita *m*

hernia /'hɜːnɪə/ *n* hernia *f*

hero /'hɪərəʊ/ *n* (*pl* -oes) héroe *m*. ~**ic** /hɪ'rəʊɪk/ *a* heroico

heroin /'herəʊɪn/ *n* heroína *f*

hero: ~**ine** /'herəʊɪn/ *n* heroína *f*. ~**ism** /'herəʊɪzm/ *n* heroísmo *m*

heron /'herən/ *n* garza *f* (real)

herring /'herɪŋ/ *n* arenque *m*

hers /hɜːz/ *poss pron* (el) suyo *m*, (la) suya *f*, (los) suyos *mpl*, (las) suyas *fpl*

herself /hɜː'self/ *pron* ella misma; (reflexive) se; (after prep) sí misma

he's /hiːz/ = **he is, he has**

hesit|ant /'hezɪtənt/ *a* vacilante. ~**ate** /-teɪt/ *vi* vacilar. ~**ation** /-'teɪʃn/ *n* vacilación *f*

heterosexual /hetərəʊ'seksjʊəl/ *a* & *n* heterosexual (*m* & *f*)

het up /het'ʌp/ *a* 🔲 nervioso

hew /hjuː/ *vt* (*pp* hewed *or* hewn) cortar; (cut into shape) tallar

hexagon /'heksəgən/ n hexágono m. ~al /-'ægənl/ a hexagonal

hey /heɪ/ int ¡eh!; (expressing dismay, protest) ¡oye!

heyday /heɪdeɪ/ n apogeo m

hi /haɪ/ int 🔳 ¡hola!

hibernat|e /'haɪbəneɪt/ vi hibernar. ~ion /-'neɪʃn/ n hibernación f

hiccough, hiccup /'hɪkʌp/ n hipo m. have (the) ~s tener hipo. ● vi hipar

hide /haɪd/ vt (pt hid, pp hidden) esconder. ● vi esconderse. ● n piel f; (tanned) cuero m. ~-and-seek /'haɪdnsi:k/ n. play ~-and-seek jugar al escondite, jugar a las escondidas (LAm)

hideous /'hɪdɪəs/ a (dreadful) horrible; (ugly) feo

hideout /'haɪdaʊt/ n escondrijo m

hiding /'haɪdɪŋ/ n (🔳, thrashing) paliza f. go into ~ esconderse. ~ place n escondite m, escondrijo m

hierarchy /'haɪərɑːkɪ/ n jerarquía f

hieroglyphics /haɪərə'glɪfɪks/ n jeroglíficos mpl

hi-fi /'haɪfaɪ/ a de alta fidelidad. ● n equipo m de alta fidelidad, hi-fi m

high /haɪ/ a (-er, -est) alto; <ideals> elevado; <wind> fuerte; (🔳, drugged) drogado, colocado 🔳; <voice> agudo; <meat> pasado. ● n alto nivel m. a (new) ~ un récord. ● adv alto. ~er education n enseñanza f superior. ~-handed /-'hændɪd/ a prepotente. ~ heels npl zapatos mpl de tacón alto. ~lands /-ləndz/ npl tierras fpl altas. ~-level a de alto nivel. ~light n punto m culminante. ● vt destacar; (Art) realzar. ~ly adv muy; <paid> muy bien. ~ly strung a nervioso. H~ness n (title) alteza f. ~-rise a <building> alto. ~ school n (Amer) instituto m, colegio m secundario. ~ street n calle f principal. ~-strung a (Amer) nervioso. ~way n carretera f

hijack /'haɪdʒæk/ vt secuestrar. ● n secuestro m. ~er n secuestrador

hike /haɪk/ n caminata f. ● vi ir de caminata. ~r n excursionista m & f

hilarious /hɪ'leərɪəs/ a muy divertido

hill /hɪl/ n colina f; (slope) cuesta f. ~side n ladera f. ~y a accidentado

hilt /hɪlt/ n (of sword) puño m. to the ~ (fig) totalmente

him /hɪm/ pron (direct object) lo, le (only Spain); (indirect object) le; (after prep) él. I know ~ lo/le conozco. ~self pron él mismo; (reflexive) se; (after prep) sí mismo

hind|er /'hɪndə(r)/ vt estorbar. ~rance /'hɪndrəns/ n obstáculo m

hindsight /'haɪnsaɪt/ n. with ~ retrospectivamente

Hindu /'hɪnduː/ n & a hindú (m & f). ~ism n hinduismo m

hinge /hɪndʒ/ n bisagra f

hint /hɪnt/ n indirecta f; (advice) consejo m. ● vi soltar una indirecta. ~ at dar a entender

hip /hɪp/ n cadera f

hippie /'hɪpɪ/ n hippy m & f

hippopotamus /hɪpə'pɒtəməs/ n (pl -muses or -mi /-maɪ/) hipopótamo m

hire /haɪə(r)/ vt alquilar <thing>; contratar <person>. ● n alquiler m. car ~ alquiler m de coches. ~ purchase n compra f a plazos

his /hɪz/ a su, sus pl. ● poss pron (el) suyo m, (la) suya f, (los) suyos mpl, (las) suyas fpl

Hispan|ic /hɪ'spænɪk/ a hispánico. ● n (Amer) hispano m. ~ist /'hɪspənɪst/ n hispanista m & f

hiss /hɪs/ n silbido. ● vt/i silbar

histor|ian /hɪ'stɔːrɪən/ n historiador m. ~ic(al) /hɪ'stɒrɪkl/ a histórico. ~y /'hɪstərɪ/ n historia f.

hit /hɪt/ vt (pt hit, pres p hitting) golpear <object>; pegarle a <person>; (collide with) chocar con; (affect) afectar. ~ it off with hacer buenas migas con. ~ on vt dar con. ● n (blow) golpe m; (success) éxito m

hitch /hɪtʃ/ vt (fasten) enganchar. ● n (snag) problema m. ~ a lift, ~ a ride (Amer) ⇨~HIKE. ~hike vi hacer autostop, hacer dedo, ir de aventón (Mex). ~hiker n autoestopista m & f

hither /'hɪðə(r)/ adv aquí, acá. ~ and thither acá y allá. ~to adv hasta ahora

hit-or-miss /ˌhɪtəˈmɪs/ *a* <*approach*> poco científico

hive /haɪv/ *n* colmena *f*

hoard /hɔːd/ *vt* acumular. ● *n* provisión *f*; (of money) tesoro *m*

hoarding /ˈhɔːdɪŋ/ *n* valla *f* publicitaria

hoarse /hɔːs/ *a* (**-er, -est**) ronco. ~**ly** *adv* con voz ronca

hoax /həʊks/ *n* engaño *m*. ● *vt* engañar

hob /hɒb/ *n* (of cooker) hornillos *mpl*, hornillas *fpl* (LAm)

hobble /ˈhɒbl/ *vi* cojear, renguear (LAm)

hobby /ˈhɒbɪ/ *n* pasatiempo *m*. ~**horse** *n* (toy) caballito *m* (de niño); (fixation) caballo *m* de batalla

hockey /ˈhɒkɪ/ *n* hockey *m*; (Amer) hockey *m* sobre hielo

hoe /həʊ/ *n* azada *f*. ● *vt* (*pres p* **hoeing**) azadonar

hog /hɒɡ/ *n* (Amer) cerdo *m*. ● *vt* (*pt* **hogged**) Ⓣ acaparar

hoist /hɔɪst/ *vt* levantar; izar <*flag*>. ● *n* montacargas *m*

hold /həʊld/ *vt* (*pt* **held**) tener; (grasp) coger (esp Spain), agarrar; (contain) contener; mantener <*interest*>; (believe) creer. ● *vi* mantenerse. ● *n* (influence) influencia *f*; (Naut, Aviat) bodega *f*. **get ~ of** agarrar; (fig, acquire) adquirir. □ ~ **back** *vt* (contain) contener. □ ~ **on** *vi* (stand firm) resistir; (wait) esperar. □ ~ **on to** *vt* (keep) guardar; (cling to) agarrarse a. □ ~ **out** *vt* (offer) ofrecer. *vi* (resist) resistir. □ ~ **up** *vt* (raise) levantar; (support) sostener; (delay) retrasar; (rob) atracar. ~**all** *n* bolsa *f* (de viaje). ~**er** *n* tenedor *m*; (of post) titular *m*; (wallet) funda *f*. ~**up** atraco *m*

hole /həʊl/ *n* agujero *m*; (in ground) hoyo *m*; (in road) bache *m*. ● *vt* agujerear

holiday /ˈhɒlɪdeɪ/ *n* vacaciones *fpl*; (public) fiesta *f*. **go on ~** ir de vacaciones. ~**maker** *n* veraneante *m & f*

holiness /ˈhəʊlɪnɪs/ *n* santidad *f*

Holland /ˈhɒlənd/ *n* Holanda *f*

hollow /ˈhɒləʊ/ *a & n* hueco (*m*)

holly /ˈhɒlɪ/ *n* acebo *m*

holocaust /ˈhɒləkɔːst/ *n* holocausto *m*

holster /ˈhəʊlstə(r)/ *n* pistolera *f*

holy /ˈhəʊlɪ/ *a* (**-ier, -iest**) santo, sagrado. **H~ Ghost** *n*, **H~ Spirit** *n* Espíritu *m* Santo. ~ **water** *n* agua *f* bendita

homage /ˈhɒmɪdʒ/ *n* homenaje *m*. **pay ~ to** rendir homenaje a

home /həʊm/ *n* casa *f*; (for old people) residencia *f* de ancianos; (native land) patria *f*. ● *a* <*cooking*> casero; (address) particular; <*background*> familiar; (Pol) interior; <*match*> de casa. ● *adv.* (**at**) ~ en casa. ~**land** *n* patria *f*. ~**less** *a* sin hogar. ~**ly** *a* (**-ier, -iest**) casero; (Amer, ugly) feo. ~**-made** *a* hecho en casa. ~ **page** *n* (Comp) página *f* frontal. ~**sick** *a*. **be ~sick** echar de menos a su familia/su país, extrañar a su familia/su país (LAm). ~ **town** *n* ciudad *f* natal. ~**work** *n* deberes *mpl*

homicide /ˈhɒmɪsaɪd/ *n* homicidio *m*

homoeopathic /ˌhəʊmɪəʊˈpæθɪk/ *a* homeopático

homogeneous /ˌhɒməʊˈdʒiːnɪəs/ *a* homogéneo

homosexual /ˌhəʊməʊˈseksjʊəl/ *a & n* homosexual (*m*)

honest /ˈɒnɪst/ *a* honrado; (frank) sincero. ~**ly** *adv* honradamente. ~**y** *n* honradez *f*

honey /ˈhʌnɪ/ *n* miel *f*. ~**comb** *n* panal *m*. ~**moon** *n* luna *f* de miel. ~**suckle** *n* madreselva *f*

honorary /ˈɒnərərɪ/ *a* honorario

honour /ˈɒnə(r)/ *n* honor *m*. ● *vt* honrar; cumplir (con) <*promise*>. ~**able** *a* honorable

hood /hʊd/ *n* capucha *f*; (car roof) capota *f*; (Amer, car bonnet) capó *m*, capote *m* (Mex)

hoodwink /ˈhʊdwɪŋk/ *vt* engañar

hoof /huːf/ *n* (*pl* **hoofs** *or* **hooves**) (of horse) casco *m*, pezuña *f* (Mex); (of cow) pezuña *f*

hook /hʊk/ *n* gancho *m*; (on garment) corchete *m*; (for fishing) anzuelo *m*. **let s.o. off the ~** dejar salir a uno del atolladero. **off the ~** <*telephone*> descolgado. ● *vt.* ~**ed on** Ⓣ adicto a.

□ ~ **up** vt enganchar. ~**ed** a <tool> en forma de gancho; <nose> aguileño

hookey /'hʊkɪ/ n. play ~ (Amer 🄸) faltar a clase, hacer novillos

hooligan /'huːlɪɡən/ n vándalo m, gamberro m

hoop /huːp/ n aro m

hooray /hʊ'reɪ/ int & n ¡viva! (m)

hoot /huːt/ n (of horn) bocinazo m; (of owl) ululato m. ● vi tocar la bocina; <owl> Ulul

Hoover /'huːvə(r)/ n (P) aspiradora f. ● vt pasar la aspiradora por, aspirar (LAm)

hooves /huːvz/ ⇒HOOF

hop /hɒp/ vi (pt hopped) saltar a la pata coja; <frog, rabbit> brincar, saltar; <bird> dar saltitos. ● n salto m; (flight) etapa f. ~(s) (Bot) lúpulo m

hope /həʊp/ n esperanza f. ● vt/i esperar. ~ **for** esperar. ~**ful** a (optimistic) esperanzado; (promising) esperanzador. ~**fully** adv con optimismo; (it is hoped) se espera. ~**less** a desesperado

horde /hɔːd/ n horda f

horizon /hə'raɪzn/ n horizonte m

horizontal /hɒrɪ'zɒntl/ a horizontal. ~**ly** adv horizontalmente

hormone /'hɔːməʊn/ n hormona f

horn /hɔːn/ n cuerno m, asta f, cacho m (LAm); (of car) bocina f; (Mus) trompa f. ~**ed** a con cuernos

hornet /'hɔːnɪt/ n avispón m

horoscope /'hɒrəskəʊp/ n horóscopo m

horrible /'hɒrəbl/ a horrible

horrid /'hɒrɪd/ a horrible

horrific /hə'rɪfɪk/ a horroroso

horrify /'hɒrɪfaɪ/ vt horrorizar

horror /'hɒrə(r)/ n horror m

hors-d'oeuvre /ɔː'dɜːvr/ n (pl -s /-'dɜːvr/ entremés m, botana f (Mex)

horse /hɔːs/ n caballo m. ~**back** n. on ~**back** a caballo. ~**power** n (unit) caballo m (de fuerza). ~**racing** n carreras fpl de caballos. ~**shoe** n herradura f

horticultur|al /hɔːtɪ'kʌltʃərəl/ a hortícola. ~**e** /'hɔːtɪkʌltʃə(r)/ n horticultura f

hose /həʊz/ n manguera f, manga f. ● vt. ~ **down** lavar (con manguera). ~**pipe** n manga f

hosiery /'həʊzɪərɪ/ n calcetería f

hospice /'hɒspɪs/ n residencia f para enfermos desahuciados

hospitable /hɒ'spɪtəbl/ a hospitalario

hospital /'hɒspɪtl/ n hospital m

hospitality /hɒspɪ'tælətɪ/ n hospitalidad f

host /həʊst/ n (master of house) anfitrión m; (Radio, TV) presentador m; (multitude) gran cantidad f; (Relig) hostia f

hostage /'hɒstɪdʒ/ n rehén m

hostel /'hɒstl/ n (for students) residencia f; (for homeless people) hogar m

hostess /'həʊstɪs/ n anfitriona f

hostil|e /'hɒstaɪl/ a hostil. ~**ity** /-'tɪlətɪ/ n hostilidad f

hot /hɒt/ a (**hotter, hottest**) caliente; <weather, day> caluroso; <climate> cálido; (Culin) picante; <news> de última hora. **be/feel** ~ tener calor. **get** ~ calentarse. **it is** ~ hace calor. ~**bed** n (fig) semillero m

hotchpotch /'hɒtʃpɒtʃ/ n mezcolanza f

hot dog n perrito m caliente

hotel /həʊ'tel/ n hotel m. ~**ier** /-ieɪ/n hotelero m

hot: ~**house** n invernadero m. ~**plate** n placa f, hornilla f (LAm). ~**-water bottle** /-'wɔːtə(r)/ n bolsa f de agua caliente

hound /haʊnd/ n perro m de caza. ● vt perseguir

hour /aʊə(r)/ n hora f. ~**ly** a <rate> por hora. ● adv (every hour) cada hora; (by the hour) por hora

house /haʊs/ n (pl -s /-'haʊzɪz/) casa f; (Pol) cámara f. ● /haʊz/ vt alojar; (keep) guardar. ~**hold** n casa f. ~**holder** n dueño m de una casa. ~**keeper** n ama f de llaves. ~**maid** n criada f, mucama f (LAm). ~**-proud** a meticuloso. ~**warming** (party) n fiesta de inauguración de una casa. ~**wife** n ama f de casa. ~**work** n tareas fpl domésticas

housing /'haʊzɪŋ/ n alojamiento m. **~ development** (Amer), **~ estate** n complejo m habitacional, urbanización f

hovel /'hɒvl/ n casucha f

hover /'hɒvə(r)/ vi <bird, threat etc> cernerse; (loiter) rondar. **~craft** n (pl invar or **-crafts**) aerodeslizador m

how /haʊ/ adv cómo. **~ about** a walk? ¿qué te parece si damos un paseo? **~ are you?** ¿cómo está Vd? **~ do you do?** (in introduction) mucho gusto. **~ long?** (in time) ¿cuánto tiempo? **~ long is the room?** ¿cuánto mide de largo el cuarto? **~ often?** ¿cuántas veces?

however /haʊ'evə(r)/ adv (nevertheless) no obstante, sin embargo; (with verb) de cualquier manera que (+ subjunctive); (with adjective or adverb) por... que (+ subjunctive). **~ much it rains** por mucho que llueva

howl /haʊl/ n aullido. ● vi aullar

hp abbr ⇒HORSEPOWER

HP abbr ⇒HIRE-PURCHASE

hub /hʌb/ n (of wheel) cubo m; (fig) centro m

hubcap /'hʌbkæp/ n tapacubos m

huddle /'hʌdl/ vi apiñarse

hue /hju:/ n (colour) color m

huff /hʌf/ n. **be in a ~** estar enfurruñado

hug /hʌg/ vt (pt **hugged**) abrazar. ● n abrazo m

huge /hju:dʒ/ a enorme. **~ly** adv enormemente

hulk /hʌlk/ n (of ship) barco m viejo

hull /hʌl/ n (of ship) casco m

hullo /hə'ləʊ/ int ⇒HELLO

hum /hʌm/ vt/i (pt **hummed**) <person> canturrear; <insect, engine> zumbar. ● n zumbido m

human /'hju:mən/ a & n humano (m). **~ being** n ser m humano. **~e** /hju:'meɪn/ a humano. **~itarian** /hju:mænɪ'teərɪən/ a humanitario. **~ity** /hju:'mænətɪ/ n humanidad f

humbl|e /'hʌmbl/ a (-er, -est) humilde. ● vt humillar. **~y** adv humildemente

humdrum /'hʌmdrʌm/ a monótono

humid /'hju:mɪd/ a húmedo. **~ity** /hju:'mɪdətɪ/ n humedad f

humiliat|e /hju:'mɪlɪeɪt/ vt humillar. **~ion** /-'eɪʃn/ n humillación f

humility /hju:'mɪlətɪ/ n humildad f

humo|rist /'hju:mərɪst/ n humorista m & f. **~rous** /-rəs/ a humorístico. **~rously** adv con gracia. **~ur** /'hju:mə(r)/ n humor m. **sense of ~ur** sentido m del humor

hump /hʌmp/ n (of person, camel) joroba f; (in ground) montículo m. ● vt encorvar. **~ (about)** (🔲, carry) cargar

hunch /hʌntʃ/ vt encorvar. ● n presentimiento m; (lump) joroba f. **~back** n jorobado m

hundred /'hʌndrəd/ a ciento, (before noun) cien. **one ~ and ninety-eight** ciento noventa y ocho. **two ~** doscientos. **three ~ pages** trescientas páginas. **four ~** cuatrocientos. **five ~** quinientos. ● n ciento m. **~s of** centenares de. **~th** a & n centésimo (m). **~weight** n 50,8kg; (Amer) 45,36kg

hung /hʌŋ/ ⇒HANG

Hungar|ian /hʌŋ'geərɪən/ a & n húngaro (m). **~y** /'hʌŋgərɪ/ n Hungría f

hung|er /'hʌŋgə(r)/ n hambre f. ● vi. **~er for** tener hambre de. **~rily** /'hʌŋgrəlɪ/ adv ávidamente. **~ry** a (-ier, -iest) hambriento. **be ~ry** tener hambre

hunk /hʌŋk/ n (buen) pedazo m

hunt /hʌnt/ vt cazar. ● vi cazar. **~ for** buscar. ● n caza f. **~er** n cazador m. **~ing** n caza f. **go ~ing** ir de caza

hurl /hɜ:l/ vt lanzar

hurrah /hʊ'rɑ:/, **hurray** /hʊ'reɪ/ int & n ¡viva! (m)

hurricane /'hʌrɪkən/ n huracán m

hurr|ied /'hʌrɪd/ a apresurado. **~iedly** adv apresuradamente. **~y** vi darse prisa, apurarse (LAm). ● vt meter prisa a, apurar (LAm). ● n prisa f. **be in a ~y** tener prisa, estar apurado (LAm)

hurt /hɜ:t/ vt (pt **hurt**) hacer daño a, lastimar (LAm). **~ s.o.'s feelings** ofender a uno. ● vi doler. **my head ~s** me duele la cabeza. **~ful** a hiriente

hurtle /'hɜːtl/ vt ir volando. ● vi. ~ **along** mover rápidamente

husband /'hʌzbənd/ n marido m, esposo m

hush /hʌʃ/ vt acallar. ● n silencio m. □ ~ **up** vt acallar <affair>. ~-**hush** a 🆃 super secreto

husk /hʌsk/ n cáscara f

husky /'hʌskɪ/ a (-ier, -iest) (hoarse) ronco

hustle /'hʌsl/ vt (jostle) empujar. ● vi (hurry) darse prisa, apurarse (LAm). ● n empuje m

hut /hʌt/ n cabaña f

hutch /hʌtʃ/ n conejera f

hybrid /'haɪbrɪd/ a & n híbrido (m)

hydrangea /haɪ'dreɪndʒə/ n hortensia f

hydrant /'haɪdrənt/ n. (fire) ~ n boca f de riego, boca f de incendios (LAm)

hydraulic /haɪ'drɔːlɪk/ a hidráulico

hydroelectric /haɪdrəʊɪ'lektrɪk/ a hidroeléctrico

hydrofoil /'haɪdrəfɔɪl/ n hidrodeslizador m

hydrogen /'haɪdrədʒən/ n hidrógeno m

hyena /haɪ'iːnə/ n hiena f

hygien|e /'haɪdʒiːn/ n higiene f. ~**ic** /haɪ'dʒiːnɪk/ a higiénico

hymn /hɪm/ n himno m

hyper... /'haɪpə(r)/ pref hiper...

hyphen /'haɪfn/ n guión m. ~**ate** /-eɪt/ vt escribir con guión

hypno|sis /hɪp'nəʊsɪs/ n hipnosis f. ~**tic** /-'nɒtɪk/ a hipnótico. ~**tism** /'hɪpnətɪzəm/ n hipnotismo m. ~**tist** /'hɪpnətɪst/ n hipnotista m & f. ~**tize** /'hɪpnətaɪz/ vt hipnotizar

hypochondriac /haɪpə'kɒn drɪæk/ n hipocondríaco m

hypocri|sy /hɪ'pɒkrəsɪ/ n hipocresía f. ~**te** /'hɪpəkrɪt/ n hipócrita m & f. ~**tical** /hɪpə'krɪtɪkl/ a hipócrita

hypodermic /haɪpə'dɜːmɪk/ a hipodérmico. ● n hipodérmica f

hypothe|sis /haɪ'pɒθəsɪs/ n (pl -theses /-siːz/) hipótesis f. ~**tical** /-ə'θetɪkl/ a hipotético

hysteri|a /hɪ'stɪərɪə/ n histerismo m. ~**cal** /-'terɪkl/ a histérico. ~**cs** /hɪ'sterɪks/ npl histerismo m. **have** ~**cs** ponerse histérico; (laugh) morir de risa

I /aɪ/ pron yo

ice /aɪs/ n hielo m. ● vt helar; glasear <cake>. ● vi. ~ **(up)** helarse, congelarse. ~**berg** /-bɜːg/ n iceberg m. ~ **box** n (compartment) congelador; (Amer 🆃, refrigerator) frigorífico m, refrigerador m (LAm). ~**cream** n helado m. ~ **cube** n cubito m de hielo

Iceland /'aɪslənd/ n Islandia f

ice: ~ **lolly** polo m, paleta f helada (LAm). ~ **rink** n pista f de hielo. ~ **skating** n patinaje m sobre hielo

icicle /'aɪsɪkl/ n carámbano m

icing /'aɪsɪŋ/ n glaseado m

icon /'aɪkɒn/ n icono m

icy /'aɪsɪ/ a (-ier, -iest) helado; (fig) glacial

I'd /aɪd/ = **I had, I would**

idea /aɪ'dɪə/ n idea f

ideal /aɪ'dɪəl/ a & n ideal (m). ~**ism** n idealismo m. ~**ist** n idealista m & f. ~**istic** /-'lɪstɪk/ a idealista. ~**ize** vt idealizar. ~**ly** adv idealmente

identical /aɪ'dentɪkl/ a idéntico. ~ **twins** npl gemelos mpl idénticos, gemelos mpl (LAm)

identif|ication /aɪdentɪfɪ'keɪʃn/ n identificación f. ~**y** /aɪ'dentɪfaɪ/ vt identificar. ● vi. ~**y with** identificarse con

identity /aɪ'dentɪtɪ/ n identidad f. ~ **card** n carné m de identidad

ideolog|ical /aɪdɪə'lɒdʒɪkl/ a ideológico. ~**y** /aɪdɪ'ɒlədʒɪ/ n ideología f

idiocy /'ɪdɪəsɪ/ n idiotez f

idiom /'ɪdɪəm/ n locución f. ~**atic** /-'mætɪk/ a idiomático

idiot /'ɪdɪət/ n idiota m & f. ~**ic** /-'ɒtɪk/ a idiota

idle /'aɪdl/ a (-er, -est) ocioso; (lazy) holgazán; (out of work) desocupado; <machine> parado. ● vi <engine> andar al ralentí. ~ness n ociosidad f; (laziness) holgazanería f

idol /'aɪdl/ n ídolo m. ~ize vt idolatrar

idyllic /ɪ'dɪlɪk/ a idílico

i.e. abbr (= id est) es decir

if /ɪf/ conj si

igloo /'ɪglu:/ n iglú m

ignite /ɪg'naɪt/ vt encender. ● vi encenderse. ~ion /-'nɪʃn/ n ignición f; (Auto) encendido m. ~ion key n llave f de contacto

ignoramus /ɪgnə'reɪməs/ n (pl -muses) ignorante

ignoran|ce /'ɪgnərəns/ n ignorancia f. ~t a ignorante

ignore /ɪg'nɔ:(r)/ vt no hacer caso de; hacer caso omiso de <warning>

ill /ɪl/ a enfermo. ● adv mal. ● n mal m

I'll /aɪl/ = I will

ill: ~-advised /-əd'vaɪzd/ a imprudente. ~ at ease /ət'i:z/ a incómodo. ~-bred /-'bred/ a mal educado

illegal /ɪ'li:gl/ a ilegal

illegible /ɪ'ledʒəbl/ a ilegible

illegitima|cy /ɪlɪ'dʒɪtɪməsɪ/ n ilegitimidad f. ~te /-ət/ a ilegítimo

illitera|cy /ɪ'lɪtərəsɪ/ n analfabetismo m. ~te /-ət/ a analfabeto

illness /'ɪlnɪs/ n enfermedad f

illogical /ɪ'lɒdʒɪkl/ a ilógico

illuminat|e /ɪ'lu:mmeɪt/ vt iluminar. ~ion /-'neɪʃn/ n iluminación f

illus|ion /ɪ'lu:ʒn/ n ilusión f. ~sory /-sərɪ/ a ilusorio

illustrat|e /'ɪləstreɪt/ vt ilustrar. ~ion /-'streɪʃn/ n ilustración f; (example) ejemplo m

illustrious /ɪ'lʌstrɪəs/ a ilustre

ill will /ɪl'wɪl/ n mala voluntad f

I'm /aɪm/ = I am

image /'ɪmɪdʒ/ n imagen f. ~ry n imágenes fpl

imagin|able /ɪ'mædʒɪnəbl/ a imaginable. ~ary a imaginario. ~ation /-'neɪʃn/ n imaginación f. ~ative a imaginativo. ~e /ɪ'mædʒɪn/ vt imaginar(se)

imbalance /ɪm'bæləns/ n desequilibrio m

imbecile /'ɪmbəsi:l/ n imbécil m & f

imitat|e /'ɪmɪteɪt/ vt imitar. ~ion /-'teɪʃn/ n imitación f. ● a de imitación. ~or n imitador m

immaculate /ɪ'mækjʊlət/ a inmaculado

immatur|e /ɪmə'tjʊə(r)/ a inmaduro. ~ity n inmadurez f

immediate /ɪ'mi:dɪət/ a inmediato. ~ly adv inmediatamente. ● conj en cuanto (+ subjunctive)

immens|e /ɪ'mens/ a inmenso. ~ely adv inmensamente; (🄴, very much) muchísimo

immers|e /ɪ'mɜ:s/ vt sumergir. ~ion /-ʃn/ n inmersión f. ~ion heater n calentador m de inmersión

immigra|nt /'ɪmɪgrənt/ a & n inmigrante (m & f). ~tion /-'greɪʃn/ n inmigración f

imminent /'ɪmɪnənt/ a inminente

immobil|e /ɪ'məʊbaɪl/ a inmóvil. ~ize /-bɪlaɪz/ vt inmovilizar

immoderate /ɪ'mɒdərət/ a inmoderado

immodest /ɪ'mɒdɪst/ a inmodesto

immoral /ɪ'mɒrəl/ a inmoral. ~ity /ɪmə'rælətɪ/ n inmoralidad f

immortal /ɪ'mɔ:tl/ a inmortal. ~ity /-'tælətɪ/ n inmortalidad f. ~ize vt inmortalizar

immun|e /ɪ'mju:n/ a inmune (to a). ~ity n inmunidad f. ~ization /ɪmjʊnaɪ'zeɪʃn/ n inmunización f. ~ize /'ɪmjʊnaɪz/ vt inmunizar

imp /ɪmp/ n diablillo m

impact /'ɪmpækt/ n impacto m

impair /ɪm'peə(r)/ vt perjudicar

impale /ɪm'peɪl/ vt atravesar (on con)

impart /ɪm'pɑ:t/ vt comunicar <news>; impartir <knowledge>

impartial /ɪm'pɑ:ʃl/ a imparcial. ~ity /-ɪ'ælətɪ/ n imparcialidad f

impassable /ɪm'pɑ:səbl/ a <barrier etc> infranqueable; <road> intransitable

impassive /ɪm'pæsɪv/ a impasible

impatien|ce /ɪm'peɪʃəns/ n impaciencia f. ~t a impaciente. **get** ~t impacientarse. ~tly adv con impaciencia

impeccable /ɪm'pekəbl/ a impecable

impede /ɪm'piːd/ vt estorbar

impediment /ɪm'pedɪmənt/ obstáculo m. (**speech**) ~ n defecto m del habla

impending /ɪm'pendɪŋ/ a inminente

impenetrable /ɪm'penɪtrəbl/ a impenetrable

imperative /ɪm'perətɪv/ a imprescindible. ● n (Gram) imperativo m

imperceptible /ɪmpə'septəbl/ a imperceptible

imperfect /ɪm'pɜːfɪkt/ a imperfecto. ~ion /ɪmpə'fekʃn/ n imperfección f

imperial /ɪm'pɪərɪəl/ a imperial. ~ism n imperialismo m

impersonal /ɪm'pɜːsənl/ a impersonal

impersonat|e /ɪm'pɜːsəneɪt/ vt hacerse pasar por; (mimic) imitar. ~ion /-'neɪʃn/ n imitación f. ~or n imitador m

impertinen|ce /ɪm'pɜːtɪnəns/ n impertinencia f. ~t a impertinente

impervious /ɪm'pɜːvɪəs/ a. ~ to impermeable a

impetuous /ɪm'petjʊəs/ a impetuoso

impetus /'ɪmpɪtəs/ n ímpetu m

implacable /ɪm'plækəbl/ a implacable

implant /ɪm'plɑːnt/ vt implantar

implement /'ɪmplɪmənt/ n instrumento m, implemento m (LAm). ● /'ɪmplɪment/ vt implementar

implicat|e /'ɪmplɪkeɪt/ vt implicar. ~ion /-'keɪʃn/ n implicación f

implicit /ɪm'plɪsɪt/ a (implied) implícito; (unquestioning) absoluto

implore /ɪm'plɔː(r)/ vt implorar

imply /ɪm'plaɪ/ vt (involve) implicar; (insinuate) dar a entender, insinuar

impolite /ɪmpə'laɪt/ a mal educado

import /ɪm'pɔːt/ vt importar. ● /'ɪmpɔːt/ n importación f; (item)

artículo m de importación; (meaning) significación f

importan|ce /ɪm'pɔːtəns/ n importancia f. ~t a importante

importer /ɪm'pɔːtə(r)/ n importador m

impos|e /ɪm'pəʊz/ vt imponer. ● vi. ~e on abusar de la amabilidad de. ~ing a imponente. ~ition /ɪmpə'zɪʃn/ n imposición f; (fig) abuso m

impossib|ility /ɪmpɒsə'bɪlətɪ/ n imposibilidad f. ~le /ɪm'pɒsəbl/ a imposible

impostor /ɪm'pɒstə(r)/ n impostor m

impoten|ce /'ɪmpətəns/ n impotencia f. ~t a impotente

impound /ɪm'paʊnd/ vt confiscar

impoverished /ɪm'pɒvərɪʃt/ a empobrecido

impractical /ɪm'præktɪkl/ a poco práctico

impregnable /ɪm'pregnəbl/ a inexpugnable

impregnate /'ɪmpregneɪt/ vt impregnar (with con, de)

impress /ɪm'pres/ vt impresionar; (make good impression) causar una buena impresión a. ● vi impresionar

impression /ɪm'preʃn/ n impresión f. ~able a impresionable. ~ism n impresionismo m

impressive /ɪm'presɪv/ a impresionante

imprint /'ɪmprɪnt/ n impresión f. ● /ɪm'prɪnt/ vt imprimir

imprison /ɪm'prɪzn/ vt encarcelar. ~ment n encarcelamiento m

improbab|ility /ɪmprɒbə'bɪlətɪ/ n improbabilidad f. ~le /ɪm'prɒbəbl/ a improbable

impromptu /ɪm'prɒmptjuː/ a improvisado. ● adv de improviso

improper /ɪm'prɒpə(r)/ a impropio; (incorrect) incorrecto

improve /ɪm'pruːv/ vt mejorar. ● vi mejorar. ~ment n mejora f

improvis|ation /ɪmprəvaɪ'zeɪʃn/ n improvisación f. ~e /'ɪmprəvaɪz/ vt/i improvisar

impuden|ce /'ɪmpjʊdəns/ *n* insolencia *f*. **~t** *a* insolente

impuls|e /'ɪmpʌls/ *n* impulso *m*. on **~e** sin reflexionar. **~ive** *a* irreflexivo

impur|e /ɪm'pjʊə(r)/ *a* impuro. **~ity** *n* impureza *f*

in /ɪn/ *prep* en; (within) dentro de. **~ a firm manner** de una manera terminante. **~ an hour('s time)** dentro de una hora. **~ doing** al hacer. **~ so far as** en la medida en que. **~ the evening** por la tarde. **~ the rain** bajo la lluvia. **~ the sun** al sol. **one ~ ten** uno de cada diez. **the best ~ the world** el mejor del mundo. ● *adv* (inside) dentro; (at home) en casa. **come ~** entrar. ● *n*. **the ~s and outs of** los detalles de

inability /ɪnə'bɪlətɪ/ *n* incapacidad *f*

inaccessible /ɪnæk'sesəbl/ *a* inaccesible

inaccura|cy /ɪn'ækjʊrəsɪ/ *n* inexactitud *f*. **~te** /-ət/ *a* inexacto

inactiv|e /ɪn'æktɪv/ *a* inactivo. **~ity** /-'tɪvətɪ/ *n* inactividad *f*

inadequa|cy /ɪn'ædɪkwəsɪ/ *a* insuficiencia *f*. **~te** /-ət/ *a* insuficiente

inadvertently /ɪnəd'vɜːtəntlɪ/ *adv* sin querer

inadvisable /ɪnəd'vaɪzəbl/ *a* desaconsejable

inane /ɪ'neɪn/ *a* estúpido

inanimate /ɪn'ænɪmət/ *a* inanimado

inappropriate /ɪnə'prəʊprɪət/ *a* inoportuno

inarticulate /ɪnɑː'tɪkjʊlət/ *a* incapaz de expresarse claramente

inattentive /ɪnə'tentɪv/ *a* desatento

inaudible /ɪn'ɔːdəbl/ *a* inaudible

inaugurate /ɪ'nɔːgjʊreɪt/ *vt* inaugurar

inborn /'ɪnbɔːn/ *a* innato

inbred /ɪn'bred/ *a* (inborn) innato; <social group> endogámico

Inc /ɪŋk/ *abbr* (Amer) (= **Incorporated**) S.A., Sociedad Anónima

incalculable /ɪn'kælkjʊləbl/ *a* incalculable

incapable /ɪn'keɪpəbl/ *a* incapaz

incapacit|ate /ɪnkə'pæsɪteɪt/ *vt* incapacitar. **~y** *n* incapacidad *f*

incarcerate /ɪn'kɑːsəreɪt/ *vt* encarcelar

incarnat|e /ɪn'kɑːnət/ *a* encarnado. **~ion** /-'neɪʃn/ *n* encarnación *f*

incendiary /ɪn'sendɪərɪ/ *a* incendiario. **~ bomb** bomba *f* incendiaria

incense /'ɪnsens/ *n* incienso *m*. ● /ɪn'sens/ *vt* enfurecer

incentive /ɪn'sentɪv/ *n* incentivo *m*

incessant /ɪn'sesnt/ *a* incesante. **~ly** *adv* sin cesar

incest /'ɪnsest/ *n* incesto *m*. **~uous** /ɪn'sestjʊəs/ *a* incestuoso

inch /ɪntʃ/ *n* pulgada *f*; (= 2,54cm). ● *vi*. **~ forward** avanzar lentamente

incidence /'ɪnsɪdəns/ *n* frecuencia *f*

incident /'ɪnsɪdənt/ *n* incidente *m*

incidental /ɪnsɪ'dentl/ *a* <effect> secundario; (minor) incidental. **~ly** *adv* a propósito

incinerat|e /ɪn'sɪnəreɪt/ *vt* incinerar. **~or** *n* incinerador *m*

incision /ɪn'sɪʒn/ *n* incisión *f*

incite /ɪn'saɪt/ *vt* incitar. **~ment** *n* incitación *f*

inclination /ɪnklɪ'neɪʃn/ *n* inclinación *f*. **have no ~ to** no tener deseos de

incline /ɪn'klaɪn/ *vt* inclinar. **be ~d to** tener tendencia a. ● *vi* inclinarse. ● /'ɪnklaɪn/ *n* pendiente *f*

inclu|de /ɪn'kluːd/ *vt* incluir. **~ding** *prep* incluso. **~sion** /-ʒn/ *n* inclusión *f*. **~sive** /-sɪv/ *a* inclusivo

incognito /ɪnkɒg'niːtəʊ/ *adv* de incógnito

incoherent /ɪnkəʊ'hɪərənt/ *a* incoherente

incom|e /'ɪnkʌm/ *n* ingresos *mpl*. **~e tax** *n* impuesto *m* sobre la renta. **~ing** *a* <tide> ascendente

incomparable /ɪn'kɒmpərəbl/ *a* incomparable

incompatible /ɪnkəm'pætəbl/ *a* incompatible

incompeten|ce /ɪn'kɒmpɪtəns/ *n* incompetencia *f*. **~t** *a* incompetente

incomplete /ɪnkəm'pliːt/ *a* incompleto

incomprehensible /ɪnkɒmprɪˈhensəbl/ *a* incomprensible

inconceivable /ɪnkənˈsiːvəbl/ *a* inconcebible

inconclusive /ɪnkənˈkluːsɪv/ *a* no concluyente

incongruous /ɪnˈkɒŋɡrʊəs/ *a* incongruente

inconsiderate /ɪnkənˈsɪdərət/ *a* desconsiderado

inconsisten|cy /ɪnkənˈsɪstənsɪ/ *n* inconsecuencia *f*. ~t *a* inconsecuente. be ~t with no concordar con

inconspicuous /ɪnkənˈspɪkjʊəs/ *a* que no llama la atención. ~ly *adv* sin llamar la atención

incontinent /ɪnˈkɒntɪnənt/ *a* incontinente

inconvenien|ce /ɪnkənˈviːnɪəns/ *a* inconveniencia *f*; (drawback) inconveniente *m*. ~t *a* inconveniente

incorporate /ɪnˈkɔːpəreɪt/ *vt* incorporar; (include) incluir; (Com) constituir (en sociedad)

incorrect /ɪnkəˈrekt/ *a* incorrecto

increas|e /ˈɪnkriːs/ *n* aumento *m* (in de). ● /ɪnˈkriːs/ *vt/i* aumentar. ~ing /ɪnˈkriːsɪŋ/ *a* creciente. ~ingly *adv* cada vez más

incredible /ɪnˈkredəbl/ *a* increíble

incredulous /ɪnˈkredjʊləs/ *a* incrédulo

incriminat|e /ɪnˈkrɪmɪneɪt/ *vt* incriminar. ~ing *a* comprometedor

incubat|e /ˈɪŋkjʊbeɪt/ *vt* incubar. ~ion /-ˈbeɪʃn/ *n* incubación *f*. ~or *n* incubadora *f*

incur /ɪnˈkɜː(r)/ *vt* (*pt* **incurred**) incurrir en; contraer <*debts*>

incurable /ɪnˈkjʊərəbl/ *a* <*disease*> incurable; <*romantic*> empedernido

indebted /ɪnˈdetɪd/ *a*. be ~ to s.o. estar en deuda con uno

indecen|cy /ɪnˈdiːsnsɪ/ *n* indecencia *f*. ~t *a* indecente

indecisi|on /ɪndɪˈsɪʒn/ *n* indecisión *f*. ~ve /-ˈsaɪsɪv/ *a* indeciso

indeed /ɪnˈdiːd/ *adv* en efecto; (really?) ¿de veras?

indefinable /ɪndɪˈfaɪnəbl/ *a* indefinible

indefinite /ɪnˈdefɪnət/ *a* indefinido. ~ly *adv* indefinidamente

indelible /ɪnˈdelɪbl/ *a* indeleble

indemni|fy /ɪnˈdemnɪfaɪ/ *vt* (insure) asegurar; (compensate) indemnizar. ~ty /-ətɪ/ *n* (insurance) indemnidad *f*; (payment) indemnización *f*

indent /ɪnˈdent/ *vt* sangrar <*text*>. ~ation /-ˈteɪʃn/ *n* mella *f*

independen|ce /ɪndɪˈpendəns/ *n* independencia *f*. ~t *a* independiente. ~tly *adv* independientemente

in-depth /ɪnˈdepθ/ *a* a fondo

indescribable /ɪndɪˈskraɪbəbl/ *a* indescriptible

indestructible /ɪndɪˈstrʌktəbl/ *a* indestructible

indeterminate /ɪndɪˈtɜːmɪnət/ *a* indeterminado

index /ˈɪndeks/ *n* (*pl* **indexes**) (in book) índice *m*; (*pl* **indexes** *or* **indices**) (Com, Math) índice *m*. ● *vt* poner índice a; (enter in index) poner en un índice. ~ **finger** *n* (dedo *m*) índice *m*. ~**-linked** /-ˈlɪŋkt/ *a* indexado

India /ˈɪndɪə/ *n* la India. ~**n** *a* & *n* indio (*m*)

indicat|e /ˈɪndɪkeɪt/ *vt* indicar. ~ion /-ˈkeɪʃn/ *n* indicación *f*. ~ive /ɪnˈdɪkətɪv/ *a* & *n* indicativo (*m*). ~or /ˈɪndɪkeɪtə(r)/ *n* indicador *m*; (Auto) intermitente *m*

indices /ˈɪndɪsiːz/ ⇒INDEX

indict /ɪnˈdaɪt/ *vt* acusar. ~ment *n* acusación *f*

indifferen|ce /ɪnˈdɪfrəns/ *n* indiferencia *f*. ~t *a* indiferente; (not good) mediocre

indigesti|ble /ɪndɪˈdʒestəbl/ *a* indigesto. ~on /-tʃən/ *n* indigestión *f*

indigna|nt /ɪnˈdɪɡnənt/ *a* indignado. ~tion /-ˈneɪʃn/ *n* indignación *f*

indirect /ɪndɪˈrekt/ *a* indirecto. ~ly *adv* indirectamente

indiscre|et /ɪndɪˈskriːt/ *a* indiscreto. ~tion /-ˈkreʃn/ *n* indiscreción *f*

indiscriminate /ɪndɪˈskrɪmɪnət/ *a* indistinto. ~ly *adv* indistintamente

indispensable /ɪndɪˈspensəbl/ *a* indispensable, imprescindible

indisposed /ɪndɪˈspəʊzd/ *a* indispuesto

indisputable /ɪndɪ'spjuːtəbl/ *a* indiscutible

indistinguishable /ɪndɪ'stɪŋwɪʃəbl/ *a* indistinguible (**from** de)

individual /ɪndɪ'vɪdjʊəl/ *a* individual. ● *n* individuo *m*. ∼**ly** *adv* individualmente

indoctrinat|e /ɪn'dɒktrɪneɪt/ *vt* adoctrinar. ∼**ion** /-'neɪʃn/ *n* adoctrinamiento *m*

indolen|ce /'ɪndələns/ *n* indolencia *f*. ∼**t** *a* indolente

indomitable /ɪn'dɒmɪtəbl/ *a* indómito

indoor /'ɪndɔː(r)/ *a* interior; <*clothes etc*> de casa; (covered) cubierto. ∼**s** *adv* dentro, adentro (LAm)

induc|e /ɪn'djuːs/ *vt* inducir. ∼**ement** *n* incentivo *m*

indulge /ɪn'dʌldʒ/ *vt* satisfacer <*desires*>; complacer <*person*>. ● *vi.* ∼ **in** permitirse. ∼**nce** /-əns/ *n* (of desires) satisfacción *f*; (extravagance) lujo *m*. ∼**nt** *a* indulgente

industrial /ɪn'dʌstrɪəl/ *a* industrial; <*unrest*> laboral. ∼**ist** *n* industrial *m & f*. ∼**ized** *a* industrializado

industrious /ɪn'dʌstrɪəs/ *a* trabajador

industry /'ɪndəstrɪ/ *n* industria *f*; (zeal) aplicación *f*

inebriated /ɪ'niːbrɪeɪtɪd/ *a* beodo, ebrio

inedible /ɪn'edɪbl/ *a* incomible

ineffective /ɪnɪ'fektɪv/ *a* ineficaz; <*person*> incompetente

ineffectual /ɪnɪ'fektjʊəl/ *a* ineficaz

inefficien|cy /ɪnɪ'fɪʃnsɪ/ *n* ineficacia *f*; (of person) incompetencia *f*. ∼**t** *a* ineficaz; <*person*> incompetente

ineligible /ɪn'elɪdʒəbl/ *a* inelegible. **be** ∼ **for** no tener derecho a

inept /ɪ'nept/ *a* inepto

inequality /ɪnɪ'kwɒlətɪ/ *n* desigualdad *f*

inert /ɪ'nɜːt/ *a* inerte. ∼**ia** /ɪ'nɜːʃə/ *n* inercia *f*

inescapable /ɪnɪ'skeɪpəbl/ *a* ineludible

inevitabl|e /ɪn'evɪtəbl/ *a* inevitable. ● *n.* **the** ∼**e** lo inevitable. ∼**y** *adv* inevitablemente

inexact /ɪnɪg'zækt/ *a* inexacto

inexcusable /ɪnɪk'skjuːsəbl/ *a* imperdonable

inexpensive /ɪnɪk'spensɪv/ *a* económico, barato

inexperience /ɪnɪk'spɪərɪəns/ *n* falta *f* de experiencia. ∼**d** *a* inexperto

inexplicable /ɪnɪk'splɪkəbl/ *a* inexplicable

infallib|ility /ɪnfælə'bɪlətɪ/ *n* infalibilidad *f*. ∼**le** /ɪn'fæləbl/ *a* infalible

infam|ous /'ɪnfəməs/ *a* infame. ∼**y** *n* infamia *f*

infan|cy /'ɪnfənsɪ/ *n* infancia *f*. ∼**t** *n* niño *m*. ∼**tile** /'ɪnfəntaɪl/ *a* infantil

infantry /'ɪnfəntrɪ/ *n* infantería *f*

infatuat|ed /ɪn'fætjʊeɪtɪd/ *a.* **be** ∼**ed with** estar encaprichado con. ∼**ion** /-'eɪʃn/ *n* encaprichamiento *m*

infect /ɪn'fekt/ *vt* infectar; (fig) contagiar. ∼ **s.o. with sth** contagiarle algo a uno. ∼**ion** /-ʃn/ *n* infección *f*. ∼**ious** /-ʃəs/ *a* contagioso

infer /ɪn'fɜː(r)/ *vt* (*pt* **inferred**) deducir

inferior /ɪn'fɪərɪə(r)/ *a & n* inferior (*m & f*). ∼**ity** /-'ɒrətɪ/ *n* inferioridad *f*

inferno /ɪn'fɜːnəʊ/ *n* (*pl* -**os**) infierno *m*

infertil|e /ɪn'fɜːtaɪl/ *a* estéril. ∼**ity** /-'tɪlətɪ/ *n* esterilidad *f*

infest /ɪn'fest/ *vt* infestar

infidelity /ɪnfɪ'delətɪ/ *n* infidelidad *f*

infiltrat|e /'ɪnfɪltreɪt/ *vt* infiltrarse en. ● *vi* infiltrarse. ∼**or** *n* infiltrado *m*

infinite /'ɪnfɪnət/ *a* infinito. ∼**ly** *adv* infinitamente

infinitesimal /ɪnfɪnɪ'tesɪml/ *a* infinitesimal

infinitive /ɪn'fɪnətɪv/ *n* infinitivo *m*

infinity /ɪn'fɪnətɪ/ *n* (infinite distance) infinito *m*; (infinite quantity) infinidad *f*

infirm /ɪn'fɜːm/ *a* enfermizo. ∼**ity** *n* enfermedad *f*

inflam|e /ɪn'fleɪm/ *vt* inflamar. ∼**mable** /ɪn'flæməbl/ *a* inflamable. ∼**mation** /-ə'meɪʃn/ *n* inflamación *f*

inflat|e /ɪnˈfleɪt/ vt inflar. ~ion /-ʃn/ n inflación f. ~ionary a inflacionario

inflection /ɪnˈflekʃn/ n inflexión f

inflexible /ɪnˈfleksəbl/ a inflexible

inflict /ɪnˈflɪkt/ vt infligir (on a)

influen|ce /ˈɪnfluəns/ n influencia f. under the ~ce (Ⅱ, drunk) borracho. ● vt influir (en). ~tial /-ˈenʃl/ a influyente

influenza /ɪnfluˈenzə/ n gripe f

influx /ˈɪnflʌks/ n afluencia f

inform /ɪnˈfɔːm/ vt informar. keep ~ed tener al corriente. ● vi. ~ on s.o. delatar a uno

informal /ɪnˈfɔːml/ a informal; <language> familiar. ~ity /-ˈmæləti/ n falta f de ceremonia. ~ly adv (casually) de manera informal; (unofficially) informalmente

inform|ation /ɪnfəˈmeɪʃn/ n información f. ~ation technology n informática f. ~ative a /ɪnˈfɔːmətɪv/ informativo. ~er /ɪbˈfɔːmə(r)/ n informante m

infrared /ɪnfrəˈred/ a infrarrojo

infrequent /ɪnˈfriːkwənt/ a poco frecuente. ~ly adv raramente

infringe /ɪnˈfrɪndʒ/ vt infringir. ~ on violar. ~ment n violación f

infuriat|e /ɪnˈfjʊərɪeɪt/ vt enfurecer. ~ing a exasperante

ingen|ious /ɪnˈdʒiːniəs/ a ingenioso. ~uity /ɪndʒɪˈnjuːəti/ n ingeniosidad f

ingot /ˈɪŋɡət/ n lingote m

ingrained /ɪnˈɡreɪnd/ a (belief) arraigado

ingratiate /ɪnˈɡreɪʃɪeɪt/ vt. ~ o.s. with congraciarse con

ingratitude /ɪnˈɡrætɪtjuːd/ n ingratitud f

ingredient /ɪnˈɡriːdɪənt/ n ingrediente m

ingrowing /ˈɪnɡrəʊɪŋ/, **ingrown** /ˈɪnɡrəʊn/ a. ~ nail n uñero m, uña f encarnada

inhabit /ɪnˈhæbɪt/ vt habitar. ~able a habitable. ~ant n habitante m

inhale /ɪnˈheɪl/ vt aspirar. ● vi (when smoking) aspirar el humo. ~r n inhalador m

inherent /ɪnˈhɪərənt/ a inherente. ~ly adv intrínsecamente

inherit /ɪnˈherɪt/ vt heredar. ~ance /-əns/ n herencia f

inhibit /ɪnˈhɪbɪt/ vt inhibir. ~ed a inhibido. ~ion /-ˈbɪʃn/ n inhibición f

inhospitable /ɪnhəˈspɪtəbl/ a <place> inhóspito; <person> inhospitalario

inhuman /ɪnˈhjuːmən/ a inhumano. ~e /ɪnhjuːˈmeɪn/ a inhumano. ~ity /ɪnhjuːˈmænəti/ n inhumanidad f

initial /ɪˈnɪʃl/ n inicial f. ● vt (pt **initialled**) firmar con iniciales. ● a inicial. ~ly adv al principio

initiat|e /ɪˈnɪʃɪeɪt/ vt iniciar; promover <scheme etc>. ~ion /-ˈeɪʃn/ n iniciación f

initiative /ɪˈnɪʃətɪv/ n iniciativa f. on one's own ~ por iniciativa propia. take the ~ tomar la iniciativa

inject /ɪnˈdʒekt/ vt inyectar. ~ion /-ʃn/ n inyección f

injur|e /ˈɪndʒə(r)/ vt herir. ~y n herida f

injustice /ɪnˈdʒʌstɪs/ n injusticia f

ink /ɪŋk/ n tinta f

ink: ~well n tintero m. ~y a manchado de tinta

inland /ˈɪnlənd/ a interior. ● /ɪnˈlænd/ adv tierra adentro. I~ Revenue /ˈɪnlənd/ n Hacienda f

in-laws /ˈɪnlɔːz/ npl parientes mpl políticos

inlay /ɪnˈleɪ/ vt (pt **inlaid**) taracear, incrustar. ● /ˈɪnleɪ/ n taracea f, incrustación f

inlet /ˈɪnlet/ n (in coastline) ensenada f; (of river, sea) brazo m

inmate /ˈɪnmeɪt/ n (of asylum) interno m; (of prison) preso m

inn /ɪn/ n posada f

innate /ɪˈneɪt/ a innato

inner /ˈɪnə(r)/ a interior; (fig) íntimo. ~most a más íntimo. ~ tube n cámara f

innocen|ce /ˈɪnəsns/ n inocencia f. ~t a & n inocente (m & f)

innocuous /ɪˈnɒkjʊəs/ *a* inocuo

innovat|e /ˈɪnəveɪt/ *vi* innovar. ~**ion** /-ˈveɪʃn/ *n* innovación *f*. ~**ive** /ˈɪnəvətɪv/ *a* innovador. ~**or** *n* innovador *m*

innuendo /ɪnjuːˈendəʊ/ *n* (*pl* **-oes**) insinuación *f*

innumerable /ɪˈnjuːmərəbl/ *a* innumerable

inoculat|e /ɪˈnɒkjʊleɪt/ *vt* inocular. ~**ion** /-ˈleɪʃn/ *n* inoculación *f*

inoffensive /ɪnəˈfensɪv/ *a* inofensivo

inopportune /ɪnˈɒpətjuːn/ *a* inoportuno

input /ˈɪnpʊt/ *n* aportación *f*, aporte *m* (LAm); (Comp) entrada *f*. ● *vt* (*pt* **input**, *pres p* **inputting**) entrar <*data*>

inquest /ˈɪnkwest/ *n* investigación *f* judicial

inquir|e /ɪnˈkwaɪə(r)/ *vt/i* preguntar. ~**e about** informarse de. ~**y** *n* pregunta *f*; (investigation) investigación *f*

inquisition /ɪnkwɪˈzɪʃn/ *n* inquisición *f*

inquisitive /ɪnˈkwɪzətɪv/ *a* inquisitivo

insan|e /ɪnˈseɪn/ *a* loco. ~**ity** /ɪnˈsænətɪ/ *n* locura *f*

insatiable /ɪnˈseɪʃəbl/ *a* insaciable

inscri|be /ɪnˈskraɪb/ *vt* inscribir <*letters*>; grabar <*design*>. ~**ption** /-ɪpʃn/ *n* inscripción *f*

inscrutable /ɪnˈskruːtəbl/ *a* inescrutable

insect /ˈɪnsekt/ *n* insecto *m*. ~**icide** /ɪnˈsektɪsaɪd/ *n* insecticida *f*

insecur|e /ɪnsɪˈkjʊə(r)/ *a* inseguro. ~**ity** *n* inseguridad *f*

insensitive /ɪnˈsensətɪv/ *a* insensible

inseparable /ɪnˈsepərəbl/ *a* inseparable

insert /ˈɪnsɜːt/ *n* materia *f* insertada. ● /ɪnˈsɜːt/ *vt* insertar. ~**ion** /ɪnˈsɜːʃn/ *n* inserción *f*

inside /ɪnˈsaɪd/ *n* interior *m*. ~ **out** al revés; (thoroughly) a fondo. ● *a* interior. ● *adv* dentro, adentro (LAm). ● *prep* dentro de. ~**s** *npl* tripas *fpl*

insight /ˈɪnsaɪt/ *n* perspicacia *f*. **gain an** ~ **into** llegar a comprender bien

insignificant /ɪnsɪgˈnɪfɪkənt/ *a* insignificante

insincer|e /ɪnsɪnˈsɪə(r)/ *a* poco sincero. ~**ity** /-ˈserətɪ/ *n* falta *f* de sinceridad

insinuat|e /ɪnˈsɪnjʊeɪt/ *vt* insinuar. ~**ion** /-ˈeɪʃn/ *n* insinuación *f*

insipid /ɪnˈsɪpɪd/ *a* insípido

insist /ɪnˈsɪst/ *vt* insistir (**that** en que). ● *vi* insistir. ~ **on** insistir en. ~**ence** /-əns/ *n* insistencia *f*. ~**ent** *a* insistente. ~**ently** *adv* con insistencia

insolen|ce /ˈɪnsələns/ *n* insolencia *f*. ~**t** *a* insolente

insoluble /ɪnˈsɒljʊbl/ *a* insoluble

insolvent /ɪnˈsɒlvənt/ *a* insolvente

insomnia /ɪnˈsɒmnɪə/ *n* insomnio *m*. ~**c** /-ˈæk/ *n* insomne *m* & *f*

inspect /ɪnˈspekt/ *vt* (officially) inspeccionar; (look at closely) revisar, examinar . ~**ion** /-ʃn/ *n* inspección *f*. ~**or** *n* inspector *m*; (on train, bus) revisor *m*, inspector *m* (LAm)

inspir|ation /ɪnspəˈreɪʃn/ *n* inspiración *f*. ~**e** /ɪnˈspaɪə(r)/ *vt* inspirar. ~**ing** *a* inspirador

instability /ɪnstəˈbɪlətɪ/ *n* inestabilidad *f*

install /ɪnˈstɔːl/ *vt* instalar. ~**ation** /-əˈleɪʃn/ *n* instalación *f*

instalment /ɪnˈstɔːlmənt/ *n* (payment) plazo *m*; (of publication) entrega *f*; (of radio, TV serial) episodio *m*

instance /ˈɪnstəns/ *n* ejemplo *m*; (case) caso *m*. **for** ~ por ejemplo. **in the first** ~ en primer lugar

instant /ˈɪnstənt/ *a* instantáneo. ● *n* instante *m*. ~**aneous** /ɪnstən ˈteɪnɪəs/ *a* instantáneo

instead /ɪnˈsted/ *adv* en cambio. ~ **of** en vez de, en lugar de

instigat|e /ˈɪnstɪgeɪt/ *vt* instigar. ~**ion** /-ˈgeɪʃn/ *n* instigación *f*

instinct /ˈɪnstɪŋkt/ *n* instinto *m*. ~**ive** *a* instintivo

institut|e /ˈɪnstɪtjuːt/ *n* instituto *m*. ● *vt* instituir; iniciar <*enquiry etc*>. ~**ion** /-ˈtjuːʃn/ *n* institución *f*. ~**ional** *a* institucional

instruct /ɪn'strʌkt/ vt instruir; (order) mandar. ~ **s.o. in sth** enseñar algo a uno. ~**ion** /-ʃn/ n instrucción f. ~**ions** npl (for use) modo m de empleo. ~**ive** a instructivo. ~**or** n instructor m

instrument /'ɪnstrəmənt/ n instrumento m. ~**al** /ɪnstrə'mentl/ a instrumental. **be** ~**al in** jugar un papel decisivo en

insubordinat|e /ɪnsə'bɔːdɪnət/ a insubordinado. ~**ion** /-'neɪʃn/ n insubordinación f

insufferable /ɪn'sʌfərəbl/ a <person> insufrible; <heat> insoportable

insufficient /ɪnsə'fɪʃnt/ a insuficiente

insular /'ɪnsjʊlə(r)/ a insular; (narrow-minded) estrecho de miras

insulat|e /'ɪnsjʊleɪt/ vt aislar. ~**ion** /-'leɪʃn/ n aislamiento m

insulin /'ɪnsjʊlɪn/ n insulina f

insult /ɪn'sʌlt/ vt insultar. ● /'ɪnsʌlt/ n insulto m. ~**ing** /ɪn'sʌltɪŋ/ a insultante

insur|ance /ɪn'ʃʊərəns/ n seguro m. ~**e** /ɪn'ʃʊə(r)/ vt (Com) asegurar; (Amer) ⇒ENSURE

insurmountable /ɪnsə'maʊntəbl/ a insuperable

intact /ɪn'tækt/ a intacto

integral /'ɪntɪɡrəl/ a integral

integrat|e /'ɪntɪɡreɪt/ vt integrar. ● vi integrarse. ~**ion** /-'ɡreɪʃn/ n integración f

integrity /ɪn'teɡrətɪ/ n integridad f

intellect /'ɪntəlekt/ n intelecto m. ~**ual** /ɪntə'lektʃʊəl/ a & n intelectual (m)

intelligen|ce /ɪn'telɪdʒəns/ n inteligencia f. ~**t** a inteligente. ~**tly** adv inteligentemente

intelligible /ɪn'telɪdʒəbl/ a inteligible

intend /ɪn'tend/ vt. ~ **to do** pensar hacer

intens|e /ɪn'tens/ a intenso; <person> apasionado. ~**ely** adv intensamente; (very) sumamente. ~**ify** /-ɪfaɪ/ vt intensificar. ● vi intensificarse. ~**ity** /-ɪtɪ/ n intensidad f

intensive /ɪn'tensɪv/ a intensivo. ~ **care** n cuidados mpl intensivos

intent /ɪn'tent/ n propósito m. ● a atento. ~ **on** absorto en. ~ **on doing** resuelto a hacer

intention /ɪn'tenʃn/ n intención f. ~**al** a intencional

intently /ɪn'tentlɪ/ adv atentamente

interact /ɪntər'ækt/ vi relacionarse. ~**ion** /-ʃn/ n interacción f

intercept /ɪntə'sept/ vt interceptar. ~**ion** /-ʃn/ n interceptación f

interchange /ɪntə'tʃeɪndʒ/ vt intercambiar. ● /'ɪntətʃeɪndʒ/ n intercambio m; (road junction) cruce m. ~**able** /-'tʃeɪndʒəbl/ a intercambiable

intercity /ɪntə'sɪtɪ/ a rápido interurbano m

intercourse /'ɪntəkɔːs/ n trato m; (sexual) acto m sexual

interest /'ɪntrest/ n interés m. ● vt interesar. ~**ed** a interesado. **be** ~**ed in** interesarse por. ~**ing** a interesante

interfere /ɪntə'fɪə(r)/ vi entrometerse. ~ **in** entrometerse en. ~ **with** afectar (a); interferir <radio>. ~**nce** /-rəns/ n intromisión f; (Radio) interferencia f

interior /ɪn'tɪərɪə(r)/ a & n interior (m)

interjection /ɪntə'dʒekʃn/ n interjección f

interlude /'ɪntəluːd/ n intervalo m; (theatre, music) interludio m

intermediary /ɪntə'miːdɪərɪ/ a & n intermediario (m)

interminable /ɪn'tɜːmɪnəbl/ a interminable

intermittent /ɪntə'mɪtnt/ a intermitente. ~**ly** adv con discontinuidad

intern /ɪn'tɜːn/ vt internar. ● /'ɪntɜːn/ n (Amer, doctor) interno m

internal /ɪn'tɜːnl/ a interno. ~**ly** adv internamente. **I**~ **Revenue Service** n (Amer) Hacienda f

international /ɪntə'næʃənl/ a internacional

Internet /'ɪntənet/ n. **the** ~ el Internet

interpret /ɪn'tɜːprɪt/ vt/i interpretar. ~**ation** /-'teɪʃn/ n interpretación f. ~**er** n intérprete m & f

interrogat|e /ɪn'terəgeɪt/ vt interrogar. **~ion** /-'geɪʃn/ n interrogatorio m. **~ive** /-'rɒgətɪv/ a interrogativo

interrupt /ɪntə'rʌpt/ vt/i interrumpir. **~ion** /-ʃn/ n interrupción f

intersect /ɪntə'sekt/ vt cruzar. ● vi <roads> cruzarse; (geometry) intersecarse. **~ion** /-ʃn/ n (roads) cruce m; (geometry) intersección f

intersperse /ɪntə'spɜ:s/ vt intercalar

interstate (**highway**) /'ɪntəsteɪt/ n (Amer) carretera f interestatal

intertwine /ɪntə'twaɪn/ vt entrelazar. ● vi entrelazarse

interval /'ɪntəvl/ n intervalo m; (theatre) descanso m. at **~s** a intervalos

interven|e /ɪntə'vi:n/ vi intervenir. **~tion** /-'venʃn/ n intervención f

interview /'ɪntəvju:/ n entrevista f. ● vt entrevistar. **~ee** /-'i:/ n entrevistado m. **~er** n entrevistador m

intestine /ɪn'testɪn/ n intestino m

intimacy /'ɪntɪməsɪ/ n intimidad f

intimate /'ɪntɪmət/ a íntimo. ● /'ɪntɪmeɪt/ vt (state) anunciar; (imply) dar a entender. **~ly** /'ɪntɪmətlɪ/ adv íntimamente

intimidat|e /ɪn'tɪmɪdeɪt/ vt intimidar. **~ion** /-'deɪʃn/ n intimidación f

into /'ɪntu:/, before consonant /'ɪntə/ prep en; <translate> a

intolerable /ɪn'tɒlərəbl/ a intolerable

intoleran|ce /ɪn'tɒlərəns/ n intolerancia f. **~t** a intolerante

intoxicat|e /ɪn'tɒksɪkeɪt/ vt embriagar; (Med) intoxicar. **~ed** a ebrio. **~ing** a <substance> estupefaciente. **~ion** /-'keɪʃn/ n embriaguez f; (Med) intoxicación f

intransitive /ɪn'trænsɪtɪv/ a intransitivo

intravenous /ɪntrə'vi:nəs/ a intravenoso

intrepid /ɪn'trepɪd/ a intrépido

intrica|cy /'ɪntrɪkəsɪ/ n complejidad f. **~te** /-ət/ a complejo

intrigu|e /ɪn'tri:g/ vt/i intrigar. ● /'ɪntri:g/ n intriga f. **~ing** /ɪn'tri:gɪŋ/ a intrigante

intrinsic /ɪn'trɪnsɪk/ a intrínseco. **~ally** adv intrínsecamente

introduc|e /ɪntrə'dju:s/ vt introducir; presentar <person>. **~tion** /ɪntrə'dʌkʃn/ n introducción f; (to person) presentación f. **~tory** /ɪntrə'dʌktərɪ/ a preliminar; <course> de introducción

introvert /'ɪntrəvɜ:t/ n introvertido m

intru|de /ɪn'tru:d/ vi entrometerse; (disturb) importunar. **~der** n intruso m. **~sion** /-ʒn/ n intrusión f. **~sive** /-sɪv/ a impertinente

intuiti|on /ɪntju:'ɪʃn/ n intuición f. **~ve** /ɪn'tju:ɪtɪv/ a intuitivo

inundat|e /'ɪnʌndeɪt/ vt inundar. **~ion** /-'deɪʃn/ n inundación f

invade /ɪn'veɪd/ vt invadir. **~r** n invasor m

invalid /'ɪnvəlɪd/ n inválido m. ● /ɪn'vælɪd/ a inválido. **~ate** /ɪn'vælɪdeɪt/ vt invalidar

invaluable /ɪn'væljʊəbl/ a inestimable, invalorable (LAm)

invariabl|e /ɪn'veərɪəbl/ a invariable. **~y** adv invariablemente

invasion /ɪn'veɪʒn/ n invasión f

invent /ɪn'vent/ vt inventar. **~ion** /-'venʃn/ n invención f. **~ive** a inventivo. **~or** n inventor m

inventory /'ɪnvəntrɪ/ n inventario m

invertebrate /ɪn'vɜ:tɪbrət/ n invertebrado m

inverted commas /ɪnvɜ:tɪd'kɒməz/ npl comillas fpl

invest /ɪn'vest/ vt invertir. ● vi. **~ in** hacer una inversión f

investigat|e /ɪn'vestɪgeɪt/ vt investigar. **~ion** /-'geɪʃn/ n investigación f. under **~ion** sometido a examen. **~or** n investigador m

inveterate /ɪn'vetərət/ a inveterado

invidious /ɪn'vɪdɪəs/ a (hateful) odioso; (unfair) injusto

invigorating /ɪn'vɪgəreɪtɪŋ/ a vigorizante; (stimulating) estimulante

invincible /ɪn'vɪnsɪbl/ a invencible

invisible /ɪn'vɪzəbl/ a invisible

invit|ation /ɪnvɪ'teɪʃn/ n invitación f. ~e /ɪn'vaɪt/ vt invitar; (ask for) pedir. ●/'ɪnvaɪt/ n 🄵 invitación f. ~ing /ɪn'vaɪtɪŋ/ a atrayente

invoice /'ɪnvɔɪs/ n factura f. ● vt. ~ s.o. (for sth) pasarle a uno factura (por algo)

involuntary /ɪn'vɒləntərɪ/ a involuntario

involve /ɪn'vɒlv/ vt (entail) suponer; (implicate) implicar. ~d in envuelto en. ~d a (complex) complicado. ~ment n participación f; (relationship) enredo m

inward /'ɪnwəd/ a interior. ● adv hacia adentro. ~s adv hacia dentro

iodine /'aɪədiːn/ n yodo m

ion /'aɪən/ n ion m

iota /aɪ'əʊtə/ n (amount) pizca f

IOU /aɪəʊ'juː/ abbr (= I owe you) pagaré m

IQ abbr (= **intelligence quotient**) CI m, cociente m intelectual

Iran /ɪ'rɑːn/ n Irán m. ~ian /ɪ'reɪnɪən/ a & n iraní (m)

Iraq /ɪ'rɑːk/ n Irak m. ~i a & n iraquí (m)

irate /aɪ'reɪt/ a colérico

Ireland /'aɪələnd/ n Irlanda f

iris /'aɪərɪs/ n (Anat) iris m; (Bot) lirio m

Irish /'aɪərɪʃ/ a irlandés. ● n (Lang) irlandés m. npl. the ~ (people) los irlandeses. ~man /-mən/ n irlandés m. ~woman n irlandesa f

iron /'aɪən/ n hierro m; (appliance) plancha f. ● a de hierro. ● vt planchar. □ ~ out vt allanar

ironic /aɪ'rɒnɪk/ a irónico. ~ally adv irónicamente

ironing board /'aɪənɪŋ/ n tabla f de planchar, burro m de planchar (Mex)

iron: ~monger /-mʌŋgə(r)/ n ferretero m. ~monger's n ferretería f

irony /'aɪərənɪ/ n ironía f

irrational /ɪ'ræʃənl/ a irracional

irrefutable /ɪrɪ'fjuːtəbl/ a irrefutable

irregular /ɪ'regjʊlə(r)/ a irregular. ~ity /-'lærətɪ/ n irregularidad f

irrelevan|ce /ɪ'reləvəns/ n irrelevancia f. ~t a irrelevante

irreparable /ɪ'repərəbl/ a irreparable

irreplaceable /ɪrɪ'pleɪsəbl/ a irreemplazable

irresistible /ɪrɪ'zɪstəbl/ a irresistible

irrespective /ɪrɪ'spektɪv/ a. ~ of sin tomar en cuenta

irresponsible /ɪrɪ'spɒnsəbl/ a irresponsable

irretrievable /ɪrɪ'triːvəbl/ a irrecuperable

irreverent /ɪ'revərənt/ a irreverente

irrevocable /ɪ'revəkəbl/ a irrevocable

irrigat|e /'ɪrɪgeɪt/ vt regar, irrigar. ~ion /-'geɪʃn/ n riego m, irrigación f

irritable /'ɪrɪtəbl/ a irritable

irritat|e /'ɪrɪteɪt/ vt irritar. ~ed a <expression> de impaciencia; <skin> irritado. be ~ed with estar irritado con. ~ing a irritante. ~ion /-'teɪʃn/ n irritación f

IRS abbr (Amer) ⇒INTERNAL REVENUE SERVICE

is /ɪz/ ⇒BE

Islam /'ɪzlɑːm/ n el Islam. ~ic /ɪz'læmɪk/ a islámico

island /'aɪlənd/ n isla f. ~er n isleño m

isolat|e /'aɪsəleɪt/ vt aislar. ~ion /-'leɪʃn/ n aislamiento m

Israel /'ɪzreɪl/ n Israel m. ~i /ɪz'reɪlɪ/ a & n israelí (m)

issue /'ɪʃuː/ n tema m, asunto m; (of magazine etc) número m; (of stamps, bank notes) emisión f; (of documents) expedición f. take ~ with discrepar de. ● vt hacer público <statement>; expedir <documents>; emitir <stamps etc>; prestar <library book>

it /ɪt/

● pronoun

····► (as subject) generally not translated. **it's huge** es enorme. **where is** it? ¿dónde está? **it's all lies** son todas mentiras

····▶ (as direct object) lo (*m*), la (*f*). **he read it to me** me lo/la leyó. **give it to me** dámelo/dámela

····▶ (as indirect object) le. **I gave it another coat of paint** le di otra mano de pintura

····▶ (after a preposition) *generally not translated*. **there's nothing behind it** no hay nada detrás

! Note, however, that in some cases *él* or *ella* must be used e.g. **he picked up the spoon and hit me with it** *agarró la cuchara y me golpeó con ella*

····▶ (at door) **who is it?** ¿quién es?. **it's me** soy yo; (on telephone) **who is it, please?** ¿quién habla, por favor?; (before passing on to sb else) ¿de parte de quién, por favor? **it's Carol** soy Carol (Spain), habla Carol

····▶ (in impersonal constructions) **it is well known that ...** bien se sabe que ... **it's five o'clock** son las cinco. **so it seems** así parece

····▶ **that's it** (that's right) eso es; (that's enough, that's finished) ya está

Italian /ɪˈtæljən/ *a & n* italiano (*m*)

italics /ɪˈtælɪks/ *npl* (letra *f*) cursiva *f*

Italy /ˈɪtəlɪ/ *n* Italia *f*

itch /ɪtʃ/ *n* picazón *f*. ●*vi* picar. **I'm ~ing to** estoy que me muero por. **my arm ~es** me pica el brazo. **~y** *a* que pica. **I've got an ~y nose** me pica la nariz

it'd /ɪtəd/ = **it had**, **it would**

item /ˈaɪtəm/ *n* artículo *m*; (on agenda) punto *m*. **news ~** *n* noticia *f*. **~ize** *vt* detallar

itinerary /aɪˈtɪnərərɪ/ *n* itinerario *m*

it'll /ˈɪtl/ = **it will**

its /ɪts/ *a* su, sus (*pl*). ●*pron* (el) suyo *m*, (la) suya *f*, (los) suyos *mpl*, (las) suyas *fpl*

it's /ɪts/ = **it is**, **it has**

itself /ɪtˈself/ *pron* él mismo, ella misma, ello mismo; (*reflexive*) se; (*after prep*) sí mismo, sí misma

I've /aɪv/ = **I have**

ivory /ˈaɪvərɪ/ *n* marfil *m*. **~ tower** *n* torre *f* de marfil

ivy /ˈaɪvɪ/ *n* hiedra *f*

Jj

jab /dʒæb/ *vt* (*pt* **jabbed**) pinchar; (thrust) hurgonear. ●*n* pinchazo *m*

jack /dʒæk/ *n* (Mec) gato *m*; (socket) enchufe *m* hembra; (Cards) sota *f*. □ **~ up** *vt* alzar con gato

jackal /ˈdʒækl/ *n* chacal *m*

jackdaw /ˈdʒækdɔː/ *n* grajilla *f*

jacket /ˈdʒækɪt/ *n* chaqueta *f*; (casual) americana *f*, saco *m* (LAm); (Amer, of book) sobrecubierta *f*; (of record) funda *f*, carátula *f*

jack: ~ knife *vi* <lorry> plegarse. **~pot** *n* premio *m* gordo. **hit the ~pot** sacar el premio gordo

jade /dʒeɪd/ *n* (stone) jade *m*

jagged /ˈdʒægɪd/ *a* <edge, cut> irregular; <rock> recortado

jaguar /ˈdʒægjʊə(r)/ *n* jaguar *m*

jail /dʒeɪl/ *n* cárcel *m*, prisión *f*. ●*vt* encarcelar. **~er** *n* carcelero *m*. **~house** *n* (Amer) cárcel *f*

jam /dʒæm/ *vt* (*pt* **jammed**) interferir con <radio>; atestar <road>. **~ sth into sth** meter algo a la fuerza en algo. ●*vi* <brakes> bloquearse; <machine> trancarse. ●*n* mermelada *f*; (Ⓘ, situation) apuro *m*

jangle /ˈdʒæŋgl/ *n* sonido *m* metálico (y áspero). ●*vi* hacer ruido (metálico)

janitor /ˈdʒænɪtə(r)/ *n* portero *m*

January /ˈdʒænjʊərɪ/ *n* enero *m*

Japan /dʒəˈpæn/ *n* (el) Japón *m*. **~ese** /dʒæpəˈniːz/ *a & n invar* japonés (*m*)

jar /dʒɑː(r)/ *n* tarro *m*, bote *m*. ●*vi* (*pt* **jarred**) <clash> desentonar. ●*vt* sacudir

jargon /ˈdʒɑːgən/ *n* jerga *f*

jaundice /ˈdʒɔːndɪs/ *n* ictericia *f*

jaunt /dʒɔːnt/ n excursión f

jaunty /'dʒɔːntɪ/ a (-ier, -iest) garboso

jaw /dʒɔː/ n mandíbula f. ~s npl fauces fpl. ~bone n mandíbula f, maxilar m; (of animal) quijada f

jay /dʒeɪ/ n arrendajo m. ~walk vi cruzar la calle descuidadamente. ~walker n peatón m imprudente

jazz /dʒæz/ n jazz m. □ ~ up vt animar. ~y a chillón

jealous /'dʒeləs/ a celoso; (envious) envidioso. ~y n celos mpl

jeans /dʒiːnz/ npl vaqueros mpl, jeans mpl, tejanos mpl, pantalones mpl de mezclilla (Mex)

Jeep (P), **jeep** /dʒiːp/ n Jeep m (P)

jeer /dʒɪə(r)/ vi. ~ at mofarse de; (boo) abuchear. ● n burla f; (boo) abucheo m

Jell-O /'dʒeləʊ/ n (P) (Amer) gelatina f (con sabor a frutas)

jelly /'dʒelɪ/ n (clear jam) jalea f; (pudding) ⇒JELL-O; (substance) gelatina f. ~fish n (pl invar or -es) medusa f

jeopardize /'dʒepədaɪz/ vt arriesgar

jerk /dʒɜːk/ n sacudida f; (▣, fool) idiota m & f. ● vt sacudir

jersey /'dʒɜːzɪ/ n (pl -eys) jersey m, suéter m, pulóver m

jest /dʒest/ n broma f. ● vi bromear

Jesus /'dʒiːzəs/ n Jesús m

jet /dʒet/ n (stream) chorro m; (plane) avión m (con motor a reacción); (mineral) azabache m. ~-black /-'blæk/ a azabache negro a invar. ~ lag n jet lag m, desfase f horario. have ~ lag estar desfasado. ~-propelled /-prə'peld/ a (de propulsión) a reacción

jettison /'dʒetɪsn/ vt echar al mar; (fig, discard) deshacerse de

jetty /'dʒetɪ/ n muelle m

Jew /dʒuː/ n judío m

jewel /'dʒuːəl/ n joya f. ~ler n joyero m. ~lery n joyas fpl

Jewish /'dʒuːɪʃ/ a judío

jiffy /'dʒɪfɪ/ n momentito m. do sth in a ~ hacer algo en un santiamén

jig /dʒɪg/ n (dance) giga f

jigsaw /'dʒɪgsɔː/ n. ~ (puzzle) rompecabezas m

jilt /dʒɪlt/ vt dejar plantado

jingle /'dʒɪŋgl/ vt hacer sonar. ● vi tintinear. ● n tintineo m; (advert) jingle m (publicitario)

job /dʒɒb/ n empleo m, trabajo m; (piece of work) trabajo m. it is a good ~ that menos mal que. ~less a desempleado

jockey /'dʒɒkɪ/ n jockey m

jocular /'dʒɒkjʊlə(r)/ a jocoso

jog /dʒɒg/ vt (pt jogged) empujar; refrescar <memory>. ● vi hacer footing, hacer jogging. ~er n persona f que hace footing. ~ging n footing m, jogging m. go ~ging salir a hacer footing or jogging

join /dʒɔɪn/ vt (link) unir; hacerse socio de <club>; hacerse miembro de <political group>; alistarse en <army>; reunirse con <another person>. ● n juntura f. ● vi. ~ together <parts> unirse; <roads etc> empalmar; <rivers> confluir. □ ~ in vi participar (en). □ ~ up vi (Mil) alistarse. ~er n carpintero m

joint /dʒɔɪnt/ a conjunto. ● n (join) unión f, junta f; (Anat) articulación f. (Culin) trozo m de carne (para asar). out of ~ descoyuntado. ~ account n cuenta f conjunta. ~ly adv conjuntamente. ~ owner n copropietario m.

joist /dʒɔɪst/ n viga f

jok|e /dʒəʊk/ n (story) chiste m; (practical joke) broma f. ● vi bromear. ~er n bromista m & f; (Cards) comodín m. ~y a jocoso

jolly /'dʒɒlɪ/ a (-ier, -iest) alegre. ● adv 🄴 muy

jolt /dʒɒlt/ vt sacudir. ● vi <vehicle> dar una sacudida. ● n sacudida f

jostle /'dʒɒsl/ vt empujar. ● vi empujarse

jot /dʒɒt/ n pizca f. ● vt (pt jotted). □ ~ down vt apuntar (rápidamente). ~ter n bloc m

journal /'dʒɜːnl/ n (diary) diario m; (newspaper) periódico m; (magazine) revista f. ~ism n periodismo m. ~ist n periodista m & f

journey /'dʒɜːnɪ/ *n* viaje *m*. **go on a** ~ hacer un viaje. ● *vi* viajar

jovial /'dʒəʊvɪəl/ *a* jovial

joy /dʒɔɪ/ *n* alegría *f*. ~**ful** *a* feliz. ~**ous** *a* feliz. ~**rider** *n* joven *m* que roba un coche para dar una vuelta. ~**stick** *n* (Aviat) palanca *f* de mando; (Comp) mando *m*, joystick *m*

jubila|nt /'dʒuːbɪlənt/ *a* jubiloso. ~**tion** /-'leɪʃn/ *n* júbilo *m*

jubilee /'dʒuːbɪliː/ *n* aniversario *m* especial

Judaism /'dʒuːdeɪɪzəm/ *n* judaísmo *m*

judge /dʒʌdʒ/ *n* juez *m*. ● *vt* juzgar. ~**ment** *n* juicio *m*

judicia|l /dʒuː'dɪʃl/ *a* judicial. ~**ry** /-ərɪ/ *n* judicatura *f*

judo /'dʒuːdəʊ/ *n* judo *m*

jug /dʒʌg/ *n* jarra *f*

juggernaut /'dʒʌgənɔːt/ *n* camión *m* grande

juggle /'dʒʌgl/ *vi* hacer malabarismos. ● *vt* hacer malabarismos con. ~**r** *n* malabarista *m* & *f*

juic|e /dʒuːs/ *n* jugo *m*, zumo *m*. ~**y** *a* jugoso, zumoso; <*story etc*> ▣ pi-cante

jukebox /'dʒuːkbɒks/ *n* máquina *f* de discos, rocola *f* (LAm)

July /dʒuː'laɪ/ *n* julio *m*

jumble /'dʒʌmbl/ *vt*. ~ **(up)** mezclar. ● *n* (muddle) revoltijo *m*. ~ **sale** *n* venta *f* de objetos usados *m*

jumbo /'dʒʌmbəʊ/ *a* gigante. ~ **jet** *n* jumbo *m*

jump /dʒʌmp/ *vt* saltar. ~ **rope** (Amer) saltar a la comba, saltar a la cuerda. ~ **the gun** obrar prematuramente. ~ **the queue** colarse. ● *vi* saltar; (start) sobresaltarse; <*prices*> alzarse. ~ **at an opportunity** apresurarse a aprovechar una oportunidad. ● *n* salto *m*; (start) susto *m*; (increase) aumento *m*. ~**er** *n* jersey *m*, suéter *m*, pulóver *m*; (Amer, dress) pichi *m*, jumper *m* & *f* (LAm). ~**er cables** (Amer), ~ **leads** *npl* cables *mpl* de arranque. ~ **rope** (Amer) comba *f*, cuerda *f*, reata *f* (Mex). ~**suit** *n* mono *m*. ~**y** *a* nervioso

junction /'dʒʌŋkʃn/ *n* (of roads, rails) cruce *m*; (Elec) empalme *m*

June /dʒuːn/ *n* junio *m*

jungle /'dʒʌŋgl/ *n* selva *f*, jungla *f*

junior /'dʒuːnɪə(r)/ *a* (in age) más joven (**to** que); (in rank) subalterno. ● *n* menor *m*

junk /dʒʌŋk/ *n* trastos *mpl* viejos; (worthless stuff) basura *f*. ● *vt* ▣ tirar. ~ **food** *n* comida *f* basura, alimento *m* chatarra (Mex). ~**ie** /'dʒʌŋkɪ/ *n* ▣ drogadicto *m*, yonqui *m* & *f* ▣. ~ **mail** *n* propaganda *f* que se recibe por correo. ~ **shop** *n* tienda *f* de trastos viejos

junta /'dʒʌntə/ *n* junta *f* militar

Jupiter /'dʒuːpɪtə(r)/ *n* Júpiter *m*

jurisdiction /dʒʊərɪs'dɪkʃn/ *n* jurisdicción *f*

jur|or /'dʒʊərə(r)/ *n* (miembro *m* de un) jurado *m*. ~**y** *n* jurado *m*

just /dʒʌst/ *a* (fair) justo. ● *adv* exactamente, justo; (barely) justo; (only) sólo, solamente. ~ **as tall** tan alto (**as** como). ~ **listen!** ¡escucha! **he has** ~ **arrived** acaba de llegar, recién llegó (LAm)

justice /'dʒʌstɪs/ *n* justicia *f*. **J**~ **of the Peace** juez *m* de paz

justif|iable /dʒʌstɪ'faɪəbl/ *a* justificable. ~**iably** *adv* con razón. ~**ication** /dʒʌstɪfɪ'keɪʃn/ *n* justi-ficación *f*. ~**y** /'dʒʌstɪfaɪ/ *vt* justi-ficar

jut /dʒʌt/ *vi* (*pt* **jutted**). ~ **(out)** sobresalir

juvenile /'dʒuːvənaɪl/ *a* juvenil; (childish) infantil. ● *n* (Jurid) menor *m* & *f*

Kk

kaleidoscope /kə'laɪdəskəʊp/ *n* caleidoscopio *m*

kangaroo /kæŋgə'ruː/ *n* canguro *m*

karate /kə'rɑːtɪ/ *n* kárate *m*, karate *m* (LAm)

keel /kiːl/ *n* (of ship) quilla *f*. □ ~ **over** *vi* volcar(se)

keen /kiːn/ *a* (**-er, -est**) <*interest, feeling*> vivo; <*wind, mind, analysis*> penetrante; <*eyesight*> agudo; (eager) entusiasta. **I'm ~ on golf** me encanta el golf. **he's ~ on Shostakovich** le gusta Shostakovich. **~ly** *adv* vivamente; (enthusiastically) con entusiasmo. **~ness** *n* intensidad *f*; (enthusiasm) entusiasmo *m*.

keep /kiːp/ *vt* (*pt* **kept**) guardar; cumplir *<promise>*; tener *<shop, animals>*; mantener *<family>*; observar *<rule>*; (celebrate) celebrar; (delay) detener; (prevent) impedir. ● *vi <food>* conservarse; (remain) quedarse; (continue) seguir. ~ **doing** seguir haciendo. ● *n* subsistencia *f*; (of castle) torreón *m*. **for ~s** 🄴 para siempre. ☐ ~ **back** *vt* retener. ● *vi* no acercarse. ☐ ~ **in** *vt* no dejar salir. ☐ ~ **off** *vt* mantenerse alejado de *<land>*. **'~ off the grass'** 'prohibido pisar el césped'. ☐ ~ **on** *vi* seguir. ~ **on doing sth** seguir haciendo. ☐ ~ **out** *vt* no dejar entrar. ☐ ~ **up** *vt* mantener. ☐ ~ **up with** *vt* estar al día en

kennel /'kenl/ *n* casa *f* del perro; (Amer, for boarding) residencia *f* canina. **~s** *n invar* residencia *f* canina

kept /kept/ ⇒KEEP

kerb /kɜːb/ *n* bordillo *m* (de la acera), borde *m* de la banqueta (Mex)

kerosene /'kerəsiːn/ *n* queroseno *m*

ketchup /'ketʃʌp/ *n* salsa *f* de tomate

kettle /'ketl/ *n* pava *f*, tetera *f* (para calentar agua)

key /kiː/ *n* llave *f*; (of computer, piano) tecla *f*; (Mus) tono *m*. **be off ~** no estar en el tono. ● *a* clave. ☐ ~ **in** *vt* teclear. **~board** *n* teclado *m*. **~hole** *n* ojo *m* de la cerradura. **~ring** *n* llavero *m*

khaki /'kɑːkɪ/ *a* caqui

kick /kɪk/ *vt* dar una patada a *<person>*; patear *<ball>*. ● *vi* dar patadas; *<horse>* cocear. ● *n* patada *f*; (of horse) coz *f*; (🄴, thrill) placer *m*. ☐ ~ **out** *vt* 🄴 echar. ☐ ~ **up** *vt* armar *<fuss etc>*. **~off** *n* (Sport) saque *m* inicial. ~ **start** *vt* arrancar (con el pedal de arranque) *<engine>*

kid /kɪd/ *n* (young goat) cabrito *m*; (🄴, child) niño *m*, chaval *m*, escuincle *m* (Mex). ● *vt* (*pt* **kidded**) tomar el pelo a. ● *vi* bromear

kidnap /'kɪdnæp/ *vt* (*pt* **kidnapped**) secuestrar. **~per** *n* secuestrador *m*. **~ping** *n* secuestro *m*

kidney /'kɪdnɪ/ *n* riñón *m*

kill /kɪl/ *vt* matar; (fig) acabar con. ● *n* matanza *f*. ☐ ~ **off** *vt* matar. **~er** *n* asesino *m*. **~ing** *n* matanza *f*; (murder) asesinato *m*. **make a ~ing** (fig) hacer un gran negocio

kiln /kɪln/ *n* horno *m*

kilo /'kiːləʊ/ *n* (*pl* **-os**) kilo *m*. **~gram(me)** /'kɪləgræm/ *n* kilogramo *m*. **~metre** /'kɪləmiːtə(r)/, /kɪ'lɒmɪtə(r)/ *n* kilómetro *m*. **~watt** /'kɪləwɒt/ *n* kilovatio *m*

kilt /kɪlt/ *n* falda *f* escocesa

kin /kɪn/ *n* familiares *mpl*

kind /kaɪnd/ *n* tipo *m*, clase *f*. ~ **of** (🄴, somewhat) un poco. **in ~** en especie. **be two of a ~** ser tal para cual. ● *a* amable

kindergarten /'kɪndəɡɑːtn/ *n* jardín *m* de infancia

kind-hearted /kaɪnd'hɑːtɪd/ *a* bondadoso

kindle /'kɪndl/ *vt* encender

kind|ly *a* (**-ier, -iest**) bondadoso. ● *adv* amablemente; (please) haga el favor de. **~ness** *n* bondad *f*; (act) favor *m*

king /kɪŋ/ *n* rey *m*. **~dom** *n* reino *m*. **~fisher** *n* martín *m* pescador. **~-size(d)** *a* extragrande

kink /kɪŋk/ *n* (in rope) vuelta *f*, curva *f*; (in hair) onda *f*. **~y** *a* 🄴 pervertido

kiosk /'kiːɒsk/ *n* quiosco *m*

kipper /'kɪpə(r)/ *n* arenque *m* ahumado

kiss /kɪs/ *n* beso *m*. ● *vt* besar. ● *vi* besarse

kit /kɪt/ *n* avíos *mpl*. **tool ~** caja *f* de herramientas. ☐ ~ **out** *vt* (*pt* **kitted**) equipar

kitchen /'kɪtʃɪn/ *n* cocina *f*

kite /kaɪt/ *n* cometa *f*, papalote *m* (Mex)

kitten /'kɪtn/ *n* gatito *m*

knack /næk/ *n* truco *m*

knapsack /'næpsæk/ *n* mochila *f*

knead /niːd/ *vt* amasar

knee /niː/ *n* rodilla *f*. **~cap** *n* rótula *f*

kneel /niːl/ *vi* (*pt* **kneeled** *or* **knelt**). **~ (down)** arrodillarse; (be on one's knees) estar arrodillado

knelt /nelt/ ⇒KNEEL

knew /njuː/ ⇒KNOW

knickers /'nɪkəz/ *npl* bragas *fpl*, calzones *mpl* (LAm), pantaletas *fpl* (Mex)

knife /naɪf/ *n* (*pl* **knives**) cuchillo *m*. ● *vt* acuchillar

knight /naɪt/ *n* caballero *m*; (Chess) caballo *m*. ● *vt* conceder el título de Sir a. **~hood** *n* título *m* de Sir

knit /nɪt/ *vt* (*pt* **knitted** *or* **knit**) hacer, tejer (LAm). ● *vi* tejer, hacer punto. **~ one's brow** fruncir el ceño. **~ting** *n* tejido *m*, punto *m*. **~ting needle** *n* aguja *f* de hacer punto, aguja *f* de tejer

knives /naɪvz/ ⇒KNIFE

knob /nɒb/ *n* botón *m*; (of door, drawer etc) tirador *m*. **~bly** *a* nudoso

knock /nɒk/ *vt* golpear; (criticize) criticar. ● *vi* golpear; (at door) llamar, golpear (LAm). ● *n* golpe *m*. □ **~ about** *vt* maltratar. □ **~ down** *vt* derribar; atropellar <*person*>. □ **~ off** *vt* hacer caer. *vi* (🔢, finish work) terminar, salir del trabajo. □ **~ out** *vt* (by blow) dejar sin sentido; (eliminate) eliminar. □ **~ over** *vt* tirar; atropellar <*person*>. **~er** *n* aldaba *f*. **~-kneed** /-'niːd/ *a* patizambo. **~out** *n* (Boxing) nocaut *m*

knot /nɒt/ *n* nudo *m*. ● *vt* (*pt* **knotted**) anudar

know /nəʊ/ *vt* (*pt* **knew**) saber; (be acquainted with) conocer. **let s.o. ~ sth** decirle algo a uno; (warn) avisarle algo a uno. ● *vi* saber. **~ how to do sth** saber hacer algo. **~ about** entender de <*cars etc*>. **~ of** saber de. ● *n*. **be in the ~** estar enterado. **~-all** *n* *n* sabelotodo *m* & *f*. **~-how** *n* know-how *m*, conocimientos *mpl* y expe-riencia *m*. **~ingly** *adv* a sabiendas. **~-it-all** (Amer) ⇒~-ALL

knowledge /'nɒlɪdʒ/ *n* saber *m*; (awareness) conocimiento *m*; (learning) conocimientos *mpl*. **~able** *a* informado

known /nəʊn/ ⇒KNOW. ● *a* conocido

knuckle /'nʌkl/ *n* nudillo *m*. □ **~ under** *vi* someterse

Korea /kə'rɪə/ *n* Corea *f*. **~n** *a* & *n* coreano (*m*)

kudos /'kjuːdɒs/ *n* prestigio *m*

Ll

lab /læb/ *n* 🔢 laboratorio *m*

label /'leɪbl/ *n* etiqueta *f*. ● *vt* (*pt* **labelled**) poner etiqueta a; (fig, describe as) tachar de

laboratory /lə'bɒrətərɪ/ *n* laboratorio *m*

laborious /lə'bɔːrɪəs/ *a* penoso

labour /'leɪbə(r)/ *n* trabajo *m*; (workers) mano *f* de obra; (Med) parto *m*. **in ~** de parto. ● *vi* trabajar. ● *vt* insistir en. **L~** *n* el partido *m* laborista. ● *a* laborista. **~er** *n* peón *m*

lace /leɪs/ *n* encaje *m*; (of shoe) cordón *m*, agujeta *f* (Mex). ● *vt* (fasten) atar

lacerate /'læsəreɪt/ *vt* lacerar

lack /læk/ *n* falta *f*. **for ~ of** por falta de. ● *vt* faltarle a uno. **he ~s confidence** le falta confianza en sí mismo. **~ing** *a*. **be ~ing** faltar. **be ~ing in** no tener

lad /læd/ *n* muchacho *m*

ladder /'lædə(r)/ *n* escalera *f* (de mano); (in stocking) carrera *f*. ● *vt* hacerse una carrera en. ● *vi* hacérsele una carrera a

laden /'leɪdn/ *a* cargado (with de)

ladle /'leɪdl/ *n* cucharón *m*

lady /'leɪdɪ/ *n* señora *f*. **young ~** señorita *f*. **~bird** *n*, **~bug** *n* (Amer) mariquita *f*, catarina *f* (Mex). **~-in-waiting** *n* dama *f* de honor. **~like** *a* fino

lag /læg/ *vi* (*pt* **lagged**). **~ (behind)** retrasarse. ● *vt* revestir <*pipes*>. ● *n* (interval) intervalo *m*

lager /'lɑːgə(r)/ *n* cerveza *f* (rubia)

lagging /'lægɪŋ/ *n* revestimiento *m*

lagoon /lə'guːn/ *n* laguna *f*

laid /leɪd/ ⇒LAY

lain /leɪn/ ⇒LIE¹

lair /leə(r)/ n guarida f

lake /leɪk/ n lago m

lamb /læm/ n cordero m

lame /leɪm/ a (-er, -est) cojo, rengo (LAm); <excuse> pobre, malo

lament /lə'ment/ n lamento m. ● vt lamentar. ~able /'læməntəbl/ a lamentable

lamp /læmp/ n lámpara f

lamp: ~post n farol m. ~shade n pantalla f

lance /lɑːns/ n lanza f

land /lænd/ n tierra f; (country) país m; (plot) terreno m. ● vt desembarcar; (obtain) conseguir; dar <blow>. ● vi (from ship) desembarcar; <aircraft> aterrizar. □ ~ up vi ir a parar. ~ing n desembarque m; (Aviat) aterrizaje m; (top of stairs) descanso m. ~lady n casera f; (of inn) dueña f. ~lord n casero m, dueño m; (of inn) dueño m. ~mark n punto m destacado. ~scape /-skeɪp/ n paisaje m. ~slide n desprendimiento m de tierras; (Pol) victoria f arrolladora

lane /leɪn/ n (path, road) camino m, sendero m; (strip of road) carril m

language /'læŋgwɪdʒ/ n idioma m; (speech, style) lenguaje m

lank /læŋk/ a <hair> lacio. ~y a (-ier, -iest) larguirucho

lantern /'læntən/ n linterna f

lap /læp/ n (of body) rodillas fpl; (Sport) vuelta f. ● vi (pt lapped) <waves> chapotear. □ ~up beber a lengüetazos; (fig) aceptar con entusiasmo

lapel /lə'pel/ n solapa f

lapse /læps/ vi (decline) degradarse; (expire) caducar; <time> transcurrir. ~ into silence callarse. ● n error m; (of time) intervalo m

laptop /'læptɒp/ n. ~ (computer) laptop m, laptop f (LAm)

lard /lɑːd/ n manteca f de cerdo

larder /'lɑːdə(r)/ n despensa f

large /lɑːdʒ/ a (-er, -est) grande, (before singular noun) gran. ● n. at ~ en libertad. ~ly adv en gran parte

lark /lɑːk/ n (bird) alondra f; (joke) broma f; (bit of fun) travesura f. □ ~ about vt hacer el tonto ⊡

larva /'lɑːvə/ n (pl -vae /-viː/) larva f

laser /'leɪzə(r)/ n láser m. ~ beam n rayo m láser. ~ printer n impresora f láser

lash /læʃ/ vt azotar. □ ~ out vi atacar. ~ out against vt atacar. ● n latigazo m; (eyelash) pestaña f; (whip) látigo m

lashings /'læʃɪŋz/ npl. ~ of (⊠, cream etc) montones de

lass /læs/ n muchacha f

lasso /læ'suː/ n (pl -os) lazo m

last /lɑːst/ a último; <week etc> pasado. ~ Monday el lunes pasado. ~ night anoche. ● adv por último; (most recently) la última vez. he came ~ llegó el último. ● n último m; (remainder) lo que queda. ~ but one penúltimo. at (long) ~ por fin. ● vi/t durar. □ ~ out vi·sobrevivir. ~ing a duradero. ~ly adv por último

latch /lætʃ/ n pestillo m

late /leɪt/ a (-er, -est) (not on time) tarde; (recent) reciente; (former) antiguo, ex. be ~ llegar tarde. in ~ July a fines de julio. the ~ Dr Phillips el difunto Dr. Phillips. ● adv tarde. ~ly adv últimamente

latent /'leɪtnt/ a latente

later /'leɪtə(r)/ adv más tarde

lateral /'lætərəl/ a lateral

latest /'leɪtɪst/ a último. ● n. at the ~ a más tardar

lathe /leɪð/ n torno m

lather /'lɑːðə(r)/ n espuma f

Latin /'lætɪn/ n (Lang) latín m. ● a latino. ~ America n América f Latina, Latinoamérica f. ~ American a & n latinoamericano f

latitude /'lætɪtjuːd/ n latitud m

latter /'lætə(r)/ a último; (of two) segundo. ● n. the ~ éste m, ésta f, éstos mpl, éstas fpl

laugh /lɑːf/ vi reír(se). ~ at reírse de. ● n risa f. ~able a ridículo. ~ing stock n hazmerreír m. ~ter n risas fpl

launch /lɔːntʃ/ vt lanzar; botar <new vessel>. ● n lanzamiento m; (of new vessel) botadura; (boat) lancha f (a motor). ~ing pad, ~ pad n plataforma f de lanzamiento

laund|er /'lɔːndə(r)/ vt lavar (y planchar). **~erette** /-et/, **L~romat** /'lɔːndrəmæt/ (Amer) (P) n lavandería f automática. **~ry** n (place) lavandería f; (dirty clothes) ropa f sucia; (clean clothes) ropa f limpia

lava /'lɑːvə/ n lava f

lavatory /'lævətərɪ/ n (cuarto m de) baño m. **public ~** servicios mpl, baños mpl (LAm)

lavish /'lævɪʃ/ a <lifestyle> de derroche; (meal) espléndido; (production) fastuoso. ● vt prodigar (**on** a)

law /lɔː/ n ley f; (profession, subject of study) derecho m. **~ and order** n orden m público. **~ court** n tribunal m

lawn /lɔːn/ n césped m, pasto m (LAm). **~mower** n cortacésped f, cortadora f de pasto (LAm)

lawsuit /'lɔːsuːt/ n juicio m

lawyer /'lɔjə(r)/ n abogado m

lax /læks/ a descuidado; <morals etc> laxo

laxative /'læksətɪv/ n laxante m

lay /leɪ/ ⇒LIE. ● vt (pt **laid**) poner <also table, eggs>; tender <trap>; formar <plan>. **~ hands on** echar mano a. **~ hold of** agarrar. ● a (non-clerical) laico; <opinion etc> profano. □ **~ down** vt dejar a un lado; imponer <condition>. □ **~ into** vt ✗ dar una paliza a. □ **~ off** vt despedir <worker>. vi 🅸 terminar. □ **~ on** vt (provide) proveer. □ **~ out** vt (design) disponer; (display) exponer; gastar <money>. **~about** n holgazán m. **~-by** n área f de reposo

layer /'leɪə(r)/ n capa f

layette /leɪˈet/ n canastilla f

layman /'leɪmən/ n (pl **-men**) lego m

layout /'leɪaʊt/ n disposición f

laz|e /leɪz/ vi holgazanear; (relax) descansar. **~iness** n pereza f. **~y** a perezoso. **~ybones** n holgazán m

lead¹ /liːd/ vt (pt **led**) conducir; dirigir <team>; llevar <life>; encabezar <parade, attack>. **I was led to believe that ...** me dieron a entender que .... ● vi (go first) ir delante; (in race) aventajar. ● n mando m; (clue) pista

f; (leash) correa f; (wire) cable m. **be in the ~** llevar la delantera

lead² /led/ n plomo m; (of pencil) mina f. **~ed** a <fuel> con plomo

lead /liːd/ **~er** n jefe m; (Pol) líder m & f; (of gang) cabecilla m. **~ership** n dirección f. **~ing** a principal; (in front) delantero

leaf /liːf/ n (pl **leaves**) hoja f. □ **~ through** vi hojear. **~let** /'liːflɪt/ n folleto m. **~y** a frondoso

league /liːg/ n liga f. **be in ~ with** estar aliado con

leak /liːk/ n (hole) agujero m; (of gas, liquid) escape m; (of information) filtración f; (in roof) gotera f; (in boat) vía f de agua. ● vi gotear; <liquid> salirse; <boat> hacer agua. ● vt perder; filtrar <information>. **~y** a <receptacle> agujereado; <roof> que tiene goteras

lean /liːn/ (pt **leaned** or **leant** /lent/) vt apoyar. ● vi inclinarse. □ **~ against** vt apoyarse en. □ **~ on** vt apoyarse en. □ **~ out** vt asomarse (**of** a). □ **~ over** vi inclinarse. ● a (**-er, -est**) <person> delga-do; <animal> flaco; <meat> magro. **~ing** a inclinado. **~-to** n colgadizo m

leap /liːp/ vi (pt **leaped** or **leapt** /lept/) saltar. ● n salto m. **~frog** n. **play ~frog** saltar al potro, jugar a la pídola, brincar al burro (Mex). ● vi (pt **-frogged**) saltar. **~ year** n año m bisiesto

learn /lɜːn/ vt/i (pt **learned** or **learnt**) aprender (**to do** a hacer). **~ed** /-ɪd/ a culto. **~er** n principiante m & f; (apprentice) aprendiz m. **~ing** n saber m

lease /liːs/ n arriendo m. ● vt arrendar

leash /liːʃ/ n correa f

least /liːst/ a (smallest amount of) mínimo; (slightest) menor; (smallest) más pequeño. ● n. **the ~** lo menos. **at ~** por lo menos. **not in the ~** en absoluto. ● adv menos

leather /'leðə(r)/ n piel f, cuero m.

leave /liːv/ vt (pt **left**) dejar; (depart from) salir de. **~ alone** dejar de tocar <thing>; dejar en paz <person>. ● vi marcharse; <train> salir. ● n permiso m. □ **~ behind** vt dejar. □ **~ out**

vt omitir. □ ~ **over** *vt.* be left over quedar. **on** ~ (Mil) de permiso

leaves /li:vz/ ⇒LEAF

lecture /'lektʃə(r)/ *n* conferencia *f*; (Univ) clase *f*; (rebuke) sermón *m*. ● *vi* dar clase. ● *vt* (scold) sermonear. ~**r** *n* conferenciante *m & f*, conferencista *m & f* (LAm); (Univ) profesor *m* universitario

led /led/ ⇒LEAD[1]

ledge /ledʒ/ *n* cornisa *f*; (of window) alféizar *m*

leek /li:k/ *n* puerro *m*

leer /'lɪə(r)/ *vi.* ~ **at** mirar impúdicamente. ● *n* mirada impúdica *f*

left /left/ ⇒LEAVE. *a* izquierdo. ● *adv* a la izquierda. ● *n* izquierda *f*. ~-**handed** /-'hændɪd/ *a* zurdo. ~ **luggage** *n* consigna *f*. ~**overs** *npl* restos *mpl*. ~-**wing** /-'wɪŋ/ *a* izquierdista

leg /leg/ *n* pierna *f*; (of animal, furniture) pata *f*; (of pork) pernil *m*; (of lamb) pierna *f*; (of journey) etapa *f*. **on its last** ~**s** en las últimas. **pull s.o.'s** ~ 🔲 tomarle el pelo a uno

legacy /'legəsɪ/ *n* herencia *f*

legal /'li:gl/ *a* (permitted by law) lícito; (recognized by law) legítimo; <*system etc*> jurídico. ~**ity** /li:'gælətɪ/ *n* legalidad *f*. ~**ize** *vt* legalizar. ~**ly** *adv* legalmente

legend /'ledʒənd/ *n* leyenda *f*. ~**ary** *a* legendario

legible /'ledʒəbl/ *a* legible

legislat|e /'ledʒɪsleɪt/ *vi* legislar. ~**ion** /-'leɪʃn/ *n* legislación *f*

legitimate /lɪ'dʒɪtɪmət/ *a* legítimo

leisure /'leʒə(r)/ *n* ocio *m*. **at your** ~ cuando le venga bien. ~**ly** *a* lento, pausado

lemon /'lemən/ *n* limón *m*. ~**ade** /-'neɪd/ *n* (fizzy) gaseosa *f* (de limón); (still) limonada *f*

lend /lend/ *vt* (*pt* **lent**) prestar. ~**ing** *n* préstamo *m*

length /leŋθ/ *n* largo *m*; (of time) duración *f*; (of cloth) largo *m*. **at** ~ (at last) por fin. **at** (**great**) ~ detalladamente. ~**en** /'leŋθən/ *vt* alargar. ● *vi* alargarse. ~**ways** *adv* a lo largo. ~**y** *a* largo

lenient /'li:nɪənt/ *a* indulgente

lens /lens/ *n* lente *f*; (of camera) objetivo *m*. (**contact**) ~**es** *npl* lentillas *fpl*, lentes *mpl* de contacto (LAm)

lent /lent/ ⇒LEND

Lent /lent/ *n* cuaresma *f*

Leo /'li:əʊ/ *n* Leo *m*

leopard /'lepəd/ *n* leopardo *m*

leotard /'li:əta:d/ *n* malla *f*

lesbian /'lezbɪən/ *n* lesbiana *f*. ● *a* lesbiano

less /les/ *a & n & adv & prep* menos. ~ **than** menos que; (with numbers) menos de. ~ **and** ~ cada vez menos. **none the** ~ sin embargo. ~**en** *vt/i* disminuir

lesson /'lesn/ *n* clase *f*

lest /lest/ *conj* no sea que (+ *subjunctive*)

let /let/ *vt* (*pt* **let**, *pres p* **letting**) dejar; (lease) alquilar. ~ **me do it** déjame hacerlo. ● *v aux.* ~'**s go!** ¡vamos!, ¡vámonos! ~'**s see** (vamos) a ver. ~'**s talk/drink** hablemos/bebamos. □ ~ **down** *vt* bajar; (deflate) desinflar; (fig) defraudar. □ ~ **go** *vt* soltar. □ ~ **in** *vt* dejar entrar. □ ~ **off** *vt* disparar <*gun*>; (cause to explode) hacer explotar; hacer estallar <*firework*>; (excuse) perdonar. □ ~ **out** *vt* dejar salir. □ ~ **through** *vt* dejar pasar. □ ~ **up** *vi* disminuir. ~**down** *n* desilusión *f*

lethal /'li:θl/ *a* <*dose, wound*> mortal; <*weapon*> mortífero

letharg|ic /lɪ'θa:dʒɪk/ *a* letárgico. ~**y** /'leθədʒɪ/ *n* letargo *m*

letter /'letə(r)/ *n* (of alphabet) letra *f*; (written message) carta *f*. ~ **bomb** *n* carta *f* bomba. ~**box** *n* buzón *m*. ~**ing** *n* letras *fpl*

lettuce /'letɪs/ *n* lechuga *f*

let-up /'letʌp/ *n* interrupción *f*

leukaemia /lu:'ki:mɪə/ *n* leucemia *f*

level /'levl/ *a* (flat, even) plano, parejo (LAm); <*spoonful*> raso. ~ **with** (at same height) al nivel de. ● *n* nivel *m*. ● *vt* (*pt* **levelled**) nivelar; (aim) apuntar. ~ **crossing** *n* paso *m* a nivel, crucero *m* (Mex)

lever /'li:və(r)/ *n* palanca *f*. ● *vt* apalancar. ~ **open** abrir haciendo palanca. ~**age** /-ɪdʒ/ *n* apalancamiento *m*

levy /'levɪ/ *vt* imponer <*tax*>. ● *n* impuesto *m*

lewd /luːd/ *a* (**-er, -est**) lascivo

liab|ility /laɪəˈbɪlətɪ/ *n* responsabilidad *f*; (回, disadvantage) lastre *m*. ∼**ities** *npl* (debts) deudas *fpl*. ∼**le** /'laɪəbl/ *a*. **be** ∼**le to do** tener tendencia a hacer. ∼**le for** responsable de. ∼**le to** susceptible de; expuesto a <*fine*>

liais|e /lɪˈeɪz/ *vi* actuar de enlace (with con). ∼**on** /-ɒn/ *n* enlace *m*

liar /'laɪə(r)/ *n* mentiroso *m*

libel /'laɪbl/ *n* difamación *f*. ● *vt* (*pt* **libelled**) difamar (por escrito)

liberal /'lɪbərəl/ *a* liberal; (generous) generoso. **L∼** (Pol) del Partido Liberal. ● *n* liberal *m & f*. ∼**ly** *adv* liberalmente; (generously) generosamente

liberat|e /'lɪbəreɪt/ *vt* liberar. ∼**ion** /-'reɪʃn/ *n* liberación *f*

liberty /'lɪbətɪ/ *n* libertad *f*. **take liberties** tomarse libertades. **take the** ∼ **of** tomarse la libertad de

Libra /'liːbrə/ *n* Libra *f*

librar|ian /laɪˈbreərɪən/ *n* bibliotecario *m*. ∼**y** /'laɪbrərɪ/ *n* biblioteca *f*

lice /laɪs/ ⇒LOUSE

licence /'laɪsns/ *n* licencia *f*, permiso *m*

license /'laɪsns/ *vt* autorizar. ● *n* (Amer) ⇒LICENCE. ∼ **number** *n* (Amer) (número *m* de) matrícula *f*. ∼ **plate** *n* (Amer) matrícula *f*, placa *f* (LAm)

lick /lɪk/ *vt* lamer; (回, defeat) dar una paliza a. ● *n* lametón *m*

licorice /'lɪkərɪs/ *n* (Amer) regaliz *m*

lid /lɪd/ *n* tapa *f*; (eyelid) párpado *m*

lie[1] /laɪ/ *vi* (*pt* **lay**, *pp* **lain**, *pres p* **lying**) echarse, tenderse; (be in lying position) estar tendido; (be) estar, encontrarse. ∼ **low** quedarse escondido. ◻∼ **down** *vi* echarse, tenderse

lie[2] /laɪ/ *n* mentira *f*. ● *vi* (*pt* **lied**, *pres p* **lying**) mentir

lie-in /laɪ'ɪn/ *n*. **have a** ∼ quedarse en la cama

lieutenant /lefˈtenənt/ *n* (Mil) teniente *m*

life /laɪf/ *n* (*pl* **lives**) vida *f*. ∼ **belt** *n* salvavidas *m*. ∼**boat** *n* lancha *f* de salvamento; (on ship) bote *m* salvavidas. ∼**buoy** *n* boya *f* salvavidas. ∼**guard** *n* salvavidas *m & f*. ∼ **jacket** *n* chaleco *m* salvavidas. ∼**less** *a* sin vida. ∼**like** *a* verosímil. ∼**line** *n* cuerda *f* de salvamento; (fig) tabla *f* de salvación. ∼**long** *a* de toda la vida. ∼ **preserver** *n* (Amer, buoy) ⇒BUOY; (jacket) ⇒∼ JACKET. ∼ **ring** *n* (Amer) ⇒∼ BELT. ∼**saver** *n* (person) salvavidas *m & f*; (fig) salvación *f*. ∼-**size(d)** *a* (de) tamaño natural. ∼**time** *n* vida *f*. ∼ **vest** *n* (Amer) ⇒∼ JACKET

lift /lɪft/ *vt* levantar. ● *vi* <*fog*> disiparse. ● *n* ascensor *m*. **give a** ∼ **to s.o.** llevar a uno en su coche, dar aventón a uno (Mex). ◻∼ **up** *vt* levantar. ∼-**off** *n* despegue *m*

light /laɪt/ *n* luz *f*; (lamp) lámpara *f*, luz *f*; (flame) fuego *m*. **come to** ∼ salir a la luz. **have you got a** ∼? ¿tienes fuego? **the** ∼**s** *npl* (traffic signals) el semáforo; (on vehicle) las luces. ● *a* (**-er, -est**) (in colour) claro; (not heavy) ligero. ● *vt* (*pt* **lit** or **lighted**) encender, prender (LAm); (illuminate) iluminar. ● *vi* encenderse, prenderse (LAm). ∼ **up** *vt* iluminar. ● *vi* iluminarse. ∼ **bulb** *n* bombilla *f*, foco *m* (Mex). ∼**en** *vt* (make less heavy) aligerar, alivianar (LAm); (give light to) iluminar; (make brighter) aclarar. ∼**er** *n* (for cigarettes) mechero *m*, encendedor *m*. ∼-**hearted** /-'hɑːtɪd/ *a* alegre. ∼**house** *n* faro *m*. ∼**ly** *adv* ligeramente

lightning /'laɪtnɪŋ/ *n*. **flash of** ∼ relámpago *m*. ● *a* relámpago

lightweight *a* ligero, liviano (LAm)

like /laɪk/ *a* parecido. ● *prep* como. ● *conj* 回 como. ● *vt*. **I** ∼ **chocolate** me gusta el chocolate. **they** ∼ **swimming** (a ellos) les gusta nadar. **would you** ∼ **a coffee?** ¿quieres un café? ∼**able** *a* simpático

like|lihood /'laɪklɪhʊd/ *n* probabilidad *f*. ∼**ly** *a* (**-ier, -iest**) probable. **he is** ∼**ly to come** es probable que venga. ● *adv* probablemente. **not** ∼**ly!** ¡ni hablar! ∼**n** *vt* comparar (**to** con, a). ∼**ness** *n* parecido *m*. **be a**

good ~**ness** parecerse mucho. ~**wise** *adv* (also) también; (the same way) lo mismo

liking /'laɪkɪŋ/ *n* (for thing) afición *f*; (for person) simpatía *f*

lilac /'laɪlək/ *a* lila. ● *n* lila *f*; (color) lila *m*

lily /'lɪlɪ/ *n* lirio *m*; (white) azucena *f*

limb /lɪm/ *n* miembro *m*. **out on a** ~ aislado

lime /laɪm/ *n* (white substance) cal *f*; (fruit) lima *f*. ~**light** *n*. **be in the** ~**light** ser el centro de atención

limerick /'lɪmərɪk/ *n* quintilla *f* humorística

limit /'lɪmɪt/ *n* límite *m*. ● *vt* limitar. ~**ation** /-'teɪʃn/ *n* limitación *f*. ~**ed** *a* limitado. ~**ed company** *n* sociedad *f* anónima

limousine /'lɪməziːn/ *n* limusina *f*

limp /lɪmp/ *vi* cojear, renguear (LAm). ● *n* cojera *f*, renguera *f* (LAm). **have a** ~ cojear. ● *a* (**-er, -est**) flojo

linden /'lɪndn/ *n* (Amer) tilo *m*

line /laɪn/ *n* línea *f*; (track) vía *f*; (wrinkle) arruga *f*; (row) fila *f*; (of poem) verso *m*; (rope) cuerda *f*; (of goods) surtido *m*; (Amer, queue) cola *f*. **stand in** ~ (Amer) hacer cola. **get in** ~ (Amer) ponerse en la cola. **cut in** ~ (Amer) colarse. **in** ~ **with** de acuerdo con. ● *vt* forrar <*skirt, box*>; bordear <*streets etc*>. □ ~ **up** *vi* alinearse; (in queue) hacer cola. *vt* (form into line) poner en fila; (align) alinear. ~**d** /laɪnd/ *a* <*paper*> con renglones; (with fabric) forrado

linen /'lɪnɪn/ *n* (sheets etc) ropa *f* blanca; (material) lino *m*

liner /'laɪnə(r)/ *n* (ship) transatlántico *m*

linger /'lɪŋɡə(r)/ *vi* tardar en marcharse. ~ (**on**) <*smells etc*> persistir. □ ~ **over** *vt* dilatarse en

lingerie /'lænʒərɪ/ *n* lencería *f*

linguist /'lɪŋɡwɪst/ *n* políglota *m* & *f*; lingüista *m* & *f*. ~**ic** /lɪŋ'ɡwɪstɪk/ *a* lingüístico. ~**ics** *n* lingüística *f*

lining /'laɪnɪŋ/ *n* forro *m*

link /lɪŋk/ *n* (of chain) eslabón *m*; (connection) conexión *f*; (bond) vínculo *m*; (transport, telecommunications) conexión *f*, enlace *m*. ● *vt* conectar; relacionar <*facts, events*>. □ ~ **up** *vt/i* conectar

lino /'laɪnəʊ/ *n* (*pl* **os**) linóleo *m*

lint /lɪnt/ *n* (Med) hilas *fpl*

lion /'laɪən/ *n* león *m*. ~**ess** /-nɪs/ *n* leona *f*

lip /lɪp/ *n* labio *m*; (edge) borde *m*. ~**read** *vi* leer los labios. ~**salve** *n* crema *f* para los labios. ~ **service** *n*. **pay** ~ **service to** aprobar de boquilla, aprobar de los dientes para afuera (Mex). ~**stick** *n* lápiz *m* de labios

liqueur /lɪ'kjʊə(r)/ *n* licor *m*

liquid /'lɪkwɪd/ *a* & *n* líquido (*m*)

liquidate /'lɪkwɪdeɪt/ *vt* liquidar

liquidize /'lɪkwɪdaɪz/ *vt* licuar. ~**r** *n* licuadora *f*

liquor /'lɪkə(r)/ *n* bebidas *fpl* alcohólicas

liquorice /'lɪkərɪs/ *n* regaliz *m*

liquor store *n* (Amer) tienda *f* de bebidas alcohólicas

lisp /lɪsp/ *n* ceceo *m*. **speak with a** ~ cecear. ● *vi* cecear

list /lɪst/ *n* lista *f*. ● *vt* hacer una lista de; (enter in a list) inscribir. ● *vi* (ship) escorar

listen /'lɪsn/ *vi* escuchar. ~ **in** (**to**) escuchar. ~ **to** escuchar. ~**er** *n* oyente *m* & *f*

listless /'lɪstlɪs/ *a* apático

lit /lɪt/ ⇒LIGHT

literacy /'lɪtərəsɪ/ *n* alfabetismo *m*

literal /'lɪtərəl/ *a* literal. ~**ly** *adv* literalmente

literary /'lɪtərərɪ/ *a* literario

literate /'lɪtərət/ *a* alfabetizado

literature /'lɪtərətʃə(r)/ *n* literatura *f*; (fig) folletos *mpl*

lithe /laɪð/ *a* ágil

litre /'liːtə(r)/ *n* litro *m*

litter /'lɪtə(r)/ *n* basura *f*; (of animals) camada *f*. ● *vt* ensuciar; (scatter) esparcir. ~**ed with** lleno de. ~ **bin** *n* papelera *f*. ~**bug**, ~**lout** *n* persona *f* que tira basura en lugares públicos

little /'lɪtl/ *a* pequeño; (not much) poco. **a** ~ **water** un poco de agua. ● *pron* poco, poca. **a** ~ un poco. ● *adv* poco.

~ **by** ~ poco a poco. ~ **finger** n (dedo m) meñique m

live /lɪv/ vt/i vivir. □ ~ **down** vt lograr borrar. □ ~ **off** vt vivir a costa de <family, friends>; (feed on) alimentarse de. □ ~ **on** vt (feed o.s. on) vivir de. vi <memory> seguir presente; <tradition> seguir existiendo. □ ~ **up** vt. ~ **it up** 🄳 darse la gran vida. □ ~ **up to** vt vivir de acuerdo con; cumplir <promise>. ● /laɪv/ a vivo; <wire> con corriente; <broadcast> en directo

livelihood /ˈlaɪvlɪhʊd/ n sustento m

lively /ˈlaɪvlɪ/ a (-ier, -iest) vivo

liven up /ˈlaɪvn/ vt animar. ● vi animar(se)

liver /ˈlɪvə(r)/ n hígado m

lives /laɪvz/ ⇒LIFE

livestock /ˈlaɪvstɒk/ n animales mpl (de cría); (cattle) ganado m

livid /ˈlɪvɪd/ a lívido; (🄳, angry) furioso

living /ˈlɪvɪŋ/ a vivo. ● n vida f. **make a** ~ ganarse la vida. ~ **room** n salón m, sala f (de estar), living m (LAm)

lizard /ˈlɪzəd/ n lagartija f; (big) lagarto m

load /ləʊd/ n (also Elec) carga f; (quantity) cantidad f; (weight, strain) peso m. ~**s of** 🄳 montones de. ● vt cargar. ~**ed** a cargado

loaf /ləʊf/ n (pl **loaves**) pan m; (stick of bread) barra f de pan. ● vi. ~ (**about**) holgazanear

loan /ləʊn/ n préstamo m. **on** ~ prestado. ● vt prestar

loath|e /ləʊð/ vt odiar. ~**ing** n odio m (of a). ~**esome** /-səm/ a repugnante

lobby /ˈlɒbɪ/ n vestíbulo m; (Pol) grupo m de presión. ● vt ejercer presión sobre. ● vi. ~ **for sth** ejercer presión para obtener algo

lobe /ləʊb/ n lóbulo m

lobster /ˈlɒbstə(r)/ n langosta f, bogavante m

local /ˈləʊkl/ a local. ~ (**phone**) **call** llamada f urbana. ● n (🄳, pub) bar m. **the** ~**s** los vecinos mpl

local: ~ **government** n administración f municipal. ~**ity**

/-ˈkælətɪ/ n localidad f. ~**ly** adv <live, work> en la zona

locat|e /ləʊˈkeɪt/ vt (situate) situar, ubicar (LAm); (find) localizar, ubicar (LAm). ~**ion** /-ʃn/ n situación f, ubicación f (LAm). **on** ~**ion** fuera del estudio. **to film on** ~**ion in Andalusia** rodar en Andalucía

lock /lɒk/ n (of door etc) cerradura f; (on canal) esclusa f; (of hair) mechón m. ● vt cerrar con llave. ● vi cerrarse con llave. □ ~ **in** vt encerrar. □ ~ **out** vt cerrar la puerta a. □ ~ **up** vt encerrar <person>; cerrar con llave <building>

locker /ˈlɒkə(r)/ n armario m, locker m (LAm). ~ **room** n (Amer) vestuario m, vestidor m (Mex)

locket /ˈlɒkɪt/ n medallón m

lock: ~**out** /ˈlɒkaʊt/ n cierre m patronal, paro m patronal (LAm). ~**smith** n cerrajero m

locomotive /ləʊkəˈməʊtɪv/ n locomotora f

lodg|e /lɒdʒ/ n (of porter) portería f. ● vt alojar; presentar <complaint>. ~**er** n huésped m. ~**ings** n alojamiento m; (room) habitación f alquilada

loft /lɒft/ n desván m, altillo m (LAm)

lofty /ˈlɒftɪ/ a (-ier, -iest) elevado; (haughty) altanero

log /lɒg/ n (of wood) tronco m; (as fuel) leño m; (record) diario m. **sleep like a** ~ dormir como un tronco. ● vt (pt **logged**) registrar. □ ~ **in**, ~ **on** vi (Comp) entrar (al sistema). □ ~ **off**, ~ **out** vi (Comp) salir (del sistema)

logarithm /ˈlɒgərɪðəm/ n logaritmo m

loggerheads /ˈlɒgəhedz/ npl. **be at** ~ **with** estar a matar con

logic /ˈlɒdʒɪk/ a lógica f. ~**al** a lógico. ~**ally** adv lógicamente

logistics /ləˈdʒɪstɪks/ n logística f. ● npl (practicalities) problemas mpl logísticos

logo /ˈləʊgəʊ/ n (pl **-os**) logo m

loin /lɔɪn/ n (Culin) lomo m. ~**s** npl entrañas fpl

loiter /ˈlɔɪtə(r)/ vi perder el tiempo

loll /lɒl/ vi repantigarse

loll|ipop /'lɒlɪpɒp/ *n* pirulí *m*. ~**y** *n* polo *m*, paleta *f* (helada) (LAm)

London /'lʌndən/ *n* Londres *m*. ●*a* londinense. ~**er** *n* londinense *m* & *f*

lone /ləun/ *a* solitario. ~**ly** *a* (**-ier, -iest**) solitario. **feel** ~**ly** sentirse muy solo. ~**r** *n* solitario *m*. ~**some** /-səm/ *a* solitario

long /lɒŋ/ *a* (**-er, -est**) largo. **a** ~ **time** mucho tiempo. **how** ~ **is it?** ¿cuánto tiene de largo? ●*adv* largo/ mucho tiempo. **as** ~ **as** (while) mientras; (provided that) con tal que (+ *subjunctive*). **before** ~ dentro de poco. **so** ~! ¡hasta luego! **so** ~ **as** (provided that) con tal que (+ *subjunctive*). □ ~ **for** *vi* anhelar. ~ **to do** estar deseando hacer. ~**-distance** /-'dɪstəns/ *a* de larga distancia. ~**-distance phone call** llamada *f* de larga distancia, conferencia *f*. ~**er** *adv*. **no** ~**er** ya no

long: ~**-haul** /-'hɔːl/ *a* de larga distancia. ~**ing** *n* anhelo *m*, ansia *f*

longitude /'lɒŋgɪtjuːd/ *n* longitud *f*

long: ~ **jump** *n* salto *m* de longitud. ~**-playing record** *n* elepé *m*. ~**-range** *a* de largo alcance. ~**-sighted** /-'saɪtɪd/ *a* hipermétrope. ~**-term** *a* a largo plazo. ~**-winded** /-'wɪndɪd/ *a* prolijo

loo /luː/ *n* 🄴 váter *m*, baño *m* (LAm)

look /lʊk/ *vt* mirar; representar <*age*>. ●*vi* mirar; (seem) parecer; (search) buscar. ●*n* mirada *f*; (appearance) aspecto *m*. **good** ~**s** belleza *f*. □ ~ **after** *vt* cuidar <*person*>; (be responsible for) encargarse de. □ ~ **at** *vt* mirar; (consider) considerar. □ ~ **down on** *vt* despreciar. □ ~ **for** *vt* buscar. □ ~ **forward to** *vt* esperar con ansia. □ ~ **into** *vt* investigar. □ ~ **like** *vt* parecerse a. □ ~ **on** *vi* mirar. □ ~ **out** *vi* tener cuidado. □ ~ **out for** *vt* buscar; (watch) tener cuidado con. □ ~ **round** *vi* volver la cabeza. □ ~ **through** *vt* hojear. □ ~ **up** *vt* buscar <*word*>; (visit) ir a ver. □ ~ **up to** *vt* admirar. ~**-alike** *n* 🄴 doble *m* & *f*. ~**out** *n* (Mil, person) vigía *m*. **be on the** ~**out for** andar a la caza de. ~**s** *npl* belleza *f*

loom /luːm/ *n* telar *m*. ●*vi* aparecerse

looney, loony /'luːnɪ/ *a* & *n* 🄴 chiflado (*m*) 🄴, loco (*m*)

loop /luːp/ *n* (shape) curva *f*; (in string) lazada *f*. ●*vt* hacer una lazada con. ~**hole** *n* (in rule) escapatoria *f*

loose /luːs/ *a* (**-er, -est**) suelto; <*garment, thread, hair*> flojo; (inexact) vago; (not packed) suelto. **be at a** ~ **end** no tener nada que hacer. ~**ly** *adv* sueltamente; (roughly) aproximadamente. ~**n** *vt* aflojar

loot /luːt/ *n* botín *m*. ●*vt/i* saquear. ~**er** *n* saqueador *m*

lop /lɒp/ *vt* (*pt* **lopped**). ~ **off** cortar

lop-sided /-'saɪdɪd/ *a* ladeado

lord /lɔːd/ *n* señor *m*; (British title) lord *m*. (**good**) **L**~! ¡Dios mío! **the L**~ el Señor. **the** (House of) **L**~**s** la Cámara de los Lores

lorry /'lɒrɪ/ *n* camión *m*. ~ **driver** *n* camionero *m*

lose /luːz/ *vt/i* (*pt* **lost**) perder. ~**r** *n* perdedor *m*

loss /lɒs/ *n* pérdida *f*. **be at a** ~ estar perplejo. **be at a** ~ **for words** no encontrar palabras

lost /lɒst/ ⇒LOSE. ●*a* perdido. **get** ~ perderse. ~ **property** *n*, ~ **and found** (Amer) oficina *f* de objetos perdidos

lot /lɒt/ *n* (fate) suerte *f*; (at auction) lote *m*; (land) solar *m*. **a** ~ (**of**) muchos. **quite a** ~ **of** 🄴 bastante. ~**s** (**of**) 🄴 muchos. **they ate the** ~ se lo comieron todo

lotion /'ləuʃn/ *n* loción *f*

lottery /'lɒtərɪ/ *n* lotería *f*

loud /laud/ *a* (**-er, -est**) fuerte; (noisy) ruidoso; (gaudy) chillón. **out** ~ en voz alta. ~**hailer** /-'heɪlə(r)/ *n* megáfono *m*. ~**ly** *adv* <*speak*> en voz alta; <*shout*> fuerte; <*complain*> a voz en grito. ~**speaker** /-'spiːkə(r)/ *n* altavoz *m*, altoparlante *m* (LAm)

lounge /laundʒ/ *vi* repantigarse. ●*n* salón *m*, sala *f* (de estar), living *m* (LAm)

lous|e /laus/ *n* (*pl* **lice**) piojo *m*. ~**y** /'lauzɪ/ *a* (**-ier, -iest**) (🄴, bad) malísimo

lout /laut/ *n* patán *m*

lov|able /'lʌvəbl/ *a* adorable. **~e**
/lʌv/ *n* amor *m*; (tennis) cero *m*. **be in
~e (with)** estar enamorado (de). **fall in
~e (with)** enamorarse (de). ● *vt* querer, amar *<person>*. **I ~e milk** me
encanta la leche. **~e affair** *n* aventura *f*, amorío *m*

lovely /'lʌvlɪ/ *a* (**-ier, -iest**) *<appear-
ance>* precioso, lindo (LAm); *<person>*
encantador, amoroso (LAm)

lover /'lʌvə(r)/ *n* amante *m & f*

loving /'lʌvɪŋ/ *a* cariñoso

low /ləʊ/ *a & adv* (**-er, -est**) bajo. ● *vi*
<cattle> mugir. **~er** *vt* bajar. **~er o.s.**
envilecerse. **~-level** *a* a ba-jo nivel.
~ly *a* (**-ier, -iest**) humilde

loyal /'lɔɪəl/ *a* leal, fiel. **~ty** *n* lealtad *f*

lozenge /'lɒzɪndʒ/ *n* (shape) rombo *m*;
(tablet) pastilla *f*

LP *abbr* (= **long-playing record**)
elepé *m*

Ltd /'lɪmɪtɪd/ *abbr* (= **Limited**) S.A.,
Sociedad Anónima

lubricate /'lu:brɪkeɪt/ *vt* lubricar

lucid /'lu:sɪd/ *a* lúcido

luck /lʌk/ *n* suerte *f*. **good ~!** ¡(buena) suerte! **~ily** *adv* por suerte. **~y** *a*
(**-ier, -iest**) *<person>* con suerte. **be
~y** tener suerte. **~y number** número
m de la suerte

lucrative /'lu:krətɪv/ *a* lucrativo

ludicrous /'lu:dɪkrəs/ *a* ridículo

lug /lʌɡ/ *vt* (*pt* **lugged**) 🄸 arrastrar

luggage /'lʌɡɪdʒ/ *n* equipaje *m*. **~
rack** *n* rejilla *f*

lukewarm /'lu:kwɔ:m/ *a* tibio; (fig)
poco entusiasta

lull /lʌl/ *vt* (soothe, send to sleep) adorme-
cer; (calm) calmar. ● *n* perio-do *m* de
calma

lullaby /'lʌləbaɪ/ *n* canción *f* de cuna

lumber /'lʌmbə(r)/ *n* trastos *mpl* viejos; (wood) maderos *mpl*. ● *vt*. **~ s.o.
with sth** 🄸 endilgar algo a uno.
~jack *n* leñador *m*

luminous /'lu:mɪnəs/ *a* luminoso

lump /lʌmp/ *n* (swelling) bulto *m*; (as
result of knock) chichón *m*; (in liquid) grumo *m*; (of sugar) terrón *m*. ● *vt*. **~
together** agrupar. **~ it** 🄸 aguantarse.
~ sum *n* suma *f* global. **~y** *a* *<sauce>*
grumoso; *<mattress, cushions>* lleno
de protuberancias

lunacy /'lu:nəsɪ/ *n* locura *f*

lunar /'lu:nə(r)/ *a* lunar

lunatic /'lu:nətɪk/ *n* loco *m*

lunch /lʌntʃ/ *n* comida *f*, almuerzo *m*.
have ~ comer, almorzar

luncheon /'lʌntʃən/ *n* comida *f*, almuerzo *m*. **~ voucher** *n* vale *m* de comida

lung /lʌŋ/ *n* pulmón *m*

lunge /lʌndʒ/ *n* arremetida *f*. ● *vi*. **~
at** arremeter contra

lurch /lɜ:tʃ/ *vi* tambalearse. ● *n*. **leave
in the ~** dejar plantado

lure /ljʊə(r)/ *vt* atraer

lurid /'ljʊərɪd/ *a* *<colour>* chillón;
(shocking) morboso

lurk /lɜ:k/ *vi* merodear; (in ambush)
estar al acecho

luscious /'lʌʃəs/ *a* delicioso

lush /lʌʃ/ *a* exuberante

lust /lʌst/ *n* lujuria *f*; (craving) deseo *m*.
● *vi*. **~ after** codiciar

lute /lu:t/ *n* laúd *m*

Luxembourg,   Luxemburg
/'lʌksəmbɜ:ɡ/ *n* Luxemburgo *m*

luxuriant /lʌɡ'zjʊərɪənt/ *a* exuberante

luxur|ious /lʌɡ'zjʊərɪəs/ *a* lujoso.
~y /'lʌkʃərɪ/ *n* lujo *m*. ● *a* de lujo

lying /'laɪɪŋ/ ⇒LIE[1], LIE[2]. ● *n* menti-ras
fpl. ● *a* mentiroso

lynch /lɪntʃ/ *vt* linchar

lyric /'lɪrɪk/ *a* lírico. **~al** *a* lírico. **~s**
npl letra *f*

Mm

MA /em'eɪ/ *abbr* ⇒MASTER

mac /mæk/ *n* 🄸 impermeable *m*

macabre /mə'kɑ:brə/ *a* macabro

macaroni /mækə'rəʊnɪ/ *n* macarrones *mpl*

mace /meɪs/ *n* (staff) maza *f*; (spice)
macis *f*. **M~** (*P*) (Amer) gas *m* para defensa personal

machine /məˈʃiːn/ n máquina f. ∼ **gun** n ametralladora f. ∼**ry** n maquinaria f; (working parts, fig) mecanismo m

mackintosh /ˈmækɪntɒʃ/ n impermeable m

macro /ˈmækrəʊ/ n (pl **-os**) (Comp) macro m

macrobiotic /mækrəʊbaɪˈɒtɪk/ a macrobiótico

mad /mæd/ a (**madder**, **maddest**) loco; (🆒, angry) furioso. be ∼ about estar loco por

madam /ˈmædəm/ n señora f

mad: ∼**cap** a atolondrado. ∼**den** vt (make mad) enloquecer; (make angry) enfurecer

made /meɪd/ ⇒MAKE. ∼**-to-measure** hecho a (la) medida

mad: ∼**house** n manicomio m. ∼**ly** adv (interested, in love etc) locamente; (frantically) como un loco. ∼**man** /-mən/ n loco m. ∼**ness** n locura f

Madonna /məˈdɒnə/ n. the ∼ (Relig) la Virgen

maestro /ˈmaɪstrəʊ/ n (pl **maestri** /-striː/ or **-os**) maestro m

Mafia /ˈmæfɪə/ n mafia f

magazine /mægəˈziːn/ n revista f; (of gun) recámara f

magenta /məˈdʒentə/ a magenta, morado

maggot /ˈmægət/ n gusano m

magic /ˈmædʒɪk/ n magia f. ● a mágico. ∼**al** a mágico. ∼**ian** /məˈdʒɪʃn/ n mago m

magistrate /ˈmædʒɪstreɪt/ n juez m que conoce de faltas y asuntos civiles de menor importancia

magnet /ˈmægnɪt/ n imán m. ∼**ic** /-ˈnetɪk/ a magnético; (fig) lleno de magnetismo. ∼**ism** n magnetismo m. ∼**ize** vt imantar, magnetizar

magnif|ication /mægnɪfɪˈkeɪʃn/ n aumento m. ∼**y** /ˈmægnɪfaɪ/ vt aumentar. ∼**ying glass** n lupa f

magnificen|ce /mægˈnɪfɪsns/ a magnificencia f. ∼**t** a magnífico

magnitude /ˈmægnɪtjuːd/ n magnitud f

magpie /ˈmægpaɪ/ n urraca f

mahogany /məˈhɒɡənɪ/ n caoba f

maid /meɪd/ n (servant) criada f, sirvienta f; (girl, old use) doncella f. **old** ∼ solterona f

maiden /ˈmeɪdn/ n doncella f. ● a <voyage> inaugural. ∼ **name** n apellido m de soltera

mail /meɪl/ n correo m; (armour) (cota f de) malla f. ● a correo. ● vt echar al correo <letter>; (send) enviar por correo. ∼**box** n (Amer) buzón m. ∼**ing list** n lista f de direcciones. ∼**man** /-mən/ n (Amer) cartero m. ∼ **order** n venta f por correo

maim /meɪm/ vt mutilar

main /meɪn/ n. (water/gas) ∼ cañería f principal. **in the** ∼ en su mayor parte. **the** ∼**s** npl (Elec) la red f de suministro. ● a principal. ∼ **course** n plato m principal, plato m fuerte. ∼ **frame** n (Comp) unidad f central. ∼**land** n. the ∼**land** la masa territorial de un país excluyendo sus islas. ● a. ∼**land China** (la) China continental. ∼**ly** adv principalmente. ∼ **road** n carretera f principal. ∼**stream** a <culture> establecido. ∼ **street** n calle f principal

maint|ain /meɪnˈteɪn/ vt mantener. ∼**enance** /ˈmeɪntənəns/ n mantenimiento m

maisonette /meɪzəˈnet/ n (small house) casita f; (part of house) dúplex m

maize /meɪz/ n maíz m

majestic /məˈdʒestɪk/ a majestuoso

majesty /ˈmædʒəstɪ/ n majestad f

major /ˈmeɪdʒə(r)/ a (important) muy importante; (Mus) mayor. **a** ∼ **road** una calle prioritaria. ● n comandante m & f, mayor m & f (LAm). ● vi. ∼ **in** (Amer, Univ) especializarse en

Majorca /məˈjɔːkə/ n Mallorca f

majority /məˈdʒɒrətɪ/ n mayoría f. ● a mayoritario

make /meɪk/ vt (pt **made**) hacer; (manufacture) fabricar; ganar <money>; tomar <decision>; llegar a <destination>. ∼ **s.o. do sth** obligar a uno a hacer algo. **be made of** estar hecho de. **I** ∼ **it two o'clock** yo tengo las dos. ∼ **believe** fingir. ∼ **do** (manage) arreglarse. ∼ **do with** (content o.s.) contentarse con. ~ it llegar; (succeed) tener éxito. ● *n* marca *f*. ~ **for** *vt* dirigirse a. □ ~ **good** *vt* compensar; (repair) reparar. □ ~ **off** *vi* escaparse (**with** con). □ ~ **out** *vt* distinguir; (understand) entender; (write out) hacer; (assert) dar a entender. *vi* (cope) arreglárselas. □ ~ **up** *vt* (constitute) formar; (prepare) preparar; inventar <*story*>; ~ **it up** (become reconciled) hacer las paces. ~ **up** (one's face) maquillarse. □ ~ **up for** *vt* compensar. **~-believe** *a* fingido, simulado. *n* ficción *f*. **~over** *n* (Amer) maquillaje *m*. **~r** *n* fabricante *m & f*. **~shift** *a* (temporary) provisional, provisorio (LAm); (improvised) improvisado. **~up** *n* maquillaje *m*. put on ~up maquillarse.

making /'meɪkɪŋ/ *n*. he has the ~s of tiene madera de. in the ~ en vías de formación

maladjusted /mælə'dʒʌstɪd/ *a* inadaptado

malaria /mə'leərɪə/ *n* malaria *f*, paludismo *m*

Malaysia /mə'leɪzɪə/ *n* Malasia *f*. **~n** *a & n* malaisio (*m*)

male /meɪl/ *a* macho; <*voice, attitude*> masculino. ● *n* macho *m*; (man) varón *m*

malevolent /mə'levələnt/ *a* malévolo

malfunction /mæl'fʌŋkʃn/ *vi* fallar, funcionar mal

malic|e /'mælɪs/ *n* mala intención *f*, maldad *f*. bear s.o. ~e guardar rencor a uno. **~ious** /mə'lɪʃəs/ *a* malintencionado. **~iously** *adv* con malevolencia

malignant /mə'lɪgnənt/ *a* maligno

mallet /'mælɪt/ *n* mazo *m*

malnutrition /mælnju:'trɪʃn/ *n* desnutrición *f*

malpractice /mæl'præktɪs/ *n* mala práctica *f* (en el ejercicio de una profesión)

malt /mɔːlt/ *n* malta *f*

Malt|a /'mɔːltə/ *n* Malta *f*. **~ese** /-'tiːz/ *a & n* maltés (*m*)

mammal /'mæml/ *n* mamífero *m*

mammoth /'mæməθ/ *n* mamut *m*. ● *a* gigantesco

man /mæn/ *n* (*pl* **men** /men/) hombre *m*; (Chess) pieza *f*. ~ **in the street** hombre *m* de la calle. ● *vt* (*pt* **manned**) encargarse de <*switchboard*>; tripular <*ship*>; servir <*guns*>

manacles /'mænəklz/ *n* (for wrists) esposas *fpl*; (for legs) grillos *mpl*

manag|e /'mænɪdʒ/ *vt* dirigir; administrar <*land, finances*>; (handle) manejar. ● *vi* (Com) dirigir; (cope) arreglárselas. **~e to do** lograr hacer. **~eable** *a* <*task*> posible de alcanzar; <*size*> razonable. **~ement** *n* dirección *f*. **~er** *n* director *m*; (of shop) encargado *m*; (of soccer team) entrenador *m*, director *m* técnico (LAm). **~eress** /-'res/ *n* encargada *f*. **~erial** /-'dʒɪərɪəl/ *a* directivo, gerencial (LAm). **~ing director** *n* director *m* ejecutivo

mandate /'mændeɪt/ *n* mandato *m*

mandatory /'mændətərɪ/ *a* obligatorio

mane /meɪn/ *n* (of horse) crin(es) *f(pl)*; (of lion) melena *f*

mangle /'mæŋgl/ *n* rodillo *m* (escurridor). ● *vt* destrozar

man: **~handle** *vt* mover a pulso; (treat roughly) maltratar. **~hole** *n* registro *m*. **~hood** *n* madurez *f*; (quality) virilidad *f*. **~-hour** *n* hora *f* hombre. **~-hunt** *n* persecución *f*

mania /'meɪnɪə/ *n* manía *f*. **~c** /-ɪæk/ *n* maníaco *m*

manicure /'mænɪkjʊə(r)/ *n* manicura *f*, manicure *f* (LAm)

manifest /'mænɪfest/ *a* manifiesto. ● *vt* manifestar. **~ation** /-'steɪʃn/ *n* manifestación *f*

manifesto /mænɪ'festəʊ/ *n* (*pl* -os) manifiesto *m*

manipulat|e /mə'nɪpjʊleɪt/ *vt* manipular. **~ion** /-'leɪʃn/ *n* manipulación *f*. **~ive** /-lətɪv/ *a* manipulador

man: **~kind** *n* humanidad *f*. **~ly** *a* viril. **~-made** *a* artificial

manner /'mænə(r)/ *n* manera *f*; (demeanour) actitud *f*; (kind) clase *f*. **~ed** *a* amanerado. **~s** *npl* modales *mpl*, educación *f*. bad ~s mala educación

manoeuvre /mə'nuːvə(r)/ *n* maniobra *f*. ● *vt/i* maniobrar

manor /'mænə(r)/ n. ~ **house** casa f solariega

manpower n mano f de obra

mansion /'mænʃn/ n mansión f

man: ~-**size(d)** a grande. ~**slaughter** n homicidio m sin premeditación

mantelpiece /'mæntlpi:s/ n repisa f de la chimenea

manual /'mænjʊəl/ a manual. ● n (handbook) manual m

manufacture /mænjʊ'fæktʃə(r)/ vt fabricar. ● n fabricación f. ~**r** n fabricante m & f

manure /mə'njʊə(r)/ n estiércol m

manuscript /'mænjʊskrɪpt/ n manuscrito m

many /'menɪ/ a & pron muchos, muchas. ~ **people** mucha gente. **a great/ good** ~ muchísimos. **how** ~? ¿cuántos? **so** ~ tantos. **too** ~ demasiados

map /mæp/ n mapa m; (of streets etc) plano m

mar /mɑː(r)/ vt (pt **marred**) estropear

marathon /'mærəθən/ n maratón m & f

marble /'mɑːbl/ n mármol m; (for game) canica f

march /mɑːtʃ/ vi (Mil) marchar. ~ **off** vi irse. ● n marcha f

March /mɑːtʃ/ n marzo m

march-past /'mɑːtʃpɑːst/ n desfile m

mare /meə(r)/ n yegua f

margarine /mɑːdʒə'riːn/ n margarina f

margin /'mɑːdʒɪn/ n margen f. ~**al** a marginal

marijuana /mærɪ'hwɑːnə/ n marihuana f

marina /mə'riːnə/ n puerto m deportivo

marine /mə'riːn/ a marino. ● n (sailor) infante m de marina

marionette /mærɪə'net/ n marioneta f

marital status /mærɪtl 'steɪtəs/ n estado m civil

mark /mɑːk/ n marca f; (stain) mancha f; (Schol) nota f; (target) blanco m. ● vt (indicate) señalar, marcar; (stain)

manchar; corregir <exam>. ~ **time** marcar el paso. □ ~ **out** vt (select) señalar; (distinguish) distinguir. ~**ed** a marcado. ~**edly** /-kɪdlɪ/ adv marcadamente. ~**er** n marcador m. ~**er** (**pen**) n rotulador m, marcador m (LAm)

market /'mɑːkɪt/ n mercado m. **on the** ~ en venta. ● vt comercializar. ~ **garden** n huerta f. ~**ing** n marketing m

marking /'mɑːkɪŋ/ n marcas fpl; (on animal, plant) mancha f

marksman /'mɑːksmən/ n (pl -**men**) tirador m. ~**ship** n puntería f

marmalade /'mɑːməleɪd/ n mermelada f (de cítricos)

maroon /mə'ruːn/ a & n granate (m). ● vt abandonar (en una isla desierta)

marquee /mɑː'kiː/ n toldo m, entoldado m; (Amer, awning) marquesina f

marriage /'mærɪdʒ/ n matrimonio m; (ceremony) casamiento m

married /'mærɪd/ a casado; <life> conyugal

marrow /'mærəʊ/ n (of bone) tuétano m; (vegetable) calabaza f verde alargada. ~ **squash** n (Amer) calabaza f verde alargada

marry /'mærɪ/ vt casarse con; (give or unite in marriage) casar. ● vi casarse. **get married** casarse (**to** con)

Mars /mɑːz/ n Marte m

marsh /mɑːʃ/ n pantano m

marshal /'mɑːʃl/ n (Mil) mariscal m; (Amer, police chief) jefe m de policía. ● vt (pt **marshalled**) reunir; poner en orden <thoughts>

marsh: ~ **mallow** /-'mæləʊ/ n malvavisco m, bombón m (LAm). ~**y** a pantanoso

martial /'mɑːʃl/ a marcial. ~ **arts** npl artes fpl marciales. ~ **law** n ley f marcial

martyr /'mɑːtə(r)/ n mártir m & f

marvel /'mɑːvl/ n maravilla f. ● vi (pt **marvelled**) maravillarse (**at** de). ~**lous** a maravilloso

Marxis|m /'mɑːksɪzəm/ n marxismo m. ~**t** a & n marxista (m & f)

marzipan /'mɑːzɪpæn/ n mazapán m

mascara /mæ'skɑːrə/ n rímel m (P)

mascot /'mæskɒt/ n mascota f

masculin|e /'mæskjʊlɪn/ a & n masculino (m). ~ity /-'lɪnətɪ/ n masculinidad f

mash /mæʃ/ n (Br 🅸, potatoes) puré m de patatas, puré m de papas (LAm). ● vt hacer puré de, moler (Mex). ~ed potatoes n puré m de patatas, puré m de papas (LAm)

mask /mɑːsk/ n máscara f; (Sport) careta f. ● vt ocultar

masochis|m /'mæsəkɪzəm/ n masoquismo m. ~t n masoquista m & f. ~tic /-'kɪstɪk/ a masoquista

mason /'meɪsn/ n (stone ~) mampostero m. M~ (freemason) masón m. ~ry /'meɪsnrɪ/ n albañilería f

masquerade /mɑːskə'reɪd/ n mascarada f. ● vi. ~ as hacerse pasar por

mass /mæs/ n masa f; (Relig) misa f; (large quantity) montón m. the ~es las masas. ● vi concentrarse

massacre /'mæsəkə(r)/ n masacre f, matanza f. ● vt masacrar

mass|age /'mæsɑːʒ/ n masaje m. ● vt masajear. ~eur /mæ'sɜː(r)/ n masajista m. ~euse /mæ'sɜːz/ n masajista f

massive /'mæsɪv/ a masivo; (heavy) macizo; (huge) enorme

mass: ~ media n medios mpl de comunicación. ~-produce /-prə'djuːs/ vt fabricar en serie

mast /mɑːst/ n mástil m; (for radio, TV) antena f repetidora

master /'mɑːstə(r)/ n amo m; (expert) maestro m; (in secondary school) profesor m; (of ship) capitán m; (master copy) original m. ~'s degree master m, maestría f. M~ of Arts (MA) poseedor m de una maestría en filosofía y letras. M~ of Science (MSc) poseedor m de una maestría en ciencias. ● vt llegar a dominar. ~key n llave f maestra. ~mind n cerebro m. ● vt dirigir. ~piece n obra f maestra. ~stroke n golpe m

de maestro. ~y n dominio m; (skill) maestría f

masturbat|e /'mæstəbeɪt/ vi masturbarse. ~ion /-'beɪʃn/ n masturbación f

mat /mæt/ n estera f; (at door) felpudo m. ● a (Amer) ⇒MATT

match /mætʃ/ n (Sport) partido m; (for fire) cerilla f, fósforo m (LAm), cerillo m (Mex); (equal) igual m. ● vt emparejar; (equal) igualar; <clothes, colours> hacer juego con. ● vi hacer juego. ~box n caja f de cerillas, caja f de fósforos (LAm), caja f de cerillos (Mex). ~ing a que hace juego. ~stick n cerilla f, fósforo m (LAm), cerillo m (Mex)

mate /meɪt/ n (of person) pareja f; (of animals, male) macho m; (of animals, female) hembra f; (assistant) ayudante m; (🅸, friend) amigo m, cuate m (Mex); (Chess) (jaque m) mate m. ● vi aparearse

material /mə'tɪərɪəl/ n material m; (cloth) tela f. ● a material. ~istic /-'lɪstɪk/ a materialista. ~ize vi materializarse. ~s npl materiales mpl

matern|al /mə'tɜːnl/ a maternal. ~ity /-ətɪ/ n maternidad f. ● a <ward> de obstetricia; <clothes> premamá, de embarazada

math /mæθ/ n (Amer) ⇒MATHS

mathematic|ian /mæθəmə'tɪʃn/ n matemático m. ~al /-'mætɪkl/ a matemático. ~s /-'mætɪks/ n matemática(s) f(pl)

maths /mæθs/ n matemática(s) f(pl)

matinée, matinee /'mætɪneɪ/ n (Theatre) función f de tarde; (Cinema) primera sesión f (de la tarde)

matrices /'meɪtrɪsiːz/ ⇒MATRIX

matriculat|e /mə'trɪkjʊleɪt/ vi matricularse. ~ion /-'leɪʃn/ n matrícula f

matrimon|ial /mætrɪ'məʊnɪəl/ a matrimonial. ~y /'mætrɪmənɪ/ n matrimonio m

matrix /'meɪtrɪks/ n (pl matrices) matriz f

matron /'meɪtrən/ n (married, elderly) matrona f; (in school) ama f de llaves; (former use, in hospital) enfermera f jefe

matt, **matte** (Amer) /mæt/ a mate

matted /'mætɪd/ a enmarañado y apelmazado

matter /'mætə(r)/ n (substance) materia f; (affair) asunto m; (pus) pus m. **as a ~ of fact** en realidad. **no ~** no importa. **what is the ~?** ¿qué pasa? **to make ~s worse** para colmo (de males). ● vi importar. **it doesn't ~** no importa. **~-of-fact** /-əv'fækt/ a <person> práctico

mattress /'mætrɪs/ n colchón m

matur|e /mə'tjʊə(r)/ a maduro. ● vi madurar. **~ity** n madurez f

maudlin /'mɔːdlɪn/ a llorón

maul /mɔːl/ vt atacar (y herir)

mauve /məʊv/ a & n malva (m)

maverick /'mævərɪk/ n inconformista m & f

maxim /'mæksɪm/ n máxima f

maxim|ize /'mæksɪmaɪz/ vt maximizar. **~um** /-əm/ a & n máximo (m)

may /meɪ/, past might

● auxiliary verb

····▸ (expressing possibility) **he ~ come** puede que venga, es posible que venga. **it ~ be true** puede ser verdad. **she ~ not have seen him** es posible que or puede que no lo haya visto

····▸ (asking for or giving permission) **~ I smoke?** ¿puedo fumar?, ¿se puede fumar? **~ I have your name and address, please?** ¿quiere darme su nombre y dirección, por favor?

····▸ (expressing a wish) **~ he be happy** que sea feliz

····▸ (conceding) **he ~ not have much experience, but he's very hardworking** no tendrá mucha experiencia, pero es muy trabajador. **that's as ~ be** puede ser

····▸ **I ~ as well stay** más vale quedarme

May /meɪ/ n mayo m

maybe /'meɪbɪ/ adv quizá(s), tal vez, a lo mejor

May Day n el primero de mayo

mayhem /'meɪhem/ n caos m

mayonnaise /meɪə'neɪz/ n mayonesa f, mahonesa f

mayor /meə(r)/ n alcalde m, alcaldesa f. **~ess** /-ɪs/ n alcaldesa f

maze /meɪz/ n laberinto m

me /miː/ pron me; (after prep) mí. **he knows ~** me conoce. **it's ~** soy yo

meadow /'medəʊ/ n prado m, pradera f

meagre /'miːgə(r)/ a escaso

meal /miːl/ n comida f. **~time** n hora f de comer

mean /miːn/ vt (pt **meant**) (intend) tener la intención de, querer; (signify) querer decir, significar. **~ to do** tener la intención de hacer. **~ well** tener buenas intenciones. **be meant for** estar destinado a. ● a (**-er**, **-est**) (miserly) tacaño; (unkind) malo; (Math) medio. ● n media f; (average) promedio m

meander /mɪ'ændə(r)/ vi <river> serpentear

meaning /'miːnɪŋ/ n sentido m. **~ful** a significativo. **~less** a sin sentido

meanness /'miːnnɪs/ n (miserliness) tacañería f; (unkindness) maldad f

means /miːnz/ n medio m. **by ~ of** por medio de, mediante. **by all ~** por supuesto. **by no ~** de ninguna manera. ● npl (wealth) medios mpl, recursos mpl. **~ test** n investigación f de ingresos

meant /ment/ ⇒MEAN

meantime /'miːntaɪm/ adv mientras tanto, entretanto. ● n. **in the ~** mientras tanto, entretanto

meanwhile /'miːnwaɪl/ adv mientras tanto, entretanto

measl|es /'miːzlz/ n sarampión m. **~y** /'miːzlɪ/ a 🄴 miserable

measure /'meʒə(r)/ n medida f; (ruler) regla f. ● vt/i medir. □ **~ up to** vt estar a la altura de. **~ment** n medida f

meat /miːt/ n carne f. **~ball** n albóndiga f. **~y** a <taste, smell> a carne; <soup, stew> con mucha carne

mechan|ic /mɪ'kænɪk/ n mecánico m. **~ical** a mecánico. **~ics** n mecánica f. **~ism** /'mekənɪzəm/ n mecanismo *m*. ~**ize** /'mekənaiz/ *vt* mecanizar

medal /'medl/ *n* medalla *f*. ~**list** /'medəlist/ *n* medallista *m* & *f*. **be a gold** ~**list** ganar una medalla de oro

meddle /'medl/ *vi* meterse, entrometerse (**in** en). ~ **with** (tinker) toquetear

media /'miːdiə/ ⇒MEDIUM. ● *npl*. the ~ los medios de comunicación

mediat|e /'miːdieɪt/ *vi* mediar. ~**ion** /-'eɪʃn/ *n* mediación *f*. ~**or** *n* mediador *m*

medical /'medikl/ *a* médico; <*student*> de medicina. ● *n* revisión *m* médica

medicat|ed /'medɪkeɪtɪd/ *a* medicinal. ~**ion** /-'keɪʃn/ *n* medicación *f*

medicin|al /mɪ'dɪsɪnl/ *a* medicinal. ~**e** /'medsɪn/ *n* medicina *f*

medieval /medɪ'iːvl/ *a* medieval

mediocre /miːdɪ'əʊkə(r)/ *a* mediocre

meditat|e /'medɪteɪt/ *vi* meditar. ~**ion** /-'teɪʃn/ *n* meditación *f*

Mediterranean /medɪtə'reɪnɪən/ *a* mediterráneo. ● *n*. the ~ el Mediterráneo

medium /'miːdɪəm/ *n* (*pl* **media**) medio *m*. **happy** ~ término *m* medio. ● *a* mediano. ~**-size(d)** /-saɪz(d)/ *a* de tamaño mediano

medley /'medlɪ/ *n* (Mus) popurrí *m*; (mixture) mezcla *f*

meek /miːk/ *a* (**-er**, **-est**) dócil

meet /miːt/ *vt* (*pt* **met**) encontrar; (bump into s.o.) encontrarse con; (fetch) ir a buscar; (get to know, be introduced to) conocer. ● *vi* encontrarse; (get to know) conocerse; (have meeting) reunirse. ~ **up** *vi* encontrarse (with con). □ ~ **with** *vt* ser recibido con; (Amer, meet) encontrarse con. ~**ing** *n* reunión *f*; (accidental between two people) encuentro *m*

megabyte /'megəbaɪt/ *n* (Comp) megabyte *m*, megaocteto *m*

megaphone /'megəfəʊn/ *n* megáfono *m*

melanchol|ic /melən'kɒlɪk/ *a* melancólico. ~**y** /'melənkɒlɪ/ *n* melancolía *f*. ● *a* melancólico

mellow /'meləʊ/ *a* (**-er**, **-est**) <*fruit*> maduro; <*sound*> dulce; <*colour*> tenue; <*person*> apacible

melodrama /'melədrɑːmə/ *n* melodrama *m*. ~**tic** /melədrə'mætɪk/ *a* melodramático

melody /'melədɪ/ *n* melodía *f*

melon /'melən/ *n* melón *m*

melt /melt/ *vt* (make liquid) derretir; fundir <*metals*>. ● *vi* (become liquid) derretirse; <*metals*> fundirse. □ ~ **down** *vt* fundir

member /'membə(r)/ *n* miembro *m* & *f*; (of club) socio *m*. ~ **of staff** empleado *m*. **M**~ **of Congress** *n* (Amer) miembro *m* & *f* del Congreso. **M**~ **of Parliament** *n* diputado *m*. ~**ship** *n* calidad *f* de socio; (members) socios *mpl*, membresía *f* (LAm)

membrane /'membreɪn/ *n* membrana *f*

memento /mɪ'mentəʊ/ *n* (*pl* **-os** *or* **-oes**) recuerdo *m*

memo /'meməʊ/ *n* (*pl* **-os**) memorándum *m*, memo *m*

memoir /'memwɑː(r)/ *n* memoria *f*

memorable /'memərəbl/ *a* memorable

memorandum /memə'rændəm/ *n* (*pl* **-ums** *or* **-da** /-də/) memorándum *m*

memorial /mɪ'mɔːrɪəl/ *n* monumento *m*. ● *a* conmemorativo

memor|ize /'meməraɪz/ *vt* aprender de memoria. ~**y** /'memərɪ/ *n* (faculty) memoria *f*; (thing remembered) recuerdo *m*. **from** ~**y** de memoria. **in** ~**y of** a la memoria de

men /men/ ⇒MAN

menac|e /'menəs/ *n* amenaza *f*; (⊞, nuisance) peligro *m* público. ● *vt* amenazar. ~**ing** *a* amenazador

mend /mend/ *vt* reparar; arreglar <*garment*>. ~ **one's ways** enmendarse. ● *n* remiendo *m*. **be on the** ~ ir mejorando

menfolk /'menfəʊk/ *n* hombres *mpl*

menial /'miːnɪəl/ *a* servil

meningitis /menɪn'dʒaɪtɪs/ *n* meningitis *f*

menopause /'menəpɔːz/ *n* menopausia *f*

menstruat|e /'menstrueɪt/ *vi* menstruar. **∼ion** /-'eɪʃn/ *n* menstruación *f*

mental /'mentl/ *a* mental; <*hospital*> psiquiátrico. **∼ity** /-'tæləti/ *n* mentalidad *f*. **∼ly** *adv* mentalmente. be **∼ly** ill ser un enfermo mental

mention /'menʃn/ *vt* mencionar. don't **∼** it! ¡no hay de qué! ● *n* mención *f*

mentor /'mentɔː(r)/ *n* mentor *m*

menu /'menjuː/ *n* menú *m*

meow /mɪ'aʊ/ *n & vi* ⇒MEW

mercenary /'mɜːsɪnərɪ/ *a & n* mercenario (*m*)

merchandise /'mɜːtʃəndaɪz/ *n* mercancías *fpl*, mercadería *f* (LAm)

merchant /'mɜːtʃənt/ *n* comerciante *m*. ● *a* <*ship, navy*> mercante. **∼ bank** *n* banco *m* mercantil

merci|ful /'mɜːsɪfl/ *a* misericordioso. **∼less** *a* despiadado

mercury /'mɜːkjʊrɪ/ *n* mercurio *m*. M**∼y** (planet) Mercurio *m*

mercy /'mɜːsɪ/ *n* compasión *f*. at the **∼** of a merced de

mere /mɪə(r)/ *a* simple. **∼ly** *adv* simplemente

merge /mɜːdʒ/ *vt* unir; fusionar <*companies*>. ● *vi* unirse; <*companies*> fusionarse. **∼r** *n* fusión *f*

meridian /mə'rɪdɪən/ *n* meridiano *m*

meringue /mə'ræŋ/ *n* merengue *m*

merit /'merɪt/ *n* mérito *m*. ● *vt* (*pt* **merited**) merecer

mermaid /'mɜːmeɪd/ *n* sirena *f*

merr|ily /'merəlɪ/ *adv* alegremente. **∼iment** /'merɪmənt/ *n* alegría *f*. **∼y** /'merɪ/ *a* (**-ier, -iest**) alegre. make **∼** divertirse. **∼-go-round** *n* tiovivo *m*, carrusel *m* (LAm). **∼y-making** *n* jolgorio *m*

mesh /meʃ/ *n* malla *f*

mesmerize /'mezməraɪz/ *vt* hipnotizar; (fascinate) cautivar

mess /mes/ *n* desorden *m*; (dirt) suciedad *f*; (Mil) rancho *m*. make a **∼** of estropear. □ **∼ up** *vt* desordenar; (dirty) ensuciar; estropear <*plans*>. □ **∼ about** *vi* tontear. □ **∼ with** *vt* (tinker with) manosear

mess|age /'mesɪdʒ/ *n* mensaje *m*; (when phoning) recado *m*. **∼enger** /'mesɪndʒə(r)/ *n* mensajero *m*

Messiah /mɪ'saɪə/ *n* Mesías *m*

Messrs /'mesəz/ *npl*. **∼** Smith los señores Smith, los Sres. Smith

messy /'mesɪ/ *a* (**-ier, -iest**) en desorden; (dirty) sucio

met /met/ ⇒MEET

metabolism /mɪ'tæbəlɪzəm/ *n* metabolismo *m*

metal /'metl/ *n* metal. ● *a* de metal. **∼lic** /mə'tælɪk/ *a* metálico

metaphor /'metəfə(r)/ *n* metáfora *f*. **∼ical** /-'fɒrɪkl/ *a* metafórico

mete /miːt/ *vt*. **∼ out** repartir; dar <*punishment*>

meteor /'miːtɪə(r)/ *n* meteoro *m*. **∼ic** /-'ɒrɪk/ *a* meteórico. **∼ite** /'miːtɪəraɪt/ *n* meteorito *m*

meteorolog|ical /miːtɪərə'lɒdʒɪkl/ *a* meteorológico. **∼ist** /-'rɒlədʒɪst/ *n* meteorólogo *m*. **∼y** /-'rɒlədʒɪ/ *n* meteorología *f*

meter /'miːtə(r)/ *n* contador *m*, medidor *m* (LAm); (Amer) ⇒METRE

method /'meθəd/ *n* método *m*. **∼ical** /mɪ'θɒdɪkl/ *a* metódico. M**∼ist** /'meθədɪst/ *a & n* metodista (*m & f*)

methylated /'meθɪleɪtɪd/ *a*. **∼ spirit(s)** *n* alcohol *m* desnaturalizado

meticulous /mɪ'tɪkjʊləs/ *a* meticuloso

metre /'miːtə(r)/ *n* metro *m*

metric /'metrɪk/ *a* métrico

metropoli|s /mɪ'trɒpəlɪs/ *n* metrópoli(s) *f*. **∼tan** /metrə'pɒlɪtən/ *a* metropolitano

mettle /'metl/ *n*. be on one's **∼** (fig) estar dispuesto a dar lo mejor de sí

mew /mjuː/ *n* maullido *m*. ● *vi* maullar

Mexic|an /'meksɪkən/ *a & n* mejicano (*m*), mexicano (*m*). **∼o** /-kəʊ/ *n* Méjico *m*, México *m*

miaow /miː'aʊ/ *n & vi* ⇒MEW

mice /maɪs/ ⇒MOUSE

mickey /'mɪkɪ/ *n*. take the **∼** out of 🄳 tomar el pelo a

micro... /'maɪkrəʊ/ *pref* micro...

microbe /'maɪkrəʊb/ n microbio m

micro: ～**chip** n pastilla f. ～**film** n microfilme m. ～**phone** n micrófono m. ～**processor** /-'prəʊsesə(r)/ n microprocesador m. ～**scope** n microscopio m. ～**scopic** /-'skɒpɪk/ a microscópico. ～**wave** n microonda f. ～**wave oven** n horno m de microondas

mid- /mɪd/ pref. in ～ air en pleno aire. in ～ March a mediados de marzo

midday /mɪd'deɪ/ n mediodía m

middl|e /'mɪdl/ a de en medio. ● n medio m. in the ～e of en medio de. ～**e-aged** /-'eɪdʒd/ a de mediana edad. **M～e Ages** npl Edad f Media. ～**e class** n clase f media. ～**e-class** a de la clase media. **M～e East** n Oriente m Medio. ～**eman** n intermediario m. ～**e name** n segundo nombre m. ～**ing** a regular

midge /mɪdʒ/ n mosquito m

midget /'mɪdʒɪt/ n enano m. ● a minúsculo

Midlands /'mɪdləndz/ npl región f central de Inglaterra

midnight /'mɪdnaɪt/ n medianoche f

midriff /'mɪdrɪf/ n diafragma m

midst /mɪdst/ n. in our ～ entre nosotros. in the ～ of en medio de

midsummer /mɪd'sʌmə(r)/ n pleno verano m; (solstice) solsticio m de verano

midway /mɪd'weɪ/ adv a mitad de camino

Midwest /mɪd'west/ región f central de los EE.UU.

midwife /'mɪdwaɪf/ n comadrona f, partera f

midwlnter /mɪd'wɪntə(r)/ n pleno invierno m

might /maɪt/ ⇒MAY. ● n (strength) fuerza f; (power) poder m. ～**y** a (strong) fuerte; (powerful) poderoso. ● adv ① muy

migraine /'mi:greɪn/ n jaqueca f

migra|nt /'maɪɡrənt/ a migratorio. ● n (person) emigrante m & f. ～ /maɪ'ɡreɪt/ vi emigrar. ～**tion** /-'ɡreɪʃn/ n migración f

mild /maɪld/ a (-er, -est) <person> afable; <climate> templado; (slight) ligero; <taste, manner> suave

mildew /'mɪldju:/ n moho m; (on plants) mildeu m, mildiu m

mildly /'maɪldlɪ/ adv (gently) suavemente; (slightly) ligeramente

mile /maɪl/ n milla f. ～**s better** ① mucho mejor. ～**s too big** ① demasiado grande. ～**age** /-ɪdʒ/ n (loosely) kilometraje m. ～**ometer** /maɪ'lɒmɪtə(r)/ n (loosely) cuentakilómetros m. ～**stone** n mojón m; (event, stage, fig) hito m

militant /'mɪlɪtənt/ a & n militante (m & f)

military /'mɪlɪtərɪ/ a militar

militia /mɪ'lɪʃə/ n milicia f

milk /mɪlk/ n leche f. ● a <product> lácteo; <chocolate> con leche. ● vt ordeñar <cow>. ～**man** /-mən/ n lechero m. ～ **shake** n batido m, (leche f) malteada f (LAm), licuado m con leche (LAm). ～**y** a lechoso. **M～y Way** n Vía f Láctea

mill /mɪl/ n molino m; (for coffee, pepper) molinillo m; (factory) fábrica f de tejidos de algodón. ● vt moler. □ ～ **about, mill around** vi dar vueltas

millennium /mɪ'lenɪəm/ n (pl **-ia** /-ɪə/ or **-iums**) milenio m

miller /'mɪlə(r)/ n molinero m

milli... /'mɪlɪ/ pref mili... ～**gram(me)** n miligramo m. ～**metre** n milímetro m

milliner /'mɪlɪnə(r)/ n sombrerero m

million /'mɪlɪən/ n millón m. a ～ **pounds** un millón de libras. ～**aire** /-'eə(r)/ n millonario m

millstone /'mɪlstəʊn/ n muela f (de molino); (fig, burden) carga f

mime /maɪm/ n mímica f. ● vt imitar, hacer la mímica de. ● vi hacer la mímica

mimic /'mɪmɪk/ vt (pt **mimicked**) imitar. ● n imitador m. ～**ry** n imitación f

mince /mɪns/ vt picar, moler (LAm) <meat>. not to ～ matters/words no andar(se) con rodeos. ● n carne f picada, carne f molida (LAm). ～ **pie** n pastelito m de Navidad (pastelito relleno de picadillo de frutos secos). ～**r** n máquina f de picar carne, máquina f de moler carne (LAm)

mind /maɪnd/ n mente f; (sanity) juicio m. to my ~ a mi parecer. be on one's mind preocuparle a uno. make up one's ~ decidirse. ● vt (look after) cuidar (de); atender <shop>. ~ the steps! ¡cuidado con las escaleras! never ~ him no le hagas caso. I don't ~ the noise no me molesta el ruido. would you ~ closing the door? ¿le importaría cerrar la puerta? ● vi. never ~ no importa, no te preocupes. I don't ~ (don't object) me da igual. do you ~ if I smoke? ¿le importa si fumo? ~ful a atento (of a). ~less a <activity> mecánico; <violence> ciego

mine¹ /maɪn/ poss pron (sing) mío, mía; (pl) míos, mías. it is ~ es mío. ~ are blue los míos/las mías son azules. a friend of ~ un amigo mío/ una amiga mía

mine² /maɪn/ n mina f; (Mil) mina f. ● vt extraer. ~field n campo m de minas. ~r n minero m

mineral /'mɪnərəl/ a & n mineral (m). ~ water n agua f mineral

mingle /'mɪŋgl/ vi mezclarse

mini... /'mɪnɪ/ pref mini...

miniature /'mɪnɪtʃə(r)/ n miniatura f. ● a en miniatura

mini: ~bus n microbús m. ~cab n taxi m (que se pide por teléfono)

minim|al /'mɪnɪml/ a mínimo. ~ize vt reducir al mínimo. ~um /-məm/ a & n (pl -ima /-mə/) mínimo (m)

mining /'maɪnɪŋ/ n minería f. ● a minero

miniskirt /'mɪnɪskɜːt/ n minifalda f

minist|er /'mɪnɪstə(r)/ n ministro m, secretario m (Mex); (Relig) pastor m. ~erial /-'stɪərɪəl/ a ministerial. ~ry n ministerio m, secretaría f (Mex)

mink /mɪŋk/ n visón m

minor /'maɪnə(r)/ a (also Mus) menor; <injury> leve; <change> pequeño; <operation> de poca importancia. ● n menor m & f de edad. ~ity /maɪ'nɒrətɪ/ n minoría f. ● a minoritario

minstrel /'mɪnstrəl/ n juglar m

mint /mɪnt/ n (plant) menta f; (sweet) pastilla f de menta; (Finance) casa f de la moneda. in ~ condition como nuevo. ● vt acuñar

minus /'maɪnəs/ prep menos; ([≡], without) sin. ● n (sign) menos m. five ~ three is two cinco menos tres is igual a dos. ~ sign n (signo m de) menos m

minute¹ /'mɪnɪt/ n minuto m. the ~s npl (of meeting) el acta f

minute² /maɪ'njuːt/ a diminuto; (detailed) minucioso

mirac|le /'mɪrəkl/ n milagro m. ~ulous /mɪ'rækjʊləs/ a milagroso

mirage /'mɪrɑːʒ/ n espejismo m

mirror /'mɪrə(r)/ n espejo m; (driving ~) (espejo m) retrovisor m. ● vt reflejar

mirth /mɜːθ/ n regocijo m; (laughter) risas fpl

misapprehension /mɪsæprɪ'henʃn/ n malentendido m

misbehav|e /mɪsbɪ'heɪv/ vi portarse mal. ~iour n mala con-ducta

miscalculat|e /mɪs'kælkjʊleɪt/ vt/i calcular mal. ~ion /-'leɪʃn/ n error m de cálculo

miscarr|iage /'mɪskærɪdʒ/ n aborto m espontáneo. ~iage of justice n injusticia f. ~y vi abortar

miscellaneous /mɪsə'leɪnɪəs/ a heterogéneo

mischie|f /'mɪstʃɪf/ n (foolish conduct) travesura f; (harm) daño m. get into ~f hacer travesuras. make ~f causar daños. ~vous /'mɪstʃɪvəs/ a travieso; <grin> pícaro

misconception /mɪskən'sepʃn/ n equivocación f

misconduct /mɪs'kɒndʌkt/ n mala conducta f

misdeed /mɪs'diːd/ n fechoría f

misdemeanour /mɪsdɪ'miːnə(r)/ n delito m menor, falta f

miser /'maɪzə(r)/ n avaro m

miserable /'mɪzərəbl/ a (sad) triste; (in low spirits) abatido; (wretched, poor) mísero; <weather> pésimo

miserly /'maɪzəlɪ/ a avariento

misery /'mɪzərɪ/ n (unhappiness) tristeza f; (pain) sufrimiento m

misfire /mɪs'faɪə(r)/ vi fallar

misfit /'mɪsfɪt/ n inadaptado m

misfortune /mɪs'fɔːtʃuːn/ *n* desgracia *f*

misgiving /mɪs'gɪvɪŋ/ *n* recelo *m*

misguided /mɪs'gaɪdɪd/ *a* equivocado

mishap /'mɪshæp/ *n* percance *m*

misinform /mɪsɪn'fɔːm/ *vt* informar mal

misinterpret /mɪsɪn'tɜːprɪt/ *vt* interpretar mal

misjudge /mɪs'dʒʌdʒ/ *vt* juzgar mal; (miscalculate) calcular mal

mislay /mɪs'leɪ/ *vt* (*pt* **mislaid**) extraviar, perder

mislead /mɪs'liːd/ *vt* (*pt* **misled** /mɪs'led/) engañar. **~ing** *a* engañoso

mismanage /mɪs'mænɪdʒ/ *vt* administrar mal. **~ment** *n* mala administración *f*

misplace /mɪs'pleɪs/ *vt* (lose) extraviar, perder

misprint /'mɪsprɪnt/ *n* errata *f*

miss /mɪs/ *vt* (fail to hit) no dar en; (regret absence of) echar de menos, extrañar (LAm); perder <*train, party*>; perder <*chance*>. **~ the point** no comprender. ● *vi* errar el tiro, fallar; <*bullet*> no dar en el blanco. ● *n* fallo *m*, falla *f* (LAm); (title) señorita *f*. □ **~ out** *vt* saltarse <*line*>. **~out on sth** perderse algo

misshapen /mɪs'ʃeɪpən/ *a* deforme

missile /'mɪsaɪl/ *n* (Mil) misil *m*

missing /'mɪsɪŋ/ *a* (lost) perdido. **be ~** faltar. **go ~** desaparecer. **~ person** desaparecido *m*

mission /'mɪʃn/ *n* misión *f*. **~ary** /'mɪʃənərɪ/ *n* misionero *m*

mist /mɪst/ *n* neblina *f*; (at sea) bruma *f*. □ **~ up** *vi* empañarse

mistake /mɪ'steɪk/ *n* error *m*. **make a ~** cometer un error. **by ~** por error. ● *vt* (*pt* **mistook**, *pp* **mistaken**) confundir. **~ for** confundir con. **~n** /-ən/ *a* equivocado. **be ~n** equivocarse

mistletoe /'mɪsltəʊ/ *n* muérdago *m*

mistreat /mɪs'triːt/ *vt* maltratar

mistress /'mɪstrɪs/ *n* (of house) señora *f*; (lover) amante *f*

mistrust /mɪs'trʌst/ *vt* desconfiar de. ● *n* desconfianza *f*. **~ful** *a* desconfiado

misty /'mɪstɪ/ *a* (**-ier, -iest**) neblinoso; <*day*> de neblina. **it's ~** hay neblina

misunderstand /mɪsʌndə'stænd/ *vt* (*pt* **-stood**) entender mal. **~ing** *n* malentendido *m*

misuse /mɪs'juːz/ *vt* emplear mal; malversar <*funds*>. ● /mɪs'juːs/ *n* mal uso *m*; (unfair use) abuso *m*; (of funds) malversación *f*

mite /maɪt/ *n* (insect) ácaro *m*

mitten /'mɪtn/ *n* mitón *m*

mix /mɪks/ *vt* mezclar. ● *vi* mezclarse; (go together) combinar. **~ with** tratarse con <*people*>. ● *n* mezcla *f*. □ **~ up** *vt* mezclar; (confuse) confundir. **~ed** *a* <*school etc*> mixto; (assorted) mezclado. **be ~ed up** estar confuso. **~er** *n* (Culin) batidora *f*; (TV, machine) mezcladora *f*. **~ture** /'mɪkstʃə(r)/ *n* mezcla *f*. **~-up** *n* lío *m*

moan /məʊn/ *n* gemido *m*. ● *vi* gemir; (complain) quejarse (**about** de)

moat /məʊt/ *n* foso *m*

mob /mɒb/ *n* turba *f*. ● *vt* (*pt* **mobbed**) acosar

mobil|e /'məʊbaɪl/ *a* móvil. **~e home** *n* caravana *f* fija, trailer *m* (LAm). **~e (phone)** *n* (teléfono *m*) móvil *m*, (teléfono *m*) celular *m* (LAm). ● *n* móvil *m*. **~ize** /'məʊbɪlaɪz/ *vt* movilizar. ● *vi* mo-vilizarse

mock /mɒk/ *vt* burlarse de. ● *a* <*anger*> fingido; <*exam*> de práctica. **~ery** /'mɒkərɪ/ *n* burla *f*. **make a ~ery of sth** ridiculizar algo

model /'mɒdl/ *n* (example) modelo *m*; (mock-up) maqueta *f*; (person) modelo *m*. ● *a* (exemplary) modelo; <*car etc*> en miniatura. ● *vt* (*pt* **modelled**) modelar. **~ s.o. on s.o.** tomar a uno como modelo

modem /'məʊdem/ *n* (Comp) módem *m*

moderat|e /'mɒdərət/ *a & n* moderado (*m*). ● /'mɒdəreɪt/ *vt* moderar. **~ely** /'mɒdərətlɪ/ *adv* (fairly) medianamente. **~ion** /-'reɪʃn/ *n* moderación *f*. **in ~ion** con moderación

modern /'mɒdn/ *a* moderno. ~**ize** *vt* modernizar

modest /'mɒdɪst/ *a* modesto. ~**y** *n* modestia *f*

modif|ication /mɒdɪfɪ'keɪʃn/ *n* modificación *f*. ~**y** /-faɪ/ *vt* modificar

module /'mɒdjuːl/ *n* módulo *m*

moist /mɔɪst/ *a* (**-er**, **-est**) húmedo. ~**en** /'mɔɪsn/ *vt* humedecer

moistur|e /'mɔɪstʃə(r)/ *n* humedad *f*. ~**ize** *vt* hidratar. ~**izer**, ~**izing cream** *n* crema *f* hidratante

mole /məʊl/ *n* (animal) topo *m*; (on skin) lunar *m*

molecule /'mɒlɪkjuːl/ *n* molécula *f*

molest /mə'lest/ *vt* abusar (sexualmente) de

mollify /'mɒlɪfaɪ/ *vt* aplacar

mollusc /'mɒləsk/ *n* molusco *m*

mollycoddle /'mɒlɪkɒdl/ *vt* mimar

molten /'məʊltən/ *a* fundido; <*lava*> líquido

mom /mɒm/ *n* (Amer, 🇺🇸) mamá *f* 🇺🇸

moment /'məʊmənt/ *n* momento *m*. **at the** ~ en este momento. **for the** ~ de momento. ~**ary** /'məʊməntərɪ/ *a* momentáneo

momentous /mə'mentəs/ *a* trascendental

momentum /mə'mentəm/ *n* momento *m*; (speed) velocidad *f*

mommy /'mɒmɪ/ *n* (Amer, 🇺🇸) mamá *m* 🇺🇸

monarch /'mɒnək/ *n* monarca *m*. ~**y** *n* monarquía *f*

monastery /'mɒnəstərɪ/ *n* monasterio *m*

Monday /'mʌndeɪ/ *n* lunes *m*

money /'mʌnɪ/ *n* dinero *m*, plata *f* (LAm). ~**box** *n* hucha *f*, alcancía *f* (LAm). ~ **order** *n* giro *m* postal

mongrel /'mʌŋgrəl/ *n* perro *m* mestizo, chucho *m* 🇺🇸

monitor /'mɒnɪtə(r)/ *n* (Tec) monitor *m*. ● *vt* observar <*elections*>; seguir <*progress*>; (electronically) monitorizar; escuchar <*broadcast*>

monk /mʌŋk/ *n* monje *m*

monkey /'mʌŋkɪ/ *n* mono *m*. ~**-nut** *n* cacahuete *m*, cacahuate *m* (Mex), maní *m* (LAm). ~**wrench** *n* llave *f* inglesa

mono /'mɒnəʊ/ *n* monofonía *f*

monologue /'mɒnəlɒg/ *n* monólogo *m*

monopol|ize /mə'nɒpəlaɪz/ *vt* monopolizar; acaparar <*conversation*>. ~**y** *n* monopolio *m*

monoton|e /'mɒnətəʊn/ *n* tono *m* monocorde. ~**ous** /mə'nɒtənəs/ *a* monótono. ~**y** *n* monotonía *f*

monsoon /mɒn'suːn/ *n* monzón *m*

monst|er /'mɒnstə(r)/ *n* monstruo *m*. ~**rous** /-strəs/ *a* monstruoso

month /mʌnθ/ *n* mes *m*. **£200 a** ~ 200 libras mensuales *or* al mes. ~**ly** *a* mensual. ~**ly payment** mensualidad *f*, cuota *f* mensual (LAm). ● *adv* mensualmente

monument /'mɒnjʊmənt/ *n* monumento *m*. ~**al** /-'mentl/ *a* monumental

moo /muː/ *n* mugido *m*. ● *vi* mugir

mood /muːd/ *n* humor *m*. **be in a good/bad** ~ estar de buen/mal humor. ~**y** *a* (**-ier**, **-iest**) temperamental; (bad-tempered) malhumorado

moon /muːn/ *n* luna *f*. ~**light** *n* luz *f* de la luna. ~**lighting** *n* pluriempleo *m*. ~**lit** *a* iluminado por la luna; <*night*> de luna

moor /mʊə(r)/ *n* páramo *m*; (of heather) brezal *m*. ● *vt* amarrar. ~**ing** *n* (place) amarradero *m*. ~**ings** *npl* (ropes) amarras *fpl*

moose /muːs/ *n invar* alce *m* americano

mop /mɒp/ *n* fregona *f*, trapeador *m* (LAm). ~ **of hair** pelambrera *f*. ● *vt* (*pt* **mopped**). ~ (**up**) limpiar

mope /məʊp/ *vi* estar abatido

moped /'məʊped/ *n* ciclomotor *m*

moral /'mɒrəl/ *a* moral. ● *n* (of tale) moraleja *f*

morale /mə'rɑːl/ *n* moral *f*

moral|ity /mə'rælətɪ/ *n* moralidad *f*. ~**ly** *adv* moralmente. ~**s** *npl* moralidad *f*

morbid /'mɔːbɪd/ *a* morboso

more /mɔː(r)/ *a* más. **two** ~ **bottles** dos botellas más ● *pron* más. **you ate** ~ **than me** comiste más que yo. **some** ~ más. ~ **than six** más de seis. **the** ~ **he has, the** ~ **he wants** cuánto más tiene, más quiere. ● *adv* más. ~ **and** ~ cada vez más. ~ **or less** más o menos. **once** ~ una vez más. **she doesn't live here any** ~ ya no vive aquí. ~**over** /mɔːˈrəʊvə(r)/ *adv* además

morgue /mɔːg/ *n* depósito *m* de cadáveres, morgue *f* (LAm)

morning /ˈmɔːnɪŋ/ *n* mañana *f*; (early hours) madrugada *f*. **at 11 o'clock in the** ~ a las once de la mañana. **in the** ~ por la mañana, en la mañana (LAm). **tomorrow/yesterday** ~ mañana/ayer por la mañana *or* (LAm) en la mañana. (good) ~! ¡buenos días!

Morocc|an /məˈrɒkən/ *a* & *n* marroquí (*m* & *f*). ~**o** /-kəʊ/ *n* Marruecos *m*

moron /ˈmɔːrɒn/ *n* imbécil *m* & *f*

morose /məˈrəʊs/ *a* taciturno

Morse /mɔːs/ *n* Morse *m*. **in** ~ **(code)** *n* en (código) morse

morsel /ˈmɔːsl/ *n* bocado *m*

mortal /ˈmɔːtl/ *a* & *n* mortal (*m*). ~**ity** /-ˈtælətɪ/ *n* mortalidad *f*

mortar /ˈmɔːtə(r)/ *n* (all senses) mortero *m*

mortgage /ˈmɔːgɪdʒ/ *n* hipoteca *f.* ● *vt* hipotecar

mortify /ˈmɔːtɪfaɪ/ *vt* darle mucha vergüenza a

mortuary /ˈmɔːtjʊərɪ/ *n* depósito *m* de cadáveres, morgue *f* (LAm)

mosaic /məʊˈzeɪk/ *n* mosaico *m*

mosque /mɒsk/ *n* mezquita *f*

mosquito /mɒsˈkiːtəʊ/ *n* (*pl* -oes) mosquito *m*, zancudo *m* (LAm)

moss /mɒs/ *n* musgo *m*

most /məʊst/ *a* la mayoría de, la mayor parte de. ~ **days** casi todos los días. ● *pron* la mayoría, la mayor parte. **at** ~ como máximo. **make the** ~ **of** aprovechar al máximo. ● *adv* más; (very) muy; (Amer, almost) casi. ~**ly** *adv* principalmente

MOT *n.* ~ **(test)** ITV *f*, inspección *f* técnica de vehículos

motel /məʊˈtel/ *n* motel *m*

moth /mɒθ/ *n* mariposa *f* de la luz, palomilla *f*; (in clothes) polilla *f*

mother /ˈmʌðə(r)/ *n* madre *f*. ● *vt* mimar. ~**-in-law** *n* (*pl* ~**s-in-law**) suegra *f*. ~**land** *n* patria *f*. ~**ly** *a*

maternal. ~**-of-pearl** *n* nácar *m*, madreperla *f*. **M**~**'s Day** *n* el día *m* de la Madre. ~**-to-be** *n* futura madre *f*. ~ **tongue** *n* lengua *f* materna

motif /məʊˈtiːf/ *n* motivo *m*

motion /ˈməʊʃn/ *n* movimiento *m*; (proposal) moción *f*. **put** *or* **set in** ~ poner algo en marcha. ● *vt/i.* ~ (**to**) **s.o. to** hacerle señas a uno para que. ~**less** *a* inmóvil

motiv|ate /ˈməʊtɪveɪt/ *vt* motivar. ~**ation** /-ˈveɪʃn/ *n* motivación *f*. ~**e** /ˈməʊtɪv/ *n* motivo *m*

motley /ˈmɒtlɪ/ *a* variopinto

motor /ˈməʊtə(r)/ *n* motor *m*. ● *a* motor; (fem) motora, motriz. ~ **bike** *n* 🄵 motocicleta *f*, moto *f* 🄵. ~ **boat** *n* lancha *f* a motor. ~ **car** *n* automóvil *m*. ~ **cycle** *n* motocicleta *f*. ~**cyclist** *n* motociclista *m* & *f*. ~**ing** *n* automovilismo *m*. ~**ist** *n* automovilista *m* & *f*. ~**way** *n* autopista *f*

motto /ˈmɒtəʊ/ *n* (*pl* -oes) lema *m*

mould /məʊld/ *n* molde *m*; (fungus) moho *m*. ● *vt* moldear; formar <*character*>. ~**ing** *n* (on wall etc) moldura *f*. ~**y** *a* mohoso

moult /məʊlt/ *vi* mudar de pelo/piel/plumas

mound /maʊnd/ *n* montículo *m*; (pile, fig) montón *m*

mount /maʊnt/ *vt* montar <*horse*>; engarzar <*gem*>; preparar <*attack*>. ● *vi* subir, crecer. ● *n.* montura *f*; (mountain) monte *m*. □ ~ **up** *vi* irse acumulando

mountain /ˈmaʊntɪn/ *n* montaña *f*. ~**eer** /maʊntɪˈnɪə(r)/ *n* alpinista *m* & *f*. ~**eering** *n* alpinismo *m*. ~**ous** *a* montañoso

mourn /mɔːn/ *vt* llorar. ● *vi* lamentarse. ~ **for s.o.** llorar a uno. ~**er** *n* doliente *m* & *f*. ~**ful** *a* triste. ~**ing** *n* duelo *m*, luto *m*. **be in** ~**ing** estar de duelo

mouse /maʊs/ *n* (*pl* **mice**) ratón *m*. ~**trap** *n* ratonera *f*

mousse /muːs/ *n* (Culin) mousse *f or* *m*; (for hair) mousse *f*

moustache /məˈstɑːʃ/ *n* bigote *m*

mouth /maʊθ/ n boca f; (of cave) entrada f; (of river) desembocadura f. ~**ful** n bocado m. ~**organ** n armónica f. ~**wash** n enjuague m bucal

move /muːv/ vt mover; (relocate) trasladar; (with emotion) conmover; (propose) proponer. ~ **the television** cambiar de lugar la televisión. ~ **house** mudarse de casa. ● vi moverse; (be in motion) estar en movimiento; (take action) tomar medidas. ● n movimiento m; (in game) jugada f; (player's turn) turno m; (removal) mudanza f. □ ~ **away** vi alejarse. □ ~ **in** vi instalarse. ~ **in with s.o.** irse a vivir con uno. □ ~ **over** vi correrse. ~**ment** n movimiento m

movie /ˈmuːvɪ/ n (Amer) película f. **the** ~**s** npl el cine. ~ **camera** n (Amer) tomavistas m, filmadora f (LAm)

moving /ˈmuːvɪŋ/ a en movimiento; (touching) conmovedor

mow /məʊ/ vt (pt **mowed** or **mown** /məʊn/) cortar <lawn>; segar <hay>. □ ~ **down** vt acribillar. ~**er** n (for lawn) cortacésped m

MP abbr ⇒MEMBER OF PARLIAMENT

Mr /ˈmɪstə(r)/ abbr (pl **Messrs**) (= **Mister**) Sr. ~ **Coldbeck** Sr. Coldbeck

Mrs /ˈmɪsɪz/ abbr (pl **Mrs**) (= **Missis**) Sra. ~ **Andrews** Sra. Andrews

Ms /mɪz/ abbr (title of married or unmarried woman)

MSc abbr ⇒MASTER

much /mʌtʃ/ a & pron mucho, mucha. ● adv mucho; (before pp) muy. ~ **as** por mucho que. ~ **the same** más o menos lo mismo. **how** ~? ¿cuánto?. **so** ~ tanto. **too** ~ demasiado

muck /mʌk/ n estiércol m; (⚅, dirt) mugre f. □ ~ **about** vi ⚅ tontear

mud /mʌd/ n barro m, lodo m

muddle /ˈmʌdl/ vt embrollar. ● n desorden m; (mix-up) lío m. □ ~ **through** vi salir del paso

muddy a lodoso; <hands etc> cubierto de lodo. ~**guard** n guardabarros m, salpicadera f (Mex)

muffle /ˈmʌfl/ vt amortiguar <sound>. ~**r** n (scarf) bufanda f; (Amer, Auto) silenciador m

mug /mʌg/ n taza f (alta y sin platillo), tarro m (Mex); (for beer) jarra f; (⚅, face) cara f, jeta f ⚄; (⚅, fool) idiota m & f. ● vt (pt **mugged**) asaltar. ~**ger** n asaltante m & f. ~**ging** n asalto m

muggy /ˈmʌgɪ/ a bochornoso

mule /mjuːl/ n mula f

mull /mʌl/ (Amer), ~ **over** vt reflexionar sobre

multi|coloured /mʌltɪˈkʌləd/ a multicolor. ~**national** /-ˈnæʃənl/ a & n multinacional (f)

multipl|e /ˈmʌltɪpl/ a múltiple. ● n múltiplo m. ~**ication** /mʌltɪplɪˈkeɪʃn/ n multiplicación f. ~**y** /ˈmʌltɪplaɪ/ vt multiplicar. ● vi (Math) multiplicar; (increase) multiplicarse

multitude /ˈmʌltɪtjuːd/ n. **a** ~ **of problems** múltiples problemas

mum /mʌm/ n ⚄ mamá f ⚄

mumble /ˈmʌmbl/ vt mascullar. ● vi hablar entre dientes

mummy /ˈmʌmɪ/ n (⚄, mother) mamá f ⚄; (archaeology) momia f

mumps /mʌmps/ n paperas fpl

munch /mʌntʃ/ vt/i mascar

mundane /mʌnˈdeɪn/ a mundano

municipal /mjuːˈnɪsɪpl/ a municipal

mural /ˈmjʊərəl/ a & n mural (f)

murder /ˈmɜːdə(r)/ n asesinato m. ● vt asesinar. ~**er** n asesino m

murky /ˈmɜːkɪ/ a (**-ier, -iest**) turbio

murmur /ˈmɜːmə(r)/ n murmullo m. ● vt/i murmurar

musc|le /ˈmʌsl/ n músculo m. ~**ular** /ˈmʌskjʊlə(r)/ a muscular; <arm, body> musculoso

muse /mjuːz/ vi meditar (**on** sobre)

museum /mjuːˈzɪəm/ n museo m

mush /mʌʃ/ n papilla f

mushroom /ˈmʌʃrʊm/ n champiñón m; (Bot) seta f. ● vi aparecer como hongos

mushy /ˈmʌʃɪ/ a blando

music /ˈmjuːzɪk/ n música f. ~**al** a musical. **be** ~ tener sentido musical.

● *n* musical *m*. ∼**ian** /mjuː'zɪʃn/ *n* músico *m*

Muslim /'mʊzlɪm/ *a & n* musulmán (*m*)

mussel /'mʌsl/ *n* mejillón *m*

must /mʌst/ *v aux* deber, tener que; (expressing supposition) deber (de). he ∼ be old debe (de) ser viejo. I ∼ have done it debo (de) haberlo hecho. ● *n*. be a ∼ ser imprescindible

mustache /'mʌstæʃ/ *n* (Amer) bigote *m*

mustard /'mʌstəd/ *n* mostaza *f*

muster /'mʌstə(r)/ *vt* reunir

musty /'mʌstɪ/ *a* (**-ier**, **-iest**) que huele a humedad

mutation /mjuː'teɪʃn/ *n* mutación *f*

mute /mjuːt/ *a* mudo

mutilate /'mjuːtɪleɪt/ *vt* mutilar

mutiny /'mjuːtɪnɪ/ *n* motín *m*. ● *vi* amotinarse

mutter /'mʌtə(r)/ *vt/i* murmurar

mutton /'mʌtn/ *n* carne *f* de ovino

mutual /'mjuːtʃʊəl/ *a* mutuo; (🇺🇸, common) común

muzzle /'mʌzl/ *n* (snout) hocico *m*; (device) bozal *m*

my /maɪ/ *a* (*sing*) mi; (*pl*) mis

myself /maɪ'self/ *pron* (*reflexive*) me; (used for emphasis) yo mismo *m*, yo misma *f*. I cut ∼ me corté. I made it ∼ lo hice yo mismo/misma. I was by ∼ estaba solo/sola

myster|ious /mɪ'stɪərɪəs/ *a* misterioso. ∼**y** /'mɪstərɪ/ *n* misterio *m*

mystical /'mɪstɪkl/ *a* místico

mystify /'mɪstɪfaɪ/ *vt* dejar perplejo

mystique /mɪ'stiːk/ *n* mística *f*

myth /mɪθ/ *n* mito *m*. ∼**ical** *a* mítico. ∼**ology** /mɪ'θɒlədʒɪ/ *n* mitología *f*

Nn

N *abbr* (= **north**) N

nab /næb/ *vt* (*pt* **nabbed**) (🔲, arrest) pescar; (snatch) agarrar

nag /næg/ *vt* (*pt* **nagged**) fastidiar; (scold) estarle encima a. ● *vi* criticar

nail /neɪl/ *n* clavo *m*; (of finger, toe) uña *f*. ∼ **polish** esmalte *m* para las uñas. ● *vt*. ∼ (**down**) clavar

naive /naɪ'iːv/ *a* ingenuo

naked /'neɪkɪd/ *a* desnudo. **to the** ∼ **eye** a simple vista

name /neɪm/ *n* nombre *m*; (of book, film) título *m*; (fig) fama *f*. **my** ∼ **is Chris** me llamo Chris. **good** ∼ buena reputación. ● *vt* ponerle nombre a; (appoint) nombrar. **a man** ∼**d Jones** un hombre llamado Jones. **she was** ∼**d after** *or* (Amer) **for her grandmother** le pusieron el nombre de su abuela. ∼**less** *a* anónimo. ∼**ly** *adv* a saber. ∼**sake** *n* (person) tocayo *m*

nanny /'nænɪ/ *n* niñera *f*

nap /næp/ *n* (sleep) sueñecito *m*; (after lunch) siesta *f*. **have a** ∼ echarse un sueño

napkin /'næpkɪn/ *n* servilleta *f*

nappy /'næpɪ/ *n* pañal *m*

narcotic /nɑː'kɒtɪk/ *a & n* narcótico (*m*)

narrat|e /nə'reɪt/ *vt* narrar. ∼**ive** /'nærətɪv/ *n* narración *f*. ∼**or** /nə'reɪtə(r)/ *n* narrador *m*

narrow /'nærəʊ/ *a* (**-er**, **-est**) estrecho, angosto (LAm). **have a** ∼ **escape** salvarse de milagro. ● *vt* estrechar; (limit) limitar. ● *vi* estrecharse. ∼**ly** *adv* (just) por poco. ∼**-minded** /-'maɪndɪd/ *a* de miras estrechas

nasal /'neɪzl/ *a* nasal; <*voice*> gangoso

nasty /'nɑːstɪ/ *a* (**-ier**, **-iest**) desagradable; (spiteful) malo (**to** con); <*taste, smell*> asqueroso; <*cut*> feo

nation /'neɪʃn/ *n* nación *f*

national /'næʃənl/ *a* nacional. ● *n* ciudadano *m*. ∼ **anthem** *n* himno *m* nacional. ~**ism** *n* nacionalismo *m*. ~**ity** /næʃəˈnæləti/ *n* nacionalidad *f*. ~**ize** *vt* nacionalizar. ~**ly** *adv* a escala nacional

nationwide /ˈneɪʃnwaɪd/ *a & adv* a escala nacional

native /ˈneɪtɪv/ *n* natural *m & f*. be a ~ **of** ser natural de. ●*a* nativo; <*country, town*> natal; <*language*> materno; <*plant, animal*> autóctono. N~ **American** indio *m* americano

nativity /nəˈtɪvəti/ *n*. the N~ la Natividad *f*

NATO /ˈneɪtəʊ/ *abbr* (= **North Atlantic Treaty Organization**) OTAN *f*

natter /ˈnætə(r)/ 🔲 *vi* charlar. ●*n* charla *f*

natural /ˈnætʃərəl/ *a* natural. ~ **history** *n* historia *f* natural. ~**ist** *n* naturalista *m & f*. ~**ized** *a* <*citizen*> naturalizado. ~**ly** *adv* (of course) naturalmente; (by nature) por naturaleza

nature /ˈneɪtʃə(r)/ *n* naturaleza *f*; (of person) carácter *m*; (of things) naturaleza *f*

naught /nɔːt/ *n* cero *m*

naughty /ˈnɔːti/ *a* (-**ier**, -**iest**) malo, travieso

nause|a /ˈnɔːzɪə/ *n* náuseas *fpl*. ~**ous** /-ɪəs/ *a* nauseabundo

nautical /ˈnɔːtɪkl/ *a* náutico. ~ **mile** *n* milla *f* marina

naval /ˈneɪvl/ *a* naval; <*officer*> de marina

nave /neɪv/ *n* nave *f*

navel /ˈneɪvl/ *n* ombligo *m*

naviga|ble /ˈnævɪɡəbl/ *a* navegable. ~**te** /ˈnævɪɡeɪt/ *vt* navegar por <*sea etc*>; gobernar <*ship*>. ●*vi* navegar. ~**tion** /-ˈɡeɪʃn/ *n* navegación *f*. ~**tor** *n* oficial *m & f* de derrota

navy /ˈneɪvi/ *n* marina *f* de guerra. ~ (**blue**) *a & n* azul (*m*) marino

NE *abbr* (= **north-east**) NE

near /nɪə(r)/ *adv* cerca. draw ~ acercarse. ●*prep*. ~ (**to**) cerca de. go ~ (**to**) sth acercarse a algo. ●*a* cercano. ●*vt* acercarse a. ~**by** *a* cercano. ~**ly** *adv* casi. he ~**ly** died por poco se muere, casi se muere. not ~**ly** ni

con mucho. ~**sighted** /-ˈsaɪtɪd/ *a* miope, corto de vista

neat /niːt/ *a* (-**er**, -**est**) <*person*> pulcro; <*room etc*> bien arreglado; (ingenious) hábil; <*whisky, gin*> solo; ~ (Amer 🔲, great) fantástico 🔲. ~**ly** *adv* pulcramente; <*organized*> cuidadosamente

necessar|ily /nesəˈserɪli/ *adv* necesariamente. ~**y** /ˈnesəseri/ *a* necesario

necessit|ate /nəˈsesɪteɪt/ *vt* exigir. ~**y** /nɪˈsesəti/ *n* necesidad *f*. the bare ~**ies** lo indispensable

neck /nek/ *n* (of person, bottle, dress) cuello *m*; (of animal) pescuezo *m*. ~ **and** ~ a la par, parejos (LAm). ~**lace** /ˈnekləs/ *n* collar *m*. ~**line** *n* escote *m*

nectar /ˈnektə(r)/ *n* néctar *m*

nectarine /ˈnektərɪn/ *n* nectarina *f*

née /neɪ/ *a* de soltera

need /niːd/ *n* necesidad *f* (**for** de). ●*vt* necesitar; (demand) exigir. you ~ not speak no tienes que hablar

needle /ˈniːdl/ *n* aguja *f*. ●*vt* (🔲, annoy) pinchar

needless /ˈniːdlɪs/ *a* innecesario

needlework /ˈniːdlwɜːk/ *n* labores *fpl* de aguja; (embroidery) bordado *m*

needy /ˈniːdi/ *a* (-**ier**, -**iest**) necesitado

negative /ˈneɡətɪv/ *a* negativo. ●*n* (of photograph) negativo *m*; (no) negativa *f*

neglect /nɪˈɡlekt/ *vt* descuidar <*house*>; desatender <*children*>; no cumplir con <*duty*>. ●*n* negligencia *f*. (**state of**) ~ abandono *m*. ~**ful** *a* negligente

neglig|ence /ˈneɡlɪdʒəns/ *n* negligencia *f*, descuido *m*. ~**ent** *a* negligente. ~**ible** /ˈneɡlɪdʒəbl/ *a* insignificante

negotia|ble /nɪˈɡəʊʃəbl/ *a* negociable. ~**te** /nɪˈɡəʊʃɪeɪt/ *vt/i* negociar. ~**tion** /-ˈeɪʃn/ *n* negociación *f*. ~**tor** *n* negociador *m*

neigh /neɪ/ *vi* relinchar

neighbour /ˈneɪbə(r)/ *n* vecino *m*. ~**hood** *n* vecindad *f*, barrio *m*. in the ~**hood of** alrededor de. ~**ing** *a* vecino

neither /'naɪðə(r)/ *a.* ~ **book** ninguno de los libros. ● *pron* ninguno, -na. ● *conj.* neither...nor ni...ni. ~ **do I** yo tampoco

neon /'ni:ɒn/ *n* neón *m.* ● *a* <*lamp etc*> de neón

nephew /'nevju:/ *n* sobrino *m*

Neptune /'neptju:n/ *n* Neptuno *m*

nerv|e /nɜ:v/ *n* nervio *m*; (courage) valor *m*; (calm) sangre *f* fría; (🅸, impudence) descaro *m.* ~**es** *npl* (before exams etc) nervios *mpl.* get on s.o.'s ~**es** ponerle los nervios de punta a uno. ~**e-racking** *a* exasperante. ~**ous** /'nɜ:vəs/ *a* nervioso. be/feel ~**ous** estar nervioso. ~**ousness** *n* nerviosismo *m.* ~**y** /'nɜ:vɪ/ *a* nervioso; (Amer 🅸) descarado

nest /nest/ *n* nido *m.* ● *vi* anidar

nestle /'nesl/ *vi* acurrucarse

net /net/ *n* red *f.* the N~ (Comp) la Red. ● *vt* (*pt* **netted**) pescar (con red) <*fish*>. ● *a* neto. ~**ball** *n* baloncesto *m*

Netherlands /'neðələndz/ *npl.* the ~ los Países Bajos

netting /'netɪŋ/ *n* redes *fpl.* wire ~ tela *f* metálica

nettle /'netl/ *n* ortiga *f*

network /'netwɜ:k/ *n* red *f*; (TV) cadena *f*

neuro|sis /njʊə'rəʊsɪs/ *n* (*pl* **-oses** /-si:z/) neurosis *f.* ~**tic** /-'rɒtɪk/ *a* & *n* neurótico (*m*)

neuter /'nju:tə(r)/ *a* & *n* neutro (*m*). ● *vt* castrar <*animals*>

neutral /'nju:trəl/ *a* neutral; <*colour*> neutro; (Elec) neutro. ~ (**gear**) (Auto) punto *m* muerto. ~**ize** *vt* neutralizar

neutron /'nju:trɒn/ *n* neutrón *m*

never /'nevə(r)/ *adv* nunca; (more emphatic) jamás; (🅸, not) no. ~ **again** nunca más. he ~ **smiles** no sonríe nunca, nunca sonríe. I ~ **saw him** 🅸 no lo vi. ~**ending** *a* interminable. ~**theless** /-ðə'les/ *adv* sin embargo, no obstante

new /nju:/ *a* (**-er**, **-est**) nuevo. ~**born** *a* recién nacido. ~**comer** *n* recién llegado *m.* ~**fangled** /-'fæŋgld/ *a* (pej) moderno. ~**ly** *adv*

recién. ~**ly-weds** *npl* recién casados *mpl*

news /nju:z/ *n.* a piece of ~ una noticia. good/bad ~ buenas/malas noticias. the ~ (TV, Radio) las noticias. ~**agent** *n* vendedor *m* de periódicos. ~**caster** *n* locutor *m.* ~**dealer** *n* (Amer) ⇨~AGENT. ~**flash** *n* información *f* de última hora. ~**letter** *n* boletín *m*, informativo *m.* ~**paper** *n* periódico *m*, diario *m.* ~**reader** *n* locutor *m*

newt /nju:t/ *n* tritón *m*

New Year /nju:'jɪə(r)/ *n* Año *m* Nuevo. N~'s Day *n* día *m* de Año Nuevo. N~'s Eve *n* noche *f* vieja, noche *f* de fin de Año

New Zealand /nju:'zi:lənd/ *n* Nueva Zeland(i)a *f*

next /nekst/ *a* próximo; <*week*, *month etc*> que viene, próximo; (adjoining) vecino; (following) siguiente. ● *adv* luego, después. ~ **to** al lado de. when you see me ~ la próxima vez que me veas. ~ **to nothing** casi nada. ~ **door** al lado (**to** de). ~**door** *a* de al lado. ~ **of kin** *n* familiar(es) *m(pl)* más cercano(s)

nib /nɪb/ *n* plumilla *f*

nibble /'nɪbl/ *vt/i* mordisquear. ● *n* mordisco *m*

Nicaragua /nɪkə'rægjʊə/ *n* Nicaragua *f.* ~**n** *a* & *n* nicaragüense (*m* & *f*)

nice /naɪs/ *a* (**-er**, **-est**) agradable; (likeable) simpático; (kind) amable; <*weather*, *food*> bueno. we had a ~ time lo pasamos bien. ~**ly** *adv* (kindly) amablemente; (politely) con buenos modales

niche /nɪtʃ, ni:ʃ/ *n* nicho *m*

nick /nɪk/ *n* corte *m* pequeño. in the ~ of time justo a tiempo. ● *vt* (🅸 steal) afanar 🅱

nickel /'nɪkl/ *n* (metal) níquel *m*; (Amer) moneda *f* de cinco centavos

nickname /'nɪkneɪm/ *n* apodo *m.* ● *vt* apodar

nicotine /'nɪkəti:n/ *n* nicotina *f*

niece /ni:s/ *n* sobrina *f*

niggling /'nɪglɪŋ/ *a* <*doubt*> constante

night /naɪt/ n noche f; (evening) tarde f. **at** ~ por la noche, de noche. **good** ~ ¡buenas noches! ● a nocturno, de noche. ~**cap** n (drink) bebida f (tomada antes de acostarse). ~**club** n club m nocturno. ~**dress** n camisón m. ~**fall** n anochecer m. ~**gown**, ~**ie** /'naɪtɪ/ 🔟 n camisón m. ~**life** n vida f nocturna. ~**ly** a de todas las noches. ~**mare** n pesadilla f. ~ **school** n escuela f nocturna. ~**-time** n noche f. ~**watchman** n sereno m

nil /nɪl/ n nada f; (Sport) cero m

nimble /'nɪmbl/ a (**-er, -est**) ágil

nine /naɪn/ a & n nueve (m). ~**teen** /naɪn'tiːn/ a & n diecinueve (m). ~**teenth** a decimonoveno. ● n diecinueveavo m. ~**tieth** /'naɪntɪəθ/ a nonagésimo. ● n noventavo m. ~**ty** a & n noventa (m)

ninth /'naɪnθ/ a & n noveno (m)

nip /nɪp/ vt (pt **nipped**) (pinch) pellizcar; (bite) mordisquear. ● vi (🔟, rush) correr

nipple /'nɪpl/ n (of woman) pezón m; (of man) tetilla f; (of baby's bottle) tetina f, chupón m (Mex)

nippy /'nɪpɪ/ a (**-ier, -iest**) (🔟, chilly) fresquito

nitrogen /'naɪtrədʒən/ n nitrógeno m

no /nəʊ/ a ninguno, (before masculine singular noun) ningún. **I have** ~ **money** no tengo dinero. **there's** ~ **food left** no queda nada de comida. **it has** ~ **windows** no tiene ventanas. **I'm** ~ **expert** no soy ningún experto. ~ **smoking** prohibido fumar. ~ **way!** 🔟 ¡ni hablar! ● adv & int no. ● n (pl **noes**) no m

noble /'nəʊbl/ a (**-er, -est**) noble. ~**man** /-mən/ n noble m

nobody /'nəʊbədɪ/ pron nadie. **there's** ~ **there** no hay nadie

nocturnal /nɒk'tɜːnl/ a nocturno

nod /nɒd/ vt (pt **nodded**). ~ **one's head** asentir con la cabeza. ● vi (in agreement) asentir con la cabeza; (in greeting) saludar con la cabeza. □ ~ **off** vi dormirse

nois|e /nɔɪz/ n ruido m. ~**ily** adv ruidosamente. ~**y** a (**-ier, -iest**) ruidoso. **it's too** ~**y here** hay demasiado ruido aquí

nomad /'nəʊmæd/ n nómada m & f. ~**ic** /-'mædɪk/ a nómada

no man's land n tierra f de nadie

nominat|e /'nɒmɪneɪt/ vt (put forward) proponer; postular (LAm); (appoint) nombrar. ~**ion** /-'neɪʃn/ n nombramiento m; (Amer, Pol) proclamación f

non-... /nɒn/ pref no ...

nonchalant /'nɒnʃələnt/ a despreocupado

non-committal /nɒnkə'mɪtl/ a evasivo

nondescript /'nɒndɪskrɪpt/ a anodino

none /nʌn/ pron ninguno, ninguna. **there were** ~ **left** no quedaba ninguno/ninguna. ~ **of us** ninguno de nosotros. ● adv no, de ninguna manera. **he is** ~ **the happier** no está más contento

nonentity /nɒ'nentətɪ/ n persona f insignificante

non-existent /nɒnɪg'zɪstənt/ a inexistente

nonplussed /nɒn'plʌst/ a perplejo

nonsens|e /'nɒnsns/ n tonterías fpl, disparates mpl. ~**ical** /-'sensɪkl/ a disparatado

non-smoker /nɒn'sməʊkə(r)/ n no fumador m. **I'm a** ~ no fumo

non-stop /nɒn'stɒp/ a <train> directo; <flight> sin escalas. ● adv sin parar; (by train) directamente; (by air) sin escalas

noodles /'nuːdlz/ npl fideos mpl

nook /nʊk/ n rincón m

noon /nuːn/ n mediodía m

no-one /'nəʊwʌn/ pron nadie

noose /nuːs/ n soga f

nor /nɔː(r)/ conj ni, tampoco. **neither blue** ~ **red** ni azul ni rojo. **he doesn't play the piano,** ~ **do I** no sabe tocar el piano, ni yo tampoco

norm /nɔːm/ n norma f

normal /'nɔːml/ a normal. ~**cy** n (Amer) normalidad f. ~**ity** /-'mælətɪ/

n normalidad *f*. **~ly** *adv* normalmente

north /nɔːθ/ *n* norte *m*. ● *a* norte. ● *adv* hacia el norte. **N~ America** *n* América *f* del Norte, Norteamérica *f*. **N~ American** *a & n* norteamericano (*m*). **~east** *n* nor(d)este *m*. ● *a* nor(d)este. ● *adv* <go> hacia el nor(d)este. **it's ~east of Leeds** está al nor(d)este de Leeds. **~erly** /'nɔːðəlɪ/ *a* <wind> del norte. **~ern** /'nɔːðən/ *a* del norte. **~erner** *n* norteño *m*. **N~ern Ireland** *n* Irlanda *f* del Norte. **N~ Sea** *n* mar *m* del Norte. **~ward** /'nɔːθwəd/, **~wards** *adv* hacia el norte. **~west** *n* noroeste *m*. ● *a* noroeste. ● *adv* hacia el noroeste

Norw|ay /'nɔːweɪ/ *n* Noruega *f*. **~egian** /-'wiːdʒən/ *a & n* noruego (*m*)

nose /nəʊz/ *n* nariz *f*. **~bleed** *n* hemorragia *f* nasal. **~dive** *vi* descender en picado, descender en picada (LAm)

nostalgi|a /nɒ'stældʒə/ *n* nostalgia *f*. **~c** *a* nostálgico

nostril /'nɒstrɪl/ *n* ventana *f* de la nariz *f*

nosy /'nəʊzɪ/ *a* (**-ier, -iest**) ⊞ entrometido, metiche (LAm)

....

not /nɒt/

Cuando **not** va precedido del verbo auxiliar **do** or **have** o de un verbo modal como **should** etc se suele emplear la forma contraída **don't, haven't, shouldn't** etc

● *adverb*

····▶ no. **I don't know** no sé. **~ yet** todavía no. **~ me** yo no

····▶ (replacing a clause) **I suppose ~** supongo que no. **of course ~** por supuesto que no. **are you going to help me or ~?** ¿me vas a ayudar o no?

····▶ (emphatic) ni. **~ a penny more!** ¡ni un penique más!

····▶ (in phrases) **certainly ~** de ninguna manera . **~ you again!** ¡tú otra vez!

....

notabl|e /'nəʊtəbl/ *a* notable; <author> distinguido. **~y** /'nəʊtəblɪ/ *adv* notablemente; (in particular) particularmente

notch /nɒtʃ/ *n* muesca *f*. □ **~ up** *vt* apuntarse

note /nəʊt/ *n* (incl Mus) nota *f*; (banknote) billete *m*. **take ~s** tomar apuntes. ● *vt* (notice) observar; (record) anotar. □ **~ down** *vt* apuntar. **~book** *n* cuaderno *m*. **~d** *a* célebre. **~paper** *n* papel *m* de carta(s)

nothing /'nʌθɪŋ/ *pron* nada. **he eats ~** no come nada. **for ~** (free) gratis; (in vain) en vano. **~ else** nada más. **~ much happened** no pasó gran cosa. **he does ~ but complain** no hace más que quejarse

notice /'nəʊtɪs/ *n* (sign) letrero *m*; (item of information) anuncio *m*; (notification) aviso *m*; (of termination of employment) preaviso *m*; **~ (of dismissal)** despido *m*. **take ~ of** hacer caso a <person>. ● *vt* notar. ● *vi* darse cuenta. **~able** *a* perceptible. **~ably** *adv* perceptiblemente. **~board** *n* tablón *m* de anuncios, tablero *m* de anuncios (LAm)

notif|ication /nəʊtɪfɪ'keɪʃn/ *n* notificación *f*. **~y** /'nəʊtɪfaɪ/ *vt* informar; (in writing) notificar. **~y s.o. of sth** comunicarle algo a uno

notion /'nəʊʃn/ *n* (concept) concepto *m*; (idea) idea *f*

notorious /nəʊ'tɔːrɪəs/ *a* notorio

notwithstanding /nɒtwɪθ'stændɪŋ/ *prep* a pesar de. ● *adv* no obstante

nougat /'nuːgɑː/ *n* turrón *m*

nought /nɔːt/ *n* cero *m*

noun /naʊn/ *n* sustantivo *m*, nombre *m*

nourish /'nʌrɪʃ/ *vt* alimentar. **~ment** *n* alimento *m*

novel /'nɒvl/ *n* novela *f*. ● *a* original, novedoso. **~ist** *n* novelista *m & f*. **~ty** *n* novedad *f*

November /nəʊ'vembə(r)/ *n* noviembre *m*

novice /'nɒvɪs/ *n* principiante *m & f*

now /naʊ/ *adv* ahora. **~ and again, ~ and then** de vez en cuando. **right ~** ahora mismo. **from ~ on** a partir de ahora. ● *conj*. **~ (that)** ahora que. **~adays** /'naʊədeɪz/ *adv* hoy (en) día

nowhere /'nəʊweə(r)/ *adv* por ninguna parte, por ningún lado; (after motion towards) a ninguna parte, a ningún lado

nozzle /'nɒzl/ *n* (on hose) boca *f*; (on fire extinguisher) boquilla *f*

nuance /'njʊɑːns/ *n* matiz *m*

nuclear /'njuːklɪə(r)/ *a* nuclear

nucleus /'njuːklɪəs/ *n* (*pl* **-lei** /-lɪaɪ/) núcleo *m*

nude /njuːd/ *a & n* desnudo (*m*). **in the ~** desnudo

nudge /nʌdʒ/ *vt* codear (ligeramente). ● *n* golpe *m* (suave) con el codo

nudi|st /'njuːdɪst/ *n* nudista *m & f.* **~ty** /'njuːdətɪ/ *n* desnudez *f*

nuisance /'njuːsns/ *n* (thing, event) molestia *f*, fastidio *m*; (person) pesado *m*

null /nʌl/ *a* nulo

numb /nʌm/ *a* entumecido. **go ~** entumecerse ● *vt* entumecer

number /'nʌmbə(r)/ *n* número *m*; (telephone number) número *m* de teléfono. **a ~ of people** varias personas. ● *vt* numerar; (count, include) contar. **~plate** *n* matrícula *f*, placa *f* (LAm)

numer|al /'njuːmərəl/ *n* número *m*. **~ical** /nju'merɪkl/ *a* numérico. **~ous** /'njuːmərəs/ *a* numeroso

nun /nʌn/ *n* monja *f*

nurse /nɜːs/ *n* enfermero *m*, enfermera *f*; (nanny) niñera *f*. ● *vt* cuidar; abrigar *<hope etc>*

nursery /'nɜːsərɪ/ *n* (for plants) vivero *m*; (day ~) guardería *f*. **~ rhyme** *n* canción *f* infantil. **~ school** *n* jardín *m* de infancia, jardín *m* infan-til (LAm)

nursing home /'nɜːsɪŋ/ *n* (for older people) residencia *f* de ancianos (*con mayor nivel de asistencia médica*)

nut /nʌt/ *n* fruto *m* seco (nuez, almendra, avellana etc); (Tec) tuerca *f*. **~ case** *n* 🔲 chiflado *m*. **~crackers** *npl* cascanueces *m*. **~meg** /-meg/ *n* nuez *f* moscada

nutri|ent /'njuːtrɪənt/ *n* nutriente *m*. **~tion** /nju'trɪʃn/ *n* nutrición *f.* **~tious** /nju'trɪʃəs/ *a* nutritivo

nuts /nʌts/ *a* (🔲, crazy) chiflado

nutshell /'nʌtʃel/ *n* cáscara *f* de nuez. **in a ~** en pocas palabras

NW *abbr* (= **north-west**) NO

nylon /'naɪlɒn/ *n* nylon *m*

oaf /əʊf/ *n* zoquete *m*

oak /əʊk/ *n* roble *m*

OAP /əʊer'piː/ *abbr* (= **old-age pensioner**) *n* pensionista *m & f*, pensionado *m*

oar /ɔː(r)/ *n* remo *m*

oasis /əʊ'eɪsɪs/ *n* (*pl* **oases** /-siːz/) oasis *m*

oath /əʊθ/ *n* juramento *m*

oat|meal /'əʊtmiːl/ *n* harina *f* de avena; (Amer, flakes) avena *f* (en copos). **~s** /əʊts/ *npl* avena *f*

obedien|ce /əʊ'biːdɪəns/ *n* obediencia *f.* **~t** *a* obediente. **~tly** *adv* obedientemente

obes|e /əʊ'biːs/ *a* obeso. **~ity** *n* obesidad *f*

obey /əʊ'beɪ/ *vt/i* obedecer

obituary /ə'bɪtʃʊərɪ/ *n* nota *f* necrológica, obituario *m*

object /'ɒbdʒɪkt/ *n* objeto *m*; (aim) objetivo *m*. ● /əb'dʒekt/ *vi* oponerse (to a). **~ion** /əb'dʒekʃn/ *n* objeción *f.* **~ionable** *a* censurable; (unpleasant) desagradable. **~ive** /əb'dʒektɪv/ *a & n* objetivo (*m*)

oblig|ation /ɒblɪ'geɪʃn/ *n* obligación *f.* **be under an ~ation to** estar obligado a. **~atory** /ə'blɪgətrɪ/ *a* obligatorio. **~e** /ə'blaɪdʒ/ *vt* obligar. **I'd be much ~ed if you could help me** le quedaría muy agradecido si pudiera ayudarme. ● *vi* hacer un favor. **~ing** *a* atento

oblique /ə'bliːk/ *a* oblicuo

obliterate /ə'blɪtəreɪt/ *vt* arrasar; (erase) borrar

oblivio|n /ə'blɪvɪən/ *n* olvido *m*. **~us** /-vɪəs/ *a* (unaware) inconsciente (to, of de)

oblong /'ɒblɒŋ/ *a* oblongo. ● *n* rectángulo *m*

obnoxious /əbˈnɒkʃəs/ a odioso

oboe /ˈəʊbəʊ/ n oboe m

obscen|e /əbˈsiːn/ a obsceno. ∼**ity** /əbˈsenətɪ/ n obscenidad f

obscur|e /əbˈskjʊə(r)/ a oscuro. ● vt ocultar; impedir ver claramente <issue>. ∼**ity** n oscuridad f

obsequious /əbˈsiːkwɪəs/ a servil

observ|ant /əbˈzɜːvənt/ a observador. ∼**ation** /ɒbzəˈveɪʃn/ n observación f. ∼**atory** /əbˈzɜːvətrɪ/ n observatorio m. ∼**e** /əbˈzɜːv/ vt observar. ∼**er** n observador m

obsess /əbˈses/ vt obsesionar. ∼**ed** /əbˈsest/ a obsesionado. ∼**ion** /-ʃn/ n obsesión f. ∼**ive** a obsesivo

obsolete /ˈɒbsəliːt/ a obsoleto

obstacle /ˈɒbstəkl/ n obstáculo m

obstina|cy /ˈɒbstɪnəsɪ/ n obstinación f. ∼**te** /-ət/ a obstinado. ∼**tely** adv obstinadamente

obstruct /əbˈstrʌkt/ vt obstruir; bloquear <traffic>. ∼**ion** /-ʃn/ n obstrucción f

obtain /əbˈteɪn/ vt conseguir, obtener. ∼**able** a asequible

obtrusive /əbˈtruːsɪv/ a <presence> demasiado prominente; <noise> molesto

obtuse /əbˈtjuːs/ a obtuso

obvious /ˈɒbvɪəs/ a obvio. ∼**ly** adv obviamente

occasion /əˈkeɪʒn/ n ocasión f. ∼**al** a esporádico. ∼**ally** adv de vez en cuando

occult /ɒˈkʌlt/ a oculto

occup|ant /ˈɒkjʊpənt/ n ocupante m & f. ∼**ation** /ɒkjʊˈpeɪʃn/ n ocupación f. ∼**ier** /ˈɒkjʊpaɪə(r)/ n ocupante m & f. ∼**y** /ˈɒkjʊpaɪ/ vt ocupar. **keep o.s.** ∼**ied** entretenerse

occur /əˈkɜː(r)/ vi (pt **occurred**) tener lugar, ocurrir; <change> producirse; (exist) encontrarse. **it** ∼**red to me that** se me ocurrió que. ∼**rence** /əˈkʌrəns/ n (incidence) incidencia f. **it is a rare** ∼**rence** no es algo frecuente

ocean /ˈəʊʃn/ n océano m

o'clock /əˈklɒk/ adv. **it is 7** ∼ son las siete. **it's one** ∼ es la una

octagon /ˈɒktəgən/ n octágono m

ootroctave /ˈɒktɪv/ n octava f

October /ɒkˈtəʊbə(r)/ n octubre m

octopus /ˈɒktəpəs/ n (pl **-puses**) pulpo m

odd /ɒd/ a (**-er, -est**) extraño, raro; <number> impar; (one of pair) desparejado. **smoke the** ∼ **cigarette** fumarse algún que otro cigarrillo. **fifty-**∼ unos cincuenta, cincuenta y pico. **the** ∼ **one out** la excepción. ∼**ity** n (thing) rareza f; (person) bicho m raro. ∼**ly** adv de una manera extraña. ∼**ly enough** por extraño que parezca. ∼**ment** n retazo m. ∼**s** npl probabilidades fpl; (in betting) apuesta f. **be at** ∼**s** estar en desacuerdo. ∼**s and ends** mpl 🔲 cosas fpl sueltas

odious /ˈəʊdɪəs/ a odioso

odometer /ɒˈdɒmətə(r)/ n (Amer) cuentakilómetros m

odour /ˈəʊdə(r)/ n olor m

....

of /ɒv/, unstressed form /əv/

● preposition

····▶ de. **a pound of cheese** una libra de queso. **it's made of wood** es de madera. **a girl of ten** una niña de diez años

····▶ (in dates) de. **the fifth of November** el cinco de noviembre

····▶ (Amer, when telling the time) **it's ten (minutes) of five** son las cinco menos diez, son diez para las cinco (LAm)

❗ ■ of is not translated in cases such as the following:
■ **colleague of mine** un colega mío; **there were six of us** éramos seis; **that's very kind of you** es Ud muy amable

....

off /ɒf/ prep (from) de. **he picked it up** ∼ **the floor** lo recogió del suelo; (distant from) **just** ∼ **the coast of Texas** a poca distancia de la costa de Tejas. **2 ft** ∼ **the ground** a dos pies del suelo; (absent from) **I've been** ∼ **work for a week** hace una semana que no voy a trabajar. ● adv (removed) **the lid was** ∼ la tapa no estaba puesta; (distant) **some way** ∼ a cierta distancia; (leaving) **I'm** ∼ me voy; (switched off) <light, TV> apagado; <water> cortado; (cancelled) *<match>* cancelado; (not on duty) *<day>* libre. ● *adj.* be ~ *<meat>* estar malo, estar pasado; *<milk>* estar cortado. **~-beat** *a* poco convencional. ~ **chance** *n.* on the ~ **chance** por si acaso

offen|ce /əˈfens/ *n* (breach of law) infracción *f*; (criminal ~ce) delito *m*; (cause of outrage) atentado *m*; (Amer, attack) ataque *m*. **take** ~**ce** ofenderse. **~d** *vt* ofender. **~der** *n* delincuente *m & f*. **~sive** /-sɪv/ *a* ofensivo; (disgusting) desagradable

offer /ˈɒfə(r)/ *vt* ofrecer. ~ **to do sth** ofrecerse a hacer algo. ● *n* oferta *f*. **on** ~ de oferta

offhand /ɒfˈhænd/ *a* (brusque) brusco. **say sth in an ~ way** decir algo a la ligera. ● *adv* de improviso

office /ˈɒfɪs/ *n* oficina *f*; (post) cargo *m*. **doctor's** ~ (Amer) consultorio *m*, consulta *m*. ~ **block** *n* edificio *m* de oficinas **~r** *n* oficial *m & f*; (police ~r) policía *m & f*; (as form of address) agente

offici|al /əˈfɪʃl/ *a* oficial. ● *n* funcionario *m* del Estado; (of party, union) dirigente *m & f*. **~ally** *adv* oficialmente. **~ous** /əˈfɪʃəs/ *a* oficioso

offing /ˈɒfɪŋ/ *n.* **in the** ~ en perspectiva

off: **~-licence** *n* tienda *f* de vinos y licores. **~-putting** *a* (disconcerting) desconcertante; (disagreeable) desagradable. **~set** *vt* (*pt* **-set**, *pres p* **-setting**) compensar. **~side** /ɒfˈsaɪd/ *a* (Sport) fuera de juego. **~spring** *n invar* prole *f*. **~stage** /-ˈsteɪdʒ/ *adv* fuera del escenario. **~-white** *a* color hueso

often /ˈɒfn/ *adv* a menudo, con frecuencia. **how ~?** ¿con qué frecuencia? **more** ~ con más frecuencia

ogle /ˈəʊgl/ *vt* comerse con los ojos

ogre /ˈəʊgə(r)/ *n* ogro *m*

oh /əʊ/ *int* ¡ah!; (expressing dismay) ¡ay!

oil /ɔɪl/ *n* aceite *m*; (petroleum) petróleo *m*. ● *vt* lubricar. **~field** *n* yacimiento *m* petrolífero. **~painting** *n* pintura *f* al óleo; (picture) óleo *m*. **~rig** *n* plataforma *f* petrolífera. **~y** *a* *<substance>* oleaginoso; *<food>* aceitoso

ointment /ˈɔɪntmənt/ *n* ungüento *m*

OK /əʊˈkeɪ/ *int* ¡vale!, ¡de acuerdo!, ¡bueno! (LAm). ● *a* ~, **thanks** bien, gracias. **the job's** ~ el trabajo no está mal

old /əʊld/ *a* (**-er**, **-est**) viejo; (not modern) antiguo; (former) antiguo; **an** ~ **friend** un viejo amigo. **how** ~ **is she?** ¿cuántos años tiene? **she is ten years** ~ tiene diez años. **his ~er sister** su hermana mayor. ~ **age** *n* vejez *f*. **~-fashioned** /-ˈfæʃənd/ *a* anticuado

olive /ˈɒlɪv/ *n* aceituna *f*.

Olympic /əˈlɪmpɪk/ *a* olímpico. **the** **~s** *npl*, **the** ~ **Games** *npl* los Juegos Olímpicos

omelette /ˈɒmlɪt/ *n* tortilla *f* francesa, omelette *m* (LAm)

omen /ˈəʊmen/ *n* agüero *m*

omi|ssion /əˈmɪʃn/ *n* omisión *f*. **~t** /əˈmɪt/ *vt* (*pt* **omitted**) omitir

on /ɒn/ *prep* en, sobre; (about) sobre. ~ **foot** a pie. ~ **Monday** el lunes. ~ **seeing** al ver. **I heard it** ~ **the radio** lo oí por la radio. ● *adv* (light etc) encendido, prendido (LAm); (machine) en marcha; (tap) abierto. ~ **and** ~ sin cesar. **and so** ~ y así sucesivamente. **have a hat** ~ llevar (puesto) un sombrero. **further** ~ un poco más allá. **what's** ~ **at the Odeon?** ¿qué dan en el Odeon? **go** ~ continuar. **later** ~ más tarde

once /wʌns/ *adv* una vez; (formerly) antes. **at** ~ inmediatamente. ~ **upon a time there was...** érase una vez.... ~ **and for all** de una vez por todas. ● *conj* una vez que

one /wʌn/ *a* uno, (before masculine singular noun) un. **the** ~ **person I trusted** la única persona en la que confiaba. ● *n* uno *m*. ~ **by** ~ uno a uno.. ● *pron* uno (*m*), una (*f*). **the blue** ~ el/la azul. **this** ~ éste/ésta. ~ **another** el uno al otro.

onerous /ˈɒnərəs/ *a* *<task>* pesado

one: **~self** /-ˈself/ *pron* (reflexive) se; (*after prep*) sí (mismo); (emphatic use) uno mismo, una misma. **by ~self** solo. **~-way** *a* *<street>* de sentido único; *<ticket>* de ida, sencillo

onion /ˈʌnɪən/ *n* cebolla *f*

onlooker /'ɒnlʊkə(r)/ *n* espectador *m*

only /'əʊnlɪ/ *a* único. she's an ~ child es hija única. ● *adv* sólo, solamente. ~ **just** (barely) apenas. I've ~ just arrived acabo de llegar. ● *conj* pero, sólo que

onset /'ɒnset/ *n* comienzo *m*; (of disease) aparición *f*

onslaught /'ɒnslɔːt/ *n* ataque *m*

onus /'əʊnəs/ *n* responsabilidad *f*

onward(s) /'ɒnwəd(z)/ *a & adv* hacia adelante

ooze /uːz/ *vt/i* rezumar

opaque /əʊ'peɪk/ *a* opaco

open /'əʊpən/ *a* abierto; <*question*> discutible. ● *n*. in the ~ al aire libre. ● *vt/i* abrir. ~**ing** *n* abertura *f*; (beginning) principio *m*. ~**ly** *adv* abiertamente. ~**-minded** /-'maɪndɪd/ *a* de actitud abierta

opera /'ɒprə/ *n* ópera *f*

operate /'ɒpəreɪt/ *vt* manejar, operar (Mex) <*machine*>. ● *vi* funcionar; <*company*> operar. ~ (on) (Med) operar (a)

operatic /ɒpə'rætɪk/ *a* operístico

operation /ɒpə'reɪʃn/ *n* operación *f*; (Mec) funcionamiento *m*; (using of machine) manejo *m*. he had an ~ lo operaron. in ~ en vigor. ~**al** *a* operacional

operative /'ɒpərətɪv/ *a*. be ~ estar en vigor

operator *n* operador *m*

opinion /ə'pɪnɪən/ *n* opinión *f*. in my ~ en mi opinión, a mi parecer

opponent /ə'pəʊnənt/ *n* adversario *m*; (in sport) contrincante *m & f*

opportun|e /'ɒpətjuːn/ *a* oportuno. ~**ist** /ɒpə'tjuːnɪst/ *n* oportunista *m & f*. ~**ity** /ɒpə'tjuːnətɪ/ *n* oportunidad *f*

oppos|e /ə'pəʊz/ *vt* oponerse a. be ~**ed to** oponerse a, estar en contra de. ~**ing** *a* opuesto. ~**ite** /'ɒpəzɪt/ *a* (contrary) opuesto; (facing) de enfrente. ● *n*. the ~**ite** lo contrario. quite the ~**ite** al contrario. ● *adv* enfrente. ● *prep* enfrente de. ~**ite number** *n* homólogo *m*. ~**ition** /ɒpə'zɪʃn/ *n* oposición *f*; (resistence) resistencia *f*

oppress /ə'pres/ *vt* oprimir. ~**ion** /-ʃn/ *n* opresión *f*. ~**ive** *a* (cruel) opresivo; <*heat*> sofocante

opt /ɒpt/ *vi*. ~ **to** optar por. □ ~ **out** *vi* decidir no tomar parte

optic|al /'ɒptɪkl/ *a* óptico. ~**ian** /ɒp'tɪʃn/ *n* óptico *m*

optimis|m /'ɒptɪmɪzəm/ *n* optimismo *m*. ~**t** *n* optimista *m & f*. ~**tic** /-'mɪstɪk/ *a* optimista

option /'ɒpʃn/ *n* opción *f*. ~**al** *a* facultativo

or /ɔː(r)/ *conj* o; (before o- and ho-) u; (*after negative*) ni. ~ **else** si no, o bien

oral /'ɔːrəl/ *a* oral. ● *n* Ⓣ examen *m* oral

orange /'ɒrɪndʒ/ *n* naranja *f*; (colour) naranja *m*. ● *a* naranja. ~**ade** /-'eɪd/ *n* naranjada *f*

orbit /'ɔːbɪt/ *n* órbita *f*. ● *vt* orbitar

orchard /'ɔːtʃəd/ *n* huerto *m*

orchestra /'ɔːkɪstrə/ *n* orquesta *f*; (Amer, in theatre) platea *f*. ~**l** /-'kestrəl/ *a* orquestal. ~**te** /-eɪt/ *vt* orquestar

orchid /'ɔːkɪd/ *n* orquídea *f*

ordain /ɔː'deɪn/ *vt* (Relig) ordenar; (decree) decretar

ordeal /ɔː'diːl/ *n* dura prueba *f*

order /'ɔːdə(r)/ *n* orden *m*; (Com) pedido *m*; (command) orden *f*. in ~ that para que. in ~ to para. ● *vt* (command) ordenar, mandar; (Com) pedir; (in restaurant) pedir, ordenar (LAm); encargar <*book*>; llamar, ordenar (LAm) <*taxi*>. ~**ly** *a* ordenado. ● *n* camillero *m*

ordinary /'ɔːdɪnrɪ/ *a* corriente; (average) medio; (mediocre) ordinario

ore /ɔː(r)/ *n* mena *f*

organ /'ɔːgən/ *n* órgano *m*

organ|ic /ɔː'gænɪk/ *a* orgánico. ~**ism** /'ɔːgənɪzəm/ *n* organismo *m*. ~**ist** /'ɔːgənɪst/ *n* organista *m & f*. ~**ization** /ɔːgənaɪ'zeɪʃn/ *n* organización *f*. ~**ize** /'ɔːgənaɪz/ *vt* organizar. ~**izer** *n* organizador *m*

orgasm /'ɔːgæzəm/ *n* orgasmo *m*

orgy /'ɔːdʒɪ/ *n* orgía *f*

Orient /'ɔːrɪənt/ *n* Oriente *m*. ~**al** /-'entl/ *a* oriental

orientat|e /'ɔːrɪənteɪt/ vt orientar. ∼**ion** /-'teɪʃn/ n orientación f

origin /'ɒrɪdʒɪn/ n origen m. ∼**al** /ə'rɪdʒənl/ a original. ∼**ally** adv originariamente. ∼**ate** /ə'rɪdʒɪneɪt/ vi. ∼**ate from** provenir de

ornament /'ɔːnəmənt/ n adorno m. ∼**al** /-'mentl/ a de adorno

ornate /ɔː'neɪt/ a ornamentado; <style> recargado

ornithology /ɔːnɪ'θɒlədʒɪ/ n ornitología f

orphan /'ɔːfn/ n huérfano m. ● vt. be ∼ed quedar huérfano. ∼**age** /-ɪdʒ/ n orfanato m

orthodox /'ɔːθədɒks/ a ortodoxo

oscillate /'ɒsɪleɪt/ vi oscilar

ostentatious /ɒsten'teɪʃəs/ a ostentoso

osteopath /'ɒstɪəpæθ/ n osteópata m & f

ostracize /'ɒstrəsaɪz/ vt hacerle vacío a

ostrich /'ɒstrɪtʃ/ n avestruz m

other /'ʌðə(r)/ a & pron otro. ∼ than aparte de. the ∼ one el otro. ∼**wise** adv de lo contrario, si no

otter /'ɒtə(r)/ n nutria f

ouch /aʊtʃ/ int ¡ay!

ought /ɔːt/ v aux. I ∼ to see it debería verlo. he ∼ to have done it debería haberlo hecho

ounce /aʊns/ n onza f (= 28.35 gr.)

our /'aʊə(r)/ a (sing) nuestro, nuestra, (pl) nuestros, nuestras. ∼**s** /'aʊəz/ poss pron (sing) nuestro, nuestra; (pl) nuestros, nuestras. ∼**s is red** el nuestro es rojo. **a friend of** ∼**s** un amigo nuestro. ∼**selves** /-'selvz/ pron (reflexive) nos; (used for emphasis and after prepositions) nosotros mismos, nosotras mismas. **we behaved** ∼**selves** nos portamos bien. **we did it** ∼**selves** lo hicimos nosotros mismos/nosotras mismas

oust /aʊst/ vt desbancar; derrocar <government>

out /aʊt/ adv (outside) fuera, afuera (LAm). (not lighted, not on) apagado; (in blossom) en flor; (in error) equivocado. **he's** ∼ (not at home) no está; **be** ∼ **to** estar resuelto a. ∼ **of** prep (from inside) de; (outside) fuera, afuera (LAm).

five ∼ **of six** cinco de cada seis. **made** ∼ **of** hecho de. **we're** ∼ **of bread** nos hemos quedado sin pan. ∼**break** n (of war) estallido m; (of disease) brote m. ∼**burst** n arrebato m. ∼**cast** n paria m & f. ∼**come** n resultado m. ∼**cry** n protesta f. ∼**dated** /-'deɪtɪd/ a anticuado. ∼**do** /-'duː/ vt (pt -**did**, pp -**done**) superar. ∼**door** a <clothes> de calle; <pool> descubierto. ∼**doors** /-'dɔːz/ adv al aire libre

outer /'aʊtə(r)/ a exterior

out: ∼**fit** n equipo m; (clothes) conjunto m. ∼**going** a <minister etc> saliente; (sociable) abierto. ∼**goings** npl gastos mpl. ∼**grow** /-'grəʊ/ vt (pt -**grew**, pp -**grown**) crecer más que <person>. **he's** ∼**grown his new shoes** le han queda-do pequeños los zapatos nuevos. ∼**ing** n excursión f

outlandish /aʊt'lændɪʃ/ a extravagante

out: ∼**law** n forajido m. ● vt proscribir. ∼**lay** n gastos mpl. ∼**let** n salida f; (Com) punto m de venta; (Amer, Elec) toma f de corriente. ∼**line** n contorno m; (summary) resumen m; (plan of project) esquema m. ● vt trazar; (summarize) esbozar. ∼**live** /-'lɪv/ vt sobrevivir a. ∼**look** n perspectivas fpl; (attitude) punto m de vista. ∼**lying** a alejado. ∼**number** /-'nʌmbə(r)/ vt superar en número. ∼-**of-date** a <ideas> desfasado; <clothes> pasado de moda. ∼**patient** n paciente m externo. ∼**post** n avanzada f. ∼**put** n pro-ducción f; (of machine, worker) rendi-miento m. ∼**right** adv comple-tamente; (frankly) abiertamente; <kill> en el acto. ● a completo; <refusal> rotundo. ∼**set** n principio m. ∼**side** a & n exterior (m). **at the** ∼**side** como máximo. ● /-'saɪd/ adv fuera, afuera (LAm). ● prep fuera de. ∼**size** a de talla gigante. ∼**skirts** npl afueras fpl. ∼**spoken** /-'spəʊkn/ a directo, franco. ∼**standing** /-'stændɪŋ/ a excepcional; <debt> pendiente. ∼**stretched** /aʊt'stretʃt/ a extendido. ∼**strip** /-'strɪp/ vt (pt -**stripped**) (run faster than) tomarle la delantera a; (exceed) sobrepasar. **~ward** /-wəd/ *a* *<appearance>* exterior; *<sign>* externo; *<journey>* de ida. **~wardly** *adv* por fuera, exteriormente. **~(s)** *adv* hacia afuera. **~weigh** /-'weɪ/ *vt* ser mayor que. **~wit** /-'wɪt/ *vt* (*pt* **-witted**) burlar

oval /'əʊvl/ *a* ovalado, oval. ● *n* óvalo *m*

ovary /'əʊvərɪ/ *n* ovario *m*

ovation /əʊ'veɪʃn/ *n* ovación *f*

oven /'ʌvn/ *n* horno *m*

over /'əʊvə(r)/ *prep* por encima de; (across) al otro lado de; (during) durante; (more than) más de. **~ and above** por encima de. ● *adv* por encima; (ended) terminado; (more) más; (in excess) de sobra. **~ again** otra vez. **~ and ~** una y otra vez. **~ here** por aquí. **~ there** por allí. **all ~** (finished) acabado; (everywhere) por todas partes

over... /'əʊvə(r)/ *pref* excesivamente, demasiado

over: **~all** /-'ɔːl/ *a* global; *<length, cost>* total. ● *adv* en conjunto. ● /'əʊvərɔːl/ *n*, **~alls** *npl* mono *m*, overol *m* (LAm); (Amer, dungarees) peto *m*, overol *m*. **~awe** /-'ɔː/ *vt* intimidar. **~balance** /-'bæləns/ *vi* perder el equilibrio. **~bearing** /-'beərɪŋ/ *a* dominante. **~board** *adv* *<throw>* por la borda. **~cast** /-'kɑːst/ *a* *<day>* nublado; *<sky>* cubierto. **~charge** /-'tʃɑːdʒ/ *vt* cobrarle de más. **~coat** *n* abrigo *m*. **~come** /-'kʌm/ *vt* (*pt* **-came**, *pp* **-come**) superar, vencer. **~crowded** /-'kraʊdɪd/ *a* abarrotado (de gente). **~do** /-'duː/ *vt* (*pt* **-did**, *pp* **-done**) exagerar; (Culin) recocer. **~dose** *n* sobredosis *f*. **~draft** *n* descubierto *m*. **~draw** /-'drɔː/ *vt* (*pt* **-drew**, *pp* **-drawn**) girar en descubierto. **be ~drawn** tener un descubierto. **~due** /-'djuː/ *a*. **the book is a month ~due** el plazo de devolución del libro venció hace un mes. **~estimate** /-'estɪmeɪt/ *vt* sobreestimar. **~flow** /-'fləʊ/ *vi* desbordarse. ● *n* /-fləʊ/ (excess) exceso *m*; (outlet) rebosadero *m*. **~grown** /-'grəʊn/ *a* demasiado grande; *<garden>* lleno de maleza. **~haul** /-'hɔːl/ *vt* revisar. ● /-hɔːl/ *n* revisión *f*.

~head /-'hed/ *adv* por encima. ● /-hed/ *a* de arriba. **~heads** /-hedz/ *npl*, **~head** *n* (Amer) gastos *mpl* indirectos. **~hear** /-'hɪə(r)/ *vt* (*pt* **-heard**) oír por casualidad. **~joyed** /-'dʒɔɪd/ *a* encantado. **~land** *a*/*adv* por tierra. **~lap** /-'læp/ *vi* (*pt* **-lapped**) traslaparse. **~leaf** /-'liːf/ *adv* al dorso. **~load** /-'ləʊd/ *vt* sobrecargar. **~look** /-'lʊk/ *vt* *<room>* dar a; (not notice) pasar por alto; (disregard) disculpar. **~night** /-'naɪt/ *adv* durante la noche. **stay ~night** quedarse a pasar la noche. ● *a* *<journey>* de noche; *<stay>* de una noche. **~pass** *n* paso *m* elevado, paso *m* a desnivel (Mex). **~pay** /-'peɪ/ *vt* (*pt* **-paid**) pagar demasiado. **~power** /-'paʊə(r)/ *vt* dominar *<opponent>*; *<emotion>* abrumar. **~powering** /-'paʊərɪŋ/ *a* *<smell>* muy fuerte; *<desire>* irrestible. **~priced** /-'praɪst/ *a* demasiado caro. **~rated** /-'reɪtɪd/ *a* sobrevalorado. **~react** /-rɪ'ækt/ *vi* reaccionar en forma exagerada. **~ride** /-'raɪd/ *vt* (*pt* **-rode**, *pp* **-ridden**) invalidar. **~riding** /-'raɪdɪŋ/ *a* dominante. **~rule** /-'ruːl/ *vt* anular; rechazar *<objection>*. **~run** /-'rʌn/ *vt* (*pt* **-ran**, *pp* **-run**, *pres p* **-running**) invadir; exceder *<limit>*. **~seas** /-'siːz/ *a* *<trade>* exterior; *<investments>* en el exterior; *<visitor>* extranjero. ● *adv* al extranjero. **~see** /-'siː/ *vt* (*pt* **-saw**, *pp* **-seen**) supervisar. **~seer** /-sɪə(r)/ *n* capataz *m* & *f*, supervisor *m*. **~shadow** /-'ʃædəʊ/ *vt* eclipsar. **~shoot** /-'ʃuːt/ *vt* (*pt* **-shot**) excederse. **~sight** /n descuido *m*. **~sleep** /-'sliːp/ *vi* (*pt* **-slept**) quedarse dormido. **~step** /-'step/ *vt* (*pt* **-stepped**) sobrepasar. **~step the mark** pasarse de la raya

overt /'əʊvɜːt/ *a* manifiesto

over: **~take** /-'teɪk/ *vt*/*i* (*pt* **-took**, *pp* **-taken**) sobrepasar; (Auto) adelantar, rebasar (Mex). **~throw** /-'θrəʊ/ *vt* (*pt* **-threw**, *pp* **-thrown**) derrocar. **~time** *n* horas *fpl* extra

overture /'əʊvətjʊə(r)/ *n* obertura *f*

over: **~turn** /-'tɜːn/ *vt* darle la vuelta a. ● *vi* volcar. **~weight** /-'weɪt/ *a* demasiado gordo. **be ~weight** pesar demasiado. **~whelm** /-'welm/ vt aplastar; (with emotion) abrumar. **~whelming** a aplastante; (fig) abrumador. **~work** /-'wɜːk/ vt hacer trabajar demasiado. ● vi trabajar demasiado. ● n agotamiento m

ow|e /əʊ/ vt deber. **~ing to** debido a

owl /aʊl/ n búho m

own /əʊn/ a propio. my ~ house mi propia casa. ● pron. it's my ~ es mío (propio)/mía (propia). on one's ~ solo. get one's ~ back 🄳 desquitarse. ● vt tener. □ ~ up vi. 🄳 confesarse culpable. **~er** n propietario m, dueño m. **~ership** n propiedad f

oxygen /'ɒksɪdʒən/ n oxígeno m

oyster /'ɔɪstə(r)/ n ostra f

····················

Pp

····················

p abbr (= **pence, penny**) penique(s) m(pl)

p. (pl **pp.**) (= **page**) pág., p.

pace /peɪs/ n paso m. keep ~ with s.o. seguirle el ritmo a uno. ● vi. ~ up and down andar de un lado para otro. **~maker** n (runner) liebre f; (Med) marcapasos m

Pacific /pə'sɪfɪk/ n. the ~ (Ocean) el (Océano) Pacífico m

pacif|ist /'pæsɪfɪst/ n pacifista m & f. **~y** /'pæsɪfaɪ/ vt apaciguar

pack /pæk/ n fardo m; (of cigarettes) paquete m, cajetilla f; (of cards) baraja f; (of hounds) jauría f; (of wolves) manada f. a ~ of lies una sarta de mentiras. ● vt empaquetar; hacer <suitcase>; (press down) apisonar. ● vi hacer la maleta, empacar (LAm). **~age** /-ɪdʒ/ n paquete m. **~age holiday** n vacaciones fpl organizadas. **~ed** /pækt/ a lleno (de gente). **~et** /'pækɪt/ n paquete m

pact /pækt/ n pacto m, acuerdo m

pad /pæd/ n (for writing) bloc m. shoulder **~s** hombreras fpl. ● vt (pt **padded**) rellenar

paddle /'pædl/ n pala f. ● vi mojarse los pies; (in canoe) remar (con pala)

paddock /'pædək/ n prado m

padlock /'pædlɒk/ n candado m. ● vt cerrar con candado

paed|iatrician /piːdɪə'trɪʃn/ n pediatra m & f. **~ophile** /'piːdəfaɪl/ n pedófilo m

pagan /'peɪɡən/ a & n pagano (m)

page /peɪdʒ/ n página f; (attendant) paje m; (in hotel) botones m. ● vt llamar por megafonía/por buscapersonas

paid /peɪd/ ⇒PAY. ● a. put ~ to 🄳 acabar con

pail /peɪl/ n balde m, cubo m

pain /peɪn/ n dolor m. I have a ~ in my back me duele la espalda. m. be in ~ tener dolores. be a ~ in the neck 🄳 ser un pesado; (thing) ser una lata. ● vt doler. **~ful** a doloroso. it's very **~ful** duele mucho. **~killer** n analgésico m. **~less** a indoloro. **~staking** /'peɪnzteɪkɪŋ/ a concienzudo

paint /peɪnt/ n pintura f. ● vt/i pintar. **~er** n pintor m. **~ing** n (medium) pintura f; (picture) cuadro m

pair /peə(r)/ n par m; (of people) pareja f. a ~ of trousers unos pantalones. □ ~off, ~ up vi formar parejas

pajamas /pə'dʒɑːməz/ npl (Amer) pijama m

Pakistan /pɑːkɪ'stɑːn/ n Pakistán m. **~i** a & n paquistaní (m & f)

pal /pæl/ n 🄳 amigo m

palace /'pælɪs/ n palacio m

palat|able /'pælətəbl/ a agradable. **~e** /'pælət/ n paladar m

pale /peɪl/ a (-er, -est) pálido. go ~, turn ~ palidecer. **~ness** n palidez f

Palestin|e /'pælɪstaɪn/ n Palestina f. **~ian** /-'stɪnɪən/ a & n palestino (m)

palette /'pælɪt/ n paleta f

palm /pɑːm/ n palma f. □ ~ off vt encajar (on a). **P~ Sunday** n Domingo m de Ramos

palpable /'pælpəbl/ a palpable

palpitat|e /'pælpɪteɪt/ vi palpitar. **~ion** /-'teɪʃn/ n palpitación f

pamper /'pæmpə(r)/ vt mimar

pamphlet /'pæmflɪt/ n folleto m

pan /pæn/ n cacerola f; (for frying) sartén f

panacea /pænə'sɪə/ n panacea f

Panama /'pænəmɑː/ n Panamá m. ∼**nian** /-'meɪnɪən/ a & n panameño (m)

pancake /'pænkeɪk/ n crep(e) m, panqueque m (LAm)

panda /'pændə/ n panda m

pandemonium /pændɪ'məʊnɪəm/ n pandemonio m

pander /'pændə(r)/ vi. ∼ **to s.o.** consentirle los caprichos a uno

pane /peɪn/ n vidrio m, cristal m

panel /'pænl/ n panel m; (group of people) jurado m. ∼**ling** n paneles mpl

pang /pæŋ/ n punzada f

panic /'pænɪk/ n pánico m. ● vi (pt **panicked**) dejarse llevar por el pánico. ∼**-stricken** a aterrorizado

panoram|a /pænə'rɑːmə/ n panorama m. ∼**ic** /-'ræmɪk/ a panorámico

pansy /'pænzɪ/ n (Bot) pensamiento m

pant /pænt/ vi jadear

panther /'pænθə(r)/ n pantera f

panties /'pæntɪz/ npl bragas fpl, calzones mpl (LAm), pantaletas fpl (Mex)

pantihose /'pæntɪhəʊz/ npl ⇒PANTYHOSE

pantomime /'pæntəmaɪm/ n pantomima f

pantry /'pæntrɪ/ n despensa f

pants /pænts/ npl (man's) calzoncillos mpl; (woman's) bragas fpl, calzones mpl (LAm), pantaletas fpl (Mex); (Amer, trousers) pantalones mpl

pantyhose /'pæntɪhəʊz/ npl (Amer) panty m, medias fpl, pantimedias fpl (Mex)

paper /'peɪpə(r)/ n papel m; (newspaper) diario m, periódico m; (exam) examen m; (document) documento m. ● vt empapelar, tapizar (Mex). ∼**back** n libro m en rústica. ∼ **clip** n sujetapapeles m, clip m. ∼**weight** n pisapapeles m. ∼**work** n papeleo m, trabajo m administrativo

parable /'pærəbl/ n parábola f

parachut|e /'pærəʃuːt/ n paracaídas m. ● vi saltar en paracaídas. ∼**ist** n paracaidista m & f

parade /pə'reɪd/ n desfile m; (Mil) formación f. ● vi desfilar. ● vt hacer alarde de

paradise /'pærədaɪs/ n paraíso m

paraffin /'pærəfɪn/ n queroseno m

paragraph /'pærəɡrɑːf/ n párrafo m

Paraguay /'pærəɡwaɪ/ n Paraguay m. ∼**an** a & n paraguayo (m)

parallel /'pærəlel/ a paralelo. ● n paralelo m; (line) paralela f

paraly|se /'pærəlaɪz/ vt paralizar. ∼**sis** /pə'ræləsɪs/ n (pl **-ses** /-siːz/) parálisis f

paranoia /pærə'nɔɪə/ n paranoia f

parapet /'pærəpɪt/ n parapeto m

paraphernalia /pærəfə'neɪlɪə/ n trastos mpl

parasite /'pærəsaɪt/ n parásito m

paratrooper /'pærətruːpə(r)/ n paracaidista m (del ejército)

parcel /'pɑːsl/ n paquete m

parch /pɑːtʃ/ vt resecar. be ∼**ed** 🄣 estar muerto de sed

parchment /'pɑːtʃmənt/ n pergamino m

pardon /'pɑːdn/ n perdón m; (Jurid) indulto m. **I beg your** ∼ perdón. (I beg your) ∼? ¿cómo?, ¿mande? (Mex). ● vt perdonar; (Jurid) indultar. ∼ **me?** (Amer) ¿cómo?

parent /'peərənt/ n (father) padre m; (mother) madre f. **my** ∼**s** mis padres. ∼**al** /pə'rentl/ a de los padres

parenthesis /pə'renθəsɪs/ n (pl **-theses** /-siːz/) paréntesis m

parenthood /'peərənthʊd/ n el ser padre/madre

Paris /'pærɪs/ n París m

parish /'pærɪʃ/ n parroquia f; (municipal) distrito m. ∼**ioner** /pə'rɪʃənə(r)/ n feligrés m

park /pɑːk/ n parque m. ● vt/i aparcar, estacionar (LAm)

parking: /'pɑːkɪŋ/∼ **lot** n (Amer) aparcamiento m, estacionamiento m (LAm). ∼ **meter** n parquímetro m

parkway /'pɑːkweɪ/ n (Amer) carretera f ajardinada

parliament /'pɑːləmənt/ n parlamento m. **~ary** /-'mentrɪ/ a parlamentario

parlour /'pɑːlə(r)/ n salón m

parochial /pə'rəʊkɪəl/ a (fig) provinciano

parody /'pærədɪ/ n parodia f. ● vt parodiar

parole /pə'rəʊl/ n libertad f condicional

parrot /'pærət/ n loro m, papagayo m

parsley /'pɑːslɪ/ n perejil m

parsnip /'pɑːsnɪp/ n pastinaca f

part /pɑːt/ n parte f; (of machine) pieza f; (of serial) episodio m; (in play) papel m; (Amer, in hair) raya f. take ~ in tomar parte en, participar en. for the most ~ en su mayor parte. ● adv en parte. ● vt separar. ● vi separarse. □ ~ with vt desprenderse de

partial /'pɑːʃl/ a parcial. be ~ to tener debilidad por. **~ly** adv parcialmente

participa|nt /pɑː'tɪsɪpənt/ n participante m & f. **~te** /-peɪt/ vi participar. **~tion** /-'peɪʃn/ n participación f

particle /'pɑːtɪkl/ n partícula f

particular /pə'tɪkjʊlə(r)/ a particular; (precise) meticuloso; (fastidious) quisquilloso. in ~ en particular. ● n detalle m. **~ly** adv particularmente; (specifically) específicamente

parting /'pɑːtɪŋ/ n despedida f; (in hair) raya f. ● a de despedida

partition /pɑː'tɪʃn/ n partición f; (wall) tabique m. ● vt dividir

partly /'pɑːtlɪ/ adv en parte

partner /'pɑːtnə(r)/ n socio m; (Sport) pareja f. **~ship** n asociación f; (Com) sociedad f

partridge /'pɑːtrɪdʒ/ n perdiz f

part-time /pɑː't'taɪm/ a & adv a tiempo parcial, de medio tiempo (LAm)

party /'pɑːtɪ/ n reunión f, fiesta f; (group) grupo m; (Pol) partido m; (Jurid) parte f

pass /pɑːs/ vt (hand, convey) pasar; (go past) pasar por delante de; (overtake) adelantar, rebasar (Mex); (approve) aprobar <exam, bill, law>; pronunciar <judgement>. ● vi pasar; <pain> pasarse; (Sport) pasar la pelota. □ ~ away vi fallecer. □ ~ down vt transmitir. □ ~ out vi desmayarse. □ ~ round vt distribuir. □ ~ up vt ⊞ dejar pasar. ● n (permit) pase m; (ticket) abono m; (in mountains) puerto m, desfiladero m; (Sport) pase m; (in exam) aprobado m. make a ~ at ⊞ intentar besar. **~able** a pasable; <road> transitable

passage /'pæsɪdʒ/ n (voyage) travesía f; (corridor) pasillo m; (alleyway) pasaje m; (in book) pasaje m

passenger /'pæsɪndʒə(r)/ n pasajero m

passer-by /pɑːsə'baɪ/ n (pl **passers-by**) transeúnte m & f

passion /'pæʃn/ n pasión f. **~ate** /-ət/ a apasionado. **~ately** adv apasionadamente

passive /'pæsɪv/ a pasivo

Passover /'pɑːsəʊvə(r)/ n Pascua f de los hebreos

pass: ~port n pasaporte m. **~word** n contraseña f

past /pɑːst/ a anterior; <life> pasado; <week, year> último. in times ~ en tiempos pasados. ● n pasado m. in the ~ (formerly) antes, antiguamente. ● prep por delante de; (beyond) más allá de. it's twenty ~ four son las cuatro y veinte. ● adv. drive ~ pasar en coche. go ~ pasar

paste /peɪst/ n pasta f; (glue) engrudo m; (wallpaper ~) pegamento m; (jewellery) estrás m

pastel /'pæstl/ a & n pastel (m)

pasteurize /'pɑːstʃəraɪz/ vt pasteurizar

pastime /'pɑːstaɪm/ n pasatiempo m

pastry /'peɪstrɪ/ n masa f; (cake) pastelito m

pasture /'pɑːstʃə(r)/ n pasto(s) mpl

pasty /'pæstɪ/ n empanadilla f, empanada f (LAm)

pat /pæt/ vt (pt **patted**) darle palmaditas. ● n palmadita f; (of butter) porción f

patch /pætʃ/ n (on clothes) remiendo m, parche m; (over eye) parche m. **a bad ~** una mala racha. ●vt remendar. □ ~ **up** vt hacerle un arreglo a

patent /'peɪtnt/ a patente. ●n patente f. ●vt patentar. ~ **leather** n charol m. ~**ly** adv. it's ~ly obvious that... está clarísimo que...

patern|al /pə'tɜːnl/ a paterno. ~**ity** /-ətɪ/ n paternidad f

path /pɑːθ/ n (pl **-s** /pɑːðz/) sendero m; (Sport) pista f; (of rocket) trayectoria f; (fig) camino m

pathetic /pə'θetɪk/ a (pitiful) patético; <excuse> pobre. **don't be so ~** no seas tan pusilánime

patien|ce /'peɪʃns/ n paciencia f. ~**t** a & n paciente (m & f). **be ~t with s.o.** tener paciencia con uno. ~**tly** adv pacientemente

patio /'pætɪəʊ/ n (pl **-os**) patio m

patriot /'pætrɪət/ n patriota m & f. ~**ic** /-'ɒtɪk/ a patriótico. ~**ism** n patriotismo m

patrol /pə'trəʊl/ n patrulla f. ●vt/i patrullar

patron /'peɪtrən/ n (of the arts) mecenas m & f; (of charity) patrocinador m; (customer) cliente m & f. ~**age** /'pætrənɪdʒ/ n (sponsorship) patrocinio m; (of the arts) mecenazgo m. ~**ize** /'pætrənaɪz/ vt ser cliente de; (fig) tratar con condescendencia. ~**izing** a condescendiente

pattern /'pætn/ n diseño m; (sample) muestra f; (in dressmaking) patrón m

paunch /pɔːntʃ/ n panza f

pause /pɔːz/ n pausa f. ●vi hacer una pausa

pave /peɪv/ vt pavimentar; (with flagstones) enlosar. ~**ment** n pavimento m; (at side of road) acera f, banqueta f (Mex)

paving stone /'peɪvɪŋstəʊn/ n losa f

paw /pɔː/ n pata f

pawn /pɔːn/ n (Chess) peón m; (fig) títere m. ●vt empeñar. ~**broker** n prestamista m & f

pay /peɪ/ vt (pt **paid**) pagar; prestar <attention>; hacer <compliment, visit>. ~ **cash** pagar al contado. ●vi pagar; (be profitable) rendir. ●n paga f. **in the ~ of** al servicio de. □ ~ **back** vt devolver; pagar <loan>. □ ~ **in** vt ingresar, depositar (LAm). □ ~ **off** vt cancelar, saldar <debt>. vi valer la pena. □ ~ **up** vi pagar. ~**able** a pagadero. ~**ment** n pago m. ~**roll** n nómina f

pea /piː/ n guisante m, arveja f (LAm), chícharo m (Mex)

peace /piːs/ n paz f. ~ **of mind** tranquilidad f. ~**ful** a tranquilo. ~**maker** n conciliador m

peach /piːtʃ/ n melocotón m, durazno m (LAm)

peacock /'piːkɒk/ n pavo m real

peak /piːk/ n cumbre f; (of career) apogeo m; (maximum) máximo m. ~ **hours** npl horas fpl de mayor demanda (o consumo etc)

peal /piːl/ n repique m. ~**s of laughter** risotadas fpl

peanut /'piːnʌt/ n cacahuete m, maní m (LAm), cacahuate m (Mex)

pear /peə(r)/ n pera f. ~ **(tree)** peral m

pearl /pɜːl/ n perla f

peasant /'peznt/ n campesino m

peat /piːt/ n turba f

pebble /'pebl/ n guijarro m

peck /pek/ vt picotear. ●n picotazo m; (kiss) besito m

peculiar /pɪ'kjuːlɪə(r)/ a raro; (special) especial. ~**ity** /-'ærətɪ/ n rareza f; (feature) particularidad f

pedal /'pedl/ n pedal m. ●vi pedalear

pedantic /pɪ'dæntɪk/ a pedante

peddle /'pedl/ vt vender por las calles

pedestal /'pedɪstl/ n pedestal m

pedestrian /pɪ'destrɪən/ n peatón m. ~ **crossing** paso m de peatones. ●a pedestre; (dull) prosaico

pedigree /'pedɪɡriː/ linaje m; (of animal) pedigrí m. ●a <animal> de raza

peek /piːk/ vi mirar a hurtadillas

peel /piːl/ n piel f, cáscara f. ●vt pelar <fruit, vegetables>. ●vi pelarse

peep /piːp/ vi. ~ **at** echarle un vistazo a. ●n (look) vistazo m; (bird sound) pío m

peer /pɪə(r)/ *vi* mirar. ∼ **at** escudriñar. ● *n* (equal) par *m* & *f*; (contemporary) coetáneo *m*; (lord) par *m*. ∼**age** /-ɪdʒ/ *n* nobleza *f*

peg /peg/ *n* (in ground) estaca *f*; (on violin) clavija *f*; (for washing) pinza *f*; (hook) gancho *m*; (for tent) estaquilla *f*. **off the** ∼ de confección. ● *vt* (*pt* **pegged**) sujetar (*con estacas, etc*); fijar <*precios*>

pejorative /pɪ'dʒɒrətɪv/ *a* peyorativo, despectivo

pelican /'pelɪkən/ *n* pelícano *m*

pellet /'pelɪt/ *n* bolita *f*; (for gun) perdigón *m*

pelt /pelt/ *n* pellejo *m*. ● *vt*. ∼ **s.o. with sth** lanzarle algo a uno. ● *vi*. ∼ **with rain**, ∼ **down** llover a cántaros

pelvis /'pelvɪs/ *n* pelvis *f*

pen /pen/ (for writing) pluma *f*; (ballpoint) bolígrafo *m*; (sheep ∼) redil *m*; (cattle ∼) corral *m*

penal /'piːnl/ *a* penal. ∼**ize** *vt* sancionar. ∼**ty** /'penltɪ/ *n* pena *f*; (fine) multa *f*; (in soccer) penalty *m*; (in US football) castigo *m*. ∼**ty kick** *n* (in soccer) penalty *m*

penance /'penəns/ *n* penitencia *f*

pence /pens/ ⇒PENNY

pencil /'pensl/ *n* lápiz *m*. ● *vt* (*pt* **pencilled**) escribir con lápiz. ∼**-sharpener** *n* sacapuntas *m*

pendulum /'pendjʊləm/ *n* péndulo *m*

penetrat|e /'penɪtreɪt/ *vt/i* penetrar. ∼**ing** *a* penetrante. ∼**ion** /-'treɪʃn/ *n* penetración *f*

penguin /'peŋgwɪn/ *n* pingüino *m*

penicillin /penɪ'sɪlɪn/ *n* penicilina *f*

peninsula /pə'nɪnsjʊlə/ *n* península *f*

penis /'piːnɪs/ *n* pene *m*

pen: ∼**knife** /'pennaɪf/ *n* (*pl* **penknives**) navaja *f*. ∼**name** *n* seudónimo *m*

penn|iless /'penɪlɪs/ *a* sin un céntimo. ∼**y** /'penɪ/ *n* (*pl* **pennies** or **pence**) penique *m*

pension /'penʃn/ *n* pensión *f*; (for retirement) pensión *f* de jubilación. ∼**er** *n* jubilado *m*

pensive /'pensɪv/ *a* pensativo

Pentecost /'pentɪkɒst/ *n* Pentecostés *m*

penthouse /'penthaʊs/ *n* penthouse *m*

pent-up /pent'ʌp/ *a* reprimido; (confined) encerrado

penultimate /pen'ʌltɪmət/ *a* penúltimo

people /'piːpl/ *npl* gente *f*; (citizens) pueblo *m*. ∼ **say (that)** se dice que, dicen que. **English** ∼ los ingleses. **young** ∼ los jóvenes. **the** ∼ (nation) el pueblo. ● *vt* poblar

pepper /'pepə(r)/ *n* pimienta *f*; (vegetable) pimiento *m*. ● *vt* (intersperse) salpicar (with de). ∼**box** *n* (Amer) pimentero *m*. ∼**corn** *n* grano *m* de pimienta. ∼**mint** *n* menta *f*; (sweet) caramelo *m* de menta. ∼**pot** *n* pimentero *m*

per /pɜː(r)/ *prep* por. ∼ **annum** al año. ∼ **cent** ⇒PERCENT. ∼ **head** por cabeza, por persona. **ten miles** ∼ **hour** diez millas por hora

perceive /pə'siːv/ *vt* percibir; (notice) darse cuenta de

percent, per cent /pə'sent/ *n* (*no pl*) porcentaje *m*. ● *adv* por ciento. ∼**age** /-ɪdʒ/ *n* porcentaje *m*

percepti|ble /pə'septəbl/ *a* perceptible. ∼**on** /-ʃn/ *n* percepción *f*. ∼**ve** /-tɪv/ *a* perspicaz

perch /pɜːtʃ/ *n* (of bird) percha *f*; (fish) perca *f*. ● *vi* <*bird*> posarse. ∼ **on** <*person*> sentarse en el borde de

percolat|e /'pɜːkəleɪt/ *vi* filtrarse. ∼**or** *n* cafetera *f* eléctrica

percussion /pə'kʌʃn/ *n* percusión *f*

perfect /'pɜːfɪkt/ *a* perfecto; <*place, day*> ideal. ● /pə'fekt/ *vt* perfeccionar. ∼**ion** /pə'fekʃn/ *n* perfección *f*. **to** ∼**ion** a la perfección. ∼**ly** /'pɜːfɪktlɪ/ *adv* perfectamente

perform /pə'fɔːm/ *vt* desempeñar <*function, role*>; ejecutar <*task*>; realizar <*experiment*>; representar <*play*>; (Mus) interpretar. ∼ **an operation** (Med) operar. ● *vi* <*actor*> actuar; <*musician*> tocar; (produce results) <*vehicle*> responder; <*company*> rendir. ∼**ance** /-əns/ *n* ejecución *f*; (of play) representación *f*; (of actor, musician) interpretación *f*; (of team) actuación *f*; (of car) rendimiento *m*. **~er** *n* (actor) actor *m*; (entertainer) artista *m* & *f*

perfume /'pɜːfjuːm/ *n* perfume *m*

perhaps /pə'hæps/ *adv* quizá(s), tal vez, a lo mejor

peril /'perəl/ *n* peligro *m*. **~ous** *a* arriesgado, peligroso

perimeter /pə'rɪmɪtə(r)/ *n* perímetro *m*

period /'pɪərɪəd/ *n* período *m*; (in history) época *f*; (lesson) clase *f*; (Amer, Gram) punto *m*; (menstruation) período *m*, regla *f*. ● *a* de (la) época. **~ic** /-'ɒdɪk/ *a* periódico. **~ical** /pɪərɪ'ɒdɪkl/ *n* revista *f*. **~ically** *adv* periódico

peripher|al /pə'rɪfərəl/ *a* secundario; (Comp) periférico. **~y** /pə'rɪfərɪ/ *n* periferia *f*

perish /'perɪʃ/ *vi* perecer; (rot) deteriorarse. **~able** *a* perecedero. **~ing** *a* 🖹 glacial

perjur|e /'pɜːdʒə(r)/ *vr*. **~e o.s.** perjurarse. **~y** *n* perjurio *m*

perk /pɜːk/ *n* gaje *m*. □ **~ up** *vt* reanimar. *vi* reanimarse

perm /pɜːm/ *n* permanente *f*. ● *vt*. **have one's hair ~ed** hacerse la permanente

permanen|ce /'pɜːmənəns/ *n* permanencia *f*. **~t** *a* permanente. **~tly** *adv* permanentemente

permissible /pə'mɪsəbl/ *a* permisible

permission /pə'mɪʃn/ *n* permiso *m*

permit /pə'mɪt/ *vt* (*pt* **permitted**) permitir. ● /'pɜːmɪt/ *n* permiso *m*

peroxide /pə'rɒksaɪd/ *n* peróxido *m*

perpendicular /pɜːpən'dɪkjʊlə(r)/ *a* & *n* perpendicular (*f*)

perpetrat|e /'pɜːpɪtreɪt/ *vt* cometer. **~or** *n* autor *m*

perpetua|l /pə'petʃʊəl/ *a* perpetuo. **~te** /pə'petʃʊeɪt/ *vt* perpetuar

perplex /pə'pleks/ *vt* dejar perplejo. **~ed** *a* perplejo

persecut|e /'pɜːsɪkjuːt/ *vt* perseguir. **~ion** /-'kjuːʃn/ *n* persecución *f*

persever|ance /pɜːsɪ'vɪərəns/ *n* perseverancia *f*. **~e** /pɜːsɪ'vɪə(r)/ *vi* perseverar, persistir

Persian /'pɜːʃn/ *a* persa. **the ~ Gulf** *n* el golfo Pérsico

persist /pə'sɪst/ *vi* persistir. **~ence** /-əns/ *n* persistencia *f*. **~ent** *a* persistente; (continual) continuo

person /'pɜːsn/ *n* persona *f*. **in ~** en persona. **~al** *a* personal; *<call>* particular; *<property>* privado. **~al assistant** *n* secretario *m* personal. **~ality** /-'næləti/ *n* personalidad *f*. **~ally** *adv* personalmente. **~nel** /pɜːsə'nel/ *n* personal *m*. **P~** (department) sección *f* de personal

perspective /pə'spektɪv/ *n* perspectiva *f*

perspir|ation /pɜːspə'reɪʃn/ *n* transpiración *f*. **~e** /pəs'paɪə(r)/ *vi* transpirar

persua|de /pə'sweɪd/ *vt* convencer, persuadir. **~e s.o. to do sth** convencer a uno para que haga algo. **~sion** *n* /-ʃn/ persuasión *f*. **~sive** /-sɪv/ *a* persuasivo

pertinent /'pɜːtɪnənt/ *a* pertinente. **~ly** *adv* pertinentemente

perturb /pə'tɜːb/ *vt* perturbar

Peru /pə'ruː/ *n* el Perú *m*

peruse /pə'ruːz/ *vt* leer cuidadosamente

Peruvian /pə'ruːvɪan/ *a* & *n* peruano (*m*)

perver|se /pə'vɜːs/ *a* retorcido; (stubborn) obstinado. **~sion** *n* perversión *f*. **~t** /pə'vɜːt/ *vt* pervertir. ● /'pɜːvɜːt/ *n* pervertido *m*

pessimis|m /'pesɪmɪzəm/ *n* pesimismo *m*. **~t** *n* pesimista *m* & *f*. **~tic** /-'mɪstɪk/ *a* pesimista

pest /pest/ *n* plaga *f*; (🖹, person, thing) peste *f*

pester /'pestə(r)/ *vt* importunar

pesticide /'pestɪsaɪd/ *n* pesticida *f*

pet /pet/ *n* animal *m* doméstico; (favourite) favorito *m*. ● *a* preferido. **my ~ hate** lo que más odio. ● *vt* (*pt* **petted**) acariciar

petal /'petl/ *n* pétalo *m*

petition /pɪ'tɪʃn/ *n* petición *f*

pet name *n* apodo *m*

petrified /'petrɪfaɪd/ a (terrified) muerto de miedo; (Geol) petrificado

petrol /'petrəl/ n gasolina f. ~ **pump** n surtidor m. ~ **station** n gasolinera f. ~ **tank** n depósito m de gasolina ~**eum** /pɪ'trəʊlɪəm/ n petróleo m.

petticoat /'petɪkəʊt/ n enagua f; (slip) combinación f

petty /'petɪ/ a (**-ier, -iest**) insignificante; (mean) mezquino. ~**y cash** n dinero m para gastos menores

petulant /'petjʊlənt/ a irritable

pew /pju:/ n banco m (de iglesia)

phantom /'fæntəm/ n fantasma m

pharma|ceutical /fɑːmə'sjuːtɪkl/ a farmacéutico. ~**cist** /'fɑːməsɪst/ n farmacéutico m. ~**cy** /'fɑːməsɪ/ n farmacia f

phase /feɪz/ n etapa f. □ ~ **out** vt retirar progresivamente

PhD abbr (= **Doctor of Philosophy**) n doctorado m; (person) Dr., Dra.

pheasant /'feznt/ n faisán m

phenomen|al /fɪ'nɒmɪnl/ a fenomenal. ~**on** /-mən/ n (pl **-ena** /-inə/) fenómeno m

philistine /'fɪlɪstaɪn/ a & n filisteo (m)

philosoph|er /fɪ'lɒsəfə(r)/ n filósofo m. ~**ical** /-ə'sɒfɪkl/ a filosófico. ~**y** /fɪ'lɒsəfɪ/ n filosofía f

phlegm /flem/ n flema f. ~**atic** /fleg'mætɪk/ a flemático

phobia /'fəʊbɪə/ n fobia f

phone /fəʊn/ n 🄸 teléfono m. ●vt/i llamar (por teléfono). ~ **back** (call again) volver a llamar; (return call) llamar (más tarde). ~ **book** n guía f telefónica, directorio m (LAm). ~ **booth**, ~ **box** n cabina f telefónica. ~ **call** n llamada f (telefónica). ~ **card** n tarjeta f telefónica. ~ **number** n número m de teléfono

phonetic /fə'netɪk/ a fonético. ~**s** n fonética f

phoney /'fəʊnɪ/ a (**-ier, -iest**) 🄸 falso

phosph|ate /'fɒsfeɪt/ n fosfato m. ~**orus** /'fɒsfərəs/ n fósforo m

photo /'fəʊtəʊ/ n (pl **-os**) 🄸 foto f. take a ~ sacar una foto. ~**copier** /-kɒpɪə(r)/ n fotocopiadora f.

~**copy** n fotocopia f. ●vt fotocopiar. ~**genic** /-'dʒenɪk/ a fotogénico. ~**graph** /-grɑːf/ n fotografía f. ●vt fotografiar, sacarle una fotografía a. ~**grapher** /fə'tɒgrəfə(r)/ n fotógrafo m. ~**graphic** /-'græfɪk/ a fotográfico. ~**graphy** /fə'tɒgrəfɪ/ n fotografía f

phrase /freɪz/ n frase f. ●vt expresar. ~ **book** n manual m de conversación

physi|cal /'fɪzɪkl/ a físico. ~**cian** /fɪ'zɪʃn/ n médico m. ~**cist** /'fɪzɪsɪst/ n físico m. ~**cs** /'fɪzɪks/ n física f. ~**ology** /fɪzɪ'ɒlədʒɪ/ n fisiología f. ~**otherapist** /fɪzɪəʊ'θerəpɪst/ n fisioterapeuta m & f. ~**otherapy** /fɪzɪəʊ'θerəpɪ/ n fisioterapia f. ~**que** /fɪ'ziːk/ n físico m

pian|ist /'pɪənɪst/ n pianista m & f. ~**o** /pɪ'ænəʊ/ n (pl **-os**) piano m

pick /pɪk/ (tool) pico m. ●vt escoger; cortar <flowers>; recoger <fruit, cotton>; abrir con una ganzúa <lock>. ~ **a quarrel** buscar camorra. ~ **holes in** criticar. □ ~ **on** vt meterse con. □ ~ **out** vt escoger; (identify) reconocer. □ ~ **up** vt recoger; (lift) levantar; (learn) aprender; adquirir <habit, etc>; contagiarse de <illness>. ●vi mejorar; <sales> subir. ~**axe** n pico m

picket /'pɪkɪt/ n (group) piquete m. ~ **line** n piquete m. ●vt formar un piquete frente a

pickle /'pɪkl/ n (in vinegar) encurtido m; (Amer, gherkin) pepinillo m; (relish) salsa f (a base de encurtidos). ●vt encurtir

pick: ~pocket n carterista m & f. ~**-up** n (truck) camioneta f

picnic /'pɪknɪk/ n picnic m

picture /'pɪktʃə(r)/ n (painting) cuadro m; (photo) foto f; (drawing) dibujo m; (illustration) ilustración f; (film) película f; (fig) descripción f. ●vt imaginarse. ~**sque** /-'resk/ a pintoresco

pie /paɪ/ n empanada f; (sweet) pastel m, tarta f

piece /piːs/ n pedazo m, trozo m; (part of machine) pieza f; (coin) moneda f; (in chess) figura f. a ~ **of advice** un consejo. a ~ **of furniture** un mueble. a ~ **of news** una noticia. take to ~s desmontar. □ ~ **together** vt juntar. ~**meal** a gradual; (unsystematic) poco sistemático. ● adv poco a poco

pier /pɪə(r)/ n muelle m; (with amusements) *paseo con atracciones sobre un muelle*

pierc|e /pɪəs/ vt perforar. ~**ing** a penetrante

piety /'paɪətɪ/ n piedad f

pig /pɪg/ n cerdo m, chancho m (LAm)

pigeon /'pɪdʒɪn/ n paloma f; (Culin) pichón m. ~**-hole** n casillero m; (fig) casilla f

piggy /'pɪgɪ/ n cerdito m. ~**back** n. give s.o. a ~**back** llevar a uno a cuestas. ~ **bank** n hucha f

pig-headed /-'hedɪd/ a terco

pigment /'pɪgmənt/ n pigmento m

pig|sty /'pɪgstaɪ/ n pocilga f. ~**tail** n (plait) trenza f; (bunch) coleta f

pike /paɪk/ n invar (fish) lucio m

pilchard /'pɪltʃəd/ n sardina f

pile /paɪl/ n (heap) montón m; (of fabric) pelo m. ● vt amontonar. ~ it on exagerar. ● vi amontonarse. □ ~ **up** vt amontonar. ● vi amontonarse. ~**s** /paɪlz/ npl (Med) almorranas fpl. ~**-up** n choque m múltiple

pilgrim /'pɪlgrɪm/ n peregrino. ~**age** /-ɪdʒ/ n peregrinación f

pill /pɪl/ n pastilla f

pillar /'pɪlə(r)/ n columna f. ~ **box** n buzón m

pillow /'pɪləʊ/ n almohada f. ~**case** n funda f de almohada

pilot /'paɪlət/ n piloto m. ● vt pilotar. ~ **light** n fuego m piloto

pimple /'pɪmpl/ n grano m, espinilla f (LAm)

pin /pɪn/ n alfiler m; (Mec) perno m. ~**s and needles** hormigueo m. ● vt (pt **pinned**) prender con alfileres; (fix) sujetar

PIN /pɪn/ n (= **personal identification number**) PIN m

pinafore /'pɪnəfɔ:(r)/ n delantal m. ~ **dress** n pichi m, jumper m & f (LAm)

pincers /'pɪnsəz/ npl tenazas fpl

pinch /pɪntʃ/ vt pellizcar; (🅴, steal) hurtar. ● vi <shoe> apretar. ● n pe-

llizco m; (small amount) pizca f. at a ~ si fuera necesario

pine /paɪn/ n pino m. ● vi. ~ **for sth** suspirar por algo. □ ~ **away** vi languidecer de añoranza. ~**apple** /'paɪnæpl/ n piña f

ping-pong /'pɪŋpɒŋ/ n ping-pong m

pink /pɪŋk/ a & n rosa (m), rosado (m)

pinnacle /'pɪnəkl/ n pináculo m

pin: ~**point** vt determinar con precisión f. ~**stripe** n raya f fina

pint /paɪnt/ n pinta f (= 0.57 litros)

pioneer /paɪə'nɪə(r)/ n pionero m

pious /'paɪəs/ a piadoso

pip /pɪp/ n (seed) pepita f; (time signal) señal f

pipe /paɪp/ n tubo m; (Mus) caramillo m; (for smoking) pipa f. ● vt llevar por tuberías. ~**-dream** n ilusión f. ~**line** n conducto m; (for oil) oleoducto m. in the ~**line** en preparación f

piping /'paɪpɪŋ/ n tubería f. ● adv. ~ hot muy caliente, hirviendo

pira|cy /'paɪərəsɪ/ n piratería f. ~**te** /'paɪərət/ n pirata m

Pisces /'paɪsiːz/ n Piscis m

piss /pɪs/ vi 🅴 mear. □ ~ **off** vi 🅴. ~ **off!** ¡vete a la mierda! ~**ed** /pɪst/ a (🅴, drunk) como una cuba; (Amer, fed up) cabreado

pistol /'pɪstl/ n pistola f

piston /'pɪstən/ n pistón m

pit /pɪt/ n hoyo m; (mine) mina f; (Amer, in fruit) hueso m

pitch /pɪtʃ/ n (substance) brea f; (degree) grado m; (Mus) tono m; (Sport) campo m. ● vt (throw) lanzar; armar <tent>. ● vi <ship> cabecear. ~**black** /-'blæk/ a oscuro como boca de lobo. ~**er** n jarra f

pitfall /'pɪtfɔ:l/ n trampa f

pith /pɪθ/ n (of orange, lemon) médula f; (fig) meollo m

pitiful /'pɪtɪfl/ a lastimoso

pittance /'pɪtns/ n miseria f

pity /'pɪtɪ/ n lástima f, pena f; (compassion) piedad f. it's a ~ you can't come es una lástima que no puedas venir. ● vt tenerle lástima a

pivot /'pɪvət/ n pivote m. ● vi pivotar; (fig) depender (**on** de)

placard /'plækɑːd/ n pancarta f; (sign) letrero m

placate /plə'keɪt/ vt apaciguar

place /pleɪs/ n lugar m; (seat) asiento m; (in firm, team) puesto m; (🏠, house) casa f. **feel out of** ∼ sentirse fuera de lugar. **take** ∼ tener lugar. ● vt poner, colocar; (identify) identificar. **be** ∼**d** (in race) colocarse. ∼**-mat** n mantel m individual

placid /'plæsɪd/ a plácido

plague /pleɪg/ n peste f; (fig) plaga f. ● vt atormentar

plaice /pleɪs/ n invar platija f

plain /pleɪn/ a (**-er**, **-est**) (clear) claro; (simple) sencillo; (candid) franco; (ugly) feo. **in** ∼ **clothes** de civil. ● adv totalmente. ● n llanura f. ∼**ly** adv claramente; (frankly) francamente; (simply) con sencillez

plait /plæt/ vt trenzar. ● n trenza f

plan /plæn/ n plan m; (map) plano m; (of book, essay) esquema f. ● vt (pt **planned**) planear; planificar <strategies>. **I'm** ∼**ning to go to Greece** pienso ir a Grecia

plane /pleɪn/ n (tree) plátano m; (level) nivel m; (Aviat) avión m; (tool) cepillo m. ● vt cepillar

planet /'plænɪt/ n planeta m. ∼**ary** a planetario

plank /plæŋk/ n tabla f

planning /'plænɪŋ/ n planificación f. **family** ∼ planificación familiar. **town** ∼ urbanismo m

plant /plɑːnt/ n planta f; (Mec) maquinaria f; (factory) fábrica f. ● vt plantar; (place in position) colocar. ∼**ation** /plæn'teɪʃn/ n plantación f

plaque /plæk/ n placa f

plasma /'plæzmə/ n plasma m

plaster /'plɑːstə(r)/ n yeso m; (on walls) revoque m; (sticking plaster) tirita f (P), curita f (P) (LAm); (for setting bones) yeso m, escayola f. ● vt revocar; rellenar con yeso <cracks>

plastic /'plæstɪk/ a & n plástico (m)

Plasticine /'plæstɪsiːn/ n (P) plastilina f (P)

plastic surgery /plæstɪk'sɜːdʒərɪ/ n cirugía f estética

plate /pleɪt/ n plato m; (of metal) chapa f; (silverware) vajilla f de plata; (in book) lámina f. ● vt recubrir (**with** de)

platform /'plætfɔːm/ n plataforma f; (Rail) andén m

platinum /'plætɪnəm/ n platino m

platitude /'plætɪtjuːd/ n lugar m común

platonic /plə'tɒnɪk/ a platónico

plausible /'plɔːzəbl/ a verosímil; <person> convincente

play /pleɪ/ vt jugar a <game, cards>; jugar a, jugar (LAm) <football, chess>; tocar <instrument>; (act role) representar el papel de. ● vi jugar. ● n juego m; (drama) obra f de teatro. □ ∼ **down** vt minimizar. □ ∼ **up** vi 🏠 <child> dar guerra; <car, TV> no funcionar bien. ∼**er** n jugador m; (Mus) músico m. ∼**ful** a juguetón. ∼**ground** n parque m de juegos infantiles; (in school) patio m de recreo. ∼**group** n jardín m de la infancia. ∼**ing card** n naipe m. ∼**ing field** n campo m de deportes. ∼**pen** n corralito m. ∼**wright** /-raɪt/ n dramaturgo m

plc abbr (= **public limited company**) S.A.

plea /pliː/ n súplica f; (excuse) excusa f; (Jurid) defensa f

plead /pliːd/ vt (Jurid) alegar; (as excuse) pretextar. ● vi suplicar. ∼ **with** suplicarle a. ∼ **guilty** declararse culpable

pleasant /'pleznt/ a agradable

pleas|e /pliːz/ int por favor. ● vt complacer; (satisfy) contentar. ● vi agradar; (wish) querer. ∼**ed** a (satisfied) satisfecho; (happy) contento. ∼**ed with** satisfecho de. ∼**ing** a agradable; (news) grato. ∼**ure** /'pleʒə(r)/ n placer m

pleat /pliːt/ n pliegue m

pledge /pledʒ/ n cantidad f prometida

plent|iful /'plentɪfl/ a abundante. ∼**y** /'plentɪ/ n abundancia f. ● pron. ∼**y of** muchos, -chas; (of sth uncountable) mucho, -cha

pliable /'plaɪəbl/ a flexible

pliers /'plaɪəz/ npl alicates mpl

plight /plaɪt/ n situación f difícil

plimsolls /'plɪmsəlz/ *npl* zapatillas *fpl* de lona

plod /plɒd/ *vi* (*pt* **plodded**) caminar con paso pesado

plot /plɒt/ *n* complot *m*; (of novel etc) argumento *m*; (piece of land) parcela *f*. ● *vt* (*pt* **plotted**) tramar; (mark out) trazar. ● *vi* conspirar

plough /plaʊ/ *n* arado *m*. ● *vt/i* arar. □ ~ **into** *vt* estrellarse contra. □ ~ **through** *vt* avanzar laboriosamente por

ploy /plɔɪ/ *n* treta *f*

pluck /plʌk/ *vt* arrancar; depilarse *<eyebrows>*; desplumar *<bird>*. ~ **up courage** to armarse de valor para. ● *n* valor *m*. ~**y** *a* (**-ier, -iest**) valiente

plug /plʌg/ *n* (in bath) tapón *m*; (Elec) enchufe *m*; (spark ~) bujía *f*. ● *vt* (*pt* **plugged**) tapar; (🄳, advertise) hacerle propaganda a. □ ~ **in** *vt* (Elec) enchufar. ~**hole** *n* desagüe *m*

plum /plʌm/ *n* ciruela *f*

plumage /'pluːmɪdʒ/ *n* plumaje *m*

plumb|er /'plʌmə(r)/ *n* fontanero *m*, plomero *m* (LAm). ~**ing** *n* instalación *f* sanitaria, instalación *f* de cañerías

plume /pluːm/ *n* pluma *f*

plump /plʌmp/ *a* (**-er, -est**) rechoncho

plunge /plʌndʒ/ *vt* hundir *<knife>*; (in water) sumergir; (into state, condition) sumir. ● *vi* zambullirse; (fall) caer. ● *n* zambullida *f*

plural /'plʊərəl/ *n* plural *m*. ● *a* en plural

plus /plʌs/ *prep* más. ● *a* positivo. ● *n* signo *m* de más; (fig) ventaja *f*

plush /plʌʃ/ *a* lujoso

Pluto /'pluːtəʊ/ *n* Plutón *m*

plutonium /pluː'təʊnɪəm/ *n* plutonio *m*

ply /plaɪ/ *vt* manejar *<tool>*; ejercer *<trade>*. ~ **s.o. with drink** dar continuamente de beber a uno. ~**wood** *n* contrachapado *m*

p.m. *abbr* (= **post meridiem**) de la tarde

pneumatic drill /njuː'mætɪk/ *a* martillo *m* neumático

pneumonia /njuː'məʊnjə/ *n* pulmonía *f*

poach /pəʊtʃ/ *vt* escalfar *<egg>*; cocer *<fish etc>*; (steal) cazar furtivamente. ~**er** *n* cazador *m* furtivo

PO box /piː'əʊ/ *n* Apdo. postal

pocket /'pɒkɪt/ *n* bolsillo *m*; (of air, resistance) bolsa *f*. ● *vt* poner en el bolsillo. ~**book** *n* (notebook) libro *m* de bolsillo; (Amer, wallet) cartera *f*; (Amer, handbag) bolso *m*, cartera *f* (LAm), bolsa *f* (Mex). ~ **money** *n* dinero *m* de bolsillo, mesada *f* (LAm)

pod /pɒd/ *n* vaina *f*

poem /'pəʊɪm/ *n* poema *f*

poet /'pəʊɪt/ *n* poeta *m*. ~**ic** /-'etɪk/ *a* poético. ~**ry** /'pəʊɪtrɪ/ *n* poesía *f*

poignant /'pɔɪnjənt/ *a* conmovedor

point /pɔɪnt/ *n* (dot, on scale) punto *m*; (sharp end) punta *f*; (in time) momento *m*; (statement) observación; (on agenda, in discussion) punto *m*; (Elec) toma *f* de corriente. **to the ~** pertinente. **up to a ~** hasta cierto punto. **be on the ~ of** estar a punto de. **get to the ~** ir al grano. **there's no ~ (in)** arguing no sirve de nada discutir. ● *vt* (aim) apuntar; (show) indicar. ● *vi* señalar. ~ **at/to sth** señalar algo. □ ~ **out** *vt* señalar. ~**-blank** *a* & *adv* a quemarropa. ~**ed** *a* (chin, nose) puntiagudo; (fig) mordaz. ~**less** *a* inútil

poise /pɔɪz/ *n* porte *m*; (composure) desenvoltura *f*

poison /'pɔɪzn/ *n* veneno *m*. ● *vt* envenenar. ~**ous** *a* venenoso; *<chemical etc>* tóxico

poke /pəʊk/ *vt* empujar; atizar *<fire>*. ● *vi* hurgar; (pry) meterse. ● *n* golpe *m*. □ ~ **about** *vi* fisgonear. ~**r** /'pəʊkə(r)/ *n* atizador *m*; (Cards) póquer *m*

poky /'pəʊkɪ/ *a* (**-ier, -iest**) diminuto

Poland /'pəʊlənd/ *n* Polonia *f*

polar /'pəʊlə(r)/ *a* polar. ~ **bear** *n* oso *m* blanco

pole /pəʊl/ *n* palo *m*; (fixed) poste *m*; (for flag) mástil *m*; (Geog) polo *m*

police /pə'liːs/ *n* policía *f*. ~**man** /-mən/ *n* policía *m*, agente *m*. ~ **station** *n* comisaría *f*. ~**woman** *n* policía *f*, agente *f*

policy /'pɒlɪsɪ/ *n* política *f*; (insurance) póliza *f* (de seguros)

polish /'pɒlɪʃ/ n (for shoes) betún m; (furniture ~) cera f para muebles; (floor ~) abrillantador m de suelos; (shine) brillo m; (fig) finura f. ● vt darle brillo a; limpiar <shoes>; (refine) pulir. □ ~ **off** vt despachar. ~**ed** a pulido

Polish /'pəʊlɪʃ/ a & n polaco (m)

polite /pə'laɪt/ a cortés. ~**ly** adv cortésmente. ~**ness** n cortesía f

politic|al /pə'lɪtɪkl/ a político. ~**ian** /pɒlɪ'tɪʃn/ n político m. ~**s** /'pɒlɪtɪks/ n política f

poll /pəʊl/ n elección f; (survey) encuesta f. ● vt obtener <votes>

pollen /'pɒlən/ n polen m

polling booth n cabina f de votar

pollut|e /pə'luːt/ vt contaminar. ~**ion** /-ʃn/ n contaminación f

polo /'pəʊləʊ/ n polo m. ~ **neck** n cuello m vuelto

poly|styrene /pɒlɪ'staɪriːn/ n poliestireno m. ~**thene** /'pɒlɪθiːn/ n plástico, polietileno m

pomp /pɒmp/ n pompa f. ~**ous** a pomposo

pond /pɒnd/ n (natural) laguna f; (artificial) estanque m

ponder /'pɒndə(r)/ vt considerar. ~**ous** a pesado

pony /'pəʊnɪ/ n poni m. ~**-tail** n cola f de caballo

poodle /'puːdl/ n caniche m

pool /puːl/ n charca f; (artificial) estanque m; (puddle) charco m. (common fund) fondos mpl comunes; (snooker) billar m americano. (**swimming**) ~ n piscina f, alberca f (Mex). ~**s** npl quinielas fpl. ● vt aunar

poor /pʊə(r)/ a (-er, -est) pobre; <quality, diet> malo. be in ~ **health** estar mal de salud. ~**ly** a 🔲 malito. ● adv mal

pop /pɒp/ n (Mus) música f pop; (Amer 🔲, father) papá m. ● vt (pt **popped**) hacer reventar; (put) poner. □ ~ **in** vi (visit) pasar por. □ ~ **out** vi saltar; <person> salir un rato. □ ~ **up** vi surgir, aparecer

popcorn /'pɒpkɔːn/ n palomitas fpl

pope /pəʊp/ n papa m

poplar /'pɒplə(r)/ n álamo m (blanco)

poppy /'pɒpɪ/ n amapola f

popular /'pɒpjʊlə(r)/ a popular. ~**ity** /-'lærətɪ/ n popularidad f. ~**ize** vt popularizar

populat|e /'pɒpjʊleɪt/ vt poblar. ~**ion** /-'leɪʃn/ n población f

porcelain /'pɔːsəlɪn/ n porcelana f

porch /pɔːtʃ/ n porche m

porcupine /'pɔːkjʊpaɪn/ n puerco m espín

pore /pɔː(r)/ n poro m

pork /pɔːk/ n carne f de cerdo m, carne f de puerco m (Mex)

porn /pɔːn/ n 🔲 pornografía f. ~**ographic** /-ə'græfɪk/ a pornográfico. ~**ography** /pɔː'nɒgrəfɪ/ n pornografía f

porpoise /'pɔːpəs/ n marsopa f

porridge /'pɒrɪdʒ/ n avena f (cocida)

port /pɔːt/ n puerto m; (Naut) babor m; (Comp) puerto m; (Culin) oporto m

portable /'pɔːtəbl/ a portátil

porter /'pɔːtə(r)/ n (for luggage) maletero m; (concierge) portero m

porthole /'pɔːthəʊl/ n portilla f

portion /'pɔːʃn/ n porción f; (part) parte f

portrait /'pɔːtrɪt/ n retrato m

portray /pɔː'treɪ/ vt representar. ~**al** n representación f

Portug|al /'pɔːtjʊgl/ n Portugal m. ~**uese** /-'giːz/ a & n portugués (m)

pose /pəʊz/ n pose f, postura f. ● vt representar <threat>; plantear <problem, question>. ● vi posar. ~ **as** hacerse pasar por

posh /pɒʃ/ a 🔲 elegante

position /pə'zɪʃn/ n posición f; (job) puesto m; (situation) situación f. ● vt colocar

positive /'pɒzətɪv/ a positivo; (real) auténtico; (certain) seguro. ● n (Photo) positiva f. ~**ly** adv positivamente

possess /pə'zes/ vt poseer. ~**ion** /-ʃn/ n posesión f; (Jurid) bien m. ~**ive** a posesivo

possib|ility /pɒsɪ'bɪlətɪ/ n posibilidad f. ~**le** /'pɒsəbl/ a posible. ~**ly** adv posiblemente

post /pəʊst/ n (pole) poste m; (job) puesto m; (mail) correo m. ● vt echar al correo <letter>; (send) enviar por correo. **keep s.o. ~ed** mantener a uno al corriente

post... /pəʊst/ *pref* post, pos

post: ~age /-ɪdʒ/ /-ɪdʒ/ *n* franqueo *m.* **~al** *a* postal. **~al order** *n* giro *m* postal. **~ box** *n* buzón *m.* **~card** *n* (tarjeta *f*) postal *f.* **~code** *n* código *m* postal

poster /'pəʊstə(r)/ *n* cartel *m*, póster *m*

posterity /pɒs'terətɪ/ *n* posteridad *f*

posthumous /'pɒstjʊməs/ *a* póstumo

post: ~man /-mən/ *n* cartero *m.* **~mark** *n* matasellos *m*

post mortem /pəʊst'mɔːtəm/ *n* autopsia *f*

post office *n* oficina *f* de correos, correos *mpl*, correo *m* (LAm)

postpone /pəʊst'pəʊn/ *vt* aplazar, posponer. **~ment** *n* aplazamiento *m*

postscript /'pəʊstskrɪpt/ *n* posdata *f*

posture /'pɒstʃə(r)/ *n* postura *f*

posy /'pəʊzɪ/ *n* ramillete *m*

pot /pɒt/ *n* (for cooking) olla *f*; (for jam, honey) tarro *m*; (for flowers) tiesto *m*; (in pottery) vasija *f.* **~s and pans** cacharros *mpl*

potato /pə'teɪtəʊ/ *n* (*pl* **-oes**) patata *f*, papa *f* (LAm)

potent /'pəʊtnt/ *a* potente; <*drink*> fuerte

potential /pəʊ'tenʃl/ *a* & *n* potencial (*m*). **~ly** *adv* potencialmente

pot: ~hole *n* cueva *f* subterránea; (in road) bache *m.* **~holing** *n* espeleología *f*

potion /'pəʊʃn/ *n* poción *f*

pot-shot *n* tiro *m* al azar

potter /'pɒtə(r)/ *n* alfarero *m.* ● *vi* hacer pequeños trabajos agradables. **~y** *n* (pots) cerámica *f*; (workshop, craft) alfarería *f*

potty /'pɒtɪ/ *a* (**-ier, -iest**) ▣ chiflado. ● *n* orinal *m*

pouch /paʊtʃ/ *n* bolsa *f* pequeña; (for correspondence) valija *f*

poultry /'pəʊltrɪ/ *n* aves *fpl* de corral

pounce /paʊns/ *vi* saltar. **~ on** abalanzarse sobre

pound /paʊnd/ *n* (weight) libra *f* (= 454g); (money) libra *f* (esterlina); (for cars) depósito *m.* ● *vt* (crush) machacar. ● *vi* aporrear; <*heart*> palpitar; <*sound*> retumbar

pour /pɔː(r)/ *vt* verter; echar <*salt*>. **~ (out)** servir <*drink*>. ● *vi* <*blood*> manar; <*water*> salir; (rain) llover a cántaros. □ **~ out** *vi* <*people*> salir en tropel. **~ing** *a.* **~ing rain** lluvia *f* torrencial

pout /paʊt/ *vi* hacer pucheros

poverty /'pɒvətɪ/ *n* pobreza *f*

powder /'paʊdə(r)/ *n* polvo *m*; (cosmetic) polvos *mpl.* ● *vt* empolvar. **~ one's face** ponerse polvos en la cara. **~y** *a* como polvo

power /'paʊə(r)/ *n* poder *m*; (energy) energía *f*; (electricity) electricidad *f*; (nation) potencia *f.* ● *vt.* **~ed by** impulsado por **~ cut** *n* apagón *m.* **~ed** *a* con motor. **~ful** *a* poderoso. **~less** *a* impotente. **~ plant**, **~-station** *n* central *f* eléctrica

PR = **public relations**

practicable /'præktɪkəbl/ *a* practicable

practical /'præktɪkl/ *a* práctico. **~ joke** *n* broma *f.* **~ly** *adv* prácticamente

practi|ce /'præktɪs/ *n* práctica *f*; (custom) costumbre *f*; (exercise) ejercicio *m*; (Sport) entrenamiento *m*; (clients) clientela *f.* **he's out of ~ce** le falta práctica. **in ~ce** (in fact) en la práctica. **~se** /'præktɪs/ *vt* practicar; ensayar <*act*>; ejercer <*profession*>. ● *vi* practicar; <*professional*> ejercer. **~tioner** /-'tɪʃənə(r)/ *n* médico *m*

prairie /'preərɪ/ *n* pradera *f*

praise /preɪz/ *vt* (Relig) alabar; (compliment) elogiar. ● *n* (credit) elogios *mpl.* **~worthy** *a* loable

pram /præm/ *n* cochecito *m*

prank /præŋk/ *n* travesura *f*

prawn /prɔːn/ *n* gamba *f*, camarón *m* (LAm)

pray /preɪ/ *vi* rezar (**for** por). **~er** /preə(r)/ *n* oración *f*

pre.. /priː/ *pref* pre...

preach /priːtʃ/ vt/i predicar. ~er n predicador m; (Amer, minister) pastor m

pre-arrange /priːəˈreɪndʒ/ vt concertar de antemano

precarious /prɪˈkeərɪəs/ a precario. ~ly adv precariamente

precaution /prɪˈkɔːʃn/ n precaución f

precede /prɪˈsiːd/ vt preceder. ~nce /ˈpresədəns/ n precedencia f. ~nt /ˈpresədənt/ n precedente m

preceding /prɪˈsiːdɪŋ/ a anterior

precept /ˈpriːsept/ n precepto m

precinct /ˈpriːsɪŋkt/ n recinto m; (Amer, police district) distrito m policial; (Amer, voting district) circunscripción f. **pedestrian** ~ zona f peatonal. ~s (of city) límites mpl

precious /ˈpreʃəs/ a precioso. ● adv 🔲 muy

precipice /ˈpresɪpɪs/ n precipicio m

precipitate /prɪˈsɪpɪteɪt/ vt precipitar. ● /prɪˈsɪpɪtət/ n precipitado m.. ● /prɪˈsɪpɪtət/ a precipitado

precis|e /prɪˈsaɪs/ a (accurate) exacto; (specific) preciso; (meticulous) minucioso. ~ely adv con precisión. ~! ¡exacto! ~ion /-ˈsɪʒn/ n precisión f

preclude /prɪˈkluːd/ vt excluir

precocious /prɪˈkəʊʃəs/ a precoz. ~ly adv precozmente

preconce|ived /priːkənˈsiːvd/ a preconcebido. ~ption /-ˈsepʃn/ n preconcepción f

precursor /priːˈkɜːsə(r)/ n precursor m

predator /ˈpredətə(r)/ n depredador m. ~y a predador

predecessor /ˈpriːdɪsesə(r)/ n predecesor m, antecesor m

predicament /prɪˈdɪkəmənt/ n aprieto m

predict /prɪˈdɪkt/ vt predecir. ~ion /-ʃn/ n predicción f

preen /priːn/ vt arreglar. ~ o.s. atildarse

prefab /ˈpriːfæb/ n 🔲 casa f prefabricada. ~ricated /-ˈfæbrɪkeɪtɪd/ a prefabricado

preface /ˈprefəs/ n prefacio m; (to event) prólogo m

prefect /ˈpriːfekt/ n (Schol) monitor m; (official) prefecto m

prefer /prɪˈfɜː(r)/ vt (pt **preferred**) preferir. ~ sth to sth preferir algo a algo. ~**able** /ˈprefrəbl/ a preferible. ~**ence** /ˈprefrəns/ n preferencia f. ~**ential** /-əˈrenʃl/ a preferente

pregnan|cy /ˈpregnənsɪ/ n embarazo m. ~t a embarazada

prehistoric /priːhɪˈstɒrɪk/ a prehistórico

prejudge /priːˈdʒʌdʒ/ vt prejuzgar

prejudice /ˈpredʒʊdɪs/ n prejuicio m. ● vt predisponer; (harm) perjudicar. ~d a lleno de prejuicios

preliminary /prɪˈlɪmɪnərɪ/ a preliminar

prelude /ˈpreljuːd/ n preludio m

premature /ˈpremətjʊə(r)/ a prematuro

premeditated /priːˈmedɪteɪtɪd/ a premeditado

premier /ˈpremɪə(r)/ n (Pol) primer ministro m

première /ˈpremɪeə(r)/ n estreno m

premise /ˈpremɪs/ n premisa f. ~s /ˈpremɪsɪz/ npl local m. on the ~s en el local

premium /ˈpriːmɪəm/ n (insurance ~) prima f de seguro. be at a ~ escasear

premonition /priːməˈnɪʃn/ n premonición f, presentimiento m

preoccup|ation /priːɒkjʊˈpeɪʃn/ n (obsession) obsesión f; (concern) preocupación f. ~ied /-ˈɒkjʊpaɪd/ a absorto; (worried) preocupado

preparat|ion /prepəˈreɪʃn/ n preparación f. ~ions npl preparativos mpl. ~ory /prɪˈpærətrɪ/ a preparatorio

prepare /prɪˈpeə(r)/ vt preparar. ● vi prepararse. ● a preparado (willing). be ~d to estar dispuesto a

preposition /prepəˈzɪʃn/ n preposición f

preposterous /prɪˈpɒstərəs/ a absurdo

prerequisite /priːˈrekwɪzɪt/ n requisito m esencial

prerogative /prɪˈrɒgətɪv/ n prerrogativa f

Presbyterian /prezbɪˈtɪərɪən/ a & n presbiteriano (m)

prescri|be /prɪˈskraɪb/ vt prescribir; (Med) recetar. ~**ption** /-ˈɪpʃn/ n (Med) receta f

presence /ˈprezns/ n presencia f. ~ **of mind** presencia f de ánimo

present /ˈpreznt/ n (gift) regalo m; (current time) presente m. **at** ~ actualmente. **for the** ~ por ahora. ● a presente. ● /prɪˈzent/ vt presentar; (give) obsequiar. ~ **s.o. with** obsequiar a uno con. ~**able** /prɪˈzentəbl/ a presentable. ~**ation** /preznˈteɪʃn/ n presentación f; (ceremony) ceremonia f de entrega. ~**er** /prɪˈzentə(r)/ n presentador m. ~**ly** /ˈprezntlɪ/ adv dentro de poco

preserv|ation /prezəˈveɪʃn/ n conservación f. ~**ative** /prɪˈzɜːvə tɪv/ n conservante m. ~**e** /prɪˈzɜːv/ vt conservar; (maintain) mantener; (Culin) hacer conserva de. ● n coto m; (jam) confitura f. **wildlife** ~**e** (Amer) reserva f de animales

preside /prɪˈzaɪd/ vi presidir. ~ **over** presidir

presiden|cy /ˈprezɪdənsɪ/ n presidencia f. ~**t** n presidente m. ~**tial** /-ˈdenʃl/ a presidencial

press /pres/ vt apretar; prensar <grapes>; (put pressure on) presionar; (iron) planchar. **be** ~**ed for time** andar escaso de tiempo. ● vi apretar; <time> apremiar; (fig) urgir. ● n (Mec, newspapers) prensa f; (printing) imprenta f. □ ~ **on** vi seguir adelante (with con). ~ **conference** n rueda f de prensa. ~ **cutting** n recorte m de periódico. ~**ing** a urgente. ~**up** n flexión f, fondo m

pressur|e /ˈpreʃə(r)/ n presión f. ● vt presionar. ~**e-cooker** n olla f a presión. ~**ize** vt presionar

prestig|e /preˈstiːʒ/ n prestigio m. ~**ious** /-ˈstɪdʒəs/ a prestigioso

presum|ably /prɪˈzjuːməblɪ/ adv. ~... supongo que..., me imagino que... ~**e** /prɪˈzjuːm/ vt suponer. ~**ptuous** /prɪˈzʌmptʃʊəs/ a impertinente

presuppose /priːsəˈpəʊz/ vt presuponer

preten|ce /prɪˈtens/ n fingimiento m; (claim) pretensión f; (pretext) pretexto m. ~**d** /-ˈtend/ vt/i fingir. ~**sion** /-ˈtenʃən/ n pretensión f. ~**tious** /-ˈtenʃəs/ a pretencioso

pretext /ˈpriːtekst/ n pretexto m

pretty /ˈprɪtɪ/ a (**-ier, -iest**) adv bonito, lindo (esp LAm)

prevail /prɪˈveɪl/ vi predominar; (win) prevalecer. □ ~ **on** vt persuadir

prevalen|ce /ˈprevələns/ n (occurrence) preponderancia f; (predominance) predominio m. ~**t** a extendido

prevent /prɪˈvent/ vt (hinder) impedir; (forestall) prevenir, evitar. ~**ion** /-ʃn/ n prevención f. ~**ive** a preventivo

preview /ˈpriːvjuː/ n preestreno m; (trailer) avance m

previous /ˈpriːvɪəs/ a anterior. ~ **to** antes de. ~**ly** adv antes

prey /preɪ/ n presa f. **bird of** ~ ave f de rapiña

price /praɪs/ n precio m. ● vt fijar el precio de. ~**less** a inestimable; (🄔, amusing) muy divertido. ~**y** a 🄔 carito

prick /prɪk/ vt/i pinchar. ● n pinchazo m

prickl|e /ˈprɪkl/ n (Bot) espina f; (of animal) púa f; (sensation) picor m. ~**y** a espinoso; <animal> con púas; (touchy) quisquilloso

pride /praɪd/ n orgullo m. ● vr. ~ **o.s. on** enorgullecerse de

priest /priːst/ n sacerdote m. ~**hood** n sacerdocio m

prim /prɪm/ a (**primmer, primmest**) mojigato; (affected) remilgado

primar|ily /ˈpraɪmərɪlɪ/ adv en primer lugar. ~**y** /ˈpraɪmərɪ/ a (principal) primordial; (first, basic) primario. ~ **school** n escuela f primaria

prime /praɪm/ vt cebar <gun>; (prepare) preparar; aprestar <surface>. ● a principal; (first rate) excelente. ● n. **be in one's** ~ estar en la flor de la vida. ~**r** n (paint) imprimación f

primeval /praɪˈmiːvl/ a primigenio

primitive /ˈprɪmɪtɪv/ a primitivo

primrose /'prɪmrəʊz/ n primavera f

prince /prɪns/ n príncipe m. ~**ss** /prɪn'ses/ n princesa f

principal /'prɪnsəpl/ a principal. ● n (of school) director m; (of university) rector m. ~**ly** /'prɪnsɪpəlɪ/ adv principalmente

principle /'prɪnsəpl/ n principio m. in ~ en principio. on ~ por principio

print /prɪnt/ vt imprimir; (write in capitals) escribir con letras de molde. ~**ed matter** impresos mpl. ● n (characters) letra f; (picture) grabado m; (Photo) copia f; (fabric) estampado m. in ~ (published) publicado; (available) a la venta. out of ~ agotado. ~**er** /'prɪntə(r)/ n impresor m; (machine) impresora f. ~**ing** n impresión f; (trade) imprenta f. ~**out** n listado m

prior /'praɪə(r)/ n prior m. ● a previo. ~ **to** antes de. ~**ity** /praɪ'ɒrətɪ/ n prioridad f. ~**y** n priorato m

prise /praɪz/ vt. ~ **open** abrir haciendo palanca

prison /'prɪzn/ n cárcel m. ~**er** n prisionero m; (in prison) preso m; (under arrest) detenido m. ~ **officer** n funcionario m de prisiones

priva|cy /'prɪvəsɪ/ n privacidad f. ~**te** /'praɪvɪt/ a privado; (confidential) personal; <lessons, house> particular. in ~**te** en privado; (secretly) en secreto. ● n soldado m raso. ~**te detective** n detective m & f privado. ~**tely** adv en privado. ~**tion** /praɪ'veɪʃn/ n privación f

privilege /'prɪvəlɪdʒ/ n privilegio m. ~**d** a privilegiado. **be** ~**d to** tener el privilegio de

prize /praɪz/ n premio m. ● a <idiot etc> de remate. ● vt estimar

pro /prəʊ/ n. ~**s and cons** los pros m y los contras

probab|ility /prɒbə'bɪlətɪ/ n probabilidad f. ~**le** /'prɒbəbl/ a probable. ~**ly** adv probablemente

probation /prə'beɪʃn/ n período m de prueba; (Jurid) libertad f condicional

probe /prəʊb/ n sonda f; (fig) investigación f. ● vt sondar. ● vi. ~ **into** investigar

problem /'prɒbləm/ n problema m. ● a difícil. ~**atic** /-'mætɪk/ a problemático

procedure /prə'siːdʒə(r)/ n procedimiento m

proceed /prə'siːd/ vi proceder; (move forward) avanzar. ~**ings** npl (report) actas fpl; (Jurid) proceso m. ~**s** /'prəʊsiːdz/ npl. **the** ~**s** lo recaudado

process /'prəʊses/ n proceso m. in **the** ~ **of** en vías de. ● vt tratar; revelar <photo>; tramitar <order>. ~**ion** /prə'seʃn/ n desfile m; (Relig) procesión f

procla|im /prə'kleɪm/ vt proclamar. ~**mation** /prɒklə'meɪʃn/ n proclamación f

procure /prə'kjʊə(r)/ vt obtener

prod /prɒd/ vt (pt **prodded**) (with sth sharp) pinchar; (with elbow) darle un codazo a. ● n (with sth sharp) pinchazo m; (with elbow) codazo m

produc|e /prə'djuːs/ vt producir; surtir <effect>; sacar <gun>; producir <film>; poner en escena <play>. ● /'prɒdjuːs/ n productos mpl. ~**er** /prə'djuːsə(r)/ n (TV, Cinema) productor m; (in theatre) director m; (manufacturer) fabricante m & f. ~**t** /'prɒdʌkt/ n producto m. ~**tion** /prə'dʌkʃn/ n (manufacture) fabricación f; (output) producción f; (of play) producción f. ~**tive** /prə'dʌktɪv/ a productivo. ~**tivity** /prɒdʌk'tɪvətɪ/ n productividad f

profess /prə'fes/ vt profesar; (pretend) pretender. ~**ion** /-'feʃn/ n profesión f. ~**ional** a & n profesional (m & f). ~**or** /-'fesə(r)/ n catedrático m; (Amer) profesor m

proficien|cy /prə'fɪʃənsɪ/ n competencia f. ~**t** a competente

profile /'prəʊfaɪl/ n perfil m

profit /'prɒfɪt/ n (Com) ganancia f; (fig) provecho m. ● vi. ~ **from** sacar provecho de. ~**able** a provechoso

profound /prə'faʊnd/ a profundo. ~**ly** adv profundamente

profus|e /prə'fjuːs/ a profuso. ~**ely** adv profusamente

prognosis /prɒg'nəʊsɪs/ n (pl -**oses**) pronóstico m

program /ˈprəʊɡræm/ n (Comp) programa m; (Amer, course) curso m. ~me /ˈprəʊɡræm/ n programa m. ● vt (pt -med) programar. ~mer n programador m

progress /ˈprəʊɡres/ n progreso m; (development) desarrollo m. make ~ hacer progresos. in ~ en curso. ● /prəˈgres/ vi hacer progresos; (develop) desarrollarse. ~ion /prəˈgreʃn/ n progresión f; (advance) evolución f. ~ive /prəˈgresɪv/ a progresivo; (reforming) progresista. ~ively adv progresivamente

prohibit /prəˈhɪbɪt/ vt prohibir; (prevent) impedir. ~ive a prohibitivo

project /prəˈdʒekt/ vt proyectar. ● vi (stick out) sobresalir. ● /ˈprɒdʒekt/ n proyecto m; (Schol) trabajo m; (Amer, housing ~) complejo m de viviendas subvencionadas. ~or /prəˈdʒektə(r)/ n proyector m

prolific /prəˈlɪfɪk/ a prolífico

prologue /ˈprəʊlɒɡ/ n prólogo m

prolong /prəˈlɒŋ/ vt prolongar

prom /prɒm/ n (Amer) baile m del colegio. ~enade /prɒməˈnɑːd/ n paseo m marítimo. ● vi pasearse.

prominen|ce /ˈprɒmɪnəns/ n prominencia f; (fig) importancia f. ~t a prominente; (important) importante; (conspicuous) destacado

promiscu|ity /prɒmɪˈskjuːətɪ/ n promiscuidad f. ~ous /prəˈmɪskjʊəs/ a promiscuo

promis|e /ˈprɒmɪs/ n promesa f. ● vt/i prometer. ~ing a prometedor; <future> halagüeño

promot|e /prəˈməʊt/ vt promover; promocionar <product>; (in rank) ascender. ~ion /-ˈməʊʃn/ n promoción f; (in rank) ascenso m

prompt /prɒmpt/ a rápido; (punctual) puntual. ● adv en punto. ● n (Comp) presto m. ● vt incitar; apuntar <actor>. ~ly adv puntualmente

prone /prəʊn/ a (tendido) boca abajo. be ~ to ser propenso a

pronoun /ˈprəʊnaʊn/ n pronombre m

pronounc|e /prəˈnaʊns/ vt pronunciar; (declare) declarar. ~ement

n declaración f. ~ed a pronunciado; (noticeable) marcado

pronunciation /prənʌnsɪˈeɪʃn/ n pronunciación f

proof /pruːf/ n prueba f, pruebas fpl; (of alcohol) graduación f normal. ● a. ~ against a prueba de. ~-reading n corrección f de pruebas

propaganda /prɒpəˈgændə/ n propaganda f

propagate /ˈprɒpəɡeɪt/ vt propagar. ● vi propagarse

propel /prəˈpel/ vt (pt propelled) propulsar. ~ler n hélice f

proper /ˈprɒpə(r)/ a correcto; (suitable) apropiado; (Gram) propio; (ⓘ, real) verdadero. ~ly adv correctamente; <eat, work> bien

property /ˈprɒpətɪ/ n propiedad f; (things owned) bienes mpl. ● a inmobiliario

prophe|cy /ˈprɒfəsɪ/ n profecía f. ~sy /ˈprɒfɪsaɪ/ vt/i profetizar. ~t /ˈprɒfɪt/ n profeta m. ~tic /prəˈfetɪk/ a profético

proportion /prəˈpɔːʃn/ n proporción f. ~al a, ~ate /-ət/ a proporcional

propos|al /prəˈpəʊzl/ n propuesta f; (of marriage) proposición f matrimonial. ~e /prəˈpəʊz/ vt proponer. ● vi. ~e to s.o. hacerle una oferta de matrimonio a una. ~ition /prɒpəˈzɪʃn/ n propuesta f; (offer) oferta f

proprietor /prəˈpraɪətə(r)/ n propietario m

pro rata /ˈprəʊˈrɑːtə/ adv a prorrata

prose /prəʊz/ n prosa f

prosecut|e /ˈprɒsɪkjuːt/ vt procesar (for por); (carry on) proseguir. ~ion /-ˈkjuːʃn/ n proceso m. the ~ (side) la acusación. ~or n fiscal m & f; (in private prosecutions) abogado m de la acusación

prospect /ˈprɒspekt/ n (possibility) posibilidad f (of de); (situation envisaged) perspectiva f. ~s (chances) perspectivas fpl. ~ive /prəˈspektɪv/ a posible; (future) futuro. ~or /prəˈspektə(r)/ n prospector m. ~us /prəˈspektəs/ n folleto m informativo

prosper /'prɒspə(r)/ vi prosperar. ~ity /-'sperətɪ/ n prosperidad f. ~ous a próspero

prostitut|e /'prɒstɪtjuːt/ n prostituta f. ~ion /-'tjuːʃn/ n prostitución f

prostrate /'prɒstreɪt/ a postrado

protagonist /prə'tægənɪst/ n protagonista m & f

protect /prə'tekt/ vt proteger. ~ion /-ʃn/ n protección f. ~ive a protector. ~or n protector m

protein /'prəʊtiːn/ n proteína f

protest /'prəʊtest/ n protesta f. in ~ (against) en señal de protesta (contra). under ~ bajo protesta. ● /prə'test/ vt/i protestar

Protestant /'prɒtɪstənt/ a & n protestante (m & f)

protester /prə'testə(r)/ n manifestante m & f

protocol /'prəʊtəkɒl/ n protocolo m

protrud|e /prə'truːd/ vi sobresalir. ~ing a <chin> prominente. ~ing eyes ojos saltones

proud /praʊd/ a orgulloso. ~ly adv con orgullo; (arrogantly) orgullosamente

prove /pruːv/ vt probar; demostrar <loyalty>. ● vi resultar. ~n a probado

proverb /'prɒvɜːb/ n refrán m, proverbio m

provide /prə'vaɪd/ vt proporcionar; dar <accommodation>. ~ s.o. with sth proveer a uno de algo. ● vi. ~ for (allow for) prever; mantener <person>. ~d conj. ~d (that) con tal de que, siempre que

providen|ce /'prɒvɪdəns/ n providencia f. ~tial /-'denʃl/ a providencial

providing /prə'vaɪdɪŋ/ conj. ~ that con tal de que, siempre que

provinc|e /'prɒvɪns/ n provincia f; (fig) competencia f. ~ial /prə'vɪnʃl/ a provincial

provision /prə'vɪʒn/ n provisión f; (supply) suministro m; (stipulation) disposición f. ~s npl provisiones fpl, víveres mpl. ~al a provisional

provo|cation /prɒvə'keɪʃn/ n provocación f. ~cative /-'vɒkətɪv/ a

provocador. ~ke /prə'vəʊk/ vt provocar

prow /praʊ/ n proa f

prowess /'praʊɪs/ n destreza f; (valour) valor m

prowl /praʊl/ vi merodear. ~er n merodeador m

proximity /prɒk'sɪmətɪ/ n proximidad f

prude /pruːd/ n mojigato m

pruden|ce /'pruːdəns/ n prudencia f. ~t a prudente. ~tly adv prudentemente

prudish /'pruːdɪʃ/ a mojigato

prune /pruːn/ n ciruela f pasa. ● vt podar

pry /praɪ/ vi curiosear. ~ into sth entrometerse en algo. vt (Amer) ⇒PRISE

PS n (postscript) P.D.

psalm /sɑːm/ n salmo m

psychiatr|ic /saɪkɪ'ætrɪk/ a psiquiátrico. ~ist /saɪ'kaɪətrɪst/ n psiquiatra m & f. ~y /saɪ'kaɪətrɪ/ n psiquiatría f

psychic /'saɪkɪk/ a para(p)sicológico

psycho|analysis /saɪkəʊə'næləsɪs/ n (p)sicoanálisis m. ~logical /saɪkə'lɒdʒɪkl/ a (p)sicológico. ~logist /saɪ'kɒlədʒɪst/ n (p)sicólogo m. ~logy /saɪ'kɒlədʒɪ/ n (p)si-cología f. ~therapy /-'θerəpɪ/ n (p)sicoterapia f

pub /pʌb/ n bar m

puberty /'pjuːbətɪ/ n pubertad f

pubic /'pjuːbɪk/ a pubiano, púbico

public /'pʌblɪk/ a público. ~an n tabernero m. ~ation /-'keɪʃn/ n publicación f. ~ holiday n día m festivo, día m feriado (LAm). ~ house n bar m. ~ity /pʌb'lɪsətɪ/ n publicidad f. ~ize /'pʌblɪsaɪz/ vt hacer público. ~ly adv públicamente. ~ school n colegio m privado; (Amer) instituto m, escuela f pública

publish /'pʌblɪʃ/ vt publicar. ~er n editor m. ~ing n publicación f. ~ing house editorial f

pudding /'pʊdɪŋ/ n postre m; (steamed) budín m

puddle /'pʌdl/ n charco m

Puerto Ric|an /pwɜːtəʊˈriːkən/ *a* & *n* portorriqueño (*m*), puertorriqueño (*m*). **~o** /-əʊ/ *n* Puerto Rico *m*

puff /pʌf/ *n* (of wind) ráfaga *f*; (of smoke) nube *f*; (action) soplo *m*; (on cigarette) chupada *f*, calada *f*. ● *vt/i* soplar. **~ at** dar chupadas a <*pipe*>. **~ out** (swell up) inflar, hinchar. **~ed** *a* (out of breath) sin aliento. **~ paste** (Amer), **~ pastry** *n* hojaldre *m*. **~y** *a* hinchado

pull /pʊl/ *vt* tirar de, jalar (LAm); desgarrarse <*muscle*>. **~ a face** hacer una mueca. **~ a fast one** hacer una mala jugada. ● *vi* tirar, jalar (LAm). **~ at** tirar de, jalar (LAm). ● *n* tirón *m*, jalón *m* (LAm); (pulling force) fuerza *f*; (influence) influencia *f*. □ **~ away** *vi* (Auto) alejarse. □ **~ back** *vi* retirarse. □ **~ down** *vt* echar abajo <*building*>; (lower) bajar. □ **~ in** *vi* (Auto) parar. □ **~ off** *vt* (remove) quitar; (achieve) conseguir. □ **~ out** *vt* sacar; retirar <*team*>. *vi* (Auto) salirse. □ **~ through** *vi* recobrar la salud. □ **~ up** *vi* (Auto) parar. *vt* (uproot) arrancar; (reprimand) regañar

pullover /ˈpʊləʊvə(r)/ *n* suéter *m*, pulóver *m*, jersey *m*

pulp /pʌlp/ *n* pulpa *f*; (for paper) pasta *f*

pulpit /ˈpʊlpɪt/ *n* púlpito *m*

pulse /pʌls/ *n* (Med) pulso *m*; (Culin) legumbre *f*

pummel /ˈpʌml/ *vt* (*pt* **pummelled**) aporrear

pump /pʌmp/ *n* bomba *f*; (for petrol) surtidor *m*. ● *vt* sacar con una bomba. □ **~ up** *vt* inflar

pumpkin /ˈpʌmpkɪn/ *n* calabaza *f*

pun /pʌn/ *n* juego *m* de palabras

punch /pʌntʃ/ *vt* darle un puñetazo a; (perforate) perforar; hacer <*hole*>. ● *n* puñetazo *m*; (vigour) fuerza *f*; (device) perforadora *f*; (drink) ponche *m*. **~ in** *vi* (Amer) fichar (al entrar al trabajo). **~ out** *vi* (Amer) fichar (al salir del trabajo)

punctual /ˈpʌŋktʃʊəl/ *a* puntual. **~ity** /-ˈælətɪ/ *n* puntualidad *f*. **~ly** *adv* puntualmente

punctuat|e /ˈpʌŋktʃʊeɪt/ *vt* puntuar. **~ion** /-ˈeɪʃn/ *n* puntuación *f*

puncture /ˈpʌŋktʃə(r)/ *n* (in tyre) pinchazo *m*. **have a ~** pinchar. ● *vt* pinchar. ● *vi* pincharse

punish /ˈpʌnɪʃ/ *vt* castigar. **~ment** *n* castigo *m*

punk /pʌŋk/ *n* punk *m* & *f*, punki *m* & *f*; (Music) punk *m*; (Amer, hoodlum) vándalo *m*

punt /pʌnt/ *n* (boat) batea *f*. **~er** *n* apostante *m* & *f*

puny /ˈpjuːnɪ/ *a* (**-ier**, **-iest**) enclenque

pup /pʌp/ *n* cachorro *m*

pupil /ˈpjuːpl/ *n* alumno *m*; (of eye) pupila *f*

puppet /ˈpʌpɪt/ *n* marioneta *f*, títere *m*; (glove **~**) títere *m*

puppy /ˈpʌpɪ/ *n* cachorro *m*

purchase /ˈpɜːtʃəs/ *vt* adquirir. ● *n* adquisición *f*. **~r** *n* comprador *m*

pur|e /ˈpjʊə(r)/ *a* (**-er**, **-est**) puro. **~ity** *n* pureza *f*

purgatory /ˈpɜːɡətrɪ/ *n* purgatorio *m*

purge /pɜːdʒ/ *vt* purgar. ● *n* purga *f*

purif|ication /pjʊərɪfɪˈkeɪʃn/ *n* purificación *f*. **~y** /ˈpjʊərɪfaɪ/ *vt* purificar

purist /ˈpjʊərɪst/ *n* purista *m* & *f*

puritan /ˈpjʊərɪtən/ *n* puritano *m*. **~ical** /-ˈtænɪkl/ *a* puritano

purple /ˈpɜːpl/ *a* morado. ● *n* morado *m*, púrpura *f*

purport /pəˈpɔːt/ *vt*. **~ to be** pretender ser

purpose /ˈpɜːpəs/ *n* propósito *m*; (determination) resolución *f*. **on ~** a propósito. **serve a ~** servir de algo. **~ful** *a* (resolute) resuelto. **~ly** *adv* a propósito

purr /pɜː(r)/ *vi* ronronear

purse /pɜːs/ *n* monedero *m*; (Amer) bolso *m*, cartera *f* (LAm), bolsa *f* (Mex)

pursu|e /pəˈsjuː/ *vt* perseguir, continuar con <*course of action*>. **~it** /pəˈsjuːt/ *n* persecución *f*; (pastime) actividad *f*

pus /pʌs/ *n* pus *m*

push /pʊʃ/ *vt* empujar; apretar (button). ● *vi* empujar. ● *n* empujón *m*; (effort) esfuerzo *m*. □ **~ back** *vt* hacer retroceder. □ **~ off** *vi* ▣ largarse. ~**chair** n sillita f de paseo, carreola f (Mex). ~**y** a (pej) ambicioso

pussy /'pʊsɪ/ (pl -**sies**), **pussycat** /'pʊsɪkæt/ n 🔟 minino m

put /pʊt/ vt (pt **put**, pres p **putting**) poner; (with care, precision) colocar; (inside sth) meter; (express) decir. ☐ ~ **across** vt comunicar. ☐ ~ **away** vt guardar. ☐ ~ **back** vt volver a poner; retrasar <clock>. ☐ ~ **by** vt guardar; ahorrar <money>. ☐ ~ **down** vt (on a surface) dejar; colgar <phone>; (suppress) sofocar; (write) apuntar; (kill) sacrificar. ☐ ~ **forward** vt presentar <plan>; proponer <candidate>; adelantar <clocks>; adelantar <meeting>. ☐ ~ **in** vt (instal) poner; presentar <claim>. ☐ ~ **in for** vt solicitar. ☐ ~ **off** vt aplazar, posponer; (disconcert) desconcertar. ☐ ~ **on** vt (wear) ponerse; poner <CD, music>; encender <light>. ☐ ~ **out** vt (extinguish) apagar; (inconvenience) incomodar; extender <hand>; (disconcert) desconcertar. ☐ ~ **through** vt (phone) poner, pasar (to con). ☐ ~ **up** vt levantar; aumentar <rent>; subir <price>; poner <sign>; alojar <guest>. ☐ ~ **up with** vt aguantar, soportar

putrid /'pju:trɪd/ a putrefacto

putt /pʌt/ n (golf) golpe m suave

puzzl|e /'pʌzl/ n misterio m; (game) rompecabezas m. ● vt dejar perplejo. ~**ed** a <expression> de desconcierto. I'm ~ed about it me tiene perplejo. ~**ing** a incomprensible; (odd) curioso

pygmy /'pɪgmɪ/ n pigmeo m

pyjamas /pə'dʒɑːməz/ npl pijama m, piyama m or f (LAm)

pylon /'paɪlɒn/ n pilón m

pyramid /'pɪrəmɪd/ n pirámide f

python /'paɪθn/ n pitón m

Qq

quack /kwæk/ n (of duck) graznido m; (person) charlatán m. ~ **doctor** n curandero m

quadrangle /'kwɒdræŋgl/ n cuadrilátero m

quadruped /'kwɒdrʊped/ n cuadrúpedo m

quadruple /'kwɒdrʊpl/ a & n cuádruplo (m). ● vt cuadruplicar

quagmire /'kwægmaɪə(r)/ n lodazal m

quaint /kweɪnt/ a (-**er**, -**est**) pintoresco; (odd) curioso

quake /kweɪk/ vi temblar. ● n 🔟 terremoto m

qualif|ication /kwɒlɪfɪ'keɪʃn/ n título m; (requirement) requisito m; (ability) capacidad f; (Sport) clasificación f; (fig) reserva f. ~**ied** /'kwɒlɪfaɪd/ a cualificado; (with degree, diploma) titulado; (competent) capacitado. ~**y** /'kwɒlɪfaɪ/ vt calificar; (limit) limitar. ● vi titularse; (Sport) clasificarse. ~**y for sth** (be entitled to) tener derecho a algo

qualit|ative /'kwɒlɪtətɪv/ a cualitativo. ~**y** /'kwɒlɪtɪ/ n calidad f; (attribute) cualidad f

qualm /kwɑːm/ n reparo m

quandary /'kwɒndrɪ/ n dilema m

quanti|fy /'kwɒntɪfaɪ/ vt cuantificar. ~**ty** /-tɪ/ n cantidad f

quarantine /'kwɒrəntiːn/ n cuarentena f. ● vt poner en cuarentena

quarrel /'kwɒrəl/ n pelea f. ● vi (pt **quarrelled**) pelearse, discutir. ~**some** /-səm/ a pendenciero

quarry /'kwɒrɪ/ n (excavation) cantera f; (prey) presa f

quart /kwɔːt/ n cuarto m de galón

quarter /'kwɔːtə(r)/ n cuarto m; (of year) trimestre m; (district) barrio m. a ~ **of an hour** un cuarto de hora. ● vt dividir en cuartos; (Mil) acuartelar. ~-**final** n cuarto m de final. ~**ly** a trimestral. ● adv trimestralmente

quartz /kwɔ:ts/ n cuarzo m

quay /ki:/ n muelle m

queasy /'kwi:zɪ/ a mareado

queen /kwi:n/ n reina f. ~ **mother** n reina f madre

queer /kwɪə(r)/ a (**-er, -est**) extraño

quench /kwentʃ/ vt quitar <*thirst*>; sofocar <*desire*>

query /'kwɪərɪ/ n pregunta f. ● vt preguntar; (doubt) poner en duda

quest /kwest/ n busca f

question /'kwestʃən/ n pregunta f; (for discussion) cuestión f. **in** ~ en cuestión. **out of the** ~ imposible. **without** ~ sin duda. ● vt hacer preguntas a; <*police etc*> interrogar; (doubt) poner en duda. ~**able** a discutible. ~ **mark** n signo m de interrogación. ~**naire** /-'neə(r)/ n cuestionario m

queue /kju:/ n cola f. ● vi (pres p **queuing**) hacer cola

quibble /'kwɪbl/ vi discutir; (split hairs) sutilizar

quick /kwɪk/ a (**-er, -est**) rápido. **be** ~! ¡date prisa! ● adv rápido. ~**en** vt acelerar. ● vi acelerarse. ~**ly** adv rápido. ~**sand** n arena f movediza. ~**tempered** /-'tempəd/ a irascible

quid /kwɪd/ n invar Ⓔ libra f (esterlina)

quiet /'kwaɪət/ a (**-er, -est**) tranquilo; (silent) callado; (discreet) discreto. ● n tranquilidad f. ● vt/i (Amer) ⇒QUIETEN. ~**en** vt calmar. ● vi calmarse. ~**ly** adv tranquilamente; (silently) silenciosamente; (discreetly) discretamente. ~**ness** n tranquilidad f

quilt /kwɪlt/ n edredón m. ~**ed** a acolchado

quintet /kwɪn'tet/ n quinteto m

quirk /kwɜːk/ n peculiaridad f

quit /kwɪt/ vt (pt **quitted**) dejar. ~ **doing** (Amer, cease) dejar de hacer. ● vi (give in) abandonar; (stop) parar; (resign) dimitir

quite /kwaɪt/ adv bastante; (completely) totalmente; (really) verdaderamente. ~ (**so!**) ¡claro! ~ **a few** bastante

quits /kwɪts/ a. **be** ~ estar en paz. **call it** ~ darlo por terminado

quiver /'kwɪvə(r)/ vi temblar

quiz /kwɪz/ n (pl **quizzes**) serie f de preguntas; (game) concurso m. ● vt (pt **quizzed**) interrogar. ~**zical** a burlón

quota /'kwəʊtə/ n cuota f

quot|ation /kwəʊ'teɪʃn/ n cita f; (price) presupuesto m. ~**ation marks** npl comillas fpl. ~**e** /kwəʊt/ vt citar; (Com) cotizar. ● n Ⓔ cita f; (price) presupuesto m. **in** ~**es** npl entre comillas

Rr

rabbi /'ræbaɪ/ n rabino m

rabbit /'ræbɪt/ n conejo m

rabi|d /'ræbɪd/ a feroz; <*dog*> rabioso. ~**es** /'reɪbiːz/ n rabia f

race /reɪs/ n (in sport) carrera f; (ethnic group) raza f. ● vt hacer correr <*horse*>. ● vi (run) correr, ir corriendo; (rush) ir de prisa. ~**course** n hipódromo m. ~**horse** n caballo m de carreras. ~ **relations** npl relaciones fpl raciales. ~**track** n hipódromo m

racial /'reɪʃl/ a racial

racing /'reɪsɪŋ/ n carreras fpl. ~ **car** n coche m de carreras

racis|m /'reɪsɪzəm/ n racismo m. ~**t** a & n racista (m & f)

rack¹ /ræk/ n (shelf) estante m; (for luggage) rejilla f; (for plates) escurreplatos m. ● vt. ~ **one's brains** devanarse los sesos

rack² /ræk/ n. **go to** ~ **and ruin** quedarse en la ruina

racket /'rækɪt/ n (for sports) raqueta; (din) alboroto m; (swindle) estafa f. ~**eer** /-ə'tɪə(r)/ n estafador m

racy /'reɪsɪ/ a (**-ier, -iest**) vivo

radar /'reɪdɑ:(r)/ n radar m

radian|ce /'reɪdɪəns/ n resplandor m. ~**t** a radiante

radiat|e /'reɪdɪeɪt/ vt irradiar. ● vi divergir. ~**ion** /-'eɪʃn/ n radiación f. ~**or** n radiador m

radical /'rædɪkl/ a & n radical (m)

radio /'reɪdɪəʊ/ n (pl **-os**) radio f or m. ● vt transmitir por radio. ~**active** /reɪdɪəʊ'æktɪv/ a radiacti·vo. ~**activity** /-'tɪvətɪ/ n radiacti·vidad f

radish /'rædɪʃ/ n rábano m

radius /'reɪdɪəs/ n (pl **-dii** /-dɪaɪ/) radio m

raffle /'ræfl/ n rifa f

raft /rɑːft/ n balsa f

rafter /'rɑːftə(r)/ n cabrio m

rag /ræg/ n andrajo m; (for wiping) trapo m. in ~s <person> andrajoso

rage /reɪdʒ/ n rabia f; (fashion) moda f. ● vi estar furioso; <storm> bramar

ragged /'rægɪd/ a <person> andrajoso; <clothes> hecho jirones

raid /reɪd/ n (Mil) incursión f; (by police, etc) redada f; (by thieves) asalto m. ● vt (Mil) atacar; <police> hacer una redada en; <thieves> asaltar. ~**er** n invasor m; (thief) ladrón m

rail /reɪl/ n barandilla f; (for train) riel m; (rod) barra f. by ~ por ferrocarril. ~**ing** n barandilla f; (fence) verja f. ~**road** n (Amer), ~**way** n ferrocarril m. ~**way station** n estación f de ferrocarril

rain /reɪn/ n lluvia f. ● vi llover. ~**bow** /-bəʊ/ n arco m iris. ~**coat** n impermeable m. ~**fall** n precipitación f. ~**y** a (**-ier, -iest**) lluvioso

raise /reɪz/ vt levantar; (breed) criar; obtener <money etc>; formular <question>; plantear <problem>; subir <price>. ● n (Amer) aumento m

raisin /'reɪzn/ n (uva f) pasa f

rake /reɪk/ n rastrillo m. ● vt rastrillar; (search) buscar en. □ ~ **up** vt remover

rally /'rælɪ/ vt reunir; (revive) reanimar. ● n reunión f; (Auto) rally m

ram /ræm/ n carnero m. ● vt (pt **rammed**) (thrust) meter por la fuerza; (crash into) chocar con

RAM /ræm/ n (Comp) RAM f

ramble /'ræmbl/ n excursión f a pie. ● vi ir de paseo; (in speech) divagar. □ ~**e on** vi divagar. ~**er** n excursionista m & f. ~**ing** a <speech> divagador

ramp /ræmp/ n rampa f

rampage /ræm'peɪdʒ/ vi alborotarse. ● /'ræmpeɪdʒ/ n. go on the ~ alborotarse

ramshackle /'ræmʃækl/ a desvencijado

ran /ræn/ ⇒RUN

ranch /rɑːntʃ/ n hacienda f

random /'rændəm/ a hecho al azar; (chance) fortuito. ● n. at ~ al azar

rang /ræŋ/ ⇒RING²

range /reɪndʒ/ n alcance m; (distance) distancia f; (series) serie f; (of mountains) cordillera f; (extent) extensión f; (Com) surtido m; (stove) cocina f económica. ● vi extenderse; (vary) variar. ~**r** n guardabosque m

rank /ræŋk/ n posición f, categoría f; (row) fila f; (for taxis) parada f. the ~ and file la masa f. ~**s** npl soldados mpl rasos. ● a (**-er, -est**) (smell) fétido; (fig) completo. ● vt clasificar. ● vi clasificarse

ransack /'rænsæk/ vt registrar; (pillage) saquear

ransom /'rænsəm/ n rescate m. hold s.o. to ~ exigir rescate por uno. ● vt rescatar; (redeem) redimir

rant /rænt/ vi despotricar

rap /ræp/ n golpe m seco. ● vt/i (pt **rapped**) golpear

rape /reɪp/ vt violar. ● n violación f

rapid /'ræpɪd/ a rápido. ~**s** npl rápidos mpl

rapist /'reɪpɪst/ n violador m

rapture /'ræptʃə(r)/ n éxtasis m. ~**ous** /-rəs/ a extático

rare /reə(r)/ a (**-er, -est**) raro; (Culin) poco hecho. ~**fied** /'reərɪfaɪd/ a enrarecido. ~**ly** adv raramente

raring /'reərɪŋ/ a 🅘. ~ to impaciente por

rarity /'reərətɪ/ n rareza f

rascal /'rɑːskl/ n granuja m & f

rash /ræʃ/ a (**-er, -est**) precipitado, imprudente. ● n erupción f

rasher /'ræʃə(r)/ n loncha f

rashly /'ræʃlɪ/ adv precipitadamente, imprudentemente

rasp /rɑːsp/ n (file) escofina f

raspberry /'rɑːzbrɪ/ n frambuesa f

rat /ræt/ n rata f

rate /reɪt/ n (ratio) proporción f; (speed) velocidad f; (price) precio m; (of interest) tipo m. **at any ~** de todas formas. **at this ~** así. **~s** npl (taxes) impuestos mpl municipales. ● vt valorar; (consider) considerar; (Amer, deserve) merecer. ● vi ser considerado

rather /'rɑːðə(r)/ adv mejor dicho; (fairly) bastante; (a little) un poco. ● int claro. **I would ~ not** prefiero no

rating /'reɪtɪŋ/ n clasificación f; (sailor) marinero m; (number, TV) índice m

ratio /'reɪʃɪəʊ/ n (pl **-os**) proporción f

ration /'ræʃn/ n ración f. **~s** npl (provisions) víveres mpl. ● vt racionar

rational /'ræʃənəl/ a racional. **~ize** vt racionalizar

rattle /'rætl/ vi traquetear. ● vt (shake) agitar; ⊞ desconcertar. ● n traqueteo m; (toy) sonajero m. □ **~ off** vt (fig) decir de corrida

raucous /'rɔːkəs/ a estridente

ravage /'rævɪdʒ/ vt estragar

rave /reɪv/ vi delirar; (in anger) despotricar. **~ about sth** poner a algo por las nubes

raven /'reɪvn/ n cuervo m

ravenous /'rævənəs/ a voraz; <person> hambriento. **be ~** morirse de hambre

ravine /rə'viːn/ n barranco m

raving /'reɪvɪŋ/ a. **~ mad** loco de atar

ravishing /'rævɪʃɪŋ/ a (enchanting) encantador

raw /rɔː/ a (**-er, -est**) crudo; <sugar> sin refinar; (inexperienced) inexperto. **~ deal** n tratamiento m injusto, injusticia f. **~ materials** npl materias fpl primas

ray /reɪ/ n rayo m

raze /reɪz/ vt arrasar

razor /'reɪzə(r)/ n navaja f de afeitar; (electric) maquinilla f de afeitar

Rd /rəʊd/ abbr (= **Road**) C/, Calle f

re /riː/ prep con referencia a. ● pref re.

reach /riːtʃ/ vt alcanzar; (extend) extender; (arrive at) llegar a; (achieve) lograr; (hand over) pasar, dar. ● vi extenderse. ● n alcance m. **within ~ of** al alcance de; (close to) a corta distancia de. □ **~ out** vi alargar la mano

react /rɪ'ækt/ vi reaccionar. **~ion** /rɪ'ækʃn/ n reacción f. **~ionary** a & n reaccionario (m). **~or** /rɪ'æktə(r)/ n reactor m

read /riːd/ vt (pt **read** /red/) leer; (study) estudiar; (interpret) interpretar. ● vi leer; <instrument> indicar. □ **~ out** vt leer en voz alta. **~able** a (clear) legible. **~er** n lector m

readily /'redɪlɪ/ adv (willingly) de buena gana; (easily) fácilmente

reading /'riːdɪŋ/ n lectura f

readjust /riːə'dʒʌst/ vt reajustar. ● vi readaptarse (**to** a)

ready /'redɪ/ a (**-ier, -iest**) listo, preparado. **get ~** prepararse. **~-made** a confeccionado

real /rɪəl/ a verdadero. ● adv (Amer ⊞) verdaderamente. **~ estate** n bienes mpl raíces, propiedad f inmobiliaria. **~ estate agent** ⇒REALTOR. **~ism** n realismo m. **~ist** n realista m & f. **~istic** /-'lɪstɪk/ a realista. **~ity** /rɪ'ælətɪ/ n realidad f. **~ization** /rɪəlaɪ'zeɪʃn/ n comprensión f. **~ize** /'rɪəlaɪz/ vt darse cuenta de; (fulfil, Com) realizar. **~ly** /'rɪəlɪ/ adv verdaderamente

realm /relm/ n reino m

realtor /'riːəltə(r)/ n (Amer) agente m inmobiliario

reap /riːp/ vt segar; (fig) cosechar

reappear /riːə'pɪə(r)/ vi reaparecer

rear /rɪə(r)/ n parte f de atrás. ● a posterior, trasero. ● vt (bring up, breed) criar. ● vi **~ (up)** <horse> encabritarse

rearguard /'rɪəgɑːd/ n retaguardia f

rearrange /riːə'reɪndʒ/ vt arreglar de otra manera

reason /'riːzn/ n razón f, motivo m. **within ~** dentro de lo razonable. ● vi razonar. **~able** a razonable. **~ing** n razonamiento m

reassur|ance /riːə'ʃʊərəns/ n promesa f tranquilizadora; (guarantee) garantía f. **~e** /riːə'ʃʊə(r)/ vt tranquilizar

rebate /'riːbeɪt/ n (discount) rebaja f

rebel /'rebl/ n rebelde m & f.
● /rɪ'bel/ vi (pt **rebelled**) rebelarse.
~**lion** /rɪ'beliən/ n rebelión f.
~**lious** a rebelde

rebound /rɪ'baʊnd/ vi rebotar; (fig)
recaer. ● /'ri:baʊnd/ n rebote m

rebuff /rɪ'bʌf/ vt rechazar. ● n desaire m

rebuild /ri:'bɪld/ vt (pt **rebuilt**) reconstruir

rebuke /rɪ'bju:k/ vt reprender. ● n
reprimenda f

recall /rɪ'kɔ:l/ vt (call s.o. back) llamar; (remember) recordar. ● n
/'ri:kɔ:l/ (of goods, ambassador) retirada f; (memory) memoria f

recap /'ri:kæp/ vt/i (pt **recapped**)
🔲 resumir

recapitulate /ri:kə'pɪtʃʊleɪt/ vt/i
resumir

recapture /ri:'kæptʃə(r)/ vt recobrar; (recall) hacer revivir

recede /rɪ'si:d/ vi retroceder

receipt /rɪ'si:t/ n recibo m. ~**s** npl
(Com) ingresos mpl

receive /rɪ'si:v/ vt recibir. ~**r** n (of
stolen goods) perista m & f; (part of
phone) auricular m

recent /'ri:snt/ a reciente. ~**ly** adv
recientemente

recept|ion /rɪ'sepʃn/ n recepción f;
(welcome) acogida f. ~**ionist** n recepcionista m & f. ~**ive** /-tɪv/ a receptivo

recess /rɪ'ses/ n hueco m; (holiday)
vacaciones fpl. ~**ion** /rɪ'seʃn/ n recesión f

recharge /ri:'tʃɑ:dʒ/ vt cargar de
nuevo, recargar

recipe /'resəpɪ/ n receta f. ~ **book**
n libro m de cocina

recipient /rɪ'sɪpɪənt/ n recipiente
m & f; (of letter) destinatario m

recit|al /rɪ'saɪtl/ n (Mus) recital m.
~**e** /rɪ'saɪt/ vt recitar; (list) enumerar

reckless /'reklɪs/ a imprudente.
~**ly** adv imprudentemente

reckon /'rekən/ vt/i calcular; (consider) considerar; (think) pensar. □ ~
on vt (rely) contar con

reclaim /rɪ'kleɪm/ vt reclamar; recuperar <land>

reclin|e /rɪ'klaɪn/ vi recostarse.
~**ing** a acostado; <seat> reclinable

recluse /rɪ'klu:s/ n ermitaño m

recogni|tion /rekəg'nɪʃn/ n reconocimiento m. **beyond** ~**tion** irreconocible. ~**ze** /'rekəgnaɪz/ vt reconocer

recoil /rɪ'kɔɪl/ vi retroceder.
● /'ri:kɔɪl/ n (of gun) culatazo m

recollect /rekə'lekt/ vt recordar.
~**ion** /-ʃn/ n recuerdo m

recommend /rekə'mend/ vt recomendar. ~**ation** /-'deɪʃn/ n recomendación f

reconcil|e /'rekənsaɪl/ vt reconciliar <people>; conciliar <facts>. ~**e
o.s.** resignarse (to a). ~**iation**
/-sɪlɪ'eɪʃn/ n reconciliación f

reconnaissance /rɪ'kɒnɪsns/ n
reconocimiento m

reconnoitre /rekə'nɔɪtə(r)/ vt
(pres p **-tring**) (Mil) reconocer

re: ~**consider** /ri:kən'sɪdə(r)/ vt
volver a considerar. ~**construct**
/ri:kən'strʌkt/ vt reconstruir

record /rɪ'kɔ:d/ vt (in register) registrar; (in diary) apuntar; (Mus) grabar. ● /'rekɔ:d/ n (document) documento m; (of events) registro m;
(Mus) disco m; (Sport) récord m. **off
the** ~ en confianza. ~**er** /rɪ'kɔ:də(r)/
n registrador m; (Mus) flauta f dulce.
~**ing** /rɪ'kɔ:dɪŋ/ n grabación f.
~**-player** /'rekɔ:d-/ n tocadiscos m
invar

recount /rɪ'kaʊnt/ vt contar, relatar

re-count /'ri:kaʊnt/ vt volver a contar; recontar <votes>. ● /'ri:kaʊnt/ n (Pol) recuento m

recover /rɪ'kʌvə(r)/ vt recuperar.
● vi reponerse. ~**y** n recuperación f

recreation /rekrɪ'eɪʃn/ n recreo m.
~**al** a de recreo

recruit /rɪ'kru:t/ n recluta m. ● vt
reclutar; contratar <staff>. ~**ment**
n reclutamiento m

rectang|le /'rektæŋgl/ n rectángulo m. ~**ular** /-'tæŋgjʊlə(r)/ a
rectangular

rectify /'rektɪfaɪ/ vt rectificar

rector /'rektə(r)/ n párroco m; (of college) rector m. ~**y** n rectoría f

recuperat|e /rɪˈkuːpəreɪt/ *vt* recuperar. ● *vi* reponerse. **~ion** /-ˈreɪʃn/ *n* recuperación *f*

recur /rɪˈkɜː(r)/ *vi* (*pt* **recurred**) repetirse. **~rence** /rɪˈkʌrns/ *n* repetición *f*. **~rent** /rɪˈkʌrənt/ *a* repetido

recycle /riːˈsaɪkl/ *vt* reciclar

red /red/ *a* (**redder**, **reddest**) rojo. ● *n* rojo. be in the ~ estar en números rojos. **~den** *vi* enrojecerse. **~dish** *a* rojizo

redecorate /riːˈdekəreɪt/ *vt* pintar de nuevo

rede|em /rɪˈdiːm/ *vt* redimir. **~mption** /-ˈdempʃn/ *n* redención *f*

red: ~-handed /-ˈhændɪd/ *a*. catch s.o. ~handed agarrar a uno con las manos en la masa. **~ herring** *n* (fig) pista *f* falsa. **~-hot** *a* al rojo vivo

red light *n* luz *f* roja

redo /riːˈduː/ *vt* (*pt* **redid**, *pp* **redone**) rehacer

redouble /rɪˈdʌbl/ *vt* redoblar

red tape /red'teɪp/ *n* (fig) papeleo *m*

reduc|e /rɪˈdjuːs/ *vt* reducir; aliviar <*pain*>. ● *vi* (Amer, slim) adelgazar. **~tion** /rɪˈdʌkʃn/ *n* reducción *f*

redundan|cy /rɪˈdʌndənsɪ/ *n* superfluidad *f*; (unemployment) despido *m*. **~t** superfluo. she was made ~t la despidieron por reducción de plantilla

reed /riːd/ *n* caña *f*; (Mus) lengüeta *f*

reef /riːf/ *n* arrecife *m*

reek /riːk/ *n* mal olor *m*. ● *vi*. ~ (of) apestar a

reel /riːl/ *n* carrete *m*. ● *vi* dar vueltas; (stagger) tambalearse. □ ~ off *vt* (fig) enumerar

refectory /rɪˈfektərɪ/ *n* refectorio *m*

refer /rɪˈfɜː(r)/ *vt* (*pt* **referred**) remitir. ● *vi* referirse. ~ to referirse a; (consult) consultar. **~ee** /refəˈriː/ *n* árbitro *m*; (for job) referencia *f*. ● *vi* (*pt* **refereed**) arbitrar. **~ence** /ˈrefrəns/ *n* referencia *f*. **~ence book** *n* libro *m* de consulta. in ~ence to, with ~ence to con referencia a; (Com) re-specto a. **~en-dum** /refəˈrendəm/ *n* (*pl* **-ums** or **-da**) referéndum *m*

refill /riːˈfɪl/ *vt* volver a llenar. ● /ˈriːfɪl/ *n* recambio *m*

refine /rɪˈfaɪn/ *vt* refinar. **~d** *a* refinado. **~ry** /-ərɪ/ *n* refinería *f*

reflect /rɪˈflekt/ *vt* reflejar. ● *vi* reflejarse; (think) reflexionar. □ ~ badly upon perjudicar. **~ion** /-ʃn/ *n* reflexión *f*; (image) reflejo *m*. **~or** *n* reflector *m*

reflex /ˈriːfleks/ *a* & *n* reflejo (*m*). **~ive** /rɪˈfleksɪv/ *a* (Gram) reflexivo

reform /rɪˈfɔːm/ *vt* reformar. ● *vi* reformarse. ● *n* reforma *f*

refrain /rɪˈfreɪn/ *n* estribillo *m*. ● *vi* abstenerse (from de)

refresh /rɪˈfreʃ/ *vt* refrescar. **~ing** *a* refrescante. **~ments** *npl* (food and drink) refrigerio *m*

refrigerat|e /rɪˈfrɪdʒəreɪt/ *vt* refrigerar. **~or** *n* frigorífico *m*, refrigerador *m* (LAm)

refuel /riːˈfjuːəl/ *vt/i* (*pt* **refuelled**) repostar

refuge /ˈrefjuːdʒ/ *n* refugio *m*. take ~ refugiarse. **~e** /refjʊˈdʒiː/ *n* refugiado *m*

refund /rɪˈfʌnd/ *vt* reembolsar. ● /ˈriːfʌnd/ *n* reembolso *m*

refusal /rɪˈfjuːzl/ *n* negativa *f*

refuse /rɪˈfjuːz/ *vt* rehusar. ● *vi* negarse. ● /ˈrefjuːs/ *n* residuos *mpl*

refute /rɪˈfjuːt/ *vt* refutar

regain /rɪˈgeɪn/ *vt* recobrar

regal /ˈriːgl/ *a* real

regard /rɪˈgɑːd/ *vt* considerar; (look at) contemplar. as ~s en lo que se refiere a. ● *n* (consideration) consideración *f*; (esteem) estima *f*. **~s** *npl* saludos *mpl*. kind ~s recuerdos. **~ing** *prep* en lo que se refiere a. **~less** *adv* a pesar de todo. **~less of** sin tener en cuenta

regatta /rɪˈgætə/ *n* regata *f*

regime /reɪˈʒiːm/ *n* régimen *m*

regiment /ˈredʒɪmənt/ *n* regimiento *m*. **~al** /-ˈmentl/ *a* del regimiento

region /ˈriːdʒən/ *n* región *f*. in the ~ of alrededor de. **~al** *a* regional

register /ˈredʒɪstə(r)/ *n* registro *m*. ● *vt* registrar; matricular <*vehicle*>; declarar <*birth*>; certificar <*letter*>; facturar <*luggage*>. ● *vi* (enrol) inscribirse; (fig) producir impresión

registrar /redʒɪ'stra:(r)/ *n* secretario *m* del registro civil; (Univ) secretario *m* general

registration /redʒɪ'streɪʃn/ *n* registración *f*; (in register) inscripción *f*. ~ **number** *n* (Auto) (número de) matrícula *f*

registry /'redʒɪstrɪ/ *n*. ~ **office** *n* registro *m* civil

regret /rɪ'gret/ *n* pesar *m*; (remorse) arrepentimiento *m*. ● *vt* (*pt* **regretted**) lamentar. I ~ **that** siento (que). ~**table** *a* lamentable

regula|r /'regjʊlə(r)/ *a* regular; (usual) habitual. ● *n* Ⓕ cliente *m* habitual. ~**rity** /-'lærətɪ/ *n* regularidad *f*. ~**rly** *adv* con regularidad. ~**te** /'regjʊleɪt/ *vt* regular. ~**tion** /-'leɪʃn/ *n* regulación *f*; (rule) regla *f*

rehears|al /rɪ'hɜ:sl/ *n* ensayo *m*. ~**e** /rɪ'hɜ:s/ *vt* ensayar

reign /reɪn/ *n* reinado *m*. ● *vi* reinar

reindeer /'reɪndɪə(r)/ *n invar* reno *m*

reinforce /ri:ɪn'fɔ:s/ *vt* reforzar. ~**ment** *n* refuerzo *m*

reins /reɪnz/ *npl* riendas *fpl*

reiterate /ri:'ɪtəreɪt/ *vt* reiterar

reject /rɪ'dʒekt/ *vt* rechazar. ● /'ri:dʒekt/ *n* producto *m* defectuoso. ~**ion** /rɪ'dʒekʃn/ *n* rechazo *m*; (after job application) respuesta *f* negativa

rejoice /rɪ'dʒɔɪs/ *vi* regocijarse

rejoin /rɪ'dʒɔɪn/ *vt* reunirse con

rejuvenate /rɪ'dʒu:vəneɪt/ *vt* rejuvenecer

relapse /rɪ'læps/ *n* recaída *f*. ● *vi* recaer; (into crime) reincidir

relat|e /rɪ'leɪt/ *vt* contar; (connect) relacionar. ● *vi* relacionarse (**to** con). ~**ed** *a* emparentado; <*ideas etc*> relacionado. ~**ion** /rɪ'leɪʃn/ *n* relación *f*; (person) pariente *m* & *f*. ~**ionship** *n* relación *f*; (blood tie) parentesco *m*; (affair) relaciones *fpl*. ~**ive** /'relətɪv/ *n* pariente *m* & *f*. ● *a* relativo. ~**ively** *adv* relativamente

relax /rɪ'læks/ *vt* relajar. ● *vi* relajarse. ~**ation** /-'seɪʃn/ *n* relajación *f*; (rest) descanso *m*; (recreation) recreo *m*. ~**ing** *a* relajante

relay /'ri:leɪ/ *n* relevo *m*. ~ (**race**) *n* carrera *f* de relevos. ● /rɪ'leɪ/ *vt* transmitir

release /rɪ'li:s/ *vt* soltar; poner en libertad <*prisoner*>; estrenar <*film*>; (Mec) soltar; publicar <*news*>. ● *n* liberación *f*; (of film) estreno *m*; (record) disco *m* nuevo

relent /rɪ'lent/ *vi* ceder. ~**less** *a* implacable; (continuous) incesante

relevan|ce /'reləvəns/ *n* pertinencia *f*. ~**t** *a* pertinente

relia|bility /rɪlaɪə'bɪlətɪ/ *n* fiabilidad *f*. ~**ble** /rɪ'laɪəbl/ *a* <*person*> de confianza; <*car*> fiable. ~**nce** /rɪ'laɪəns/ *n* dependencia *f*; (trust) confianza *f*. ~**nt** /rɪ'laɪənt/ *a* confiado

relic /'relɪk/ *n* reliquia *f*

relie|f /rɪ'li:f/ *n* alivio *m*; (assistance) socorro *m*. **be on** ~**f** (Amer) recibir prestaciones de la seguridad social. ~**ve** /rɪ'li:v/ *vt* aliviar; (take over from) relevar. ~**ved** *a* aliviado. **feel** ~**ved** sentir un gran alivio

religio|n /rɪ'lɪdʒən/ *n* religión *f*. ~**us** /rɪ'lɪdʒəs/ *a* religioso

relinquish /rɪ'lɪŋkwɪʃ/ *vt* abandonar, renunciar

relish /'relɪʃ/ *n* gusto *m*; (Culin) salsa *f*. ● *vt* saborear

reluctan|ce /rɪ'lʌktəns/ *n* desgana *f*. ~**t** *a* mal dispuesto. **be** ~**t to** no tener ganas de. ~**tly** *adv* de mala gana

rely /rɪ'laɪ/ *vi*. ~ **on** contar con; (trust) fiarse de; (depend) depender

remain /rɪ'meɪn/ *vi* (be left) quedar; (stay) quedarse; (continue to be) seguir. ~**der** *n* resto *m*. ~**s** *npl* restos *mpl*; (left-overs) sobras *fpl*

remand /rɪ'mɑ:nd/ *vt*. ~ **in custody** mantener bajo custodia. ● *n*. **on** ~ en prisión preventiva

remark /rɪ'mɑ:k/ *n* observación *f*. ● *vt* observar. ~**able** *a* notable

remarry /ri:'mærɪ/ *vi* volver a casarse

remedy /'remədɪ/ *n* remedio *m*. ● *vt* remediar

remember /rɪ'membə(r)/ *vt* acordarse de, recordar. ● *vi* acordarse

remind /rɪ'maɪnd/ *vt* recordar. ~**er** *n* recordatorio *m*

reminisce /remɪˈnɪs/ vi rememorar los viejos tiempos. ~**nces** /-ənsɪz/ npl recuerdos mpl. ~**nt** /-ˈnɪsnt/ a. be ~nt of recordar

remnant /ˈremnənt/ n resto m; (of cloth) retazo m; (trace) vestigio m

remorse /rɪˈmɔːs/ n remordimiento m. ~**ful** a arrepentido. ~**less** a implacable

remote /rɪˈməʊt/ a remoto. ~ **control** n mando m a distancia. ~**ly** adv remotamente

remov|able /rɪˈmuːvəbl/ a (detachable) de quita y pon; <handle> desmontable. ~**al** n eliminación f; (from house) mudanza f. ~**e** /rɪˈmuːv/ vt quitar; (dismiss) destituir; (get rid of) eliminar

render /ˈrendə(r)/ vt rendir <homage>; prestar <help etc>. ~ sth useless hacer que algo resulte inútil

rendezvous /ˈrɒndɪvuː/ n (pl -vous /-vuːz/) cita f

renegade /ˈrenɪgeɪd/ n renegado

renew /rɪˈnjuː/ vt renovar; (resume) reanudar. ~**al** n renovación f

renounce /rɪˈnaʊns/ vt renunciar a

renovat|e /ˈrenəveɪt/ vt renovar. ~**ion** /-ˈveɪʃn/ n renovación f

renown /rɪˈnaʊn/ n renombre m. ~**ed** a de renombre

rent /rent/ n alquiler m. ●vt alquilar. ~**al** n alquiler m. car ~ (Amer) alquiler m de coche

renunciation /rɪnʌnsɪˈeɪʃn/ n renuncia f

reopen /riːˈəʊpən/ vt volver a abrir. ●vi reabrirse

reorganize /riːˈɔːgənaɪz/ vt reorganizar

rep /rep/ n (Com) representante m & f

repair /rɪˈpeə(r)/ vt arreglar, reparar; arreglar <clothes, shoes>. ●n reparación f; (patch) remiendo m. in good ~ en buen estado. it's beyond ~ ya no tiene arreglo

repatriate /riːˈpætrɪeɪt/ vt repatriar

repay /riːˈpeɪ/ vt (pt repaid) reembolsar; pagar <debt>; corresponder a <kindness>. ~**ment** n pago m

repeal /rɪˈpiːl/ vt revocar. ●n revocación f

repeat /rɪˈpiːt/ vt repetir. ●vi repetir(se). ●n repetición f. ~**edly** adv repetidas veces

repel /rɪˈpel/ vt (pt repelled) repeler. ~**lent** a repelente

repent /rɪˈpent/ vi arrepentirse. ~**ant** a arrepentido

repercussion /riːpəˈkʌʃn/ n repercusión f

repertoire /ˈrepətwɑː(r)/ n repertorio m

repetit|ion /repɪˈtɪʃn/ n repetición f. ~**ious** /-ˈtɪʃəs/ a, ~**ive** /rɪˈpetətɪv/ a repetitivo

replace /rɪˈpleɪs/ vt reponer; cambiar <battery>; (take the place of) sustituir. ~**ment** n sustitución f; (person) sustituto m

replay /ˈriːpleɪ/ n (Sport) repetición f del partido; (recording) repetición f inmediata

replenish /rɪˈplenɪʃ/ vt reponer

replica /ˈreplɪkə/ n réplica f

reply /rɪˈplaɪ/ vt/i responder, contestar. ~ **to sth** responder a algo, contestar algo. ●n respuesta f

report /rɪˈpɔːt/ vt <reporter> informar sobre; informar de <accident>; (denounce) denunciar. ●vi informar; (present o.s.) presentarse. ●n informe m; (Schol) boletín m de notas; (rumour) rumor m; (in newspaper) reportaje m. ~ **card** (Amer) n boletín m de calificaciones. ~**edly** adv según se dice. ~**er** n periodista m & f, reportero m

reprehensible /reprɪˈhensəbl/ a reprensible

represent /reprɪˈzent/ vt representar. ~**ation** /-ˈteɪʃn/ n representación f. ~**ative** a representativo. ●n representante m & f; (Amer, in government) diputado m

repress /rɪˈpres/ vt reprimir. ~**ion** /-ʃn/ n represión f. ~**ive** a represivo

reprieve /rɪˈpriːv/ n indulto m; (fig) respiro m. ●vt indultar

reprimand /ˈreprɪmɑːnd/ vt reprender. ●n represión f

reprisal /rɪˈpraɪzl/ n represalia f

reproach /rɪˈprəʊtʃ/ vt reprochar. ●n reproche m. ~**ful** a de reproche

reproduc|e /riːprəˈdjuːs/ vt reproducir. ●vi reproducirse. ~**tion**

/-'dʌkʃn/ n reproducción f. ~tive /-'dʌktɪv/ a reproductor

reprove /rɪ'pruːv/ vt reprender

reptile /'reptaɪl/ n reptil m

republic /rɪ'pʌblɪk/ n república f. ~an a & n republicano (m). R~ a & n (in US) republicano (m)

repugnan|ce /rɪ'pʌgnəns/ n repugnancia f. ~t a repugnante

repuls|e /rɪ'pʌls/ vt rechazar, repulsar. ~ion /-ʃn/ n repulsión f. ~ive a repulsivo

reput|able /'repjʊtəbl/ a acreditado, reputado. ~ation /repjʊ'teɪʃn/ n reputación f

request /rɪ'kwest/ n petición f. ● vt pedir

require /rɪ'kwaɪə(r)/ vt requerir; (need) necesitar; (demand) exigir. ~d a necesario. ~ment n requisito m

rescue /'reskjuː/ vt rescatar, salvar. ● n rescate m. ~r n salvador m

research /rɪ'sɜːtʃ/ n investigación f. ● vt investigar. ~er n investigador m

resembl|ance /rɪ'zembləns/ n parecido m. ~e /rɪ'zembl/ vt parecerse a

resent /rɪ'zent/ vt guardarle rencor a <person>. she ~ed his success le molestaba que él tuviera éxito. ~ful a resentido. ~ment n resentimiento m

reserv|ation /rezə'veɪʃn/ n reserva f; (booking) reserva f. ~e /rɪ'zɜːv/ vt reservar. ● n reserva f; (in sports) suplente m & f. ~ed a reservado. ~oir /'rezəvwɑː(r)/ n embalse m

reshuffle /riː'ʃʌfl/ n (Pol) reorganización f

residen|ce /'rezɪdəns/ n residencia f. ~t a & n residente (m & f). ~tial /rezɪ'denʃl/ a residencial

residue /'rezɪdjuː/ n residuo m

resign /rɪ'zaɪn/ vt/i dimitir. ~ o.s. to resignarse a. ~ation /rezɪg'neɪʃn/ n resignación f; (from job) dimisión f. ~ed a resignado

resilien|ce /rɪ'zɪlɪəns/ n elasticidad f; (of person) resistencia f. ~t a elástico; <person> resistente

resin /'rezɪn/ n resina f

resist /rɪ'zɪst/ vt resistir. ● vi resistirse. ~ance n resistencia f. ~ant a resistente

resolut|e /'rezəluːt/ a resuelto. ~ion /-'luːʃn/ n resolución f

resolve /rɪ'zɒlv/ vt resolver. ~ to do resolver a hacer. ● n resolución f

resort /rɪ'zɔːt/ n recurso m; (place) lugar m turístico. in the last ~ como último recurso. □ ~ to vt recurrir a.

resource /rɪ'sɔːs/ n recurso m. ~ful a ingenioso

respect /rɪ'spekt/ n (esteem) respeto m; (aspect) respecto m. with ~ to con respecto a. ● vt respetar. ~able a respetable. ~ful a respetuoso. ~ive a respectivo. ~ively adv respectivamente

respiration /respə'reɪʃn/ n respiración f

respite /'respaɪt/ n respiro m

respon|d /rɪ'spɒnd/ vi responder. ~se /rɪ'spɒns/ n respuesta f; (reaction) reacción f

responsib|ility /rɪspɒnsə'bɪlətɪ/ n responsabilidad f. ~le /rɪ'spɒnsəbl/ a responsable; <job> de responsabilidad. ~ly adv con formalidad

responsive /rɪ'spɒnsɪv/ a que reacciona bien. ~ to sensible a

rest /rest/ vt descansar; (lean) apoyar. ● vi descansar; (lean) apoyarse. ● n descanso m; (Mus) pausa f; (remainder) resto m, lo demás; (people) los demás, los otros mpl. to have a ~ tomarse un descanso. □ ~ up vi (Amer) descansar

restaurant /'restərɒnt/ n restaurante m

rest: ~ful a sosegado. ~ive a impaciente. ~less a inquieto

restor|ation /restə'reɪʃn/ n restablecimiento m; (of building, monarch) restauración f. ~e /rɪ'stɔː(r)/ vt restablecer; restaurar <building>; devolver <confidence, health>

restrain /rɪ'streɪn/ vt contener. ~ o.s. contenerse. ~ed a (moderate) moderado; (in control of self) comedido. ~t n restricción f; (moderation) compostura f

restrict /rɪˈstrɪkt/ vt restringir. ∼**ion** /-ʃn/ n restricción f. ∼**ive** a restrictivo

rest room n (Amer) baño m, servicio m

result /rɪˈzʌlt/ n resultado m. **as a** ∼ **of** como consecuencia de. ● vi. ∼ **from** resultar de. ∼ **in** dar como resultado

resume /rɪˈzjuːm/ vt reanudar. ● vi reanudarse

résumé /ˈrezjʊmeɪ/ n resumen m; (Amer, CV) curriculum m, historial m personal

resurrect /rezəˈrekt/ vt resucitar. ∼**ion** /-ʃn/ n resurrección f

resuscitat|e /rɪˈsʌsɪteɪt/ vt resucitar. ∼**ion** /-ˈteɪʃn/ n resucitación f

retail /ˈriːteɪl/ n venta f al por menor. ● a & adv al por menor. ● vt vender al por menor. ● vi venderse al por menor. ∼**er** n minorista m & f

retain /rɪˈteɪn/ vt retener; conservar <heat>

retaliat|e /rɪˈtælɪeɪt/ vi desquitarse; (Mil) tomar represalias. ∼**ion** /-ˈeɪʃn/ n represalias fpl

retarded /rɪˈtɑːdɪd/ a retrasado

rethink /riːˈθɪŋk/ vt (pt **rethought**) reconsiderar

reticen|ce /ˈretɪsns/ n reticencia f. ∼**t** a reticente

retina /ˈretɪnə/ n retina f

retinue /ˈretɪnjuː/ n séquito m

retir|e /rɪˈtaɪə(r)/ vi (from work) jubilarse; (withdraw) retirarse; (go to bed) acostarse. ∼**ed** a jubilado. ∼**ement** n jubilación f. ∼**ing** a retraído

retort /rɪˈtɔːt/ vt/i replicar. ● n réplica f

retrace /riːˈtreɪs/ vt. ∼ **one's steps** volver sobre sus pasos

retract /rɪˈtrækt/ vt retirar <statement>. ● vi retractarse

retrain /riːˈtreɪn/ vi hacer un curso de reciclaje

retreat /rɪˈtriːt/ vi retirarse. ● n retirada f; (place) refugio m

retrial /riːˈtraɪəl/ n nuevo juicio m

retriev|al /rɪˈtriːvl/ n recuperación f. ∼**e** /rɪˈtriːv/ vt recuperar. ∼**er** n (dog) perro m cobrador

retro|grade /ˈretrəgreɪd/ a retrógrado. ∼**spect** /-spekt/ n. **in** ∼ en retrospectiva. ∼**spective** /-ˈspektɪv/ a retrospectivo

return /rɪˈtɜːn/ vi volver, regresar; <symptom> reaparecer. ● vt devolver; corresponder a <affection>. ● n regreso m, vuelta f; (Com) rendimiento m; (to owner) devolución f. **in** ∼ **for** a cambio de. **many happy** ∼**s!** ¡feliz cumpleaños! ∼ **ticket** n billete m or (LAm) boleto m de ida y vuelta, boleto m redondo (Mex). ∼**s** npl (Com) ingresos mpl

reun|ion /riːˈjuːnɪən/ n reunión f. ∼**ite** /riːjuːˈnaɪt/ vt reunir

rev /rev/ n (Auto, 🚗) revolución f. ● vt/i. ∼ **(up)** (pt **revved**) (Auto, 🚗) acelerar(se)

reveal /rɪˈviːl/ vt revelar. ∼**ing** a revelador

revel /ˈrevl/ vi (pt **revelled**) tener un jolgorio. ∼ **in** deleitarse en. ∼**ry** n jolgorio m

revelation /revəˈleɪʃn/ n revelación f

revenge /rɪˈvendʒ/ n venganza f. **take** ∼ vengarse. ● vt vengar

revenue /ˈrevənjuː/ n ingresos mpl

revere /rɪˈvɪə(r)/ vt venerar. ∼**nce** /ˈrevərəns/ n reverencia f.

Reverend /ˈrevərənd/ a reverendo

reverent /ˈrevərənt/ a reverente

reverie /ˈrevərɪ/ n ensueño m

revers|al /rɪˈvɜːsl/ n inversión f. ∼**e** /rɪˈvɜːs/ a inverso. ● n contrario m; (back) revés m; (Auto) marcha f atrás. ● vt invertir; anular <decision>; (Auto) dar marcha atrás a. ● vi (Auto) dar marcha atrás

revert /rɪˈvɜːt/ vi. ∼ **to** volver a; (Jurid) revertir a

review /rɪˈvjuː/ n revisión f; (Mil) revista f; (of book, play, etc) crítica f. ● vt examinar <situation>; reseñar <book, play, etc>; (Amer, for exam) repasar

revis|e /rɪˈvaɪz/ vt revisar; (Schol) repasar. ∼**ion** /rɪˈvɪʒn/ n revisión f; (Schol) repaso m

revive /rɪ'vaɪv/ *vt* resucitar *<person>*

revolt /rɪ'vəʊlt/ *vi* sublevarse. ● *n* revuelta *f*. **~ing** *a* asqueroso

revolution /revə'luːʃn/ *n* revolución *f*. **~ary** *a* & *n* revolucionario (*m*). **~ize** *vt* revolucionar

revolv|e /rɪ'vɒlv/ *vi* girar. **~r** *n* revólver *m*. **~ing** /rɪ'vɒlvɪŋ/ *a* giratorio

revue /rɪ'vjuː/ *n* revista *f*

revulsion /rɪ'vʌlʃn/ *n* asco *m*

reward /rɪ'wɔːd/ *n* recompensa *f*. ● *vt* recompensar. **~ing** *a* gratificante

rewrite /riː'raɪt/ *vt* (*pt* **rewrote**, *pp* **rewritten**) volver a escribir *or* redactar; (*copy out*) escribir otra vez

rhetoric /'retərɪk/ *n* retórica *f*. **~al** /rɪ'tɒrɪkl/ *a* retórico

rheumatism /'ruːmətɪzəm/ *n* reumatismo *m*

rhinoceros /raɪ'nɒsərəs/ *n* (*pl* **-oses** *or invar*) rinoceronte *m*

rhubarb /'ruːbɑːb/ *n* ruibarbo *m*

rhyme /raɪm/ *n* rima *f*; (*poem*) poesía *f*. ● *vt/i* rimar

rhythm /'rɪðəm/ *n* ritmo *m*. **~ic(al)** /'rɪðmɪk(l)/ *a* rítmico

rib /rɪb/ *n* costilla *f*

ribbon /'rɪbən/ *n* cinta *f*

rice /raɪs/ *n* arroz *m*. **~ pudding** *n* arroz con leche

rich /rɪtʃ/ *a* (**-er**, **-est**) rico. ● *n* ricos *mpl*. **~es** *npl* riquezas *fpl*

ricochet /'rɪkəʃeɪ/ *vi* rebotar

rid /rɪd/ *vt* (*pt* **rid**, *pres p* **ridding**) librar (of de). **get ~ of** deshacerse de. **~dance** /'rɪdns/ *n*. **good ~dance!** ¡adiós y buen viaje!

ridden /'rɪdn/ ⇒RIDE

riddle /'rɪdl/ *n* acertijo *m*. ● *vt* acribillar. **be ~d** with estar lleno de

ride /raɪd/ *vi* (*pt* **rode**, *pp* **ridden**) (*on horseback*) montar a caballo; (*go*) ir (en bicicleta, a caballo etc). ● *vt* montar a *<horse>*; ir en *<bicycle>*; (Amer) ir en *<bus, tren>*; recorrer *<distance>*. ● *n* (on horse) cabalgata *f*; (in car) paseo *m* en coche. **take s.o. for a ~** 🗊 engañarle a uno. **~r** *n* (on horse) jinete *m*; (cyclist) ciclista *m* & *f*

ridge /rɪdʒ/ *n* (of hills) cadena *f*; (hilltop) cresta *f*

ridicul|e /'rɪdɪkjuːl/ *n* burlas *fpl*. ● *vt* ridiculizar. **~ous** /rɪ'dɪkjʊləs/ *a* ridículo

rife /raɪf/ *a* difundido

rifle /'raɪfl/ *n* fusil *m*

rift /rɪft/ *n* grieta *f*; (fig) ruptura *f*

rig /rɪg/ *vt* (*pt* **rigged**) (pej) amañar. ● *n* (at sea) plataforma *f* de perforación. □ **~ up** *vt* improvisar

right /raɪt/ *a* *<answer>* correcto; (morally) bueno; (not left) derecho; (suitable) adecuado. **be ~** *<person>* tener razón; *<clock>* estar bien. **it is ~** (just, moral) es justo. **put ~** rectificar. **the ~ person for the job** la persona indicada para el puesto. ● *n* (entitlement) derecho *m*; (not left) derecha *f*; (not evil) bien *m*. **~ of way** (Auto) prioridad *f*. **be in the ~** tener razón. **on the ~** a la derecha. ● *vt* enderezar; (fig) reparar. ● *adv* a la derecha; (directly) derecho; (completely) completamente. **~ away** *adv* inmediatamente. **~ angle** *n* ángulo *m* recto. **~eous** /'raɪtʃəs/ *a* recto; *<cause>* justo. **~ful** /'raɪtfl/ *a* legítimo. **~-handed** /-'hændɪd/ *a* diestro. **~-hand man** *n* brazo *m* derecho. **~ly** *adv* justamente. **~ wing** *a* (Pol) derechista

rigid /'rɪdʒɪd/ *a* rígido

rig|orous /'rɪgərəs/ *a* riguroso. **~our** /'rɪgə(r)/ *n* rigor *m*

rim /rɪm/ *n* borde *m*; (of wheel) llanta *f*; (of glasses) montura *f*

rind /raɪnd/ *n* corteza *f*; (of fruit) cáscara *f*

ring¹ /rɪŋ/ *n* (circle) círculo *m*; (circle of metal etc) aro *m*; (on finger) anillo *m*; (on finger with stone) sortija *f*; (Boxing) cuadrilátero *m*; (bullring) ruedo *m*; (for circus) pista *f*; ● *vt* cercar

ring² /rɪŋ/ *n* (of bell) toque *m*; (tinkle) tintineo *m*; (telephone call) llamada *f*. ● *vt* (*pt* **rang**, *pp* **rung**) hacer sonar; (telephone) llamar por teléfono. **~ the bell** tocar el timbre. ● *vi* sonar. **~ back** *vt/i* volver a llamar. □ **~ up** *vt* llamar por teléfono

ring: ~leader /'rɪŋliːdə(r)/ *n* cabecilla *m* & *f*. **~ road** *n* carretera *f* de circunvalación

rink /rɪŋk/ *n* pista *f*

rinse /rɪns/ *vt* enjuagar. ● *n* aclarado *m*; (of dishes) enjuague *m*; (for hair) tintura *f* (no permanente)

riot /ˈraɪət/ *n* disturbio *m*; (of colours) profusión *f*. **run** ~ desenfrenarse. ● *vi* causar disturbios

rip /rɪp/ *vt* (*pt* **ripped**) rasgar. ● *vi* rasgarse. ● *n* rasgón *m*. □ ~ **off** *vt* (pull off) arrancar; (🅧, cheat) robar

ripe /raɪp/ *a* (**-er, -est**) maduro. ~**n** /ˈraɪpn/ *vt/i* madurar

rip-off /ˈrɪpɒf/ *n* 🅧 timo *m*

ripple /ˈrɪpl/ *n* (on water) onda *f*

ris|e /raɪz/ *vi* (*pt* **rose**, *pp* **risen**) subir; <*sun*> salir; <*river*> crecer; <*prices*> subir; <*land*> elevarse; (get up) levantarse. ● *n* subida *f*; (land) altura *f*; (increase) aumento *m*; (to power) ascenso *m*. **give** ~**e to** ocasionar. ~**er** *n*. **early** ~**er** *n* madrugador *m*. ~**ing** *n*. ● *a* <*sun*> naciente; <*number*> creciente; <*prices*> en alza

risk /rɪsk/ *n* riesgo *m*. ● *vt* arriesgar. ~**y** *a* (**-ier, -iest**) arriesgado

rite /raɪt/ *n* rito *m*

ritual /ˈrɪtʃʊəl/ *a & n* ritual (*m*)

rival /ˈraɪvl/ *a & n* rival (*m*). ~**ry** *n* rivalidad *f*

river /ˈrɪvə(r)/ *n* río *m*

rivet /ˈrɪvɪt/ *n* remache *m*. ~**ing** *a* fascinante

road /rəʊd/ *n* (in town) calle *f*; (between towns) carretera *f*; (route, way) camino *m*. ~ **map** *n* mapa *m* de carreteras. ~**side** *n* borde *m* de la carretera. ~**works** *npl* obras *fpl*. ~**worthy** *a* <*vehicle*> apto para circular

roam /rəʊm/ *vi* vagar

roar /rɔː(r)/ *n* rugido *m*; (laughter) carcajada *f*. ● *vt/i* rugir. ~ **past** <*vehicles*> pasar con estruendo. ~ **with** **laughter** reírse a carcajadas. ~**ing** *a* <*trade etc*> activo

roast /rəʊst/ *vt* asar; tostar <*coffee*>. ● *a & n* asado (*m*). ~ **beef** *n* rosbif *m*

rob /rɒb/ *vt* (*pt* **robbed**) atracar, asaltar <*bank*>; robarle a <*person*>. ~ **of** (deprive of) privar de. ~**ber** *n* ladrón *m*; (of bank) atracador *m*. ~**bery** *n* robo *m*; (of bank) atraco *m*

robe /rəʊb/ *n* bata *f*; (Univ etc) toga *f*

robin /ˈrɒbɪn/ *n* petirrojo *m*

robot /ˈrəʊbɒt/ *n* robot *m*, autómata *m*

robust /rəʊˈbʌst/ *a* robusto

rock /rɒk/ *n* roca *f*; (crag, cliff) peñasco *m*. ● *vt* mecer; (shake) sacudir. ● *vi* mecerse; (shake) sacudirse. ● *n* (Mus) música *f* rock. ~**-bottom** /-ˈbɒtəm/ *a* 🅘 bajísimo

rocket /ˈrɒkɪt/ *n* cohete *m*

rock: ~**ing-chair** *n* mecedora *f*. ~**y** *a* (**-ier, -iest**) rocoso; (fig, shaky) bamboleante

rod /rɒd/ *n* vara *f*; (for fishing) caña *f*; (metal) barra *f*

rode /rəʊd/ →RIDE

rodent /ˈrəʊdnt/ *n* roedor *m*

rogue /rəʊg/ *n* pícaro *m*

role /rəʊl/ *n* papel *m*

roll /rəʊl/ *vt* hacer rodar; (roll up) enrollar; allanar <*lawn*>; aplanar <*pastry*>. ● *vi* rodar; <*ship*> balancearse; (on floor) revolcarse. **be** ~**ing** **in money** 🅘 nadar en dinero ● *n* rollo *m*; (of ship) balanceo *m*; (of drum) redoble *m*; (of thunder) retumbo *m*; (bread) panecillo *m*, bolillo *m* (Mex). □ ~ **over** *vi* (turn over) dar una vuelta. □ ~ **up** *vt* enrollar; arremangar <*sleeve*>. *vi* 🅘 llegar. ~**-call** *n* lista *f*

roller /ˈrəʊlə(r)/ *n* rodillo *m*; (wheel) rueda *f*; (for hair) rulo *m*. ~**-coaster** *n* montaña *f* rusa. ~**-skate** *n* patín *m* de ruedas. ~**-skating** patinaje *m* (sobre ruedas)

rolling /ˈrəʊlɪŋ/ *a* ondulado. ~**-pin** *n* rodillo *m*

ROM /rɒm/ *n* (= **read-only memory**) ROM *f*

Roman /ˈrəʊmən/ *a & n* romano (*m*). ~ **Catholic** *a & n* católico (*m*) (romano)

romance /rəʊˈmæns/ *n* novela *f* romántica; (love) amor *m*; (affair) aventura *f*

Romania /ruːˈmeɪnɪə/ *n* Rumania *f*, Rumanía *f*. ~**n** *a & n* rumano (*m*)

romantic /rəʊˈmæntɪk/ *a* romántico

Rome /rəʊm/ *n* Roma *f*

romp /rɒmp/ *vi* retozar

roof /ru:f/ n techo m, tejado m; (of mouth) paladar m. ●vt techar. ~**rack** n baca f. ~**top** n tejado m

rook /rʊk/ n grajo m; (in chess) torre f

room /ru:m/ n cuarto m, habitación f; (bedroom) dormitorio m; (space) espacio m; (large hall) sala f. ~**y** a espacioso

roost /ru:st/ vi posarse. ~**er** n gallo m

root /ru:t/ n raíz f. **take** ~ echar raíces; <idea> arraigarse. ●vi echar raíces. ~ **about** vi hurgar. □ ~ **for** vt 🇺🇸 alentar. □ ~ **out** vt extirpar

rope /rəʊp/ n cuerda f. **know the** ~**s** estar al corriente. ●vt atar; (Amer, lasso) enlazar. □ ~ **in** vt agarrar

rose¹ /rəʊz/ n rosa f; (nozzle) roseta f

rose² /rəʊz/ ⇒RISE

rosé /ˈrəʊzeɪ/ n (vino m) rosado m

rot /rɒt/ vt (pt **rotted**) pudrir. ●vi pudrirse. ●n putrefacción f

rota /ˈrəʊtə/ n lista f (de turnos)

rotary /ˈrəʊtərɪ/ a rotatorio

rotat|e /rəʊˈteɪt/ vt girar; (change round) alternar. ●vi girar; (change round) alternarse. ~**ion** /-ʃn/ n rotación f

rote /rəʊt/ n. **by** ~ de memoria

rotten /ˈrɒtn/ a podrido; 🇺🇸 pésimo 🇺🇸; <weather> horrible

rough /rʌf/ a (-**er**, -**est**) áspero; <person> tosco; (bad) malo; <ground> accidentado; (violent) brutal; (approximate) aproximado; <diamond> bruto. ●adv duro. ~ **copy**, ~ **draft** borrador m. ●vt. ~ **it** vivir sin comodidades. ~**age** /ˈrʌfɪdʒ/ n fibra f. ~**-and-ready** a improvisado. ~**ly** adv bruscamente; (more or less) aproximadamente

roulette /ru:ˈlet/ n ruleta f

round /raʊnd/ a (-**er**, -**est**) redondo. ●n círculo m; (of visits, drinks) ronda f; (of competition) vuelta f; (Boxing) asalto m. ●prep alrededor de. ●adv alrededor. ~ **about** (approximately) aproximadamente. **come** ~ **to**, **go** ~ **to** (a friend etc) pasar por casa de. ●vt doblar <corner>. □ ~ **off** vt terminar; redondear <number>. □ ~ **up** vt rodear <cattle>; hacer una redada de <suspects>. ~**about** n tiovivo m, carrusel m (LAm); (for traffic) glorieta f, rotonda f. ●a in directo. ~ **trip** n viaje m de ida y vuelta. ~**-up** n resumen m; (of suspects) redada f

rous|e /raʊz/ vt despertar. ~**ing** a enardecedor

route /ru:t/ n ruta f; (Naut, Aviat) rumbo m; (of bus) línea f

routine /ru:ˈti:n/ n rutina f. ●a rutinario

row¹ /rəʊ/ n fila f. ●vi remar

row² /raʊ/ n (🇬🇧, noise) bulla f 🇬🇧; (quarrel) pelea f. ●vi 🇬🇧 pelearse

rowboat /ˈrəʊbəʊt/ (Amer) n bote m de remos

rowdy /ˈraʊdɪ/ a (-**ier**, -**iest**) escandaloso, alborotador

rowing /ˈrəʊɪŋ/ n remo m. ~ **boat** n bote m de remos

royal /ˈrɔɪəl/ a real. ~**ist** a & n monárquico (m). ~**ly** adv magníficamente. ~**ty** n realeza f

rub /rʌb/ vt (pt **rubbed**) frotar. □ ~ **out** vt borrar

rubber /ˈrʌbə(r)/ n goma f, caucho m, hule m (Mex); (eraser) goma f (de borrar). ~ **band** n goma f (elástica). ~**-stamp** vt (fig) autorizar. ~**y** a parecido al caucho

rubbish /ˈrʌbɪʃ/ n basura f; (junk) trastos mpl; (fig) tonterías fpl. ~ **bin** n cubo m de la basura, bote m de la basura (Mex). ~**y** a sin valor

rubble /ˈrʌbl/ n escombros mpl

ruby /ˈru:bɪ/ n rubí m

rucksack /ˈrʌksæk/ n mochila f

rudder /ˈrʌdə(r)/ n timón m

rude /ru:d/ a (-**er**, -**est**) grosero, mal educado; (improper) indecente; (brusque) brusco. ~**ly** adv groseramente. ~**ness** n mala educación f

rudimentary /ru:dɪˈmentrɪ/ a rudimentario

ruffian /ˈrʌfɪən/ n rufián m

ruffle /ˈrʌfl/ vt despeinar <hair>; arrugar <clothes>

rug /rʌg/ n alfombra f, tapete m (Mex); (blanket) manta f de viaje

rugged /ˈrʌgɪd/ a <coast> escarpado; <landscape> escabroso

ruin /'ru:ɪn/ n ruina f. ● vt arruinar; (spoil) estropear

rul|e /ru:l/ n regla f; (Pol) dominio m. **as a ~** por regla general. ● vt gobernar; (master) dominar; (Jurid) dictaminar. **~e out** vt descartar. **~ed paper** n papel m rayado. **~er** n (sovereign) soberano m; (leader) gobernante m & f; (measure) regla f. **~ing** a <class> dirigente. ● n decisión f

rum /rʌm/ n ron m

rumble /'rʌmbl/ vi retumbar; <stomach> hacer ruidos

rummage /'rʌmɪdʒ/ vi hurgar

rumour /'ru:mə(r)/ n rumor m. ● vt. **it is ~ed that** se rumorea que

rump steak /rʌmpsteɪk/ n filete m de cadera

run /rʌn/ vi (pt ran, pp run, pres p running) correr; <water> correr; (function) funcionar; (melt) derretirse; <makeup> correrse; <colour> desteñir; <bus etc> circular; (in election) presentarse. ● vt correr <race>; dirigir <business>; correr <risk>; (move, pass) pasar; tender <wire>; preparar <bath>. **~ a temperature** tener fiebre. ● n corrida f, carrera f; (outing) paseo m (en coche); (ski) pista f. **in the long ~** a la larga. **be on the ~** estar prófu-go. □ **~ away** vi huir, escaparse. □ **~ down** vi bajar corriendo; <battery> descargarse. vt (Auto) atrope-llar; (belittle) denigrar. □ **~ in** vi entrar corriendo. □ **~ into** vt to-parse con <friend>; (hit) chocar con. □ **~ off** vt sacar <copies>. □ **~ out** vi salir corriendo; <liquid> salirse; (fig) agotarse. □ **~ out of** vt que-darse sin. □ **~ over** vt (Auto) atrope-llar. □ **~ through** vt (review) ensa-yar; (rehearse) repasar. □ **~ up** vt ir acumulando <bill>. vi subir corrien-do. **~away** n fugitivo m. **~ down** a <person> agotado

rung[1] /rʌŋ/ n (of ladder) peldaño m

rung[2] /rʌŋ/ ⇒RING

run: **~ner** /'rʌnə(r)/ n corredor m; (on sledge) patín m. **~ner bean** n judía f escarlata. **~ner-up** n. **be ~er up** quedar en segundo lugar. **~ning** n. **be in the ~ning** tener posibilida-des de ganar. ● a <water> corriente; <commentary> en directo. **four times**

~ning cuatro veces seguidas. **~ny** /'rʌnɪ/ a líquido; <nose> que moquea. **~way** n pista f de aterrizaje

rupture /'rʌptʃə(r)/ n ruptura f. ● vt romper

rural /'ruərəl/ a rural

ruse /ru:z/ n ardid m

rush /rʌʃ/ n (haste) prisa f; (crush) bullicio m; (plant) junco m. ● vi precipitarse. ● vt apresurar; (Mil) asaltar. **~-hour** n hora f punta, hora f pico (LAm)

Russia /'rʌʃə/ n Rusia f. **~n** a & n ruso (m)

rust /rʌst/ n orín m. ● vt oxidar. ● vi oxidarse

rustle /'rʌsl/ vt hacer susurrar; (Amer) robar. ● vi susurrar □ **~ up** vt 🄯 preparar.

rust: **~proof** a inoxidable. **~y** (**-ier, -iest**) oxidado

rut /rʌt/ n surco m. **be in a ~** estar anquilosado

ruthless /'ru:θlɪs/ a despiadado

rye /raɪ/ n centeno m

Ss

S abbr (= **south**) S

sabot|age /'sæbətɑːʒ/ n sabotaje m. ● vt sabotear. **~eur** /-'tɜː(r)/ n saboteador m

saccharin /'sækərɪn/ n sacarina f

sachet /'sæʃeɪ/ n bolsita f

sack /sæk/ n saco m. **get the ~** 🄯 ser despedido. ● vt 🄯 despedir.

sacrament /'sækrəmənt/ n sacramento m

sacred /'seɪkrɪd/ a sagrado

sacrifice /'sækrɪfaɪs/ n sacrificio m. ● vt sacrificar

sacrileg|e /'sækrɪlɪdʒ/ n sacrilegio m. **~ious** /-'lɪdʒəs/ a sacrílego

sad /sæd/ a (**sadder**, **saddest**) triste. **~den** vt entristecer

saddle /'sædl/ n silla f de montar.
● vt ensillar <horse>. ∼ s.o. with sth
(fig) endilgarle algo a uno

sadist /'seɪdɪst/ n sádico m. ∼tic
/sə'dɪstɪk/ a sádico

sadly /'sædlɪ/ adv tristemente; (fig)
desgraciadamente. ∼ness n tristeza f

safe /seɪf/ a (-er, -est) seguro; (out of
danger) salvo; (cautious) prudente. ∼
and sound sano y salvo. ● n caja f
fuerte.' ∼ deposit n caja f de seguridad. ∼guard n salvaguardia f. ● vt
salvaguardar. ∼ly adv sin peligro;
(in safe place) en lugar seguro. ∼ty n
seguridad f. ∼ty belt n cinturón m
de seguridad. ∼ty pin n imperdible
m

sag /sæg/ vi (pt **sagged**) <ceiling>
combarse; <bed> hundirse

saga /'sɑːgə/ n saga f

Sagittarius /sædʒɪ'teərɪəs/ n Sagitario m

said /sed/ ⇒SAY

sail /seɪl/ n vela f; (trip) paseo m (en
barco). set ∼ zarpar. ● vi navegar;
(leave) partir; (Sport) practicar la vela;
(fig) deslizarse. go ∼ing salir a navegar. vt gobernar <boat>. ∼boat n
(Amer) barco m de vela. ∼ing n
(Sport) vela f. ∼ing boat n, ∼ing
ship n barco m de vela. ∼or n marinero m

saint /seɪnt/, before name /sənt/ n
santo m. ∼ly a santo

sake /seɪk/ n. for the ∼ of por. for
God's ∼ por el amor de Dios

salad /'sæləd/ n ensalada f. ∼ bowl
n ensaladera f. ∼ dressing n aliño
m

salary /'sælərɪ/ n sueldo m

sale /seɪl/ n venta f; (at reduced prices)
liquidación f. for ∼ (sign) se vende.
be for ∼ estar a la venta. be on ∼
(Amer, reduced) estar en liquidación.
∼able a vendible. (for sale) estar a la
venta. ∼s clerk n (Amer) dependiente m, dependienta f. ∼sman /-mən/
n vendedor m; (in shop) dependiente
m. ∼swoman n vendedora f; (in
shop) dependienta f

saliva /sə'laɪvə/ n saliva f

salmon /'sæmən/ n invar salmón m

saloon /sə'luːn/ n (on ship) salón m;
(Amer, bar) bar m; (Auto) turismo m

salt /sɔːlt/ n sal f. ● vt salar. ∼ cellar n salero m. ∼y a salado

salute /sə'luːt/ n saludo m. ● vt saludar. ● vi hacer un saludo

Salvadorean, Salvadorian
/sælvə'dɔːrɪən/ a & n salvadoreño
(m)

salvage /'sælvɪdʒ/ vt salvar

salvation /sæl'veɪʃn/ n salvación f

same /seɪm/ a igual (as que); (before
noun) mismo (as que). at the ∼ time
al mismo tiempo. ● pron. the ∼ lo
mismo. all the ∼ de todas formas.
● adv. the ∼ igual

sample /'sɑːmpl/ n muestra f. ● vt
degustar <food>

sanct|ify /'sæŋktɪfaɪ/ vt santificar.
∼ion /'sæŋkʃn/ n sanción f. ● vt
sancionar. ∼uary /'sæŋktʃʊərɪ/ n
(Relig) santuario m; (for wildlife) reserva f; (refuge) asilo m

sand /sænd/ n arena f. ● vt pulir
<floor>. □ ∼ down vt lijar <wood>

sandal /'sændl/ n sandalia f

sand: ∼castle n castillo m de arena. ∼paper n papel m de lija. ● vt
lijar. ∼storm n tormenta f de arena

sandwich /'sænwɪdʒ/ n bocadillo
m, sandwich m. ● vt. be ∼ed between <person> estar apretujado
entre

sandy /'sændɪ/ a arenoso

sane /seɪn/ a (-er, -est) <person>
cuerdo; (sensible) sensato

sang /sæŋ/ ⇒SING

sanitary /'sænɪtrɪ/ a higiénico;
<system etc> sanitario. ∼ towel, ∼
napkin n (Amer) compresa f (higiéni-
ca)

sanitation /sænɪ'teɪʃn/ n higiene f;
(drainage) sistema m sanitario

sanity /'sænɪtɪ/ n cordura f; (good
sense) sensatez f

sank /sæŋk/ ⇒SINK

Santa (Claus) /'sæntə(klɔːz)/ n
Papá m Noel

sap /sæp/ n (in plants) savia f. ● vt (pt
sapped) minar

sapling /'sæplɪŋ/ n árbol m joven

sapphire /'sæfaɪə(r)/ n zafiro m

sarcas|m /'sɑːkæzəm/ n sarcasmo m. **~tic** /-'kæstɪk/ a sarcástico

sardine /sɑː'diːn/ n sardina f

sash /sæʃ/ n (over shoulder) banda f; (round waist) fajín m.

sat /sæt/ ⇒SIT

satchel /'sætʃl/ n cartera f

satellite /'sætəlaɪt/ n & a satélite (m). **~ TV** n televisión f por satélite

satin /'sætɪn/ n raso m. ● a de raso

satir|e /'sætaɪə(r)/ n sátira f. **~ical** /sə'tɪrɪkl/ a satírico. **~ize** /'sætəraɪz/ vt satirizar

satis|faction /sætɪs'fækʃn/ n satisfacción f. **~factorily** /-'fæktərɪlɪ/ adv satisfactoriamente. **~factory** /-'fæktərɪ/ a satisfactorio. **~fy** /'sætɪsfaɪ/ vt satisfacer; (convince) convencer. **~fying** a satisfactorio

saturat|e /'sætʃəreɪt/ vt saturar. **~ed** a saturado; (drenched) empapado

Saturday /'sætədeɪ/ n sábado m

Saturn /'sætən/ n Saturno m

sauce /sɔːs/ n salsa f; (cheek) descaro m. **~pan** /'sɔːspən/ n cazo m, cacerola f. **~r** /'sɔːsə(r)/ n platillo m

saucy /'sɔːsɪ/ a (-ier, -iest) descarado

Saudi /'saʊdɪ/ a & n saudita (m & f). **~ Arabia** /-ə'reɪbɪə/ n Arabia f Saudí

sauna /'sɔːnə/ n sauna f

saunter /'sɔːntə(r)/ vi pasearse

sausage /'sɒsɪdʒ/ n salchicha f

savage /'sævɪdʒ/ a salvaje; (fierce) feroz. ● n salvaje m & f. ● vt atacar. **~ry** n ferocidad f

sav|e /seɪv/ vt (rescue) salvar; ahorrar <money, time>; (prevent) evitar; (Comp) guardar. ● n (football) parada f. ● prep salvo, excepto. □ **~e up** vi/t ahorrar. **~er** n ahorrador m. **~ing** n ahorro m. **~ings** npl ahorros mpl

saviour /'seɪvɪə(r)/ n salvador m

savour /'seɪvə(r)/ vt saborear. **~y** a (appetizing) sabroso; (not sweet) no dulce

saw¹ /sɔː/ ⇒SEE¹

saw² /sɔː/ n sierra f. ● vt (pt sawed, pp sawn) serrar. **~dust** n serrín m. **~n** /sɔːn/ ⇒SAW²

saxophone /'sæksəfəʊn/ n saxofón m, saxófono m

say /seɪ/ vt/i (pt said /sed/) decir; rezar <prayer>. ● n. have a **~** expresar una opinión; (in decision) tener voz en capítulo. have no **~** no tener ni voz ni voto. **~ing** n refrán m

scab /skæb/ n costra f; (🔲, blackleg) esquirol m

scaffolding /'skæfəldɪŋ/ n andamios mpl

scald /skɔːld/ vt escaldar

scale /skeɪl/ n (also Mus) escala f; (of fish) escama f. ● vt (climb) escalar. **~ down** vt reducir (a escala) <drawing>; recortar <operation>. **~s** npl (for weighing) balanza f, peso m

scallion /'skæljən/ n (Amer) cebolleta f

scalp /skælp/ vt quitar el cuero cabelludo a

scamper /'skæmpə(r)/ vi. **~ away** irse correteando

scan /skæn/ vt (pt scanned) escudriñar; (quickly) echar un vistazo a; <radar> explorar

scandal /'skændl/ n escándalo m; (gossip) chismorreo m. **~ize** vt escandalizar. **~ous** a escandaloso

Scandinavia /skændɪ'neɪvɪə/ n Escandinavia f. **~n** a & n escandinavo (m)

scant /skænt/ a escaso. **~y** a (-ier, -iest) escaso

scapegoat /'skeɪpgəʊt/ n cabeza f de turco

scar /skɑː(r)/ n cicatriz f

scarc|e /skeəs/ a (-er, -est) escaso. be **~e** escasear. make o.s. **~e** 🔲 mantenerse lejos. **~ely** adv apenas. **~ity** n escasez f

scare /skeə(r)/ vt asustar. be **~d** tener miedo. be **~d of sth** tenerle miedo a algo. ● n susto m. **~crow** n espantapájaros m

scarf /skɑːf/ n (pl scarves) bufanda f; (over head) pañuelo m

scarlet /'skɑːlət/ a escarlata f. **~ fever** n escarlatina f

scarves /skɑːvz/ ⇒SCARF

scary /'skeərɪ/ a (**-ier, -iest**) que da miedo

scathing /'skeɪðɪŋ/ a mordaz

scatter /'skætə(r)/ vt (throw) esparcir; (disperse) dispersar. ● vi dispersarse. ~**ed** /'skætəd/ a disperso; (occasional) esporádico

scavenge /'skævɪndʒ/ vi escarbar (en la basura)

scenario /sɪ'nɑːrɪəʊ/ n (pl **-os**) perspectiva f; (of film) guión m

scen|e /siːn/ n escena f; (sight) vista f; (fuss) lío m. **behind the ~es** entre bastidores. ~**ery** /'siːnərɪ/ n paisaje m; (in theatre) decorado m. ~**ic** /'siːnɪk/ a pintoresco

scent /sent/ n olor m; (perfume) perfume m; (trail) pista f. ● vt intuir; (make fragrant) perfumar

sceptic /'skeptɪk/ n escéptico m. ~**al** a escéptico. ~**ism** /-sɪzəm/ n escepticismo m

sceptre /'septə(r)/ n cetro m

schedule /'ʃedjuːl, 'skedjuːl/ n programa f; (timetable) horario m. **behind ~** atrasado. **it's on ~** va de acuerdo a lo previsto. ● vt proyectar. ~**d flight** n vuelo m regular

scheme /skiːm/ n proyecto m; (plot) intriga f. ● vi (pej) intrigar

schizophrenic /skɪtsə'frenɪk/ a & n esquizofrénico (m)

scholar /'skɒlə(r)/ n erudito m. ~**ly** a erudito. ~**ship** n erudición f; (grant) beca f

school /skuːl/ n escuela f; (Univ) facultad f. ● a <age, holidays, year> escolar. ● vt instruir; (train) capacitar. ~**boy** n colegial m. ~**girl** n colegiala f. ~**ing** n instrucción f. ~**master** n (primary) maestro m; (secondary) profesor m. ~**mistress** n (primary) maestra f; (secondary) profesora f. ~**teacher** n (primary) maestro m; (secondary) profesor m

scien|ce /'saɪəns/ n ciencia f. **study ~ce** estudiar ciencias. ~**ce fiction** n ciencia f ficción. ~**tific** /-'tɪfɪk/ a científico. ~**tist** /'saɪəntɪst/ n científico m

scissors /'sɪsəz/ npl tijeras fpl

scoff /skɒf/ vt 🄓 zamparse. ● vi. ~ **at** mofarse de

scold /skəʊld/ vt regañar

scoop /skuːp/ n pala f; (news) primicia f. □ ~ **out** vt sacar; excavar <hole>

scooter /'skuːtə(r)/ n escúter m; (for child) patinete m

scope /skəʊp/ n alcance m; (opportunity) oportunidad f

scorch /skɔːtʃ/ vt chamuscar. ~**ing** a 🄓 de mucho calor

score /skɔː(r)/ n tanteo m; (Mus) partitura f; (twenty) veintena f. **on that ~** en cuanto a eso. **know the ~** 🄓 saber cómo son las cosas. ● vt marcar <goal>; anotarse <points>; (cut, mark) rayar; conseguir <success>. ● vi marcar

scorn /skɔːn/ n desdén m. ● vt desdeñar. ~**ful** a desdeñoso

Scorpio /'skɔːpɪəʊ/ n Escorpio m, Escorpión m

scorpion /'skɔːpɪən/ n escorpión m

Scot /skɒt/ n escocés m. ~**ch** /skɒtʃ/ n whisky m, güisqui m

scotch /skɒtʃ/ vt frustrar; acallar <rumours>

Scotch tape n (Amer) celo m, cinta f Scotch

Scot: ~land /'skɒtlənd/ n Escocia f. ~**s** a escocés. ~**tish** a escocés

scoundrel /'skaʊndrəl/ n canalla f

scour /'skaʊə(r)/ vt fregar; (search) registrar. ~**er** n estropajo m

scourge /skɜːdʒ/ n azote m

scout /skaʊt/ n explorador m. **Boy S~** explorador m

scowl /skaʊl/ n ceño m fruncido. ● vi fruncir el ceño

scram /skræm/ vi 🄓 largarse

scramble /'skræmbl/ vi (clamber) gatear. ● n (difficult climb) subida f difícil; (struggle) rebatiña f. ~**d egg** n huevos mpl revueltos

scrap /skræp/ n pedacito m; (🄓, fight) pelea f. ● vt (pt **scrapped**) desechar. ~**book** n álbum m de recortes. ~**s** npl sobras fpl

scrape /skreɪp/ n (fig) apuro m. ● vt raspar; (graze) rasparse; (rub) rascar. □ ~ **through** vi/t aprobar por los pelos <exam>. □ ~ **together** vt reunir. ~**r** n rasqueta f

scrap: ~**heap** n montón m de deshechos. ~ **yard** n chatarrería f

scratch /skrætʃ/ vt rayar <furniture, record>; (with nail etc) arañar; rascarse <itch>. ●vi arañar. ●n rayón m; (from nail etc) arañazo m. **start from** ~ empezar desde cero. **be up to** ~ dar la talla

scrawl /skrɔːl/ n garabato m. ●vt/i garabatear

scream /skriːm/ vt/i gritar. ●n grito m

screech /skriːtʃ/ vi chillar; <brakes etc> chirriar. ●n chillido m; (of brakes etc) chirrido m

screen /skriːn/ n pantalla f; (folding) biombo m. ●vt (hide) ocultar; (protect) proteger; proyectar <film>

screw /skruː/ n tornillo m. ● vt atornillar. □~ **up** vt atornillar; entornar <eyes>; torcer <face>; (⌧, ruin) fastidiar. ~**driver** n destornillador m

scribble /skrɪbl/ vt/i garrabatear. ●n garrabato m

script /skrɪpt/ n escritura f; (of film etc) guión m

scroll /skrəʊl/ n rollo m (de pergamino)

scrounge /skraʊndʒ/ vt/i gorronear. ~**r** n gorrón m

scrub /skrʌb/ n (land) maleza f. ●vt/i (pt **scrubbed**) fregar

scruff /skrʌf/ n. **by the** ~ **of the neck** por el pescuezo. ~**y** a (-**ier**, -**iest**) desaliñado

scrup|le /skruːpl/ n escrúpulo m. ~**ulous** /-jʊləs/ a escrupuloso

scrutin|ize /skruːtɪnaɪz/ vt escudriñar; inspeccionar <document>. ~**y** /skruːtɪnɪ/ n examen m minucioso

scuffle /skʌfl/ n refriega f

sculpt /skʌlpt/ vt/i esculpir. ~**or** n escultor m. ~**ure** /-tʃə(r)/ n escultura f. ●vt/i esculpir

scum /skʌm/ n espuma f; (people, pej) escoria f

scupper /skʌpə(r)/ vt echar por tierra <plans>

scurry /skʌrɪ/ vi corretear

scuttle /skʌtl/ n cubo m del carbón. ●vt barrenar <ship>. ●vi. ~ **away** escabullirse rápidamente

scythe /saɪð/ n guadaña f

SE abbr (= **south-east**) SE

sea /siː/ n mar m. **at** ~ en el mar; (fig) confuso. **by** ~ por mar. ~**food** n mariscos mpl. ~ **front** n paseo m marítimo, malecón m (LAm). ~**gull** n gaviota f. ~**horse** n caballito m de mar

seal /siːl/ n sello m; (animal) foca f. ●vt sellar. □~ **off** vt acordonar <area>

sea level n nivel m del mar

sea lion n león m marino

seam /siːm/ n costura f; (of coal) veta f

seaman /siːmən/ n (pl -**men**) marinero m

seamy /siːmɪ/ a sórdido

seance /seɪɑːns/ n sesión f de espiritismo

search /sɜːtʃ/ vt registrar; buscar en <records>. ●vi buscar. ●n (for sth) búsqueda f; (of sth) registro m; (Comp) búsqueda f. **in** ~ **of** en busca de. □~ **for** vt buscar. ~**ing** a penetrante. ~**light** n reflector m. ~ **party** n partida f de rescate

sea: ~**shore** n orilla f del mar. ~**sick** a mareado. **be** ~**sick** marearse. ~**side** n playa f

season /siːzn/ n estación f; (period) temporada f. **high/low** ~ temporada f alta/baja. ●vt (Culin) sazonar. ~**al** a estacional; <demand> de estación. ~**ed** a (fig) avezado. ~**ing** n condimento m. ~ **ticket** n abono m (de temporada)

seat /siːt/ n asiento m; (place) lugar m; (in cinema, theatre) localidad f; (of trousers) fondillos mpl. **take a** ~ sentarse. ●vt sentar; (have seats for) <auditorium> tener capacidad para; <bus> tener asientos para. ~**belt** n cinturón m de seguridad

sea: ~**urchin** n erizo m de mar. ~**weed** n alga f marina. ~**worthy** a en condiciones de navegar

seclu|ded /sɪkluːdɪd/ a aislado. ~**sion** /-ʒn/ n aislamiento m

second /'sekənd/ a & n segundo (m). on ~ thoughts pensándolo bien. ● adv (in race etc) en segundo lugar. ● vt secundar. ~s npl (goods) artículos mpl de segunda calidad; (Ⓑ, more food) have ~s repetir. ● /sɪ'kɒnd/ vt (transfer) trasladar temporalmente. ~ary /'sekəndrɪ/ a secundario. ~ary school n instituto m (de enseñanza secundaria)

second: ~-class a de segunda (clase). ~-hand a de segunda mano. ~ly adv en segundo lugar. ~-rate a mediocre

secre|cy /'si:krəsɪ/ n secreto m. ~t a & n secreto (m). in ~t en secreto

secretar|ial /sekrə'teərɪəl/ a de secretario; <course> de secretariado. ~y /'sekrətrɪ/ n secretario m. S~y of State (in UK) ministro m: (in US) secretario m de Estado

secretive /'si:krɪtɪv/ a reservado

sect /sekt/ n secta f. ~arian /-'teərɪən/ a sectario

section /'sekʃn/ n sección f; (part) parte f

sector /'sektə(r)/ n sector m

secular /'sekjʊlə(r)/ a secular

secur|e /sɪ'kjʊə(r)/ a seguro; <shelf> firme. ● vt asegurar; (obtain) obtener. ~ely adv seguramente. ~ity n seguridad f; (for loan) garantía f

sedat|e /sɪ'deɪt/ a reposado. ● vt sedar. ~ion /sɪ'deɪʃn/ n sedación f. ~ive /'sedətɪv/ a & n sedante (m)

sediment /'sedɪmənt/ n sedimento m

seduc|e /sɪ'dju:s/ vt seducir. ~er n seductor m. ~tion /sɪ'dʌkʃn/ n seducción f. ~tive /sɪ'dʌktɪv/ a seductor

see /si:/ ● vt (pt saw, pp seen) ver; (understand) comprender; (escort) acompañar. ~ing that visto que. ~ you later! ¡hasta luego! ● vi ver. □ ~ off vt (say goodbye to) despedirse de. □ ~ through vt llevar a cabo; calar <person>. □ ~ to vt ocuparse de

seed /si:d/ n semilla f; (fig) germen m; (Amer, pip) pepita f. go to ~ granar; (fig) echarse a perder. ~ling n planta f de semillero. ~y a (-ier, -iest) sórdido

seek /si:k/ vt (pt sought) buscar; pedir <approval>. □ ~ out vt buscar

seem /si:m/ vi parecer

seen /si:n/ ⇒SEE

seep /si:p/ vi filtrarse

see-saw /'si:sɔ:/ n balancín m

seethe /si:ð/ vi (fig) estar furioso. I was seething with anger me hervía la sangre

see-through /'si:θru:/ a transparente

segment /'segmənt/ n segmento m; (of orange) gajo m

segregat|e /'segrɪgeɪt/ vt segregar. ~ion /-'geɪʃn/ n segregación f

seiz|e /si:z/ vt agarrar; (Jurid) incautar. ~e on vt aprovechar <chance>. □ ~e up vi (Tec) agarrotarse. ~ure /'si:ʒə(r)/ n incautación f; (Med) ataque m

seldom /'seldəm/ adv rara vez

select /sɪ'lekt/ vt escoger; (Sport) seleccionar. ● a selecto; (exclusive) exclusivo. ~ion /-ʃn/ n selección f. ~ive a selectivo

self /self/ n (pl selves). he's his old ~ again vuelve a ser el de antes. ~-addressed a con el nombre y la dirección del remitente. ~-catering a con facilidades para cocinar. ~-centred a egocéntrico. ~-confidence n confianza f en sí mismo. ~-confident a seguro de sí mismo. ~-conscious a cohibido. ~-contained a independiente. ~-control n dominio m de sí mismo. ~-defence n defensa f propia. ~-employed a que trabaja por cuenta propia. ~-evident a evidente. ~-important a presumido. ~-indulgent a inmoderado. ~-interest n interés m (personal). ~ish a egoísta. ~ishness n egoísmo m. ~-pity n autocompasión. ~-portrait n autorretrato m. ~-respect n amor m propio. ~-righteous a santurrón. ~-sacrifice n abnegación f. ~-satisfied a satisfecho de sí mismo. ~-serve (Amer), ~-service a & n autoservicio (m). ~-sufficient a independiente

sell /sel/ vt (pt **sold**) vender. ● vi venderse. □ ~ **off** vt liquidar. ~ **out** vi. we've sold out of gloves los guantes están agotados. ~**by date** n fecha f límite de venta. ~**er** n vendedor m

Sellotape /'seləteɪp/ n (P) celo m, cinta f Scotch

sell-out /'selaʊt/ n (performance) éxito m de taquilla; (🅸, betrayal) capitulación f

semblance /'sembləns/ n apariencia f

semester /sɪ'mestə(r)/ n (Amer) semestre m

semi... /'semɪ/ pref semi...

semi|breve /-briːv/ n redonda f. ~**circle** n semicírculo m. ~**colon** /-'kəʊlən/ n punto m y coma. ~**detached** /-dɪ'tætʃt/ a <house> adosado. ~**final** /-'faɪml/ n semifinal f

seminar /'semɪnɑː(r)/ n seminario m

senat|e /'senɪt/ n senado m. the S~e (Amer) el Senado. ~**or** /-ətə(r)/ n senador m

send /send/ vt/i (pt **sent**) mandar, enviar. □ ~ **away** vt despedir. □ ~ **away for** vt pedir (por correo). □ ~ **for** vt enviar a buscar. □ ~ **off for** vt pedir (por correo). □ ~ **up** vt 🅸 parodiar. ~**er** n remitente m. ~**off** n despedida f

senile /'siːnaɪl/ a senil

senior /'siːnɪə(r)/ a mayor; (in rank) superior; <partner etc> principal. ● n mayor m & f. ~ **citizen** n jubilado m. ~ **high school** n (Amer) colegio m secundario. ~**ity** /-'ɒrətɪ/ n antigüedad f

sensation /sen'seɪʃn/ n sensación f. ~**al** a sensacional

sens|e /sens/ n sentido m; (common sense) juicio m; (feeling) sensación f. **make** ~**e** vt tener sentido. **make** ~**e of sth** entender algo. ~**eless** a sin sentido. ~**ible** /'sensəbl/ a sensato; <clothing> práctico. ~**itive** /'sensɪtɪv/ a sensible; (touchy) susceptible. ~**itivity** /-'tɪvətɪ/ n sensibilidad f. ~**ual** /'senʃʊəl/ a sensual. ~**uous** /'sensʊəs/ a sensual

sent /sent/ ⇒SEND

sentence /'sentəns/ n frase f; (judgment) sentencia f; (punishment) condena f. ● vt. ~ **to** condenar a

sentiment /'sentɪmənt/ n sentimiento m; (opinion) opinión f. ~**al** /-'mentl/ a sentimental. ~**ality** /-'tælətɪ/ n sentimentalismo m

sentry /'sentrɪ/ n centinela f

separa|ble /'sepərəbl/ a separable. ~**te** /'sepərət/ a separado; (independent) independiente. ● vt /'sepərət/ separar. ● vi separarse. ~**tely** /'sepərətlɪ/ adv por separado. ~**tion** /-'reɪʃn/ n separación f. ~**tist** /'sepərətɪst/ n separatista m & f

September /sep'tembə(r)/ n se(p)tiembre m

septic /'septɪk/ a séptico

sequel /'siːkwəl/ n continuación f; (later events) secuela f

sequence /'siːkwəns/ n sucesión f; (of film) secuencia f

Serb /sɜːb/ a & n ⇒SERBIAN. ~**ia** /'sɜːbɪə/ n Serbia f ~**ian** a & n serbio (m)

serenade /serə'neɪd/ n serenata f. ● vt dar serenata a

serene /sɪ'riːn/ a sereno

sergeant /'sɑːdʒənt/ n sargento m

serial /'sɪərɪəl/ n serie f. ~**ize** vt serializar

series /'sɪəriːz/ n serie f

serious /'sɪərɪəs/ a serio. ~**ly** adv seriamente; (ill) gravemente. **take** ~**ly** tomar en serio

sermon /'sɜːmən/ n sermón m

serum /'sɪərəm/ n (pl **-a**) suero m

servant /'sɜːvənt/ n criado m

serve /sɜːv/ vt servir; servir a <country>; cumplir <sentence>. ~ **as** servir de. it ~**s you right** ¡bien te lo mereces! ● vi servir; (in tennis) sacar. ● n (in tennis) saque m. ~**r** n (Comp) servidor m

service /'sɜːvɪs/ n servicio m; (of car etc) revisión f. ● vt revisar <car etc>. ~ **charge** n (in restaurant) servicio m. ~**s** npl (Mil) fuerzas fpl armadas. ~ **station** n estación f de servicio

serviette /sɜːvɪ'et/ n servilleta f

servile /'sɜːvaɪl/ a servil

session /'seʃn/ n sesión f

set /set/ *vt* (*pt* **set**, *pres p* **setting**) poner; poner en hora *<clock etc>*; fijar *<limit etc>*; (typeset) componer. ~ **fire to** prender fuego a. ~ **free** *vt* poner en libertad. ● *vi <sun>* ponerse; *<jelly>* cuajarse. ● *n* serie *f*; (of cutlery etc) juego *m*; (tennis) set *m*; (TV, Radio) aparato *m*; (in theatre) decorado *m*; (of people) círculo *m*. ● *a* fijo. **be** ~ **on** estar resuelto a. □ ~ **back** *vt* (delay) retardar; (🅣, cost) costar. □ ~ **off** *vi* salir. *vt* hacer sonar *<alarm>*; hacer explotar *<bomb>*. □ ~ **out** *vt* exponer *<argument>*. *vi* (leave) salir. □ ~ **up** *vt* establecer. ~**back** *n* revés *m*

settee /se'ti:/ *n* sofá *m*

setting /'setɪŋ/ *n* (of dial, switch) posición *f*

settle /'setl/ *vt* (arrange) acordar; arreglar *<matter>*; resolver *<dispute>*; pagar *<bill>*; saldar *<debt>*. ● *vi* (live) establecerse. □ ~ **down** *vi* calmarse; (become more responsible) sentar (la) cabeza. □ ~ **for** *vt* aceptar. □ ~ **up** *vi* arreglar cuentas. ~**ment** *n* establecimiento *m*; (agreement) acuerdo *m*; (of debt) liquidación *f*; (colony) colonia *f*. ~**r** *n* colono *m*

set: ~**to** *n* pelea *f*. ~**up** *n* 🅣 sistema *m*; (con) tinglado *m*

seven /'sevn/ *a & n* siete (*m*). ~**teen** /sevn'ti:n/ *a & n* diecisiete (*m*). ~**teenth** *a* decimoséptimo. ● *n* diecisietavo *m*. ~**th** *a & n* séptimo (*m*). ~**tieth** /'sevntɪɪθ/ *a* septuagésimo. ● *n* setentavo *m*. ~**ty** /'sevntɪ/ *a & n* setenta (*m*)

sever /'sevə(r)/ *vt* cortar; (fig) romper

several /'sevrəl/ *a & pron* varios

sever|e /sɪ'vɪə(r)/ *a* (**-er, -est**) severo; (serious) grave; *<weather>* riguroso. ~**ely** *adv* severamente. ~**ity** /sɪ'verətɪ/ *n* severidad *f*; (seriousness) gravedad *f*

sew /səʊ/ *vt/i* (*pt* **sewed**, *pp* **sewn**, *or* **sewed**) coser. □ ~ **up** *vt* coser

sew|age /'su:ɪdʒ/ *n* aguas *fpl* residuales. ~**er** /'su:ə(r)/ *n* cloaca *f*

sewing /'səʊɪŋ/ *n* costura *f*. ~ **machine** *n* máquina *f* de coser

sewn /səʊn/ ⇒SEW

sex /seks/ *n* sexo *m*. **have** ~ tener relaciones sexuales. ● *a* sexual. ~**ist** *a* & *n* sexista (*m & f*). ~**ual** /'sekʃʊəl/ *a* sexual. ~**ual intercourse** *n* relaciones *fpl* sexuales. ~**uality** /-'ælətɪ/ *n* sexualidad *f*. ~**y** *a* (**-ier, -iest**) excitante, sexy, provocativo

shabby /'ʃæbɪ/ *a* (**-ier, -iest**) *<clothes>* gastado; *<person>* pobremente vestido

shack /ʃæk/ *n* choza *f*

shade /ʃeɪd/ *n* sombra *f*; (of colour) tono *m*; (for lamp) pantalla *f*; (nuance) matiz *m*; (Amer, over window) persiana *f*

shadow /'ʃædəʊ/ *n* sombra *f*. ● *vt* (follow) seguir de cerca a. ~**y** *a* (fig) vago

shady /'ʃeɪdɪ/ *a* (**-ier, -iest**) sombreado; (fig) turbio; *<character>* sospechoso

shaft /ʃɑ:ft/ *n* (of arrow) astil *m*; (Mec) eje *m*; (of light) rayo *m*; (of lift, mine) pozo *m*

shaggy /'ʃægɪ/ *a* (**-ier, -iest**) peludo

shake /ʃeɪk/ *vt* (*pt* **shook**, *pp* **shaken**) sacudir; agitar *<bottle>*; (shock) desconcertar. ~ **hands with** estrechar la mano a. ~ **one's head** negar con la cabeza; (Amer, meaning yes) asentir con la cabeza. ● *vi* temblar. □ ~ **off** *vi* deshacerse de. ● *n* sacudida *f*

shaky /'ʃeɪkɪ/ *a* (**-ier, -iest**) tembloroso; *<table etc>* inestable

shall /ʃæl/ *v aux*. **we** ~ **see** veremos. ~ **we go to the cinema?** ¿vamos al cine?

shallow /'ʃæləʊ/ *a* (**-er, -est**) poco profundo; (fig) superficial

sham /ʃæm/ *n* farsa *f*. ● *a* fingido

shambles /'ʃæmblz/ *npl* (🅣, mess) caos *m*

shame /ʃeɪm/ *n* (feeling) vergüenza *f*. **what a** ~! ¡qué lástima! ● *vt* avergonzar. ~**ful** *a* vergonzoso. ~**less** *a* desvergonzado

shampoo /ʃæm'pu:/ *n* champú *m*. ● *vt* lavar

shan't /ʃɑ:nt/ = **shall not**

shape /ʃeɪp/ *n* forma *f*. ● *vt* formar; determinar *<future>*. ● *vi* tomar forma. ~**less** *a* informe

share /ʃeə(r)/ n porción f; (Com) acción f. ● vt compartir; (divide) dividir. ● vi compartir. ~ in sth participar en algo. □~ **out** vt repartir. ~**holder** n accionista m & f. ~**out** n reparto m

shark /ʃɑːk/ n tiburón m

sharp /ʃɑːp/ a (-**er**, -**est**) <knife etc> afilado; <pin etc> puntiagudo; <pain, sound> agudo; <taste> ácido; <bend> cerrado; <contrast> marcado; (clever) listo; (Mus) sostenido. ● adv en punto. **at seven o'clock** ~ a las siete en punto. ● n (Mus) sostenido m. ~**en** vt afilar; sacar punta a <pencil>. ~**ener** n (Mec) afilador m; (for pencils) sacapuntas m. ~**ly** adv bruscamente

shatter /ʃætə(r)/ vt hacer añicos. **he was** ~**ed by the news** la noticia lo dejó destrozado. ● vi hacerse añicos. ~**ed** /ʃætəd/a (exhausted) agotado

shav|e /ʃeɪv/ vt afeitar, rasurar (Mex). ● vi afeitarse, rasurarse (Mex). ● n afeitada f, rasurada f (Mex). **have a** ~**e** afeitarse. ~**er** n maquinilla f (de afeitar). ~**ing brush** n brocha f de afeitar. ~**ing cream** n crema f de afeitar

shawl /ʃɔːl/ n chal m

she /ʃiː/ pron ella

sheaf /ʃiːf/ n (pl **sheaves** /ʃiːvz/) gavilla f

shear /ʃɪə(r)/ vt (pp **shorn** or **sheared**) esquilar. ~**s** /ʃɪəz/ npl tijeras fpl grandes

shed /ʃed/ n cobertizo m. ● vt (pt **shed**, pres p **shedding**) perder; derramar <tears>; despojarse de <clothes>. ~ **light on** arrojar luz sobre

she'd /ʃiː(ə)d/ = **she had, she would**

sheep /ʃiːp/ n invar oveja f. ~**dog** n perro m pastor. ~**ish** a avergonzado

sheer /ʃɪə(r)/ a (as intensifier) puro; (steep) perpendicular

sheet /ʃiːt/ n sábana f; (of paper) hoja f; (of glass) lámina f; (of ice) capa f

shelf /ʃelf/ n (pl **shelves**) estante m. **a set of shelves** unos estantes

shell /ʃel/ n concha f; (of egg) cáscara f; (of crab, snail, tortoise) caparazón m or f; (explosive) proyectil m, obús m. ● vt pelar <peas etc>; (Mil) bombardear

she'll /ʃiː(ə)l/ = **she had, she would**

shellfish /ʃelfɪʃ/ n invar marisco m; (collectively) mariscos mpl

shelter /ʃeltə(r)/ n refugio m. **take** ~ refugiarse. ● vt darle cobijo a <fugitive>; (protect from weather) resguardar. ● vi refugiarse. ~**ed** /ʃeltəd/ a <spot> abrigado; <life> protegido

shelv|e /ʃelv/ vt (fig) dar carpetazo a. ~**ing** n estantería f

shepherd /ʃepəd/ n pastor m. ~**ess** /-ˈdes/ n pastora f

sherbet /ʃɜːbət/ n (Amer, water ice) sorbete m

sheriff /ʃerɪf/ n (in US) sheriff m

sherry /ʃeri/ n (vino m de) jerez m

she's /ʃiːz/ = **she is, she has**

shield /ʃiːld/ n escudo m. ● vt proteger

shift /ʃɪft/ vt cambiar; correr <furniture etc>. ● vi <wind> cambiar; <attention, opinion> pasar a; (Amer, change gear) cambiar de velocidad. ● n cambio m; (work) turno m; (workers) tanda f. ~**y** a (-**ier**, -**iest**) furtivo

shilling /ʃɪlɪŋ/ n chelín m

shimmer /ʃɪmə(r)/ vi rielar, relucir

shin /ʃɪn/ n espinilla f

shine /ʃaɪn/ vi (pt **shone**) brillar. ● vt sacar brillo a. ~ **a light on sth** alumbrar algo con una luz. ● n brillo m

shingle /ʃɪŋɡl/ n (pebbles) guijarros mpl

shin|ing /ʃaɪnɪŋ/ a brillante. ~**y** /ʃaɪni/ a (-**ier**, -**iest**) brillante

ship /ʃɪp/ n barco m, buque m. ● vt (pt **shipped**) transportar; (send) enviar; (load) embarcar. ~**building** n construcción f naval. ~**ment** n envío m. ~**ping** n transporte m; (ships) barcos mpl. ~**shape** a limpio y ordenado. ~**wreck** n naufragio m. ~**wrecked** a naufragado. **be** ~**wrecked** naufragar. ~**yard** n astillero m

shirk /ʃɜːk/ vt esquivar

shirt /ʃɜːt/ n camisa f. **in** ~-**sleeves** en mangas de camisa

shit /ʃɪt/ n & int (vulg) mierda (f). ● vi (vulg) (pt **shat**, pres p **shitting**) cagar

shiver /'ʃɪvə(r)/ vi temblar. ● n escalofrío m

shoal /ʃəʊl/ n banco m

shock /ʃɒk/ n (of impact) choque m; (of earthquake) sacudida f; (surprise) shock m; (scare) susto m; (Elec) descarga f; (Med) shock m. get a ~ llevarse un shock. ● vt escandalizar; (appal) horrorizar. ~**ing** a escandaloso; ⊞ espantoso

shod /ʃɒd/ ⇒SHOE

shoddy /'ʃɒdɪ/ a (-ier, -iest) mal hecho, de pacotilla

shoe /ʃuː/ n zapato m; (of horse) herradura f. ● vt (pt **shod**, pres p **shoeing**) herrar <horse>. ~**horn** n calzador m. ~**lace** n cordón m (de zapato). ~ **polish** n betún m

shone /ʃɒn/ ⇒SHINE

shoo /ʃuː/ vt ahuyentar

shook /ʃʊk/ ⇒SHAKE

shoot /ʃuːt/ vt (pt **shot**) disparar; rodar <film>. ● vi (hunt) cazar. ● n (Bot) retoño m. □ ~ **down** vt derribar. □ ~ **out** vi (rush) salir disparado. □ ~ **up** vi <prices> dispararse; (grow) crecer mucho

shop /ʃɒp/ n tienda f. go to the ~s ir de compras. talk ~ hablar del trabajo. ● vi (pt **shopping**) hacer compras. go ~**ping** ir de compras. □ ~ **around** vi buscar el mejor precio. ~ **assistant** n dependiente m, dependienta f, empleado m, empleada f (LAm). ~**keeper** n comerciante m, tendero m. ~**lifter** n ladrón m (que roba en las tiendas). ~**lifting** n hurto m (en las tiendas). ~**per** n comprador m. ~**ping** n (purchases) compras fpl. do the ~**ping** hacer la compra, hacer el mandado (Mex). ~**ping bag** n bolsa f de la compra. ~**ping cart** n (Amer) carrito m (de la compra). ~**ping centre**, ~**ping mall** (Amer) n centro m comercial. ~**ping trolley** n carrito m de la compra. ~ **steward** n enlace m sindical. ~ **window** n escaparate m, vidriera f (LAm), aparador m (Mex)

shore /ʃɔː(r)/ n orilla f

shorn /ʃɔːn/ ⇒SHEAR

short /ʃɔːt/ a (-er, -est) corto; (not lasting) breve; <person> bajo; (curt) brusco. a ~ time ago hace poco. be ~ of time/money andar corto de tiempo/dinero. Mick is ~ for Michael Mick es el diminutivo de Michael. ● adv <stop> en seco. we never went ~ of food nunca nos faltó comida. ● n. in ~ en resumen. ~**age** /-ɪdʒ/ n escasez f, falta f. ~**bread** n galleta f (de mantequilla). ~ **circuit** n cortocircuito m. ~**coming** n defecto m. ~ **cut** n atajo m. ~**en** vt acortar. ~**hand** n taquigrafía f. ~**ly** adv (soon) dentro de poco. ~**ly before midnight** poco antes de la medianoche. ~**s** npl pantalones m cortos, shorts mpl; (Amer, underwear) calzoncillos mpl. ~**-sighted** /-'saɪtɪd/ a miope

shot /ʃɒt/ ⇒SHOOT. ● n (from gun) disparo m; tiro m; (in soccer) tiro m, disparo m; (in other sports) tiro m; (Photo) foto f. be a good/poor ~ ser un buen/mal tirador. be off like a ~ salir disparado. ~**gun** n escopeta f

should /ʃʊd, ʃəd/ v aux. I ~ go debería ir. you ~n't have said that no deberías haber dicho eso. I ~ like to see her me gustaría verla. if he ~ come si viniese

shoulder /'ʃəʊldə(r)/ n hombro m. ● vt cargar con <responsibility>; ponerse al hombro <burden>. ~ **blade** n omóplato m

shout /ʃaʊt/ n grito m. ● vt/i gritar. ~ at s.o. gritarle a uno

shove /ʃʌv/ n empujón m. ● vt empujar; (⊞, put) poner. ● vi empujar. □ ~ **off** vi ⊞ largarse

shovel /'ʃʌvl/ n pala f. ● vt (pt **shovelled**) palear <coal>; espalar <snow>

show /ʃəʊ/ vt (pt **showed**, pp **shown**) mostrar; (put on display) exponer; poner <film>. I'll ~ you to your room lo acompaño a su cuarto. ● vi (be visible) verse. ● n muestra f; (exhibition) exposición f; (in theatre) espectáculo m; (on TV, radio) programa m; (ostentation) pompa f. be on ~ estar expuesto. □ ~ **off** vt (pej) lucir; presumir de. vi presumir, lucirse.

□ ~ **up** *vi* (be visible) notarse; (arrive) aparecer. *vt* (reveal) poner de manifiesto; (embarrass) hacer quedar mal. ~**case** *n* vitrina *f*. ~**down** *n* confrontación *f*

shower /'ʃaʊə(r)/ *n* (of rain) chaparrón *m*; (for washing) ducha *f*. **have a** ~, **take a** ~ ducharse. ● *vi* ducharse

showjumping *n* concursos *mpl* hípicos.

shown /ʃəʊn/ ⇒SHOW

show: ~**-off** *n* fanfarrón *m*. ~**room** *n* sala *f* de exposición *f*. ~**y** *a* (**-ier, -iest**) llamativo; (attractive) ostentoso

shrank /ʃræŋk/ ⇒SHRINK

shred /ʃred/ *n* pedazo *m*; (fig) pizca *f*. ● *vt* (*pt* **shredded**) hacer tiras; destruir, triturar <*documents*>. ~**der** *n* (for paper) trituradora *f*; (for vegetables) cortadora *f*

shrewd /ʃruːd/ *a* (**-er, -est**) astuto

shriek /ʃriːk/ *n* chillido *m*; (of pain) alarido *m*. ● *vt/i* chillar

shrift /ʃrɪft/ *n*. **give s.o. short** ~ despachar a uno con brusquedad. **give sth short** ~ desestimar algo de plano

shrill /ʃrɪl/ *a* agudo

shrimp /ʃrɪmp/ *n* gamba *f*, camarón *m* (LAm); (Amer, large) langostino *m*

shrine /ʃraɪn/ *n* (place) santuario *m*; (tomb) sepulcro *m*

shrink /ʃrɪŋk/ *vt* (*pt* **shrank**, *pp* **shrunk**) encoger. ● *vi* encogerse; <*amount*> reducirse; retroceder (recoil)

shrivel /'ʃrɪvl/ *vi* (*pt* **shrivelled**). ~ (**up**) <*plant*> marchitarse; <*fruit*> resecarse y arrugarse

shroud /ʃraʊd/ *n* mortaja *f*; (fig) velo *m*. ● *vt* envolver

Shrove /ʃrəʊv/ *n*. ~ **Tuesday** *n* martes *m* de carnaval

shrub /ʃrʌb/ *n* arbusto *m*

shrug /ʃrʌg/ *vt* (*pt* **shrugged**) encogerse de hombros

shrunk /ʃrʌŋk/ ⇒SHRINK. ~**en** *a* encogido

shudder /'ʃʌdə(r)/ *vi* estremecerse. ● *n* estremecimiento *m*

shuffle /'ʃʌfl/ *vi* andar arrastrando los pies. ● *vt* barajar <*cards*>. ~ **one's feet** arrastrar los pies

shun /ʃʌn/ *vt* (*pt* **shunned**) evitar

shunt /ʃʌnt/ *vt* cambiar de vía

shush /ʃʊʃ/ *int* ¡chitón!

shut /ʃʌt/ *vt* (*pt* **shut**, *pres p* **shutting**) cerrar. ● *vi* cerrarse. ● *a*. be ~ estar cerrado. □ ~ **down** *vt/i* cerrar. □ ~ **up** *vt* cerrar; 🎦 hacer callar. *vi* callarse. ~**ter** *n* contraventana *f*; (Photo) obturador *m*

shuttle /'ʃʌtl/ *n* lanzadera *f*; (Aviat) puente *m* aéreo; (space ~) transbordador *m* espacial. ● *vi*. ~ (**back and forth**) ir y venir. ~**cock** *n* volante *m*. ~ **service** *n* servicio *m* de enlace

shy /ʃaɪ/ *a* (**-er, -est**) tímido. ● *vi* (*pt* **shied**) asustarse. ~**ness** *n* timidez *f*

sick /sɪk/ *a* enfermo; <*humour*> negro; (🎦, fed up) harto. **be** ~ estar enfermo; (vomit) vomitar. **be** ~ **of** (fig) estar harto de. **feel** ~ sentir náuseas. **get** ~ (Amer) caer enfermo, enfermarse (LAm). ~ **leave** *n* permiso *m* por enfermedad, baja *f* por enfermedad. ~**ly** /'sɪklɪ/ *a* (**-lier, -liest**) enfermizo; <*taste, smell etc*> nauseabundo. ~**ness** /'sɪknɪs/ *n* enfermedad *f*

side /saɪd/ *n* lado *m*; (of hill) ladera *f*; (of person) costado *m*; (team) equipo *m*; (fig) parte *f*. ~ **by** ~ uno al lado del otro. **take** ~**s** tomar partido. ● *a* lateral. □ ~ **with** *vt* ponerse de parte de. ~**board** *n* aparador *m*. ~ **dish** *n* acompañamiento *m*. ~**-effect** *n* efecto *m* secundario; (fig) consecuencia *f* indirecta. ~**line** *n* actividad *f* suplementaria. ~ **road** *n* calle *f* secundaria. ~**-step** *vt* eludir. ~**-track** *vt* desviar del tema. ~**walk** *n* (Amer) acera *f*, vereda *f* (LAm), banqueta *f* (Mex). ~**ways** *a* & *adv* de lado

siding /'saɪdɪŋ/ *n* apartadero *m*

sidle /'saɪdl/ *vi*. ~ **up to** s.o. acercarse furtivamente a uno

siege /siːdʒ/ *n* sitio *m*

sieve /sɪv/ *n* tamiz *m*. ● *vt* tamizar, cernir

sift /sɪft/ vt tamizar, cernir. ● vi. ~ **through sth** pasar algo por el tamiz

sigh /saɪ/ n suspiro. ● vi suspirar

sight /saɪt/ n vista f; (spectacle) espectáculo m; (on gun) mira f. **at first** ~ a primera vista. **catch** ~ **of** ver; (in distance) avistar. **lose** ~ **of** perder de vista. **see the** ~**s** visitar los lugares de interés. **within** ~ **of** (near) cerca de. ● vt ver; divisar <land>. ~**-see-ing** n. **go** ~ ir a visitar los lugares de interés. ~**seer** /-siːə(r)/ n turista m & f

sign /saɪn/ n (indication) señal f, indicio m; (gesture) señal f, seña f; (notice) letrero m; (Astr) signo m. ● vt firmar. □ ~ **on** vi (for unemployment benefit) anotarse para recibir el seguro de desempleo

signal /'sɪgnəl/ n señal f. ● vt (pt **signalled**) señalar. ● vi. ~ (**to s.o.**) hacer señas (a uno); (Auto) poner el intermitente, señalizar

signature /'sɪgnətʃə(r)/ n firma f. ~ **tune** n sintonía f

significan|ce /sɪg'nɪfɪkəns/ n importancia f. ~**t** a (important) importante; <fact, remark> significativo

signify /'sɪgnɪfaɪ/ vt significar

signpost /'saɪnpəʊst/ n señal f, poste m indicador

silen|ce /'saɪləns/ n silencio m. ● vt hacer callar. ~**cer** n (on gun and on car) silenciador m. ~**t** a silencioso; <film> mudo. **remain** ~**t** quedarse callado. ~**tly** adv silenciosamente

silhouette /sɪluː'et/ n silueta f. ● vt. **be** ~**d** perfilarse (**against** contra)

silicon /'sɪlɪkən/ n silicio m. ~ **chip** n pastilla f de silicio

silk /sɪlk/ n seda f. ~**y** a (of silk) de seda; (like silk) sedoso

silly /'sɪlɪ/ a (**-ier, -iest**) tonto

silt /sɪlt/ n cieno m

silver /'sɪlvə(r)/ n plata f. ● a de plata. ~**-plated** a bañado en plata, plateado. ~**ware** /-weə(r)/ n platería f

simil|ar /'sɪmɪlə(r)/ a parecido, similar. ~**arity** /-'lærətɪ/ n parecido m. ~**arly** adv de igual manera. ~**e** /'sɪmɪlɪ/ n símil m

simmer /'sɪmə(r)/ vt/i hervir a fuego lento. □ ~ **down** vi calmarse

simpl|e /'sɪmpl/ a (**-er, -est**) sencillo, simple; <person> (humble) simple; (backward) simple. ~**e-minded** /-'maɪndɪd/ a ingenuo. ~**icity** /-'plɪsətɪ/ n simplicidad f, sencillez f. ~**ify** /'sɪmplɪfaɪ/ vt simplificar. ~**y** adv sencillamente, simplemente; (absolutely) realmente

simulate /'sɪmjʊleɪt/ vt simular

simultaneous /sɪml'teɪnɪəs/ a simultáneo. ~**ly** adv simultáneamente

sin /sɪn/ n pecado m. ● vi (pt **sinned**) pecar

since /sɪns/

● preposition

····▸ desde. **he's been living here** ~ **1991** vive aquí desde 1991. ~ **Christmas** desde Navidad. ~ **then** desde entonces. **I haven't been feeling well** ~ **Sunday** desde el domingo que no me siento bien. **how long is it** ~ **your interview?** ¿cuánto (tiempo) hace de la entrevista?

● adverb

····▸ desde entonces. **I haven't spoken to her** ~ no he hablado con ella desde entonces

● conjunction

····▸ desde que. **I haven't seen her** ~ **she left** no la he visto desde que se fue. ~ **coming to Manchester** desde que vine (or vino etc) a Manchester. **it's ten years** ~ **he died** hace diez años que se murió

····▸ (because) como, ya que. ~ **it was quite late, I decided to stay** como or ya que era bastante tarde, decidí quedarme

sincer|e /sɪn'sɪə(r)/ a sincero. ~**ely** adv sinceramente. **yours** ~**ely**, ~**ely** (**yours**) (in letters) (saluda) a usted atentamente. ~**ity** /-'serətɪ/ n sinceridad f

sinful /'sɪnfl/ a <person> pecador; <act> pecaminoso

sing /sɪŋ/ vt/i (pt **sang**, pp **sung**) cantar

singe /sɪndʒ/ *vt* (*pres p* **singeing**) chamuscar

singer /'sɪŋə(r)/ *n* cantante *m & f*

single /'sɪŋgl/ *a* solo; (not double) sencillo; (unmarried) soltero; <*bed, room*> individual, de una plaza (LAm); <*ticket*> de ida, sencillo. **not a ~ house** ni una sola casa. **every ~ day** todos los días sin excepción. ● *n* (ticket) billete *m* sencillo, boleto *m* de ida (LAm). □ ~ **out** *vt* escoger; (distinguish) distinguir. ~**-handed** /-'hæn dɪd/ *a & adv* sin ayuda. ~**s** *npl* (Sport) individuales *mpl*

singular /'sɪŋgjʊlə(r)/ *n* singular *f*. ● *a* singular; (unusual) raro; <*noun*> en singular

sinister /'sɪnɪstə(r)/ *a* siniestro

sink /sɪŋk/ *vt* (*pt* **sank**, *pp* **sunk**) hundir. ● *vi* hundirse. ● *n* fregadero *m* (Amer, in bathroom) lavabo *m*, lavamanos *m*. □ ~ **in** *vi* penetrar

sinner /'sɪnə(r)/ *n* pecador *m*

sip /sɪp/ *n* sorbo *m*. ● *vt* (*pt* **sipped**) sorber

siphon /'saɪfən/ *n* sifón *m*. ~ (**out**) sacar con sifón. □ ~ **off** *vt* desviar <*money*>.

sir /sɜː(r)/ *n* señor *m*. **S~** *n* (title) sir *m*. **Dear S~,** (in letters) De mi mayor consideración:

siren /'saɪərən/ *n* sirena *f*

sister /'sɪstə(r)/ *n* hermana *f*; (nurse) enfermera *f* jefe. ~**-in-law** *n* (*pl* ~**s-in-law**) cuñada *f*

sit /sɪt/ *vi* (*pt* **sat**, *pres p* **sitting**) sentarse; <*committee etc*> reunirse en sesión. **be ~ting** estar sentado. ● *vt* sentar; hacer <*exam*>. □ ~ **back** *vi* (fig) relajarse. □ ~ **down** *vi* sentarse. **be ~ting down** estar sentado. □ ~ **up** *vi* (from lying) incorpo-rarse; (straighten back) ponerse dere-cho. ~**-in** *n* (strike) encierro *m*, ocupación *f*

site /saɪt/ *n* emplazamiento *m*; (piece of land) terreno *m*; (archaeological) yacimiento *m*. **building ~** *n* solar *m*. ● *vt* situar

sit: ~**ting** *n* sesión *f*; (in restaurant) turno *m*. ~**ting room** *n* sala *f* de estar, living *m*

situat|e /'sɪtjʊeɪt/ *vt* situar. ~**ion** /-'eɪʃn/ *n* situación *f*

six /sɪks/ *a & n* seis (*m*). ~**teen** /sɪk'stiːn/ *a & n* dieciséis (*m*). ~**teenth** *a* decimosexto. ● *n* dieciseisavo *m*. ~**th** *a & n* sexto (*m*). ~**tieth** /'sɪkstɪɪθ/ *a* sexagésimo. ● *n* sesentavo *m*. ~**ty** /'sɪkstɪ/ *a & n* sesenta (*m*)

size /saɪz/ *n* tamaño *m*; (of clothes) talla *f*; (of shoes) número *m*; (of problem, operation) magnitud *f*. **what ~ do you take?** (clothes) ¿qué talla tiene?; (shoes) ¿qué número calza?. □ ~ **up** *vt* 🄸 evaluar <*problem*>; calar <*person*>

sizzle /'sɪzl/ *vi* crepitar

skat|e /skeɪt/ *n* patín *m*.● *vi* patinar. ~**eboard** *n* monopatín *m*, patineta *f* (Mex). ~**er** *n* patinador *m*. ~**ing** *n* patinaje *m*. ~**ing-rink** *n* pista *f* de patinaje

skeleton /'skelɪtn/ *n* esqueleto *m*. ~ **key** *n* llave *f* maestra

sketch /sketʃ/ *n* (drawing) dibujo *m*; (rougher) esbozo *m*; (TV, Theatre) sketch *m*. ● *vt* esbozar. ● *vi* dibujar. ~**y** *a* (**-ier, -iest**) incompleto

ski /skiː/ *n* (*pl* **skis**) esquí *m*. ● *vi* (*pt* **skied**, *pres p* **skiing**) esquiar. **go ~ing** ir a esquiar

skid /skɪd/ *vi* (*pt* **skidded**) patinar. ● *n* patinazo *m*

ski: ~**er** *n* esquiador *m*. ~**ing** *n* esquí *m*

skilful /'skɪlfl/ *a* diestro

ski-lift /'skiːlɪft/ *n* telesquí *m*

skill /skɪl/ *n* habilidad *f*; (technical) destreza *f*. ~**ed** *a* hábil; <*worker*> cualificado

skim /skɪm/ *vt* (*pt* **skimmed**) espumar <*soup*>; desnatar, descremar <*milk*>; (glide over) pasar casi rozando. ~ **milk** (Amer), ~**med milk** *n* leche *f* desnatada, leche *f* descremada. ~ **through** *vt* leer por encima

skimp /skɪmp/ *vi*. ~ **on sth** escatimar algo. ~**y** *a* (**-ier, -iest**) escaso; <*skirt, dress*> brevísimo

skin /skɪn/ *n* piel *f*. ● *vt* (*pt* **skinned**) despellejar. ~**-deep** *a* superficial. ~**-diving** *n* submarinismo *m*. ~**ny** *a* (**-ier, -iest**) flaco

skip /skɪp/ *vi* (*pt* **skipped**) *vi* saltar; (with rope) saltar a la comba, saltar a la cuerda. ● *vt* saltarse *<chapter>*; faltar a *<class>*. ● *n* brinco *m*; (container) contenedor *m* (*para escombros*). ~**per** *n* capitán *m*. ~**ping-rope**, ~**rope** (Amer) *n* comba *f*, cuerda *f* de saltar, reata *f* (Mex)

skirmish /'skɜːmɪʃ/ *n* escaramuza *f*

skirt /skɜːt/ *n* falda *f*. ● *vt* bordear; (go round) ladear. ~**ing-board** *n* rodapié *m*, zócalo *m*

skittle /'skɪtl/ *n* bolo *m*

skive off /skaɪv/ (*vi* ⊞, disappear) escurrir el bulto; (stay away from work) no ir a trabajar

skulk /skʌlk/ *vi* (hide) esconderse. ~ **around** *vi* merodear

skull /skʌl/ *n* cráneo *m*; (remains) calavera *f*

sky /skaɪ/ *n* cielo *m*. ~**lark** *n* alondra *f*. ~**light** *n* tragaluz *m*. ~**scraper** *n* rascacielos *m*

slab /slæb/ *n* (of concrete) bloque *m*; (of stone) losa *f*

slack /slæk/ *a* (**-er**, **-est**) flojo; *<person>* poco aplicado; *<period>* de poca actividad. ● *vi* flojear. ~**en** *vt* aflojar. ● *vi <person>* descansar. □ ~**en off** *vt/i* aflojar

slain /sleɪn/ ⇨SLAY

slake /sleɪk/ *vt* apagar

slam /slæm/ *vt* (*pt* **slammed**). ~ **the door** dar un portazo. ~ **the door shut** cerrar de un portazo. ~ **on the brakes** pegar un frenazo; (⊞, criticize) atacar violentamente. ● *vi* cerrarse de un portazo

slander /'slɑːndə(r)/ *n* calumnia *f*. ● *vt* difamar

slang /slæŋ/ *n* argot *m*

slant /slɑːnt/ *vt* inclinar. ● *n* inclinación *f*

slap /slæp/ *vt* (*pt* **slapped**) (on face) pegarle una bofetada a; (put) tirar. ~ **s.o. on the back** darle una palmada a uno en la espalda ● *n* bofetada *f*; (on back) palmada *f*. ● *adv* de lleno. ~**dash** *a* descuidado; *<work>* chapucero

slash /slæʃ/ *vt* acuchillar; (fig) rebajar drásticamente. ● *n* cuchillada *f*

slat /slæt/ *n* tablilla *f*

slate /sleɪt/ *n* pizarra *f*. ● *vt* ⊞ poner por los suelos

slaughter /'slɔːtə(r)/ *vt* matar salvajemente; matar *<animal>*. ● *n* carnicería *f*; (of animals) matanza *f*

slave /sleɪv/ *n* esclavo *m*. ● *vi* ~ (away) trabajar como un negro. ~**driver** *n* ⊞ negrero *m*. ~**ry** /-əri/ *n* esclavitud *f*

slay /sleɪ/ *vt* (*pt* **slew**, *pp* **slain**) dar muerte a

sleazy /'sliːzi/ *a* (**-ier**, **-iest**) ⊞ sórdido

sled /sled/ (Amer), **sledge** /sledʒ/ *n* trineo *m*

sledge-hammer *n* mazo *m*, almádena *f*

sleek /sliːk/ *a* (**-er**, **-est**) liso, brillante

sleep /sliːp/ *n* sueño *m*. **go to** ~ dormirse. ● *vi* (*pt* **slept**) dormir. ● *vt* poder alojar. ~**er** *n* (on track) traviesa *f*, durmiente *m*. **be a light/heavy** ~**er** tener el sueño ligero/pesado. ~**ing bag** *n* saco *m* de dormir. ~**ing pill** *n* somnífero *m*. ~**less** *a*. **have a** ~**less night** pasar la noche en blanco. ~**walk** *vi* caminar dormido. ~**y** *a* (**-ier**, **-iest**) soñoliento. **be/feel** ~**y** tener sueño

sleet /sliːt/ *n* aguanieve *f*

sleeve /sliːv/ *n* manga *f*; (for record) funda *f*, carátula *f*. **up one's** ~ en reserva. ~**less** *a* sin mangas

sleigh /sleɪ/ *n* trineo *m*

slender /'slendə(r)/ *a* delgado; (fig) escaso

slept /slept/ ⇨SLEEP

slew /sluː/ ⇨SLAY

slice /slaɪs/ *n* (of ham) lonja *f*; (of bread) rebanada *f*; (of meat) tajada *f*; (of cheese) trozo *m*; (of sth round) rodaja *f*. ● *vt* cortar (en rebanadas, tajadas etc)

slick /slɪk/ *a <performance>* muy pulido. ● *n*. (oil) ~ marea *f* negra

slid|e /slaɪd/ *vt* (*pt* **slid**) deslizar. ● *vi* (intentionally) deslizarse; (unintentionally) resbalarse; (in playground) tobogán *m*, resbaladilla *f* (Mex); (for hair) pasador *m*, broche *m* (Mex); (Photo) diapositiva *f*. ~**ing scale** *n* escala *f* móvil

slight /slaɪt/ *a* (**-er, -est**) ligero; (slender) delgado. ● *vt* desairar. ● *n* desaire *m*. ∼**est** *a* mínimo. **not in the** ∼**est** en absoluto. ∼**ly** *adv* un poco, ligeramente

slim /slɪm/ *a* (**slimmer, slimmest**) delgado. ● *vi* (*pt* **slimmed**) (become slimmer) adelgazar; (diet) hacer régimen

slim|e /slaɪm/ *n* limo *m*; (of snail, ⊠lug) baba *f*. ∼**y** *a* viscoso; (fig) excesivamente obsequioso

sling /slɪŋ/ *n* (Med) cabestrillo *m*. ● *vt* (*pt* **slung**) lanzar

slip /slɪp/ *vt* (*pt* **slipped**) deslizar. ∼ **s.o.'s mind** olvidársele a uno. ● *vi* resbalarse. **it** ∼**ped out of my hands** se me resbaló de las manos. **he** ∼**ped out the back door** se deslizó por la puerta trasera ● *n* resbalón *m*; (mistake) error *m*; (petticoat) combinación *f*; (paper) trozo *m*. **give s.o. the** ∼ lograr zafarse de uno. ∼ **of the tongue** *n* lapsus *m* linguae. □ ∼ **away** *vi* escabullirse. □ ∼ **up** *vi* ⊞ equivocarse

slipper /'slɪpə(r)/ *n* zapatilla *f*

slippery /'slɪpərɪ/ *a* resbaladizo

slip: ∼ **road** *n* rampa *f* de acceso. ∼**shod** /'slɪpʃɒd/ *a* descuidado. ∼**-up** *n* ⊞ error *m*

slit /slɪt/ *n* raja *f*; (cut) corte *m*. ● *vt* (*pt* **slit**, *pres p* **slitting**) rajar; (cut) cortar

slither /'slɪðə(r)/ *vi* deslizarse

slobber /'slɒbə(r)/ *vi* babear

slog /slɒg/ *vt* (*pt* **slogged**) golpear. ● *vi* caminar trabajosamente. ● *n* golpetazo *m*; (hard work) trabajo *m* penoso. □ ∼ **away** *vi* sudar tinta ⊞

slogan /'sləʊgən/ *n* eslogan *m*

slop /slɒp/ *vt* (*pt* **slopped**) derramar. ● *vi* derramarse

slop|e /sləʊp/ *vi* inclinarse. ● *vt* inclinar. ● *n* declive *m*, pendiente *f*. ∼**ing** *a* inclinado

sloppy /'slɒpɪ/ *a* (**-ier, -iest**) <work> descuidado; <person> desaliñado

slosh /slɒʃ/ *vi* ⊞ chapotear

slot /slɒt/ *n* ranura *f*. ● *vt* (*pt* **slotted**) encajar

slot-machine *n* distribuidor *m* automático; (for gambling) máquina *f* tragamonedas

slouch /slaʊtʃ/ *vi* andar cargado de espaldas; (in chair) repanchigarse

Slovak /'sləʊvæk/ *a* & *n* eslovaco (*m*). ∼**ia** *n* Eslovaquia *f*

slovenly /'slʌvnlɪ/ *a* <work> descuidado; <person> desaliñado

slow /sləʊ/ *a* (**-er, -est**) lento. **be** ∼ <clock> estar atrasado. **in** ∼ **motion** a cámara lenta. ● *adv* despacio. ● *vt* retardar. ● *vi* ir más despacio. □ ∼ **down**, ∼ **up** *vt* retardar. *vi* ir más despacio. ∼**ly** *adv* despacio, lentamente

sludge /slʌdʒ/ *n* fango *m*

slug /slʌg/ *n* babosa *f*. ∼**gish** *a* lento

slum /slʌm/ *n* barrio *m* bajo

slumber /'slʌmbə(r)/ *vi* dormir

slump /slʌmp/ *n* baja *f* repentina; (in business) depresión *f*. ● *vi* bajar repentinamente; (collapse) desplomarse

slung /slʌŋ/ ⇒SLING

slur /slɜː(r)/ *vt* (*pt* **slurred**). ∼ **one's words** arrastrar las palabras. ● *n*. **a racist** ∼ un comentario racista

slush /slʌʃ/ *n* nieve *f* medio derretida

sly /slaɪ/ *a* (**slyer, slyest**) (crafty) astuto. ● *n*. **on the** ∼ a hurtadillas. ∼**ly** *adv* astutamente

smack /smæk/ *n* manotazo *m*. ● *adv* ⊞ ∼ **in the middle** justo en el medio. **he went** ∼ **into a tree** se dio contra un árbol. ● *vt* pegarle a (*con la mano*)

small /smɔːl/ *a* (**-er, -est**) pequeño, chico (LAm). ● *n*. **the** ∼ **of the back** la región lumbar. ∼ **ads** *npl* anuncios *mpl* (clasificados), avisos *mpl* (clasificados) (LAm). ∼ **change** *n* suelto *m*. ∼**pox** /-pɒks/ *n* viruela *f*. ∼ **talk** *n* charla *f* sobre temas triviales

smart /smɑːt/ *a* (**-er, -est**) elegante; (clever) listo; (brisk) rápido. ● *vi* escocer. □ ∼**en up** *vt* arreglar. *vi* <person> mejorar su aspecto, arreglarse. ∼**ly** *adv* elegantemente; (quickly) rápidamente

smash /smæʃ/ *vt* romper; (into little pieces) hacer pedazos; batir <record>. ● *vi* romperse; (collide) chocar (**into**

con). ● *n* (noise) estrépito *m*; (collision) choque *m*; (in sport) smash *m*. □ ~ **up** *vt* destrozar. ~**ing** *a* 🇬🇧 estupendo

smattering /'smætərɪŋ/ *n* nociones *fpl*

smear /smɪə(r)/ *vt* untar (**with** de); (stain) manchar (**with** de); (fig) difamar. ● *n* mancha *f*

smell /smel/ *n* olor *m*; (sense) olfato *m*. ● *vt* (*pt* **smelt**) oler; *<animal>* olfatear. ● *vi* oler. ~ **of** sth oler a algo. ~**y** *a* maloliente. be ~**y** oler mal

smelt /smelt/ ⇒SMELL. ● *vt* fundir

smile /smaɪl/ *n* sonrisa *f*. ● *vi* sonreír. ~ **at** s.o. sonreírle a uno

smirk /smɜːk/ *n* sonrisita *f* (*de suficiencia etc*)

smith /smɪθ/ *n* herrero *m*

smithereens /smɪðə'riːnz/ *npl.* smash sth to ~ hacer algo añicos

smock /smɒk/ *n* blusa *f*, bata *f*

smog /smɒg/ *n* smog *m*

smok|e /sməʊk/ *n* humo *m*. ● *vt* fumar *<tobacco>*; ahumar *<food>*. ● *vi* fumar. ~**eless** *a* que arde sin humo. ~**er** *n* fumador *m*. ~**y** *a* *<room>* lleno de humo

smooth /smuːð/ *a* (**-er**, **-est**) *<texture/stone>* liso; *<skin>* suave; *<movement>* suave; *<sea>* tranquilo. ● *vt* alisar. □ ~ **out** *vt* allanar *<problems>*. ~**ly** *adv* suavemente; (without problems) sin problemas

smother /'smʌðə(r)/ *vt* asfixiar *<person>*. ~ **s.o. with kisses** cubrir a uno de besos

smoulder /'sməʊldə(r)/ *vi* arder sin llama

smudge /smʌdʒ/ *n* borrón *m*. ● *vi* tiznarse

smug /smʌg/ *a* (**smugger**, **smuggest**) pagado de sí mismo; *<expression>* de suficiencia

smuggl|e /'smʌgl/ *vt* pasar de contrabando. ~**er** *n* contrabandista *m* & *f*. ~**ing** *n* contrabando *m*

snack /snæk/ *n* tentempié *m*. ~ **bar** *n* cafetería *f*

snag /snæg/ *n* problema *m*

snail /sneɪl/ *n* caracol *m*. at a ~'s pace a paso de tortuga

snake /sneɪk/ *n* culebra *f*, serpiente *f*

snap /snæp/ *vt* (*pt* **snapped**) (break) romper. ~ **one's fingers** chasquear los dedos. ● *vi* romperse; *<dog>* intentar morder; (say) contestar bruscamente. ~ **at** *<dog>* intentar morder; (say) contestar bruscamente. ● *n* chasquido *m*; (Photo) foto *f*. ● *a* instantáneo. □ ~ **up** *vt* no dejar escapar *<offer>*. ~**py** *a* (**-ier**, **-iest**) 🇬🇧 rápido. make it ~**py!** ¡date prisa! ~**shot** *n* foto *f*

snare /sneə(r)/ *n* trampa *f*

snarl /snɑːl/ *vi* gruñir

snatch /snætʃ/ *vt.* ~ sth from s.o. arrebatarle algo a uno; (steal) robar. ● *n* (short part) fragmento *m*

sneak /sniːk/ *n* soplón *m*. ● *vi* (*past* & *pp* **sneaked** *or* 🇬🇧 **snuck**) ~ **in** entrar a hurtadillas. ~ **off** escabullirse. ~**ers** /'sniːkəz/ *npl* zapatillas *fpl* de deporte. ~**y** *a* artero

sneer /snɪə(r)/ *n* expresión *f* desdeñosa. ● *vi* hacer una mueca de desprecio. ~ **at** hablar con desprecio a

sneeze /sniːz/ *n* estornudo *m*. ● *vi* estornudar

snide /snaɪd/ *a* insidioso

sniff /snɪf/ *vt* oler. ● *vi* sorberse la nariz

snigger /'snɪgə(r)/ *n* risilla *f*. ● *vi* reírse (*por lo bajo*)

snip /snɪp/ *vt* (*pt* **snipped**) dar un tijeretazo a. ● *n* tijeretazo *m*

sniper /'snaɪpə(r)/ *n* francotirador *m*

snippet /'snɪpɪt/ *n* (of conversation) trozo *m*. ~**s of information** datos *mpl* aislados

snivel /'snɪvl/ *vi* (*pt* **snivelled**) lloriquear

snob /snɒb/ *n* esnob *m* & *f*. ~**bery** *n* esnobismo *m*. ~**bish** *a* esnob

snooker /'snuːkə(r)/ *n* snooker *m*

snoop /snuːp/ *vi* 🇬🇧 husmear

snooze /snuːz/ *n* sueñecito *m*. ● *vi* dormitar

snore /snɔː(r)/ *n* ronquido *m*. ● *vi* roncar

snorkel /'snɔːkl/ *n* esnórkel *m*

snort /snɔːt/ *n* bufido *m*. ● *vi* bufar

snout /snaʊt/ n hocico m

snow /snəʊ/ n nieve f. ● vi nevar. be ~ed in estar aislado por la nieve. be ~ed under with work estar agobiado de trabajo. ~ball n bola f de nieve. ~drift n nieve f amontonada. ~fall n nevada f. ~flake n copo m de nieve. ~man n muñeco m de nieve. ~plough n quitanieves m. ~storm n tormenta f de nieve. ~y a <day, weather> nevoso; <landscape> nevado

snub /snʌb/ vt (pt snubbed) desairar. ● n desaire m. ~-nosed a chato

snuck /snʌk/ ⇒SNEAK

snuff out /snʌf/ vt apagar <candle>

snug /snʌg/ a (snugger, snuggest) cómodo; (tight) ajustado

snuggle (up) /'snʌgl/ vi acurrucarse

so /səʊ/ adv (before a or adv) tan; (thus) así. ● conj (therefore) así que. ~ am I yo también. ~ as to para. ~ far adv (time) hasta ahora. ~ far as I know que yo sepa. ~ long! ¡hasta luego! and ~ on, and ~ forth etcétera (etcétera). I think ~ creo que sí. or ~ más o menos. ~ that conj para que.

soak /səʊk/ vt remojar. ● vi remojarse. □ ~ in vi penetrar. □ ~ up vt absorber. ~ing a empapado

so-and-so /'səʊənsəʊ/ n fulano m

soap /səʊp/ n jabón m. ● vt enjabonar. ~ opera n telenovela f, culebrón m. ~ powder n jabón m en polvo. ~y a jabonoso

soar /sɔː(r)/ vi <bird/plane> planear; (rise) elevarse; <price> dispararse. ~ing a <inflation> galopante

sob /sɒb/ n sollozo m. ● vi (pt sobbed) sollozar

sober /'səʊbə(r)/ a (not drunk) sobrio

so-called /'səʊkɔːld/ a llamado; (pej) supuesto

soccer /'sɒkə(r)/ n fútbol m, futbol m (Mex)

sociable /'səʊʃəbl/ a sociable

social /'səʊʃl/ a social; (sociable) sociable. ~ism n socialismo m. ~ist a & n socialista (m & f). ~ize vt socializar. ~ security n seguridad f social. ~ worker n asistente m social

society /sə'saɪətɪ/ n sociedad f

sociolog|ical /səʊsɪə'lɒdʒɪkl/ a sociológico. ~ist n /-'ɒlədʒɪst/ n sociólogo m. ~y /-'ɒlədʒɪ/ n sociología f

sock /sɒk/ n calcetín m

socket /'sɒkɪt/ n (of joint) hueco m; (of eye) cuenca f; (wall plug) enchufe m; (for bulb) portalámparas m

soda /'səʊdə/ n soda f. ~-water n soda f

sodium /'səʊdɪəm/ n sodio m

sofa /'səʊfə/ n sofá m

soft /sɒft/ a (-er, -est) blando; <light, colour> suave; (gentle) dulce, tierno; (not strict) blando. ~ drink n refresco m. ~en /'sɒfn/ vt ablandar; suavizar <skin>. ● vi ablandarse. ~ly adv dulcemente; <speak> bajito. ~ware /-weə(r)/ n software m

soggy /'sɒgɪ/ a (-ier, -iest) empapado

soil /sɔɪl/ n tierra f; (Amer, dirt) suciedad f. ● vt ensuciar

solar /'səʊlə(r)/ a solar

sold /səʊld/ ⇒SELL

solder /'sɒldə(r)/ vt soldar

soldier /'səʊldʒə(r)/ n soldado m. □ ~ on vi 🔳 seguir al pie del cañón

sole /səʊl/ n (of foot) planta f; (of shoe) suela f. ● a único, solo. ~ly adv únicamente

solemn /'sɒləm/ a solemne

solicitor /sə'lɪsɪtə(r)/ n abogado m; (notary) notario m

solid /'sɒlɪd/ a sólido; <gold etc> macizo; (unanimous) unánime; <meal> sustancioso. ● n sólido m. ~s npl alimentos mpl sólidos. ~arity /sɒlɪ'dærətɪ/ n solidaridad f. ~Ify /sə'lɪdɪfaɪ/ vi solidificarse

solitary /'sɒlɪtrɪ/ a solitario

solitude /'sɒlɪtjuːd/ n soledad f

solo /'səʊləʊ/ n (pl -os) (Mus) solo m. ~ist n solista m & f

solstice /'sɒlstɪs/ n solsticio m

solu|ble /'sɒljʊbl/ a soluble. ~tion /sə'luːʃn/ n solución f

solve /sɒlv/ vt solucionar <problem>; resolver <mystery>. ~nt /-vənt/ a & n solvente (m)

sombre /'sɒmbə(r)/ a sombrío

some /sʌm/, *unstressed form* /səm/

● *adjective*

····➤ (unspecified number) unos, unas. he ate ~ olives comió unas aceitunas

····➤ (unspecified amount) *not translated*. I have to buy ~ bread tengo que comprar pan. would you like ~ coffee? ¿quieres café?

····➤ (certain, not all) algunos, -nas. I like ~ modern writers algunos escritores modernos me gustan

····➤ (a little) algo de. I eat ~ meat, but not much como algo de carne, pero no mucho

····➤ (considerable amount of) we've known each other for ~ time ya hace tiempo que nos conocemos

····➤ (expressing admiration) that's ~ car you've got! ¡vaya coche que tienes!

● *pronoun*

····➤ (a number of things or people) algunos, -nas, unos, unas. ~ are mine and ~ aren't algunos *or* unos son míos y otros no. aren't there any apples? we bought ~ yesterday ¿no hay manzanas? compramos algunas ayer

····➤ (part of an amount) he wants ~ quiere un poco. ~ of what he said parte *or* algo de lo que dijo

····➤ (certain people) algunos, -nas . ~ say that... algunos dicen que...

● *adverb*

····➤ (approximately) unos, unas, alrededor de. there were ~ fifty people there había unas cincuenta personas, había alrededor de cincuenta personas

some: ~**body** /-bədɪ/ *pron* alguien. ~**how** *adv* de algún modo. ~**how or other** de una manera u otra. ~**one** *pron* alguien

somersault /'sʌməsɔːlt/ *n* salto *m* mortal. ● *vi* dar un salto mortal

some: ~**thing** *pron* algo *m*. ~**thing like** (approximately) alrededor de. ~**time** *a* ex. ● *adv* algún día. ~**time next week** un día de la semana que viene. ~**times** *adv* a veces. ~**where** *adv* en alguna parte, en ~gún lado

son /sʌn/ *n* hijo *m*

sonata /sə'nɑːtə/ *n* sonata *f*

song /sɒŋ/ *n* canción *f*

sonic /'sɒnɪk/ *a* sónico

son-in-law /'sʌnɪnlɔː/ *n* (*pl* **sons-in-law**) yerno *m*

sonnet /'sɒnɪt/ *n* soneto *m*

son of a bitch *n* (*pl* **sons of bitches**) (esp Amer 🗷) hijo *m* de puta

soon /suːn/ *adv* (**-er, -est**) pronto; (in a short time) dentro de poco. ~ **after** poco después. ~**er or later** tarde o temprano. **as** ~ **as** en cuanto; **as** ~ **as possible** lo antes posible. **the** ~**er the better** cuanto antes mejor

soot /sʊt/ *n* hollín *m*

sooth|e /suːð/ *vt* calmar; aliviar *<pain>*. ~**ing** *a* *<medicine>* calmante; *<words>* tranquilizador

sooty /'sʊtɪ/ *a* cubierto de hollín

sophisticated /sə'fɪstɪkeɪtɪd/ *a* sofisticado; (complex) complejo

sophomore /'sɒfəmɔː(r)/ *n* (Amer) estudiante *m & f* de segundo curso (*en la universidad*)

sopping /'sɒpɪŋ/ *a*. ~ (wet) empapado

soppy /'sɒpɪ/ *a* (**-ier, -iest**) 🗉 sentimental

soprano /sə'prɑːnəʊ/ *n* (*pl* **-os**) soprano *f*

sordid /'sɔːdɪd/ *a* sórdido

sore /sɔː(r)/ *a* (**-er, -est**) dolorido; (Amer 🗉, angry) **be** ~ **at s.o.** estar picado con uno. ~ **throat** *n* dolor *m* de garganta. **I've got a** ~ **throat** me duele la garganta. ● *n* llaga *f*.

sorrow /'sɒrəʊ/ *n* pena *f*, pesar *m*

sorry /'sɒrɪ/ *a* (**-ier, -ier**) arrepentido; (wretched) lamentable. **I'm** ~ lo siento. **be** ~ **for s.o.** (pity) compadecer a uno. **I'm** ~ **you can't come** siento que no puedas venir. **say** ~ pedir perdón. ~**!** (apologizing) ¡lo siento! ¡perdón!. ~**?** (asking s.o. to repeat) ¿cómo?

sort /sɔːt/ *n* tipo *m*, clase *f*; (🗉, person) tipo *m*. **a** ~ **of** una especie de. ● *vt* clasificar. □ ~ **out** *vt* (organize) ordenar; organizar *<finances>*; (separate out) separar; solucionar *<problem>*

so-so /'səʊsəʊ/ *a* regular

soufflé /'su:fleɪ/ n suflé m

sought /sɔ:t/ ⇒SEEK

soul /səʊl/ n alma f

sound /saʊnd/ n sonido m; (noise) ruido m. ●vt tocar. ●vi sonar; (seem) parecer (**as if** que). **it ~s interesting** suena interesante.. ●a (**-er, -est**) sano; *<argument>* lógico; (secure) seguro. ●adv. **~ asleep** profundamente dormido. **~ barrier** n barrera f del sonido. **~ly** adv sólidamente; (asleep) profundamente. **~proof** a insonorizado. **~track** n banda f sonora

soup /su:p/ n sopa f

sour /'saʊə(r)/ a (**-er, -est**) agrio; *<milk>* cortado

source /sɔ:s/ n fuente f

south /saʊθ/ n sur m. ●a sur a *invar*; *<wind>* del sur. ●adv *<go>* hacia el sur. **it's ~ of** está al sur de. **S~ Africa** n Sudáfrica f. **S~ America** n América f (del Sur), Sudamérica f. **S~ American** a & n sudamericano (m). **~-east** n sudeste m, sureste m. **~erly** /'sʌðəlɪ/ *<wind>* del sur. **~ern** /'sʌðən/ a del sur, meridional. **~erner** n sureño m. **~ward** /-wəd/, **~wards** adv hacia el sur. **~-west** n sudoeste m, suroeste m

souvenir /su:və'nɪə(r)/ n recuerdo m

sovereign /'sɒvrɪn/ n & a soberano (m)

Soviet /'səʊvɪət/ a (History) soviético. **the ~ Union** n la Unión f Soviética

sow[1] /səʊ/ vt (pt **sowed**, pp **sowed** or **sown** /səʊn/) sembrar

sow[2] /saʊ/ n cerda f

soy (esp Amer), **soya** /'sɔɪə/ n. **~ bean** n soja f

spa /spɑ:/ n balneario m

space /speɪs/ n espacio m; (room) espacio m, lugar m. ●a *<research etc>* espacial. ●vt espaciar. □ **~ out** vt espaciar. **~craft, ~ship** n nave f espacial

spacious /'speɪʃəs/ a espacioso

spade /speɪd/ n pala f. **~s** npl (Cards) picas fpl

spaghetti /spə'getɪ/ n espaguetis mpl

Spain /speɪn/ n España f

span /spæn/ n (of arch) luz f; (of time) espacio m; (of wings) envergadura f. ●vt (pt **spanned**) extenderse sobre. ●a ⇒SPICK

Spaniard /'spænjəd/ n español m

spaniel /'spænjəl/ n spaniel m

Spanish /'spænɪʃ/ a español; (Lang) castellano, español. ●n (Lang) castellano m, español m. npl. **the ~** (people) los españoles

spank /spæŋk/ vt pegarle a (*en las nalgas*)

spanner /'spænə(r)/ n llave f

spare /speə(r)/ vt. **if you can ~ the time** si tienes tiempo. **can you ~ me a pound?** ¿tienes una libra que me des? **~ no effort** no escatimar esfuerzos. **have money to ~** tener dinero de sobra. ●a (not in use) de más; (replacement) de repuesto; (free) libre. **~ (part)** n repuesto m. **~ room** n cuarto m de huéspedes. **~ time** n tiempo m libre. **~ tyre** n neumático m de repuesto

sparingly /'speərɪŋlɪ/ adv *<use>* con moderación

spark /spɑ:k/ n chispa f. ●vt provocar *<criticism>*; suscitar *<interest>*. **~ing plug** n (Auto) bujía f

sparkl|e /'spɑ:kl/ vi centellear. ●n destello m. **~ing** a centelleante; *<wine>* espumoso

spark plug n (Auto) bujía f

sparrow /'spærəʊ/ n gorrión m

sparse /spɑ:s/ a escaso. **~ly** adv escasamente

spasm /'spæzəm/ n espasmo m; (of cough) acceso m. **~odic** /-'mɒdɪk/ a espasmódico; (Med) irregular

spat /spæt/ ⇒SPIT

spate /speɪt/ n racha f

spatial /'speɪʃl/ a espacial

spatter /'spætə(r)/ vt salpicar (**with** de)

spawn /spɔ:n/ n huevas fpl. ●vt generar. ●vi desovar

speak /spi:k/ vt/i (pt **spoke**, pp **spoken**) hablar. **~ for s.o.** hablar en nombre de uno. □ **~ up** vi hablar más fuerte. **~er** n (in public) orador m; (loudspeaker) altavoz m; (of language) hablante m & f

spear /spɪə(r)/ n lanza f. ~**head** vt (lead) encabezar

special /'speʃl/ a especial. ~**ist** /'speʃəlɪst/ n especialista m & f. ~**ity** /-ɪ'ælətɪ/ n especialidad f. ~**ization** /-əlaɪ'zeɪʃn/ n especialización f. ~**ize** /-əlaɪz/ vi especializarse. ~**ized** a especializado. ~**ly** adv especialmente. ~**ty** n (Amer) especialidad f

species /'spiːʃiːz/ n especie f

specif|ic /spə'sɪfɪk/ a específico. ~**ically** adv específicamente; <state> explícitamente. ~**ication** /-ɪ'keɪʃn/ n especificación f. ~**y** /'spesɪfaɪ/ vt especificar

specimen /'spesɪmɪn/ n muestra f

speck /spek/ n (of dust) mota f; (in distance) punto m

specs /speks/ npl 🔲 ⇒SPECTACLES

spectac|le /'spektəkl/ n espectáculo m. ~**les** npl gafas fpl, lentes fpl (LAm), anteojos mpl (LAm). ~**ular** /-'tækjʊlə(r)/ a espectacular

spectator /spek'teɪtə(r)/ n espectador m

spectr|e /'spektə(r)/ n espectro m. ~**um** /'spektrəm/ n (pl -**tra** /-trə/) espectro m; (of views) gama f

speculat|e /'spekjʊleɪt/ vi especular. ~**ion** /-'leɪʃn/ n especulación f. ~**or** n especulador m

sped /sped/ ⇒SPEED

speech /spiːtʃ/ n (faculty) habla f; (address) discurso m. ~**less** a mudo

speed /spiːd/ n velocidad f; (rapidity) rapidez f. ●vi (pt **speeded**) (drive too fast) ir a exceso de velocidad. □ ~ **off**, ~ **away** (pt **sped**) vi alejarse a toda velocidad. □ ~ **by** (pt **sped**) vi <time> pasar volando. □ ~ **up** (pt **speeded**) vt acelerar. vi acelerarse. ~**boat** n lancha f motora. ~ **limit** n velocidad f máxima. ~**ometer** /spiː'dɒmɪtə(r)/ n velocímetro m. ~**way** n (Amer) autopista f. ~**y** a (-**ier**, -**iest**) rápido

spell /spel/ n (magic) hechizo m; (of weather, activity) período m. **go through a bad** ~ pasar por una mala racha. ●vt/i (pt **spelled** or **spelt**) escribir. □ ~ **out** vt deletrear; (fig) explicar. ~**ing** n ortografía f

spellbound /'spelbaʊnd/ a embelesado

spelt /spelt/ ⇒SPELL

spend /spend/ vt (pt **spent** /spent/) gastar <money>; pasar <time>; dedicar <care>. ●vi gastar dinero

sperm /spɜːm/ n (pl **sperms** or **sperm**) esperma f; (individual) espermatozoide m

spew /spjuː/ vt/i vomitar

spher|e /sfɪə(r)/ n esfera f. ~**ical** /'sferɪkl/ a esférico

spice /spaɪs/ n especia f

spick /spɪk/ a. ~ **and span** limpio y ordenado

spicy /'spaɪsɪ/ a picante

spider /'spaɪdə(r)/ n araña f

spik|e /spaɪk/ n (of metal etc) punta f. ~**y** a puntiagudo

spill /spɪl/ vt (pt **spilled** or **spilt**) derramar. ●vi derramarse. ~ **over** vi <container> desbordarse; <liquid> rebosar

spin /spɪn/ vt (pt **spun**, pres p **spinning**) hacer girar; hilar <wool>; centrifugar <washing>. ●vi girar. ●n. **give sth a** ~ hacer girar algo. **go for a** ~ (Auto) ir a dar un paseo en coche

spinach /'spɪnɪdʒ/ n espinacas fpl

spindly /'spɪndlɪ/ a larguirucho

spin-drier /spɪn'draɪə(r)/ n centrifugadora f (de ropa)

spine /spaɪn/ n columna f vertebral; (of book) lomo m; (on animal) púa f. ~**less** a (fig) sin carácter

spinning wheel /'spɪnɪŋ/ n rueca f

spin-off /'spɪnɒf/ n resultado m indirecto; (by-product) producto m derivado

spinster /'spɪnstə(r)/ n soltera f

spiral /'spaɪərəl/ a espiral; <shape> de espiral. ●n espiral f. ●vi (pt **spiralled**) <unemployment> escalar; <prices> dispararse. ~ **staircase** n escalera f de caracol

spire /'spaɪə(r)/ n aguja f

spirit /'spɪrɪt/ n espíritu m. **be in good** ~s estar animado. **in low** ~s abatido. ~**ed** a animado, fogoso. ~**s** npl (drinks) bebidas fpl alcohólicas (de *alta graduación).* ~**ual** /'spɪrɪtjʊəl/ *a* espiritual

spit /spɪt/ *vt* (*pt* **spat** *or* (Amer) **spit**, *pres p* **spitting**) escupir. ● *vi* escupir. it's ~ting caen algunas gotas. ● *n* saliva *f*; (for roasting) asador *m*

spite /spaɪt/ *n* rencor *m*. in ~ of a pesar de. ● *vt* fastidiar. ~**ful** *a* rencoroso

spittle /'spɪtl/ *n* baba *f*

splash /splæʃ/ *vt* salpicar. ● *vi* <*person*> chapotear. ● *n* salpicadura *f*. a ~ of paint un poco de pintura. □ ~ **about** *vi* chapotear. □ ~ **down** <*spacecraft*> amerizar. □ ~ **out** *vi* gastarse un dineral (**on** en)

splendid /'splendɪd/ *a* espléndido. ~**our** /-ə/ *n* esplendor *m*

splint /splɪnt/ *n* tablilla *f*

splinter /'splɪntə(r)/ *n* astilla *f*. ● *vi* astillarse

split /splɪt/ *vt* (*pt* **split**, *pres p* **splitting**) partir; fisionar <*atom*>; reventar <*trousers*>; (divide) dividir. ● *vi* partirse; (divide) dividirse. a ~ting headache un dolor de cabeza espantoso. ● *n* (in garment) descosido *m*; (in wood, glass) rajadura *f*. □ ~ **up** *vi* separarse. ~ **second** *n* fracción *f* de segundo

splutter /'splʌtə(r)/ *vi* chisporrotear; <*person*> farfullar

spoil /spɔɪl/ *vt* (*pt* **spoilt** *or* **spoiled**) estropear, echar a perder; (indulge) consentir, malcriar. ~**s** *npl* botín *m*. ~**-sport** *n* aguafiestas *m* & *f*

spoke¹ /spəʊk/ ⇒SPEAK

spoke² /spəʊk/ *n* (of wheel) rayo *m*

spoken /spəʊkən/ ⇒SPEAK

spokesman /'spəʊksmən/ *n* (*pl* **-men**) portavoz *m*

sponge /spʌndʒ/ *n* esponja *f*. ● *vt* limpiar con una esponja. ~ **off**, ~ **on** *vt* vivir a costillas de. ~ **cake** *n* bizcocho *m*

sponsor /'spɒnsə(r)/ *n* patrocinador *m*; (of the arts) mecenas *m* & *f*; (surety) garante *m*. ● *vt* patrocinar. ~**ship** *n* patrocinio *m*; (of the arts) mecenazgo *m*

spontaneous /spɒn'teɪnɪəs/ *a* espontáneo. ~**ously** *adv* espontáneamente

spoof /spuːf/ *n* 🄴 parodia *f*

spooky /'spuːkɪ/ *a* (**-ier**, **-iest**) 🄴 espeluznante

spool /spuːl/ *n* carrete *m*

spoon /spuːn/ *n* cuchara *f*. ~**ful** *n* cucharada *f*

sporadic /spə'rædɪk/ *a* esporádico

sport /spɔːt/ *n* deporte *m*. ~**s car** *n* coche *m* deportivo. ~**s centre** *n* centro *m* deportivo. ~**sman** /-mən/ *n*, (*pl* **-men**), ~**swoman** *n* deportista *m* & *f*

spot /spɒt/ *n* mancha *f*; (pimple) grano *m*; (place) lugar *m*; (in pattern) lunar *m*. be in a ~ 🄴 estar en apuros. on the ~ allí mismo; <*decide*> en ese mismo momento. ● *vt* (*pt* **spotted**) manchar; (🄴, notice) ver, divisar; descubrir <*mistake*>. ~ **check** *n* control *m* hecho al azar. ~**less** *a* <*clothes*> impecable; <*house*> limpísimo. ~**light** *n* reflector *m*; (in theatre) foco *m*. ~**ted** *a* moteado; <*material*> de lunares. ~**ty** *a* (**-ier**, **-iest**) <*skin*> lleno de granos; <*youth*> con la cara llena de granos

spouse /spaʊz/ *n* cónyuge *m* & *f*

spout /spaʊt/ *n* pico *m*; (jet) chorro *m*

sprain /spreɪn/ *vt* hacerse un esguince en. ● *n* esguince *m*

sprang /spræŋ/ ⇒SPRING

spray /spreɪ/ *n* (of flowers) ramillete *m*; (from sea) espuma *f*; (liquid in spray form) espray *m*; (device) rociador *m*. ● *vt* rociar

spread /spred/ *vt* (*pt* **spread**) (stretch, extend) extender; desplegar <*wings*>; difundir <*idea, news*>. ~ **butter on a piece of toast** untar una tostada con mantequilla. ● *vi* extenderse; <*disease*> propagarse; <*idea, news*> difundirse. ● *n* (of ideas) difusión *f*; (of disease, fire) propagación *f*; (🄴, feast) festín *m*. □ ~ **out** *vi* (move apart) desplegarse

spree /spriː/ *n*. go on a shopping ~ ir de expedición a las tiendas

sprightly /'spraɪtlɪ/ *a* (**-ier**, **-iest**) vivo

spring /sprɪŋ/ n (season) primavera f; (device) resorte m; (in mattress) muelle m, resorte m (LAm); (elasticity) elasticidad f; (water) manantial m. ● a primaveral. ● vi (pt **sprang**, pp **sprung**) saltar; (issue) brotar. ~ **from sth** <problem> provenir de algo. □ ~ **up** vi surgir. ~**board** n trampolín m. ~**clean** /-'kliːn/ vi hacer una limpieza general. ~ **onion** n cebolleta f. ~**time** n primavera f. ~**y** a (-**ier**, -**iest**) <mattress, grass> mullido

sprinkle /'sprɪŋkl/ vt salpicar; (with liquid) rociar. ● n salpicadura f; (of liquid) rociada f. ~**r** n regadera f

sprint /sprɪnt/ n carrera f corta. ● vi (Sport) esprintar; (run fast) correr. ~**er** n corredor m

sprout /spraʊt/ vi brotar. ● n brote m. (**Brussels**) ~**s** npl coles fpl de Bruselas

sprung /sprʌŋ/ ⇒SPRING

spud /spʌd/ n 🄴 patata f, papa f (LAm)

spun /spʌn/ ⇒SPIN

spur /spɜː(r)/ n espuela f; (stimulus) acicate m. **on the ~ of the moment** sin pensarlo. ● vt (pt **spurred**). ~ (**on**) espolear; (fig) estimular

spurn /spɜːn/ vt desdeñar; (reject) rechazar

spurt /spɜːt/ vi <liquid> salir a chorros. ● n chorro m; (of activity) racha f

spy /spaɪ/ n espía m & f. ● vt descubrir, ver. ● vi espiar. ~ **on s.o.** espiar a uno

squabble /'skwɒbl/ vi reñir

squad /skwɒd/ n (Mil) pelotón m; (of police) brigada f; (Sport) equipo m. ~ **car** m coche m patrulla. ~**ron** /'skwɒdrən/ n (Mil, Aviat) escuadrón m; (Naut) escuadra f

squalid /'skwɒlɪd/ a miserable

squall /skwɔːl/ n turbión m

squalor /'skwɒlə(r)/ n miseria f

squander /'skwɒndə(r)/ vt derrochar; desaprovechar <opportunity>

square /skweə(r)/ n cuadrado m; (in town) plaza f. ● a cuadrado; <meal> decente; (🄸, old-fashioned) chapado a la antigua. ● vt (settle) arreglar; (Math) elevar al cuadrado. ● vi (agree)

cuadrar. □ ~ **up**. vi arreglar cuentas (**with** con). ~**ly** adv directamente

squash /skwɒʃ/ vt aplastar; (suppress) acallar. ● n. **it was a terrible** ~ íbamos (or iban) terriblemente apretujados; (drink) **orange** ~ naranjada f; (Sport) squash m; (vegetable) calabaza f. ~**y** a blando

squat /skwɒt/ vi (pt **squatted**) ponerse en cuclillas; (occupy illegally) ocupar sin autorización. ● a rechoncho y bajo. ~**ter** n ocupante m & f ilegal, okupa m & f

squawk /skwɔːk/ n graznido m. ● vi graznar

squeak /skwiːk/ n chillido m; (of door) chirrido m. ● vi chillar; <door> chirriar; <shoes> crujir. ~**y** a chirriante

squeal /skwiːl/ n chillido m ● vi chillar

squeamish /'skwiːmɪʃ/ a impresionable, delicado

squeeze /skwiːz/ vt apretar; exprimir <lemon etc>. ● vi. ~ **in** meterse. ● n estrujón m; (of hand) apretón m

squid /skwɪd/ n calamar m

squiggle /'skwɪgl/ n garabato m

squint /skwɪnt/ vi bizquear; (trying to see) entrecerrar los ojos. ● n estrabismo m

squirm /skwɜːm/ vi retorcerse

squirrel /'skwɪrəl/ n ardilla f

squirt /skwɜːt/ vt <liquid> echar un chorro de. ● vi salir a chorros. ● n chorrito m

St /sənt/ abbr (= **saint**) /sənt/ S, San (to); (= **street**) C/, Calle f

stab /stæb/ vt (pt **stabbed**) apuñalar. ● n puñalada f; (pain) punzada f. **have a ~ at sth** intentar algo

stabili|ty /stə'bɪlətɪ/ n estabilidad f. ~**ze** /'steɪbɪlaɪz/ vt/i estabilizar

stable /'steɪbl/ a (-**er**, -**est**) estable. ● n caballeriza f, cuadra f

stack /stæk/ n montón m. ● vt. ~ (**up**) amontonar

stadium /'steɪdɪəm/ n (pl -**diums** or -**dia** /-dɪə/) estadio m

staff /stɑːf/ n (stick) palo m; (employees) personal m. **teaching** ~ personal m docente. **a member of** ~ un empleado

stag /stæg/ n ciervo m. **~-night**, **~-party** n (before wedding) fiesta f de despedida de soltero; (men-only party) fiesta f para hombres

stage /steɪdʒ/ n (in theatre) escenario f; (platform) plataforma f; (phase) etapa f. **the ~** (profession, medium) el teatro. ● vt poner en escena <play>; (arrange) organizar; (pej) orquestar. **~coach** n diligencia f

stagger /'stægə(r)/ vi tambalearse. ● vt dejar estupefacto; escalonar <holidays etc>. **~ing** a asombroso

stagna|nt /'stægnənt/ a estancado. **~te** /stæg'neɪt/ vi estancarse

staid /steɪd/ a serio, formal

stain /steɪn/ vt manchar; (colour) teñir. ● n mancha f; (dye) tintura f. **~ed glass window** n vidriera f de colores. **~less steel** n acero m inoxidable. **~ remover** n quitamanchas m

stair /steə(r)/ n escalón m. **~s** npl escalera f. **~case**, **~way** n escalera f

stake /steɪk/ n estaca f; (wager) apuesta f; (Com) intereses mpl. **be at ~** estar en juego. ● vt estacar; jugarse <reputation>. **~ a claim** reclamar

stala|ctite /'stæləktaɪt/ n estalactita f. **~gmite** /'stæləgmaɪt/ n estalagmita f

stale /steɪl/ a (-er, -est) no fresco; <bread> duro; <smell> viciado. **~mate** n (Chess) ahogado m; (deadlock) punto m muerto

stalk /stɔːk/ n tallo m. ● vt acechar. ● vi irse indignado

stall /stɔːl/ n (in stable) compartimiento m; (in market) puesto m. **~s** npl (in theatre) platea f, patio m de butacas. ● vt parar <engine>. ● vi <engine> pararse; (fig) andar con rodeos

stallion /'stæljən/ n semental m

stalwart /'stɔːlwət/ a <supporter> leal, incondicional

stamina /'stæmɪnə/ n resistencia f

stammer /'stæmə(r)/ vi tartamudear. ● n tartamudeo m

stamp /stæmp/ vt (with feet) patear; (press) estampar; (with rubber stamp) sellar; (fig) señalar. ● vi dar patadas en el suelo. ● n sello m, estampilla f

(LAm), timbre m (Mex); (on passport) sello m; (with foot) patada f; (mark) marca f, señal f. **□ ~ out** vt (fig) erradicar. **~ed addressed envelope** n sobre m franqueado con su dirección

stampede /stæm'piːd/ n estampida f. ● vi salir en estampida

stance /stɑːns/ n postura f

stand /stænd/ vi (pt **stood**) estar de pie, estar parado (LAm); (rise) ponerse de pie, pararse; (be) encontrarse; (Pol) presentarse como candidato (**for** en). **the offer ~s** la oferta sigue en pie. **~ to reason** ser lógico. ● vt (endure) soportar; (place) colocar. **~ a chance** tener una posibilidad. ● n posición f, postura f; (for lamp etc) pie m, sostén m; (at market) puesto m; (booth) quiosco m; (Sport) tribuna f. **make a ~ against** sth oponer resistencia a algo. **□ ~ back** vi apartarse. **□ ~ by** vi estar preparado. vt (support) apoyar. **□ ~ down** vi retirarse. **□ ~ for** vt significar. **□ ~ in for** vt suplir a. **□ ~ out** vi destacarse. **□ ~ up** vi ponerse de pie, pararse (LAm). **□ ~ up for** vt defender. **□ ~ up for oneself** defenderse. **□ ~ up to** vt resistir a

standard /'stændəd/ n norma f; (level) nivel m; (flag) estandarte m. ● a estándar a invar, normal. **~ize** vt estandarizar. **~ lamp** n lámpara f de pie. **~s** npl principios mpl

stand: ~-by n (at airport) stand-by m. **be on ~-by** <police> estar en estado de alerta. **~-in** n suplente m & f. **~ing** a de pie, parado (LAm); (permanent) permanente f. ● n posición f; (prestige) prestigio m. **~off** n (Amer, draw) empate m; (deadlock) callejón m sin salida. **~point** n punto m de vista. **~still** n. **be at a ~still** estar paralizado. **come to a ~still** <vehicle> parar; <city> quedar paralizado

stank /stæŋk/ ⇒STINK

staple /'steɪpl/ a principal. ● n grapa f. ● vt sujetar con una grapa. **~r** n grapadora f

star /stɑː(r)/ n (incl Cinema, Theatre) estrella f; (asterisk) asterisco m. ● vi (pt **starred**). **~ in a film** protagonizar una película. **~board** n estribor m.

starch /stɑːtʃ/ n almidón m; (in food)
fécula f. ● vt almidonar. ∼y a *‹food›*
a base de féculas

stardom /'stɑːdəm/ n estrellato m

stare /steə(r)/ n mirada f fija. ● vi. ∼
(at) mirar fijamente

starfish /'stɑːfɪʃ/ n estrella f de mar

stark /stɑːk/ a (-er, -est) escueto.
● adv completamente

starling /'stɑːlɪŋ/ n estornino m

starry /'stɑːrɪ/ a estrellado

start /stɑːt/ vt empezar, comenzar;
encender *‹engine›*; arrancar *‹car›*;
(cause) provocar; abrir *‹business›*.
● vi empezar; *‹car etc›* arrancar;
(jump) dar un respingo. to ∼ with (as
linker) para empezar. ∼ off by doing
sth empezar por hacer algo. ● n
principio m; (Sport) ventaja f; (jump)
susto m. make an early ∼ (on journey)
salir temprano. ∼er n (Auto) motor
m de arranque; (Culin) primer plato
m. ∼ing-point n punto m de partida

startle /'stɑːtl/ vt asustar

starv|ation /stɑː'veɪʃn/ n hambre f,
inanición f. ∼e /stɑːv/ vt hacer morir de hambre. ● vi morirse de
hambre. I'm ∼ing me muero de
hambre

state /steɪt/ n estado m. be in a ∼
estar agitado. the S∼ los Estados
mpl Unidos. ● vt declarar; expresar
‹views›; (fix) fijar. ● a del Estado;
(Schol) público; (with ceremony) de gala.
∼ly a (-ier, -iest) majestuoso. ∼ly
home n casa f solariega. ∼ment n
declaración f; (account) informe m.
∼sman /-mən/ n estadista m

static /'stætɪk/ a estacionario. ● n
(interference) estática f

station /'steɪʃn/ n estación f; (on
radio) emisora f; (TV) canal m. ● vt colocar; (Mil) estacionar. ∼ary a estacionario. ∼er's (shop) n papelería
f. ∼ery n artículos mpl de papelería.
∼ wagon n (Amer) ranchera f, (coche m) familiar m, camioneta f (LAm)

statistic /stə'tɪstɪk/ n estadística f.
∼al a estadístico. ∼s n (science)
estadística f

statue /'stætʃuː/ n estatua f

stature /'stætʃə(r)/ n talla f, estatura f

status /'steɪtəs/ n posición f social;
(prestige) categoría f; (Jurid) estado m

statut|e /'stætʃuːt/ n estatuto m.
∼ory /-ʊtrɪ/ a estatutario

staunch /stɔːnʃ/ a (-er, -est) leal

stave /steɪv/ n (Mus) pentagrama m.
□ ∼ off vt evitar

stay /steɪ/ n (of time) estancia f, estadía f (LAm); (Jurid) suspensión f. ● vi
quedarse; (reside) alojarse. ∼ing
in a hotel estoy en un hotel. □ ∼ in vi
quedarse en casa. □ ∼ up vi quedarse levantado

stead /sted/ n. in s.o.'s ∼ en lugar
de uno. stand s.o. in good ∼ re-
sultarle muy útil a uno. ∼ily adv
firmemente; (regularly) regularmente.
∼y a (-ier, -iest) firme; (regular) regular; *‹flow›* continuo; *‹worker›* serio

steak /steɪk/ n. a ∼ un filete. some
∼ carne para guisar

steal /stiːl/ vt (pt stole, pp stolen)
robar. ∼ in vi entrar a hurtadillas

stealth /stelθ/ n. by ∼ sigilo-
samente. ∼y a sigiloso

steam /stiːm/ n vapor m. let off ∼
(fig) desahogarse. ● vt (cook) cocer al
vapor. ● vi echar vapor. □ ∼ up vi
empañarse. ∼ engine n máquina f
de vapor. ∼er n (ship) barco m de vapor. ∼roller n apisonadora f. ∼y a
lleno de vapor

steel /stiːl/ n acero m. ● vt. ∼ o.s.
armarse de valor. ∼ industry n
industria f siderúrgica

steep /stiːp/ ● a (-er, -est) empi-
nado; *‹increase›* considerable;
‹price› 🔢 excesivo

steeple /'stiːpl/ n aguja f, campanario m

steeply /'stiːplɪ/ adv abruptamente;
‹increase› considerablemente

steer /stɪə(r)/ vt dirigir; gobernar
‹ship›. ● vi (in ship) estar al timón. ∼
clear of evitar. ∼ing n (Auto) dirección f. ∼ing wheel n volante m

stem /stem/ n (of plant) tallo m; (of
glass) pie m; (of word) raíz f. ● vt (pt
stemmed) contener *‹bleeding›*.
● vi. ∼ from provenir de

stench /stentʃ/ n hedor m

stencil /'stensl/ n plantilla f

stenographer /ste'nɒɡrəfə(r)/ n estenógrafo m

step /step/ vi (pt **stepped**). ~ in sth pisar algo. □ ~ **aside** vi hacerse a un lado. □ ~ **down** vi retirarse. □ ~ **in** vi (fig) intervenir. □ ~ **up** vt intensificar; redoblar <security>. ● n paso m; (stair) escalón m; (fig) medida f. **take** ~**s** tomar medidas. **be in** ~ llevar el paso. **be out of** ~ no llevar el paso. ~**brother** n hermanastro m. ~**daughter** n hijastra f. ~**father** n padrastro m. ~**ladder** n escalera f de tijera. ~**mother** n madrastra f. ~**ping-stone** n peldaño m. ~**sister** n hermanastra f. ~**son** n hijastro m

stereo /'steriəʊ/ n (pl **-os** estéreo m. ● a estéreo a invar. ~**type** n estereotipo m

steril|e /'sterail/ a estéril. ~**ize** /'sterilaiz/ vt esterilizar

sterling /'stɜːlɪŋ/ n libras fpl esterlinas. ● a <pound> esterlina

stern /stɜːn/ n (of boat) popa f. ● a (**-er, -est**) severo

stethoscope /'steθəskəʊp/ n estetoscopio m

stew /stjuː/ vt/i guisar. ● n estofado m, guiso m

steward /'stjuːəd/ n administrador m; (on ship) camarero m; (air steward) sobrecargo m, aeromozo m (LAm). ~**ess** /-'des/ n camarera f; (on aircraft) auxiliar f de vuelo, azafata f

stick /stɪk/ n palo m; (for walking) bastón m; (of celery etc) tallo m. ● vt (pt **stuck**) (glue) pegar; (🆗, put) po-ner; (thrust) clavar; (🆗, endure) so-portar. ● vi pegarse; (jam) atascarse. ~ **out** vi sobresalir. □ ~ **to** vt ce-ñirse a. □ ~ **up for** vt 🆗 defender. ~**er** n pegatina f. ~**ing plaster** n esparadrapo m; (individual) tirita f, cu-rita f (LAm). ~**ler** /'stɪklə(r)/ n. **be a** ~**ler for** insistir en. ~**y** /'stɪkɪ/ a (**-ier, -iest**) <surface> pegajoso; <label> engomado

stiff /stɪf/ a (**-er, -est**) rígido; <joint, fabric> tieso; <muscle> entumecido; (difficult) difícil; <manner> estirado; <drink> fuerte. **have a** ~ **neck** tener tortícolis. ~**en** vi (become rigid) agarrotarse; (become firm) endurecerse. ~**ly** adv rígidamente.

stifl|e /'staifl/ vt sofocar. ~**ing** a sofocante

stiletto (heel) /stɪ'letəʊ/ n (pl **-os**) tacón m de aguja

still /stɪl/ a inmóvil; (peaceful) tranquilo; <drink> sin gas. **sit** ~, **stand** ~ quedarse tranquilo. ● adv todavía, aún; (nevertheless) sin embargo. ~**born** a nacido muerto. ~ **life** n (pl **-s**) bodegón m. ~**ness** n tranquilidad f

stilted /'stɪltɪd/ a rebuscado; <conversation> forzado

stilts /stɪlts/ npl zancos mpl

stimul|ant /'stɪmjʊlənt/ n estimulante m. ~**ate** /-leit/ vt estimular. ~**ation** /-'leiʃn/ n estímulo m. ~**us** /-əs/ n (pl **-li** /-lai/) estímulo m

sting /stɪŋ/ n picadura f; (organ) aguijón m. ● vt/i (pt **stung**) picar

stingy /'stɪndʒɪ/ a (**-ier, -iest**) tacaño

stink /stɪŋk/ n hedor m. ● vi (pt **stank** or **stunk**, pp **stunk**) apestar, oler mal

stipulat|e /'stɪpjʊleit/ vt/i estipular. ~**ion** /-'leiʃn/ n estipulación f

stir /stɜː(r)/ vt (pt **stirred**) remover, revolver; (move) agitar; estimular <imagination>. ● vi moverse. ~ **up trouble** armar lío 🆗. ● n revuelo m, conmoción f

stirrup /'stɪrəp/ n estribo m

stitch /stɪtʃ/ n (in sewing) puntada f; (in knitting) punto m; (pain) dolor m costado. **be in** ~**es** 🆗 desternillarse de risa. ● vt coser

stock /stɒk/ n (Com, supplies) existencias fpl; (Com, variety) surtido m; (livestock) ganado m; (Culin) caldo m. ~**s and shares**, ~**s and bonds** (Amer) acciones fpl. **out of** ~ agotado. **take** ~ **of sth** (fig) hacer un balance de algo. ● a estándar a invar; (fig) trillado. ● vt surtir, abastecer (**with** de). □ ~ **up** vi abastecerse (**with** de). ~**broker** /-brəʊkə(r)/ n corredor m de bolsa. **S**~ **Exchange** n bolsa f. ~**ing** n media f. ~**pile** n reservas *fpl.* ● *vt* almacenar. **~-still** *a* inmóvil. **~-taking** *n* (Com) inventario *m*. **~y** *a* (**-ier, -iest**) bajo y fornido

stodgy /'stɒdʒɪ/ (**-dgier, -dgiest**) *a* pesado

stoke /stəʊk/ *vt* echarle carbón (*or* leña) a

stole /stəʊl/ ⇒STEAL

stolen /'stəʊlən/ ⇒STEAL

stomach /'stʌmək/ *n* estómago *m*. ● *vt* soportar. **~-ache** *n* dolor *m* de estómago

ston|e /stəʊn/ *n* piedra *f*; (in fruit) hueso *m*; (weight, *pl* **stone**) *unidad de peso equivalente a 14 libras o 6,35 kg*. ● *a* de piedra. ● *vt* apedrear. **~e-deaf** *a* sordo como una tapia. **~y** *a* <*silence*> sepulcral

stood /stʊd/ ⇒STAND

stool /stuːl/ *n* taburete *m*

stoop /stuːp/ *vi* agacharse; (fig) rebajarse. ● *n.* **have a ~** ser cargado de espaldas

stop /stɒp/ *vt* (*pt* **stopped**) (halt, switch off) parar; (cease) terminar; (prevent) impedir; (interrupt) interrumpir. **~ doing sth** dejar de hacer algo. **~ it!** ¡basta ya! ● *vi* <*bus*> parar, detenerse; <*clock*> pararse. **it's ~ped raining** ha dejado de llover. ● *n* (bus etc) parada *f*; (break on journey) parada *f*. **put a ~ to sth** poner fin a algo. **come to a ~** detenerse. **~gap** *n* remedio *m* provisional. **~over** *n* escala *f*. **~page** /'stɒpɪdʒ/ *n* suspensión *f*, paradero *m* (LAm); (of work) huelga *f*, paro *m* (LAm); (interruption) interrupción *f*. **~per** *n* tapón *m*. **~watch** *n* cronómetro *m*

storage /'stɔːrɪdʒ/ *n* almacenamiento *m*

store /stɔː(r)/ *n* provisión *f*; (depot) almacén *m*; (Amer, shop) tienda *f*; (fig) reserva *f*. **in ~** en reserva. ● *vt* (for future) poner en reserva; (in warehouse) almacenar. □ **~ up** *vt* (fig) ir acumulando. **~keeper** *n* (Amer) tendero *m*, comerciante *m & f*. **~room** *n* almacén *m*; (for food) despensa *f*

storey /'stɔːrɪ/ *n* (*pl* **-eys**) piso *m*, planta *f*

stork /stɔːk/ *n* cigüeña *f*

storm /stɔːm/ *n* tempestad *f*. ● *vi* rabiar. ● *vt* (Mil) asaltar. **~y** *a* tormentoso; <*sea, relationship*> tempestuoso

story /'stɔːrɪ/ *n* historia *f*; (in newspaper) artículo *m*; (rumour) rumor *m*; (🆃, lie) mentira *f*, cuento *m*. **~-teller** *n* cuentista *m & f*

stout /staʊt/ *a* (**-er, -est**) robusto, corpulento. ● *n* cerveza *f* negra

stove /stəʊv/ *n* estufa *f*

stow /stəʊ/ *vt* guardar; (hide) esconder. □ **~ away** *vi* viajar de polizón. **~away** *n* polizón *m & f*

straggl|e /'strægl/ *vi* rezagarse. **~y** *a* desordenado

straight /streɪt/ *a* (**-er, -est**) recto; (tidy) en orden; (frank) franco; <*hair*> lacio; (🆃, conventional) convencional. **be ~** estar derecho. ● *adv* <*sit up*> derecho; (direct) directamente; (without delay) inmediatamente. **~ away** en seguida, inmediatamente. **~ on** todo recto. **~ out** sin rodeos. ● *n* recta *f*. **~en** *vt* enderezar. □ **~en up** *vt* ordenar. **~forward** /-'fɔːwəd/ *a* franco; (easy) sencillo

strain /streɪn/ *n* (tension) tensión *f*; (injury) torcedura *f*. ● *vt* forzar <*voice, eyesight*>; someter a demasiada tensión <*relations*>; (sieve) colar. **~ one's back** hacerse daño en la espalda. **~ a muscle** hacerse un esguince. **~ed** *a* forzado; <*relations*> tirante. **~er** *n* colador *m*. **~s** *npl* (Mus) acordes *mpl*

strait /streɪt/ *n* estrecho *m*. **be in dire ~s** estar en grandes apuros. **~jacket** *n* camisa *f* de fuerza

strand /strænd/ *n* (thread) hebra *f*. **a ~ of hair** un pelo. ● *vt.* **be ~ed** <*ship*> quedar encallado. **I was left ~ed** me abandonaron a mi suerte

strange /streɪndʒ/ *a* (**-er, -est**) raro, extraño; (not known) desconocido. **~ly** *adv* de una manera rara. **~ly enough** aunque parezca mentira. **~r** *n* desconocido *m*; (from another place) forastero

strangle /'stræŋgl/ *vt* estrangular

strap /stræp/ *n* correa *f*; (of garment) tirante *m*. ● *vt* (*pt* **strapped**) atar con una correa

strat|egic /strə'ti:dʒɪk/ *a* estratégico. **~egy** /'strætədʒɪ/ *n* estrategia *f*

straw /strɔ:/ *n* paja *f*; (drinking ~) pajita *f*, paja *f*, popote *m* (Mex). **the last ~** el colmo. **~berry** /-bərɪ/ *n* fresa *f*; (large) fresón *m*

stray /streɪ/ *vi* (wander away) apartarse; (get lost) extraviarse; (deviate) desviarse (**from** de). ● *a* *<animal>* (without owner) callejero; (lost) perdido. ● *n* (without owner) perro *m*/gato *m* callejero; (lost) perro *m*/gato *m* perdido

streak /stri:k/ *n* lista *f*, raya *f*; (in hair) reflejo *m*; (in personality) veta *f*

stream /stri:m/ *n* arroyo *m*; (current) corriente *f*. **a ~ of abuse** una sarta de insultos. ● *vi* correr. □ **~ out** *vi* *<people>* salir en tropel. **~er** *n* (paper) serpentina *f*; (banner) banderín *m*. **~line** *vt* dar línea aerodinámica a; (simplify) racionalizar. **~lined** *a* aerodinámico

street /stri:t/ *n* calle *f*. **~car** *n* (Amer) tranvía *m*. **~ lamp** *n* farol *m*. **~ map**, **~ plan** *n* plano *m*

strength /streŋθ/ *n* fuerza *f*; (of wall etc) solidez *f*. **~en** *vt* reforzar *<wall>*; fortalecer *<muscle>*

strenuous /'strenjʊəs/ *a* enérgico; (arduous) arduo; (tiring) fatigoso

stress /stres/ *n* énfasis *f*; (Gram) acento *m*; (Mec, Med, tension) tensión *f*. ● *vt* insistir en

stretch /stretʃ/ *vt* estirar; (extend) extender; forzar *<truth>*; estirar *<resources>*. ● *vi* estirarse; (when sleepy) desperezarse; (extend) extenderse; (be elastic) estirarse. ● *n* (period) período *m*; (of road) tramo *m*. **at a ~** sin parar. □ **~ out** *vi* *<person>* tenderse. **~er** *n* camilla *f*

strict /strɪkt/ *a* (**-er, -est**) estricto; *<secrecy>* absoluto. **~ly** *adv* con severidad; *<rigorously>* terminantemente. **~ly speaking** en rigor

stridden /strɪdn/ ⇒STRIDE

stride /straɪd/ *vi* (*pt* **strode**, *pp* **stridden**) andar a zancadas. ● *n* zancada *f*. **take sth in one's ~** tomarse algo con calma. **~nt** /'straɪdnt/ *a* estridente

strife /straɪf/ *n* conflicto *m*

strike /straɪk/ *vt* (*pt* **struck**) golpear; encender *<match>*; encontrar *<gold, oil>*; *<clock>* dar. **it ~s me as odd** me parece raro. ● *vi* golpear; (go on strike) declararse en huelga; (be on strike) estar en huelga; (attack) atacar; *<clock>* dar la hora. ● *n* (of workers) huelga *f*, paro *m*; (attack) ataque *m*. **come out on ~** ir a la huelga. □ **~ off**, **~ out** *vt* tachar. **~ up a friendship** trabar amistad. **~r** *n* huelguista *m & f*; (Sport) artillero *m*

striking /'straɪkɪŋ/ *a* *<resemblance>* sorprendente; *<colour>* llamativo

string /strɪŋ/ *n* cordel *m*, mecate *m* (Mex); (Mus) cuerda *f*; (of lies, pearls) sarta *f*; (of people) sucesión *f*. □ **~ along** *vt* 🄚 engañar

stringent /'strɪndʒənt/ *a* riguroso

strip /strɪp/ *vt* (*pt* **stripped**) desnudar *<person>*; deshacer *<bed>*. ● *vi* desnudarse. ● *n* tira *f*; (of land) franja *f*. **~ cartoon** *n* historieta *f*

stripe /straɪp/ *n* raya *f*. **~d** *a* a rayas, rayado

strip lighting *n* luz *f* fluorescente

strive /straɪv/ *vi* (*pt* **strove**, *pp* **striven**). **~ to** esforzarse por

strode /strəʊd/ ⇒STRIDE

stroke /strəʊk/ *n* golpe *m*; (in swimming) brazada *f*; (Med) ataque *m* de apoplejía; (of pen etc) trazo *m*; (of clock) campanada *f*; (caress) caricia *f*. **a ~ of luck** un golpe de suerte. ● *vt* acariciar

stroll /strəʊl/ *vi* pasearse. ● *n* paseo *m*. **~er** *n* (Amer) sillita *f* de paseo, cochecito *m*

strong /strɒŋ/ *a* (**-er, -est**) fuerte. **~hold** *n* fortaleza *f*; (fig) baluarte *m*. **~ly** *adv* (greatly) fuertemente; *<protest>* enérgicamente; (deeply) profundamente. **~room** *n* cámara *f* acorazada

strove /strəʊv/ ⇒STRIVE

struck /strʌk/ ⇒STRIKE

structur|al /'strʌktʃərəl/ *a* estructural. **~e** /'strʌktʃə(r)/ *n* estructura *f*

struggle /'strʌgl/ *vi* luchar; (thrash around) forcejear. ● *n* lucha *f*

strum /strʌm/ *vt* (*pt* **strummed**) rasguear

strung /strʌŋ/ ⇒STRING

strut /strʌt/ n (in building) puntal m. ● vi (pt **strutted**) pavonearse

stub /stʌb/ n (of pencil, candle) cabo m; (counterfoil) talón m; (of cigarette) colilla. □~ **out** (pt **stubbed**) vt apagar

stubble /'stʌbl/ n rastrojo m; (beard) barba f de varios días

stubborn /'stʌbən/ a terco

stuck /stʌk/ ⇒STICK. ● a. the drawer is ~ el cajón se ha atascado. the door is ~ la puerta se ha atrancado. ~-**up** a 🔟 estirado

stud /stʌd/ n tachuela f; (for collar) gemelo m.

student /'stju:dənt/ n estudiante m & f; (at school) alumno m. ~ **driver** n (Amer) persona que está aprendiendo a conducir

studio /'stju:dɪəʊ/ n (pl -os) estudio m. ~ **apartment**, ~ **flat** n estudio m

studious /'stju:dɪəs/ a estudioso

study /'stʌdɪ/ n estudio m. ● vt/i estudiar

stuff /stʌf/ n 🔟 cosas fpl. what's this ~ called? ¿cómo se llama esta cosa?. ● vt rellenar; disecar <animal>; (cram) atiborrar; (put) meter de prisa. ~ o.s. 🔟 darse un atracón. ~ing n relleno m. ~y a (-ier, -iest) mal ventilado; (old-fashioned) acartonado. it's ~y in here está muy cargado el ambiente

stumble /'stʌmbl/ vi tropezar. ~e **across**, ~e **on** vt dar con. ~ing-**block** n tropiezo m, impedimento m

stump /stʌmp/ n (of limb) muñón m; (of tree) tocón m

stun /stʌn/ vt (pt **stunned**) (daze) aturdir; (bewilder) dejar atónito. ~ning a sensacional

stung /stʌŋ/ ⇒STING

stunk /stʌŋk/ ⇒STINK

stunt /stʌnt/ n 🔟 ardid m publicitario. ● vt detener, atrofiar. ~ed a (growth) atrofiado; (body) raquítico. ~man n especialista m. ~woman n especialista f

stupendous /stju:'pendəs/ a estupendo

stupid /'stju:pɪd/ a (foolish) tonto; (un-

intelligent) estúpido. ~ity /-'pɪdətɪ/ n estupidez f. ~ly adv estúpidamente

stupor /'stju:pə(r)/ n estupor m

sturdy /'stɜːdɪ/ a (-ier, -iest) robusto

stutter /'stʌtə(r)/ vi tartamudear. ● n tartamudeo m

sty /staɪ/ n (pl **sties**) pocilga f; (Med) orzuelo m

styl|e /staɪl/ n estilo m; (fashion) moda f; (design, type) diseño m. in ~ a lo grande. ~ vt diseñar. ~ish a elegante. ~ist n estilista m & f. **hair** ~ist estilista m & f

stylus /'staɪləs/ n (pl -**uses**) aguja f (de tocadiscos)

suave /swɑːv/ a elegante y desenvuelto

subconscious /sʌb'kɒnʃəs/ a & n subconsciente (m)

subdivide /sʌbdɪ'vaɪd/ vt subdividir

subdued /səb'dju:d/ a apagado

subject /'sʌbdʒɪkt/ a sometido. ~ to sujeto a. ● n (theme) tema m; (Schol) asignatura f, materia f (LAm); (Gram) sujeto m; (Pol) súbdito m. ● /səb'dʒekt/ vt someter. ~ive /səb'dʒektɪv/ a subjetivo

subjunctive /səb'dʒʌŋktɪv/ a & n subjuntivo (m)

sublime /sə'blaɪm/ a sublime

submarine /sʌbmə'ri:n/ n submarino m

submerge /səb'mɜːdʒ/ vt sumergir. ● vi sumergirse

submi|ssion /səb'mɪʃn/ n sumisión f. ~t /səb'mɪt/ vt (pt sub-**mitted**) (subject) someter; presentar <application>. ● vi rendirse

subordinate /sə'bɔːdɪnət/ a & n subordinado (m). ● /sə'bɔːdɪneɪt/ vt subordinar

subscri|be /səb'skraɪb/ vi suscribir. ~be to suscribirse a <magazine>. ~ber n suscriptor m. ~ption /-rɪpʃn/ n (to magazine) suscripción f

subsequent /'sʌbsɪkwənt/ a posterior, subsiguiente. ~ly adv posteriormente

subside /səb'saɪd/ vi <land> hundirse; <flood> bajar; <storm, wind>

amainar. **~nce** /'sʌbsɪdəns/ *n* hundimiento *m*

subsidiary /səb'sɪdɪərɪ/ *a* secundario; <*subject*> complementario. ●*n* (Com) filial

subsid|ize /'sʌbsɪdaɪz/ *vt* subvencionar, subsidiar (LAm). **~y** /'sʌbsədɪ/ *n* subvención *f*, subsidio *m*

substance /'sʌbstəns/ *n* sustancia *f*

substandard /sʌb'stændəd/ *a* de calidad inferior

substantial /səb'stænʃl/ *a* (sturdy) sólido; <*meal*> sustancioso; (considerable) considerable

substitut|e /'sʌbstɪtjuːt/ *n* (person) substituto *m*; (thing) sucedáneo *m*. ●*vt/i* sustituir. **~ion** /-'tjuːʃn/ *n* sustitución *f*

subterranean /sʌbtə'reɪnjən/ *a* subterráneo

subtitle /'sʌbtaɪtl/ *n* subtítulo *m*

subtle /'sʌtl/ *a* (**-er, -est**) sutil; (tactful) discreto. **~ty** *n* sutileza *f*

subtract /səb'trækt/ *vt* restar. **~ion** /-ʃn/ *n* resta *f*

suburb /'sʌbɜːb/ *n* barrio *m* residencial de las afueras, colonia *f*. **the ~s** las afueras *fpl*. **~an** /sə'bɜːbən/ *a* suburbano. **~ia** /sə'bɜːbɪə/ *n zonas residenciales de las afueras de una ciudad*

subversive /səb'vɜːsɪv/ *a* subversivo

subway /'sʌbweɪ/ *n* paso *m* subterráneo; (Amer) metro *m*

succeed /sək'siːd/ *vi* <*plan*> dar resultado; <*person*> tener éxito. **~ in doing** lograr hacer. ●*vt* suceder

success /sək'ses/ *n* éxito *m*. **~ful** *a* <*person*> de éxito, exitoso (LAm). **the ~ful applicant** el candidato que obtenga el puesto. **~fully** *a* satisfactoriamente. **~ion** /-ʃn/ *n* sucesión *f*. **for 3 years in ~ion** durante tres años consecutivos. **in rapid ~ion** uno tras otro. **~ive** *a* sucesivo. **~or** *n* sucesor *m*

succulent /'sʌkjʊlənt/ *a* suculento

succumb /sə'kʌm/ *vi* sucumbir

such /sʌtʃ/ *a* tal (+ *noun*), tan (+ *adj*). **~ a big house** una casa tan grande. ●*pron* tal. **~ and ~** tal o

cual. **~ as** como. **~ as it is** tal como es

suck /sʌk/ *vt* chupar <*sweet, thumb*>; sorber <*liquid*>. □ **~ up** *vt* <*vacuum cleaner*> aspirar; <*pump*> succionar. □ **~ up to** *vt* Ⓔ dar coba a. **~er** *n* (plant) chupón *m*; (Ⓔ, person) imbécil *m*

suckle /'sʌkl/ *vt* amamantar

suction /'sʌkʃn/ *n* succión *f*

sudden /'sʌdn/ *a* repentino. **all of a ~** de repente. **~ly** *adv* de repente

suds /sʌdz/ *npl* espuma *f* de jabón

sue /suː/ *vt* (*pres p* **suing**) demandar (**for** por)

suede /sweɪd/ *n* ante *m*

suet /'suːɪt/ *n* sebo *m*

suffer /'sʌfə(r)/ *vt* sufrir; (tolerate) aguantar. ●*vi* sufrir; (be affected) resentirse

suffic|e /sə'faɪs/ *vi* bastar. **~ient** /sə'fɪʃnt/ *a* suficiente, bastante. **~iently** *adv* (lo) suficientemente

suffix /'sʌfɪks/ *n* (*pl* **-ixes**) sufijo *m*

suffocat|e /'sʌfəkeɪt/ *vt* asfixiar. ●*vi* asfixiarse. **~ion** /-'keɪʃn/ *n* asfixia *f*

sugar /'ʃʊgə(r)/ *n* azúcar *m* & *f*. **~ bowl** *n* azucarero *m*. **~y** *a* azucarado.

suggest /sə'dʒest/ *vt* sugerir. **~ion** /-tʃən/ *n* sugerencia *f*

suicid|al /suːɪ'saɪdl/ *a* suicida. **~e** /'suːɪsaɪd/ *n* suicidio *m*. **commit ~e** suicidarse

suit /suːt/ *n* traje *m*; (woman's) traje *m* de chaqueta; (Cards) palo *m*; (Jurid) pleito *m*. ●*vt* venirle bien a, convenirle a; <*clothes*> quedarle bien a; (adapt) adaptar. **be ~ed to** <*thing*> ser apropiado para. **I'm not ~ed to this kind of work** no sirvo para este tipo de trabajo. **~able** *a* apropiado, adecuado. **~ably** *adv* <*dressed*> apropiadamente; <*qualified*> adecuadamente. **~case** *n* maleta *f*, valija *f* (LAm)

suite /swiːt/ *n* (of furniture) juego *m*; (of rooms) suite *f*

sulk /sʌlk/ *vi* enfurruñarse

sullen /'sʌlən/ *a* hosco

sulphur /'sʌlfə(r)/ n azufre m. ∼**ic acid** /sʌl'fjʊərɪk/ n ácido m sulfúrico

sultan /'sʌltən/ n sultán m

sultana /sʌl'tɑ:nə/ n pasa f de Esmirna

sultry /'sʌltrɪ/ a (**-ier, -iest**) <weather> bochornoso; (fig) sensual

sum /sʌm/ n (of money) suma f, cantidad f; (Math) suma f. ● □ ∼ **up** (pt **summed**) vt resumir. ● vi recapitular

summar|ily /'sʌmərɪlɪ/ adv sumariamente. ∼**ize** vt resumir. ∼**y** n resumen m

summer /'sʌmə(r)/ n verano m. ∼ **camp** n (in US) colonia f de vacaciones. ∼**time** n verano m. ∼**y** a veraniego

summit /'sʌmɪt/ n (of mountain) cumbre f. ∼ **conference** n conferencia f cumbre

summon /'sʌmən/ vt llamar; convocar <meeting, s.o. to meeting>; (Jurid) citar. □ ∼ **up** vt armarse de. ∼**s** n (Jurid) citación f. ● vt citar

sumptuous /'sʌmptjʊəs/ a suntuoso

sun /sʌn/ n sol m. ∼**bathe** vi tomar el sol, asolearse (LAm). ∼**beam** n rayo m de sol. ∼**burn** n quemadura f de sol. ∼**burnt** a quemado por el sol

Sunday /'sʌndeɪ/ n domingo m

sunflower /'sʌnflaʊə(r)/ n girasol m

sung /sʌŋ/ ⇒SING

sunglasses /'sʌnglɑ:sɪz/ npl gafas fpl de sol, lentes mpl de sol (LAm)

sunk /sʌŋk/ ⇒SINK. ∼**en** /'sʌŋkən/ ● a hundido

sun: ∼**light** n luz f del sol. ∼**ny** a (**-ier, -iest**) <day> de sol; (place) soleado. **it is** ∼**ny** hace sol. ∼**rise** n. at ∼**rise** al amanecer. salida f del sol. ∼**roof** n techo m corredizo. ∼**set** n puesta f del sol. ∼**shine** n sol m. ∼**stroke** n insolación f. ∼**tan** n bronceado m. **get a** ∼**tan** broncearse. ∼**tan lotion** n bronceador m

super /'su:pə(r)/ a 🖪 genial, super a invar

superb /su:'pɜ:b/ a espléndido

supercilious /su:pə'sɪlɪəs/ a desdeñoso

superficial /su:pə'fɪʃl/ a superficial

superfluous /su:'pɜ:flʊəs/ a superfluo

superhighway /'su:pəhaɪweɪ/ n (Amer, Auto) autopista f; (Comp) **information** ∼ autopista f de la comunicación

superhuman /su:pə'hju:mən/ a sobrehumano

superintendent /su:pərɪn'tendənt/ n director m; (Amer, of building) portero m; (of police) comisario m; (in US) superintendente m & f

superior /su:'pɪərɪə(r)/ a & n superior (m). ∼**ity** /-'ɒrətɪ/ n superioridad f

superlative /su:'pɜ:lətɪv/ a inigualable. ● n superlativo m

supermarket /'su:pəmɑ:kɪt/ n supermercado m

supernatural /su:pə'nætʃrəl/ a sobrenatural

superpower /'su:pəpaʊə(r)/ n superpotencia f

supersede /su:pə'si:d/ vt reemplazar, sustituir

supersonic /su:pə'sɒnɪk/ a supersónico

superstitio|n /su:pə'stɪʃn/ n superstición f. ∼**us** a /-əs/ supersticioso

supervis|e /'su:pəvaɪz/ vt supervisar. ∼**ion** /-'vɪʒn/ n supervisión f. ∼**or** n supervisor m

supper /'sʌpə(r)/ n cena f (ligera), comida f (ligera) (LAm)

supple /sʌpl/ a flexible

supplement /'sʌplɪmənt/ n suplemento m; (to diet, income) complemento m. ● vt complementar <diet, income>. ∼**ary** /-'mentərɪ/ a suplementario

suppl|ier /sə'plaɪə(r)/ n (Com) proveedor m. ∼**y** /sə'plaɪ/ vt suministrar; proporcionar <information>. ∼**y s.o. with sth** <equipment> proveer a uno de algo; (in business) abastecer a uno de algo. ● n ministro m. ∼**y and demand**

oferta f y demanda. ~ies npl provisiones mpl, víveres mpl; (Mil) pertrechos mpl. **office** ~ies artículos mpl de oficina

support /sə'pɔːt/ vt (hold up) sostener; (back) apoyar; mantener <family>. ● n apoyo m; (Tec) soporte m. ~er n partidario m; (Sport) hincha m & f

suppos|e /sə'pəuz/ vt suponer, imaginarse; (think) creer. **I'm ~ed to start work at nine** se supone que tengo que empezar a trabajar a las nueve. ~**edly** adv supuestamente. ~**ition** /sʌpə'zɪʃn/ n suposición f

suppress /sə'pres/ vt reprimir <feelings>; sofocar <rebellion>. ~**ion** /-ʃn/n represión f

suprem|acy /su:'preməsɪ/ n supremacía f. ~**e** /su:'priːm/ a supremo

sure /ʃuə(r)/ a (-er, -est) seguro. **make ~ that** asegurarse de que. ● adv ¡claro!. ~**ly** adv (undoubtedly) seguramente; (gladly) desde luego. ~**ly you don't believe that!** ¡no te creerás eso! ~**ty** /-ətɪ/ n garantía f

surf /sɜːf/ n oleaje m; (foam) espuma f. ● vi hacer surf. ● vt (Comp) surfear, navegar

surface /'sɜːfɪs/ n superficie f. ● a superficial. ● vt recubrir (**with** de). ● vi salir a la superficie; <problems> aflorar

surfboard /'sɜːfbɔːd/ n tabla f de surf

surfeit /'sɜːfɪt/ n exceso m

surf: ~**er** n surfista m & f ~**ing** n surf m

surge /sɜːdʒ/ vi <crowd> moverse en tropel; <sea> hincharse. ● n oleada f; (in demand, sales) aumento m

surg|eon /'sɜːdʒən/ n cirujano m. ~**ery** n cirugía f; (consulting room) consultorio m; (consulting hours) consulta f. ~**ical** a quirúrgico

surly /'sɜːlɪ/ a (-ier, -iest) hosco

surmise /sə'maɪz/ vt conjeturar

surmount /sə'maunt/ vt superar

surname /'sɜːneɪm/ n apellido m

surpass /sə'pɑːs/ vt superar

surplus /'sɜːpləs/ a & n excedente (m)

surpris|e /sə'praɪz/ n sorpresa f. ● vt sorprender. ~**ed** a sorprendido.

~**ing** a sorprendente. ~**ingly** adv sorprendentemente

surrender /sə'rendə(r)/ vt entregar. ● vi rendirse. ● n rendición f

surreptitious /sʌrəp'tɪʃəs/ a furtivo

surround /sə'raund/ vt rodear; (Mil) rodear, cercar. ~**ing** a circundante. ~**ings** npl alrededores mpl; (environment) ambiente m

surveillance /sɜː'veɪləns/ n vigilancia f

survey /'sɜːveɪ/ n inspección f; (report) informe m; (general view) vista f general. ● /sə'veɪ/ vt inspeccionar; (measure) medir; (look at) contemplar. ~**or** n topógrafo m, agrimensor m; (of building) perito m

surviv|al /sə'vaɪvl/ n supervivencia f. ~**e** /sə'vaɪv/ vt/i sobrevivir. ~**or** n superviviente m & f

susceptible /sə'septəbl/ a. ~ **to** propenso a

suspect /sə'spekt/ vt sospechar; sospechar de <person>. ● /'sʌspekt/ a & n sospechoso (m)

suspen|d /sə'spend/ vt suspender. ~**ders** npl (Amer, braces) tirantes mpl. ~**se** /-s/ n (in film etc) suspense m, suspenso m (LAm). **keep s.o.** ~**se** mantener a uno sobre ascuas. ~**sion** /-ʃn/ n suspensión f. ~**sion bridge** n puente m colgante

suspici|on /sə'spɪʃn/ n (belief) sospecha f; (mistrust) desconfianza f. ~**ous** /-ʃəs/ a desconfiado; (causing suspicion) sospechoso

sustain /sə'steɪn/ vt sostener; mantener <conversation, interest>; (suffer) sufrir

SW abbr (= **south-west**) SO

swab /swɒb/ n (specimen) muestra f, frotis m

swagger /'swægə(r)/ vi pavonearse

swallow /'swɒləu/ vt/i tragar. ● n trago m; (bird) golondrina f

swam /swæm/ ⇒SWIM

swamp /swɒmp/ n pantano m, ciénaga f. ● vt inundar. ~**y** a pantanoso

swan /swɒn/ n cisne m

swap /swɒp/ vt/i (pt **swapped**) intercambiar. ∼ **sth for sth** cambiar algo por algo. ● n cambio m

swarm /swɔːm/ n enjambre m. ● vi <bees> enjambrar; (fig) hormiguear

swarthy /ˈswɔːðɪ/ a (**-ier, -iest**) moreno

swat /swɒt/ vt (pt **swatted**) matar (con matamoscas etc)

sway /sweɪ/ vi balancearse; (gently) mecerse. ● vt (influence) influir en

swear /sweə(r)/ vt/i (pt **swore**, pp **sworn**) jurar. ∼**word** n palabrota f

sweat /swet/ n sudor m, transpiración f. ● vi sudar

sweat|er /ˈswetə(r)/ n jersey m, suéter m. ∼**shirt** n sudadera f. ∼**suit** n (Amer) chándal m, equipo m de deportes

swede /swiːd/ n nabo m sueco

Swede /swiːd/ n sueco m. ∼**n** /ˈswiːdn/ n Suecia f. ∼**ish** a sueco. ● n (Lang) sueco m. ● npl. the ∼ (people) los suecos

sweep /swiːp/ vt (pt **swept**) barrer; deshollinar <chimney>. ● vi barrer. ● n barrido m. ∼ **away** vt (carry away) arrastrar; (abolish) erradicar. ∼**er** n barrendero m. ∼**ing** a <gesture> amplio; <changes> radical; <statement> demasiado general

sweet /swiːt/ a (**-er, -est**) dulce; (fragrant) fragante; (pleasant) agradable; (kind, gentle) dulce; (cute) rico. **have a** ∼ **tooth** ser dulcero. ● n caramelo m, dulce m (Mex); (dish) postre m. ∼**en** vt endulzar. ∼**heart** n enamorado m; (as form of address) amor m. ∼**ly** adv dulcemente. ∼ **potato** n boniato m, batata f

swell /swel/ vt (pt **swelled**, pp **swollen** or **swelled**) hinchar; (increase) aumentar. ● vi hincharse; (increase) aumentar. ● a (Amer 🆒) fenomenal. ● n (of sea) oleaje m. ∼**ing** n hinchazón m

sweltering /ˈsweltərɪŋ/ vi sofocante

swept /swept/ ⇒SWEEP

swerve /swɜːv/ vi virar bruscamente

swift /swɪft/ a (**-er, -est**) veloz, rápido; <reply> rápido. ● n (bird) vencejo m. ∼**ly** adv rápidamente

swig /swɪg/ vt (pt **swigged**) 🆒 beber a grandes tragos. ● n 🆒 trago m

swim /swɪm/ vi (pt **swam**, pp **swum**) nadar. ● n baño m. ∼**mer** n nadador m. ∼**ming** n natación f. ∼**ming bath(s)** n(pl) piscina f cubierta, alberca f techada (Mex). ∼**ming pool** n piscina f, alberca f (Mex). ∼**ming trunks** npl bañador m, traje m de baño ∼**suit** n traje m de baño, bañador m

swindle /ˈswɪndl/ vt estafar. ● n estafa f. ∼**r** n estafador m

swine /swaɪn/ npl cerdos mpl. ● n (pl **swine**) (🆒, person) canalla m & f

swing /swɪŋ/ vt (pt **swung**) balancear; (object on rope) hacer oscilar. ● vi (dangle) balancearse; (swing on a swing) columpiarse; <pendulum> oscilar. ∼ **open/shut** abrirse/cerrarse. ● n oscilación f, vaivén m; (seat) columpio m; (in opinion) cambio m. **in full** ∼ en plena actividad

swipe /swaɪp/ vt darle un golpe a; (🆒, snatch) birlar. ● n golpe m

Swiss /swɪs/ a suizo (m). ● npl. the ∼ los suizos

switch /swɪtʃ/ n (Elec) interruptor m; (exchange) intercambio m; (Amer, Rail) agujas fpl. ● vt cambiar; (deviate) desviar. □ ∼ **off** vt (Elec) apagar <light, TV, heating>; desconectar <electricity>. □ ∼ **on** vt encender, prender (LAm); arrancar <engine>. ∼**board** n centralita f

Switzerland /ˈswɪtsələnd/ n Suiza f

swivel /ˈswɪvl/ vi (pt **swivelled**) girar. ● vt hacer girar

swollen /ˈswəʊlən/ ⇒SWELL. ● a hinchado

swoop /swuːp/ vi <bird> abatirse; <police> llevar a cabo una redada. ● n (of bird) descenso m en picado or (LAm) en picada; (by police) redada f

sword /sɔːd/ n espada f

swore /swɔː(r)/ ⇒SWEAR

sworn /swɔːn/ ⇒SWEAR. ● a <enemy> declarado; <statement> jurado

swot /swɒt/ *vt/i* (*pt* **swotted**) (Schol, 🇬🇧) empollar, estudiar como loco. ● *n* (Schol, 🇬🇧) empollón *m*, ma-tado *m* (Mex)

swum /swʌm/ ⇒SWIM

swung /swʌŋ/ ⇒SWING

syllable /ˈsɪləbl/ *n* sílaba *f*

syllabus /ˈsɪləbəs/ *n* (*pl* **-buses**) plan *m* de estudios; (of a particular subject) programa *m*

symbol /ˈsɪmbl/ *n* símbolo *m*. ∼**ic(al)** /-ˈbɒlɪk(l)/ *a* simbólico. ∼**ism** *n* simbolismo *m*. ∼**ize** *vt* simbolizar

symmetr|ical /sɪˈmetrɪkl/ *a* simétrico. ∼**y** /ˈsɪmətrɪ/ *n* simetría *f*

sympath|etic /sɪmpəˈθetɪk/ *a* comprensivo; (showing pity) compasivo. ∼**ize** /ˈsɪmpəθaɪz/ *vi* comprender; (commiserate) ∼**ize with s.o.** compadecer a uno. ∼**y** /ˈsɪmpəθɪ/ *n* comprensión *f*; (pity) compasión *f*; (condolences) pésame *m*

symphony /ˈsɪmfənɪ/ *n* sinfonía *f*

symptom /ˈsɪmptəm/ *n* síntoma *m*. ∼**atic** /-ˈmætɪk/ *a* sintomático

synagogue /ˈsɪnəgɒg/ *n* sinagoga *f*

synchronize /ˈsɪŋkrənaɪz/ *vt* sincronizar

syndicate /ˈsɪndɪkət/ *n* agrupación *f*; (Amer, TV) agencia *f* de distribución periodística

synonym /ˈsɪnənɪm/ *n* sinónimo *m*. ∼**ous** /-ˈnɒnɪməs/ *a* sinónimo

syntax /ˈsɪntæks/ *n* sintaxis *f*

synthesi|s /ˈsɪnθəsɪs/ *n* (*pl* **-theses** /-siːz/) síntesis *f*. ∼**ze** /-aɪz/ *vt* sintetizar

synthetic /sɪnˈθetɪk/ *a* sintético

syringe /ˈsɪrɪndʒ/ *n* jeringa *f*, jeringuilla *f*

syrup /ˈsɪrəp/ *n* (sugar solution) almíbar *m*; (with other ingredients) jarabe *m*; (medicine) jarabe *m*

system /ˈsɪstəm/ *n* sistema *m*, método *m*; (Tec, Mec, Comp) sistema *m*. **the digestive** ∼ el aparato digestivo. ∼**atic** /-əˈmætɪk/ *a* sistemático. ∼**atically** /-əˈmætɪklɪ/ *adv* sistemáticamente. ∼**s analyst** *n* analista *m* & *f* de sistemas

Tt

tab /tæb/ *n* (flap) lengüeta *f*; (label) etiqueta *f*

table /ˈteɪbl/ *n* mesa *f*; (list) tabla *f*. ∼**cloth** *n* mantel *m*. ∼ **mat** *n* salvamanteles *m*. ∼**spoon** *n* cuchara *f* grande; (measure) cucharada *f* (grande)

tablet /ˈtæblɪt/ *n* pastilla *f*; (pill) comprimido *m*

table tennis *n* tenis *m* de mesa, ping-pong *m*

tabloid /ˈtæblɔɪd/ *n* tabloide *m*

taboo /təˈbuː/ *a* & *n* tabú (*m*)

tacit /ˈtæsɪt/ *a* tácito

taciturn /ˈtæsɪtɜːn/ *a* taciturno

tack /tæk/ *n* tachuela *f*; (stitch) hilván *m*. ● *vt* clavar con tachuelas; (sew) hilvanar. ● *vi* (Naut) virar □ ∼ **on** *vt* añadir.

tackle /ˈtækl/ *n* (equipment) equipo *m*; (soccer) entrada *f* fuerte; (US football, Rugby) placaje *m*. **fishing** ∼ aparejo *m* de pesca. ● *vt* abordar <*problem*>; (in soccer) entrarle a; (in US football, Rugby) placar

tacky /ˈtækɪ/ *a* pegajoso

tact /tækt/ *n* tacto *m*. ∼**ful** *a* diplomático

tactic|al /ˈtæktɪkl/ *a* táctico. ∼**s** *npl* táctica *f*

tactless /ˈtæktləs/ *a* indiscreto

tadpole /ˈtædpəʊl/ *n* renacuajo *m*

tag /tæg/ *n* (label) etiqueta *f*. □ ∼ **along** (*pt* **tagged**) *vt* 🇬🇧 seguir

tail /teɪl/ *n* (of horse, fish, bird) cola *f*; (of dog, pig) rabo *m*. ∼**s** *npl* (tailcoat) frac *m*; (of coin) cruz *f*. ● *vt* seguir. □ ∼ **off** *vi* disminuir.

tailor /ˈteɪlə(r)/ *n* sastre *m*. ∼**ed** /ˈteɪləd/ *a* entallado. ∼**-made** *n* hecho a (la) medida

taint /teɪnt/ *vt* contaminar

take /teɪk/ *vt* (*pt* **took**, *pp* **taken**) tomar, coger (esp Spain), agarrar (esp LAm); (capture) capturar; (endure) aguantar; (require) requerir; llevar

<time>; tomar *<bath>*; tomar *<medicine>*; (carry) llevar; aceptar *<cheque>*. **I ~ a size 10** uso la talla 14. ● *n* (Cinema) toma *f*. □ ~ **after** *vt* parecerse a. □ ~ **away** *vt* llevarse; (confiscate) quitar. □ ~ **back** *vt* retirar *<statement etc>*. □ ~ **in** *vt* achicar *<garment>*; (understand) asimilar; (deceive) engañar. □ ~ **off** *vt* (remove) quitar, sacar; quitarse *<shoes, jacket>*; (mimic) imitar. *vi* (Aviat) despegar. □ ~ **on** *vt* contratar *<employee>*. □ ~ **out** *vt* sacar. □ ~ **over** *vt* tomar posesión de; hacerse cargo de *<job>*. *vi* (assume control) asumir el poder. □ ~ **up** *vt* empezar a hacer *<hobby>*; aceptar *<challenge>*; subir *<hem>*; llevar *<time>*; ocupar *<space>*. **~-off** *n* despegue *m*. **~-over** *n* (Com) absorción *f*

takings /'teɪkɪŋz/ *npl* recaudación *f*; (at box office) taquilla *f*

talcum powder /'tælkəm/ *n* polvos *mpl* de talco, talco *m* (LAm)

tale /teɪl/ *n* cuento *m*

talent /'tælənt/ *n* talento *m*. **~ed** *a* talentoso

talk /tɔːk/ *vt/i* hablar. **~ to s.o.** hablar con uno. **~ about** hablar de. ● *n* conversación *f*; (lecture) charla *f*. □ ~ **over** *vt* discutir. **~ative** /-ətɪv/ *a* hablador

tall /tɔːl/ *a* (**-er, -est**) alto. **~ story** *n* 🗊 cuento *m* chino

tally /'tælɪ/ *vi* coincidir (**with** con)

talon /'tælən/ *n* garra *f*

tambourine /tæmbə'riːn/ *n* pandereta *f*

tame /teɪm/ *a* (**-er, -est**) *<animal>* (by nature) manso; (tamed) domado. ● *vt* domar *<wild animal>*

tamper /'tæmpə(r)/ *vi*. **~ with** tocar; (alter) alterar, falsificar

tampon /'tæmpɒn/ *n* tampón *m*

tan /tæn/ *vi* (*pt* **tanned**) broncearse. ● *n* bronceado *m*. **get a ~** broncearse. ● *a* habano

tang /tæŋ/ *n* sabor *m* fuerte

tangent /'tændʒənt/ *n* tangente *f*

tangerine /tændʒə'riːn/ *n* mandarina *f*

tangible /'tændʒəbl/ *a* tangible

tangle /'tæŋgl/ *vt* enredar. **get ~d (up)** enredarse. ● *n* enredo *m*, maraña *f*

tango /'tæŋgəʊ/ *n* (*pl* **-os**) tango *m*

tank /tæŋk/ *n* depósito *m*; (Auto) tanque *m*; (Mil) tanque *m*

tanker /'tæŋkə(r)/ *n* (ship) buque *m* cisterna; (truck) camión *m* cisterna

tantrum /'tæntrəm/ *n* berrinche *m*, rabieta *f*

tap /tæp/ *n* grifo *m*, llave *f* (LAm); (knock) golpecito *m*. ● *vt* (*pt* **tapped**) (knock) dar un golpecito en; interceptar *<phone>*. ● *vi* dar golpecitos (**on** en). **~ dancing** *n* claqué *m*

tape /teɪp/ *n* cinta *f*; (Med) esparadrapo *m*. ● *vt* (record) grabar. **~-measure** *n* cinta *f* métrica

taper /'teɪpə(r)/ *vt* afilar. ● *vi* afilarse. □ ~ **off** *vi* disminuir

tape recorder *n* magnetofón *m*, magnetófono *m*

tapestry /'tæpɪstrɪ/ *n* tapiz *m*

tar /tɑː(r)/ *n* alquitrán *m*. ● *vt* (*pt* **tarred**) alquitranar

target /'tɑːgɪt/ *n* blanco *m*; (fig) objetivo *m*

tarmac /'tɑːmæk/ *n* pista *f*. **T~** *n* (Amer, P) asfalto *m*

tarnish /'tɑːnɪʃ/ *vt* deslustrar; empañar *<reputation>*

tart /tɑːt/ *n* pastel *m*; (individual) pastelillo *m*; (🗷, woman) prostituta *f*, fulana *f* 🗊. ● *vt*. **~ o.s. up** 🗊 engalanarse. ● *a* (**-er, -est**) ácido

tartan /'tɑːtn/ *n* tartán *m*, tela *f* escocesa

task /tɑːsk/ *n* tarea *f*. **take to ~** reprender

tassel /'tæsl/ *n* borla *f*

tast|e /teɪst/ *n* sabor *m*, gusto *m*; (liking) gusto *m*. ● *vt* probar. ● *vi*. **~ of** saber a. **~eful** *a* de buen gusto. **~eless** *a* soso; (fig) de mal gusto. **~y** *a* (**-ier, -iest**) sabroso

tat /tæt/ ⇒TIT FOR TAT

tatter|ed /'tætəd/ *a* hecho jirones. **~s** /'tætəz/ *npl* andrajos *mpl*

tattoo /tæ'tuː/ *n* (on body) tatuaje *m*. ● *vt* tatuar

tatty /'tætɪ/ *a* (**-ier, -iest**) gastado, estropeado

taught /tɔːt/ ⇒TEACH

taunt /tɔːnt/ vt provocar mediante burlas. ● n pulla f

Taurus /'tɔːrəs/ n Tauro m

taut /tɔːt/ a tenso

tavern /'tævən/ n taberna f

tax /tæks/ n impuesto m. ● vt imponer contribuciones a <person>; gravar <thing>; (strain) poner a prueba. ~**able** a imponible. ~**ation** /-'seɪʃn/ n impuestos mpl; (system) sistema m tributario. ~ **collector** n recaudador m de impuestos. ~**free** a libre de impuestos

taxi /'tæksɪ/ n (pl **-is**) taxi m. ● vi (pt **taxied**, pres p **taxiing**) <aircraft> rodar por la pista

taxpayer /'tækspeɪə(r)/ n contribuyente m & f

tea /tiː/ n té m; (afternoon tea) merienda f, té m. ~ **bag** n bolsita f de té

teach /tiːtʃ/ vt (pt **taught**) dar clases de, enseñar <subject>; dar clase a <person>. ~ **school** (Amer) dar clase(s) en un colegio. ● vi dar clase(s). ~**er** n profesor m; (primary) maestro m. ~**ing** n enseñanza f. ● a docente

tea: ~**cup** n taza f de té. ~ **leaf** n hoja f de té

team /tiːm/ n equipo m. □ ~ **up** vi asociarse (with con). ~ **work** n trabajo m de equipo

teapot /'tiːpɒt/ n tetera f

tear[1] /teə(r)/ vt (pt **tore**, pp **torn**) romper, rasgar. ● vi romperse, rasgarse. ● n rotura f; (rip) desgarrón m. □ ~ **along** vi ir a toda velocidad. □ ~ **apart** vt desgarrar. □ ~ **off**, ~ **out** vt arrancar. □ ~ **up** vt romper

tear[2] /tɪə(r)/ n lágrima f. be in ~s estar llorando. ~**ful** a lloroso <farewell> triste. ~ **gas** n gas m lacrimógeno

tease /tiːz/ vt tomarle el pelo a

tea: ~ **set** n juego m de té. ~**spoon** n cucharita f, cucharilla f; (amount) cucharadita f

teat /tiːt/ n (of animal) tetilla f; (for bottle) tetina f

tea towel /'tiːtaʊəl/ n paño m de cocina

techni|cal /'teknɪkl/ a técnico. ~**cality** n /-'kælətɪ/ n detalle m técnico. ~**cally** adv técnicamente. ~**cian** /tek'nɪʃn/ n técnico m. ~**que** /tek'niːk/ n técnica f

technolog|ical /teknə'lɒdʒɪkl/ a tecnológico. ~**y** /tek'nɒlədʒɪ/ n tecnología f

teddy bear /'tedɪ/ n osito m de peluche

tedi|ous /'tiːdɪəs/ a tedioso. ~**um** /'tiːdɪəm/ n tedio m

teem /tiːm/ vi abundar (**with** en), estar repleto (**with** de)

teen|age /'tiːneɪdʒ/ a adolescente; (for teenagers) para jóvenes. ~**ager** n adolescente m & f. ~**s** /tiːnz/ npl adolescencia f

teeny /'tiːnɪ/ a (**-ier**, **-iest**) 🄴 chiquito

teeter /'tiːtə(r)/ vi balancearse

teeth /tiːθ/ ⇒TOOTH. ~**e** /tiːð/ vi. he's ~ing le están saliendo los dientes. ~**ing troubles** npl (fig) problemas mpl iniciales

tele|communications /telɪkə mjuːnɪ'keɪʃnz/ npl telecomunicaciones fpl. ~**gram** /'telɪɡræm/ n telegrama m. ~**pathic** /telɪ'pæθɪk/ a telepático. ~**pathy** /tə'lepəθɪ/ n telepatía f

telephon|e /'telɪfəʊn/ n teléfono m. ● vt llamar por teléfono. ~**e booth**, ~**e box** n cabina f telefónica. ~**e call** n llamada f telefónica. ~**e directory** n guía f telefónica. ~**e exchange** n central f telefónica. ~**ist** /tɪ'lefənɪst/ n telefonista m & f

tele|sales /'telɪseɪlz/ npl televentas fpl. ~**scope** n telescopio m. ~**scopic** /-'skɒpɪk/ a telescópico. ~**text** n teletex(to) m

televis|e /'telɪvaɪz/ vt televisar. ~**ion** /'telɪvɪʒn/ n (medium) televisión f. ~**ion** (set) n televisor m

telex /'teleks/ n télex m

tell /tel/ vt (pt **told**) decir; contar <story, joke>; (distinguish) distinguir. ~ **the difference** notar la diferencia. ~ **the time** decir la hora. ● vi (produce an effect) tener efecto; (know) saber. □ ~ **off** vt regañar. ~**ing** a revelador. **∼-tale** n soplón m. ● a revelador

telly /'telɪ/ n 🔲 tele f

temp /temp/ n empleado m eventual or temporal

temper /'tempə(r)/ n (mood) humor m; (disposition) carácter m; (fit of anger) cólera f. **be in a ∼** estar furioso. **lose one's ∼** perder los estribos. **∼ament** /'temprəmənt/ n temperamento m. **∼amental** /-'mentl/ a temperamental. **∼ate** /'tempərət/ a templado. **∼ature** /'temprɪtʃə(r)/ n temperatura f. **have a ∼ature** tener fiebre

tempestuous /tem'pestjʊəs/ a tempestuoso

temple /'templ/ n templo m; (Anat) sien f

tempo /'tempəʊ/ n (pl **-os** or **tempi**) ritmo m

temporar|ily /'tempərərəlɪ/ adv temporalmente, temporariamente (LAm). **∼y** /'tempərərɪ/ a temporal, provisional; <job> eventual, temporal

tempt /tempt/ vt tentar. **∼ation** /-'teɪʃn/ n tentación f. **∼ing** a tentador

ten /ten/ a & n diez (m)

tenaci|ous /tɪ'neɪʃəs/ a tenaz. **∼ty** /tɪ'næsətɪ/ n tenacidad f

tenan|cy /'tenənsɪ/ n inquilinato m. **∼t** n inquilino m, arrendatorio m

tend /tend/ vi. **∼ to** tender a. ● vt cuidar (de). **∼ency** /'tendənsɪ/ n tendencia f

tender /'tendə(r)/ a tierno; (painful) sensible. ● n (Com) oferta f. **legal ∼** n moneda f de curso legal. ● vt ofrecer, presentar. **∼ly** adv tiernamente

tendon /'tendən/ n tendón m

tennis /'tenɪs/ n tenis m

tenor /'tenə(r)/ n tenor m

tens|e /tens/ a (**-er, -est**) (taut) tenso, tirante; <person> tenso. ● n (Gram) tiempo m. **∼ion** /'tenʃn/ n tensión f; (between two parties) conflicto m

tent /tent/ n tienda f (de campaña), carpa f (LAm)

tentacle /'tentəkl/ n tentáculo m

tentative /'tentətɪv/ a <plan> provisional; <offer> tentativo; <person> indeciso

tenterhooks /'tentəhʊks/ npl. **be on ∼** estar en ascuas

tenth /tenθ/ a & n décimo (m)

tenuous /'tenjʊəs/ a <claim> poco fundado; <link> indirecto

tenure /'tenjʊə(r)/ n tenencia f; (period of office) ejercicio m

tepid /'tepɪd/ a tibio

term /tɜːm/ n (of time) período m; (Schol) trimestre m; (word etc) término m. **∼s** npl condiciones fpl; (Com) precio m. **on good/bad ∼s** en buenas/malas relaciones. ● vt calificar de

termin|al /'tɜːmɪnl/ a terminal. ● (transport) terminal f; (Comp, Elec) terminal m. **∼ate** /-eɪt/ vt poner fin a; poner término a <contract>; (Amer, fire) despedir. ● vi terminarse. **∼ology** /-'nɒlədʒɪ/ n terminología f

terrace /'terəs/ n terraza f; (houses) hilera f de casas

terrain /tə'reɪn/ n terreno m

terrestrial /tɪ'restrɪəl/ a terrestre

terribl|e /'terəbl/ a espantoso. **∼y** adv terriblemente

terrif|ic /tə'rɪfɪk/ a (🔲, excellent) estupendo; (🔲, huge) enorme. **∼ied** /'terɪfaɪd/ a aterrorizado. **∼y** /'terɪfaɪ/ vt aterrorizar. **∼ying** a aterrador

territor|ial /terɪ'tɔːrɪəl/ a territorial. **∼y** /'terɪtrɪ/ n territorio m

terror /'terə(r)/ n terror m. **∼ism** n terrorismo m. **∼ist** n terrorista m & f. **∼ize** vt aterrorizar

terse /tɜːs/ a seco, lacónico

test /test/ n (of machine, drug) prueba f; (exam) prueba f, test m; (of blood) análisis m; (for eyes, hearing) examen m. ● vt probar, poner a prueba <product>; hacerle una prueba a <student>; evaluar <knowledge>; examinar <sight>

testament /'testəmənt/ n (will) testamento m. **Old/New T∼** Antiguo/Nuevo Testamento

testicle /'testɪkl/ n testículo m

testify /'testɪfaɪ/ vt atestiguar. ● vi declarar

testimon|ial /testɪˈməʊnɪəl/ *n* recomendación *f*. **~y** /ˈtestɪmənɪ/ *n* testimonio *m*

test: **~ match** *n* partido *m* internacional. **~ tube** *n* tubo *m* de ensayo, probeta *f*

tether /ˈteðə(r)/ *vt* atar. ● *n*. be at the end of one's **~** no poder más

text /tekst/ *n* texto *m*. **~book** *n* libro *m* de texto

textile /ˈtekstaɪl/ *a & n* textil (*m*)

texture /ˈtekstʃə(r)/ *n* textura *f*

Thames /temz/ *n* Támesis *m*

than /ðæn, ðən/ *conj* que; (with quantity) de

thank /θæŋk/ *vt* darle las gracias a, agradecer. **~ you** gracias. **~ful** *a* agradecido. **~fully** *adv* (happily) gracias a Dios. **~less** *a* ingrato. **~s** *npl* agradecimiento *m*. **~s!** Ⓘ ¡gracias!. **~s to** gracias a

Thanksgiving (Day) /θæŋks ˈɡɪvɪŋ/ *n* (in US) el día de Acción de Gracias

that /ðæt, ðət/ *a* (*pl* those) ese, aquel, esa, aquella. ● *pron* (*pl* those) ése, aquél, ésa, aquélla. **~ is** es decir. **~'s not true** eso no es cierto. **~'s why** por eso. **is ~ you?** ¿eres tú? **like ~** así. ● *adv* tan. ● *rel pron* que; (with prep) el que, la que, el cual, la cual. ● *conj* que

thatched /θætʃt/ *a* <roof> de paja; <cottage> con techo de paja

thaw /θɔː/ *vt* descongelar. ● *vi* descongelarse; <snow> derretirse. ● *n* deshielo *m*

....

the *before vowel* /ðɪ/, *before consonant* /ðə/, *stressed form* /ðiː/

● *definite article*

····▸ el (*m*), la (*f*), los (*mpl*), las (*fpl*). **~ building** el edificio. **~ windows** las ventanas

❗ Feminine singular nouns beginning with a stressed or ■ accented *a* or *ha* take the article *el* instead of *la*, e.g. **~ soul** *el alma;* **~ axe** *el hacha.* **~ eagle** *el águila*

Note that when *el* follows the prepositions *de* and *a*, it combines

to form *del* and *al,* e.g. **of ~ group** *del grupo.* **I went to ~ bank** *fui al banco*

····▸ (before an ordinal number in names, titles) *not translated.* **Henry ~ Eighth** Enrique Octavo. **Elizabeth ~ Second** Isabel Segunda

····▸ (in abstractions) lo. **~ impossible** lo imposible

....

theatr|e /ˈθɪətə(r)/ *n* teatro *m*; (Amer, movie theater) cine *m*. **~ical** /-ˈætrɪkl/ *a* teatral

theft /θeft/ *n* hurto *m*

their /ðeə(r)/ *a* su, sus *pl.* **~s** /ðeəz/ *poss pron* (el) suyo *m*, (la) suya *f*, (los) suyos *mpl*, (las) suyas *fpl*

them /ðem, ðəm/ *pron* (accusative) los *m*, las *f*; (dative) les; (after prep) ellos *m*, ellas *f*

theme /θiːm/ *n* tema *m*. **~ park** *n* parque *m* temático. **~ song** *n* motivo *m* principal

themselves /ðəmˈselvz/ *pron* ellos mismos *m*, ellas mismas *f*; (reflexive) se; (after prep) sí mismos *m*, sí mismas *f*

then /ðen/ *adv* entonces; (next) luego, después. **by ~** para entonces. **now and ~** de vez en cuando. **since ~** desde entonces. ● *a* entonces

theology /θɪˈɒlədʒɪ/ *n* teología *f*

theor|etical /θɪəˈretɪkl/ *a* teórico. **~y** /ˈθɪərɪ/ *n* teoría *f*

therap|eutic /θerəˈpjuːtɪk/ *a* terapéutico. **~ist** /ˈθerəpɪst/ *n* terapeuta *m & f*. **~y** /θerəpɪ/ *n* terapia *f*

there /ðeə(r)/ *adv* ahí; (further away) allí, ahí; (less precise, further) allá. **~ is**, **~ are** hay. **~ it is** ahí está. **down ~** ahí abajo. **up ~** ahí arriba. ● *int*. **~!** **that's the last box** ¡listo! ésa es la última caja. **~, ~, don't cry!** vamos, no llores. **~abouts** *adv* por ahí. **~fore** /-fɔː(r)/ *adv* por lo tanto.

thermometer /θəˈmɒmɪtə(r)/ *n* termómetro *m*

Thermos /ˈθɜːməs/ *n* (P) termo *m*

thermostat /ˈθɜːməstæt/ *n* termostato *m*

thesaurus /θɪˈsɔːrəs/ *n* (*pl* -ri /-raɪ/) diccionario *m* de sinónimos

these /ðiːz/ a estos, estas. ● *pron* éstos, éstas

thesis /ˈθiːsɪs/ n (*pl* **theses** /-siːz/) tesis f

they /ðeɪ/ *pron* ellos m, ellas f. ~ **say that** dicen *or* se dice que

they'd /ðeɪ(ə)d/ = **they had**, **they would**

they'll /ðeɪl/ = **they will**

they're /ðeɪə(r)/ = **they are**

they've /ðeɪv/ = **they have**

thick /θɪk/ a (**-er**, **-est**) <*layer*, *sweater*> grueso, gordo; <*sauce*> espeso; <*fog*, *smoke*> espeso, denso; <*fur*> tupido; (🇮, *stupid*) burro. ● *adv* espesamente, densamente. ● *n*. in the ~ of en medio de. ~**en** *vt* espesar. ● *vi* espesarse. ~**et** /-ɪt/ n matorral m. ~**ness** n (of fabric) grosor m; (of paper, wood, wall) espesor m

thief /θiːf/ n (*pl* **thieves** /θiːvz/) ladrón m

thigh /θaɪ/ n muslo m

thimble /ˈθɪmbl/ n dedal m

thin /θɪn/ a (**thinner**, **thinnest**) <*person*> delgado, flaco; <*layer*, *slice*> fino; <*hair*> ralo

thing /θɪŋ/ n cosa f. **it's a good ~ (that)**... menos mal que.... **just the ~** exactamente lo que se necesita. **poor ~!** ¡pobrecito!

think /θɪŋk/ *vt* (*pt* **thought**) pensar, creer. ● *vi* pensar (**about** en); (carefully) reflexionar; (imagine) imaginarse. **I ~ so** creo que sí. ~ **of** s.o. pensar en uno. **I hadn't thought of that** eso no se me ha ocurrido. ~ **over** *vt* pensar bien. ~ **up** *vt* idear, inventar. ~**er** n pensador m. ~**-tank** n gabinete m estratégico

third /θɜːd/ a tercero, (before masculine singular noun) tercer. ● n tercio m, tercera parte f. ~ (**gear**) n (Auto) tercera f. ~**-rate** a muy inferior. **T~ World** n Tercer Mundo m

thirst /θɜːst/ n sed f. ~**y** a sediento. **be ~y** tener sed

thirt|een /θɜːˈtiːn/ a & n trece (m). ~**teenth** a decimotercero. ● n treceavo m ~**ieth** /ˈθɜːtɪəθ/ a trigésimo. ● n treintavo m. ~**y** /ˈθɜːtɪ/ a & n treinta (m)

this /ðɪs/ a (*pl* **these**) este, esta. ~ **one** éste, ésta. ● *pron* (*pl* **these**) éste, ésta, esto. **like ~** así

thistle /ˈθɪsl/ n cardo m

thong /θɒŋ/ n correa f; (Amer, sandal) chancla f

thorn /θɔːn/ n espina f. ~**y** a espinoso

thorough /ˈθʌrə/ a <*investigation*> riguroso; <*cleaning etc*> a fondo; <*person*> concienzudo. ~**bred** /-bred/ a de pura sangre. ~**fare** n vía f pública; (street) calle f. **no ~fare** prohibido el paso. ~**ly** *adv* <*clean*> a fondo; <*examine*> minuciosamente; (completely) perfectamente

those /ðəʊz/ a esos, esas, aquellos, aquellas. ● *pron* ésos, ésas, aquéllos, aquéllas

though /ðəʊ/ *conj* aunque. ● *adv* sin embargo. **as ~** como si

thought /θɔːt/ ⇒THINK. ● n pensamiento m; (idea) idea f. ~**ful** a pensativo; (considerate) atento. ~**fully** *adv* pensativamente; (considerately) atentamente. ~**less** a desconsiderado

thousand /ˈθaʊznd/ a & n mil (m). ~**th** a & n milésimo (m)

thrash /θræʃ/ *vt* azotar; (defeat) derrotar

thread /θred/ n hilo m; (of screw) rosca f. ● *vt* enhebrar <*needle*>; ensartar <*beads*>. ~**bare** a gastado, raído

threat /θret/ n amenaza f. ~**en** *vt/i* amenazar. ~**ening** a amenazador

three /θriː/ a & n tres (m). ~**fold** a triple. ● *adv* tres veces

threshold /ˈθreʃhəʊld/ n umbral m

threw /θruː/ ⇒THROW

thrift /θrɪft/ n economía f, ahorro m. ~**y** a frugal

thrill /θrɪl/ n emoción f. ● *vt* emocionar. ~**ed** a contentísimo (**with** con). ~**er** n (book) libro m de suspense *or* (LAm) suspenso; (film) película f de suspense *or* (LAm) suspenso. ~**ing** a emocionante

thriv|e /θraɪv/ *vi* prosperar. ~**ing** a próspero

throat /θrəʊt/ n garganta f

throb /θrɒb/ vi (pt **throbbed**) palpitar; (with pain) dar punzadas; <engine> vibrar. **~bing** a <pain> punzante

throes /θrəʊz/ npl. **be in one's death ~** estar agonizando

throne /θrəʊn/ n trono m

throng /θrɒŋ/ n multitud f

throttle /'θrɒtl/ n (Auto) acelerador m (que se acciona con la mano). ● vt estrangular

through /θru:/ prep por, a través de; (during) durante; (by means of) a través de; (Amer, until and including) **Monday ~ Friday** de lunes a viernes. ● adv de parte a parte, de un lado a otro; (entirely) completamente; (to the end) hasta el final. **be ~** (finished) haber terminado. ● a <train etc> directo. **no ~ road** calle sin salida. **~out** /-'aʊt/ prep por todo; (time) durante todo. **~out his career** a lo largo de su carrera

throve /θrəʊv/ ⇒THRIVE

throw /θrəʊ/ vt (pt **threw**, pp **thrown**) tirar, aventar (Mex); lanzar <grenade, javelin>; (disconcert) desconcertar; 🔲 hacer, dar <party>. ● n (of ball) tiro m; (of dice) tirada f. □ **~ away** vt tirar. □ **~ up** vi (vomit) vomitar.

thrush /θrʌʃ/ n tordo m

thrust /θrʌst/ vt (pt **thrust**) empujar; (push in) clavar. ● n empujón m; (of sword) estocada f

thud /θʌd/ n ruido m sordo

thug /θʌɡ/ n matón m

thumb /θʌm/ n pulgar m. ● vt. **~ a lift** ir a dedo. **~tack** n (Amer) chincheta f, tachuela f, chinche f (Mex)

thump /θʌmp/ vt golpear. ● vi <heart> latir fuertemente. ● n golpazo m

thunder /'θʌndə(r)/ n truenos mpl, (of traffic) estruendo m. ● vi tronar. **~bolt** n rayo m. **~storm** n tormenta f eléctrica. **~y** a con truenos

Thursday /'θɜːzdeɪ/ n jueves m

thus /ðʌs/ adv así

thwart /θwɔːt/ vt frustrar

tic /tɪk/ n tic m

tick /tɪk/ n (sound) tic m; (insect) garrapata f, (mark) marca f, visto m, palomita f (Mex); (🔲, instant) momentito m. ● vi hacer tictac. ● vt. **~ (off)** marcar

ticket /'tɪkɪt/ n (for bus, train) billete m, boleto m (LAm); (for plane) pasaje m, billete m; (for theatre, museum) entrada f; (for baggage, coat) ticket m; (fine) multa f. **~ collector** n revisor m. **~ office** n (transport) mostrador m de venta de billetes or (LAm) boletos; (in theatre) taquilla f, boletería f (LAm)

tickl|e /'tɪkl/ vt hacerle cosquillas a. ● n cosquilleo m. **~ish** /'tɪklɪʃ/ a. be **~ish** tener cosquillas

tidal wave /'taɪdl/ n maremoto m

tide /taɪd/ n marea f. **high/low ~** marea alta/baja. □ **~ over** vt ayudar a salir de un apuro

tid|ily /'taɪdɪlɪ/ adv ordenadamente. **~iness** n orden m. **~y** a (-ier, -iest) ordenado. ● vt/i **~y (up)** ordenar, arreglar

tie /taɪ/ vt (pres p **tying**) atar, amarrar (LAm); hacer <knot>. ● vi (Sport) empatar. ● n (constraint) atadura f; (bond) lazo m; (necktie) corbata f; (Sport) empate m. □ **~ in with** vt concordar con. □ **~ up** vt atar. **be ~d up** (busy) estar ocupado

tier /tɪə(r)/ n hilera f superpuesta; (in stadium etc) grada f; (of cake) piso m

tiger /'taɪɡə(r)/ n tigre m

tight /taɪt/ a (-er, -est) <clothes> ajustado, ceñido; (taut) tieso; <control> estricto; <knot, nut> apretado; (🔲, drunk) borracho. **~en** vt apretar. □ **~en up** vt hacer más estricto. **~-fisted** /-'fɪstɪd/ a tacaño. **~ly** adv bien, fuerte; <fastened> fuertemente. **~rope** n cuerda f floja. **~s** npl (for ballet etc) leotardo(s) m(pl); (pantyhose) medias fpl

tile /taɪl/ n (decorative) azulejo m; (on roof) teja f; (on floor) baldosa f. ● vt azulejar; tejar <roof>; embaldosar <floor>

till /tɪl/ prep hasta. ● conj hasta que. ● n caja f. ● vt cultivar

tilt /tɪlt/ vt inclinar. ● vi inclinarse. ● n inclinación f

timber /'tɪmbə(r)/ n madera f (para construcción)

time /taɪm/ n tiempo m; (moment) momento m; (occasion) ocasión f; (by clock) hora *f*; (epoch) época *f*; (rhythm) compás *m*. at **~s** a veces. for the **~** being por el momento. from **~** to **~** de vez en cuando. have a good **~** divertirse, pasarlo bien. in a year's **~** dentro de un año. in no **~** en un abrir y cerrar de ojos. in **~** a tiempo; (eventually) con el tiempo. arrive on **~** llegar a tiempo. it's **~** we left es hora de irnos. ● *vt* elegir el momento; cronometrar *<race>*. **~ bomb** *n* bomba *f* de tiempo. **~ly** *a* oportuno. **~r** *n* cronómetro *m*; (Culin) avisador *m*; (with sand) reloj *m* de arena; (Elec) interruptor *m* de reloj. **~s** /'taɪmz/ *prep*. 2 **~s** 4 is 8 2 (multiplicado) por 4 son 8. **~table** *n* horario *m*

timid /'tɪmɪd/ *a* tímido; (fearful) miedoso

tin /tɪn/ *n* estaño *m*; (container) lata *f*. **~ foil** *n* papel *m* de estaño

tinge /tɪndʒ/ *vt*. be **~d** with sth estar matizado de algo. ● *n* matiz *m*

tingle /'tɪŋgl/ *vi* sentir un hormigueo

tinker /'tɪŋkə(r)/ *vi*. **~** with juguetear con

tinkle /'tɪŋkl/ *vi* tintinear

tinned /tɪnd/ *a* en lata, enlatado

tin opener *n* abrelatas *m*

tint /tɪnt/ *n* matiz *m*

tiny /'taɪnɪ/ *a* (**-ier, -iest**) minúsculo, diminuto

tip /tɪp/ *n* punta *f*. ● *vt* (*pt* **tipped**) (tilt) inclinar; (overturn) volcar; (pour) verter; (give gratuity to) darle (una) propina a. □ **~ off** *vt* avisar. □ **~ out** *vt* verter. □ **~ over** *vi* caerse. **~** propina *f*; (advice) consejo *m* (práctico); (for rubbish) vertedero *m*. **~ped** *a* *<cigarette>* con filtro

tipsy /'tɪpsɪ/ *a* achispado

tiptoe /'tɪptəʊ/ *n*. on **~** de puntillas

tiptop /'tɪptɒp/ *a* ⬛ de primera. in **~** condition en excelente estado

tire /'taɪə(r)/ *n* (Amer) ⇒TYRE. ● *vt* cansar. ● *vi* cansarse. **~d** /'taɪəd/ *a* cansado. get **~d** cansarse. **~d of** harto de. **~d out** agotado. **~less** *a* incansable; *<efforts>* inagotable. **~some** /-səm/ *a* *<person>* pesado; *<task>* tedioso

tiring /'taɪərɪŋ/ *a* cansado, cansador (LAm)

tissue /'tɪʃu:/ *n* (Anat, Bot) tejido *m*; (paper handkerchief) pañuelo *m* de papel. **~ paper** *n* papel *m* de seda

tit /tɪt/ *n* (bird) paro *m*; (🗙, breast) teta *f*

titbit /'tɪtbɪt/ *n* exquisitez *f*

tit for tat *n*: it was **~** fue ojo por ojo, diente por diente

title /'taɪtl/ *n* título *m*

to /tu:, tə/ *prep* a; (towards) hacia; (in order to) para; (as far as) hasta; (of) de. give it **~** me dámelo. what did you say **~** him? ¿qué le dijiste?; I don't want **~** no quiero. it's twenty **~** seven (by clock) son las siete menos veinte, son veinte para las siete (LAm). ● *adv*. pull **~** cerrar. **~ and fro** *adv* de un lado a otro

toad /təʊd/ *n* sapo *m*. **~stool** *n* hongo *m* (*no comestible*)

toast /təʊst/ *n* pan *m* tostado, tostadas *fpl*; (drink) brindis *m*. a piece of **~** una tostada, un pan tostado (Mex). drink a **~** to brindar por. ● *vt* (Culin) tostar; (drink to) brindar por. **~er** *n* tostadora *f* (eléctrica), tostador *m*

tobacco /tə'bækəʊ/ *n* tabaco *m*. **~nist** /-ənɪst/ *n* estanquero *m*

toboggan /tə'bɒgən/ *n* tobogán *m*

today /tə'deɪ/ *n* & *adv* hoy (*m*)

toddler /'tɒdlə(r)/ *n* niño *m* pequeño (*entre un año y dos años y medio de edad*)

toe /təʊ/ *n* dedo *m* (del pie); (of shoe) punta *f*. big **~** dedo *m* gordo (del pie). on one's **~s** (fig) alerta. ● *vt*. **~** the line acatar la disciplina

toffee /'tɒfɪ/ *n* toffee *m* (*golosina hecha con azúcar y mantequilla*)

together /tə'geðə(r)/ *adv* juntos; (at same time) a la vez. **~** with junto con

toil /tɔɪl/ *vi* afanarse. ● *n* trabajo *m* duro

toilet /'tɔɪlɪt/ *n* servicio *m*, baño *m* (LAm). **~ paper** *n* papel *m* higiénico. **~ries** /'tɔɪlɪtrɪz/ *npl* artículos *mpl* de tocador. **~ roll** *n* rollo *m* de papel higiénico

token /'təʊkən/ *n* muestra *f*; (voucher) vale *m*; (coin) ficha *f*. ● *a* simbólico

told /təʊld/ ⇒TELL

tolera|ble /'tɒlərəbl/ *a* tolerable; (not bad) pasable. **~nce** /'tɒlərəns/ *n* to-lerancia *f*. **~nt** *a* tolerante. **~te** /-reɪt/ *vt* tolerar. **~tion** /-'reɪʃən/ *n* tolerancia *f*

toll /təʊl/ *n* (on road) peaje *m*, cuota *f* (Mex). **death ~** número *m* de muer-tos. **~ call** *n* (Amer) llamada *f* inte-rurbana, conferencia *f*. ● *vi* doblar, tocar a muerto

tomato /tə'mɑːtəʊ/ *n* (*pl* -oes) to-mate *m*, jitomate *m* (Mex)

tomb /tuːm/ *n* tumba *f*, sepulcro *m*. **~stone** *n* lápida *f*

tomorrow /tə'mɒrəʊ/ *n* & *adv* ma-ñana (*f*). **see you ~!** ¡hasta mañana!

ton /tʌn/ *n* tonelada *f* (= 1,016kg). **~s of** ☐ montones de. **metric ~** tonela-da *f* (métrica) (= 1,000kg)

tone /təʊn/ *n* tono *m*. ☐ **~ down** *vt* atenuar; moderar <*language*>. **~-deaf** *a* que no tiene oído (mu-sical)

tongs /tɒŋz/ *npl* tenacillas *fpl*

tongue /tʌŋ/ *n* lengua *f*. **say sth ~ in cheek** decir algo medio burlándose. **~-tied** *a* cohibido. **~-twister** *n* trabalenguas *m*

tonic /'tɒnɪk/ *a* tónico. ● *n* (Med, fig) tónico *m*. **~ (water)** *n* tónica *f*

tonight /tə'naɪt/ *adv* & *n* esta noche (*f*); (evening) esta tarde (*f*)

tonne /tʌn/ *n* tonelada *f* (métrica)

tonsil /'tɒnsl/ *n* amígdala *f*. **~litis** /-'laɪtɪs/ *n* amigdalitis *f*

too /tuː/ *adv* (excessively) demasiado; (also) también. **I'm not ~ sure** no estoy muy seguro. **~ many** demasia-dos. **~ much** demasiado

took /tʊk/ ⇒TAKE

tool /tuːl/ *n* herramienta *f*

tooth /tuːθ/ *n* (*pl* **teeth**) diente *m*; (molar) muela *f*. **~ache** *n* dolor *m* de muelas. **~brush** *n* cepillo *m* de dientes. **~paste** *n* pasta *f* dentífri-ca, pasta *f* de dientes. **~pick** *n* pali-llo *m* (de dientes)

top /tɒp/ *n* parte *f* superior, parte *f* de arriba; (of mountain) cima *f*; (of tree) co-pa *f*; (of page) parte *f* superior; (lid, of bottle) tapa *f*; (of pen) capuchón *m*; (spinning **~**) trompo *m*, peonza *f*. **be ~ of the class** ser el primero de la cla-

se. **from ~ to bottom** de arriba abajo. **on ~ of** encima de; (besides) además de. ● *a* más alto; <*shelf*> superior; <*speed*> máximo; (in rank) superior; (leading) más destacado. ● *vt* (*pt* **topped**) cubrir; (exceed) exceder. ☐ **~ up** *vt* llenar. **~ floor** *n* último piso *m*. **~ hat** *n* chistera *f*. **~-heavy** /-'hevɪ/ *a* inestable (*por ser más pesado en su parte superior*)

topic /'tɒpɪk/ *n* tema *m*. **~al** *a* de actualidad

topless /tɒples/ *a* topless

topple /'tɒpl/ *vi* (Pol) derribar; (over-turn) volcar. ● *vi* caerse

top secret /tɒp'siːkrɪt/ *a* secreto, reservado

torch /tɔːtʃ/ *n* linterna *f*; (flaming) antorcha *f*

tore /tɔː(r)/ ⇒TEAR[1]

torment /'tɔːment/ *n* tormento *m*. ● /tɔː'ment/ *vt* atormentar

torn /tɔːn/ ⇒TEAR[1]

tornado /tɔː'neɪdəʊ/ *n* (*pl* -oes) tornado *m*

torpedo /tɔː'piːdəʊ/ *n* (*pl* -oes) torpedo *m*. ● *vt* torpedear

torrent /'tɒrənt/ *n* torrente *m*. **~ial** /tə'renʃl/ *a* torrencial

torrid /'tɒrɪd/ *a* tórrido; <*affair*> apasionado

tortoise /'tɔːtəs/ *n* tortuga *f*. **~shell** *n* carey *m*

tortuous /'tɔːtjʊəs/ *a* tortuoso

torture /'tɔːtʃə(r)/ *n* tortura *f*. ● *vt* torturar

Tory /'tɔːrɪ/ *a* & *n* tory *m* & *f*

toss /tɒs/ *vt* tirar, lanzar <*ball*>; (shake) sacudir. ● *vi*. **~ and turn** (in bed) dar vueltas

tot /tɒt/ *n* pequeño *m*; (☐, of liquor) tra-go *m*. ● *vt* (*pt* **totted**). **~ up** ☐ su-mar

total /'təʊtl/ *a* & *n* total (*m*). ● *vt* (*pt* **totalled**) ascender a un total de; (add up) totalizar. **~itarian** /təʊtælɪ'teərɪən/ *a* totalitario. **~ly** *adv* totalmente

totter /'tɒtə(r)/ *vi* tambalearse

touch /tʌtʃ/ *vt* tocar; (move) conmo-ver; (concern) afectar. ● *vi* tocar; <*wires*> tocarse. ● *n* toque *m*; (sense) tacto *m*; (contact) contacto *m*. **be/get/**

stay in ~ **with** estar/ponerse/mantenerse en contacto con. □ ~ **down** *vi* <*aircraft*> aterrizar. □ ~ **up** *vt* retocar. ~**ing** *a* enternecedor. ~**y** *a* quisquilloso

tough /tʌf/ *a* (**-er, -est**) duro; (strong) fuerte, resistente; (difficult) difícil; (severe) severo. ~**en.** ~ (**up**) *vt* endurecer; hacer más fuerte <*person*>

tour /tʊə(r)/ *n* viaje *m*; (visit) visita *f*; (excursion) excursión *f*; (by team etc) gira *f*. **be on** ~ estar de gira. ● *vt* recorrer; (visit) visitar. ~ **guide** *n* guía de turismo

touris|m /'tʊərizəm/ *n* turismo *m*. ~**t** /'tʊərɪst/ *n* turista *m* & *f*. ● *a* turístico. ~**t office** *n* oficina *f* de turismo

tournament /'tɔːnəmənt/ *n* torneo *m*

tousle /'taʊzl/ *vt* despeinar

tout /taʊt/ *vi.* ~ (**for**) solicitar

tow /təʊ/ *vt* remolcar. ● *n* remolque *m*

toward(s) /tə'wɔːd(z)/ *prep* hacia. **his attitude** ~ **her** su actitud para con ella

towel /'taʊəl/ *n* toalla *f*

tower /'taʊə(r)/ *n* torre *f*. ● *vi.* ~ **above** <*building*> descollar sobre; <*person*> destacar sobre. ~ **block** *n* edificio *m or* bloque *m* de apartamentos. ~**ing** *a* altísimo; <*rage*> violento

town /taʊn/ *n* ciudad *f*; (smaller) pueblo *m*. **go to** ~ 🔢 no escatimar dinero. ~ **hall** *n* ayuntamiento *m*

toxic /'tɒksɪk/ *a* tóxico

toy /tɔɪ/ *n* juguete *m*. □ ~ **with** *vt* juguetear con <*object*>; darle vueltas a <*idea*>. ~**shop** *n* juguetería *f*

trac|e /treɪs/ *n* señal *f*, rastro *m*. ● *vt* trazar; (draw) dibujar; (with tracing paper) calcar; (track down) localizar. ~**ing paper** *n* papel *m* de calcar

track /træk/ *n* pista *f*, huellas *fpl*; (path) sendero *m*; (Sport) pista *f*. **the** ~(**s**) la vía férrea; (Rail) vía *f*. **keep** ~ **of** seguirle la pista a <*person*>. ● *vt* seguirle la pista a. □ ~ **down** *vt* localizar. ~ **suit** *n* equipo *m* (de deportes), chándal *m*

tract /trækt/ *n* (land) extensión *f*; (pamphlet) tratado *m* breve

traction /'trækʃn/ *n* tracción *f*

tractor /'træktə(r)/ *n* tractor *m*

trade /treɪd/ *n* comercio *m*; (occupation) oficio *m*; (exchange) cambio *m*; (industry) industria *f*. ● *vt.* ~ **sth for sth** cambiar algo por algo. ● *vi* comerciar. □ ~ **in** *vt* (give in part-exchange) entregar como parte del pago. ~ **mark** *n* marca *f* (de fábrica). ~**r** *n* comerciante *m* & *f*. ~ **union** *n* sindicato *m*

tradition /trə'dɪʃn/ *n* tradición *f*. ~**al** *a* tradicional

traffic /'træfɪk/ *n* tráfico *m*. ● *vi* (*pt* **trafficked**) comerciar (in en). ~ **circle** *n* (Amer) glorieta *f*, rotonda *f*. ~ **island** *n* isla *f* peatonal. ~ **jam** *n* embotellamiento *m*, atasco *m*. ~ **lights** *npl* semáforo *m*. ~ **warden** *n* guardia *m*, controlador *m* de tráfico

trag|edy /'trædʒɪdɪ/ *n* tragedia *f*. ~**ic** /'trædʒɪk/ *a* trágico

trail /treɪl/ *vi* arrastrarse; (lag) rezagarse. ● *vt* (track) seguir la pista de. ● *n* (left by animal, person) huellas *fpl*; (path) sendero *m*. **be on the** ~ **of s.o./ sth** seguir la pista de uno/algo ~**er** *n* remolque *m*; (Amer, caravan) caravana *f*, rulot *m*; (film) avance *m*

train /treɪn/ *n* (Rail) tren *m*; (of events) serie *f*; (of dress) cola *f*. ● *vt* capacitar <*employee*>; adiestrar <*soldier*>; (Sport) entrenar; educar <*voice*>; guiar <*plant*>; amaestrar <*animal*>. ● *vi* estudiar; (Sport) entrenarse. ~**ed** *a* (skilled) cualificado, calificado; <*doctor*> diplomado. ~**ee** /treɪ'niː/ *n* aprendiz *m*; (Amer, Mil) recluta *m* & *f*. ~**er** *n* (Sport) entrenador *m*; (of animals) amaestrador *m*. ~**ers** *mpl* zapatillas *fpl* de deporte. ~**ing** *n* capacitación *f*; (Sport) entrenamiento *m*

trait /treɪ(t)/ *n* rasgo *m*

traitor /'treɪtə(r)/ *n* traidor *m*

tram /træm/ *n* tranvía *m*

tramp /træmp/ *vi.* ~ (**along**) caminar pesadamente. ● *n* vagabundo *m*

trample /'træmpl/ *vt* pisotear. ● *vi.* ~ **on** pisotear

trampoline /'træmpəli:n/ n trampolín m

trance /trɑ:ns/ n trance m

tranquil /'træŋkwɪl/ a tranquilo. ～**lity** /-'kwɪləti/ n tranquilidad f; (of person) serenidad f. ～**lize** /'træŋkwɪlaɪz/ vt sedar, dar un sedante a. ～**lizer** n sedante m, tranquilizante m

transaction /træn'zækʃən/ n transacción f, operación f

transatlantic /trænzət'læntɪk/ a transatlántico

transcend /træn'send/ vt (go beyond) exceder

transcript /'trænskrɪpt/ n transcripción f

transfer /træns'fɜ:(r)/ vt (pt transferred) trasladar; traspasar <player>; transferir <funds, property>; pasar <call>. ●vi trasladarse. ●/'trænsfɜ:(r)/ n traslado m; (of player) traspaso m; (of funds, property) transferencia f; (paper) calcomanía f

transform /træns'fɔ:m/ vt transformar. ～**ation** /-ə'meɪʃn/ n transformación f. ～**er** n transformador m

transfusion /træns'fju:ʒn/ n transfusión f

transient /'trænzɪənt/ a pasajero

transistor /træn'zɪstə(r)/ n transistor m

transit /'trænsɪt/ n tránsito m. ～**ion** /træn'zɪʒn/ n transición f. ～**ive** /'trænsɪtɪv/ a transitivo

translat|e /trænz'leɪt/ vt traducir. ～**ion** /-ʃn/ n traducción f. ～**or** n traductor m

transmission /træns'mɪʃn/ n transmisión f

transmit /trænz'mɪt/ vt (pt transmitted) transmitir. ～**ter** n transmisor m

transparen|cy /træns'pærənsɪ/ n transparencia f; (Photo) diapositiva f. ～**t** a transparente

transplant /træns'plɑ:nt/ vt trasplantar. ●/'trænsplɑ:nt/ n trasplante m

transport /træn'spɔ:t/ vt transportar. ●/'trænspɔ:t/ n transporte m. ～**ation** /-'teɪʃn/ n transporte m

trap /træp/ n trampa f. ●vt (pt trapped) atrapar; (jam) atascar; (cut off) bloquear. ～**door** n trampilla f

trapeze /trə'pi:z/ n trapecio m

trash /træʃ/ n basura f; (Amer, worthless people) escoria f. ～ **can** n (Amer) cubo m de la basura, bote m de la basura (Mex). ～**y** a <souvenir> de porquería; <magazine> malo

travel /'trævl/ vi (pt travelled) viajar; <vehicle> desplazarse. ●vt recorrer. ●n viajes mpl. ～ **agency** n agencia f de viajes. ～**ler** n viajero m. ～**ler's cheque** n cheque m de viaje or viajero. ～**ling expenses** npl gastos mpl de viaje

trawler /'trɔ:lə(r)/ n barca f pesquera

tray /treɪ/ n bandeja f

treacher|ous a traidor; (deceptive) engañoso. ～**y** n traición f

treacle /'tri:kl/ n melaza f

tread /tred/ vi (pt trod, pp trodden) pisar. ～ **on** sth pisar algo. ～ **carefully** andarse con cuidado. ●n (step) paso m; (of tyre) banda f de rodamiento

treason /'tri:zn/ n traición f

treasur|e /'treʒə(r)/ n tesoro m. ～**ed** /'treʒəd/ a <possession> preciado. ～**er** /'treʒərə(r)/ n tesorero m. ～**y** n erario m, tesoro m. the T～**y** el fisco, la hacienda pública. **Department of the T～y** (in US) Departamento m del Tesoro

treat /tri:t/ vt tratar; (Med) tratar. ～ **s.o.** (to meal etc) invitar a uno. ●n placer m; (present) regalo m

treatise /'tri:tɪz/ n tratado m

treatment /'tri:tmənt/ n tratamiento m

treaty /'tri:tɪ/ n tratado m

treble /'trebl/ a triple; <clef> de sol; <voice> de tiple. ●vt triplicar. ●vi triplicarse. ●n tiple m & f

tree /tri:/ n árbol m

trek /trek/ n caminata f. ●vi (pt trekked) caminar

trellis /'trelɪs/ n enrejado m

tremble /'trembl/ vi temblar

tremendous /trɪ'mendəs/ a formidable; (fam, huge) tremendo. ～**ly** adv tremendamente

tremor /'tremə(r)/ n temblor m

trench /trentʃ/ n zanja f; (Mil) trinchera f

trend /trend/ n tendencia f; (fashion) moda f. **~y** a (**-ier, -iest**) Ⓘ moderno

trepidation /trepɪ'deɪʃn/ n inquietud f

trespass /'trespəs/ vi. **~ on** entrar sin autorización (en propiedad ajena). **~er** n intruso m

trial /'traɪəl/ n prueba f; (Jurid) proceso m, juicio m; (ordeal) prueba f dura. **by ~ and error** por ensayo y error. **be on ~** estar a prueba; (Jurid) estar siendo procesado

triang|le /'traɪæŋgl/ n triángulo m. **~ular** /-'æŋgjʊlə(r)/ a triangular

trib|al /'traɪbl/ a tribal. **~e** /traɪb/ n tribu f

tribulation /trɪbjʊ'leɪʃn/ n tribulación f

tribunal /traɪ'bjuːnl/ n tribunal m

tributary /'trɪbjʊtrɪ/ n (Geog) afluente m

tribute /'trɪbjuːt/ n tributo m; (acknowledgement) homenaje m. **pay ~ to** rendir homenaje a

trick /trɪk/ n trampa f, ardid m; (joke) broma f; (feat) truco m; (in card games) baza f. **play a ~ on** gastar una broma a. ● vt engañar. **~ery** n engaño m

trickle /'trɪkl/ vi gotear. **~ in** (fig) entrar poco a poco

trickster /'trɪkstə(r)/ n estafador m

tricky /'trɪkɪ/ a delicado, difícil

tricycle /'traɪsɪkl/ n triciclo m

tried /traɪd/ ⇒TRY

trifl|e /'traɪfl/ n nimiedad f; (Culin) postre de bizcocho, jerez, frutas y nata. ● vi. □ **~e with** vt jugar con. **~ing** a insignificante

trigger /'trɪgə(r)/ n (of gun) gatillo m. ● vt. **~ (off)** desencadenar

trim /trɪm/ a (**trimmer, trimmest**) (slim) esbelto; (neat) elegante. ● vt (pt **trimmed**) (cut) recortar; (adorn) adornar. ● n (cut) recorte m. **in ~** en buen estado. **~mings** npl recortes mpl

trinity /'trɪnɪtɪ/ n. **the (Holy) T~** la (Santísima) Trinidad

trinket /'trɪŋkɪt/ n chuchería f

trio /'triːəʊ/ n (pl **-os**) trío m

trip /trɪp/ (pt **tripped**) vt **~ (up)** hacerle una zancadilla a, hacer tropezar. ● vi tropezar. ● n (journey) viaje m; (outing) excursión f; (stumble) traspié m

tripe /traɪp/ n callos mpl, mondongo m (LAm), pancita f (Mex); (Ⓘ, nonsense) paparruchas fpl

triple /'trɪpl/ a triple. ● vt triplicar. ● vi triplicarse. **~t** /'trɪplɪt/ n trillizo m

triplicate /'trɪplɪkət/ a triplicado. **in ~** por triplicado

tripod /'traɪpɒd/ n trípode m

trite /traɪt/ a trillado

triumph /'traɪʌmf/ n triunfo m. ● vi triunfar (**over** sobre). **~al** /-'ʌmfl/ a triunfal. **~ant** /-'ʌmfnt/ a <troops> triunfador; <moment> triunfal; <smile> de triunfo

trivial /'trɪvɪəl/ a insignificante; <concerns> trivial. **~ity** /-'ælətɪ/ n trivialidad f

trod, trodden /trɒd, trɒdn/ ⇒TREAD

trolley /'trɒlɪ/ n (pl **-eys**) carretón m; (in supermarket, airport) carrito m; (for food, drink) carrito m, mesa f rodante. **~ car** n (Amer) tranvía f

trombone /trɒm'bəʊn/ n trombón m

troop /truːp/ n compañía f; (of cavalry) escuadrón m. ● vi. **~ in** entrar en tropel. **~ out** salir en tropel. **~er** n soldado m de caballería; (Amer, state police officer) agente m & f. **~s** npl (Mil) tropas fpl

trophy /'trəʊfɪ/ n trofeo m

tropic /'trɒpɪk/ n trópico m. **~al** a tropical. **~s** npl trópicos mpl

trot /trɒt/ n trote m. ● vi (pt **trotted**) trotar

trouble /'trʌbl/ n problemas mpl; (awkward situation) apuro m; (inconvenience) molestia f. **be in ~** estar en apuros. **get into ~** meterse en problemas. **look for ~** buscar camo-rra. **take the ~ to do sth** molestarse en hacer algo. ● vt (bother) molestar; (worry) preocupar. **~-maker** n alborotador m. **~some** /-səm/ a problemático. ~ **spot** *n* punto *m* conflictivo

trough /trɒf/ *n* (for drinking) abrevadero *m*; (for feeding) comedero *m*

troupe /tru:p/ *n* compañía *f* teatral

trousers /'traʊzəz/ *npl* pantalón *m*, pantalones *mpl*

trout /traʊt/ *n* (*pl* **trout**) trucha *f*

trowel /'traʊəl/ *n* (garden) desplantador *m*; (for mortar) paleta *f*

truant /'tru:ənt/ *n*. **play** ~ hacer novillos

truce /tru:s/ *n* tregua *f*

truck /trʌk/ *n* camión *m*; (Rail) vagón *m*, furgón *m*; (Amer, vegetables, fruit) productos *mpl* de la huerta. ~ **driver**, ~**er** (Amer) *n* camionero *m*. ~**ing** *n* transporte *m* por carretera

trudge /trʌdʒ/ *vi* andar penosamente

true /tru:/ *a* (**-er**, **-est**) verdadero; <*story, account*> verídico; <*friend*> auténtico, de verdad. ~ **to** s/th/s.o. fiel a algo/uno. **be** ~ ser cierto. **come** ~ hacerse realidad

truffle /'trʌfl/ *n* trufa *f*; (chocolate) trufa *f* de chocolate

truly /'tru:lɪ/ *adv* verdaderamente; (sincerely) sinceramente. **yours** ~ (in letters) cordiales saludos

trump /trʌmp/ *n* (Cards) triunfo *m*; (fig) baza *f*

trumpet /'trʌmpɪt/ *n* trompeta *f*. ~**er** *n* trompetista *m* & *f*, trompeta *m* & *f*

truncheon /'trʌntʃən/ *n* porra *f*

trunk /trʌŋk/ *n* (of tree) tronco *m*; (box) baúl *m*; (of elephant) trompa *f*; (Amer, Auto) maletero *m*, cajuela *f* (Mex). ~**s** *npl* bañador *m*, traje *m* de baño

truss /trʌs/. **truss (up)** *vt* atar

trust /trʌst/ *n* confianza *f*; (money, property) fondo *m* de inversiones; (institution) fundación *f*. **on** ~ a ojos cerrados; (Com) al fiado. ● *vi*. ~ **in** s.o./s/th confiar en uno/algo. ● *vt* confiar en; (in negative sentences) fiarse; (hope) esperar. ~**ed** *a* leal. ~**ee** /trʌ'sti:/ *n* fideicomisario *m*. ~**ful** *a* confiado. ~**ing** *a* confiado. ~**worthy**, ~**y** *a* digno de confianza

truth /tru:θ/ *n* (*pl* **-s** /tru:ðz/) verdad *f*; (of account, story) veracidad *f*. ~**ful** *a* veraz.

try /traɪ/ *vt* (*pt* **tried**) intentar; probar <*food, product*>; (be a strain on) poner a prueba; (Jurid) procesar. ~ **to do sth** tratar de hacer algo, intentar hacer algo. ~ **not to forget** procura no olvidarte. ● *n* tentativa *f*, prueba *f*; (Rugby) ensayo *m*. □ ~ **on** *vt* probarse <*garment*>. □ ~ **out** *vt* probar. ~**ing** *a* duro; (annoying) molesto

tsar /zɑ:(r)/ *n* zar *m*

T-shirt /'ti:ʃɜ:t/ *n* camiseta *f*

tub /tʌb/ *n* cuba *f*; (for washing clothes) tina *f*; (bathtub) bañera *f*; (for ice cream) envase *m*, tarrina *f*

tuba /'tju:bə/ *n* tuba *f*

tubby /'tʌbɪ/ *a* (**-ier**, **-iest**) rechoncho

tube /tju:b/ *n* tubo *m*; (🇬🇧, Rail) metro *m*; (Amer 🇬🇧, television) tele *f*. **inner** ~ *n* cámara *f* de aire

tuberculosis /tju:bɜ:kjʊˈləʊsɪs/ *n* tuberculosis *f*

tub|ing /'tju:bɪŋ/ *n* tubería *f*. ~**ular** /-jʊlə(r)/ *a* tubular

tuck /tʌk/ *n* (fold) jareta *f*. ● *vt* plegar; (put) meter. □ ~ **in(to)** *vi* (🇬🇧, eat) ponerse a comer. □ ~ **up** *vt* arropar <*child*>

Tuesday /'tju:zdeɪ/ *n* martes *m*

tuft /tʌft/ *n* (of hair) mechón *m*; (of feathers) penacho *m*; (of grass) mata *f*

tug /tʌg/ *vt* (*pt* **tugged**) tirar de. ● *vi*. ~ **at sth** tirar de algo. ● *n* tirón *m*; (Naut) remolcador *m*. ~**-of-war** *n* juego de tira y afloja

tuition /tju:'ɪʃn/ *n* clases *fpl*

tulip /'tju:lɪp/ *n* tulipán *m*

tumble /'tʌmbl/ *vi* caerse. ● *n* caída *f*. ~**down** *a* en ruinas. ~**-drier** *n* secadora *f*. ~**r** *n* (glass) vaso *m* (*de lados rectos*)

tummy /'tʌmɪ/ *n* 🇬🇧 barriga *f*

tumour /'tju:mə(r)/ *n* tumor *m*

tumult /'tju:mʌlt/ *n* tumulto *m*. ~**uous** /-'mʌltjʊəs/ *a* <*applause*> apoteósico

tuna /'tju:nə/ *n* (*pl* **tuna**) atún *m*

tune /tju:n/ *n* melodía *f*; (piece) tonada *f*. **be in** ~ estar afinado. **be out of** ~ estar desafinado. ● *vt* afinar, sintonizar <*radio, TV*>; (Mec) poner a punto. ●*vi*. ~ **in** (**to**) sintonizar (con). □ ~ **up** *vt/i* afinar. ~**ful** *a* melodioso. ~**r** *n* afinador *m*; (Radio) sintonizador *m*

tunic /'tju:nɪk/ *n* túnica *f*

tunnel /'tʌnl/ *n* túnel *m*. ●*vi* (*pt* **tunnelled**) abrir un túnel

turban /'tɜːbən/ *n* turbante *m*

turbine /'tɜːbaɪn/ *n* turbina *f*

turbo /'tɜːbəʊ/ *n* (*pl* **-os**) turbo(compresor) *m*

turbulen|ce /'tɜːbjʊləns/ *n* turbulencia *f*. ~**t** *a* turbulento

turf /tɜːf/ *n* (*pl* **turfs** *or* **turves**) césped *m*; (segment of grass) tepe *m*. □ ~ **out** *vt* 🄴 echar

turgid /'tɜːdʒɪd/ *a* <*language*> ampuloso

turkey /'tɜːkɪ/ *n* (*pl* **-eys**) pavo *m*

Turk|ey /'tɜːkɪ/ *f* Turquía *f*. ~**ish** *a & n* turco (*m*)

turmoil /'tɜːmɔɪl/ *n* confusión *f*

turn /tɜːn/ *vt* hacer girar; volver <*head, page*>; doblar <*corner*>; (change) cambiar; (deflect) desviar. ~ **sth into sth** convertir *or* transformar algo en algo. ●*vi* <*handle*> girar, dar vueltas; <*person*> volverse, darse la vuelta. ~ **right** girar *or* doblar *or* torcer a la derecha. ~ **red** ponerse rojo. ~ **into sth** convertirse en algo. ●*n* vuelta *f*; (in road) curva *f*; (change) giro *m*; (sequence) turno *m*; (🄴, of illness) ataque *m*. **good** ~ favor *m*. **in** ~ a su vez. □ ~ **down** *vt* (fold) doblar; (reduce) bajar; (reject) rechazar. □ ~ **off** *vt* cerrar <*tap*>; apagar <*light, TV, etc*>. *vi* (from road) doblar. □ ~ **on** *vt* abrir <*tap*>; encender, prender (LAm) <*light etc*>. □ ~ **out** *vt* apagar <*light etc*>. *vi* (result) resultar. □ ~ **round** *vi* darse la vuelta. □ ~ **up** *vi* aparecer. *vt* (find) encontrar; levantar <*collar*>; subir <*hem*>; acortar <*trousers*>; poner más fuerte <*gas*>. ~**ed-up** *a* <*nose*> respingón. ~**ing** *n* (in town) bocacalle *f*. **we've missed the ~ing** nos hemos pasado la calle (*or* carretera). ~**ing-point** *n* momento *m* decisivo.

turnip /'tɜːnɪp/ *n* nabo *m*

turn: ~**over** *n* (Com) facturación *f*; (of staff) movimiento *m*. ~**pike** *n* (Amer) autopista *f* de peaje. ~**stile** *n* torniquete *m*. ~**table** *n* platina *f*. ~**-up** *n* (of trousers) vuelta *f*, valenciana *f* (Mex)

turquoise /'tɜːkwɔɪz/ *a & n* turquesa (*f*)

turret /'tʌrɪt/ *n* torrecilla *f*

turtle /'tɜːtl/ *n* tortuga *f* de mar; (Amer, tortoise) tortuga *f*

turves /tɜːvz/ ⇒TURF

tusk /tʌsk/ *n* colmillo *m*

tussle /'tʌsl/ *n* lucha *f*

tutor /'tjuːtə(r)/ *n* profesor *m* particular

tuxedo /tʌk'siːdəʊ/ *n* (*pl* **-os**) (Amer) esmoquin *m*, smoking *m*

TV /tiː'viː/ *n* televisión *f*, tele *f* 🄴

twang /twæŋ/ *n* tañido *m*; (in voice) gangueo *m*

tweet /twiːt/ *n* piada *f*. ●*vi* piar

tweezers /'twiːzəz/ *npl* pinzas *fpl*

twel|fth /twelfθ/ *a* duodécimo. ●*n* doceavo *m*. ~**ve** /twelv/ *a & n* doce (*m*)

twent|ieth /'twentɪəθ/ *a* vigésimo. ●*n* veinteavo *m*. ~**y** /'twentɪ/ *a & n* veinte (*m*)

twice /twaɪs/ *adv* dos veces. ~ **as many people** el doble de gente

twiddle /'twɪdl/ *vt* (hacer) girar

twig /twɪg/ *n* ramita *f*. ●*vi* (*pt* **twigged**) 🄴 caer, darse cuenta

twilight /'twaɪlaɪt/ *n* crepúsculo *m*

twin /twɪn/ *a & n* gemelo (*m*), mellizo (*m*) (LAm)

twine /twaɪn/ *n* cordel *m*, bramante *m*

twinge /twɪndʒ/ *n* punzada *f*; (of remorse) punzada *f*

twinkle /'twɪŋkl/ *vi* centellear. ●*n* centelleo *m*; (in eye) brillo *m*

twirl /twɜːl/ *vt* (hacer) girar. ●*vi* girar. ●*n* vuelta *f*

twist /twɪst/ *vt* retorcer; (roll) enrollar; girar <*knob*>; tergiversar <*words*>; (distort) retorcer. ~ **one's ankle** torcerse el tobillo. ●*vi* <*rope, wire*> enrollarse; <*road, river*> serpentear. ●*n* torsión *f*; (curve) vuelta *f*

twit /twɪt/ *n* 🔢 imbécil *m*

twitch /twɪtʃ/ *vi* moverse. ● *n* tic *m*

twitter /'twɪtə(r)/ *vi* gorjear

two /tu:/ *a & n* dos (*m*). ~**-bit** *a* (Amer) de tres al cuarto. ~**-faced** *a* falso, insincero. ~**fold** *a* doble. ● *adv* dos veces. ~**pence** /'tʌpəns/ *n* dos peniques *mpl*. ~**-piece** (**suit**) *n* traje *m* de dos piezas. ~**-way** *a* <*traffic*> de doble sentido

tycoon /taɪ'ku:n/ *n* magnate *m*

tying /'taɪɪŋ/ ⇒TIE

type /taɪp/ *n* tipo *m*. ● *vt/i* escribir a máquina. ~**-cast** *a* <*actor*> encasillado. ~**script** *n* texto *m* me-canografiado, manuscrito *m* (*de una obra, novela etc*). ~**writer** *n* máqui-na *f* de escribir. ~**written** *a* escrito a máquina, mecanografiado

typhoon /taɪ'fu:n/ *n* tifón *m*

typical /'tɪpɪkl/ *a* típico. ~**ly** *adv* típicamente

typify /'tɪpɪfaɪ/ *vt* tipificar

typi|ng /'taɪpɪŋ/ *n* mecanografía *f*. ~**st** *n* mecanógrafo *m*

tyran|nical /tɪ'rænɪkl/ *a* tiránico. ~**ny** /'tɪrənɪ/ *n* tiranía *f*. ~**t** /'taɪərənt/ *n* tirano *m*

tyre /'taɪə(r)/ *n* neumático *m*, llanta *f* (LAm)

....

U u

....

udder /'ʌdə(r)/ *n* ubre *f*

UFO /'ju:fəʊ/ *abbr* (= **unidentified flying object**) OVNI *m* (*objeto volante no identificado*)

ugly /'ʌglɪ/ *a* (**-ier, -iest**) feo

UK /ju:'keɪ/ *abbr* (= **United Kingdom**) Reino *m* Unido

Ukraine /ju:'kreɪn/ *n* Ucrania *f*

ulcer /'ʌlsə(r)/ *n* úlcera *f*; (external) llaga *f*

ultimate /'ʌltɪmət/ *a* (eventual) final; (utmost) máximo. ~**ly** *adv* en última instancia; (in the long run) a la larga

ultimatum /ʌltɪ'meɪtəm/ *n* (*pl* **-ums**) ultimátum *m*

ultra... /'ʌltrə/ *pref* ultra... ~**violet** /-'vaɪələt/ *a* ultravioleta

umbilical cord /ʌm'bɪlɪkl/ *n* cordón *m* umbilical

umbrella /ʌm'brelə/ *n* paraguas *m*

umpire /'ʌmpaɪə(r)/ *n* árbitro *m*. ● *vt* arbitrar

umpteen /'ʌmpti:n/ *a* 🔢 tropecientos 🔢. ~**th** *a* 🔢 enésimo

un... /ʌn/ *pref* in..., des..., no, poco, sin

UN /ju:'en/ *abbr* (= **United Nations**) ONU *f* (*Organización de las Naciones Unidas*)

unable /ʌn'eɪbl/ *a*. be ~ **to** no poder; (be incapable of) ser incapaz de

unacceptable /ʌnək'septəbl/ *a* <*behaviour*> inaceptable; <*terms*> inadmisible

unaccompanied /ʌnə'kʌmpənɪd/ *a* <*luggage*> no acompañado; <*person, instrument*> solo; <*singing*> sin acompañamiento

unaccustomed /ʌnə'kʌstəmd/ *a* desacostumbrado. be ~ **to** *a* no estar acostumbrado a

unaffected /ʌnə'fektɪd/ *a* natural

unaided /ʌn'eɪdɪd/ *a* sin ayuda

unanimous /ju:'nænɪməs/ *a* unánime. ~**ly** *adv* unánimemente; <*elect*> por unanimidad

unarmed /ʌn'ɑ:md/ *a* desarmado

unattended /ʌnə'tendɪd/ *a* sin vigilar

unattractive /ʌnə'træktɪv/ *a* poco atractivo

unavoidabl|e /ʌnə'vɔɪdəbl/ *a* inevitable. ~**y** *adv*. I was ~y delayed no pude evitar llegar tarde

unaware /ʌnə'weə(r)/ *a*. be ~ **of** ignorar, no ser consciente de. ~**s** /-eəz/ *adv* desprevenido

unbearabl|e /ʌn'beərəbl/ *a* insoportable, inaguantable. ~**y** *adv* inaguantablemente

unbeat|able /ʌn'bi:təbl/ *a* <*quality*> insuperable; <*team*> invencible. ~**en** *a* no vencido; <*record*> insuperado

unbelievable /ˌʌnbɪˈliːvəbl/ *a* increíble. **~y** *adv* increíblemente

unbiased /ʌnˈbaɪəst/ *a* imparcial

unblock /ʌnˈblɒk/ *vt* desatascar

unbolt /ʌnˈbəʊlt/ *vt* descorrer el pestillo de

unborn /ʌnˈbɔːn/ *a* que todavía no ha nacido

unbreakable /ʌnˈbreɪkəbl/ *a* irrompible

unbroken /ʌnˈbrəʊkən/ *a* (intact) intacto; (continuous) ininterrumpido

unbutton /ʌnˈbʌtn/ *vt* desabotonar, desabrochar

uncalled-for /ʌnˈkɔːldfɔː(r)/ *a* fuera de lugar

uncanny /ʌnˈkænɪ/ *a* (**-ier, -iest**) raro, extraño

uncertain /ʌnˈsɜːtn/ *a* incierto; (hesitant) vacilante. **be ~ of/about sth** no estar seguro de algo. **~ty** *n* incertidumbre *f*

uncharitable /ʌnˈtʃærɪtəbl/ *a* severo

uncivilized /ʌnˈsɪvɪlaɪzd/ *a* incivilizado

uncle /ˈʌŋkl/ *n* tío *m*

unclean /ʌnˈkliːn/ *a* impuro

unclear /ʌnˈklɪə(r)/ *a* poco claro

uncomfortable /ʌnˈkʌmfətəbl/ *a* incómodo

uncommon /ʌnˈkɒmən/ *a* poco común

uncompromising /ʌnˈkɒmprəmaɪzɪŋ/ *a* intransigente

unconcerned /ʌnkənˈsɜːnd/ *a* indiferente

unconditional /ʌnkənˈdɪʃənl/ *a* incondicional

unconnected /ʌnkəˈnektɪd/ *a* (unrelated) sin conexión. **the events are ~** estos acontecimientos no guardan ninguna relación (entre sí)

unconscious /ʌnˈkɒnʃəs/ *a* (Med) inconsciente. **~ly** *adv* inconscientemente

unconventional /ʌnkənˈvenʃənl/ *a* poco convencional

uncork /ʌnˈkɔːk/ *vt* descorchar

uncouth /ʌnˈkuːθ/ *a* zafio

uncover /ʌnˈkʌvə(r)/ *vt* destapar; revelar <*plot, scandal*>

undaunted /ʌnˈdɔːntɪd/ *a* impertérrito

undecided /ʌndɪˈsaɪdɪd/ *a* indeciso

undeniable /ʌndɪˈnaɪəbl/ *a* innegable. **~y** *adv* sin lugar a dudas

under /ˈʌndə(r)/ *prep* debajo de; (less than) menos de; <*heading*> bajo; (according to) según; (expressing movement) por debajo de. ● *adv* debajo, abajo

under... *pref* sub...

under: **~carriage** *n* (Aviat) tren *m* de aterrizaje. **~charge** *vt* /-ˈtʃɑːdʒ/ cobrarle de menos a. **~clothes** *npl* ropa *f* interior. **~coat**, **~coating** (Amer) *n* (paint) pintura *f* base; (first coat) primera mano *f* de pintura. **~cover** *a* /-ˈkʌvə(r)/ secreto. **~current** *n* corriente *f* submarina. **~dog** *n*. **the ~dog** el que tiene menos posibilidades. **the ~dogs** *npl* los de abajo. **~done** *a* /-ˈdʌn/ <*meat*> poco hecho. **~estimate** /-ˈestɪmeɪt/ *vt* (underrate) subestimar. **~fed** /-ˈfed/ *a* subalimentado. **~foot** /-ˈfʊt/ *adv* debajo de los pies. **~go** *vt* (*pt* **-went**, *pp* **-gone**) sufrir. **~graduate** /-ˈgrædjʊət/ *n* estudiante *m & f* universitario (no licenciado). **~ground** /-ˈgraʊnd/ *adv* bajo tierra; (in secret) clandestinamente. ● /-ˈgraʊnd/ *a* subterráneo; (secret) clandestino. ● *n* metro *m*. **~growth** *n* maleza *f*. **~hand** /-ˈhænd/ *a* (secret) clandestino; (deceptive) fraudulento. **~lie** /-ˈlaɪ/ *vt* (*pt* **-lay**, *pp* **-lain**, *pres p* **-lying**) subyacer a. **~line** /-ˈlaɪn/ *vt* subrayar. **~lying** /-ˈlaɪɪŋ/ *a* subyacente. **~mine** /-ˈmaɪn/ *vt* socavar. **~neath** /-ˈniːθ/ *prep* debajo de, abajo de (LAm). ● *adv* por debajo. **~paid** /-ˈpeɪd/ *a* mal pagado. **~pants** *npl* calzoncillos *mpl*. **~pass** *n* paso *m* subterráneo; (for traffic) paso *m* inferior. **~privileged** /-ˈprɪvəlɪdʒd/ *a* desfavorecido. **~rate** /-ˈreɪt/ *vt* subestimar. **~rated** /-ˈreɪtɪd/ *a* no debidamente apreciado. **~shirt** *n* (Amer) camiseta *f* (interior).

understand /ʌndəˈstænd/ *vt* (*pt* **-stood**) entender; (empathize with) comprender, entender. ● *vi* entender, comprender. ~**able** *a* comprensible. ~**ing** *a* comprensivo. ● *n* (grasp) entendimiento *m*; (sympathy) comprensión *f*; (agreement) acuerdo *m*

under: ~**statement** *n* subestimación *f*. ~**take** /-'teɪk/ (*pt* -**took**, *pp* -**taken**) emprender *<task>*; asumir *<responsibility>*. ~**take to do sth** comprometerse a hacer algo. ~**taker** *n* director *m* de pompas fúnebres. ~**taking** /-'teɪkɪŋ/ *n* empresa *f*; (promise) promesa *f*. ~**tone** *n*. **in an** ~**tone** en voz baja. ~**value** /-'vælju:/ *vt* subvalorar. ~**water** /-'wɔːtə(r)/ *a* submarino. ● *adv* debajo del agua. ~**wear** *n* ropa *f* interior. ~**weight** /-'weɪt/ *a* de peso más bajo que el normal. ~**went** /-'went/ ⇒UNDERGO. ~**world** *n* (criminals) hampa *f*. ~**write** /-'raɪt/ *vt* (*pt* -**wrote**, *pp* -**written**) (Com) asegurar; (guarantee financially) financiar

undeserved /ʌndɪ'zɜːvd/ *a* inmerecido

undesirable /ʌndɪ'zaɪərəbl/ *a* indeseable

undignified /ʌn'dɪɡnɪfaɪd/ *a* indecoroso

undisputed /ʌndɪs'pjuːtɪd/ *a* *<champion>* indiscutido; *<facts>* innegable

undo /ʌn'duː/ *vt* (*pt* -**did**, *pp* -**done**) desabrochar *<button, jacket>*; abrir *<zip>*; desatar *<knot, laces>*

undoubted /ʌn'daʊtɪd/ *a* indudable. ~**ly** *adv* indudablemente, sin duda

undress /ʌn'dres/ *vt* desvestir, desnudar. ● *vi* desvestirse, desnudarse

undue /ʌn'djuː/ *a* excesivo

undulate /'ʌndjʊleɪt/ *vi* ondular

unduly /ʌn'djuːlɪ/ *adv* excesivamente

unearth /ʌn'ɜːθ/ *vt* desenterrar; descubrir *<document>*

unearthly /ʌn'ɜːθlɪ/ *a* sobrenatural. **at an** ~ **hour** a estas horas intempestivas

uneasy /ʌn'iːzɪ/ *a* incómodo

uneconomic /ʌniːkə'nɒmɪk/ *a* poco económico

uneducated /ʌn'edjʊkeɪtɪd/ *a* sin educación

unemploy|ed /ʌnɪm'plɔɪd/ *a* desempleado, parado. ~**ment** *n* desempleo *m*, paro *m*

unending /ʌn'endɪŋ/ *a* interminable, sin fin

unequal /ʌn'iːkwəl/ *a* desigual

unequivocal /ʌnɪ'kwɪvəkl/ *a* inequívoco

unethical /ʌn'eθɪkl/ *a* poco ético, inmoral

uneven /ʌn'iːvn/ *a* desigual

unexpected /ʌnɪk'spektɪd/ *a* inesperado; *<result>* imprevisto. ~**ly** *adv* *<arrive>* de improviso; *<happen>* de forma imprevista

unfair /ʌn'feə(r)/ *a* injusto; improcedente *<dismissal>*. ~**ly** *adv* injustamente

unfaithful /ʌn'feɪθfl/ *a* infiel

unfamiliar /ʌnfə'mɪlɪə(r)/ *a* desconocido. **be** ~ **with** desconocer

unfasten /ʌn'fɑːsn/ *vt* desabrochar *<clothes>*; (untie) desatar

unfavourable /ʌn'feɪvərəbl/ *a* desfavorable

unfeeling /ʌn'fiːlɪŋ/ *a* insensible

unfit /ʌn'fɪt/ *a*. **I'm** ~ no estoy en forma. ~ **for human consumption** no apto para el consumo

unfold /ʌn'fəʊld/ *vt* desdoblar; desplegar *<wings>*; (fig) revelar. ● *vi* *<leaf>* abrirse; *<events>* desarrollarse

unforeseen /ʌnfɔː'siːn/ *a* imprevisto

unforgettable /ʌnfə'ɡetəbl/ *a* inolvidable

unforgivable /ʌnfə'ɡɪvəbl/ *a* imperdonable

unfortunate /ʌn'fɔːtʃənət/ *a* desafortunado; (regrettable) lamentable. ~**ly** *adv* desafortunadamente; (stronger) por desgracia, desgraciadamente

unfounded /ʌn'faʊndɪd/ *a* infundado

unfriendly /ʌn'frendlɪ/ *a* poco amistoso; (stronger) antipático

unfurl /ʌn'fɜːl/ *vt* desplegar

ungainly /ʌn'geɪnlɪ/ a desgarbado

ungrateful /ʌn'greɪtfl/ a desagradecido, ingrato

unhapp|iness /ʌn'hæpɪnes/ n infelicidad f, tristeza f. **~y** a (**-ier, -iest**) infeliz, triste; (unsuitable) inoportuno. **be ~y about sth** no estar contento con algo

unharmed /ʌn'hɑːmd/ a <person> ileso

unhealthy /ʌn'helθɪ/ a (**-ier, -iest**) <person> de mala salud; <complexion> enfermizo; <conditions> poco saludable

unhurt /ʌn'hɜːt/ a ileso

unification /juːnɪfɪ'keɪʃn/ n unificación f

uniform /'juːnɪfɔːm/ a & n uniforme (m). **~ity** /-'fɔːmətɪ/ n uniformidad f

unify /'juːnɪfaɪ/ vt unir

unilateral /juːnɪ'lætərəl/ a unilateral

unimaginable /ʌnɪ'mædʒɪnəbl/ a inimaginable

unimaginative /ʌnɪ'mædʒɪnətɪv/ a <person> poco imaginativo

unimportant /ʌnɪm'pɔːtnt/ a sin importancia

uninhabited /ʌnɪn'hæbɪtɪd/ a deshabitado; <island> despoblado

unintelligible /ʌnɪn'telɪdʒəbl/ a ininteligible

unintentional /ʌnɪn'tenʃənl/ a involuntario

union /'juːnjən/ n unión f; (trade union) sindicato m; (student ~) asociación f de estudiantes. **U~ Jack** bandera f del Reino Unido

unique /juː'niːk/ a único

unison /'juːnɪsn/ n. **in ~** al unísono

unit /'juːnɪt/ n unidad f; (of furniture etc) módulo m; (in course) módulo m

unite /juː'naɪt/ vt unir. ● vi unirse. **U~d Kingdom** n Reino m Unido. **U~d Nations** n Organización f de las Naciones Unidas (ONU). **U~d States (of America)** n Estados mpl Unidos (de América)

unity /'juːnɪtɪ/ n unidad f

univers|al /juːnɪ'vɜːsl/ a universal. **~e** /'juːnɪvɜːs/ n universo m

university /juːnɪ'vɜːsətɪ/ n universidad f. ● a universitario

unjust /ʌn'dʒʌst/ a injusto. **~ified** /-ɪfaɪd/ a injustificado

unkind /ʌn'kaɪnd/ a poco amable; (cruel) cruel; <remark> hiriente

unknown /ʌn'nəʊn/ a desconocido

unlawful /ʌn'lɔːfl/ a ilegal

unleaded /ʌn'ledɪd/ a <fuel> sin plomo

unleash /ʌn'liːʃ/ vt soltar

unless /ʌn'les, ən'les/ conj a menos que, a no ser que

unlike /ʌn'laɪk/ prep diferente de. (in contrast to) a diferencia de. **~ly** a improbable

unlimited /ʌn'lɪmɪtɪd/ a ilimitado

unlisted /ʌn'lɪstɪd/ a (Amer) que no figura en la guía telefónica, privado (Mex)

unload /ʌn'ləʊd/ vt descargar

unlock /ʌn'lɒk/ vt abrir (con llave)

unluck|ily /ʌn'lʌkɪlɪ/ adv desgraciadamente. **~y** a (**-ier, -iest**) <person> sin suerte, desafortunado. **be ~y** tener mala suerte; (bring bad luck) traer mala suerte

unmarried /ʌn'mærɪd/ a soltero

unmask /ʌn'mɑːsk/ vt desenmascarar

unmentionable /ʌn'menʃənəbl/ a inmencionable

unmistakable /ʌnmɪ'steɪkəbl/ a inconfundible

unnatural /ʌn'nætʃərəl/ a poco natural; (not normal) anormal

unnecessar|ily /ʌn'nesəsərɪlɪ/ adv innecesariamente. **~y** a innecesario

unnerve /ʌn'nɜːv/ vt desconcertar

unnoticed /ʌn'nəʊtɪst/ a inadvertido

unobtainable /ʌnəb'teɪnəbl/ a imposible de conseguir

unobtrusive /ʌnəb'truːsɪv/ a discreto

unofficial /ʌnə'fɪʃl/ a no oficial. **~ly** adv extraoficialmente

unpack /ʌn'pæk/ vt sacar las cosas de <bags>; deshacer, desempacar (LAm) <suitcase>. ● vi deshacer las maletas

unpaid /ʌn'peɪd/ a <work> no retribuido, no remunerado; <leave> sin sueldo

unperturbed /ʌnpə'tɜ:bd/ a impasible. **he carried on** ~ siguió sin inmutarse

unpleasant /ʌn'pleznt/ a desagradable

unplug /ʌn'plʌg/ vt desenchufar

unpopular /ʌn'pɒpjʊlə(r)/ a impopular

unprecedented /ʌn'presɪdentɪd/ a sin precedentes

unpredictable /ʌnprɪ'dɪktəbl/ a imprevisible

unprepared /ʌnprɪ'peəd/ a no preparado; (unready) desprevenido

unprofessional /ʌnprə'feʃənəl/ a poco profesional

unprofitable /ʌn'prɒfɪtəbl/ a no rentable

unprotected /ʌnprə'tektɪd/ a sin protección; <sex> sin el uso de preservativos

unqualified /ʌn'kwɒlɪfaɪd/ a sin título; (fig) absoluto

unquestion|able /ʌn'kwestʃən əbl/ a incuestionable, innegable. ~**ing** a <obedience> ciego; <loyalty> incondicional

unravel /ʌn'rævl/ vt (pt un-ravelled) desenredar; desentrañar <mystery>

unreal /ʌn'rɪəl/ a irreal. ~**istic** /-'lɪstɪk/ a poco realista

unreasonable /ʌn'ri:zənəbl/ a irrazonable

unrecognizable /ʌnrekəg 'naɪzəbl/ a irreconocible

unrelated /ʌnrɪ'leɪtɪd/ a <facts> no relacionados (entre sí); <people> no emparentado

unreliable /ʌnrɪ'laɪəbl/ a <person> informal; <machine> poco fiable; <information> poco fidedigno

unrepentant /ʌnrɪ'pentənt/ a impenitente

unrest /ʌn'rest/ n (discontent) descontento m; (disturbances) disturbios mpl

unrivalled /ʌn'raɪvld/ a incomparable

unroll /ʌn'rəʊl/ vt desenrollar. ●vi desenrollarse

unruffled /ʌn'rʌfld/ <person> sereno

unruly /ʌn'ru:lɪ/ a <class> indisciplinado; <child> revoltoso

unsafe /ʌn'seɪf/ a inseguro

unsatisfactory /ʌnsætɪs'fæktərɪ/ a insatisfactorio

unsavoury /ʌn'seɪvərɪ/ a desagradable

unscathed /ʌn'skeɪðd/ a ileso

unscheduled /ʌn'ʃedju:ld/ a no programado, no previsto

unscrew /ʌn'skru:/ vt destornillar; desenroscar <lid>

unscrupulous /ʌn'skru:pjʊləs/ a inescrupuloso

unseemly /ʌn'si:mlɪ/ a indecoroso

unseen /ʌn'si:n/ a <danger> oculto; (unnoticed) sin ser visto

unselfish /ʌn'selfɪʃ/ a <act> desinteresado; <person> nada egoísta

unsettle /ʌn'setl/ vt desestabilizar <situation>; alterar <plans>. ~**d** a agitado; <weather> inestable; (undecided) pendiente (de resolución)

unshakeable /ʌn'ʃeɪkəbl/ a inquebrantable

unshaven /ʌn'ʃeɪvn/ a sin afeitar, sin rasurar (Mex)

unsightly /ʌn'saɪtlɪ/ a feo

unskilled /ʌn'skɪld/ a <work> no especializado; <worker> no cualificado, no calificado

unsociable /ʌn'səʊʃəbl/ a insociable

unsolved /ʌn'sɒlvd/ a no resuelto; <murder> sin esclarecerse

unsophisticated /ʌnsə'fɪstɪkeɪ tɪd/ a sencillo

unsound /ʌn'saʊnd/ a poco sólido

unspecified /ʌn'spesɪfaɪd/ a no especificado

unstable /ʌn'steɪbl/ a inestable

unsteady /ʌn'stedɪ/ a inestable, poco firme

unstuck /ʌn'stʌk/ a despegado. **come** ~ despegarse; (fail) fracasar

unsuccessful /ʌnsək'sesfʊl/ a <attempt> infructuoso. **be** ~ no tener éxito, fracasar

unsuitable /ʌn'su:təbl/ a <*clothing*> poco apropiado, poco adecuado; <*time*> inconveniente. **she is ∼ for the job** no es la persona indicada para el trabajo

unsure /ʌn'ʃʊə(r)/ a inseguro

unthinkable /ʌn'θɪŋkəbl/ a inconcebible

untid|iness /ʌn'taɪdnəs/ n desorden m. **∼y** a (**-ier**, **-iest**) desordenado; <*appearance, writing*> descuidado

untie /ʌn'taɪ/ vt desatar, desamarrar (LAm)

until /ən'tɪl, ʌn'tɪl/ prep hasta. ● conj hasta que

untold /ʌn'təʊld/ a incalculable

untouched /ʌn'tʌtʃt/ a intacto

untried /ʌn'traɪd/ a no probado

untrue /ʌn'tru:/ a falso

unused /ʌn'ju:zd/ a nuevo. ● /ʌn'ju:st/ a. **∼ to** no acostumbrado a

unusual /ʌn'ju:ʒʊəl/ a poco común, poco corriente. **it's ∼ to see so many people** es raro ver a tanta gente. **∼ly** adv excepcionalmente, inusitadamente

unveil /ʌn'veɪl/ vt descubrir

unwanted /ʌn'wɒntɪd/ a superfluo; <*child*> no deseado

unwelcome /ʌn'welkəm/ a <*news*> poco grato; <*guest*> inoportuno

unwell /ʌn'wel/ a indispuesto

unwieldy /ʌn'wi:ldɪ/ a pesado y difícil de manejar

unwilling /ʌn'wɪlɪŋ/ a mal dispuesto. **be ∼** no querer

unwind /ʌn'waɪnd/ vt (pt **unwound**) desenrollar. ● vi (⯃, relax) relajarse

unwise /ʌn'waɪz/ a poco sensato

unworthy /ʌn'wɜ:ðɪ/ a indigno

unwrap /ʌn'ræp/ vt (pt **unwrapped**) desenvolver

unwritten /ʌn'rɪtn/ a no escrito; <*agreement*> verbal

up /ʌp/ adv arriba; (upwards) hacia arriba; (higher) más arriba. **∼ here** aquí arriba. **∼ there** allí arriba. **∼ to** hasta. **he's not ∼ yet** todavía no se ha levantado. **be ∼ against** enfren-

tarse con. **come ∼** subir **go ∼** subir. **he's not ∼ to the job** no tiene las condiciones necesarias para el trabajo. **it's ∼ to you** depende de ti. **what's ∼?** ¿qué pasa? ● prep. **go ∼ the stairs** subir la escalera. **it's just ∼ the road** está un poco más allá. ● vt (pt **upped**) aumentar. ● n. **∼s and downs** npl altibajos mpl; (of life) vicisitudes fpl. **∼bringing** /'ʌpbrɪŋɪŋ/ n educación f. **∼date** /ʌp'deɪt/ vt poner al día. **∼grade** /ʌp'greɪd/ vt elevar de categoría <*person*>; mejorar <*equipment*>. **∼heaval** /ʌp'hi:vl/ n trastorno m. **∼hill** /ʌp'hɪl/ adv cuesta arriba. **∼hold** /ʌp'həʊld/ vt (pt **upheld**) mantener <*principle*>; confirmar <*decision*>. **∼holster** /ʌp'həʊlstə(r)/ vt tapizar. **∼holstery** n tapicería f. **∼keep** n mantenimiento m. **∼-market** /ʌp'mɑ:kɪt/ a de categoría

upon /ə'pɒn/ prep sobre. **once ∼ a time** érase una vez

upper /'ʌpə(r)/ a superior. **∼ class** n clase f alta

up: ∼right a vertical; <*citizen*> recto. **place sth ∼right** poner algo de pie. **∼rising** /'ʌpraɪzɪŋ/ n levantamiento m. **∼roar** n tumulto m

upset /ʌp'set/ vt (pt **upset**, pres p **upsetting**) (hurt) disgustar; (offend) ofender; (distress) alterar; desbaratar <*plans*>. ● a (hurt) disgustado; (distressed) alterado; (offended) ofendido; (disappointed) desilusionado. ● /'ʌpset/ n trastorno m. **have a stomach ∼** estar mal del estómago

up: ∼shot n resultado m. **∼side down** /ʌpsaɪd'daʊn/ adv al revés (con la parte de arriba abajo); (in disorder) patas arriba. **turn sth ∼side down** poner algo boca abajo. **∼stairs** /ʌp'steəz/ adv arriba. **go ∼stairs** subir. ● /'ʌpsteəz/ a de arriba. **∼start** n advenedizo m. **∼state** adv (Amer). **I live ∼state** vivo en el norte del estado. **∼stream** /ʌp'stri:m/ adv río arriba. **∼take** n. **be quick on the ∼take** agarrar las cosas al vuelo. **∼-to-date** /ʌptə'deɪt/ a al día; <*news*> de última hora. **∼turn** n repunte m, mejora f.

~ward /'ʌpwəd/ a *<movement>* ascendente; *<direction>* hacia arriba. ● *adv* hacia arriba. **~wards** *adv* hacia arriba

uranium /jʊ'reɪnɪəm/ n uranio m

Uranus /'jʊərənəs/, /jʊə'reɪnəs/ n Urano m

urban /'ɜːbən/ a urbano

urchin /'ɜːtʃɪn/ n pilluelo m

urge /ɜːdʒ/ vt instar. **~ s.o. to do sth** instar a uno a que haga algo. ● n impulso m; (wish, whim) ganas fpl. □ **~ on** vt animar

urgen|cy /'ɜːdʒənsɪ/ n urgencia f. **~t** a urgente. **~tly** adv urgentemente, con urgencia

urin|ate /'jʊərɪneɪt/ vi orinar. **~e** /'jʊərɪn/ n orina f

Uruguay /'jʊərəgwaɪ/ n Uruguay m. **~an** a & n uruguayo (m)

us /ʌs, əs/ pron nos; (after prep) nosotros m, nosotras f

US(A) /ju:es'eɪ/ abbr (= **United States (of America)**) EE.UU. (only written), Estados mpl Unidos

usage /'ju:zɪdʒ/ n uso m

use /ju:z/ vt usar; utilizar *<service, facilities>*; consumir *<fuel>*. ● /ju:s/ n uso m, empleo m. **be of ~** servir. **it is no ~** es inútil. □ **~ up** vt agotar, consumir. **~d** /ju:zd/ a usado. ● /ju:st/ v mod **~ to**. he **~d to say** decía, solía decir. **there ~d to be** (antes) había. ● a /ju:st/. **be ~d to** estar acostumbrado a. **~ful** /'ju:sfl/ a útil. **~fully** adv útilmente. **~less** a inútil; *<person>* incompetente. **~r** /-zə(r)/ n usuario m. **drug ~** n consumidor m de drogas

usher /'ʌʃə(r)/ n (in theatre etc) acomodador m. □ **~ in** vt hacer pasar; marcar el comienzo de *<new era>*. **~ette** /-'ret/ n acomodadora f

USSR abbr (History) (= **Union of Soviet Socialist Republics**) URSS

usual /'ju:ʒʊəl/ a usual; (habitual) acostumbrado, habitual; *<place, route>* de siempre. **as ~** como de costumbre, como siempre. **~ly** adv normalmente. **he ~ly wakes up early** suele despertarse temprano

utensil /ju:'tensl/ n utensilio m

utilize /'ju:tɪlaɪz/ vt utilizar

utmost /'ʌtməʊst/ a sumo. ● n. **do one's ~** hacer todo lo posible (**to** para)

utter /'ʌtə(r)/ a completo. ● vt pronunciar *<word>*; dar *<cry>*. **~ly** adv totalmente

U-turn /'ju:tɜːn/ n cambio m de sentido

···

Vv

···

vacan|cy /'veɪkənsɪ/ n (job) vacante f; (room) habitación f libre. **~t** a *<building>* desocupado; *<seat>* libre; *<post>* vacante; *<look>* ausente

vacate /və'keɪt/ vt dejar

vacation /və'keɪʃn/ n (Amer) vacaciones fpl. **go on ~** ir de vacaciones. **~er** n (Amer) veraneante m & f

vaccin|ate /'væksɪneɪt/ vt vacunar. **~ation** /-'neɪʃn/ n vacunación f. **~e** /'væksi:n/ n vacuna f

vacuum /'vækjʊəm/ n vacío m. **~ cleaner** n aspiradora f

vagina /və'dʒaɪnə/ n vagina f

vague /veɪg/ a (**-er, -est**) vago; *<outline>* borroso; *<person, expression>* despistado. **~ly** adv vagamente

vain /veɪn/ a (**-er, -est**) vanidoso; (useless) vano. **in ~** en vano

Valentine's Day /'væləntaɪnz/ n el día de San Valentín

valiant /'vælɪənt/ a valeroso

valid /'vælɪd/ a válido. **~ate** /-eɪt/ vt dar validez a; validar *<contract>*. **~ity** /-'ɪdətɪ/ n validez f

valley /'vælɪ/ n (pl **-eys**) valle m

valour /'vælə(r)/ n valor m

valu|able /'væljʊəbl/ a valioso. **~ables** npl objetos mpl de valor. **~ation** /-'eɪʃn/ n valoración f. **~e** /'vælju:/ n valor m. ● vt valorar; tasar, valorar, avaluar (LAm) *<property>*. **~e added tax** n impuesto m sobre el valor añadido

valve /vælv/ n válvula f

vampire /'væmpaɪə(r)/ *n* vampiro *m*

van /væn/ *n* furgoneta *f*, camioneta *f*; (Rail) furgón *m*

vandal /'vændl/ *n* vándalo *m*. ~**ism** *n* vandalismo *m*. ~**ize** *vt* destruir

vanilla /və'nɪlə/ *n* vainilla *f*

vanish /'vænɪʃ/ *vi* desaparecer

vanity /'vænɪtɪ/ *n* vanidad *f*. ~ **case** *n* neceser *m*

vapour /'veɪpə(r)/ *n* vapor *m*

varia|ble /'veərɪəbl/ *a* variable. ~**nce** /-əns/ *n*. **at** ~**ce** en desacuerdo. ~**nt** *n* variante *f*. ~**tion** /-'eɪʃn/ *n* variación *f*

vari|ed /'veərɪd/ *a* variado. ~**ety** /və'raɪətɪ/ *n* variedad *f*. ~**ety show** *n* espectáculo *m* de variedades. ~**ous** /'veərɪəs/ *a* (several) varios; (different) diversos

varnish /'vɑːnɪʃ/ *n* barniz *m*; (for nails) esmalte *m*. ● *vt* barnizar; pintar *<nails>*

vary /'veərɪ/ *vt/i* variar

vase /vɑːz/, (Amer) /veɪs/ *n* (for flowers) florero *m*; (ornamental) jarrón *m*

vast /vɑːst/ *a* vasto, extenso; *<size>* inmenso. ~**ly** *adv* infinitamente

vat /væt/ *n* cuba *f*

VAT /viːeɪ'tiː/ *abbr* (= **value added tax**) IVA *m*

vault /vɔːlt/ *n* (roof) bóveda *f*; (in bank) cámara *f* acorazada; (tomb) cripta *f*. ● *vt/i* saltar

VCR *n* = **videocassette recorder**

VDU *n* = **visual display unit**

veal /viːl/ *n* ternera *f*

veer /vɪə(r)/ *vi* dar un viraje, virar

vegeta|ble /'vedʒɪtəbl/ *a* vegetal. ● *n* verdura *f*. ~**rian** /vedʒɪ'teərɪən/ *a* & *n* vegetariano (*m*). ~**tion** /vedʒɪ'teɪʃn/ *n* vegetación *f*

vehement /'viːəmənt/ *a* vehemente. ~**tly** *adv* con vehemencia

vehicle /'viːɪkl/ *n* vehículo *m*

veil /veɪl/ *n* velo *m*

vein /veɪn/ *n* vena *f*; (in marble) veta *f*

velocity /vɪ'lɒsɪtɪ/ *n* velocidad *f*

velvet /'velvɪt/ *n* terciopelo *m*

vendetta /ven'detə/ *n* vendetta *f*

vend|ing machine /'vendɪŋ/ *n* distribuidor *m* automático. ~**or** /'vendə(r)/ *n* vendedor *m*

veneer /və'nɪə(r)/ *n* chapa *f*, enchapado *m*; (fig) barniz *m*, apariencia *f*

venerate /'venəreɪt/ *vt* venerar

venereal /və'nɪərɪəl/ *a* venéreo

Venetian blind /və'niːʃn/ *n* persiana *f* veneciana

Venezuela /venə'zweɪlə/ *n* Venezuela *f*. ~**n** *a* & *n* venezolano (*m*)

vengeance /'vendʒəns/ *n* venganza *f*. **with a** ~ (fig) con ganas

venom /'venəm/ *n* veneno *m*. ~**ous** *a* venenoso

vent /vent/ *n* (conducto *m* de) ventilación; (air ~) respiradero *m*. **give** ~ **to** dar rienda suelta a. ● *vt* descargar

ventilat|e /'ventɪleɪt/ *vt* ventilar. ~**ion** /-'leɪʃn/ *n* ventilación *f*

ventriloquist /ven'trɪləkwɪst/ *n* ventrílocuo *m*

venture /'ventʃə(r)/ *n* empresa *f*. ● *vt* aventurar. ● *vi* atreverse

venue /'venjuː/ *n* (for concert) lugar *m* de actuación

Venus /'viːnəs/ *n* Venus *m*

veranda /və'rændə/ *n* galería *f*

verb /vɜːb/ *n* verbo *m*. ~**al** *a* verbal.

verdict /'vɜːdɪkt/ *n* veredicto *m*; (opinion) opinión *f*

verge /vɜːdʒ/ *n* borde *m*. □ ~ **on** *vt* rayar en

verify /'verɪfaɪ/ *vt* (confirm) confirmar; (check) verificar

vermin /'vɜːmɪn/ *n* alimañas *fpl*

versatil|e /'vɜːsətaɪl/ *a* versátil. ~**ity** /-'tɪlətɪ/ *n* versatilidad *f*

verse /vɜːs/ *n* estrofa *f*; (poetry) poesías *fpl*. ~**d** /vɜːst/ *a*. **be well-**~**ed in** ser muy versado en. ~**ion** /'vɜːʃn/ *n* versión *f*

versus /'vɜːsəs/ *prep* contra

vertebra /'vɜːtɪbrə/ *n* (*pl* -**brae** /-briː/) vértebra *f*. ~**te** /-brət/ *n* vertebrado *m*

vertical /'vɜːtɪkl/ *a* & *n* vertical (*f*). ~**ly** *adv* verticalmente

vertigo /'vɜːtɪɡəʊ/ *n* vértigo *m*

verve /vɜːv/ *n* brío *m*

very /'verɪ/ *adv* muy. ~ **much** muchísimo. ~ **well** muy bien. **the** ~ **first**

el primero de todos. ● *a* mismo. **the ~ thing** exactamente lo que hace falta

vessel /'vesl/ *n* (receptacle) recipiente *m*; (ship) navío *m*, nave *f*

vest /vest/ *n* camiseta *f*; (Amer) chaleco *m*.

vestige /'vestɪdʒ/ *n* vestigio *m*

vet /vet/ *n* veterinario *m*; (Amer 🄝, veteran) veterano *m*. ● *vt* (*pt* **vetted**) someter a investigación *<applicant>*

veteran /'vetərən/ *n* veterano *m*

veterinary /'vetərɪnərɪ/ *a* veterinario. **~ surgeon** *n* veterinario *m*

veto /'vi:təʊ/ *n* (*pl* **-oes**) veto *m*. ● *vt* vetar

vex /veks/ *vt* fastidiar

via /'vaɪə/ *prep* por, por vía de

viable /'vaɪəbl/ *a* viable

viaduct /'vaɪədʌkt/ *n* viaducto *m*

vibrat|e /vaɪ'breɪt/ *vt/i* vibrar. **~ion** /-ʃn/ *n* vibración *f*

vicar /'vɪkə(r)/ *n* párroco *m*. **~age** /-rɪdʒ/ *n* casa *f* del párroco

vice /vaɪs/ *n* vicio *m*; (Tec) torno *m* de banco

vice versa /vaɪsɪ'vɜːsə/ *adv* viceversa

vicinity /vɪ'sɪnɪtɪ/ *n* vecindad *f*. **in the ~ of** cerca de

vicious /'vɪʃəs/ *a* *<attack>* feroz; *<dog>* fiero; *<rumour>* malicioso. **~ circle** *n* círculo *m* vicioso

victim /'vɪktɪm/ *n* víctima *f*. **~ize** *vt* victimizar

victor /'vɪktə(r)/ *n* vencedor *m*

Victorian /vɪk'tɔːrɪən/ *a* victoriano

victor|ious /vɪk'tɔːrɪəs/ *a* *<army>* victorioso; *<team>* vencedor. **~y** /'vɪktərɪ/ *n* victoria *f*

video /'vɪdɪəʊ/n (*pl* **-os**) vídeo *m*, video *m* (LAm). **~ camera** *n* videocámara *f*. **~(cassette) recorder** *n* magnetoscopio *m*. **~tape** *n* videocassette *f*

vie /vaɪ/ *vi* (*pres p* **vying**) rivalizar

Vietnam /vjet'næm/ *n* Vietnam *m*. **~ese** *a* & *n* vietnamita (*m* & *f*)

view /vju:/ *n* vista *f*; (mental survey) visión *f* de conjunto; (opinion) opinión *f*. **in my ~** a mi juicio. **in ~ of** en vista de. **on ~** expuesto. ● *vt* ver *<scene,*

property>; (consider) considerar. **~er** *n* (TV) televidente *m* & *f*. **~finder** *n* visor *m*. **~point** *n* punto *m* de vista

vigilance *n* vigilancia *f*. **~ant** *a* vigilante

vigo|rous /'vɪgərəs/ *a* enérgico; *<growth>* vigoroso. **~ur** /'vɪgə(r)/ *n* vigor *m*

vile /vaɪl/ *a* (base) vil; *<food>* asqueroso; *<weather, temper>* horrible

village /'vɪlɪdʒ/ *n* pueblo *m*; (small) aldea *f*. **~r** *n* vecino *m* del pueblo; (of small village) aldeano *m*

villain /'vɪlən/ *n* maleante *m* & *f*; (in story etc) villano *m*

vindicate /'vɪndɪkeɪt/ *vt* justificar

vindictive /vɪn'dɪktɪv/ *a* vengativo

vine /vaɪn/ *n* (on ground) vid *f*; (climbing) parra *f*

vinegar /'vɪnɪgə(r)/ *n* vinagre *m*

vineyard /'vɪnjəd/ *n* viña *f*

vintage /'vɪntɪdʒ/ *n* (year) cosecha *f*. ● *a* *<wine>* añejo; *<car>* de época

vinyl /'vaɪnɪl/ *n* vinilo *m*

viola /vɪ'əʊlə/ *n* viola *f*

violat|e /'vaɪəleɪt/ *vt* violar. **~ion** /-'leɪʃn/ *n* violación *f*

violen|ce /'vaɪələns/ *n* violencia *f*. **~t** *a* violento. **~tly** *adv* violentamente

violet /'vaɪələt/ *a* & *n* violeta (*f*); (colour) violeta (*m*)

violin /'vaɪəlɪn/ *n* violín *m*. **~ist** *n* violinista *m* & *f*

VIP /vi:aɪ'pi:/ *abbr* (= **very important person**) VIP *m*

viper /'vaɪpə(r)/ *n* víbora *f*

virgin /'vɜːdʒɪn/ *a* & *n* virgen (*f*)

Virgo /'vɜːgəʊ/ *n* Virgo *f*

virile /'vɪraɪl/ *a* viril

virtual /'vɜːtʃʊəl/ *a*. **traffic is at a ~ standstill** el tráfico está prácticamente paralizado. **~ reality** *n* realidad *f* virtual. **~ly** *adv* prácticamente

virtue /'vɜːtʃu:/ *n* virtud *f*. **by ~ of** en virtud de

virtuous /'vɜːtʃʊəs/ *a* virtuoso

virulent /'vɪrʊlənt/ *a* virulento

virus /'vaɪərəs/ *n* (*pl* **-uses**) virus *m*

visa /'vi:zə/ *n* visado *m*, visa *f* (LAm)

vise /vaɪs/ *n* (Amer) torno *m* de banco

visib|ility /vɪzɪ'bɪlətɪ/ n visibilidad f. ~**le** /'vɪzɪbl/ a visible; <sign, improvement> evidente

vision /'vɪʒn/ n visión f; (sight) vista f

visit /'vɪzɪt/ vt visitar; hacer una visita a <person>. ● vi hacer visitas. ~ **with s.o.** (Amer) ir a ver a uno. ● n visita f. **pay s.o. a** ~ hacerle una visita a uno. ~**or** n visitante m & f; (guest) visita f

visor /'vaɪzə(r)/ n visera f

visual /'vɪʒʊəl/ a visual. ~**ize** vt imaginar(se); (foresee) prever

vital /'vaɪtl/ a (essential) esencial; <factor> de vital importancia; <organ> vital. ~**ity** /vaɪ'tælətɪ/ n vitalidad f

vitamin /'vɪtəmɪn/ n vitamina f.

vivacious /vɪ'veɪʃəs/ a vivaz

vivid /'vɪvɪd/ a vivo. ~**ly** adv intensamente; (describe) gráficamente

vivisection /vɪvɪ'sekʃn/ n vivisección f

vocabulary /və'kæbjʊlərɪ/ n vocabulario m

vocal /'vəʊkl/ a vocal. ~**ist** n cantante m & f

vocation /vəʊ'keɪʃn/ n vocación f. ~**al** a profesional

vociferous /və'sɪfərəs/ a vociferador

vogue /vəʊg/ n moda f, boga f

voice /vɔɪs/ n voz f. ● vt expresar

void /vɔɪd/ a (not valid) nulo. ● n vacío m

volatile /'vɒlətaɪl/ a volátil; <person> imprevisible

volcan|ic /vɒl'kænɪk/ a volcánico. ~**o** /vɒl'keɪnəʊ/ n (pl -**oes**) volcán m

volley /'vɒlɪ/ n (pl -**eys**) (of gunfire) descarga f cerrada; (sport) volea f. ~**ball** n vóleibol m

volt /vəʊlt/ n voltio m. ~**age** /-ɪdʒ/ n voltaje m

volume /'vɒljuːm/ n volumen m; (book) tomo m

voluntar|ily /'vɒləntərəlɪ/ adv voluntariamente. ~**y** a voluntario; <organization> de beneficencia

volunteer /vɒlən'tɪə(r)/ n voluntario m. ● vt ofrecer. ● vi. ~ (**to**) ofrecerse (a)

vomit /'vɒmɪt/ vt/i vomitar. ● n vómito m

voracious /və'reɪʃəs/ a voraz

vot|e /vəʊt/ n voto m; (right) derecho m al voto; (act) votación f. ● vi votar. ~**er** n votante m & f. ~**ing** n votación f

vouch /vaʊtʃ/ vi. ~ **for s.o.** responder por uno. ~**er** /-ə(r)/ n vale m

vow /vaʊ/ n voto m. ● vi jurar

vowel /'vaʊəl/ n vocal f

voyage /'vɔɪɪdʒ/ n viaje m; (by sea) travesía f

vulgar /'vʌlgə(r)/ a (coarse) grosero, vulgar; (tasteless) de mal gusto. ~**ity** /-'gærətɪ/ n vulgaridad f

vulnerable /'vʌlnərəbl/ a vulnerable

vulture /'vʌltʃə(r)/ n buitre m

vying /'vaɪɪŋ/ ⇒VIE

Ww

W abbr (= **West**) O

wad /wɒd/ n (of notes) fajo m; (tied together) lío m; (papers) montón m

waddle /'wɒdl/ vi contonearse

wade /weɪd/ vi caminar (por el agua etc)

wafer /'weɪfə(r)/ n galleta f de barquillo

waffle /'wɒfl/ n 🅑 palabrería f. ● vi 🅑 divagar; (in essay, exam) meter paja 🅑. ● n (Culin) gofre m, wafle m (LAm)

waft /wɒft/ vi flotar

wag /wæg/ vt (pt **wagged**) menear. ● vi menearse

wage /weɪdʒ/ n sueldo m. ~**s** npl salario m, sueldo m. ~**r** n apuesta f

waggle /'wægl/ vt menear. ● vi menearse

wagon /'wægən/ n carro m; (Rail) vagón m; (Amer, delivery truck) furgoneta f de reparto

wail /weɪl/ vi llorar

waist /weɪst/ n cintura f. ~**coat** n chaleco m. ~**line** n cintura f

wait /weɪt/ *vi* esperar; (at table) servir. **~ for** esperar. **~ on s.o.** aten-der a uno. ● *vt* (await) esperar *<chance, turn>*. **~ table** (Amer) servir a la mesa. **I can't ~ to see him** me muero de ganas de verlo. ● *n* espera *f*. **lie in ~** acechar

waiter /'weɪtə(r)/ *n* camarero *m*, mesero *m* (LAm)

wait: ~ing-list *n* lista *f* de espera. **~ing-room** *n* sala *f* de espera

waitress /'weɪtrɪs/ *n* camarera *f*, mesera *f* (LAm)

waive /weɪv/ *vt* renunciar a

wake /weɪk/ *vt* (*pt* **woke**, *pp* **woken**) despertar. ● *vi* despertarse. ● *n* (Naut) estela *f*. **in the ~ of** como resultado de. □ **~ up** *vt* despertar. *vi* despertarse

Wales /weɪlz/ *n* (el país de) Gales

walk /wɔːk/ *vi* andar, caminar; (not ride) ir a pie; (stroll) pasear. ● *vt* andar por *<streets>*; llevar de paseo *<dog>*. ● *n* paseo *m*; (long) caminata *f*; (gait) manera *f* de andar. □ **~ out** *vi* salir; *<workers>* declararse en huelga. □ **~ out on** *vt* abandonar. **~er** *n* excursionista *m & f*

walkie-talkie /wɔːkɪ'tɔːkɪ/ *n* walkie-talkie *m*

walk: ~ing-stick *n* bastón *m*. **W~man** /-mən/ *n* Walkman *m* (P). **~-out** *n* retirada en señal de protesta; (strike) abandono *m* del trabajo

wall /wɔːl/ *n* (interior) pared *f*; (exterior) muro *m*

wallet /'wɒlɪt/ *n* cartera *f*, billetera *f*

wallop /'wɒləp/ *vt* (*pt* **walloped**) 🔲 darle un golpazo a.

wallow /'wɒləʊ/ *vi* revolcarse

wallpaper /'wɔːlpeɪpə(r)/ *n* papel *m* pintado

walnut /'wɔːlnʌt/ *n* nuez *f*; (tree) nogal *m*

walrus /'wɔːlrəs/ *n* morsa *f*

waltz /wɔːls/ *n* vals *m*. ● *vi* valsar

wand /wɒnd/ *n* varita *f* (mágica)

wander /'wɒndə(r)/ *vi* vagar; (stroll) pasear; (digress) divagar. ● *n* vuelta *f*, paseo *m*. **~er** *n* trotamundos *m*

wane /weɪn/ *vi* *<moon>* menguar; *<interest>* decaer. ● *n*. **be on the ~** *<popularity>* estar decayendo

wangle /'wæŋgl/ *vt* 🔲 agenciarse

want /wɒnt/ *vt* querer; (need) necesitar. ● *vi*. **~ for** carecer de. ● *n* necesidad *f*; (lack) falta *f*. **~ed** *a <criminal>* buscado

war /wɔː(r)/ *n* guerra *f*. **at ~** en guerra

warble /'wɔːbl/ *vi* trinar, gorjear

ward /wɔːd/ *n* (in hospital) sala *f*; (child) pupilo *m*. □ **~ off** *vt* conjurar *<danger>*; rechazar *<attack>*

warden /'wɔːdn/ *n* guarda *m*

warder /'wɔːdə(r)/ *n* celador *m* (de una cárcel)

wardrobe /'wɔːdrəʊb/ *n* armario *m*; (clothes) guardarropa *f*, vestuario *m*

warehouse /'weəhaʊs/ *n* depósito *m*, almacén *m*

wares /weəz/ *npl* mercancía(s) *f(pl)*

war: ~fare *n* guerra *f*. **~head** *n* cabeza *f*, ojiva *f*

warm /wɔːm/ *a* (**-er, -est**) *<water, day>* tibio, templado; *<room>* caliente; *<climate, wind>* cálido; *<clothes>* de abrigo; *<welcome>* caluroso. **be ~** *<person>* tener calor. **it's ~ today** hoy hace calor. ● *vt*. **~ (up)** calentar *<room>*; recalentar *<food>*; (fig) animar. ● *vi*. **~ (up)** calentarse; (fig) animarse. **~-blooded** /-'blʌdɪd/ *a* de sangre caliente. **~ly** *adv* (heartily) calurosamente. **~th** *n* calor *m*; (of colour, atmosphere) calidez *f*

warn /wɔːn/ *vt* advertir. **~ing** *n* advertencia *f*; (notice) aviso *m*

warp /wɔːp/ *vt* alabear. **~ed** /'wɔːpt/ *a <wood>* alabeado; *<mind>* retorcido

warrant /'wɒrənt/ *n* orden *f* judicial; (search ~) orden *f* de registro; (for arrest) orden *f* de arresto. ● *vt* justificar. **~y** *n* garantía *f*

warrior /'wɒrɪə(r)/ *n* guerrero *m*

warship /'wɔːʃɪp/ *n* buque *m* de guerra

wart /wɔːt/ *n* verruga *f*

wartime /'wɔːtaɪm/ *n* tiempo *m* de guerra

wary /'weərɪ/ *a* (**-ier, -iest**) cauteloso. **be ~ of** recelar de

was /wəz/, wɒz/ ⇒BE

wash /wɒʃ/ *vt* lavar; fregar, lavar (LAm) *<floor>*. **~ one's face** lavarse la cara. ● *vi* lavarse. ● *n* (in washing machine) lavado *m*. **have a ~** lavarse. **I gave the car a ~** lavé el coche. □ **~ out** *vt* (clean) lavar; (rinse) enjuagar. □ **~ up** *vi* fregar los platos, lavar los trastes (Mex); (Amer, wash face and hands) lavarse. **~able** *a* lavable. **~basin, ~bowl** (Amer) *n* lavabo *m*. **~er** *n* arandela *f*. **~ing** *n* lavado *m*; (dirty clothes) ropa *f* para lavar; (wet clothes) ropa *f* lavada. **do the ~ing** lavar la ropa, hacer la colada. **~ing-machine** *n* máquina *f* de lavar, lavadora *f*. **~ing-powder** *n* jabón *m* en polvo. **~ing-up** *n*. **do the ~ing-up** lavar los platos, fregar (los platos). **~ing-up liquid** *n* lavavajillas *m*. **~out** *n* 🔲 desastre *m*. **~room** *n* (Amer) baños *mpl*, servicios *mpl*

wasp /wɒsp/ *n* avispa *f*

waste /weɪst/ ● *a* <*matter*> de desecho; <*land*> (barren) yermo; (uncultivated) baldío. ● *n* (of materials) desperdicio *m*; (of time) pérdida *f*; (refuse) residuos *mpl*. ● *vt* despilfarrar <*electricity, money*>; desperdiciar <*talent, effort*>; perder <*time*>. ● *vi*. **~-disposal unit** *n* trituradora *f* de desperdicios. **~ful** *a* poco económico; <*person*> despilfarrador. **~-paper basket** *n* papelera *f*

watch /wɒtʃ/ *vt* mirar; observar <*person, expression*>; ver <*TV*>; (keep an eye on) vigilar; (take heed) tener cuidado con. ● *vi* mirar. ● *n* (observation) vigilancia *f*; (period of duty) guardia *f*; (timepiece) reloj *m*. **~ out** *vi* (be careful) tener cuidado; (look carefully) estarse atento. **~dog** *n* perro *m* guardián. **~man** /-mən/ *n* (*pl* **-men**) vigilante *m*.

water /ˈwɔːtə(r)/ *n* agua *f*. ● *vt* regar <*plants etc*>. ● *vi* <*eyes*> llorar. **make s.o.'s mouth ~** hacérsele la boca agua, hacérsele agua la boca (LAm). **~ down** *vt* diluir; aguar <*wine*>. **~-colour** *n* acuarela *f*. **~cress** *n* berro *m*. **~fall** *n* cascada *f*; (large) catarata *f*. **~ing-can** *n* regadera *f*. **~lily** *n* nenúfar *m*. **~logged** /-lɒgd/ *a* anegado; <*shoes*> empapado. **~proof** *a* impermeable; <*watch*> sumergible. **~-skiing** *n* esquí *m*

acuático. **~tight** *a* hermético; <*boat*> estanco; <*argument*> irrebatible. **~way** *n* canal *m* navegable. **~y** *a* acuoso; <*eyes*> lloroso

watt /wɒt/ *n* vatio *m*

wave /weɪv/ *n* onda *f*; (of hand) señal *f*; (fig) oleada *f*. ● *vt* agitar; (curl) ondular <*hair*>. ● *vi* (signal) hacer señales con la mano; ondear <*flag*>. **~band** *n* banda *f* de frecuencia. **~length** *n* longitud *f* de onda

waver /ˈweɪvə(r)/ *vi* (be indecisive) vacilar; (falter) flaquear

wavy /ˈweɪvɪ/ *a* (**-ier, -iest**) ondulado

wax /wæks/ *n* cera *f*. ● *vi* <*moon*> crecer. **~work** *n* figura *f* de cera. **~works** *npl* museo *m* de cera

way /weɪ/ *n* (route) camino *m*; (manner) manera *f*, forma *f*, modo *m*; (direction) dirección *f*; (habit) costumbre *f*. **it's a long ~ from here** queda muy lejos de aquí. **be in the ~** estorbar. **by the ~** a propósito. **either ~** de cualquier manera. **give ~** (collapse) ceder, romperse; (Auto) ceder el paso. **in a ~** en cierta manera. **in some ~s** en ciertos modos. **make ~** dejar paso a. **no ~!** ¡ni hablar! **on my ~ to** de camino a. **out of the ~** remoto; (extraordinary) fuera de lo común. **that ~** por allí. **this ~** por aquí. **~ in** *n* entrada *f*. **~lay** /weɪˈleɪ/ *vt* (*pt* **-laid**) abordar. **~ out** *n* salida *f*. **~-out** *a* ultramoderno, original. **~s** *npl* costumbres *fpl*

we /wiː/ *pron* nosotros *m*, nosotras *f*

weak /wiːk/ *a* (**-er, -est**) débil; <*structure*> poco sólido; <*performance, student*> flojo; <*coffee*> poco cargado; <*solution*> diluido; <*beer*> suave; (pej) aguado. **~en** *vt* debilitar. ● *vi* <*resolve*> flaquear. **~ling** *n* alfeñique *m*. **~ness** *n* debilidad *f*

wealth /welθ/ *n* riqueza *f*. **~y** *a* (**-ier, -iest**) rico

weapon /ˈwepən/ *n* arma *f*

wear /weə(r)/ *vt* (*pt* **wore**, *pp* **worn**) llevar; vestirse de <*black, red, etc*>; (usually) usar. **I've got nothing to ~** no tengo nada que ponerme. ● *vi* (through use) gastarse; (last) durar. ● *n* uso *m*; (damage) desgaste *m*; **~ and tear** desgaste *m* natural. □ **~**

out *vt* gastar; (tire) agotar. *vi* gastarse

weary /'wɪərɪ/ *a* (**-ier, -iest**) cansado. ● *vt* cansar. ● *vi* cansarse. ~ **of** cansarse de

weather /'weðə(r)/ *n* tiempo *m*. what's the ~ like? ¿qué tiempo hace?. the ~ was bad hizo mal tiempo. be under the ~ 🄵 no andar muy bien 🄵. ● *vt* (survive) sobrellevar. ~**-beaten** *a* curtido. ~ **forecast** *n* pronóstico *m* del tiempo. ~**-vane** *n* veleta *f*

weave /wiːv/ *vt* (*pt* **wove**, *pp* **woven**) tejer; entretejer *<threads>*. ~ **one's way** abrirse paso. ● *vi* *<person>* zigzaguear; *<road>* serpentear. ~**r** *n* tejedor *m*

web /web/ *n* (of spider) telaraña *f*; (of intrigue) red *f*. ~**b site** *n* (Comp) sitio web *m*

wed /wed/ *vt* (*pt* **wedded**) casarse con. ● *vi* casarse.

we'd /wiːd/, /wɪəd/ = **we had, we would**

wedding /'wedɪŋ/ *n* boda *f*, casamiento *m*. ~**cake** *n* pastel *m* de boda. ~**ring** *n* anillo *m* de boda

wedge /wedʒ/ *n* cuña *f*

Wednesday /'wenzdeɪ/ *n* miércoles *m*

wee /wiː/ *a* 🄵 pequeñito. ● *n*. have a ~ 🄵 hacer pis 🄵

weed /wiːd/ *n* mala hierba *f*. ● *vt* desherbar. □ ~ **out** *vt* eliminar. ~**killer** *n* herbicida *m*. ~**y** *a* *<person>* enclenque; (Amer, lanky) larguirucho 🄵

week /wiːk/ *n* semana *f*. ~**day** *n* día *m* de semana. ~**end** *n* fin *m* de semana. ~**ly** *a* semanal. ● *n* semanario *m*. ● *adv* semanalmente

weep /wiːp/ *vi* (*pt* **wept**) llorar

weigh /weɪ/ *vt/i* pesar. ~ **anchor** levar anclas. □ ~ **down** *vt* (fig) oprimir. □ ~ **up** *vt* pesar; (fig) considerar

weight /weɪt/ *n* peso *m*; (sport) pesa *f*. put on ~ engordar. lose ~ adelgazar. ~**lifting** *n* halterofilia *f*, levantamiento *m* de pesos

weir /wɪə(r)/ *n* presa *f*

weird /wɪəd/ *a* (**-er, -est**) raro, extraño; (unearthly) misterioso

welcom|e /'welkəm/ *a* bienvenido. you're ~**e!** (after thank you) ¡de nada! ● *n* bienvenida *f*; (reception) acogida *f*. ● *vt* dar la bienvenida a; (appreciate) alegrarse de. ~**ing** *a* acogedor

weld /weld/ *vt* soldar. ● *n* soldadura *f*. ~**er** *n* soldador *m*

welfare /'welfeə(r)/ *n* bienestar *m*; (aid) asistencia *f* social. **W~ State** *n* estado *m* benefactor

well /wel/ *adv* (**better, best**) bien. ~ **done!** ¡muy bien!, ¡bravo! as ~ también. as ~ as además de. we may as ~ go tomorrow más vale que vayamos mañana. do ~ (succeed) tener éxito. very ~ muy bien. ● *a* bien. I'm very ~ estoy muy bien. ● *int* (introducing, continuing sentence) bueno; (surprise) ¡vaya!; (indignation, resignation) bueno. ~ **I never!** ¡no me digas! ● *n* pozo *m*

we'll /wiːl/, /wɪəl/ = **we will**

well: ~-behaved /-bɪ'heɪvd/ *a* que se porta bien, bueno. ~**-educated** /-'edʒʊkeɪtɪd/ *a* culto.

wellington (boot) /'welɪŋtən/ *n* bota *f* de goma *or* de agua; (Amer, short boot) botín *m*

well: ~-known /-'nəʊn/ *a* conocido. ~ **off** *a* adinerado. ~**-stocked** /-'stɒkt/ *a* bien provisto. ~**-to-do** /-tə'duː/ *a* adinerado

Welsh /welʃ/ *a & n* galés (*m*). the ~ *n* los galeses

went /went/ ⇒**GO**

wept /wept/ ⇒**WEEP**

were /wɜː(r), wə(r)/ ⇒**BE**

we're /wɪə(r)/ = **we are**

west /west/ *n* oeste *m*. the **W~** el Occidente *m*. ● *a* oeste; *<wind>* del oeste. ● *adv* *<go>* hacia el oeste, al oeste. it's ~ of York está al oeste de York. ~**erly** /-əlɪ/ *a* *<wind>* del oeste. ~**ern** /-ən/ *a* occidental. ● *n* (film) película *f* del Oeste. ~**erner** *n* occidental *m & f*. **W~ Indian** *a & n* antillano (*m*). **W~ Indies** *npl* Antillas *fpl*. ~**ward(s)** /-wəd(z)/ *adv* hacia el oeste

wet /wet/ *a* (**wetter, wettest**) mojado; (rainy) lluvioso; (🄵, person) soso. '~ **paint**' 'pintura fresca'. get ~ mojarse. he got his feet ~ se mojó los pies. ● *vt* (*pt* **wetted**) mojar; (dampen) humedecer. ~ **o.s.** orinarse.

~ **blanket** n aguafiestas m & f. ~ **suit** n traje m de neopreno

we've /wi:v/ = WE HAVE

whack /wæk/ vt ① golpear. ● n ① golpe m.

whale /weɪl/ n ballena f. **we had a** ~ **of a time** ① lo pasamos bomba ①

wham /wæm/ int ¡zas!

wharf /wɔːf/ n (pl **wharves** or **wharfs**) muelle m

what /wɒt/

● adjective

····▸ (in questions) qué. ~ **perfume are you wearing?** ¿qué perfume llevas?. ~ **colour are the walls?** ¿de qué color son las paredes?

····▸ (in exclamations) qué. ~ **a beautiful house!** ¡qué casa más linda!. ~ **a lot of people!** ¡cuánta gente!

····▸ (in indirect speech) qué. **I'll ask him** ~ **bus to take** le preguntaré qué autobús hay que tomar. **do you know** ~ **time it leaves?** ¿sabes a qué hora sale?

● pronoun

····▸ (in questions) qué. ~ **is it?** ¿qué es? ~ **for?** ¿para qué?. ~'**s the problem?** ¿cuál es el problema? ~'**s he like?** ¿cómo es? **what?** (say that again) ¿cómo?, ¿qué?

····▸ (in indirect questions) qué. **I didn't know** ~ **to do** no sabía qué hacer

····▸ (relative) lo que. **I did** ~ **I could** hice lo que pude. ~ **I need is a new car** lo que necesito es un coche nuevo

····▸ (in phrases) ~ **about me?** ¿y yo qué? ~ **if she doesn't come?** ¿y si no viene?

whatever /wɒt'evə(r)/ a cualquiera. ● pron (todo) lo que, cualquier cosa que

whatsoever /wɒtsəʊ'evə(r)/ a & pron = **whatever**

wheat /wi:t/ n trigo m

wheel /wi:l/ n rueda f. **at the** ~ al volante. ● vt empujar <bicycle etc>; llevar (en silla de ruedas etc) <person>. ~**barrow** n carretilla f. ~**chair** n silla f de ruedas

wheeze /wi:z/ vi respirar con dificultad

when /wen/ adv cuándo. ● conj cuando. ~**ever** /-'evə(r)/ adv (every time that) cada vez que, siempre que; (at whatever time) **we'll go** ~**ever you're ready** saldremos cuando estés listo

where /weə(r)/ adv & conj donde; (interrogative) dónde. ~ **are you going?** ¿adónde vas? ~ **are you from?** ¿de dónde eres?. ~**abouts** /-əbaʊts/ adv en qué parte. ● n paradero m. ~**as** /-'æz/ conj por cuanto; (in contrast) mientras (que). ~**ver** /weər'evə(r)/ adv (in questions) dónde; (no matter where) en cualquier parte. ● conj donde (+ subjunctive), dondequiera (+ subjunctive)

whet /wet/ vt (pt **whetted**) abrir <appetite>

whether /'weðə(r)/ conj si. **I don't know** ~ **she will like it** no sé si le gustará. ~ **you like it or not** te guste o no te guste

which /wɪtʃ/ a (in questions) (sing) qué, cuál; (pl) qué, cuáles. ~ **one** cuál. ~ **one of you** cuál de ustedes. ● pron (in questions) (sing) cuál; (pl) cuáles; (relative) que; (object) el cual, la cual, lo cual, los cuales, las cuales. ~**ever** /-'evə(r)/ a cualquier. ● pron cualquiera que, el que, la que; (in questions) cuál; (pl) cuáles

while /waɪl/ n rato m. **a** ~ **ago** hace un rato. ● conj mientras; (although) aunque. □ ~ **away** vt pasar <time>

whilst /waɪlst/ conj ⇒WHILE

whim /wɪm/ n capricho m

whimper /'wɪmpə(r)/ vi gimotear. ● n quejido m

whine /waɪn/ vi <person> gemir; <child> lloriquear; <dog> aullar

whip /wɪp/ n látigo m; (for punishment) azote m. ● vt (pt **whipped** /wɪpt/) fustigar, pegarle a (con la fusta) <horse>; azotar <person>; (Culin) batir

whirl /wɜːl/ vi girar rápidamente. ~**pool** n remolino m. ~**wind** n torbellino m

whirr /wɜː(r)/ n zumbido m. ● vi zumbar

whisk /wɪsk/ vt (Culin) batir. ● n (Culin) batidor m. ~ **away** llevarse

whisker /'wɪskə(r)/ n pelo m. ~**s** npl (of cat etc) bigotes mpl

whisky /'wɪskɪ/ n whisky m, güisqui m

whisper /'wɪspə(r)/ vt susurrar. ● vi cuchichear. ● n susurro m

whistle /'wɪsl/ n silbido m; (loud) chiflado m; (instrument) silbato m, pito m. ● vi silbar; (loudly) chiflar

white /waɪt/ a (-er, -est) blanco. **go ~** ponerse pálido. ● n blanco; (of egg) clara f. **~ coffee** n café m con leche. **~-collar worker** n empleado m de oficina. **~ elephant** n objeto m inútil y costoso. **~-hot** a <metal> al rojo blanco. **~ lie** n mentirijilla f. **~n** vt/i blanquear. **~wash** n cal f; (cover-up) tapadera f 🔲. ● vt blanquear, encalar

Whitsun /'wɪtsn/ n Pentecostés m

whiz /wɪz/ vi (pt **whizzed**). **~ by, ~ past** pasar zumbando. **~-kid** n 🔲 lince m 🔲

who /huː/ pron (in questions) quién; (pl) quiénes; (as relative) que; **the girl ~ lives there** la chica que vive allí. **those ~ can't come tomorrow** los que no puedan venir mañana. **~ever** /huː'evə(r)/ pron quienquiera que; (interrogative) quién

whole /həʊl/ a. **the ~ country** todo el país. **there's a ~ bottle left** queda una botella entera. ● n todo m, conjunto m; (total) total m. **on the ~** en general. **~-hearted** /-'hɑːtɪd/ a <support> incondicional; <approval> sin reservar. **~meal** a integral. **~sale** n venta f al por mayor. ● a & adv al por mayor. **~some** /-səm/ a sano

wholly /'həʊlɪ/ adv completamente

whom /huːm/ pron que, a quien; (in questions) a quién

whooping cough /'huːpɪŋ/ n tos f convulsa

whore /hɔː(r)/ n puta f

whose /huːz/ pron de quién; (pl) de quiénes. ● a (in questions) de quién; (pl) de quiénes; (relative) cuyo; (pl) cuyos

why /waɪ/ adv por qué. **~ not?** ¿por qué no? **that's ~ I couldn't go** por eso no pude ir. ● int ¡vaya!

wick /wɪk/ n mecha f

wicked /'wɪkɪd/ a malo; (mischievous) travieso; (🔲, very bad) malísimo

wicker /'wɪkə(r)/ n mimbre m & f. ● a de mimbre. **~work** n artículos mpl de mimbre

wicket /'wɪkɪt/ n (cricket) rastrillo m

wide /waɪd/ a (-er, -est) ancho; <range, experience> amplio; (off target) desviado. **it's four metres ~** tiene cuatro metros de ancho. ● adv open **~!** abra bien la boca. **~ awake** a completamente despierto; (fig) despabilado. **I left the door ~ open** dejé la puerta abierta de par en par. **~ly** adv extensamente; (believed) generalmente; (different) muy. **~n** vt ensanchar. ● vi ensancharse. **~spread** a extendido; (fig) difundido

widow /'wɪdəʊ/ n viuda f. **~er** n viudo m.

width /wɪdθ/ n anchura f. **in ~** de ancho

wield /wiːld/ vt manejar; ejercer <power>

wife /waɪf/ n (pl **wives**) mujer f, esposa f

wig /wɪg/ n peluca f

wiggle /'wɪgl/ vt menear. ● vi menearse

wild /waɪld/ a (-er, -est) <animal> salvaje; <flower> silvestre; <country> agreste; (enraged) furioso; <idea> extravagante; (with joy) loco. **a ~ guess** una conjetura hecha totalmente al azar. **I'm not ~ about the idea** la idea no me enloquece. ● adv en estado salvaje. **run ~** <children> criarse como salvajes. **~s** npl regiones fpl salvajes. **~erness** /'wɪldənɪs/ n páramo m. **~fire** n. **spread like ~fire** correr como un reguero de pólvora. **~-goose chase** n empresa f inútil. **~life** n fauna f. **~ly** adv violentamente; (fig) locamente

....

will /wɪl/

● auxiliary verb

past **would**; contracted forms **I'll, you'll, etc = I will, you will, etc.; won't = will not**

····▷ (talking about the future)

The Spanish future tense is not always the first option for translating the English future tense. The present tense of *ir* + *a* + *verb* is commonly used instead, particularly in Latin American countries. **he'll be here on Tuesday** *estará el martes, va a estar el martes;* **she won't agree** *no va a aceptar, no aceptará*

····➤ (in invitations and requests) ∼ **you have some wine?** ¿quieres (un poco de) vino? **you'll stay for dinner, won't you?** te quedas a cenar, ¿no?

····➤ (in tag questions) **you ∼ be back soon, won't you?** vas a volver pronto, ¿no?

····➤ (in short answers) **will it be ready by Monday? - yes, it ∼** ¿estará listo para el lunes? - sí

● *noun*

····➤ (mental power) voluntad *f*

····➤ (document) testamento *m*

willing /'wɪlɪŋ/ *a* complaciente. ∼ **to** dispuesto a. ∼**ly** *adv* de buena gana

willow /'wɪləʊ/ *n* sauce *m*

will-power /'wɪlpaʊə(r)/ *n* fuerza *f* de voluntad

wilt /wɪlt/ *vi* marchitarse

win /wɪn/ *vt* (*pt* **won**, *pres p* **winning**) ganar; (achieve, obtain) conseguir. ● *vi* ganar. ● *n* victoria *f*. □ ∼ **over** *vt* ganarse a

wince /wɪns/ *vi* hacer una mueca de dolor

winch /wɪntʃ/ *n* cabrestante *m*. ● *vt* levantar con un cabrestante

wind[1] /wɪnd/ *n* viento *m*; (in stomach) gases *mpl*. ∼ **instrument** instrumento *m* de viento. ● *vt* dejar sin aliento; <*blow*> cortarle la respiración a

wind[2] /waɪnd/ *vt* (*pt* **wound**) (wrap around) enrollar; dar cuerda a <*clock etc*>. ● *vi* <*road etc*> serpentear. □ ∼ **up** *vt* dar cuerda a <*watch, clock*>; (fig) terminar, concluir

wind /wɪnd/ : ∼**-cheater** *n* cazadora *f*. ∼**fall** *n* (fig) suerte *f* inesperada

winding /'waɪndɪŋ/ *a* tortuoso

windmill /'wɪndmɪl/ *n* molino *m* (de viento)

window /'wɪndəʊ/ *n* ventana *f*; (in shop) escaparate *m*, vitrina *f* (LAm), vidriera *f* (LAm), aparador *m* (Mex); (of vehicle, booking-office) ventanilla *f*; (Comp) ventana *f*, window *m*. ∼ **box** *n* jardinera *f*. ∼**-shop** *vi* mirar los escaparates. ∼**sill** *n* alféizar *m* or repisa *f* de la ventana

wind /wɪnd/: ∼**pipe** *n* tráquea *f*. ∼**screen** *n*, ∼**shield** *n* (Amer) parabrisas *m*. ∼**screen wiper** *n* limpiaparabrisas *m*. ∼**swept** *a* azotado por el viento. ∼**y** *a* (**-ier**, **-iest**) <*day*> ventoso, de viento. **it's** ∼**y** hace viento

wine /waɪn/ *n* vino *m*. ∼**-cellar** *n* bodega *f*. ∼**-glass** *n* copa *f* de vino. ∼**-growing** *n* vinicultura *f*. ● *a* vinícola. ∼ **list** *n* lista *f* de vinos. ∼**-tasting** *n* cata *f* de vinos

wing /wɪŋ/ *n* ala *f*; (Auto) aleta *f*. **under one's** ∼ bajo la protección de uno. ∼**er** *n* (Sport) ala *m & f*. ∼**s** *npl* (in theatre) bastidores *mpl*

wink /wɪŋk/ *vi* guiñar el ojo; <*light etc*> centellear. ● *n* guiño *m*. **not to sleep a** ∼ no pegar ojo

win: ∼**ner** *n* ganador *m*. ∼**ning-post** *n* poste *m* de llegada. ∼**nings** *npl* ganancias *fpl*

wint|er /'wɪntə(r)/ *n* invierno *m*. ● *vi* invernar. ∼**ry** *a* invernal

wipe /waɪp/ *vt* limpiar, pasarle un trapo a; (dry) secar. ∼ **one's nose** limpiarse la nariz. ● *n*. **give sth a** ∼ limpiar algo, pasarle un trapo a algo. □ ∼ **out** *vt* (cancel) cancelar; (destroy) destruir; (obliterate) borrar. □ ∼ **up** *vt* limpiar

wir|e /'waɪə(r)/ *n* alambre *m*; (Elec) cable *m*. ∼**ing** *n* instalación *f* eléctrica

wisdom /'wɪzdəm/ *n* sabiduría *f*. ∼ **tooth** *n* muela *f* del juicio

wise /waɪz/ *a* (**-er**, **-est**) sabio; (sensible) prudente; <*decision, choice*> acertado. ∼**ly** *adv* sabiamente; (sensibly) prudentemente

wish /wɪʃ/ *n* deseo *m*; (greeting) saludo *m*. **make a** ∼ pedir un deseo. **best** ∼**es, John** (in letters) saludos de

John, un abrazo de John. ● *vt* desear. ~ **s.o. well** desear buena suerte a uno. I ~ I **were rich** ¡ojalá fuera rico! **he ~ed he hadn't told her** lamentó habérselo dicho. ~**ful thinking** *n* ilusiones *fpl*

wistful /'wɪstfl/ *a* melancólico

wit /wɪt/ *n* gracia *f*; (intelligence) ingenio *m*. **be at one's ~s' end** no saber más qué hacer

witch /wɪtʃ/ *n* bruja *f*. ~**craft** *n* brujería *f*.

with /wɪð/ *prep* con; (cause, having) de. **come ~ me** ven conmigo. **take it ~ you** llévalo contigo; (formal) llévelo consigo. **the man ~ the beard** el hombre de la barba. **trembling ~ fear** temblando de miedo

withdraw /wɪð'drɔː/ *vt* (*pt* **withdrew**, *pp* **withdrawn**) retirar. ● *vi* apartarse. ~**al** *n* retirada *f*. ~**n** *a* <*person*> retraído

wither /'wɪðə(r)/ *vi* marchitarse

withhold /wɪð'həʊld/ *vt* (*pt* **withheld**) retener; (conceal) ocultar (**from** a)

within /wɪð'ɪn/ *prep* dentro de. ● *adv* dentro. ~ **sight** a la vista

without /wɪð'aʊt/ *prep* sin. ~ **paying** sin pagar

withstand /wɪð'stænd/ *vt* (*pt* **-stood**) resistir

witness /'wɪtnɪs/ *n* testigo *m*; (proof) testimonio *m*. ● *vt* presenciar; atestiguar <*signature*>. ~**-box** *n* tribuna *f* de los testigos

wit|icism /'wɪtɪsɪzəm/ *n* ocurrencia *f*. ~**y** /'wɪtɪ/ *a* (**-ier**, **-iest**) gracioso

wives /waɪvz/ ⇒WIFE

wizard /'wɪzəd/ *n* hechicero *m*

wizened /'wɪznd/ *a* arrugado

wobbl|e /'wɒbl/ *vi* <*chair*> tambalearse; <*bicycle*> bambolearse; <*voice, jelly, hand*> temblar. ~**y** *a* <*chair etc*> cojo

woe /wəʊ/ *n* aflicción *f*

woke /wəʊk/, **woken** /'wəʊkən/ ⇒WAKE

wolf /wʊlf/ *n* (*pl* **wolves** /wʊlvz/) lobo *m*

woman /'wʊmən/ *n* (*pl* **women**) mujer *f*

womb /wuːm/ *n* matriz *f*

women /'wɪmɪn/ *npl* ⇒WOMAN

won /wʌn/ ⇒WIN

wonder /'wʌndə(r)/ *n* maravilla *f*; (bewilderment) asombro *m*. **no ~** no es de extrañarse (**that** que). ● *vt* (ask oneself) preguntarse. I ~ **whose book this is** me pregunto de quién será este libro; (in polite requests) I ~ **if you could help me?** ¿me podría ayudar? ~**ful** *a* maravilloso. ~**fully** *adv* maravillosamente

won't /wəʊnt/ = **will not**

wood /wʊd/ *n* madera *f*; (for burning) leña *f*; (area) bosque *m*. ~**ed** *a* poblado de árboles, boscoso. ~**en** *a* de madera. ~**land** *n* bosque *m*. ~**wind** /-wɪnd/ *n* instrumentos *mpl* de viento de madera. ~**work** *n* carpintería *f*; (in room etc) maderaje *m*. ~**worm** *n* carcoma *f*. ~**y** *a* leñoso

wool /wʊl/ *n* lana *f*. **pull the ~ over s.o.'s eyes** engañar a uno. ~**len** *a* de lana. ~**ly** *a* (**-ier**, **-iest**) de lana; (unclear) vago. ● *n* jersey *m*

word /wɜːd/ *n* palabra *f*; (news) noticia *f*. **by ~ of mouth** de palabra. I **didn't say a** ~ yo no dije nada. **in other ~s** es decir. ● *vt* expresar. ~**ing** *n* redacción *f*; (of question) formulación *f*. ~ **processor** *n* procesador *m* de textos. ~**y** *a* prolijo

wore /wɔː(r)/ ⇒WEAR

work /wɜːk/ *n* trabajo *m*; (arts) obra *f*. **be out of ~** estar sin trabajo, estar desocupado. ● *vt* hacer trabajar; manejar <*machine*>. ● *vi* trabajar; <*machine*> funcionar; <*student*> estudiar; <*drug etc*> surtir efecto. □ ~ **off** *vt* desahogar. □ ~ **out** *vt* resolver <*problem*>; (calculate) calcular; (understand) entender. *vi* (succeed) salir bien; (Sport) entrenarse. □ ~ **up** *vt*. **get ~ed up** exaltarse. ~**able** *a* <*project, solution*> factible. ~**er** *n* trabajador *m*; (manual) obrero *m*; (in office, bank) empleado *m*. ~**ing** *a* <*day*> laborable; <*clothes etc*> de trabajo. **in ~ing order** en estado de funcionamiento. ~**ing class** *n* clase *f* obrera. ~**ing-class** *a* de la clase obrera. ~**man** /-mən/ *n* (*pl* **-men**) obrero *m*. ~**manship** *n* destreza *f*. ~**s** *npl* (building) fábrica *f*;

(Mec) mecanismo *m*. ∼**shop** *n* taller *m*

world /wɜːld/ *n* mundo *m*. out of this ∼ maravilloso. ● *a* mundial. **W**∼ **Cup** *n*. the **W**∼ **Cup** la Copa del Mundo. ∼**ly** *a* mundano. ∼**wide** *a* universal. **W**∼ **Wide Web** *n* World Wide Web *m*

worm /wɜːm/ *n* gusano *m*, lombriz *f*

worn /wɔːn/ ⇒WEAR. ● *a* gastado. ∼**-out** *a* gastado; <*person*> rendido

worr|ied /'wʌrɪd/ *a* preocupado. ∼**y** /'wʌrɪ/ *vt* preocupar; (annoy) molestar. ● *vi* preocuparse. ● *n* preocupación *f*. ∼**ying** *a* inquietante

worse /wɜːs/ *a* peor. get ∼ empeorar. ● *adv* peor; (more) más. ∼**n** *vt/i* empeorar

worship /'wɜːʃɪp/ *n* culto *m*; (title) Su Señoría. ● *vt* (*pt* **worshipped**) adorar

worst /wɜːst/ *a* peor. he's the ∼ in the class es el peor de la clase. ● *adv* peor. ● *n*. the ∼ lo peor

worth /wɜːθ/ *n* valor *m*. ● *a*. be ∼ valer. it's ∼ trying vale la pena probarlo. it was ∼ my while (me) valió la pena. ∼**less** *a* sin valor. ∼**while** /-'waɪl/ *a* que vale la pena. ∼**y** /'wɜːðɪ/ *a* meritorio; (respectable) respetable; (laudable) loable

would /wʊd/ *v aux*. (in conditional sentences) ∼ **you** go? ¿irías tú? he ∼ **come if he could** vendría si pudiera; (in reported speech) I **thought you'd forget** pensé que te olvidarías; (in requests, invitations) ∼ **you come here, please?** ¿quieres venir aquí? ∼ **you switch the television off?** ¿podrías apagar la televisión?; (be prepared to) he ∼**n't listen to me** no me quería escuchar

wound¹ /wuːnd/ *n* herida *f*. ● *vt* herir

wound² /waʊnd/ ⇒WIND²

wove, woven /wəʊv, 'wəʊvn/ ⇒WEAVE

wow /waʊ/ *int* ¡ah!

wrangle /'ræŋgl/ *vi* reñir. ● *n* riña *f*

wrap /ræp/ *vt* (*pt* **wrapped**) envolver. ● *n* bata *f*; (shawl) chal *m*. ∼**per** *n*, ∼**ping** *n* envoltura *f*

wrath /rɒθ/ *n* ira *f*

wreak /riːk/ *vt* sembrar. ∼ **havoc** causar estragos

wreath /riːθ/ *n* (*pl* **-ths** /-ðz/) corona *f*

wreck /rek/ *n* (ship) restos *mpl* de un naufragio; (vehicle) restos *mpl* de un avión siniestrado. be a **nervous** ∼ tener los nervios destrozados. ● *vt* provocar el naufragio de <*ship*>; destrozar <*car*>; (Amer, demolish) demoler; (fig) destrozar. ∼**age** /-ɪdʒ/ *n* restos *mpl*; (of building) ruinas *fpl*

wrench /rentʃ/ *vt* arrancar; (sprain) desgarrarse; dislocarse <*joint*>. ● *n* tirón *m*; (emotional) dolor *m* (*causado por una separación*); (tool) llave *f* inglesa

wrestl|e /'resl/ *vi* luchar. ∼**er** *n* luchador *m*. ∼**ing** *n* lucha *f*

wretch /retʃ/ *n* (despicable person) desgraciado *m*; (unfortunate person) desdichado *m* & *f*. ∼**ed** /-ɪd/ *a* desdichado; <*weather*> horrible

wriggle /'rɪgl/ *vi* retorcerse. ∼ **out of** escaparse de

wring /rɪŋ/ *vt* (*pt* **wrung**) retorcer <*neck*>. ∼ **out of** (obtain from) arrancar. □ ∼ **out** *vt* retorcer

wrinkl|e /'rɪŋkl/ *n* arruga *f*. ● *vt* arrugar. ● *vi* arrugarse. ∼**y** *a* arrugado

wrist /rɪst/ *n* muñeca *f*. ∼**watch** *n* reloj *m* de pulsera

writ /rɪt/ *n* orden *m* judicial

write /raɪt/ *vt/i* (*pt* **wrote**, *pp* **written**, *pres p* **writing**) escribir. □ ∼ **down** *vt* anotar. □ ∼ **off** *vt* cancelar <*debt*>. ∼**-off** *n*. the car was a ∼**-off** el coche fue declarado un siniestro total. ∼**r** *n* escritor *m*

writhe /raɪð/ *vi* retorcerse

writing /'raɪtɪŋ/ *n* (script) escritura *f*; (handwriting) letra *f*. in ∼ por escrito. ∼**s** *npl* obra *f*, escritos *mpl*. ∼ **desk** *n* escritorio *m*. ∼ **pad** *n* bloc *m*. ∼ **paper** *n* papel *m* de escribir

written /'rɪtn/ ⇒WRITE

wrong /rɒŋ/ *a* equivocado, incorrecto; (not just) injusto; (mistaken) equivocado. be ∼ no tener razón; (be mistaken) equivocarse. what's ∼? ¿qué pasa? it's ∼ to steal robar está mal. what's ∼ with that? ¿qué hay de malo en eso?. ● *adv* mal. **go ~** equivocarse; *<plan>* salir mal. ● *n* injusticia *f*; (evil) mal *m*. **in the ~** equivocado. ● *vt* ser injusto con. **~ful** *a* injusto. **~ly** *adv* mal; (unfairly) injustamente

wrote /rəʊt/ ⇒WRITE

wrought iron /rɔːt/ *n* hierro *m* forjado

wrung /rʌŋ/ ⇒WRING

wry /raɪ/ *a* (**wryer, wryest**) irónico. **make a ~ face** torcer el gesto

X x

xerox /ˈzɪərɒks/ *vt* fotocopiar, xerografiar

Xmas /ˈkrɪsməs/ *n abbr* (**Christmas**) Navidad *f*

X-ray /ˈeksreɪ/ *n* (ray) rayo *m* X; (photograph) radiografía *f*. **~s** *npl* rayos *mpl*. ● *vt* hacer una radiografía de

xylophone /ˈzaɪləfəʊn/ *n* xilofón *m*, xilófono *m*

Y y

yacht /jɒt/ *n* yate *m*. **~ing** *n* navegación *f* a vela

yank /jæŋk/ *vt* tirar de (violentamente)

Yankee /ˈjæŋkɪ/ *n* yanqui *m & f*

yap /jæp/ *vi* (*pt* **yapped**) *<dog>* ladrar (*con ladridos agudos*)

yard /jɑːd/ *n* patio *m*; (Amer, garden) jardín *m*; (measurement) yarda *f* (= 0.9144 metre)

yarn /jɑːn/ *n* hilo *m*; (, tale) cuento *m*

yawn /jɔːn/ *vi* bostezar. ● *n* bostezo *m*

year /jɪə(r)/ *n* año *m*. **be three ~s old** tener tres años. **~ly** *a* anual. ● *adv* cada año

yearn /ˈjɜːn/ *vi*. **~ to do sth** anhelar hacer algo. **~ for sth** añorar algo. **~ing** *n* anhelo *m*, ansia *f*

yeast /jiːst/ *n* levadura *f*

yell /jel/ *vi* gritar. ● *n* grito *m*

yellow /ˈjeləʊ/ *a & n* amarillo (*m*)

yelp /jelp/ *n* gañido *m*. ● *vi* gañir

yes /jes/ *int & n* sí (*m*)

yesterday /ˈjestədeɪ/ *adv & n* ayer (*m*). **the day before ~** anteayer *m*. **~ morning** ayer por la mañana, ayer en la mañana (LAm)

yet /jet/ *adv* todavía, aún; (already) ya. **as ~** hasta ahora; (as a linker) sin embargo. ● *conj* pero

Yiddish /ˈjɪdɪʃ/ *n* yídish *m*

yield /jiːld/ *vt* (surrender) ceder; producir *<crop/mineral>*; dar *<results>*. ● *vi* ceder. '**yield**' (Amer, traffic sign) ceda el paso. ● *n* rendimiento *m*

yoga /ˈjəʊgə/ *n* yoga *m*

yoghurt /ˈjɒgət/ *n* yogur *m*

yoke /jəʊk/ *n* (fig also) yugo *m*

yokel /ˈjəʊkl/ *n* palurdo *m*

yolk /jəʊk/ *n* yema *f* (de huevo)

you /juː/

● *pronoun*

····► (as the subject) (familiar form) (*sing*) tú, vos (River Plate and parts of Central America); (*pl*) vosotros, -tras (Spain), ustedes (LAm); (formal) (*sing*) usted; (*pl*) ustedes

! In Spanish the subject pronoun is usually only used ■ to give emphasis or mark contrast.

····► (as the direct object) (familiar form) (*sing*) te; (*pl*) os (Spain), los, las (LAm); (formal) (*sing*) lo *or* (Spain) le, la; (*pl*) los *or* (Spain) les, las. **I love ~** te quiero

····► (as the indirect object) (familiar form) (*sing*) te; (*pl*) os (Spain), les (LAm); (formal) (*sing*) le; (*pl*) les. **I sent ~ the book yesterday** te mandé el libro ayer

! The pronoun *se* replaces the indirect object pronoun *le* or ■ *les* when the latter is used with the direct object pronoun (*lo, la* etc), e.g. **I gave it to** ~ *se lo di*

····▶ (when used after a preposition) (familiar form) (*sing*) ti, vos (River Plate and parts of Central America); (*pl*) vosotros, -tras (Spain), ustedes (LAm); (formal) (*sing*) usted; (*pl*) ustedes

····▶ (generalizing) uno, tú (esp Spain). ~ **feel very proud** uno se siente muy orgulloso, te sientes muy orgulloso (esp Spain). ~ **have to be patient** hay que tener paciencia

you'd /juːd/, /jʊəd/ = **you had**, **you would**

you'll /juːl/, /jʊəl/ = **you will**

young /jʌŋ/ *a* (**-er, -est**) joven. **my** ~**er sister** mi hermana menor. **he's a year** ~**er than me** tiene un año menos que yo. ~ **lady** *n* señorita *f*. ~ **man** *n* joven *m*. ~**ster** /-stə(r)/ *n* joven *m*

your /jɔː(r)/ *a* (belonging to one person) (*sing, familiar*) tu; (*pl, familiar*) tus; (*sing, formal*) su; (*pl, formal*) sus; (belonging to more than one person) (*sing, familiar*) vuestro, -tra, su (LAm); (*pl, familiar*) vuestros, -tras, sus (LAm); (*sing, formal*) su; (*pl, formal*) sus

you're /jʊə(r)/, /jɔː(r)/ = **you are**

yours /jɔːz/ *poss pron* (belonging to one person) (*sing, familiar*) tuyo, -ya; (*pl, familiar*) tuyos, -yas; (*sing, formal*) suyo, -ya; (*pl, formal*) suyos, -yas. (belonging to more than one person) (*sing, familiar*) vuestro, -tra; (*pl, familiar*) vuestros, -tras, suyos, -yas (LAm); (*sing, formal*) suyo, -ya; (*pl, formal*) suyos, -yas **an aunt of** ~ una tía tuya; ~ **is here** el tuyo está aquí

yourself /jɔːˈself/ *pron* (*reflexive*). (emphatic use) 🅴 tú mismo, tú misma; (formal) usted mismo, usted misma. **describe** ~**f** descríbete; (Ud form) descríbase. **stop thinking about** ~**f** deja de pensar en tí mismo; (formal) deje de pensar en sí mismo; **by** ~**f** solo, sola. ~**ves** /jɔːˈselvz/ *pron* vosotros mismos, vosotras mismas (familiar), ustedes mismos, ustedes mismas (LAm familiar), ustedes mismos, ustedes mismas (formal); (*re-*

flexive). **behave** ~**ves** ¡portaos bien (familiar), ¡pórtense bien! (LAm familiar), ¡pórtense bien! (formal). **by** ~**ves** solos, solas

youth /juːθ/ *n* (*pl* **youths** /juːðz/) (early life) juventud *f*; (boy) joven *m*; (young people) juventud *f*. ~**ful** *a* joven, juvenil. ~ **hostel** *n* albergue *m* juvenil

you've /juːv/ = **you have**

Yugoslav /ˈjuːɡəslɑːv/ *a & n* yugoslavo (*m*). ~**ia** /-ˈslɑːvɪə/ *n* Yugoslavia *f*

Zz

zeal /ziːl/ *n* fervor *m*, celo *m*

zeal|ot /ˈzelət/ *n* fanático *m*. ~**ous** /-əs/ *a* ferviente; (worker) que pone gran celo en su trabajo

zebra /ˈzebrə/ *n* cebra *f*. ~ **crossing** *n* paso *m* de cebra

zenith /ˈzenɪθ/ *n* cenit *m*

zero /ˈzɪərəʊ/ *n* (*pl* **-os**) cero *m*

zest /zest/ *n* entusiasmo *m*; (peel) cáscara *f*

zigzag /ˈzɪɡzæɡ/ *n* zigzag *m*. ● *vi* (*pt* **zigzagged**) zigzaguear

zilch /zɪltʃ/ *n* 🅰 nada de nada

zinc /zɪŋk/ *n* cinc *m*

zip /zɪp/ *n* cremallera *f*, cierre *m* (LAm), zíper *m* (Mex). ● *vt*. ~ (up) cerrar (la cremallera). **Z**~ **code** *n* (Amer) código *m* postal. ~ **fastener** *n* cremallera *f*. ~**per** *n*/*vt* ⇒ZIP

zodiac /ˈzəʊdɪæk/ *n* zodíaco *m*, zodiaco *m*

zombie /ˈzɒmbɪ/ *n* zombi *m & f*

zone /zəʊn/ *n* zona *f*. **time** ~ *n* huso *m* horario

zoo /zuː/ *n* zoo *m*, zoológico *m*. ~**logical** /zuːəˈlɒdʒɪkl/ *a* zoológico. ~**logist** /zuːˈɒlədʒɪst/ *n* zoólogo *m*. ~**logy** /zuːˈɒlədʒɪ/ *n* zoología *f*

zoom /zuːm/ *n*. □ ~ **in** *vi* (Photo) hacer un zoom in (**on** sobre). □ ~ **past** *vi*/*t* pasar zumbando. ~ **lens** *n* teleobjetivo *m*, zoom *m*

zucchini /zʊˈkiːnɪ/ *n* (*invar or* ~**s**) (Amer) calabacín *m*

Numbers · Números

English		Spanish
zero	0	cero
one (first)	1	uno (primero)
two (second)	2	dos (segundo)
three (third)	3	tres (tercero)
four (fourth)	4	cuatro (cuarto)
five (fifth)	5	cinco (quinto)
six (sixth)	6	seis (sexto)
seven (seventh)	7	siete (séptimo)
eight (eighth)	8	ocho (octavo)
nine (ninth)	9	nueve (noveno)
ten (tenth)	10	diez (décimo)
eleven (eleventh)	11	once (undécimo)
twelve (twelfth)	12	doce (duodécimo)
thirteen (thirteenth)	13	trece (decimotercero)
fourteen (fourteenth)	14	catorce (decimocuarto)
fifteen (fifteenth)	15	quince (decimoquinto)
sixteen (sixteenth)	16	dieciséis (decimosexto)
seventeen (seventeenth)	17	diecisiete (decimoséptimo)
eighteen (eighteenth)	18	dieciocho (decimoctavo)
nineteen (nineteenth)	19	diecinueve (decimonoveno)
twenty (twentieth)	20	veinte (vigésimo)
twenty-one (twenty-first)	21	veintiuno (vigésimo primero)
twenty-two (twenty-second)	22	veintidós (vigésimo segundo)
twenty-three (twenty-third)	23	veintitrés (vigésimo tercero)
twenty-four (twenty-fourth)	24	veinticuatro (vigésimo cuarto)
twenty-five (twenty-fifth)	25	veinticinco (vigésimo quinto)
twenty-six (twenty-sixth)	26	veintiséis (vigésimo sexto)
thirty (thirtieth)	30	treinta (trigésimo)
thirty-one (thirty-first)	31	treinta y uno (trigésimo primero)
forty (fortieth)	40	cuarenta (cuadragésimo)
fifty (fiftieth)	50	cincuenta (quincuagésimo)
sixty (sixtieth)	60	sesenta (sexagésimo)
seventy (seventieth)	70	setenta (septuagésimo)
eighty (eightieth)	80	ochenta (octogésimo)

English	Number	Español
ninety (ninetieth)	90	noventa (nonagésimo)
a/one hundred (hundredth)	100	cien (centésimo)
a/one hundred and one (hundred and first)	101	ciento uno (centésimo primero)
two hundred (two hundredth)	200	doscientos (ducentésimo)
three hundred (three hundredth)	300	trescientos (tricentésimo)
four hundred (four hundredth)	400	cuatrocientos (cuadringentésimo)
five hundred (five hundredth)	500	quinientos (quingentésimo)
six hundred (six hundredth)	600	seiscientos (sexcentésimo)
seven hundred (seven hundredth)	700	setecientos (septingentésimo)
eight hundred (eight hundredth)	800	ochocientos (octingentésimo)
nine hundred (nine hundredth)	900	novecientos (noningentésimo)
a/one thousand (thousandth)	1000	mil (milésimo)
two thousand (two thousandth)	2000	dos mil (dos milésimo)
a/one million (millionth)	1,000,000	un millón (millonésimo)

Spanish Verbs · Verbos españoles

Regular verbs:
in **-ar** (*e.g.* **comprar**)
Present; compr|o, ~as, ~a, ~amos, ~áis, ~an
Future: comprar|é, ~ás, ~á, ~emos, ~éis, ~án
Imperfect: compr|aba, ~abas, ~aba, ~ábamos, ~abais, ~aban
Preterite: compr|é, ~aste, ~ó, ~amos, ~asteis, ~aron
Present subjunctive: compr|e, ~es, ~e, ~emos, ~éis, ~en
Imperfect subjunctive: compr|ara, ~aras ~ara, ~áramos, ~arais, ~aran
compr|ase, ~ases, ~ase, ~ásemos, ~aseis, ~asen
Conditional: comprar|ía, ~ías, ~ía, ~íamos, ~íais, ~ían
Present participle: comprando
Past participle: comprado
Imperative: compra, comprad

in **-er** (*e.g.* **beber**)
Present: beb|o, ~es, ~e, ~emos, ~éis, ~en
Future: beber|é, ~ás, ~á, ~emos, ~éis, ~án
Imperfect: beb|ía, ~ías, ~ía, ~íamos, ~íais, ~ían
Preterite: beb|í, ~iste, ~ió, ~imos, ~isteis, ~ieron
Present subjunctive: beb|a, ~as, ~a, ~amos, ~áis, ~an
Imperfect subjunctive: beb|iera, ~ieras, ~iera, ~iéramos, ~ierais, ~ieran
beb|iese, ~ieses, ~iese, ~iésemos, ~ieseis, ~iesen
Conditional: beber|ía, ~ías, ~ía, ~íamos, ~íais, ~ían
Present participle: bebiendo
Past participle: bebido
Imperative: bebe, bebed

in **-ir** (*e.g.* **vivir**)
Present: viv|o, ~es, ~e, ~imos, ~ís, ~en
Future: vivir|é, ~ás, ~á, ~emos, ~éis, ~án
Imperfect: viv|ía, ~ías, ~ía, ~íamos, ~íais, ~ían
Preterite: viv|í, ~iste, ~ió, ~imos, ~isteis, ~ieron
Present subjunctive: viv|a, ~as, ~a, ~amos, ~áis, ~an
Imperfect subjunctive: viv|iera, ~ieras, ~iera, ~iéramos, ~ierais, ~ieran
viv|iese, ~ieses, ~iese, ~iésemos, ~ieseis, ~iesen
Conditional: vivir|ía, ~ías, ~ía, ~íamos, ~íais, ~ían
Present participle: viviendo
Past participle: vivido
Imperative: vive, vivid

Irregular verbs:
[1] cerrar
Present: cierro, cierras, cierra, cerramos, cerráis, cierran
Present subjunctive: cierre, cierres, cierre, cerremos, cerréis, cierren
Imperative: cierra, cerrad

[2] contar, mover
Present: cuento, cuentas, cuenta, contamos, contáis, cuentan
muevo, mueves, mueve, movemos, movéis, mueven
Present subjunctive: cuente, cuentes, cuente, contemos, contéis, cuenten
mueva, muevas, mueva, movamos, mováis, muevan
Imperative: cuenta, contad
mueve, moved

[3] jugar
Present: juego, juegas, juega, jugamos, jugáis, juegan
Preterite: jug|ué, jugaste, jugó, jugamos, jugasteis, jugaron
Present subjunctive: juegue, juegues, juegue, juguemos, juguéis, jueguen

[4] sentir
Present: siento, sientes, siente, sentimos, sentís, sienten
Preterite: sentí, sentiste, sintió, sentimos, sentisteis, sintieron
Present subjunctive: sienta, sientas, sienta, sintamos, sintáis, sientan
Imperfect subjunctive: sint|iera, ~ieras, ~iera, ~iéramos, ~ierais, ~ieran

sint|iese, ~ieses, ~iese,
~iésemos, ~ieseis, ~iesen
Present participle: sintiendo
Imperative: siente, sentid

[5] pedir
Present: pido, pides, pide, pedimos,
  pedís, piden
Preterite: pedí, pediste, pidió,
  pedimos, pedisteis, pidieron
Present subjunctive: pid|a, ~as, ~a,
  ~amos, ~áis, ~an
Imperfect subjunctive: pid|iera,
  ~ieras, ~iera, ~iéramos,
  ~ierais, ~ieran
  pid|iese, ~ieses, ~iese,
  ~iésemos, ~ieseis, ~iesen
Present participle: pidiendo
Imperative: pide, pedid

[6] dormir
Present: duermo, duermes, duerme,
  dormimos, dormís, duermen
Preterite: dormí, dormiste, durmió,
  dormimos, dormisteis, durmieron
Present subjunctive: duerma,
  duermas, duerma, durmamos,
  durmáis, duerman
Imperfect subjunctive: durm|iera,
  ~ieras, ~iera, ~iéramos,
  ~ierais, ~ieran
  durm|iese, ~ieses, ~iese,
  ~iésemos, ~ieseis, ~iesen
Present participle: durmiendo
Imperative: duerme, dormid

[7] dedicar
Preterite: dediqué, dedicaste, dedicó,
  dedicamos, dedicasteis, dedicaron
Present subjunctive: dediqu|e, ~es,
  ~e, ~emos, ~éis, ~en

[8] delinquir
Present: delinco, delinques, delinque,
  delinquimos, delinquís, delinquen
Present subjunctive: delinc|a, ~as,
  ~a, ~amos, ~áis, ~an

[9] vencer, esparcir
Present: venzo, vences, vence,
  vencemos, vencéis, vencen
  esparzo, esparces, esparce,
  esparcimos, esparcís, esparcen
Present subjunctive: venz|a, ~as, ~a,
  ~amos, ~áis, ~an
  esparz|a, ~as, ~a, ~amos, ~áis,
  ~an

[10] rechazar
Preterite: rechacé, rechazaste,
  rechazó, rechazamos, rechazasteis,
  rechazaron
Present subjunctive: rechac|e, ~es,
  ~e, ~emos, ~éis, ~en

[11] conocer, lucir
Present: conozco, conoces, conoce,
  conocemos, conocéis, conocen
  luzco, luces, luce, lucimos, lucís,
  lucen
Present subjunctive: conozc|a, ~as,
  ~a, ~amos, ~áis, ~an
  luzc|a, ~as, ~a, ~amos, ~áis,
  ~an

[12] pagar
Preterite: pagué, pagaste, pagó,
  pagamos, pagasteis, pagaron
Present subjunctive: pagu|e, ~es, ~e,
  ~emos, ~éis, ~en

[13] distinguir
Present: distingo, distingues,
  distingue, distinguimos,
  distinguís, distinguen
Present subjunctive: disting|a, ~as,
  ~a, ~amos, ~áis, ~an

[14] acoger, afligir
Present: acojo, acoges, acoge,
  acogemos, acogéis, acogen
  aflijo, afliges, aflige, afligimos,
  afligís, afligen
Present subjunctive: acoj|a, ~as, ~a,
  ~amos, ~áis, ~an
  aflij|a, ~as, ~a, ~amos, ~áis,
  ~an

[15] averiguar
Preterite: averigüé, averiguaste,
  averiguó, averiguamos,
  averiguasteis, averiguaron
Present subjunctive: averigü|e, ~es,
  ~e, ~emos, ~éis, ~en

[16] agorar
Present: agüero, agüeras, agüera,
  agoramos, agoráis, agüeran
Present subjunctive: agüere, agüeres,
  agüere, agoremos, agoréis, agüeren
Imperative: agüera, agorad

[17] huir
Present: huyo, huyes, huye, huimos,
  huís, huyen

Preterite: huí, huiste, huyó, huimos,
  huisteis, huyeron
Present subjunctive: huy|a, ~as, ~a,
  ~amos, ~áis, ~an
Imperfect subjunctive: huy|era,
  ~eras, ~era, ~éramos, ~erais,
  ~eran
  huy|ese, ~eses, ~ese, ~ésemos,
  ~eseis, ~esen
Present participle: huyendo
Imperative: huye, huid

[18] creer

Preterite: creí, creíste, creyó,
  creímos, creísteis, creyeron
Imperfect subjunctive: crey|era,
  ~eras, ~era, ~éramos, ~erais,
  ~eran
  crey|ese, ~eses, ~ese, ~ésemos,
  ~eseis, ~esen
Present participle: creyendo
Past participle: creído

[19] argüir

Present: arguyo, arguyes, arguye,
  argüimos, argüís, arguyen
Preterite: argüí, argüiste, arguyó,
  argüimos, argüisteis, arguyeron
Present subjunctive: arguy|a, ~as,
  ~a, ~amos, ~áis, ~an
Imperfect subjunctive: arguy|era,
  ~eras, ~era, ~éramos, ~erais,
  ~eran
  arguy|ese, ~eses, ~ese,
  ~ésemos, ~eseis, ~esen
Present participle: arguyendo
Imperative: arguye, argüid

[20] vaciar

Present: vacío, vacías, vacía,
  vaciamos, vaciáis, vacían
Present subjunctive: vacíe, vacíes,
  vacíe, vaciemos, vaciéis, vacíen
Imperative: vacía, vaciad

[21] acentuar

Present: acentúo, acentúas, acentúa,
  acentuamos, acentuáis, acentúan
Present subjunctive: acentúe,
  acentúes, acentúe, acentuemos,
  acentuéis, acentúen
Imperative: acentúa, acentuad

[22] atañer, engullir

Preterite: atañ|í, ~iste, ~ó, ~imos,
  ~isteis, ~eron
  engull|í ~iste, ~ó, ~imos,
  ~isteis, ~eron

Imperfect subjunctive: atañ|era,
  ~eras, ~era, ~éramos, ~erais,
  ~eran
  atañ|ese, ~eses, ~ese, ~ésemos,
  ~eseis, ~esen
  engull|era, ~eras, ~era,
  ~éramos, ~erais, ~eran
  engull|ese, ~eses, ~ese,
  ~ésemos, ~eseis, ~esen
Present participle: atañendo
  engullendo

[23] aislar, aullar

Present: aíslo, aíslas, aísla, aislamos,
  aisláis, aíslan
  aúllo, aúllas, aúlla, aullamos
  aulláis, aúllan
Present subjunctive: aísle, aísles,
  aísle, aislemos, aisléis, aíslen
  aúlle, aúlles, aúlle, aullemos,
  aulléis, aúllen
Imperative: aísla, aislad
  aúlla, aullad

[24] abolir, garantir

Present: abolimos, abolís
  garantimos, garantís
Present subjunctive: not used
Imperative: abolid
  garantid

[25] andar

Preterite: anduv|e, ~iste, ~o,
  ~imos, ~isteis, ~ieron
Imperfect subjunctive: anduv|iera,
  ~ieras, ~iera, ~iéramos,
  ~ierais, ~ieran
  anduv|iese, ~ieses, ~iese,
  ~iésemos, ~ieseis, ~iesen

[26] dar

Present: doy, das, da, damos, dais, dan
Preterite: di, diste, dio, dimos, disteis,
  dieron
Present subjunctive: dé, des, dé,
  demos, deis, den
Imperfect subjunctive: diera, dieras,
  diera, diéramos, dierais, dieran
  diese, dieses, diese, diésemos,
  dieseis, diesen

[27] estar

Present: estoy, estás, está, estamos,
  estáis, están
Preterite: estuv|e, ~iste, ~o, ~imos,
  ~isteis, ~ieron
Present subjunctive: esté, estés, esté,
  estemos, estéis, estén

Imperfect subjunctive: estuv|iera,
~**ieras,** ~**iera,** ~**iéramos,**
~**ierais,** ~**ieran**
estuv|iese, ~**ieses,** ~**iese,**
~**iésemos,** ~**ieseis,** ~**iesen**
Imperative: está, estad

[28] caber
Present: quepo, cabes, cabe, cabemos,
cabéis, caben
Future: cabr|é, ~**ás,** ~**á,** ~**emos,**
~**éis,** ~**án**
Preterite: cup|e, ~**iste,** ~**o,** ~**imos,**
~**isteis,** ~**ieron**
Present subjunctive: quep|a, ~**as,** ~**a,**
~**amos,** ~**áis,** ~**an**
Imperfect subjunctive: cup|iera,
~**ieras,** ~**iera,** ~**iéramos,**
~**ierais,** ~**ieran**
cup|iese, ~**ieses,** ~**iese,**
~**iésemos,** ~**ieseis,** ~**iesen**
Conditional: cabr|ía, ~**ías,** ~**ía,**
~**íamos,** ~**íais,** ~**ían**

[29] caer
Present: caigo, caes, cae, caemos,
caéis, caen
Preterite: caí, caiste, cayó, caímos,
caísteis, cayeron
Present subjunctive: caig|a, ~**as,** ~**a,**
~**amos,** ~**áis,** ~**an**
Imperfect subjunctive: cay|era,
~**eras,** ~**era,** ~**éramos,** ~**erais,**
~**eran**
cay|ese, ~**eses,** ~**ese,** ~**ésemos,**
~**eseis,** ~**esen**
Present participle: cayendo
Past participle: caído

[30] haber
Present: he, has, ha, hemos, habéis,
han
Future: habr|é, ~**ás,** ~**á,** ~**emos,**
~**éis,** ~**án**
Preterite: hub|e, ~**iste,** ~**o,** ~**imos,**
~**isteis,** ~**ieron**
Present subjunctive: hay|a, ~**as,** ~**a,**
~**amos,** ~**áis,** ~**an**
Imperfect subjunctive: hub|iera,
~**ieras,** ~**iera,** ~**iéramos,**
~**ierais,** ~**ieran**
hub|iese, ~**ieses,** ~**iese,**
~**iésemos,** ~**ieseis,** ~**iesen**
Conditional: habr|ía, ~**ías,** ~**ía,**
~**íamos,** ~**íais,** ~**ían**

[31] hacer
Present: hago, haces, hace, hacemos,
hacéis, hacen
Future: har|é, ~**ás,** ~**á,** ~**emos,**
~**éis,** ~**án**
Preterite: hice, hiciste, hizo, hicimos,
hicisteis, hicieron
Present subjunctive: hag|a, ~**as,** ~**a,**
~**amos,** ~**áis,** ~**an**
Imperfect subjunctive: hic|iera,
~**ieras,** ~**iera,** ~**iéramos,**
~**ierais,** ~**ieran**
hic|iese, ~**ieses,** ~**iese,**
~**iésemos,** ~**ieseis,** ~**iesen**
Conditional: har|ía, ~**ías,** ~**ía,**
~**íamos,** ~**íais,** ~**ían**
Past participle: hecho
Imperative: haz, haced

[32] placer
Preterite: plació/plugo
Present subjunctive: plazca
Imperfect subjunctive:
placiera/pluguiera
placiese/pluguiese

[33] poder
Present: puedo, puedes, puede,
podemos, podéis, pueden
Future: podr|é, ~**ás,** ~**á,** ~**emos,**
~**éis,** ~**án**
Preterite: pud|e, ~**iste,** ~**o,** ~**imos,**
~**isteis,** ~**ieron**
Present subjunctive: pueda, puedas,
pueda, podamos, podáis, puedan
Imperfect subjunctive: pud|iera,
~**ieras,** ~**iera,** ~**iéramos,**
~**ierais,** ~**ieran**
pud|iese, ~**ieses,** ~**iese,**
~**iésemos,** ~**ieseis,** ~**iesen**
Conditional: podr|ía, ~**ías,** ~**ía,**
~**íamos,** ~**íais,** ~**ían**
Past participle: pudiendo

[34] poner
Present: pongo, pones, pone,
ponemos, ponéis, ponen
Future: pondr|é, ~**ás,** ~**á,** ~**emos,**
~**éis,** ~**án**
Preterite: pus|e, ~**iste,** ~**o,** ~**imos,**
~**isteis,** ~**ieron**
Present subjunctive: pong|a, ~**as,** ~**a,**
~**amos,** ~**áis,** ~**an**
Imperfect subjunctive: pus|iera,
~**ieras,** ~**iera,** ~**iéramos,**
~**ierais,** ~**ieran**
pus|iese, ~**ieses,** ~**iese,**
~**iésemos,** ~**ieseis,** ~**iesen**

Conditional: pondr|ía, ∼ías, ∼ía,
  ∼íamos, ∼íais, ∼ían
Past participle: puesto
Imperative: pon, poned

[35] querer
Present: quiero, quieres, quiere,
  queremos, queréis, quieren
Future: querr|é, ∼ás, ∼á, ∼emos,
  ∼éis, ∼án
Preterite: quis|e, ∼iste, ∼o, ∼imos,
  ∼isteis, ∼ieron
Present subjunctive: quiera, quieras,
  quiera, queramos, queráis, quieran
Imperfect subjunctive: quis|iera,
  ∼ieras, ∼iera, ∼iéramos,
  ∼ierais, ∼ieran
  quis|iese, ∼ieses, ∼iese,
  ∼iésemos, ∼ieseis, ∼iesen
Conditional: querr|ía, ∼ías, ∼ía,
  ∼íamos, ∼íais, ∼ían
Imperative: quiere, quered

[36] raer
Present: raigo/rayo, raes, rae,
  raemos, raéis, raen
Preterite: raí, raíste, rayó, raímos,
  raísteis, rayeron
Present subjunctive: raig|a, ∼as, ∼a,
  ∼amos, ∼áis, ∼an
  ray|a, ∼as, ∼a, ∼amos, ∼áis,
  ∼an
Imperfect subjunctive: ray|era,
  ∼eras, ∼era, ∼éramos, ∼erais,
  ∼eran
  ray|ese, ∼eses, ∼ese, ∼ésemos,
  ∼eseis, ∼esen
Present participle: rayendo
Past participle: raído

[37] roer
Present: roo/roigo/royo, roes, roe,
  roemos, roéis, roen
Preterite: roí, roíste, royó, roímos,
  roísteis, royeron
Present subjunctive: roa/roiga/roya,
  roas, roa, roamos, roáis, roan
Imperfect subjunctive: roy|era,
  ∼eras, ∼era, ∼éramos, ∼erais,
  ∼eran
  roy|ese, ∼eses, ∼ese, ∼ésemos,
  ∼eseis, ∼esen
Present participle: royendo
Past participle: roído

[38] saber
Present: sé, sabes, sabe, sabemos,
  sabéis, saben

Future: sabr|é, ∼ás, ∼á, ∼emos,
  ∼éis, ∼án
Preterite: sup|e, ∼iste, ∼o, ∼imos,
  ∼isteis, ∼ieron
Present subjunctive: sep|a, ∼as, ∼a,
  ∼amos, ∼áis, ∼an
Imperfect subjunctive: sup|iera,
  ∼ieras, ∼iera, ∼iéramos,
  ∼ierais, ∼ieran
  sup|iese, ∼ieses, ∼iese,
  ∼iésemos, ∼ieseis, ∼iesen
Conditional: sabr|ía, ∼ías, ∼ía,
  ∼íamos, ∼íais, ∼ían

[39] ser
Present: soy, eres, es, somos, sois, son
Imperfect: era, eras, era, éramos,
  erais, eran
Preterite: fui, fuiste, fue, fuimos,
  fuisteis, fueron
Present subjunctive: se|a, ∼as, ∼a,
  ∼amos, ∼áis, ∼an
Imperfect subjunctive: fu|era, ∼eras,
  ∼era, ∼éramos, ∼erais, ∼eran
  fu|ese, ∼eses, ∼ese, ∼ésemos,
  ∼eseis, ∼esen
Imperative: sé, sed

[40] tener
Present: tengo, tienes, tiene, tenemos,
  tenéis, tienen
Future: tendr|é, ∼ás, ∼á, ∼emos,
  ∼éis, ∼án
Preterite: tuv|e, ∼iste, ∼o, ∼imos,
  ∼isteis, ∼ieron
Present subjunctive: teng|a, ∼as, ∼a,
  ∼amos, ∼áis, ∼an
Imperfect subjunctive: tuv|iera,
  ∼ieras, ∼iera, ∼iéramos,
  ∼ierais, ∼ieran
  tuv|iese, ∼ieses, ∼iese,
  ∼iésemos, ∼ieseis, ∼iesen
Conditional: tendr|ía, ∼ías, ∼ía,
  ∼íamos, ∼íais, ∼ían
Imperative: ten, tened

[41] traer
Present: traigo, traes, trae, traemos,
  traéis, traen
Preterite: traj|e, ∼iste, ∼o, ∼imos,
  ∼isteis, ∼eron
Present subjunctive: traig|a, ∼as, ∼a,
  ∼amos, ∼áis, ∼an
Imperfect subjunctive: traj|era,
  ∼eras, ∼era, ∼éramos, ∼erais,
  ∼eran

traj|ese, ~eses, ~ese, ~ésemos,
~eseis, ~esen
Present participle: trayendo
Past participle: traído

[42] valer
Present: valgo, vales, vale, valemos,
valéis, valen
Future: vald|ré, ~ás, ~á, ~emos,
~éis, ~án
Present subjunctive: valg|a, ~as, ~a,
~amos ~áis, ~an
Conditional: vald|ría, ~ías, ~ía,
~íamos, ~íais, ~ían
Imperative: val/vale, valed

[43] ver
Present: veo, ves, ve, vemos, veis, ven
Imperfect: ve|ía, ~ías, ~ía, ~íamos,
~íais, ~ían
Preterite: vi, viste, vio, vimos, visteis,
vieron
Present subjunctive: ve|a, ~as, ~a,
~amos, ~áis, ~an
Past participle: visto

[44] yacer
Present: yazco/yazgo/yago, yaces,
yace, yacemos, yacéis, yacen
Present subjunctive:
yazca/yazga/yaga, yazcas,
yazca, yazcamos, yazcáis, yazcan
Imperative: yace/yaz, yaced

[45] asir
Present: asgo, ases, ase, asimos, asís,
asen
Present subjunctive: asg|a, ~as, ~a,
~amos, ~áis, ~an

[46] decir
Present: digo, dices, dice, decimos,
decís, dicen
Future: dir|é, ~ás, ~á, ~emos,
~éis, ~án
Preterite: dij|e, ~iste, ~o, ~imos,
~isteis, ~eron
Present subjunctive: dig|a, ~as, ~a,
~amos, ~áis, ~an
Imperfect subjunctive: dij|era, ~eras,
~era, ~éramos, ~erais, ~eran
dij|ese, ~eses, ~ese, ~ésemos,
~eseis, ~esen
Conditional: dir|ía, ~ías, ~ía,
~íamos, ~íais, ~ían
Present participle: dicho

Imperative: di, decid

[47] reducir
Present: reduzco, reduces, reduce,
reducimos, reducís, reducen
Preterite: reduj|e, ~iste, ~o, ~imos,
~isteis, ~eron
Present subjunctive: reduzc|a, ~as,
~a, ~amos, ~áis, ~an
Imperfect subjunctive: reduj|era,
~eras, ~era, ~éramos, ~erais,
~eran
reduj|ese, ~eses, ~ese,
~ésemos, ~eseis, ~esen

[48] erguir
Present: irgo, irgues, irgue, erguimos,
erguís, irguen
yergo, yergues, yergue, erguimos,
erguís, yerguen
Preterite: erguí, erguiste, irguió,
erguimos, erguisteis, irguieron
Present subjunctive: irg|a, ~as, ~a,
~amos, ~áis, ~an
yerg|a, ~as, ~a, ~amos, ~áis,
~an
Imperfect subjunctive: irgu|iera,
~ieras, ~iera, ~iéramos,
~ierais, ~ieran
irgu|iese, ~ieses, ~iese,
~iésemos, ~ieseis, ~iesen
Present participle: irguiendo
Imperative: irgue/yergue, erguid

[49] ir
Present: voy, vas, va, vamos, vais, van
Imperfect: iba, ibas, iba, íbamos,
ibais, iban
Preterite: fui, fuiste, fue, fuimos,
fuisteis, fueron
Present subjunctive: vay|a, ~as, ~a,
~amos, ~áis, ~an
Imperfect subjunctive: fu|era, ~eras,
~era, ~éramos, ~erais, ~eran
fu|ese, ~eses, ~ese, ~ésemos,
~eseis, ~esen
Present participle: yendo
Imperative: ve, id

[50] oír
Present: oigo, oyes, oye, oímos, oís,
oyen
Preterite: oí, oíste, oyó, oímos, oísteis,
oyeron
Present subjunctive: oig|a, ~as, ~a,
~amos, ~áis, ~an

Imperfect subjunctive: oy|era, **~eras, ~era, ~éramos, ~erais, ~eran** oy|ese, **~eses, ~ese, ~ésemos, ~eseis, ~esen**
Present participle: oyendo
Past participle: oído
Imperative: oye, oíd

[51] **reír**
Present: río, ríes, ríe, reímos, reís, ríen
Preterite: reí, reíste, rió, reímos, reísteis, rieron
Present subjunctive: ría, rías, ría, riamos, riáis, rían
Present participle: riendo
Past participle: reído
Imperative: ríe, reíd

[52] **salir**
Present: salgo, sales, sale, salimos, salís, salen
Future: saldr|é, **~ás, ~á, ~emos, ~éis, ~án**

Present subjunctive: salg|a, **~as, ~a, ~amos, ~áis, ~an**
Conditional: saldr|ía, **~ías, ~ía, ~íamos, ~íais, ~ían**
Imperative: sal, salid

[53] **venir**
Present: vengo, vienes, viene, venimos, venís, vienen
Future: vendr|é, **~ás, ~á, ~emos, ~éis, ~án**
Preterite: vin|e, **~iste, ~o, ~imos, ~isteis, ~ieron**
Present subjunctive: veng|a, **~as, ~a, ~amos, ~áis, ~an**
Imperfect subjunctive: vin|iera, **~ieras, ~iera, ~iéramos, ~ierais, ~ieran** vin|iese, **~ieses, ~iese, ~iésemos, ~ieseis, ~iesen**
Conditional: vendr|ía, **~ías, ~ía, ~íamos, ~íais, ~ían**
Present participle: viniendo
Imperative: ven, venid

Verbos Irregulares Ingleses

Infinitivo	*Pretérito*	*Participio pasado*
arise	arose	arisen
awake	awoke	awoken
be	was	been
bear	bore	borne
beat	beat	beaten
become	became	become
befall	befell	befallen
beget	begot	begotten
begin	began	begun
behold	beheld	beheld
bend	bent	bent
beset	beset	beset
bet	bet, betted	bet, betted
bid	bade, bid	bidden, bid
bind	bound	bound
bite	bit	bitten
bleed	bled	bled
blow	blew	blown
break	broke	broken
breed	bred	bred
bring	brought	brought
broadcast	broadcast(ed)	broadcast
build	built	built
burn	burnt, burned	burnt, burned
burst	burst	burst
buy	bought	bought
cast	cast	cast
catch	caught	caught
choose	chose	chosen
cleave	clove, cleft, cleaved	cloven, cleft, cleaved
cling	clung	clung
clothe	clothed, clad	clothed, clad
come	came	come
cost	cost	cost
creep	crept	crept
crow	crowed, crew	crowed
cut	cut	cut
deal	dealt	dealt
dig	dug	dug
do	did	done
draw	drew	drawn
dream	dreamt, dreamed	dreamt, dreamed
drink	drank	drunk
drive	drove	driven
dwell	dwelt	dwelt
eat	ate	eaten
fall	fell	fallen
feed	fed	fed
feel	felt	felt
fight	fought	fought
find	found	found

Infinitivo	*Pretérito*	*Participio pasado*
flee	fled	fled
fling	flung	flung
fly	flew	flown
forbear	forbore	forborne
forbid	forbad(e)	forbidden
forecast	forecast(ed)	forecast(ed)
foresee	foresaw	foreseen
foretell	foretold	foretold
forget	forgot	forgotten
forgive	forgave	forgiven
forsake	forsook	forsaken
freeze	froze	frozen
gainsay	gainsaid	gainsaid
get	got	got, gotten
give	gave	given
go	went	gone
grind	ground	ground
grow	grew	grown
hang	hung, hanged	hung, hanged
have	had	had
hear	heard	heard
hew	hewed	hewn, hewed
hide	hid	hidden
hit	hit	hit
hold	held	held
hurt	hurt	hurt
inlay	inlaid	inlaid
keep	kept	kept
kneel	knelt	knelt
knit	knitted, knit	knitted, knit
know	knew	known
lay	laid	laid
lead	led	led
lean	leaned, leant	leaned, leant
leap	leaped, leapt	leaped, leapt
learn	learned, learnt	learned, learnt
leave	left	left
lend	lent	lent
let	let	let
lie	lay	lain
light	lit, lighted	lit, lighted
lose	lost	lost
make	made	made
mean	meant	meant
meet	met	met
mislay	mislaid	mislaid
mislead	misled	misled
misspell	misspelt	misspelt
mistake	mistook	mistaken
misunderstand	misunderstood	misunderstood
mow	mowed	mown
outbid	outbid	outbid
outdo	outdid	outdone
outgrow	outgrew	outgrown
overcome	overcame	overcome

Infinitivo	Pretérito	Participio pasado
overdo	overdid	overdone
overhang	overhung	overhung
overhear	overheard	overheard
override	overrode	overridden
overrun	overran	overrun
oversee	oversaw	overseen
overshoot	overshot	overshot
oversleep	overslept	overslept
overtake	overtook	overtaken
overthrow	overthrew	overthrown
partake	partook	partaken
pay	paid	paid
prove	proved	proved, proven
put	put	put
quit	quitted, quit	quitted, quit
read /ri:d/	read /red/	read /red/
rebuild	rebuilt	rebuilt
redo	redid	redone
rend	rent	rent
repay	repaid	repaid
rewrite	rewrote	rewritten
rid	rid	rid
ride	rode	ridden
ring	rang	rung
rise	rose	risen
run	ran	run
saw	sawed	sawn, sawed
say	said	said
see	saw	seen
seek	sought	sought
sell	sold	sold
send	sent	sent
set	set	set
sew	sewed	sewn, sewed
shake	shook	shaken
shear	sheared	shorn, sheared
shed	shed	shed
shine	shone	shone
shoe	shod	shod
shoot	shot	shot
show	showed	shown, showed
shrink	shrank	shrunk
shut	shut	shut
sing	sang	sung
sink	sank	sunk
sit	sat	sat
slay	slew	slain
sleep	slept	slept
slide	slid	slid
sling	slung	slung
slit	slit	slit
smell	smelt, smelled	smelt, smelled
smite	smote	smitten
sow	sowed	sown, sowed
speak	spoke	spoken

Infinitivo	Pretérito	Participio pasado
speed	speeded, sped	speeded, sped
spell	spelt, spelled	spelt, spelled
spend	spent	spent
spill	spilled, spilt	spilled, spilt
spin	spun	spun
spit	spat	spat
split	split	split
spoil	spoilt, spoiled	spoilt, spoiled
spread	spread	spread
spring	sprang	sprung
stand	stood	stood
steal	stole	stolen
stick	stuck	stuck
sting	stung	stung
stink	stank, stunk	stunk
strew	strewed	strewn, strewed
stride	strode	stridden
strike	struck	struck
string	strung	strung
strive	strove	striven
swear	swore	sworn
sweep	swept	swept
swell	swelled	swollen, swelled
swim	swam	swum
swing	swung	swung
take	took	taken
teach	taught	taught
tear	tore	torn
tell	told	told
think	thought	thought
thrive	thrived, throve	thrived, thriven
throw	threw	thrown
thrust	thrust	thrust
tread	trod	trodden, trod
unbend	unbent	unbent
undergo	underwent	undergone
understand	understood	understood
undertake	undertook	undertaken
undo	undid	undone
upset	upset	upset
wake	woke, waked	woken, waked
waylay	waylaid	waylaid
wear	wore	worn
weave	wove	woven
weep	wept	wept
win	won	won
wind	wound	wound
withdraw	withdrew	withdrawn
withhold	withheld	withheld
withstand	withstood	withstood
wring	wrung	wrung
write	wrote	written